HUMANS:
from the beginning

by CHRISTOPHER SEDDON

~ From the first apes to the first cities ~

GLANVILLE PUBLICATIONS

First published in eBook in 2014 by Glanville Publications.

This revised paperback edition 2015 by Glanville Publications.

ISBN 978-0-9927620-4-9

Contents

Acknowledgements

I should like to thank Vici MacDonald, Chris Bruce, Robert Lovejoy, Tony Richards and Dr Leszek Zdunek for their immense and invaluable encouragement, advice, suggestions and general input, without which this book could never have been written.

Introduction

This book 'does what it says on the cover': it is a history of the human world from the time of the first apes to the time of the first cities. It is intended for anybody who is interested in the origins of the human species and how we subsequently went on to populate the world, discover agriculture and eventually build cities. This vast span of time covers all but that tenth of one percent of the human story that we know as 'recorded history'. The reader will learn that today's complex societies are fundamentally no different to those of later prehistory; and that their ultimate origins go back millions of years. Many contemporary concerns also have deep roots: climate change has long played a pivotal role in our affairs and those of our ancestors. Habitat destruction, loss of biodiversity and failed states are also nothing new.

Within my lifetime, our knowledge the distant past has been greatly increased by modern science. The invention of radiocarbon dating in the 1950s essentially rewrote the prehistory of Europe. More recently, genetic techniques have demonstrated our close evolutionary relationship to chimpanzees and the recent African origin of modern humans. Much vital albeit less headline-making work is carried out using methods that would not be practical without computers. We should remember, though, that the study of prehistory is a fairly recent discipline. That there was even such a thing as prehistory was not widely recognised until Darwin's time.

Human evolution and prehistory is now a fast-moving and dynamic field. As recently as 2009, when I commenced work on this book, there was still no strong evidence that modern humans had interbred with Neanderthals. The enigmatic Denisovans – an archaic human species that apparently also interbred with modern humans – had yet to be discovered, as had *Australopithecus sediba*, a South African species that might be the direct ancestor of the first humans. Many long-established scholarly paradigms have been called into question by recent findings. Such discoveries are widely reported in the media, reflecting the level of public interest in our origins and our past.

The field is of course well-covered by a wide range of books covering every major topic and aimed at specialists, non-specialists and general readers alike. What does not exist is a single volume, single author book that covers the whole story: human evolution from the first apes to modern humans; the dispersal of modern humans from Africa to every habitable continent; the adoption of agriculture in many parts of the world at the end of the last Ice Age; and finally the appearance of state-level societies not too dissimilar to the modern nation state. In short, a one-stop guide to prehistory; a book not just for students and specialists but also for those wishing to know more about the subject but not quite knowing where to start.

It is this gap that I have set out to address with my book. To write such a book was certainly not easy: in addition to the sheer volume of material, the number of academic disciplines involved is considerable and includes anthropology, archaeology, sociology, evolutionary biology, zoology, botany, genetics, geography, climatology, geology and physics. I have tried to make it accessible to all while maintaining the fullest standards of academic rigour. Above all I have tried to avoid writing a textbook. In a textbook, a chapter is formally structured, with overviews, summaries and conclusions. Just as Stephen Hawking was advised that equations would hurt sales of his *A Brief*

History of Time, I felt that such an approach would reduce the appeal of my book to the general reader. My priority has been to present the facts in the context of a readable, flowing narrative.

What is a hominin?

The characters in our story are a group of two-legged apes known as the hominins, of which modern humans (*Homo sapiens*) are but the most recent. The hominin line came into existence in Africa around seven to eight million years ago, when our ancestors diverged from those of our closest living ape relatives, the chimpanzees. Today, we are the only hominin species in existence, but this is actually unusual. For most of the period with which we are concerned, there were several hominin species in existence in various places at the same time. Not all of these hominins were our direct ancestors; many were evolutionary cul-de-sacs that died out completely. Rather than an orderly procession of ever-more 'advanced' species, leading inexorably towards *Homo sapiens*, the hominin family tree has been likened to a tangled bush.

The exact number of hominin species within this 'bush' remains uncertain. The first – and perhaps most obvious reason – is that many hominin species may remain undiscovered to this day, even assuming that any of their fossilised remains have survived to be discovered. The second, less obvious, reason is that palaeoanthropologists frequently disagree on just how many distinct species are represented by the fossil record. The two rival schools of thought are known informally as the 'Lumpers' and the 'Splitters': the 'Lumpers' try shoehorn as many fossils into a single species, while the 'Splitters' need very little excuse to proclaim new species or even new genera for each new fossil discovery.

What is becoming clear is that there were three main 'phases' in the evolution of the hominins after they diverged from chimpanzees. The hominins from the earliest phase – lasting from around seven up to 4.2 million years ago – were 'dual-purpose' apes with brains no larger than those of chimpanzees, and adaptations for both tree-climbing and two-legged walking. We are fortunate in that we have a remarkably-complete 4.4-million-year-old hominin skeleton belonging to the species *Ardipithecus ramidus*. The skeleton, popularly known as 'Ardi', was discovered in Ethiopia in 1994, and has greatly increased our knowledge of this period of hominin evolution. Ardi retained tree-climbing adaptations including an opposable big toe and thumb; later hominins (including ourselves) retained only the opposable thumb. We also have remains of an earlier *Ardipithecus* species, *Ardipithecus kadabba*, which lived from 5.8 to 5.2 million years ago; and two even earlier species, *Orrorin tugenensis* and *Sahelanthropus tchadensis*, which may push the hominin fossil record right back to the split with chimpanzees.

The hominins from the second phase – lasting from around 4.2 to 2.0 million years ago – are known as australopithecines. Their brains were again no larger than those of chimpanzees, and they probably still spent time in the trees, but they were now better adapted to walking upright. The opposable big toe gave way to the modern in-line big toe; the foot was arched; and there were other adaptations to the striding gait of a modern human. The australopithecines were widely distributed in Africa, though lumpers and splitters argue over just how many species there were. It is generally accepted that the first humans evolved from australopithecines, though from which species and where remains disputed. The australopithecines probably made and used stone tools, though the evidence is rather limited.

The third and final phase lasted from 2.0 million to around 200,000 years ago, and it was during this period that the first humans emerged. A 'human', in this context, means any hominin belonging to Genus *Homo*. Just how many human species there have been is a field in which the lumpers and splitters have had a field day, but most agree that the number is at least six: *Homo habilis*, *Homo erectus*,

Homo heidelbergensis, *Homo neanderthalensis* (the Neanderthals), *Homo floresiensis* (the diminutive 'hobbit people' from the island of Flores) and *Homo sapiens* (modern humans). Non-modern humans are often referred to as 'archaic humans'. The earliest humans were only slightly larger-brained than the australopithecines, and not was not until around 600,000 years ago that brain size began to approach modern proportions. Humans are thought to have been the first hominins to leave Africa (though this is by no means certain), and by one million years ago, were widely distributed throughout the Old World.

Our own species, *Homo sapiens*, is now believed to have emerged in Africa at the end of this third phase, before 'going global' and replacing the archaic human populations throughout the Old World. A rival point of view, now largely abandoned, is that the archaic humans were actually early forms of *Homo sapiens*, and that modern humans emerged gradually from these regional populations. The two theories are known respectively as the Replacement (or Out of Africa) and Multiregional continuity hypotheses. In fact, it now seems that modern humans did interbreed with at least two archaic human species, so neither view should really be thought of as wholly right or wrong.

It is important to bear in mind that the three phases of hominin evolution did not each lead to 'new, improved models'; hominins living four or five million years ago were as well-adapted to their environment as any that came after them. It is easy to take the conceited, human-centric view that large-brained, two-legged humans must be an 'improvement' upon small-brained tree-climbing apes, but even if that were so, evolution does not 'plan ahead'. When the first hominins emerged, nobody was thinking in terms of what features might be included in the second or third generation models. Rather, hominin species evolved in response to competition from other species and changing environmental conditions; these are the same processes that have always shaped living organisms.

How to use this book

The primer that follows this section provides an introduction to some of the more technical subjects in the book. If the reader does not wish to take on board too much 'techie' material at once, they may skip the primer and rely on the glossary items as they are encountered. These provide the same information, but in smaller doses.

Good luck and enjoy what I am certain you will find to be a fascinating journey into the human past.

Technical primer

Unpicking the strands

In order to make sense of the 'tangled bush' of hominin evolution, palaeoanthropologists often make use of a technique known as cladistic analysis. In evolutionary biology, cladistics is a method of analysing evolutionary relationships between organisms. It entails identifying one or more characteristics that are unique to an evolutionary lineage, for example the vertebrate backbone. A group of organisms are said to form a 'clade' if they all share a common ancestor that itself possessed these characteristics. The term 'clade' comes from the Greek word *klados*, meaning a branch. A clade can include many species (for example vertebrates, mammals and primates all represent clades), or a group within a single species sharing a particular characteristic, such as a specific genetic lineage.

Characteristics are said to be either primitive or derived. 'Primitive' in this context does not mean a characteristic is backward or poorly-adapted. It simply means that it is shared by all members of a clade, having arisen before the clade's common ancestor. 'Derived', on the other hand, refers to traits that are unique to a particular clade. Thus the five-digit limbs of humans and other primates are primitive, because they are shared with the earliest mammals. Conversely, toe and finger nails are derived, because early mammals had claws rather than nails. Similarly, a horse's hooves are derived. Horses have shed all but the third digit of each of their limbs. Most species possess a mosaic or mixture of primitive and derived traits. It is important to note that characteristics are primitive and derived only in relation to the group under consideration. The five-digit limb is derived when considering all vertebrates, because it was not present in the earliest vertebrates. Similarly, toe and finger nails are primitive when considering hominins, because they appeared much earlier on in primate evolution.

Cladistics is based on the assumption that the appearance of derived characteristics reflects evolutionary relationships. For example, apes and humans lack the characteristic primate tail, hinting at the existence of a common ancestor that lost its tail. In order to unpick the strands that make up the hominin 'bush', palaeoanthropologists must work at much finer resolutions than presence or absence of gross anatomical features such as tails or toenails. Subtle metrical differences between fossilised bones and teeth from different hominin species must be considered. Specialist computer software is then used to construct a diagram known as a 'cladogram', which is best thought of as an evolutionary family tree of the lineage under consideration.

Icehouse Earth

The whole of the hominin story is set within a period of climate change, and the last third of it has taken place against the background of the Quaternary Ice Age, the first ice age for a quarter of a billion years. Climate change, of such concern to us today, is therefore nothing new, and has always played a role in hominin affairs. It may come as a surprise to learn that the Earth is still technically in this ice age, which began at the start of the Pleistocene epoch, 2,588,000 years ago. Ever since then, the planet has alternated between periods of cool, arid and warm, wet climatic conditions as ice sheets ebbed and flowed in higher latitudes. During cold periods, the ice sheets locked up vast amounts of fresh water that might otherwise have fallen as rain.

The cold spells are often referred to as 'ice ages', and in particular the end of the most recent glacial period, 11,600 years ago,[1] is popularly known as the end of the last Ice Age. These warm spells – known as interglacials - are no more than breaks in an on-going ice age. The current Holocene epoch, following on from the last glacial period, is such a break. In theory, glacial conditions will one day return, though the effects of the current global warming makes this uncertain. Glacial periods are not necessarily periods of unremitting cold, but alternate between colder and warmer intervals known respectively as stadials and interstadials.

The idea that there were periods when glaciers extended beyond their present-day limits gradually emerged during the first half of the nineteenth century. Geologists sought to explain such phenomena as rock scouring and scratching, the cutting of valleys, the existence of whale-shaped hills known as drumlins and the presence of erratic boulders and ridges of rocky debris known as moraines. The phenomenon was first described as Eiszeit ('ice age') by the German botanist Karl Friedrich Schimper in 1837. The cause of these ice ages was not at first known, but in the 1860s the Scottish scholar and businessman James Croll suggested that they might be caused by periodic changes in the Earth's orbit around the Sun. His work attracted some interest, but was not widely believed. However, the theory was revived early in the twentieth century by the Serbian civil engineer Milutin Milanković, who carried out much of his research while interned in Budapest during World War I, and proposed that the changes in climate are driven by what are now known as the Milanković cycles, which affect the Earth's orbit and its axis of day-night rotation.

The Earth does not travel around the Sun in a perfectly circular path; instead the orbit is slightly elliptical, meaning that at some times of the year it is closer to the Sun than at others. The extent by which the orbit differs from a perfect circle (known as the orbital eccentricity) varies over the course of a cycle of around 100,000 years; at times of high eccentricity, the Earth will experience greater extremes of temperature over the course of a year. As well as this, the tilt of the Earth's axis varies on a 41,000 year cycle, affecting seasonal variations in temperature. There will be only a minor difference between summer and winter when the axial tilt is low, but when it is high the difference will be greater. The Earth also 'wobbles' slowly, like a gyroscope or spinning-top (a phenomenon known as precession), on a cycle of 26,000 years. The effect of this 'wobbling' is that the distance from the Sun when the particular seasons fall varies over the course of the 26,000 year cycle, again affecting their intensity. Thus, for example, winters will be harsher if they fall when the Earth is further away from the Sun; currently, this is the case for the Southern Hemisphere.

Milanković believed that the net effect of the cycles was to cause the amount and distribution of solar energy reaching Earth to vary in a predictable if complex manner. If the energy received from the sun in higher latitudes during the summer months is insufficient to melt snow accumulating during the previous winter, glaciers will advance as the ice builds up. At other times, though, energy received from the sun will increase, and the ice will melt.[2] The theory, like its predecessor, was largely ignored for decades and did not begin to gain acceptance until the late 1960s. By that time, evidence had begun to accumulate that the timing of glacial periods matched those predicted by Milanković. Unfortunately, Milanković did not live to see his theory vindicated, having died in 1958.

Evidence for past ice ages can be detected in core samples taken from the seabed, which contain the shells of microscopic marine organisms known as *Foraminifera*. The carbonate in these shells contains two main isotopes of oxygen: ^{16}O and ^{18}O. Isotopes are atoms that are identical chemically but differ slightly in mass; the superscripted numbers refer to the 'atomic weight' of the isotopes. Water containing the lighter isotope ^{16}O evaporates from oceans more rapidly than that containing the heavier ^{18}O, so water falling as rain will contain more of the lighter ^{16}O than do oceans. During an ice age, it is this ^{16}O-rich water that becomes locked up in the ice sheets, while ^{18}O-rich water remains in the oceans. Consequently, *Foraminifera* that lived during an ice age will contain more ^{18}O in their shells than those that lived during warmer periods.

When the ratios of ^{18}O to ^{16}O in the shells are plotted on a graph for core samples of different ages, distinct peaks and troughs can be seen to have occurred over the course of several hundred thousand years. These peaks and troughs correspond to past episodes of warming and cooling, and are known as marine isotope stages (MIS). These are numbered, with MIS 1 being the most recent. Some stages are subdivided with a suffixed letter, for example MIS 5e. Over the last 200,000 years, there have been three major cold periods (corresponding to Marine Isotope Stages 2, 4 and 6) alternating with warmer periods (Marine Isotope Stages 1, 3, and 5).

At the present time, we are living in a warm interglacial period: MIS 1. This was preceded by the glacial MIS 2, which lasted from 24,000 to 11,600 years ago. The peak of this cold period lasted from 22,000 to 18,000 years ago, and is known as the Last Glacial Maximum (LGM). MIS 3, from 59,000 to 24,000 years ago, was warmer but less so than today, and is classed as an interstadial. MIS 4, from 74,000 to 59,000 years ago, was cold, though less so than MIS 2. MIS 5 was the last full interglacial before the present one, and lasted from 130,000 to 74,000 years ago; it was preceded by another glacial period, MIS 6, from 190,000 to 130,000 years age.[3,1]

It is unlikely to be a coincidence that the hominins emerged into a world of deteriorating climate, or that the first humans appeared soon after the downturn became a full-blown ice age. There is also little doubt that the history of our own species, *Homo sapiens*, has been profoundly affected by the climatic cycles of the last 200,000 years. Their coming and going dictated the timing of human migrations round the world, and it not until the onset of the current interglacial did the climate become sufficiently stable to permit agriculture, thus making possible cities and the world with which we are now familiar.

Roadmaps of prehistory

The events described in this book occur deep in archaeological and geological time, and it is necessary to make use of the timescales used by both geologists and archaeologists. Unfortunately, the two systems differ from one another, as archaeologists are interested in artefacts, whereas geologists concern themselves with rocks. Also, lengthy though archaeological time is, it is still only tiny fraction of the age of the Earth.

Archaeologists still use the familiar Three Age system, devised by Christian Jürgensen Thomsen in the early nineteenth century. Archaeological eras are denoted by the technology predominantly used, thus the Stone Age was followed by the Bronze Age and finally the Iron Age. However, the system has been extended to reflect the fact that the Stone Age lasted for around 2.5 million years and encompasses all but the last five or six millennia. In the 1860s, Sir John Lubbock subdivided the Stone Age into the Palaeolithic ('Old Stone Age') and Neolithic ('New Stone Age') with the latter following the transition to farming. Later workers split the Palaeolithic into Lower, Middle and Upper periods and also introduced the Mesolithic ('Middle Stone Age') between the Palaeolithic and Neolithic. In addition, the terms Epipalaeolithic and Chalcolithic ('Copper and Stone') are sometimes used, to cater for early adopters of agriculture and metallurgy respectively. In Africa, a rather simpler system of Early, Middle and Late Stone Ages is used.

Geologists originally divided geological time into four periods, although only the two most recent remain in use, the Tertiary and the Quaternary. The Tertiary began approximately 65 million years ago, with the extinction of the dinosaurs. The start of the Quaternary is far more recent, beginning with the onset of the Quaternary Ice Age 2,588,000 years ago. The Tertiary and Quaternary are further subdivided into epochs as follows:

Tertiary (Paleogene)
   Palaeocene ('Ancient', 65 to 56 million years ago.
   Eocene ('Dawn', 55 to 33.9 million years ago)
   Oligocene ('Few', 33.9 to 23 million years ago)

Tertiary (Neogene)
   Miocene ('Less Recent', 23,030,000 to 5,332,000 years ago).
   Pliocene ('More Recent', 5,332,000 to 2,588,000 years ago)

Quaternary
   Pleistocene ('Most Recent', 2,588,000 to 11,600 years ago.
   Holocene ('Wholly Recent', from 11,600 years ago)

In this book, we shall be largely concerned with events from the Late Miocene/Early Pliocene onwards, and modern humans did not appear until near the end of the Middle Pleistocene.

Deciphering the past

The last fifty years have seen our understanding of the past transformed by the invention of various means to determine the age of fossils and archaeological discoveries. One of the biggest problems faced by prehistorians has always been how place fossils and artefacts in time. If we think of the timescales described above as roadmaps, how are we to find where our fossils and artefacts belong on these maps?

Relative dating of artefacts along the lines of 'x' is older than 'y' is relatively straightforward. Provided an archaeological site has remained undisturbed (which is not always the case), the deeper that artefacts and remains are buried, the older they are. The problem is to put actual dates on x and y, and this is rather more difficult. Before the introduction of radiometric dating in the 1950s, dating was a rather haphazard affair, commonly involving assumptions about the diffusion of ideas and artefacts from places where written records were kept and reasonably accurate dates were known. For example, it was assumed – quite incorrectly as it later turned out - that Stonehenge was more recent than the great civilisation of Mycenaean Greece.

The idea behind radiometric dating is that radioactive material present in a fossil, artefact or other sample can be used as a 'clock' to determine its age. The material decays at a known rate and by measuring the amount present in the sample, its age can be calculated. Decay rates are usually quoted as 'half-lives', i.e. the time it will take half of the material in question to decay. Often, the material under consideration is an unstable isotope of an element that is normally stable; for example, radiocarbon dating relies on the unstable carbon isotope, ^{14}C.

^{14}C has a half-life of 5,730 years, decaying to nitrogen. This is an infinitesimally short time in comparison to the age of the Earth, and one might have expected all the ^{14}C to have long since decayed. In fact, the terrestrial supply is constantly being replenished from the action of cosmic rays upon the upper atmosphere, and so atmospheric carbon dioxide (CO_2) contains a small percentage of ^{14}C. All living things absorb carbon, either directly (by photosynthesis) or indirectly (via the food chain); thus they will also contain a small percentage of ^{14}C. Once a plant or animal dies, it ceases to absorb fresh carbon, and the percentage of ^{14}C begins to fall in comparison to living organisms. By comparing this figure with the percentage present in living things, the time since death occurred can be established.

The technique was developed by the American chemist Willard Libby in 1949 and it revolutionised archaeology, earning Libby the Nobel Prize for Chemistry in 1960. However, there are limitations. Firstly, it can only be used for human, animal or plant remains – the ages of stone tools and other artefacts can only be inferred from organic remains, if any, that are buried in the same archaeological context. Secondly, it only has a limited 'range'. Beyond 45,000 years, the percentage of ^{14}C remaining is too small to be measured, even with modern techniques such as accelerator mass spectrometry (AMS). Another problem is the cosmic ray flux that produces ^{14}C in the upper atmosphere is not constant as was once believed, and variations have to be compensated for by using charts known calibration curves. These are based on samples that have an age that can be measured by independent means, such as by dendrochronology (counting tree-rings). Calibration curves are constantly being refined, so dates are often left uncalibrated in scientific literature and quoted as radiocarbon years before present (BP), or YBP uncalibrated. 'Present' is taken to be 1950, and readers can obtain calibrated dates using calibration curves compiled long after the article was published. In this book, where literature is cited that gives only the uncalibrated dates, these have been calibrated using a computer program and the uncalibrated literature dates added in brackets.

If it is necessary to go back beyond the range of radiocarbon dating, then other radiometric methods must be used. The potassium-argon and argon-argon methods rely on the decay of the potassium isotope ^{40}K to ^{40}Ar, and it is particularly useful for dating volcanic lava flows and tuffs (ash). Before rocks solidify from a molten state, any ^{40}Ar will be driven off, but ^{40}Ar produced after they crystallize will remain trapped. The ratio of ^{40}K to trapped ^{40}Ar in the sample can thus be used to determine when the sample crystallised from the molten state. The argon-argon method is a variant in which irradiation is used to convert non-radioactive ^{39}K to ^{39}Ar, and the ratio of ^{39}Ar to ^{40}Ar is then measured. Unlike the potassium-argon method, where the amounts of potassium and argon have to be measured separately, the argon-argon method requires a single measurement and is hence less susceptible to errors. These methods are particularly useful for dating fossil remains or stone tools; the age can be estimated from the position in relation to underlying and/or overlying volcanic material.

Another radiometric technique is the uranium series method, which relies on the decay of ^{234}U to the thorium isotope ^{230}Th. The method is used to date calcium carbonate materials such as speleothem (stalagmites and stalactites), which precipitate from natural water. Uranium is slightly soluble in water, and such materials contain uranium in small amounts; but thorium is insoluble, and will not be present in freshly-precipitated speleothem. The amount of thorium present in a sample will, therefore, serve as a measure of how much time has passed since it was precipitated.

Cosmogenic radionuclide dating is a related technique that relies on radioactive isotopes in an artefact arising in minute quantities through exposure to cosmic rays. Isotopes are produced at a known rate, but production will cease if the artefact becomes buried. By measuring the amounts present of various isotopes, and exploiting their known decay rate, the time since burial can be determined.

Recently, archaeologists have been able to draw on a new high-tech method known as luminescence dating, used for samples containing crystalline materials. The underlying principle is that any buried object will gradually accumulate a radiation 'dose' from the weak, naturally-occurring radioactivity of surrounding materials. This dose takes the form of electrons trapped by defects in the material's crystalline lattice, and if the quantity of these can be measured and the background radiation levels are known, then the time it has taken the electrons to accumulate can be calculated.

Measuring the quantity of trapped electrons can be done by one of three methods, the choice of which will depend on the type of material to be dated. Thermoluminescence (TL) involves heating a sample to expel the trapped electrons, which emit light as they escape; this provides a measure of their quantity. Optically Stimulated Luminescence (OSL) works on the same principle except the electrons are expelled by an intense light source. Electron Spin Resonance (ESR) involves direct measurement of the magnetic 'signal' of the trapped electrons.

TL is used mainly for materials such as ceramics and bricks, in which any initially trapped electrons were driven off by the intense heat of firing, and so setting the 'clock' running. OSL is used for quartz and sand grains, in which exposure to sunlight drove off any initially trapped electrons; here the 'clock' starts running when the material is buried or otherwise ceases to be exposed to sunlight. ESR is mainly used for dental enamel, which is precipitated during life and accumulates very few trapped electrons during that period.

Another useful technique is palaeomagnetic dating, which relies on periodic changes in polarity of the Earth's magnetic field. During intervals of 'reversed' (as opposed to 'normal') polarity, a compass needle will point south rather than north. The frequency with which reversals occur has varied considerably: at times the same polarity has been maintained for tens of millions of years; at others a change has occurred after just 50,000 years. There is no preferred polarity and the present state of affairs is only considered normal because the last switch occurred 780,000 years ago – long before the invention of the compass.

Ancient polarities can be detected in volcanic rock and fine-grained sediments that settled into place relatively slowly. Ferromagnetic particles in these materials will preserve a record of the polarity at the time of cooling or settling. The sequence of polarity changes is well known, especially over the last five million years, by means of paired potassium-argon and palaeomagnetic readings on volcanic rocks. Geomagnetic reversals are infrequent, and the resolution of dates obtained by this method is fairly low. It is therefore generally used in conjunction with other methods.

Finally, faunal dating is a low-tech but effective method that relies on finding animal remains in the same archaeological context as the artefacts or fossils under consideration. Knowledge of the dates when these animals were likely to have been present in the general region near an archaeological site implies a date range for the artefacts or fossils.

Genetic studies

A very different but no less powerful tool for studying the distant past is genetics. The genome of any living organism is often described as a set of genetic instructions for making that organism, but it may also be thought of as a remarkably detailed history book. Encoded in DNA within the genome of each human alive today is the story of every migration involving that individual's forbears going back to the emergence of *Homo sapiens*; and before that an evolutionary history of our species that stretches back through its hominin, primate and mammal ancestry, to the very origins of life on this planet.[4]

Genetic differences arise because genetic material undergoes occasional random changes known as mutations, often as a result of DNA copying errors during cell division. If a mutation occurs in reproductive cells, it will be passed on to the next generation; thus over many generations, mutations will accumulate in genetic sequences. The resulting variation within a population is known as genetic diversity. Generally speaking, the genetic diversity of a large, well-established population will be higher than that of a small, recently-established population.

A very important tool for geneticists is the so-called 'molecular clock', which is based on the principle that mutations occur at a roughly constant rate. When two populations become separated, each begins to pick up its own distinct set of mutations. By determining the differences between equivalent genetic sequences in the two populations, it is possible to estimate the time since they diverged from one another. The molecular clock principle can be applied to long-separated human groups (for example Aboriginal Australians and Native Americans), or to species (for example modern humans and chimpanzees).

Geneticists use the term 'haplogroup' to describe particular sets of mutations within a genetic sequence. Haplogroups may be thought of as genetic lineages, and the presence or absence of particular haplogroups in a population can be used to make inferences about the history and origins of that population. Although any set of mutations on any genetic sequence could be used to define a haplogroup, research often focuses on two 'types' of DNA: Y-chromosomal and mitochondrial.

Most of the DNA making up the human genome resides in the nuclei of cells, where it makes up 23 pairs of chromosomes: one sex-determining pair and 22 non-sex-determining or autosomal pairs. In men, the sex-determining pair comprises one X and one Y-chromosome; women have two X-chromosomes. With the exception of the Y-chromosome, all nuclear DNA recombines, i.e. one of it is inherited from each parent; but because women lack a Y-chromosome, men inherit their Y-chromosomal DNA solely from their fathers. Consequently, it is far easier to track genetic lineages over many generations with Y-chromosomal DNA than it is with autosomal DNA. The drawback is that only paternal lineage can be traced, and studies can only be performed with men.

In addition to nuclear DNA, a small amount of DNA resides in small, membrane-enclosed bodies known as mitochondria. These are again found inside the cells of living organisms, and carry out a number of functions, but their principle role is to generate a substance known as ATP that is used as used as a source of chemical energy. For this reason, mitochondria are often described as the cell's 'batteries'. They are believed to have once been free-living bacteria that took up residence inside cells about two billion years ago, and established a symbiotic relationship with them.[5] Although they have long since ceased to be capable of an independent existence, mitochondria have retained a small amount of their own DNA, known as mitochondrial DNA (mtDNA), to distinguish it from nuclear DNA. All mammals, including humans, inherit mitochondrial DNA solely from their mothers, because the mitochondria in a sperm cell are located in the whiplash tail. This is discarded after fertilisation, and so it never becomes part of the fertilized ovum. Mitochondrial DNA is thus useful for tracing maternal lineages, and unlike Y-chromosomal methods, can be used with both sexes.

PART I:

THE SYMBOLIC APE

30 MILLION TO 60,000 YEARS AGO

1: A very remote period indeed

Just another species of African ape

The idea that humans are apes isn't exactly new; over forty years ago Desmond Morris[1] described us as 'naked apes'. More recently, science author Jared Diamond[2] referred to us as the 'third chimpanzee', noting that the two species of chimpanzee ('common' chimps and bonobos) are more closely related to us than they are to anything else. Our close affinities to the apes have been generally accepted since Darwin's time, but they were hinted at in the mid-eighteenth century when the term 'primate' was coined for the mammal group that includes apes, monkeys and humans.

As Diamond has pointed out, were you to swap a group of humans' clothes for fur and put them in an enclosure in a zoo near the chimps and gorillas, nobody would dispute that the three species all look very similar. Even our more distant cousins, the Old and New World monkeys look far more like humans than they do cats, sheep, elephants, or anything else that we customarily label as 'animals'. Yet the view persists that we are somehow 'different', and in a way that is more fundamental than anything distinguishing chimps and gorillas from other animals.

It is true that no other ape uses laptops, iPhones, or Facebook; it took humans to paint the Sistine Chapel, write Shakespeare's sonnets and compose Beethoven's Ninth Symphony; and Neil Armstrong's 'giant leap' on the surface of the Moon was for mankind, not chimpkind or gorillakind. However, these differences are less important than one may think. Apes were social networking long before Facebook. Laptops and iPhones are tools and, as primatologist Jane Goodall first noted in the 1960s, other apes make and use tools. Shakespeare's sonnets and the Ninth Symphony are, above all, expressions of human emotion; and we share the same range of emotions as other apes. Even the Moon landing in 1969 was first and foremost about politics; and chimps are also political animals.

It is obvious, though, that these differences are not entirely a matter of degree. Art, literature and science are all consequences of a behavioural package anthropologists refer to as 'modern human behaviour'. These things would not be possible without our ability to use symbols to convey information. Symbols can take the form of sounds, images or objects. They may refer directly to an object or idea, for example a representational image; or they may be totally abstract, such as spoken or written words. Thus for example a drawing of a cat, the sound 'cat' or the written letters 'c-a-t' may all be used to refer to a cat.

Syntactic language is a system of communication that enables an effectively infinite range of meanings to be conveyed, but it is only one component of our ability to use symbols – an ability we do not share with our fellow apes. We use symbols all the time – whenever we read a newspaper, check the time, consult a map or admire a painting or sculpture. All of these activities involve symbolic behaviour: human society could not function without it.

Thus on one hand we seem to be very similar to other apes; on the other very different. How did the differences arise? Are they really something fundamental, or are they no more than the continuation of earlier evolutionary trends? Are the differences between us and the other apes more important than what we share with them, or is it the other way round? Can we be sure that we are nothing more than apes? If so why did we – and no other species of ape past or present – end up with all the trappings of what we call 'civilisation'?

Paradigm shift

From our vantage point of the twenty-first century, it is strange to recall that a little over two centuries ago, most people believed that the Bible and the works of Classical scholars contained everything there was to know about human origins. Few doubted that the Earth and every living thing upon it had been created, by God, out of nothing. It was widely believed that this had happened in 4004 BC, a date computed by Archbishop James Ussher of Armagh in 1650 from purely Biblical sources. There was by definition no such thing as prehistory. This viewpoint started to unravel during the latter part of the eighteenth century when geologists began to understand the processes that had shaped the surface of the Earth. It also became clear that the fossil record contained evidence of life forms that no longer existed, implying a sequence of events more complex than could be explained by the Biblical account of a single great flood.

The English canal engineer William Smith and French naturalist Georges Cuvier were among those who recognised that rocks of different ages preserved different assemblages of fossils. 'Strata' Smith, as he was known, proposed the Law of Faunal Succession, which was based on the observation that sedimentary rock strata contain fossilised flora and fauna. These fossils succeed each other vertically in a specific, reliable order that can be identified over wide horizontal distances. Thus, for example, fossilised mammoths would never be found with dinosaurs because they lived millions of years apart in different geological eras. Smith collated the first geological maps of England and Wales, but his work was only recognised towards the end of his life, and he even spent time in a debtors' prison.

Meanwhile, across the Channel, Georges Cuvier demonstrated that fossil mammoths did not correspond to any living species of elephant. This was a problem for those who believed that God's creation had been too perfect for anything to simply become extinct. However, Cuvier did not abandon creationism. He proposed that extinctions had been caused by periodic catastrophes, of which Noah's flood was the most recent, and the only one where humans had been present. In each case, God had created new species, to replace those that had been wiped out. No species contemporary with humans had ever become extinct, as breeding stock of all of these had been taken aboard Noah's Ark.

A rather different approach was taken by the Scottish geologist James Hutton, who argued that geological principles do not change with time and have remained the same throughout Earth's history. He suggested that changes in the Earth's geology occurred gradually, and were driven by volcanic action, deposition of sediment, and erosion by wind and rain, rather than by floods and other biblical catastrophes. Hutton realised that these processes would have required far longer than 6,000 years to shape the Earth as we know it. Unfortunately his writing style was at best obscure, and his work attracted little interest in his lifetime. It was not until the 1830s that his theories were popularised by fellow Scot Sir Charles Lyell. Nevertheless Hutton's approach, for which Lyell coined the term 'uniformitarian', is now considered to be the foundation of modern geology.

Another man whose work was overlooked for decades was John Frere, father of the Napoleonic-era diplomat John Hookham Frere. In 1797, Frere presented evidence suggesting that humans had been contemporary with now-extinct animals. He wrote to the Society of Antiquaries of London submitting some flint artefacts found at Hoxne, Suffolk. Similar stone artefacts had been known for centuries, but their significance was not widely appreciated. Indeed, many people believed they were thunderbolts or the work of elves rather than of human origin. The Hoxne artefacts – now known to be 400,000-year-old hand-axes – had been found twelve feet below the ground and were associated with bones of extinct animals. Frere suggested that they were *"weapons of war, fabricated and used by a people who had not the use of metals. The situation in which these weapons were found may tempt us to refer them to a very remote period indeed, even beyond that of the present world"*. Although Frere was not the first to suggest a human origin for the stone artefacts, he was the first to use archaeological context to attest to their great antiquity and – by implication – that of humanity.

It would take more than sixty years for Frere's radical suggestion to become widely accepted, as the majority of his contemporaries still preferred to hold on to Biblical explanation. Nevertheless, evidence continued to accumulate for a greater human antiquity than that allowed by James Ussher's chronology. In 1813, the Danish historian Lauritz Schebye Vedel-Simonsen noted that the earliest inhabitants of Scandinavia had used weapons and implements that were originally made from wood and stone. Later artefacts were made from copper, and only the latest were of iron. The idea was soon taken up by Christian Jürgensen Thomsen, Curator of the Danish National Museum of Antiquities. Thomsen faced the task of putting the museum's large and growing collection into order, and he arranged them by the now-familiar Ages of Stone, Bronze and Iron. Thomsen's Three Age system was widely adopted, especially after his guidebook to the museum's collection was translated into English. Some years later, Sir John Lubbock subdivided the Stone Age into two periods, an older period characterised by flaked tools and a later period of more sophisticated, polished artefacts. He termed the two periods the Palaeolithic and Neolithic, or the Old Stone Age and New Stone Age.

The decisive moment came in 1859, a year that saw two events pivotal in our understanding of human prehistory. The first came in April of that year when geologist Joseph Prestwich and antiquarian John Evans visited customs official Jacques Boucher de Perthes at Abbeville in northern France. Boucher de Perthes had collected stone implements from gravel pits in the Somme valley and, some years earlier, he had published his conclusions regarding the association of these artefacts with the bones of extinct animals. His views had attracted little support and his main advocate was a former critic, Dr Marcel-Jérôme Rigollot of Amiens, who recovered similar artefacts from gravels at Saint-Acheul in northern France. However, Prestwich and Evans were convinced. On returning to Britain, they delivered presentations in London at the Royal Society and at the Society of Antiquaries in which they publicly supported Boucher de Perthes' claim. What they termed the Antiquity of Man was accepted at last, so establishing 'prehistory' as a valid concept.

Just how this new perspective on the human past might have fared in isolation will never be known, because it was followed only months later by the publication of Charles Darwin's *On the Origin of Species by Means of Natural Selection, or the Preservation of Favoured Races in the Struggle for Life*, to give the work its full title. Darwin was certainly not the first to think of evolution; the idea had been proposed by others decades earlier, most notably the French biologist Jean-Baptiste Lamarck. Indeed early editions of *Origin* avoided the word 'evolution' altogether, using instead the term 'descent with modification'. What Darwin proposed was 'natural selection', a process whereby differences between individuals of the same species mean that some will fare better than others. The more successful individuals are better able to evade predators and compete effectively for limited resources; accordingly they stand a better chance of reproducing and passing on their advantageous traits to their offspring.

The classic example of natural selection, which creationists have spent the last 150 years trying in vain to debunk, is the Peppered moth (*Biston betularia*). This insect exists in both speckled light grey and all-black varieties. Originally the light-coloured form was the most common, but the pollution of the Industrial Revolution led to many of the trees on which the moths rested becoming blackened by soot. This meant that the dark-coloured moths were better camouflaged from predators, and were consequently more likely to reproduce and pass their colour scheme on to their offspring. During the mid-nineteenth century, numbers of the dark-coloured moths began to rise, and by 1895 some 98 percent of moths in the Manchester area were dark-coloured.

Darwin developed the theory of natural selection between 1844 and 1858, but it was independently proposed by the Welsh naturalist and explorer Alfred Russel Wallace. This served as a wake-up call to Darwin and prompted him to publish. In 1858, a synopsis of Darwin's work was presented to the

Linnaean Society of London, jointly with Wallace's paper. Wallace's independent endorsement of Darwin's work leant much weight to it. Happily, there were none of the unseemly squabbles over priorities that have bedevilled so many joint discoveries down the centuries. *Origin* was published the following year, and the first edition promptly sold out.

Darwin was not the first to propose that humans evolved from apes. In *Origin* he only hints that the theory may cast light on human origins. It was left to his friend and self-styled 'bulldog' Thomas Henry Huxley to present anatomical and other evidence for the evolution of man and apes from a common ancestor. Huxley, grandfather of *Brave New World* author Aldous Huxley, published *Evidence as to Man's Place in Nature* in 1863. This book – the first ever to be devoted to the topic of human evolution – appeared eight years before Darwin's *Descent of Man* and cemented mankind's place in the animal kingdom. Finally, in 1871, with the publication of *Descent of Man*, Darwin proposed that humans were most closely related to African apes.

The transformation was complete: from chosen beings created in 4004 BC in God's image, to an ape that had evolved in Africa at some unknown time in the distant past. Science had triumphed over superstition, to reveal the existence of an eerie forgotten world that lay far beyond the comforting reach of the Old Testament and the texts of ancient Greek and Roman historians.

Ever since the 1850s, anthropologists, archaeologists and scientists from many other disciplines have all tried to piece together the events of this long, formative period. They have drawn together strands of evidence from many diverse sources. These include fossils, archaeological remains, indicators of ancient climate change, languages that have not been spoken for millennia, and even the molecules of which our bodies are composed. Their findings cover a span of time so vast that recorded history is but an instant in comparison. They have revealed a story that began over 30 million years ago with the rise of our distant ancestors, on a planet barely recognisable as Earth.

2: The rise and fall of the Planet of the Apes

Missing Link

They lived in the forests of Africa around five to seven million years ago. They were apes, but they lived at a time when the heyday of the apes already lay millions of years in the past. Across Africa and Eurasia, climate change had driven much of a once-diverse lineage into extinction. No fossil remains of these apes, popularly known as the Missing Link, have ever been found. Yet they must have existed, because if they hadn't, neither would we. At some point during the Late Miocene epoch, they underwent a lineage split. How and why remains the subject of intense study, but the fate of the two lineages could not have been more different. From one eventually arose the two species of chimpanzee now living. From the second arose mankind. These apes were the ancestors of Aristotle, Alexander the Great, Julius Caesar, Michelangelo, Shakespeare, Galileo, Newton, Beethoven, Einstein and every human alive today.

Although Darwin proposed that humans were descended from African apes as far back as 1871, there was at that time no fossil evidence to support the view. The first Neanderthal fossils had been found a few years before the publication of *Origin of Species*, but it was clear even then that they were far closer to humans than they were to apes. Darwin mentions them only briefly in *The Descent of Man*. The only fossil ape known at the time was *Dryopithecus* – an ape that lived in Eurasia, not Africa. Darwin's view would not be confirmed for almost a hundred years.

In fact, for much of the last century, it was widely believed that gorillas, 'common' chimps and bonobos were far more closely related to the orang-utans of Asia than any of these species were to humans. The four were lumped together as the 'Great Apes' (gibbons and siamangs being regarded as the 'lesser' apes). It was thought that humans had diverged from them as long ago as around 15 to 20 million years ago, or possibly even earlier. The fossil ape *Ramapithecus*, known from the Siwalik Hills of India, was touted as a likely human ancestor. This suggested an Asian rather than African origin for humans. The main problem was a lack of evidence to the contrary in the form of fossils, as the African ape fossil record is poor.

In the 1960s, the emerging science of molecular biology changed the picture radically. It was discovered that in all living organisms, genetic material undergoes occasional random changes known as mutations, often as a result of DNA copying errors during cell division. If a mutation occurs in reproductive cells, it will be passed on to the next generation; thus over many generations, mutations will accumulate in genetic sequences and the proteins they produce. As explained in the technical primer, the mutations occur at a roughly constant rate and hence the 'genetic distance' between two species (the differences between equivalent genetic sequences or their corresponding proteins) will be related to the time since these species last shared a common ancestor, or 'divergence time'. This principle is known as the 'molecular clock'.

To obtain actual divergence times in calendar years, it is necessary to calibrate the molecular clock, i.e. determine the rate at which genetic distances increase with time. The most common approach is to look at genetic distances for species where actual divergence times are known from the fossil record. In principle it is then straightforward to calculate divergence times for other species. The main problem with this approach is that it relies on an accurate and correctly-dated fossil record. An alternative is to compare genome sequences between children and their parents and obtain mutation rates per generation directly. The molecular clock is then calibrated from the generation times, i.e. the average ages at reproduction of the lineages under consideration.

Researchers initially worked with protein molecules, and results showed that Darwin was right after all. Humans and African apes were closely related to each other – it was the orang-utans who were the outliers. Towards the end of the decade, using blood serums, geneticists Vincent Sarich and Allan Wilson[1] obtained a time for the divergence of humans from African apes of just five million years ago, far more recently than had been previously thought.

Predictably, this challenge to paleontological orthodoxy was met with scepticism and downright disbelief, but subsequent work vindicated Sarich and Wilson's findings. These findings raised the obvious question: which ape was our closest relative – was it the chimpanzee or the gorilla? To answer the question, improved sequencing methods were developed, enabling the direct study of DNA itself, rather than DNA products such as proteins. It turned out to be a pretty close call, but these studies showed that we are slightly more closely related to chimpanzees than we are to gorillas.[2]

Current estimates for when we diverged from chimpanzees vary, but most are in the region of between five and seven million years ago. Figures are typically in the lower part of this range, in fact little changed from Sarich and Wilson's initial estimate.[3,4,5,6] However, a recent estimate relying on direct measurements of the mutation rate per generation suggests that seven to eight million years ago might in fact be a minimum figure.[7] Estimates for gorillas indicate that they diverged from humans about 10 million years ago.[8]

The implications of these findings are that that humans and chimpanzees are descended from a species of African ape that lived millions of years ago – the Last Common Ancestor (LCA) or, in popular parlance, the Missing Link. Our relationship to the two species of chimpanzee is so close that Jared Diamond suggested we be classed as a third species of chimpanzee. If this scheme is followed, then the LCA should really be called the Zeroth Chimpanzee, though we shall see presently that there are doubts as to whether it was particularly chimplike. Regardless of which, humans are to all intents and purposes just another species of African ape. What else do we have in common with our fellow primates, and what light they can shed on human origins?

Killer App

The terms 'primate' and '*Homo sapiens*' were both coined by the Swedish naturalist Carl Linnaeus in 1758. 'Primate' means 'of first rank', reflecting Linnaeus's view that this group ranked first in God's grand scheme of things. Linnaeus did not believe in evolution (to recall, few people did in the mid-eighteenth century) and – never the most modest of men – claimed that "*God creates, Linnaeus arranges*". He was nevertheless criticised for daring to suggest any connection between humans and mere animals.

The primates are a diverse and successful group of mammals comprising over 370 species,[9] including *Homo sapiens*. Traditionally, they are broken into two groups: the anthropoids (apes, monkeys and humans) and the less human-looking prosimians (tarsiers, lemurs, lorises and a number of smaller groups). In fact, the tarsiers are thought to be more closely related to the anthropoids than they are to other prosimians,[10] but this need not concern us. Primates are typically arboreal (tree-dwelling) and live in the tropics and subtropics of Africa, Asia and South America. They are primarily dependent on sight rather than smell, and possess stereoscopic (3d) vision. Unlike most mammals, they often have good colour vision. Curiously, primates lack an obvious defining physical feature, unlike many other mammals such as bats, whales or elephants.[11] They don't have an obvious 'killer app' like the bat's echolocation, the elephant's trunk, or the ruminant's digestive system. What they do have is larger brains than other equivalently-sized mammals. Why should this be so?

One possibility is that primates need large brains to manage complex relationships within social groups. Primates, for the most part, are social animals, living in groups that usually possess a clear social hierarchy. While sociality is common throughout the animal kingdom, few species enter into the kind of complex social relationships that are normal to primates. A major benefit of group living is that it provides a powerful defence against predators. Many species of primate are capable of mounting an effective group defence against predators far larger than themselves, and in such circumstances a predator will often decide to try its luck elsewhere. In situations involving predators that cannot be deterred by strength in numbers, more eyes on the ground can provide early warning of an approaching lion or tiger, giving the group time to take to the trees or scatter. Usually, everybody will have time to get away.[12] Even if the worst comes to worst, the larger the group, the better one's chances are of not being the unlucky one that gets caught. The benefits of sociality are not limited to mutual protection and cooperative behaviours such as food-sharing have been documented for some of the higher primates, including chimpanzees, bonobos and capuchin monkeys.[13]

However, group living also has its disadvantages. Just as tensions can build up among any close-knit human group, so the same thing can happen in non-human primate societies. The solution is for small groups to form coalitions within the larger overall living group. Such alliances are built around the ability of animals to make informed choices about potential allies on the basis of individual characteristics such as reliability and which other group members they would be likely to beat in a fight.

While the nature of these alliances varies from species to species, in all cases the key to maintaining them is grooming. This is a social activity in which animals remove fleas, lice, dead skin, leaves, dirt, twigs, and other detritus from each other's fur. Grooming is a pleasurable activity for primates, releasing endorphins in addition to its utilitarian function, but it is time-consuming and can take up as much as 20 percent of the day.[14] Within primate societies, it is largely confined to 'grooming cliques'. Members of a clique are far more likely to back up fellow members than non-members in any fighting with third parties.[12]

Grooming appears to be pivotal in holding primate coalitions together,[12] although it is not the only social tool that has been observed. Food-sharing also plays an important role. Male chimpanzees exchange meat for support against adversaries[15] and have also been known to raid domestic crops for items that may be traded against favours.[16] In addition to food, mating opportunities are also traded. Alpha male chimpanzees monopolise access to ovulating females, but they will tolerate mating attempts by males that regularly back them in conflicts.[17]

Within primate coalitions and within the broader groups, individuals are constantly having to balance conflicting interests, playing one individual off against another and keeping as many happy as possible.[12] In short, they have to play primate politics. It certainly does not appear too far removed from the political shenanigans that go on in the workplace, in government, or indeed in international relations. As in human societies, the rewards of getting to the top are high. Dominant individuals enjoy greater reproductive success,[18] and better access to food.[19]

In the 1980s, British psychologists Dick Byrne and Andrew Whiten[20] proposed what became known as the 'Machiavellian intelligence hypothesis', although it now goes by the less dramatic appellation of 'social brain hypothesis'. The theory states that the large brains of primates enable them to use knowledge about the social behaviour of their fellows for predicting their likely future behaviour. They then base relationships upon these predictions. The suggestion of a link between the complexity of primate societies and brain size was not new, but it had been largely overlooked in favour of a rival theory that related brain size to fruit eating. The fruit eating theory states that because fruit-bearing trees come into fruit at different times, larger brains are required to keep track of what fruits are available at any given time and place. The main problem with this theory is that it fails to explain why some fruit eaters have bigger brains than others.[12]

British anthropologist Robin Dunbar[21,22,23] later tested the social brain hypothesis by considering neocortex size as a percentage of overall brain size. It is the neocortex or 'grey matter' that is used for higher-level brain functions, including thinking – hence the oft-heard exhortation to 'use your grey matter'. The relative size of the neocortex in mammals typically ranges from 10 to 40 percent, but in primates this rises to a range from between 50 to 80 percent. Dunbar found that there was a good correlation between relative neocortex size and both overall group and 'grooming clique' sizes. The grooming clique was found to be larger in cases where the overall group size was also large. Dunbar believes that it is actually grooming clique size that influences neocortex size. As overall group size increases, so larger coalitions are required for mutual protection – and so more 'grey matter' is required to handle the politics.

Sociality is prevalent among diverse primate groups, suggesting that it appeared very early on in primate history. That it has persisted for so long suggests that it has played a pivotal role in the success of the primates as a group – the primate 'killer app'. Dunbar also believes that it was the driving force behind the evolution of language in humans, a topic to which we shall return in Chapter 11. It is tempting, therefore, to view the LCA as a gregarious ape on the cusp of humanity, needing only to add language to its repertoire. In reality, the truth is far more complicated.

Dire straits

Molecular and taxonomic evidence suggests that primates evolved and indeed became quite diverse as far back as the Late Cretaceous period, the tail end of the dinosaur era.[24,25,26,10] Unfortunately, fossil evidence is lacking, although this is not too surprising. It has been estimated that only around seven percent of all primate species that have ever existed are known from the fossil record, and the oldest-known primate fossils date back to no further than the Early Eocene, 55 million years ago.[27,28] Accordingly, we know very little about the earliest primates. It is commonly supposed that they were small and nocturnal, as many prosimians are today. Both characteristics would have been an advantage in a world dominated by dinosaurs, but even this has been called into question. Genetic data from retinal proteins in various primate species suggests that nocturnality arose on several occasions from ancestors that were not nocturnal.[29]

Anthropoids probably diverged from prosimians no later than Early Eocene[30] and possibly much earlier,[26,10] although they are not known from the fossil record until the Middle Eocene. Where they originated remains uncertain; early fossil anthropoids are documented for both Afro-Arabia and Asia. At that time, Africa and Arabia formed a single continent, separated from Eurasia by the Tethys Sea. The two landmasses remained separate until 17 million years ago, but evidently this was not an impenetrable barrier to mammalian dispersal.[31]

The oldest currently-known fossil anthropoid is *Eosimias* ('dawn monkey'), which lived in China 45 million years ago,[32] but the earliest African anthropoid, *Biretia*, is only about 37 million years old.[33,31] However, the discovery of a diverse assemblage of fossil anthropoids, including *Biretia*, at Dur At-Talah in central Libya,[34] indicates that there was already considerable anthropoid diversity in Africa by this time. One possible explanation is that anthropoids were present in Africa much earlier than is currently known from the fossil record. Another possibility is that there were migrations of already-diverse anthropoids into Africa from Asia. Regardless of origin, these early anthropoids were fairly generalised. They were neither apes nor monkeys, but had features common to both.[35]

Apes are comparative newcomers to the primate family. Genetic data has tended to indicate a divergence between apes and their cousins the Old World monkeys around 21 to 25 million years ago,[36] but one study pushed the date back to around 29.2 to 34.5 million years ago.[37] Confirmatory evidence of these dates was lacking until 2009, when the partial skull of a fossil primate was found at Harrat Al Ujayfa, Al Hijaz Province in Saudi Arabia. Ironically, the discovery was made by a team searching for fossil whales from an era when the region was underwater. The remains are about 28 to 29 million years old, dating to near the start of the Late Oligocene, and were described as *Saadanius hijazensis*. Living in warm damp forest near what is now the Red Sea, the baboon-sized *Saadanius* shares characteristics with the *Propliopithecoidea*, a primate family that existed more than 30 million years ago. The *Propliopithecoidea* are believed to be early members of the Catarrhini, a primate grouping that contains both the apes and the Old World monkeys. *Saadanius* also shared characteristics with more recent apelike primates found to have lived from 23 to 20 million years ago: it lacked the advanced sinuses of the modern apes and Old World monkeys, but had a bony ear tube that was not yet fully developed in the *Propliopithecoidea*. *Saadanius* was still a 'halfway house' between an Old World monkey and an ape, but the fossil evidence suggested that the two groups had diverged soon after. The time lies roughly midway between the two sets of dates obtained from genetic data.[38]

One of the best-known early apes is *Proconsul*, discovered in 1909 and named in 1931. *Proconsul* is known from a number of Early Miocene sites in western Kenya dating from between 22 and 18 million years old.[39] The name is a reference to it having evolved before chimpanzees; 'Consul' was a common name for chimpanzees at that time, including one at London Zoo. Several species of *Proconsul* are known, ranging in size from present-day gibbons to female gorillas, though none were as large as a male silverback gorilla.[40] Like modern apes, *Proconsul* lacked a tail. Its brain was larger than a comparably-sized monkey, and its dentition and facial structure suggest that its diet consisted largely of fruit.[41,42] *Proconsul* still shared many features with monkeys, such as arms and legs that were of almost equal length. Its torso was deep and narrow, like that of a monkey or indeed like most four-legged animals such as cats or dogs. This shape differs from that of the human or modern ape torso, which is broad from side to side and shallow from front to back. The lumbar region of *Proconsul's* back was longer than that of a modern ape, and the shoulder-blades were positioned on the side of the body, in contrast to a human or modern ape, where they are positioned on the back. In consequence, its arms were far more restricted in their range of movement than those of a human or a modern ape. All this suggests that it moved with its body horizontal to the ground like a monkey, unlike a modern ape where the body is more vertical to the ground. When in the trees it probably walked on all fours along the branches, whereas a modern ape moves suspended below the branches. It might have come down to the ground to get from one tree to another, rather than leap from tree to tree.[39] On the ground *Proconsul* probably walked on its palms,[11] whereas chimpanzees and gorillas walk on their knuckles.

Besides *Proconsul*, several other apes are known from East Africa, mostly from the period between 16 to 18 million years ago.[40] These include the gibbon-like *Dendropithecus* ('Tree Ape'), the diminutive *Micropithecus*, the chimp-sized *Morotopithecus* from Moroto, Uganda, the gorilla-sized *Afropithecus* ('African Ape') and *Turkanapithecus* ('Ape of Lake Turkana'). The latter two come from sites in northern Kenya, where *Proconsul* is unknown. It is clear that Early Miocene apes were more diverse and successful than their present-day (non-human) counterparts.[11]

These events were taking place against a background of long-term climate change, shaped by the gradual movement of continents. During the Eocene, South America and Australia were still joined to Antarctica. Ocean currents transported heat from equatorial to polar latitudes, equalising temperatures worldwide and warm, wet climate and forest vegetation extended from the equator to the poles.[42] However, 41 million years ago, the Drake Passage opened up between South America and Antarctica. This was followed by the deepening of the Tasmanian Gateway from 35.5 to 33.5

million years ago, during the transition from the Eocene to the Oligocene. The isolation of Antarctica resulted in the establishment of the Antarctic Circumpolar Current, which cut off the heat transport from the equator.[43] Large ice sheets first appeared on Antarctica 34 million years ago, locking up vast amounts of water and resulting in cooler, dryer weather worldwide.[44]

The climate became more seasonal, with hotter summers and colder winters. From the Early Miocene, the rainforest belt that covered most of Africa began to break up into distinct ecological niches. Increasingly, the vast tracts of rainforest were interrupted by patches of woodland and grassland. Much of Eurasia was covered with evergreen forests, scrub and woodlands, associated with increased seasonality and aridity.[11,42]

Although early anthropoids are known on both sides of the Tethys Sea, no apes are known from outside the Afro-Arabian continent until it came into contact with Eurasia at the beginning of the Middle Miocene, 17 to 18 million years ago.[39] Subsequently, about 15 to 16 million years ago, the apes extended their range into Eurasia. This expansion coincided with the Middle Miocene climatic optimum, a period of climatic revival that allowed tropical and subtropical mammals to extend their ranges northward. The earliest Eurasian apes, *Griphopithecus* and *Kenyapithecus*, are known from sites in Turkey and Central Europe. Like their African contemporaries, they had thick enamelled molars and sturdy jaws, adaptations for exploiting a broad spectrum of seasonally available foods. Between 13 and 9 million years ago, the diversity of the apes increased across the whole of Eurasia, from Southern Europe to China.[11,45]

Probably the most-studied genus from this era is *Dryopithecus* ('Oak ape'), discovered in France in the 1850s. *Dryopithecus* was more 'apelike' than *Proconsul* and might have been an early hominid, the primate family that includes present-day great apes and humans. It had a broad, flattened, apelike torso, and the shoulder-blades were positioned on the back of the body. The arms had the same range of movement as humans and modern apes, implying *Dryopithecus* had the posture and under-branch suspensory locomotion characteristic of modern apes. *Dryopithecus* was about the size of a chimpanzee, and is known from sites in Central and Western Europe from 14 to 8 million years ago.[11] Other possible early hominids include *Pierolapithecus* and *Anoiapithecus*, both of which lived in Spain around 12 million years ago.[46,47]

Whether the hominids originated in Eurasia or Africa remains uncertain. At the same time apes were diversifying in Eurasia, environments were becoming dryer and increasingly more seasonal in Africa.[45] Globally, the climatic optimum had petered out and temperatures were declining again.[44] In Africa the problems were exacerbated by the uplifting of the Ethiopian Plateau and the opening of the Great Rift Valley down the eastern side of the continent. The elevated highlands blocked moisture from the Atlantic Ocean, casting a 'rain shadow' across much of East Africa. The rain shadow first appeared 15 million years ago and intensified throughout the Miocene and into the Pliocene.[41,48]

In Africa, there is a scarcity of fossil evidence for the period from 16 to 10 million years ago, and the 'In and out of Africa' theory proposed that apes might simply have disappeared from Africa after 16 million years ago. On this view, the hominids arose in Eurasia and gave rise to the orang-utans there, but one group returned to Africa 10 million years ago and subsequently gave rise to the present-day African apes, including us.[49] More recently, though, fossil apes have been found in Kenya and Ethiopia dating to the latter part of the supposedly 'blank' period. The diversity of these apes has cast doubt on the view that apes were ever absent from Africa. We are still a long way from identifying the course of events in the Miocene that eventually led to the present-day African apes, including ourselves.[50,51]

The climate took another turn for the worse nine million years ago when the main phase of uplifting of the Himalayas and the Tibetan Plateau initiated a monsoonal climate in South Asia. The weathering of the freshly-exposed rocks resulted in a significant reduction of atmospheric CO_2, causing a further drop in global temperatures.[52] In Western and Central Europe, this led to greater seasonality and a shift from subtropical evergreen forests to predominantly deciduous broadleaved woodlands. By five million years ago, Eurasian apes had been reduced to their present-day range of southern China and Southeast Asia.[45]

Finally, 5.6 million years ago, the Mediterranean Sea became disconnected from the world's oceans and dried up, depriving Africa and Eurasia of an important moisture source. This episode is known as the Messinian salinity crisis and it lasted until 5.33 million years ago, when the Atlantic broke through what is now the Strait of Gibraltar and rapidly refilled the Mediterranean. In turn, this latter event might have triggered further climatic shocks.[53] The increasingly arid conditions caused the continuous forests favoured by apes to break up and be replaced by more open woodland and grassland savannah, especially east of the Great Rift Valley.[41] In addition, apes faced competition from monkeys, who can digest unripe fruit and will thus eat it before it becomes suitable for ape consumption.[12] It was during these less than propitious times that the Last Common Ancestor lived. It was as likely to lead to an evolutionary cul-de-sac as it was to become the progenitor of mankind.

A tangled bush

The idea that there was a now-extinct 'Missing Link' between apes and present-day humans goes back to Huxley and Darwin's time when, as noted, fossil evidence was non-existent. In fact, the view that just a single extinct species separates us from the other apes has been long recognised as simplistic. We now know that several species of human lived before the rise of *Homo sapiens*. They were preceded by many species of 'upright ape'; biped apes that walked on two legs like humans, yet had brains no larger than chimpanzees.

The technical term for the group that includes the various species of upright ape and human is 'hominin'. Most researchers don't include anything either past or present from the chimpanzee side in this grouping; basically it includes just us and anything more closely related to us than are chimpanzees. Unfortunately, 'hominin' is confusingly similar to the term 'hominid' which it superseded. It is recognised that we are African apes, so 'hominid' has been expanded in scope to include the great apes and their extinct relatives as well as humans, though it does not include gibbons and siamangs.

Of all the hominin species that have ever existed, only one now remains – *Homo sapiens*. However, the present situation where we are the only existing hominin species is not the norm. For most of the last four or five million years, there have been more than one hominin species living contemporaneously. Even we modern humans have shared the planet with other hominins such as the Neanderthals for much of our existence. We can categorically rule out the view that there has been a simple evolutionary progression from one species to another all the way from the LCA to *Homo sapiens*. Not all the hominins were our direct ancestors; many were evolutionary cul-de-sacs, and died out without issue. In fact, early hominin evolution has been likened more to a tangled bush than to a simple tree.[54] Our knowledge about this 'bush' has emerged only gradually over many decades; but it is clear that there was nothing inevitable about humanity emerging from one particular strand of this bush.

Relics

Homo sapiens are large-brained bipeds whereas the Last Common Ancestor was small-brained and it was not a biped. Chimpanzees on the face of it would seem to be less changed from the LCA than we are, but is this actually the case? The conventional view is that as the forests shrank, our ancestors were forced out onto the savannahs and the changes they underwent were adaptations to this new way of life. Meanwhile, the ancestors of the chimpanzees and gorillas remained in the forests. As they did not leave their ancestral habitat, they were under less pressure to adapt and remained more or less unchanged. Thus, it is reasoned, the LCA must have resembled a chimpanzee. Accordingly, chimpanzees are often used as a 'proxy' for the LCA to draw inferences about its lifestyle, diet, social dynamics and mating strategies. Many theories about how humans came to walk on two legs rather than four have envisaged chimpanzee-like apes as an evolutionary starting-point. Is this reasoning correct?

It may be simplistic to assume that only hominins have undergone evolutionary change since the split with chimpanzees; the African fossil record suggests that very few, if any mammalian lineages have remained unchanged since the Late Miocene.[55] Unfortunately, we are hampered by the lack of fossil evidence; to date only one fossil chimpanzee has ever been found.[56] 'Common' chimpanzees and bonobos diverged from one another about 1.3 million years ago,[57] too recently to confirm that the LCA was chimplike.

On the other hand, chimpanzees do appear to have much in common with gorillas. It is often assumed that features they share evolved only once, and were already present when gorillas diverged from the line leading to chimpanzees and humans. It follows that such features were also shared with the LCA, and can thus be used to draw inferences about it and the early days of hominin evolution. The rationale behind this view is known as the parsimony principle, or Ockham's razor, after the fourteenth century philosopher William of Ockham to whom it is attributed. This simply states that any hypothesis should make as few assumptions as possible. When assumptions do need to be made, the simplest or most plausible should be chosen. For example, if we assume that the construction of Stonehenge and the Pyramids was within the capability of Neolithic and Bronze Age people, we can reject explanations involving lost civilisations or ancient alien astronauts. Similarly, in evolutionary biology, explanations that involve a particular feature evolving only once are usually favoured.

However, Ockham's razor is not infallible. If an explanation is 'more parsimonious', it doesn't necessarily mean it is correct. There are limits to how far we can take the assumption that shared similarities imply shared ancestry.[55] One feature shared between chimpanzees and gorillas is that they 'knuckle-walk' when on the ground. Knuckle-walking is a form of quadrupedal locomotion in which the forelimbs hold the fingers in a partially flexed posture that allows body weight to press down on the ground through the knuckles. Until recently, it was widely believed that knuckle-walking evolved only once (at some time prior to when gorillas diverged from chimpanzees and humans), and that humans must have evolved from a knuckle-walking ancestor.[58,59]

In fact, more recent evidence suggests that knuckle-walking evolved separately in chimpanzees and gorillas.[60] If so, then we cannot assume that the Last Common Ancestor was a knuckle-walker, and theories that assume that it was are therefore suspect. It could be that hominin bipedalism and the knuckle-walking of chimpanzees and gorillas were three distinct adaptations to the deteriorating climatic conditions of the Late Miocene. Indeed, chimpanzees and gorillas may have undergone as pronounced a series of evolutionary changes since that time as have humans. Rather than a true reflection of a once-mighty primate family, they may be relics, owing their survival to a suite of specialist adaptations. For all our genetic similarity to chimpanzees, it is therefore unlikely that the LCA resembled a chimpanzee.[61] We can be certain, though, that the LCA did exist – and that it did so at a time when the future of the African apes hung in the balance.

The symbolic ape

3: Down from the trees

In search of the earliest hominins

Although remains of humans clearly more primitive than those living today started to come to light in the late nineteenth century, it was not until the 1920s that more apelike hominins started to turn up. The first of these was *Australopithecus africanus* ('Southern ape of Africa'), discovered by Australian anatomist Raymond Dart in South Africa. Dart's findings were challenged at first, but many more discoveries followed in subsequent decades. The australopithecines were bipeds like humans, but their brains were no larger than those of chimpanzees. Up until the 1990s, the earliest known species was *Australopithecus afarensis*, known from 3.9 to 2.8 million years ago. The famous 'Lucy', a 3.2-million-year-old skeleton of a female, belongs to this species. However, even *Australopithecus afarensis* lived well after the presumptive time of the Last Common Ancestor. Not until the 1990s were fossils found that provided tangible evidence of the earliest phase of hominin evolution, at the start of the Pliocene, 5.332 million years ago.

The discovery that would open up a whole new chapter in our evolutionary history was made in the Afar region of Ethiopia. In the south of the region is Awash River, which provides a narrow green belt for the Afar people. The Afar people are nomadic, raising sheep and goats on the banks of the Awash and moving to higher ground during the rainy season each November. The Afar region has been occupied by *Homo sapiens* since our species first emerged; before that by earlier humans; and before that by pre-human hominins. Consequently, it is one of the most important archaeological sites in the world, providing a rich fossil record of hominin history.

The Middle Awash is a study area located along the Awash River Valley. Most of its fossil-bearing sediment outcrops are small, and they are scattered over a wide area. It is at one such site, near the small village of Aramis, that the first discovery was made of a hominin predating the australopithecines. Between 1992 and 1993 a research team headed by palaeoanthropologist Tim White recovered fragments probably representing seventeen individuals from the locality. These appeared to be more primitive and apelike than any known australopithecine, and were recognised as a new species. The remains were dated to 4.4 million years old, and the new species was at first classed as an australopithecine, *Australopithecus ramidus*; 'ramid' means 'root' in the Afar language.[1] Subsequently, it was assigned a new genus, *Ardipithecus*, on the basis that it was thought to represent an earlier hominin adaptive plateau than that of the australopithecines; 'ardi' means 'ground' or 'floor' in Afar.

Much more was to come. In November 1994, one of White's students, Yohannes Haile-Selassie, found what he immediately recognised as hominin finger bones. More bones were soon recovered, but they were in poor condition and preservatives had to be promptly applied to prevent them from crumbling to dust. Parts had been trampled and scattered into more than 100 fragments, and the skull was crushed to 4 cm (1.5 in.) in height. The researchers decided to remove entire blocks of sediment, cover them in plaster, and move them to the National Museum of Ethiopia in Addis Ababa to finish the work of excavation. This painstaking work and the subsequent reconstruction of the remains would take many years. Nevertheless, Haile-Selassie had been responsible for the discovery of the oldest and most complete hominin skeleton found to date.[2] For a palaeoanthropologist, it was the equivalent of winning the National Lottery jackpot on a triple rollover.

With the work on the skeleton still in progress, Haile-Selassie was involved with a further discovery of *Ardipithecus* remains. These later samples were also found at Middle Awash and recovered between 1997 and 1999. They represented five individuals, and were older than the 1994 findings. On the basis of its more primitive dental characteristics, the remains were eventually assigned to a second, earlier species of *Ardipithecus*. *Ardipithecus kadabba* lived from 5.8 to 5.2 million years ago, pushing the hominin lineage back into the Late Miocene.[3] Subsequently, more *Ardipithecus ramidus* finds were made in 2005 at the nearby site of As Duma. This new find comprised nine individuals and was dated by argon-argon and palaeomagnetic techniques to around 4.32 to 4.51 million years old.[4]

It would be fifteen years before all the findings on *Ardipithecus* were published. By this time, two even earlier possible hominins had come to light. The first of these was *Orrorin tugenensis* ('Original Man of Tugen' in the local Tugen language), discovered in 2000 in central Kenya at a site in the Tugen Hills that run for approximately 100 km (60 miles) along the Great Rift Valley.[5] The find – immediately dubbed 'Millennium Man' – comprised the six million years old remains of at least five individuals, including a thigh bone and a number of teeth. Associated animal remains included impala and colobus monkeys, suggesting that *Orrorin* had lived in open woodland with some denser stands of trees – an environment not unlike that of *Ardipithecus*. Further remains, including two more thigh bones, were later recovered from four sites in the region.

Computerised tomography scans and other studies of the thigh bone suggested that *Orrorin* was a biped, although like *Ardipithecus* it retained adaptations to life in the trees. More controversially, it was suggested that the thigh bone was more humanlike than that of *Ardipithecus* or the australopithecines and a similar claim was made for the small and thick-enamelled molar teeth. These are claimed to be more humanlike than either the thin-enamelled molars of *Ardipithecus* or the thick-enamelled but large molars of australopithecines. Accordingly, it was claimed, neither *Ardipithecus* nor the australopithecines could have been human ancestors. Indeed, it was suggested that *Ardipithecus* could have been on the evolutionary line leading to gorillas.[6,7]

Predictably, this claim attracted heated criticism,[3,8,9] but later work has failed to resolve matters. One study concluded that the *Orrorin* thigh bone most closely resembles those of the australopithecines, thus refuting the suggestion that it was more closely related to humans.[10] However, a second concluded that the thumb of *Orrorin* is also more humanlike than that of the australopithecines, and that it displays typical humanlike features related to precision grasping.[11]

Also controversial has been an even earlier possible hominin find, reported in 2001 from the Djurab Desert in northern Chad. The discovery was made by French palaeontologist Michel Brunet[12] and comprises a near-complete skull, fragmentary lower jawbone and several teeth. However, no postcranial (below the neck) remains were found. The remains were given the nickname Toumai (meaning 'hope of life' in the local language), and described as *Sahelanthropus tchadensis* ('Sahel Man of Chad'). Toumai was estimated by faunal dating to be around six to seven million years old.[13]

This find has also been dismissed as an early gorilla,[14] but other studies concluded that on the basis of its cranial features, it was indeed a hominin.[15,16,17] If so, then an age range of six to seven million years does not sit very well with genetic estimates that humans diverged from chimpanzees somewhere between five and seven million years ago, particularly as these estimates tend to favour the lower end of the date range. A possible solution to the problem is that after the split, members of the human and chimpanzee lineages continued to interbreed for a while, before separating for good. The genetic date would then reflect the latter event rather than the former.[18] A more likely explanation is inaccuracy of the fossil dates used to calibrate the molecular clock. A recent study, based on directly-measured inter-generational mutation rates (see Chapter 2) and using new figures for the generation times of chimpanzees, gorillas and humans, concluded that seven to eight million years ago was probably a minimum estimate for when humans diverged from chimpanzees.[19]

Given that the material from both *Orrorin* and *Sahelanthropus* is very fragmentary, some feel it is too soon to be drawing anything other than tentative conclusions,[20] and such caution is probably justified. It should also be borne in mind that hominin-like features are not necessarily diagnostic of hominin status. As was probably the case with knuckle-walking, they could have evolved more than once.[21]

Can the erection of these two new genera be justified? Are *Orrorin* and *Sahelanthropus* sufficiently distinct from *Ardipithecus* and from each other to each require a new genus? As noted in the introduction to this book, there are two rival schools of taxonomic 'bookkeeping' known as the 'Splitters' and the 'Lumpers'. Splitters need very little excuse for erecting new species or genera, while Lumpers try to shoehorn species into as few categories as possible. Palaeoanthropologists tend to be Splitters and are prone to erect new genera for each new discovery, for example *Plesianthropus*, *Pithecanthropus* and *Sinanthropus*. Then, every few decades, the Lumpers decide it's time to tidy things up – for example *Plesianthropus transvaalensis*, a female hominin popularly known as Mrs Ples, was later determined to be an australopithecine. Similarly, *Pithecanthropus erectus* and *Sinanthropus pekinensis* are now both classified as *Homo erectus*.

So, to rephrase the question in plainer terms: was hominin diversity in the Late Miocene and Early Pliocene as great as is implied by the existence of three distinct genera? In a classic case of lumping, Tim White and his colleagues[22] claimed that a comparison of the dentition of *Orrorin* and *Sahelanthropus* with that of *Ardipithecus kadabba* cast doubt on whether they represented three distinct genera or even three distinct species. On the other hand, given the diversity of apes in Africa and Eurasia during the Late Miocene, it would not be unexpected to have multiple genera represented.[21] It is therefore remains to be seen whether *Orrorin* and *Sahelanthropus* will one day follow *Plesianthropus*, *Pithecanthropus* and *Sinanthropus* into taxonomic oblivion.

Ardi revealed

In October 2009, after fifteen years of study, Tim White and his colleagues finally published a 108-page report on *Ardipithecus ramidus*. At the same time, a collection of eleven articles was published in the journal *Science*. Much of the work centred on the skeleton discovered by Haile-Selassie, now nicknamed 'Ardi' and believed to have been female. White's collaborators in the lengthy project included anthropologist Owen Lovejoy, whose previous work had included the reconstruction of the skeleton of Lucy.

Weighing an estimated 50 kg (110 lb.) and standing 1.2 m (4 ft. 0 in.) high,[23] Ardi was roughly the size of a chimpanzee. Her brain was fairly small at 300 to 350 cc, similar to that of a bonobo or a female common chimpanzee.[24] Based on animal and plant fossil evidence, it appears that she and her kind had lived in a woodland setting with small forest patches.[25,26,27] Dental evidence suggests that the *Ardipithecus* diet was that of a generalised omnivore, eating fruit, nutritious plants, mushrooms, invertebrates and possibly small vertebrates. Ardi's teeth lacked the specialised adaptations of chimpanzees and gorillas, which rely on soft ripe fruit and fibrous plant foods respectively.[28]

Ardipithecus was a facultative biped, meaning that it was capable of walking on two legs, but it also spent time in the trees. The foramen magnum (the hole in the base of the skull through which the spinal column enters) was positioned in the centre of the skull; a hominin adaptation for walking upright that is not seen in other apes. However, it lacked the more advanced adaptations to bipedality that were present in later hominins, and was a less efficient walker than a human. The thigh bone and pelvis were adapted for upright walking, but also retained apelike adaptations for climbing. In addition, unlike any later hominin, *Ardipithecus* had opposable big toes.[1,29,30,31] Opposable thumbs and big toes are helpful for climbing and life in the trees, and they are a common primate feature. Chimpanzees and gorillas have them, but humans and australopithecines later lost the opposable big toe. The opposable thumb was not lost because it is useful for grasping things and without it, tool-making would be difficult if not impossible.

Ardipithecus's opposable big toe was a feature persisting from pre-hominin times and further demonstrates that its ability to walk upright was comparatively primitive. However, the foot did show humanlike adaptations for upright walking. The other four toes were shortened in comparison to those of present-day African apes, and the foot was arched. Overall *Ardipithecus* had a 'dual-purpose' foot for both upright walking and climbing in trees. The morphology of its hands, arms, feet, pelvis and legs imply that it moved in the trees on its feet and palms – like *Proconsul* – rather than clinging to the undersides of branches like a modern ape. *Ardipithecus* did not knuckle-walk like present-day African apes, and lacked virtually all of the specialisations that protect the hands of these apes from injury while they climb and feed in trees.[23,32,31] Recall, though, that modern apes are not the only apes ever to have got about in the trees by under-branch suspensory locomotion; *Dryopithecus* was doing so 14 million years ago. This implies that the under-branch suspensory locomotion of *Dryopithecus* must have evolved separately to that of chimpanzees and gorillas – another example of an ape method of locomotion evolving more than once.[29] When it came to primates, Nature clearly didn't share William of Ockham's enthusiasm for parsimony.

If *Ardipithecus* was still moving around on its palms when in the trees like *Proconsul*, then the implication was that the Last Common Ancestor had done so also. Owen Lovejoy claims that the picture emerging from the *Ardipithecus* evidence is that the LCA had limb proportions more like those of monkeys than apes; that its feet functioned more like those of monkeys and early apes such as *Proconsul* than like modern apes; and none of the changes that modern apes have evolved to stiffen their hands for suspension and vertical climbing were present. Accordingly, its locomotion did not resemble that of any present-day ape.[29] These conclusions, if correct, more or less put paid to the notion of the LCA being chimplike,[23] and this was not the only major surprise to emerge from the *Ardipithecus* data.

Till death us do part

In a sexually-reproducing species, the term sexual dimorphism refers to the physical differences between the two sexes. The classic example is the angler fish: the tiny male attaches itself to the much larger female, and lives out the remainder of its life as a parasite. It becomes incapable of independent existence, serving only to fertilise the female. Sexual dimorphism is common in primates, and typically manifests itself not just in body size but also in dental differences. In many species males have enlarged canine teeth, used for threat displays in order to gain social dominance.

Among the living primates, a strong correlation between mating strategy and sexual dimorphism has been found. This in turn is related to male-on-male aggression. In species that are monogamous, such as gibbons, inter-male aggression is fairly limited. Other than their primary sexual characteristics, there is not much difference between males and females. On the other hand, in polygamous species, there is a tendency for male-on-male aggression when competing for access to females. Males are under pressure to get ahead of the rest, and one solution is to be bigger than the other guys. This is the case with gorillas, where males weigh in at almost twice the size of their female counterparts. However, size isn't the only possibility. Male common chimpanzees are only about 35 percent larger by body weight than females,[33] but they also have enlarged canine teeth in comparison to females.

Gorillas live in groups of various sizes and typically these groups consist of a single dominant male, a harem of females and their offspring, and sometimes subordinate males are also present. Females typically migrate from their group of birth to join another group, thereby avoiding inbreeding. Males either stay with their group of birth or start a new group by going off on their own. In the first case, mating opportunities are limited until the dominant male dies or they can depose him. The second, however, offers the possibility of attracting young adult females dispersing from other groups. In both these scenarios, whether it is trying to get to the top or simply trying to stay there, big burly males will be at a clear advantage over smaller, weaker ones.[34,35]

Chimpanzees live in groups comprising multiple males and multiple females. Mating is promiscuous, whereby any male will mate with any female. Again, females tend to disperse from their group of birth, but males usually remain with their birth group for life. However, there are some behavioural differences between 'common' chimpanzees and bonobos. Common chimpanzees form loosely-knit communities that vary in size from twenty to over a hundred individuals. Females tend to forage small territories either alone or with dependant young, but the kin-related males tend to form bands that patrol the territories of the females and fend off males from neighbouring groups. Here again the environment is very competitive for males, both from the point of view of maintaining one's own position within the group and keeping outsiders away from the local females. However, because they are kin-related, there is a degree of kin-bonding and hence cooperation between the males in a group.[34]

Bonobos on the other hand tend to forage in small mixed-sex groups. Bonobo society is based on strong bonding between the females and weaker bonding among the males, despite the lack of kin-relatedness between the former.[34] Bonobos indulge in a variety of sexual activity matched only by humans, including face-to-face copulation, tongue kissing, oral sex and same-sex genital rubbing. It is thought that bonobos use sex in preference to aggression as a means of conflict resolution. This apparent tendency to 'make love not war' has meant that they are less sexually dimorphic than common chimpanzees.[36]

Modern human society is widely based upon the concept of pair bonding for life, and extramural sexual activity is frowned upon. Yet modern humans are mildly sexually dimorphic and males are about 20 percent larger by body weight.[33] Men possess greater physical strength than women, and on average are taller. This suggests that strict monogamy may not be the natural mating strategy of *Homo sapiens*, and that the true strategy is based on pair bonding with a slight tendency for male infidelity. Whether such a line of argument would cut much ice in divorce proceedings is doubtful.

Theories about the origins of our distinctive reproductive strategy tend to concentrate on the extensive post-natal care human infants require in comparison to those of other mammals. A human baby is virtually helpless during the early stages of its life. During this period it is obviously in the woman's best interest if she continues to receive support from the baby's father, something that is most likely to happen in a monogamous relationship. On the other hand, a man can improve his reproductive chances by fathering additional children with other women. This carries a considerable reward for very little effort, albeit there is the risk of detection.[37] On-going sexual receptivity in women probably evolved to strengthen pair-bonding and counter the appeal of infidelity.

One feature of human reproductive biology that is highly uncommon among mammals is concealed ovulation. In most mammal species, females are only fully sexually receptive when ovulating and hence able to conceive. At such times they give visual, olfactory or other cues to advertise their condition to the males. In both species of chimpanzee, for example, the genitals turn bright red. There are no equivalent cues in our species, but copulations take place throughout a woman's menstrual cycle, and she has no need to advertise when she was ovulating. The typical primate visual cues probably disappeared because there were no evolutionary pressures maintaining them, rather than because of a specific need to conceal ovulation.[38] However, there are other possibilities. If a woman is going to be unfaithful, advertising the only times she can fall pregnant could cause problems.

The long-standing view is that that monogamy and other distinctive features of human reproductive biology did not arise until the first humans emerged around two million years ago. This view was based on the assumption that Last Common Ancestor was chimp-like, and was supported by estimated average body weights of the australopithecines, which before the 1990s were the earliest-known hominins. Although trying to calculate body weights from the available fossil evidence is rather problematic, anthropologist Henry McHenry[33] obtained figures that suggested males of *Australopithecus afarensis* were about 50 percent larger by body weight than females. With *Australopithecus africanus* the figure was slightly less at around 35 percent, comparable to common chimpanzees. McHenry's figures, if correct, are consistent with a social structure of large groupings of kin-related males and unrelated females,[39] similar to that of chimpanzees. Mating would have been promiscuous, with females dispersing to join other groups on reaching sexual maturity. If fact, more recent estimates suggest that *Australopithecus afarensis* was less sexually dimorphic than McHenry believed.[40] Furthermore, *Ardipithecus* has thrown a major spanner in the works.

In terms of body size it appears to have been only minimally dimorphic,[23] and its canine teeth were only slightly more dimorphic than those of modern humans. All known non-hominin apes possess a honing C/P3 dental complex. This means that the pointed-shaped upper canine fits in with the lower canine and lower third premolar in a way that it is constantly honed, or sharpened. Generally speaking, this feature is more developed in males than in females, and the dagger-like upper canines are important in male-on-male aggression.

However, in *Ardipithecus*, not only were male and female canines similar in size, but the male canine had been dramatically 'feminised' in shape. The crown of the upper canine was altered from the pointed shape seen in apes to a less threatening diamond shape in both males and females. Furthermore, there was no evidence of honing.[28] Overall, this suggested a reduction in male-on-male aggression and a largely monogamous species, implying that the mating strategy of modern humans emerged fairly early on in hominin history – long before large brains evolved. Owen Lovejoy believes that the explanation might have been connected to the emergence of bipedalism.

Four legs good, two legs better

Human bipedalism is one of the most unusual ways of getting about, shared with no other living species. Nearly all bipeds – such as kangaroos – move with their backs close to horizontal, using their tails as a counterweight. In common with other apes, we lack a tail. Chimpanzees waddle when walking upright, but humans walk with a striding gait. This is a process requiring split-second timing. It involves a series of actions divided into two alternating phases, the swing phase and the stance phase. Assisted by the big toe, the leg in the swing phase pushes off from the ground ('toe-off'), swings under the body while slightly flexed ('mid-stance'), and finally straightens out again prior to the foot hitting the ground heel-first ('heel-strike'). It then remains in the extended position, providing support (the stance phase), while the other leg goes through the swing phase as the body continues to move forward. The British anthropologist John Napier once remarked that human walking is a risky business, and it is hard to disagree. For it to have evolved at all, the advantages must have been considerable. Not only that, but it requires extensive anatomical adaptations.

These include:

1. A curved lower spine;
2. A shorter, broader pelvis and thigh bone angled inwards, allowing it to swing under the body (the chimpanzee thigh bone is not angled);
3. Longer lower limbs (chimpanzees have short lower limbs);
4. The ability to fully straighten the leg (chimpanzees cannot do this);
5. An enlarged, in-line big toe (chimpanzees have opposable big toes);
6. A repositioning of the foramen magnum from the rear to the centre of the skull; with present-day apes, it is positioned at the rear, but with humans and other hominins, it is centrally-placed.

On the face of it, one may wonder what evolutionary forces could possibly select for such a radical series of transformations.[39] An obvious possibility is that bipedalism freed our hands for other purposes, such as tool-making. This is an attractive theory, because our hands have proved useful ever since. However, evolution does not work that way and features don't evolve because of what they might enable to happen in the future. Our hands weren't freed from locomotive purposes to enable us to manufacture stone tools – or to build skyscrapers, aeroplanes and computers. The human hand was a useful spin-off from something else, but what?

During the twentieth century, many theories were proposed. Some of these understandably focused on food procurement strategies. The 'Man the Hunter' theory, popular in the 1960s, saw bipedalism as an adaptation for hunting. Although bipeds are slower and less energy efficient than quadrupeds at top speed, at lower speeds they possess greater stamina, a feature that is useful for tracking and killing prey. A variant on the theory was 'Man the Scavenger'. This model also saw advantages in the superior biped endurance, this time for following migrating herds and scavenging carcasses. Both theories sound plausible, but the evidence of *Ardipithecus* suggests that bipedalism considerably predates the large-scale consumption of meat.

Other theories emphasised posture rather than locomotion. One suggestion considered hominin threat displays, where individuals stand erect in aggressive encounters. The idea was that the taller you are, the more impressive you look, and the more likely a potential opponent will be to back down.[41] Another theory considered field studies of chimpanzees showing that 80 percent of bipedal behaviour was related to stationary feeding of fruit from bushes and low branches in small trees. Only four percent was observed while walking. It was proposed that bipedalism was initially a feeding adaptation that only later became a locomotion adaptation. Both these theories suggest standing upright preceded bipedal walking.[42]

In the 1980s, two very plausible and complimentary theories were proposed. The first, the 'Efficient Biped' model put forward by anthropologists Peter Rodman and Henry McHenry,[43] suggests that bipedalism evolved in response to the climate change of the Late Miocene. This caused continuous forests to be replaced by more open woodland and grassland savannah, and sources of food became more thinly dispersed as a result. Although early hominins such as *Ardipithecus* lived in the remaining forests and woodlands, they would often have had to walk long distances between wooded patches in order to obtain a meal. From an evolutionary point of view, more energy-efficient ways of getting about would be favoured. Rodman and McHenry noted that humans are at least as energy-efficient as conventional quadrupeds at walking speeds, albeit they are less so when running. They also noted that the human gait is much more energy-efficient than either the knuckle-walking or bipedal locomotion of chimpanzees.

As proposed, the theory was over-simplified. Firstly, early hominins such as *Ardipithecus* were less efficient bipeds than modern humans. Secondly, to recall from Chapter 2, chimpanzee knuckle-walking evolved separately from that of gorillas. Human bipedalism and the two types of knuckle-walking were all separate evolutionary developments. However, if each evolved from something less efficient, then it remains possible that energy considerations were driving the evolutionary processes.

Even if the advantages were at first only slight, then more dispersed and otherwise unreachable food sources provided the evolutionary pressure for more efficient bipedalism, thus enabling biped apes to extend their range. Complimentary to the theory is a proposal made by evolutionary biologist Peter Wheeler.[44] He suggested that bipedalism arose from the need to reduce exposure to the sun while foraging, particularly at noon. Upright apes have less of their body surface exposed to the sun than those going about on all fours, and they can thus continue to forage for a longer portion of the day. Furthermore, when higher up off the ground they can gain more benefit from cooling breezes. Bipedalism would be a win-win situation. Not only would biped apes use up less energy getting about; they would be less exposed to the effects of the sun when out in the open, crossing between wooded patches. The added attraction of these theories is that they suggest that the switch to bipedalism was simply an evolutionary response to climate change.

Owen Lovejoy[45] has put forward a completely different suggestion – the 'Man the Provisioner' model. Once again, the switch to bipedalism was an evolutionary response to the need to forage further afield due to food sources becoming more dispersed during the Late Miocene. The difference is that according to this model, bipedalism also liberated the forelimbs, enabling males to carry food items back to a home base and share them with females and their offspring. This strategy increased the reproductive potential of a female in three ways. Firstly, it ensured that she and her offspring were well-fed; secondly it gave her more time to devote to parental care; and thirdly, being well-nourished reduced the time between successive pregnancies. For the males to benefit in terms of reproductive potential it was necessary for them to provision only their own offspring. They could only be reasonably sure they were doing this if they were in a monogamous relationship. This pair-bonding was reinforced by females remaining continually sexually receptive; and moreover, concealed ovulation meant that regular copulation was necessary in order to conceive.

The weak dimorphism of *Ardipithecus* fits the theory, but the stronger dimorphism of the later australopithecines is a problem. If humans evolved from australopithecines, and australopithecines from *Ardipithecus*, then the implication is that the weak sexual dimorphism and monogamy of modern humans was a later development. However, Lovejoy[46] has questioned the importance of body size dimorphism in primates in relation to a promiscuous mating strategy. He points out that in many primate species male body size is related to factors other than mate competition. Also, though there is intense inter-male competition with both gorillas and chimpanzees, the latter are far less dimorphic in term of body size. He argues, therefore, that canine size is more important than body size in primate mating strategies. Given that canine dimorphism was small in not just *Ardipithecus* but also the australopithecines, Lovejoy reasoned that the mating strategies of these early hominins were similar to those of modern humans.

Lovejoy's findings are not universally accepted, but comparative studies of the human and chimpanzee Y-chromosomes have provided support for his view. The Y-chromosome is one of the two sex-determining chromosomes in most mammals, containing the SRY (sex determining Y) gene that triggers the development of male gonads. Given that chimpanzees are so closely related to humans, one would expect to see little difference between the Y chromosomes of the two species. In fact, studies suggest that there are considerable differences, and that most of the changes have occurred on the chimpanzee side. These changes may reflect the prominent role of the Y-chromosome in sperm production, and its importance in a promiscuous mating strategy.[47,48] The implication is that it is the chimpanzee rather than human mating strategy that is most changed since the time of the Last Common Ancestor, and that the mating strategy of the latter was therefore more humanlike than chimplike. If correct, this is consistent with the suggestion that *Ardipithecus* was monogamous in its mating habits.

However, the matter is far from settled one way or the other. Despite the fresh insight that has been gained from *Ardipithecus*, our knowledge of this earliest period in hominin evolution is far from complete. We can be hopeful, though, that evidence will continue to emerge that will increase our understanding. With this in mind, let us move on to consider the putative descendants of *Ardipithecus*, the australopithecines.

4: The southern apes

Did Ardi meet Lucy?

The australopithecines are the best-known and best-understood of the pre-human hominins, and the first discoveries go back to the 1920s. Finds include 'Lucy', a remarkably complete 3.2-million-year-old female, but the picture is nevertheless still frustratingly incomplete. Even now it's been said that the whole of the hominin fossil record could be fitted into the back of a pickup truck.[1] The oldest-known australopithecine remains are around 4.1 to 4.2 million years old;[2,3] this is just 200,000 years after *Ardipithecus*. Moreover, given uncertainties in dating, and the near-certainty that we don't have the remains of the last-ever *Ardipithecus* or the first-ever australopithecine, there is a good chance the two lived even closer together in time, possibly even overlapping. Did the australopithecines evolve from *Ardipithecus*? Did the two species ever meet?

It seems likely – though by no means certain – that the australopithecines did evolve from *Ardipithecus*. What is not known is how the evolutionary change proceeded, and there are two hypotheses that fit the fossil data. The first invokes an evolutionary process known as 'punctuated gradualism'. It suggests that over the course of 200,000 years *Ardipithecus ramidus* evolved fairly rapidly until it had become *Australopithecus anamensis*, the earliest-known australopithecine species. Bear in mind that while 200,000 years may seem like a long time, from an evolutionary point of view it is little more than the blink of an eye. The second hypothesis involves 'punctuated equilibrium' and it proposes that the lineage of the early *Ardipithecus* species *Ardipithecus kadabba* split at some point. One lineage went on to become *Australopithecus anamensis*; the other, less-changed lineage became Ardi's species, *Ardipithecus ramidus*.[3,4]

'Punctuated gradualism' and 'punctuated equilibrium' are two comparatively recent alternatives to the traditional view that rates of evolutionary change are constant and that species evolve only very slowly. Biologists Nils Eldredge and Stephen Jay Gould[5] have proposed that evolution proceeds by long periods of stasis, when little or no evolutionary change occurs. This is punctuated by rapid bursts of speciation, during which lineages split and new species emerge. They termed this process punctuated equilibrium. Punctuated gradualism is a half-way house in which there are again long periods of stasis, followed by rapid change. Here though, there are no lineage splits and one species simply evolves, rapidly, into another. Both models account for the lack of fossils intermediate between earlier and later species by the transformation being too rapid to be visible in the fossil record.

To some extent, it is debatable as to whether 'punctuation' models should be regarded as being at odds with conventional evolutionary theory. As biologist Richard Dawkins[6] has pointed out, nobody has ever claimed that the rate of evolutionary change is completely uniform. For now, though, the term 'punctuated event' will be used to describe the relatively rapid appearance of a new species. It should also be noted that punctuated changes are only rapid in geological terms. An increase of 30 cm (1 ft.) in adult height, occurring over 60,000 years, would correspond to an average height increase of a millimetre (1/25th in.) every ten generations, assuming a generation time of 20 years. 60,000 years is an infinitesimally short period of geological time.

Which (if either) model is correct? In 2012, Ardi's discoverer Yohannes Haile-Selassie reported the find of a 3.4-million-year-old partial hominin foot at the Afar site of Woranso-Mille. The date is well after the emergence of the australopithecines, but the big toe is opposable, suggesting affinities to *Ardipithecus*. This suggests that the lineage-split view is correct and that after the split, *Ardipithecus*-type hominins continued until well into the time of the australopithecines. Ardi's descendants presumably encountered them, although Lucy herself lived around 200,000 years later. A word of caution is that the fourth metatarsal of the Woranso-Mille foot is longer than the first and second. Metatarsals are the five long bones in the forefoot which connect the ankle bones to those of the toes. Long fourth metatarsals are not seen in any other hominin or in existent apes, though they are seen in some Miocene apes.[7] We cannot therefore rule out the possibility that the foot is from a non-hominin ape. The discovery highlights just how little we really know about this period, and the likelihood that there were many hominin species that have left absolutely no trace in the fossil record.

The walkers

In comparison to *Ardipithecus*, the australopithecines were more evolved in the direction of modern humans, though they still retained many apelike features. The teeth of the australopithecines were humanlike, though the back teeth were larger than those of a human. The face was apelike, with a prominent browridge and lower jaw jutting forward. However, the spinal column entered the skull through a centrally-placed foramen magnum, as was the case with *Ardipithecus*,[8] differing from the rear positioning seen in apes. This, as we saw in Chapter 3, is an adaptation to walking upright.

The brain was still only slightly larger than that of a chimpanzee and barely a third the size of that of a modern human. The early species *Australopithecus afarensis* had a cranial capacity that ranged from 380 to 485 cc. The cranial capacity of a primate is defined as the internal volume of its braincase, and is as such a measure of the size of its brain. The later *Australopithecus africanus* showed a modest increase in cranial capacity to a range of 430 to 520 cc, and some of the so-called robust australopithecines ranged from 500 to 545 cc. By comparison, the range for a present-day chimpanzee is 280 to 450 cc, and the average size for a modern human is 1,350 cc.[8]

The limb proportions remained apelike, with very short thighs, powerful arms and forearms long in proportion to upper arms.[9] These, together with the curved bones of the hands and feet suggest the australopithecines retained adaptations to tree-climbing, possibly for escaping predators, for sleeping and for foraging.[10] However, the australopithecine ankle lacked the range of movement of that of a present-day chimpanzee, and was poorly-adapted for modern apelike vertical climbing.[11] In addition, the opposable big toe of *Ardipithecus* was replaced with an in-line big toe;[9,10] the australopithecine feet were arched, like those of humans;[12] and the squatter, broader pelvis was more humanlike than that of *Ardipithecus*. Unlike *Ardipithecus*, the thigh bone angled inwards, like a human. This allowed the feet to swing below the below the body's centre of gravity and implies a humanlike striding walk, unlike the waddling motion of modern apes[13] (see Chapter 3).

The shape of the australopithecine ribcage has been the subject of debate for many years. One view is that it was funnel-shaped, like that of an ape; a possible adaptation to under-branch suspensory locomotion.[9] Alternatively, a more humanlike barrel shape has been suggested.[14] Recent work suggests an intermediate position. The upper part was narrow and apelike, but the lower part was more humanlike and less flared than that of an ape.[15]

Recently, it has been suggested that the hearing abilities of australopithecines differed from those of modern humans, although they were evolving in the human direction. The three middle ear auditory ossicles (malleus, incus and stapes) are the smallest bones in the human body, and serve to transmit sounds from the air to the fluid-filled labyrinth of the inner ear. Due to their tiny size, they are rarely found with early hominin fossils, but examples have been recovered from South African australopithecine remains. They show that the malleus was humanlike in its proportions, but the incus and stapes were still apelike.[16]

The shift from an arboreal lifestyle may well have been linked to another important development. It has long been recognised that newborn human babies are larger in relation to their mothers than the offspring of apes. The infant-mother mass ratio (IMMR) for humans ranges from 4.8 to 6.5 percent, almost double the figure of 3.3 percent for chimpanzees. Based on known relationships in anthropoids between adult brain mass, newborn infant brain mass, and newborn infant body size, estimates have been obtained for the birth weights of extinct hominin species. A figure of 2.1 to 3.2 percent was obtained for *Ardipithecus*, within the range of modern apes. However, *Australopithecus* came in at 4.0 to 6.7 percent, an average of greater than five percent. This is only just below the range for modern humans. These results suggest that the humanlike trend towards bigger babies began with the australopithecines. Possibly, carrying such large babies around restricted the tree-climbing activities of nursing mothers.[17] Conversely, a more terrestrial lifestyle might have released the constraints on IMMR, enabling larger babies to be born. It is something of a chicken-and-egg situation.

You are what you eat

Long-held views on australopithecine diet have come under scrutiny in recent years. The australopithecines had a distinctive suite of dental features generally thought to imply strict vegetarianism, including small or moderate-sized incisors and large, thick-enamelled, flat molars. This type of dentition is not well suited for eating tough fruits or leaves, and lacks the shearing potential needed for processing meat. On the other hand, it is ideal for breaking down hard, brittle food items including nuts and some fruits. The large flat molars served well for crushing, and the thick enamel would have withstood abrasion and fracture. The thick tooth-bearing portion of the australopithecine lower jaws was able to withstand the strains generated by chewing such foods. However, it is likely that the australopithecines preferred soft, sugar-rich fruits, only falling back on the hard, brittle food items when nothing else was available. Microwear patterns on their teeth are similar to those of modern-day seed and soft fruit eaters.[18,19,20] Chips on the dental enamel of back teeth indicate that the australopithecines used high bite forces, similar to those of modern seed-eating mammals such as orang-utans and peccaries.[21] Overall, their dental adaptations suited them for life in a variety of habitats, ranging from gallery forest (forest forming as corridors along rivers or wetlands in landscapes that are otherwise sparse in trees) to open savannah.[18]

However, recent studies using a technique known as stable isotope analysis suggest that the picture might not be so straightforward. Carbon has two stable (i.e. non-radioactive) isotopes, ^{12}C and ^{13}C, both of which are absorbed by plants in the form of atmospheric CO_2 through photosynthesis. However, plants take up proportionally less ^{13}C than ^{12}C, meaning that if the two isotopes were present in equal amounts in the atmosphere, a plant would absorb more ^{12}C than ^{13}C (in fact ^{13}C is scarcer than ^{12}C in the atmosphere, but the proportion absorbed by plants is even less). Although all plants favour ^{12}C, the extent to which they do so depends on the method of photosynthesis they use. There are two main photosynthetic processes: the C3 process employed by trees, bushes and shrubs, and the C4 process employed by plants such as grasses and sedges. The C4 process takes up slightly more atmospheric ^{13}C than does the C3 process.

Animals incorporate carbon from their food into their bones, teeth and body tissues and hence the isotopic composition of these will provide an indication of diet; lower ^{13}C levels will indicate a diet of trees, bushes and shrubs. The old adage 'you are what you eat' is literally true. Analysis of the carbon isotopes present in australopithecine dental enamel has hinted at possible consumption of meat. The dental enamel was taken from molar teeth of four fossil *Australopithecus africanus* from the Makapansgat Valley in South Africa. It was found that their diet included around 25 to 50 percent of tropical grasses and sedges, although the region was at that time rich in trees, bushes and shrubs. Why would the australopithecines shun this rich source of food? One possibility was to avoid competition, but it is also possible that their diet included animals that ate tropical grasses and sedges, such as termites or young antelope.[22]

Clues about the diet of *Australopithecus africanus* have also been obtained from measurements of strontium and barium levels in dental enamel. Strontium (Sr) and barium (Ba) are elements with similar chemical properties to calcium and find their way into dental enamel and bone via the food chain, though in far smaller amounts than calcium. The abundance of these elements relative to calcium depends upon the diet: Sr/Ca and Ba/Ca ratios are lower in carnivores than they are in herbivores. Results suggest that *Australopithecus africanus* might have eaten a seasonally-varying diet that alternated between meat and plant food.[23] Given the lack of dental adaptations for meat-eating, one possible interpretation of these results is that australopithecines used stone tools for processing meat. As we shall see presently, there is evidence to suppose that this was indeed the case.

The use of such techniques is not restricted to learning about diet; they can also help identify where individuals have spent their lives. Stable isotope analysis has been used to infer that like female chimpanzees, female australopithecines migrated from their group of birth to join another group. Strontium exists in a number of isotopic forms, but the abundance of these varies. In particular, the abundance of isotope ^{87}Sr in relation to ^{86}Sr is sensitive to local geology and the ^{87}Sr/^{86}Sr ratio of dental strontium can therefore help identify where an individual grew up. It was found that males had lived and died in the region where their remains were found, whereas the females had grown up outside the region. The implication is that the australopithecine social structure was similar to that of chimpanzees, where females disperse from their group of birth (see Chapter 3).[24]

Lucy and her relatives

The oldest australopithecine species so far recognised is *Australopithecus anamensis*, known from finds going back to the 1960s at sites near Lake Turkana, Kenya, but not recognised as a new species until 1995.[25] Subsequently, fossils were also discovered in Ethiopia at Middle Awash.[3] The species is known from 4.2 to 3.9 million years ago,[8] and takes its name from the word for 'lake' in the local Turkana language. Lake Turkana, formerly known as Lake Rudolf, is the largest of a series of lakes that have formed in troughs within the Great Rift Valley, crossing into Ethiopia at its far northern end. It is the world's largest alkaline desert lake and its waters, though drinkable, are rather unpalatable. The surrounding region is arid and classed as desert and dry shrub land. Though inhospitable today, the region was once a varied mixture of habitats and while *Australopithecus anamensis* appears to have favoured forest conditions, remains have also been found in areas containing wooded, bushland, grassland and open environments.[25] Apparently, australopithecines were able to adapt to a wider range of habitats than *Ardipithecus*.

Although classed as a separate species, it is likely that *Australopithecus anamensis* was simply an earlier form of *Australopithecus afarensis*,[3] known in the fossil record from 3.9 to 3.0 million years ago.[8] *Australopithecus afarensis* was discovered in the 1970s in Ethiopia at Hadar, a village on the southern edge of the Afar Triangle. The initial discovery comprised a knee joint,[26] but other finds soon followed. The first of these was 'Lucy', the oldest and most complete early hominin skeleton found up to that point. This diminutive female lived around 3.2 million years ago, stood 1.1 m (3 ft. 8 in.)

tall, and weighed about 30 kg (66 lb.).[9] She gained her nickname from the Beatles song *Lucy in the Sky with Diamonds*, played at a party held to mark the discovery.

Shortly after the discovery of Lucy, the team found a fossil bed containing 333 separate fragments. The site was accordingly dubbed Locality 333, a label that gives little hint of the disastrous sequence of events that unfolded there millions of years ago. The remains were associated with a group of at least thirteen *Australopithecus afarensis* individuals including males, females and four or more infants who had met with a sudden end. It is believed that the group – now known as the First Family – were drowned by a flash flood, as there is no evidence that they were attacked by predators. If they were indeed all members of a single social group, it suggests *Australopithecus afarensis* lived in relatively large groups of mixed sexes and ages. Like Lucy, the First Family lived around 3.2 million years ago.[27] We can but wonder about what happened on that day, now so long ago. Was there any warning? Were there any survivors? If so, they must certainly have felt a sense of loss, even if it wasn't mourning in the sense that we understand it.

In 1978, a set of hominin footprints were discovered that had been preserved for 3.66 million years in volcanic ash at Laetoli in Tanzania.[28] Again, they are a mute testament to a drama that played out in the distant past – the hominins were walking through muddy ash following an eruption of Mt. Sadiman, 20 km (12 miles) away, and they would have been able to see the volcano smouldering menacingly on the horizon. Their footprints were captured like a plaster casting. The mud must have had time to harden before further eruptions covered the footprints in a layer of ash, from which they would not emerge until the present day. One of the wonderful dioramas in the American Museum of Natural History in New York records the scene, in which a life-sized male is displayed with a protective arm around the shoulder of the female. It is apparently untrue that they were only posed that way to stop the female figure from toppling over.[1]

Generally attributed to *Australopithecus afarensis*, the footprints were made by three bipedal individuals, all walking in the same direction. The footprints confirmed that these hominins had humanlike arched feet and lacked the opposable big toe of *Ardipithecus*.[12] Deep heel impressions in relation to those made by the toes suggest that the Laetoli hominins were walking fully upright. Comparisons with impressions made by modern humans, bonobos and orang-utans confirm that the footprints are generally modern in aspect.[28]

Australopithecus afarensis differed only slightly from its presumed predecessor *Australopithecus anamensis*, differences being mainly confined to the teeth, shape of the chin and the tympanic plate in the middle ear.[8] However, research into the shape and form of the carpal bones (the bones connecting the hand to the forearm) of *Australopithecus anamensis* suggests that it might have spent more time in the trees than *Australopithecus afarensis*.[29] According to Henry McHenry's calculations (see Chapter 3), *Australopithecus afarensis* showed considerable sexual dimorphism; males measured 1.51 m (5 ft. 0 in.) tall and weighed 45 kg (99 lb.) whereas females measured just 1.05 m (3 ft. 6 in.) and weighed only 29 kg (64 lb.).[30] If these figures are correct, then *Australopithecus afarensis* was even more sexually dimorphic than chimpanzees, and some have suggested that the 'males' and 'females' actually represent two different species. However, recent estimates cast doubt on them and suggest that *Australopithecus afarensis* was less sexually dimorphic than McHenry believed.[31] *Australopithecus afarensis* was capable of occupying a range of habitats. At Hadar, Lucy and her folk apparently lived in woodland, but at Laetoli the environment was a much more open grassland savannah.[10]

Australopithecus afarensis and *Australopithecus anamensis* are known from the East African countries of Ethiopia, Kenya and Tanzania, but in 1993 the partial lower jawbone of an australopithecine, complete with teeth, was found by Michel Brunet in the Bahr el Ghazal valley in northern Chad. The remains were named Abel in memory of Brunet's friend and colleague Abel Brillanceau, who had died of malaria in 1989. Estimated to be from 3.5 to 3.0 million years old, the remains differed from

Australopithecus afarensis both dentally and in the chin region. Accordingly, the remains were assigned to a new species, *Australopithecus bahrelghazali*.[32,8]

The deposits in which Abel was found suggest *Australopithecus bahrelghazali* inhabited a lakeside environment incorporating rivers and streams with associated woodland.[10] Given that Abel remains the only known example of *Australopithecus bahrelghazali*, our knowledge is understandably very limited. We cannot really say whether it is indeed a distinct species, or simply a western offshoot of *Australopithecus afarensis*. Only further fossil evidence can confirm the situation.[8] If *Australopithecus anamensis*, *Australopithecus afarensis* and *Australopithecus bahrelghazali* were indeed all variants of the same species, the fact that they colonised a wide range of habitats suggests considerable behavioural flexibility.

Despite these discoveries, some anthropologists believed that hominin diversity in East Africa should have been greater during the period from four to three million years ago, noting that an apparent increase is seen after three million years ago. Between 1998 and 1999, a team carried out field work on the western shore of Lake Turkana to see if this really was the extent of Middle Pliocene hominin diversity in the region. They recovered a number of hominin remains aged between 3.3 and 3.5 million years old, including a largely-complete but distorted skull. On the basis of its distinctive flat-faced anatomy, the skull was assigned to its own genus and described as *Kenyanthropus platyops* ('flat-faced man of Kenya'). The team claimed the skull as evidence of the missing hominin diversity. They also noted similarities between the skull's facial architecture and that of *Homo rudolfensis*, a much-debated possible early human species that we shall encounter in Chapter 5.[33]

The assignment of the skull to a new genus was not universally accepted. Some believed that the apparent shape of the skull arose from its distortion, and that '*Kenyanthropus*' may simply be an early Kenyan variant of *Australopithecus afarensis*.[34] It could be that the only hominins from this period were *Australopithecus afarensis* and possibly late survivors of *Ardipithecus*, but new hominin species were about to come onto the scene.

The First of the Great South Africans

The first ever discovery of a bipedal ape was made in South Africa in 1924, so starting an as yet unresolved battle with the East African countries to be recognised as the birthplace of the human lineage. Two years earlier, a talented young Australian anatomist named Raymond Dart had accepted the position of Professor of Anatomy at the newly-founded University of Witwatersrand in Johannesburg. Dart seems to have had an unorthodox turn of mind and is said to have had a "*scorn for accepted opinion*". These qualities did not endear him to the scientific establishment and were probably what led to his being offered a position far from mainstream academe. The facilities at his new post were somewhat basic and while doing everything he could to improve matters in the University's anatomy department, he soon turned to non-medical interests including anthropology.[35]

Investigating a box of fossil-bearing rock from a limestone quarry in Taung in North West Province, Dart discovered fossilised remains of a juvenile apelike creature. The remains comprised the face, part of the skull, the complete lower jaw and a brain endocast (a cast of the inside of the braincase), the latter forming naturally when material within the skull hardened to rock. The brain was small, like that of an ape, but the foramen magnum was placed centrally, which as we saw in Chapter 3 implied that the animal was a biped. The teeth were more humanlike than apelike. Dart described what became known as the Taung Child in February 1925 in the journal *Nature*, naming it *Australopithecus africanus* ('Southern ape of Africa').[36]

Dart's claim was strongly criticised at the time, largely because it flew in the face of the then-accepted 'brains first' model. In the early part of the last century there was much debate about which came first; small-brained bipedal apes or smart tree-climbing apes. In the 1920s, prevailing academic opinion supported the 'brains first' model. Its proponents included the prominent Scottish anthropologist Sir Arthur Keith, and Henry Fairfield Osborn, director of the American Museum of Natural History. They were supported by the supposed evidence of *Eoanthropus Dawsoni* ('Dawson's Dawn Man), better known as Piltdown Man, a humanlike skull with an apelike jaw.[10] As early as 1923, the German anatomist Franz Weidenreich exposed the now-notorious Piltdown Man as a hoax, but his conclusions were not widely accepted for another thirty years.

Dart's find was widely dismissed as a fossilised ape and he was even criticised for introducing the term *Australopithecus*, which critics complained was a mishmash of Latin and Greek. However, in 1936 the Scottish palaeontologist Robert Broom, a long-time supporter of Dart, instigated new searches for early human fossils. He soon discovered the braincase of an adult specimen in a set of limestone caves at Sterkfontein near Krugersdorp, 25 km (15 miles) northwest of Johannesburg. Further finds followed at nearby Kromdraai in 1938, but then World War II intervened and the sites were closed down for the duration of hostilities. Broom (who was in his seventies) spent the war years preparing a monograph on the finds. This was published in 1946, after which the australopithecines were generally accepted as bipedal apes. Broom assigned his finds to two species, *Plesianthropus transvaalensis* ('Near-man from the Transvaal') and *Paranthropus robustus* ('robust alongside-man'). After the war, now assisted by palaeontologist John T. Robinson, Broom resumed his excavations, and in April 1947, the pair discovered the nearly complete adult skull of a female *Plesianthropus* that became popularly known as Mrs Ples. A fossilised pelvis, vertebral column and fragmentary rib and thigh bone were also discovered by Broom in 1947 at Sterkfontein, and these may be part of the same individual as Mrs Ples. *Plesianthropus transvaalensis* is now regarded as the same species as *Australopithecus africanus*.[9]

Australopithecus africanus lived rather later than *Australopithecus afarensis*, and is known from 2.8 to 2.3 million years ago.[8] The species is known only from four sites, all in South Africa. Its habitat ranged from wet forest with high rainfall to dry partially-wooded savannah.[27] It might have evolved from *Australopithecus afarensis* though this is by no means certain,[26] and its relationship (if any) to later hominins is also uncertain.

Australopithecus africanus is a puzzling mixture of humanlike and apelike characteristics. The skull and dentition are more humanlike than those of *Australopithecus afarensis*; but *Australopithecus africanus* is more apelike in its limb proportions. Its arms are longer than its legs, suggesting that it was a more proficient tree climber than the earlier species.[8] Even at this comparatively late stage, it seems, hominins were spending a significant amount of time in the trees. According to Henry McHenry's calculations, *Australopithecus africanus* was still sexually dimorphic, but less so than *Australopithecus afarensis*. Males were estimated to measure 1.38 m (4 ft. 6 in.) tall and weigh 41 kg (90 lb.); females measured 1.15 m (3 ft. 9 in.) tall and weighed 30 kg (66 lb.).[30] Given that doubts have been raised about McHenry's dimorphism estimates for *Australopithecus afarensis*, it is probably wise to be cautious about these figures, although no revised estimates are yet available for *Australopithecus africanus*.

Sterkfontein has continued to yield hominin fossils. It is now part of the Cradle of Humankind, a World Heritage Site named by UNESCO in 1999. In 2004, Mrs Ples made the Top 100 in SABC3's television series *Great South Africans*, placing her in the company of Nelson Mandela, Steve Biko and Dr Christiaan Barnard.

Confusion grows over human ancestry

As by now will be apparent, the evolutionary history of the australopithecines is nowhere near fully understood, and it is also far from clear where the earliest humans fit into the picture. Even the

The symbolic ape

geographical location of where the earliest humans emerged remains uncertain, with rival claims being made for East Africa and South Africa. The traditional claimants are *Australopithecus afarensis* from East Africa versus *Australopithecus africanus* from South Africa. From one of these two, it is commonly supposed that the first human species, *Homo habilis*, arose. This in turn gave rise to the more modern *Homo erectus*.

Matters have become increasingly confused since the latter part of the last century, with two new species claimed as ancestral to the earliest humans. The first discovery was made in Ethiopia. Between 1996 and 1998, a team excavating the Bouri Formation at Middle Awash recovered a number of hominin remains including a partial skeleton. Together with remains recovered in 1990, they were ascribed to a new species of australopithecine, which received the name *Australopithecus garhi*; 'garhi' means 'surprise' in the Afar language. The remains were 2.5 million years old; very close in time to the emergence of the first humans. Its discoverers claimed that that it evolved from *Australopithecus afarensis*, with which it had similarities. However, there were also significant differences, including the positioning of its cheekbones and its larger back teeth. The cranial capacity remained apelike, at 450 cc; nevertheless its discoverers suggested that it was in the right place at the right time to be the ancestor of the first humans, and that there was nothing to preclude it from that status. They added, though, that *Australopithecus africanus* could not be ruled out as a human ancestor.[37]

South Africa's claimant is *Australopithecus sediba*, a new australopithecine species announced in 2010. The discovery was made at Malapa, part of a now-eroded cave system located in the Cradle of Humankind World Heritage Site about 15 km (9.3 miles) northeast of the hominid-bearing sites of Sterkfontein and Swartkrans, and about 45 km (28 miles) from Johannesburg.[38] The recovery effort was led by Lee Berger, a palaeoanthropologist at the University of the Witwatersrand, Johannesburg. The find was made when Matthew, Lee's nine-year-old son, discovered a hominin collar bone embedded in a rock.[39]

The find comprised two extremely well-preserved partial skeletons that were initially thought be somewhere between 1.78 and 1.95 million years old,[40] later revised to 1.977 million years.[41] These estimates were obtained with a combination of uranium series, palaeomagnetic and faunal dating methods. The skeletons belonged to a juvenile male (MH1) aged 12 to 13 at time of his death, and an adult female (MH2).[38] They were found together buried in alluvial sediment, along with the remains of wildcats, hyenas and a number of other mammals. It is thought that on the ground above the cave system were a number of 'death traps', or long vertical shafts, down which the animals fell, probably attracted by the smell of damp. The pair – possibly mother and son – might have fallen to their deaths while searching for water. The sediments imply that subsequent high-volume water inflow, perhaps the result of a large storm, caused a debris flow. This carried the bodies deeper into the cave, to deposit them along a subterranean stream.[40]

The finds were assigned to a new australopithecine species, *Australopithecus sediba*; the word 'sediba' means 'fountain' or 'wellspring' in the Sotho language. The more complete skull of the juvenile MH1 has a capacity of 420 cc, probably at least 95 percent of adult size. The remains share many similarities with *Australopithecus africanus*, but there are also significant differences. Humanlike features include smaller molars and premolars; less pronounced cheekbones; and certain features of the pelvis. The lower-to-upper limb bone proportions are also similar to those of later humans such as *Homo erectus* – and indeed are unlike the more apelike proportions of *Homo habilis*. The anatomy of its hip, knees and ankles suggest that *Australopithecus sediba* was a habitual biped. Overall, it was claimed that *Australopithecus sediba* shares more derived (non-apelike) features with early humans than it does with other australopithecines. However, Berger decided to classify the new discovery as an australopithecine rather than a human.[38]

The initial announcement of *Australopithecus sediba* attracted extensive news coverage, but not everybody was convinced by the claims made for it. Australian anthropologist Darren Curnoe was reported[42] as claiming that *Australopithecus sediba* is in the wrong place at the wrong time to be a human ancestor. He noted that *Homo habilis* emerged in East Africa well before the time of *Australopithecus sediba*. However, his argument does assume that *Homo habilis* is indeed an early human. As we shall see in Chapter 5, this may not be the case. On the other hand, it is possible that at least some of *Australopithecus sediba*'s humanlike features evolved independently. Thus they may not necessarily imply shared ancestry.[43]

Nevertheless, subsequent studies do support Berger's initial claims. They suggest that aspects of the brain, dentition, pelvis, hand and foot of *Australopithecus sediba* could indeed be interpreted as incipient humanlike features. A virtual endocast of the brain, obtained from x-ray tomography, revealed an australopithecine-like size and pattern of convolutions. However, the orbitofrontal region (located behind the eyes) shows possible development towards humanlike frontal lobes. The frontal lobes are located at the front of the brain, behind the eyes and forehead, and in modern humans they are responsible for many of the higher brain functions, including planning and reasoning. Possibly some neural reorganization of the brain preceded its later size increase in early humans.[44]

The teeth are a mosaic of primitive and derived traits. Cladistic analysis of 22 dental traits suggests that *Australopithecus sediba* was a sister species of *Australopithecus africanus* (i.e. the two shared a common ancestor) and that the two were further evolved in the direction of early humans than were the australopithecines from East Africa.[45] However, the lower jawbone and dentition (especially canines and premolars) are below the size range for *Australopithecus africanus* and inside the size range for early humans. This confirms that *Australopithecus sediba* was a distinct species from *Australopithecus africanus* and not merely a late-surviving form of that species.[46]

The upper ribcage of *Australopithecus sediba* exhibits an apelike funnel shape, unlike the barrel shape associated with *Homo*. The funnel shape, as previously noted, may be an adaptation to under-branch suspensory locomotion. The barrel shape may be associated with the increased chest volume and lung function necessary for endurance walking and running. The lower thorax, however, appears less flared than that of apes and more closely approximates the form found in humans.[15] The spine is long and flexible, a form that has more in common with early *Homo* than with other australopithecines; curvature of the lower spine is a hallmark of walking upright.[47]

The upper limbs are still predominantly apelike, suggesting the retention of substantial climbing and suspensory abilities.[48] The hands show a mixture of australopithecine and human features. They retain adaptations for tree-climbing, but there is also a long thumb and shorter fingers, suggesting precision gripping of the type associated with tool manufacture and use.[49]

The pelvis and foot are a mosaic of apelike and humanlike characteristics that have not been seen in other hominins. These have been interpreted as adaptations to bipedalism, while retaining a degree of arboreal ability that would have aided survival in a dual terrestrial/arboreal world. However, the bipedal mechanics of *Australopithecus sediba* differed both from those of humans and those reconstructed for other australopithecines, suggesting that there might have been several forms of hominin bipedalism at this time.[50,51,52]

Although the evidence that *Australopithecus sediba* was a human ancestor is compelling, it is certainly not conclusive. Were we to have contemporary hominin fossils from East Africa in a comparable state of preservation, matters might become clearer, but unfortunately, this is not the case. We shall return to *Australopithecus sediba* and its possible relationship to early humans in Chapters 5 and 6.

A hominin dead end

If we accept that either *Australopithecus garhi* or *Australopithecus sediba* were on the line of evolution leading to the first humans, then what of *Paranthropus robustus*, the species discovered in South Africa by Robert Broom before World War II? The discovery was the first of what became known as a robust australopithecine. The australopithecines are traditionally divided into two 'types', the gracile (slender-built) australopithecines and the robust (big-boned) australopithecines. In addition to *Paranthropus robustus*, two other species are considered to be robust. *Paranthropus boisei* was discovered at Olduvai Gorge, Tanzania in 1959 by anthropologists Louis and Mary Leakey (we shall meet the Leakeys again in Chapter 5). The species was originally designated *Zinjanthropus boisei*; 'Zinj' is an ancient Arabic word for the coast of East Africa, and the name also honours expedition sponsor Charles Boise. The initial find comprised a skull, which was given the affectionate nickname of 'Dear Boy' by Mary Leakey. The third robust species, *Paranthropus aethiopicus*, was discovered in 1968, but not described as a separate species until 1985. In that year, the American anthropologist Alan Walker recovered a skull at a site on the western shore of Lake Turkana that became known as the Black Skull, as it had been stained black by the high manganese content of the material from which it was recovered. *Paranthropus robustus* is known from two sites in South Africa dating from 1.8 to 1.0 million years ago or possibly later, and *Paranthropus boisei* is known from sites in Tanzania, Kenya and Ethiopia dating from 2.3 to 1.2 million years ago or possibly later. The oldest (and last to be discovered) is *Paranthropus aethiopicus*, known from sites in Kenya and Ethiopia dating from 2.7 to 2.3 million years ago.[8]

The robust australopithecines emerged fairly late in the australopithecine era, and indeed for much of their career they were contemporary with early humans. While they probably evolved from a gracile ancestor, unfortunately much about their evolutionary history remains unclear.[9,53] Affinities with *Australopithecus afarensis* have been suggested on the basis of similarities of the lower jawbone,[54] and many schemes propose *Paranthropus aethiopicus* as the common ancestor of the other two.[55]

The term 'robust' is somewhat misleading. In comparison to the gracile australopithecines, the robust australopithecines had powerful jaws and large grindstone-like back teeth, but both types were otherwise very similar. The conventional explanation is that these features were adaptations to eating increased quantities of coarse fibrous gritty plant material such as seeds, roots and tubers – foods that the dentition of earlier australopithecines could not readily process. By now – the later part of the Pliocene – the climate of Africa had become increasingly arid and seasonal as the long-term global cooling continued. The ability to process tough food items is assumed have been essential to survive the dry season.[10,55] It is commonly supposed that the robust australopithecines were over-specialised, and lacked the flexible subsistence strategy needed to survive in the increasingly unstable climatic conditions that followed the onset of the Pleistocene.[27]

The true picture may be more complex. Carbon isotope data from the dental enamel of *Paranthropus robustus* individuals suggests that the species was not a dietary specialist. While grasses and sedges made up an important part of its diet, the intake of these foodstuffs was subject to considerable short-term variation. Not only was there seasonal change, but also variation from year to year. The latter might have reflected yearly differences in rainfall-affected foods, or possibly migration between wooded and more open environments.[56] Studies of dental microwear have suggested that tough food items were not eaten regularly and instead of specialising in such foods, the robust australopithecines relied on them only as a fallback.[57]

Despite this, measurements of strontium and barium levels relative to calcium in dental enamel suggest that diet of *Paranthropus robustus* was less varied than that of *Australopithecus africanus*, and did not include meat. By contrast, the diet of early humans was based more on meat, though it too was less varied than that of *Australopithecus africanus*. Thus a possible scenario is that the broad-based dietary strategy of the gracile australopithecines became split between plant-eating robust australopithecines and meat-eating humans.[23] In the long run, the latter proved to be the better bet. The robust australopithecines survived for a very long time, but they were ultimately a dead end in the hominin story.

Mother of Invention

Could australopithecines have made and used stone tools? On the face of it, there is absolutely no reason why not. In the 1960s, primatologist Jane Goodall discovered that chimpanzees make use of tools, selecting and sometimes modifying particular objects for particular tasks – a behaviour previously thought to be unique to humans. The best known example of tool use is for 'termite-fishing', where small sticks or plant stems are inserted into a termite mound. When termites bite on the stick or plant stem, it is slowly withdrawn and the clinging termites may then be eaten. Sometimes, chimpanzees deliberately fray the ends of their tools before use, a technique that increases the number of termites caught.[58] Other objects used as tools include leaves for making sponges to extract water from deep holes, and stones for cracking nuts;[59] and chimpanzees appear to be capable of learning novel tool usages from their companions rather than having to re-invent these for themselves.[60] If chimpanzees and humans both make tools, then it is likely that the Last Common Ancestor (LCA) did also and by implication, the earliest hominins. Evidence for termite sticks will clearly not have survived, but how about early stone tools?

The oldest unequivocal stone artefacts currently known anywhere in the world are tools from the Gona River drainage region of Ethiopia, dated to 2.5 to 2.6 million years old by argon-argon and palaeomagnetic methods. Recovered between 1992 and 1994, the Gona tools are admittedly very basic, being little more than sharp-edged flakes together with the cores from which the flakes were removed. In addition to serving as a source for the flakes, the cores show evidence of pitting and bruising, suggesting that they were used as multi-purpose tools, possibly for hammering and pounding. The tools are similar to those of Oldowan tool industry, which are believed to be of human origin.[61,62]

No hominin remains were recovered in association with the tools, but in 1999, anthropologists working at the nearby Bouri Formation reported the discovery of large mammal bones bearing cut-marks apparently made by stone tools, possibly as a result of dismembering and filleting carcasses. Animals appeared to have been defleshed, and their long bones broken open, presumably to extract marrow. The bones were found in association with 2.5-million-year-old australopithecine remains, thought to be of *Australopithecus garhi*.[63]

Although *Australopithecus garhi* is one of the most recently-known australopithecine species, its brain was no larger than that of earlier australopithecines, and there is no reason to suppose that it was any more cognitively advanced. If it was capable of making stone tools, then earlier australopithecines should also have been capable of doing so. Direct evidence is lacking, but it has been claimed that 3.39-million-year-old animal bones from Dikika, Ethiopia, show stone tool cut-marks for flesh removal, and signs of having been struck with hammerstones to extract bone marrow.[64] In the absence of any associated tools, there is no way to tell whether the cut-marks were produced with specially-made tools or naturally-sharp pieces of stone. Some are sceptical and argue that as the bones were buried in coarse-grained, sandy deposits, it is likely that trampling by animals produced the marks.[65] Unambiguous evidence for carcass processing by hominins does not occur in the archaeological record until around two million years ago.[66]

If australopithecine tool use was widespread, then one might perhaps have expected unambiguous evidence to have by now come to light. Stone tools are far more durable than animal remains and therefore turn up more frequently. Yet no pre-Gona artefacts have yet been found, and even the Gona artefacts lack a direct association with australopithecines. Could australopithecines really have made and used stone tools?

In the 1980s, archaeologist Nicholas Toth[67] carried out experiments in replicating Oldowan artefacts. Although technically crude, regular production of such stone tools does require a certain amount of skill. There are a number of possible techniques for stone knapping or obtaining stone flakes from a core, but experiments have shown that the most efficient method is one known as percussion knapping. Three conditions must be met to successfully produce flakes. Firstly, a core must be chosen that has an edge with an acute angle (less than 90 degrees), near which a hammer blow can be struck; secondly, the core must be struck a glancing blow about 1 cm (0.4 in.) away from the edge; and thirdly, the blow must be directed through an area of high mass such as a ridge or a bulge. Toth's studies of cores and flakes at archaeological sites suggested that early tool-makers had indeed mastered percussion knapping and used it to the exclusion of the other less efficient techniques.

The big question was, could such a technique be mastered by an ape? If so, there would be no reason to suppose that Oldowan stone tools could not have been made by australopithecines. Archaeologist Thomas Wynn and primatologist William McGrew[68] posed the question as to whether, given opportunity and motivation, an ape could make Oldowan tools. They concluded that the skills were no more demanding than those demonstrated by chimpanzees when making tools from twigs.

The next step was to test the theory experimentally. Nicholas Toth collaborated with primatologist Sue Savage-Rumbaugh, who had spent many years working with a male bonobo named Kanzi.[69] Kanzi had learned to use a large vocabulary of words displayed on a keyboard, and to understand complex English sentences. Toth encouraged Kanzi to make sharp stone flakes that could then be used to obtain a food reward from a box secured with string. Kanzi was able to make flakes and obtain his reward, but only by knocking cobbles together or smashing them against another hard object. He never used percussion knapping, despite being shown the technique.

It is uncertain if Kanzi's unimpressive performance arose from cognitive limitations, anatomical limitations of arms, wrists and hands (compared with a human), or simple lack of motivation given the cruder flakes he produced were fit for the purpose of obtaining the food reward. However, the fact that he did obtain usable flakes does suggest that early hominins might have done the same. Unfortunately, flakes and battered rocks of the type that resulted from Kanzi's tool-making activities can also be produced by purely natural forces. It would therefore be hard to demonstrate that such items were genuine artefacts. On the other hand, evidence for the use of such tools would show up in the form of cut-marks on animal bones arising from butchery practices. This appears to be so, albeit the evidence is confined to just the two cases.

It could be that meat-eating and hence tool use were infrequent practices, possibly only adopted in times and places where other food sources were scarce. This does beg the question as to why only *Australopithecus garhi* made recognisable tools, assuming that it was responsible for the Gona artefacts. The answer may be connected to the increasingly arid and seasonal climate of Late Pliocene Africa. Faced with reduced and seasonal availability of traditional food items, *Australopithecus garhi* and indeed other late australopithecines might have responded by adding more meat to their diet. The increased requirements to butcher carcasses led, over time, to the refinement of tool-making techniques, and eventually recognizable artefacts were produced. Hominins had always possessed the ability, but never before the need to make such tools. However, when faced with the need, necessity proved to be the mother of invention.

Did the australopithecines leave Africa?

The generally accepted view is that the australopithecines remained confined to Africa throughout their long career. It is certainly true that no australopithecine remains have ever been found in Asia, but absence of evidence is not evidence of absence. Very few fossils of any vertebrate species have been found for the Late Pliocene and Early Pleistocene of Southwest Asia, despite this region being larger than Kenya, Ethiopia and Tanzania combined. For millions of years, Africa and Eurasia have formed a single landmass, and it is purely by convention that we regard Europe, Asia and Africa as separate continents. Early hominins are unlikely to have made the distinction, being guided purely by bio-geographical considerations. In fact, three million years ago, the grassland savannahs of Africa extended all the way from West Africa to northern China, and there are no obvious reasons why the australopithecines could not have expanded their range there. It is true that there is no evidence that they did, but this could simply reflect lack of preservation or even lack of fieldwork in what is after all a very large area.[70] As we shall see in subsequent chapters, there is good reason to suppose that early hominins did leave Africa ahead of the first generally-accepted migrant, *Homo erectus*. For now, though, we shall stay in Africa: we have reached the point in the human story where the first commonly-recognised human species, *Homo habilis*, makes its appearance.

5: Becoming human

Discoveries at Olduvai Gorge

Olduvai Gorge, Tanzania, is probably the best-known fossil hominin site in the world, and it has been instrumental in advancing our knowledge of early human evolution. Like Sterkfontein, it is often described as the Cradle of Mankind, and it too is now a UNESCO World Heritage Site. Running for 50 km (30 miles) along the eastern Serengeti, the steep-sided 100 m (330 ft.) deep ravine was discovered in 1911 by entomologist Wilhelm Kattwinkel, and takes its name from the Maasai word for the wild sisal plant growing in the gorge, 'oldupai'. Both Olduvai and the gorge's original name Oldoway are thought to be mispronunciations; locally it is referred to as Oldupai Gorge.

Today the region is largely dry, but just over two million of years ago, the Olduvai Basin contained a broad, shallow alkaline lake, around 3 m (10 ft.) in depth and varying in diameter from 7 to 15 km (4 to 9 miles). Over time, seasonal fluctuations in the water level deposited fine layers of ash from the volcanoes to the east, laying down successive strata along the shoreline. Eventually the lake dried up, but more recently a river cut through the layers of rock laid down by the ancient lake, revealing seven main layers or beds in the walls of the gorge. The earliest archaeological deposit, known as Bed I, has produced evidence of campsites and living floors along with stone tools.

From 1913 onwards, the German prehistorian Hans Reck led a number of expeditions to the gorge, and reported fossils that later attracted the interest of Louis Leakey, a research fellow of St. John's College Cambridge. Leakey first investigated the site in 1931, and recovered a number of artefacts. These included a stone chopping tool now on display in the British Museum, one of the oldest objects in the museum's collection at 1.8 million years old. Leakey classed the artefacts as Oldowan, for the then still-current name Oldoway Gorge.

The following year, after returning to England and in need of an illustrator for his book *Adam's Ancestors*, Leakey was introduced to Mary Nichol, who had illustrated tools found at Hembury, a Neolithic site near Honiton, Devon. Soon afterwards, Leakey left his wife Frida for Mary. While this would hardly lead to a raised eyebrow now, in the 1930s it caused a major scandal. It effectively ended Leakey's career at Cambridge, and it was not until 1935 that he was able to return to Olduvai. After obtaining his divorce from Frida, he and Mary were married on Christmas Eve 1936, so establishing a dynasty of fossil-hunters spanning three generations, whose work continues to the present day. The outbreak of war forced the Leakeys to curtail their work at Olduvai Gorge, but they returned in 1951. They continued to make regular visits throughout the 1950s, recovering large samples of artefacts and animal bones, in addition to the robust australopithecine skull 'Dear Boy' described in Chapter 4.

By 1960, the Leakeys had been joined in the field by their son Jonathan. In November of that year Jonathan and Mary found a lower jawbone with 13 teeth still in place, together with finger, hand and wrist bones. The find was the first example of a large-brained hominin that the Leakeys would eventually describe as a new human species. Over the next three years further fossils were recovered and analysed with the help of primatologist John Napier and anthropologist Phillip Tobias. The new species was announced in the journal *Nature* early in 1964[1] and given a name suggested by Raymond Dart – *Homo habilis* ('Handy Man').

The first human species

As is so often the case with new scientific discoveries, *Homo habilis* caused a rumpus in the anthropological community, and it remains poorly-understood to this day. The fossils recovered from Olduvai Gorge are now known to be around 1.8 million years old. Similar fossils, aged 1.89 million years, have been recovered from Koobi Fora on the eastern shores of Lake Turkana, Kenya.[2] A problem is the lack of unequivocal fossil material: we have only eight skulls or partial skulls; postcranial remains are restricted to the hands, portions of a right arm and both legs, and a reasonably-complete foot. The latter is believed to have been parted from its owner by a crocodile. Most of the fossil material has been found in East Africa, but the skull STW 53 from Sterkfontein, South Africa, may also be *Homo habilis*.[3] The species has not been found outside Africa, and like the australopithecines, it is widely assumed that it never left there. However, as we shall see in Chapter 6, recent discoveries have led to suggestions that it might have reached the Caucasus, or even Southeast Asia. The oldest, albeit tentative, fossil evidence for *Homo habilis* to date is AL 666-1, a 2.33-million-year-old upper jawbone recovered at Hadar, Ethiopia, and dated by the argon-argon method. However, its describers have urged caution, and stress that its assignment to *Homo habilis* is only provisional.[4] The most recent *Homo habilis* fossil currently known is a 1.44-million-year-old partial upper jawbone from Koobi Fora.[5] If AL 666-1 is accepted, the species spans almost a million years in the fossil record, but the oldest uncontested *Homo habilis* remains are only 1.9 million years old.[6]

The cranial capacity ranges from 500 to 700 cc, though some commentators set the upper limit at around 600 cc.[7] *Homo habilis* is thus rather better endowed than the gracile australopithecines, whose cranial capacity never exceeded 520 cc, but it barely attained half the 1,350 cc average of a modern human. In comparison to the australopithecines, the skull of *Homo habilis* was less massively-built, and the upper and lower jawbones were within the human size range. The feet were humanlike, as were the thumb joints.[8]

Homo habilis did retain a number of australopithecine-like features such as proportionately long arms and short legs, and while these could have been rarely-needed vestigial relics of an australopithecine past, the long arms, together with hand bones do suggest *Homo habilis* might have retained some apelike tree-climbing ability.[9] There was a degree of sexual dimorphism not seen in later hominins. Males are estimated to have averaged around 1.57 m (5 ft. 1 in.) tall and weighed around 52 kg (114 lb.), whereas females were only around 1.25 m (4 ft. 1 in.) tall on average, with a weight of around 32 kg (70 lb.).[10] As with the australopithecines, though, these estimates should be treated with caution.

It is possible that some remains currently assigned to *Homo habilis* could actually belong to late australopithecines. In particular, it has been suggested that the Sterkfontein skull STW 53 is more primitive than that of *Australopithecus sediba*. It may therefore represent *Australopithecus africanus* and not *Homo habilis*. This in turn would cast doubt on other fossils assigned to *Homo habilis* on the basis of comparisons to the Sterkfontein skull.[11] Making accurate diagnoses of fragmentary remains is often problematic and it should be remembered that fossils such as 'Lucy' and *Australopithecus sediba* are very much the exception. Unfortunately, we do not currently have an example of *Homo habilis* in anything like such a state of preservation.

Was there a second species?

Overall, there is considerable variability within the material broadly assigned to *Homo habilis*, and there has been a long-running suspicion that it actually represents more than one species. In 1986,

Soviet anthropologist Valery Alekseyev proposed assigning a 1.89-million-year-old fossil skull from Koobi Fora to a new human species, *Homo rudolfensis*. The name comes from Lake Rudolf, which was the former name for Lake Turkana. Discovered in 1972, the skull had previously been assigned to *Homo habilis*, but Alekseyev noted that it has a flatter, broader face and larger teeth.[8,7] The cranial capacity has recently been estimated at 700 cc,[12] right at the upper end of the range for *Homo habilis*. However, when related to estimates of body mass based on eye socket size, the brain is not unduly large for an archaic hominin.[7]

Following the 1986 announcement, a number of fossils were reassigned to *Homo rudolfensis*, including other specimens from Koobi Fora, some from Chemeron in Kenya, and some from Uraha in Malawi. Unfortunately, these did not include any postcranial remains.[13,7] The existence of *Homo rudolfensis* as a separate species has remained controversial, although fossils recovered at Koobi Fora in 2012 are said to confirm its distinctiveness from *Homo habilis*. The fossils range in age from 1.78 to 1.95 million years old, and include the well-preserved face of an adolescent, a nearly-complete lower jawbone, and a fragment of a lower jawbone. The face shares many of the features that distinguish the original 1972 find from other specimens of early *Homo*.[14]

It remains an open question as to where *Homo rudolfensis* belongs in the scheme of human evolution. It shares facial similarities with the flat-faced 3.5-million-year-old *Kenyanthropus platyops* skull, the evolutionary significance of which remains unclear.[15] However, on that basis Australian anthropologists David Cameron and Colin Groves[2] reject *Homo* status for *Homo rudolfensis* altogether. They accept that it is a genuine species, but suggest that it probably evolved from *Kenyanthropus platyops*. Cameron and Groves do not feel *Homo rudolfensis* is part of *Homo* and suggest that it be reclassified as *Kenyanthropus rudolfensis*, completely removing it from the human line.

Humanity questioned

Is *Homo habilis* genuinely human? This really depends on what you mean by 'human', and part of the controversy attending the 1964 announcement arose from its brain size being rather smaller than the 750 cc proposed as the human minimum by Sir Arthur Keith. Its retention of apelike limbs and tree-climbing abilities has led some to doubt whether it should be classed within Genus *Homo*,[16] the grouping that includes all human species. Indeed, some literature does refer to it as *Australopithecus habilis*.[17,18] Could *Homo habilis* become the anthropological equivalent of the now ex-planet Pluto?

A key question is whether or not *Homo* as currently constituted represents a clade (i.e. a genuine lineage) within the hominins. For *Homo* to be a clade, firstly, it must contain all the recognised members and only the recognised members, including *Homo habilis* (and *Homo rudolfensis*); secondly, there must be a common ancestor that itself is a member of *Homo*; and thirdly, all the descendants of that common ancestor must also be members of *Homo*, i.e. they cannot be australopithecines. To determine whether or not this is the case is easier stated than accomplished. A grouping like *Homo* requires much finer resolution than broader groupings such as vertebrates, mammals or primates. To obtain a set of features unique to *Homo* means that a large number of anatomical details must be considered in minute detail. Matters are not helped by the fact that all but a single species within *Homo* are now extinct.

A number of studies have been conducted using cladistic analysis, but they have proved inconclusive. Some have suggested that *Homo* is only a valid lineage if *Homo habilis* and *Homo rudolfensis* are removed.[19] Others exclude only *Homo rudolfensis*, leaving *Homo habilis* within *Homo*.[2] A wide-ranging cladistic study of skull characteristics suggested that both *Homo habilis* and *Homo rudolfensis* can both be accommodated within *Homo* without having to include any of the australopithecines.[20] However, anthropologist Bernard Wood[7,21] believes that clades should not be the only consideration.

To be included in *Homo*, he argues, hominins must be of a similar 'grade' in terms of diet and locomotion. The comparisons should be made with reference to the first species to have been included in *Homo*, i.e. *Homo sapiens*. Wood believes that *Homo habilis* differs so greatly from *Homo sapiens* in terms of dentition and limb proportions that it should not be included in *Homo*.

Even if *Homo habilis* is accepted as a member of *Homo*, it remains uncertain whether or not it was the ancestor of any later hominins, and its own ancestry is also the subject of widespread disagreement. The traditional view is that it arose from either *Australopithecus afarensis* or *Australopithecus africanus*. More recently, as we saw in Chapter 4, *Australopithecus garhi* has been proposed as a possible ancestor. *Homo habilis* is commonly thought to have given rise to the undisputedly-human *Homo erectus*, but as we shall see in Chapter 6 there are a number of other possibilities, including the recently-discovered *Australopithecus sediba*.

Cognitive abilities of *Homo habilis*

There is no evidence in *Homo habilis* for the range of complex behaviours associated with modern humans, although it has been suggested that the species might have employed some form of language. Phillip Tobias[22] examined an endocast (in this case a plaster cast of the inside of the braincase) of a well-preserved *Homo habilis* skull from Koobi Fora. He concluded that the brain's sulcal and gyral patterns (these are the ridges and furrows that give the human brain its wrinkled look) were more humanlike than apelike. He also found that the frontal and the parietal lobes were enlarged, and that the Broca's Area was expanded in comparison to the same region in australopithecines and modern apes. The frontal lobes, which control higher brain functions including planning and reasoning, are located at the front of the brain. Behind them, on the top and on each side of the brain are the parietal lobes, which carry out a wide range of functions including spatial awareness and the processing of sensory information.

In modern humans, the Broca's Area is a region of the brain known since the nineteenth century to be associated with speech. It is located in the frontal lobe of the brain's left hemisphere and is named for Paul Broca, a French physician who noted a connection between damage to this area and the condition now known as Broca's Aphasia. This is a language disorder that leaves patients unable to speak in a grammatically-correct manner.[23] Understandably, these suggestions have proved controversial, and some reject endocast evidence altogether.[7] Given the current state of our understanding of the factors controlling brain growth and shape, and that the cognitive implications of these changes in brain shape are almost entirely unknown, it is best to be cautious.[24]

It should be noted that *Homo habilis* and modern humans have far smaller brains than do elephants and whales. The obvious question, then, is why are they not as intelligent as we are? The answer is that the absolute brain size of an animal is not a wholly-reliable guide to its 'braininess'. Elephants and whales are far larger than humans and need larger brains to co-ordinate body movements and perform various 'housekeeping' tasks such as breathing and maintaining correct body temperature. There isn't any capacity left over for more advanced behaviours.

A more reliable guide to brainpower is the encephalization quotient (EQ), a function of brain size in relation to the size of the animal as a whole. Various formulae are used to calculate the EQ and some calculations are based on the neocortex or 'grey matter' rather than total brain mass. Regardless of the method used, mammals tend to have higher EQs than other vertebrates such as fish and reptiles; and primates in turn tend to have higher EQs than other mammals. Based on his body mass calculations, Henry McHenry[10] estimated the EQ for a number of early hominins. The australopithecines ranged from 2.4 to 3.1, but *Homo habilis*, at 3.1, did no more than hit the top end of the australopithecine range. For comparison, chimpanzees are 2.0 and modern humans come in at 5.8. However, calculations based on neocortex ratios do put *Homo habilis* slightly ahead of the australopithecines, ranging from 3.30 to 3.49 in comparison to 3.15 to 3.33.[25] Given the inherent problems of trying to estimate body masses and cranial capacities from the very limited fossil material available, one should be cautious about drawing too many inferences from these figures. However, it is probably reasonable to conclude that in cognitive terms, *Homo habilis* was an incremental rather than step improvement on earlier hominins.

The Oldowan tool industry

Homo habilis is associated with the Oldowan tool industry, the oldest and most primitive of all stone tool industries, beginning about 2.5 to 2.6 million years ago and persisting for over a million years. If it did start with *Homo habilis*, the Oldowan tool industry was certainly not unique to them and was continued by subsequent hominins, both in Africa and later in Eurasia. As we saw in Chapter 4, though, it is possible that stone tools were also produced by late australopithecines using similar techniques. In all probability the Oldowan wasn't a single 'industry' as such, and was re-invented on many occasions.

The Oldowan is characterised by simple cores (cobbles), sharp-edged flakes that have been detached from such cobbles, and hammerstones. The flakes were occasionally retouched (intentionally reshaped) by striking off small chips to sharpen or reshape the edges.[26] Tools of this type are also categorised as Mode 1 under a scheme proposed by British archaeologist Sir Grahame Clark, whereby stone tools are classified into five categories or modes that range from the simplest (Mode 1) to the most advanced (Mode 5).[27] An archaeologist devising such a scheme now would probably use the word 'generation' instead of 'mode'. Thus Oldowan artefacts may be thought of as first generation stone tools; later stone tools are second through to fifth generation.

Initially, Oldowan artefacts were categorised by Mary Leakey into a range of types including choppers, scrapers, awls, anvils and hammerstones. However, Nicholas Toth's experiments with replicating Oldowan artefacts (see Chapter 4) showed that all these so-called 'types' can result from simply flaking stone cobbles to produce sharp stone flakes. Toth also managed to show that while the flakes are useful cutting tools, the cores are of little value. This suggests that the cores were not finished tools but merely by-products left over from the production of the flakes, and that the flakes were the most important tools, used for animal butchery. The hammerstones might have been used to detach flakes from cores, and also to break open animal bones to extract bone marrow.[28]

Food for Thought?

As we have just seen, *Homo habilis* represented an advance in brainpower over earlier hominins, albeit a modest one. The question is why did it need to wise up? Over-sized brains might sound like a good idea, but the same could be said of owning a Rolls-Royce. The problem in both cases is that they are expensive to run, and there is a pretty good case for trying to get by without. Brain tissue requires over 22 times as much energy as an equivalent amount of muscle tissue. In a modern human, the brain uses around 16 percent of the body's energy budget despite making up just 2 percent of the body's overall mass. While the energy costs of the smaller *Homo habilis* brain were less, they were still considerable.

Before asking why such a brain evolved, we should ask how it was possible in the first place. In 1995, Leslie Aiello and Peter Wheeler proposed the expensive tissue hypothesis. They argued that to compensate for the energy used by an over-sized brain, another part of the body would have to cut down its energy consumption. It turns out that the brain isn't the only 'gas guzzling' organ; the heart, liver, kidneys and gut also consume disproportionally large amounts of energy. Of these, the size of the heart, liver and kidneys is more or less determined by the size of the organism. The theory goes on to claim that only in the gut is there any scope for downsizing. In other words you can have a big brain or a big gut, but you can't have both.[29]

Animals subsisting on a diet of low-quality hard to digest foods require large guts with complex fermenting chambers, ruling out any possibility of big brains. Only those whose diets are high in sugars and proteins can downsize to smaller simpler guts, and so sustain the energy costs of a large brain; this in turn implies a diet of high-quality foods. Meat is ideal, being nutritious with high protein content. The expensive tissue hypothesis meshed well with the then-current view that the small-brained australopithecines were vegetarians with large guts. Large-brained humans, on the other hand, ate meat and hence required smaller guts. The theory was originally tested across a wide range of anthropoid primates, and took into account the differing body sizes of the species tested.

The expensive tissue hypothesis is widely accepted, but recent work has cast some doubt upon it. The original calculations did not take into account body fat, variations in which can considerably affect overall body mass, as any weight-watcher will be aware. When fat-free body mass was considered, it was claimed that no correlation could be found between small guts and large brains. Instead, it was argued, brain enlargement must have come about through either a net increase in energy intake or for savings to be made elsewhere. Such measures might indeed have included an energy-rich meat-based diet. Others include food-sharing and other cooperative behaviours that reduce the per-calorie cost of obtaining food.[30]

Cooperative behaviours do suggest a link to brain size. Recall that the social brain hypothesis (see Chapter 2) proposes a link between primate brain size and social complexity. Could the increased brain size of *Homo habilis* have been associated with such increased social complexity and enabled it to live in larger groups? We saw that there was a relationship between group size and the relative size of the neocortex, but while we can measure the latter in existent species, it is rather harder for those that are long extinct. Fortunately, it turns out that for some groups of mammals, including primates, there is a simple relationship between neocortex size and overall brain size. Since overall brain size can often be estimated for extinct hominins, neocortex size can be calculated. In the case of *Homo habilis*, social group size was estimated to be 80, rather larger than the 60 to 70 estimated for the australopithecines.[25]

Living in larger social groups might have facilitated larger brains by reducing food costs through cooperative behaviours, though this leaves unexplained how and why larger social groups came about in the first place. Were smaller group sizes (requiring smaller brains) no longer adequate? If not, why not? The answer to this question may lie with climate change.

Hunter or scavenger?

At the onset of the Pleistocene, 2,588 million years ago, the Earth tipped into the Quaternary Ice Age. It followed 50 million years of climatic downturn, and was the first full-blown ice age for a quarter of a billion years. Cooler, arid conditions alternated with warm, wet conditions as ice sheets ebbed and flowed in higher latitudes. It is surely no coincidence that the appearance of larger-brained hominins followed so closely on the heels of the new ice age. For *Homo habilis*, behavioural flexibility would have been a considerable advantage in the face of the now constantly-changing availability and distribution of sources of food, and it is likely that both bigger brains and a greater number of individuals cooperating played a part. These factors evidently gave *Homo habilis* the edge over the robust australopithecines, for the simple reason that humans are here today and the robust australopithecines are not, but how did *Homo habilis* set about obtaining the high-quality food needed for its 'expensive' and/or 'social' brain?

Fifty years ago, the accepted view was that humans have always been hunter-gatherers. At a symposium held in Chicago in 1966 entitled '*Man the Hunter*', anthropologist Marshall Sahlins put forward the view that hunter-gatherers were the 'original affluent society', contradicting the then-popular view that hunter-gather societies were always near the brink of starvation. Sahlins' theory was based on the view that ethnographic data suggested hunter-gatherers had more leisure time than those living in an industrial society. Sahlins' theory has been criticised for a variety of reasons, but in any case his model cannot really be applied to hominin evolution. Modern hunter-gatherers have weaponry that can kill prey at a distance, such as the bow and arrow and the atlatl (spear-thrower); technology that was not available to early humans. Consequently, they would have been far less effective as hunters than modern hunter-gatherers.

The Chicago conference also identified the technical and organisational demands of hunting as being the driving force of hominin evolution. In this model, bipedal locomotion, tool manufacture and use, increased intelligence, and social cooperation were all tied up in an adaptation involving efficient hunting of mammals of all sizes.[27,26] However, in the late 1970s, the publications of South African archaeologist Glynn Isaac[31] brought about a paradigm shift. He proposed the food-sharing hypothesis, a theory that stated that hominins require a 'home base' for eating. The idea of food sharing and cooperation was central to the model, which also suggested that there was a division of labour between males and females. Males hunted large animals and scavenged carcasses, while females and juveniles concentrated on opportunistic hunting of small animals and gathering edible plants. Isaac later replaced this model with the central place foraging model. On this view, the main emphasis was on a safe refuge, with secondary importance given to food sharing. Isaac went on to become Professor of Anthropology at Harvard University, but sadly he died two years later aged just 46.

In the meantime, the American archaeologist Louis Binford[32] had put forward a rival theory. Binford was one of the founding fathers of the 'New Archaeology' movement of the 1960s, now known as processual archaeology. Processual archaeologists believe that they can interpret past cultural systems through archaeological evidence. Binford applied this approach to the early hominin sites at Olduvai Gorge. He compared these with carnivore scavenger sites, and assumed that any difference between the two could be attributed to hominin activity. He concluded that hominins were scavenging the kills and death sites of other predator-scavengers for low food value items. They were earning a living as lowly marginal scavengers, feeding on whatever was left over by lions, hyenas and vultures. On the basis of these findings he proposed the Scavenging hypothesis. This model stated that early hominins did not hunt at all, but roamed the savannah scavenging kills from other carnivores, thus obtaining only low-value food items.

One problem with the Isaac theory is that the 'home base' sites of modern hunter-gatherers differ from the Olduvai sites. Hunter-gatherers tend to use a site as a safe haven and occupy it for only a few weeks before moving on. However, at the Olduvai sites, material accumulated over five to ten years, and they were visited by carnivores that left tooth-marks on animal bones – hardly a safe haven. Some of the tooth-marks overlap cut-marks made by hominins with stone tools, implying the hominins got to the bones first. Other tooth-marks are overlapped by cut-marks, implying hominin scavenging from carnivore kills.[33]

In response to this problem, anthropologist Richard Potts[34] proposed the stone caching hypothesis. He noted that some rocks found at Olduvai sites do not occur naturally in the region, and must therefore have been brought in from further afield. He suggested that early hominins built up caches of stone for tool-making at convenient places, to which animal carcasses could be brought for butchery. Another theory,[35] proposed at about the same time, was that early hominins exploited woodlands near water sources. These locations provided medium-sized carcasses that could be scavenged for head contents and bone marrow, both of which would be left by other (non-tool-using) scavengers.

Despite all this research, our understanding of the subsistence strategies of *Homo habilis* remains limited, and there is no consensus as to which if any of the competing theories are correct. Archaeologist Steven Mithen[36] has suggested two factors for the lack of consensus. Firstly, the archaeological record is too poorly-preserved to draw definite conclusions. Secondly, *Homo habilis* was likely to have been flexible in its behaviour, switching between hunting and scavenging and between sharing food and simply eating it as circumstances dictated.

In conclusion, it remains uncertain how many species the *habilis* type represents, and how they should be categorised. What is clear is that they were larger-brained hominins that depended for their survival upon a high-quality diet and the ability to make and use tools. That they might have existed for as long as a million years is a testament to their success.

6: The first Diaspora – or was it?

About a boy

He lived 1.56 million years ago and based on dental considerations, he was probably somewhere from 8 ½ to slightly over 9 ½ years old when he died.[1] What were the circumstances of his untimely death? Were others left who mourned his passing? We simply don't know. All we know is that he died, and was rapidly buried by natural processes on the edge of a marsh. In August 1984, his remains came to light when fossil-hunter Kamoya Kimeu was prospecting for fossils along the south bank of the Nariokotome River, 5 km (3 miles) west of Lake Turkana. Kimeu was a long-time assistant of Richard and Meave Leakey, and his team was planning to move camp next day after failing to discover any hominin remains. While carrying out a final search of the area on his own, he came across a small skull-fragment that he recognised to be of human origin. Together with anthropologist Alan Walker, the Leakeys spent the next four years excavating the find spot, and they eventually recovered a complete skull and most of the skeleton. When it was found to represent an adolescent male, the skeleton was dubbed the 'Turkana Boy' by its discoverers. It is even more complete than Lucy, with only some small hand and foot bones missing.[2]

We saw in Chapter 5 that there is doubt as to whether *Homo habilis* should be classified in *Homo*, but the Turkana Boy was unquestionably human. He was 1.62 m (5 ft. 3 in.) tall at the time of his death, and had he lived to adulthood it is estimated that he would have attained a height of 1.85 m (6 ft. 1 in.) or more, tall even by modern standards.[3] His short arms, in relation to his legs, were like those of a modern human. Unlike *Homo habilis*, he had abandoned any residual reliance on tree-climbing. His narrowed pelvis increased the energy efficiency of his leg muscles, and the lower part of his ribcage was narrowed accordingly. To compensate in terms of chest volume and lung function, the upper part of his ribcage expanded to give him the characteristic barrel-shaped chest of a modern human.[2]

Although the Turkana Boy's feet were not perfectly preserved, there is reason to suppose that they were essentially modern. Hominin footprints have been found preserved in two sedimentary layers near the town of Ileret, Kenya. They are 1.51 to 1.53 million years old, contemporary with the Turkana Boy and second in age only to the Laetoli footprints in Tanzania. The prints appear to have been made by a modern humanlike foot, arched with an in-line big toe. The prints reflect a movement and pressure distribution characteristic of modern human walking. The size of the prints is consistent with stature and body mass estimates of the Turkana Boy's people.[4]

The Turkana Boy was not entirely like a modern human and he possessed a mosaic of archaic and modern features. His braincase was long and low, a characteristic feature of early hominins, but differing from the globular braincase of modern humans. He had a flat and receding forehead and a prominent browridge over the eyes. His nose projected forward, with downward-orientated nostrils, similar to a modern human, unlike the more apelike *Homo habilis*. He was completely chinless, with massive, jutting jaws, and his teeth were intermediate in size between *Homo habilis* and modern humans. He had a pronounced occipital torus or horizontal ridge at the back of the head for the attachment of neck muscles.[5,2]

The Turkana Boy had a much narrower thoracic vertebral canal than a modern human. The vertebral canal is the space in the vertebral column through which the nerve-bearing spinal cord passes, and the thoracic vertebrae are those located between the neck and the base of the rib cage. The nerves passing through this region control breathing, and he might therefore have lacked the fine breathing control necessary for modern speech.[6] Like *Homo habilis*, the Turkana Boy's people were probably fairly limited in their use of language.

Another difference was that the Turkana Boy's overall rate of development and maturation were more rapid than those of a modern human. In primates, a strong correlation has been found between rate of dental development (ages when crown formation and root formation is completed) and overall development (characteristics such as adult brain weight, age of sexual maturity, and lifespan). Modern humans have a more prolonged dental development, reach sexual maturity later, and live longer than other primates.[7]

Dental enamel on a growing tooth is laid down in a 24-hourly growth cycle that remains preserved in the hard tissues of the crown and roots.[8,9] With the aid of suitable scanning techniques, growth increments can be counted rather like tree rings, and thus serve as a 'clock' to determine the time since eruption.[9,10] By using this technique, it has been shown that australopithecines and early humans had faster, more apelike rates of dental enamel growth than modern humans. Crown formation times for the Turkana Boy's back teeth were similar to those of the australopithecines, i.e. rather more rapid than those of modern humans. On this basis, his age has been estimated at 8 rather than 12 years old. The slow maturation of modern humans was evidently a later development.[1]

The Turkana Boy belongs to a species originally referred to as *Homo erectus*, but which many now class as a different species, *Homo ergaster* ('working man'). On the original definition, *Homo erectus* was a widespread and diverse species known from Africa and Eurasia,[11] but the tendency now is to reserve that term for the Eurasian fossil remains. There were dental differences between the two populations,[12] and African populations were also distinguished from their Eurasian counterparts by higher-domed and thinner-walled crania and less massive faces and browridges.[2] It remains disputed as to whether or not these differences justify the recognition of two separate species.[12] Here, the term *Homo erectus* is used for both, qualified as 'African' or 'Asian' where necessary. By whatever name however, the conventional view is that the Turkana Boy's people were the first hominins to leave Africa. Recent evidence has cast doubt on this view, as we shall see.

The oldest undisputed example of African *Homo erectus* is a 1.78-million-year-old skull from Koobi Fora, East Turkana, although the earliest evidence for the species may be a 1.87-million-year-old skull fragment.[13] African *Homo erectus* persisted until around 600,000 years ago.[5] These hominins colonised dryer, more seasonal African environments, where there was relatively little surface water or shade. Their physique was not unlike that of present-day humans living in equatorial East Africa, who have slim bodies and long limbs. This body-shape gives a higher surface area to volume ratio than the stockier build of, say, an Inuit, and is more efficient at dissipating (as opposed to conserving) heat. Another adaptation to the dry hot climate was the projecting, modern-like nose, which acted as a condenser, preventing moisture from being exhaled and so wasted. It is also likely that African *Homo erectus* was almost hairless, like a modern human, but unlike any previously-existing hominin including, in all probability, *Homo habilis*. This would have greatly aided heat dissipation.[2]

The degree of sexual dimorphism in *Homo erectus* was no greater than that of modern humans, suggesting a similar mating strategy (although as we saw in Chapter 3, the trend towards long-term and mutually-supportive relationships between males and females might have begun much earlier). It has also been suggested that the present-day helplessness of newborn babies might have had its origins with the Turkana Boy's people. In modern humans, the long-standing view is that pelvic constraints restrict brain growth before birth. Thus the narrowed pelvis of *Homo erectus* implies a lifestyle based on some form of mutually-supportive parenting.[14,2] In fact, recent work suggests that brain growth before birth may be constrained by energetic rather than pelvic factors. Comparisons with other primates suggest that there is a limit to how large a foetus can become in the womb before its metabolic needs become too great for the mother to support; birth must occur before this limit is exceeded.[15] The result, however, is the same in both cases: a limit to brain growth before birth, and the lengthy dependency of a newborn baby on its parents.

The fate of an adult female found at Koobi Fora provides evidence of a very different kind for mutually-supportive relationships among *Homo erectus*. Her partially-complete skeleton was discovered by Kamoya Kimeu eleven years before his discovery of the Turkana Boy. She lived around 1.7 million years ago[5] and shortly before her death, her bones had become brittle, fibrous and coarse-textured, suggesting a breakdown within the bone-forming cycle.[16] Such pathological symptoms are associated with a lethal condition known as hypervitaminosis A. This results from an excessive intake of vitamin A, such as may arise from eating the liver of a carnivore. It would have taken weeks if not months for pathological condition of the Koobi Fora female's bones to manifest itself, and throughout that time she could not have survived on her own. Somebody must have been feeding her, providing her with water and protecting her from carnivores – a human story the details of which we shall never know.[3]

That the livers of certain animals including dogs and polar bears are unsafe to eat has long been appreciated by people native to Polar Regions, such as the Inuit. Unfortunately, Europeans seem to have been rather slower to cotton on. In 1913, the Swiss explorer Xavier Mertz died and his colleague Douglas Mawson became gravely ill on an Antarctic expedition as a result of eating the liver of their sled dogs. This measure was forced upon them after most of their supplies fell into a crevasse.

Cognitive abilities of *Homo erectus*

The Turkana Boy's brain, though close to adult size, was just 880 cc, only slightly above the top end of the range for *Homo habilis*. The adult cranial capacity of African *Homo erectus* was around 900 cc.[5] This is just two-thirds of the average size for a modern human, although the latter does vary considerably. Even this slender advantage over *Homo habilis* was largely swallowed up by the greater size of African *Homo erectus*; in terms of encephalization quotient there was a modest increase to an estimated value of 3.3 based on Henry McHenry's calculations.[17] A more recent estimate, based on the Turkana Boy, suggests that the value was between 2.71 and 3.78;[18] only slightly above the 3.49 estimated maximum figure for *Homo habilis*.

Despite this, tool use by African *Homo erectus* was more sophisticated than that of *Homo habilis*, implying some increase in brainpower. By one million years ago, they had colonised large parts of Africa. The dispersal was certainly not a planned affair. From time to time, groups living on the periphery of the expansion outgrew available food and other essentials, and 'overspills' from such groups would migrate into a vacant territory. In most cases this probably did not involve moving very far, but over many generations these small moves added up to long-distance migrations. Their presence in diverse habitats such as the dryer peripheries of lake basins on the floor of the Great Rift Valley and the Ethiopian high plateau suggests that they were more flexible in their behaviour than *Homo habilis*, and able colonise regions that the latter could not.[5,2]

By 500,000 years ago, tantalising evidence emerges of symbolic behaviour in Asian *Homo erectus*.[19] Archaeologists studying freshwater mussel shells excavated in the nineteenth century at Trinil, Java discovered a geometric pattern of grooves engraved into one of the shells. The pattern, which was probably made with a shark's tooth, appears to have been intentionally-made and consists of a zigzag line with three sharp turns producing an 'M' shape, a set of more superficial parallel lines, and a zigzag with two turns producing a back-to-front 'N'. Another shell had been sharpened and polished for use as a cutting tool: the earliest-known example of the use of shells for tool-making.

In addition, the number of large adult mussels in the shell assemblage suggests that they were intentionally collected for eating. Seafood is a dietary adaptation was once thought to be exclusive to modern humans, beginning around 165,000 years ago. Subsequently it was discovered that Neanderthals were exploiting seafood on the Malaga coast 150,000 years ago. The Trinil shells show that the use of seafood by humans was a much earlier development. Seafood is nutritious and rich in fatty acids, which are essential to the developing brain of young mammals. Indeed, it has been suggested that access to such foods was essential to the evolutionary development of the human brain.[20]

The shells were excavated by Dutch anthropologist Eugene Dubois in 1891 during the course of his work in Java, which led to the discovery of *Homo erectus*. They now form part of the Dubois Collection in the Naturalis Biodiversity Centre in Leiden. Researchers dated sediments within the shells with argon-argon and luminescence methods to obtain an age range of 540,000 to 430,000 years old. Overall, the Trinil shells suggest that *Homo erectus* possessed a far greater behavioural flexibility than previously believed in terms of both tool-making technology and subsistence strategies. The engraved geometric pattern suggest that at least some capacity for symbolic thought was already present in early humans 500,000 years ago.

Marathon man

At the London 2012 Summer Olympics, Usain Bolt successfully defended his 100 and 200 metre titles, recording times of 9.63 and 19.32 seconds. Bolt has been hailed as the greatest sprint runner of all time, but humans are actually mediocre sprinters. Bolt sustained a speed of just over 10 m/sec (22 mph) for fractionally under 20 seconds in the 200 metre. These performances compare poorly with animals such as horses, greyhounds and antelopes, which can sustain a gallop of up to double the speed of Usain Bolt for several minutes. Furthermore, humans are energetically-inefficient runners. They use roughly twice the metabolic energy over the same distance than is typical for a mammal of equal size. For this reason, running has generally been considered to have played no major role in human evolution. What has been largely overlooked is the fact that humans are excellent endurance runners, able to cover long distances over extended time periods. At London 2012, gold medallist Mo Farah recorded a time of 27 min 30.42 sec in the 10,000 metre, or just over 6 m/sec (13.4 mph). Even an amateur jogger can average 3.2 to 4.2 m/sec (7.2 to 9.4 mph) for 10 km (6.2 miles) or more. This ability is not shared with other primates, and is rare among quadrupedal mammals. Even horses can only sustain a canter at 5.8 m/sec (13 mph) over long distances. That humans are so good at endurance running suggests that it is rather more than a spinoff from the evolution of bipedalism.

Biologists Dennis Bramble and Daniel Lieberman[21] have examined derived (in this case not shared with apes) human skeletomuscular features associated with running and walking. The features fall into four categories: energy efficiency, shock absorption, stability and temperature regulation. Around half of the features are useful only for endurance running, including a long Achilles tendon (a tendon passing behind the ankle); an enlarged gluteus maximus (the large muscle in the buttock); the ability of the shoulders to rotate independently of the head to allow better balance; and a more balanced head with a nuchal ligament (located at the back of the neck) to counter its tendency to pitch forward when running. Of the remaining features, nearly all benefit endurance running more than walking. These include larger surface areas in the ankle, knee and hip joints, and larger lumbar vertebrae, to provide enhanced shock absorption; and a tall, narrow body to help dissipate heat. Only

The symbolic ape

one feature provides equal benefit to both running and walking: longer legs, to enable a longer, more energy-efficient stride. Overall, the implication is that at some time in the past, endurance running – today no more than a form of exercise and recreation – was once necessary for survival.

Nearly all the features listed were present in *Homo erectus*. Some, such as the presence of a long Achilles tendon, cannot be verified due to incomplete fossil evidence. A few features were also present in *Homo habilis*. Bramble and Lieberman concluded that endurance running was an adaptation that was limited to *Homo* and appeared fairly early on, originating about two million years ago. The obvious question is, why, when walking is easier, safer and more energy-efficient? Bramble and Lieberman were unable to provide a definite answer, but suggested a role for either hunting or scavenging. Hunters might have run down their prey before killing it with close-range weapons. Although endurance running is uncommon among present-day hunter-gatherers, it has become largely unnecessary since the invention of long-range weapons such as the bow and arrow. Endurance running might also have helped early *Homo* to compete more effectively with other scavengers, including other hominins.

Today, the ultimate test of an endurance runner is to compete in the marathon. Indeed, the word 'marathon' has become synonymous with any lengthy or difficult task or operation. The marathon event takes its name from the story of the Greek soldier Pheidippides, who purportedly died of exhaustion after running to Athens to report a Greek victory at the Battle of Marathon, but the true origins of the marathon may be considerably more ancient.

Uncertainty over origins of *Homo erectus*

Once thought to be fairly straightforward, the origin of *Homo erectus* is now a subject of increasing controversy. The conventional view, still widely held, is that it evolved from *Homo habilis*, despite the marked contrasts between the two species. African *Homo erectus* might have appeared in a sudden 'punctuated' evolutionary event, triggered by increasingly fluctuating climatic conditions from around 1.7 to 1.9 million years ago.[22,2] By this time, the environment inside the East African Rift Valley had begun to vary rapidly between sustained wet and sustained arid conditions as a result of shifting wind patterns.[23]

Recent discoveries now pose a challenge to the view that *Homo erectus* evolved from *Homo habilis*. A report published in 2007 claimed that the two species had been sympatric (i.e. lived in the same or overlapping geographic regions) in the basin of Lake Turkana for almost half a million years. This conclusion was largely based on a 1.55-million-year-old skull and a 1.44-million-year-old partial upper jawbone, both recovered from Koobi Fora. The skull, known as KNM-ER 42700, was assigned to *Homo erectus*, although it was closer in size to *Homo habilis* with a cranial capacity of just 691 cc. The jawbone, known as KNM-ER 42703, was assigned to *Homo habilis*, implying that this species had survived until much more recently than had been previously believed. The report suggested that it was implausible for *Homo erectus* to have evolved from *Homo habilis*, since this evidence showed that the latter species had survived alongside its supposed successor.[24]

A possible scenario is that *Homo habilis* and *Homo erectus* both arose from a yet-to-be identified common ancestor. One problem is that the earliest fossil evidence for African *Homo erectus* does not appear until almost 1.9 million years ago, much later than that of *Homo habilis*. However, this would be much less of a problem if the AL 666-1 upper jawbone, supposedly from *Homo habilis* (see Chapter 5) does eventually turn out to be from something else, so virtually eliminating the gap between the first appearances of the two species.

If on the other hand the 'tangled bush' model (see Chapter 2) is correct and there were many branches of early hominin evolution, then *Homo habilis* and *Homo erectus* (and possibly *Homo rudolfensis*) could have emerged from separate branches at some time around two million years ago. This second view is consistent with the *Australopithecus sediba* evidence announced in 2010. As we saw in Chapter 4, its lower-to-upper limb bone proportions are closer to those of later *Homo* than they are to the more apelike proportions of *Homo habilis*. The implication – with the caveat that these features might have evolved more than once – is that *Australopithecus sediba* is a more plausible ancestor of *Homo erectus* than is *Homo habilis*.

A long production run

Buy a computer, a camera or a television set, and within a year at the most, something newer and better will be on the market. Not only do the products get updated, but every so often a completely new technology comes along, such as the smartphone, the tablet, or cloud computing. Against this background, the mature technology used in mechanical wristwatches has in recent years led to an astonishing revival in their popularity at the expense of the far more accurate and reliable quartz watch. Many expensive watches employ movements that have been in production for decades.

So imagine a technology that remained in use, with little change, for almost one and a half million years; that is to say, three-fifths of the entire span of human prehistory. Although the earliest African *Homo erectus* remains are associated with the same primitive Mode 1 Oldowan tools as *Homo habilis*, these soon gave way to the distinctive teardrop-shaped Acheulean 'hand-axes'. This tool type is named for Saint-Acheul in northern France, where examples were found in the mid-nineteenth century. It is artefacts of this type that John Frere and Jacques Boucher de Perthes first cited as evidence of the great time depth of human prehistory. In fact, these European examples are actually only about a quarter the age of the earliest-known Acheulean hand-axes, which are the 1.76 million years old examples found at Kokiselei, West Turkana. Oldowan tools have also been recovered from the same archaeological context, suggesting that both technologies were, for a while at least, in use at the same time.[25] Slightly younger Acheulean artefacts are known from East Turkana, from Konso in Ethiopia and from Peninj, near Olduvai Gorge.[2] The oldest-known non-African examples are the artefacts from Attirampakkam in southeast India, recently-dated by cosmogenic radionuclide techniques, and thought to be around 1.51 million years old.[26]

Acheulean tools are classified as Mode 2 on Sir Grahame Clark's tool complexity scheme, and may be thought of as second generation stone tools. The signature hand-axes were flat cobbles or large flakes that were completely flaked over on both sides to produce a sharp edge around the entire periphery. They are sometimes referred to as bifaces, although this term is applicable to any piece that has been worked on two sides. Many were teardrop-shaped, narrowing from a broad base at one end to a rounded point at the other. In addition to teardrops, other forms were often produced, including ovals and triangles. Some pieces had a sharp edge rather than a point opposite the base and are referred to as cleavers rather than hand-axes. The hand-axes, unlike Oldowan artefacts, were the first tools to be clearly beyond the abilities of non-human apes, requiring tool makers to concern themselves with overall shape of the finished artefact. Rather than simply producing sharp flakes, it was necessary to trim the hand-axe to produce cutting edges, and sides that converged to a pointed tip. Often, too, the hand-axes were symmetrical in two dimensions, with trimming on one edge being placed to match the opposite edge.[2,27]

From its beginning until it was finally abandoned 250,000 years ago, the Acheulean hand-axe industry displayed very little variation, although it wasn't entirely static. The later hand-axes do tend to be more refined and symmetrical than earlier ones, which are often much thicker and less extensively trimmed. However, by that time the makers were hominins with larger brains than *Homo erectus*. We shall return to the connection between brain size and this possible refinement of hand-axe manufacture in Chapter 7.[2,27]

Experiments have shown the hand-axes to be effective for butchery purposes. Some might have been used as a discus for bringing down prey, and others could have been used for chopping and scraping wood. Anthropologist Richard Klein[2] likens the Acheulean hand-axe to a Swiss army knife that could have been used for a multitude of purposes. Nevertheless, much about the possible functions of these often beautifully-crafted artefacts remains speculative. At some sites such as Melka Kunture in Ethiopia, Olorgesailie in Kenya, Isimila in Tanzania and Kalambo Falls on the border of Zambia and Tanzania, hand-axes occur in large numbers, but appear to have been discarded soon after manufacture. They show no sign of wear, suggesting that they were never used. Another major puzzle is that they are often too large and unwieldy to be useful. The Natural History Museum in London has a fine example of a 'Size XXL' hand-axe, measuring 30 cm (1 ft.) in length and weighing 2.8 kg (6 lb 2 oz.). One interesting theory proposes that the axes were made to impress prospective mates. When a female saw a large, symmetrical axe, she might have concluded that its maker possessed the right attributes to father successful offspring. The axe, having served its purpose (or not) would then be discarded. This proposal has inevitably become known as the 'sexy hand-axe' theory.[28]

Another issue is that while the hand-axes are ubiquitous in Africa, Europe and Southwest Asia, they are very rare further east where simple Oldowan-type flake and core artefacts predominate. The boundary between the two regions is known as the Movius Line, after the American archaeologist Hallam Movius who first noted the discontinuity in 1948. The Movius Line has been almost universally accepted ever since. It has been variously suggested that the ancestors of those living east of the Movius Line had already left Africa by the time the hand-axes were invented;[29] or that not every hominin group in Africa adopted Acheulean technology, and that the original migrants were among those lacking it;[25] or that the population sizes at the extremities of the migration were too low to keep the skills necessary for hand-axe production alive from one generation to the next.[30]

Another scenario is that the migrants passed through a region lacking suitable raw materials to make the hand-axes and were forced to look to alternatives for tool-making. One suggestion is they switched to bamboo and either forgot how to make hand-axes or were happy to continue using bamboo even when suitable stone was available.[2] Perhaps they simply discovered that readily-available bamboo was a more convenient tool-making material than stone.[3,31,32] Either possibility would be invisible in the archaeological record, as bamboo implements would be most unlikely to be preserved.

But is the Movius Line real? Archaeologist Robin Dennell[33] argues that it is not. He notes that none of the Mainland Southeast Asian flake and core industries cited by Movius can be unambiguously shown to be contemporary with the Acheulean industries to the west, and that there is no firm evidence that hominins were present in the region at all prior to one million years ago. The scarcity of hand-axes in China could be apparent rather than actual and might reflect an incomplete archaeological record. Rather than two monolithic cultures of hand-axe users and non-hand-axe users, Dennell suggests that true picture is a mosaic in which both Oldowan and Acheulean technologies were in use in the same regions. It should also be borne in mind that although no bamboo implements have been found, we do have the shell cutting tool from Trinil, Java – a region where suitable stone is scarce.[19] At minimum, this demonstrates that *Homo erectus* in the East was capable of utilising raw materials other than stone for tool-making where necessary; they were in no sense the 'backward cousins' of the hand-axe using populations to the west.

The gift of Prometheus

There is little doubt that fire use was a key breakthrough for early humans. Fire can be used to deter predators, to provide heat and lighting, and for cooking. Human activities can be carried on through the hours of darkness, and fire would certainly have been an asset in the colder regions beyond Africa. The British primatologist Richard Wrangham[34] has argued that the ability to cook food played a crucial role in human evolution. When food is cooked, it becomes more palatable, and the amount of available nutrient is increased. Wrangham believes that once humans were able to cook food, the gut could become smaller. As we have seen, the resulting energy savings in terms of reduced metabolic activity might have offset the energetic 'expense' of larger brains. On the Wrangham view, we would expect the first evidence for use of fire to coincide with the emergence of *Homo habilis* or *Homo erectus*, i.e. around two million years ago. In fact, clear signs of use of fire do not show up in the archaeological record until rather later.

Finding incontrovertible evidence is problematic: unlike stone tools, a fire is transient and can only be inferred from clear signs of burning having occurred. Distinguishing controlled use of fire from natural wildfire is also a problem, at least in Africa where lightning-induced wildfire is very common. Nevertheless, such is the importance of early use of fire that palaeontologist Travis Pickering has insisted that "*extraordinary evidence*" is required for its acceptance.[35] Evidence of hearths would qualify as 'extraordinary', but unfortunately this is lacking from the earliest candidate sites.

The earliest archaeological evidence for fire use in Africa is inconclusive. Localised red patches of oxidised sediment found at the site of Koobi Fora (FxJj20) in Kenya date to around 1.6 million years ago and are thought to be remains from fire use by early humans. Similar evidence has been reported from the slightly younger site of Chesowanja, also in Kenya. Stronger evidence has been found at Swartkrans Cave, near Sterkfontein, South Africa, which is about 1.0 to 1.5 million years old. There, archaeologists have recovered 270 burned animal bones from the uppermost level, Member 3. Hominin remains found at the site include both *Homo erectus* and the australopithecine species *Paranthropus robustus*; while it is generally assumed that only the former were responsible for the fires, this cannot be proved from the evidence.[36]

A complication is that the burned bones were probably moved a short distance away from where they were burned: it cannot be ruled out that wildfires ignited flammable material, including the bones, which lay on the floor of the cave mouth, and that these were later washed by rainfall deeper into the gully where Member 3 formed.[35] Against that, palaeontologist Bob Brain argues that while the burned bones are found throughout the 6 m (19 ft. 8 in.) thick Member 3, hardly any have been found in the earlier Members 1 and 2, despite these containing vertebrate fossils in large quantities. If wildfire had been responsible for the burned bones, they would have been found in all three levels. Nevertheless, it is fair to say that while Swartkrans Cave demonstrates fire use on the balance of probabilities, it does not do so beyond reasonable doubt.

The earliest currently-known evidence for fire use that does qualify as 'extraordinary' is that from Wonderwerk Cave, an Acheulean-era site in Northern Cape Province, South Africa, dating to approximately one million years ago. Using a technique known as micromorphological analysis and Fourier transform infrared microspectroscopy, a team lead by archaeologist Francisco Berna investigated a habitation layer known as Stratum 10. This was found to contain ash, minute bone fragments, and complete or fragmented bones that show signs of burning. This material was associated with Acheulean artefacts, and it persists through the whole of Stratum 10. Overall, it suggests that fires occurred in the cave with a frequency too great to be accounted for by natural causes. Any lingering doubt is banished by the cave entrance being 30 m (100 ft.) from the excavation area, and it was still further away at the time Stratum 10 was laid down – much too far for the burnt material to been blown in or washed in from outside. Berna's team were even able to rule out the possibility of spontaneous combustion of bat guano, which though rare has been known to occur in caves.[37]

This evidence tells us that African *Homo erectus* was making use of fire no later than one million years ago, and probably earlier. What we don't know is if early humans at that time knew how to actually produce fire, or if they were simply making opportunistic use of wildfire to start their own fires. The evidence from Eurasia suggests the latter. Once humans had left Africa, the controlled use of fire would have been a very powerful resource in the often challenging environments, in particular that of Early Pleistocene Europe. In fact, although humans were widely dispersed across Eurasia by one million years ago, prior to 400,000 years ago, evidence for use of fire in Europe is non-existent and the evidence from Asia comes from just two sites.[38]

The first of these is Locality 1 at Zhoukoudian, near Beijing. The archaeological layers at this much-investigated cave site accumulated between 500,000 and 200,000 years ago. Burnt bones and stone tools have been recovered from Layer 10, the lowest and oldest layer, and evidence of hearths has long been claimed. However, work in the late 1990s failed to find any traces of the wood ash and charcoal that would be expected at an archaeological hearth site.[39]

Rather more convincing is the evidence from Gesher Benot Ya'aqov, a 790,000-year-old site on the shores of the now-drained Lake Huleh, Israel. Burned wood and small burned flint fragments found at the site may indicate the locations of hearths. Although it is an outdoor site, wildfire is unlikely to account for the burning: electrical storms in the region mainly occur during the wet season, making lightning-induced wildfire uncommon, and fire started by humans is a likely explanation.[40]

Elsewhere, though, there is nothing. No evidence for use of fire has been found at any European site from the Early or Middle Pleistocene. Not until 400,000 years ago do the first signs emerge at the British site of Beeches Pit and the German site of Schöningen, where charred wood, heated sediments and the possible remains of hearths have been found. From then on, however, evidence for use of fire becomes increasingly widespread throughout Europe, Asia and Africa. In Europe and Western Asia, use of fire by Neanderthals was widespread, and it must therefore be assumed that they had developed the means to produce fire rather than having to wait for a convenient lightning strike. That such evidence is not seen earlier suggests that until 400,000 years ago, there was no habitual as opposed to opportunistic use of fire, and that humans were able to occupy northern latitudes without it.[38] Such timings make Richard Wrangham's cooking hypothesis look improbable. Notably, by this time *Homo erectus* had given way to the larger-brained *Homo heidelbergensis*, suggesting that bigger brains led to the use of fire, rather than the other way around.

The first Out of Africa

The former Soviet republic of Georgia is located at the crossroads of Europe and Asia. Lying on the eastern shores of the Black Sea, it was the destination of Jason and the Argonauts in their quest for the Golden Fleece, but long before this it was a stopping point for the earliest-known hominin migration out of Africa. In 1984, stone tools were discovered at the small medieval town of Dmanisi in the southeast of the country, 93 km (58 miles) southwest of the capital, Tbilisi. Archaeologists broke through the foundations of a medieval building into an ancient river deposit, where simple Oldowan-like tools were found with the bones of extinct mammals.

During the 1990s, the remains of early humans were recovered, including two partial skulls and a lower jawbone. The fossils were dated by palaeomagnetic, potassium-argon and argon-argon methods, giving an age for the remains of 1.77 million years old.[41] Subsequent dating of the stone tools indicated that the site was first occupied 1.85 million years ago, and that repeated occupations continued over a period of 80,000 years. There was evidently a long-term human presence in the

Caucasus at around or possibly even before the time of the earliest evidence for *Homo erectus* in Africa.[42]

There have been a number of subsequent discoveries of human remains at the site. These include the skull, lower jawbone and partial skeleton of an adolescent;[43,18] the skulls and lower jawbones of two adults;[44,45] and postcranial bones from three other individuals, all adults.[18] One of the skulls belonged to an elderly male who had lost all but one of his teeth some years prior to his death. Like the vitamin A-poisoned Koobi Fora female, he could not have survived unaided and must have been cared for by his companions throughout those last years of his life.[46,44] The other skull, the fifth to be discovered at the site and hence known as Skull 5, is characterised by a large face and thick browridges. Skull 5 is complete and undeformed; it is the only known fully-preserved adult hominin skull from the early Pleistocene.[45]

From the various remains, body size metrics have been estimated for the Dmanisi hominins. They were 1.45 to 1.66 m (4 ft. 9 in. to 5 ft. 5 in.) tall and weighed 40.0 to 50.0 kg (88 to 110 lb.). The cranial capacities of the five skulls range from 546 to 730 cc, about half that of a modern human. The encephalization quotient lies in the range from 2.4 to 3.13; a figure that is at the lower end of the estimates for the Turkana Boy, and is more comparable to that of *Homo habilis* or the australopithecines.[18,45]

The Dmanisi hominins display a mosaic of primitive (resembling earlier hominins) and derived (more modern) features. Their limb proportions were similar to those of a modern human. The lower limbs and feet were essentially modern, although the feet turned slightly inwards. On the other hand, the forearm lacked what is known as humeral torsion. In modern humans, the elbow joint is typically rotated relative to the shoulder joint, so that the forearm naturally hangs with the palms facing inwards; but the Dmanisi forearm lacked this rotation, so their palms were oriented more forwards. The inward-turning feet, lack of humeral torsion, small body size and small brain size may be seen as primitive traits, sharing more with *Homo habilis* than with *Homo erectus*.[47,18]

Initially assigned to African *Homo erectus*,[43] the Dmanisi hominins were later put forward as a new human species, *Homo georgicus*;[48] though this proposal has since been retracted.[45] As already noted, there is absolutely no reason why pre-*erectus* hominins could not have left Africa, but the Dmanisi hominins are probably better thought of as an early form of African *Homo erectus*. Notably, the 691 cc cranial capacity of the diminutive 1.55-million-year-old KNM-ER 42700 skull from Koobi Fora lies within the Dmanisi range. It could be that early African *Homo erectus* was not only quite widespread, but also unusually variable in both body and brain size, and also less modern than sometimes supposed.[47]

More radically, it has been suggested that *Homo habilis* and *Homo rudolfensis* might also have been early forms of *Homo erectus*, and that early *Homo* was a single evolving lineage rather than multiple species. This conclusion is based on a claim that shape variation between the five Dmanisi skulls is roughly the same as that seen among the various early *Homo* skulls from East Africa, even though the former represents a single species and the latter are generally thought to represent several.[45] Another interpretation is that there were actually two hominin species at Dmanisi, adapted to different feeding niches.[49]

Even more controversial, as we shall see presently, is the possibility that the first humans appeared in Asia rather than Africa. In any case, at about the same time that the Dmanisi people were living in Georgia or shortly thereafter, there is evidence for the presence of other early humans in Southeast Asia and China.

Dubois' odyssey

It was on the Indonesian island of Java in 1891 that a young Dutch army doctor named Eugene Dubois made the first discovery of an extinct human species that had lived significantly before *Homo sapiens*. Dubois was an anatomist who became fascinated with the subject of human origins. He had been an avid fossil-collector from childhood, and believed that fossils provided the best way of exploring evolutionary history, although this approach was not universally accepted at the time. Dubois believed that fossil origins of mankind would be found in the tropics, where present-day apes live. Unlike Darwin, he believed that humans were more closely related to Asian orang-utans and gibbons than they were to African apes, making the Far East the best place to look for early human fossils. To this end he joined the Dutch army as a doctor, had himself posted to the Dutch East Indies, and arrived in Sumatra in December 1887. The demands of his day job meant it was quite a while before he could begin his search of the many caves in Sumatra, where he believed the fossil evidence would be found. Eventually, though, he was able to investigate the caves at Lida Adjer and duly began to unearth the bones of various mammals. Armed with this evidence, he managed to persuade the Dutch government to relieve him of his medical duties and allow him work full time on his fossil hunting. He was also assigned the services of fifty convicts to help him with his excavations.[50]

After failing to discover any human fossils in Sumatra, Dubois received permission in April 1890 to transfer his work to neighbouring Java. He began searching cave sites, again without success, so he began investigating open sites as well. Finally, in October 1891, at Trinil in the eastern part of the island, he recovered a low-domed angular thick-walled human skullcap with a large shelf-like brow ridge. In August 1892, he recovered a humanlike thigh bone from what he believed to be the same individual. Convinced that he had found what had already become known as the missing link, Dubois at first proposed the name *Anthropithecus erectus* ('erect man-ape'). This he based on what he believed were the apelike proportions of its brain – which he estimated at 700 cc – and the modernity of the thigh bone. However, in November 1892 he revised the cranial capacity upwards to 900 cc, closer to that of a modern human than an ape. Accordingly, he renamed the fossil *Pithecanthropus erectus* ('erect ape-man').[50]

In 1895 Dubois returned to Europe and embarked on a tour to promote his claim to have found the missing link. Although the scientific community was intrigued by his discoveries, his conclusions were generally rejected. Disappointed, he eventually accepted a position as professor of geology at the University of Amsterdam. He refused to allow any examination of his fossils until, under increasing pressure to grant access, he finally relented in 1923. His motives have been questioned: the popular view is that he was acting out of pique, but it is more likely that he was simply protecting his intellectual property. Two years after his return to Europe, he had permitted Gustav Schwalbe of the University of Strasburg to make a cast of the skullcap. To Dubois's undoubted frustration, Schwalbe's subsequent monograph was far more sympathetically received than any of his own work.[50]

By the 1920s, excavations had begun in China and further human fossils soon came to light. Similarities between these finds and *Pithanthropus* were noted, but Dubois rejected any connection. Then, in 1936 palaeontologist Ralph von Koenigswald made a further discovery on Java itself. Excavating near Mojokerto, eastern Java, in 1936, von Koenigswald recovered a juvenile skull later known as the Mojokerto Child, and now thought to have been about a year to 18 months old at death.[51] The following year, von Koenigswald made further discoveries at Sangiran, central Java, after promising to pay local people 10 cents for each find. The finds included fragments making up an almost-complete skull, though von Koenigswald's delight at this discovery was somewhat tempered when he learned his helpers were breaking larger finds into smaller pieces to maximise their bounty.[50]

Dubois again rejected any affinities between the new Javanese finds and *Pithecanthropus*. He argued his find was more apelike than the later discoveries, leading to the popular misconception that he had repudiated his claim that it was an intermediate form between apes and modern humans. He died in December 1940, having arguably done himself few favours in the last four decades of his life. Sir Arthur Keith, writing in an obituary notice, observed that Dubois was *"an idealist who held his ideas so firmly that he tended to bend the facts rather than alter his ideas to fit them"*.[50] Others take a more positive view: in June 2009, fellow Dutchman Marco Langbroek named the asteroid (206241) Dubois in his honour.

In 1927, the Canadian anthropologist Davidson Black described the Chinese discoveries as *Sinanthropus pekinensis* ('Chinese man of Peking'). His conclusions were based on an examination of two teeth recovered from the cave site of Zhoukoudian in Dragon Bone Hill, near Beijing (then known in the West as Peking). The find became popularly known as Peking Man. Several skullcaps were recovered from the same site in subsequent years. Both Black and the German anatomist Franz Weidenreich noted similarities between the Zhoukoudian finds and *Pithanthropus*, but as noted above Dubois rejected the similarities.[5]

Unfortunately, the Zhoukoudian fossils were lost during World War II. Work at the site was halted by the Japanese invasion in 1937, but the fossils remained at the Cenozoic Research Laboratory of the Peking Union Medical College until 1941. Following the American entry into the war, an attempt was made to transfer them to the United States for safekeeping. In an episode reminiscent of the adventures of Indiana Jones, a group of US marines were tasked with getting the priceless fossils out of China, but before they could do so they were captured by the enemy. The fossils were never seen again and their fate remains a mystery to this day. One theory is that they went down with the *Awa Maru*, an ocean liner requisitioned by the Japanese military and sunk by a US submarine in March 1945. Recently, it has been suggested that the marines came under attack from Chinese communist rebels at Qinhuagdao, 300 km (185 miles) east of Beijing, and buried the fossils at what is now a car park.[52] Fortunately, Weidenreich had made plaster casts, now kept at the American Museum of Natural History, and copies of the casts are held by the Institute of Vertebrate Palaeontology and Palaeoanthropology in Beijing. After the war, excavation resumed at Zhoukoudian and a number of discoveries have been made since, including two skull fragments. Zhoukoudian became a World Heritage site in 1987.[5]

It is now generally accepted that the Javanese and Chinese fossils belong to the same species. In 1950 both were reclassified as *Homo erectus* by the German biologist Ernst Mayr as part of a general lumping exercise of the bewildering plethora of hominin genera and species then recognised.[5] The Mojokerto Child was once thought to be 1.81 million years old[29] but has since been shown to be no older than 1.49 million years.[53] The Sangiran fossils have been dated to 1.51 million years old with the argon-argon method.[54] A *Homo erectus* fossil skull from Gongwangling, Shaanxi Province in North China has recently been dated to around 1.63 million years old,[55] and stone tools from the Nihewan Basin, 150 km (90 miles) west of Beijing, have been dated to as far back as 1.66 million years old.[56,57] In relative terms, these Chinese dates are only slightly more recent than that of the Dmanisi hominins.

Another recent finding is that computerised tomography has shown that the development of the Mojokerto Child is more consistent with an age of one year to 18 months old at death than the four to six years once believed. The brain of the Mojokerto Child had attained 72 to 84 percent of adult size, suggesting that the Asian *Homo erectus* pattern of brain growth was still more rapid and apelike than that of modern humans. For a modern one-year-old child, the figure is only 50 percent of adult size, whereas for chimpanzees it is 80 percent.[51] This result is consistent with the apelike development and maturation of the Turkana Boy implied from dental studies.

As discussed above, many researchers differentiate between African and Asian *Homo erectus*, and the orthodox position is that the former evolved from *Homo habilis* in Africa and later migrated to

Asia. In the process, it underwent sufficient evolutionary change for it to be considered a separate species. The Dmanisi hominins are a strong hint that matters were not in fact so straightforward, and further evidence for the complexity of picture emerged in 2004, when it was discovered that dwarf hominins had been living on the island of Flores until just 12,000 years ago.

The 'hobbit people' of Flores

The Indonesian island of Flores is part of the Lesser Sunda, an archipelago in Island Southeast Asia. The name comes from the Portuguese word 'flowers' and is a legacy of Portugal's colonial influence in the region between the sixteenth and mid-nineteenth century. The island is popular with tourists and its best-known attraction is Mt. Kelimutu, an active volcano with three brightly-coloured crater lakes located on its eastern summit; the colours are caused by dissolved volcanic gases reacting with minerals in the lake basins.

Tourists are not the only people with an interest in Flores. Anthropologists believe the first modern human settlers of Australia 'island hopped' through the Indonesian archipelago, and in 2003 a joint Australian and Indonesian team of anthropologists were investigating Liang Bua, a limestone cave. They were looking for evidence of the original migration, but instead, they discovered a largely-complete skeleton now known formally as LB1, but almost immediately nicknamed Flo. Accompanied by a complete lower jawbone known as LB2, the 18,000-year-old skeleton was extremely fragile, but was not fossilised. This was notable in itself, but the most remarkable thing about it was its size – or lack thereof. The discoverers, led by anthropologists Peter Brown and Michael Morwood, claimed that Flo had been a 30-year-old human female – but she stood no more than 1.06 m (3 ft. 6 in.) tall. Her weight was estimated to be somewhere between 16 and 36 kg (35 and 79 lb.). She had a cranial capacity of just 380 cc, comparable to that of an australopithecine. Yet she was apparently human: she lacked the large back teeth of an australopithecine, the proportions of her facial skeleton were those of a human, and she appeared to be a humanlike fully-committed biped. Accordingly, Brown and Morwood classed her as belonging to a new human species, *Homo floresiensis*.[58] More material, representing at least nine individuals, was recovered in 2004, together with Oldowan-type stone tools. Some of these were dated to around 74,000 to 95,000 years old; others were more recent at 12,000 years old. The dates were obtained by radiocarbon, luminescence, uranium series and electron spin resonance methods. The tools were accompanied by animal remains, indicating that the area was a focus for a range of hominin activities.[59,60]

The small size of *Homo floresiensis* was, the team claimed, a result of a phenomenon known as insular dwarfism. Animals living on an island where food is relatively scarce and predators are few or absent will 'downsize' over many generations, in order to reduce calorific requirements. What is actually happening is that evolution is favouring the smaller offspring in each generation. If predators do not pose a threat, any advantages in being large will be outweighed by poorer fuel-economy. Before modern humans reached Flores, the island met both conditions: relatively little animal life, and a lack of any predators other than the Komodo dragon. The only other large animals on Flores were extinct elephants known as *Stegodon sondaari*, which had undergone insular dwarfism of the kind proposed for *Homo floresiensis*. The term is relative, though, as these animals were still comparable in size to a water buffalo. If hominins such as *Homo erectus* had reached Flores, then possibly the same could have happened to them, eventually leading to *Homo floresiensis*. The team claimed that despite its tiny apelike brain, *Homo floresiensis* had an encephalization quotient comparable to that of *Homo habilis* and *Homo erectus*. They were capable of complex behaviour and cognition, and were probably the makers of the tools. Oldowan-type technology would be well within their capabilities, although as we saw in Chapter 4 this might also have been true of the earliest hominins.

The discovery attracted considerable publicity, and *Homo floresiensis* was immediately nicknamed the Flores Hobbit, to Brown's reported annoyance.[61] However, doubts as to whether it was genuinely a new human species emerged almost immediately. The Indonesian anthropologist Teuku Jacob claimed that Flo was a modern human suffering from microcephaly, a developmental disorder leading to a smaller brain. Jacob claimed Flo was a modern human of Australomelanesian extraction,[62] and he was supported by primatologist Robert Martin[63] of the Field Museum, Chicago. Following Jacob's death in 2007, his co-workers revived the theory, this time claiming that Flo had suffered from Down syndrome.[64,65]

However, the majority of workers rejected the microcephaly theory and accepted *Homo floresiensis* as a new human species.[66,67,68,69,70] Studies mainly considered the metrics of Flo in comparison to microcephalic humans, pygmies, early human species and australopithecines. The general conclusion was that *Homo floresiensis* showed a better fit with the various extinct hominins than it did with the microcephalic or normal modern humans: for example Flo's long, low cranial vault is not a feature shared with modern humans, microcephalic or not.[70] Her wrist was more primitive that of a modern human.[69] Other pathological explanations such as Laron syndrome (a form of dwarfism related to a genetic disorder) and cretinism were also rejected.[70]

If we accept that *Homo floresiensis* is indeed a new species, then what did it evolve from? The most obvious possibility is Asian *Homo erectus*, chiefly because we do know it was present in Asia. However, studies have noted that while the cranial metrics were consistent with *Homo erectus*, the limb proportions of *Homo floresiensis* had more in common with *Australopithecus garhi*[66] and the feet were a mosaic of primitive apelike and derived humanlike features. The big toe was fully in-line, albeit short, and the metatarsals followed a humanlike sequence in which the 1st (innermost) was the most robust (sturdily-built), followed by the 5th (outermost), then 4th, 3rd, and finally 2nd. The foot, though, was disproportionately long in comparison to that of a modern human; the lesser metatarsals (2nd to 5th) were long; and the outer toes were long and curved, unlike the short, straight toes of a modern human.[71] The fact that the feet and limb proportions of *Homo erectus* were modern suggests that *Homo floresiensis* evolved from a species that was more primitive, such as *Homo habilis*. Another possibility is that *Homo floresiensis* evolved from an early and less modern type of African *Homo erectus*, probably similar to the Dmanisi hominins.[72]

These possibilities are supported by studies that considered how insular dwarfism may affect brain size. The studies concluded that the smaller-brained *Homo habilis* or the Dmanisi hominins are more plausible ancestors than Asian *Homo erectus*.[73] Even with a revised estimate of 420 cc for the brain size of *Homo floresiensis*, not all of the brain reduction from Asian *Homo erectus* can be explained in terms of a simple downsizing model, and a *habilis*-like ancestor is a better fit.[74]

The next big question is how did these ancestors – whoever they were – reach Flores in the first place? Unlike Java and many other islands in the Indonesian archipelago, Flores was never connected to the mainland. This was the case even during the maximum extent of the ice ages, when sea-levels dropped. Consequently, there has been popular speculation that Flo's forebears must have had the ability to build boats. There is no direct evidence in the form of artefacts to suggest that humans built boats until very late in the prehistoric era. We know that modern humans must have used boats to cross the sea from the Southeast Asian archipelago to Australia, but could earlier hominins have made sea crossings by boat? There have been suggestions that African *Homo erectus* could have dispersed into Eurasia not just overland through the Levant, but across the Strait of Gibraltar, across the Bab el-Mandeb Strait at the southern end of the Red Sea, and across the Mediterranean via Sicily.[2] However, the construction of a suitable watercraft and the navigational skills required to make a voyage across the open sea are generally accepted to have been beyond the abilities of early humans.[75] In the case of the migration of early humans from Africa, most anthropologists take the view that purely overland routes were used, but in the case of Flores, no overland route has ever existed.

Both Sherlock Holmes and *Star Trek's* Mr Spock maintained that when you have eliminated the impossible, whatever remains, however improbable, must be the truth. Does this mean that the first settlers must have reached Flores using some form of primitive watercraft – possibly logs lashed together – or is there something else 'improbable' we need to consider first? In fact, there is – the settlers could have been swept out to sea and stranded on Flores by a natural occurrence such as a flash-flood or a tsunami, possibly on a raft of matted vegetation. This is believed to have been way the ancestors of the New World monkeys reached South America from Africa; nobody is suggesting that these early monkeys built boats. Accidental stranding seems to be the likeliest explanation for the early human presence on Flores.

We don't know when this happened, but it has been suggested that artefacts from the sites of Mata Menge and Wolo Sege in central Flores show technological continuity with the *Homo floresiensis* artefacts from Liang Bua. Unfortunately, no hominin remains have been recovered from either site. The Mata Menge artefacts are 880,000 years old and those from Wolo Sege are at least at least a million years old, suggesting that Flo's distant forbears were on Flores by that time. They could of course have been there much earlier.[76,77]

Assuming its encephalization quotient was comparable to that of *Homo habilis* and *Homo erectus*, *Homo floresiensis* probably possessed similar cognitive abilities. Like these species, it would have lacked the complex language of modern humans, though it might have had a limited form of language. A clue to the possibly advanced cognitive abilities of *Homo floresiensis* is that the prefrontal cortex and temporal lobes corresponding to a region known as Brodmann area 10 are expanded in comparison to other fossil hominins.[67] The prefrontal cortex is the frontmost part of the frontal lobes; the temporal lobes are located on both of the lower sides of the brain, below the parietal lobes. The function of Brodmann area 10 is not well understood, but it may be involved in processes such as taking initiatives and planning future activities. If so, it implies that *Homo floresiensis* was able to plan, respond to situations, use memories, and communicate information among group members.[66]

Probably the most controversial idea is that *Homo floresiensis* survived into modern times and is the origin of tales about the Ebu Gogo. These small, humanlike folk are said to have been living on Flores when the Portuguese arrived 400 years ago. Some claim they were still being seen as recently as 100 years ago. It was also suggested that similar folk are the basis of legends such as the Orang Pendek from Sumatra, and even leprechauns in Ireland. It is probably as well to be sceptical, because 'little people' are so prevalent in world folk traditions. If these were all due to actual hominins, concrete evidence would surely have emerged by now. However, if endemic dwarf hominins can arise on Flores, there is certainly no reason to suppose similar species could not arise elsewhere. It is quite possible that evidence from similarly isolated locations may come to light in the future.

In fact, it is notable that the most recent artefacts are 12,000 years old, because this coincides with both a volcanic eruption and the disappearance from the fossil record of the dwarf elephants. These animals might have been an important source of food,[59] and it seems too much of a coincidence for the two events not to be linked. Even if the eruption did not directly bring about the demise of *Homo floresiensis*, it killed off a food source that they were dependent on and were unable to survive without. It therefore seems unlikely that the Ebu Gogo were *Homo floresiensis*. It remains an open question whether or not these diminutive beings ever came into contact with modern humans or indeed any other hominins during their million year sojourn on Flores.

An Asian origin?

Up until now, we have followed the more or less conventional view that the earliest representatives of *Homo* lived in Africa: this view is one of the most fundamental paradigms in the study of human evolution. However, the last few chapters have shown that some of the underlying assumptions are questionable: that *Homo habilis* was the first human species; that *Homo habilis* was the first hominin to make and use stone tools; that African *Homo erectus* evolved from *Homo habilis*; that African *Homo erectus* was the first hominin species to leave Africa; and that the Dmanisi and Flores hominins evolved from either African or Asian *Homo erectus*. If all of these assumptions are false, we are left with a plausible scenario in which tool-making australopithecines left Africa and colonised the grasslands of Western, South and Central Asia 2.6 million years or even earlier.[78]

We can now go further and envisage a scenario in which the first human species arose from an australopithecine ancestor in Asia rather than Africa. It most closely resembled the Dmanisi hominins, and may indeed have been the same species. It existed some time prior to the earliest recorded dates for African *Homo erectus* (1.87 million years ago), the Dmanisi hominins (1.85 million years ago) and Asian *Homo erectus* (1.63 million years ago). A more modern form evolved from it, and migrated to Africa some time before 1.87 million years ago (African *Homo erectus*) and Java some time before 1.63 million years ago (Asian *Homo erectus*). However, the more primitive form persisted at Dmanisi, and on Flores.[13] This scenario eliminates the need for *Homo floresiensis* to be a 'downsized' form of Asian *Homo erectus*, or for the Dmanisi hominins to be an early form of African *Homo erectus*. An Asian origin for *Homo erectus* also eliminates the problem of it coexisting with *Homo habilis* in Africa. Whether or not this scenario will gain acceptance, only time and further fossil evidence will tell.

The pioneers

Regardless of whether humans evolved in Africa or Asia, they have been present in the latter for at least 1.85 million years. Establishing a permanent presence in Europe apparently took longer. This was probably due to the episodes of glaciation that periodically gripped the continent.[2] Evidence of what seems to have been an ultimately doomed venture into Europe began to emerge in the mid-1990s from the Sierra de Atapuerca, near the city of Burgos in northern Spain.

The Gran Dolina ('Great Depression') is a large cave, one of several discovered as a consequence of the construction of a railway for the transport of minerals at the end of the nineteenth century. The systematic excavation of the site started in 1981, but it was not until 1993 that a survey pit was started, and the layer known as TD6 was reached the following year.[2] Finds included 87 hominin bone fragments, corresponding to at least six individuals of different ages and sexes. A total of 268 flaked stone artefacts were also recovered, all of which were simple Oldowan-style tools. As was the case with the Dmanisi hominins, no Acheulean hand-axes were found.[79,80] Subsequent excavations have continued to yield hominin fossils, and to date the remains of ten individuals have been identified.[81]

The TD6 hominins had a cranial capacity of over 1,000 cc, compared to the 900 cc of *Homo erectus*. The midface was fully-modern (the midface is the middle of the face including the nose and its associated bony structures) and dental traits were also said to distinguish them from African *Homo erectus*. They were allocated their own species, *Homo antecessor* ('Pioneer Man') by their discoverers, who initially claimed that the TD6 hominins were a possible common ancestor of the Neanderthals and modern humans.[82] This claim was later withdrawn, although the discoverers still maintained that *Homo antecessor* was closely related to the lineage leading to *Homo sapiens*.[83]

Based on uranium series and electron spin resonance results, the TD6 fossils and artefacts are thought to be somewhere from 780,000 to 857,000 years old.[84] In 2007, a fragment of a lower jawbone and an isolated lower left fourth premolar, both from the same individual, were recovered from the nearby Sima del Elefante ('Pit of the Elephant') site. These were also assigned to *Homo antecessor* and were dated by palaeomagnetic and cosmogenic radionuclide techniques to around 1.1 to 1.2 million years old, suggesting that the species was present in the region for 400,000 years.[85] This is an impressive period of time: almost ten times the length of our own tenure in Europe.

The origins of *Homo antecessor* are uncertain. One possibility is that it is an offshoot of African *Homo erectus* that migrated into Europe and ultimately died out, unable to adapt to the harsh conditions of one of the glacial episodes.[2] Another is that the species could be a European population of Asian *Homo erectus* associated with a migration from Asia. A lower jawbone recovered from TD6 in 2003 is said to resemble lower jawbones from Chinese *Homo erectus*.[83] Studies of *Homo antecessor* dental characteristics also suggest that it is more closely related to Asian hominins of that period than it is to any African species.[86,87] If correct, this might explain the lack of Acheulean technology. Indeed, an Asian origin for *Homo antecessor* was once reasoned for purely on the basis of its lack of Acheulean technology, then thought to be absent from Asia 1.2 million years ago.[88] However, Acheulean artefacts dating to 1.51 million years ago have since been found at Attirampakkam in India, as previously noted.

Homo antecessor fossils have not been found anywhere else, and it is therefore very uncertain as to where it fits into the broader picture. If, as seems likely, it did not contribute to later human evolution, what happened to it? A clue to the possible fate of the TD6 people is that around 25 percent of the bones found at Gran Dolina show signs of damage that includes chop-marks and cut-marks, peeling where bones have been broken and bent, and marks where bones have been splintered for marrow extraction. All of which adds up to a compelling case for cannibalism. Furthermore, the extent and pattern of the damage marks suggests butchery for food purposes rather than ritual cannibalism.[89] Perhaps things got so bad for the TD6 people that they ended up eating each other; an ignominious end to a group of pioneers who maintained a foothold in Europe for so long.

Back to Africa

If *Homo antecessor* is indeed of Asian origin, it might have been just part of a more general dispersal of *Homo erectus* from Asia. It has been suggested that two fossils from Olduvai Gorge resemble 'classic' Asian *Homo erectus* more closely than they do African *Homo erectus*, suggesting they might also have been of Asian origin.[90] Another possible migrant from Asia was discovered at Middle Awash in 2002. Known as the 'Daka Cranium', the find comprised a one-million-year-old skullcap and some other remains. The skullcap's describers noted a strong resemblance to Asian *Homo erectus* and claimed it had attributes placing it firmly within the range of its Asian counterparts.[22] These possible migrations have been dubbed 'Back to Africa',[3] although the use of the term does of course presuppose that the forebears of these hominins originated from there in the first place.

Whether we regard African and Asian *Homo erectus*, *Homo antecessor* and the Dmanisi hominins as regional populations (sometimes known as 'demes'), species, or something in between (such as sub-species), is to some extent moot. The distinction between these categories is actually quite vague, and there is no consensus on how to best define 'species'. The problem was noted by Darwin in *The Origin of Species*, and matters are little improved to this day. Even the common-sense definition that two animals are the same species if they can interbreed in the wild and produce fertile offspring is fraught with difficulties. For example, wolves (*Canis lupus*) can interbreed with coyotes (*Canis latrans*) and jackals (*Canis aureus*), even though all three are regarded as separate species. Which if any of the various hominin species could interbreed we have no way of knowing. If the remains of a cross-bred hominin from this period were to be recovered, it is doubtful that we would be able to unambiguously identify it as such. Even interbreeding between modern humans and Neanderthals, though inferred from genetic evidence, has not been convincingly demonstrated in terms of fossilised remains. This is in spite of a far more extensive fossil record than those we have considered so far. Accordingly, some authorities prefer to think in terms of populations rather than species.[91]

However, there is one interesting possibility. If the Acheulean hand-axes were indeed part of a courtship ritual, then it is one that 'Back to Africa' migrants from east of the Movius Line would have been unaware of. Female descendants of the immigrants, when presented with a freshly-made Acheulean hand-axe by local suitors would not know how to respond and males, on failing to make such an offering, would be clueless as to why their advances had been spurned. We have no way of knowing if this ever occurred, but the possibility is explored in the novel *Evolution* by the British author Stephen Baxter.[92] Though primarily a work of science fiction, much of the action is set in prehistoric times and is based firmly upon our current knowledge. While Baxter's novel suggested the problem was purely cultural, it is possible that if the 'sexy hand-axe' theory is correct, such behaviour was instinctive and would have prevented the locals from mating with the newcomers. In that event, the two really were different species, as what is known as a 'reproductive isolation mechanism' was in operation; an incompatibility between two organisms that prevents them from reproducing. In fact, it is quite common for animals to be classed as different species because subtle differences in their courtship rituals prevent them from mating.[93]

The first Britons

It is likely that the actual picture of population movements between Africa and Eurasia is more complicated than that suggested even by the current fossil evidence. Although *Homo antecessor* was associated with Oldowan tools, recent re-dating of Acheulean hand-axes excavated from two western Mediterranean sites in Spain suggests that some of these were around 900,000 years old,[94] making them roughly contemporary with *Homo antecessor*. So other, Acheulean-using, hominin groups must also have also been in Europe at the time, possibly arising from migrations from Africa.

It also seems that European hominins of this time were not confined to Mediterranean climates. Between 2005 and 2013, evidence emerged of an early human presence in Britain – at this time connected to the mainland and lying on the southern edge of the forests of northwestern Europe. In 2005, flint artefacts believed to be 700,000 years old were reported from Pakefield in Suffolk. Made from good quality black flint, they were provisionally categorised as simple Oldowan-style tools, although the sample size of 32 artefacts was too small for a more definite diagnosis to be made. The date was 200,000 years before the previous earliest-known human presence in northwestern Europe,[95] but in 2010 even earlier artefacts were reported from the coastal village of Happisburgh, Norfolk (pronounced 'Hazebrough'). Based on palaeomagnetic and faunal considerations, the flint artefacts, 78 in all, were estimated to be at least 780,000 years old and possibly as much as one million years old.[96]

In May 2013, hominin footprints were discovered on the beach at Happisburgh. Thought to be the same age as the flint artefacts, they are the earliest-known direct evidence for the presence of humans in Northern Europe. The footprints briefly emerged at low tide, having being exposed by rough seas. Within a fortnight, they had vanished again – but not before a team led by Nick Ashton from the British Museum had obtained plaster casts and 3d images. A total of 152 footprints were recorded, of which twelve yielded complete outlines suitable for analysis. It is thought that these twelve footprints represented five individuals ranging in height from 0.93 to 1.73 m (3 ft. 0 in. to 5 ft. 8 in.), suggesting the presence of both adults and children. The estimated foot size, foot area and stature of the Happisburgh hominins is consistent with estimates for *Homo antecessor*, though at this stage it is probably best to regard affinities to the TD6 hominins as tentative.[97]

The symbolic ape

The Happisburgh people occupied the edges of a confer-dominated forest close to where the Thames flowed into the North Sea, about 150 km (95 miles) north of the present estuary. Analysis of animal remains suggests that they lived towards the end of an interglacial period, although which interglacial is uncertain. There were warm periods from 866,000 to 814,000 years ago, and from 970,000 to 936,000 years ago.[96]

The climate was similar to that of today and while comfortable by British standards, it would have been chilly for those used to a Mediterranean climate. The implication is that Early Pleistocene humans were much more adaptable to ever-changing climatic conditions than was previously thought, although it remains unclear whether expansion into northern latitudes with lower winter temperatures required human physical adaptation, seasonal migration or developments in technology such as hunting, clothing, or the use of shelters.[95,96,98]

If, for the moment at least, we use the unqualified term *Homo erectus* to describe all these hominins, then the picture is of a species that was sufficiently flexible in its behaviour to spread across much of the Old World, colonising the whole of Africa and much of Asia. Only in Europe was the climate so variable that they were unable to maintain a permanent toehold, despite excursions as far north as Britain. Physically they were committed bipeds, having shed all vestiges of their ancestral life in the trees. Although they did not appear across the full extent of the *Homo erectus* range, the Acheulean hand-axes were the first technology unquestionably beyond the reach of earlier hominins, implying a definite increase in brainpower.

Around 600,000 years ago, the African and Asian populations began to diverge from each other: in Africa and Europe, bigger-brained hominins start to appear in the fossil record. Asian *Homo erectus* seems to have remained largely unchanged until its final disappearance, although just when this was is uncertain. In 1996, ages as recent as 27,000 years old were claimed for remains from Ngandong and Sambungmacan in Java,[99] but recent argon-argon and electron spin resonance dating suggests that they are at least 143,000 years old and possibly as much as 546,000 years old.[100] Even the more recent date is around 100,000 years before modern humans reached Southeast Asia, so it now looks less likely that modern humans ever encountered *Homo erectus* there. Nevertheless, as we shall see in Chapter 8, other archaic humans were present in Southeast Asia around 50,000 years ago; and they did encounter modern humans.

7: The archaics

Muddle in the Middle

On October 21 1907, a quarry worker named Daniel Hartmann recovered a virtually complete human lower jawbone from a sandpit near the village of Mauer, in southwest Germany, 10 km (6 miles) from the historic city of Heidelberg. The teeth were clearly human, but the jawbone was thick and lacked a chin. Hartmann showed the find to Professor Otto Schoetensack, an anthropologist at the University of Heidelberg. Schoetensack subsequently named the discovery *Homo heidelbergensis* ('Heidelberg Man'). The Mauer Mandible, as it is now known, has been dated by electron spin resonance, uranium series and infrared radio-fluorescence techniques, and is 609,000 ± 40,000 years old.[1]

Although few took the new species seriously at the time,[2] further discoveries followed. In 1921, a skull and a number of other bones were found in an iron and zinc mine in Broken Hill, Northern Rhodesia (now Kabwe, Zambia) by a Swiss miner named Tom Zwiglaar. Characterised by its heavy browridges, the Kabwe skull was at the time also assigned to a new species, *Homo rhodesiensis* ('Rhodesian Man'). Its cranial capacity is around 1,280 cc,[3] well within the modern range. However, we have only a very rough estimate of its age, as the mining activity largely destroyed geological evidence that would have enabled accurate dating. An age of around 300,000 years old has been suggested.[4] Following these discoveries, many similar finds were made in Europe and Africa, and also at two sites in China: Dali and Jinniu Shan.

An important find, now thought to shed light on the origins of *Homo heidelbergensis*, is a human skullcap recovered in 1994 during excavations for the construction of a highway near the Italian town of Ceprano. Unfortunately, it was shattered by a bulldozer immediately prior to its discovery. Originally thought to be from 800,000 to 900,000 years old,[5] it was variously proposed as a new human species, *Homo cepranensis*,[6] or as a European population of *Homo erectus* associated with a migration from Asia.[7] However, recent work suggests that the skullcap is far younger, and dates of 450,000[8] and 385,000 years old[9] have been obtained by palaeomagnetic and potassium-argon dating respectively. A re-evaluation of the skullcap found a combination of primitive *erectus*-like and derived *heidelbergensis*-like traits, suggesting that it might have been an early form of *Homo heidelbergensis*.[10] A recently-discovered partial lower jawbone from Mala Balanica, Serbia, displays a similar combination of traits,[11] and at 397,000 to 525,000 years old, is about the same age as the Ceprano skullcap.[12]

The oldest accurately-dated examples of *Homo heidelbergensis* are a 600,000-year-old skull found at Bodo, Ethiopia in 1976,[13] and the Mauer Mandible itself. The Chinese specimens, though usually classed as an eastern offshoot of *Homo heidelbergensis*, are considerably more recent, ranging from 200,000 to 300,000 years old.[14]

Homo heidelbergensis predates the appearance of both modern humans in Africa and the Neanderthals in Europe. The average cranial capacity is only slightly less than that of a modern human, so it was once considered to be an early form of our own species and classed as Archaic *Homo sapiens*. Modern humans in Africa and the Neanderthals in Europe were simply regarded as later subspecies of *Homo sapiens*, and the term '*Homo heidelbergensis*' fell into disuse. Since the mid-1990s, however, the tendency has been to regard 'archaics', Neanderthals and modern humans as

The symbolic ape

separate species, and revive the original name of *Homo heidelbergensis* for 'Archaic *Homo sapiens*'.[15] *Homo heidelbergensis* is seen as the common ancestor of Neanderthals and modern humans. This view is really little more than a change in the bookkeeping,[16] as both schemes have Neanderthals and modern humans evolving from the same earlier group. The case for adopting the new scheme really rests on the assumption that the differences between 'archaics', Neanderthals and modern humans are sufficient to justify classifying them all as separate species, something that not everybody accepts.[17] It has also been argued that the Chinese specimens do not belong in *Homo heidelbergensis* and should (since their true affinities remain unclear) continue to be termed Archaic *Homo sapiens*.[14]

The latter point does illustrate a continuing problem with *Homo heidelbergensis*: as Archaic *Homo sapiens* it came to be used as a dumping ground for any Middle Pleistocene hominin that wasn't *Homo erectus*, a Neanderthal, or a modern human.[4] Consequently, it tends to be defined in terms of features intermediate between *Homo erectus* and later humans, whereas a species should be defined in terms of unique traits.[18] There is also much debate as to whether *Homo heidelbergensis* is indeed a single species; a situation that anthropologist Phillip Rightmire[15] has referred to as the "*muddle in the middle*".

Rightmire[19] has proposed two scenarios. The first is that the European and African populations represent two distinct species, *Homo heidelbergensis* in Europe and *Homo rhodesiensis* in Africa, with the European species evolving from a single population that migrated from Africa. On this view, *Homo heidelbergensis* is actually an early form of Neanderthal and *Homo rhodesiensis* is the ancestor of modern humans. This scenario can be shown to be correct if derived 'proto-Neanderthal' features show up in the early European *Homo heidelbergensis* populations, and these features are not shared with the corresponding African populations. The second scenario proposes that *Homo heidelbergensis* is a single species that spread widely across Africa and Western Eurasia at the beginning of the Middle Pleistocene, and only later differentiated into Neanderthals in Western Eurasia and modern humans in Africa. A third scenario, considered problematic by Rightmire, is that *Homo antecessor* diverged from *Homo erectus* to become the common ancestor of *Homo heidelbergensis* and *Homo rhodesiensis*; the latter two were essentially early forms of Neanderthals and *Homo sapiens* respectively.

Both scenarios propose a single African origin for European Middle Pleistocene hominins and that any earlier hominins simply died out. However, matters might not have been so straightforward. A problem is that European *Homo heidelbergensis* is highly variable in terms of the morphology of its skull, lower jawbone, dentition and postcranial anatomy. Fossils exhibit a mosaic of primitive and derived characteristics that cannot be organised into consistent geographical or chronological 'demes'. A possible solution is the 'sources and sinks' model, which proposes that Europe was a population 'sink' that became largely depopulated during adverse climatic episodes. Each time the climate improved, the continent was repopulated from 'sources', or refugia that had remained habitable. Such refugia might have existed in Iberia, Italy and the Balkans, although it is possible that on occasions even these became uninhabitable and repopulation occurred from the Levant or the Caucasus. The refugia were only capable of supporting their existing populations: they could not serve as 'arks' where other populations could seek refuge, with the consequence that these died out. During glacial periods, distinct demes emerged within the isolated populations; during warmer spells populations expanded and came into contact with one another to produce a 'mix and match' of morphological characteristics. It is also possible that demes of earlier hominins such as *Homo antecessor* persisted and interbred with *Homo heidelbergensis*. This could explain the primitive characteristics of fossils such as the Ceprano skullcap.[20]

With the limited amount of fossil material available it is very difficult to obtain a definitive answer as to which scenario is correct. A cladistic study of skull characteristics supported the two species scenario. It found that *Homo heidelbergensis* and the Neanderthals were part of a single lineage, and that *Homo rhodesiensis* (represented by the Kabwe skull) formed a separate lineage.[21] Conversely, an analysis performed using skull 'landmarks' supported the single species scenario. Landmarks are anatomical points that are equivalent for all the specimens under consideration. Skulls were chosen from Africa, Asia and Africa, and they included Kabwe, Dali, Jinniu Shan, and the newly-recruited Ceprano skullcap. An association was found between the skulls from all three continents, suggesting that they all belong to a single species.[10] Clearly, matters remain far from resolved, but for now the term '*Homo heidelbergensis*' is used here for both African and Eurasian populations without necessarily endorsing any particular model.

Bigger brains – but why?

Homo heidelbergensis retained much of the primitive aspect of *Homo erectus*, including a large forwardly-projecting face, a massive chinless lower jaw, heavy browridges, low flattened forehead, and a marked occipital torus at the back of the head, to which were attached the rear neck muscles. However, the typical cranial capacity was around 90 percent of that of modern humans, a considerable increase on that of earlier humans.[22] Much of the increase was in the parietal lobes,[3] which process sensory information and are responsible for spatial awareness. The jump in cranial capacity appears quite suddenly in the fossil record and suggests *Homo heidelbergensis* emerged in a rapid 'punctuated' event, like the one that might have been responsible for African *Homo erectus*.[22]

Why did this increase in brain power happen in the first place? We have seen that larger brains of *Homo habilis* may be associated with an increase in group sizes, and the *Homo heidelbergensis* increase may signal a further jump. Calculations based on the social brain hypothesis (see Chapter 2) yield an estimated group size of around 120 to 130 individuals.[23] Did a situation arise where such an increase became advantageous? *Homo heidelbergensis* appears soon after the onset of the Middle Pleistocene Transition, when swings in climate were becoming even larger,[24] with severe environmental consequences. The effects of climate change were at their greatest in Europe, but Africa was not spared: during warm periods the Sahara supported rich, well-watered and varied environments, where hominin populations might have been widespread; on the other hand during glacial periods, the Sahara became an arid wilderness, incapable of sustaining human life. Only in Asia did the climate remain relatively stable. Possibly this explains the lengthy persistence of the smaller-brained *Homo erectus* in Southeast Asia and China.[25] In these challenging conditions, what advantage would larger group size have conferred? One possibility is that food and water became more widely dispersed. One way of ensuring continued access to these essentials was to maintain good relations with other human groups.[26]

Retiring the Acheulean hand-axe

Homo heidelbergensis continued to make Acheulean hand-axes, but its appearance coincides with a tendency to more refined artefacts. Later Acheulean hand-axes are thinner, more extensively trimmed and more symmetrical, often in three dimensions. The 3d symmetry of these axes suggests a cognitive advance whereby a tool-maker could hold a mental image of the finished tool while it was still a block of unworked stone, and 'rotate' it in their mind's eye.[22]

Did this refinement coincide with the brain expansion associated with *Homo heidelbergensis*? If so, one could expect to see two periods of stasis representing early and late Acheulean, with a period of rapid change at 600,000 years ago corresponding to *Homo heidelbergensis*. It would be difficult to confirm, because many Acheulean artefacts are only weakly dated. In fact, it seems more likely that the refinement was gradual, and there was no rapid change. It is not known exactly when various refinements in knapping techniques occurred, and they might not all have appeared at the same time.[22,3] Some, indeed, might have predated the emergence of *Homo heidelbergensis*. In 2009, palaeomagnetic dates of 900,000 years and 760,000 years were reported for Acheulean hand-axes from two sites in Spain.[27] These had been previously assigned to Late Acheulean on the basis of supposed degree of refinement, but turned out to be much older than 600,000 years. Supposed levels of tool refinement may reflect differences in the availability of suitable raw materials as much as the cognitive abilities of their makers.[22]

The overall picture appears to be one of slow technological change over the course of around 300,000 years rather than a quantum leap arising from the larger brain of *Homo heidelbergensis*. Nevertheless, by 500,000 years ago tools were coming into use that implied techniques beyond the abilities of earlier hominins. Stone points from the archaeological site of Kathu Pan 1 (KP 1) in South Africa might have been used as spear tips. Some exhibit fractures to their ends, bases and edges that are consistent with a weapon striking a target – but not with use for cutting or scraping. The points are shaped near the base in a way that suggests that they were hafted to wooden spears. Experiments with replicas of the KP 1 points, made from similar raw materials, suggest that they made effective spear tips: the earliest-known multi-component tools.[28]

In 1995, the remains of four wooden spears were discovered at an open cast mine near the town of Schöningen in Germany. The spears are around 400,000 years old, and they were associated with carcasses of horses. Although as we saw in Chapter 5, even *Homo habilis* probably hunted to some extent, this combination of spears and their probable victims is the earliest unequivocal evidence of hunting by humans of large mammals. Each spear was over 2 m (6 ft. 6 in.) long, sharpened at both ends, and scraped smooth with stone tools.[29] The KP 1 and the Schöningen artefacts were probably used as thrusting spears rather than as projectile weapons, which did not come into use until around 280,000 years ago.[30] The production of these early spears was nevertheless a more complex process than making a hand-axe.[3]

The long age of the Acheulean hand-axe finally drew to a close with the advent of the Middle Stone Age in Africa and the Middle Palaeolithic in Europe. In Africa, the Acheulean/Middle Stone Age transition began 300,000 years ago and was largely completed by 200,000 years ago,[31] though transitional assemblages with elements from both Acheulean and Middle Stone Age are known from later.[32] In Europe the transition occurred slightly later, around 250,000 to 200,000 years ago.[33] The Middle Stone Age and Middle Palaeolithic are both characterised by prepared-core industries, although these had their origins in the late Acheulean from as early as 400,000 years ago.[34] Prepared-core techniques entail shaping a stone core to a pre-planned form, from which flakes of a desired size and shape are then struck. Depending on the shape of the core, the resulting flakes may be oval or triangular. They may then require retouching to improve their cutting edge. Such techniques are economical in their use of raw materials, because many flakes may be struck from the same core. Unlike the multi-purpose Acheulean hand-axe, they enable tools to be fashioned for specific purposes.[35] Prepared-core industries are classified as Mode 3 in Sir Grahame Clark's scheme: third generation industries lying midway in complexity between the earliest stone tools and those of late prehistory.

Prepared-core industries are now thought to have arisen independently in Africa and Eurasia.[36] They might have arisen when it was realised that flakes produced as a by-product of hand-axe manufacture could sometimes be useful as tools in their own right. Gradually, the emphasis shifted to the flakes themselves becoming the main product. Methods include the Levallois technique, named for the Parisian suburb of Levallois-Perret where examples of such prepared cores were discovered in the nineteenth century. It involves at least five or six clearly separate stages, each of which requires careful preplanning. Flakes were first struck off around the periphery of a raw stone nodule; the scars from this process were then used as striking platforms (the point where a stone core is struck by a hammerstone) to remove flakes from one surface of the nodule. From the resulting core, one or more flakes could now be detached, the shape and size of which being predetermined by the core preparation.[37] Flakes so produced were fashioned into as many as forty distinct tool types, each with its own specific cutting, scraping or piercing function. There was a much greater standardisation in the form of the tools made, indicating a clearer mental template and greater manipulative skill applied to their manufacture.[35]

No place like home

The earliest tentative evidence for purpose-built dwellings in Europe comes from the sites of Bilzingsleben in Germany and Terra Amata, near Nice, southern France, both of which are thought to be roughly 400,000 to 300,000 years old. Bilzingsleben is located alongside a stream that flowed from a nearby spring to a small lake; the finds comprise three concentrations of artefacts and fragmentary animal bones. Each of these is accompanied by large stones and bones that could have been used to build a wall, and is close to a spread of charcoal that might have been a fire hearth. Terra Amata is thought to be a seasonal occupation site where free-standing shelters were built, and in common with Bilzingsleben, there is evidence for the use of fire and the construction of hearths. Traces of posts suggest that saplings were embedded in the ground, bent towards the middle, and tied off to form rudimentary huts measuring around 8 m by 4 m (26 ft. by 13 ft.).[4,22,38]

At both sites, the evidence for shelter building is inconclusive, and there is certainly no sign the kind of well-organised substantial huts that were much later built by early modern humans in Europe. Nevertheless, these remains do suggest that *Homo heidelbergensis* was able to utilise technology and materials that extended beyond stone tool use, and this helped them to master the challenging conditions of Pleistocene Europe.[3] However, there is no evidence for fire use anywhere in Europe prior to 400,000 to 300,000 years ago, despite its obvious advantages in a region where winter temperatures fall below freezing.[38]

The Boxgrove people

The village of Boxgrove is located 5 km (3.5 miles) to the northeast of Chichester in West Sussex, and is noted for its ruined priory and thirteenth century parish church. The census of 2001 showed a population of fewer than a thousand people, but Acheulean hand-axes from the nearby Eartham Quarry suggest that people have been living in the area for a very long time indeed. In 1985 a team from University College London began excavating the quarry. The project grew in scope and eventually involved over 40 specialists and a large number of excavators. No human remains were found until late 1993, when a volunteer named Roger Pedersen spotted what turned out to be a human shin bone. Subsequently, two incisor teeth were found. The remains are 500,000 years old, making them the earliest-known human remains from Great Britain. The shin bone is the only postcranial element of *Homo heidelbergensis* to have been found in Northern Europe, and it is one of the most massive leg bones of an early human ever found. Its owner was probably a man on the basis of its size and thickness: he was powerfully-built, weighing over 90 kg (200 lb.) and standing at least 1.8 m (5 ft. 11 in.) tall. He was nicknamed Roger in honour of Roger Pedersen, and was probably around forty at the time of his death – a respectable age for the time. There were no indications as to the cause of death, though the shin bone had been gnawed, probably by wolves. The site has also yielded over 300 Acheulean hand-axes, together with debitage (the waste material left over from their production), and also the butchered remains of horse and rhinoceros.[2,39]

Today, the quarry is located 10 km (6 miles) from the coast, but half a million years ago the sea was much closer. At the time this part of Britain was connected to mainland Europe, and West Sussex was probably one of the most westerly points remaining above water. Massive chalk cliffs, 100 m (330 ft.) high, ran along an indented shoreline of beaches and tidal lagoons. Boxgrove was a coastal plain of salt marshes and grasslands, grazed by red deer, bison, horses, elephants and rhinoceros. Predators included wolves, hyenas, lions – and humans. For the latter, there was the added attraction of flint in the chalk cliffs: a perfect material for tool-making.[2,39]

Boxgrove has provided a wealth of data on the behaviour of hominins from this era. The scatter of artefacts is overlain by fine silt deposits that have frozen them in time for half a million years. Exact places where people made hand-axes have been preserved, with flakes of flint struck off lying where they fell.[39] The patterns of scattered debitage even make it possible to observe the arrangement of a tool-maker's legs while they went about their work. In some cases it has been possible to 'refit' flakes to the original hand-axe, yielding the exact sequence in which they had been removed, and shedding much light upon the stone knapping techniques used by *Homo heidelbergensis*. Also important is that the silt deposits overlying the artefacts accumulated over just 20 to 100 years, possibly only a single generation. Sites from the Middle Pleistocene are usually separated by thousands of years and archaeologists can rarely associate more than one location used by a specific group. At Boxgrove, however, they have been able to identify several associated sites, presumably used by the same group of people. It is thus possible to piece together a coherent picture of site usage by the Boxgrove people.[3]

It appears that hand-axes were not the only stone artefacts produced at Boxgrove. At one site of hand-axe manufacture, beside the other debitage was a small pile of larger flakes that had been set aside for possible use as tools in their own right – presaging the later Middle Stone Age and Middle Palaeolithic flaked tool industries. Refitting suggests that there were even larger flakes that are now missing, and were presumably taken away for tool use. A significant implication is that the tool-maker was able to concentrate on more than one goal at a time, i.e. both the hand-axe and the possibility of obtaining usable flakes as a by-product.[3]

One site of operations was the base of the cliff. Flint nodules were tested for quality by striking off a few flakes and discarded if of poor quality. Otherwise they were either knapped into hand-axes on the spot or removed for future use. A few hundred metres away from the cliff, the butchered remains of a horse were found. There are ten discrete debitage piles where, by refitting, archaeologists deduced that hand-axes had been produced, presumably to butcher the carcass of horse. The hand-axes themselves were not found and were presumably taken away when the job was complete. Each debitage pile seems to have been produced by an individual, not a group.[3]

A third site was located at the edge of a freshwater pond that served as a water hole. A large number of hand-axes and smaller tools were found, together with the butchered remains of many animals. The hand-axes were in some cases only partially formed. It appears that the group carried both cores and hand-axes around from place to place, with the latter in varying degrees of completion. The incomplete hand-axes were used not only as tools but as a source of flakes for making the smaller tools. The fact that hand-axes were left at the water hole but not at the site of the butchered horse carcass suggests that the former was a place of ongoing operations where tools were left for future use, whereas butchering the horse carcass was a one-off activity. This pattern of temporary and re-used sites suggests the Boxgrove people stuck to habitual patterns of action rather than performing activities on an *ad hoc* basis.[3]

The dawn of art and language

If *Homo heidelbergensis* was more cognitively advanced than *Homo erectus*, how close was the species to the behavioural pattern of modern humans? As with the earlier species, there is some evidence that *Homo heidelbergensis* was capable of some form of symbolic behaviour, though it was still probably fairly limited. The Berekhat Ram pebble is a small lump of volcanic lava that some believe is a female figurine. It was excavated in 1981 at the Late Acheulean site of Berekhat Ram on the Golan Heights in the Levant, in a level sealed between two basalt flows. Accurate dating of these permitted the age of the artefact to be estimated at around 250,000 to 280,000 years old. The object had been incised, probably with a sharp-edged flake tool. It was claimed that the intention was to represent the female form, with indications of head, neck, arms, shoulders and breasts.[40] Sceptics point out that the resemblance to a woman is poor[3] and it certainly bears very little resemblance to the finely-crafted 'Venus' figurines that are known from Europe after 40,000 years ago. Nevertheless, the pebble is undoubtedly a human-modified object that possesses no obvious utilitarian function.

To some extent the controversy over the nature of the Berekhat Ram pebble reflects the two rival schools of thought over the emergence of modern human behaviour, which we shall consider in detail in Chapter 11. One view is that it emerged quite suddenly in a cognitive 'human revolution', possibly as a result of a genetic mutation that somehow 'rewired' the human brain as recently as 50,000 years ago.[41] This 'smartness mutation' conferred an enormous survival advantage on its possessors, and rapidly swept through the human population. The event has been referred to as the Great Leap Forward, a term coined by Jared Diamond[42] in reference to the (disastrous) economic and social plan implemented between 1958 and 1961 in China by Mao Zedong.

Others, though, believe that there was no Great Leap Forward and that the elements of modern human behaviour emerged only very gradually over tens and possibly hundreds of millennia.[31] If the latter view is correct, it is likely that the Berekhat Ram pebble is indeed an attempt to portray a woman. This would make it the world's earliest-known example of representational art. Crude as it is, it could represent the earliest glimmerings of a sculptural tradition that would one day lead to the Venus de Milo, Michelangelo's *David* and Rodin's *The Thinker*.

While the Berekhat Ram pebble could be evidence of an early and quite possibly isolated creative spark, it is not by itself evidence for the behavioural modernity of *Homo heidelbergensis*. However, further evidence comes from Twin Rivers, a complex of caves in southern Zambia. The site was studied as far back as the 1950s, but in 1999 British archaeologist Larry Barham led an investigation and recovered over 300 pieces of haematite, limonite and specularite, ranging in age from 266,000 to 400,000 years old. These minerals can be used to produce a range of colours including red, yellow, brown and purple, and are known collectively as ochres. It seems very likely that the pieces found at the site were used as pigments; they are not naturally present in deposits at the site and must therefore have been brought in from elsewhere, and some of the specularite pieces showed signs of grinding. Specularite is harder than other ochres and more effort is required to obtain powder for pigments.[43]

We don't know for certain that the ochres were used as pigments. Simple utilitarian explanations are also possible, such as for medicinal purposes and for use in hide processing. However, the range of colours seen at Twin Rivers, the effort put into obtaining the different materials, and in particular to grinding the specularite suggests that such functional explanations are inadequate. Barham believes that the ochres were used primarily for ritual body painting and perhaps for cave painting as well, although no direct evidence remains after so long. Barham also believes that pigment use implies language. Unlike the carving of artefacts, rituals are group activities. Their meaning and significance is most effectively communicated by the use of language.[44]

This brings us to the question of whether or not *Homo heidelbergensis* had language. An endocast of the inside of the Kabwe skull has shown that the Broca's Area, a region of the brain linked with speech in modern humans (see Chapter 5), was enlarged relative to the corresponding area in the right hemisphere, which does suggest a degree of linguistic competence. However, it cannot tell us if *Homo heidelbergensis* used the complex grammatical language of modern humans. It has been suggested that grammatical language was necessary to provide verbal instruction in tool-making techniques, these having become too complex to be learned solely by observing others. An alternative viewpoint is that the key to learning was for the teacher to use pointing gestures and simple, non-grammatical instructions. Grammatical language might not have been necessary.[3]

The bottom line is that while methods of tool production had become more sophisticated than those of *Homo erectus*, the tools themselves were little changed. This suggests that the range of tasks performed did not change, but *Homo heidelbergensis* became more efficient at carrying them out. Technology had improved, but its role in the hominin way of life might not have changed significantly. The species was clearly able to fine-tune the technologies and expertise of *Homo erectus*, but it was not able to move these onto a new level. The ability of modern humans to innovate was still lacking in the people that lived during the period between 600,000 and 250,000 years ago.[3]

Florisbad

By 260,000 years ago, there is evidence to suggest that the anatomical condition of hominins in Africa was becoming increasingly modern. Unfortunately the evidence is sparse, comprising only a few specimens. The best known is the partial skull that was recovered in 1932 from the depths of the hot spring at Florisbad, some 50 km (30 miles) from Bloemfontein, South Africa. The town of Florisbad is named for Floris Venter, a local entrepreneur who in 1912 enlarged the pools at the spring for use as a spa. Later that year an earthquake caused a new spring to open up, revealing stone tools and fossils. The fossils were later described in a paper by Raymond Dart's future ally, Robert Broom.[45]

In 1932, zoologist Thomas F. Dreyer and his assistant Alice Lyle carried out excavations in the vicinity of the spring. They were funded by a Captain Robert E. Helme and the excavations produced further quantities of animal fossils. Venter feared loss of revenue if his baths were temporarily drained and Dreyer and Lyle had to wade around in the waters and grope for bones. On one such occasion, Dreyer plunged his hand into the spring deposits underwater and – rather in the manner of Little Jack Horner – pulled out part of a human skull, with his fingers stuck between its eyes. The skull comprises the right side of the face, most of the forehead and portions of the roof and sidewalls. A single upper right wisdom tooth was also found with the skull.[41] Two small samples of enamel from the tooth have been dated at 259,000 years old using electron spin resonance techniques.[46] In 1935, Dreyer described the find as *Homo helmei* ('Helme's Man'), to mark its distinctiveness from other fossil *Homo sapiens* and to acknowledge Helme's sponsorship that had made the discovery possible in the first place. *Homo helmei* is not widely accepted, largely because it is still known only from this one specimen, and it is usually 'lumped' into *Homo heidelbergensis*.

Nevertheless, the Florisbad skull does seem to represent an intermediate between *Homo heidelbergensis* and *Homo sapiens*. In comparison to that of a modern human, it is thick-walled and the face is broad and massive; but although there is thickening above the eye sockets, the browridge is less prominent, the forehead is relatively steep, and the face is flat and tucked in beneath the front part of the braincase.[41] These latter features contrast with the heavy browridges, low flattened forehead and long low braincase characteristic of *Homo heidelbergensis* and other early humans. In 1992 a skull and thigh bone, thought to be around 270,000 to 300,000 years old, were found at Ileret, northeast of Lake Turkana.[47] Both the skull and a similar example from Laetoli, Tanzania, are also intermediate in form between *Homo heidelbergensis* and *Homo sapiens*, and they may belong to the same 'group' as the Florisbad skull.[48]

For the time being, though, we shall leave Africa. While the African population was apparently evolving in the direction of modern humans, another group was emerging in Europe – the Neanderthals.

8: The other people

Please don't call us football hooligans

Of all early humans, none have captured the public imagination to anywhere near the extent of the Neanderthals. Indeed, with the possible exception of the dinosaurs, no extinct species is so deeply rooted in our popular culture. The idea that tens of thousands of years ago, people very much like ourselves shared the planet with another human species is one that intrigues many. Although like 'dinosaur', the term 'Neanderthal' is all-too-often used in a pejorative sense, in literature Neanderthals have generally been portrayed in a sympathetic light; for example *The Inheritors* by William Golding; Jean M. Auel's *Clan of the Cave Bear* series; and *The Ugly Little Boy* by Isaac Asimov. *The Neanderthal Parallax* is an award-winning trilogy by Canadian SF writer Robert Sawyer about a team of scientists who accidentally make contact with a parallel universe, in which Neanderthals rather than *Homo sapiens* became the dominant life form on Earth.

The term 'Neanderthal' comes from Neander Thal (Neander Valley), near Dusseldorf, Germany, where the first recognised specimen Neanderthal 1 was discovered at Feldhofer Cave in 1856. The German spelling was changed to Neander Tal in 1901, hence the commonly-used variant spelling Neandertal. The scientific name, *Homo neanderthalensis*, was unaffected by the change, as it is not permitted to alter the formal names of species once they have been assigned. The Neander Valley is named for Joachim Neander, a seventeenth century Calvinist theologian who is best known for composing the popular hymn *Praise to the Lord, the Almighty*. 'Neander' is a classicised form of the German surname Neumann (Newman in English). Ironically, therefore, the literal meaning of Neanderthal is New Man's Valley.

Discovery and rediscovery

Neanderthal 1 was not actually the first discovery of a Neanderthal, as specimens had previously been recovered in Ennis Cave, Belgium between 1829 and 1830 and Forbes Cave, Gibraltar in 1848. Unlike Neanderthal 1, however, their significance was not immediately recognised, so the Feldhofer Cave discovery was the first fossil to be recognised as a non-modern human.[1]

The fossils recovered at Feldhofer Cave include a skullcap, two thigh bones, three bones from the right arm, two from the left arm, part of the left ilium (upper pelvic bone), fragments of a shoulder blade, and ribs. The cave was located in a limestone gorge and the remains were recovered by quarry workers in August 1856. As it would later turn out, they inadvertently discarded further remains and possibly also stone tools.[2] The find was examined by a local schoolteacher and amateur naturalist, Johann Karl Fuhlrott, who noted that the remains were unlike those of modern humans. Fuhlrott passed the remains on to Hermann Schaaffhausen, Professor of Anatomy at the University of Bonn, and the pair jointly announced the discovery in 1857. However, Schaaffhausen considered the Neanderthals to represent an ancient Northern European race predating the Germans and the Celts. That they might represent a new species of human was first suggested in 1864 by the Irish anatomist William King, who proposed the name *Homo neanderthalensis*.[2] King's suggestion was not widely accepted at first and, foreshadowing the debate over the Flores hominins almost a century and a half later, the Prussian pathologist Rudolf Virchow dismissed the Feldhofer remains as belonging to a modern human affected by disease.[1]

Archaeologists eventually did return to the quarry, only to find that the cave had been destroyed. The whole area had been excavated for its limestone, needed for the steel industry as the Industrial Revolution transformed Dusseldorf into a boom town. In the 1920s the area was turned into a park. The cave remained lost to science until 1997, when Ralf Schmitz and Jürgen Thissen from the Rhineland Archaeological Service relocated it with old maps, and nineteenth century paintings of the site in which they recognised a rock that still stood in the Neander Park. They then dug exploratory trenches nearby, and on sifting through the debris they found bat teeth and pieces of stalactites – items that are only found in caves.[3]

Realising they had located the site of Feldhofer Cave, Schmitz and Thissen continued their investigations. Eventually, they unearthed 62 human skeletal fragments. A number of cranial pieces were found to either fit or represent elements missing from the skull of the original nineteenth century find. Another small piece of bone exactly fitted its left knee joint. It was established that the finds represent three individuals – two adults (including the 1856 find) and one adolescent. In addition, the team recovered a large number of stone tools and animal remains showing evidence of butchery. Radiocarbon dating of the remains indicates that the Feldhofer Cave Neanderthals lived 42,000 years ago.[4]

Our distinctive cousins

We know far more about Neanderthals we do about any other extinct hominins. It has certainly helped that the prehistory of Europe has been more extensively investigated than that of any other region. No less important, the Neanderthals and their immediate precursors were the first hominins known to intentionally bury their dead. Consequently, many remains have been recovered from burial sites. It has also proved possible to extract genetic material from Neanderthal remains in many cases, from which we have learned much about their evolutionary history and their way of life.

Anatomically, Neanderthals were quite distinct not only from modern humans, but also from any earlier hominins. The 'classic' Neanderthals that had emerged in Europe by 130,000 years ago retained the forwardly-projecting face, chinless lower jaw, pronounced browridge and low flattened forehead of *Homo heidelbergensis*. However, the braincase was distinct from that of the earlier species, being higher, more rounded, and having a cylindrical shape when viewed from the rear.[1] It was still long and low in comparison to the globular skull of a modern human. The cranial capacity was very large, varying from 1,245 to 1,740 cc, with an average of about 1,520 cc,[2] somewhat larger than the 1,350 cc average of a present-day human. However, modern humans from the period 75,000 to 27,000 years ago had roughly the same cranial capacity as contemporary Neanderthals.[5] The smaller brain size of present-day humans reflects the fact that we are rather less massive and powerfully built than modern humans from that era.

In stature, Neanderthals were rather shorter than modern humans, with males averaging from 1.64 to 1.68 m (5 ft. 4½ in. to 5 ft. 6 in.) and females 1.52 to 1.56 m (5 ft. to 5 ft. 1½ in.) tall.[6] However, they were stocky and powerfully-built, with a wide pelvis and short, heavily-muscled limbs.[1] A typical male weighed about 80 kg (176 lb.), in the region of twenty percent more than a modern man of the same height.[7] The large wide chest of Neanderthals might have been related to the increased oxygen consumption associated with the higher energy demands of a larger body.[8] Their wrists and hands were big-boned and muscular, and anthropologist Glenn Conroy[9] has noted that Neanderthals probably didn't do limp hand-shakes.

The symbolic ape

The powerful biting musculature and large size and pattern of wear of their front teeth suggests that Neanderthals might have used their jaws as a vice-like tool, possibly for gripping mammal hides while skinning them with stone tools.[1,10] Certain features of the Neanderthal lower jawbone are unique to Neanderthals. The corresponding features in modern humans are actually a primitive legacy from *Homo erectus*, ruling out the once-popular view that modern humans evolved from Neanderthals.[11]

The large nose and sinuses of the Neanderthals might have been a climatic adaptation that helped to warm and moisten the dry, cold air of northern latitudes, in turn protecting the brain and aiding respiration.[10] Limb proportions were probably also adaptations to the problem of retaining body heat in cold climates. They are mirrored to some extent by those of present-day Inuit and Sami people. Interestingly, Neanderthals were more extreme in their limb proportions, despite living in more moderate conditions. This suggests they were more reliant on their physiology to combat the cold than any modern human.[2] Having evolved in Africa, the first modern humans in Europe found themselves poorly-adapted to the harsh conditions there. Unable to adapt their bodies, they adapted their technology, and thus became more reliant on it than were the Neanderthals. However, technological change can greatly outpace evolutionary change, and that in the long run might have been a factor giving modern humans a competitive edge over Neanderthals.

The Neanderthal humerus (upper arm) was typically far more massive on the right than on the left. Such asymmetry also exists in modern humans, but typically does not exceed 5 to 14 percent. In Neanderthals the range was from 24 to 57 percent, similar to that of modern cricketers and tennis players. The traditional explanation is that this arose from regular underhanded spear-thrusting at close quarters. In such activities (assuming a right-handed individual), the right arm is positioned towards the back, while the left arm is positioned towards the front and serves to guide and stabilise the spear. It has been generally assumed that the bulk of the spear-thrusting force would be supplied by the right arm, but it has been found that muscular activity of the chest and shoulder is actually greater on the left hand side of the body. It has been found that because the left hand is the closest point of contact, the reaction force as the spear makes impact with the target is countered by the muscles on the left side of the body. Instead of spear-thrusting, it has been suggested that the massive right arm arose from scraping animal hides – an activity that probably consumed many hours a week.[12]

A Neanderthal adaptation that has been the subject of much interest is the superior pubic ramus (forming part of the pubic bone located at the front and base of both halves of the pelvis), which is longer than that of a modern human. In the 1980s, palaeoanthropologist Erik Trinkaus[13] suggested that in females, this indicated a wider birth canal. In turn, he claimed, this implied that the gestation period of Neanderthals was longer than that of modern humans, possibly as long as 12 to 14 months. This figure was obtained by comparing brain size versus gestation period in other mammals. Consequently, he argued, Neanderthal infants were born more developed and less helpless than present-day infants. Trinkaus believed the necessary levels of parental care only became possible after 30,000 years ago, after which time the anomalously-short gestation period of modern humans became advantageous, as it reduced the energy costs to the mother of carrying over a longer term, and possibly reduced the intervals between births.

Trinkaus' brain size versus gestation period calculations were criticised because they were based on a survey that that was not specific to primates and included only a few primate species: later work has shown that in primates, birth weight rather than brain size is a better indicator of gestation period.[14] He also followed the then-current view that modern humans evolved from Neanderthals around 30,000 years ago, and saw the shorter gestation period was just one of a number of evolutionary changes. We now know that modern humans did not evolve from Neanderthals and, as we have seen, the lengthy dependency of newborn babies on their parents probably goes back much further than 30,000 years. We have also seen that there is a limit to how long a growing foetus can remain in the womb before its metabolic needs become too great for the mother to support.[15]

Other theories were later proposed to explain the supposedly-wider birth canal. One suggestion was that it simply reflected the greater size of the head in comparison to the relatively short stature.[16] Another proposal was that the brain grew faster *in utero* compared with modern humans.[17] That the birth canal actually *was* wider was challenged in 1987, when an analysis was published of the pelvis of the Kebara 2 skeleton from Kebara Cave, Mount Carmel, in Israel. It showed that the pelvic inlet was comparable to that of a modern human, and that the length of the superior pubic ramus was simply due to the Neanderthal hip bone, which is externally rotated (turned outwards from the midline of the body) to a greater extent than the modern hip bone. It has now been suggested that the differences between the Neanderthal and the modern pelvis are related to locomotion and posture, rather than the need for an enlarged birth canal. Unfortunately, the Kebara 2 pelvis, one of the most complete ever found, was from a male, so an enlarged Neanderthal birth canal could not be entirely ruled out.[18]

However, more recent research, using virtual reconstruction techniques, has provided fresh insight. It turns out that the Neanderthal gestation period was similar to that of modern humans, but the birth canal was different to that of a modern woman. The techniques were used to estimate the brain size of a newborn infant from Mezmaiskaya Cave in Russia, who had died just one or two weeks after birth. By assuming a modern rate of brain growth after birth, researchers established that the brain size at birth was comparable to that of a modern human. This in turn suggested that the Neanderthal gestation period was also similar.[19]

Researchers have also used tomography scans to construct a virtual reconstruction of the birth canal of a female Neanderthal from Tabun in Israel. They found that the overall size was comparable to that of a modern woman – suggesting that Neanderthal childbirth was equally problematic – but that the shape of the canal differed. In both modern humans and Neanderthals, the outlet from the birth canal is oval-shaped, but whereas in a modern woman the oval is aligned vertically, in a Neanderthal woman it was aligned horizontally. It was suggested that the horizontal alignment of the Neanderthal birth canal was the original hominin condition. When brain size began to increase relative to body size in the Middle Pleistocene, there were two evolutionary solutions to the problem. One was simply a wider pelvis. Such a solution posed no problems for the stocky, cold-adapted Neanderthals. However, in Africa, where there was a need for efficient heat dissipation, it was essential to retain a slim build. Consequently, the vertical alignment evolved, necessitating the rotation of the infant while passing through the birth canal, as in modern childbirth.[20]

After birth, Neanderthal brain development differed from that of modern humans. Virtual reconstruction of two infants from Dederiyeh Cave in Syria, aged 1.6 and 2 years old, showed a cranial capacity at the high end of what is normal for present-day children of the same age, suggesting a faster growth rate during infancy.[19] Similar techniques have also been used to show that the development of the Neanderthal brain also differed from that of modern humans. During infancy, cranial bones are thin, and bone tissue formation is not yet complete. Shape changes of the frontal and parietal bones, which form the front, and the roof and sides of the skull, are largely driven by the increase in brain volume. Thus the development of the brain case reflects that of the brain itself. At birth, modern humans have relatively elongated braincases, similar to those of Neanderthals. Only later, between the age of one and two years old, does the braincase of a modern infant take on the characteristic globular shape that distinguishes *Homo sapiens* from other human species. However, this 'globularization' phase did not occur with Neanderthal infants, and they retained the long, low-shaped brain case into adulthood.[21]

Another question is whether or not Neanderthals reached maturity earlier than modern humans. The larger adult size of the Neanderthal brain was balanced by a faster growth rate in childhood, meaning that adult size was attained at about the same age.[19] As we saw in Chapter 6, a direct correlation between rates of dental development and age of maturation has been used to infer that early humans matured faster than modern humans. However, for Neanderthals, such studies have produced contradictory results. One study found rates more comparable to earlier humans,[22] but another obtained rates closer to those of modern humans (although the root growth followed a different pattern).[23] More recently, data from the teeth of six juvenile Neanderthals has suggested an intermediate position; Neanderthal dental development was more prolonged than that of earlier humans, but it was still more rapid than that of modern humans.[24]

Meet Wilma

In 2008, in a long-overdue attempt to dispel widespread perception of Neanderthals as brutish troll-like beings, the *National Geographic* commissioned a full-sized reconstruction of a Neanderthal woman.[25] The project drew on the latest information from genetics, fossil evidence, and archaeology. The starting point of the reconstruction was a 'feminised' cast of a composite male Neanderthal skeleton originally assembled from various specimens at the American Museum of Natural History. In some cases, male body parts were swapped for the female equivalent, where this was available. For example, the Kebara 2 pelvis used in the original composite was substituted for a female pelvis from Tabun. Where no appropriate female body part was available, the male part was rescaled to female proportions. The skull was constructed from scratch, using only female specimens. The skeleton was then fleshed out using modelling clay and from this model a silicone cast was made, painted up and given red hair from Highland cattle. The result was a sturdy and rather careworn woman, having a bad hair day. She was given the name Wilma, after the *Flintstones* character. While her appearance is a little strange to our eyes, there is absolutely no doubting her humanity.

Genetic studies suggest that Neanderthals might have had pale skin and red hair. Humans, in common with many other living organisms, owe their skin, hair and eye colour to a pigment known as melanin, which is produced by cells known as melanocytes. In modern humans, a gene known as melanocortin 1 receptor (MC1R) is responsible for individual coloration, and red hair and pale skin is associated with certain alleles (variant forms) of this gene. Genetic testing of two Neanderthal individuals found at Monte Lessini in Italy and at the El Sidrón cave in northern Spain showed they both possessed an allele of the MC1R gene not found in modern humans, but when it was inserted into a modern human melanocyte cell, it was found to produce the same effects as modern alleles associated with red hair and pale skin. This does not prove that all Neanderthals had red hair and pale skin, as other individuals might have had different alleles of MC1R. However, it does mean Neanderthals probably had the same range of skin and hair colour as modern humans.[26]

In present-day human populations, skin and hair colour are adaptations to latitude. In equatorial regions, dark skin and hair are essential to block out the Sun's ultraviolet rays and guard against skin cancer. In higher latitudes, where lower levels of ultraviolet are normal, this is less critical. Furthermore, people with pale skin are able to generate Vitamin D more efficiently. So while mutations in MC1R leading to pale skin in Africa would be adverse and selected against, in higher latitudes the reverse would be the case. This would lead to the range of skin and hair colours seen in present-day human populations. Assuming the same happened in the case of the Neanderthals, the Northern European populations would have had pale skins, and those living in southerly locations would have been more olive-skinned.

Origins: The Pit of Bones

With the successful extraction of genetic material from Neanderthal remains, it has been possible to use the molecular clock method to put a date on when the most recent common ancestor of Neanderthals and modern humans lived. Studies have focussed on both nuclear DNA and mitochondrial DNA.

Mitochondrial studies have yielded a date of 660,000 ± 140,000 years ago.[27] Studies based on nuclear DNA indicate that the populations that gave rise to Neanderthals and modern humans began to diverge from one another about 700,000 years ago. The populations became distinct species 370,000 years ago.[28] These dates broadly correspond to when *Homo heidelbergensis* lived in Europe and Africa, though, as we saw in Chapter 7, there are doubts as to whether the European and African populations are actually the same species. The timing nevertheless rules out the possibility that modern humans evolved from Neanderthals 30,000 years ago.

'Classic' Neanderthals, i.e. humans possessing the full suite of Neanderthal characteristics, do not appear in the fossil record until 130,000 years ago. However, French palaeoanthropologist Jean-Jacques Hublin[29] has proposed that Neanderthal characteristics appeared gradually over time, in a piecemeal fashion. Thus, for example if Feature X appeared in one population and Feature Y in another, then interbreeding between the two populations would have resulted in a population possessing both Features X and Y. Over time, populations gradually acquired the full suite of Neanderthal characteristics by a process of accretion, resulting in a gradual transition from *Homo heidelbergensis* to Neanderthal. In fact, Hublin goes further and argues that European *Homo heidelbergensis* are actually early Neanderthals. This is basically the same as the first of Philip Rightmire's two scenarios discussed in Chapter 7, in which European and African *Homo heidelbergensis* are seen as two separate species, with the latter receiving the name *Homo rhodesiensis*; except that Hublin proposes doing away with the name *Homo heidelbergensis* altogether. The accretion model explains 'proto-Neanderthal' features seen on certain fossils dating to the period prior to the appearance of the 'classic' Neanderthals. These include a 400,000-year-old fragmentary skull from Swanscombe in England and the 225,000-year-old Steinheim skull from Stuttgart, Germany. The accretion model also dovetails with the 'sources and sinks' model outlined in Chapter 7, which sees demes possessing different proto-Neanderthal features 'mixing and matching' until the 'classic' Neanderthal form emerged.

Some of the distinctive Neanderthal features might have resulted from the effects of genetic drift on the small isolated populations.[30] Genetic drift refers to random inter-generational changes in the frequency with which an allele occurs in a population. Even if none of the resulting characteristics (hair colour, blood group, etc.) confers any particular advantage, these changes will occur because some individuals will have more children than others. In a small population, this can result in some characteristics becoming very common, and others disappearing altogether. An analogy for genetic drift is seen in small isolated villages where everybody ends up with the same surname. If for example Mr and Mrs Smith are the only Smiths in the village and they have only daughters, then the surname Smith will disappear from the next generation. Over enough generations, the villagers will 'drift' to just one surname.

Genetic drift fits the accretion model, as it requires Neanderthal characteristics to appear gradually rather than all at once. To test the theory, researchers obtained a divergence time for Neanderthals from modern humans using a statistical comparison of skull characteristics. If the theory is correct, there should be a close correspondence between this figure and those obtained by genetic methods. The date obtained was 373,000 years ago, very close to the genetic result of 370,000 years ago, and thus supporting the accretion model.[31]

The symbolic ape

Much of the evidence we have regarding Neanderthal origins comes from a single site in the Sierra de Atapuerca of northern Spain, near the city of Burgos: a Middle Pleistocene human burial pit known as Sima de los Huesos. The name translates – rather appropriately – as 'the Pit of Bones'. Sima de los Huesos is a small muddy chamber lying at the bottom of a 13 m (43 ft.) chimney, lying deep within the Cueva Mayor system of caves. Unlike the nearby Gran Dolina, the Cueva Mayor was not exposed by the cutting of a railway trench. Graffiti found in the cave system suggests adventurous young men from Burgos have been exploring it with ropes and torches since the late thirteenth century. Some supposedly ventured into the dark caverns in search of fossil cave bear teeth to impress their girlfriends, and in the twentieth century the site also became popular with amateur fossil hunters. However, it did not receive professional attention until 1976, when a student named Trinidad Torres discovered a human lower jawbone while searching for cave bear fossils. Torres realised the significance of finding human remains in association with Middle Pleistocene cave bear fossils. He showed his find to palaeontologist Emiliano Aguirre, who confirmed that the jawbone was typical for hominins from this era.

Investigation of the site has proved to be long and difficult. The most immediate problems are logistical. The cramped site is located more than 500 m (⅓ mile) from the mouth of the Cueva Mayor and is hard to access, necessitating at times crawling on the stomach. Another problem is the disturbance to the site caused by the many generations of souvenir and fossil hunters. Systematic excavation commenced in 1984 and has continued ever since. To date, over 2,000 fragmentary hominin fossils have been recovered, including three skulls. In total, the remains are thought to represent at least 32 individuals of both sexes. It is likely that the site was simply used for the hygienic disposal of the dead, because there is no evidence to suppose that any of the individuals were deliberately killed and the bones show no sign of injuries caused by spears or clubs. Unlike the *Homo antecessor* remains from the nearby Gran Dolina site, there is no evidence of cannibalism. Barring a single hand-axe, no artefacts have been recovered from the site, suggesting that it was not a place of ritual or other regular activity. Many of the remains are of adolescents and young adults, leading some to suppose the deaths did not result from everyday events. Possibilities include epidemic disease and massacre by a rival group, even though evidence for the latter is lacking. In fact, the pattern of mortality was probably quite normal for the time, and a similar peak in adolescence has been found at a site at Krapina in Croatia. The deaths could simply be the result of hunting accidents and childbirth complications. Hunting accidents were probably not uncommon among inexperienced young hunters, and women likely fell pregnant soon after commencing menstruation.[10]

Study of this enormous collection of bones is still in progress, and is likely to continue for some time yet as the site yields further fossils. However, it has become clear that the fossils show a mixture of *Homo heidelbergensis* and Neanderthal characteristics, just as would be expected if the accretion model is correct. The key question is how old is the site? Age estimates have varied: an early study using uranium series dating suggested that it was approximately 350,000 years old,[32] but later work, using higher-resolution uranium series techniques, suggested that the remains were at least 530,000 years old.[33] This older date would be problematic, as it would make the Sima people earlier than some *Homo heidelbergensis* remains from Southern Europe and the Balkan region that show no incipient Neanderthal characteristic features. More recently however, it has been suggested that the hominin-bearing layer at Sima is only 430,000 years old; this is in better agreement with the accretion hypothesis.[34]

The world of the Neanderthals

There is little doubt that Neanderthal life was very harsh. Studies of their remains suggest that few lived beyond their early forties, though they probably had a potential lifespan comparable to that of modern humans.[1] Many remains show healed fractures, particularly to parts of the upper body, suggesting injuries incurred in close range hunting of large mammals. Malnutrition, arthritis and periodontal gum disease were common. Neanderthals lived hard and died young.[2,10] It would, however, be a mistake to think of the world they inhabited as solely an icy wilderness. The era in which they lived was not one of consistent cold, and the more southerly populations in the Levant and southwest Europe enjoyed tolerably warm conditions even during glacial epochs. Only the populations from the more recent European sites lived under the harsh Ice Age conditions of popular imagination.[1]

Two prolonged glacial periods occurred during the Middle Stone Age in Africa and Middle Palaeolithic in Europe. The first of these was the Riss Glacial from 190,000 to 126,000 years ago (broadly corresponding to Marine Isotope Stage 6), and the second was the Würm Glacial or last glacial period ('the last Ice Age') from 110,000 to 11,650 years ago. Between the two was a warm interval, the Eemian Interglacial from 126,000 to 110,000 years ago (roughly spanning the last two-thirds of Marine Isotope Stage 5e and first third of Marine Isotope Stage 5d).[35,36,37] During the Eemian, forest and narrow-nosed rhinoceros, straight-tusked elephants, hippopotamus, lions and hyenas could be found even in northwestern and Central Europe.[38]

The Würm Glacial that followed was initially punctuated by warm interstadials, but the onset of Marine Isotope Stage 4, 74,000 years ago,[35] saw Europe plunged into a prolonged deep freeze. During this period, glaciers covered most of Scandinavia, Britain and Ireland, and steppe and steppe-tundra covered much of Northern and Central Europe. Forests were confined to Southern Europe,[39] but the steppe and steppe-tundra provided an abundance of herd animals. Hunting these was probably easier than hunting the deer and boar that inhabited the thick forests further south.[1] Even the warmer intervals were on occasions punctuated by abrupt cooling episodes known as Heinrich events. These cold snaps were associated with ice sheet instability, and resulted in the launching of 'iceberg armadas' into the North Atlantic.[40] The Heinrich events might each have lasted for around 250 years.[41]

The world of the Neanderthals, as established from numerous sites, stretched from Britain in the northwest, Israel in the south, and Gibraltar in the southwest. The partial skeleton of an eight-to-ten-year-old child discovered in the late 1930s in Teshik-Tash Cave, Uzbekistan, was until recently thought to represent the easternmost extent of the Neanderthal range. However, mitochondrial and nuclear DNA recovered from remains found at the sites of Okladnikov Cave and Denisova Cave in the Altai Mountains has now been found to be of Neanderthal origin, extending their range at least 2,000 km (1,250 miles) further east, into southern Siberia.[42,43] In all probability, though, the extent of the Neanderthal range fluctuated in accordance with the climate, shifting further south during cold episodes.[44]

Data from mitochondrial DNA recovered from Neanderthals suggests that the Neanderthal population was divided into at least three distinct geographical groups: a western group living in a region stretching from the Atlantic coast to the Baltic and to the Caspian Sea; a southern group in Southern and Southeastern Europe; and an eastern group in Western Asia. Populations might not have been constant over time, and some inter-group migration might have occurred.[45] The mitochondrial data also suggests that Neanderthal population sizes were very low. Genetic diversity in mitochondrial DNA recovered from Neanderthals living from 38,000 to 70,000 years ago has been found to have been just a third that of present-day modern human populations. The genetic diversity of a population is related to its size, and from this result it has been estimated that the population

The symbolic ape

included fewer than 3,500 females of child-bearing age.[46] Low population size is also implied by genetic data from one of the Altai specimens, which showed that inbreeding was common.[43]

It is likely that the western population suffered a collapse approximately 48,000 years ago. Genetic diversity of the later members of this population was very low, even by Neanderthal standards. The result may be interpreted as a population bottleneck, followed by recovery. The timing corresponds with several brief episodes of extremely low temperature, the effects of which were particularly severe in Western Europe. As conditions improved, the region was re-colonised, either from a small western refugium, or from the east.[47]

A Spanish site, El Sidrón, in the north of the country has provided disturbing insights into Neanderthal family life – and death. El Sidrón is an extensive system of limestone caves in the Asturias region. Human remains were first discovered in 1994, and systematic excavations commenced in 2000, and to date, around 1,800 hominin skeletal fragments and 400 stone tools have been recovered. The human remains represent twelve Neanderthal individuals, including three adult males, three adult females, three male adolescents, two juveniles, and an infant of unknown sex. They are thought to be part of a single group, all of whom died at around the same time. The remains and accompanying tools were found in a side gallery deep within the cave complex, and were probably brought down from the surface when a violent storm caused an upper gallery or a series of fissures to collapse.[48,49] The whole assemblage is around 49,000 years old.[50]

The low temperature of the side gallery meant that genetic material has survived, and mitochondrial DNA was successfully extracted from each of the individuals. It was found that the genetic diversity of the group was lower than would be expected for unrelated Neanderthals, suggesting that they were related to one another. All three of the adult males carried the same mitochondrial lineage, whereas the three adult females all carried different lineages. As mitochondrial DNA is inherited solely from the maternal line, the males must all have shared the same maternal lineages. However, the females all had different maternal lineages, suggesting that in Neanderthal groups, mature males remained within their family birth group, but females came from outside. The term 'patrilocality' is applied to social systems where men remain in the family home, but women move to the home of their new husband upon marriage.[49]

There also emerged a darker side to the discoveries. All the El Sidrón individuals had suffered from stunted growth, presumably arising from malnutrition. This was indicated by deficiencies in dental enamel formation, known as hypoplasias, which occur when growth is arrested. Hypoplasias were present on over 50 percent of the group members' incisors, canines and premolars, and over 30 percent of their molars. Five of the members had experienced two episodes of growth arrest, and one adult had experienced four. It is clear that for this extended Neanderthal family, life was very difficult – and in the end, it seems, this group met a grim fate. Many of the bones have been cut with stone tools or smashed open for their marrow – in other words, cannibalism. We shall never know exactly what happened, but it is likely that the El Sidrón Neanderthals were killed and eaten by members of a neighbouring group who were themselves on the brink of starvation.[48]

This grisly incident aside, it is not known to what extent Neanderthal groups interacted with each other, if at all. Evidence for long-distance social networking is only very tentative. In southwest France, sources for stone artefacts found at Neanderthal sites, when identified, have in most cases turned out to be local. However, a small amount of material, rarely exceeding one or two percent of the total, has been traced to sources up to 100 km (60 miles) away. This is far too distant to have simply been recovered during the course of daily foraging. Could the material have arrived on the site via some form of social interaction with other Neanderthal groups? Intriguing as this thought may be, it is not the only possibility. One is that Neanderthal groups were involved in a series of far-ranging annual movements, probably in response to shifting seasonal distributions of animal herds or other sources of food. If the various seasonal migrations all began and ended at a given site location, then over time materials from distant sources would end up on the site. Another possible explanation is that in the course of their seasonal migrations, a number of different groups all used the same site at different times of the year. There is also the problem that, in southwest France at least, high-quality raw material is so abundant that it unlikely to have been the subject of long-distance trade.[51]

Much of our knowledge of the Neanderthal lifestyle comes from their sites, which have been extensively studied over many decades. From them have been teased clues about food-procurement, diet, tool-making technologies and mortuary practices. Much work has focused on the caves and rock shelters in southwest France, some of which remained in use for over 60,000 years. It is their apparent propensity for caves and rock shelters that has given rise to the public perception of Neanderthals as 'cave men', though many open-air sites are also known. The cave and rock shelter sites are typically well-sheltered locations on south or southeast-facing flanks of river valleys, commanding extensive views over adjacent valley habitats. Such sites offered obvious advantages for observing distribution and movement of game animals, while benefiting from more sunlight and increased protection from prevailing winds. A further consideration was ease of access to raw material for tool-making. Accordingly, many sites are located close to limestone outcrops yielding abundant, accessible high-quality flints. Sheltered valley habitats provided refuge for several species of game animals during glacial periods and were herd migration routes. The valleys of minor tributaries seem to have been preferred to those of major rivers, probably because narrow valleys afford better protection from the elements. However, sites were typically close to a confluence with larger valleys, providing easy access to the sources of food available within the wider and more exposed floodplains of major rivers.[51]

The caves and rock shelters were probably living places rather than just places for killing animals and butchery. A sleeping and rest area has been identified at Abric Romaní, a 55,000-year-old rock shelter near Barcelona and traces of hearths of one form or another have been found at many sites. The fires would have been used for cooking food and to provide warmth, light and protection from predators. Though some hearths were underlain by rocks, they are generally fairly unsophisticated and lacked the means to control airflow and heat dissipation.[2,52] There is only limited evidence of other forms of site modification, such as walls and paved floors, but there is better evidence for dug pits that might have been used for food storage. In frozen soil, a pit could have acted as a refrigerator to store frozen meat for weeks if not months. Not all these cave and rock shelter sites necessarily served as living places. Some were located at higher elevations, and could only be reached by a strenuous climb. These might have been only sporadically occupied, probably for observation purposes.[51]

Open-air sites are nearly always found close to springs, streams or lakes. Such locations were favourable places for camping or obtaining food. Some sites are near sources of stone raw materials and have extensive flaking debris, suggesting that they were used as stone tool workshops. Others have scatters of artefacts and animal bones, suggesting either a camp or a site where animals were killed and butchered.[2] Most open-air sites were probably only briefly occupied in order to carry out short term activities, but a few seem to have been the focus of intensive and wide-ranging activities, extending over substantial areas of the surrounding terrain.[51]

The Neanderthals are generally associated with the Mousterian industry, a prepared-core industry that takes its name from Le Moustier, a rock shelter in the Dordogne region of southwest France. The Mousterian is classed as Mode 3 in Sir Grahame Clark's scheme; a third generation prepared-core tool-making technology that was more sophisticated than the earlier Acheulean hand-axes, but not too dissimilar to the tool-making technologies of later *Homo heidelbergensis*. It emerged between 250,000 and 200,000 years ago,[2] and characteristic tool types included single-edged pieces known as side scrapers, tooth-edged 'denticulates', 'notches' (featuring a single indentation), backed knives (which were sharp on one edge and blunted on the other like a penknife), points, and hand-axes.[10]

Microwear studies of the side scrapers suggest that they were used to cut and slice wood, meat or skin, as well as for scraping hide or bone. To what use the notched and tooth-edged pieces were put is less clear. Microwear analysis suggests suggest that some were used as planes or scrapers for shaping wooden stakes or shafts. Some might also have been used on skins, meat or soft plant material. The points were probably hafted to wooden spears using pitch obtained from birch bark. The penknife-like backed knives seem to have been intended for cutting, with pressure attached to the blunt edge. They were probably used on wood, plant material and processing animal products. On the other hand, the hand-axes seem to have been a continuation of the earlier Acheulean industry.[51,53] The Neanderthal tool production repertoire also included blades.[51] A blade is defined as a flake struck from a prepared stone core and that is more than twice as long as is broad. Blades can be retouched to produce a wide range of tools including knives, awls, points and scrapers. The term 'bladelet' is used to describe small blades measuring around 1 to 4 cm (0.4 to 1.6 in.) in length.[54]

Neanderthals also made specialised bone tools. Two sites in the Dordogne Valley have yielded four nearly identical deer rib fragments with smoothed edges. These have been interpreted as being a type of tool known as a *lissoir* (French 'to make smooth') used for preparing animal hides. The *lissoir* is used by present-day leather-workers to make hides softer, tougher and more waterproof. Their manufacture entailed polishing and grinding the rib fragments to a predetermined size and shape, implying that Neanderthals knew how to exploit the specific properties of bone both for shaping and for use. A date of 51,500 years old has been obtained for one of the artefacts using optically stimulated luminescence, making these tools the earliest-known specialised bone tools in Europe.[55]

A question that remains unresolved is the Neanderthal use of clothing. Even during warm Eemian Interglacial, Neanderthals must have faced a considerable heat-loss problem in winter. Wearing animal skins across the shoulder would have been insufficient to cope with the temperatures of even an averagely cold winter and body cooling caused by wind-chill. Clothing and footwear would have had to be sewn together tightly in order to keep out snow and water.[56] However, definite evidence for tailored clothing is lacking prior to the arrival of modern humans in Europe, and is only found at sites associated with modern humans.[2,57]

Earning a crust

There is no lack of clues in the archaeological record as to how Neanderthals went about getting their next meal, but making sense of them has never been easy. The traditional view of Neanderthals is that they were predominantly meat eaters, and indeed stable isotope analysis does support that view. Carbon and nitrogen isotope data for Neanderthal remains from sites in Belgium, France, Croatia and Germany suggests a diet heavily dependent on meat from herbivores.[58,59] Animal remains found at Neanderthal sites suggest that their meat came primarily from five main species: reindeer, red deer, horses, aurochs (cattle) and steppe bison.[51]

The conventional view is that Neanderthals hunted close up to their prey with heavy-duty thrusting spears rather than projectile spears.[44,10] Recently, however, this view has been challenged. A Neanderthal left upper arm found at Tourville-la-Rivière, Normandy was found to have an abnormality that might have resulted from trauma connected to repetitive movements similar to those seen for professional throwing athletes.[60] Another strong hint is the discovery of 280,000-year-old projectile points in Ethiopia. Made from local volcanic obsidian, the points predate the emergence of modern human by 80,000 years. Although they were not made by Neanderthals, they demonstrate that archaic humans could make long-range projectile weapons.[61]

Despite these findings, it seems likely that Neanderthals did frequently engage their prey at close quarters. Indirect evidence for this comes from the high incidence of healed upper body fractures seen in many Neanderthal remains. These injuries are not unlike those suffered by present-day rodeo riders, who also handle large animals at close quarters.[10] The physical strength and anatomical robustness of both sexes suggests that they shared hunting activities.[44] Some Neanderthal groups used sharpened sticks as spears, but others used spears tipped with hafted stone points. A site at the Cotte de St Brelade in Jersey (then part of the French mainland) has yielded stone points with impact damage consistent with use as spear tips. The most dramatic evidence for Neanderthal hunting comes from the 130,000-year-old site of Lehringen in Germany, where a wooden spear with a fire-hardened tip was found lodged between the ribs of a mammoth. Neanderthals clearly weren't afraid to take on the largest of mammals.[51,1]

What was hunted varied from site to site, and even at the same site over time. Some of this variation was undoubtedly due to which animal species were available for hunting at a given location. Availability probably varied as a result of climate change occurring over the lengthy periods of occupation. For example, Combe Grenal in the Dordogne Valley was occupied from 115,000 until 50,000 years ago, during which time there were no fewer than 55 distinct episodes of occupation. From the considerable amount of animal remains accumulated over that time, it has been noted that during warm intervals red deer were common. During cold spells, reindeer predominated.[51]

As we shall see in Chapter 12, the Levant underwent alternating periods of occupation by Neanderthals and modern humans, with the latter first taking up residence around 120,000 years ago. Today the Levantine Middle Stone Age sites are of great interest as they provide an opportunity to compare and contrast patterns of behaviour by the two sets of 'tenants'. Although the tool-making technologies of both Neanderthals and modern humans in the Levant were comparable, anthropologists Daniel Lieberman and John Shea[62] suggest that hunting strategies between the two species differed. They analysed growth patterns in gazelle teeth by examining acellular cementum, which is a bone-like tissue that anchors tooth roots to the surrounding socket and forms in successive bands. Thicker bands are formed during the wet season, and thinner bands are formed during the dry season. The technique is not unlike counting tree rings, and analysis of the outermost band can reveal the time of the year death occurred to within two months. It was discovered that at the modern human site of Jebel Qafzeh, in Israel, gazelles were killed only in the dry season, whereas at the nearby Neanderthal site of Kebara, they were killed all the year round. These results were interpreted to mean that Neanderthals primarily organised their activities from large general-purpose sites. More specialised or seasonal activities were probably carried out at smaller sites on the periphery of the main one, although none of these have been found. By contrast, the modern humans lived at different sites at different times of the year to facilitate exploitation of seasonal food sources.

Both approaches have their pros and cons. The Neanderthal strategy permitted an increased capacity for storage and investment in material culture. The main problem is that food sources around the central camp would have become depleted due to year-long exploitation, and a law of diminishing returns would have begun to effect hunting and foraging activities. The approach adopted by the modern humans avoided these problems by relocating to sites near periodically abundant food sources. After the group have moved on to the next site, these then have a year to recover. The drawback would have been that the group had to do without items that could not readily be moved from site to site. Lieberman and Shea interpreted the difference as reflecting behavioural differences between the two species; but they may simply reflect the differing environmental conditions prevailing during Neanderthal and modern human periods of occupation.[2]

In recent years it has become clear that the Neanderthals were not restricted to reliance on large herbivores. At Bajondillo Cave on the Malaga coast, the fractured remains of mussel shells and other molluscs show that Neanderthals were harvesting shellfish 150,000 years ago.[63] Rather later, at the coastal sites of Vanguard Cave and Gorham's Cave, Gibraltar, the remains of seals, dolphins, fish and shellfish suggest that Neanderthals exploited coastal environments, probably making seasonal visits to the coast. The shellfish were found associated with ash, implying that they had been heated over a fire in order to open the shells.[64] At Gorham's Cave, heat-discoloured pigeon bones suggest that the Neanderthals living there also caught and roasted pigeons.[65] The ability to exploit seafood and catch birds was once thought to be restricted to modern humans, although we now know that the former goes back to the time of *Homo erectus*.

Evidence obtained from studying dental microwear[66] and from chemical analysis of coprolites (fossilised faeces)[67] suggests that the Neanderthal diet was highly varied, and included plant as well as animal foods.[66] Studies of fossilised dental calculus (hardened plaque) suggest that Neanderthals were capable of harvesting and processing plant foods.[68] Researchers took samples from individuals who lived in two very different climates: Shanidar 3 from Shanidar Cave, Iraq, and Spy 1 and Spy 2 from Spy Cave, Belgium, and in both cases starch grains were recovered. Those from Shanidar 3 originated from wild cereals and legumes, many of which were gelatinised (a process that occurs when starchy foods such as pasta are cooked in boiling water). The starch grains from the two Spy Cave Neanderthals originated from tubers (possibly water-lily roots) and sorghum, which today is an important cereal crop in many parts of the world. A number of microscopic silica bodies known as phytoliths were also recovered from the Shanidar 3 samples. Phytoliths improve the structural rigidity of plants and also make them distasteful to predators. Those from Shanidar 3 originated predominantly from date palms; dates are nutritious and would certainly have been a useful addition to the Neanderthal diet.

It is also notable that date palms have different harvest seasons to barley and legumes, suggesting seasonal rounds of collecting and scheduled returns to different harvesting areas. Anthropologists have long been interested in the timing of two major hominin dietary adaptations: the cooking of plant foods and an increase in the diversity of food-types exploited. That the Neanderthals mastered both adaptations in two very different climates – Mediterranean and northern oceanic – is further proof of their sophistication.

Burial of the dead

It is widely believed that Neanderthals intentionally buried their dead, and there is evidence of Neanderthal burials from many sites in Europe and Western Asia. Such graves present the best case for Neanderthal spirituality or religion, but they might have simply been dug to remove corpses from habitation areas. On the other hand, the fact that individuals and small groups are usually interred in these sites does suggest a contrast with the *Homo heidelbergensis*/proto-Neanderthal burial site at Sima de los Huesos, where bodies might simply have been dumped unceremoniously. Such sites include La Ferrassie, near the town of Les Eyzies in the Dordogne Valley. Discovered by two local men in September 1909, the 70,000-year-old site is a rock shelter where a group of two adults and five children – possibly a family – were buried. The burials were aligned in an east-west direction with the exception of an infant burial located at the back of the cave; this was aligned in a north-south direction.[1,2]

One of the best-known Neanderthal burial sites is Shanidar Cave in the Zagros Mountains in Iraqi Kurdistan, which was excavated by Ralph Solecki between 1953 and 1960. The limestone cave is 760 m (2,500 ft.) above sea level and overlooks the Great Zab River, a tributary of the Tigris. The ceiling, which is up to 15 m (45 ft.) above the floor at its highest place, is soot-blackened from the fires of Kurdish goatherds and their families who, at the time of the excavation, were still living in huts in the cave during the winter months. The remains of nine Neanderthal individuals were recovered during the excavations, comprising groups found on two different levels of the excavation. The individuals in the uppermost level were found immediately below rock-fall debris, and had apparently been killed by a cave-in 60,000 years ago. One of the victims of this disaster, an elderly male known as Shanidar 1, was found lying on his back, legs fully extended and arms folded across his chest, covered with small pieces of limestone. This suggests that others – possibly survivors of the cave-in – later returned to the cave and attempted to bury him. No less significant was his long-term physical condition before his death. The numerous injuries he had sustained to the left side of his face suggest that he was probably blind in one eye. He had also suffered a massive injury to the right side of his body that had caused arthritic degeneration of the right knee and ankle. In addition, there were fractures and the possible loss of part of the right forearm. That these injuries had subsequently healed imply that they had been sustained before his death in the cave-in. In turn, this suggests that other members of his group must have cared for him during periods of convalescence.[9,1] As we have already seen, there is much earlier evidence for care of sick and injured individuals, so we should not regard this as a novel development.

In lower levels of the excavation, dating from around 80,000 to 70,000 years ago, more remains were found. The individuals in this group appeared to have been intentionally buried.[1] The grave of one individual, a male aged from 30 to 45 years old known as Shanidar 4, was found in 1960 and yielded thought-provoking evidence that floral tributes might have been placed in his grave. Soil samples gathered from around the body were later analysed for pollen, in an attempt to reconstruct the climatic and vegetation history of the site. In addition to the usual pollen found throughout the site, some samples yielded whole clumps of pollen. It has been suggested that entire flowering plants entered the grave deposit, presumably placed there by grieving relatives.[69] However, it is also possible that the pollen was introduced into the burial by a gerbil-like rodent known as the Persian Jird. This species is known to store large numbers of seeds and flowers at certain points in their burrows. This, together with the lack of ritual treatment of other remains in the cave, suggests that the pollen had natural origins.[70]

Evidence of funerary rites has been claimed from a number of other Neanderthal sites. Artefacts and once-meaty bones have been found in burial infill, and are often claimed as grave goods. The bones were supposedly intended to ensure that the deceased did not get too peckish *en route* to the next world, although it is just as likely that these items were accidentally introduced when the grave was filled in after the bodies were interred. Grotta Guattari, discovered in 1939, was once thought to make the best case for ceremonial treatment of Neanderthal bones. The cave is located at Monte Circeo, an isolated promontory on the southwest coast of Italy, 100 km (60 miles) from Rome. The site was discovered by construction workers after having been sealed by rock debris for perhaps 50,000 years. On the floor of the cave was found an irregular ring of rocks surrounding a Neanderthal skull. Unfortunately, the position of the skull inside the ring is open to question, as it was moved and replaced before it was first seen by experts. Both positioning and skull damage are now thought be a result of hyena activity. The skull of the young boy found at Cave, Uzbekistan was surrounded by five or six pairs of ibis (mountain goat) horns. However, such horns also occurred throughout the deposit associated with the site, and there is nothing to suppose those found with the skull had been deliberately placed.[51,2,1]

In fact, there is no conclusive evidence of any ritual or symbolic behaviour at any Neanderthal site. Nevertheless, the purpose of the burials must have been more than simply disposing of dead bodies, as there are far simpler ways of achieving this. We must assume that there were strong social and emotional bonds in Neanderthal society, dictating that the remains of close kin should be preserved after death. Even if Neanderthals lacked symbolic behaviour, there is no reason to suppose that they felt the loss of kin or friends any less keenly than do modern people.

Were they really dimwits?

Were the Neanderthals behaviourally modern? In other words, were they capable of using symbols such as the spoken word to organise their thoughts and their behaviour? As we saw in Chapter 7, the possible use of ochre for ornamentation and body painting hints that *Homo heidelbergensis* might have some capacity for symbolic behaviour. The evidence for such a capacity in Neanderthals is stronger, but interpretations of the available data are still hotly disputed. As we have just seen, evidence for funerary rites has been claimed for a number of Neanderthal burials, but in all cases, other explanations are more likely. Less equivocal is evidence for ochre use. Finds at the Dutch site of Maastricht-Belvédère confirm that red ochre was being used at least 200,000 to 250,000 years ago and, as was the case at the *Homo heidelbergensis* Twin Rivers site in Zambia (see Chapter 7), was a non-local material that had been brought to the site from sources at least 40 km (25 miles) away.[71] Again, though, we cannot be certain that the ochre was used as pigment for ornamentation or body painting.

Some of the most compelling – yet controversial – evidence for symbolic behaviour in Neanderthals comes from a number of sites located in a restricted area of northern Spain, and in western and central France, west of the River Rhône. The sites are associated with the Châtelperronian people, and span a period from around 45,000 to perhaps 36,000 years ago.[72] The Châtelperronian is named for La Grotte des Fées, at Châtelperron, Allier in central France, where characteristic artefacts were first identified. Other Châtelperronian sites include the Grotte du Renne at Arcy-sur-Cure in north-central France and Saint Césaire in southwest France.[2] The Châtelperronian was confirmed as a Neanderthal culture after human remains found at Grotte du Renne were found to be of Neanderthal and not modern human origin.[73] However, associated stone artefacts combine typical Neanderthal Mousterian stone tools with articles more typical of modern humans such as end scrapers, which are long flakes or blades with a sharp, retouched edge at one end, used for working animal hide; and burins (chisels) for working wood, bone and antler. Other seemingly modern items include worked bone artefacts such as projectile points, awls, pins and burnishing tools; and beads and pendants made from grooved or pierced animal teeth, ivory, bone, or shell.[74]

At Grotte du Renne, Neanderthals were manufacturing bone artefacts and ornaments, and they also modified the living space to an extent usually associated only with modern humans. There are traces of several huts, including a rough circle of eleven postholes that possibly once supported mammoth tusks. This encloses an area of 3 to 4 m (10 to 13 ft.) across, partially paved with limestone plaques.[2,72] The Châtelperronian people, in short, showed evidence of modern human behaviour – but was it of independent Neanderthal origin?

The Châtelperronian is located very close in time to the transition from the Middle to Upper Palaeolithic, the time when modern humans finally reached Europe. The Aurignacian, a modern human culture named for Aurignac in southwest France, spread rapidly across Europe in the period from 46,000 to 41,000 years ago,[75] and would certainly have come into contact with the Neanderthal population. Could the Neanderthals have simply borrowed their innovative technology from their new neighbours? Anthropologists Richard Klein and Blake Edgar[72] think so and claim that the most persuasive elements of the Châtelperronian only appear towards its end, suggesting an Aurignacian influence. Archaeologists Sir Paul Mellars[76,77] and Steven Mithen[78] both agree with this view, and they dismiss as entirely implausible the coincidence of Neanderthals independently starting to use beads and other behaviourally-modern paraphernalia just before the appearance on the scene of modern humans.

Mellars[77] attributes the Châtelperronian to what he terms a 'bow wave effect', i.e. technological and cultural diffusion from the modern human populations in North Africa and Asia, some way in advance of the actual dispersal of modern humans into Europe. He notes such chains of connection have been widely documented among recent hunter-gatherer groups, which have carried both technological ideas and cultural elements over distances of up to several thousand kilometres. Examples of the latter include prized species of marine shells and especially-valued raw materials.

The issue really turns on whether the Châtelperronian can be shown to pre-date any Aurignacian influence. Unfortunately, the evidence from two of the classic Châtelperronian sites is far from clear-cut. La Grotte des Fées was discovered and extensively excavated in the nineteenth century, but the most recent and important work on the site was carried out by Henri Delporte from 1951 to 1955 and in 1962. Delporte's work suggested that while the lowest layers are unquestionably Mousterian, the Châtelperronian layers are interposed between layers containing artefacts associated with the Aurignacian culture. In 2005, radiocarbon dates were published that were claimed to support Delporte's conclusions.[79] If these conclusions are accepted, they suggest that the site was alternately occupied by Neanderthals and modern humans. The periodic changes in tenancy probably reflected the vicissitudes of climatic instability, but regardless of which, the implication is that there was close contact between the Neanderthal and modern populations.

In 2006, archaeologist João Zilhão, who has long championed an independent Neanderthal origin for the Châtelperronian, claimed that the Aurignacian artefacts had been accidentally forced downwards into the earlier Châtelperronian layers by the original nineteenth century excavations at the site. Accordingly, he argued, the deepest Châtelperronian layers actually predate the Aurignacian, and hence cannot be the result of contact with modern humans.[80] The authors of the original 2005 report then published a rebuttal in which they claimed to have refuted Zilhão's views, and to have confirmed their original findings.[81]

The battleground then shifted to the Grotte du Renne. A report published in 2010 claimed that mixing of archaeological materials had occurred, and that the association between Châtelperronian artefacts and Neanderthals was suspect.[82] Sir Paul Mellars,[83] one of the authors of the earlier Grotte des Fées reports, claimed that the one of the most important pillars of evidence for Neanderthal symbolic behaviour had effectively collapsed. Zilhão's team duly published their own report into the Grotte du Renne, rejecting claims that the site had been disturbed.[84] Both sides in the debate seemed to take the view that if a site failed to back their argument, it must be suspect. In this case, however, Zilhão was backed by an independent study in which radiocarbon dates were obtained for bone fragments recovered from the various levels of Grotte du Renne. The dates suggested that the site had not been disturbed, supporting a Neanderthal origin for the Châtelperronian. Had any bone fragment moved from its original layer, it would have yielded an anomalously young or old date. However, it was found that the oldest Châtelperronian levels were only 44,500 to 45,000 years old.[85] More recently, new radiocarbon dates for the Châtelperronian across the whole of its range suggest that it did not begin until around 45,000 years ago, placing it entirely within the period after modern humans entered Europe.[86] Even a 'bow wave effect' is not necessary to invoke the possibility of an Aurignacian influence.

By this time, Zilhão's team had moved on to other lines of evidence in support of their views.[87] A 43,500-year-old broken King Scallop (*Pecten maximus*) shell was recovered at the Neanderthal site of Cueva Antón in the Region of Murcia, southeast Spain. The shell had been perforated and painted on its exterior side with mix of yellow goethite and red hematite, possibly to match the red colour of the interior side. It could have been used as an item of body decoration, which was discarded after having been accidentally broken. At Cueva de los Aviones, also in the Region of Murcia, a large number of marine shells were found, mainly of edible species. The shells are between 50,000 and 45,000 years old, and most had been collected as food (itself an advanced behaviour once thought to be beyond the abilities of Neanderthals).

However, some cockle shells (*Acanthocardia tuberculata* and *Glycymeris insubrica*) had been coloured with pigment and perforated for use as ornaments. The upper valve of a spiny oyster shell (*Spondylus gaederopus*) contained residues of the red mineral lepidocrocite mixed with ground particles of charcoal, dolomite, hematite and pyrite. The shell had apparently been used as a container for the storage of the colourants, or as a paint cup for their preparation. The additives, when fresh, have a brilliant black, reflective appearance, and may have been used as a cosmetic preparation. *Spondylus* shells might have been chosen for this purpose because of their striking colours, typically crimson red, or violet. They are known to have been used for symbolic or ritual-related purposes in Neolithic Europe and pre-Columbian America.

Also discovered at Cueva de los Aviones were lumps of red and yellow colourants that were found to contain a number of iron-based minerals. None of these minerals occur naturally in the cave, or nearby. The yellow mineral natrojarosite was used in Ancient Egypt as a cosmetic or for the representation of female skin in painting. The natrojarosite found at the site might have been the contents of a small purse made of perishable material. Was this the powder compact of its day? The discoveries were widely reported, and Zilhão made it clear that he thought it was time for negative public perceptions of Neanderthals to change.[88]

Evidence for Neanderthal use of ornaments has also been found in northern Italy. At Grotta di Fumane, a cave site near Verona, some 660 bird bones were recovered from Mousterian layers dating to around 44,000 years ago. Cut-marks and other signs of damage to wing bones were apparently caused by the removal of flight feathers. Although 22 bird species were present in the assemblage, feathers had only been removed from certain species, including the Lammergeier (Bearded Vulture), the Red-footed Falcon, the Eurasian Black Vulture, the Alpine Chough and the Common Wood Pigeon. The larger flight feathers from the first three of these species are too long for use as fletching elements on spears, suggesting they were collected for ornamental purposes.[89] A broader survey of bird remains found at Neanderthal sites does back up this conclusion. The wing-bones of raptors, crows, magpies and jays occurred more often, and displayed cut-marks more often than other bones. As none of these species have food value, the observations could only be explained by removal of their flight feathers.[90]

Possibly the most compelling evidence yet for Neanderthal symbolic behaviour is the 39,000-year-old rock engraving identified at Gorham's Cave.[91] The deeply-etched cross-hatched pattern is carved into the dolomite bedrock of the cave, and was wholly-covered by an undisturbed archaeological level containing Mousterian artefacts. As these are of purely Neanderthal origin, the association of the engraving with Neanderthals is secure.

Researchers carried out a number of tests to demonstrate that the engraving was intentional. They used a variety of tools and cutting actions on blocks of dolomite rock similar to the rock face at Gorham's Cave and found that results best matching the engraving were achieved by using a pointed tool to create and enlarge a groove. Considerable care and physical effort was required to produce similar markings. The researchers also used the sharp tools to cut pork skin on a dolomite slab to rule out the possibility that the pattern had been produced accidentally while cutting meat or working animal hides.

What remains unproven is that these developments were of entirely independent Neanderthal origin; even the earliest dates do not significantly predate the presence of modern humans in Europe,[92,93] and the 'bow wave' model certainly cannot be ruled out. Even so, Italian cognitive researcher Francesco d'Errico believes that the archaeological record of modern humans in Middle Stone Age Africa and Neanderthals in Middle Palaeolithic Europe does not provide evidence of any dramatic cognitive differences between the two species. He suggests that behavioural modernity may not be unique to our species and could have arisen over a long period among different human types, including Neanderthals.

D'Errico[74,94] maintains that the Châtelperronian and other late Neanderthal technologies have nothing in common with the technology that modern humans introduced into Europe. Instead, they appear as independent developments from local industries. They also argue that even if one accepts the 'bow wave' argument, it would actually reinforce the notion that Neanderthals were behaviourally modern and able to incorporate external elements into their culture.[95,96] However, Sir Paul Mellars[77] believes that any technology exchanged between Neanderthals and modern humans would not necessarily have had the same social and cognitive meanings for the two species.

Even if one accepts that the Cueva de los Aviones and Grotta di Fumane artefacts are of independent Neanderthal origin, does it necessarily prove that at Neanderthals possessed the full range of mental faculties that are seen in modern humans? In particular, did they possess the same linguistic abilities? For a long time, it was believed that they did not. Based on the analysis of Neanderthal specimen from La Chapelle-aux-Saints, France, it was claimed that the Neanderthal larynx was positioned high in the throat, like a chimpanzee (or a modern human baby), making it impossible for Neanderthals to produce the modern range of vocalisations.[97] However, the hyoid bone of Kebara 2 provided new evidence. The hyoid is a small U-shaped bone that lies between the root of the tongue and the larynx, anchoring the muscles required for speech. The Kebara 2 hyoid is within the modern range in morphology and internal bone structure. Furthermore, by analysis of patterns of muscle attachment, researchers were able to show that the placement of the Neanderthal larynx was similar to that of a modern human, low in the throat.[98,99,100]

3d modelling work has supported these conclusions. Data from a number of Neanderthal skulls was used to reconstruct the vocal tract. The estimated hyoid position fell within the modern range and acoustic analysis shows that Neanderthals were able to make the quantal vowel sounds (/a/, /i/ and /u/) that are present in all modern human languages. The Neanderthal /i/ and /u/ sounds are within the modern range; /a/ falls just outside[101] (by convention, phonetic sounds are enclosed in slashes).

Two more anatomical features have been prominent in the debate over Neanderthal speech. The first of these is the thoracic vertebral canal, which as we saw in Chapter 6 is the space in the vertebral column though which pass the nerves associated with the control of breathing. In the case of *Homo erectus*, the nerve canal was narrower than that of a modern human, but in the case of Neanderthals the canal is within the modern range. This suggests that Neanderthals did have the fine control of breathing that is necessary for modern speech.[102] The second feature is the hypoglossal canal, which is a passage in the base of the skull through which pass the nerves controlling the tongue. The Neanderthal hypoglossal canal diameter is within the modern range[103] and this was initially taken as evidence for finer control of the tongue, and hence speech capability. However, later work on extinct hominins, modern humans, and a range of other living primates has shown that the size of the hypoglossal nerve is unrelated to the size of the canal, thus taking it out of the debate.[104]

Overall, Neanderthals appear to have had all the anatomical features required for speech, but did they possess the cognitive ability to handle grammatical language? Skeletal and dental evidence suggests that around 90 percent of Neanderthals were right-handed – similar to the 9:1 ratio observed for modern humans. This implies that their brains were lateralised like those of modern humans.[105] In modern humans, many higher brain functions – including those governing speech – are predominantly located in one hemisphere or the other. However, lateralisation may considerably predate the Neanderthals. As we saw in Chapters 5 and 7, *Homo habilis* and *Homo heidelbergensis* might have possessed the equivalent of the speech-related Broca's Area. While lateralisation might well be a necessary condition for modern speech, it might not be a sufficient condition.

There are in any case reasons to suppose that the neural organisation of the Neanderthal brain differed from that of modern humans. As we shall see in Chapter 11, the globular shape of the *Homo sapiens* braincase may be related to the development of modern speech. If so, the Neanderthals with their long, low braincases might have lacked language as we know it. Steven Mithen[78] believes that Neanderthals communicated with a 'holistic' language in which single utterances conveyed meanings

The symbolic ape

in much the same way as sentences do in modern speech. Such a language was limited in terms of the range of meanings and concepts that could be expressed. We shall return to Mithen's theory in Chapter 12.

Another factor is that in comparison to a modern human brain, a greater proportion of the Neanderthal brain might have been dedicated to the visual cortex. Living at high latitudes, Neanderthals experienced lower light levels than people living in the tropics, and larger eyes might have been an evolutionary response. Recent work, based on the assumption that the size of the eye socket is related to the size of the eye itself has confirmed that Neanderthals did indeed have larger eyes than modern humans. If more of the brain was required for body and visual systems, then less was available for other functions. It has been suggested that Neanderthals were less able than modern humans to maintain the complex social networks required to manage long-distance trade networks effectively, and learn about the existence of distant foraging areas unaffected by local shortages. Furthermore, their ability to develop and pass on innovations might have been limited in comparison to modern humans. An evolutionary response to high latitude conditions based upon visual acuity was initially very effective, but in the long term the modern human response of enhanced sociability proved a better bet in the unstable climate of Ice Age Europe.[5]

In conclusion, it is reasonably safe to conclude that Neanderthals were not the dimwits of popular imagination. However, their cognitive abilities and neural organisation almost certainly differed from those of modern humans. The case for behavioural modernity remains unproven; there are reasonably sound arguments both for and against.

The Million Dollar Question

A topic of perennial interest to scholars and laypeople alike is did Neanderthals and modern humans interbreed? Until recently, there was no strong evidence one way or another, although there was no reason to suppose that they did not. While Neanderthals would certainly have appeared strange to modern humans and vice versa, they would not necessarily have seemed unattractive to each other. For a present-day human, having sex with a Neanderthal could be a somewhat hazardous affair, given the considerably superior physical strength of the latter. To the rather more powerfully-built *Homo sapiens* of that era, it might have been less of an issue. There is no reason to suppose that such a union would not have led to viable and probably fertile offspring; as noted in Chapter 6, this is often the case among closely related species.

However, prior to 2010, there was no definite evidence for or against interbreeding. Erik Trinkaus[106] has claimed there was evidence to show that Neanderthals and modern humans did interbreed up to Gravettian times. Trinkaus compared remains of early European modern humans with early modern humans from Africa. He claimed that the European fossils exhibit a number of distinctive Neanderthal traits, but that these features were not present among the African samples. This, Trinkaus believes, is best explained by the assimilation of some Neanderthals into early modern human populations as the latter dispersed westwards across Europe.

This claim notwithstanding, no convincing fossil evidence of a Neanderthal/modern hybrid has ever come to light. Claims that the 24,500-year-old skeleton of a 4-year-old child found at Abrigo do Lagar Velho, Portugal in 1998 is an example of a hybrid[107] have not been widely accepted. Notably, the burial was typical of the Gravettian, a culture that is firmly associated with modern humans. It is possible that the infant was simply an unusually stocky modern human juvenile, or a 'chunky child' as one critic put it.[108] Recently, it been claimed that a Neanderthal lower jawbone from Riparo Mezzena, northern Italy, shows some modern traits, including an incipient chin that might have arisen from interbreeding with modern humans,[109] possibly living at the nearby site of Grotta di Fumane.[110]

In the absence of unequivocal fossil evidence, researchers turned to genetics. Initially, the evidence was negative. Studies of mitochondrial DNA samples obtained from Neanderthal and contemporary modern human remains in Europe found no evidence for interbreeding between the two.[111,112,113] Computer simulations of modern human migration into Europe suggested that any interbreeding must have been minimal; or otherwise the modern genome would have become progressively diluted by that of Neanderthals as the modern populations moved westwards. By the time the migrants reached the northwestern corner of Europe, they would have been close to 100 percent Neanderthal.[114]

In 2006, researchers claimed that an allele of the gene microcephalin (MCPH1) had entered the modern human genome as a result of interbreeding with extinct humans, quite possibly Neanderthals. Microcephalin is linked with brain size and haplogroup D, as this allele is known, is now the most common form throughout the world, except in sub-Saharan Africa. Haplogroup D first appeared 37,000 years ago, at a time when modern humans had reached Europe and had presumably encountered Neanderthals.[115] The claim seemed plausible, but subsequent work showed that that Neanderthals actually had an ancestral form of microcephalin. The haplogroup D allele almost certainly arose as a mutation purely within the *Homo sapiens* lineage.[116,117]

However, over the next three years, tentative genetic evidence began to emerge for interbreeding between modern and archaic humans. Researchers investigated genetic sequence data from Europeans, East Asians and West Africans and found traces of an archaic contribution to the modern genome. No particular archaic species could be identified, but a Neanderthal contribution, at least to the European genome, seemed likely.[118,119] This conclusion was soon vindicated. A project to sequence the Neanderthal genome was commenced in 2006 at the Max Planck Institute for Evolutionary Anthropology,[120,27] and in May 2010, researchers published a first draft of the Neanderthal genome.[121]

With the initial announcement came the dramatic news that made headlines around the world. It turned out that between one and four percent of the genome of modern non-Africans was derived from Neanderthals. In other words, the answer to the million dollar question was 'yes, they did interbreed – but not in Africa'. The researchers compared the Neanderthal genome with those of five present-day individuals: two indigenous Africans (one San from South Africa and one Yoruba from West Africa) and three Eurasians (one from Papua New Guinea, one from China and one from France). The results showed that Neanderthals were more closely related to non-Africans than to Africans. This is not particularly surprising, as Neanderthals are not known to have lived in Africa. Any interbreeding has generally been supposed to have occurred within the known range of the Neanderthals, in Europe and Western Asia. What was unexpected was that no difference was found between Papua New Guinean, Chinese and French individuals in terms of their degree of relatedness to Neanderthals.

However, the authors of the Max Planck report could not rule out the possibility that their results reflected substructure in the early modern human population of Africa rather than interbreeding; in other words the splitting of the population into smaller sub-populations that were isolated from one another by barriers such as mountain ranges, rivers, or the appearance of deserts during periods of low rainfall. It was suggested that such conditions might have existed in Africa after Neanderthals diverged from modern humans, leaving some groups more closely related to Neanderthals than others. If members one of these were the ancestors of present-day non-Africans, then this would also be consistent with the genetic findings.

Although the Max Planck group felt that this scenario was less likely than the interbreeding hypothesis, independent researchers later claimed that the substructure model is a more realistic scenario. They used a mathematical model to represent a connected string of regional populations spanning Africa and Eurasia. After the string split, the Eurasian and African parts of the range subsequently evolved into Neanderthals and modern humans respectively. For the latter, groups geographically closest to the split (i.e. in North Africa) remained more closely related to Neanderthals than those further south.[122]

Assuming that Neanderthals and modern humans did interbreed, the implication was that it must have happened at a time before the ancestors of the present-day Asian, Australasian and European populations diverged from one another – presumably soon after modern humans first left Africa, and long before they reached Europe. If the population that left Africa was small, only limited interbreeding would be necessary to leave the Neanderthal contribution fixed in the modern non-African genome for all time, as numbers increased during the subsequent peopling of the world. Conversely, later encounters, for example in Europe, would leave little genetic trace. Modern populations were by that time large in comparison to Neanderthal groups.

Subsequent work by independent researchers initially appeared to back this conclusion,[123] and it was suggested that the interbreeding had occurred in Southwest Asia from 47,000 to 65,000 years ago.[124] These dates were later refined using ancient DNA obtained from early modern human remains from two Eurasian sites: Ust'-Ishim in western Siberia and Kostenki in in southern Russia. The Ust'-Ishim remains are 45,000 years old; those from Kostenki date from 38,700 to 36,200 years old. The two sets of results were very consistent: the Ust'-Ishim data indicated that interbreeding between Neanderthals and this individual's ancestors had occurred from 7,000 to 13,000 years earlier, i.e. 52,000 to 58,000 years ago;[125] Kostenki yielded a date of 54,000 years ago.[126] Researchers also demonstrated that the substructure model was unlikely to explain genetic similarities between Neanderthals and modern non-African populations.[124,127]

However, later reports found that non-Africans were not, after all, equally related to Neanderthals, and that there are higher levels of Neanderthal ancestry in East Asians than in Europeans.[128,129,130] Given that Neanderthals lived in Europe but are not known from East Asia, this was an unexpected development. It was also reported that North Africans *do* carry a Neanderthal genetic signature,[131,129] although this is less mysterious as it is believed that some modern pre-Neolithic people later migrated back to Africa from Southwest Asia.[132,133] One interpretation of the East Asian data is that after the ancestors of present-day Europeans and East Asians had separated from one another, the latter encountered and interbred with a second, more easterly population of Neanderthals. As noted above, the latter are now known from as far to the east as the Altai Mountains, and it is possible that their range also extended further south.

In fact, the differences between present-day European and East Asian populations are probably more related to differing effects of natural selection in the two regions than they are to additional episodes of interbreeding in the East. The latest research suggests that around 20 percent of the Neanderthal genome survives in the present-day population, although individuals each only possess a small fraction of this amount.[130] Many useful Neanderthal genes have been incorporated into the modern genome; for example those involved with the production of keratin, a protein that is used in skin, hair and nails.[134] In East Asian populations, many genes involved with protection from the sun's UV rays are of Neanderthal origin.[135] It is likely that the transfer of Neanderthal genes helped modern humans to adapt to conditions away from their African homeland

Curiously, some deleterious genes also have a Neanderthal connection, including those implicated in type 2 diabetes and in Crohn's disease. Possibly, these genes were once advantageous, and it is only our changed diet since the advent of agriculture that has triggered these adverse effects. Significantly, Neanderthal DNA was largely absent from the X chromosome and genes associated with modern testes. The implication is that Neanderthal DNA in these regions led to reduced male fertility, or sterility,[134] suggesting that Neanderthals and modern humans were at the limits of biological compatibility.

The non-random distribution of Neanderthal DNA in the modern genome suggests that natural selection has had a significant role to play determining present-day Neanderthal gene frequencies. Beneficial genes would have been selected for whereas adverse ones would have been selected against. Whether the effects of a particular gene was beneficial, neutral or adverse would in many cases have depended upon local conditions, and this is probably what was responsible for the higher incidence of Neanderthal DNA in East Asian populations.

The possibility of increased male sterility is a complication if we are talking about only one or two episodes of interbreeding. Some believe that instead of one-off 'pulses', interbreeding occurred throughout the Neanderthal range – but only very occasionally. Mathematical studies suggest that the Neanderthal component of the modern genome could be accounted for even if interbreeding only occurred once every 70 to 80 generations. Such a low rate could be due either to social factors or to a very limited reproductive compatibility between the two species. Such a scenario would also account for the absence of a Neanderthal contribution to the modern mitochondrial gene pool, as Neanderthal mitochondrial DNA would be rapidly eliminated by genetic drift.[136,137] This model might turn out to be a more realistic scenario than the 'pulse' model.

The Denisovans

In 2008, a distal phalanx (fingertip) bone from a hominin little finger was recovered from Denisova Cave in the Altai Mountains. The cave is named for a hermit called Dionisij (Denis) who is supposed to have lived there in eighteenth century, but if this is true he was only the latest in a long line of inhabitants. In April 2010, it was reported that the phalanx had belonged to a hitherto-unknown human species.[138]

The small bone is 30,000 to 48,000 years old, and is believed to have belonged to a child aged between five and seven years old. Due to the cool, dry climate, it was possible to extract DNA from the bone, isolate mitochondrial DNA fragments, and sequence the entire mitochondrial genome. As we inherit our mitochondrial DNA solely from our mothers, this led to the find being dubbed X Woman, despite being a juvenile of unknown gender.

Neanderthals, identified as such by their mitochondrial DNA, were known to have been living less than 100 km (60 miles) away at Okladnikov Cave (they had still at this point to be identified at Denisova Cave itself). In addition, there is archaeological evidence to suggest that modern humans were in the Altai before 40,000 years ago. The expectation, therefore, was that the mitochondrial DNA from the bone would match that of either Neanderthals or modern humans, but neither turned out to be the case. Instead, sequencing revealed that X Woman had last shared a common ancestor with Neanderthals and modern humans about a million years ago.

X Woman clearly wasn't a Neanderthal or a modern human, but what was she (if indeed she was a 'she')? One possibility was *Homo heidelbergensis*, the presumptive common ancestor of the Neanderthals and modern humans, but as we saw in Chapter 7, this species probably appeared no earlier than 600,000 years ago, and was too recent to be associated with X Woman's ancestors. On the other hand, one million years ago was too recent for X Woman to be a late-surviving descendant of the first wave of *Homo erectus* to reach Southeast Asia and China.

Towards the end of 2010, it was reported that X Woman's nuclear genome had been sequenced.[139] It turned out that X-Woman lacked a Y-chromosome and therefore was indeed female. The discovery of an upper molar tooth from a young adult was also reported and the sequencing of mitochondrial DNA from the tooth confirmed that it had belonged to a different individual to the phalanx. For this reason, the term 'X-Woman' was dropped in favour of 'Denisovan'.

The nuclear data allowed more detailed estimates to be made regarding the relatedness of Denisovans, Neanderthals and modern humans. It was found that the Denisovans diverged from Neanderthals 640,000 years ago, and from present-day Africans 804,000 years ago. The two Eurasian species (Denisovans and Neanderthals) were thus more closely related to one another than they were to modern humans (an African species), as might be expected.[139]

What was entirely unexpected was the finding that 4.8 percent of the nuclear genome of present-day New Guineans derives from Denisovans, greater than the Neanderthal contribution of 2.5 percent.[139] The implication was that the Denisovan range had once extended from the deciduous forests of Siberia to the tropics. This is a wider ecological and geographic region than any other hominin species, with the exception of modern humans.[140] Overall, the data was consistent with a scenario in which modern humans, on leaving Africa, interbred with Neanderthals and then, at some subsequent point, the ancestors of present-day New Guineans interbred with Denisovans.

Follow-up studies confirmed the presence of Denisovan genetic material in some other modern populations of Island Southeast Asia, and also in Aboriginal Australians, Fijians and Polynesians. Significantly, though, it was largely absent from mainland populations. The small Denisovan component found there is likely to have been introduced by modern humans migrating from Island Southeast Asia. The most logical explanation is that the present-day population of Mainland Southeast Asia are descended from a second group of migrants that arrived after the Denisovans had become extinct.[140,141,128,43] As we shall see in Chapter 13, this is likely to be the correct explanation.

We have already seen that modern humans 'imported' advantageous genes from Neanderthals, which might have helped them to adapt to local conditions. Similarly, interbreeding with Denisovans might have boosted the immune systems of some modern populations. The human leucocyte antigen (HLA) helps the immune system to recognise and combat pathogens. There are three genes known as HLA-A, HLA-B and HLA-C, and it believed that a number of alleles of these genes are of Denisovan origin. These alleles could have conferred immunity to pathogens to which the incoming modern population had not been previously exposed, and given a survival advantage to those acquiring them from the Denisovans.[142]

It has been suggested, on the basis of allele comparison with modern humans, that the Denisovans were dark-skinned, with brown eyes and hair.[128] Other than that, and beyond their genetic impact on modern populations, we still know very little about them. The Middle Pleistocene fossil record of Southeast and East Asia is very sparse and the Denisovan tooth, probably a third or possibly second left upper molar, fails to support a connection with any of the few remains that have been found. The tooth is fairly large, lying within the size range of *Homo erectus* and *Homo habilis*. It is above the size range typical for Neanderthals, early modern humans, and the very few third upper molars that have been recovered from other late archaic hominins in the region. The tooth shares no recent features with Neanderthals or modern humans, hinting at the distinctiveness of the Denisovans.[139] On the other hand, the report failed to note that some early modern human teeth are also very large, such as those associated with the 35,000-year-old lower jawbone from Peştera cu Oase in Romania.[143,144] Size alone probably does not tell us very much.[145]

The most recent genetic work indicates that the Denisovans interbred with other human species as well as our own. They interbred with Neanderthals in the Altai region, and they also interbred with an unidentified species of archaic hominin. Given that the Denisovans and Neanderthals diverged from one another after they diverged from modern humans, one would expect the two species to be equally genetically distinct from our own species. However, this is not the case; the Denisovans are more genetically distinct than are the Neanderthals. It turns out that scattered fragments amounting to around one percent of their genome is much older than the rest of it. This is best explained by the

Denisovans interbreeding with archaic hominins whose ancestors split from the common ancestor of the Neanderthals, Denisovans and modern humans 1.1 to 4.0 million years ago. No particular species has been identified, but the timing would suggest Asian *Homo erectus*.[43]

The Denisovans' place in the human evolutionary story – already far from clear – became further confused with the successful extraction of mitochondrial DNA from the thigh bone of a hominin recovered from the Sima de los Huesos site in Spain. An estimated age of 400,000 years was obtained by comparison with other, younger ancient DNA sequences dated by direct means. As the Sima de los Huesos hominins have been described as proto-Neanderthals, the expectation was that the material would show affinity to genetic sequences obtained from later Neanderthal remains. Instead, it more closely resembled ancestral Denisovan mitochondrial DNA.[146] One possible interpretation is that that mitochondrial lineages originally present in the Denisovan/Neanderthal common ancestor subsequently disappeared from the Neanderthal line, but persisted in the Denisovans. It and other genetic lineages could have been lost in a population bottleneck of the type known to have affected Neanderthal populations.

It is now clear that the view of modern humans entirely replacing archaic populations is not correct, either in or out of Africa. There is certainly an element of truth to the multiregional model. It is, however, only an element. The range of variation between modern and archaic humans is greater than that in any existing primate species. We should not think of Denisovans and Neanderthals as simply variant forms of *Homo sapiens*.[147]

The fate of the Neanderthals

Ever since the nineteenth century, the fate of the Neanderthals has gripped the imagination of scientists and lay people alike. Superbly adapted to the harsh, glacial conditions of Europe and Western Asia, they had lived there for over 300,000 years – only to disappear abruptly, soon after arrival of modern humans 46,000 years ago. Estimates as to just how long the Neanderthals survived after the arrival modern humans in Europe have varied over the years, ranging from as 10,000 years to no more than a few centuries.[75] The latest radiocarbon dating of Neanderthal sites suggest that they went extinct between 41,000 and 39,000 years ago, about 5,000 years after the first modern humans arrived.[86]

A factor in these revisions has been the improved accuracy of both radiocarbon dates and calibration data. Not only do the newer radiocarbon dates suggest that many supposedly-late Neanderthals are actually older than was originally believed, but it also turns out that the calibration data used to convert them to calendar years was resulting in systematic underestimates. Many supposedly-late Neanderthals have now been shown to be much older than first believed. For example, two specimens from Vindija Cave in Croatia were originally thought to be from 32,000 to 33,000 years old (28,000 to 29,000 radiocarbon years BP),[148] but these dates are now thought to be nearer 36,000 to 37,000 years old (32,000 to 33,000 radiocarbon years BP).[149] Similarly, an infant from Mezmaiskaya Cave in the northern Caucasus, once believed to be a late survivor from 29,000 years ago, is now believed to be have lived more like 40,000 years ago.[150]

At the peripheries of Europe, Neanderthals might have persisted for rather longer than elsewhere. Possible late survival is documented from two very different settings: Gorham's Cave, Gibraltar, and Byzovaya, in the western foothills of the northernmost Urals. Gorham's Cave seems to have been a favoured location that was visited repeatedly over many thousands of years. Natural light penetrates deep into the cave, and a high ceiling permits ventilation of smoke from the hearths that were repeatedly made there. Neanderthal occupation of the cave continued until 33,000 years ago (28,000 radiocarbon years BP), and possibly until as recently as 29,000 years ago (24,000 radiocarbon years

BP), and the site was later used by modern humans right up until Phoenician and Carthaginian times. However, there was a 5,000 years hiatus after the last Neanderthal occupation before the first modern humans took up residence.[151,152]

At Byzovaya, a total of 313 stone artefacts have been collected over the years, all reflecting typical Middle Palaeolithic tool production techniques characteristic of Neanderthal Mousterian industries, and ranging from 31,000 to 34,000 years old.[153] As no human remains have been recovered, we cannot be certain that the tool-makers were definitely Neanderthals. If they were, however, proof that Neanderthals were capable of living inside the Arctic Circle would refute any theories linking their disappearance to the deteriorating climate.

Indeed, such climate change might have been responsible for the late survival of Neanderthals in the Iberian Peninsula. The Ebro River in northern Spain might have represented an ecological barrier to the expansion of modern humans into the region,[74] although some apparently did penetrate further south.[107,152] The cold, arid conditions of Heinrich Event 4, which occurred 40,000 years ago, might also have delayed expansion of modern humans into Iberia. The effects were probably exacerbated by the Campanian Ignimbrite eruption in southern Italy, which coincided with Heinrich Event 4, and was the largest volcanic eruption of the last 200,000 years in the Mediterranean area. It ejected 250 to 300 cubic km (60 to 72 cubic miles) of ash, or 50 to 60 times the amount ejected by Vesuvius in AD 79.[154,155] Computer simulations show that the Iberian inland became a semi-desert, which formed a buffer zone between the two populations. With the advance of modern humans temporarily halted, the south became a refugium for late-surviving Neanderthals.[156]

It must be noted that recent work has cast doubt on late Neanderthal survival even in the Iberian Peninsula and that here, too, dates have been underestimated. Researchers used a technique known as ultra-filtration to remove traces of modern contaminants (for example preservatives and glues) from fossil bone collagens (proteins making up the bone matrix) prior to radiocarbon dating. Without this process, it is claimed that the contaminants make samples appear younger than they actually are. For example, a carbon contamination of just one percent will make a 50,000-year-old sample appear to be just 37,000 years old. Unfortunately, the majority of bones do not contain enough collagen for the technique to be used, but bones recovered from Jarama VI and Cueva del Boquet Zafarraya suggested that the Neanderthal remains there were at least 10,000 years older than previously believed.[157] Should other dates for the Iberian Neanderthals turn out to have been similarly understated, then it would suggest that they died out before modern humans arrived. However, the authors of the Gorham's Cave report had previously considered and ruled out the possibility of contamination affecting their results.[152]

If we assume that at least some of the Iberian Neanderthals did survive up to and possibly beyond 32,000 years ago, was the Aurignacian advance south a genocidal onslaught, as some believe?[54,158] It is all too easy to invoke the horrors of the last hundred years and suggest that the Neanderthals were victims of genocide. *Homo sapiens* do not have a particularly good record, even with members of their own species. Is there any reason, though, to suppose that relations between a group of modern humans and Neanderthals would be any more or any less friendly than those between two groups of modern humans?

We don't know, because there is very little evidence of either inter-personal or inter-communal violence prior to Neolithic times, although it undoubtedly occurred from time to time. The earliest evidence of possible inter-species violence between modern humans and Neanderthals comes from Shanidar Cave; the alleged victim is a Neanderthal male, Shanidar 3. Thought to be in his early 40s, Shanidar 3 suffered a penetrating injury to his ninth rib shortly before his death. The injury had partially healed, suggesting that he survived the initial incident. However, he died before healing was completed, probably within two months of sustaining the injury. Death came either as a consequence, or from some unrelated cause – possibly the same cave-in that killed the elderly male, Shanidar 1.

Even before the injury, Shanidar 3 was not in the best of health and was suffering from a degenerative joint disease of the right foot. This would certainly have hampered any attempt to get out of the way of falling rocks.

To try to gain insight into Shanidar 3's injury, researchers carried out controlled stabbing experiments with replicas of Mousterian and Levallois points on the ribcages of pig carcasses. The stabs were conducted with a crossbow at different draw weights in an effort to replicate the impact forces associated with both thrusting spears and long-range projectiles. Although not ruling out the possibility that Shanidar 3 had been either attacked or accidentally injured with a hand held weapon, results suggested that his injuries were most consistent with him having been struck by a long-range projectile weapon. It was assumed that Neanderthals lacked such weaponry, and that therefore Shanidar 3 must have been attacked by a modern human.[159] As we have seen, however, recent evidence has cast doubt on this assumption.

In addition to this 'new evidence', there is a possible alibi for *Homo sapiens*. The suggestion that modern humans were present at the scene of crime is based on uncalibrated radiocarbon dates of 46,900 and 50,600 BP for material recovered from just above Shanidar 3. These dates were obtained in the 1960s, and the actual date is now thought to be nearer 60,000 years ago.[1] During this period, it is not thought that any modern humans were present in the region. No jury would convict on the evidence presented.

The only other clearly-documented case of violence involving Neanderthals is St. Césaire 1, the skeleton of a young adult Neanderthal, which was discovered in 1979. Thought to be around 36,000 years old, the skeleton and some associated Châtelperronian artefacts were recovered at the site of La Roche à Pierrot, a collapsed rock shelter near the village of St. Césaire in southwest France. Tomography and computer reconstruction techniques have been used to construct a virtual model of St. Césaire 1's skull, and it was found that there was a healed fracture at the apex on the cranial vault – an injury that had resulted from St. Césaire 1 being struck with a sharp object, probably by an assailant. Accidental injury, such as falling onto a sharp edge, a rock-fall, or an unintentional blow, for example as resulting from a hunting incident, were thought to be less likely, as these injuries typically affect the side rather than the apex of the cranial vault. However, the injury was not fatal and St Césaire 1 survived for at least several months after the attack.[160]

Who was the attacker? Unlike the much earlier Shanidar Cave incident, there is no doubt that modern humans were in France by 36,000 years ago. However, is thought more likely that a member of the same group was responsible for the attack. Either the attack was a premeditated assault, or the result of an argument. The cause might have been a potential mate, or status within the group. Population densities were low and potential conflicts between groups of either species were probably best resolved by simply keeping out of each other's way. On the other hand, it is possible that food shortages might have led to inter-group conflict, as was probably the case at El Sidrón.[160]

These two incidents fall rather short of evidence for genocide. Jared Diamond[161] has suggested that the Neanderthals suffered the same fate that would much later befall the Native Americans, Aboriginal Australians and other indigenous people after the arrival of European colonists, and were wiped out by a combination of disease, killing and displacement. This view draws on another less-than-meritorious aspect of the European colonial era: as is well known, the diseases the Europeans brought with them proved even more destructive than their desire for conquest and gold. The main problem with this view is that diseases such as smallpox, flu, tuberculosis, measles and cholera all originally affected animals. They only crossed the species barrier when humans began living in large numbers in close proximity to animals – in other words, with the advent of farming. Hunter-gatherers would have had little or no exposure to such diseases. Furthermore, on the rare occasions infection did occur – assuming that it ever did – the population density was far too small for it to become an epidemic. It should also be appreciated that as hunter-gatherers, the Aurignacian and Gravettian people lived in relatively small groups. They were not Conquistadors.

If we accept that modern humans were responsible for the demise of the Neanderthals – and the evidence is only circumstantial – then a scenario in which modern humans simply outcompeted with Neanderthals for the same resources seems far more likely than any involving genocide and conquest. The question, then, is what gave modern humans the edge? Were they simply smarter than the Neanderthals? Richard Klein[2] has little doubt that this was the case. To Klein, every aspect of the archaeological record suggests that Neanderthals were behaviourally less advanced than modern humans. This includes artefacts, site modification, ability to adapt to extreme environments, and subsistence. In a similar vein, Steven Mithen[78] claims that Neanderthals were held back by the lack of modern language. To Mithen, the immense stability and conservatism of Neanderthal culture argues against them possessing such a language. The Neanderthals had a clear need for bows and arrows, means of storing food, and needles and threads, but without language, such things remained beyond them.

But does this argument hold water? A recent survey of explanations based around a reading of the archaeological record suggests that it does not: apart from evidence for symbolic behaviour, Neanderthals enjoyed a diet as diverse as that of modern humans and their hunting techniques and capacity for innovation were not obviously inferior. Sophisticated Neanderthal technologies included manufacturing pitch for hafting spear points and making specialised bone tools for working animal hides. The survey also disputed the common view that modern humans had larger social networks than Neanderthals, claiming that there was no evidence for this in the archaeological records of Middle Stone Age Africa and Middle Palaeolithic Europe.[162]

It could be argued that Neanderthals were over-reliant on their cold-adapted physiology. Technology can adapt far faster than evolutionary processes, and the first modern humans in Europe had already had to adapt to a variety of environments very different to their original African homeland. However, this does not necessarily tell us anything about cognitive differences between the two species. It is probably best to set aside arguments that focus too heavily on cognitive differences between Neanderthals and modern humans, and concentrate on other lines on enquiry.

Computer simulations have been used to analyse the relationship between high-resolution climate data for specific periods and the geographical distribution of archaeological sites associated with Neanderthal and modern human populations. This data was used to reconstruct regions that the two populations could potentially have occupied. The simulations used a program known as GARP, which has also been used to study the impact of climate change on biodiversity. The program is capable of 'learning' to refine its predictions of regions occupied until they match the known archaeological data. From this, predictions can be made about the regions occupied by the two populations at different times, under different climatic conditions, and whether they were expanding or contracting. For example, the program does correctly predict that during the cold Heinrich Event 4, the Ebro River Valley represented a southerly limit to modern human expansion.

Simulations were run for various climate phases of the Upper Palaeolithic. It was found in each case the geographical range of the Neanderthals contracted, but that that of the incoming modern humans expanded. This was the case even during Greenland Interstadial 8 (GI8), when the climate was favourable and Neanderthals could have expanded their range. The obvious implication is that competition with modern humans was responsible for the range contraction and ultimate extinction of the Neanderthals.[163] In this respect, it is almost certainly relevant that modern humans significantly outnumbered Neanderthals. Archaeological evidence based on site numbers suggests that the ratio might have been as high as 10:1 in favour of the incoming modern population.[164] Sheer weight of numbers might have enabled the modern humans to expand their overall territory at the expense of the Neanderthals.

However, the exact circumstances of the Neanderthal extinction remain uncertain, as does how the two populations interacted with each other. Unless the Châtelperronian beads and sophisticated tools were of completely independent Neanderthal origin – something that admittedly cannot be ruled out – the implication is that there was some form of interaction. It is in any case difficult to believe that the two populations shunned each other completely.

Once they were gone from their southern Iberian refugium, the long story of the Neanderthals was at an end. Or was it? As we have seen, around 20 percent of the Neanderthal genome survives in the present-day population. With a current world population of seven billion, there is now more Neanderthal DNA in existence than ever before. The Neanderthals are far from extinct.

9: Enter *Homo sapiens*

Johnny-come-lately

Homo sapiens – the species to which we all belong – is believed to have emerged in Africa about 200,000 years ago. While that may seem like a long time, it represents just ten percent of the span of time since the first undisputedly human species, *Homo erectus*, emerged in Africa. It is only one percent of the time that has passed since the era of the early apes such as *Proconsul*. Even that is a fairly recent event in terms of primate evolution. *Homo sapiens* are a Johnny-come-lately species, the most recent of all humans. We are only the latest in a long line of African apes.

Understandably, the circumstances in which our species first appeared are of considerable interest to palaeoanthropologists. Although they have differing views on what unique anatomical traits should be used to define *Homo sapiens*, there is agreement that the modern human skull is distinct from that of earlier hominins. Rather than jutting forward, the face and eyes are tucked under the braincase, which is globular rather than rather than long, low and oval-shaped. The forehead is steep rather than flat and receding, and the chin is prominent.[1,2] The changes leading to the distinctive skull shape of modern humans might actually not have been that dramatic. They might have arisen from nothing more than a reduction in the length of the sphenoid bone, which is the central bone of the cranial base from which the face grows forward.[3]

Currently, the oldest fossil remains recognised as belonging to *Homo sapiens* are from three sites, all in Africa. These are Omo and Herto, both in Ethiopia, and Jebel Irhoud, in Morocco. The Omo and Jebel Irhoud remains were discovered in the 1960s, but their age was not accurately determined until recently. The Herto remains were discovered in the late 1990s, and for a while were thought to be the earliest examples of *Homo sapiens* until a re-evaluation of the Omo remains showed that these are older still.

Omo: earliest modern humans

The Omo remains were discovered in 1967, when a team led by Richard Leakey recovered human fossils from two sites in the basin of the Omo River in southwest Ethiopia. Although the sites were located on opposite sides of the river, both were found in the same geological stratum: Member I of a 100 m (330 ft.) thick layer of sediment known as the Kibish Formation. Omo I comprises a fragmentary skull together with some postcranial remains, and Omo II is an almost-intact skull.[4,5]

Both skulls are modern in appearance. The reconstructed skull of Omo I has a globular braincase and steep forehead. It has a prominent chin, small browridges, a rounded occipital region (the back of skull), and the teeth are modern in shape and size. Although it is still more robust than many modern skulls, it unmistakably belongs to *Homo sapiens*. The cranial capacity of Omo II is a hefty 1435 cc, larger than the present day average, the braincase is long but domed, and the browridges are small. Unlike Omo I, Omo II retains some primitive features, notably a more receding forehead, a more angular occipital region, a prominent occipital torus for the attachment of the rear neck muscles, and a slight ridge along the midline of the braincase known as sagittal keeling.[6]

Omo I and Omo II were originally believed to be around 130,000 years old, but in 2005 they were revealed to be far older. A team lead by geologist Ian McDougall from the Australian National University, Canberra, revisited the recovery sites, and used the original site documentation to pinpoint the exact locations of the two fossil finds. Bone fragments missed in the 1967 excavations were recovered from the Omo I site and found to fit the Omo I skull, thus confirming that the investigators were at the right spot. It turned out that the geological stratum in which the fossils were found was sandwiched between two layers of volcanic tuffs (ash) from nearby eruptions, and the both fossils had lain just above the lower layer of tuff. Volcanic ash can be readily dated by the argon-argon technique, and by dating the lower ash layer it was found that the remains were actually 195,000 years old.[7,8] This makes them at least 35,000 years older than any other modern human remains found to date.

It is probable that the two individuals were not exact contemporaries, and that they actually lived centuries apart. While it is unlikely that significant evolutionary change could have occurred during the time that separated Omo I from Omo II, they could have belonged to two different populations, each of which lived in the region at a different time. Omo I represents a modern or near-modern human, but the more primitive Omo II could be a late-surviving member of a more archaic lineage.[9]

Rituals at Herto?

The Herto remains reveal tantalising hints of ancient mortuary rituals of a type still practiced in some parts of the world today. The remains were recovered in 1997 by a team led by Tim White, who had previously headed up the team responsible for the discovery of *Ardipithecus*. The find was made in the Upper Herto Member, a geological stratum in the Bouri Formation at Middle Awash, and comprised three well-preserved skulls plus fragmentary remains.[10] These were dated by argon-argon dating of volcanic material found in the geological stratum containing the remains, and found to be between 154,000 and 160,000 years old.[11] All three of the skulls show cut-marks indicative of some form of mortuary ritual: the earliest example of such practice documented for modern humans.

Two of the skulls belonged to adult males; the third to a six-year-old child. The cranial capacity of the better-preserved adult skull is 1,450 cc and again, this is pretty respectable, lying at the high end of the modern human range. Although the finds are close enough to present-day humans to be considered the same species, they still possess some primitive features. These include more robust facial features and a longer braincase. Accordingly, White and his colleagues proposed a new subspecies for the remains, *Homo sapiens idaltu*. The word 'idaltu' means 'elder' or 'first-born' in the Afar language. On the basis of comparison with other fossils, they claimed that *Homo sapiens idaltu* evolved from *Homo rhodesiensis* (or African *Homo heidelbergensis*), and that it was the ancestor of fully-modern *Homo sapiens*.[10]

Archaeological evidence suggests that the Upper Herto people lived by the edge of a freshwater lake, but the associated remains of hippopotamus, cattle, antelope, cane-rat, wildebeest and horses suggest that grasslands were also close at hand. There is evidence for the repeated butchery of large mammal carcasses, particularly hippopotamus. In addition, 640 stone artefacts were recovered from the same geological stratum as the fossils. They included Levallois flakes and points normally associated with the Middle Stone Age, but less technologically-advanced Acheulean artefacts were also present. Such tool industries are traditionally classified as final or transitional Acheulean. The Upper Herto people were not the first humans in the region; the Upper Herto Member overlies a 260,000-year-old layer known as the Lower Herto Member. Unfortunately, no human remains have been found in this layer, although there are late Acheulean-type tools and evidence of carcass butchery.[11]

The better-preserved of the two Upper Herto adult skulls was reconstructed from scattered fragments, and was found to bear cut-marks made with stone tools. Some of these are deep marks typical of de-fleshing, but most are more superficial, and suggest repetitive scraping. The latter are not seen on animal remains processed for food, ruling out cannibalism as a cause. The child's skull also exhibits cut-marks, in this case made by a very sharp stone flake deep in its base. The rear part of the base was broken away, and the broken edges polished. The sides of the skull also show a deep polish; this might have formed from repeated handling of the skull in rituals. The other adult skull was the least modified, bearing just two cut-marks.[11]

There is ethnographic evidence from several cultures for similar treatment and preservation of skulls as part of their mortuary rituals. For example, some New Guinean skulls show cut-marks, decoration and polishing reminiscent of the traces seen on the Upper Herto skulls. The implications are that the Upper Herto people might have had similar rituals and a complex belief system: these are considered to be one of the hallmarks of modern human behaviour.[11]

The Jebel Irhoud child

Recent dating of fossil evidence from Morocco suggests that modern humans were also present in North Africa at around the same time that the Upper Herto people lived. Jebel Irhoud is a cave site located about 100 km (60 miles) west of Marrakech. The remains were originally thought to be anything from 190,000 to 90,000 years old, but this has now been pinned down by uranium series and electron spin resonance methods to around 160,000 years old.[12] To date, remains corresponding to seven individuals have been recovered, including two partial skulls. The better-preserved of these, Irhoud 1, discovered in 1961, has primitive features including moderately-developed browridges and a long, low cranial vault. However, the forehead is within the modern range, and it lacks an occipital torus. The cranial capacity of 1,300 to 1,480 cc also falls within the range of early modern humans. The second skull, Irhoud 2, discovered in 1962, is less complete but is broadly similar to Irhoud 1. Irhoud 3, a child's lower jawbone, was discovered in 1968. While it is more robust than that of present-day people, it has a distinct, modern-like chin.[4,13,5]

As we have seen in earlier chapters, there is a strong correlation in primates between rates of dental development and age of maturation, and this has been used to show that archaic humans matured earlier than modern humans. Studies of three teeth preserved in the Irhoud 3 jawbone suggest that that the child's rate of dental development was similar to that of a modern child, implying a similar rate of maturation. Thus it seems that the lengthy maturation of modern people had emerged by no later than 160,000 years ago.[12]

Hiatus

Although there is no fossil evidence for modern humans in South Africa prior to around 120,000 years ago,[14] there is archaeological evidence for their presence there by 165,000 years ago.[15] Thus it appears that by around this time, modern humans had spread across the whole continent.

The earliest modern human remains found outside Africa are rather more recent, probably dating to around 115,000 years ago. The remains were found at two sites in Israel, Mugharet es-Skhul and Jebel Qafzeh during excavations conducted by British archaeologist Dorothy Garrod and palaeontologist Dorothea Bate between 1929 and 1934. Though they still retain archaic features such as robustness, the Skhul and Qafzeh people are essentially modern with a high and well-rounded skull, and pronounced chins.[5] They show some resemblance to the Jebel Irhoud people, suggesting that they were of North African descent,[9] but at that time Earth was in the middle of the warm, wet Eemian interglacial that preceded the last Ice Age. 'Humid corridors' existed through the normally-inhospitable Sahara,[16] opening up access to the Levant and effectively making it an eastern extension of North Africa.[17,18]

Away from the neighbourhood of Africa, there is no convincing evidence for modern human remains until around 60,000 years ago. The Liujiang Skull, discovered in 1958 at Tongtianyan Cave, southern China, has been claimed to be as much as much as 111,000 to 139,000 years old on the basis of uranium series methods,[19] but the exact geological position of the find was not documented, and the skull could be as little as 30,000 years old.[20] A lower jawbone from Zhirendong ('*Homo sapiens* cave') in Guizhou Province, southern China, has been securely dated to 106,000 years old,[21] but it is uncertain whether it is from a modern human or simply a member of a late *Homo erectus* population.[22]

Currently, the earliest human remains known that are not African or Levantine; are undisputedly modern; and have been reliably dated, are in the order of 65,000 to 40,000 years old. These are the fossil finds from Lake Mungo in southern New South Wales, Australia; from Tam Pa Ling ('Cave of the Monkeys') in Huà Pan Province, Laos; and from Tabon Cave in the Philippines. The Australian finds comprise the remains of three individuals, including a partial skeleton known informally as 'Mungo Lady'. They are thought to be around 42,000 years old,[23] and possibly as much as 62,000 years old.[24] A partial skull found at Tam Pa Ling is about the same age, estimated to be from 46,000 to 63,000 years old;[25] the Tabon Cave find, a shin bone, is slightly younger and is between 37,000 and 58,000 years old.[26] No European finds are greater than around 45,000 years old.[27,28,29]

Unless one accepts the disputed 139,000 year date for the Liujiang Skull, there is no clear fossil evidence for modern humans outside Africa and the Levant until at least 130,000 years after their first appearance at Omo. The simplest explanation for this hiatus is that modern humans evolved in Africa and only later migrated to other parts of the Old World.

The Time Machine

Although a comparatively recent African origin for *Homo sapiens* is now generally accepted, this was not always the case. Much of the fossil evidence favouring an African origin only come to light or was accurately dated in the last twenty years or so, and prior to the 1980s it was commonly believed that modern humans had evolved from archaic humans in various parts of the world. Thus Neanderthals in Europe, *Homo heidelbergensis* (or *rhodesiensis*) in Africa and *Homo erectus* in Asia were simply all early forms of *Homo sapiens*; our species was thought to be almost two million years old rather than around 200,000 years old. The two rival models became known as the Out of Africa and Multiregional continuity hypotheses.

Unable to resolve matters with the fossil evidence then available, researchers turned to genetics to try and solve the problem. Most of the studies involved nuclear DNA, but the first breakthrough came from geneticist Allan Wilson and two of his PhD students at the University of California, Berkeley, Rebecca Cann and Mark Stoneking. They studied patterns of mitochondrial DNA variation in 147 people, drawn from five geographic populations around the world: Africa, Asia, Australia, Europe and New Guinea.

Mitochondrial DNA is distinct from ordinary nuclear DNA, and it is inherited solely from the maternal line. As a tool for studying human populations, it has two major advantages over nuclear DNA. The first, as noted above, is that it is inherited exclusively from the maternal line and does not recombine with paternal DNA, making it far easier to track mitochondrial lineages over many generations. The second advantage is that mitochondrial DNA accumulates mutations ten times faster than nuclear DNA. This means that over a comparatively short period of time, distinct genetic lineages known as haplogroups will emerge. In turn, genetic diversity will increase within these haplogroups, and eventually lineages appearing within them will diverge from one another to form daughter haplogroups. Haplogroups are defined in terms of particular genetic mutations known as markers.

By sampling mitochondrial DNA from various populations around the world, it is possible to determine where particular haplogroups originated. The longer a haplogroup has been present in a particular region, the greater will be its genetic diversity. Provided it is still present in the region it originated, the genetic diversity will be at a maximum there, and the age of the haplogroup can then be determined by use of the molecular clock principle. Statistical methods can be applied to the data and used to estimate population sizes. These techniques can be used to map out prehistoric demographics and migrations around the world; in theory at least they are investigative tools only slightly less powerful than handing anthropologists the keys to Dr Who's *Tardis*.

In practice, though, matters are rather more complicated. As noted in Chapter 2, calibrating the molecular clock is far from straightforward, and genetic dates are usually subject to considerable uncertainty.[30] Also, there are disagreements as to the effects of natural selection on haplogroup distribution; it is possible that some haplogroups are better suited than others for survival in various environments around the world.[31,32] Another complication is that migrations occurring in historical times can erase traces of those occurring in prehistoric times.[33] Consequently, as we shall see in later chapters, genetic material obtained from actual prehistoric human remains (so-called ancient DNA or aDNA) often gives quite different results to those obtained by studying present-day populations. With these caveats in mind, population genetics is nevertheless a powerful tool in studies of human prehistory.

Mitochondrial Eve

In January 1987, Wilson's team published their mitochondrial results in the journal *Nature*. They had discovered that the entire human population of the world could be arranged into a single family tree with 133 different maternal lineages. The tree showed a distinct split between the African and non-African populations, with the former showing the greater number of lineages; thus the greatest genetic diversity was found in Africa. This result implied that the African population was the longest established, as would be expected if modern humans originated there. The team were also able to estimate the extent to which the various genetic lineages had diverged from one another since the time of their common ancestor, taken to be one woman. By applying the molecular clock principle, they were able to show that this had been about 200,000 years ago. In other words, everybody living in the world today can trace their mitochondrial DNA to one African woman who lived about 200,000 years ago.[34]

The story made the front cover of *Newsweek*, under the headline "*The Search for Adam and Eve*". Inevitably, this one woman soon became known as 'Mitochondrial Eve', but the term is rather misleading; if other parts of the human genome had been used, they would have yielded genetic lineages that traced back to different ancestors.[35] It is also untrue that Mitochondrial Eve was the only woman alive at the time; there were others, but their mitochondrial lineages all ended at some point with women who failed to have any daughters. This is an example of genetic drift (see Chapter 8) where in a small population, the various mitochondrial lineages 'drifted' down to just the one – that of Mitochondrial Eve.

In 1992, Wilson's statistical techniques were challenged on technical grounds, and it was also noted that his team had examined only a small portion of the mitochondrial DNA genome. However, subsequent studies have confirmed the original result. More extensive regions of the mitochondrial DNA genome have been studied; the results confirm that the mitochondrial genetic diversity of Africans is far greater than that of non-Africans, and suggest that Mitochondrial Eve lived about 170,000 to 200,000 years ago.[36,37,38]

By around 2000, genetic techniques had advanced to the point where it had become practical to study the male sex-determining Y-chromosome, which in common with mitochondrial DNA, does not recombine. In this case however, because only men have a Y-chromosome; Y-chromosomal DNA is inherited exclusively from the paternal line. A consequence – and drawback – is that Y-chromosomal studies can only be carried out with men. Y-chromosomal studies likewise backed an African origin for modern humans, showing that Africans possess greater genetic diversity than non-Africans and that the ancestry of all existent Y-chromosomal lineages can be traced back to Africa.[39,37,40,41,42,43] It was also now possible to study ordinary recombining DNA, and once again, the results backed an African origin for modern humans, showing that genetic diversity decreases with geographical distance from Africa.[37,44,45,46,47]

With most palaeoanthropologists now accepting an African origin for *Homo sapiens*, the next task was to try and pinpoint in which part of Africa Mitochondrial Eve lived. Unfortunately, mitochondrial studies cannot provide a fine enough geographical resolution to settle matters, and can only tell us that she was part of a fairly small population[48] that lived in either East Africa or South Africa.[49] However, a recent study of autosomal genetic diversity supports a South African origin.[50] If this conclusion is correct, then modern human fossils older than the Omo remains may await discovery in South Africa.

Modernising humanity

Having answered the question of when and where modern humans emerged, the next key question is how? One possibility is that they emerged in one place among a single isolated African population, from whence they spread across the whole of Africa and replaced the various archaic populations as they did so. The second possibility is that that the accretion model proposed for the Neanderthals in Europe (see Chapter 8) may also be applicable to Africa. If so, the anatomical and behavioural features now associated with modern humans might have appeared at different times and places across Africa, until what we see today emerged. As with the model proposed for Neanderthals, isolated human populations, each possessing some modern characteristics, periodically encountered one another and interbred. Over time, more and more of these characteristics began accumulate in single populations, until eventually a population bearing the full *Homo sapiens* 'package' emerged.[51,52,53,54]

The fossil evidence does suggest that humans in Africa were only gradually 'modernised' after the split with the Neanderthals. Fossil remains begin to show increasing modern characteristics between 300,000 to 200,000 years ago, before entering the modern range between 200,000 and 100,000 years ago. During this second period, while clearly representing modern humans, fossil remains were still more robust than any living people, and it is only after 35,000 years ago that people with the more gracile, fully modern skeletal form make their appearance.[55,9] Overall, this is what would be expected if the accretion model is correct.

Genetic data from living populations also supports the accretion model. It suggests that modern humans are descended from multiple archaic human populations that existed in isolation in Africa for long periods, before coming into contact and interbreeding.[56] This process might not have ended with the emergence of *Homo sapiens*. Researchers have also found that approximately two percent of the genome of the present-day sub-Saharan African population derives from interbreeding between modern and archaic humans that occurred as recently 35,000 years ago. The archaic species concerned has not yet been identified, but they diverged from modern humans 700,000 years ago and are thought to have lived in Central Africa.[57] If this conclusion is correct, it means that archaic humans persisted alongside modern humans in Africa for at over 150,000 years. As yet, though, there is no fossil evidence for archaic humans surviving in Africa for this long.

A possible scenario is that while the accretion process was gradual and geographically-widespread, only one relatively localised population eventually acquired the full *Homo sapiens* 'package', giving it a competitive edge over other human populations. It is this population, possibly numbering between 2,000 and 10,000 individuals, from which the world's current population is largely descended.[58] As we shall see in Chapter 11, it is possible that the package included features linked to the emergence of modern human behaviour. Once it had come together, the full package enabled these early modern humans to spread across the rest of Africa, although they continued to encounter and interbreed with archaic populations.

How, why and when modern human behaviour emerged is one of the key questions of human prehistory. Before we can examine these issues in detail, we must first take a look at the later part of the African Middle Stone Age, from 190,000 to around 40,000 years ago. Far from being 'the early days of *Homo sapiens*', this period spans three-quarters of the history of our species.

10: The long African dawn

The first 150,000 years

How can we build up a picture of what happened in Africa during this lengthy formative period? In addition to the fossil evidence reviewed in Chapter 9, we can draw on archaeological, genetic, climatic and even linguistic data, although the last of these is rather speculative. The archaeological record gives the appearance of a strange mixture of innovation and conservatism. The technology of early modern humans does not for the most part appear notably different from that of the Neanderthals, but there are sporadic exceptions that suggest *Homo sapiens* were behaviourally modern more or less from the outset. What is remarkable is that innovative technologies repeatedly appeared, only to disappear after a fairly short period; a pattern that was repeated until the onset of the Late Stone Age. These technologies included tools made from bone or antler, and stone tool-types that did not come into widespread use until much later. After each burst of innovation, there was an apparent reversion to more conservative technologies, and hi-tech solutions that would not be seen again for tens of thousands of years were seemingly abandoned.

Two population expansions have been revealed by studies of mitochondrial DNA data from present-day populations, both of which took place within Africa before the peopling of the non-African world. The first was fairly modest, and involved the small founding group of modern humans that emerged around 190,000 years ago. The genetic footprint and – more speculatively – the linguistic footprint of this first expansion can still be discerned in the African population to this day. The second expansion, which was much larger than the first, did not occur until around 80,000 to 60,000 years ago.[1]

These technological and demographic developments were set against a background of climate change and recurring episodes of extreme drought. The Middle Stone Age saw two glacial episodes: the Riss from 190,000 to 126,000 years ago, and the Würm ('the last Ice Age') from 110,000 to 11,650 years ago. Between the two glacial periods was a warm interglacial, the Eemian, from 126,000 to 110,000 years ago. However, tropical Africa additionally suffered recurring episodes of extreme drought, occurring during three main periods: from 132,000 to 127,000 years ago; from 111,000 to 108,000 years ago; and from 105,000 to 95,000 years ago. Lesser episodes of aridity occurred thereafter, continuing until 70,000 years ago.[2]

The aridity is clearly documented by core samples from the Great Lakes of the Rift Valley. The data from Lake Malawi from these periods reveals that pollen levels dropped, and that there was a lack of charcoal particles of the type that would result from flash fires. It is implied that the region around the lake had become a near-desert, with vegetation too sparse to sustain flash fires. The lake itself became shallow and saline as its water level, currently 706 m (2,316 ft.) deep, dropped to just 125 m (410 ft.), and the volume was reduced by 95 percent. Data from nearby Lake Tanganyika and from Lake Bosumtwi in Ghana reveals a similar picture.[2,3]

Not until the coldest part of the Last Glacial Maximum, from 17,000 to 16,000 years ago, would conditions again be so arid.[4] The existence of our forebears throughout the Middle Stone Age was ever precarious.

The symbolic ape

Pinnacle Point

At Pinnacle Point on the southern coast of South Africa, evidence has been found of an innovative cultural 'package' 165,000 years ago, including the harvesting of seafood, manufacture of sophisticated stone tools, and the use of red ochre pigment. The stone tools, known as microliths, appear almost 100,000 years earlier than once thought. Pinnacle Point is a golf course near the town of Mossel Bay, Western Cape Province. In 2000, as part of the preparatory work for the construction of the golf course, a survey was made of a series of caves in the nearby coastal cliffs, and it was discovered that they held a wealth of artefacts and animal remains going back to the early part of the Middle Stone Age. The caves were subsequently investigated by an international team, led by anthropologist Curtis Marean from the Institute of Human Origins of Arizona State University.

The lowest levels of the cave known as PP13B were dated by optically stimulated luminescence, and are 164,000 ± 12,000 years old. Although no human remains were recovered from these levels, they are very close to the same age as the Upper Herto and Jebel Irhoud remains from Ethiopia and Morocco. By this time, apparently, modern humans had already dispersed across much of Africa. In the PP13B levels were found evidence for the use of ochre, sophisticated stone tools, and harvesting of seafood, all of which are considered to be markers of modern human behaviour. There were almost sixty pieces of red ochre, some of which showed signs of grinding or scraping. Notably, there was a preference for the reddest, most chromatic ochre and Marean believed it showed all the signs of being used as pigment for body-painting and possibly the colouring of animal hides. Also found were a total of 1,836 flaked stone artefacts, including a significant number of microliths.[5]

Microliths are small blades with a width of less than 10 mm (0.375 in.), and their first appearance was once thought to be around 70,000 years ago.[6] They were commonly used in hafted tools and weapons, i.e. set into bone or wooden handles, or the shafts or tips of spears. Rather than having to repair or discard an entire tool when worn or damaged, only the affected microlith would need to be repaired or replaced. Microliths are classed as Mode 5, the most advanced tool technology on Sir Grahame Clark's scale, and they have been described by archaeologist Steven Mithen[7] as the 'plug-in pull-out' technology of the Stone Age. The Pinnacle Point people thus apparently bypassed the use of technologies based on larger blades (Mode 4 technologies). Another refinement, again once thought to be a much later development, was the use of heat treatment to improve the flaking properties of the source materials used for tools.[8]

Another significant discovery at Pinnacle Point is evidence for the use of seafood. Remains included fifteen types of marine invertebrate, including whelks, limpets, mussels and periwinkles. Seafood was an excellent alternative to savannah and steppe herbivores from a nutritional point of view,[9] and had the advantage of being easier to obtain. Its availability was also less affected by the kind of arid conditions that were then prevailing in South Africa during the Riss Glacial Period. Marean and his colleagues[5] speculated that seafood might have been crucial to the survival of these early modern humans as their traditional food sources became scarce, forcing them to expand their home ranges to include Africa's coastline. Shellfish collecting is often associated with more complex and sedentary societies; and at Pinnacle Point, this might have been a stimulus for symbolic expression through ochre use.

Shell middens and river fishing

Despite seafood's many benefits, the next evidence for its usage in Africa is 40,000 years after Pinnacle Point, at a site on the west coast of the Buri Peninsula in Eritrea. There, 125,000-year-old middens have been found, containing the discarded shells of oysters, clams and crabs, as well as the remains of rhinoceros, elephants and hippopotamus. The dates were obtained by uranium series techniques. As with Pinnacle Point, no actual human remains have been recovered, but some stone tools were found in the middens. These appear to be a mixture of old and new technologies, including both teardrop-shaped hand-axes and obsidian flake and blade tools.[10] There may be a simple explanation for the apparent hiatus, as it is likely that much of the evidence from the intervening period has been lost. Coastal sites of human occupation during glacial periods are rare because sea levels were much lower than today, and evidence was submerged when sea levels rose again. Losses may include isolated settlements contemporary with Pinnacle Point.[5] It is probably no coincidence that the Eritrean shell middens date to the Eemian Interglacial, when sea levels were comparable to those of today.

Another site where modern humans were utilising advanced technologies and behaviours is at Katanda on the Upper Semliki River in the Democratic Republic of the Congo. Evidence has been found that there was a well-developed fishing industry at three locations there 90,000 years ago. A number of bone artefacts have been recovered, including both barbed and unbarbed points, and a long tapering pointed piece of unknown function. Possibly, it was a dagger or knife, or even a blank for making barbed points. The pieces are well made, and were finished with a stone grinder. It is possible that they were used for river fishing, making them the earliest-known fishing-tackle.[11]

The use of 'organic technologies' such as bone and antler is thought to be one of the archaeological signals of modern human behaviour.[12] Bone and antler tools, particularly ground and polished points, represent high-performance technologies. Their initial production is time-expensive because of the grinding they require.[13] Such tools do not become common in the archaeological record until around 40,000 years ago in Europe and 25,000 years ago in Africa; this has been cited as one strand of evidence supporting a Great Leap Forward in brainpower 50,000 years ago. It is supposed that anatomically modern humans living prior to then were cognitively incapable of using these materials.[14]

The Katanda sites have yielded extensive remains of large catfish (*Clarias*), all adults, weighing over 35 kg (77 lb.). The absence of younger fish indicates that fishing was carried out exclusively at the beginning of the rainy season, when *Clarias* is known to spawn near the shore. This suggests that exploitation took place as part of a specialised seasonal strategy, rather than on an *ad hoc* basis. Furthermore, the scarcity of fish vertebrae implies that edible portions were separated from heads at the site, and removed to be eaten elsewhere. The Katanda people were evidently competent hunters and fishers who planned their settlement choices around the seasonal availability of game and fish.[11,12]

Why, then, was this precocious technology seemingly no more than a flash in the pan? After Katanda, bone tools are not seen again for more than 10,000 years. One possibility is that the bone artefacts are actually no more than around 12,000 years old, but disturbances of the site forced them downwards into the archaeological layers associated with the Middle Stone Age.[15] The problem with this theory is that it fails to explain the other advanced behaviours implied by the catfish remains.

Blombos Cave

Blombos Cave, on the southern coast of South Africa, is one of the of the most extensively-studied African Middle Stone Age sites. The cave has yielded many artefacts, most notably two 73,000-year-old engraved pieces of ochre, which may be the oldest examples of abstract art anywhere in the world. The site is located in a limestone cliff 35 m (115 ft.) above sea level, and is currently 100 m (330 ft.) from the shore. However, for much of the time that it was in use, lower sea levels meant that the shore was further away. The site was discovered by archaeologist Christopher Henshilwood in 1991, and it has been excavated regularly since.[16]

Three major phases of occupation have been identified, known as M1, M2 and M3. Optically stimulated luminescence and thermoluminescence dating shows that the M1 phase occurred 73,000 years ago; M2 is divided into an upper phase 77,000 years ago and a lower phase 80,000 years ago; and M3 spanned a period from 143,000 to 125,000 years ago, although there are uncertainties of several millennia in all of these dates. Each phase contains a number of occupation layers, most of which are quite shallow. These suggest that the cave was occupied only sporadically, and for relatively short periods of time.[17,18,19,20,21] All three phases of occupation have evidence to suggest the people living there enjoyed a varied diet, including large fish, shellfish, seals and dolphins. Land mammals were extensively hunted, and Henshilwood[22] claims that baked mole-rats made a frequent appearance on the menu. The latter were apparently cooked over a fire in a manner still favoured by local farm workers, who regard these large burrowing rodents as a delicacy. That fire was regularly used for cooking purposes is apparent from the wood-ash scattered throughout the occupation layers.[23]

The M1 and the upper M2 phases have yielded artefacts associated with the Stillbay tool industry, named for the nearby village of Still Bay, where the first examples were identified in the 1920s. This industry is noted for its distinctive Still Bay points, which are finely-worked elliptical or lanceolate (leaf-shaped) in shape, sharply-pointed at each apex. They are usually executed on high-quality raw materials including chert, quartzite and silcrete. The latter is a concrete-like material formed from silica and soil grains. The increased use of finer-grained stone, relative to earlier Middle Stone Age phases, is a characteristic of the Stillbay industry, and the use of silcrete is particularly predominant in the M1 phase. Tool types include end scrapers and burins, similar to those of the much later European Upper Palaeolithic.[23] End scrapers are elongated flakes or blades with retouched edge at one end, used for scraping animal skins. The chisel-like burins were specifically intended for working bone and antler materials.[24]

The Blombos people also made use of bone tools, and twenty-eight of these have been recovered from the M1 and M2 phases – the largest collection of such artefacts so far found at an African Middle Stone Age site. The majority are shaped on bone fragments or splinters removed from long bone shafts, although in some cases the whole bone is shaped. Cattle and wildebeest bone is most widely used, but marine mammal bone and in one case bird bone were also employed.[23] Most of these tools are quite crudely finished, and were probably used as awls to perforate fairly soft material such as well-worked hides, possibly during the manufacture of clothing and carrying bags. A few are more finely-worked, symmetrical in shape, and are circular in cross-section; these are thought to have been projectile points. Both awls and projectile points resemble those known from later African prehistory, and from ethnographic collections.[14] They were extensively used after manufacture, and in many cases they were sharpened and re-used after tip breakage. A bone tool was probably only discarded if the breakage occurred near the midpoint rather than the tip, making it too small to hold.[14,20]

Two further examples of advanced Stillbay technology are the use of compound adhesives and pressure flaking. A compound adhesive is one in which two or more components are mixed before use, and traces of such an adhesive, comprised of red ochre and plant gum, have been found on Stillbay points at another South African site, Sibudu Cave, 40 km (25 miles) from Durban. The points are roughly 70,000 years old, and show micro-fractures consistent with hafting for use as spear tips. Experiments have shown that the ochre/gum adhesive forms a tough bond, preventing the stone insert from breaking away from its haft when used. Evidence for the possible use of this technology has also been found at a number of other sites, although not at Blombos. To use compound adhesives satisfactorily, considerable experimentation is necessary to find the right ingredients, and fire must be used to dry the adhesive after application.[25] The use of adhesives 70,000 years ago confirms that at least some elements of modern cognition must have been present by then.[26]

Pressure flaking is a technique used for finishing a stone artefact by exerting a pressure with the sharp end of a tool close to the unfinished edges of the piece. The technique requires the prior use of heat treatment to improve flaking properties, and was once thought to have been used no earlier than European Solutrean industry, about 20,000 years ago. However, experimental techniques and microscopic study has shown that that it was used at Blombos, during the final shaping of Stillbay points made on heat-treated silcrete.[27]

Blombos Cave has also provided further evidence for what Henshilwood and his team claim is strong evidence for early symbolic behaviour. Finds include 41 beads, several thousand pieces of ochre and two 'toolkits' for processing ochre. The beads were made from perforated shells of the marine snail *Nassarius kraussianus* ('tick shell'), which occur only in estuaries. They were probably brought to the site from the Duiwenhoks and Goukou Rivers, which are located around 20 km (12 miles) from the cave, and are too far away for the shells to have been deposited at the cave by non-human predators. While it is possible that the tick shells were collected as food, the time taken to extract the small edible content of each shell makes this unlikely given the availability of larger shellfish and fish. The shells are all adults, indicating that they were selected for size, and the perforations appear to be artificial rather than the result of some natural process. A sharp tool, elliptical in section, was most likely used to make the perforations. The beads show signs of wear from rubbing against thread or contact with human skin, suggesting they were worn as bracelets or necklaces. Traces of ochre have been found on the shells suggesting the possible colouring of the beads, though it could also have come from body-paint. The beads were found in groups displaying similar size, colour, perforation type and use-wear pattern, suggesting such groups represented single beadwork items. Again, Henshilwood believes that wearing of such personal ornaments implies the existence of modern fully-syntactical language.[28,29,20]

The use of beads might have been widespread across Africa by this time. Beads made from the marine snails *Nassarius gibbosulus* and possibly *Nassarius circumcinctus* have been reported from a number of North African sites, including Oued Djebbana in Algeria[30] and the Moroccan sites of Grotte des Pigeons, Rhafas, Ifri n'Ammar and Contrebandiers. The Moroccan shells range from 70,000 to 85,000 years old, and were worn as stung beads. Some show residues of red ochre, suggesting that they were coloured with pigments.[31,32]

In 2002, Henshilwood reported the two pieces of engraved ochre from the 73,000-year-old M1 phase. The two pieces of engraved ochre, catalogued as AA 8937 and AA 8938, have been described as the world's oldest examples of abstract art. The pieces have both been engraved with cross-hatched patterns. In addition, on AA 8938 the pattern is bounded top and bottom by parallel lines, with a third parallel line running through the middle. The fact that the two pieces are so similar suggests a deliberate intent, rather somebody absent-mindedly scratching away at the pieces with a sharp object. Somebody who knew just what they were doing must have sat down and engraved the two pieces. Henshilwood argues that this implies the existence of modern fully-syntactical language.[17,20] Other engraved ochres were later identified, although they were less spectacular than AA 8937 and AA 8938. They came from all three phases of the site, and some were over 100,000 years old.[21]

Henshilwood dismisses other possible explanations for the marks on the ochres. For example, he claims that they could not be the by-product of testing for the quality of powder that could be obtained from the ochres, as only a few lines would be required for this purpose. He also believes that the marks are unlikely to have been the result of absent-minded doodling because great care was taken in completing the patterns and ensuring the incisions matched up. Furthermore, engraving lines on hard pieces of ochre requires full concentration in order to apply the right pressure and keep the depth of incision constant. He believes that not only were the marks on the ochres made with deliberate intent, but recurring motifs on ochres found in all three of the Middle Stone Age phases are evidence of a tradition of engraved geometric patterns that began more than 100,000 years ago and persisted for tens of millennia.[21]

The two M3 phase 'toolkits', designated Tk1 and Tk2, are 101,000 years old. The toolkits comprise abalone shells, each of which contained a mixture of ochre, charcoal and crushed bone. Tk1 was found with a quartzite cobble, which was stained with red ochre and showed signs of having been used for pounding and grinding. An animal bone was found with ochre residues, which had probably been used as a stirrer and for transferring some of the mixture from the shells. What the mixture was used for is uncertain. There is no resin or wax to suggest that it was used as an adhesive. Possibly it was used to paint a surface in order to protect it – or maybe to decorate it. Tk1 and Tk2 were found in close proximity to one another, suggesting that they were used at the same time. The fact that there are few other archaeological remains in the same layer suggests that at this point in its long history, Blombos Cave was being used as a workshop. It was abandoned shortly after the compounds were made; and long before the cave was next occupied, sand blew in from outside and buried the toolkits for the next 100,000 years.[21]

Graphic art at Diepkloof Rock Shelter

Diepkloof Rock Shelter, Western Cape Province, has provided further evidence for the existence of graphic tradition, spanning many generations, in the African Middle Stone Age.[33] Like many other South African sites, Diepkloof Rock Shelter was repeatedly occupied over tens of millennia. People lived there from before 130,000 years ago to about 45,000 years ago. Occupation of the cave encompassed the pre-Stillbay, Stillbay, Howieson's Poort, and post-Howieson's Poort periods. It was from 60,000-year-old Howieson's Poort layers that researchers recovered 270 engraved fragments of ostrich eggshell, representing at least 25 eggshells. It seems likely that the decorated eggshells were used as water flasks, a purpose for which indigenous Kalahari people use them to this day. A 12 mm (½ in.) diameter hole was punched in one piece that came from the apex of the eggshell. Ostrich eggs are well-suited for this purpose, being larger than the eggs of any other living bird species. They are by necessity sturdy, as they have to endure being sat on by a 100 kg (220 lb.) female ostrich.

Two principal designs seem to have been favoured by the Diepkloof people. The first was a hatched band motif consisting of two long parallel lines, intersected at roughly right angles by shorter, regularly spaced lines. Within this style, craftspeople exercised a certain amount of variation of both the width of the bands and the spacing of the hatching. The design was later replaced by one featuring parallel or slightly diverging lines, suggesting that the dominant styles changed over time. The engravings were clearly standardised, showing repetitive patterns made in accordance with a set of rules, although there was scope for individual expression within these rules.

The most obvious question is what was the significance of these geometric patterns? Christopher Henshilwood notes that the Christian cross would appear equally abstract to somebody unfamiliar with religious iconography. It is possible that the patterns meant something quite specific to the people who made them, though just what we simply don't know and probably never will know. Another question is if humans were able to produce abstract art over 100,000 years ago, why was figurative art not seen until so much later? One possibility is that humans were still not behaviourally fully modern and were not at this stage able to make figurative images, though Henshilwood rejects this possibility. He notes that there are many cultures that do not make figurative art, and many others do so using perishable materials that would not survive for tens of thousands of years.[34]

Even if Henshilwood is right, does the archaeological record of the Middle Stone Age indicate only gradually increasing symbolic behaviour, not reaching maturity until around 100,000 to 60,000 years ago? Use of pigment is attested well before the earliest use of beads, and this in turn precedes the Blombos engraved ochres and the Diepkloof Rock Shelter engraved ostrich eggs. Should we even be equating these things with modern human behaviour?

It could of course simply be the case that we haven't yet found examples of beads and artwork from earlier times, possibly because the relevant sites are now underwater. However, archaeologist Larry Barham[35] believes that there is another explanation. Citing ethnographic research,[36] he notes that among recent hunter-gatherers in New Guinea, there were pronounced social differences between groups relying on land and tree-based game, and those dependent on fish and other aquatic foods. The former were highly mobile, egalitarian, and had few forms of physical expression other than body painting, dancing and singing. On the other hand, the latter were densely packed, sedentary and socially stratified. Hierarchy was often pronounced, with some villages even exhibiting hereditary rankings. These groups had complex rituals, involving elaborate visual arts. Barham speculates that long-standing ochre use without other material culture would be consistent with small, widely scattered groups that have little need to engage in elaborate social signalling.

Anthropologists Steven Kuhn and Mary Stiner[37] have noted that beads have a number of advantages over pigment use for conveying status. They are more durable than body-painting (tattooing excepted); more costly in terms of materials and time needed for their manufacture and hence more prestigious; and they can be used as part of a social exchange network. Kuhn and Stiner believe that the presence of beads is a marker of increased social complexity, and that they possibly first appeared in response to heightened levels of intra-group competition.

Regardless of which, psychologist Frederick Coolidge and anthropologist Thomas Wynn[38] remain unconvinced that beads and the use of pigments equate to language and modern human behaviour. They suggest that these things could simply be markers of one's status within a group. Users could be aware of how they were perceived by others, but not necessarily behaviourally modern.

Stillbay, Howieson's Poort and long-distance trade

The Stillbay industry was widespread and not confined to the region around Blombos Cave and Still Bay.[39] However, it might have been comparatively short-lived, lasting for less than thousand years from 71,900 to 71,000 years ago. Though these dates are not strictly consistent with those proposed for the M1 and M2 phases of Blombos Cave, the associated degree of uncertainty is such that they probably do overlap. Problems arise when trying to establish a precise timeline because of the chronological 'haze' that results from different sites being dated by means of different methods. There is also the near-certainty that we do not have the earliest and latest artefacts associated with any one industry. What is curious is that the Stillbay did not give way to a comparable industry. After this high-tech millennium, there was a return to typical Middle Stone Age prepared-core industries that lasted for around 6,000 years.[40]

At the end of this period, another advanced industry arose, known as Howieson's Poort. This is characterised by small crescent-shaped and trapezoidal microliths that were probably hafted into wood or bone handles, or used as spear tips.[41,42] Innovation might not have been limited to tool technology. Dense accumulations of burnt plant remains have been claimed as evidence that Howieson's Poort people used the controlled burning of vegetation to promote the growth of root vegetables; a practice that can increase productivity five to ten-fold.[43]

Howieson's Poort was current from around 64,800 to 59,500 years ago[40] before it too disappeared, and once again there was a return to more typical Middle Stone Age technologies. The Howieson's Poort industry was also widespread, and industries conforming closely to variations of it are well represented over large areas of Central and southern Africa to the south of the Zambezi. A remarkable feature of both the Stillbay and Howieson's Poort industries is that the dates of their start and dates of their disappearance were more or less simultaneous at archaeological sites spread across a region of 2,000,000 sq. km (775,000 sq. miles).[44] Clearly, both were associated with far-ranging social networks.

Direct evidence of trade and long-distance interactions during the Howieson's Poort era has been provided by the Klasies River site, where around a quarter of the artefacts were made from non-local materials such as silcrete in preference to the locally-available quartzite. The use of high-quality non-local raw materials for the manufacture of microliths might have played a major role in the maintenance of social networks. Silcrete is not superior to quartzite as a tool-making material, and there are no practical reasons to choose it; but the use of a more costly raw material rendered the finished object more valuable as an item in an exchange network. Such objects are used today in the ritual hxaro exchange system of the present-day San people of Namibia and Botswana, a system of establishing long-distance social relationships by exchanging gifts.[12]

The use of non-local materials during the African Middle Stone Age, while uncommon, has been identified at many sites, not just in South Africa. Obsidian, a naturally-occurring volcanic glass, is a high-quality material that is well suited for the production of implements with an extremely sharp cutting edge.[7] Obsidian tends to have a unique chemical signature that can be related to its source. It has thus been possible to show that in many cases, implements have been manufactured from obsidian obtained from distant sources. In one case, seven pieces of obsidian from the Mumba Rock Shelter in northern Tanzania were found to be derived from an outcrop that lies 320 km (200 miles) from the shelter. Although it is thought that mobile foraging groups might have ranged as far afield as 100 km (60 miles), it is unlikely that transport of obsidian over more than three times the distance, as at Mumba, could be the result of deliberate collecting forays. It seems more likely that the explanation is increased interaction and exchange among various groups.[12]

As one may expect, at sites where obsidian is plentiful, most of the raw material is locally-sourced, but even in these cases material from distant sources has been used. In one case, the inhabitants of Prolonged Drift in Kenya seemed to show a definite preference for imported obsidians. Nearly 90 percent of the obsidian was imported from sources at Sonanchi and Njorowa Gorge, about 50 km (30 miles) from the site, whereas only a few specimens have been found from the much nearer Maasai Gorge outcrops near Mount Eburru. An interesting though speculative possibility is that groups controlled these valuable obsidian sources and denied access to others.[12]

The overall picture is one of technologically-sophisticated people interacting over long distances, but why were the Stillbay and Howieson's Poort industries both apparently abandoned in favour of less advanced tool technologies? Were these advanced tool-types repeatedly invented, only for the technology to be lost on each occasion?[45] If so, then why? A possibility is that the appearances and subsequent disappearances of these innovative technologies reflect expansions and contractions in the population. When populations fell to a level where social networks could no longer be sustained, technological innovations could no longer be transmitted. Consequently, innovations and sophisticated stone tool technology disappeared.[44,46]

The problem with this view, at least in the case of the Howieson's Poort era, is that there is no evidence for a social collapse at its end. Howieson's Poort sites do not seem to have been abandoned at any stage. In some cases, possible Howieson's Poort and post-Howieson's Poort artefacts have been found together in the same archaeological layer. Furthermore, the change to less refined knapping techniques and artefacts is very gradual, and occurs in parallel at many widely separated sites such as Klasies River and Rose Cottage, lying about 600 km (370 miles) apart. These gradual, parallel changes suggest the evolutionary development of a different style of weapons and domestic tools rather than the collapse of social systems and breakdown of cultural transmission.[47]

The solution to the puzzle may be that the loss of technology is apparent rather than actual. Recent work at the Pinnacle Point site PP5-6 has revealed a microlithic industry originating approximately 71,000 years ago, predating Howieson's Poort by six millennia. Together with the much earlier presence of microliths at Pinnacle Point site PP13B, the PP5-6 discovery suggests that microlithic technology was an early and enduring development. The apparent appearance and disappearance of complex technologies may be nothing more than a reflection of the small number of sites excavated in Africa.[48]

There may also be a problem with the assumption that Stillbay and Howieson's Poort technologies were necessarily 'better' than those that followed. Possibly the technologies during the South African Middle Stone Age are better seen as a series of adaptations to changing environments rather than being judged as being 'more advanced' or 'less advanced' than their predecessors.[49] Animal remains from the site of Sibudu Cave, KwaZulu-Natal suggest a gradual change from those preferring closed woodland such as pigs, duiker, bushbuck and other small mammals, to buffalo and wildebeest, which favour open environments. The technological change could simply reflect changes in the environment and the types of animals available as prey. Perhaps the less complex technologies were simply better suited to the job.[50]

If indeed the successor technologies really were less complex. Again, this may be more apparent than real. Archaeologists have recently identified a new tool tradition at Sibudu Cave, the Sibudan, which dates from around 58,000 years ago, or just after the end of the Howieson's Poort era. Though similar in many ways to typical African Middle Stone Age, the Sibudan is distinct from them. Artefacts recovered from six archaeological layers were linked by common features, which identify them as a distinct tradition. Many of these features are considered to be hallmarks of a sophisticated stone tool-making technology, including standardised tool types and methods of production. Overall, the Sibudan suggests that post-Howieson's Poort tool technologies were far from rudimentary or unsophisticated.[51]

A lengthy isolation

Khoisan is the collective name for two groups of indigenous Africans: the Khoi Khoi of South Africa (once known as the Hottentots), who live as nomadic pastors; and the San or Bushmen of Namibia and Botswana, who live as hunter-gatherers. The San people are distinguished by their 'non-African' physical appearance, at least in comparison to the Bantu features of Central African, African-Caribbean and African-American people. The San are smaller, with lighter skin, more tightly-curled hair and an epicanthic fold over the eye that also characterises people from East Asia. Some believe the epicanthic fold was an ancestral characteristic of our species that was later lost in Western Asian and Bantu populations, though this remains largely speculative.[52]

The Khoisan, together with the Hadza (or Hadzabe) and Sandawe of Tanzania, are among a number indigenous peoples living in South Africa and East Africa who speak a highly-distinctive form of language known as click consonant languages. The characteristic 'clicks' are made by snapping the tongue away from the teeth or hard palate.[53] They are used as consonants, unlike other languages where they are used only as interjections – for example the 'tut-tut' sound used in English to express disapproval. Click consonant languages are among the richest of all human languages in terms of the distinct units of sound (phonemes) that are used to make up words. A click consonant is usually written as an exclamation mark.

Little is known about the history of African click-speaking populations, but linguists have classified their languages into five groups: the Khoisan Ju, !Ui-Taa and Khoe, together with Sandawe and Hadza. They disagree on whether there are any deeper links between these groups, though the first three are often thought to be related and Sandawe may also belong to this group. However, possible relationships between Sandawe and Hadza are more controversial, even though the two populations live within 150 km (100 miles) of each other. Nevertheless, the case for a common origin is strengthened by the great rarity of click languages outside Africa. Out of all the thousands of non-African languages, clicks feature in only one – the Damin ritual language of Australia.[54]

If one accepts this argument, then the implication is that the various click language speakers in South Africa and East Africa must all be descended from a single population. A view long popular with scholars is that click-speakers once occupied a broad region stretching from South Africa to Ethiopia and Sudan. Their range was then reduced by the far more recent expansion of Bantu farmers from Cameroon between 3000 BC and AD 500[55] (see Chapter 21). If this view is correct, it would be expected that their genetic heritage would show a recent common ancestry. In fact, studies of mitochondrial DNA and Y-chromosome divergence have found deep genetic divergences between the Khoisan and the Tanzanian click-speakers, and likewise between Ethiopians and Khoisan. This suggests a very early separation between these populations, possibly predating the dispersal of modern humans from Africa. If the click languages do indeed have a common origin, the implication is that they are a very ancient element of human language.[56,57,54]

A deep separation between the Khoisan people and other African populations was also indicated by a report on early population movements within Africa, released in 2008 by the Genographic Project, a collaborative venture between the National Geographic Society, IBM and the Waitt Family Foundation. The report, entitled *The Dawn of Human Matrilineal Diversity*,[1] concluded that from a time between 90,000 and 144,000 years ago, the Khoisan population was cut off from the human population in the rest of Africa, and remained isolated for as long as 100,000 years.

Geneticists believe that the entire human mitochondrial DNA phylogeny – effectively the family tree of humanity – has two principle branches, known as L0 and L1-6 respectively. The latter is by far the more geographically widespread, giving rise to the great majority of mitochondrial DNA haplogroups found today. It gave rise to six 'daughter' haplogroups known as L1 to L6, of which L1 is the oldest. However, it is L0 that predominates among the Khoisan. The L0 daughter haplogroups L0d and L0k account for 60 percent of the Khoisan mitochondrial gene pool, although they are rare among non-Khoisan people. L0 also has other branches, found elsewhere in Africa. L0d and L0k are very ancient and are thought to have diverged from L0 around 150,000 years ago.

Within a haplogroup, there will be a certain amount of genetic diversity; individuals with the same mitochondrial haplogroup will not have identical mitochondrial genomes, unless they share a very recent maternal ancestor. The longer a particular haplogroup is present in a population, the greater will be its genetic diversity. L0d and L0k show more genetic diversity among Khoisan people than in non-Khoisan people; but other haplogroups show less genetic diversity among Khoisan people than they do elsewhere. This suggests that the Khoisan mitochondrial DNA gene pool originally comprised just L0d and L0k, together possibly with haplogroups that have since become extinct. Only later did additional lineages enter the Khoisan mitochondrial DNA gene pool from elsewhere. At the same time, L0d and L0k entered the non-Khoisan gene pool.

Two scenarios were put forward in order to put a date on the Khoisan isolation. The first proposed that an ancestral Khoisan population, containing both the L0 and L1-6 mitochondrial branches, became isolated in South Africa. Genetic drift subsequently eliminated all but L0d and L0k. Statistical analysis showed that for this to occur, the isolation must have happened at least 90,000 years ago. The second scenario proposed that the division between the L0 and L1-6 mitochondrial branches occurred as a result of an early split in the then still very small modern human population. The split left an L0 population in South Africa and an L1-6 population in East Africa. Subsequently, a group bearing the haplogroup L0abf – the precursor to L0a, L0b and L0f – migrated back to East Africa, explaining the presence of these L0 daughter haplogroups outside South Africa. This migration must have occurred before L0k diverged from L0abf 144,000 years ago, or else L0k would not have remained confined to South Africa.

While unable to reliably identify a specific cause for the split, the authors of the report noted that severe drought conditions were probably responsible, and that their eventual easing ended the isolation. Other than L0d and L0k, the oldest haplogroups to be found in the Khoisan mitochondrial DNA gene pool are only 40,000 years old, corresponding to the onset of the African Late Stone Age. The implication is at this point, the Khoisan came into renewed contact with other Africans. A similar maximum age was found for the non-Khoisan branches of L0d and L0k, consistent with their introduction into the non-Khoisan population at that time.

A separate study, considering both mitochondrial and Y-chromosomal data, found that the Khoisan had diverged from the Sandawe and Hadza of Tanzania around 35,000 years ago.[54] The result would suggest that the Sandawe and Hadza are likely descended from a group that migrated from South Africa to Tanzania at that time; the date is consistent with the Genographic Project report. The overall picture is that there were no population exchanges (at least of women) between the Khoisan and other Africans until 40,000 years ago.

The publication of the Genographic Project report generated considerable media interest of a more-or-less sensational nature including claims that the human line had 'nearly split in two'. This is certainly wide of the mark, and the Khoisan isolation is best seen in the context of the overall picture of isolated regional-local populations throughout Africa generally. Indeed, the Genographic Project report noted another mitochondrial DNA study, also published in 2008, that focused on the Pygmy hunter-gathers of western Central Africa. This study concluded that the ancestors of the present-day Pygmies diverged from an ancestral population approximately 70,000 years ago. They, too, went through a lengthy period of isolation, which continued until around 40,000 years ago.[58]

In fact, it is unlikely that humans in South Africa were totally isolated from the outside world, as small groups arriving from elsewhere would probably leave no trace in the present-day gene pool. However, if there was no large scale immigration into South Africa during the latter part of the Middle Stone Age, it is certainly possible that the Khoisan people are the descendants of early settlers of South Africa, such as the Blombos and Klasies River people. In addition, if click languages only arose once, the implication is that they must have already been in use when the Khoisan diverged from the Sandawe and Hadza. The Genographic Project's report stated that it was 'tempting' to link early South African settlements to ancestors of the Khoisan, but admitted that their data could not prove it. Further advances in linguistics and genetics may eventually provide more definitive answers, though much will remain speculation unless human DNA is one day recovered from a South African Middle Stone Age site. Unfortunately, conditions in Africa do not favour the preservation of DNA, and this possibility is remote.

The question also remains as to why click consonant languages are practically unknown away from Africa. The clue may be in the fact that they are known only among African hunter-gatherers. It is possible that in this environment, click systems confer an advantage when hunting. For example, when stalking prey, some Khoisan groups revert to a hushed whisper-like communication. Speech is devoiced and consists almost entirely of clicks.[57] If the first migrants from Africa passed through an environment where click consonants were less useful, then possibly over time they gradually dropped out of use, and were never re-invented.

Things can only get better

Around 95,000 years ago the climatic conditions in tropical Africa began to improve, although sporadic episodes of drought continued until 70,000 years ago. Africa was also probably affected by the eruption of the Toba supervolcano, 73,000 years ago (see Chapter 12). Although lake levels increased, they did not reach present-day levels until 60,000 years ago. Paradoxically, the easing of arid conditions in tropical Africa coincided with their onset elsewhere on the continent, and in the Levant. Their cause was the onset of a severe cold period (Marine Isotope Stage 4) 74,000 years ago, which brought harsh, dry conditions to regions outside the tropics. Tropical Africa was spared these effects because its climate depends more on the African monsoon than it does global temperatures. However, between 90,000 and 70,000 years ago, there was a 'crossover' period when reasonably favourable rainfall conditions prevailed throughout the whole of Africa; these might have been played a crucial role in human expansions.[2,3]

The human population, reduced to small isolated groups during the arid periods, began to expand. The expansion is associated with the mitochondrial haplogroup L3, which is now distributed across the whole of the continent. L3 is thought to have originated in East Africa, where both its highest occurrence and its oldest daughter haplogroups (L3a and L3h) are found.[55,59] Two other L3 daughter haplogroups, M and N, have a global distribution, implying that the L3 expansion was ultimately responsible for the peopling of the non-African world.[1]

Early work suggested a date from 80,000 to 60,000 years ago for the L3 expansion, and a possible origin with a small group in East Africa.[60] More recent research has used a statistical technique known as Bayesian inference, named for the eighteenth century mathematician Rev. Thomas Bayes. It is a powerful but computational-intensive statistical method that has been brought to the fore by the increased 'number-crunching' abilities of modern computers. The technique was used to estimate prehistoric human population sizes in Africa from mitochondrial genetic diversity. The results were consistent with those obtained by the earlier study, and indicated an L3 expansion beginning between 86,000 and 61,000 years ago.[61]

What caused the L3 expansion? An obvious possibility was the improving climatic situation,[62] but while this undoubtedly played a part, it leaves unexplained why East African populations carrying other haplogroups[55] failed to expand. Possibly an initially small L3-carrying group gained a technological advantage over others, allowing it to out-compete rival groups.[61] This advantage might have been the invention of tailored clothing, the appearance of which is thought to coincide closely with the initial dispersal of modern humans from Africa.[63]

Regardless of cause, the L3 expansion is generally believed to have led to the peopling of the non-African world. Before we look at this, though, we shall turn our attention to the emergence of modern human behaviour. How, why and when did it emerge? How do we define it or recognise it in the archaeological record? What clues can be gleaned from the lengthy period we have just reviewed?

11: The making of the modern mind

The Great Leap Forward

What is modern human behaviour and how does it differ from the behaviour of earlier humans? As noted in Chapter 1, human society could not function without our ability to use symbols in the form of sounds, images or objects to convey information. It is the ability to use symbols to organise both our thoughts and our actions that sets us apart from our fellow African apes, and indeed from the rest of the animal kingdom.

When and under what circumstances modern human behaviour emerged are understandably key questions for anthropologists, as indeed is why it emerged at all. Most agree that there is a connection with the origin of modern syntactic language, but there is as yet no consensus about the latter. There is also no agreement as to whether modern human behaviour is confined to modern humans, or whether our ability to use symbols was shared with some archaic humans; in particular the Neanderthals.

Much debate has centred on when behavioural modernity emerged in relation to anatomical modernity. On the face of it, it seems logical to suppose that they both emerged at the same time; the alternative is that the first anatomically modern humans were somehow *not* behaviourally-modern. Why should this be so? If a child from 200,000 years ago was raised from birth in our modern society, is there any reason to suppose they would differ mentally from anybody else?

As far back as the nineteenth century, it was noticed that there is a sharp discontinuity in the archaeological record of Western Europe, corresponding to the arrival of modern humans at start of what is now known as the Upper Palaeolithic. The artefacts preceding this transition are for the most part purely functional and, as we saw in Chapter 8, the few exceptions are hotly disputed. From around 45,000 years ago, there is a dramatic change as the archaeological record is transformed by the appearance of artefacts that are unquestionably the work of modern minds. These include the magnificent polychrome animal paintings at sites such as Lascaux and Chauvet; ivory sculptures and bas reliefs of human and animal subjects; and enigmatic large-breasted 'Venus' figurines.

Although there is evidence for symbolic expression in Africa well before European Upper Palaeolithic, we saw in Chapter 10 that it is both sporadic and disputed. Why is the first unequivocal evidence for modern human behaviour not seen until around 150,000 years after our species first emerged? British archaeologist Colin Renfrew[1,2,3] has described the conundrum as the Sapient Paradox: how to reconcile an early appearance of anatomical modernity with a much later appearance for the first clear markers of behavioural modernity. A possible explanation is that behavioural modernity trailed anatomical modernity by tens of thousands of years. This implies that while the humans from Omo, Herto, Jebel Irhoud and Skhul might have looked modern, mentally they had not yet quite 'got there': we might see them as simple-minded folk, who in all probability lacked our complex, syntactic language. Only much later did modern human behaviour emerge in the wake of a 'human revolution' or, as Jared Diamond[4] put it, a Great Leap Forward.

A leading proponent of this view is anthropologist Richard Klein,[5] who claims that the revolution in Africa took place with the transition from the Middle to Late Stone Age, about 40,000 years ago. Klein argues that prior to this date, modern human technology was indistinguishable from that of the Neanderthals, and that Middle Stone Age people were less effective hunters than their Late Stone Age counterparts. He notes that there is only limited evidence of fishing and fowling prior to the Late Stone Age; and that abundant but dangerous buffalo and wild boar were often shunned in favour of rarer but harmless eland. He believes that the mental and organisational skills required for these activities were still lacking from otherwise-modern people at that time. If he is correct, there must have been profound mental differences between Middle Stone Age and present-day people, despite the outward resemblance. How could such a counter-intuitive state of affairs have come about?

One possibility is that the earliest modern humans lacked language, at least as we know it. Klein believes modern language came about as a result of a favourable genetic mutation affecting the brain which, he claims, occurred about 50,000 years ago.[5] Klein's original 'prime suspect' was a gene known as FOXP2, or Forkhead Box P2. This regulates a number of other genes, some of which are believed to play a role in the development of the parts of the brain associated with speech, although the exact genes involved are not known. The FOXP2 gene is not unique to humans and exists with very few differences in other animals. The first clue that it could be a 'speech gene' came from studies of Family KE, an extended British family living in London (their actual identity is not in the public domain). Some members of the family have problems with aspects of grammar, including the use of inflexions in tenses. They also have difficulty in producing the fine movements of the tongue and lips required for normal speech. The problem affects three generations of the family and has been studied since the 1990s. In 2001, geneticists determined that the affected members of the family all have a defective version of the FOXP2 gene.[6]

In 2002, a team at the Max Planck Institute for Evolutionary Anthropology in Leipzig, Germany compared the human version of the FOXP2 gene with that of the chimpanzee, gorilla, orang-utan, rhesus macaque and mouse. They found that only three changes to the gene have occurred since humans diverged from mice, although two of these had occurred since the far more recent split between humans and chimps. They suggested that these two changes might have been critical to the development of speech and language, and that they had occurred at some stage in the last 200,000 years.[7]

Klein believed the actual date would turn out to be 50,000 years and that FOXP2 was the 'smoking gun' responsible for the Great Leap Forward. Then in 2007 came a fresh announcement from the Max Planck Institute. Their work with the Neanderthal genome had shown that Neanderthals possessed exactly the same version of FOXP2 as do modern humans.[8] The implication was that the changes to FOXP2 must have occurred before the two species diverged from one another, which was at least 370,000 years ago.

Although FOXP2 has failed to support Klein's argument, it does not necessarily mean that he is wrong; an as-yet undiscovered 'language gene' could still exist. Alternatively, the capacity for language might have existed prior to 50,000 years ago, but for some reason language itself did not appear until then.

Down with the Revolution

The idea that there was a Great Leap Forward sometime after the emergence of anatomical modernity is doubted by some. Anthropologists Sally McBrearty and Alison Brooks[9,10] have argued that modern human behaviour is characterised by four traits: abstract thinking, the ability to plan ahead, the ability to innovate, and symbolic behaviour. They suggest that the Great Leap Forward is an illusion that stemmed from a Eurocentric bias and an incomplete appreciation of the African archaeological record. They note that many of the components of the supposed revolution may be found tens of thousands of years earlier in the form of innovative technologies and behaviours at various African Middle Stone Age sites, as described in Chapter 10.

McBrearty and Brooks have also challenged Richard Klein's assertions about the effectiveness of Middle Stone Age hunters. Their argument is why would these hunters go to all the effort of obtaining food from difficult sources if there was enough readily-available food to go round? During the Middle Stone Age, population densities were probably low enough for food shortages not to be a problem. However, population densities increased during the Late Stone Age, and people now had to consider food sources that had not always been worth the extra effort in the past, such as difficult-to-catch fish and birds and dangerous buffalo and wild boar.

A major problem for scholars of modern human behaviour is to find a means to unequivocally recognise it in the archaeological record. For example, as we have seen, ochre has been associated with *Homo heidelbergensis* and the Neanderthals, as well as early modern humans, and beads are known from 110,000 to 90,000 years ago. However, some are sceptical that these are proof of symbolic behaviour. Even the engraved ochres at Blombos Cave do not convince everybody.[11] Cognitive researcher Francesco d'Errico,[12] while broadly in agreement with McBrearty and Brooks, has expressed concern over their choice of traits that characterize modern behaviour and believes that they were influenced by their knowledge of the African Middle Stone Age. He argues that other researchers, with other areas of expertise, may choose different criteria to define modernity, and that there is no reason why these should not be considered to be equally valid. D'Errico believes that what we perceive as modern human behaviour was not the result of a single revolution. Rather it was the product of a number of developments that occurred in different places, at different times, and over different time-scales.[13]

Even if we accept that the innovation associated with the European Upper Palaeolithic really was absent from the African Middle Stone Age, it doesn't necessarily prove that the modern humans of that era were incapable of modern human behaviour. The lag between anatomical and behavioural modernity – even if real – may owe more to demographic than to cognitive factors. Populations may have needed to reach a certain density before newly-learned skills could be accumulated and shared with neighbouring groups, or passed on to succeeding generations, to the extent that they left clear archaeological evidence of modernity. Prior to this 'tipping point' being reached, innovations might have been as likely to die out as they were to be enhanced and developed.[14]

Shaping up

Consistent with this last point, archaeologists Christopher Henshilwood and Curtis Marean[15,16] believe that the key criterion for modern human behaviour is not merely the capacity for symbolic thought, but also its use in day-to-day life. They argue that only when anatomically modern humans made full use of their capacity for symbolic thinking could they be considered fully modern from a behavioural perspective.

Henshilwood and Marean believe that modern human behaviour was restricted to *Homo sapiens* and favour the term 'fully symbolic *sapiens* behaviour' rather than 'modern human behaviour' to describe it. They see it as the culmination of a long line of developments toward modernity, going back tens or possibly hundreds of millennia. They nevertheless believe that the neurological and anatomical changes associated with modernity occurred at the same time, and that there was no subsequent 'smartness mutation' affecting the brain.

As we have seen in earlier chapters, the globular braincase of *Homo sapiens* differs in shape from the long, low braincase of earlier humans. In the case of the Neanderthals at least, this appears to reflect differences in brain development between the ages of one and two years old. At birth, modern humans have relatively elongated braincases, similar to those of Neanderthals. Only later, between the age of one and two years old, does the braincase of a modern infant take on a characteristic globular shape, but with Neanderthal infants this change did not occur. Although the cranial capacity of *Homo heidelbergensis* and the Neanderthals was larger than that of *Homo erectus*, the braincase – and by implication the brain itself – was simply an enlarged version of that of the earlier species.[17] By contrast, the braincase of *Homo sapiens* reflects a change in the actual proportions of the brain, with expansion of the parietal lobes. Located at the top and on each side of the brain, the parietal lobes carry out functions including the processing of speech-related sounds (or written words), and their development might have played a crucial role in the development of language.[11]

It should be noted that other explanations for the distinctive shape of the modern human cranium and face have been proposed. These include a reduction in facial size because cooked food required less chewing; changing the head's centre of gravity to help stop it from pitching up and down when running; more efficient regulation of body temperature when running; and physical adaptations for speech production.[17] However, while it is possible that these factors did play a part, in the light of evidence presented in this and preceding chapters, it seems unlikely that they did so to the exclusion of brain shape. It could be that the emergence of the modern human brain marked the key step in 'modernising' humans, giving them a decisive advantage over those with the archaic-type brains.

If we accept the Henshilwood and Marean view that fully symbolic *sapiens* behaviour was at first only latent, then when did it actually emerge? Could it only have come to fruition as recently as 50,000 years ago, as suggested by Richard Klein? Taking the evidence presented in the previous chapter into consideration, it seems likely that behavioural modernity emerged before that time. Even if beads and ochre can be challenged as markers of modernity, the engraved ochres and other evidence from Blombos Cave, the Katanda fishing-tackle, and the engraved ostrich eggshells from Diepkloof cannot all be dismissed, nor can the clear evidence of long-distance interactions indicated during the Stillbay and Howieson's Poort eras. These developments only push behavioural modernity back to around 70,000 years, but the microliths, ochre and seafood at Pinnacle Point, 165,000 years ago, strongly hints at a much earlier origin. Nevertheless, the view that anatomical modernity preceded behavioural modernity cannot be ruled out. Even the Pinnacle Point evidence is around 30,000 years more recent than the first anatomically modern humans at Omo.

The language instinct

Henshilwood and Marean see language as an integral part of modern human behaviour,[15] and it is reasonable to suppose that the origins of the two are closely linked. It is now widely believed that modern language, with its immense complexity, arises from an innate capacity of the human brain. This idea can be traced back to the thinking of eighteenth century philosopher Emmanuel Kant, but in its modern form it has been championed by linguists Noam Chomsky and Steven Pinker.

In the 1960s, Chomsky suggested that without an instinctive linguistic ability, young children could never master all the intricacies of a language simply by hearing adults speaking it. He suggested there must instead be an innate 'universal grammar' at the root of human language, providing structural constraints on what is and isn't valid usage of words. In his 1994 book *The Language Instinct*, Steven Pinker[18] proposed that there is a 'language acquisition device' that makes possible the rapid learning of language during early childhood. According to Pinker, the 'language acquisition device' only remains functional during a specific critical period of childhood. Subsequently, it is dismantled in order to free up resources needed by an energy-hungry brain, and hence it is never possible in later life to learn to speak further languages as fluently as do native speakers.

Modern syntactic language probably evolved gradually in a series of increasingly complex systems of communication used by our various hominin ancestors. Such systems are commonly referred to as 'protolanguage', but just what their nature is and how they originated are areas of major disagreement among academics.[19] There are two competing theories: one states that protolanguage was 'compositional', or made up of distinct words; the other that it was 'holistic', and that an entire message was contained in a single utterance. Which theory is correct?

Tittle-tattle

A convincing argument for why language came about is made by anthropologist Robin Dunbar,[20] who believes that it enabled humans to live together in ever-increasing group sizes. Without language, he claims, it was impossible for these groups to maintain social cohesion. As we already seen in Chapter 2, the social brain hypothesis proposes a link between primate brain size and social group size, and so group sizes can be predicted for extinct hominins. An obvious question is: what is the predicted group size for modern humans? The number turns out to be approximately 150, and it has come to be known as Dunbar's Number. Dunbar claims that numbers close to 150 come up repeatedly when considering group sizes in traditional societies, such as clans within hunter-gather groups, horticulturalists in Indonesia, the Philippines and South America, and also the estimated sizes of Neolithic farming villages. He also claims that the number can be discerned in a modern society, even though millions of people live together in cities. He notes that small and medium-sized businesses with fewer than 150 to 200 employees tend to be arranged on informal lines, but larger companies become increasingly hierarchical, and require formal management structures in order to function efficiently.

By comparison, the group sizes of other primate species do not typically exceed the 50 to 55 characteristic of baboons and chimpanzees. As we have seen, the increase in group size might have come about as early humans had to cope with increasingly challenging environmental conditions, but larger groups would have brought a fresh problem. As we saw in Chapter 2, non-human primate coalitions are maintained by grooming. The larger the group size, the more time has to be devoted to grooming: even if numbers do not exceed 50 to 55, it still takes up about 20 percent of the daylight hours. This is a considerable overhead, and it is clear that there must be a limit, or there would not be enough hours left in the day to forage for food.

With a group size of 150, how much time would modern humans need to spend on grooming? Based on comparisons of group sizes and grooming time for other primates, the estimated figure for modern humans is a prohibitive 42 percent.[21] Dunbar believes that language provided a means of reducing this massive overhead to manageable proportions. He notes that while many primates use calls to warn their fellows of approaching predators, this isn't their sole function: they also call out to keep in touch with their preferred grooming partners in what is essentially 'vocal grooming'. These calls are holistic, and convey the whole meaning of the message in a single utterance. Dunbar argues that they were the protolanguage from which modern language eventually developed.

Dunbar has also made the observation that when humans talk, most of the conversation is social tittle-tattle. Even in common-rooms of universities, conversations about cultural, political, philosophical and scientific matters account for no more than a quarter of the conversation. Newspapers reflect this trend. He noted that a copy of the *Sun* devoted 78 percent of its column-inches of text to 'human interest' stories. While this may seem unremarkable, even the more highbrow *Times* only devoted 57 percent of its column-inches to serious matters.

Dunbar believes that in human society, social chatter serves as vocal grooming and that this has replaced physical grooming in all but the most intimate situations. At any one time, only one person will normally be speaking and the others will be listening, just as at any one time only one ape or monkey will be doing the grooming. If the speaker corresponds to the 'groomer' then they are 'grooming' several people at once instead of just one. Dunbar notes that the maximum number of people who can hold a conversation is four, assuming the participants are standing in a circle with typical background noise. When the number increases beyond four, it becomes difficult for everybody remain within easy hearing distance of everybody else. However, with one person able to 'groom' up three others, group size could potentially treble without any increase in grooming time. The group size of 55 for chimps and baboons becomes very close to Dunbar's Number of 150.

Dunbar believes that the ability to exchange social information about the behaviour and relationships of third parties within such large groups of early humans was essential to maintain social cohesion, and that this is the reason language evolved. The critical point was reached with the emergence of *Homo heidelbergensis*, when grooming time is estimated to have reached 33 to 37 percent, based on a predicted group size of 125 to 130.[21] A language with sufficient flexibility to manage social relationships within a group was required, although at this stage not necessarily the symbolic language of modern humans.

A mammoth problem

Although Dunbar's 'grooming and gossip' theory has proved popular with anthropologists, not everybody accepts it. British-born linguist Derek Bickerton[22] claims that for language to evolve at all, it would need to be useful even with a very restricted vocabulary. With such limitations, any gossip that could be passed on would probably not hold anybody's attention for very long.

Bickerton[23] also rejects the view that human language is in any way connected to the communication systems employed by other animals, regardless of how advanced some of these may seem to be. He notes, for example, that vervet monkeys have distinct alarm calls for leopards, snakes and eagles, each of which triggers a different threat response. However, these calls convey the whole meaning of the message in a single utterance, and thus are still holistic. They do not contain the nature of the threat (for example a leopard) and the appropriate action (up into the trees) as separate concepts. The calls are simply intended to trigger a hard-wired threat response when heard; the actual sighting of a predator triggers the slightly different response of first giving the relevant warning call.

This is very different to human language. Language is symbolic, can deal with concepts, and can deal with subject matter that is not rooted in the here and now. While it is certainly possible to shout a warning to get up the nearest tree if a leopard appears, it is not necessary for a leopard to be present in order to think about them. Language can be used to express an effectively infinite range of ideas. By contrast, the best a vervet monkey can do is to warn its fellows about leopards, snakes and eagles. How did we get from one to the other? Bickerton's view is that we didn't.

In his 1990 work *Language and Species* Bickerton[23] suggested that modern language originated from a protolanguage resembling the stripped-down 'pidgins' that develop as a *lingua franca* when two or more groups do not have a language in common – for example Chinese, Korean, Japanese and Filipino sugar plantation workers in Hawaii during the late nineteenth century. Pidgins are far simpler than full-blown languages, and generally have limited vocabularies and very little grammar. They lack such features as articles, prepositions, and markers of case, tense, and aspect. They are nevertheless a considerable advance on vervet monkey warnings, as they permit separate expression of concepts such as 'leopard' and 'tree'. Like full language, a pidgin is compositional: a message is made up of distinct words rather than a single utterance.

Bickerton[23,24,25,26] has put forward various theories for the origins of a pidgin-like compositional protolanguage and its subsequent evolution into full-blown language, but in his 2009 work *Adam's*

Tongue[22] he proposes that modern language arose not from primate calls but from the needs of early human scavengers to communicate with their fellows. Groups needed to split up when searching for carcasses, but they had to regroup in order to exploit substantial finds. They did have one advantage over other scavengers in that they had tools that could cut through the tough hides of the carcasses to get to the meat, rather than having to wait for putrefying bacteria to do the job for them. The problem was how to let everybody else know that you'd found a fresh carcass, and to exploit it before other scavengers did. There was a need to break free from the here and now and convey information along the lines of 'I saw a freshly-dead mammoth over by the stream half an hour ago'.

Bickerton believes that the capacity for protolanguage was already present in early hominins. Although apes do not use any form of language in the wild, they can be taught to use sign language and computer keyboards. In an experiment carried out in the 1960s, Beatrice and Allen Gardner trained a female chimpanzee named Washoe to use around 250 signs. Washoe was able to connect these signs in a meaningful way; for example she signed 'water bird' upon seeing a picture of a swan. The ability to connect things is what distinguishes protolanguage from predator alarm calls. However, the capacity for protolanguage never developed any further in non-human apes, because from an evolutionary point of view, there was no requirement for it. It was not until early humans began to scavenge the carcasses of large mammals that the need arose for the first time.

Early humans might have at first communicated their carcass finds by a combination of pointing and imitating animal sounds, but given that the capacity for protolanguage was also present, simple phrases would soon have followed. Humans would then have been able to form simple concepts like 'mammoth' or 'stream', and use them to make sentences. Increasingly complex speech then followed, and eventually modern language emerged.

It all sounds very plausible, but it does not explain Robin Dunbar's observation that so much conversation today is social. Bickerton dismisses this objection as the 'fallacy of first use': whatever something is first used for will be its main use now. If this were the case, Bickerton argues, computers would have first been used for email and web browsing. This argument is not entirely convincing, to some extent because of the choice of analogy. For one thing, computers did not evolve: they were invented by humans, and subsequent innovations were due to humans. Computers were first used to process data, and this is largely what they are used for to this day. While they are no longer restricted to running the humble office payroll program, and no longer rely on punch-cards for data input, computers are still predominantly data processing devices. Amazon and eBay could not function without the ability to process the terabytes of data flowing hourly through their sites. Search engines like Google must process vast amount of data in order to return search results.

However, Bickerton poses two very important questions, which need to be answered. Firstly, assuming that the vocabularies of the first languages were fairly small, how could gossip of any real interest be passed on? Secondly, if holistic primate calls were, after all, the root of modern language, then the question of how we got from one to the other remains to be addressed.

The caves are alive with the sound of music

A possible answer to the second question has been proposed by linguist Alison Wray,[27] who believes that protolanguage was holistic rather than compositional, and that like the vervet monkey alarm calls, it comprised single utterances conveying complete messages. Such utterances, though holistic, could be polysyllabic, and it sometimes happened that two utterances would share not only a syllable but also a meaning: for examples, suppose 'gizfood' meant 'give me the food' and 'gizwater' meant 'give me the water' (these were not the examples Wray used), then both share the syllable 'giz' and

The symbolic ape

the meaning 'give me'. By such means, Wray believes that holistic but polysyllabic utterances were gradually split up or 'segmented' into nouns and verbs.

It may seem implausible that two random utterances with a common syllable or syllables that happened to mean the same thing could occur often enough for a meaningful vocabulary to emerge. Indeed, this is Bickerton's view.[22] However, computer simulations by Simon Kirby,[28] Professor of Language Evolution at Edinburgh University, do support Wray's conclusions. The results suggest that over many generations, associations between particular syllables and meanings become established, and eventually an entire compositional language arises.

Archaeologist Steven Mithen, a pioneer in the field of 'cognitive archaeology', has built on the holistic protolanguage theory, stressing the role of music in the evolution of modern language.[19,29] Mithen notes that music has been largely ignored by linguists, but claims that it may give us an insight into how early hominins communicated with one another. Central to Mithen's theory is emotion, which plays a crucial survival role in the lives of animals. A fear response, for example, is necessary to make an animal flee from a dangerous predator. Conversely, happiness is a 'reward' for successfully completing a task. Psychologists recognise four basic emotions – happiness, sadness, fear and anger, with more complex emotions such as shame and jealousy being composites of these four. Experiments suggest that we share these emotions with other primates and, by implication, with early hominins. Emotions were crucial for the development of modern human behaviour, and indeed are essential for the survival of any sentient species. For example, without the fear response when faced with a dangerous predator, you are likely to end up as dinner.

Mithen pulls together two ideas. The first is that music can be used to both express and manipulate human emotions; the second that the utterances of primates serve much the same function. Mithen describes primate utterances as 'holistic and manipulative': for example the vervet monkey alarm calls manipulate emotions by inducing fear of a specific predator (leopards, snakes or eagles), in turn triggering the appropriate survival response. Mithen believes that the group living of early hominins, coupled with the increased use of gestural communications, led to an extension of this communication mode into what he terms 'Hmmmmm' (five 'm's). This stands for Holistic, manipulative, multi-modal, musical and mimetic', with dance and mime being added to the repertoire. As with the utterances of vervet monkeys, Hmmmmm was intended to manipulate the actions of others. It was more complex than the vocalisations of any present-day non-human primate, but less so than that of present-day humans. Mithen suggests that Hmmmmm emerged with *Homo erectus*, though the form used by later, larger brained humans such as the Neanderthals was more complex. Hmmmmm was also used by modern humans when they first emerged.

The musical qualities of Hmmmmm may also address objections to the 'grooming and gossip' theory. Mithen raises basically the same objection as Bickerton, i.e. how could the limited range of words available in the earliest stages of language be used to exchange information about social commitments and third-party relationships? He also raises a second issue: even if such gossip was possible, would it be as pleasurable as grooming? He argues that this objection might not apply if vocal grooming took the form of song rather than speech. Even today, singing is a form of social bonding seen everywhere from church congregations to football grounds.

Mind-reading

Despite its pivotal role in the emergence of modern human behaviour, language is not the whole story. Another behaviour which emerged at some stage during our hominin past is mind-reading. What psychologists refer to rather confusingly as 'theory of mind' is the ability to understand what another individual is thinking, and to realise that they can have desires, beliefs and intentions that differ from one's own. We are not born with this ability: it normally develops during early childhood at between four to four-and-a-half years of age. Autism, while not fully understood, appears to involve impairment to the proper functioning of theory of mind.

Children below the age of around four to five years old will fail what is known as the false belief test. A common version of this test uses two dolls named 'Sally' and 'Anne' (these were the names used by the original researchers).[30] Sally has a basket; Anne has a box. The child is shown a scene in which Sally puts a marble in her basket and then leaves the room. While Sally is out of the room, Anne takes the marble out of Sally's basket and puts it into her box. Sally then returns and the child is asked where they think she will look for the marble. The child is said to have 'passed' the test if they understand that Sally will probably look inside her basket before realising that the marble is no longer there. Young children fail to realise that Sally has no way of knowing that the marble has been moved, and say that she will look in Anne's box.

Theory of mind is as ubiquitous in human society as any other aspect of modern human behaviour: in juggling the sometimes conflicting needs of family, friends and workplace; in politics ranging from the office to national and international; and in more or less any form of sport where there is a need to second-guess the intentions of opponents. The classic submarine drama *The Enemy Below* demonstrates how theory of mind functions in wartime as US Navy destroyer captain Robert Mitchum and U-boat commander Kurt Jürgens engage in a deadly battle of wits.

To what extent do other primates have theory of mind? Deception appears to be common among apes and the more socially-advanced of the Old World monkeys, but rare or absent from other primates. Robin Dunbar[20] cites a particularly ingenious example of deception in which a juvenile male baboon named Paul made a loud shriek, of the type usually made by juveniles if attacked by somebody much larger than themselves. His mother promptly rushed to his aid and launched herself at a nearby female, Mel, who had been innocently digging up an edible tuber. During the ensuing commotion, Paul made off with the tuber. In other examples of deception, female baboons have been known to illicitly mate with low-ranked males: offending couples deliberately concealed their activities from disapproving harem males by refraining from the customary loud copulation shrieks that would give the game away.

However, deception is not quite the same as theory of mind. To test theory of mind in chimpanzees, researchers devised a variation of the Sally and Anne test. The chimpanzees were allowed to see four identical boxes, one of which a researcher would mark with a peg and subsequently bait with a food reward. The boxes were designed so that the researcher could not see the peg when baiting the chosen box; and the chimpanzees could not see which box was actually baited. Once the chimpanzees had learned to choose the box with the peg, a trick was introduced: the peg was moved while the researcher was out of sight. To collect the reward, the chimpanzees had to choose the box where the peg had originally been left and not the one that it had been moved to. Their performance was not outstanding – they did better than autistic adults, but nowhere near as well as children aged five to six years old. The implication is that chimpanzees do have theory of mind, but it is less advanced than that of humans.[20]

Cognitive fluidity

Language and theory of mind are two major components of the human mental landscape. What other components might there be, and how were they assembled into the cognitive package we term 'modern human behaviour'? One of the most plausible scenarios describing the cognitive development of archaic and modern humans was proposed by Steven Mithen in his 1996 work *The Prehistory of the Mind: a search for the origins of art, religion and science*,[31] which he put forward as an archaeologist's approach to a problem normally tackled by psychologists and neurologists. In addition to archaeology, Mithen drew on evidence from psychology, linguistics, anthropology, observations of the behaviour of chimpanzees, and a variety of other sources.

Mithen proposed that the human mind is made up of a number of 'cognitive domains' or specialist intelligences that are dedicated to various tasks: a 'linguistic intelligence' for language; a 'social intelligence' for handling social interactions; a 'natural history intelligence' for dealing with such matters as animal behaviour, weather and local geography; and a 'technical intelligence' for tool-making. Underlying these specialist intelligences is a core of 'general intelligence'. In the behaviourally-modern mind, the various intelligences are linked by a process Mithen terms 'cognitive fluidity'. However, according to Mithen's theory, this was not always the case, and early humans were literally incapable of joined-up thinking.

The theory is to some extent a synthesis of earlier 'modular' theories about the mind's function, its development from childhood, and the nature of creative thought.[32,33,34,35] The modular picture views the human brain as a series of 'modules' that perform various tasks. They vary considerably in their nature; some are hard-wired and fully-functional from birth, such as those handling sensory input (sight, hearing, taste, smell and touch). Others contain the basic data needed to assist a child's learning processes.

In addition to the modules for developing linguistic competence and theory of mind, Mithen suggests that children are born with modules that are 'pre-loaded' with data about both the physical and biological world. Children instinctively understand concepts such as solidity, gravity and inertia, and they are aware of the difference between living things and inanimate objects. Mithen notes that among all known cultures, certain biological concepts are universal: for example birds, fish, trees, flowering plants and grass – knowledge that is essential to hunter-gatherers. Similarly, intuitive physics is an aid to tool-making.

Mithen believes that the modern human mind emerged in stages over many millions of years. The earliest primate minds had only a general intelligence. The next step was the addition of the specialist intelligences, although these did not all appear at the same time. The first to develop was the social intelligence, evidence of which is seen in the highly-developed social skills of chimpanzees. After humans diverged from chimpanzees, the other three specialist intelligences followed.

These minds still lacked cognitive fluidity – that is to say, most of the various intelligences could not interact with one another. The exception was the linguistic intelligence, which was tied in with the social intelligence and was used in social interaction. The natural history and technical intelligences remained isolated, meaning that individuals could not share knowledge about matters such as animal behaviour or tool-making. Early humans, including Neanderthals, possessed minds of this type, though the various intelligences became more sophisticated over time.

Mithen believes consciousness was initially a mechanism that enabled an individual to predict how other group members might behave in certain situations. At some stage humans became able to look into their own thoughts about how they themselves would behave in such situations. What they could still not do at this stage was to think consciously about non-social matters. What they experienced when foraging or making a stone tool might have been similar to what we often experience when driving a car along a familiar route. Mithen notes that we can function on 'autopilot', driving with due care and attention to other road-users, roundabouts, junctions and traffic-lights – but have no memory of having done so at the end of the journey.

The final steps to behavioural modernity came about as a result of cognitive fluidity, which was attained when the various intelligences all began to interact with one another. The key was language, which as we have just seen was originally restricted to aiding social interactions. Use of language for other purposes was initially very limited, but such fragmentary conversations about non-social matters did eventually break down the barriers between the domains; it was clearly very useful to be able to share information about tool-making or hunting.

Mithen's work recalled a controversial theory proposed twenty years earlier by American psychologist Julian Jaynes,[36] who claimed that until around 3,000 years ago, humans possessed what he termed 'bicameral minds' that did not experience consciousness as we know it. Responses to situations arose in the right hemisphere of the brain and were 'heard' in the left hemisphere as a voice or 'god' giving advice or commands. Unaware that they were actually hearing their own thoughts, people would heed and obey without question. However, the increased social complexity of the Late Bronze Age caused a 'breakdown' of the bicameral mind, and people became fully aware of their own thought processes.

The Mithen theory is complemented by that of psychologist Frederick Coolidge and anthropologist Thomas Wynn,[37,11] who propose that modern human behaviour arose from a small but significant increase in what is termed the 'working memory' of the brain. This is the ability to consciously hold and manipulate information – basically the ability to think about complex ideas. Like Klein, they believe that this resulted from a genetic mutation, although rather earlier than 50,000 years ago. Coolidge and Wynn believe that it was this 'memory upgrade' that unlocked the full power of language, hence making cognitive fluidity possible. However, according to Mithen's later theories, the actual emergence of full cognitive fluidity only occurred later, and without any further changes to brain's workings.

Mithen proposed his cognitive fluidity theory before he developed the idea of the multi-medium protolanguage Hmmmmm, and at the time he also followed Richard Klein in the view that modern human behaviour emerged rather suddenly, around 50,000 years ago. However, he now accepts an earlier date and a gradual emergence between 200,000 and 70,000 years ago.[29] The transformation of Hmmmmm into modern language came about through the gradual splitting of holistic utterances into smaller components, as proposed by Wray and Kirby, and did not involve any rewiring of the brain or 'smartness mutations'.[19]

'Hmmmmm' never entirely disappeared, and music retains many of its features. On this timescale, according to Mithen, the Skhul and Qafzeh people were probably still using Hmmmmm. Eventually, though, the process was completed and modern language appeared. This in turn broke down the barriers between the various cognitive domains, and brought about full cognitive fluidity.[19] The Neanderthals, for their part, continued to use Hmmmmm and – so to speak – never made the connection. As noted in Chapter 8, Mithen does not accept that the Neanderthals were capable of behavioural modernity, but it would not require a major revision to his theory for full language to have emerged from Hmmmmm independently in more than one human species.

One thing that should be emphasised about these theories that in the case of modern humans at least, Hmmmmm-speakers were not 'simple-minded' – their lack of behavioural modernity stemmed purely from lack of exposure at birth to a modern language. A young child from Hmmmmm-speaking modern parents would, if raised among language-speakers, itself become a fully-competent language-speaker.

Mithen believes that the transformation from Hmmmmm to modern language might have begun when the earliest modern human communities within Africa began to adopt specialised economic roles and social positions, leading to trade and exchange with other communities. Communicating with strangers became a regular occurrence, and brought about the need to exchange information efficiently. Probably there was a feedback between the development of language and trade, with the two processes reinforcing each other. Mithen believes that the gradual nature of the transformation explains the slow rate of increase in the pace of innovation during the African Middle Stone Age.[29]

It is possible that to the language and trade Mithen postulates may be added the effects of 'stress' factors such as climatic and population pressures. These could have provided the incentive for greater cooperation between groups, thereby kick-starting the whole process. We should note, though, that the seemingly-modern technologies and behaviours seen at Pinnacle Point suggest that the transformation from Hmmmmm to full language might have been rather more rapid than Mithen suggests. On the other hand, it is possible that modern language did not become widespread until 70,000 years ago, but did emerge in some isolated populations much earlier. Possibly the greater social complexity of coastal societies such as Pinnacle Point played a part.

Tools and language

In addition to the various possibilities discussed above, could other factors have played a part in the development of the human brain and the emergence of language? Almost certainly, the answer is 'yes', and one factor that might have had a significant role is tool-making. Neurologists believe that Broca's Area and other parts of the brain long viewed as 'language areas' are in fact involved with other functions, including tool use. Recently, it has been suggested that tool-making was the original function of these areas of the brain, but parts of them were later repurposed as language areas.[38]

Two studies were carried out in which subjects carried out tool-making tasks while undergoing a brain imaging scan to record the areas of the brain in which activity was triggered. In the first study, individuals used a hammer stone to strike flakes from a flint core, so replicating Oldowan tool-making techniques.[39] In the second study, subjects were asked to produce both Oldowan tools and Acheulean hand-axes.[40]

In both studies, the Oldowan tool-making triggered activity in the left ventral premotor cortex. This region of the brain is known to be involved in coordinating hand movements, but it also includes Broca's Area. The second study found that Acheulean tool-making triggered activity in this region, but it also triggered activity in the right hemisphere of the brain in regions associated with language. Further studies, in which a wired-up glove was used to record hand movements while a subject carried out tool-making activities, have shown that in terms of manual dexterity, an Acheulean hand-axe is no more difficult to make than the far simpler Oldowan tools.[41]

The results suggest that the step up from Oldowan to Acheulean technologies required an increase in brainpower rather than in manual dexterity, and that there was a link between the appearance of more complex tool-making techniques and the evolution of language. Interestingly, as we saw in Chapter 5, the Broca's Area of *Homo habilis* was expanded in comparison to the same region in the australopithecines. These experimental results suggest that the expansion might have been linked to the appearance of better tool-making skills as well as or possibly instead of the use of language by *Homo habilis*.

The origins of religion

For the final section of this brief study of the human mind and its development, we turn to what is certainly its most contentious topic. Religion is universal in human society, and it appears to be a fundamental part of the human condition.[42] Why should people all over the world believe in a supernatural being or beings inhabiting a realm detached from our day-to-day existence? Though religions differ considerably throughout the world, a belief in such beings is a very common aspect of them. The supernatural is not confined to religion, and entities unconstrained by conventional laws of physics and biology have featured in literature going back to the time of Homer. In *The Odyssey*, Odysseus encounters various spirits, including Agamemnon, Achilles, and his own mother who died during his lengthy absence from his kingdom in Ithaca. The literature of subsequent millennia abounds with tales of ghosts, invisible beings, werewolves and the like. Anthropomorphism – the attribution of human characteristics to non-human things – is a common feature of both religion and story-telling. If we accept that religion is indeed a product of the way the human brain works, the obvious question is why? Is religion useful, or is a 'misfiring by-product' of something more useful, as Richard Dawkins[43] has suggested?

Robin Dunbar[44,45] has noted that both religion and story-telling are universal to human culture. He claims that the social brain hypothesis provides an explanation as to why this is so. As we have seen, theory of mind refers to the ability to anticipate the thoughts of others. However, it is actually no more than a restricted case of what philosophers have termed 'intentionality': awareness of mind-states such as knowing, thinking, believing, desiring or intending. Simple organisms such as bacteria completely lack self-awareness and are said to possess zero-order intentionality. Anything that is aware of what it is thinking possesses first-order intentionality. Organisms possessing brains, such as vertebrates and the more complex invertebrates, are capable of first-order intentionality. To have a belief about somebody else's belief, such as 'I *believe* (1) that Sally *thinks* (2) the marble is still in her basket' requires second-order intentionality. Thus theory of mind may be described as second-order intentionality.

For day-to-day purposes, humans typically use up to three orders of intentionality, for example 'I *think* (1) Sally *believes* (2) that Fred *wants* (3) to leave her for Anne'. In fact we can do considerably better, and are capable of fifth and sixth-order. Dunbar suggests that in writing *Othello*, Shakespeare would have required six levels in order to keep track of the plot. Even if their camp-fire stories never quite matched the works of Shakespeare, early story-tellers would have required similar levels of intentionality if they were going to hold their audiences. Dunbar believes that a functioning religion also requires similar levels of intentionality.

From this, Dunbar suggests that the capacity for story-telling and religion must be advantageous from an evolutionary point of view. He notes that to power all this extra intentionality requires energetically-expensive brain power (see Chapter 5) and suggests that for this capacity to have evolved at all, the advantages must have been considerable. He notes that in small-scale societies, such as those of hunter-gatherers, story-telling plays an important role in social bonding. He argues that religion is an even more powerful bonding device, creating a sense of unity strong enough to enforce cohesion in a large group.

However, there are problems with this view. It assumes that the capacity for higher-order intentionality resulted directly from evolutionary pressures and that it was not simply a spin-off from something else. Even with five or six levels of intentionality, religion as we know it could not function without modern language; this in turn, as we saw, might have required an increase in 'working memory'. Such a 'hardware upgrade' could also have allowed the brain to keep track of what was happening at higher levels of intentionality. If so, it seems likely that higher-order intentionality was simply a spin-off of the evolutionary processes that led to modern language. If it did indeed lead to religion, then it would support Dawkins' 'misfiring by-product' view.

Theories advocating religion and ritual as a means of creating social cohesion were first advocated by the French sociologist Émile Durkheim.[46] Though they are widely accepted, such theories have been criticised on the grounds that they invoke 'functionalism'. In sociology, structural functionalism is a model that sees society as composed of institutions that function for the common good. While a fuller discussion is beyond the scope of this work, critics of functionalism argue that it downplays conflict and inequality. They also suggest that functionalism is logically flawed and begins by assuming the very thing it sets out to prove. Religion and ritual do indeed create social cohesion – but this, critics argue, is more a description rather than an explanation. It doesn't tell us why religion and ritual exist, unless one supposes that people consciously invented them for that purpose. It is very difficult to argue that the tribal elders of early settlements sat down to discuss introducing rituals that would bind their society together, in case it became more complex in the future. While Dunbar is not suggesting that this was actually the case, we need to ask just how and why religious rituals actually came about.[47,48]

We must also not forget that for all its perceived advantages, religion has been a deeply-divisive force throughout human history. It has been responsible for countless wars, oppression and bloodshed, all of which continue unabated to this day. Furthermore, as we shall see in Chapter 14, it is possible that religion was dividing society as long ago as 40,000 years. While the social brain hypothesis provides a plausible link between brain size, social group size, and the emergence of language, it may be pushing the model too far to link it directly to the emergence of religion.

South African cognitive archaeologist David Lewis-Williams believes that that many aspects of religion can be explained in terms of the neurological architecture of the human brain. In his book *The Mind in the Cave: Consciousness and the Origins of Art* and follow-up works,[49,47,50] Lewis-Williams notes that many religions centre on a belief in a multi-tiered cosmos with other realms located 'above' and 'below' that of our every-day experience; Heaven and Hell are only one example of such a cosmology. He suggests that widespread belief in the existence of these other realms arises from visions and hallucinations experienced in altered states of consciousness. These may be induced by meditation, use of psychotropic substances, and other ritual practices. All human brains are wired up the same way, and hence all experience broadly the same visions and hallucinations. How they are interpreted varies from culture to culture.

According to Lewis-Williams, the earliest religions were shamanistic and involved individuals entering altered states of consciousness. Present-day shamanistic religions are based on the belief that shamans are able to leave their bodies and travel to other realms of existence, where they can communicate directly with powerful spirits. Shamans thus act as mediators between the living and the spirit worlds. The word 'shaman' originally came from the language of the Tungus of Siberia, but shamanism is now used as a generic term for such belief systems.

Human consciousness may be thought of as a spectrum, along which the brain's state of consciousness is constantly shifting. At one end of the spectrum is the alert, outward-directed consciousness that we use to relate to our environment and to solve problems. As we move along the spectrum, we reach more introverted states where we solve problems by inward-directed thought. Further on, we reach a state of day-dreaming or reverie, and beyond this the brain normally reaches the boundary between wakefulness and sleep (known as the hypnagogic state) before entering a state of dreaming.

However, there is also a second, 'intensified trajectory', involving altered states of consciousness. This trajectory is typically associated with psychotropic substances, but it may also be induced by intense concentration, chanting, clapping, drumming, prolonged rhythmic movement, or hyperventilation. Those who have experienced it report that it leads through three stages. In Stage 1, an individual experiences phenomena including grids, sets of parallel lines, bright dots, thin, meandering lines, zigzag lines, and 'fortification' patterns. The latter, familiar to sufferers of migraine with aura, comprise arcs of shimmering zigzag lines, often resembling the battlements of a castle. During Stage 2, the brain attempts to interpret these phenomena by construing them as objects with personal significance, for example emotional or religious manifestations. As individuals pass from Stage 2 to Stage 3, they often pass through a vortex or tunnel, at the end of which is bright light. On the internal surface of the vortex there is sometimes a grid upon which appear hallucinogenic images of people, animals and monsters. There is often a sensation of flying at this point. Finally, Stage 3 is reached, and at this point individuals find themselves in a bizarre, ever-changing world of hallucinations. This stage is comparable to normal dreaming, but is more intense, memorable and prolonged. Hallucinations are not just visual; individuals may hear voices or experience sensations such changing into animals.

Lewis-Williams believes that the phenomena experienced in this intensified trajectory are what give rise to perceptions of an alternative reality. Shamanistic practices are based on the belief that people with special powers and skills have access to these realms. In actuality, they are experiencing illusions resulting from the behaviour of the human nervous system in altered states of consciousness. These illusions may be what is being depicted in the cave art of the European Upper Palaeolithic, and could lie at the root of all belief systems from these times to the present day.

Lewis-Williams' theories are compelling and we shall encounter them again in later chapters. First, however, we must consider what archaeology, genetics and climate change can tell us about the circumstances in which *Homo sapiens* left Africa and went on to colonise the rest of the world.

The symbolic ape

PART II:

OUT OF AFRICA

127,000 TO 14,600 YEARS AGO

12: Going global

To leave Africa

It is widely accepted that the non-African world is largely populated by the descendants of a small group of modern humans thought to have left Africa around 65,000 years ago. Were they the first to leave, and if not what happened to their forerunners? How, when and under what circumstances did this pioneering group leave Africa? To leave Africa there are theoretically four routes into Eurasia: from Morocco across the Straits of Gibraltar; from Tunisia to Sicily and thence to Italy; from Egypt across the Sinai desert into the Levant; and across the Bab el-Mandeb Strait between the Red Sea and the Gulf of Aden.[1] In practice there are only the last two, as the navigation of the Mediterranean was apparently beyond the capability of even early modern humans,[2] and there are climate-related issues with both of these routes.

The Sahara and Sinai can only be crossed during interglacials, when warm, wet climatic conditions cause these normally inhospitable regions to green, and the Levant becomes a northeasterly extension of Africa.[3,4] Three periods have been identified in the last 200,000 years when the central Sahara and Sahel contained trees, indicating substantially wetter conditions than at present. The presence of trees was inferred from carbon isotope analysis of individual plant leaf waxes, which were recovered from a marine sediment core containing windblown dust from the Sahara (as we saw in Chapter 4, the isotope ^{13}C occurs at lower levels in trees and bushes than in other vegetation). It was found that the first wet phase occurred from 120,000 to 110,000 years ago during the Eemian Interglacial; the second from 50,000 to 45,000 years ago during the warm Marine Isotope Stage 3 interstadial; and the third during the early part of the current Holocene period. During the wet phases, humans were able to cross this currently inhospitable region.[5]

Satellite radar images have revealed networks of now-buried river channels that extend across the Sahara desert to the Mediterranean coast. Geochemical data has shown that water in these systems originated from the south during wet episodes. During the period from 120,000 to 110,000 years ago, the channel network penetrated all the way to the Mediterranean, and provided an uninterrupted freshwater corridor across what is now arid desert. By travelling along this humid, life-sustaining corridor, it was possible to leave Africa.[6,7]

Outside one of these windows, people would not have been able to reach further into Asia, even if they could reach the Levant. Except during an interglacial, there are a variety of geographical barriers to movement between the Levant and the rest of Asia. To the north lies the Taurus mountain chain in southern Turkey, running along a curve from Lake Eğirdir in the west to the upper reaches of the Euphrates and Tigris in the east. To the east the Zagros mountain chain runs some 1,800 km (1,100 miles) from near the Turkish border, running southeast along the western border of Iran and down to the Straits of Hormuz. Together with the Syrian and Arabian deserts, these form an impenetrable barrier between the Levant and the rest of Asia. To the west of the Syrian Desert and to the north and east of the Tigris and Euphrates valleys is the hilly arc known as the Fertile Crescent. It offers a way to reach the South Asian coast, but it is completely inhospitable during cold, arid periods.[8,9]

The northern route is the most obvious way out of Africa, as it does not involve any form of water crossing. During interglacials, the Levant serves as a staging point for onward dispersals into Europe and Asia, and it is by this route that earlier human species are assumed to have left Africa.[2] However, 65,000 years ago, when modern humans are thought to have left Africa, the Earth was experiencing the cold, arid conditions of Marine Isotope Stage 4. For this reason, the widely accepted view is that the peopling of the non-African world did not involve this route.

The Bab el-Mandeb Strait – meaning 'The Gate of Tears' – is a narrow waterway at the southern end of the Red Sea, separating Djibouti from Yemen. At times of cold, dry conditions, such as those prevailing 65,000 years ago, it is just 11 km (6.8 miles) across. Even when sea levels are high (as they are at present), it is only 18 km (11 miles) across at its narrowest point, about half the width of the Strait of Dover. On a clear day, Yemen is clearly visible from the shores of Djibouti. The crossing is nevertheless treacherous, with swift-running currents that could have swept primitive watercraft out into the Indian Ocean. Not for nothing is it known as the Gate of Tears. Crossing is therefore problematic, though it is unlikely to have been beyond the abilities of African Middle Stone Age seafarers.[10,11]

To people able to make the crossing, this southern route offers a very attractive lifestyle – that of beachcombing. As we saw in Chapter 10, modern humans were harvesting seafood at Pinnacle Point 165,000 years ago. It provides a good quality diet, and is far easier to obtain than savannah game. Once migrants had crossed the Red Sea, they would have found such a food supply available to them all the way along the coast of the Indian Ocean. They could have moved along the southern Asian coast through Yemen and Oman, and then onwards to India and Southeast Asia.[8,9]

The time sharers

Long before this presumed southern migration, probably around 115,000 years ago, modern humans took advantage of the Saharan 'humid corridor' to extend their range into the Levant. Early fossil evidence for this excursion comes from two sites in Israel, Mugharet es-Skhul and Jebel Qafzeh. As noted in Chapter 9, the Skhul and Qafzeh people still retain archaic features such as robustness, but they are essentially modern with a high and well-rounded skull and a pronounced chin.[12] Their resemblance to the Jebel Irhoud people of Morocco suggests that they originated from North Africa.[13]

Mugharet es-Skhul ('Cave of the Kids') is a cave site on the western slopes of Mount Carmel, 3 km (2 miles) south of Haifa. The caves of Mount Carmel were discovered by chance by British engineers planning a road to Haifa, and between 1929 and 1934 they were excavated by British archaeologist Dorothy Garrod, accompanied by palaeontologist Dorothea Bate from the Natural History Museum in London. Garrod, who later became the first woman professor at Cambridge University, employed an excavation team consisting almost entirely of women. Men were only drafted in for the more strenuous tasks, such as drilling by hand and lifting slabs of limestone.[14]

The cave contains three main layers and from the second of these, Layer B, Garrod's team recovered the remains of nine individuals (Skhul I-IX), most of which had been intentionally buried. The lower jawbone of a large boar was found enclosed in the arms of the skeleton Skhul V.[15] Recently, two shells of species *Nassarius gibbosulus*, perforated to serve as beads, have been shown to have come from the Skhul V burial layer. The beads had been in storage at the Natural History Museum in London since their recovery by Garrod's team, and their origin was confirmed by an analysis of material still adhering to them.[16] The implication in terms of symbolic behaviour, as noted in Chapter 10 for bead use in Africa, would of course also apply to these Levantine examples. The boar's jawbone and the beads have been interpreted as possible grave goods. More contentious is a flint scraper found between the hands of skeleton Skhul IV, but this could have just happened to be in the soil that was heaped on top of the body at burial.[14]

Dating the Skhul remains has long been an issue, and in 2005 attempts were made to resolve this. Four fossils of reasonably-secure provenance were dated by electron spin resonance and uranium series techniques. The fossils chosen were a molar tooth from Skhul II, bone fragments from Skhul IX, a tooth from the Skhul boar jawbone, and another tooth from an ox associated with Skhul IX. Researchers concluded that provided the burials all took place within a relatively short time span, then the best age estimate lies between 100,000 and 135,000 years old. They could not be certain that the time span had been short,[15] but the date range is consistent with an arrival of modern humans in the Levant during the time that the Saharan humid corridor was open, from 120,000 to 110,000 years ago.

The second site, Jebel Qafzeh, is a cave located near Mount Precipice, south of Nazareth. It was first excavated between 1933 and 1934, and then later between 1965 and 1979.[17] Five partial skeletons and fragments of as many as ten other individuals have been recovered.[18] Again, there is evidence of deliberate burial and of grave goods, with one adolescent buried with an antler placed directly on their chest.[17] Another grave contained the remains of a woman and child, apparently buried together.[12] Once again, we can only speculate as to whether the woman was the mother of the child, and to the circumstances of their deaths.

In addition to the burials, the lower layers of the site contained a series of hearths, stone artefacts, animal bones, a collection of marine shells, and lumps of red ochre. The marine shells were recovered from layers earlier than most of the graves, except for one burial. The shells are naturally-perforated *Glycymeris* bivalves, which must have been collected and brought from the Mediterranean shore, some 35 km (22 miles) away. Several shells show traces of having been strung, and a few had been stained with red and yellow ochre. Naturally-perforated *Glycymeris* shells are almost as common as non-perforated ones, and were presumably selected for this reason. The ochre is thought to have been brought from outcrops located from 8 to 60 km (5 to 37 miles) away from the site.

The need to make special trips to obtain shells and other items not related to immediate survival is a behaviourally-modern trait. While the purpose of expeditions to the coast was probably not just to acquire the shells, it is possible that they served as a reminder of the risks and dangers of the undertaking, and that they were souvenirs as well as just ornaments.[17] Once again, there is uncertainty about the age of this site. One estimate, obtained by electron spin resonance dating of associated mammal remains, is that it is $115,000 \pm 15,000$ years old;[19] again, this time fits in with when the Saharan humid corridor was open.

The technology of the Skhul and Qafzeh people was dominated by the use of the Levallois technique,[12] a prepared-core technology that differed little from those of the Neanderthals. There is no hint of the microlith technology of the Pinnacle Point people who lived 50,000 years earlier. Nevertheless, there are elements of modern human behaviour, expressed through symbolic burials.[15] Unfortunately, no typological connection is apparent between the Levantine stone tools and those from North Africa,[20] which would then tie in with the fossil evidence for a North African origin.

Were the modern humans alone in the region? In particular, could the Skhul people have had Neanderthal neighbours? A short distance from Skhul is Tabun Cave, which Dorothy Garrod also excavated. Findings included the partial skeleton of a Neanderthal woman. The age of Tabun C1, as the skeleton is known, is subject to a good deal of uncertainty, partly due to doubts as to its exact provenance. Garrod recovered it from near the top of the cave's Layer C, but believed it to have been buried from the Layer B immediately above. C1 has been dated to $122,000 \pm 16,000$ years old by uranium series techniques, and similar dates have been obtained for animal remains from Layer B. The results suggest that Garrod was correct and that Tabun C1 lived around 122,000 years ago.[21]

It is sorely tempting to imagine modern humans and Neanderthals living peacefully side-by-side in a part of the world where modern humans have subsequently failed, quite woefully, to live in peace with their own kind. In reality, the huge uncertainties in the dating mean that the Tabun, Skhul and Qafzeh people were probably separated from each other by many millennia, but at the moment we simply don't know for certain, one way or another.

However, modern humans did not remain in the Levant any later than 75,000 years ago,[22] and fossil evidence suggests that Neanderthals returned to the region at about the same time. Neanderthal burials are known from the lower levels of Shanidar Cave in northern Iraq, dating from 70,000 to 80,000 years ago; and from another Mount Carmel site, Kebara Cave, dating from 50,000 to 60,000 years ago. The Neanderthal site of Dederiyeh Cave in Syria may be as recent as 45,000 years old.[23,12] All of this points to a lengthy re-occupation of the region by Neanderthals. Was this a Neanderthal conquest? Were the modern humans driven out of the Levant by Neanderthals?

A likelier explanation is that the excursion of modern humans into the Levant was terminated by a return to cooler, dryer climate. There was an abrupt cold, dry period from 90,000 to 85,000 years ago known as Heinrich Event 7,[24] followed 74,000 years ago by the onset of the prolonged glacial conditions of Marine Isotope Stage 4. The ranges of modern humans and Neanderthals might have ebbed and flowed in accordance with climate change. The two human species 'time shared' the Levant: whenever the climate was warm, the region was occupied by modern humans; when it was cool it was occupied by Neanderthals. Animal remains show that in cooler times, Arctic fauna spread down from Europe, but when the climate warmed they would be replaced by Afro-tropical fauna. Like any other animal species, modern humans and Neanderthals merely 'went with the flow', probably following herd animals that, in the case of African species, migrated south as their existing pastures disappeared.[23,14] In a sense, the Levantine people had never really left Africa. As previously noted, the Levant of that time is better thought of as a northeasterly extension of that continent.

Before it was possible to establish a chronology for the Levant, it had been assumed that the Skhul and Qafzeh people had gone on to colonise Europe, but the discovery that they were replaced by Neanderthals makes this unlikely. Given the previously-noted geographical and climatic obstacles to doing so, is it also unlikely that they moved on into South Asia. If the Skhul and Qafzeh people went anywhere at all, it was back to Africa. The only other possibility is that they died out completely. The latter, grimmer, scenario is actually the likeliest. According to one estimate, the total Levantine population was just over 500 and, as such, was barely viable.[22]

It has been suggested that the migration to the Levant failed because the Skhul and Qafzeh people were not yet fully modern.[25] However, this ignores the question as to why even fully modern people would push on into mountainous inhospitable terrain, when it was far easier to migrate back into Africa. Bear in mind that the Levantine people of that time probably had no recollection that their forbears had started out from Africa thousands of years earlier. If they did make it back to Africa, they would therefore not have seen their return there as a 'retreat', or their time in the Levant as part of a 'failed' migration. Modern humans did not return to the Levant until around 50,000 years ago. By then, their technology was considerably more advanced, and was associated with the Upper Palaeolithic.[18] This enabled them to overcome the harsh conditions that had ultimately defeated their predecessors tens of thousands of years earlier.

Onwards to China?

Could modern humans have moved on from the Levant before the cold set in 90,000 years ago, either east towards India and China, or south into the Arabian Peninsula? There is no reason why not, but the fossil evidence for an early modern human presence in China is controversial. An age of between 111,000 and 139,000 years old has been claimed for the Liujiang Skull from Tongtianyan Cave in southern China. The dates were obtained by uranium series methods,[26] although there are concerns about the geological integrity of the site, and the skull may actually be only 30,000 years old.[27] Also contentious are the fossilised lower jawbone and two molar teeth found at Zhirendong ('*Homo sapiens* cave'), a small cave in Guizhou Province, southern China. Here there is no dispute about the age of the remains, which were discovered in 2007 and found by uranium series methods to be 106,000 years old; this age is also supported by associated animal remains. The lower jawbone has been described as exhibiting a mixture of archaic and modern features: its robustness suggests that it is from an archaic human, but it has a modern human chin. Such a mixture of archaic and modern features has been interpreted as possibly representing a population of modern humans who reached China and interbred with the local archaic population.[28]

On the other hand, the Zhirendong remains could simply represent a late *Homo erectus* population whose lower jaw had over time become more like that of a modern human. Unfortunately, there is no relevant fossil evidence for this period from anywhere between the Levantine/African region and Borneo, making it difficult to choose between the two possibilities. We should therefore reserve judgment until more is known about the typical lower jawbone of Chinese *Homo erectus*.[29,11]

Evidence for dispersal from Africa 65,000 years ago

The widely accepted view, based on genetic evidence, is that modern humans dispersed from Africa in a single migration sometime around 65,000 years ago.[30,31] Taking the southern route, they crossed the Bab el-Mandeb Strait and then rapidly made their way along the southern Asian coast, reaching Australia around 50,000 years ago. It is supposed that any earlier migrations eventually died out.

The fossil and archaeological evidence suggests that early migrants reached East Asia and Australia before Europe. As noted in Chapter 9, the earliest reliably-dated fossil evidence we have for undisputedly-modern humans outside Africa and the Levant is in the order of 65,000 to 40,000 years old. The Australian 'Mungo Lady' from New South Wales is thought to be around 42,000 years old,[32] and possibly as much as 62,000 years old;[33] and remains from East Asia may be of similar age.[34,35] No European finds are greater than around 45,000 years old.[36,37,38] The archaeological record suggest that modern humans were at Lake Mungo 46,000 to 50,000 years ago,[32] and in Europe 46,000 years ago.[39] While the later dates from both East Asia and Australia are close to the European dates, humans must have arrived in northern Australia well before they reached New South Wales. Even if the Lake Mungo artefacts are only 46,000 years old, a conservative estimate would suggest that humans reached Australia at least 50,000 years ago.[40]

These dates don't tell us when modern humans first left Africa, but they suggest that it was a long time after the early Levantine migration. The genetic evidence paints a similar picture. The bulk of the world's non-African mitochondrial haplogroups are represented by just two major branches of the African haplogroup L3: the daughter haplogroups M and N. Various estimates suggest that L3 appeared between 85,000 and 70,000 years ago,[41,42,43,44] in East Africa.[45] As we saw in Chapter 10, the subsequent expansion of L3 is thought to have been aided by improving climatic conditions in tropical Africa, and possibly by technological innovation.

M and N are both in the region of 55,000 to 65,000 years old.[46,41,47] Haplogroup R diverged from N very early on, and is regarded as a third founding haplogroup. All three probably originated somewhere between East Africa and the Persian Gulf,[48] though there is an east/west split in their present-day distribution. M is more or less absent from Europe, but all three haplogroups occur further east.[49]

If we accept a non-African origin for M and N, their appearance between 65,000 and 55,000 years ago roughly dates the migration out of Africa. Unfortunately, no early 'pre-M' or 'pre-N' lineages have been found in either Africa or the Arabian Peninsula. These would make it far easier to pinpoint the origins of M and N, but in both East Africa[50] and Arabia[51,52,43] the mitochondrial gene pool is dominated by haplogroups relating to much later migrations.

Interestingly, these dates are close to those obtained by researchers who used the body louse (*Pediculus humanus corporis*) to estimate when tailored clothing came into use. They worked on the assumption that the body louse diverged from the head louse at about this time, taking advantage of the new niche that had opened up. The researchers used data from mitochondrial and nuclear DNA to show that the body louse originated in Africa 72,000 years ago, and they suggested that there might be a link between the invention of tailored clothing and the migration of modern humans from Africa.[53]

It is widely believed that there was just the one migration from Africa, and that the founder haplogroups M, N and R were associated with it. All three are roughly the same age, whereas had they been associated with separate migrations at different times, it would be expected that their ages would reflect the various dates of the migrations.[41] Estimates based on mitochondrial genetic data suggest that the initial migratory group included no more than 500 to 2000 reproductively-active women.[54,41] Of course the total number of men, women and children taking part in the migration would have been greater, and a total founding population of around 3,000 has been suggested.[55]

Having left Africa, the migrants are thought to have dispersed along the southern Asian coast. Throughout Southeast Asia, scattered along the route of the projected beachcomber migration, are isolated populations of so-called Negritos (the term means 'little black people'; although originally coined by European explorers, it is still used by anthropologists and is not considered derogatory). These people have long been thought to be aboriginal because their culture and appearance marks them out from surrounding people. They closely resemble Khoisan Africans, being short in stature with tightly curled hair and an epicanthic fold. They include the inhabitants of the Andaman Islands in the Bay of Bengal, the Semang from the Malay Peninsula, the Mani people of Thailand and a number of indigenous groups in the Philippines.[4]

Mitochondrial DNA studies have shown that the Andaman Islanders, the Semang and aboriginal New Guineans and Aboriginal Australian all possess localised but very ancient branches of the three founder haplogroups M, N and R. The implication is that these groups settled along the coastline of the Indian Ocean a long time ago, and that they have remained in more or less the same place ever since. Researchers applied a statistical technique known as founder analysis to the genetic data, with the aim of identifying and dating migrations into new territory. The results suggest that the settlement took place at least 60,000 years ago, and that these peoples are indeed the relict populations left over from the original migration out of Africa.[41,56]

Following the initial migration, the world's non-African population grew rapidly. According to estimates based on mitochondrial genetic diversity, the population of South and Southeast Asia had increased fivefold by around 52,000 years ago. By 45,000 years ago, Africa had been overtaken: more than half the world's population lived on the Indian subcontinent, and in the Thai and Malay peninsulas.[47]

The physical logistics of the migration has been described as the coastal 'express train' scenario. It proposes that migrants from Africa moved swiftly along the shorelines of Arabia and the Indian Ocean Rim to Southeast Asia and Australia. Already adapted to the beachcombing lifestyle and migrating at up to 4 km (2.5 miles) each year along the shorelines, they could have progressed all the way to Indonesia given the low sea level. At most it is thought that the process would have taken 15,000 years, and probably less than 10,000 years. As beachcombers, the migrants could also have largely avoided the climate change-related problems faced by inland populations during the rapid climatic fluctuations of the Late Pleistocene.

While archaeological evidence in support of this hypothesis is lacking, it is likely that it has been lost as a result of sea level rises. Coastal migration may also explain why the migrants did not immediately replace archaic peoples living inland, such as those known from Ngandong in Indonesia. It would also conveniently explain the early dates for human presence in Australia, and the presence of the relict Negrito populations discussed above.[57,54,41,58]

A problem with the scenario as proposed is that it lacks a convincing rationale for the ever-eastwards movement of the migrants. David Bulbeck[59] has suggested that the migrants adapted to living in river estuaries, and that a tradition of seeking out suitable estuarine habitats provided the main impetus for the migratory movement. The dispersal was aided by the use of watercraft that could transport colonists together with sufficient food, water, and other supplies needed to traverse long stretches of inhospitable coast. Bulbeck argues that the migrants were long familiar with watercraft, which facilitated the exploitation of niches such as reefs and marine shallows. Estuarine habitats along the rim of the Indian Ocean provided the migrants good access to drinking water, food and timber. These rich resources supported healthy population growth and led eventually to crowded conditions, even if the surrounding stretches of land remained uninhabited. It was overcrowding that stimulated the search for new estuarine habitats further along the coast, but watercraft enabled onward migrants to keep in touch with their parent communities, and resulted in a chain of interlinked settlements.

It is possible that migrants also followed rivers inland from time to time. Computer simulations suggest that populations could have followed a number of routes, both coastal and inland. Both the coasts and the interior of the Indian subcontinent would have been attractive to mobile parties of hunter-gatherers, who could have moved rapidly inland via river corridors such as the Indus River and Narmada River valleys and the Ganges–Brahmaputra Delta. Indeed, large river deltas would have represented significant barriers, forcing migratory groups far inland in order to cross.[1,60] The presence of a fossil skull at the Tam Pa Ling cave site in Laos, located well away from the coast, confirms that inland migration routes were followed at least some of the time.[34]

This, then, is the standard model of how modern humans came to populate the world. It is supported by both fossil and genetic evidence, and popularised by many books and television series. A criticism is that it remains largely untestable, because any archaeological evidence of a coastal migration is assumed to have been submerged at the end of the last Ice Age. However, it is becoming increasingly clear that populations of modern humans were established in Arabia well before 65,000 years ago. Furthermore, the founding mitochondrial haplogroup L3 that went on to populate the world might not even have originated in Africa.

Early migrations into Arabia

Until fairly recently, it was believed that the Levantine excursion was the only early migration of modern humans from Africa. It now appears that at least one and probably two culturally-distinct groups from East Africa established themselves in Arabia during the period from 127,000 to 106,000 years ago. The Arabian Peninsula is more than ten times the size of Britain and because it occupies its own tectonic plate, it is technically a subcontinent. Today, it is largely arid desert: the Rub' al-Khali Desert in the south and the Great Nafud Desert to the north. Running through the centre of the Peninsula is a highland region known as the Nejd Plateau. Arabia has not always been so inhospitable, and periodically it has been transformed by warm and wet climate phases into a fertile, habitable ecosystem;[10] there are widespread indications of now dried-up lakes and rivers.[61] During these wet phases, the limit of monsoon rainfall was lifted far north of its present position and its intensity in Arabia increased. Several such phases have been identified over the last 330,000 years. They correspond to warm interglacial or interstadial periods, as identified in the marine oxygen isotope record. The main wet phase of the Late Pleistocene was the Eemian Interglacial, but there were also significant wet periods during Marine Isotope Stage 5c and Marine Isotope Stage 5a. The subsequent onset of the cold Marine Isotope Stage 4, 74,000 years ago, saw a return to prolonged aridity.[62,63,64,65] During favourable periods, the whole of the Arabian Peninsula might have acted as a 'pump', drawing in populations from the Levant, India and East Africa; conversely, dry, cold periods would have seen these populations largely die out.[10]

Archaeologist Jeffrey Rose[64] has suggested that some populations survived by retreating to refugia that remained habitable throughout arid periods, and continued to provide reliable sources of food and drinking water. These included the Red Sea basin and Yemeni highlands, and the southeast Arabian coastal zone. In addition, large portions of the Persian Gulf were exposed by the reduced sea levels. The appearance of freshwater springs in the exposed basin might have transformed the Gulf into a coastal oasis of 200,000 sq. km. (77,000 square miles) – comparable in size to Great Britain. The mosaic landscape of freshwater springs, river floodplains, mangrove swamps and estuaries would have been very attractive to human settlers.

A large number of archaeological sites are known in Arabia, and others may lie buried beneath the sands or submerged by rising sea levels. The sites are often associated with rivers, streams and lakes. Some are located along the margins of the Red Sea, and might have been associated with migrations. Others are located inland, suggesting that favourable conditions existed at the time of occupation. Unfortunately, few reliable age estimates exist.[66] A number of Middle Palaeolithic prepared-core tool industries have been documented, and associations between them and industries in the Levant, India and East Africa have been proposed on the grounds of tool typology. In the absence of secure dating, such associations are no more than tentative. Even the tool-makers are uncertain; no human fossil remains have ever been found, and the level of technology could imply that the tools were made by Neanderthals or late archaic humans rather than modern humans.[66,10] More definite information has recently begun to emerge from the region. Secure dates have been obtained for Middle Palaeolithic artefacts from Jebel Faya in the United Arab Emirates.[67] and the Dhofar region of southwest Oman[20] These findings pose a significant challenge for the standard model of a single Out of Africa migration 65,000 years ago.

Jebel Faya is a mountain lying due south of the Straits of Hormuz and is equidistant from the Gulf of Oman and the Persian Gulf. The finds were made in a rock shelter known as FAY-NE1, located 180 m (600 ft.) above sea level at the northeast end of the mountain. The rock shelter contains archaeological layers dating from the Iron and Bronze Ages all the way back to the Middle Palaeolithic. Artefacts from the latter have been found in three layers and optically stimulated luminescence dating showed that artefacts from the oldest layer, Layer C, range from 127,000 to 95,000 years old. The Jebel Faya Layer C artefacts were manufactured using a range of methods, and include small hand-axes, small thick leaf-shaped pieces known as foliates, end scrapers, side scrapers and denticulates. It was suggested that in terms of typology and manufacturing techniques, the tools were unrelated to those of Levant; and that the manufacturing techniques suggest a connection with East Africa.

It was proposed that modern humans crossed the Bab el-Mandeb Strait just before the start of the warm Eemian Interglacial, while sea levels were still low, and it could still be readily crossed. Having occupied the southern Yemeni coast, groups were able to spread out both along the coast and inland. The warm, wet conditions of the Eemian transformed the now-arid Nejd Plateau from a geographical barrier to a region of abundant vegetation and readily-available water, enabling the migrants to expand all the way to Jebel Faya. However, during the subsequent cooler, arid periods that followed the Eemian, it is possible that the corridor across the Nejd Plateau closed, cutting off the Jebel Faya people from groups living further south.

One problem is that the Jebel Faya artefacts cannot be associated with any specific East African tool industry, and Sir Paul Mellars has expressed scepticism. He does not believe that there is any evidence that the tool style is explicitly African, or that the tools were even made by modern humans. He noted that the Jebel Faya bifaces are stouter than those common in Africa at the time.[68]

These objections could not be made for Dhofar findings, which were announced just under a year later. They have been firmly associated with the Nubian Complex, a mainly Levallois prepared-core Middle Stone Age industry from the Middle and Lower Nile Valley. The Nubian Complex is divided into Early and Late phases, and is characterised by a regional variant of the Levallois technique. It was first reported from northern Sudan in the 1960s. In Africa, Nubian artefacts have been found from Sinai to the Horn of Africa, with dates ranging from roughly 120,000 to 100,000 years old. Following tentative reports of Nubian artefacts in Yemen, the Dhofar Archaeological Project (DAP) was initiated in 2010 to explore the Late Pleistocene archaeological record of the Dhofar region.

Two seasons of fieldwork were conducted over the winters of 2010 and 2011, and over a hundred finds of artefacts were made, ranging from isolated cores to high-density scatters. The finds all were made on the Nejd Plateau, mostly near streams, channels and rocky outcrops of suitable raw material. The most common tool types found were points, flakes and blades. A number of retouched tools were also found, including side scrapers, end scrapers, denticulates, notches, and a small number of burins and perforators. The same tool types, occurring at similar frequencies, are found within Late Nubian Complex assemblages in Africa. On the basis of these typological similarities, and the use of Levallois techniques, the Dhofar assemblages were classified as Late Nubian Complex. At the open-air site of Aybut Al Auwal, a mean age of $106,600 \pm 6,400$ years old was obtained for artefact-bearing sediment, using optically stimulated luminescence dating. This date is consistent with Nubian Complex dates from Africa, but it slightly predates the earliest African dates for the Late Nubian. While there insufficient evidence to state that the Late phase originated in Arabia and later spread back to East Africa, it remains a possibility.

The Dhofar findings provide clear evidence of cultural exchange across the Red Sea by modern humans some 40,000 years before modern humans were supposed to have made the crossing. Even if an African origin for the Jebel Faya artefacts is rejected, the Dhofar evidence cannot be so readily dismissed. We must accept that modern humans were on the Arabian Peninsula well before the canonical date for the migration from Africa of around 65,000 years ago.

Another widely accepted view to come under scrutiny is the *tabula rasa* model, which supposes that the human populations of Arabia were extinguished by periods of widespread desiccation.[10] The *tabula rasa* view can rescue the single Out of Africa migration model by supposing that the Jebel Faya and Dhofar populations died out, either during the intermittent cold periods between 110,000 and 74,000 years ago, or during the protracted and severe cold period that followed (Marine Isotope Stage 4). However, recent evidence suggests that human populations were able to survive the periodic hyper-arid climatic oscillations by retreating to refugia where human life could still be sustained.[64]

One such site is Shi'bat Dihya 1 (SD1) in western Yemen.[69] Optically stimulated luminescence dating has shown that it is 55,000 years old, making it slightly later than the supposed migration from Africa. The site is located in the Wadi Surdud basin, in the foothills of the western Yemeni highlands along the Tihama coastal plain. It is some 50 km (31 miles) from the present-day Red Sea coast, but at the time of occupation, it was 120 km (75 miles) inland. Over 30,000 stone artefacts have been recovered, including blades, pointed blades, pointed flakes, and Levallois-like flakes with long unworked cutting edges. The artefacts were made mainly from rhyolite, a high-quality fine-grained material that is locally available in large quantities. Other materials used included basalt and sandstone. The manufacturing techniques used are similar to those seen at contemporary sites in southern Arabia, the Levant, the Horn of Africa and North Africa, but typologically the tools do not resemble any from these regions.

At the time of occupation, in the early stages of the mild, semi-wet Marine Isotope Stage 3, the region was semi-arid to arid. Animal remains at Shi'bat Dihya 1 include the onager, a species that lives in arid steppe environments, and is no longer found on the Arabian Peninsula. Wadi Surdud would nevertheless have been an attractive habitat, suitable for long-term human settlement. Even during arid periods, the foothills of the western Yemeni highlands provide reliable sources of water, and the region is roamed by herbivores. Similar ecological niches may also be found on the east of the Peninsula, in the foothills of the Al Hajar Mountains. It seems likely that such regions acted as refugia for human populations when climatic conditions deteriorated.

Once again, no human remains are associated with Shi'bat Dihya 1. Given their lack of obvious affinities to other contemporary industries, it is impossible to say whether the Shi'bat Dihya 1 artefacts were made by modern or archaic humans. They are well within range of Neanderthal technological capability, and indeed Levantine Neanderthal artefacts from Tabun B are said to show a higher degree of technical sophistication. Shi'bat Dihya 1 could thus represent a southern extension of the Neanderthal range.

A key question now is whether modern humans have continuously occupied parts of the Arabian Peninsula since just before the start of Eemian Interglacial, 126,000 years ago. There is still far too little evidence to provide a definitive answer. However, the later occupation levels at Jebel Faya that follow Layer C do suggest the emergence and development of local tool industries. In turn, this supports the notion of a continuous occupation by descendants of the initial migrants, rather than a re-occupation by later migratory groups.

Surviving Toba

73,000 years ago, the Earth experienced the largest volcanic event of the last two million years when a supervolcano beneath Lake Toba in northern Sumatra erupted with a Volcanic Explosivity Index intensity of 8 ('Ultra-Plinian'), ejecting 2,500 to 3,000 cubic km (600 to 720 cubic miles) of magma.[70] In comparison, historical eruptions such as Krakatau, Tambora and Pinatubo were mere firecrackers. The largest of these, Tambora in 1815, ejected just 50 cubic km (12 cubic miles) of magma. Even the last eruption of the Yellowstone Caldera, 640,000 years ago, ejected far less material.[70]

Around 800 cubic km (190 cubic miles) of ejected magma fell as ash.[71] The resulting deposits are now known as Youngest Toba Tuff (YTT). Much of the Indian subcontinent was blanketed in ash to a depth of 10 to 15 cm (4 to 6 in.). In places, drifting caused the ash to pile up to depths of up to 6m (19 ft. 8 in.). Ash also fell on the Malay Peninsula, in the Indian Ocean, the Arabian Sea, and the East China Sea.[72,73] The dispersal of ashes from Sumatra in both western and eastern directions indicates two contrasting wind directions, and suggests that the Toba eruption probably happened during the Southeast Asian summer monsoon season.[74]

The plume from the eruption was 27 to 37 km (16 to 23 miles) high, creating dense stratospheric dust and aerosol clouds. The increase in atmospheric opacity might have produced a brief pronounced volcanic winter regionally or possibly even globally. Sulphuric acid aerosols corresponding to the eruption have been detected in Greenland ice core samples. The aerosols remained present in the atmosphere for at least six years, suggesting the eruption might have involved several phases over a number of years. Subsequently, temperatures might have fallen by 3 to 5 degrees Celsius, accelerating the shift to colder conditions already underway at that time.[75,76]

Anthropologist Stanley H. Ambrose[77] has suggested that the eruption caused a bottleneck in human populations across the world. He proposed a number of scenarios, but his favoured scenario assumed modern humans had left Africa before the eruption took place. Ambrose suggests that the various ethnicities seen today arose from genetic drift among the diminished populations. The bottleneck theory is supported by a more recent work involving a series of climate model simulations in which varying amounts of sulphur dioxide were injected into the upper atmosphere. Cooling of up to 10 degrees Celsius was predicted, although recovery occurred within a few years, and none of the simulations led to the onset of glaciation. Even so, it was concluded that the effects upon humanity were severe.[78] However, other studies have suggested that the effects of the eruption were rather less deleterious. One suggested that the temperature drop was no more than 1 degree Celsius.[79] Another claimed that no evidence has been found that any animal species suffered extinction or decline, and concluded that Toba did not cause bottlenecks in human, animal or plant populations.[80]

The Indian subcontinent would certainly not have been the healthiest of places to be. Nevertheless, there is reason to suppose that modern humans were there at the time, and that they survived the catastrophe. This further complication for the standard model emerged in 2007, when artefacts were reported from India that date to the time of the eruption. They thus predate the canonical African exodus date of after 65,000 years ago by at least eight millennia, and the date of the exodus itself would of course have to have been earlier still.

The stone artefacts were recovered from both above and below a 2.55 m (8 ft. 0 in.) thick ash deposit near Jwalapuram, an archaeological study area in the Jurreru River valley of Andhra Pradesh, southern India. The date of the eruption is known with reasonable accuracy, so we can be fairly confident about the age of the artefacts. The two sets of artefacts have enough in common to suggest that their makers survived the catastrophe. Clearly the artefacts were made by humans, but were they modern humans? Tools included blades, end scrapers and burins, together with cores from which blades had been struck. One piece of red ochre, showing signs of use, was also found. The tools and tool-making technology bore a closer resemblance to African Middle Stone Age industries such as Howieson's Poort than to the prepared-core industries typical of the Eurasian Middle Palaeolithic. This, together with the behavioural flexibility needed to survive the eruption and its aftermath, suggests that modern humans were already in India at the time of the eruption – and that at least some of them lived through it.[81,82] One problem, shared with the various Arabian artefacts, is the lack of associated human remains, and some have expressed scepticism that modern humans were responsible for the Jurreru artefacts.[31]

A pre-Toba exit from Africa can be just about accommodated within the range of the genetic dates given for a migration from Africa, albeit at the upper end. A number of estimates have also been obtained for the dates of the earliest Indian-specific branches of the mitochondrial haplogroup M: 73,000 years ago does lie within the range of some of these,[83,49,84] but others are more recent.[85,43] However, it is possible that estimates of mitochondrial haplogroup ages obtained from present-day populations do not tell the full story about earlier Late Pleistocene populations due to sampling problems, the small size of the original populations, and population increases and replacements during the later stages of the Late Pleistocene and the Holocene.[82]

Towards a new model

The question now, of course, is how can we reconcile the emerging picture with the single Out of Africa model, as derived from genetic data? The simplest answer is to suppose that the early Levantine and Arabian migrants – and possibly the Jwalapuram people as well – all died out. One could even suppose that Shi'bat Dihya 1 is evidence that relict populations from Eemian persisted at inland locations and did not take part in the exodus. Perhaps the beachcombers passed by along the coast without even being aware of their existence.

Another possibility is that there is something wrong with the genetic methods upon which the entire Out of Africa 2 edifice rests. Maybe the dates are being distorted by a systematic factor that nobody has taken into account. Perhaps it is simply unrealistic to draw inferences from present-day populations about migrations that took place many tens of millennia ago.

A more balanced position would be to view Out of Africa 2 as not so much incorrect as incomplete. Archaeologists Robin Dennell and Michael Petraglia[86] note that when proposed it was a useful model for interpreting a very small amount of data. The data, though still sparse, is now much improved. They suggest that there are benefits to be gained from widening the range of possible hypotheses. A good place to start is with two components of the southern coastal Out of Africa 2 scenario that are not necessarily invalidated by the new data.

The first of these is the expansion of mitochondrial haplogroup L3. There is strong evidence to support an origin for this haplogroup between 70,000 and 85,000 years ago, with a subsequent expansion of branches both inside and outside of Africa. The second is the coastal express train scenario. Regardless of its exact point of departure or whether it was the first dispersal, this scenario provides a parsimonious explanation for the presence of modern humans in Australia before they reached Europe, as indicated by fossil, archaeological and genetic evidence.

The first departure from the standard model is to suppose that from the Eemian Interglacial onwards, modern humans in East Africa extended their range into the Arabian Peninsula, and were as widespread there as in East Africa. In the early stages of the L3 expansion, prior to the onset of the cold Marine Isotope Stage 4, 74,000 years ago, early L3 lineages were distributed across both East Africa and Arabia. It is probable that mitochondrial lineages other than L3 were also present in smaller amounts in Arabia, associated with groups that had been living in the region since the Eemian. Conceivably, L3 arose in Arabia rather than East Africa, but it is not necessary to suppose that it did.

With the shift to cold, arid climatic conditions at the start of Marine Isotope Stage 4, human groups might have retreated to the three ecological refugia, as proposed by Jeffrey Rose above. Rose[64] suggests that in addition, hunter-gatherers began to increasingly rely on coastal resources rather than big- and medium-game hunting in the Arabian interior. This would have left a situation where human groups were largely concentrated in three isolated refugia, including the expanded coastal oasis of the Persian Gulf.

It is likely that the Persian Gulf refugium attracted Neanderthals as well as modern humans. If it is the case that modern humans interbred with Neanderthals shortly after leaving Africa, and if the Persian Gulf refugium model is correct, then Neanderthals would have moved south from the Levant, encountering modern populations in the north of the refugium.[87] As we have seen, Shi'bat Dihya 1 could represent a southern extension of the Neanderthal range, and if so, it is unlikely to have been the only one.

After this encounter, it can be envisaged that a modern population of beachcombers in the north of the refugium began to expand along the coastline of Iran, Pakistan, India, and eastwards. The group – from which the world's current non-African population is largely descended – was initially small enough for genetic drift to eliminate all mitochondrial lineages except for two emerging branches of the dominant L3 haplogroup. These eventually became M, N, and subsequently R. Early branches of L3 continued to exist in all three Arabian refugia, but they were probably erased by later population bottlenecks and/or more recent population movements.[64]

The timescale for these events is after the onset of cold, arid conditions, 74,000 years ago, making it a borderline case as to whether the descendants of this group had reached India before the Toba eruption even if the genetic dates can be stretched to accommodate the possibility. If not, perhaps the Jurreru people descend from an earlier migration, either from Arabia or the Levant. Even if they survived the Toba eruption, the mitochondrial genomes of these and other early Eurasian populations of modern humans might subsequently have been overwhelmed by later migrations and lost to genetic drift so that no trace of it remains in present-day populations. That does not necessarily mean that the Jurreru people themselves died out: it is entirely possible that portions of their nuclear genome survive, along with those of other possible early migrants.[88] Being inherited from both parents, these would have been less susceptible to the effects of genetic drift than the mitochondrial lineages. Whether or not this is actually the case we don't yet know.

The scenario outlined here is very unlikely to represent the complete picture, if indeed subsequent discoveries do not show it to be partly or wholly incorrect. For now, though, it provides as good a framework as any to accommodate our growing body of knowledge about this crucial period in human history.

13: Two waves

East of India

Beyond India and Bangladesh, beachcombers moving along the rim of the Indian Ocean would find themselves in the region known today as Southeast Asia, comprising the countries east of India and south of China. In addition to the Asian mainland, the region includes Island Southeast Asia, a series of archipelagos to the east and southeast of the mainland. These comprise around 25,000 islands, including Borneo, Sumatra, Java, Bali and the Philippines. Many of these islands, together with the Malay Peninsula, are part of the Sunda shelf, an extension of the continental shelf of Southeast Asia. During times of low sea levels, they all become part of a large peninsular region known as Sundaland.

At such times, the adjacent Sahul continental shelf forms a greater Australian landmass including Australia, Tasmania and New Guinea. Between the two is an archipelago of deep-water islands that never become a part of either landmass. They are known collectively as Wallacea after Darwin's rival Alfred Russel Wallace, and include Lombok, Sumbawa, Komodo, Flores, Sumba and Timor. The Philippines and the Melanesian islands east of New Guinea also remain insular at these times. Nevertheless, the sea crossings required to reach all of these places are greatly reduced in length.

Sea levels began to drop sharply 70,000 years ago, reaching a minimum 65,000 years ago and then recovering sharply 59,000 years ago, as the cold of Marine Isotope Stage 4 gave way to the warmer conditions of Marine Isotope Stage 3.[1] A date obtained from genetic data of 62,000 to 75,000 years ago suggests that it was probably during the low sea level window that the first of two waves of modern human settlers arrived in the region.[2] They established themselves in Sundaland, and island-hopped to the Philippines and Sahul – but at least one species of archaic humans were already in the region. As we saw in Chapter 8, the migrants encountered and interbred with the Denisovans, possibly 'importing' immune system-enhancing genes in the process. It is also possible that the Denisovans were not the only late surviving archaic people in East Asia.

The Red Deer Cave People

The complexity of the human evolutionary history of East Asia was further underlined by a discovery announced less than two years after that of the Denisovans. Human remains outside the range of variation of early East Asian *Homo sapiens* were reported from two sites in southwest China: Longlin Cave in Guangxi Province, and Maludong ('Red Deer Cave') in Yunnan Province.[3] Radiocarbon dating has yielded ages of 11,500 and 14,000 years old respectively for the two sites, which are located 300 km (185 miles) apart. The hominins, popularly reported as the Red Deer Cave people, are believed to represent a single population. The remains include two partial skulls that present a mixture of modern and archaic features, together with some that appear to be unique. Overall, the Red Deer Cave people are very robust. The cheek bones are broad and flared sideways, giving the skulls a strong facial resemblance to Darth Vader. The browridges are conspicuous and the chin is less prominent than that of a modern human.

Like the Denisovans, the remains may represent a late surviving archaic population. However, there is another possibility. A considerable degree of variability has been found in the braincase shape of early modern humans in Africa, possibly as a result of populations becoming isolated from one another for extended periods.[4] It is possible that the Red Deer Cave people represent a previously-unknown human migration from Africa to East Asia that might or might not have contributed to the genetic makeup of the region's present-day populations. The extraction of ancient DNA from the remains would undoubtedly shed more light on the matter, but attempts have so far proved unsuccessful.

Hog-roasts in Sundaland

The first discovery of modern human fossil remains in this vast region was made in Malaysian Borneo at the Niah Caves, a complex of large limestone caverns set in the forested Niah National Park 16 km (10 miles) from the north coast of Sarawak. The West Mouth entrance to the main cave, Niah Great Cave, has indications of sporadic human presence during the Late Pleistocene. Subsequently, during the Neolithic period from 3000 to 500 BC, the caves were used as a burial ground. During the 1950s and 1960s, the Sarawak Museum carried out a series of archaeological excavations of the caves under the direction of its curator, British anthropologist Tom Harrisson and his wife Barbara. Harrisson was one of the creators of the Mass Observation social research project that began in 1937 in the United Kingdom with the aim of recording everyday British life through untrained volunteer observers. During World War II, he served in the Army Reconnaissance Corps and in 1945 he was parachuted into Borneo on special operations behind Japanese lines. He took up his post at the museum in 1947 and, inspired by Eugene Dubois' 'Java Man', began excavations in search of 'Borneo Man'.[5,6]

In 1958, what became known as Deep Skull was discovered in a deep trench known as 'Hell' because of the hot, humid conditions. The Deep Skull was originally reported to be 40,000 years old; a date obtained by the then new technique of radiocarbon dating. The discovery attracted considerable interest at the time as it was not then thought that modern humans had been in the region so early. Unfortunately, Harrisson never wrote up a full report on the site, and in 2000 the Niah Caves Project was set up to resolve lingering questions from the original excavations. A major objective was to attempt to confirm the age of Deep Skull.[6] As a result of this work, the skull was found to be slightly younger at 35,000 years old.[5] It is thought to have belonged to a young adult aged from 20 to 30 years old, probably female.[7]

Subsequent finds of modern human remains have included a fragmented left thigh bone from an individual aged from 18 to 25 years old, and a fragment of a right shin bone. In addition, 27 skull fragments from the earlier excavations were discovered at the Museum's archives in 2005. The fragments were not found in the Hell trench itself, but they came from the same geological layers. Red pigment, found on the interior surface of three of the fragments, turned out not to be ochre but a plant product, possibly a tree resin.[5]

The Niah Caves Project also considered animal remains found in the Hell trench in layers, which dated over a lengthy period from 45,000 to 33,000 years ago. These have yielded insight into the diet of the cave's inhabitants and included abundant pig remains. In present-day Borneo, 'pig booms' occur every few years in response to flowering and fruiting of locally-abundant tropical *Dipterocarp* trees. These in turn are triggered by the Southern hemisphere oscillations of the El Nino weather phenomenon. On such occasions, pig populations may increase tenfold, and it is possible that hunter-gather groups converged on the region to take advantage of this bounty. The whole or partial carcasses of pigs and other animal were brought to the cave for butchery, and there is evidence of worked bone pieces being used for this purpose. However, these implements were crudely made and were probably manufactured *in situ* for single use.[5]

For a long time, the Deep Skull was the earliest definite evidence for modern humans in Southeast Asia, although it is far more recent than the arrival dates suggested by genetic studies. However, uranium series and electron spin resonance dates of some recent fossil discoveries are more consistent with the genetic dates. Currently the oldest is the partial skull found at Tam Pa Ling ('Cave of the Monkeys') in the Huà Pan Province of Laos, which could be as old 63,000 years. Even its minimum age of 46,000 years would make it significantly older than the Deep Skull.[8]

Two early fossil human finds have been reported from the Philippines. The first is a shin bone found with other human remains at Tabon Cave on the island of Palawan, in the Philippines, which dates from 37,000 to 58,000 years old.[9] The other find is a human third metatarsal from Callao Cave in northern Luzon, which predates both the Tam Pa Ling and Tabon Cave finds and has been dated to 67,000 years old. The find indicates that humans could make sea crossings at this time, but it is not certain that this fossil represents a modern human. The bone is gracile, suggestive of a Filipino Negrito, but it is also within the range of *Homo habilis* and of *Homo floresiensis* – the 'hobbit people' of Flores, which lies over 2,500 km (1,500 miles) to the south.[10] This raises many interesting possibilities, but is it is probably too soon to jump to any conclusions.

Sulawesi cave art

As we shall see in Chapter 14, the arrival of modern humans in Europe was marked by the appearance in the archaeological record of a sophisticated artistic tradition, which includes both portable art objects and cave art. Archaeologists have long been puzzled by an apparent lack of antecedents for this artwork, either in Africa or along early migration routes. It is difficult to see how a seemingly mature artistic tradition could arise *de novo* in Upper Palaeolithic Europe – but if the 40,000-year-old cave paintings at sites such as Altamira and El Castillo really were the earliest cave art anywhere in the world, this would have to have been the case.

In the 1950s, rock art was reported from limestone caves in the Maros and Pangkep regions of the island of Sulawesi, Indonesia. Over 90 rock art sites are known, which have been extensively studied by Indonesian scholars and appear to belong two distinct periods. The art of the earlier period comprises hand stencils produced by spraying pigment over hands pressed against rock surface, together with a smaller number of large, naturalistic paintings of large Sulawesi mammals, including the anoa (a small bovid), the Celebes warty pig and the babirusa (a member of the pig family). The artwork of the later period is typified by small anthropomorphic depictions and a wide range of geometric signs, typically drawn using a black pigment. This later period has been associated with Austronesian migrants on stylistic grounds, and is thought to be no more than a few thousand years old.

The art of the earlier period, though much older than that of the later period, was still thought to be less than 10,000 years old. However, recently-reported uranium series dates obtained for 14 paintings (12 hand stencils and two animal paintings) located at seven different cave sites indicate that it is much older. The oldest hand stencil is at least 39,900 years old and the oldest animal painting is at least 35,700 years old. The most recent hand stencil dates to no earlier than 27,200 years ago, suggesting a tradition that endured for at least 13,000 years – comparable to the duration of the European cave painting era.[11]

That contemporary traditions of cave art occurred in two regions as far apart as Europe and Indonesia implies either independent development or a common origin dating much further back in time. If the latter was the case, it is possible that even earlier examples of cave art still await discovery.

Dating the first Australians

It is probable that the first humans to reach the Sahul continent did so after settlers had been island-hopping across the Wallacean archipelago for some time, and had established a chain of colonies that stretched back to the Asian mainland. This process of colonisation probably required not only a founding population, but also continued contact with parent communities and other outside groups in order to avoid the problems of inbreeding and unbalanced sex ratios. To build, provision, and navigate vessels capable of making frequent voyages between the various islands implies that the colonists possessed an effective boat-building technology.[12] Such technology must by then have been well established; even without David Bulbeck's estuarine theory, it is likely the coastal migrants needed boats to ford rivers or extend coastal foraging areas.[13]

There are two main routes by which it is possible to island hop from Sundaland to Sahul: an eastern route via Maluku to what is now New Guinea, and a southern route via Timor to Arnhem Land in the Northern Territory, Australia. Either route requires at least eight to seventeen separate crossings, including at least three of 30 km (18 miles) or more and one of 70 km (44 miles) or more.[14,12] At the mid-point of such a voyage, even on a clear day, the land in both directions would be below the horizon – a daunting prospect even if you know that there is land where you are going. Much later, the Polynesians would learn to recognise characteristic cloud formations that betray the presence of land, and possibly this is how the colonists located islands that lay over the horizon.

The date of the first settlement of Australia and New Guinea has been the subject of a long-running debate. Some argue for a 'long chronology' of 60,000 years or more; others for a 'short chronology' of around 40,000 years. Even the more recent figure is pushing the limits of radiocarbon dating, but dates obtained by other methods have proved controversial. The earliest site in the New Guinea highlands has been dated to between 49,000 and 44,000 years old[15] and a majority now agree that people were present on the Sahul continent at least 45,000 years ago.

What are Australia's oldest-known human remains were found at Lake Mungo, one of a series of 19 dried up lakes making up the Willandra Lakes system. The Willandra Lakes Region is a World Heritage Site that covers 2,400 sq. km (925 sq. miles) in southwest New South Wales, about 1,000 km (620 miles) west of Sydney. The water levels in the lakes remained high until 45,000 years ago and then began to decline. They dried up completely 22,000 years ago and have remained dry ever since.[16]

The remains include the world's oldest cremation and the world's oldest ritual ochre burial. The burnt human remains of two individuals, Mungo 1 and Mungo 2 (or WLH 1 and 2), were discovered in 1969 by archaeologist Jim Bowler. The finds, reconstructed in the lab by anthropologist Alan Thorne, comprise about 25 percent of a lightly built female skeleton – informally known as 'Mungo Lady' – and a few fragments of a second individual. In 1974, Bowler discovered a full skeleton, Mungo 3 (WLH 3), within the same geological stratum, only 450 m (1,500 ft.) from the cremation site. He and Thorne excavated the remains, which had been covered in ochre. Mungo 3 is again lightly built, but male, and is known inevitably as Mungo Man. In 1992, Mungo Lady was returned into the keeping of local Aboriginal groups, though in practice her remains are kept under lock and key at the Mungo National Park museum.[17,6]

The Lake Mungo remains were initially thought to be about 30,000 years old on the basis of radiocarbon dating. More recently, Thorne[18] used electron spin resonance and uranium series techniques on Mungo 3, and optically stimulated luminescence on sand grains from sediments below the level of remains. He obtained a date of 62,000 years old. These findings were subsequently challenged by Bowler and his colleagues,[17] who noted that the sand grains used in Thorne's studies had been collected from sediments 300 m (1,000 ft.) from the burial. Using sediment samples from a more secure context, they obtained an age of 42,000 years for both Mungo 1 and Mungo 3. Dates were also obtained for silcrete artefacts that were found below the burial layers. These provide the earliest evidence for human occupation at the site, and were claimed to be no older than between 46,000 and 50,000 years.

Also controversial is the claim that mitochondrial DNA recovered from Mungo 3 belongs to a haplogroup no longer present in the human population, and that it diverged from the mitochondrial DNA sequences of living humans before the time of Mitochondrial Eve.[19] The claim has been disputed because, it is argued, the warm climate prevalent at Lake Mungo caused degradation of the DNA to occur.[20]

It is a similar picture at other key sites in Australian and New Guinea where the long chronologists and short chronologists continue to battle it out. In addition to Lake Mungo, the long chronologists base their case around the sites of Nauwalabila and Malakunanja in the Northern Territory, Devil's Lair in Western Australia and Huon Peninsula in Papua New Guinea. The Nauwalabila I and Malakunaja II rock shelters in Kakadu National Park, Arnhem Land, Northern Territory have yielded a number of stone artefacts, and a series of studies using thermoluminescence and optically stimulated luminescence dating of sand surrounding these artefacts have suggested that they are between 50,000 and 60,000 years old.[21,22,23] However, short chronologists are sceptical and argue that termite activity could have affected the results by bringing sand grains to the surface and shifting artefacts downwards. They believe that the sites are no more than 42,000 to 45,000 years old, and that there is no good evidence for a human presence in Australia much before this date.[24,25] Uncertainty over much of the earliest data stems from questions over the reliability of the archaeological context of artefacts rather than the dating technologies used.[26,27]

It should be noted that the original colonists in all probability inhabited coastal sites that were later submerged as sea levels rose. It is only to be expected that inland sites would show more recent dates. Even if the short chronologists are right about the dating of currently-known sites, there are no grounds for ruling out an earlier arrival. Overall, we have almost no knowledge of where people first reached the Sahul coast, nor do we know how long it took for people to subsequently spread from presumed landing sites in the north of Australia to sites like Lake Mungo in the southeast. If, however, we accept that the latter was settled at least 46,000 years ago, even a conservative estimate would suggest that humans reached Australia at least 50,000 years ago.[27]

Just one migration

Another bone of contention over the years has been the number of migrations into Australia. Differences in body size and skin colour among various present-day Aboriginal populations, and the supposed presence of both 'gracile' and 'robust' types in the fossil record has been taken by some to imply that there were at least two colonisation events. Mungo Lady and Mungo Man are slightly-built but fully modern in appearance, with a rounded skull, reduced browridges and a flat face lying below the forehead. These features are shared with other, less-complete specimens from Willandra Lakes, and also a skull from Keilor, Melbourne. However, other remains have been found that are more robust in appearance, with large jaws and teeth, thick skull bones, prominent continuous browridges and flat, receding foreheads. These 'robust' people have been found at Kow Swamp, which was once a lake on the margin of the floodplain of the Murray River in northern Victoria, and at Coobool Creek in New South Wales. A robust skull, WLH 50, has also been found at Willandra Lakes.

The Kow Swamp people are more recent than Mungo Lady and Mungo Man, although there is again a discrepancy between dates obtained from radiocarbon and optical dating. Radiocarbon dating of the Kow Swamp people has yielded an age range of 9,000 to 15,000 years, but optically stimulated luminescence suggests they are older and lived between 19,000 and 22,000 years ago, during the Last

Glacial Maximum. This earlier date seems the likelier, as shoreline silt in which most of the Kow Swamp people were interred was deposited by high lake levels between 26,000 and 19,000 years ago.[28]

Alan Thorne[29] believes that the gracile and robust forms represent two distinct types and that Australia was colonised by two distinct migration episodes. First came the 'gracile populations', from China and then, rather later, the 'robust populations' from Indonesia. The latter, he argued, have features that are characteristic of and represent continuity with Java *Homo erectus*. Thorne's model was essentially an updated version of an earlier proposal by the American anthropologist Joseph Birdsell,[30] who studied Aboriginal Australians in different parts of the country and noted variations in height build and skin colour. Birdsell ascribed the differences to three distinct races that had populated Australia at different times. However, genetic evidence fails to support either the Birdsell or the Thorne proposals.

Mitochondrial DNA isolated from 'robust' specimens at Kow Swamp and more recent 'gracile' specimens from Willandra Lakes have been found to share a common origin with that of the present-day Aboriginal Australians, ruling out differing origins.[19] Genetic studies of living populations suggest that there was a single founding migration around 58,000 years ago, followed by a lengthy period of isolation from the rest of the world. Nearly all Aboriginal Australian mitochondrial lineages are either unique to Australia or shared only with New Guineans and Melanesians. The lineages do not share a common ancestor with any Asian lineage more recent than the time of the initial dispersal along the rim of the Indian Ocean.[31] That Aboriginal Australians and New Guineans have nearly identical proportions of Denisovan genetic material also suggests a single common origin for the two populations.[32]

However, the high degree of genetic diversity found in the present-day Aboriginal populations of Australia and New Guinea suggests that the founding population was relatively large, probably comprising several thousand individuals. Rather than a single large group, it is possible that the first Australians arrived in smaller groups spread over the course of a few generations.[33,34]

These results firmly suggest that the Willandra and Kow Swamp populations are descended from the same founding group, leaving us to look elsewhere for an explanation of the differences between the two. Suggestions put forward have involved cultural, evolutionary and environmental factors. Firstly, it is possible that the archaic-looking flattened receding foreheads of the Kow Swamp people were artificially deformed by a cultural practice that involved swaddling from birth. Unable to expand in one direction, the brain is forced to grow in a different direction in order to reach full size. Skull growth modifies in order to accommodate it, resulting in a radically different skull shape. The practice was the past performed in many parts of the world, including France, South America and the Pacific islands (although it is not known among current Aboriginal Australian populations). In the 1980s, anthropologist Peter Brown compared artificially-deformed skulls from the Melanesian island of Arawe with the Kow Swamp crania. He was able to show that the flat receding foreheads observed in the latter were also the result of intentional deformation.[35,27]

Brown was not able to explain all the Kow Swamp features said to be shared with *Homo erectus*, including the well-developed browridges, large molars and premolars and large robust lower jaws. However, the differences between the Kow Swamp people and other Pleistocene humans in Australia emerged as full glacial conditions developed. The robust form was probably an evolutionary response to the harsh conditions by a population isolated in a similar manner to the Khoisan during the African megadrought episodes (see Chapter 10).[28]

That variations in body size and form for a single, geographically-widespread species can be driven by climate has been understood since the nineteenth century. Bergmann's Rule, published in 1847 by German biologist Christian Bergmann, states that in the warmer part of the species' range, populations will be smaller-bodied than those living in colder regions. Allen's Rule, published in 1877 by American zoologist Joel Asaph Allen, states that the populations living in warmer regions will be longer-limbed than those living in colder regions.[36] Taken together, these rules predict people will be short and stocky during glacial periods, and longer-limbed and more gracile during warmer periods.

In addition, local conditions might have played a part. It has been noted that present-day Aboriginal populations living in desert conditions are more slightly-built than those living in the Murray Valley. This pattern might also have existed in the Pleistocene, with the early Lake Mungo form being an adaptation to an arid environment, and the Kow Swamp form reflecting a temperate riverine environment. It is likely that the differences between the Lake Mungo and Kow Swamp populations can be explained in terms of a combination of these factors. In conclusion, then, the evidence suggests that Australia was settled just once, at least 50,000 years ago. Over time, the descendants of the original founding population adapted to a wide range of habitats, producing the physical diversity seen among Aboriginal Australians today.[27]

Into the interior

Once they reached the Sahul coast, the settlers probably maintained a beachcomber lifestyle and until the 1980s, it was widely believed that this had persisted until the end of the last Ice Age 11,600 years ago, when rising sea levels drowned coastal plains and drove foragers inland. At that time, few inland sites were known, although settlers must surely have occupied sites in the Australian interior before they reached Lake Mungo. Other early inland sites include Puritjarra, a large rock shelter in Cleland Hills, Northern Territory, close to a large, reliable source of water at Murantji Rockhole, and first occupied 39,000 years ago.[27]

Two complimentary models have been proposed to describe how the Australian interior was originally settled. The first is a 'refuge, corridor and barrier' model, proposed by Australian anthropologist Peter Veth.[37] Veth suggests that less marginal habitats with reliable water supplies were occupied first, and served as refuges during adverse climatic periods. Settlers favoured piedmont/montane uplands and riverine/gorge systems. Such locations provided reliable water sources, and were less sensitive to climate change. The settlers avoided sand-ridge deserts such as the Great Sandy Desert, the Great Victoria Desert, and the Simpson Desert. The deserts were resource-poor, lacked reliable sources of water, and acted as 'barriers' to hunter-gatherers. However, during times of wetter climate, 'corridors' between the refuges became habitable, and were intermittently occupied.

Limited occupation of sand-ridge desert occurred after 25,000 years ago, but the only evidence of earlier human activities in such regions comes from sites located near montane environments, where it is likely the hunter-gatherers were based. This implies that the hunter-gatherers of this time lacked a settlement system like that of twentieth century Aboriginal Australians in the sandy deserts. The latter, though, rely on an intimate knowledge of landscapes and long-distance social and reciprocal exchange networks. The initial colonisation of inland Australia was accomplished by people who had none of these things. Accordingly, their economy must have differed from that of Aboriginal Australians in the historic period.[27]

The 'desert transformation' model was put forward by archaeologists Peter Hiscock and Lynley Wallis.[38,27] It proposed that the interior was occupied during a period of higher rainfall, more abundant surface water and food sources. Only later did climate change transform these regions into arid desert. In other words, hunter-gatherers did not move into a desert; the desert came to them, forcing them to adapt to the more extreme conditions. In many desert regions, seasonal floods and large standing bodies of water were common until about 40,000 to 45,000 years ago. These regions, though they were still deserts, were more hospitable than today because of the presence of these large permanent bodies of water.[27]

The migration of hunter-gatherers into unfamiliar, relatively well-watered inland regions prior to 40,000 years ago was probably the basis for later survival as conditions deteriorated. Following the initial settlement of the interior, rainfall diminished and permanent surface water became scarce. Though access to reliable sources of water remained crucial, people were able to adjust to the harsher conditions because by that time they had local knowledge, and social networks had been established. Furthermore, the more desert-focused lifestyle now enabled hunter-gatherers to settle even harsher environments that they had previously shunned.[27]

A trend to cold, dry climates began about 45,000 years ago and intensified rapidly after 30,000 years ago. During the Last Glacial Maximum from 26,500 to 19,000 years ago, rainfall dropped to about half of today's levels, lakes dried up and deserts expanded. Upland areas became cold, dry and treeless. Reduced vegetation cover triggered a phase of sand-dune building and intense dust storms. Overall, conditions became harsher than at any time since the arrival of humans in Australia.[27]

Many sites were abandoned during the Last Glacial Maximum, but human presence continued at inland refugia in upland regions with water sources charged by aquifers, and at sites like Colless Creek in Lawn Hill Gorge, Queensland, where water remained available all the year round. People confined their activities to small and better-watered parts, abandoning the more arid regions. There was a shift to using locally-sourced stone and ochre in preference to higher-quality but more distant materials.[38]

That local areas and entire regions were abandoned during the Last Glacial Maximum is an indication of how precarious existence was during the Pleistocene. It is possible that some populations died out entirely. Life remained possible within the refugia, but it is likely that populations there came under considerable pressure from outsiders forced to abandon their own territories. We can only speculate on the humanitarian crisis the Last Glacial Maximum must have triggered across much of Australia.

The second wave

While some groups of settlers were island-hopping their way to what are now New Guinea and Australia, many others presumably continued with the beachcomber habit that had by now been a way of life for many millennia. What these people apparently did not do is participate in the settlement of East Asia, at least not in large numbers. This unexpected conclusion was suggested by a genetic study carried out in 2011.[2] Researchers obtained permission to extract and sequence genetic material from a lock of hair from an Aboriginal Australian man who died early in the last century. The reason was to overcome the problems arising from recent intermarriage between Europeans and Aboriginal Australians. Principal component analysis of the whole genome confirmed, not unexpectedly, that Aboriginal Australians were closely related to New Guineans. The significant discovery came when researchers compared the genome to those of Han Chinese, Europeans and Africans. They found that Han are more closely related to Europeans than they are to Aboriginal Australians. The split between the Han and Australian populations occurred 62,000 to 75,000 years ago; but the European and Han populations did not separate until 25,000 to 38,000 years ago. The latter date range must be an underestimate, because as we have seen, modern humans were in Europe around 46,000 years ago. This date is nevertheless long after the Han/Australian split.

If Australia and East Asia were settled by offshoots of the same migration, one would expect on geographical grounds for a Han/Australia split to occur in Southeast Asia, at some time after the migrants there had parted company with those who would go on to colonise Europe. That the reverse is true implies that Australia was settled by a first wave of migrants, and East Asia was not settled until rather later, and by a second wave of migrants. On the other hand, the study did find that the non-African groups were equally distant in their relatedness to Africans, confirming that both migratory waves derived ultimately from the same small founder population. What should we make of this?

Mitochondrial genetic diversity data suggests that by 52,000 years ago, the populations of South and Southeast Asia had increased fivefold since the first wave of colonisation,[39] so it is likely that by that time population pressures were triggering a fresh round of migrations. Some groups migrated towards Europe, while others retraced the route of the original beachcombers eastwards. Archaeological evidence suggests that by 43,000 years ago, modern humans had also begun to exploit the rich resources of what American biologist Dale Guthrie has termed the Mammoth Steppe.

The Mammoth Steppe

Guthrie[40] suggests that modern humans adapted to the arid, cold and windy conditions of the Eurasian Steppe, a series of ecoregions that stretch from the Great Hungarian Plain to Mongolia. In historical times, the overland trade routes of the Silk Road ran through it, connecting Europe to India and China. In Palaeolithic times, the region supported herds of large herbivores, including mammoths, woolly rhinos, wild horses, reindeer, musk-oxen and saiga antelopes. At that time, the steppe covered much of northern Eurasia; the southern limit roughly coincided with the 35th Parallel, the Himalayas and the Tibetan plateau. The Mammoth Steppe's warmer southern fringes of Xinjiang, Mongolia and the Lake Baikal region of Siberia are regions that now contain large expanses of desert. However, 40,000 to 50,000 years ago, these regions offered limitless hunting opportunities to hunter-gatherers who were able to adapt to the hostile conditions – and indeed overcome considerable problems of getting there at all.[14]

Groups trying to reach the steppe from the south faced major obstacles in the form of mountains and deserts that stretch from Afghanistan to Chengdu in China. Mobile hunter-gatherers always need to follow three simple rules: stay near reliable sources of water, follow the movements of herd animals, and avoid deserts and mountains. By following rivers and exploiting their resources, these criteria can be met. With this in mind, Stephen Oppenheimer[14] suggested that the Mammoth Steppe and East Asia were colonised in a pincer movement from the Indian subcontinent, Southeast Asia and China. Although Oppenheimer was thinking in terms of a single wave of migrants from Africa, there is no reason why his scenario would not be applicable to a second wave, occurring long after the settlement of Australia.

As we have seen, it is likely that settlers used river systems to penetrate into the heartland of South Asia. Oppenheimer believes that these also provided access to the Mammoth Steppe. The Indus may be followed up to the eastern and of the Khyber Pass and round the western side of the Himalayas. From there, settlers could move northeast to the Russian Altai, and then east through southern Siberia via a series of lakes and waterways, passing north of Sinkiang and Mongolia, eventually reaching the Lake Baikal region. This route was passable during the milder climatic phases from 50,000 to 30,000 years ago, when it consisted of grassland and open woodland. Settlers could also have followed the Ganges-Brahmaputra, Salween, Mekong and Yangtze Rivers northwards to their sources in Tibet, this time skirting the eastern side of the Himalayas. Finally, any groups who moved north along the coast from Southeast Asia to northern China could then move inland along the future Silk Road to reach Mongolia, Sinkiang and southern Siberia.

Archaeological evidence does point to an early occupation of the Mammoth Steppe. At the site of Kara-Bom in the Russian Altai, typical Upper Palaeolithic artefacts, 43,000 years old, have been recovered, including end scrapers and retouched blades and bladelets. These blade-based industries overlay earlier Levallois-dominated Middle Palaeolithic layers that go back as far as 62,000 to 72,000 years ago. A key issue is whether or not the Upper Palaeolithic industries there are indigenous. Did they arise from the earlier Middle Palaeolithic industries, as some believe, or were they are intrusive, with modern humans replacing an earlier and presumably archaic population? If the indigenous picture is correct, the implication is that modern humans were in the Altai region long before 43,000 years ago. Unfortunately, no fossil remains have been found with any of the Middle Palaeolithic artefacts.[41,42]

Upper Palaeolithic technology subsequently spread across southern Siberia, reaching Makarovo on the western side of Lake Baikal 39,000 years ago, and Varvarina Gora and Tolbaga on the eastern side of Lake Baikal 35,000 to 30,000 years ago. Sites are mainly concentrated in the Altai Mountains and the Trans-Baikal region to the east of Lake Baikal, but the presence of some sites in the Yenisei, Angara and Upper Lena River basins suggest an occupation of the whole southern Siberia at this time.[43] Meanwhile, groups migrating along the coast from Southeast Asia had reached northeastern Russia by 38,000 years ago and Japan by 37,000 years ago.[44] If one accepts that the Upper Palaeolithic artefacts at Kara-Bom represent the earliest presence of modern humans in Siberia, then this pattern is consistent with Oppenheimer's view of a pincer movement onto the Mammoth Steppe.

At first, settlers did not venture above latitudes of 55°N,[45] but by around 30,000 years ago they had apparently learned how to live in the extreme conditions of the Russian Arctic. The Yana Rhinoceros Horn site is located along the Lower Yana River and lies at 71°N, well above the Arctic Circle. Artefacts recovered at this site include spear foreshafts made from rhinoceros and mammoth horn, and a wide variety of tools and flakes.[46] Subsequently, during the Last Glacial Maximum, the expansion slowed and perhaps stalled. Based on a scarcity of sites, it appears that Northeast Asia had only a sparse human presence during that time.[45,47]

Unfortunately, there are very few human remains from this period. The earliest found so far are the 45,000-year-old left thighbone found near Ust'-Ishim in western Siberia in 2008,[48] and remains from two Chinese sites: the 39,000 to 42,000-year-old Tianyuan 1 remains from Tianyuan Cave, Zhoukoudian,[49] and the 38,500 to 44,000-year-old skull fragments from Laibin in central China.[50] These apart, no other securely-dated and undisputedly-modern human remains from East Asia are more than 30,000 years old.[51] To further investigate the initial settlement of the Mammoth Steppe and East Asia, we must consider the genetic evidence.

The big picture, as indicated by mitochondrial genetic diversity data, is that a population expansion began in Central and Northern Asia about 49,000 years ago,[39] a result that is consistent with the idea that people were exploiting the Mammoth Steppe. Mitochondrial data also allows us to examine the process in more detail. The principle mitochondrial haplogroups in East Asia and Siberia are C, D, E, G and Z (daughters of M); A, X and Y (daughters of N); and B and F (daughters of R). These may be thought of as the 'limbs and boughs' of the M, N and R 'trunks', and smaller subgroups (B4b1, M8a, Y1, etc.) as 'twigs' on the mitochondrial 'tree'.[52] A northward expansion from Southeast Asia was indicated by even the earliest studies, which found that the greatest mitochondrial genetic diversity (and hence age) occurs in Vietnam.[53] More recent studies suggest a similar picture: the oldest branches are M7, F and B. All three are around 50,000 years old,[54] and originated in Southeast Asia or southern China.[55,52]

However, the picture is more complex than a simple northward migration or migrations. There is a considerable variation in the frequency at which different mitochondrial haplogroups occur in different places: for example A, C, D, G, Y and Z are the main northern haplogroups; but in the south, C, Y and Z are rare, and B and F predominate. 'Twigs' are highly localised, for example Y1 is restricted to Northeast Asian populations, and the indigenous Ainu people of the northern Japan islands. This latter finding is consistent with archaeological evidence for a migration route between the two.[52] Haplogroups C and Z are thought to be sister groups, deriving from a common ancestor,

CZ, that in turn derived from a haplogroup denoted M8.[55] Stephen Oppenheimer[14] believes that the origin of the M8/CZ complex is to be found on the Indian subcontinent, and that these were the people who reached the Russian Altai, 43,000 years ago before moving east onto the Mammoth Steppe.

The Y-chromosomal evidence broadly supports the pincer movement model. Early studies indicated an initial colonisation of Southeast Asia, followed by a northwards migration. It was found that Y-chromosomal genetic diversity is at its highest in Southeast Asia, and that haplogroups in the north were only a subset of those found in the south.[56] In addition, northern regions of East Asia received a significant genetic contribution from Central Asia.[57] Thus at least two populations were converging on the Mammoth Steppe. Later research suggested that northern populations underwent expansion earlier than those in the south, which did not begin to expand until after the Last Glacial Maximum. The implication, again, is that the resources available on the Mammoth Steppe initially aided the northern expansion. Only the warmer, more stable post-Last Glacial Maximum climate enabled the southern populations to expand, although they then grew more rapidly than those in the north.[58]

Recently, it has been suggested that there were two northwards expansions into East Asia.[59,60] The first occurred approximately 60,000 years ago and involved the Y-chromosomal haplogroup D (M174). This haplogroup now has a very fragmented distribution across the East Asia, averaging 9.60 percent in the general population, but peaking at 41.31 in Tibet, 35.08 percent in Japan, and 56.25 percent in the Andaman Islands. The high incidence among Andaman Islanders – believed to be a relict population little changed since the initial migration out of Africa – suggests that some of the first wave of beachcombers did, after all, reach East Asia. A northwards expansion 60,000 years ago also suggests that the Middle Palaeolithic artefacts at Kara-Bom were produced by modern humans.

The second, likely much larger expansion, occurred 25,000 to 30,000 years ago and involved the Y-chromosomal haplogroup O3 (M122), a branch of the dominant East Asian-specific haplogroup O (M175). This second northward expansion was presumably associated with the second wave eastward migration, after the settlement of Australia. The fragmented distribution of D (M174) today is probably a consequence of the later expansion, and that of the Neolithic Han Chinese.

This two migrations picture is supported by ancient DNA obtained from the Ust'-Ishim thighbone. Sequencing of the Ust'-Ishim individual's genome suggests that the population to which they belonged diverged from the ancestors of present-day west Eurasians and east Eurasians before the latter two diverged from one another. The implication is that there was an early migration, occurring prior to 45,000 years ago, and that possibly it was members of this population that were responsible for the Kara-Bom Middle Palaeolithic industries.[48]

In summary, it is likely that the peopling of the East Asia was far more complex than can be explained by simple models,[57] and it is also likely that local movements since the end of the Pleistocene has significantly obscured the picture.[61] Nevertheless, the big picture is reasonably clear. By 40,000 years ago, modern humans had colonised Australia and were widespread across the southern and eastern parts of the Eurasian landmass. They had encountered and interbred with at least two archaic populations. As we shall now see, they had by this time also begun to make inroads into Europe, where the Neanderthals had hitherto remained unchallenged.

14: An inaccessible peninsula

We have invented nothing

In September 1940, less than three months after the fall of France, four teenage boys and a small dog named Robot made one of the greatest archaeological discoveries of the last century. The group were walking through the sloping woods above Lascaux Manor, near the town of Montignac, which lies on the Vézère River, Dordogne. They were investigating a local legend about an old tunnel, said to connect Lascaux Manor to the ruined Château de Montignac on the other side of the river. Robot was running on ahead of the boys, and was attracted to a deep hole in the ground. Covered with overgrowth, it had been exposed by the falling of a tree.

Accounts vary as to what happened next. According to some versions, the little dog fell into the hole and had to be rescued. Other versions claim that the boys used their penknives to enlarge the hole, cutting away earth and removing stones; and others suggest that the boys first equipped themselves with picks, shovels and lighting before returning to investigate further. Whichever version is correct, they enlarged the hole and at length they were able to slide through feet-first, one by one, along a stalagmite-embedded, semi-vertical shaft, to reach a dark underground chamber. There, in the flickering glow of their oil-lamp, they saw multicoloured paintings of horses, cattle and herds of deer, unseen by human eyes for at least 18,000 years.

Despite the unhappy times, news of the discovery spread rapidly. Villagers flocked to the caves and they soon drew visitors from further afield. Among these was the Catholic priest and archaeologist Abbé Henri Breuil, who was able to attest to the great antiquity of the caves and described them as 'The Sistine Chapel of Prehistory'. Another early visitor was Pablo Picasso, who on emerging from the cave, is said to have remarked – in reference to modern art – "*We have invented nothing*".

In 1948, the site's landowners opened the caves as a tourist attraction, and soon they were attracting a quarter of a million visitors annually. Unfortunately, by 1955 the CO_2 exhaled by the large numbers of visitors was promoting the growth of algae, causing significant damage to the paintings. In 1963, after a number of unsuccessful attempts to ameliorate the problem, the caves were taken over by the French Ministry of Cultural Affairs and closed to the public. Only five people a day are now admitted, and scholars wishing to visit the caves for research purposes face a lengthy wait for a twenty-minute slot. Ordinary visitors have to make do with Lascaux II, a facsimile of the original that opened in 1983.

The paintings are now believed to be between 18,000 and 19,000 years old – four times older than the Pyramids – and are associated with the Solutrean or early Magdalenian period. There are 915 animals depicted, mainly horses, deer, aurochs (wild cattle) and bison – animals that at that time roamed wild on the steppes of Ice Age Europe.[1] Despite their great antiquity, the Lascaux cave paintings are certainly not the earliest cave paintings known: the oldest artworks in the Altamira and El Castillo caves in northern Spain have been dated by uranium series methods to 36,000 and 40,800 years old respectively.[2] The cave paintings at these and many other sites are perhaps the most spectacular examples of Ice Age art; art that proclaims the arrival of modern humans in Europe.

Transition

The archaeological record of Europe is marked by a dramatic discontinuity that first appeared in the Balkans about 46,000 years ago and spread across the continent over the next 5,000 years.[3] Below the transition point are the purely utilitarian artefacts of the Middle Palaeolithic; above these we see for the first time art objects that nobody disputes are the works of modern minds: ivory sculptures, engraved stone blocks and bas reliefs. The Upper Palaeolithic is characterised not just by cave art but by statuettes of animal, human and anthropomorphic figures, representations of both male and female sex organs, and so-called 'Venus' figurines. Although much earlier examples of abstract and graphic art are known from the African Middle Stone Age, there is no fully representational figurative art from that era.[4,5]

Upper Palaeolithic tools are classed as Mode 4 in Sir Grahame Clark's tool-complexity scheme. Blades now predominate over flakes, albeit the latter remained in use. The Levallois technique gradually gave way to the striking of blades from long prismatic stone cores. End scrapers and burins became more widespread, and more finely-worked.[6,7] Certain tool types made an appearance in Europe for the first time: 'carinate' (keel-shaped) and 'nosed' scrapers; small bladelets known as Dufour and Font-Yves forms that probably served as the tips and barbs of composite spears or arrowheads; and spearhead points carved from bone and antler, split at the base to permit hafting.[8,4]

High-quality flint, shells, and ivory beads began to circulate over long distances. They provide the first unequivocal evidence for well-established exchange networks in Europe.[8,7] Settlement patterns also attest to high levels of social organisation. Sites were concentrated in locations along the migration trails of the herds of large herbivores, implying that hunters were able to anticipate the migratory behaviour of particular species and co-ordinate their activities accordingly. Animal remains indicate a strong preference for a single animal species, though the particular species targeted varied from region to region. Reindeer and horses were the prey of choice in the tundra-dominated landscapes of Western Europe. In Eastern and Central Europe, the more steppe-adapted species such as steppe bison, ass and woolly mammoth were preferred. In the more forested south, the emphasis was on red deer, chamois and ibis. Reindeer predominated at sites in the Périgord region in southwest France.[8]

The first discovery of Upper Palaeolithic human remains was made by railway workers at the rock-shelter of Abri de Crô-Magnon near Les Eyzies-de-Tayac-Sireuil, Dordogne in 1868. An excavation by geologist Louis Lartet showed that the fossils came from a layer that also contained the remains of lions, mammoths and reindeer, together with numerous artefacts including stone tools, perforated sea shells and animal teeth. The human remains represented between five and eight individuals, including a middle-aged man, two younger men, a young woman and an infant;[9] and just as Neander Thal gave its name to the Neanderthals, so these people became known as the Cro-Magnons.

In fact, we now know that the people from Abri de Crô-Magnon lived in the Gravettian period, almost 20,000 years after modern humans first reached Europe.[10] Anthropologists recognise four main periods in the European Upper Palaeolithic: the Aurignacian, the Gravettian, the Solutrean (overlapping in time with the later Gravettian or Epigravettian), and the Magdalenian. These early modern Europeans are still informally referred to as Cro-Magnons. However, the first modern people in Europe are more correctly referred to as Aurignacian.

The Aurignacian takes its name from the site of Aurignac in the lower Pyrenees, which was excavated by Louis Lartet in 1860. Supposedly-Aurignacian sites are widespread, being known from the Atlantic coast of Spain to the Levant, and possibly as far east as the Zagros Mountains. As we shall see, though, it is questionable as to whether everything that has been described as 'Aurignacian' in the past can be assigned to a single, homogenous culture.

Currently, the earliest-known fossil remains of modern humans in Europe are milk teeth from Grotta del Cavallo in southern Italy that are from 43,000 to 45,000 years old,[11] and an upper jawbone from Kents Cavern, England, now believed to be from 41,500 to 44,200 years old.[12] The Grotta del Cavallo teeth were excavated in 1964 and for a long time it was thought that they were Neanderthal, but they are now believed to be modern. The Kents Cavern upper jawbone is an even earlier find, reported by Sir Arthur Keith in 1927, and until recently it was thought to be no more than 36,400 years old.

More comprehensive assemblages of modern human remains do not show up until slightly later. Remains of three individuals recovered from Peștera cu Oase ('Cave with Bones') in Romania include a largely-complete lower jawbone, the near-complete skull of a 15-year-old adolescent, and a left temporal bone (the temporal bones are situated at the sides and base of the skull, alongside the temporal lobes of the brain). The remains are believed to be from 39,000 to 41,000 years old (34,000 to 36,000 radiocarbon years BP)[13,14] and exhibit a mosaic of modern and archaic features. Modern features include the absence of browridges, a narrow nasal aperture, and a prominent chin; but there are also archaic features such as a wide dental arcade and very large molars.[15] Nevertheless, there is little doubt that they are modern humans and not Neanderthals.[16]

The Mladeč Caves, Moravia in the Czech Republic have yielded not only a large number of modern human remains, but also an association with Aurignacian artefacts. The remains are 35,000 years old (31,000 radiocarbon years BP), and include numerous remains of adults and juveniles of both sexes. The artefacts include stone tools, bone points and awls, and perforated teeth. The Mladeč Caves people lived fairly late on in the Aurignacian period, but the discovery confirms that the Aurignacian culture was associated with modern humans rather than Neanderthals.[17]

We must remember that the modern populations were not moving into an empty continent. The archaeological discontinuity between the Middle and Upper Palaeolithic bears mute testament to what happened when two human species – Neanderthals and *Homo sapiens* – briefly coexisted in Europe. The most recent radiocarbon dates suggest that Neanderthals died out about 5,000 years after the first modern humans arrived.[18] The demise of the Neanderthals is unlikely to have been the result of a deliberate pogrom by the modern populations, and contacts might not necessarily have been unfriendly. More likely, the Neanderthals were unable to compete for food and other resources against a demographic avalanche of newcomers that, on the basis of site sizes and numbers, might have outnumbered them by as much as ten to one.[19]

Just how and to what extent the Neanderthal and modern populations interacted with one another is not known with any certainty. There is only very limited evidence for them both being present at sites in the same region at the same time.[20] That there was some interaction seems likely, although the evidence is largely indirect. In Chapter 8, we reviewed evidence for symbolic behaviour at Neanderthal sites in France, Spain and northern Italy. The evidence at these sites includes beads, pendants, skin colourants and decorative feathers, recovered from layers that in some cases clearly predate the arrival of modern humans. Even so, we cannot rule out the possibility that long-range scouting parties made contact with Neanderthals ahead of larger-scale migrations. Such contacts could have resulted in the latter acquiring beads and elements of Upper Palaeolithic technology. Regardless of arguments concerning Neanderthal cognitive abilities, it does seem to be rather a coincidence that these items do not appear in the Neanderthal archaeological record until shortly before the arrival of modern humans.[21,22,23]

Who were the Aurignacians?

On the face of it, given its geographical proximity to Africa, it may seem surprising that Europe was not settled by modern humans until many millennia after the initial 'beachcomber' dispersal along the rim of the Indian Ocean. As viewed from Asia, though, Europe is an inaccessible peninsula in the northwestern corner of the Eurasian landmass.[24] There are only two ways into Europe from Asia: a northern route from Central Asia, around the northern margins of the Black Sea,[25] and a southern route via the Levant.[24] However, in the case of the northern route, Neanderthals survived in the Caucasus until fairly late. Had modern humans taken that route, the Neanderthals would probably have disappeared before their counterparts further west, and this route therefore seems less likely than the southern route.[26]

The southern route is consistent with a scenario in which some descendants of the original Out of Africa migration moved into the Levant from India, and then proceeded onwards into Europe – but opportunities for such a migration are rare. The Taurus and Zagros mountain ranges are major obstructions, as are the Syrian and Arabian Deserts. The only route into the Levant is via the Fertile Crescent, and this is only passable during warm, wet periods.[24] During the cold Marine Isotope Stage 4, it was an inhospitable wasteland, but after 59,000 years ago the climate improved to an extent.[27] Marine Isotope Stage 3 was a period of climatic instability that saw a succession of rapid oscillations between warm and cold conditions, interspersed with more severe cold Heinrich ('iceberg armada') events.[28,29,30] During the warmer intervals, the Fertile Crescent greened and access to the Levant was possible.

Based on the most recent radiocarbon data, it is believed that modern humans entered southeastern Europe 46,000 years ago.[3] Genetic data is broadly consistent with this date: mitochondrial genetic diversity data indicates that a rapid expansion of the modern population of Europe began 42,000 years ago.[31] Groups dispersed rapidly from east to west across Central and Western Europe, reaching Spain by 41,000 years ago.[3] Meanwhile, other groups migrated northwards onto the East European Plain, to reach Kostenki on the River Don in southern Russia between 42,000 and 45,000 years ago.[32] Some groups might have moved as far north as the Arctic Circle. Evidence of human occupation 40,000 years ago has been found at the Russian site of Mamontovaya Kurya ('Mammoth Curve'), though it cannot be ruled out that these people were Neanderthals.[33]

The westwards migration proceeded along two routes: a northern route along the Danube, and a southern route along the rim of the Mediterranean.[4] In all probability, these dispersals were linked to the interstadials GI11 (46,500 years ago) and GI10 (43,000 years ago), both of which led to substantially warmer conditions.[30] Temperatures might have risen by 5 to 8 degrees Celsius, resulting in a replacement of tundra or steppe in Western Europe with a partially-wooded landscape.[16] However, a major climatic downturn, Heinrich Event 4 (HE4), then set in around 38,000 years ago.[34]

The Danubian route is represented by the distribution of the so-called classic Aurignacian technologies, as originally noted at Aurignac itself. These include split-base bone and antler points, carinate and nosed scrapers, and 'Aurignacian' blades which are heavily retouched along their edges. These artefacts have been found at sites across Western, Central and Southeastern Europe. The Mediterranean route is represented by what are sometimes referred to as the Proto-Aurignacian technologies. These are mainly concentrated along the Mediterranean coast of Europe, from northeastern Italy to northern Catalonia, and then across the Pyrenees to the Atlantic coast of northern Spain. They differ from the classic Aurignacian, and are dominated by the Dufour and Font-Yves bladelets.[4,16] The tool assemblages at Kostenki are thought to be related to the Proto-Aurignacian.[26]

The Danubian and Mediterranean migration paths converged in southwest France roughly 40,000 to 41,000 years old (35,000 to 36,000 radiocarbon years BP). Proto-Aurignacian bladelet artefacts have been found at the site Le Piage, in the Lot region. Not too far away, in the Dordogne region, are the sites of Abri Castanet, Abri Blanchard, La Ferrassie and Abri Pataud. There, both stone tools and carved ivory artefacts show close analogies with classic Aurignacian artefacts from sites in Central Europe, including Geißenklösterle and Keilberg-Kirche in Germany, and Willendorf in Austria. These Central European sites are two to three thousand years older than the French sites dating to around 43,000 years ago; these older dates are consistent with an east to west migration.[16,35]

There may be a connection between the arrival of classic Aurignacian industries in southwest France and the Heinrich Event 4 cold snap: the onset of extremely severe winters in Central Europe might have forced a southwards migration.[16] Although the dates don't match up exactly, one must remember that there is always a degree of uncertainty in the dating artefacts and events from this far back in time.

It all sounds fairly straightforward, but in reality things may be more complicated than a single bifurcating and re-converging migration across Europe. The first appearance of Proto-Aurignacian and classic Aurignacian industries represents a sharp break with earlier industries wherever they are found.[36,4] There is therefore no doubt that they are intrusive, but from where did they originate, and can they both be lumped together as a single industry? To answer these questions, we must attempt to unravel a complex archaeological trail that begins in Asia and leads into the Levant before connecting to the European Aurignacian.

Zagros origins

In the late 1950s, the American archaeologist Ralph Solecki identified an early Upper Palaeolithic industry at Shanidar Cave in northern Iraq. He was struck by similarities it showed with the Aurignacian, but was persuaded by Dorothy Garrod that it was sufficiently different to warrant its own designation. Solecki named it the Baradostian after Baradost Mountain, which forms part of the Zagros mountain chain. The Baradostian was subsequently identified at a number of Zagros sites in Iran. These include Warwasi, a rock-shelter site located north of Kermanshah in the west of the country. The subsequent troubles in the region have understandably caused problems for Western scholars, but fortunately the finds at Warwasi were subsequently housed at the University of Pennsylvania.[37]

Warwasi and other Baradostian sites are characterised by Aurignacian-like artefacts, including end scrapers, burins, Font-Yves points and Dufour bladelets. At Warwasi, flake-based artefacts predominate in the lower, earlier layers, but these give way to blade-based artefacts in the upper, later layers. Archaeologists Deborah Olszewski and Harold Dibble believe that Solecki's first impression was right, and that the Baradostian is an Aurignacian industry. They have proposed renaming it the Zagros Aurignacian, divided into Early (predominantly flake-based) and Late (blade and bladelet-based) stages. They have also noted some continuity between the Baradostian and the earlier Middle Palaeolithic industries at Warwasi, which is quite unlike the discontinuity seen between Upper and Middle Palaeolithic industries in Europe. This is important, because the lack of a clear break suggests that the Baradostian evolved *in situ*. If it really was an Aurignacian precursor industry, the implication is that the ultimate origin of the Aurignacian was in the Zagros region.[37,38,25]

Unfortunately, proof is lacking. Very few Zagros sites have been excavated, and radiocarbon dates for those that have were obtained in the 1950s and 1960s. Techniques at that time were far less sophisticated than those now in use, and such dates are not considered as reliable as those obtained by using modern AMS methods. The oldest Baradostian radiocarbon dates range from 36,000 to in excess of 40,000 years, but these may be underestimated.[37,38] For the Baradostian to be a precursor to Aurignacian industries further west, it would need to be around 50,000 years old.

Back to the Levant

The evidence that emerges as we follow the trail into the Levant is less tentative. It confirms a return of modern humans after an absence of more than 40,000 years. This time, they were here to stay, and they have lived in the region ever since. Much crucial data has emerged from Ksar Akil, a large rock-shelter in Lebanon, located just inland from the coast near Beirut. Ksar Akil was first excavated in the late 1930s by a group of American Jesuits turned archaeologists. Led by Fathers J. Franklin Ewing and Joseph Doherty, the group excavated 19 m (62 ft.) of artefact-bearing deposits, spanning the later Middle Palaeolithic through to the Epipalaeolithic. They found 25 Upper Palaeolithic layers, divided into six stages, overlaying a series of layers containing typical late Middle Palaeolithic industries. The oldest Upper Palaeolithic layer is estimated to be between 43,000 and 49,500 years old.[3]

In Layer XVII of Stage 2 (the second lowest Upper Palaeolithic stage), Ewing and Doherty found a burial containing the remains of a child, estimated by Ewing to be eight years old, and the fragmentary remains of a second individual. The child was named 'Egbert' and was originally thought to be male, though its gender is uncertain. Egbert's skull was given to the Beirut National Museum, but the fate of the other remains is unknown. In 1989, based on casts of Egbert's skull held at the Natural History Museum in London, anthropologist Chris Stringer confirmed that Egbert was a modern human, with a globular skull and a pronounced chin. Stringer felt that Egbert might have been female. Based on dental eruption, Egbert was between seven and nine years old at the time of death.[39]

The Stage 1 layers are associated with an industry known as the Emiran. Emiran artefacts are known other sites in Southwest Asia, including Boker Tachtit in the Negev Desert, where they range from 43,000 to 50,000 years old.[3] The Emiran is characterised by the use of the Middle Palaeolithic Levallois method rather than prismatic core technology, but it does include typical Upper Palaeolithic retouched tools including end scrapers and chisel-like burins. The Emiran thus incorporates a combination of Middle and Upper Palaeolithic technologies, and is often labelled a 'transitional' industry. While the presence of Middle Palaeolithic elements implies that the Emiran did at some point evolve from a Middle Palaeolithic industry, it does not imply that this necessarily happened *in situ*, and some prefer the more neutral term Initial Upper Palaeolithic industry.[40]

There is actually little evidence for continuity between the Emiran and earlier local Middle Palaeolithic industries, and its origins remain unclear. On the other hand, continuity between it and the later Ahmarian industries is reasonably well documented.[41,42] Ahmarian artefacts show up in the Stage 2 layers at Ksar Akil, and are characterised by the gradual replacement of the Levallois technique by more typical Upper Palaeolithic prismatic core technologies. Artefacts include end scrapers and a variety of retouched and pointed blades.[40,42] The discovery of Egbert in the Stage 2 layers at Ksar Akil unambiguously associates the Ahmarian with modern humans. Although no such association is known for the Emiran, the continuity between it and the Ahmarian confirms that it is also associated with modern humans.[26]

Above the Stage 2 layers at Ksar Akil is a 7 m (23 ft.) sequence with three sub-phases, A, B and C, which were originally all classified as Levantine Aurignacian. It was thought that this had gradually developed *in situ* from the Ahmarian. However, most scholars now regard the Levantine Aurignacian intrusive and technologically distinct from the Ahmarian,[43] which is thought to have persisted in the region long after the arrival of the Levantine Aurignacian.[16] It is also now believed that the A and B sub-phases represent a continuation of the Ahmarian, and that only sub-phase C is Levantine Aurignacian. The A and B sub-phases contain large numbers of small retouched bladelets and sharply-pointed artefacts resembling the Dufour bladelets and Font Yves points known from

European sites. They are named El Wad forms after the Israeli site where they were first excavated by Dorothy Garrod.[16]

Sub-phase C is between 35,000 and 36,000 years old (31,000 and 32,000 radiocarbon years BP), and contains artefacts most closely resembling the classic Aurignacian as recognised in southwest France.[16] The Levantine Aurignacian is known from sites in Israel, Syria, Lebanon and Iran. Similarities between the two were recognised as far back as the 1930s, but the relationship was only confirmed with the discovery of split-base bone and antler spearhead points at the sites of Hayonim, Kebara Cave and El Quseir. The most reliably-dated of these are two examples excavated from the early Levantine Aurignacian level at Kebara Cave, which date to between 39,000 and 41,000 years old (34,000 and 36,000 radiocarbon years BP). The split-base points are considered to be archetypal Aurignacian artefacts, and were at one time referred to as the 'pointe d'Aurignac'.[16]

Following the archaeological trail northwards into Turkey is difficult, as early Upper Palaeolithic sites there are scarce. Most of the central Anatolian plateau lies more than 1,000 m (3,200ft) above sea level, and it might have supported only very low population densities. In Western Europe, cave sites more than 500 m (1,600 ft.) above sea level were seldom if ever occupied during the Upper Palaeolithic. During cold, dry periods, people were probably attracted to milder coastal Mediterranean habitats. Consequently, many sites may now be underwater, submerged by rising sea levels at the end of the last Ice Age.[44]

Nevertheless, Turkey does have one very important Upper Palaeolithic site, Üçağızlı Cave, located on Mediterranean coast of the country, near the border with Syria. It lies roughly 250 km (155 miles) to the north of Ksar Akil, not far from Antakya, or Antioch as it was known in antiquity. Üçağızlı is the collapsed remnant of what must once have been a much larger cave system, and its name simply means 'Three Mouths Cave'. It was discovered in the 1980s and excavated by anthropologist Angela Minzoni-Deroche in the 1990s. Stone tools from the lower layers are Emiran; those from upper layers Ahmarian. However, there are no Levantine Aurignacian artefacts.[40,42]

At both Üçağızlı Cave and Ksar Akil, shells used as ornaments have been found in large numbers. Those at Üçağızlı may be between 41,000 and 43,000 years old; those at Ksar Akil even older. The inhabitants of both sites were selective in their choice of shells, preferring those that were either luminous white, brightly-coloured, or attractively patterned. Although a variety of species were used as ornaments at both sites, the most commonly-used were the marine snails *Nassarius gibbosula* and *Columbella rustica* and the marine bivalve *Glycmeris*. At Üçağızlı, shells of the freshwater snail *Theodoxus jordani* were also used. Most of the shells were pierced near the lip for use as beads, either by scratching or by punching with pointed tool.[40]

Ethnographic comparisons with recent societies suggest that beads might have been symbols of group affiliation, gender and marital status. Although beads first appeared much earlier, their use in the Upper Palaeolithic of Southwest Asia might have the crossing of a demographic threshold as populations reached levels at which new statements of identity became necessary.[40] It is therefore not surprising that modern humans continued to migrate westwards towards Europe, aided in all probability by the warm climatic episode GI12, about 48,000 years ago.[30,16]

Putting it all together

To sum up the evidence so far: in the Zagros there is an Aurignacian-like industry known as the Baradostian that appears to have arisen *in situ*, raising the possibility that it might be the Aurignacian mother culture. Uncertainties in the dating mean that this cannot be confirmed; the published dates of around 40,000 years old are too recent, but they could understate the age of the Baradostian.

In the Levant and Turkey, the earliest Upper Palaeolithic industry is the Emiran, a non-indigenous industry that nevertheless combines elements of Middle and Upper Palaeolithic technology. The Emiran developed *in situ* into the Ahmarian, in which Middle Palaeolithic techniques were gradually phased out. The Ahmarian is unambiguously associated with modern humans, as by implication is the Emiran. A third Levantine industry, the Levantine Aurignacian, has the clearest affinities to the classic Aurignacian in Europe, but it appears to be intrusive upon the region.

Together with clear markers of behavioural modernity such as beads, this data fits a broad picture of a dispersal of modern humans from India into the Levant, onwards into Anatolia, and finally Europe. In Europe, there are two dispersal routes: a northern route along the Danube, and a southern route along the rim of the Mediterranean. The northern route is associated with the classic Aurignacian; the southern route with a bladelet-dominated industry known as the Proto-Aurignacian. Are these two both part-and-parcel of the same migration, or do they represent two completely separate migrations?

Sir Paul Mellars[16] believes the latter and suggests that the Proto-Aurignacian Mediterranean bladelet industries should be renamed 'Fumanian' for the Italian site Grotta di Fumane. If we accept this view, where are the origins of the two migrations to be found? Mellars notes the similarities of the Dufour bladelets and Font Yves points with the El Wad artefacts found in the sub-phases A and B at Ksar Akil, and at other Levantine sites such as Boker Tachtit. A date of 41,500 years old (39,000 radiocarbon years BP) has been obtained from the latter. Further east, similar bladelets and points are found at Warwasi and other Baradostian sites. By comparison, their counterparts from the French Mediterranean and northern Spain are younger at between 39,000 and 38,000 years old (38,000 and 36,000 radiocarbon years BP). This would suggest that the origin of the Proto-Aurignacian/ Fumanian lies with either the later Ahmarian in the Levant or possibly the Baradostian in the Zagros.[16]

The classic Aurignacian might have arisen from the Late Zagros Aurignacian phase of the Baradostian, reaching Europe via the Levant. Another possibility is that it originated in the Balkans. Bacho Kiro Cave is a 46,000-year-old[3] cave site in Bulgaria, and gives its name to the Bachokirian, an Upper Palaeolithic industry first identified by Polish archaeologist Janusz Kozlowski in 1982. As is usual for Upper Palaeolithic industries, the Bachokirian layers at Bacho Kiro Cave contrast sharply with underlying Mousterian layers, and are clearly intrusive. Kozlowski subsequently identified the Bachokirian at another Bulgarian site, Temnata Cave. Here, however, a precursor Levallois industry was present in the lower layers of the site. This earlier industry was again intrusive upon Mousterian industries, and shows affinities to the Emiran in the Levant[45] or possibly to the Early Zagros Aurignacian phase of the Baradostian.[38]

Later levels at Temnata show a transition from Levallois to typical Upper Palaeolithic prismatic core techniques for blade manufacture. According to Kozlowski, the same transition is also seen at a number of sites in southern Moravia, Upper Silesia, eastern Slovakia, and western Ukraine. These industries also appear to be of non-local origin. Accordingly, Kozlowski has concluded that the classic Aurignacian emerged *in situ* in the Balkans and Middle Danube region from precursor Levallois-based industries that can be traced to Initial Upper Palaeolithic industries in the Levant or the Zagros, and are presumably associated with a westwards migration from there.[45]

What of the Levantine Aurignacian? Kozlowski's model fits well with the view that this is intrusive upon the region, and is more recent than the European Aurignacian. It might therefore have arisen from a back-migration from Europe into the Levant, possibly driven by the onset of the Heinrich Event 4 cold snap.[16,43]

The Gravettian

Around 33,000 years ago, the climate started to deteriorate and ice sheets began to advance in the long slow build-up to the Last Glacial Maximum.[46] Trees disappeared from all but the most southerly parts of Europe, leaving vast open landscapes dominated by grasses, mosses and other herbaceous plants. These steppe and tundra conditions provided a rich environment for numerous species of cold-adapted herd animals such as reindeer, steppe bison, mammoths and woolly rhinoceros.[8]

The middle Upper Palaeolithic is set against this climatic background, and is marked by the appearance and spread of a culture known as the Gravettian. Named for the type site of La Gravette in the Dordogne, the Gravettian appeared around 29,000 years ago, and had replaced the Aurignacian by 28,000 years ago.[7] The Gravettian was characterised by a number of innovations, including semi-sedentism, elaborate mortuary practices, and advances in projectile technology. Gravettian tool technology was characterised by pointed blades, often backed (blunted on one edge like a penknife blade) to facilitate hafting. Weapon tips produced from antler were in some cases small enough to suggest the use of the bow and arrow and the atlatl,[7] though such weapon systems are not directly attested until rather later.[47] These technological advances might have been a response to the onset of the colder climate.[48]

In Central Europe, particularly in Moravia and Slovakia, Gravettian settlements along rivers such as were occupied for several months of the year. Much effort was invested in the construction of dwellings.[7] At sites including Pavlov and Dolní Věstonice in Moravia, post-holes and stone foundations surrounding large central hearths suggest that substantial houses were constructed. At some sites, such as Kostenki, where wood was lacking, the tusks, jaws, ribs, and leg bones of mammoths were used as construction materials.[8,7] At Kostenki and a number of other sites, large pits were cut into the permafrost – early examples of refrigeration units. They were probably used during warmer months for cold storage of meat, or of animal bones kept for fuel. Another innovation seen at Kostenki and elsewhere on the East European Plain is the eyed needle. Examples range in age from 35,000 to 30,000 years old at Kostenki, and from 35,000 to 28,000 years old at Tolbaga, which lies to the southeast of Lake Baikal.[47]

The diet of the Gravettian people was not confined to large herbivores: the remains of fish and other small animals have been found at Gravettian sites,[7] and stable isotope analysis of human remains from a number of sites in Romania, France, Britain, Italy, the Czech Republic and Russia suggest the Gravettian diet included fish, shellfish and waterfowl. At Kostenki, such items accounted for well over 50 percent of the dietary protein intake.[49,50]

Overall, the large sites suggest that the population of Europe increased during the Gravettian. This might have been the result of the rich steppe environment that emerged ahead of the steadily-advancing glaciers and which the Gravettians were well-equipped to exploit with their innovative technology.[47] The emergence of larger social units led to greater social complexity and a greater degree of specialisation by individuals. Some worked as tool-makers, others as hunters. It is likely that a decision-making hierarchy was required to co-ordinate the activities of groups as a whole.[8]

Over forty Gravettian burials are known, at locations from France to Russia, including some double and even two triple interments. Most of the burials include ornamentation with ochre and grave offerings.[7] At Sungir in Russia, a boy and girl, both between 11 and 13 years old, were buried in a long, narrow grave, covered with red ochre and accompanied by a spectacular collection of grave goods. These included thousands of ivory beads, hundreds of fox teeth, ivory pins, pendants and animal carvings, and spears made from mammoth tusk, one of which was 2.4 m (7 ft. 11 in.) long.[51] Such elaborate burials probably reflect greater social complexity and the emergence of high-status individuals.[8] The child burials at Sungir suggest that such status might have been inherited.[52] A rather more macabre possibility is human sacrifice.[51]

In locations with reliable sources of food and water, populations might have been living at higher densities, leading to 'crowding stress' affecting relationships between separate groups. Under such conditions, these groups might have been forced to establish distinct territories to avoid disputes over access to hunting grounds and sources of raw material for tool-making. In turn, this might have resulted in expressions of group identity, possibly reflected in particular styles of art, ornamentation or even utilitarian artefacts such as spearheads or knives. This could explain the diverse range of artefacts seen in Europe at different places and different times during the Upper Palaeolithic. If so, these could represent expressions of distinct ethnicity,[8] and a continuation of the trend that began with the beads found at Üçağızlı and Ksar Akil.

However, it is likely that the scattered human groups on the whole maintained positive relations between one another. Given the unpredictable climatic and environmental conditions, there was no guarantee that heavy snowfall, over-grazing, or fire would not disrupt the migratory routes. The non-appearance of migratory herds upon which groups depended could prove disastrous. To mitigate these effects, long-distance contact and co-operation between the groups were essential as a hedge against local failure of food supplies. Trade networks, existent since the Aurignacian, became more conspicuous during the Last Glacial Maximum, when food supply reliability was at its most precarious.[8]

While many features of Gravettian culture are thought to be local adaptations, the ultimate origin of the Gravettian remains uncertain. It might have arisen among indigenous late Aurignacian populations, probably in Central Europe.[7] On the other hand, archaeologist Jiří Svoboda[53] believes that it was intrusive. He claims that Gravettian tools are typologically unrelated to those of the Aurignacian, and sees a connection to the Ahmarian industries of the Levant. Although the Ahmarian considerably predate the Gravettian as it generally recognised, he believes that an early Gravettian industry with Ahmarian affinities is to be found at the 36,000 to 39,000-year-old cave site of Kozarnika, near Belogradchik in Bulgaria.

Lion-men and flutes of the Jura Mountains

The Löwenmensch (Lion-man) of Hohlenstein-Stadel is one of the earliest-known examples of what is unequivocally figurative art. The 30 cm (11.8 in.) high figurine is carved from mammoth ivory and is a therianthropic (part human, part animal) figurine of a human figure with a lion's head. The figurine's gender is uncertain: it lacks male genitalia, but the body proportions and lack of breasts suggest that it is male. Slanting marks on its left arm have been interpreted as tattoos. Regardless of gender, the figure is clearly both human and feline at the same time.[1]

The Löwenmensch is around 36,500 years old (31,000 to 32,000 radiocarbon years BP)[54] and was discovered in fragments in 1939 at Hohlenstein-Stadel, an Aurignacian cave site in the Lone Valley of the Swabian Jura Mountains of southwest Germany. Following the outbreak of World War II, it was then forgotten for thirty years. Reconstruction did not begin until 1969 and was not completed until 1988.[1]

Jean Clottes,[1] one of France's most eminent prehistorians, believes that the Löwenmensch reinforces the importance of felines to Upper Palaeolithic people, and also highlights the fluid nature of their belief systems in which the borders separating humans from animals were easy to cross. He speculates that the Löwenmensch could represent a shaman partially transformed into a lion. It could also be a mythical being or a supernatural spirit.

Out of Africa

The case for such an interpretation was strengthened with the discovery in 2003 of a similar figurine at Hohle Fels Cave in the Ach Valley, only a short distance from Lone Valley. Like the original Löwenmensch, the Hohle Fels figurine depicts a mixture of feline and human traits, and again no sexual characteristics can be discerned. However, it is considerably smaller, measuring only 2.55 cm (1 in.). It is around 37,000 years old (31,000 to 33,000 radiocarbon years BP), roughly the same age as its Hohlenstein-Stadel counterpart. The implication is that the people of the Ach and Lone Valleys shared a belief system connected with therianthropic images of felines and humans. This would be consistent with the view proposed by David Lewis-Williams that much European Upper Palaeolithic art can be explained in terms of shamanistic practices, as we shall see shortly. The Hohle Fels Löwenmensch was found with a bird-like figurine of about the same age that probably represents a cormorant or a duck. Also found was a figurine of a horse's head, which at around 35,000 years old (30,000 radiocarbon years BP) is more slightly recent than the other two.[54]

The people of the Swabian Jura region also made the world's earliest-known musical instruments. A total of eight flutes have been recovered from the caves of Geißenklösterle, Hohle Fels and Vogelherd since 1995. The flutes were originally all thought to be around 36,000 years old, but revised dates of 42,000 to 43,000 years old have since been obtained for those from Geißenklösterle. It is possible that the ages of other artefacts from the region have also been understated.[35]

Four flutes are carved from hollow bird bones and the other four from mammoth ivory. The latter type would have been the harder to make, necessitating the shaping of the flute from a piece of mammoth ivory, then splitting it in half, hollowing it out and carving holes, and finally re-joining the halves with air-tight seals. One of the ivory flutes, from Geißenklösterle, has dozens of finely-carved notches along the edges of the two halves to facilitate binding and sealing. A three-holed bird bone flute from the same site has been found to produce four basic notes and three overtones, comparable to many modern types of flute. The flutes have a range of diameters, to produce different tones. Music was clearly important to the Swabian Jura people, though whether it was for ritual purposes or simply for entertainment is not known. Most of the flutes were found with stone tools and animal remains, suggesting that they were used in a diverse range of social and cultural situations.[55] One of the Hohle Fels flutes was played by flautist Bernadette Käfer for a film featured at the dOCUMENTA (13) contemporary art exhibition at Kassel, Germany, in 2012.

Venus figurines and other portable art

Hohle Fels has also yielded the earliest-yet known example of a so-called 'Venus' figurine. The mammoth ivory piece is at least 35,000 years old and was discovered in six fragments in 2008, in close proximity to a flute.[56] Similar female carvings are known throughout the European Upper Palaeolithic, although they are chiefly associated with the Gravettian period. They are collectively known as Venus figurines, despite predating the Roman goddess by tens of millennia. Typically lozenge-shaped, they are characterised by exaggerated sexual characteristics, with very large breasts, accentuated hips, thighs and buttocks, and large, explicit vulvas. Other anatomical details tend to be neglected, especially arms and feet. The heads generally lack facial detail. The contrast with the classical portrayal of Venus could not be greater.

The figurines were carved from materials including mammoth ivory, serpentine, steatite or limestone, and were often coloured with ochre. Others were made from fired clay, making them among the earliest-known ceramics.[57] In total, over a hundred are known, ranging in size from 4 to 25 cm (1 ½ to 10 in.) high. Many have engraved or incised patterns, which may represent hair and clothing. Most are from the Gravettian, and it was widely believed that the 'Venus' tradition originated that period, but the Hohle Fels discovery confirms an Aurignacian origin and suggests that there was at least some degree of cultural continuity between the Aurignacian and Gravettian.

Since the first examples were discovered in the nineteenth century, many have attained iconic status. These include the Venus of Willendorf, which is 11.1 cm (4.4 in.) high and carved from oolitic limestone. The statue was discovered in 1908 by archaeologist Josef Szombathy near the village of Willendorf in Austria, and now resides in the Natural History Museum, Vienna. Others include the ceramic Black Venus of Dolní Věstonice in the Czech Republic, the serpentine Venus of Galgenberg, Austria, and the ivory Venus of Lespugue from the Pyrenees.

The figurines are often interpreted as fertility figures or mother goddesses, but their real function is unknown. One novel suggestion, by anthropologists Leroy McDermott and Catherine Hodge McCoid,[58,59] is that they may be self-portrayals of pregnant women. They note likenesses between a photograph of a 'Venus' figurine viewed from above and one of a pregnant woman standing with her feet together, viewed from her own perspective looking down on her breasts and abdomen. The theory has met with a certain amount of scepticism, but McDermott and McCoid argue that it explains the features found in representations of the female form from the Upper Palaeolithic.

It may be simplistic to assume that the Venus figurines had only one function and it could be they had a variety of regional-specific meanings within an overall theme.[7] Explicit sexual imagery was not confined to the female form: some sites have yielded equally explicit phallic representations, carved out of bone, ivory or, in one case, the horn core of a bison. While their function is not known for certain, Sir Paul Mellars[5] has refused to rule out the possibility that they are Upper Palaeolithic sex toys.

The greatest range of portable art is from the latter part of Upper Palaeolithic, dating from 15,000 to 12,000 years ago. Many items have been found at Magdalenian sites in the Franco-Cantabrian region (a region comprising northern Spain and southwest France), and contemporary sites in southern Germany. Animals depicted include reindeer, horses, ibex, mammoths, fish, birds and seals. The images are highly naturalistic and are either engraved on bone or stone, or carved from fragments of these materials.[8] A notable recent find was the engraved deer shoulder blade found at El Mirón Cave in Spain. On the flat surface is an engraved image of the head, neck, and part of the dorsal line of a red deer hind, including such details as a nostril, an eye and the base of an ear. A small slate plaque pendant, engraved with the image of a horse, was also found at this site.[60] Human subjects are also depicted, though these are generally more stylised.[8,7] These include a mysterious bone plaque, found at the Laugerie-Basse rock-shelter in the Dordogne, portraying a pregnant woman apparently lying at the feet of a reindeer.[1] Utilitarian objects too, such as atlatls, harpoons and spatulas, were sometimes beautifully carved and engraved with both naturalistic and geometric designs.[8,1]

The wrong time of the month

Could some portable art objects have actually been Upper Palaeolithic calendars and if so, then what was being recorded? In 1972 the American researcher Alexander Marshack examined just about every prehistoric artefact he could lay his hands on for calendrical notches. He published his findings in a book entitled *The Roots of Civilization*[61] in which he claimed that Upper Palaeolithic people in Europe were making records of the phases of the Moon. On the face of it, this seems highly plausible. There is little doubt that Upper Palaeolithic people were aware that the phase of the Moon changes from night to night in a predictable manner.

There are two problems, though. Firstly, it seems unnecessary to record, say, the days since the last full moon when one can simply look at the Moon, note the current phase, and work forward to when the next full moon will occur. If, for example, a waxing half-moon was seen in the evening sky, then Upper Palaeolithic people would certainly have been aware that it would be full in another seven days. The second problem is the tallies vary in numbers of days by more than can be explained by the small seasonal variations in the length of the lunar cycle, or by observational error. However, there is another cycle with an average length almost identical to that of the lunar cycle that does show a certain amount of variation – the human menstrual cycle. It is likely that this is what was being recorded, since the advantages of knowing when that time of the month is approaching are fairly obvious, and this was probably also the case 30,000 years ago.

That the human menstrual cycle is almost exactly one lunar month in duration is now thought to be pure co-incidence, but it is one that was noticed many thousands of years ago. The words 'moon', 'month', 'menstruate' and 'measure' (time) all have the same ancient root in the Indo-European language family, predating the emergence of Greek, Latin and Sanskrit.

The Mind in the Cave

Despite the large numbers of figurines and other portable art objects that have been found, the best-known form of artistic expression during the Upper Palaeolithic is the remarkable cave art known from Lascaux, Chauvet, Cosquer, Pech-Merle and Niaux in France, Altamira and El Castillo in Spain, and many other sites, mainly located in southwest France and in Cantabria. In all, around 320 sites have been discovered in this region since the mid-nineteenth century. The artwork consists overwhelmingly of depictions of animals: chiefly those that the people of Ice Age Europe relied upon for food, such as reindeer, horses, bison, aurochs, ibex and mammoths. Other species were also represented though, including birds, rhinos, felines, bears and wolves.[8,1]

Humans were depicted only very rarely, and fewer than twenty portrayals are known. Some are therianthropic, such as the highly-stylised, bird-headed, male figure in the Shaft of the Dead Man at Lascaux. However, the stencilled outlines and positive prints of human hands are fairly common, chiefly from the earlier caves, and feature the hands of both adults and children. Female genitalia also occur frequently during the early period, but also appear during the Solutrean and Magdalenian. In addition, there are various purely abstract symbols including meandering rows of dots or circles, linear 'macaroni' engravings, and triangular and rectangular tectiform (roof-shaped) designs.[8,1]

Techniques included both engraving and painting. The latter entailed applying pigment to the rock surface by a variety of techniques, including direct application with fingers, brushes, or stump drawing (application with the hand or a piece of animal hide), or by spray-painting through a tube or by spitting directly from the mouth. Pigments used included ochre to produce a range of colours from yellow to deep maroon, and black manganese dioxide. Sometimes mixtures of the two were used. Generally far from natural daylight, the artists obviously required artificial illumination, and this was provided by torches and animal-grease lamps. Torches were often made from Sylvester Pine and lamps were usually ordinary stones with a natural hollow that contained grease and a wick, though more skilfully-made, decorated examples are known.[8,62,1]

Although some engravings are known from open-air sites, much of the artwork is located deep inside the caves, often in narrow and inaccessible passages. At Lascaux, for example, the Shaft of the Dead Man is accessible only via a 6 m (17 ft.) deep shaft, and Cosquer is accessed via a 120 m (395 ft.) long tunnel. Currently, the entrance to this tunnel lies 37 m (121 ft.) below the surface of the Mediterranean, and Cosquer can only be accessed by scuba divers. However, during the Upper Palaeolithic, when sea-levels were lower, the entrance to the cave was some way from the shore.[1]

There have of course been many attempts to interpret the motives that lay behind the creation of the cave art. Originally it was thought to be *art pour l'art*, or art for the sake of art. The caves were seen as Upper Palaeolithic art galleries, created and appreciated by people with time on their hand for activities beyond the daily round of hunting, gathering, and tool-making. The problem with this view is that much of the art is located in the depths of the caves, far from where it could easily be appreciated.[62]

Throughout the first half of the twentieth century, explanations tended to focus on totemism and hunting magic. Totemism is a belief system in which a group of humans such as a clan is represented by a particular species of animal or plant, thus the 'Eagle People', 'Bear People', etc. The word 'totem' is derived from the North American Indian Ojibwe word 'odoodem', meaning clan or kinship group. It was suggested that the cave images could be the equivalent of a totem pole, but the problem with this view is that the caves invariably portray multiple species rather than just one species, as might be expected for totemic cultures.[62]

The Abbé Henri Breuil and others proposed explanations based on hunting magic, which is a belief that an image of an animal or person can influence the subject portrayed. Though specifics differ between cultures, hunting magic is a belief common in traditional small-scale societies. The view was that if people went deep underground to make images, it could only be for magical purposes, as their work could not readily be seen by others. It was the act of making the image that was important, and its purpose was to ensure successful hunting. Images of felines and other dangerous predators were explained in terms of the artists hoping to acquire the strength and hunting skill of these animals. Abstract images were said to represent traps, weapons or hunters' hides.[8,62,1]

Later explanations emphasised structuralism, a philosophical movement that originated early in the twentieth century with the work of the Swiss linguist Ferdinand de Saussure. It was later applied to anthropology by the French anthropologist Claude Levi-Strauss, who proposed that the language, kinship systems, and mythology of any human culture can be explained in terms of 'binary opposites' (for example up/down, life/death and male/female), and the relationships between them. The French archaeologists Andre Leroi-Gourhan and Annette Laming-Emperaire then sought binary opposites in cave art, and viewed the images both of animals and abstract designs as either male or female symbols. For example, horses and stags are male symbolisations whereas bison and aurochs are female. Similarly, line or arrow-like figures are male, and broader triangular designs female, in both cases representing genitalia.[62]

Some believe that that it is pointless to try and interpret the art itself. While there are no shortages of plausible hypotheses, it is difficult to test them adequately. Also, different interpretations might have been valid at different times and places during the Upper Palaeolithic. Rather than try to explain the motivation for producing the art, it is argued that the emphasis should be on explaining its distribution geographically and over time, and the social and environmental contexts in which it was produced.[63,8] It is immediately obvious that the cave art is concentrated in a highly localised region – the Périgord, with 60 or more sites, and adjacent areas of southwest France, the Pyrenees and northwestern Spain. In fact, 90 percent of all known cave art is found in the Franco-Cantabrian region. There are other regions of Europe with limestone caves suitable for cave art, but very little has been found there.[8,1] The cave art is also concentrated in time as well as geographically, peaking during the Last Glacial Maximum, at a time when northern and Central Europe was uninhabitable. As conditions improved after the Last Glacial Maximum, cave art finally disappeared.[63]

It has been proposed that the high concentration of art in the Franco-Cantabrian region can explained in terms of high population density and 'crowding stress' that, as noted above, might have led to a need for distinct territories. The Franco-Cantabrian region lies at what was the most southerly part of the open tundra and steppe environment in Ice Age Europe. It thus supported the highest concentrations of herd animals, whose migration trails followed predictable routes through major river valleys flowing westwards from the Massif Central and northwards from the Cantabrian Mountains. The conditions were ideal for aggregations of large human groups to exploit migrating herds, and more people were forced southwards into the region as the climate steadily deteriorated up to the Last Glacial Maximum.[8]

Accordingly, cave art could have been a response to the population crowding. This created a need for ritual and ceremonial activities to maintain social cohesion, and enforce territorial boundaries. Such a need had always existed in the densely-populated Franco-Cantabrian region, but the problems were exacerbated during the Last Glacial Maximum. On this view, cave art might have been an integral part of the ideology of Ice Age hunter-gatherers, a social and cultural adaptation to the extreme conditions. Possibly major centres such as Lascaux and Altamira served as ritualistic or ceremonial centres during annual gatherings by various groups. Another possibility is that the production of the art was controlled by chiefs or religious leaders who used its creation and associated ceremony to reinforce their roles of power and authority within the societies. During the subsequent climatic upturn, populations spread out once more, repopulating Northern and Central Europe. The 'crowd stress' eased and with it the need for tightly-demarcated territories of exploitation. After 20,000 years, the era of cave art was at an end.[63,8,48]

This view is widely accepted, although models that posit religion and ritual as a means of creating social cohesion have been criticised on the grounds that they are more descriptive than explanatory (see Chapter 11). An alternative explanation has been put forward by David Lewis-Williams.[62] Drawing on ethnographic studies of present-day South African and North American rock art and traditions, he suggests that Upper Palaeolithic cave art was created as part of a shamanistic belief system. Lewis-Williams has proposed that the universal belief in a multi-tiered cosmos is rooted in the very structure of the human brain, and that in altered states of consciousness, people can experience journeys to realms other than that of our everyday existence. While such altered states are associated with psychotropic substances, they may be induced by other means including intense concentration, chanting, clapping, drumming, prolonged rhythmic movement and hyperventilation. Sensory deprivation, of the type that may be experienced in the depths of the cave networks, also induces hallucinations (see Chapter 11).

The spread of shamanistic religions across the northern hemisphere and the New World suggests that shamanism is based on a very ancient set of beliefs, diffusing from a common source and possibly brought to America by the earliest settlers there. There is, however, another possibility and that is that the similarity of these traditions arises from the universality of the human neural system's capacity to generate entoptic images while in altered states of consciousness. While probably not identical to any ethnographically-recorded shamanistic tradition, Upper Palaeolithic belief systems might have had comparable core features. These belief systems probably did not remain static throughout the whole of the Upper Palaeolithic, but they remained essentially shamanistic.

Lewis-Williams views the cave art representing visions experienced by people in altered states of consciousness. Shamans saw both images of animals and geometrical patterns apparently 'projected' onto the walls of the caves, and the paintings represented the 'fixing' of these images. Indeed, the images might have been seen as entities released from or coaxed from the living membrane between the image maker and the spirit world. Even the paint used to make the images probably had its own significance and potency as a power-impregnated solvent, which dissolved the rock and allowed images of the other world to pass through. Notably, the images lack any naturalistic setting; there are no trees, rivers or grassy plains, suggesting that they are mental images, unconstrained by the natural world. Some images might have been painted while the artist remained in an altered state of consciousness. Hand prints, too, might have been more than just signatures of artists or the Upper Palaeolithic equivalent of 'Kilroy was here'. When a hand is put against the wall and sprayed with paint, it blends into the rock, to all intents and purposes disappearing into the wall. Again, paint was probably significant in this context, facilitating intimate contact with the realm behind it.

In altered states of consciousness, all the senses hallucinate, not just sight, and in shamanistic belief systems, visions are not silent. They speak, make animal sounds and communicate with the shamans. In addition to these neurologically-induced sensations, other sounds would have been made by people to accompany the rituals. Possibly, the Jura Mountain bone flutes described above were used in such rituals. Lighting, too, might have played a ritual as well as purely functional role. In contrast to modern electric lighting, the light of oil lamps and torches only illuminates portions of the wall; the images of animals would have seemingly materialised out of the darkness. Some of the lamps found in the caves are engraved with animal motifs or geometric designs similar to those occurring on the walls of caves, suggesting that they were more than just means of illumination.

To early modern humans, living in Europe during the Upper Palaeolithic, the subterranean passages and chambers that made up the caves were seen as the entrails of the spirit world. To enter them was to physically enter a nether realm where they could see the 'fixed' visions of the spirit-animals that empowered the shamans, and possibly experience the same visions for themselves. However, Lewis-Williams goes further and suggests that the origins of social stratification may also be found in such belief systems. Those able to master the techniques necessary to enter the altered states of consciousness and thus access the spirit world were set apart from those who could not. The cramped nature of the caves themselves suggests such a structure. At Lascaux, for example, only the Hall of the Bulls is large enough to have accommodated communal ritual activity. The carefully-composed images there must have been the result of a communal effort, albeit involving highly-skilled people and use of scaffolding. Notably, this hall is the nearest part of the complex to the surface, and it might have served as an antechamber into deeper parts of subterranean realm.

Possibly the most thought-provoking section of Lascaux is the Shaft of the Dead Man, often simply referred to as the Shaft. It is a deep shaft, accessible only by ropes and ladders. Floor space is limited, and very few people could have occupied it at a time. In the Shaft is portrayed a highly stylised man, who has the head of a bird, four-fingered birdlike hands, and a prominent phallus. He is apparently confronting a partially-eviscerated bison. Below him, a bird is perched atop a post. With its back to this scene and its tail raised is a rhinoceros, and on the opposite side is a black horse. These images may be interpreted as shamanistic: the death of the bison parallels the metaphorical 'death' of a shaman as he enters the spirit world and his fusion with his spirit-helper, a bird. Interestingly, the Shaft is characterised by high levels of naturally-occurring CO_2, which might have induced altered states if people stayed down there long enough.

However, in other lower levels at Lascaux, individual images do not appear to form parts of larger compositions, and are often superimposed upon each other. To Lewis-Williams, this suggests uncoordinated participation by different isolated individuals at different times, probably over a long period. It is in such regions of cave complexes that entoptic images were 'fixed'. In moving through these narrow passages, people might have felt that they were passing through the vortex experienced when in altered states of consciousness.

Only a few select individuals might have been permitted to enter the cramped lower levels of Lascaux and other caves. The use of inaccessible regions of the caves that could only accommodate a few people at a time was probably deliberate. Even areas where communal rituals took place might have been off limits to the majority of the population. Art and religion might thus have been born in a process of social stratification.

The Big Freeze

Between 26,500 and 22,000 years ago, the advancing glaciers had reached their Last Glacial Maximum full extent. The Scandinavian ice sheet blanketed Northern and Central Europe to depths of up to 5 km (3 miles), with the southern extent of the glaciation passing through Germany and Poland. Meanwhile, ice sheets covered the whole of Iceland and much of Britain and Ireland, which at that time were both still part of the European mainland. Further south, the mountainous regions of Europe were also icebound, including the Pyrenees, the Alps and the Carpathians.[64,46] While northern areas of Europe were never entirely abandoned, the greater part of the human population had by this time retreated to isolated refugia[65] including Franco-Cantabrian region, the Italian and Balkan peninsulas and a 'Periglacial Zone' on East European Plain.[66,67] The population of Western Europe might have fallen to as low as 17,000, including 10,000 in the Franco-Cantabrian refugium.[65]

Largely isolated from one another, the human populations in these regions underwent marked regionalisation. In some regions, the Gravettian continued; for example, in Italy it persisted until after the end of the Last Glacial Maximum.[7] Ceramic figurines found at the cave site of Vela Spila in Croatia have been dated to between 15,000 and 17,500 years old.[68] These later Gravettian industries are often referred to as Epigravettian.[7]

In other regions, new industries arose, such as the Solutrean, which is named after the type-site of Solutré, near Mâcon in eastern France. The Solutrean is known from sites in the Franco-Cantabrian region, characterised by finely-made leaf-shaped weapon tips. These appear to have been precisely made in terms of size and weight, reflecting the demands of hafting and aerodynamic efficiency. They were probably used as the tips of atlatl-propelled javelins; some of the smaller pieces might have been used as arrowheads. The leaf-points were often made with pressure flaking techniques, using flints that had been heat-treated to improve fracture dynamics.[7] The high-quality raw materials used to make these technologically-complex tools were often transported over long distances.[69]

The Solutrean is thought to have arisen in Iberia, and it briefly expanded north of the Pyrenees into Aquitaine before retreating back into its southern refugium. Its place on the French reindeer steppes was taken by an industry known as the Badegoulian.[65,70] The roots of the Badegoulian are uncertain. Some see it as purely a French phenomenon, though unrelated to the Solutrean.[69] Others believe that it originated in Central or Eastern Europe.[71,65,70] It is distinguished from the Solutrean by its generally cruder tool-making technology and the use of locally-sourced raw materials.[69]

The ice sheets began to retreat from Last Glacial Maximum levels 19,000 years ago, although there was another cold snap, Heinrich Event 1, 17,000 years ago. Thereafter, the climate began to improve and there was an abrupt warming with the onset of the Bølling-Allerød Interstadial, 14,500 years ago.[64,46,72] Although the ice age was by not yet over, populations now began to expand from their refugia.[65] A new culture known as the Magdalenian appeared in southern France, probably derived from the Badegoulian.[71,69]

The Magdalenian is named for the type site of La Madeleine, a rock-shelter in the Dordogne. It spread eastwards to Russia, across southern Europe and eventually, as conditions continued to improve, to Northern Europe. It reached Britain in the guise of the Creswellian 14,000 years ago. In Eastern Europe it is often referred to as the Moldovan. Extensive social networks were established and stone tools and marine shells were traded over long distances, in some cases up to 700 km (435 miles). In the still-cold environment, reindeer, bison, and aurochs remained key sources of food, though river fish were also important. Innovations such as the harpoon appeared for the first time in the later part of the Magdalenian. Some Magdalenian sites were very large, and were probably occupied for several months in the year; for example the La Madeleine rock-shelter is more than 180 m (595 ft.) long. In Eastern Europe, large semi-permanent dwellings were constructed from mammoth bones at sites such as Mezhirich and Mezine in central Ukraine and Yudinovo in Russia. The Magdalenian was the last cultural period of Ice Age Europe: the continent would undergo one final cold snap in the form of the Younger Dryas stadial before the Ice Age ended, bringing the Upper Palaeolithic to a close.[7]

Genetics: the Big Bounce

What can genetics tell us about the European Upper Palaeolithic? Trying to unravel the genetic history of Europe is not an easy matter. As Stephen Oppenheimer[24] has pointed out, there is no 'genetic history book' in which particular genetic lineages can be neatly assigned to dates and events. The wars, invasions, and general to-ings and fro-ings of more recent historical times have seen to that. Margins of uncertainty become problematic when trying to pin down age estimates for particular haplogroups in relation to tightly-constrained events such as the Last Glacial Maximum and the end of the last Ice Age. While most studies have involved living populations, ancient DNA has also obtained from prehistoric human remains. Recently, whole genome sequencing of this genetic material has added considerably to our knowledge concerning the early peopling of Europe. Before considering these latest developments, we shall review what has been learned from earlier studies of mitochondrial and Y-chromosomal DNA.

Most modern Europeans can be assigned to nine principal mitochondrial haplogroups: H, V, U, K, J, T, I, W and X.[73] H and V are sister haplogroups that derive from a common ancestor known as HV; J and T are similarly derived from JT; but K is actually a member of the U family tree. The haplogroups were assigned letters before the relationships between them were fully understood, otherwise a different system would have undoubtedly been adopted. The two most important Upper Palaeolithic haplogroups are U and HV.

The oldest mitochondrial haplogroup in Europe is U5. Although found elsewhere, U5 is thought to have evolved in Europe.[74] A range of estimates exist for its age, mostly lying between 50,000 and 25,000 years old.[74,75,76,77] The earlier part of this age range would be consistent with an Aurignacian origin. The Aurignacian people might also have brought the Y-chromosomal haplogroup R1 (M173) to Europe. It is of very ancient Eurasian origin, and has been present in Europe since Upper Palaeolithic times.[78,79]

U5 can also provide an insight into events in Southwest Asia immediately prior to the initial migrations into Europe. Haplogroup U6 is the sister group of U5 and it, together with M1, is common in North Africa, both having arrived there about 40,000 to 45,000 years ago in a back-migration from Asia.[80,81] A possible scenario is that populations harbouring precursors to M1, U6, and U5 were all living in the same broad geographic area of Southwest Asia, possibly in separate regional enclaves. These populations then expanded and migrated in response to the improved climate that opened the way into the Levant, and hence to both Europe and North Africa. Subsequently, populations bearing U5 went on to colonise Europe, while those with M1 and U6 entered North Africa.[80] Y-chromosomal data also supports an ancient Asian back-migration into Africa.[82,83] Thus populations returned to Africa twenty or more millennia after their distant forebears left.

To date, only one sample of ancient DNA from the Aurignacian period has been securely assigned to a mitochondrial haplogroup. A full mitochondrial sequence was obtained from 37,500-year-old human remains at Kostenki and identified as U2 rather than U5.[84] U2 is around 50,000 years old, and originated in either India or Southwest Asia,[85,86] but more ancient DNA results are needed from this period before we can start to draw any conclusions. The occurrence of U5 in present-day European populations is fairly modest at around seven to ten percent,[87,88] and U2 is also rare.[85,86] We must assume, therefore, that later events had a far greater bearing on the genetic makeup of modern Europeans.

Among contemporary populations, H is by far the most common mitochondrial haplogroup in both Europe and Southwest Asia. It is also fairly common in North Africa, Central Asia and Pakistan. In Europe, frequencies are typically around 40 percent, rising to 50 percent in the Basque Country. In Southwest Asia and the Caucasus, the frequency drops off to around 25 to 10 percent.[89,90] It has more subhaplogroups than any other European haplogroup, many of which can be further subdivided into minor branches.[91,92]

V, the sister haplogroup of H, is rather less common. Occurrence ranges from between 2.5 to 5 percent among most European populations,[93] although higher levels occur in northern Spain.[94,95] and among the Sami people of Scandinavia.[96,97]

Various estimates for the age of H range from 25,000 to 30,000 years old. It is believed to have diverged from the ancestral haplogroup HV in Southwest Asia and reached Europe somewhere between 20,000 and 25,000 years ago, subsequently dispersing to the southwest of the continent.[96,74,89,98] HV0, the precursor of V,[92] probably entered Europe from the east at the same time;[98] but V did not emerge until between 11,000 to 16,000 years ago, in Iberia.[97,90,77]

The dispersal of H and HV0 occurred at about the same time as an expansion from the Levant into the Mediterranean basin of the Y-chromosomal haplogroup F (M89), from which haplogroup I (M170) subsequently arose *in situ* in Europe.[78,79] The dates coincide fairly closely to the peak of the Last Glacial Maximum, arguably a less than propitious time to migrate into Europe. However, if one accepts an eastern origin for the Badegoulian, then such migrations were clearly still possible and may have brought H, HV0 and F (M89) to Europe.[65,70]

The postglacial repopulation of Europe from the Franco-Cantabrian refugium has been associated with V, H1, H2, and U5b1b, all of which are around the same age.[90,75,98] All four haplogroups have been found in Northwest Africa, suggesting that the postglacial expansion also took people across the Strait of Gibraltar into Africa.[75,99] Meanwhile, U5b3 expanded from the Italian refugium[100] and U4 and U5a from the Periglacial Zone refugium.[101,76] A similar picture is seen for Y-chromosomal lineages: the haplogroup I1b2 (M26) is associated with the expansion from Franco-Cantabria; I1b* (P37) from either the Balkans or the Periglacial Zone.[102]

Although there is no supporting archaeological evidence, it is possible that Southwest Asia also participated in the repopulation of Europe. The mitochondrial haplogroups J and T have long been associated with the dispersal of Neolithic farmers into Europe, but it has recently been claimed that they reached Europe earlier, as part of a postglacial expansion from a Southwest Asian refugium.[103]

Mitochondrial genetic diversity data confirms a rebounding of the population of Europe during the period from 15,000 to 10,000 years ago.[31] Overall, it has been suggested that the postglacial repopulation contributed 70 percent to the mitochondrial gene pool of present-day Europe. By contrast, the Neolithic component is only 20 percent.[88] Similarly, the Neolithic component of the Y-chromosomal gene pool is only 22 percent.[78] As we shall see in Chapter 19, the suggestion of such a low Neolithic component was controversial when first proposed in the 1990s.

However, it would be dangerous to think that genetic studies tell the whole story. Although the postglacial repopulation theory is firmly supported by archaeological evidence,[65] recent high-resolution mitochondrial studies of the Franco-Cantabrian region suggest that we may not yet have a full understanding of all the demographic processes involved.[95,104,105]

We should also be careful about relating the ages of specific haplogroups to particular demographic events in prehistory. Just because a haplogroup is now common in particular place, it doesn't necessarily mean that it was present there when it first arose.[106,107,108] An example is the complete absence of haplogroup V from a sample size of 121 taken from four Late Neolithic/Early Bronze Age sites in the Basque Country.[109] Occurrence among present-day Basques is around 10 to 12 percent.[97,94] This high incidence may be due to the effects of genetic drift, or to the cumulative genetic impact of the Roman, Visigoth and Vandal invasions in historical times.[110] Its absence in prehistoric times means that the role of V in the repopulation of postglacial Europe has to be questioned.[109]

Other ancient DNA results also suggest that we may not yet have the full genetic picture. Mitochondrial DNA obtained from individuals at postglacial hunter-gatherer sites shows a north-south divide between H and U: there is a preponderance of H at sites in Portugal,[111] but U5b1, U5b2, U5a and U4 predominate at sites in Central Europe and southeastern Russia. In addition, two individuals from the Magdalenian site of Hohler Fels in Germany were broadly identified as belonging to haplogroup U. The high incidence of U-based lineages suggests that these were more common at the time of the repopulation of Central Europe than they are today.[112]

Recently, ancient DNA recovered from individuals who lived far apart both geographically and in time has provided a fresh insight into the early settlement of Europe by modern humans. Researchers sequenced the genome of the Kostenki individual[113] and that of MA-1, a boy who lived 24,000 years ago at Mal'ta in southern central Siberia.[114] It was found that both possess close genetic affinities to present-day Europeans and western Siberians, though not to eastern Eurasians. The Mal'ta boy was also closely related to present-day Native Americans. These results suggest the existence of scattered, genetically-linked Upper Palaeolithic populations stretching from Europe to Central Asia, and that present-day Europeans derive a part of their ancestry from these populations. Thus it appears that some modern humans did after all reach Europe via the northern route discussed above.

We shall return to Europe in Chapter 19, when we consider the Mesolithic period and the subsequent spread of agriculture in to Europe. First we shall turn our attention to the settlement of New World, a place that no humans had previously reached, and where our closest relatives were monkeys whose ancestors were fortuitously rafted across the Atlantic from Africa 35 million years ago.

15: The final frontier

The peopling of the New World

The New World was the last habitable part of the globe to be settled by humans. In South America, the only primates were the New World monkeys; and no primates of any description had lived in North America since the Eocene period. Today, Alaska is separated from eastern Siberia by the Bering Strait, which is 55 km (18 miles) wide, but this has not always been the case. Throughout the period from 25,000 years ago until as late as 10,000 years ago, sea levels were so low that the strait and parts of the adjoining Chukchi and Bering Seas became dry land. The result was a landmass stretching from the Verkhoyansk Range in eastern Siberia to the Mackenzie River in northwestern Canada.[1] Known as Beringia, this so-called 'land bridge' was 1,600 km (1,000 miles) from north to south and linked Asia to North America. The region remained dry and cold, but free of ice. It is thought to have been an open landscape covered with grasses and herbaceous tundra and steppe vegetation.[2,3] It is via the Beringia land bridge that humans are long believed to have first reached the New World, but the number of migrations and their timing have been hotly debated for many decades.

As we saw in Chapter 13, humans had adapted to the extreme conditions of the Russian Arctic by around 30,000 years ago, but no unequivocal evidence has yet been found for a human presence east of the Yana Rhinoceros Horn site until much later. This site lies some 1,200 km (750 miles) west of the Bering Strait. There are hints of an early human presence, including 28,000-year-old mammoth bone flakes and fragments recovered from Bluefish Caves in Yukon Territory, and even older bone materials from along the nearby Old Crow River. Unfortunately, these bones lack associated stone artefacts, and may be the result of natural processes such as trampling by animals. The earliest reliable archaeological evidence comes from Swan Point in central Alaska, where a distinctive microlith and burin industry dates to 14,000 years ago. The Swan Point artefacts share many technological qualities with late Upper Palaeolithic sites in central Siberia, suggesting an eastward dispersal across Beringia during the late glacial period.[4]

After 14,000 years ago, a human presence in Beringia becomes well-established in the archaeological record. The best-known industries are the Nenana of central Alaska and the Ushki of Kamchatka. Both date to the period from 13,800 to 13,000 years ago. They are characterised by small pieces made from blades and flakes, but they lack microliths and burins. Also well-documented, but apparently distinct, is the Sluiceway-Tuluaq industry of northwestern Alaska, which is dated to 13,200 years ago and is associated with large lanceolate pieces. However, by 12,500 to 12,000 years ago, the region saw a change to technologies based upon microliths and burins; these changes were probably responses to the rapidly changing shrub-tundra environment of late-glacial Beringia.[4,5]

Expansion into the New World was undoubtedly delayed by two ice sheets that blanketed North America: the Laurentide across eastern Canada, and the Cordilleran along the Rocky Mountains. When it was at its maximum extent, from 21,000 to 14,000 years ago, the Laurentide extended from the Mackenzie River in northwestern Canada, blanketed the Canadian Arctic Archipelago and Greenland, and reached as far south as Pennsylvania and Cape Cod.[6] The Cordilleran was smaller, extending along the Rockies and down to Washington State.[7]

After the Last Glacial Maximum, the ice retreated sufficiently to create two ice-free routes along which migrations could have proceeded. The first was along the Pacific Coast; the second was a corridor through the Cordilleran and Laurentide ice sheets, lying east of the Canadian Rockies. Both routes were closed during the Last Glacial Maximum, but re-opened towards the end of the last Ice Age. Timing of the reopening of the two routes is still debated, because of imprecise dating and because the various Cordilleran glaciers reacted differently to climate change. Nonetheless, the Pacific route appears to have become deglaciated and thus open to human habitation no later than 15,000 years ago. On the other hand, the Cordilleran-Laurentide corridor might not have opened until as late as 14,000 to 13,500 years ago.[4]

Over the years, there has been much debate over which of these two routes could have provided the resources necessary to sustain a human migration from Beringia: the Cordilleran-Laurentide corridor might not have been repopulated by plant and animal life until several thousand years after it reopened.[8] The archaeological records of both routes are still inadequate for addressing questions about the initial peopling of the New World. However, the presence of 13,100 to 13,000-year-old human remains at Arlington Springs, on Santa Rosa Island off the coast of California, suggests the migrants used watercraft.[4] If the coastal route was taken, a problem is that much evidence could have long ago been submerged by rising post-glacial sea levels.[9]

A three-stage model

So far, this all sounds reasonably straightforward. However, genetic data rules out a simple migration from East Asia.[10] Analysis of Native American mitochondrial DNA originally identified four founding haplogroups in the population, A, B, C and D. All four are of Asian origin, but B is absent from the indigenous eastern Siberian populations that are the most obvious candidates to have been the source population for the migration.[11,12]

One interpretation is that B arrived in a separate migration to the other three haplogroups,[13] but it seems more likely that the founding population of the New World originated from a location where all four haplogroups are present – ruling out eastern Siberia. Despite their ubiquity in the New World, A, B, C and D are relatively uncommon in Asia, and occur together only in parts of Central Asia. Consistent with this view, later work has demonstrated that the New World mitochondrial haplogroups show closer genetic affinity to those of populations in eastern Central Asia than those of indigenous eastern Siberians.[14] In addition, the recent ages of some mitochondrial haplogroups present in eastern Siberia suggest that the present population arose from a later migration into the region, after Beringia had already been settled.[15,10,16]

The discovery of a fifth New World mitochondrial haplogroup, X,[17] initially led to confusion, as it occurs at low frequency in Europe.[18] However, it soon became clear that the European and New World variants of X are distinct from one another and that the latter's origins again lie in eastern Central Asia, in the region of the Altai Mountains.[19,20] Y-chromosomal data also suggests that Native Americans can trace their origins to Central Asia. The two founding haplogroups are Q1a3a (M3) and C3b (P39), both of which originated in the Altai region.[21,22] The recently-sequenced genome of the 24,000-year-old MA-1 juvenile remains from Mal'ta in southern central Siberia indicates that 14 to 38 percent of Native American ancestry may be traced back to the ancient population to which he belonged. Notably, this population showed no close affinity to present-day East Asians, though it did contribute to European ancestry. The latter finding indicates that the European genetic signal in Native American populations is not wholly of post-Columbian origin, as has long been thought.[23]

To accommodate these findings, a three-stage scenario has been proposed. The first stage was a period of gradual population growth as the ancestors of the first Americans diverged from the Central

Asian gene pool and moved to the northeast. This was followed by a lengthy period of isolation in Beringia, and finally there was a single, rapid population expansion into North America from Beringia.[24] Mitochondrial genetic diversity data suggests that the occupation of Beringia occurred approximately 30,000 years ago.[25]

During the Last Glacial Maximum, Beringia acted as a refugium for human populations, but the way into North America was blocked by the ice sheets blanketing the continent; and the way back into Asia was barred by arid wastelands. Mitochondrial genetic diversity data indicates that a moderate contraction of the population probably occurred between 23,000 and 19,000 years ago.[26,27] While the population remained isolated, the founder mitochondrial haplogroups differentiated from their Asian sisters. The founders have been identified as A2, B2, C1b, C1c, C1d, D1 and X2a, plus a number of minor haplogroups.[28,29,30]

As conditions again began to expand. A migration from Beringia into the New World began around 18,000 years ago, probably via the Pacific coastal route.[31,26,27] Estimates as to the size of the founding population range from as many as 10,000[32,24] to as few as 70 individuals.[33]

This three-stage model is supported by archaeological evidence. A statistical technique known as diffusion analysis was applied to the distribution of Siberian and Alaskan Upper Palaeolithic sites both geographically and over time in order to track population expansions. The results suggested an initial expansion that began in the Altai Mountains 46,000 years ago, and continued until 32,000 years ago. This period coincides with the favourable conditions of the warm Marine Isotope Stage 3 interstadial. The expansion was then followed by a lengthy hiatus coinciding with the Last Glacial Maximum, but a second expansion eventually began roughly 16,000 years ago as conditions improved. This second expansion led to the colonisation of Alaska and subsequently the rest of the New World.[34]

The first Americans

Until fairly recently, the popular view was the earliest Paleoindians – that is to say the first peoples who entered and subsequently populated the New World – were the Clovis people. The 'Clovis First' view supposed that these people made their way into the continent via the Laurentide-Cordilleran ice corridor, before spreading out rapidly across the United States. The Clovis culture is named for Clovis, New Mexico, where distinctive stone projectile points were first found in the 1930s. Recent work suggests that the earliest reliably-dated Clovis sites may be no older than 13,250 years old.[35] These dates are rather more recent than the 18,000 and 16,000 years ago proposed for the three-stage model discussed above.

The 'Clovis First' view began to crumble as long ago as the mid-1970s, although for a long time, the evidence was controversial, and it is still disputed by some. Part of the problem was a lack of unequivocal pre-Clovis sites in North America where logically one would expect to find the earliest evidence of settlement. The best-known possible pre-Clovis site is Meadowcroft Rockshelter, near Avella, Pennsylvania, which was excavated between 1973 and 1978. Artefacts from this site have been bracketed by dates of 15,200 and 13,400 years old, obtained from radiocarbon-dated charcoal fragments recovered from layers above and below them. The older of these two dates considerably predates Clovis, but it is regarded as suspect. These doubts have long hampered full acceptance of the site by an archaeological community that remains sceptical of pre-Clovis claims.[8,4]

More recently, though, evidence for a pre-Clovis occupation of North America has begun to emerge from a number other sites. These include Buttermilk Creek (Texas), Manis (Washington State), Paisley Cave (Oregon), Cactus Hill (Virginia) and Topper (South Carolina). The evidence from first three of these sites is probably the most convincing. Buttermilk Creek is located along a small valley, close to the Clovis site of Gault. Lying below a Clovis horizon of 2.5 cm (1 in.) has been found a 20 cm (8 in.) layer containing stone tools and debitage that represented repeated tool manufacturing and use at the site over a period of time. Ages ranging from 13,200 to 15,500 years old have been obtained for the artefacts by optically stimulated luminescence dating.[36]

At Manis, the tip of a bone projectile point has been found embedded in the rib of a mastodon, which was excavated from sediment at the base of a pond between 1977 and 1979. The rib, probably the 14th (of 19) had been penetrated to a depth of 2.15 cm (0.85 in.) by the projectile, which would also have penetrated hair, skin and up to 30 cm (1 ft.) of muscle. There is no evidence for bone regrowth, suggesting that the mastodon died soon after being attacked. Recently-obtained radiocarbon dates suggest the kill took place 13,800 years ago, centuries before Clovis.[37]

At Paisley Cave, human coprolites (fossilised faeces) have been radiocarbon dated to between 14,000 and 14,270 years old, at least 750 years before Clovis. Mitochondrial DNA obtained from the coprolites has been identified as belonging to haplogroups A2 and B2. Both are founding New World mitochondrial haplogroups, and thus confirm the human origin of the coprolites.[38] Sediments and animal faeces around the coprolites were later tested for human genetic material to rule out the possibility of later contamination caused by people urinating in the cave; none was found.[39]

The evidence from the other two sites is more equivocal. Cactus Hill, near Richmond, Virginia, is a sand-dune site with Clovis and more recent levels. Potentially-older stone artefacts, including small prismatic blade cores, blades, and two points have been recovered from below the Clovis level. A number of radiocarbon dates have been obtained, including three pre-Clovis dates ranging from 18,000 to 20,000 years old, but some are more recent. However, optically stimulated luminescence dates do tie in with the older radiocarbon dates.[4]

Topper, on the Savannah River, South Carolina, is a sandy deposit that overlies a clay terrace. Small flakes and larger unworked cobbles have been found beneath a possible Clovis layer, separated from it by a thick layer of clay. Some have argued that the flakes are microliths or burins, but it is also possible that they were produced by purely natural processes, such as variations in temperature causing material to crack and break off from the cobbles. Dating these supposed artefacts has been problematic. It has been claimed that some of the material is as old as 50,000 years, but this seem highly improbable.[9,4]

In addition to these sites, there is evidence from a number of locations for butchery and other exploitation of mammoth carcasses well before Clovis. In Wisconsin, strong evidence has been found that mammoths were hunted and/or scavenged close to the southern margins of the Laurentide ice sheet between 14,200 and 14,800 years ago. At the sites of Schaefer and Hebior, mammoth remains were found, together with stone artefacts. The remains bear cut-marks consistent with butchery with stone tools. Even earlier are the 16,000-year-old lower limb bones from a mammoth recovered at Mud Lake, Kenosha County, Wisconsin, which also bear cut-marks – though in this case no stone tools have been found.[4,5]

Mammoth and mastodon bones might also have been used as raw material for tool-making. At Page-Ladson, Florida, a 14,400-year-old mastodon tusk has been found, together with stone tools. The tusk bears deep grooves, apparently made as it was removed from its socket. Earlier but less secure evidence has been found at two sites in the Midwest: La Sena, Nebraska and Lovewell, Kansas. At these sites, mammoth leg bones have been found with impact marks and signs of flaking. The bones were probably quarried and flaked within a few years of the deaths of the animals, a practice documented for both the Clovis and Beringia people. La Sena is between 20,000 and 22,000 years old, and Lovewell is about 19,000 years old. Unfortunately, no stone tools have been found at either site.[4,5]

Does the combined weight of evidence from these sites mean that it really is time to abandon 'Clovis First'? Anthropologist Robert Kelly[9] believes that the evidence is insufficient to break the

'Clovis Barrier'. While they are interesting, these finds may represent nothing more than unsuccessful pioneering groups that became extinct long before Clovis. Kelly suggests that if there was a sustained human presence in North America 14,000 to 16,000 years ago, many more early-dated sites would by now have been found. A major problem for Kelly's viewpoint is that it ignores the evidence for a sustained pre-Clovis human presence in South America. To have reached South America from Siberia, migrants presumably must have first passed through North America.

Evidence from South America

Several South American sites predate the Clovis barrier, most notably Monte Verde in southern Chile, where there is evidence of human occupation from 14,600 years ago. The site is a peat bog located in the terraces of a small creek in the Maullín river basin, midway between the Pacific coast and the Andean mountains. Evidence of human occupation has been well preserved, and excavation was carried out between 1977 and 1985 under the direction of anthropologist Tom Dillehay. Finds from the lower layer of the site include wooden tent remains, the foundations and floors of huts, hearths and braziers, wooden lances, mortars and digging sticks, human footprints and numerous stone tools. These items suggest that the site was occupied all year round. Animal and plant remains suggest food was obtained from a wide variety of habitats, both on the coast and in the mountains. These include marshes, wetlands, forests, estuaries, and rocky and sandy shorelines. The remains include mastodon and now-extinct llama species, wild potatoes, and edible and medicinal plants and seaweeds. The coast would have yielded pebbles for tool manufacture, and bitumen used as adhesive for hafting tools.[40]

More recently, a range of marine, shoreline and estuarine seaweeds have also been recovered from an upper occupational layer known as Monte Verde II. All contain iodine, iron, zinc and a wide range of trace elements, particularly cobalt, copper, boron, and manganese. They are said to aid cholesterol metabolism, increase the calcium uptake of bones, and increase the body's ability to fight infection. Two of the species are non-edible, and were evidently used solely for medicinal purposes. They are today used by local indigenous people to treat various ailments, including digestive problems, stomach ulcers, skin rashes, inflammations, abscesses, eye infections and gout.[41]

Further evidence for maritime-based activity by early South American settlers has been found at two coastal sites in southern Peru. At the site of Quebrada Tacahuay, which is between 12,500 and 12,700 years old, remains of seabirds and fish have been recovered, including anchovies. The remains of these small, schooling fish suggest that the Quebrada Tacahuay people had specialised nets for fishing. Other recovered materials include a hearth, cutting tools and flakes. Quebrada Tacahuay is now located 300 to 400 m (330 to 440 yards) from the shore, but when it was occupied it was probably a kilometre (0.6 mile) or more inland due to lower sea levels.[42]

A short distance northwest along the Peruvian coast is the site of Quebrada Jaguay 280 (QJ 280), which lies 2 km (1.25 miles) inland. Again, when occupied it was further from the coast, in this case 7 to 8 km (4.3 to 5 miles) inland. The site is between 11,000 and 13,000 years old. Finds include petrified wood, small pieces of obsidian, and the abundant remains of fish, crustaceans and marine molluscs. The fish were predominantly small drum, which were probably harvested with nets. The QJ 280 people also seem to have ventured some way inland: the chemical composition of the obsidian suggests that it originated 130 km (80 miles) away, in the Andean highlands. It has been suggested that the QJ 280 people based their foraging around an annual cycle in which they spent part of the year in the highlands and the remainder on the coast.[43] Quebrada Santa Julia in central Chile is another coastal site where tools were made from non-local materials; quartz was obtained from sources up to 30 km (18 miles) inland.[44]

The overall picture from South America is a pre-Clovis settlement by versatile bands of semi-sedentary hunter-gatherers. It remains unknown whether the settlers at Monte Verde and elsewhere reached South America via a coastal or inland route. However, if the coastal route was taken, groups travelling along the Pacific coast might have migrated slowly all the way from Alaska to Tierra del Fuego. In all probability, they used boats in the manner described in Chapter 12, and exploited the interior river basins as they moved south.[41]

The Pacific coastal route is supported by genetic evidence obtained by sampling Native American populations from North, Central and South America. Mesoamerican and Andean populations are fairly similar in genetic terms, and genetic diversity in South America decreases from west to east. Both observations are consistent with an initial dispersal along the Pacific coast, followed by the settlement of the eastern tropical lowlands.[45] The Pacific scenario is also backed by the very presence of humans in South America prior to 14,000 years ago. As noted above, the Cordilleran-Laurentide ice corridor was likely to have been impassable until rather later.

The Clovis culture

Although the 'Clovis First' view has, strictly speaking at least, been disproved, Clovis remains the earliest distinct culture clearly documented in the archaeological record of the New World. The signature Clovis points are lanceolate stone projectile points, fluted (grooved) on each face, with the fluting generally extending about one-third to one-half the length of the face. Finished points are blunted along the edges where they were hafted to the spear, to prevent the binding material from being inadvertently cut during use. Although all Clovis points share these features, there is a degree of regional variety. This probably came about through changes in knapping styles and techniques over time in different parts of the continent. Other elements of the Clovis tool kit include end and side scrapers, gravers, knives, and occasional bone tools. The Clovis tool-makers relied almost exclusively on high-quality material, including chert, jasper, chalcedony and obsidian. The stone was usually acquired at bedrock outcrops rather than from secondary sources such as river or glacial gravels, suggesting that the Clovis people had an extensive knowledge of the geology of the region. To those who knew where to look, raw material from outcrops had the advantage that it was more likely to be of adequate size and quality for tool-making.[8]

Decorative art is very rare among Clovis sites. A few dozen specimens of limestone incised with parallel or intersecting lines have been found, all but two of which were found at Gault, Texas. There is nothing comparable to the cave paintings and portable art of Upper Palaeolithic Europe.[8] However, it is possible that many of the Clovis points might have been more than purely utilitarian objects. The materials from which they made are often strikingly coloured, such as red jasper, black obsidian, and multicoloured chalcedony. Among Aboriginal Australians, deep red cherts were thought to have been formed from the blood of ancestral beings, and it is possible the coloured raw material had a similar significance for the Clovis people.[46]

Clovis artefacts and sites have been found across the contiguous United States in a variety of environments, from the rich grasslands of the western Plains to the forests of the Southeastern United States. No subsequent North American occupation was so widespread or occupied such diverse habitats, albeit many areas appear to have been only sparsely occupied. The Clovis people inhabited the Great Basin, the Columbia and Colorado Plateaus, northern Great Plains, northern Rockies and the uppermost and lowermost reaches of the Mississippi Valley, and they inhabited Central America as far south as Panama. However, they have not been found in Alaska or northwestern Canada.[8,5]

Clovis sites are often small and typically represent short-term camps, caches and kill sites. However, there is evidence for longer-term habitation at sites in Texas and the Southeastern United States, where large numbers of Clovis artefacts have been found. These may represent quarry and habitation sites habitually used by Clovis people, from which they did not range great distances. The great majority of the artefacts were made from locally or near-locally-sourced materials. For example at Gault, 99 percent of the artefacts were made from local on-site chert.[4]

It remains disputed as to whether the Clovis people were generalists or primarily big-game specialists. Animal remains from 33 Clovis sites have been claimed to support the big-game view, and that the incidence of mammoth and mastodon remains was greater than would be expected if there was an equal emphasis on all available prey animals.[47] However, the number of Clovis kill sites has been challenged. For example, a mastodon kill site in Hiscock, NY has now been re-interpreted as a quarry from which mastodon bone and ivory was obtained from geological deposits. In all, the number of supposed kill sites in North America has fallen from 75 to just 14 for which there is secure, unambiguous evidence of hunting activities.[48,49,8]

Crucial to understanding the Clovis phenomenon is when and where did it originate, and how fast did it spread? Does it represent an actual expansion of people across North America, or was it simply a cultural phenomenon? Based on ages of reliably-dated sites, Clovis first appeared between 13,100 and 13,250 years ago, during the latter part of the warm Bølling-Allerød Interstadial, and it came to an end between 12,925 and 12,800 years ago, soon after the start of the subsequent Younger Dryas cold interval. This gives Clovis a span of just 200 to 450 years, suggesting a rapid expansion across much of North America.[35]

Dates in various regions of North America overlap with one another, making it difficult to determine the point of origin and direction taken by the Clovis expansion.[4] The traditional view is that the Clovis people came through the Cordilleran-Laurentide corridor, subsequently spreading southwards and eastwards. It has been claimed that statistical analysis of Clovis site dates supports this view, and shows a 'wave of advance' spreading from the mouth of the ice corridor 13,400 years ago.[50] This date gives a good fit with dates for the opening of the corridor, 13,500 years ago, but as noted above there are questions as to how soon it could have supported a human migration. Other possibilities are an inland migration from the West Coast, which is consistent with view that the first Paleoindians took a coastal route all the way south to Tierra del Fuego. It could be that sizable populations were established in South America first, with the Clovis expansion later occurring northwards from Central America. This would be consistent with the bulk of the pre-Clovis sites being located in South America.[50]

A rather more unorthodox idea, known as the Solutrean Hypothesis, has been put forward by archaeologists Bruce Bradley and Dennis Stanford,[51] who claim that the New World was settled not from Siberia but from Europe. They note that the fluted Clovis points, while lacking antecedents in the archaeological record of Upper Palaeolithic Siberia, do closely resemble leaf-shaped projectile points of the Solutrean culture from the Franco-Cantabrian region of late Upper Palaeolithic Europe. Other similarities between the Clovis and Solutrean cultures include shared tool-making techniques and the use of high-quality materials such as quartz.

To explain what they describe as an 'extraordinary convergence', Stanford and Bradley suggest that the Solutrean people used boats to hunt northward-migrating seals along the margins of the sea ice. During the Last Glacial Maximum, this formed much further south than is now the case, covered major portions of the North Atlantic, and formed an 'ice bridge' between Europe and North America. Eventually, they claim, some groups followed the ice bridge all the way to America, a distance of around 2,500 km (1,550 miles), which is a shorter distance than the historical Thule Inuit migrations from Alaska to Greenland. The Solutrean disappeared from Europe well before Clovis, but Stanford and Bradley suggest that the pre-Clovis sites fill this time gap and that their technologies are transitional between the two. They also note that sites like Meadowcroft and Page-Ladson are located close to the Atlantic coast of North America.

Others are sceptical and anthropologists Lawrence Straus, David Meltzer and Ted Goebel[52] have emphasised the differences rather than the similarities between the two cultures. They note, for instance, that Solutrean points lack the signature fluting of their Clovis counterparts, and the Clovis people for their part lacked anything corresponding to the portable and cave art of Upper Palaeolithic Europe. It is also questionable whether the Solutrean people hunted seals and other aquatic mammals. Technology such as the harpoon did not appear in Europe until much later. Straus, Meltzer and Goebel believe that technological convergence between the two cultures, while real, is hardly extraordinary. Another problem for the Solutrean hypothesis is that it is completely unsupported by the genetic evidence which, as we saw above, indicates an ultimate origin for the first Americans in eastern Central Asia.

The sheer speed of the Clovis expansion coupled with the existence of pre-Clovis sites has led to the suggestion that the Clovis phenomenon may simply represent a spread of technology among pre-existing population rather than an actual movement of people.[35,53] It is important to realise that the spread of innovations doesn't always correspond to the spread of people, as we shall see in later chapters. More evidence is needed to clarify whether or not this was the case for Clovis.[54]

Regardless of its origin, the speed of the Clovis expansion meant that the population soon become thinly-stretched across a continent the size of North America. It would have been important for the distantly-scattered Clovis groups to maintain cooperative relations and open social networks with one another. By so doing, they were able to maximize their effective gene pool and thus avoid the problems of inbreeding, at the same time pooling knowledge about local conditions and availability of resources.[8]

The end of the Clovis period coincides closely with the onset of the Younger Dryas cold period and while it might have been a factor, it is unlikely to have been the only cause. The Clovis culture was replaced by more regionally-specific traditions including the Folsom culture, named for Folsom, New Mexico. There, characteristic stone projectile points, smaller and thinner than the Clovis points, were first discovered in 1927. These later tool forms do appear to correspond to new and sometimes locally-specific or prey-specific hunting strategies: the Folsom occupations, for example, appeared on the Plains and Rocky Mountains of western North America, where bison were abundant. The shift from the single widespread Clovis form to multiple regional forms might have come about as colonists settled in specific areas. In many places, there was a greater reliance on locally-available stone, suggesting that groups were now less mobile. As local populations grew, they became less demographically-vulnerable and, over time, lost the pressure to maintain contact with distant groups. Given the vastness of North America and its topographic and geographic barriers, this had never been easy.[8]

Who was Kennewick Man?

A topic generating almost as much controversy as Clovis First is the number of prehistoric migrations into the New World. Did the founding population of Native Americans arrive in just one post-glacial period migration, or did other migrants arrive during the early and middle Holocene?

In 1996, a human skull was found in the Columbia River, Kennewick, Washington State, and more skeletal remains were later recovered, including the pelvis in which a stone spear tip was embedded. Radiocarbon dating established the remains to be 8,400 years old. The remains belonged to a man who had died aged between 40 and 55 years old, but he did not resemble a Native American. His skull was long and narrow, face narrow, and his chin jutted. He looked more like a European than a broad-headed and broad-faced Native American. A facial reconstruction by physical anthropologist James Chatters is said to bear a startling resemblance to actor Sir Patrick Stewart, best known for his role as Captain Jean-Luc Picard in *Star Trek*. As many *Star Trek* stories have involved time-travel, there have invariably been suggestions that Kennewick Man actually *was* Picard, who had failed to return from one of his missions.

In fact, the skull was not European and its teeth suggested an Asian origin. Studies revealed that the skull features were most like those of the Ainu people of Japan and indigenous people of the South Pacific. It was also learned that Kennewick Man's life had been arduous. In addition to the spear injury, he had suffered many injuries and bone fractures. On the other hand, he had eaten well and enjoyed a diet that included salmon. Unfortunately, attempts to extract DNA from the bones were unsuccessful.[55]

Kennewick Man was not alone. The skull shape of ancient Paleoindians differs from those of present-day Native Americans; the latter form is generally supposed not to have appeared until around 5,000 years ago.[55] It has been suggested that the differences are best accounted by two successive migrations, with the Paleoindians arriving first and later being replaced by ancestors of modern Native Americans.[56] Another suggestion is that the Native American skull shape arose *in situ* from that of the Paleoindians by a process of local microevolution, possibly driven by changes in diet associated with the change from hunter-gathering to farming between 8,000 and 2,000 years ago.[57]

However, the likeliest explanation is that the skull data has simply been misinterpreted. For example, the 9,225-year-old male skull from Wizards Beach, Nevada, falls easily within the range of variation of Santa Cruz, Sioux and Blackfoot Native Americans.[58] Principal component analysis has been applied to large numbers of Late Pleistocene, Early Holocene and present-day human skulls from Africa, Eurasia and the New World. The results suggested that when variations in skull shape were considered over a wide geographical range (such as from Australia to South America), or over a wide span of time (from the Late Pleistocene to the present day), the skulls could not be grouped into discrete categories, but instead formed a continuous spectrum of variation. When applied to New World groups alone, the same continuous pattern was seen. The supposed Paleoindian and Native American forms were no more than extremes at opposite ends of a continuum, and most of the New World samples fell well between the two extremes.[59]

Three language families

In 1986, the American linguist Joseph Greenberg[60] used comparative linguistics in an attempt to identify the number of migrations into the New World. It has long been known that languages evolve over time, and that there are language 'families' or groups of languages that share common origins. For example French, Spanish, Portuguese, Italian, Romanian and Catalan, together with numerous other less commonly-spoken tongues, all derive from Latin (strictly speaking, from Vulgar Latin, the term given to the colloquial forms used throughout the Roman Empire), and are known as the Romance languages. Greenberg began by assuming each group of migrants spoke their own language and that over time a language family arose from each founding language. In theory at least, it is only be necessary to determine how many Native American language families there are, and that will correspond to the number of migrations. In earlier work going back to the 1960s, Greenberg claimed that there were three language families: Amerind, Na-Dene and Aleut-Eskimo. He concluded, therefore, that there had been three migrations.

The great majority of languages spoken by Native Americans are Amerind. The second group, Na-Dene, comprises languages spoken mainly in northwestern Canada, Alaska and along the Pacific

Coast; and Aleut-Eskimo is restricted to the Aleutian Islands and the Arctic. As Amerind is the most diverse family, Greenberg suggested that it corresponded to the earliest migration. It was followed by the Na-Dene, and finally the Aleut-Eskimo migrations. Greenberg went on to use a method known as glottochronology to try and put a timescale on the three migrations. This method was first devised in the 1950s by the American linguist Morris Swadesh, and relies on two assumptions. The first is that in any language there will be a core vocabulary of commonly-used words (now known as the Swadesh List). The second is that words are lost from this vocabulary at a constant rate over time; a figure of 86 percent word retention over 1,000 years is commonly used.

Unfortunately, as Greenberg himself observed, there are a number of problems with the method. Certain types of word, such as personal pronouns, are retained for much longer than others. There are difficulties in deciding which words should be included in the lists themselves. Even if these difficulties are overcome, there are limits to how far back in time one can go. After around 10,000 years, the number of retained words is too small for a meaningful judgement. With these caveats in mind, Greenberg nevertheless suggested a date of 4,000 years ago for Aleut-Eskimo, 9,000 years ago for Na-Dene, and in excess of 11,000 years ago for Amerind. The last date is beyond the useful limits of glottochronology.

At best, these conclusions could be regarded as tentative. Another problem is that a figure of just three Native American language families is widely seen as a gross underestimate. Some linguists claim that that the true number is over 160.[55] However, it turns out that Greenberg could have been right after all.

Genetic studies vindicate Greenberg

The mitochondrial 'big picture' argues against multiple migrations. The New World mitochondrial haplogroups, while ubiquitous there, are only a subset of those seen in Asia, where they are fairly uncommon. It is highly unlikely that multiple migrations into the New World would repeatedly introduce that same set of rare haplogroups and no others.[14,61] That these haplogroups have similar genetic dates also points to a single common origin.[17]

However, the supposed Na-Dene and Aleut-Eskimo migrations were small in comparison to comparison to earlier Amerind migration. Could the 'big picture' be missing some fine detail? The answer appears to be 'yes'. Some of the minor mitochondrial haplogroups show evidence for Holocene migrations in both directions across the Bering Strait. Haplogroup D2 consists of two sister haplogroups, D2a and D2b. The former is restricted to Aleut-Eskimos, whereas the latter is found only in Siberia. The absence of D2 from other Native American populations suggests that it reached the New World in a later migration. Haplogroup D3, which has been reported in Canada and Greenland, might be another Holocene arrival from Siberia. All was not one-way traffic, as the presence of New World-derived haplogroups in Siberia suggests that back-migrations from Alaska also occurred.[29]

Y-chromosomal studies have drawn mixed conclusions. The two founding haplogroups are Q1a3a (M3) and C3b (P39). The former, occurring in over three-quarters of Native American males, is far more prevalent than the latter, which has an incidence of around five percent. As previously noted, the origin of both can be traced back to the Altai region of Central Asia. It has been suggested that the pair represent the major and minor components of the same migration, and that other Y-chromosomal haplogroups present in the population are of recent European origin.[21] However, it has also been proposed that each haplogroup represented a separate migration,[62] and that some of the supposedly-European lineages are actually of Central Asian and eastern Siberian origin, thus indicating at least two migrations.[63,64]

A more definitive answer has had to await the development of techniques that can make use of genome-wide data. The results have apparently vindicated Greenberg and shown that there were indeed three migrations: a major migration, followed by two smaller ones. It was found that most Native American populations are descended from a single ancestral population. However, Aleut-Eskimo speakers inherit almost half their ancestry from a second migratory group. Meanwhile, the Na-Dene-speaking Chipewyan from Canada inherit roughly one-tenth of their ancestry from a third migration. These results are entirely consistent with Greenberg's conclusions.[65] Later work with ancient DNA confirmed these findings, but also showed that the prehistoric Saqqaq culture from Greenland represented a fourth migration into the New World.[66]

What these studies do not show is evidence of a population replacement around 5,000 years ago and indeed suggest that the bulk of Native Americans are descended from the original pioneers who entered the New World during the latter part of the last Ice Age. This conclusion has been reinforced by ancient DNA recovered from the remains of a young male interred at a Clovis burial site in Montana and from the 13,000-year-old skeleton of an adolescent female found in a cave in the Yucatan Peninsula, Mexico. The young male's genome was sequenced and it showed that he belonged to a population directly ancestral to many present-day Native Americans.[67] The adolescent female, whose skull was typical of the Paleoindian form, was found to belong to mitochondrial haplogroup D1, which occurs only among present-day Native Americans.[68] Both results are consistent with the view that there was continuity between Paleoindians and present-day Native Americans.

The settlement of the New World meant that modern humans were now established on every habitable continental landmass, something no species of large mammal had ever previously accomplished. The whole process, from leaving Africa, had possibly taken as little as 50,000 years – in geological terms, no more than the blink of an eye. As modern humans prospered though, other large mammals were less fortunate, and by 10,000 years ago at least two-thirds of them had become extinct. How did this come about? The prime suspect is *Homo sapiens*.

The final frontier   **207**

16: Humanity in the dock

A Pleistocene whodunit

The Pleistocene world was dominated by large mammals, flightless birds and reptiles. In North America, these included mammoths, mastodons, giant ground sloths, camels, sabre-tooth cats, and giant beavers. In Eurasia, woolly mammoth and rhinoceros, and giant deer with antlers spanning 3 m (10 ft.) were common. South American species included the glyptodont, a giant relative of the armadillo, and the litoptern, which resembled a cross between a horse and a camel (though unrelated to either). Finally, in Australia, there lived the hippopotamus-sized *Diprotodon optatum* that weighed in at 2.8 tonnes, and was the largest marsupial of all time. These animals are collectively known as the megafauna, a term applied to animals with an adult weight of 45 kg (100 lb.) or more. Humans are just large enough to be considered megafauna.

Between 50,000 and 10,000 years ago, many of these great beasts vanished in one of the largest extinction events since the demise of the dinosaurs. Australia and the New World were hardest hit, but no habitable continent remained unscathed. Overall, about 180 large mammal species and over 100 entire genera perished. Though by no means the largest mass extinction in Earth's history, it was the first to occur after the appearance of humans, and its timing coincides closely with the dispersal of modern humans around the world.[1,2,3,4] Usually referred to as the Late Quaternary extinction event, it was recognised by early geologists towards the end of the eighteenth century. By the early nineteenth century, two possible causes were being proposed as possible causes for the extinctions – climate change and human activity. The latter became popular after 1860, and by the 1870s it was being referred to as 'the favourite hypothesis'. By then, it was accepted that humans had once coexisted with the megafauna,[5] but is the 'favourite hypothesis' correct? Humanity is in the dock, but were our ancestors guilty?

Overkill and other human causes

The simplest human-causation model is known as the 'overkill' or 'blitzkrieg' hypothesis. This model views early human groups as big-game hunters that rapidly hunted the megafauna into extinction. It was proposed its present form by Paul Martin,[6,7] a geoscientist at the University of Arizona. In essence, the overkill hypothesis is based on five observations:

1. Rates of megafaunal extinction were much higher on landmasses only colonised by hunter-gathers in the last 60,000 years or so than they were in Africa, where humans evolved;
2. Remote island species, not previously exposed to humans, are highly vulnerable to human predation;
3. Ethnographic data and theoretical modelling suggest that hunter-gatherers preferentially select large prey;
4. The Quaternary extinctions took a significantly higher toll on large animals than on small;

5. Climate fluctuated widely throughout the Pleistocene without producing comparable mass extinctions of megafauna – hence climate change can be eliminated from the short-list of alternative causes.

From this, it is implied that selective over-hunting of large, slow-breeding animals, facilitated by their naiveté to the threat posed by humans, resulted in rapid mass extinctions. These occurred wherever hunter-gatherers colonised new landmasses, and once human populations had reached densities at which they were killing the megafauna faster than the latter could breed.[6,7,8,9,2]

However, there are a number of problems with the assumptions underlying the overkill theory. In particular, it is questionable whether the extinction of remote island species through human predation is relevant when considering continental-scale extinctions. Remote islands are generally free of predators, making fauna naive to any form of predation, not just by humans. This, together with restricted ranges and small populations, renders island fauna unusually vulnerable to invading predators.

The overkill theory probably exaggerates the hunting efficiency of colonising human groups. Also, as we have seen in earlier chapters, it is unlikely that Upper Palaeolithic peoples relied solely on big-game hunting. Consistent with this, studies have shown that present-day hunter-gatherers do not universally target the largest species available to them.[9]

Overkill is not the only human-causation theory, and human activities other than hunting have also been put forward as possible causes. These include habitat destruction as a result of human activity; introduction of invasive predatory species; and the introduction of virulent diseases.

Prehistoric extinctions in Holocene times have occurred on islands as a result of habitat alteration by land clearance and use of fire; for example in Hawaii,[10] New Zealand and other Pacific islands,[11] and Madagascar.[12] Present-day hunter-gatherers burn off vegetation for a variety of reasons, such as clearing passageways, hunting along the fire front, signalling to distant groups, and promoting the growth of particular plants.[13] Compared with undisturbed woodland, the post-fire grow-back vegetation contains a far greater range and quality of edible plant foods for both humans and potential prey animals.[14] However, as we shall see presently, there are reasons to doubt that human habitat alteration could have led to extinctions on a continent-wide scale.

Similarly, the effect of introduced predators on native species is well documented; rats, cats, dogs, pigs and foxes are particularly destructive. When the first Polynesian settlers arrived on the Pacific islands, they brought pigs and dogs with them, and inadvertently introduced rats. All these new predators had a disastrous impact on native island fauna. Prey naiveté was a major factor, as many islands lacked native predators; but the effects were less severe on islands that already had predators.[15,9] The role of introduced predators in Australia and the New World is less clear, but is unlikely to explain the Late Quaternary extinctions. Dingoes did not reach Australia until well after the extinctions, and although domesticated dogs were brought to the New World by the first human settlers, wolves and coyotes had already been preying on megafauna for at least a million years.[3] Wolves, domestic dogs and dingoes are all the same species, *Canis lupus*.

The third possibility, a virulent 'hyper-disease', is rather more speculative. Ross MacPhee, a palaeontologist at the American Museum of Natural History and virologist Preston Marx[16] believe that a virus jumped from human colonists to megafauna, with devastating results. In a kind of *The War of the Worlds* scenario in reverse, the megafauna succumbed to a disease to which the human invaders were immune. To cause the sudden collapse of so many species though, such diseases would have to be an entirely new pathogen on the affected landmasses, jump between species easily and kill infected species rapidly. Such a combination seems to be unlikely, and such extremely lethal, cross-species pathogens are not known today. Overall, this makes the hyper-disease theory unlikely.[3]

There is no doubt that human activity, particularly since the beginning of the industrial era, has led to a profoundly worrying loss of biodiversity. Theories that implicate humans in the Quaternary Extinction Event are understandably popular with environmental campaigners, who see it as a harbinger of worse to come if humanity does not mend its ways. However, it is quite simply bad science to extrapolate recent biodiversity losses back to the Late Pleistocene without further evidence, or without considering alternatives such as climate change. We must also beware of assuming that the extinctions, worldwide, had a single cause or even a single combination of causes.

Climate change

Nineteenth century climate change theories were based around either sudden catastrophic deep freeze or drought,[5] but modern hypotheses emphasise ecological effects. The models fall into three main types, known as 'habitat loss', 'nutrient mosaic', and 'coevolutionary disequilibrium'.[3]

The habitat loss model assumes that climate change caused areas with conditions capable of supporting megafauna to either disappear or break up into zones too small to support viable populations.[17] The nutrient mosaic model is a special case of habitat loss; it postulates that climate change resulted in a shortening of the growing season, leading to a reduction in local plant diversity. This in turn impacted herbivore species that rely on a diverse range of plant foods in their diet.[18] Coevolutionary disequilibrium proposes that the herbivore diversity was maintained by highly complex habitats in which plant and animal species had evolved together (coevolution). Rapid climate change from glacial to interglacial conditions resulted in a reorganisation of the flora, disrupting the delicate equilibrium of these ecosystems.[19]

A common argument against climate change-related theories is that megafauna were able to survive previous episodes of climate change throughout the Pleistocene, which saw around twenty glacial-interglacial cycles. Only the most recent cycle saw mass extinctions occur. Notably, this was the first where modern humans were present.[2] On the face of it, this is a perfectly reasonable point, but maybe we should be looking at the bigger picture. Palaeontologist Philip Gingerich[20] notes that since the extinction of the dinosaurs, the rate of appearance of new mammalian genera has been closely matched by the rate at which other genera become extinct. Faunal turnover has varied, but the overall diversity over time has remained fairly constant. The Early Pleistocene saw the appearance of a large number of new genera. Gingerich argues that the subsequent extinctions were an inevitable sequel as equilibrium was restored; a mammalian boom-to-bust.

Deep Impact

One of the more controversial theories, first proposed in 2007, is that around 12,900 years ago, Earth suffered multiple airbursts and surface impacts from fragments of a comet or asteroid that had previously broken up in space. In North America, the bombardment caused devastating shock-waves and continent-wide forest fires that brought about the extinction of the megafauna. While the overall effects were far less severe than those of the impact now believed to have killed off the dinosaurs, they were still sufficient to trigger a global 'impact winter'. This in turn precipitated Younger Dryas climatic downturn.

Evidence for the supposed impact was claimed in the form of a 12,900-year-old carbon-rich layer or 'black mat'. The layer has been identified at around fifty Clovis sites in North America. It is said to contain material consistent with an impact, including magnetic mineral grains, soot, carbon spherules and so-called nanodiamonds. The latter are minute diamonds formed when carbon particles are subjected to intense heat and pressure by an explosion. [21,22,23] More recently, evidence for impacts has also been claimed from Younger Dryas boundary sites in Mexico, Belgium, the Netherlands, Germany and Syria.[24,25] Anomalous levels of platinum, said to be due to the impact of a large iron meteorite, have also been reported from Greenland ice core samples dating to the Younger Dryas boundary.[26]

In theory this is all sounds highly feasible, but in practice the timing is a little suspicious. Other factors were in play at the time, and it is not necessary to invoke an extraterrestrial impact to explain the onset of the Younger Dryas. Named for the arctic-alpine flowering plant *Dryas octopetala* that flourished in the northern tundra at that time, the Younger Dryas marks the final stage of the Pleistocene. It lasted from 12,900 until 11,600 years ago and both its onset and termination were fairly abrupt.[27,28] During the preceding Bølling-Allerød warm period, the North American ice sheets retreated. The resulting meltwater formed a vast glacial lake known as Lake Agassiz, larger than all the modern Great Lakes put together. Beginning 13,000 years ago, Lake Agassiz released a series of freshwater discharges into the Arctic Ocean, through what is now the drainage basin of the Mackenzie River.[29] The conventional view is that the great volume of freshwater disrupted the Gulf Stream, halting the flow of warm seawater from the tropics to higher latitudes. The result was to plunge the Northern Hemisphere back into glacial conditions. Effects in the Southern Hemisphere are less certain, though evidence of cooling has been found there also.[30]

That an extraterrestrial impact should occur at more or less the same time as the freshwater discharge seems to be a rather implausible coincidence. It should also be noted that other studies have failed to find evidence for the nanodiamonds,[31] and that there is no evidence for the continent-wide conflagration supposedly triggered by the impact.[32] Evidence for burning is better attributed to climate change-generated increases in natural wildfires.[33] Similarly, the magnetic grains can be accounted for by a constant influx of micrometeorites from space.[34] The 'black mats' do not occur throughout the whole of North America, but rather are located predominantly in the west. They may be algal mats or ancient soils associated with regional increases in moisture.[35] The source of platinum anomaly may be extraterrestrial, but this remains unproven and more evidence is needed. All in all, it is probably best to be sceptical about the impact theory, although it cannot be ruled out.

It is now time for us to take a look at the extinctions on a case by case basis, and see which if any of the above theories best explains them.

Australia: Reasonable doubt

Before the first settlers reached Australia, the dominant mammalian lifeforms were marsupials, which arrived there at least 55 million years ago. Current evidence suggests that the extant Australian marsupial orders evolved from an ancestor or ancestors that dispersed from South America, via Antarctica, at a time when these three continents were still connected.[36] Australia suffered a major loss of not just large but also medium-sized mammals in the Late Pleistocene. All marsupials exceeding 100 kg (220 lb.), 19 species in all, became extinct; as did 22 out of 38 species weighing between 10 and 100 kg (22 and 220 lb.); along with three large reptiles and the flightless ostrich-sized bird *Genyornis newtoni*. Two other large flightless birds, the emu and the cassowary, survived. More than 85 percent of Australian megafauna were lost.[37] In addition, many animals 'downsized'. For example, based on tooth size, present-day Red and Grey kangaroos are about a third smaller than their Late Pleistocene counterparts.[38]

The 'overkill' hypothesis, as applied to Australia, is claimed to explain not only these extinctions, but also the size reduction of many species. It is supposed that the ponderous, lumbering megafauna were relatively easy for early human settlers to pursue.[7] In some cases, though, hunters ignored smaller adults. Accordingly, small size conferred a reproductive advantage and some species survived, but were diminished in size.[39] However, overkill has been criticised on a number of grounds. One of these is the lack of archaeological evidence. There are no kill sites or campsites anywhere in Australia containing bones of extinct megafauna, and none of the older sites has any evidence for butchery and consumption of large animals.[38] To Martin,[7] though, this was not a problem. His view was that vulnerable prey was exterminated so rapidly by invading human hunter-gatherers that the chances of now being able to find appreciable evidence are small. A problem with this line of reasoning is that it cannot be falsified.[40] It should also be noted that in other parts of the world such as Late Pleistocene Europe, there is ample evidence for the killing of large mammals by humans.

Two further criticisms have also been levelled at Martin's hypothesis. The first is the assumption that Australian megafauna were naive to the dangers posed by human predators. Present-day kangaroos display predator-avoidance behaviours even when faced with an unfamiliar predator. There have always been large, effective predators in Australia, such as the marsupial lion, which preyed on large kangaroos. It is therefore unlikely that the response of Australian megafauna to human predation was comparable to that of species living on remote islands with no predators.[9,38]

The second objection is that the original settlers might have lacked stone-tipped spears, atlatls and other technology necessary for efficient big-game hunting. They do not show up in archaeological record of Australia until well into the Holocene, and in their absence it is difficult to see how either the first Australians or their immediate descendants could have hunted megafauna with the efficiency required to bring about a geologically-instantaneous mass extinction across a landmass the size of Australia.[9]

There have been a number of studies purporting to demonstrate overkill, but all have been criticised for various reasons. In the first of these, geologists Gifford Miller and John Magee[37] obtained an extinction date for *Genyornis newtoni*. They used a variety of techniques to obtain dates for eggshells of *Genyornis* and the emu over a period from 120,000 years ago at Lake Eyre, in the central deserts of South Australia. It was found that while the eggshell record of the emu was continuous, that of *Genyornis* disappeared 50,000 years ago, implying its extinction. Two other sites were also sampled and extinction was also indicated at these, but only approximate dates were obtained. Miller and Magee noted that the extinction predated the onset of colder, more arid conditions, leading them to conclude that humans were responsible. Critics point out that Miller and Magee assume that firstly, the extinction at these three sites was repeated across the whole of Australia; that secondly, in the absence of major climate change, humans must have been responsible; and thirdly, if humans were culpable for the demise of *Genyornis*, they must have been responsible for all the other extinctions as well.[9,38]

A more comprehensive study by geologist Richard Roberts and palaeontologist Tim Flannery[41] covered 28 widely distributed sites. Roberts and Flannery used optically stimulated luminescence dating techniques on megafauna-bearing sediment, and uranium series dating of flowstones present at some of the sites. They obtained extinction dates for a wide range of species, including giant wombats (*Diprotodon*) and giant kangaroos (*Procoptodon*, *Protemnodon* and *Simosthenurus*). They concluded these and other megafauna had died out around 46,000 years ago, in a continent-wide extinction event. The disappearance was sudden, with the data indicating that a relatively diverse group of fauna had survived until close to the time of the extinction. Here, too, the conclusion was that a human 'blitzkrieg' had been responsible.

However, Roberts and Flannery have been criticised for omitting some age estimates considered to be unreliable, and ignoring broken-up skeletal remains on the grounds that these were assumed to have been disturbed. Another problem is the considerable delay before the extinction event if it is accepted that the first humans reached Australia prior to 50,000 years ago.[38] On the other hand, it could be argued that the human population needed to reach a certain density before hunting began to seriously affect the megafauna.[8]

A third study, by biologist Susan Rule and colleagues,[42] used the fungus *Sporormiella* to indicate the presence of large herbivores. *Sporormiella* requires herbivore digestion to complete its life cycle, and produces spores on their dung, and consequently the presence of the spores can be used to track ancient herbivore populations. This method has been successfully applied to sites in various parts of the world, including North America. The study also used pollen and charcoal levels to reconstruct vegetation, fires and climate change. The study area was the Lynch's Crater swamp in Queensland, and two core samples were analysed, spanning the periods from 130,000 to 24,000 and from 54,000 to 3,000 years ago. The samples cover the fluctuating climate of the Late Pleistocene, and document commensurate changes in vegetation. During arid periods, mixed rainforest gave way to sclerophyllous (dry country) vegetation, including eucalyptus and acacia. By 55,000 years ago, the region had changed from a shallow lake to a swamp. High *Sporormiella* counts suggest that large herbivores ranged very close to or over the swamp surface.

Around 41,000 years ago, the *Sporormiella* counts fell to near zero, implying megafaunal extinction. The date is fairly close to that obtained by Roberts and Flannery for their proposed continent-wide extinction event. The *Sporormiella* decline was followed roughly 100 years later by an increase in charcoal levels, and over the next 1,500 years patchy rainforest was gradually replaced by grasses and sclerophyllous forest. Unlike previous advances in sclerophyllous vegetation, these changes were claimed to have had no climatic cause; and the earlier changes were not accompanied by *Sporormiella* declines. The suggestion is that that once the megafauna were extinct, reduced consumption of vegetation led to an increase in natural fires. These in turn led to the replacement of the fire-sensitive rainforest with fire-tolerant grasses and sclerophyllous vegetation. The sequencing of these events, with the megafaunal extinction preceding the vegetation changes, is interpreted to imply human causation.

Archaeologist Judith Field[43] has noted that contrary to what is claimed, the period in question (Marine Isotope Stage 3) was a period of climatic instability[44] and that there is evidence for increased aridity in Australia after 45,000 years ago.[45] Field also questions the assumption that the megafauna were present in such great numbers that their sudden disappearance would trigger the vegetation changes described in the report.

On the basis of the evidence presented, the case for overkill is unproven; at very least there is reasonable doubt. Turning to indirect human causes, could the extinctions be a consequence of fire-starting by the first Australian settlers? A number of researchers have suggested that human fire-starting differed in both timing and frequency from natural fire cycles, resulting in the replacement of a drought-adapted mosaic of trees, shrubs and palatable nutrient-rich grasslands with the modern fire-adapted grasslands and desert scrub. These changes in turn impacted the megafauna, many of which were browsers. Among herbivores, grazers feed predominantly on grasses whereas browsers favour leaves, shoots and shrubs. The specialised herbivores became extinct, though more flexible feeders, such as the emu, were able to survive. The loss of the herbivores also had the knock-on effect of depriving large non-human predators of prey, so resulting in their extinction.[46,37,13]

It sounds very plausible and it is true that present-day Aboriginal Australians use what is known as 'fire-stick farming'; but such activities, intended to increase overall foraging efficiency, do so by promoting rather than damaging biodiversity. Furthermore, it has been questioned as to whether the early human populations in Australia were sufficiently dense in numbers to be able to bring about habitat change on a continent-wide scale. It therefore seems doubtful that fire-starting brought about an ecological catastrophe soon after humans arrived in Australia.[47,48] A recent study of continent-wide charcoal records over the last 70,000 years found that biomass burning increased during warm climatic periods and decreased when the climate turned colder – just as would be expected if natural causes were responsible. There was no evidence for a fundamental shift that could be associated with the arrival of human colonists.[49]

In the 1980s, biologist David Horton[47] proposed a model to explain the selective extinction of megafauna based solely on the effects of climate change, without the need to assume any form of human causation. Using the palaeoclimate data available at the time, together with climate and vegetation data for present-day Australia, Horton noted that rainfall follows a concentric pattern. Coastal regions receive the highest average rainfall, but it declines steadily further inland, and the interior is arid. This is reflected in the habitat arrangement of Australia, which is also concentric, with woodland being distributed around the coast. The size of the arid zone will vary in accordance with global climatic conditions. In the build-up to the Last Glacial Maximum it expanded outwards from the centre, increasingly restricting the number of sources of free water.

For small animals, who obtain sufficient water from their food, this is not a problem. However, large animals need to remain within range of reliable sources of water. Normally, this was not a problem for the megafauna, but in times of drought, many water sources dried up, and those remaining were spaced farther apart. Animals at one water source would often have no others within range. In such cases, they would be restricted to sources of food that they could reach and still return to the water source. When such sources, already reduced in quantity and quality by the drought, were exhausted, the animals would die despite the continued availability of water. With no additional supplies of water in range, they were trapped, unable to look for fresh sources of food, or retreat in advance of the expanding arid zone. Horton suggested that it was only in the last glacial period that the arid core region expanded far enough to eliminate the megafauna, reaching a critical point between 26,000 and 15,000 years ago.

In 2006, biologist Stephen Wroe and archaeologist Judith Field[50] updated the Horton model to take into account more recent evidence. This included better age estimates that only become available after around 2000,[38] and palaeoclimate data. The latter suggests a trend towards arid and erratic conditions in Australia after about 400,000 to 300,000 years ago, with aridity increasing after 100,000 years ago. Some of the most important evidence comes from Cuddie Springs in New South Wales, now an ephemeral lake that only fills after heavy rainfall. 40,000 years ago, when people first used the area, the environment comprised a large, full lake surrounded by open shrublands that provided excellent conditions for both large animals and humans.[38] Stone tools and animal remains recovered at the site suggest that humans and megafauna coexisted for 15,000 years or more, and that the extinctions occurred gradually, against a background of climatic deterioration.[51,52,53,54]

Based on this new data, Wroe and Field claimed that the megafaunal extinctions began much earlier than the 46,000 years ago suggested by proponents of the overkill model, and that they were brought on by the effects of longer term climate change. They found that of 68 species of megafauna that were supposedly driven to extinction by humans, only 21 can be shown to have survived the severe cold period of the Penultimate Glacial Maximum, 130,000 years ago. In other words, the remaining 39 species of megafauna might have become extinct 80,000 years before the arrival of humans in Australia, assuming a date of 50,000 years ago for the latter. Of these, only thirteen species (eight were initially claimed) were still present when humans reached Australia[55] and four or more of these survived until the onset of the Last Glacial Maximum.[50] This suggests a staggered pattern in which most megafaunal extinctions predated human arrival, and in which the influence of people was a minor factor in a broader trend that began much earlier, in Middle Pleistocene times.

However, a few notes of caution should be sounded. Some authorities claim that the remains at Cuddie springs have been mixed up, rendering dates unreliable.[41,56] It is also important to bear in mind once more that absence of evidence is not evidence of absence. Just because remains of species are not known after a certain date, it does not necessarily mean that they did not exist. We must treat with caution claims that such and such a species was extinct by such and such a date.

Evidence from southern Australia suggests fauna there were adapted to aridity. In 2002, extensive Middle Pleistocene animal remains were recovered from the Thylacoleo Caves beneath the arid Nullarbor Plain, a treeless (as suggested by the name) steppe on the coast of the Great Australian Bight. A total of 69 species, including eight previously-unknown species of kangaroo, were represented by the remains; 21 of these species failed to survive the Pleistocene. A team lead by palaeontologist Gavin Prideaux[57] analysed the carbon and oxygen stable isotope ratios of dental enamel obtained from the fossils. These can provide an indication of the type of vegetation eaten, which in turn would have been influenced by the climatic conditions prevailing at the time. The results were similar to those obtained for present-day kangaroos and wombats from southern Australia, indicating that the climatic conditions of the Nullarbor Plain were similar to those of today, and that the now-extinct megafauna living there were adapted to arid conditions.

In a follow-up study, Prideaux and his colleagues[58] considered *Procoptodon goliah*, a large kangaroo species that became extinct about 50,000 to 45,000 years ago. Microwear and carbon stable isotope analysis of the teeth of fossil remains suggests that it was a browser, unlike large present-day kangaroos, all of which are grazers. The diet of *Procoptodon goliah* consisted of saltbush and other chenopods, suggesting it was adapted to arid and semiarid shrublands. However, oxygen stable isotope data suggests that it drank more water than contemporary grazing kangaroos. This would have affected local populations of *Procoptodon goliah* in times of drought, but it was argued that the species had survived repeated periods of drought throughout the Pleistocene. Moreover, its extinction did not occur during a particularly arid period.

Prideaux claimed that adaptation of the megafauna to arid conditions disproved the aridity hypothesis, but neither study put forward any specific points that refute the Horton model of animals being tethered to single water sources. However, the timing of the extinction of *Procoptodon goliah*, at a time of mild conditions, means that in its case at least, the effects of human predation cannot be ruled out. On the other hand, both studies noted that chenopod shrub steppe is fairly fire-resistant. If chenopods were an important food item for the megafauna, it would weaken the argument that human fire-starting was a factor driving species to extinction.[58]

Overall, it seems unlikely that widely dispersed hunter-gatherer groups could either exterminate entire species across a landmass the size of Australia, or bring about significant continent-wide environmental changes. On the other hand, it is possible that these were factors in the decline of the megafauna still present when humans reached Australia. Possibly a combination of factors were responsible for the final extinction, including hunting, climate change, and changes in natural fire activity.[59]

The New World: Open verdict

In North America, 33 genera of megafauna went extinct, a loss of 72 percent; and in South America, the losses were even more severe with 50 genera lost, or 83 percent. Unlike Australia, though, some genera did survive elsewhere in the world.[1] The timing of these extinction broadly coincides with the arrival of humans and overkill proponent Paul Martin long argued for a connection between the two.

In the 1970s, Martin[6] suggested that after making their way through the Cordilleran and Laurentide ice sheets, the Clovis people (see Chapter 15) found the conditions so favourable in terms of prey availability that the population grew explosively, doubling in as little as every 20 to 50 years. At this rate of growth, it took no more than a millennium to fully populate the New World. With no perceived need to avoid wasteful consumption, big-game hunters killed prey animals faster than they could reproduce, resulting in their rapid extinction. Prey naiveté is supposed to have played a major role: prey species had no experience of being hunted by humans, and the more vulnerable animals were killed off before they could learn defensive behaviours. More recently, Martin's conclusions have been supported by a computer simulation of human and large herbivore population dynamics in North America at the end of the Pleistocene. The simulation correctly predicted the extinction or survival of 32 out of 41 prey species, suggesting that human population growth and hunting almost invariably leads to a mass extinction.[60]

However, things may not be as simple as they seem. A criticism of the overkill theory is that megafaunal kills are unequivocally associated with just fourteen Clovis sites. Of these, twelve are associated with mammoth remains and the other two with mastodon. No other megafauna appear to have been hunted, despite the greater abundance of camels and horses. Martin's view, as with Australia, was that the extinction was simply too rapid to leave any evidence; the same criticisms apply. Another problem is that some of the extinctions occurred in places where there were no humans. In Alaska, horses declined in size, then in numbers, and finally became extinct – but the extinction occurred some 500 years before the first humans arrived.[61]

As with Australia, the notion of prey naiveté has been criticised. In present-day North America, wolves and brown bears are returning to areas from which they were eliminated many decades ago. Along re-colonisation fronts, 'naive' moose are vulnerable to the returning predators, but behind this front, surviving populations quickly adjust. They are no more susceptible than populations that have always been familiar with bears and wolves. It has been suggested that this model serves as an analogy for the megafauna, and that for animal populations ahead of the human expansion to remain naive, every single animal encountering human hunters would have to be killed, including entire herds.[9]

Indirect causation by fire-starting has been proposed for North America, at least as a partial cause. It has been suggested that human fire-starting might have affected vegetation by compounding the effects of natural flash fires, thus contributing to the megafaunal extinctions.[62,63] Evidence of possible human fire-starting has also been reported from the Chilean Lake District.[64] However, there is no clear-cut evidence that fire use by humans led to any major habitat alterations in the New World at the time of the extinctions.[3]

Turning to theories based on the impact of climate change, mammoth-steppe proponent Dale Guthrie[18] has put forward an ecological theory now known as the nutrient mosaic hypothesis. As noted above, this is a special case of the habitat loss model. Guthrie has suggested that the cause of the extinctions was a trend towards shorter annual growing seasons for plants, and increasing seasonality of climate, particularly in respect of rainfall. These trends were brought about by the long-term decline in global temperatures that began in the Late Eocene. They resulted in the gradual breakup of an almost global closed-canopy forest landscape into a more open mosaic of trees, shrubs and herbs. However, this landscape was quite unlike any existing today. Instead of inhabiting distinct biomes such as woodlands, grasslands, savannah and tundra, diverse plant species could all be found together across large regions Guthrie refers to as 'plaids'. The resulting vegetation diversity was particularly favourable for large herbivores, but it did not last. With the transition from the Pleistocene to the Holocene, growing seasons became ever more constricted, increasing competition between plants. Individual species became restricted to habitats that particularly favoured them, and to where they had the edge over other species not quite so well adapted. Consequently, local vegetation diversity declined as the 'plaids' were subsumed into larger, more homogenous vegetation zones.

Large non-ruminating herbivores such as horses, rhinos, mammoths and mastodons were particularly hard hit. These animals rely on a great diversity of plant forms in their diet to provide a balanced mixture of carbohydrate, protein, fat, vitamins, minerals and fibre. They lack the complex stomachs of the ruminants, which can break down the toxins present in many plants, and can synthesise most of the essential amino acids, fatty acids and vitamins. Competition with the ruminants, possibly combined with the effects of human predation, made extinction inevitable. In less biodiverse vegetation zones that replaced the 'plaids', specialised feeders came to the fore. In the northern tundra, these were caribou, which are able to feed on lichen. In the deciduous forests, the previously uncommon moose and small and medium-sized deer selectively browsed on the most nutritious portions of shrubs, and on the plains and prairies of the south, bison took advantage of the abundant grasses.

A slightly different approach is the coevolutionary disequilibrium model. Palaeontologists Russell Graham and Ernest Lundelius[19] have put forward a model based on an analogy with the grazing successions of present-day African savannahs, where annually-migrating savannah herbivores graze on specific plant species. This stimulates the growth and development of other plant species that will be eaten by subsequent migratory waves of herbivores. Thus annually, the growth of food sources for one species depends on the activities of the preceding species. Such a sequence, known as a 'grazing succession', allows many herbivore species to co-exist, but to maintain it they must follow specific migration routes at specific times, and the plant species available at these times and places must be of nutritional value. This finely-balanced equilibrium can be disturbed, for example by a change in the migratory behaviour of the animals or of the distribution of plant species.

Graham and Lundelius proposed that climate change brought about such a disturbance in North America, leading to extinction for many of the large herbivores. They suggested that generalists were particularly vulnerable because they were forced to develop new feeding strategies, and modify their mixed foliage intake accordingly. Their enzyme systems had to adjust to the changes. This might sometimes have resulted in their losing the ability to break down toxins to which they had previously been adapted, hence poisoning themselves into extinction. Another problem was increased competition for the same resources, leading to extinction for all but those species best adapted to the new ecological patterns. Eventually, the latter were able to take over vacated niches and expand their own populations.

In choosing between these various human and climate-based hypotheses, it is obviously crucial to learn as much as we can about the timing and tempo of the extinctions. Were they more or less simultaneous, or did they occur step-wise, over a longer period of time? Recent work has produced contradictory results. One study considered the last occurrence dates in the fossil record of 16 of the extinct genera. These dates, considered secure, all lie between 11,400 and 13,800 years ago. There are no dates available for the remainder, which are less abundant in the fossil record. Simulations using statistical techniques were carried out and these suggested that the observed extinction chronology is fully consistent with the simultaneous extinction of at least 31 genera in a single event.[65]

However, a second study, using *Sporormiella* spores, reached a very different conclusion.[63] The spores, which have been found in mammoth dung, were again used to track ancient herbivore populations. This study, which preceded the Australian study described above, concerned spores on dung excreted within a lake watershed. The spores are eventually washed into the lake, and thus *Sporormiella* spore levels in lake sediments will be an indicator of the local herbivore population. Samples were taken from an 11.5 m (38 ft.) sediment core extracted from Appleman Lake, Indiana. It was found that *Sporormiella* levels were initially high, but began to decline 14,800 years ago, and fell below levels indicating megafaunal extinction 13,700 years ago. This data suggests a decline culminating in local extinction of the megafauna, occurring over the course of 1,100 years. If the megafauna persisted in other parts of North America until 11,400 years ago, then the overall picture is one of a gradual decline over the course of at least 3,400 years. The evidence thus rules out sudden-extinction models, such as an extraterrestrial impact or a blitzkrieg by Clovis hunters.

The same study went on to consider vegetation in the Appleman Lake region, using pollen data. It was found that that there was an increase in black ash and hop-hornbeam about 13,700 years ago. These hardwood trees coexisted with spruce, a combination of species not seen today. 11,900 years ago, spruce was replaced with pine, and after 11,000 years ago there was a rapid increase in the abundance of oak, marking the establishment of Holocene deciduous forests. These shifts began well after the beginning of the megafaunal decline, suggesting that climate-forced changes in vegetation were not a factor in the extinctions. In summary, the study leaves unresolved the debate over human versus climatic causation (or both) of the North American megafaunal extinctions. Accordingly, an open verdict must be returned.

Extinctions in Eurasia and Africa

Fewer genera were lost in Eurasia than in Australia or the New World, though losses were still significant. In Europe and Northern Asia, a total of nine genera of megafauna went extinct, amounting to 36 percent. Of these, four genera survived elsewhere in the world.[1] The species lost included the woolly mammoth, the woolly rhinoceros, the steppe bison and the so-called Irish elk or giant deer. Horses disappeared from higher latitudes, and the musk ox survived only in North America.

The complex history of the last 30,000 years of the woolly mammoth and giant deer emphasizes the complex nature of the megafaunal extinctions in northern Eurasia, in which different species went extinct at different times, and in different regions. Widely distributed before about 20,000 years ago, these two species underwent successive contractions in range. These occurred at different times, and from each of which they made only partial recoveries. Finally, in the Holocene, both were confined to one or more relatively small areas before becoming extinct.[66]

Before their extinction, the giant deer and the woolly mammoth underwent dramatic shifts in distribution, driven by climate and vegetation changes. The two species responded differently. About 14,000 years ago the woolly mammoth disappeared from most of northern Eurasia as forests spread at the onset of the warm Bølling-Allerød Interstadial. It became restricted to the far north of Siberia, where open steppe-tundra environments persisted. Woolly mammoths persisted in mainland Siberia on the Taymyr Peninsula until 9,000 years ago (9,600 radiocarbon years BP) and on St Paul Island in the Bering Sea until 6,700 years ago (7,900 radiocarbon years BP). Teeth from dwarf mammoths have been found on Wrangel Island in the Arctic Ocean over a period from 7,000 to 4,000 years ago, confirming that in this isolated part of the world, mammoths persisted into the time of the Egyptian Pharaohs.[67,68,66]

Unlike the woolly mammoth, the giant deer was not an inhabitant of treeless steppe-tundra. Comparable in size to a present-day moose, it had a shoulder height of up to 2.1 m (6 ft. 10 in.) with an antler span of up to 3.6 m (11 ft. 9 in.). It was probably a mixed feeder (i.e. both a browser and a grazer), and males required an environment capable of sustaining the annual growth of their huge antlers. Until 22,000 years ago (20,000 radiocarbon years BP), its range extended across the middle latitudes of Eurasia from Ireland to east of Lake Baikal. During the Last Glacial Maximum, it vanished from Western and Central Europe and became restricted to refugia that included parts of Southeast Europe and southern Central Asia, probably in areas where tree and shrub vegetation persisted.[66]

After the Last Glacial Maximum the giant deer returned to parts of northwestern Europe. During the period from 14,500 to 14,000 years ago (12,500 to 12,000 radiocarbon years BP), the species re-colonised the Isle of Man, Britain, Ireland, southern Scandinavia and northern Germany. The warmer conditions resulted in the replacement of steppe-tundra with open herbaceous vegetation and some birch trees. However, it did not return to southern or central parts of Western Europe, despite similar changes to the vegetation. It is possible that the post-Last Glacial Maximum re-expansion of human populations from the south was a factor. Although people were present in small numbers in northwestern Europe, they clearly did not affect its re-colonising the region. Further south, however, human populations were denser, and this may be why the giant deer failed to return to these regions.[66]

Around 12,600 years ago (10,700 radiocarbon years BP), during the Younger Dryas, the giant deer population in the northwest collapsed dramatically. The probable cause was a marked deterioration of the vegetation that saw the landscape return to open steppe-tundra, although the giant deer might have survived for a while in Scotland. Humans were not present in Britain, Ireland or the Isle of Man during the Younger Dryas, so the cause in this case was almost certainly climate and vegetation change.[66]

On the boundary between Europe and Asia in the Urals and western Siberia, the giant deer survived rather longer. It appeared in this region about 12,700 years ago (10,800 radiocarbon years BP), having probably migrated from Southeast Europe or western Central Asia, rather than from the more distant northwestern Europe. In contrast to the harsh conditions in Europe during the Younger Dryas, the eastern slopes of the Urals saw the persistence of a favourable habitat of grass-shrub vegetation and open woodland. In a region where it was relatively safe from human predation, the giant deer survived until about 7,700 years ago (6,900 radiocarbon years BP). Its ultimate demise might have come when changes in vegetation forced it out on to the adjacent West Siberian plain, where it became vulnerable to increased hunting activities.[66]

Marked shifts in the distributions of both giant deer and woolly mammoth were driven by climate-induced changes in vegetation. However, giant deer not only survived earlier Pleistocene glacial episodes, it also expanded its European range and thrived during interglacials. If one assumes that Holocene climate and vegetation is similar to that of previous interglacials, then why did the giant deer fail to re-expand as before? Here, one has to suspect the one new factor, absent in previous interglacials – modern humans. However, it is important to bear in mind that the evidence is only circumstantial. More work is needed to clarify the pattern of extinctions, changes in vegetation, and human activities in Eurasia.[66]

Africa experienced the lowest extinction rates of any major landmass. Eight genera were lost, including three that survived elsewhere. The percentage loss of just 18 percent was half of that for Eurasia.[1] The explanation favoured by overkill proponents is that because humans evolved in Africa, prey animals there were wary of them and therefore less vulnerable. The timing of the extinctions that did occur also fits well with a Great Leap Forward in human cognition, 50,000 years ago. It is argued that prior to then humans were not smart enough to hunt megafauna efficiently,[69] although as we saw in Chapter 11, these ideas have been challenged.

In fact, there are good reasons to suppose that Africa would be less affected by the Late Quaternary extinctions than other continents. In comparison to other continents, Africa has a greater available habitat area, greater long-term climatic stability, a greater equatorial region, and a greater mammalian diversity. These factors may explain the resistance of African species to extinction more adequately than gradual acclimation to human predation.[9]

Partly because it straddles the equator, Africa has been less affected by climate change than the New World and Australia. Glaciers have encompassed as much as 56 percent of North America over this time. As much as 60 percent of Australia has been overrun by windswept sand-dunes. Many large African species underwent major range contractions during Pleistocene glacial maxima, but Africa is large enough to suffer vast loss of habitable area and still sustain refugia extensive enough to sustain large species. African species could survive climatic conditions that most species elsewhere would not, and on this basis alone a lower rate of megafaunal extinction in Africa would be expected.[9]

In summary, it is very hard to make a convincing case for either climate change or human predation being solely responsible for the Late Quaternary extinctions on a worldwide basis. Clearly, different factors operated in different places and at different times. If the re-expansion of the giant deer in post-Last Glacial Maximum Europe was inhibited by the spread of humans, it is possible that variations of this scenario played out elsewhere. However, one thing is clear. Irrespective of whether or not humans played a role in the extinctions, their subsequent activities from the early Holocene onwards has meant that a return to the biodiversity of the Pleistocene is impossible. As we shall now see, the end of the Ice Age triggered a sequence of events that were to lead to the domination of Earth's biosphere by just one species – *Homo sapiens*.

PART III:

THE NEOLITHIC REVOLUTION

22,000 BC TO AD 500

17: Feed the World

The ice melts

In this work to date, we have hitherto considered periods spanning millions of years. Even the career of our own species, *Homo sapiens*, covers around 200,000 years. These timescales are so vast that a few millennia are neither here nor there, but as the Earth warmed from the Last Glacial Maximum, the tempo of change began to increase. The era of cave painting in Europe is delineated by two of its most famous sites, Altamira and Lascaux; the former dating to the early part of the Upper Palaeolithic, the latter to its waning years. The two are separated by 18,000 years; before another 18,000 years had passed, humans had landed on the Moon. Our understanding of this latter period of human prehistory, while far from complete, is more extensive than that of earlier times.

The Pleistocene finally came to an end around 9600 BC. The Younger Dryas represented the final chilly blast of the Ice Age; the unstable and often cold, arid conditions were replaced by the warm, wet, and ultimately stable conditions of the Holocene. Sea levels had been gradually rising ever since the Last Glacial Maximum, although by 9000 BC they remained 50 m (165 ft.) below those of today.[1] In more northerly locations that had lain beneath the glaciers, the rise in sea level was more than outweighed by the land itself 'rebounding' as the great weight of ice was lifted. Nevertheless, the gradual inundation of low-lying areas began to reshape the geography of the entire planet. The subcontinent of Beringia disappeared beneath the waves, separating Eurasia from North America; Britain and Ireland were separated from mainland Europe; Japan from mainland Asia; and New Guinea and Tasmania from Australia. More than half of the huge Pleistocene landmass of Sundaland was submerged, and by 6500 BC only the present-day Island Southeast Asian archipelago remained above water.[2]

In Europe and North America, the forests of birch and pine retreated northwards and open tundra shrank. Over several centuries, these by now more temperate latitudes were filled with deciduous woodland of oak, elm and beech. The Inter-Tropical Convergence Zone, which carries rain through tropical Africa and across the Indian Ocean, moved north to pass over the Sahara, transforming it into a region of lakes within extensive savannah grassland.[1] In Southwest Asia, the previously inhospitable Fertile Crescent greened. The region became one of several foci of a fundamentally new way of life, characterised by Australian archaeologist and linguist V. Gordon Childe as the 'Neolithic Revolution'.

Childe was one of the most influential prehistorians of the last century. He was a committed socialist, who was active in the New South Wales labour movement before moving to Britain in 1921, and his thinking about prehistory was influenced by Friedrich Engels' 1884 work *Origin of the Family, Private Property and the State*, which in turn drew heavily from the work of American anthropologist Lewis Henry Morgan. The Morgan-Engels scheme proposed an economically-determined progression from hunter-gatherer 'savagery', through agricultural 'barbarism', to the urban-based 'civilisations' of Egypt, Mesopotamia, Greece and Rome.

Drawing an analogy with the Industrial Revolution in Europe, which took place during the latter part of the eighteenth century and the early nineteenth century, Childe[3] proposed that there had been a 'Neolithic Revolution' which saw hunter-gatherer societies transformed into farming communities. This in turn was followed by an 'Urban Revolution' that transformed the farming communities into complex urban societies. Although contemporary models have progressed beyond Childe's theories, there is no doubt that he correctly identified two of the most profound social transformations prior to the Industrial Revolution.

Agriculture and domestication

The *Concise Oxford Dictionary* defines agriculture as "*The science or practice of cultivating the soil and rearing animals*". Agriculture, in its broadest sense, means food production. Agriculture can mean either arable farming or pastoralism, but in both cases domestication is also involved. Domesticated plants and animals are raised in a human-managed environment, and have often undergone biological change in comparison to their wild counterparts. These changes make them more suitable for human exploitation, but in the case of plants, can also make them unable to reproduce without human intervention. It remains contentious the degree to which human intentions played a role in such changes; also whether the changes can be attributed solely to the process of domestication; and indeed whether the process of domestication necessarily involves any biological change at all.[4] There is no universally-agreed definition of domestication,[5] although ongoing human intervention is regarded as a key feature.[6] It is generally accepted that agricultural societies have a degree of dependency on domesticated species, though it is disputed just how dependent a society must be before it is considered agricultural.[7]

Where biological change has occurred with domesticated species, the processes are reasonably well understood. The classic case is that of the cereals, members of the grass family (*Poaceae*). These include wheat, barley, millet, sorghum, rice and maize. Ears of wild cereals are held together by small, brittle structures known as rachis that shatter when ripe, so that the grains can disperse. Unless wild cereals are harvested before they fully ripen, much of the grain will be lost, but in domesticated cereals the rachis is toughened and the ear remains intact until it is harvested and threshed. Such variants occur in the wild from time to time as a result of genetic mutation, but they invariably fail to reproduce, as evidenced by the lack of feral domestic cereals. On the other hand, they would be more likely to have been successfully harvested by early farmers than the normal shattering varieties. When wild cereals are harvested by either uprooting or sickle reaping, significant grain spillage is likely to occur with the normal, shattering ears, but this does not happen with the rare non-shattering variants. Thus the latter will be unintentionally selected for by human activities and, over successive cycles of harvesting and sewing, become increasingly common. Eventually, the shattering variety will be completely eliminated. The seed stock held for replanting is at this point considered to be domesticated. In addition to the cereals, domesticated plants include tubers (potato, sweet potato, taro, yams, manioc (cassava), and a number of minor crops); squashes (including butternut, marrow, and pumpkin); legumes (beans, peas, lentils and vetch); sugarcane; and many fruits and nuts.

A sequence of events leading to domestication can be set in motion if hunter-gatherers begin to cultivate wild cereals, instead of simply harvesting them from naturally-occurring wild stands. Archaeologist Gordon Hillman and botanist Stuart Davies[8] have demonstrated that by using harvesting methods available to early farmers, wild wheats and barley could have been domesticated within a few centuries, or possibly even decades. They concluded that for the selective process to occur, farmers needed to harvest their crops by either sickle-reaping or uprooting before they had fully ripened. Harvesting while not fully ripe would mitigate, but not eliminate, losses due to shattering, but such losses would select strongly in favour of the non-shattering variety. It was necessary to use sickles or uprooting to harvest the crop, because the alternative method of shaking or beating ears of grain into collecting baskets would favour collection of the shattering rather than non-shattering variety. In fact, beating or shaking only works well if the ripe ears of grain are in the process of shattering, and would not have been used for unripe crops. Sickle-reaping and uprooting have the additional advantage of yielding straw as a by-product, which can be used as a building material or as fuel.

Although domestic cereal strains eventually arose as a result of the practices outlined above, it is dangerous to assume that their appearance in the archaeological record is a reliable marker for the beginnings of arable farming. If early farmers did not follow the harvesting practices outlined above, the cereals they cultivated would have remained indistinguishable from wild varieties. The appearance of domesticated varieties, possibly millennia later, would then indicate nothing more than a change in the management or harvesting practices of cultivated crops.[9]

It is nevertheless important for archaeologists to be able to reliably categorise cereal remains as either wild or domesticated. Cereal grains only preserve if charred, and remains – if not charred – are often badly decomposed.[10] Categorisation on the basis of the physical characteristics of grain or rachis can be problematic. Fortunately, there are other aids to recognition. Starch grains from domesticated cereals have a smooth surface, whereas those from wild varieties are rough,[11] and phytoliths differ in size and shape between domesticated and wild cereal varieties.[10,12] The presence or absence of various molecules can also be used as a diagnostic tool.[13] In recent years, these techniques have been used to study millet domestication in China.

Plant domestication is just half of the story, but curiously only a few animals have been successfully domesticated. The most important large domesticated mammals are the 'Major Five' of cattle, sheep, goats, pigs and horses. There is also the 'Minor Nine' of Arabian and Bactrian camels, donkey, reindeer, water buffalo, yak, llama, alpaca and two relatives of the wild aurochs – the banteng and the gaur.[14] Smaller herbivores include chickens, turkeys, rabbits and guinea pigs.[1] However, these fourteen large herbivores represent only a small fraction of 148 worldwide that could potentially be domesticated.[14] Why so few? For domestication to be successful, an animal must possess certain characteristics. Firstly, it must be a herd animal. In a herd, some animals are dominant, but most are subordinate – and can transfer their submissive behaviours to humans. While the Asian mouflon (*Ovis ares*) displays such behaviours, the North American bighorn sheep (*Ovis canadensis*) does not, and was never domesticated by Native Americans. Secondly, animals must not be territorial, or have strong flight reflexes. This has ruled out the domestication of gazelles and other antelopes, and deer. With the exception of the reindeer, all of these animals are too nervous to be managed. The third and probably most obvious requirement is that animals must breed readily in captivity. As zoo keepers will testify, with many species this can be a problem.[15]

Animal domestication might have involved a greater degree of human selection than was the case for plant domestication. Early pastoral herders might have bred from smaller and more docile animals, resulting in time in herded animals becoming smaller than their wild counterparts. Again, though, there must be caveats to using evidence of reduced size as a marker for domestication. Factors such as climate and environment are known to influence body size in animals, as are the differing culling strategies of hunters and herders. Hunters will preferentially target larger animals, which accordingly predominate in animal remains. Conversely, herders tend to cull young males but keep females alive until they have passed their reproductive peak. Since females are usually smaller than males, this gives an illusion that the domesticated animals are smaller. A more reliable approach, therefore, is to look for evidence that assemblages are dominated by the remains of young males and older females. Another marker of domestication is the appearance of features that are accidental by-products of the relaxation of natural selection in the human-controlled environment, such as changes in the shape and size of goat horns.[16,4,17,9]

Agricultural packages

To establish a successful agricultural economy, Neolithic farmers needed to assemble a 'package' combining sources of carbohydrate (cereals and tubers) and protein (pulses and animals), together with attendant technologies such as pottery and tools for processing seeds. Packages are sometimes considered to include items such as particular prestige or cult objects, architectural styles and settlement layouts.[18] They varied considerably from region to region, dictated by local occurrence of species suitable for domestication. Southwest Asia undoubtedly had the strongest package, comprising emmer and einkorn wheat, barley, lentils, peas, chickpeas, bitter vetch, flax, sheep, goats, pigs and cattle. Conversely, Mexico and North America lacked large mammals suitable for domestication. Most parts of the world lacked any suitable indigenous species, and had to import domesticated species from elsewhere in order to establish an agricultural economy.

Agriculture was not adopted by everybody at once. Instead, it arose in relatively few places, and then spread out from these primary centres. It is thought to have emerged independently in Southwest Asia, the Middle Yangtze and Yellow Rivers of China, the Highlands of New Guinea, the Andes, Mesoamerica, and the Eastern Woodlands of the United States. Claims have also been made for limited developments in central sub-Saharan Africa, southern India, and the Murray Valley region of Australia. All these developments occurred at different times between 9600 and 2000 BC, and involved different combinations of plants and/or animals. Furthermore, the spread of agricultural systems varied greatly in both speed and extent. Some expanded rapidly and widely, some hardly expanded at all.[19,20] Agriculture spread rapidly east and west from Southwest Asia to Europe, Egypt and the Indus Valley, averaging 1 km (0.7 miles) per year. Even faster was the spread east from the Philippines to Polynesia, which averaged 5 km (3.2 miles) per year. On the other hand, north-south spreads were slower, less than 0.8 km (0.5 miles) per year for maize and beans from Mexico to the Southwestern United States, and less than 0.5 km (0.3 miles) per year to the Eastern United States. Llamas spread north from Peru to Ecuador at just 0.3 km (0.2 miles) per year. Agriculture failed to reach Native American California at all from the Southwestern United States, or to reach Australia from New Guinea or Indonesia.[14]

Some agricultural packages spread more or less in their entirety, such as that of Southwest Asia. Others were modified as new crops and animals were added to the roster while some of the older ones were dropped. For example, as farmers spread from China into Island Southeast Asia and Oceania, they gradually phased out rice and foxtail millet in favour of crops less susceptible to rain shortfall, such as taro and other tubers.[21] In the New World, some components simply failed to spread. The guinea pig and llama never reached Mesoamerica from the Andes, although manioc, sweet potatoes and peanuts did.[14]

Overall, the Southwest Asian package spread faster and more completely than any of the others. This was in part due to the combination of herd animals, cereals and pulses, which together provide great nutritional benefits. The cereals and pulses are suited to storage, and provide both carbohydrate and protein. Conversely, tree crops and tubers yield mainly carbohydrate, and agricultural systems based on these do not provide a nutritionally balanced diet. Protein must in many cases be obtained from fish and wild game, limiting the potential for expansion.[22,23] Geographical factors also may play a part. In particular, Jared Diamond[14] has suggested that it is easier for agriculture to spread in an east-west direction than north-south, as we shall see in Chapter 24.

Regardless of these issues, the consequences were the same in all cases. Food production, as opposed to food collection, means that far more people can be supported per unit area. A family of hunter-gatherers may require several square kilometres of territory for subsistence, whereas a family of irrigation farmers can get by with less than a single hectare of farmland. Thus in general less land is needed to feed a unit of farmers than a unit of hunter-gatherers. Hunter-gatherers range from one to a maximum of ten people per square kilometre, but non-urban farmers range from three to a hundred people per square kilometre. Irrigation farmers can achieve even higher densities. Agriculture has served as the economic foundation for the last 10,000 years of human population growth, and has enabled – if not actually brought about – the rise of civilisation as we know it.[19]

The origins of agriculture

Even if one accepts the view that humans did not become behaviourally modern until around 70,000 years ago or even later, they still got along without agriculture for the bulk of that time. Why did agriculture not start earlier? It could be – and until the late 1960s was – argued that until about 10,000 years ago, humans lacked the social complexity and technological sophistication to make agriculture possible. Both arable faming and pastoralism involve a considerable investment in terms of planning and labour. Arable farming entails tillage of fields, sowing, harvesting, storage of the harvest, and retention of seed stock for replanting; and pastoralism entails managing and breeding livestock. In fact, there was a more fundamental reason: the unstable climate of the Pleistocene made agriculture impossible. It was only the climatic amelioration and stability of the Holocene that allowed agriculture to emerge, and then only where plant and animal species suitable for domestication could be found.[24] However, this presents us with a second question. Why in many cases did agriculture not start until many millennia after the Pleistocene to Holocene transition, even where suitable wild precursors were present?

Two of the better-known early theories are the 'Oasis Theory', summarised by V. Gordon Childe in his 1936 book *Man Makes Himself* [3] and the 'Hilly Flanks Hypothesis' proposed by Robert Braidwood in the late 1940s.[25] The Oasis Theory maintains that as the climate in Southwest Asia became dryer at the end of the Pleistocene, humans and animals were forced into close association round oases, and gradually became accustomed to each other. Some animals became tame. By only killing off the more intractable individuals, hunter-gatherers set in motion the process that led to domestication. The theory did not explain plant cultivation, but the main problem is that we now know that the Early Holocene climate became wetter, not dryer.

The Hilly Flanks Hypothesis asserted that agriculture began on the hilly flanks of the Fertile Crescent, regions that were the natural habitat zone for both plants and animals with the potential for domestication. While not offering a specific reason for why domestication occurred, Braidwood suggested that by the end of the Pleistocene, humans were technologically and culturally ready to begin domestication, and were sufficiently familiar with the species that were to be domesticated.

Both Childe and Braidwood focused predominantly on Early Holocene Southwest Asia, where agriculture began almost immediately. Their theories did not explain the delays in other parts of the world where suitable wild species were available. They also assumed – as most scholars had done since Victorian times – that agriculture is 'a good thing', bringing enormous advantages. The view was that early human societies simply lacked the know-how to put it into practice, and consequently were forever on the brink of starvation.[1] This picture was finally challenged by a number ethnographic studies carried out in the 1960s. One of the most influential of these was that of Canadian anthropologist Richard Lee. His 1968 paper[26] on the contemporary hunter-gatherers of the Kalahari Desert showed these people kept their populations well within the capacity of the available food supply. They had no problem with finding enough to eat, exploiting seasonally-available food sources with a highly organised schedule of movements. If preferred foods were scarce, they would simply fall back on less-favoured items. Furthermore, foraging took up only a few hours of the day and they enjoyed far more leisure time than farmers or indeed factory workers.

Having to work harder was not the extent of the difficulties faced by early agricultural communities. The adoption of agriculture was generally accompanied by a decline in health and probably in life expectancy. Skeletal and dental evidence from sites in both the Old and New World have been cited as painting a picture of increasing incidence of anaemia, bone disease, tuberculosis, leprosy and malnutrition. Teeth show signs of dental enamel hypoplasias and enamel micro-defects, implying episodes of poor health; and skeletal evidence suggests delayed juvenile growth and for juvenile osteoporosis.[27] However, the reliability of inferring prehistoric health from skeletal data has been challenged on the grounds that cemetery populations may not fairly represent the health of the population as a whole. For example, the skeletal pathology of somebody who died at the age of 20 was probably not typical of that of 20-year-olds who did not die. Indeed, it has been suggested that the higher frequency of skeletal lesions in early agricultural samples could reflect the fact people were living longer and were now surviving illnesses that did not leave such obvious physical markers.[28]

Nevertheless, Jared Diamond[15,14] paints a stark picture of some of the more deleterious effects of agriculture, and argues that livestock and crops are connected to disease. Smallpox, influenza, tuberculosis, malaria, bubonic plague, measles and cholera are diseases that evolved from those infecting farm animals, and they could not flourish among dispersed hunter-gatherers. They arose with the advent of agriculture, and accelerated with the subsequent rise of cities. Measles, tuberculosis and smallpox came from cattle; influenza from pigs and ducks; and pertussis (whooping cough) from pigs and dogs. The close proximity in which humans lived to their animals enabled diseases to cross the species barrier. This remains a factor to this day, resulting in the flu pandemics that periodically kill millions across the globe. Other factors in early agricultural settlements included poor hygiene from accumulated sewage that non-sedentary groups could simply leave behind, and disease-transmitting rodents attracted to stored food. Diamond also suggests that diet was generally poorer than that of hunter-gatherers, and that this affected adult stature. In Greece and Turkey, at the end of the Pleistocene, men averaged 1.78 m (5 ft. 10 in.) and women 1.68 m (5 ft. 6 in.). However, with the coming of agriculture, heights fell dramatically. By 4000 BC males were averaging 1.60 m (5 ft. 3 in.) and females 1.55 m (5 ft. 1 in.). Not until classical times did average height begin to increase, but it has still not reached hunter-gatherer levels.

These issues may offer an explanation for the delayed transitions to agriculture, but we are now faced with a third question: why did it start at all? If agriculture is unnecessary to avoid starvation, and requires a greater *per capita* labour input than hunter-gathering, then why would anybody choose it as a subsistence strategy? In the late 1960s, there was a paradigm shift away from agriculture as a natural step in human progress, to trying to identify factors that might have necessitated its adoption. As noted in Chapter 5, it was during the 1960s that the movement known as New Archaeology or processual archaeology came into its own. Processual archaeologists look to interpret cultures in terms of systems of social and economic behaviour, and explanations for culture change are sought in terms of either external factors such as environmental change, or the impact of new technologies; or in terms of internal factors such as population stress. Great emphasis is placed on testability, whereby hypotheses are proposed and then tested against archaeological evidence. Much use is made of statistical and computational techniques, and ethnographic parallels are often used to interpret features found in the archaeological record.[29]

Prior to the 1960s, many explanations for evidence of social change in the archaeological record were based on the notion of prehistoric migrations and conquests. Pottery styles, in particular, were seen as evidence of migration. For example, the distinctive Bell Beaker style that became widespread in the Late Neolithic was presumed to be associated with warlike 'Beaker Folk'. Given that in the historical period, Britain (for example) was successively invaded by Romans, Anglo-Saxons, Vikings and Normans, it was perhaps not unreasonable to assume that similar events had occurred in prehistoric times. Another key concept was diffusion, whereby innovations diffused by trade and cultural contact between 'higher' civilisations and the more 'backward' societies around them. In particular, it was generally assumed that major advances in European prehistory resulted from the diffusion of ideas from the classical civilisations of the Levant, the Mediterranean, and Egypt. This view was known as *Ex Oriente Lux* ('Light from the East').

However, by the end of the 1950s, it was becoming clear that such explanations were unsatisfactory. The advent of radiocarbon dating in the late 1950s and 1960s rewrote the chronology of European prehistory, and many cultures and innovations were found to be too old to have been influenced by developments in the East.[30] For example, Stonehenge turned out to be far older than the Mycenaean civilisation of Greece, previously believed to have been an influence on its construction. Consequently, explanations based on migrations and conquests fell out of favour, to be replaced by those based on a model Colin Renfrew[31] has described as 'peer polity interaction'.

A polity is a politically-autonomous community, and can be any size. In Renfrew's model, a number of polities interact, none of which are more prominent than any of the others. Within a given region, the highest-order social units in terms of scale and organisational complexity are considered to be polities. The peer polity interaction model states that if significant organisational change or increase in complexity occurs within one polity, it will likely be reflected in some neighbouring polities. In addition to innovations such as agriculture, changes may include building styles, objects deemed to be of high status or burial customs. Such innovations will not be attributable to any particular site, but will appear within several different polities at about the same time. Renfrew suggested a number of mechanisms by which innovations might have been transmitted, including trade, competitive emulation and warfare.

The latter two have long been powerful drivers of innovation. Competitive emulation basically means getting ahead of the other polities with ever more impressive displays of wealth and power. Examples include the statues of Easter Island, and the rivalry between medieval Florence and Pisa that led to the construction of the immense cathedrals in these two cities. More recently, competition between the Soviet Union and the United States led to the 'space race' of the 1960s. Many of the technological advances of the last century were driven by the needs of the military. Without the impetus of World War I, aviation might have taken decades to progress beyond the early flying machines of the Wright Brothers, Louis Blériot and A.V. Roe. Without the drive to develop weapons of mass destruction, nuclear fission might have remained a laboratory curiosity. Similarly, the Beaker phenomenon was found to be better explained by peer polity interaction than by the existence of 'Beaker Folk'.[32] One has only to imagine archaeologists a few millennia hence seeking to interpret the early twenty-first century in terms of 'iPhone Folk' to appreciate the attractions of the peer polity viewpoint.

One of the first topics to come under the scrutiny of the processualists was the origins of agriculture. The term 'Neolithic', as introduced by Sir John Lubbock in 1865, originally referred solely to stone tool technology. However, by the twentieth century, it had broadened to include sedentary village life and agriculture. The processual school of thought narrowed the definition once more, so that it referred purely to the agricultural mode of subsistence.[33] With this in mind, they considered the possibility that the shift to a new mode of subsistence might have been driven by demographic stress. On this picture, increasing population levels in the Late Pleistocene and Early Holocene brought about food shortages, and people were forced to turn to agriculture to make up the shortfall. American archaeologist Lewis Binford[34] suggested that in favourable coastal regions, ready availability of fish and other seafood encouraged the development of relatively sedentary communities. Such communities will experience faster population growth than more mobile societies. Women living in nomadic groups must space out birth intervals to four years or more, because a mother shifting camp can carry only one infant or slow toddler; but those living in sedentary communities are not subject to this constraint.[35] Binford argued that as populations grew, so some people were forced to move inland into less populated zones. The numbers of migrants soon pushed population levels there to above the carrying capacity – i.e. the maximum population that can be sustained by a particular habitat. Existing subsistence systems of gathering wild cereals had to be intensified to increase the food supply, leading to the development of cereal cultivation. Archaeologist Kent Flannery[36] further suggested that such intensification would only be required in marginal areas on the fringes of the ranges of the wild cereals. It would be in these regions, rather than in regions where the cereals were plentiful, that people would be forced to start cultivation.

Following on from this, anthropologist Mark Cohen[37] put forward the argument that events leading to the emergence of agriculture in various parts of the world had much in common. Local factors played a part in different regions, but in each case the underlying general cause was population pressure. The improving climatic conditions towards the end of Pleistocene led to continuous population growth, which in turn led to a dietary shift from large game to more readily available food sources, such as seafood, small game and cereals. As the population density grew, suitable territory shrank and hunter-gatherer groups were essentially forced into sedentism. This promoted a higher birth rate, so further increasing the population. Eventually, people were forced to cultivate cereals, simply to feed the growing population. Animal domestication followed later, as game animals declined in numbers.

Later theories have emphasised the role of climate change during the latter part of the Pleistocene. One possibility is that climatic stress of the Younger Dryas was a contributing factor in the subsequent development of agriculture.[38,39] Another possibility is that the climatic amelioration of the preceding Bølling-Allerød warm period led to the emergence of semi-sedentary and fully sedentary communities, leading in turn to growing populations being forced to turn to cultivation.[40]

An alternative to demographic stress models are those based on social stress. In these, the driving force behind the adoption of agriculture is competition between ambitious individuals and groups. Canadian archaeologist Brian Hayden[41] believes that among larger, more complex hunter-gatherer groups, one way to get ahead was to stage an extravagant feast. This would maintain prestige and assert dominance over those attending who were unable to hold events on the same scale. Hayden emphasises that this would only be possible among sedentary communities living in relatively rich environments, where the necessary food surpluses could be acquired and stored, and where there was no pressure to share food within the group. Such food sharing is regarded as almost mandatory among present-day hunter-gatherers who, for the most part, live in regions with a limited and fluctuating food supply. It is likely, therefore, that such an ethic was present among earlier hunter-gatherer groups living in poorer environments.

A rather different point of view is that neither social nor population pressures were involved, nor indeed any conscious awareness or choice by human populations. Rather, plants have co-evolved with humans for as long as they have been used as sources of food. American archaeologist David Rindos[42] has proposed a three-stage evolutionary sequence leading to plant domestication. 'Incidental domestication' occurred when people protected wild plants in the general environment. This was followed by 'specialised domestication', when people began to depend on wild species and consciously propagated them. At this stage, Rindos suggested, the plants began to undergo changes as they adapted to human intervention. 'Agricultural domestication' was the culmination of the co-evolutionary process, producing plants adapted to a special set of humanly-produced conditions. Rindos denied human intentionality in the process, which he saw purely as an outcome of unconscious Darwinian selection. People could not intentionally domesticate crops, but they could and did favour plants most useful to them.

Processualism remained to the fore of archaeological theory until the late 1980s, when a rival school of thought emerged. Post-processual archaeologists reject the view that we can ever gain an objective view of the past, believing instead that there may be several equally valid interpretations that can be put on archaeological data. Emphasis is placed the importance of symbolism and belief systems in human societies. The name notwithstanding, post-processualism has not replaced processualism and many archaeologists draw on both schools of thought.[29] However, the two view the emergence of agriculture very differently. Whereas processual archaeologists view the Neolithic as an economic phenomenon, to post-processualists it was ideological in nature, representing new ways of thinking and changes in material culture. On this view, the subsistence economy was only one aspect of a bigger picture, no more fundamental than any other aspect.[33]

British archaeologist Graeme Barker[20] notes that there are profound differences between the world view of present-day hunter-gatherer groups and that of subsistence farmers, and believes this also to have been the case in prehistoric times. Prehistoric hunter-gatherers probably saw themselves as a part of the cosmos, along with the animals and plants they relied on (see Chapter 14). However, when they adopted agriculture, their view of the natural world changed from something to that they were a part of to something that they sought to control. As we shall see in subsequent chapters, burial practices became increasing elaborate. The final resting places of ancestors became an important means by which farmers signified their new relationship to the land. Barker poses an important question: were the new ideologies a cause of or a consequence of hunter-gatherers adopting agriculture? Did they bring about behavioural changes that lead to farming, or were they the result of the shift in mind-set associated with becoming a farmer? British archaeologist Ian Hodder[43] believes that it was the former, with ideology change serving as the driver of subsistence change. He sees agriculture the culmination of social and symbolic processes relating to how people viewed themselves with respect to the natural world.

Perhaps unsurprisingly, there remains no consensus on how and why agriculture arose. It is unlikely that the same explanations are applicable in each and every case[4] although it is probable that sedentism was an important factor. Many believe that agriculture, especially in Southwest Asia, could only have arisen among sedentary rather than seasonally mobile groups.[19] Sedentism and the concomitant population increase placed a strain on food supplies and other resources in the immediate vicinity of a settlement. This pressure, possibly combined with elements of social competition as outlined in Brian Hayden's Feasting Hypothesis, might have provided the stimulus leading to agriculture.[19,1]

Australian archaeologist Peter Bellwood[19] believes that there might have been an additional factor in the mix: that of risk management. He notes that Early Holocene climates were never completely stable and that periods of plenty might have alternated with periods of mild climatic stress. While the climatic instability of the Pleistocene did not permit agriculture at all, absolute stability would have left no need for it. In 'risky' but highly productive Early Holocene environments, such as the Levant, periodic fluctuations in food supplies might have led to early experiments with agriculture.

British archaeologist Chris Scarre[1] believes that agriculture did not arise from a single cause, but was a series of adjustments and adaptations by hunter-gatherer communities in response to particular social, demographic and environmental conditions. Hunter-gatherers were not 'passive bystanders', and the process of domestication was not an abrupt transition at the start of Holocene. Instead, it was a gradual process stretching way back into the Upper Palaeolithic.

Transitions to agriculture

Did the spread of agriculture involved farmers, or merely farming? In other words, did farming populations expand from the primary centres where agriculture had initially emerged, and replace indigenous hunter-gatherer people as they colonised new territory; or did indigenous people learn about agriculture from farmers, and then take it up themselves? The two models are known respectively as demic diffusion and cultural diffusion. Unsurprisingly, there are conflicting views about the relative importance of the two.

Peter Bellwood[19] is pessimistic about the prospects of hunter-gatherers making the switch to agriculture. He is unconvinced by any evidence that purports to show continuity from a hunter-gatherer to a farming economy, and notes that there is little in the ethnographic record to suggest that hunter-gatherers ever succeeded in adopting agriculture in a manner that led to a population expansion. If hunter-gatherers lived in a region unsuitable for agriculture (such as semi-desert or rainforest), they would become surrounded by dispersing farming populations, but would unable to emulate their new neighbours. In addition, such groups tend to be mobile, multi-family bands, egalitarian in social structure, and lacking the hierarchical structure associated with complex pre-agricultural societies. Bellwood argues that such groups lack the collective mind-set to make a shift to agriculture.

Conversely, hunter-gatherers living in more favourable conditions would in the first instance lack any great motivation to switch to agriculture, even though such societies often possess the required degree of organisation and social complexity to make such a switch feasible. Unfortunately for them, after coming into contact with farmers they would only have a limited window of opportunity to adopt agriculture before the farming population grows to the extent that they take over all the suitable farmland, leaving nothing for the hunter-gatherers.

Bellwood does stress that there are limits to what may be inferred on the basis of ethnographic evidence, and that it cannot be stated with confidence that indigenous adoption never occurred in prehistoric times. However, he does note the low status of African Khoisan hunter-gatherers who live alongside Bantu farmers, and suggests that the low status of hunter-gatherers probably goes back to prehistoric times. Given such a relationship between hunter-gatherers and farmers, the former would be more likely end up being employed as labourers on the farms of the latter than be encouraged to adopt agriculture for themselves.

Nevertheless, archaeologists Peter Rowley-Conwy[33] and Marek Zvelebil[44] have both outlined a possible scenario by which hunter-gatherers made the transition to agriculture. They have argued strongly for such a scenario in the Baltic region, though in principle it could be applied elsewhere. Rowley-Conwy and Zvelebil proposed a three-stage model, with each stage defined by archaeological evidence on a regional level. The model considers a frontier between the hunter-gatherer and farming communities, across which there are contacts and exchanges. During the first phase, the hunter-gatherers learn about farming and exchange materials and information with farmers. However, they do not adopt agriculture, and the two societies remain culturally and economically independent. This phase ends with the hunter-gatherers adopting at least some major elements of farming, although at this stage they are only producing around five percent of their food. During the second phase, farming practices begin to replace hunter-gathering, but at this stage agriculture is still just a part of an overall hybrid foraging and farming strategy, and accounts for less than 50 percent of the subsistence economy. Not until the third and final phase is there a shift to a full dependence on agriculture.

Low-level food production

A subject of much debate among anthropologists is whether or not there are stable (as opposed to transitional) 'middle ground' economies between hunter-gathering and farming. Peter Bellwood[19] is dubious and has drawn on the *Ethnographic Atlas*, a database of societies from around the world, compiled by American anthropologist George Murdock in the 1960s. He notes that in the Old World, very few ethnographically-documented societies combine agriculture with a major dependency on hunter-gathering. Most of the exceptions are Pacific Island communities, which lack major herd animals, and rely heavily on fishing. In general, hunter-gatherers only practice a small amount of agriculture, and farmers only practice a small amount of hunter-gathering. There is almost no middle ground of, say, 30 percent agriculture and 70 percent hunter-gathering. Although the situation in the New World is less clear-cut, due to the absence of large domesticated meat animals, middle-ground societies appear to be largely absent. It is Bellwood's view that the middle ground is not stable. Societies practice either hunter-gathering or agriculture; being good at one is better than trying to balance the needs of both. Marek Zvelebil[44] suggests that any transition from a hunter-gatherer to an agricultural economy is likely to be of short duration.

Anthropologist Bruce Smith[7] believes that the apparent lack of middle-ground societies in the *Ethnographic Atlas* demonstrates only that, by the time it was compiled, there were very few middle-ground societies left. Most had been either replaced by or absorbed into fully agricultural societies. Smith notes that such societies did exist in prehistoric times, such as the Jōmon culture of Japan. As we shall see in Chapter 22, the Jōmon was a hunter-gatherer culture that existed for 10,000 years, although food production was an integral if not major part of their subsistence.[45] Smith has proposed that such societies should be classed as low-level food producers; low-level food production may involve the cultivation of either domesticated or wild crops.

In the next few chapters, we shall see how agriculture arose and spread in many parts of the world. We shall look at how this spread affected the genetic makeup of many present-day populations, and possibly even the languages they now speak. Space does not permit a full treatment, but this work will endeavour to present at least some of the many different ways in which people around the world responded to the coming of agriculture.

18: Assembling the package

Epipalaeolithic roots

The world's first agricultural revolution took place in Southwest Asia, and the events leading up to the transition can be traced far further back in time than anywhere else. Once believed to be a fairly brief episode at the close of the Upper Palaeolithic, the Epipalaeolithic is now known to have extended back to around 22,000 BC, when the Last Glacial Maximum was at its height. It lasted until 9600 BC, when the Younger Dryas ended, and the world emerged into the present Holocene epoch. In the Levant, it is divided between Early and Late, with the emergence of the Natufian culture around 13,000 BC being taken as the boundary between the two.[1] It is during this period of rather more than ten millennia that there was an increasing shift towards sedentism, which was a pivotal factor in the emergence of agriculture. However, its ending did not complete the transition. Mixed farming systems, incorporating both domesticated crops and livestock, did not begin to emerge for more than another millennium.

The theatre in which the world's earliest transition to agriculture was enacted was named the Fertile Crescent in 1906 by American academic James Henry Breasted; an arc of hilly country comprising the Levant to the west and Mesopotamia to the east. What is currently among the most politically-sensitive regions in the world includes significant territory within Iraq, Syria, Lebanon, Jordan, Palestine and Israel, together with the southeastern borders of Turkey, and the western borders of Iran.[2]

The Levant itself is a relatively small region of Southwest Asia. It is bounded by the Taurus and Zagros mountains to the north, the Mediterranean coastline to the west, the Sinai Peninsula to the south, and the Syrian Desert to the east. The region is approximately 1,000 km (620 miles) from north to south, and up to 400 km (250 miles) from east to west. It is characterised by a mosaic of markedly-varying rainfall and vegetation zones:[3] in the north and west, there are regions of moist steppe and woodland that receive over 200 mm of rainfall per annum, but to the southeast there is a 'Marginal Zone' of dry steppe and sub-desert.[4]

During the Last Glacial Maximum, the Fertile Crescent, in common with other regions, experienced a cold, dry climate. Pollen records suggest that woodland and forest-steppe was confined mostly to the Mediterranean coastal region, with perhaps a few isolated refugia surviving in the northern Zagros. The rest of the region was steppe and desert-steppe. Hunter-gatherers were able to collect acorns, almonds, barley, and emmer wheat in the woodland and forest-steppe regions, and barley and emmer wheat could also be found in the steppe regions in patchily-distributed stands. The steppes also offered a range of tubers and edible seeds, especially oil-rich chenopods.[5] The area was rich in game, including sheep, goat, aurochs, wild boar, gazelle and deer.[2] The hunter-gatherer populations of the Levant during this period have been termed Kebaran, and those in the Zagros the Zarzian.

The Kebaran was so named in 1931 by Dorothy Garrod, following her excavations at Kebara Cave in Mount Carmel, Israel, a site we have already encountered several times in earlier chapters. Prior to the 1960s, archaeological efforts focused on cave sites and rock shelters in the Mediterranean woodland zone in Israel, but archaeologists have since found Kebaran sites in the Negev and Sinai

Deserts, and the semi-arid steppe deserts of Jordan and Syria.[6] There is a considerable variation in the size of Kebaran sites. Some, mainly found on the steppes, are as small as 25 sq. m. (270 sq. ft.), and were probably used by small groups for short-term seasonal occupation. Most sites are around 100 to 150 sq. m. (1,070 to 1,600 sq. ft.) and a few are far larger, ranging from 500 to 1,500 sq. m. (5,380 to 16,000 sq. ft.).[2] The larger sites were mainly located in coastal and upland regions, and in the Jordan Valley. Implements for pounding and grinding have been found, mainly at the larger sites, and include hammerstones, grinding slabs, mortars and pestles. However, no sickles have been found at Kebaran sites.[6,2]

Much of our understanding of the Early Epipalaeolithic has come from Ohalo II, a large and now-submerged site in the Sea of Galilee. It was discovered by archaeologist Dani Nadel in 1989 when water levels in the lake temporarily dropped by several metres during a period of drought. The site was occupied around 23,000 years ago,[7] at which time the Sea of Galilee formed the northern part of the much larger Lake Lisan ('tongue' in Arabic). The Ohalo II site covered 2,000 sq. m. (21,500 sq. ft.), around 500 sq. m. (5,380 sq. ft.) of which has been excavated. Remains include six brushwood huts, with walls of oak branches, tamarisk and willow. The huts were roughly oval in shape, with a north-south long axis, and they had apparently burned down. It is not known whether the burning of the huts was accidental or intentional.[8]

Water levels in the lake were rising, and the fire might have been a ritual act prior to abandoning the site. Regardless of the circumstances, the fire was a boon to archaeologists. The heat dried out the many plant remains in the huts and then, not long afterwards, the rising water levels submerged the charred remains of the site, sealing it under a layer of silt and clay; a combination of events that preserved the huts and botanical remains for twenty-three millennia.

The Kebaran saw a 'spectrum shift' from big game to smaller animals, in particular gazelle.[9] In addition, at Ohalo II, people hunted deer and caught hare and birds, and the large numbers of fish bones recovered suggest they also caught fish from the lake.[10] Plant remains at the site suggest that the Ohalo II people made use of a wide range of plants. No fewer than 142 different species have been identified, including emmer wheat, barley, brome and other small-grained grasses, acorns, almonds, pistachios, olives, legumes, raspberries, figs and grapes. These were collected from a range of habitats, including the nearby Mount Tabor.[11]

Also found at the site were the remains of a man in a shallow burial pit. He was buried in a supine position, with hands crossed over his chest, legs flexed and heels touching the pelvis. Three stones were set under the head to support it, and a small gazelle bone was also placed near it. The man was aged about 35 to 40 years old at death, and he had been suffering from severe physical disabilities in later life. These included a chronic bone infection of his lower ribcage, and an atrophied upper arm. The latter might have been caused by traumatic nerve palsy, in turn the result of a shoulder injury. This is interpreted as reflecting social commitment to such members of the local social group.[12,13,14,10] As we have seen though, evidence of caring for the sick and disabled goes back much further in time.

Much information has been obtained from the remains of Hut 1, a kidney-shaped structure with a floor space of 12 sq. m (130 sq. ft.).[15,16] Archaeologists considered the distribution and type of almost 60,000 seeds and fruits and the distribution of around 8,000 stone tools, chips and fragments of the floor of the hut. From this, they showed that the use of domestic space inside the hut was consciously planned rather than haphazard, and that food preparation, tool-making and sleeping were carried on in different parts of the structure. In this respect, these humble brushwood huts were no different to a modern dwelling.

The most prominent artefact was a 40 cm (19 inch) long slab of basalt, which was embedded in the floor in the northern part of the hut for use as a grinding stone and work surface. Scattered around this was a U-shaped distribution of plant remains, suggesting that somebody had squatted by the grinding stone while using it for food processing. The plants processed included cereal grains and fruits with known medicinal properties, although there was no proof that the latter had actually been used for this purpose. Other seed and fruit remains on the hut floor probably came from building and roofing materials, and seeds of grasses thought to have been used for bedding were found in the southern part of the hut. The bedding was arranged around the walls, with a hearth in the centre.

Flint-knapping debris was concentrated near the entrance to the hut in a pattern which suggests that two or three individuals sat facing the light from the door while they knapped stone tools. Also found near the entrance were the remains of flowers which – barring the disputed Neanderthal floral tributes at Shanidar Cave – is the earliest-known use of flowers. Most local plants flower in spring, suggesting that this was when the fire happened.

Outside the hut, finds included six open-air hearths,[15] and a group of burned stones covered with ash that might be the remains of an oven. Combined with the evidence for processing cereals with the grinding stone, this suggests that the Ohalo II people baked dough made from grain flour.[17]

Three lines of evidence suggest that Ohalo II was probably occupied for much of the year. Firstly, the differing ripening seasons of the grains and fruits harvested at the site suggests that it was occupied at least during spring and autumn.[18] The second line of evidence is growth patterns in the teeth of gazelle remains found at the site. These can be determined by examining acellular cementum, which is the bone-like tissue anchoring tooth roots to the surrounding socket. It is formed in successive bands, with thicker bands forming during the wet season, and thinner bands during the dry season. The technique is not unlike counting tree rings, and analysis of the outermost band can reveal the time of the year death occurred to within two months. From this, it was shown that the animals were hunted in winter and spring.[19] Finally, based on their present-day migratory patterns, birds whose remains were found at the site were caught between September and November, and between February and April.[20] Overall, it is safe to conclude that Ohalo II was not a temporary seasonal camp, and was used as a year-round base.[10]

After 16,000 BC, an archaeological complex known as the Geometric Kebaran developed in the southern Levant, named for the culture's characteristic geometric microlithic stone tools.[3] These people lived in caves and in small camps, mostly 300 sq. m. (3,230 sq. ft.) in size or smaller, although some were larger. It is thought that they were seasonally mobile, possibly moving between winter lowland camps and summer camps at higher altitude. Like their predecessors, they used stone grinding implements and harvested wild cereals, but they still lacked sickles.[21] It is possible that during the Early Epipalaeolithic, people simply collected the wild grain from the ground, after it had been shed. Studies suggest that continual collection from the ground between May and October could have provided a ready source of food through the summer months, and provided a surplus to last through to the following spring.[22]

A key site from the later Early Epipalaeolithic is Neve David, located on the western slopes of Mount Carmel. Here, small semi-subterranean circular huts with stone foundations have been found, anticipating the similar dwellings of the Natufian culture that was to follow. There was also a burial with stone grinding implements as grave goods, presaging the elaborate burials often found at Natufian sites.[6] The site also yielded beads made from tooth-shaped dentalium shells.[23] Again, these would later feature prominently in Natufian mortuary practices. The later Early Epipalaeolithic also saw the earliest-known cemetery in the Levant. At 'Uyun al-Hammam in Jordan, the remains of at least eleven individuals have been found, interred in eight graves. In two of these, the remains of foxes were also found, attesting to increasingly complex mortuary rituals.[24]

The Zarzian culture of the Zagros Mountains is named for the cave of Zarzi in Iraq. It was contemporary with the Kebaran, but it is much less well understood. Nearly all data derives from excavations in late 1950s and early 1960s at Shanidar and other sites. Political unrest in the region has placed it largely off limits to archaeologists since the late 1960s. Zarzian tool-making technology included blades, bladelets, small scrapers and geometric microliths. Small coarse grinding stones have also been found; these were mainly used for grinding pigments. Plant food was less plentiful than in the Levant, and the Zarzian people relied heavily on hunting. Goats seem to have been the most important species, but sheep, deer and wild boar were also hunted. The Zarzian people also made use of riverine foods, including fish, waterfowl, and river clams.[2]

The Natufian

Around 12,500 BC,[25] the Bølling-Allerød Interstadial brought a warmer, wetter and more seasonal climate to Southwest Asia. These more benign conditions favoured the spread of deciduous woodland from their glacial refugia, along with annual grasses including wild cereals. Park woodland, a mix of oak woodland and grassland, now expanded rapidly from the southern Levant out over the uplands and steppes of the northern Fertile Crescent, preceded by a 'bow wave' of annual plants.[5] The first appearance of the Natufian culture, dated to around 12,900 BC,[3] slightly predates the onset of the Bølling-Allerød. While improving conditions undoubtedly favoured the Natufian people, it was apparently not the trigger for their emergence as a distinct culture.[26]

The Natufian was first identified in 1928, when Dorothy Garrod excavated the cave site of Shuqbah. This site is located in Wadi en-Natuf, a dry valley in the Mount Carmel hills, near the Palestinian town of Shuqbah. Further sites were discovered in the 1930s. The findings at these sites suggested a radical transformation in material culture, with the appearance of houses, elaborate burials, and tools for harvesting and processing cereals. Artefacts of limestone, basalt, sandstone and bone, often beautifully decorated, have been found at many sites. Some of these were purely utilitarian, such as bone tools for hunting, fishing and hide working, ground-stone implements (tools in which grinding plays a key role in manufacture) for use as mortars and pounding tools, heavy-duty scrapers, whetstones and hammerstones.[27] Other artefacts were ornamental or decorative. These included beads and pendants of limestone, basalt, malachite and other green stones, bone, teeth and dentalium shells, animal figurines, and carvings of animals and of abstract designs.[28,29,30,31]

So striking were the apparent changes that Garrod[32] even suggested that the Natufians might have been an intrusive people. In fact, the discoveries at Ohalo II and other sites suggest that many elements of Natufian culture were already present in the Kebaran, including semi-subterranean circular dwellings, grinding implements, burials with grave goods, and dentalium beads. The Natufian is therefore likely to have been a continuation of the Kebaran. Nevertheless, it has become clear that the Natufian emerged quite rapidly throughout the Levant, probably within a few centuries. Sites are far larger than those of the Geometric Kebaran, and occur in greater numbers, suggesting that the indigenous population had increased rapidly.[2]

The Natufian is divided into two phases, Early and Late, corresponding closely (but not exactly) to the Bølling-Allerød warm period (12,500 to 10,900 BC) and Younger Dryas (10,900 to 9600 BC) respectively. The Early Natufian saw the appearance of village communities located in the oak-pistachio woodlands of the Mediterranean coast and Jordan Valley, where herbaceous undergrowth contained abundant cereals.[33] Two sites have also been discovered in the Euphrates Valley in northern Syria: Abu Hureyra, and the later site of Mureybet 1A. These are contemporary with the Natufian, but it is disputed as to whether they should be 'lumped' with it or classified as belonging to a distinct Middle Euphrates culture of their own.[34]

Many Natufian villages were located in regions between thick woodland and forest steppe. Such locations, known as ecotones, provided access to edible plants from two contrasting habitats, and were likely to have permanent water supplies.[8] While some caves were used, most sites were open-air, ranging in size from under 350 sq. m. (3,770 sq. ft.) to over 5,000 sq. m. (53,800 sq. ft.). Most are around 1,000 to 2,000 sq. m. (10,760 to 21,520 sq. ft.), five to ten times larger than typical Kebaran sites. Populations several hundred strong have been estimated for the largest villages, but communities of around 50 people were more typical. Smaller sites on the steppes adjacent to the Natufian heartland were probably used as campsites by hunting and gathering parties, making brief sorties to obtain food supplies for the main settlements.[2]

Early Natufian houses were substantial semi-subterranean circular or oval structures, typically 3 to 6 m (10 to 20 ft.) in diameter. They were set in dry-stone walled pits cut into the subsoil, with stone-lined floors. Larger houses had internal wooden posts to support a roof that was probably made of wood, brushwood and thatch. Houses were entered through a doorway and down two or three steps, and a hearth of stone slabs was often set in the centre of the floor.[35,33,6] In one small building at the site of 'Ain Mallaha in northern Israel, a rounded bench covered with lime plaster was found. The building could have been used for ritual purposes by the village's leader or possibly shaman.[36]

The Natufian toolkit was very similar to that of earlier Epipalaeolithic cultures in the Levant, with one important addition – the sickle. Another change was that the geometric microliths of the Geometric Kebaran largely gave way to crescent-shaped microliths known as lunates. Food-processing equipment has been found at many Natufian sites, chiefly the larger ones. These include portable mortars, bowls, querns, slabs and pestles. Many of these implements were made from basalt, a material commonly only available from sources some distance away. Bowls and mortars were often decorated with carved geometric designs or raised reliefs. It is thought that the mortars and pestles were used mainly for grinding nuts, and the querns and slabs for seeds.[6,2]

That the Natufians used sickles has been implied from the tell-tale presence of sickle gloss on microliths that were evidently hafted as elements in sickles. Sickle gloss is a polish that occurs when blades are used to cut large numbers of plant stems, and is produced by silica present in these stems. Experiments using flint blades specially knapped for the purpose have shown that a smoother, brighter gloss develops when sickles are used to harvest semi-ripe cereals. This gloss is similar to that seen on Natufian microliths, suggesting that they harvested their cereals before they had fully ripened and before the rachis could shatter.[37,38]

The Natufians exploited a wide range of plants. At Abu Hureyra, for example, they collected over 150 plant species from the valley, steppe, and forest edge zones, all of which were within walking distance of the site. The plants included einkorn wheat, rye, barley, fruit, nuts, legumes and tubers. Other plants were probably used for flavouring, as dyes, and for medicinal purposes.[39]

What the Natufians apparently failed to do, in at least during the Early Natufian period, was to domesticate the wild cereals they harvested. As we saw in Chapter 17, grain harvested with sickles will become enriched with seed from non-shattering plants, and repeatedly re-sowing such seed will eventually result in domestication. However, research suggests that grain harvested when semi-ripe is still viable, and that sufficient will fall to the ground during harvest to re-seed a stand of wild cereal. It was found that within three years of harvesting, a stand would grow back to its original density.[37] Consequently, the Early Natufians had no need to sow fields with their own seed stock, and the process leading to domestication was thus never set in motion. On the other hand, the Early Natufians were not pure hunter-gatherers. They are probably best categorised as low-level food producers, as defined by Bruce Smith[40] (see Chapter 17).

The Natufian has often been called the 'gazelle culture', a reference to the ubiquity of gazelle remains at Natufian sites. However, wild boar, aurochs and deer made significant contributions to their diet.[41] Water fowl were also important, especially in sites along the Jordan Valley, where both migratory and nesting ducks gathered. At 'Ain Mallaha, freshwater fish were caught seasonally in the now-drained Lake Huleh.[36] The gazelle, however, was the overwhelming prey of choice, valued not just for meat and hides, but also bone marrow.[42] At many sites, such as 'Ain Mallaha and Hayonim, 50 km (32 miles) to the southwest, gazelle remained in the vicinity of the settlements all year.

However, at Abu Hureyra, they formed large herds that passed close to the site in late spring each year, during their northward migrations.[43] Kills at other times of the year were modest in comparison. Considerable planning was therefore required to kill and butcher the animals, and process the meat and skins for later use. These annual gazelle hunts were clearly successful, since they were maintained with little variation throughout the life of the Abu Hureyra settlement.[34]

A notable feature of Natufian gazelle exploitation is that males were preferentially targeted. Remains at a number of sites reveal that at various times and places, between 60 and 80 percent of the animals killed were males. It is likely that this was an attempt at herd management, or rather game management, as in theory only a few males are required to maintain the herds. Unfortunately, the Natufians made the mistake of killing the largest animals they could find. The females were now forced to mate with the smaller males that would not previously have been their first choice, resulting smaller offspring. 30 percent of modern gazelles reach maximum size, but this number fell to 20 percent and finally only two percent at Natufian sites.[41]

It is possible that dogs were used by Natufian hunters. At 'Ain Mallaha, one grave contained the remains of a woman who had been buried with a dog, and dog burials have also been found at Hayonim. In both cases, the remains appear to be of domesticated dogs as opposed to tamed wolves.[44] The domestic dog's wild ancestor is thought to be the Eurasian grey wolf (*Canis lupus*), with which it can to this day interbreed. Just when domestication occurred is still uncertain: dates of between 15,000 and 40,000 years ago have been suggested.[45,46,47,48] Where domestication occurred is also uncertain, though some genetic studies have suggested that the domestic dog originated in East Asia, south of the Yangtze River.[46,49]

It is likely that wolves were attracted to pre-agricultural settlements, which offered excellent opportunities for scavenging. Wolves would have been valued by the inhabitants, who might have begun to tame and keep them for hunting, as guard dogs to warn of approaching strangers, and simply for companionship. Once isolated from the native lupine population, these animals became subject to artificial rather than natural selection. Wolf pups became socialised to humans, and unconsciously and unintentionally selected for decreased flight behaviour and increased sociality – two key aspects of tameness.[50]

Sedentism, ritual and social organisation

While there is little doubt that the major Early Natufian sites were more than just transient settlements, it remains uncertain as to whether they were occupied for the whole year, or just for a part of it. Were the Natufians fully sedentary, or did they disperse from their large settlements, with groups spending much of the year at smaller satellite camps? It seems unlikely that they would go to the trouble of building substantial houses that were only used for a small part of the year. Another point is that sedentism enables women to have children at shorter intervals, and thus provides an explanation for the rapid increase in population seen during the Natufian (see Chapter 17).

Cementum growth studies of gazelle teeth found at Natufian sites again indicate that the animals were hunted throughout the year, supporting claims that the Natufians were sedentary.[19] Another possible line of evidence is the presence of bones of rats, mice and sparrows at Natufian sites. Commensal strains of these species appeared for the first time during the Natufian, and it is argued that they were exploiting the new niche created by permanent human settlements.[51,52] Unfortunately, the reliability of such animal remains as a marker of sedentism is questionable. It has been reported that some present-day mobile groups will repeatedly return to the same location before they are eventually forced to move on for good by rising numbers of rodents and other pests attracted to site rubbish.[53]

The scarcity of dedicated storage installations at Natufian sites has been cited as evidence against sedentism. Rare examples include a paved bin in Hayonim Terrace, and a number of plastered pits at 'Ain Mallaha. If people were staying at the sites on a year-round basis, one might expect to see more evidence of granaries and other facilities for storing food. However, it is possible that baskets were used for such purposes. Bone tools found at Natufian sites are similar to those known from ethnographic studies to be used for basket-making. If baskets were used for storing food, they would have long since rotted away.[36]

A plausible scenario was proposed by Francois Valla,[54] who led a French excavation team at 'Ain Mallaha. Drawing on ethnographic data, he suggested that Natufian village life emerged from seasonal gatherings of Kebaran hunter-gatherers. Members of widely dispersed groups took part in religious rituals, enjoyed feasts, and exchanged marriage partners before going their separate ways. However, the highly favourable conditions of the Bølling-Allerød enabled the groups to extend these gatherings, until eventually they were living together for the whole year in villages such as 'Ain Mallaha, Abu Hureyra and Mureybet.

Burial practices are certainly consistent with sedentism. Although burial of dead in cemeteries, as noted above, predates the Natufian era, it was only then that the practice became widespread. Some Natufian cemeteries contain large numbers of burials, for example at Wadi-en-Natuf the remains of almost 100 individuals were found. At 'Ain Mallaha and Hayonim, many graves were dug in deserted dwellings and outside of houses, although not under the floors of active households. One building at 'Ain Mallaha – designated Structure 131 by archaeologists – contained twelve burials. It was semi-circular and rather larger than average at 9 m (30 ft.) across, with a roof supported on posts and three hearths: one located close to the straight wall and the two others close together at the rear of the building.[36] Some burials are single inhumations, although around 80 per cent are group graves. In the latter case, individuals of both sexes and of all ages, including infants, were typically buried together. Such burials probably reflect descent groups, either nuclear or extended families. Many individuals were buried wearing items of personal ornamentation, mostly made from dentalium shells.[55] The increase in the number of cemetery burials may reflect an increasing sense that people belonged to a village community, as well as to a family or extended family unit.[3] Cemeteries may also reflect a need to mark a territory as belonging to villagers by establishing an ancestor presence there.[56]

Dentalium shells are in many cases found at sites far from the coast and must therefore have been obtained by trade. The existence of geographically wide-ranging exchange networks in the Natufian is implied by the presence of not only dentalium shells, but also artefacts of basalt and coloured minerals at locations far from any sources for these materials.[1,3] Although the trade in dentalium shells predated the Natufian, there is a dramatic increase in their numbers in comparison to earlier periods.[57,58] Steven Mithen[8] has suggested that the dentalium jewellery denoted social identity. He believes that sedentism provided the opportunity for some individuals to acquire surpluses of food and goods. Control of the trading relationships might have been the key to wealth and power. Mithen speculated that the key to maintaining these might have been to limit the number of shells in circulation at any given time. The most effective way of doing so was to bury large quantities of them with the dead. Those remaining in circulation would thus confer status or prestige on their owners.

Mithen's view does seem highly plausible. As we saw in Chapter 10, ethnographic evidence suggests that sedentary hunter-gatherer groups tend to be socially stratified, whereas highly mobile groups are more egalitarian. In Chapter 14 we saw that the first appearance of shell beads in the Levant, thousands of years before the Natufian period, might have been linked to a need to display group affiliation and status. Given the increase in both social complexity and long-distance exchange during the Natufian, the need to display individual status might have become ever more pressing. Individuals would have had to assert their status not only within their own group, but possibly among members of neighbouring groups as well.[1]

Yet differences in Natufian mortuary practices do not appear to highlight social hierarchies or the existence of any form of elite. A comprehensive survey of Natufian burials was carried out by anthropologists Bryan Byrd and Christopher Monahan,[55] who considered grave goods, burial site complexity, and a number of other factors. They found that there was a lack of any standardised Natufian regional burial tradition and failed to find any correlations that would identify high status individuals or kin groups. They concluded that Natufian villages were not chiefdoms with hereditary elites.

In fact, both social organisation and the degree of sedentism probably varied from site to site. Some Natufian groups might have continued to be organised along the lines of small-scale bands, with the nuclear family as the basic unit. However, in more favourable settings, where the larger settlements were located, social complexity was undoubtedly greater, and quite different patterns were probably adopted. These might have been based on extended families or moieties. In the latter, a society is divided into two descent groups, and members of each group will always take marriage partners from the other group.[1]

Life in the Early Natufian does seem to have been on the whole peaceful, and evidence for violence is very rare.[59] The Natufian people showed few signs of physical trauma such as healed fractures, nutritional deficiencies or infectious diseases. There was no evidence for dietary stress, such as may be indicated by dental enamel hypoplasias (see Chapter 8).[59] Matters were not perfect – their teeth were worn down by the grit from stone grinding equipment that found its way into the ground seeds and nuts that they ate.[60] Tooth loss was very common in older individuals, and dental caries affected young and old alike.[61] Overall, though, life was good for the Early Natufian villagers; but it was not to last.

Hard times

Around 10,900 BC, the Younger Dryas plunged the Earth back into renewed cold and aridity. The woodlands and cereals, so vital to the Natufian way of life, retreated,[5] and foraging returns declined accordingly. Did this bring to an end the Natufian experiment with village living? In fact, recent work suggests that the transition from Early to Late Natufian might have slightly preceded the Younger Dryas.[26] If so, then possibly the over-exploitation of wild plants and animals by a burgeoning population led to the collapse of village living. Regardless of cause, many sites were abandoned and the Natufians returned to a more mobile way of life. At 'Ain Mallaha, there was no longer a permanent settlement. The large houses gave way to far less substantial structures, occupied only seasonally. The site continued to be used for burials, possibly now regarded as a sacred place where the dead were united with their ancestors.[35]

With these changes came significant shifts in mortuary practices. People were now very rarely buried with grave goods, and when they were it was usually without the once-ubiquitous body ornaments of dentalium shells. There was also a switch away from group burials to single interments. Another change was that graves were frequently re-opened to remove skulls and long bones for reburial elsewhere, a practice known as secondary burial.[55] Many of these practices, in particular skull removal, would be continued into Neolithic times.[62] The changed circumstances of the Natufians almost certainly led to changes in their world view and belief systems, in turn leading to changes in their mortuary practices. However, the latter are open to conflicting interpretation.

Steven Mithen[8] believes that the collapse of village living meant the end of the power base for the elite who controlled the distribution of the dentalium shells. Without this control over their availability, the shells became worthless – as gold or diamonds would if they became freely available. Mithen sees Late Natufian society as more egalitarian than that of the Early Natufian period. To him, the switch away from kin-based group burials reflects the reduced importance of lineage. People were judged instead on their achievements in life and their personal qualities. In addition, Mithen suggests that the increase in secondary burial probably came about because the majority of people died away from their ancestral homes, and now-dispersed groups periodically returned with the remains of the recently-deceased for re-interment. Bryan Byrd and Christopher Monahan[55] also see single interments as reflecting a growing emphasis on the importance of the individual over the group, although as discussed above, they have raised doubts about the existence of high-status kin groups during the Early Natufian.

Anthropologist Ian Kuijt[62] takes a rather different view. To him, secondary burials, single interments and the lack of grave goods reflect the development of community-based mortuary rituals intended to cut across household and kin group lines, and emphasize the importance of group membership over the status of individuals. Differences within the community, whether actual or merely perceived, were minimised by ensuring similar mortuary treatment for all its members. These practices arose from a desire to maintain solidarity and to provide an important stabilising force during a period of significant economic change. However, we should again note the criticism that has been made of models positing ritual as a means of promoting social cohesion (see Chapters 11 and 14), albeit these are widely accepted.

In fact, recent discoveries suggest that our understanding of Late Natufian mortuary practices, and indeed society, is far from complete. Hilazon Tachtit is a small cave located in the Galilee region of Israel. The site appears to have been a dedicated burial ground, and at least 28 individuals were interred there. The site is 10 km (6 miles) from Hayonim, the nearest domestic Natufian site. Of particular interest is the 12,000-year-old grave of a 45-year-old woman, which has been interpreted as a shaman burial. The slightly-built woman, who suffered from disabilities, was clearly a person of some importance. Considerable effort had gone into the preparation of her grave, which was hollowed out of the cave's bedrock, plastered with clay, and lined with limestone slabs. She was buried with highly unusual grave goods comprising over 70 tortoise shells, the tail of an aurochs, the pelvis of a leopard, the forelimb of a wild boar, the wingtip of a golden eagle, a basalt bowl, and a complete human foot. The latter came from an individual rather larger than herself. Tortoises, the tails of cattle, eagle wings and fur-bearing animals continue to play important symbolic and shamanistic roles among traditional societies to this day. The presence of such grave goods suggests that the woman was perceived as being in a close relationship with these animal spirits.[63]

The tortoises appear to have been roasted in their shells, and the meat carefully removed so as not to damage the carapaces, prior to their being placed in the grave with the woman's remains. In a second pit, located near to the grave, the remains of at least three aurochs that had been processed for their meat and marrow were found. It is not known whether these animals were killed at the same time as the woman's burial, but the tortoise meat alone would have fed at least 35 people. The collection of so many tortoises for a specific event would have been a significant undertaking. Notwithstanding the loss of village life, it is clear that considerable social complexity still existed in the Late Natufian. Elements of the feasting event at Hilazon Tachtit anticipate those of later cultural traditions. In particular, the use of wild cattle in feasting and other ritual events was particularly prevalent in the Neolithic period across Southwest Asia.[64]

Despite this evidence for ritual feasting and social complexity, life during the Younger Dryas was harsh. There is evidence that the health of the Natufians began to suffer. At 'Ain Mallaha and Hayonim, tooth loss and dental caries show an increase in the Late Natufian in comparison to the Early Natufian.[61] At the site of Nahal Oren, south of Haifa, average heights were rather less than those of the Early Natufian inhabitants of 'Ain Mallaha. The difference in height between men and women also decreased. Both are possible indicators of poor diet, leading to reduced growth.[59] Another hint at food shortages has come from studying strontium levels in skeletal remains. Cereals

The Neolithic Revolution

are rich in strontium, and the low strontium levels found in some Late Natufian remains suggests a reduction in cereal foods during this period.[65]

Faced with these problems, the Late Natufians responded in a variety of ways. In the Negev and Sinai Deserts, survival depended on improved hunting techniques to kill what game was available. It is from here that we have the some of the earliest unequivocal evidence for the use of bows and arrows. Stone points from the sites of Harif and Shunera appear, on the basis of weight, aerodynamic shape, and impact fractures, to have been used as arrowheads.[66] At settlements further north, there is evidence that they widened the range of animals that they hunted. At the Late Natufian sites of Hatula, near Jerusalem, and Salibiya I in the Lower Jordan Valley, smaller game such as hare was taken, although gazelle continued to account for 80 to 90 percent of the animal remains. Notably though, at Salibiya I, gazelle age profiles are consistent with those of modern herds, with high proportions of juvenile animals. Instead of the selective targeting of adult males, entire herds were now killed. Possibly, hunting methods involving game drives and nets were used.[67,68] At Hatula, also, there is a much-reduced bias towards males, and a high proportion of juveniles among the animals killed.[41,9]

Experiments with herding and agriculture

Curiously, as many Natufian groups were forced to abandon village life, in the foothills of the Taurus and Zagros mountains groups were establishing villages for the first time. Hallan Çemi Tepesi is a small settlement in southeastern Turkey that was occupied during the latter part of the Epipalaeolithic. The villagers built substantial circular stone houses, suggesting that the site was rather more than a seasonal hunter-gatherer camp. Two of the buildings are thought to have been public. Much larger than the domestic dwellings, they each contained semi-circular stone benches set against the wall, and the floors were surfaced with a mixture of sand and plaster. An aurochs skull was found in one of the buildings that had evidently hung upon the wall – an early indication of the significance that the aurochs would later acquire in Neolithic belief systems. The significance of the aurochs was underlined by the discovery of several small ground-stone objects resembling miniature stylised bucrania, or carved ox's skull and horns. The site's inhabitants possessed a rich material culture that also included stone bowls incised with elaborate geometric and naturalistic designs, and stone pestles sculpted with animal designs. The presence of obsidian and copper ore, neither of which are locally available, implies that the Hallan Çemi Tepesi people engaged in long-distance trade.[69]

However, it is their subsistence economy that is of the greatest interest. Cereals appear to be absent, but lentils, bitter vetch, almonds and pistachios were collected, and animal remains include sheep, goats, pigs, deer, turtle, birds, fish and clams. Growth bands on the shells of the clams have enabled the time of year that they were collected to be determined. From this it is apparent that Hallan Çemi Tepesi was occupied throughout the year. There are also intriguing hints that the pigs were being herded. Remains found suggest that less than a third of the pigs reached an age of three years, a proportion similar to that observed at sites where domesticated pig remains have been found. Furthermore, an analysis of the molar sizes of the pigs has shown that they were mid-way in size between wild and domesticated pigs. Such a reduction in molar size is considered to be a sign that pigs are in the early stages of domestication. A note of caution should be sounded though, as only a small number of molars have been analysed. Sheep and goat remains also indicate management strategies. These animals remained undomesticated, and in cases where ages could be determined, approximately two-thirds of them were at least 3 ½ years old. This is entirely consistent with them being hunted from a wild population, but there is a strong bias towards males – suggesting attempts at game management similar to that practiced by the Natufians with gazelle herds.[70,69]

Assembling the package   **243**

At Abu Hureyra there was a highly significant development – one of the world's first examples of cereal domestication. With the onset of the Younger Dryas, the landscape around the site slid rapidly into aridity, and availability of wild foods declined. The site's archaeological record provides a mute testament to the struggle the villagers must have faced to keep their settlement viable. Edible woodland fruits were an early casualty, followed lentils and other large-seeded legumes. Soon afterwards, wheat, rye, and even hardy drought-resistant chenopods went into decline. By this point, the landscape had become an arid and increasingly treeless steppe. Only periodic flooding of the Euphrates allowed edible club rush and Euphrates knotgrass to grow in substantial quantities.

Rather than try to find somewhere else to live, the villagers apparently began to cultivate wild wheat and rye. Long after these cereals had ceased to be available locally, they persisted in reduced quantities in the archaeological record of Abu Hureyra. They are accompanied by weeds normally found on arable land – an important indication of cultivation practices. A century or so later, by around 10,700 BC, domesticated rye appeared, the unintentional product of cultivation. This was followed a further two or three centuries later by the sudden reappearance of lentils and other large-seeded legumes. The Younger Dryas continued to maintain its cold, arid grip, and these plants would not have been locally available in the wild.[71]

This early experiment with agriculture ultimately failed. Even domestic crops could not support Abu Hureyra, and it was eventually abandoned. The domesticated rye, unable to reproduce without human intervention, died out. Rye never became a major part of the agricultural package that later emerged in Southwest Asia. In comparison to wheat, rice, maize and barley, rye remains a relatively minor agricultural crop to this day. However, the villagers at Abu Hureyra had provided a foretaste of what was to come.

Eventually, around 9600 BC, the Younger Dryas came to an abrupt end. Temperatures rose between 5 and 10 degrees Celsius in less than a decade, and in the early centuries of the new Holocene epoch, carried on rising. The climate was now not only warm and wet; it was also very stable, without the rapid oscillations that characterised the Late Pleistocene.[72] In Southwest Asia, experiments with agriculture were resumed, and this time they did not fail.

The Walls of Jericho

The city of Jericho is thought to be the oldest continuously inhabited city in the world. Like Homer's Troy, Jericho inevitably attracted the interest of nineteenth century archaeologists, in search of evidence for walls supposedly destroyed by Joshua's invading Israelite army. The mound of Tell es-Sultan, in the Jordan Valley, has long been equated with the Biblical city, and was first investigated in 1873. More extensive excavations followed during the first half of the twentieth century, revealing a series of Early and Middle Bronze Age walls and ramparts, beneath which lay even older remains dating to the early Neolithic. Even this is not the earliest occupation of the site. The oldest remains date back to the Early Natufian, although this was followed by a lengthy hiatus. Dating the beginning of the Neolithic occupation is problematic, but the oldest radiocarbon date, for Sample P-378, suggests that the site was in use by 9250 BC (7825 radiocarbon years BC).[73]

The Neolithic layers were first fully investigated by British archaeologist Kathleen Kenyon, who excavated the site between 1952 and 1958. Kenyon was one of the most notable archaeologists of the last century and, like Dorothy Garrod, her achievements came in an era when the field was still largely male-dominated. Her excavations at Jericho revealed the existence of a Neolithic settlement of 2.4 ha (6 acres), as large as the Bronze Age city. Kenyon found no sign of pottery in the early levels at Jericho, so she named the two main Neolithic phases Pre-Pottery Neolithic A (PPNA) and

Pre-Pottery Neolithic B (PPNB). These names remain in use, although some prefer to lump the two together as the Aceramic Neolithic.

Population estimates for the PPNA phase at Jericho range from 400 to 900 inhabitants.[73] The western side of the site was enclosed by a stone wall 3.8 m (12 ft. 6 in.) high and 1.8 m (5 ft. 11 in.) wide at base, tapering to 1.1 m (3 ft. 7 in.) at the top. Attached to the inside of the wall was a large circular tower, 8.2 m (26 ft. 11 in.) high, 9 m (29 ft. 6 in.) in diameter at the bases, tapering to 7 m (23 ft.) at the top, with 22 stone steps inside.[73]

Kenyon thought, perhaps not unreasonably, that this structure was defensive, but this view raises a number of questions. Firstly, who was the enemy? While it is probable that life in the PPNA was not entirely pacific, there is little evidence for widespread conflict in the Levant prior to the sixth millennium BC. There are no mass graves, or settlements destroyed by fire. Why were no other sites fortified? If the Jericho wall was defensive, why was the tower on the inside rather than the outside, as might have been expected? Another point is that after a few centuries, debris from demolished houses and other rubbish almost reached the top of the tower, yet neither it nor the wall were rebuilt. Israeli archaeologist Ofer Bar-Yosef[73] has noted that the site is located on a sloping plain. He believes that the walls might have been defences against floods and landslides from the Palestine Hills. The accumulation of debris eventually raised the level of the settlement so much that the wall became redundant. The role of the tower remains unknown, but Bar-Yosef suggests that it was a 'special structure', possibly intended for ritual.

Kenyon's findings disproved V. Gordon Childe's view that pottery was an essential component of a 'Neolithic Revolution', and showed that agriculture did not necessarily arrive in a single, indivisible package. However, it is only recently that that we have come to appreciate just how complex and protracted the transition was.[74] The PPNA is generally taken to have begun with the transition to the Holocene at around 9600 BC, although a possible precursor phase known as the Khiamian, characterised by the El-Khiam stone point, was slightly earlier. In comparison to the Natufian, the PPNA was a relatively brief phenomenon, lasting for little over a millennium before giving way to the PPNB around 8500 BC. The PPNB lasted rather longer, continuing until about 6500 BC. It is often divided into an Early (8500 to 8100 BC), a Middle (8100 to 7500 BC), a Late (7500 to 6750 BC) and a Final (6750 to 6500 BC).[3,1,26] Note that these dates are only approximate. The Final PPNB is sometimes referred to as the PPNC, though Kenyon never used this term.

With climatic conditions now very favourable, there was a return to the sedentism of the Early Natufian. Most of the PPNA settlements were located within the Levantine Corridor, a narrow belt running north-to-south along today's boundary between the Mediterranean and the Iranian steppe regions. In addition to Jordan Valley sites such as Jericho, the PPNA encompasses sites such as Mureybet, Abu Hureyra, and Jerf el-Ahmar in northern Syria. During the Early Holocene, this region lay within the Mediterranean woodland, and was rich in plant foods and game animals.[36] PPNA sites were larger than their Natufian predecessors, suggesting that the population had begun to increase. The largest, including Mureybet, Jericho, Netiv Hagdud, Gilgal and Dra, were from three to eight times larger than the largest Natufian sites.[36,33] A typical medium-sized settlement was between 2,000 and 3,000 sq. m. (21,500 to 32,300 sq. ft.) in extent, though a few such as Jericho and Mureybet were considerably larger.[2]

Houses were typically round or oval semi-subterranean structures. They were similar to those of the Early Natufian, but more substantial in construction. They were built with stone-lined foundations and superstructures built of loaf-shaped sun-baked mud bricks. At Netiv Hagdud, 20 km (12 miles) north of Jericho, houses were large and oval, ranging in size from 5 to 10 m (16 to 32 ft.) in length. They had plastered floors, internal hearths and, it is thought, conical roofs. Some might have comprised two rooms. There were significant differences in layout between the large villages and small hamlets. At the former, including Netiv Hagdud, Jericho and Mureybet, there were open spaces where some of the domestic activities took place. On the other hand, at smaller sites such as Nahal Oren, the houses were all the same size and were clustered together, like the compound of an extended family.[30,36,2] The stone tool-making technology of the PPNA continued the Natufian use of microliths and sickles, but there were many more heavy-duty tools such as picks, adzes, planes, and a variety of grinding equipment. Querns and hand stones gradually replaced mortars and pestles as cereal dependency increased.[2]

Burial practices appear to have been fairly standardised throughout the PPNA. Like the Late Natufian, graves were very simple and grave goods largely absent. The practice of secondary burial also continued from the Late Natufian, with the majority of PPNA adults having their skulls removed for subsequent reburial elsewhere in the village. The primary burials were generally under the floors of houses, or in courtyards between buildings. Skull removal was rare in the case of children, who account for around 40 percent of all burials for the PPNA period. One exception was a cache of five infant skulls placed in a pit below a plastered basin at Jericho. Kenyon found a total of 276 burials at Jericho. Most appear to be associated with residential buildings, although a number of individuals were also buried in the tower.[62]

The population increase of the PPNA seems to have been greatest in the north, and this may well be the 'core area' from which subsequent population expansions occurred. It is thought that groups 'budded off' to found settlements in new territories around the Mediterranean.[33,1] However, the south was not a backwater, and Jericho and other major sites might have been functioned as centres for the exchange of agricultural surpluses and certain minerals, such as salt, obsidian and malachite.[1]

Salt has long been valued as a food additive and preservative. Roman legionnaires are popularly supposed to have been on occasions paid in salt, giving rise to the term 'salary' (Latin '*salarium*'). Obsidian, as we have seen, has been prized since Palaeolithic times as a tool-making material. The increased importance of malachite and other green stones for making beads and pendants, a trend first seen in the Late Natufian, may reflect the growing importance of agriculture. Green mimics the colour of young leaves, which signify germination. The green stone beads and pendants might have been used as amulets intended to protect farmers and bring about successful harvests.[75] Exchanges of these items might have formed the basis of an early market economy, where forces of supply and demand had begun to operate.[1]

Jericho is by far the largest PPNA site in the Levant, and for this reason it was for a long time widely assumed that the Levantine Neolithic originated in the Jordan Valley. In fact, as we shall see, recent discoveries suggest that the region might have been quite peripheral to the social and economic developments of the early Neolithic.[8]

Granaries and figs

Until the end of the last century, it was widely believed that crop domestication had originated during the PPNA in a core region around the Jordan Valley, before spreading rapidly to the rest of the Fertile Crescent. The domestication of animals was thought to have been delayed until around 8000 BC, during the Middle PPNB. This view has since changed: it is now thought that both crop and livestock domestication occurred at roughly the same time, and that the process occurred across the whole of the Fertile Crescent rather than in just a core region. A factor in this changed perspective is that it is now recognised that we cannot necessarily assume the presence of domesticated species in the archaeological record represents the earliest beginning of agricultural practices. Instead, it is thought that any manifestation of archaeologically-visible change in crops and livestock was preceded by a long period – possibly more than 1,000 years – of increasingly intensive human management.[74]

Aside from the changes associated with domestication, there are three strong archaeological indications that crop management practices are taking place. Firstly, the presence of seeds in quantities greater than could have been harvested from local stands of wild cereals; secondly, evidence of storage facilities; and thirdly, the presence of seeds of commonly-occurring weeds mixed in with the grain. In recent years, such evidence has been found at a number of PPNA sites.

Seeds in great quantities have been found at the sites of Gilgal and Netiv Hagdud, both of which are located in the Jordan Valley within 20 km (12 miles) of Jericho. A large cache comprising 260,000 wild barley grains and 120,000 wild oat grains, dating from 9400 to 9200 BC, has been found at Gilgal. Such vast quantities could not have been harvested from naturally-occurring sources. No cereals grow in the saline deposits to the east of the site, and only moderate amounts can be collected in good years in the wadi floodplains to the west. Within a few years, local cereal stands would have been depleted by overexploitation. It is a similar picture at nearby Netiv Hagdud, where a large quantity of wild barley has been found.[76] Evidence for small clay storage bins has also been found at Netiv Hagdud. It is likely, though not certain, that these bins were used for storing food.[77]

Unequivocal evidence of storage facilities has been found at the site of Dhra', which lies to the south of the Dead Sea. It is fairly large at 6,500 sq. m. (70,000 sq. ft.),[78] though it is still far smaller than Jericho. At Dhra', excavations have revealed the remains of at least four purpose-built communal granaries, located between residential buildings. The latter doubled as food-processing installations, with grindstones set into the floors. Some of the granaries are built over earlier structures, and the earliest phase of construction dates to between 9300 and 9200 BC. These granaries are the first large, dedicated food-storage facilities known anywhere in the world. They were circular, about 3 m (10 ft.) across, built with mud walls, and some also had outer retaining walls of stone. Inside, stone pillars were used to support a wooden floor, suspended above the ground for air circulation, and for protection against insects and rodents. The floor had a slope, to aid runoff of water, and grain was probably stored in baskets. Although no roofing materials have been found, it is thought that they were topped with a flat roof of wood and reeds, covered with a thick coating of mud for protection against rain. The granaries were probably used for no more than about fifty years before having to be rebuilt.[77]

Finally, agricultural weeds have been found at the site of Jerf el-Ahmar in Syria. Here, wild emmer wheat and rye remains dating to about 9250 BC (9800 to 9700 radiocarbon years BP) were found associated with the remains of weeds commonly associated with agriculture, suggesting that these cereals, though not domesticated, were under cultivation.[79] In addition, small rooms in a large communal building at the site might have been used for cereal storage.[80]

While many of the crops under cultivation during the PPNA were still not domesticated, some might have been undergoing transformation to the domestic varieties at this time. Although the first fully-domesticated lentils do not occur until around 6800 BC, there is evidence that lentil cultivation was widespread much earlier. Over two hundred lentil seeds were found at Netiv Hagdud and a similar amount were found at Jerf el-Ahmar. The seeds, dating to around 9000 BC, were still wild, but it is thought that they were on the way to becoming domesticated. About 90 percent of wild lentil seeds were dormant, that is to say they do not germinate readily after sowing. Domestication involves the loss of this dormancy and the development of a non-shattering seed pod. It is thought that the seeds found at Netiv Hagdud and Jerf el-Ahmar, though not non-shattering, must have been of a low dormancy variety in order to make cultivation practical.[76] Wild lentil populations from northern Syria and southern Turkey have been suggested as the possible genetic stock of the cultivated lentil.[81] If this is correct, then it is likely that the first stage of lentil domestication – loss of dormancy – occurred there. It then quickly spread south to the Jordan Valley, along trade routes that brought materials such as obsidian all the way from Anatolia to Jericho.[76]

The fig tree might also have been domesticated during the PPNA. Remains of fig fruits, dating from 9400 BC to 9200 BC, have been found at Gilgal and a number of other Levantine PPNA sites. The fruits are of the domestic variety, and outnumber the remains of any other fruit. Among wild fig trees, a small genetic change can lead to a variety that yields seedless fruit. Unlike the unfertilised fruits of the normal variety, these fruits are not shed but are retained until they become soft and sweet. The seedless fig tree cannot reproduce in nature, but it can be propagated very easily by cutting and planting branches. The ease with which edible fruit can thus be produced probably explains the early domestication of the fig tree.[82]

Overall, PPNA societies were still low-level food producers rather than fully-fledged agriculturalists. As far as animals are concerned, the emphasis continued to be on hunting rather than herding. Hunters continued to favour the gazelle, though remains suggest that younger animals were now killed. This, together with an increasing shift to smaller mammals, birds and fish suggest that gazelle was now becoming scarce, possibly because there were now simply more mouths to feed.[9]

First came the temple, then the city

780 km (485 miles) to the northeast of Jericho is a site unlike any other known in the early Neolithic world of Southwest Asia. Göbekli Tepe is thought to be the world's oldest temple. It comprises a series of stone circles that draw superficial comparison to Stonehenge, but it predates the well-known Salisbury Plain monument by seven millennia. Located on a limestone ridge 15 km (9 miles) from the town of Şanlıurfa in southeastern Turkey, it was noted as far back as the early 1960s, but was largely ignored for thirty years. However, in 1994 it was visited by German archaeologist Klaus Schmidt, who believed that the site was Neolithic. He began excavating there the following year, and excavations have been ongoing ever since.

At the lowest level of the site, Layer III, Schmidt discovered a series of semi-submerged circular or oval enclosures. Each comprises a dry-stone wall, into which up to twelve T-shaped limestone pillars are set, often joined to one another by stone benches. At the centre of each enclosure are two more pillars, which tend to be larger than the surrounding ones. The pillars range in height from 3 to 5 m (10 to 16 ft.) and weigh up to 10 tonnes. They were quarried from limestone plateaus close to the site, where a number of incomplete pillars remain *in situ*. One weighs over 50 tonnes, larger than any of the finished pillars so far excavated. Currently, four enclosures, designated A to D, are undergoing excavation, but geomagnetic surveys suggest that least twenty exist. Many of the pillars are carved with bas-reliefs of animals, including snakes, wild boar, foxes, lions, aurochs, wild sheep, gazelle, onager, birds, various insects, spiders, and scorpions. Where sexual characteristics are present, they are always male. The images are large, often life-size, and semi-naturalistic in style. Some pillars exhibit pairs of human arms and hands, suggesting that they represent stylised anthropomorphic beings. However, it is unclear as to whether they represent gods, shamans, ancestors, or even demons. There are also a number of mysterious abstract symbols that have been interpreted as pictograms.[83,84,85,86,87]

Pictograms are graphic symbols used to convey meaning, often by pictorial resemblance to a physical object. They are widely used in present-day road and other public signage to denote traffic lights, pedestrian crossings, speed cameras, etc. Some pictograms are entirely abstract, for example the 'Radiation Hazard' trefoil symbol. Pictograms can also combine pictorial and abstract motifs; for example the use of a circle containing an image struck out with a diagonal bar to denote interdiction. Pictograms can thus encode and convey information. As we shall see in Chapter 26, they form the basis of a form of writing known as semasiography. If the Göbekli Tepe symbols were indeed pictograms, then the origins of writing may extend back into the early Neolithic, thousands of years before the appearance of writing systems such as cuneiform and hieroglyphic script.

No traces of houses have been found and there is little doubt that Göbekli Tepe was a ritual centre, possibly the first of its kind.[84] Unlike Stonehenge, the people who built Göbekli Tepe lacked a mixed farming economy. This overturned the conventional wisdom going back to the time of V. Gordon Childe that such major projects could only be realised by fully-established farming communities. "*First came the temple, then the city*", as Schmidt put it. How are we to interpret this temple?

One possibility is that the animals depicted in the various enclosures are totemic. It could be that the site was frequented by a number of groups, each of which identified itself with a different animal or animals and travelled to the site to perform rituals in its own particular enclosure.[87] Another possibility is that like the painted caves of Upper Palaeolithic Europe, Göbekli Tepe was associated with shamanistic practices.[88]

However, there is an important difference between the cave paintings of Lascaux, Cosquer and Chauvet, and Göbekli Tepe. The former were the works of a few talented artists, but a project on the scale of Göbekli Tepe would have required a large number of labourers and craftsmen. Coordinating the activities of all these people, to say nothing of providing them all with food and shelter, would have been a major undertaking. It should also be remembered that unlike the builders of Stonehenge, the Göbekli Tepe people were still not yet full agriculturalists. Such an undertaking was almost certainly beyond the capabilities of a few shamans and their communities. Instead, it seems likely that the monument was constructed by a hierarchical, stratified society, with powerful rulers. The shamans might have had more in common with priests.[87] The link between rulers and religion, so prevalent in later times, might have already started to take shape. However, we cannot be certain. As we shall see in Chapter 19, even the construction of Stonehenge might not necessarily have involved a hierarchical society.

The totemic and shamanistic explanations are not necessarily mutually exclusive, and if the totemic view is correct, then it possible that animals depicted in each enclosure could provide clues as to the origins of particular groups. For example, wild boar depictions predominate in Enclosure C. This suggests a group originating from the north, where pigs account for up to 40 percent of the animal remains found at PPNA sites. Combinations of wild boar with aurochs and cranes, as seen in Enclosure D, suggest an ecotone of steppe and river valley, such as along most water courses in the Euphrates and Tigris drainage regions.[87]

Eventually, the enclosures at Göbekli Tepe complex were filled in and buried with debris. Animal remains and stone artefacts mixed in with the soil suggest that the filling material came from a typical late PPNA settlement refuse dump. The settlement has not been found, but the amount of debris involved suggests that it was not far away. Subsequently, a far less impressive complex was constructed over the first, comprising rectangular pits with smaller pillars, averaging about 1.5 m (5 ft.).[87]

Establishing a chronology for Göbekli Tepe has proved difficult, so it is not clear just when the various phases of construction took place. Steven Mithen[8] has suggested that the earliest monuments were constructed very soon after 9600 BC. Plant remains from the settlement debris have been dated to around 9000 BC,[89] but this does not tell us when the site was first occupied. Assuming that the debris accumulated while the Layer III site was in use, the first occupation of the site would be no later than this date. Based on dates for soil overlaying the filling debris, the Layer III complex was probably buried around 8000 BC.[87] Dates for carbonates formed on the stone walls as a result of their burial suggest it could have been no later than 7700 BC.[90]

Just why the Layer III complex was buried and the Layer II complex built over it is not known. A possible clue comes from the site of Nevali Çori, 30 km (18 miles) away. Unfortunately, this site was submerged following the construction of the Atatürk Dam, which is named for the pre-war Turkish leader Mustafa Kemal Atatürk. Prior to flooding, the site was excavated between 1983 and 1991 by Harold Hauptmann from the University of Heidelberg. The site was first occupied around 8500 BC, at the start of the PPNB, and occupation spanned three phases before final abandonment around 7600 BC.[91] It comprised some 29 rectangular multi-roomed houses and a 'cult building' – marking a shift from circular houses to the rectangular constructions that have largely characterised human dwellings ever since. The cult building dates to the site's second and third phases. It was approximately square, measuring 13.9 by 13.5 m (45 ft. 7 in. by 45 ft. 4 in.), and was cut about 3 m (10 ft.) into the slope behind it. Access was via two downward steps. A stone bench ran all the way around the interior, broken by pillars similar to those at Göbekli Tepe and again surrounding a central pair, although they resembled the Hebrew letter ٦ (daleth) rather than the letter T.[87,88] There is clearly a connection between the two sites, and possibly the shift to rectangular architecture is why Göbekli Tepe was filled in and rebuilt along rectangular lines.

Sacred and profane architecture of the PPNA

Another site with a possible connection to Göbekli Tepe is Jerf el-Ahmar, which lies 100 km (62 miles) to the southwest. This small PPNA village is located on the west bank of the Euphrates and was discovered in the late 1980s. It was excavated throughout the following decade by French archaeologist Danielle Stordeur. Since 1999, it has lain underwater, following the completion of the Tichrine Dam on the Middle Euphrates. Built on the slopes of two adjacent hills, the village demonstrates a considerable degree of planning, with houses and communal buildings built on a series of terraces. They varied considerably in plan, ranging from small circular and single-roomed to larger, roughly-rectangular and multi-roomed. On the western side of the village stood a large, circular communal building, surrounded by smaller residential buildings. It is rounded and semi-submerged, with thick stone retaining walls 2.3 m (7 ft. 6 in.) deep. Inside, there are six small rooms and two benches surrounding a central space, in which was found a headless skeleton. This building might have been a multi-purpose village hall that combined the functions of a communal food store and a ritual centre. As noted above, the small cells might have been used for cereal storage, while meetings and rituals probably took place in the central space. A connection with the aurochs iconography at Göbekli Tepe was found in a small round building on the eastern side of the village that had been deliberately burned down. Inside the remains were found the skulls of four aurochs that had once hung on the walls.[80] The find also recalls the aurochs skull at the Epipalaeolithic site of Hallan Çemi Tepesi.[8]

Among the richly engraved and carved stone artefacts found at Jerf el-Ahmar were four small, oval stones that had been engraved with snakes, foxes, owls, eagles, insects and abstract symbols. Like the symbols at Göbekli Tepe, these carvings have also been interpreted as pictograms. There is a similarity between the pictograms at the two sites, and the snake and fox motif echoes that at Göbekli Tepe. While the connection with Göbekli Tepe remains unproven, these elements do make it seem highly plausible.[92,8,87]

Another PPNA site where rituals might have taken place is WF16 (Wadi Faynan) in southern Jordan. Most of the buildings excavated to date are semi-subterranean circular dwellings, typical of the PPNA. However, there are also three larger buildings, designated Structures O75, O45 and O12. The last two of these have been interpreted as granaries, but the function of O75 is uncertain. It comprises an amphitheatre-like main floor, surrounded by benches, and large postholes suggest that the structure was at least partially covered. Set into slightly raised platforms on the floor are two cup-hole mortars, of a type typically used for crop processing. It has been suggested that crop processing was carried out as a ritualistic activity, witnessed by members of the community. Broken bowls found near the mortars may reflect associated feasting .[93]

If this interpretation is correct, then O75 represents an even more intimate mixing of domestic and ritual activities than the western communal building at Jerf el-Ahmar. We should not be unduly surprised at this, as there is no reason to suppose that the present-day dichotomy between sacred and profane existed in early Neolithic society. The construction and maintenance of O75 was a major undertaking, possibly involving the entire community. Together with the granaries at Dhra', the communal buildings at Jerf el-Ahmar and WF16 suggest that the focus of life in the PPNA might have been on the community rather than individual households.[6,77,93]

Transition to the PPNB

Around 8500 BC, just over 1,000 years after the end of the Younger Dryas, the PPNA gave way to the PPNB. In the north, there was direct continuity between the two, but in the south there appears to have been a crisis. Most sites were abandoned, possibly because wild animals had been over-exploited, or harvest yields were declining through soil exhaustion. Another possibility is that villages were struck by outbreaks of contagious disease. The PPNB was characterised by the gradual emergence and spread of a fully-fledged mixed farming economy throughout and indeed beyond the Fertile Crescent, with accompanying social and demographic changes. The PPNB was greater in extent than the PPNA, eventually incorporating the whole of the Levant, central Anatolia, and Cyprus.[3]

On average, during the Early PPNB, sites were three times larger than their PPNA predecessors, and by the Late PPNB, they were ten times larger, with average populations of over 3,000. 'Ain Ghazal, on the outskirts of Amman, reached 4.5 ha (11 acres) – almost twice the size of Jericho – during the Middle PPNB, and it eventually attained a size of 12 ha (30 acres). Sites such as Basta, south of Petra, and Çatalhöyük on the Konya Plane in central Anatolia were even larger. A notable feature of the PPNB is a shift from circular single-roomed houses to rectangular, multi-roomed buildings. As settlement sizes grew, so living spaces became ever more compartmentalised. This trend may reflect the increased stress of living in large communities and a greater desire for privacy, or the growing emphasis on personal goods and ownership, or in all probability a combination of these and other factors.[94]

Another development was the appearance of two-storey buildings. The lower storey was used as a dedicated storage area and the main living-quarters were located on the upper storey. The change was probably related to the same factors as the increase in compartmentalisation. In particular, the shift from communal granaries to household storage systems may reflect a change from community to household levels of economic organisation during the PPNB.[94,77,95]

Mortuary practices showed continuity with those of the PPNA. The predominant practice continued to be single inhumations, often below the floors of residential buildings, with little or no grave goods. Skulls continued to be removed for secondary burial, but now the practice arose of modelling facial features on the skull in plaster. Plastered skulls were first found at Jericho by Kenyon, who found seven in a single pit and a number of isolated skulls below house floors. They have since been found at numerous sites, each settlement making them in a subtly different manner, though conforming to the same basic design. In some cases, only part of the skull was plastered, but in others, natural features such as ears, nose, eyes and mouth were modelled with clay. With some skulls, clay has been used to represent eyes, with others such as at Jericho, marine shells were used. It is likely that the plastered skulls were not intended to accurately portray the deceased. Many have missing features such as ears or the lower jaw, or anatomical impossibilities such as the nose superimposed over the mouth. The range of variation of facial types in skulls from a given site is far smaller than that seen in living populations. The skulls therefore seem to reflect a system of idealised representation rather than an attempt to represent historical people. As fewer than five percent of skulls were plastered, it can be assumed that only certain individuals were so treated, probably tribal elders or other people of importance.[96]

The emergence of mixed farming

While cereals and legumes were extensively cultivated during the PPNA, it is not until the PPNB that fairly clear-cut evidence for domesticated varieties first emerges. The earliest convincing examples of wheat domestication are remains of emmer and einkorn from Çayönü Tepesi and Cafer Höyük in southeastern Turkey. They date from 8600 to 7900 BC, and possess the characteristic tough, non-shattering rachis. Subsequently, domesticated emmer is reported at Tell Aswad near Damascus between 8500 and 8200 BC, and became widespread across the whole of the Levant between 8100 and 6700 BC. Domesticated einkorn reached Tell Aswad between 8200 and 7550 BC, and spread south to Jericho within the same timescale. The earliest domesticated barley dates to between 8200 and 7550 BC at Tell Aswad, and between 7450 and 7300 BC at Jarmo, Iraq.[97]

Semi-domesticated peas and chickpeas have been found at Çayönü Tepesi, again dated to between 8600 and 7900 BC. The peas still had a rough seed coating, typical of wild peas, and the chickpeas were smaller than the fully domesticated variety. Fully-domesticated peas first appeared at a number of Turkish sites, including Çayönü Tepesi, around 7500 BC, and subsequently occur in large quantities at many Levantine sites.[97]

Genetics has proved to be of great value in increasing our understanding of the domestication of a number of plant species. Studies are based on the assumption that wild plants will show the greatest genetic similarity to their domesticated counterparts in the region where domestication occurred. Researchers sampled wild einkorn from a wide range of locations within the Fertile Crescent. They found that wild strains from the Karacadag Mountains of southeastern Turkey are the most genetically similar to domesticated einkorn. Accordingly, they concluded that it had been domesticated there and that domestication had occurred only once.[98,99]

The Karacadag Mountains are a range of hills no more than 30 km (18 miles) from Göbekli Tepe, and this has led Steven Mithen[8] to suggest that the monument played a pivotal role in the origin and spread of domestic cereals in Southwest Asia. Mithen proposed that the need to provide food for the hundreds of people who gathered for ceremonies at Göbekli Tepe might have led to intensive cultivation of wild cereals, leading in turn to the first domestic strains. The grain at Göbekli Tepe soon became known for their high yields, leading visitors to take home bags of seed for sowing on their own plots. Thus domesticated cereals reached sites such as Jerf el-Ahmar, and eventually the obsidian trade routes spread them south, possibly all the way to the Jordan Valley.

The theory has the appeal that it sidesteps explanations involving population pressure or climate change. The case for southeastern Turkey being an epicentre for crop domestication is strengthened by genetic results for emmer wheat that suggest that it too was domesticated in southeastern Turkey.[100] Barley on the other hand has been pinpointed to the Israel/Jordan region,[101] where it was already being extensively harvested as a wild crop. It has been suggested that domestication might have been achieved with the aid of technology imported from southeastern Turkey.[100]

More recently, studies have suggested that einkorn, emmer and barley might have been domesticated more than once. Researchers identified a wild strain of einkorn, known as race β, as being the most similar to domestic einkorn. Race β occurs only in the Karacadag and Kartal-Karadag mountain regions. Unexpectedly, though, it turned out that domesticated einkorn has a higher genetic diversity than race β einkorn. If einkorn was domesticated only once, it would have experienced a population bottleneck, leading to loss of genetic diversity. The researchers suggested, therefore, that einkorn had been domesticated several times from race β. They proposed that race β einkorn was initially cultivated in Natufian times and then transferred to other locations within the Fertile Crescent in a semi-domesticated state. Gradually, in several areas, variants of race β einkorn emerged with fully-domesticated traits. Each of these domesticated strains experienced a loss of genetic diversity, but this was offset by their large number.[102] It was suggested that the race β einkorn was transferred either by migrating PPNA farmers or by exchange, but Mithen's suggestion of people transferring seed from Göbekli Tepe also fits the model well. A similar multiple-domestication scenario has also been proposed for emmer wheat.[103] For barley, a second independent domestication has been identified 1,500 to 3,000 km (930 to 1,860 miles) east of the Fertile Crescent.[104]

The focus of animal domestication, likewise, appears to have been in southeastern Turkey. We have already seen that there is evidence that domesticated pigs were being farmed at Hallan Çemi Tepesi in the Late Epipalaeolithic. There are a greater number of pig remains at Çayönü Tepesi and Cafer Höyük, allowing a more convincing case to be made. At Çayönü Tepesi, reduction in molar tooth sizes and ages at slaughter is thought to reflect a gradual process during the course of the Middle PPNB, in which pigs moved from a wild to fully-domesticated status.[105] Similar studies at Cafer Höyük have led to the conclusion that domesticated pigs were being kept there by 8300 BC.[74]

Pigs then gradually spread through the Fertile Crescent. Domestic pigs are thought to have been present in Middle PPNB levels at Aswad, but they did not reach the southernmost end of the Levantine corridor until about 7000 to 6500 BC or the Zagros until 7000 BC.[74] Mitochondrial DNA evidence suggests that the wild boar originated in Island Southeast Asia and subsequently dispersed across Eurasia. Multiple independent domestication events have been identified: one in Southeast Asia, at least one in East Asia, another in India, and at least two in Europe.[106] Curiously, the mitochondrial haplogroups of wild boar from Southwest Asia have not been found among modern domestic pigs, although mitochondrial DNA recovered from pig remains found at Neolithic sites in Europe does contain these haplogroups. Evidently in later prehistory, European domestic pigs spread eastwards, and completely replaced earlier domestic pigs of Southwest Asian origin.[107]

We have already seen that herds of wild sheep and goats were managed at Hallan Çemi Tepesi in the Late Epipalaeolithic. However, the earliest evidence for actual goat herding comes from the site of Ganj Dareh in the central Zagros, dating to 7900 BC. Goat remains show the tell-tale presence of young males and older females; this resulted from the systematic culling of young males at ages between one and two years, while females were kept alive until past prime breeding age.[108] Ganj Dareh lies within the highland natural habitat of wild goats, but by 7500 BC the first goats appeared outside their natural habitat – at Ali Kosh on the lowland piedmont of southwest Iran. These, too, display the same pattern of young males and older females. Progressive changes in the size and shape of goat horns have also been noted over the 1,000-year occupation of this site, as selective pressures for large horns were eliminated. Thereafter, goats spread rapidly south, supplanting the once-ubiquitous gazelle. However, the latter continued to be hunted on the Mediterranean coastal plain until the end of the PPNB.[74]

Recently, genetics have been used to investigate the origins of domesticated goats. Researchers sampled mitochondrial DNA from domesticated goats from locations across Eurasia and North Africa, and identified six mitochondrial haplogroups, A, B, C, D, F and G (there was initially an E, but it was later found to be a subgroup of A). These lineages are not closely related, and it has been estimated that they diverged from one another anywhere from 100,000 to 600,000 years ago. They therefore existed long before domestication, and each represents a different domesticated segment of a larger wild goat population. A is by far the most abundant lineage, accounting for over 90 percent of the total. B and C account for all but a tiny portion of the remainder. This has been interpreted to mean that goats were domesticated three times. There is no strong geographical pattern to the distribution of the six lineages, which may reflect movements of domestic goats due to human migration and trade.[109,110]

In order to trace the actual geographical locations where goat domestication occurred, researchers carried out a genetic analysis of a large sample of wild goats, or bezoars, from Turkey, Iran and Iraq. They found that the mitochondrial haplogroup C is widespread among wild goats in southern Zagros and central Iranian Plateau region. Similarly, haplogroup A is widespread in eastern Anatolia. They concluded that goats had been domesticated in both regions. They also found evidence for a population expansion associated with haplogroup C, which they attributed to several centuries or even millennia of management of wild herds before the managed animals were completely isolated from the wild ones. The overwhelming predominance of haplogroup A today is interpreted as a successful expansion of farmers from Anatolia. Goats initially domesticated in Anatolia were transferred by herders from their place of domestication, and eventually they replaced the domesticated herds in the southern Zagros and central Iranian Plateau. Further support from this view is provided by the finding that domestic goats belonging to haplogroup C are more closely related to wild goats of that lineage from southeastern Turkey than they are to those from the Zagros.[111]

After Hallan Çemi Tepesi, the earliest evidence for sheep management is at Körtik Tepe, 50 km (30 miles) to the south, where wild sheep were apparently managed around 8900 BC.[112] Soon afterwards, the first possible signs of domesticated sheep appear in the archaeological record. Sheep remains dating from 8600 BC to 8300 BC at Nevali Çori indicate significantly smaller animals than those present at the contemporary sites of Göbekli Tepe and Cafer Höyük, hinting at domestication.[113] The spread of managed sheep occurred after that of goats; sheep arrived in the Levant after 7200 BC and the Zagros after 7000 BC.[74] Mitochondrial studies indicate that sheep were domesticated on at least three occasions from the wild mouflon, which has a current range from Turkey to Iran.[114,115]

The domestication of cattle from wild aurochs occurred rather later than that of pigs, goats and sheep. Remains from the Upper Euphrates Valley from the Early and Middle PPNB, dating from 9000 to 8000 BC, are still within the size range of wild aurochs. A high degree of sexual dimorphism, consistent with wild aurochs, has been found in cattle remains from sites such as Mureybet, Jerf el-Ahmar and Göbekli Tepe. However, at the sites of Halula and Dja'de el-Mughara in northern Syria, cows are closer in size to bulls, suggesting that the process of domestication was underway there. Domesticated cattle eventually did spread out from this region, reaching the southern Levant and the Zagros no earlier than 7500 BC.[74]

The genetic picture is widely accepted to indicate two domestication events, one of taurine cattle (*Bos taurus*) in the Fertile Crescent, and one of zebu cattle (*Bos indicus*) in South Asia. Although European cattle are thought to have originated from Southwest Asia,[116] lineages native to Europe have also been found. This has been interpreted as evidence of interbreeding between domesticated cattle and wild European aurochs. Another possibility is that some European cattle can trace their origins to an independent domestication there.[117,118]

Meat, of course, is not the only 'product' that can be obtained from animals. Animals can yield milk and wool, and can be used for traction. These 'secondary products' have the advantage (certainly from the animal's point of view) that they can be obtained without killing the animal. The 'secondary products revolution' theory was first advanced by British archaeologist Andrew Sherratt,[119] who believed that it coincided with the appearance of woolly breeds of sheep, the introduction of ploughing, and the invention of wheeled vehicles. These innovations do not appear until after 4000 BC.

In fact, we now know that the earliest evidence for the use of secondary products goes back much further. As we have seen, inferences about herd management and domestication can be made from animal remains found at sites. Similarly, clues about just how domestic herds were exploited can be teased out of slaughtering patterns by age and sex. These vary according to whether herds were exploited for meat, milk, fleece, traction, or any of these in combination. For instance, in the 1970s, studies of modern shepherding in Turkey found that meat production entails extensive slaughter of sub-adult males aged between six to eighteen months; for dairy shepherding, half of the lambs are killed when less than two months old; and wool exploitation is accompanied the frequent slaughter of both sexes.

However, these patterns might not have applied in early Neolithic times. Later workers found that semi-nomadic Kurdish dairy shepherds keep the lambs alive until they can be killed for meat; thus there are two methods of dairy shepherding with quite different slaughter profiles. Similar models have also been identified for goats. For cattle, models have to take into account that there would have been a need to keep many calves alive until weaned. Wild aurochs cows require physical contact with their calves in order to produce milk, although this trait has been bred out of modern dairy cattle. Using such methods, archaeologists have inferred that sheep and goats were being exploited for meat, milk and fleece in Southwest Asia from the Middle PPNB onwards.[120]

Direct evidence for dairy farming is lacking from the Pre-Pottery Neolithic. However, analysis of lipid residues taken from pottery vessels from sites in Southwest Asia and southeastern Europe has confirmed that the use of milk was already widespread by the start of the ceramic period. It was particularly important in northwestern Anatolia, a region favourable for grazing cattle. Notably, in comparison to other domestic animals, a higher proportion of cattle remains are found in this region than at sites elsewhere, where milk was less important.[121]

It is believed that the lipid residues were from processed milk in the form of cheese, ghee, etc., rather than fresh milk. Such products could be stored for use throughout the year. The use of processed milk would also have been a solution to the problem of lactose intolerance.[121] Most mammals lose the ability to digest the lactose sugar in fresh milk soon after weaning because the body stops producing lactase, the enzyme required to break down lactose in the digestive system. However, in European human populations, lactase production is retained into adulthood. The failure to 'switch off' lactase production came about as a result of a chance mutation, which in hunter-gatherer societies conferred little benefit. In agricultural societies, however, it was highly beneficial and swept through the population. Based on living populations, genetic estimates for the time of appearance of this mutation are within the last 10,000 to 5,000 years,[122] but analysis of ancient DNA recovered at a 5,000-year-old Neolithic necropolis in France found that those buried there did not possess it.[123] It is likely, therefore, that the Neolithic populations of Southwest Asia were still lactose intolerant, though consuming processed milk products would have presented less of a problem to them.

The overall picture is of the gradual emergence of a fully-developed Neolithic economy of domesticated cereals, legumes and animals. The economies of the Early and Middle PPNB were still characterised by low-level food production, rather than fully-fledged agriculture. The transition to the latter did not occur until the Late PPNB. Although southeastern Turkey was the focal point of many important developments, the PPNB was not a single, unified cultural phenomenon that started in one place and subsequently spread. Rather it is best thought of as an 'interaction sphere' in which various innovations, cultural ideas and practices spread between communities via trade networks.[124] The concept of the PPNB interaction sphere is basically an example of the peer polity interaction model described in Chapter 17. The site of Çayönü Tepesi and the island of Cyprus have given archaeologists a considerable insight into social complexity and the emergence of mixed farming during the PPNB.

Çayönü Tepesi

One of the most extensively investigated PPNB sites is Çayönü Tepesi in southeastern Turkey, which was first excavated in 1964. The 4.5 ha (11 acres) site is located by a stream at the foot of the Taurus Mountains, near to the headwaters of the Tigris River.[125] It was first occupied during the later PPNA, around 8600 BC,[91] with occupation continuing throughout the PPNB. The site thus provides a series of snapshots of village life during this period, giving us a powerful insight into the social, cultural and economic changes that occurred over the course of more than two millennia. A total of six sub-phases of occupation have been identified, each named for a characteristic architectural style.

The vicinity of the site was probably covered with open forest, consisting mainly of oak, pistachio and almond. To the east, there was an area covered with steppe vegetation. There was a small stream or a swamp on the northern side that probably attracted wild animals, especially wild boar. Thus, the site was located in a rich, diverse environment that provided the inhabitants with a wide range of plant and animal foods.[126] A rich material culture has been identified, and artefacts found include clay figurines, mostly of animals, with a few of humanoid form. Other finds include stone tools of flint and obsidian, ground-stone artefacts, and hafts for flint knives of bone and horn. Also of interest are beads and hooks made from hammered native copper. The latter are among the earliest recorded metal artefacts.[125]

The architectural changes of the PPNB are well documented at Çayönü Tepesi. The Round Building sub-phase was a fairly typical PPNA village, comprising circular wattle-and-daub houses on stone foundations. However, towards the end of the PPNA, these gave way to the long rectangular buildings of the Grill Building sub-phase. These buildings were all aligned roughly north-south, had similar dimensions of about 5.5 by 11 m (18 by 36 ft.), and were built on a tripartite plan. The north-facing living area was built upon grill-like parallel stone foundations, upon which was laid a floor of mud plaster and brushwood. Over this, a wattle-and-daub superstructure was erected. The channels between the foundations probably helped to keep the house ventilated and the floors dry in wet weather. Attached to the living area was an enclosed central courtyard, typically containing a paved hearth, and a storage area of small rooms. The Grill Building style continued into the Middle PPNB, when the 'grills' were replaced by broader foundations separated by narrow drainage channels. This new style is referred to as the Channelled Building sub-phase. A significant change is that all hearths, pits and working areas were moved to open yards outside the houses. In the following Cobbled-Paved Building sub-phase, the parallel wall foundation concept was abandoned altogether, and was replaced with a paved floor. Substantial walls replaced those of wattle and daub, and the interior space was subdivided. It is probable that improved roofing techniques had made the drainage channels unnecessary. Towards the end of the Middle PPNB, these buildings were replaced by the much larger buildings of the Cell Building sub-phase. These comprised a series of interconnected cell-like storage rooms, and living quarters on a second storey. The cells had no external doors and were accessed through the floor of the second storey. The final sub-phase is the Large Room Building sub-phase, in which rooms became considerably larger than the cells of the preceding sub-phase.[127,128]

A striking feature of the settlement is the uniformity of the buildings in each sub-phase. Not only were the buildings completely standardised in design, but their orientation was the same and their location predetermined to the point that archaeologists could predict just where the next building would occur. It has been suggested that on a number of occasions, the entire settlement was demolished and rebuilt according to a definite plan.[127]

Later phases of the site were built around a central plaza, measuring 50 by 30 m (165 by 100 ft.) and probably intended for public meetings and ceremonies. A huge grooved stone, probably a communal axe-sharpening facility, was found in the plaza. The earliest signs of a public space are to be found in the Channelled Building and Cobbled-Paved sub-phases, but it was fully developed during the Cell Building sub-phase. Along the northern side of the plaza were a group of buildings in which a number of unusual artefacts were found. These included a clay model of a house, and elegantly worked beads and pendants of semi-precious stones. The houses themselves were built on the same uniform plan as contemporary buildings on the site, but they were larger, with more massive walls. It is notable that the plaza was first constructed at around the same time as workshop areas are separated from residential areas. These developments suggest that the Channelled Building sub-phase was a period of growing social stratification that continued into subsequent sub-phases.[127,128]

There were four public buildings at Çayönü Tepesi, although they did not all exist at the same time, and their relationship to each other and to the houses of the various sub-phases is uncertain. However, they do provide a tantalising glimpse into the belief systems of the PPNB period. The earliest is thought to be the 'flagstone building', which existed in the Grill phase. This building has a floor of large, flat flagstones into which three monoliths are set, but unlike Göbekli Tepe and Nevali Çori, they are not carved. Presumably, though, it was also a cult building. The 'bench building' is smaller than the other buildings, comprising a single room with massive stone benches running along its walls. It might have been used as a meeting room and it could have been built any time from the later Grill to the Cobbled-Paved sub-phase. Although it came later than the 'flagstone building', the latter might still have been in use at that time. The 'skull building' was evidently a charnel house. At one end are three square cells in which were found 70 skulls and the remains of at least 400 individuals. Also found within the skull building was the skull and horns of an aurochs. The building underwent at least five rebuilding phases, but was eventually abandoned. Later versions date to the Cobbled-Paved sub-phase, but the original construction probably dates to the Channelled Building sub-phase or possibly earlier. The most recent building, dating to the Cell Building sub-phase, was the 'terrazzo building'. This is named for its terrazzo floor, built in two layers above a hard packed layer of stone. The top layer consists of limestone stained with red iron oxide and set in burned and slaked limestone mortar. The floor was polished after the hardening of the mortar.[127,128]

The aurochs skull and horns found in the skull building is another early indicator of the significance the aurochs came to hold in belief systems during the Southwest Asian Neolithic. A further clue that the building might have been more than a simple repository for the dead came to light in the 1980s. Blood residues were recovered from a stone slab making up part of the floor of the main room in the skull building, and from artefacts including a flint knife. When analysed, these were found to have come from aurochs, sheep, goats – and humans. The most obvious interpretation is human sacrifice, but there are other possibilities such as an intermediate stage of a secondary burial. The body of the deceased might have been placed on the stone slab, and some form of ritual dismemberment then occurred prior to interment in the small rooms at the north end of the building.[129]

Çayönü Tepesi documents a gradual and rather piecemeal transition from sedentary hunter-gathering to a fully-functional mixed farming economy, via a period of low-level food production. Plant remains at the site are scarce,[126] but include emmer and einkorn wheat, and peas, chickpeas and lentils, dating to between 8600 and 7900 BC. These, as noted above, are among the earliest examples of plant domestication in Southwest Asia.[97] The abundance of grinding tools and sickles in the Cell Building sub-phase suggests that domesticated cereals became increasingly important at that time. However, pistachio, almond, and wild barley remained important elements of the overall subsistence economy.[126]

Animal remains at the site are more abundant, and have been extensively studied. During the PPNA and Early PPNB, people living at settlements in southeastern Turkey tended to specialise in whichever large animal species was most abundant at the site. At Hallan Çemi Tepesi, for example, wild sheep were preferred. At Cafer Höyük, located closer to the higher elevations of Taurus

Mountains, wild goats were the prey of choice. Gazelles were targeted at sites located close to the Harran Plain. Wild boar accounted for about 40 percent of the animal remains at Çayönü Tepesi right up to the Channelled Building sub-phase. The 'big four' of pigs, sheep, goats and aurochs accounted for about 60 percent of the animal remains, but a wide range of other wild species were also hunted, including gazelle, deer, hare, birds, tortoise and fish. Around 8200 BC, at the start of the Cobbled-Paved sub-phase, there was a shift away from broad-spectrum hunting and an increasing dependency on the 'big four'. Totals increased to 75 percent in the Late PPNB Cell sub-phase, and to just below 90 percent in the Large Room sub-phase.[130]

Pig remains are abundant in all of the Pre-Pottery Neolithic sub-phases at Çayönü Tepesi. Although wild pigs continued to be hunted, the remains have enabled researchers to document a gradual process of pig domestication, occurring over the lengthy period the site was occupied. The process began with a reduction in molar tooth size in the Cobbled-Paved and later sub-phases; this was followed by body size reduction in the Cell Building and Large Room sub-phases, with the size range of pig remains in the latter being comparable to a modern population. The age at which animals were slaughtered also show a shift towards that which may be expected from a domestic population, where the majority are killed before reaching adulthood. The number of pigs surviving into adulthood fell from 60 percent in the PPNA Round building sub-phase to 25 percent in the Cobbled-Paved sub-phase, and to just 10 percent by the Cell Building sub-phase.[105,126]

While pigs remained an important source of meat at Çayönü Tepesi throughout the Pre-Pottery Neolithic, their pre-eminence was gradually eclipsed by sheep and goats. During the PPNA, these accounted for below seven percent of the animal remains, but the figure rose progressively during the PPNB. Sheep and goats reach 23 percent by the Channelled Building sub-phase and 54 percent in the Large Room sub-phase, suggesting that herds of the animals were being kept at the site.[130] There was also a marked shift in size distribution to smaller animals, though it occurred sooner for goats than for sheep. Smaller goats started to appear in the Channelled Building sub-phase, and the trend continued in the Cobbled-Paved and Cell Building sub-phases. The end result was a size distribution comparable to that of a domestic population. However, with sheep this shift did not occur until the Large Room sub-phase, and as with pigs some wild animals continued to be hunted.[126] Another trend is an increase over time in the number of sheep over goats, which might have been a response to damage to woodland vegetation caused by keeping large numbers of goats.[131]

There is also evidence that domestic cattle were eventually kept at Çayönü Tepesi, although sample sizes are smaller than for pigs, sheep and goats. During the PPNA, and the Early PPNB Grill sub-phase, size distributions were consistent with wild aurochs. There was a slight decrease during the Middle PPNB Channelled Building and Cobbled-Paved sub-phases, but a decisive shift did not occur until the Late/Final PPNB Large Room sub-phase, at which point remains were within the size range of domestic cattle. Part of the overall diminution reflects an increase in the number of females, which is consistent with a domestic herd. Also consistent is that as with pigs, slaughter patterns show that fewer animals survived until adulthood. Notably, red deer from the same time span show no decrease in size. Both red deer and aurochs are large forest-dwelling herbivores and natural factors such as climate change would be expected to affect both species equally. In addition, stable-isotope analysis for carbon and nitrogen in red deer do not show any significant variation, as might have been expected if climate change had affected their diet. It therefore seems likely that the decrease in size seen with aurochs was the result of domestication.[126,130]

In summary, the domestication of the 'big four' at Çayönü Tepesi began in the Middle PPNB, during the Channelled Building sub-phase. The first smaller-sized pigs appeared, and there was a shift to slaughtering younger animals. This coincided with the shift away from broad-spectrum hunting and an increase in the importance of sheep and goats. There was also an increase in social complexity, as evidenced by the appearance of specialised workshop areas and public spaces within the site. At first, keeping animals might only have been an additional subsistence option. Possibly, it increased in importance as centuries of intensive hunting began to exhaust the supply of wild game. Subsequently, there was an increased reliance on domestic animals, especially sheep and goats; the evidence for which is seen in a shift to smaller animals of all four species, and finally an increase in the number of females. The process of domestication was completed in the Late PPNB and this, combined with the cultivation of by now fully-domesticated crops, meant that Çayönü Tepesi had a fully-functioning mixed farming economy; one of the first in the world.[130]

The settlement of Cyprus

The piecemeal and indeed haphazard nature of the transition to agriculture in Southwest Asia is also very well illustrated by events in Cyprus. Although conventionally considered to be a part of Europe, Cyprus lies off the Anatolian coast. The island's minimum distance from the mainland is 69 km (43 miles), but on a clear day it can be seen from the Taurus Mountains and people would have long been aware of its existence. It has never been connected to the mainland, and in the Late Pleistocene there were very few indigenous mammalian species. The only large mammals were dwarf hippos and elephants.[132] Humans first visited Cyprus during the Late Natufian. At Aetokremnos, a rock-shelter at Akrotiri, on the southern coast of the island, there is evidence of human activity dating to between 10,800 and 10,500 BC[132] and at the same site, the remains of pigs dating from 9700 to 9400 BC have been found. The pigs were apparently brought to the island and subsequently managed by hunter-gatherers. Although pigs are strong swimmers, it is not thought that they could have reached Cyprus by themselves in sufficient numbers to form a permanent population.[133] It has been claimed that humans hunted the Cypriot dwarf hippos into extinction,[134] although they might have been already extinct by the time the first hunter-gatherers arrived.[132] Hunter-gatherers continued to frequent Cyprus until the arrival of the first farmers, though it is not known whether or not they established permanent settlements on the island.[135,132] Sites from the later part of the period have Late PPNA/Early PPNB tool assemblages, but their subsistence was based on hunting the wild pigs rather than farming.[132]

The first undisputedly-permanent settlements in Cyprus appeared around 8500 BC, at a time corresponding to the PPNA/PPNB transition on the mainland. The sites of Mylouthkia and Shillourokambos are contemporary with Tell Aswad, Nevali Çori, and later phases at Çayönü Tepesi and Jerf el-Ahmar. At Mylouthkia, near Kissonerga in the southwest of the island, some of the earliest water wells in the world have been discovered. Three wells are known, the largest of which is 8.5 m (28 ft.) deep and 2.25 m (7 ft. 4 in.) in diameter.[136] The wells were not all in use at the same time; Well 116 dates to around 8500 BC, but Well 133 is more recent, dating to around 7100 BC.[137] The wells are a local innovation, with no equivalent on the mainland.[135]

Shillourokambos is 6 km (3.5 miles) from Limassol in southern Cyprus, and was first occupied from around 8400 BC. Several phases of occupation have been documented through to 7000 BC, although there was a hiatus of several decades around 8000 BC.[132] Most of the buildings on the site are poorly preserved, but a large number of animal remains and stone artefacts have been recovered. Numerous burials have also been excavated. In one of these, dating from between 7500 and 7200 BC, an 8-month-old cat was found buried with its owner and grave goods; possibly the cat was killed on the death of its owner.[138] Cats reached Cyprus no later than 8500 BC, having probably been imported to deal with mice. Mice were repeatedly introduced in Cyprus, presumably reaching the island as stowaways. It is interesting to note that foxes were introduced to Cyprus around 8000 BC. Possibly, during the Pre-Pottery Neolithic, farmers used a number of small predatory species to combat mice.[132]

The domestic cat (*Felis silvestris catus*) is descended from the Near Eastern wildcat (*Felis silvestris lybica*), and was initially domesticated in Southwest Asia. Domestication probably occurred soon after the appearance of commensal strains of rats, mice and sparrows in human settlements. To cats, these pests were a reliable source of food. Cats were initially commensals themselves, their presence tolerated by humans rather than actively sought out as domestic pets. In time, though, villagers probably came to value cats as mousers. The Shillourokambos burial is the earliest evidence for the long association between cats and humans.[139,50]

Mylouthkia and Shillourokambos have provided an important perspective on low-level food production, and the subsequent transition to agriculture. Plant remains at both include emmer and einkorn wheat, and barley. At Mylouthkia, all three were probably domesticated, but at Shillourokambos the barley was of the wild variety and it has not been determined if the wheat was wild or domesticated. The wild barley there could have been of local origin or introduced. Wild barley grows in Cyprus, but it also occurs at a number of mainland sites. On the other hand, wild emmer and einkorn do not occur in Cyprus, and the Shillourokambos examples were probably domesticated. Lentils and peas were also introduced to Cyprus although transplanting them from the mainland would have been difficult. Pulses contain symbiotic nitrogen-fixing rhizobium bacteria in their roots and a culture of the bacteria, specific to the pulse, is required if it is to be successfully transplanted.[140]

At Shillourokambos, much valuable data has been obtained by analysis of animal remains. The data shows that there were considerable changes in animal husbandry strategies over time. During the earliest phases of the site (corresponding to the Early PPNB on the mainland), most meat came from hunting the previously-introduced wild pigs. Goats – possibly feral domesticated animals – were also hunted in small numbers. Domesticated cattle were present from the start, but never made a major contribution to the meat supply. Later phases (corresponding to the Middle PPNB on the mainland) saw the introduction of domesticated sheep and pigs, the latter distinct from their wild cousins already on the island. Wild fallow deer were also introduced, and were hunted until the later phases of the site. Goats continued to be hunted, and around half the pigs were also obtained by hunting. The sheep, on the other hand, were exploited for both meat and milk. However, overall meat production at this stage was probably still less than 50 percent of the meat consumed.[132]

Around 7500 BC (corresponding to the start of the Late PPNB on the mainland), a rapid decrease in size and skeletal evidence for malnutrition suggests that an environmental crisis affected the animal herds. In response, farmers appear to have re-domesticated the feral goats. Later, pig breeding was stepped up, and fresh sheep were imported from the mainland. Meat production gradually increased, although it probably never exceeded 60 to 75 percent of the meat consumed. Even if milk production is factored in, the overall picture at Shillourokambos is one of a long period of low-level food production, followed by a slow transition to farming. The former was unstable and opportunistic, and was based on rapidly-changing combinations of hunting, management of wild/feral animals, and livestock breeding. These developments broadly mirror those at mainland sites such as Çayönü Tepesi during the PPNB.[132]

Despite the ongoing contacts between Cypriot and mainland groups, some cultural developments were slow to reach the island. The largest Neolithic site in Cyprus is Khirokitia, located on the slope of a hill in the valley of the Maroni River, about 6 km from the southern coast. The site is rather later than Mylouthkia and Shillourokambos, dating to around 7000 BC, and it comprises a large number of circular houses of stone and mud brick that range in diameter from 2.3 to 9.8 m (7 ft. 6 in. to 32 ft.). Circular houses, similar to those of the PPNA, persisted in Cyprus long after the switch to rectangular buildings on the mainland.[141]

Another possible architectural link to the PPNA has been found at the site of Tenta, near Larnica. In addition to circular dwellings, there is a larger circular building comprising small cells that surround a larger central area.[142] Archaeologist Edgar Peltenburg[135] has likened this structure to the large communal building at Jerf el-Ahmar, and claims that the Tenta layout and circular buildings are architectural retentions from the PPNA. Although Jerf el-Ahmar is too far inland to have been the origin for the Cypriot colonists, it is possible that they came from a settlement on the Syrian coast with similar cultural and architectural traditions. This settlement, if it existed, has probably since been submerged by rising sea levels. Once arriving, the colonists maintained their cultural traditions for millennia, long after these had gone out of fashion on the mainland.[8]

The forked mound

As noted above, by the Late PPNB, some settlements were becoming very large. One of the most notable of these 'mega sites' is Çatalhöyük, located on the Konya Plain in central Anatolia, which was 13.5 ha (33 acres) in extent and had a population that ranged from 3,000 to 8,000 people. The settlement was first occupied in 7400 BC, long after Çayönü Tepesi, and making it something of a latecomer in Neolithic terms. Occupation spanned 1,400 years up to 6000 BC, taking it into the Pottery Neolithic. The site comprises two mounds: the larger East Mound comprises the Neolithic occupation, but there was also a later, smaller West Mound dating to the Chalcolithic. Some 18 levels of occupation have been identified in the East Mound, corresponding to roughly one level every 70 to 80 years, and there are some 21 m (69 ft.) of occupation debris.[143]

Çatalhöyük means 'forked mound' in Turkish. Long before it came to the attention of Western scholars, the site was known to the local community, who named it. The term probably refers to the fact that the path from the town of Çumra to the south divides into three at the site. One path goes to the east, another to the west, and the other passes between the two mounds. The site first came to the attention of British archaeologist James Mellaart in 1952, but he was unable to investigate further until 1958. Even then his work at another site did not permit him to commence excavations until 1961. Mellaart worked at the site until 1965, and discovered spectacular painted walls, burials and figurines. He believed that Çatalhöyük had been a cult centre of a great mother goddess, a forerunner of the Anatolian earth mother goddess Cybele, who was prominent in Classical times. Despite the global attention attracted by Mellaart's findings, no further excavations were carried out until 1993 when a team lead by his former student Ian Hodder commenced a program of excavation, site conservation, and research that will continue for many years to come. The many discoveries at the site are described in his book *Çatalhöyük: The Leopard's Tale*.[143]

The Konya Plain lies in the middle of the Anatolian Plateau at an elevation of 1,000 m (3,300 ft.), and has just 350 mm (14 in.) of rainfall annually. Although the climate was wetter in the Early Holocene, conditions were still semi-arid, with moist winters and summer drought. However, rivers flowing onto the plain formed alluvial fans suitable for agriculture, and in addition there were marshlands and seasonal lakes. The environment comprised a complex mosaic of grassy steppe around the marshlands, shrubs on better-drained soils, and trees along river margins. While much of the region was unsuitable for agriculture, Çatalhöyük is located in the centre of the largest of the fertile alluvial fans, the Çarsamba Fan. This lies on the southern margin of the plain, and is fed by the Çarsamba River from the southwest.

Çatalhöyük is strikingly different to sites such as Çayönü Tepesi. It completely lacked public buildings and despite its size, there were no streets or approaches at ground level. Instead, the rectangular houses directly abutted one another honeycomb style, and were accessed via a trapdoor in the roof. The only way of getting about was to walk over the flat roofs of neighbouring houses. Ladders were used to get in and out of the houses, and the settlement itself. Archaeological surveys of the Konya Plain have suggested that there were a number of settlements in the region before Çatalhöyük was established, and that others were established after the Neolithic site was abandoned

– but that none coexisted with it. There is no indication that communities needed to congregate to make use of localised resources; indeed the people of Çatalhöyük made use of a very wide environment. The question is what drew people together to create a single, densely-packed community at this one place?

The houses were built with mud brick walls, supported by timber posts. Internally, they comprised a main room for living, working, cooking, eating and sleeping. There were also one or more side rooms for storage, entered through low openings from the main room. Low platforms ran around the walls, which probably served as benches and work spaces. The entry ladder was usually set into the south wall of the dwelling, leading down into the main living area. An oven was sited directly below the ladder, so the trapdoor entrance also served as a chimney. The interior walls and floors were plastered and interior features such as basins and bins were also sometimes plastered. Unlike the hard lime plaster found at many other sites, a soft lime-rich mud plaster was used that required regular resurfacing, typically on an annual basis. The successive layers of plaster on the walls could build up to as much as 7.5 cm (3 in.) thick, and in one case a wall was found to have 450 layers of plaster. In warm and dry weather, many activities probably took place on the roofs of the houses, and there might have been areas in which animals were penned. At the end of its life of around 70 to 80 years, a house would be demolished and rebuilt. The roof was dismantled and the main structural timber supports were removed. Finally, the walls were dismantled, leaving the interior filled with rubble. This was levelled and a new house constructed on top.

The interior walls of the houses were richly decorated with paintings and moulded reliefs, mainly of wild animals including leopards, bulls, deer, goats and vultures. Reliefs of leopards frequently feature a pair of animals standing head to head. Some paintings depict human figures, including one apparently wearing a leopard skin; others depict hunting scenes. In many houses, the skulls and horns of bulls and other animals were plastered and set into the walls or placed on pillars. Most of the wall decorations are found on the north wall, opposite the entrance ladder. A large number of clay and figurines have also been found. Some are crudely made quadruped animals, which may be cattle. The better-executed figurines include female statuettes, of which the best-known is that of a woman seated between a pair of felines. Some of female figures are very plump, recalling the 'Venus' figurines of Upper Palaeolithic Europe. Other figurines depict both men and women standing beside or seated on large felines. Many burials have been found under the floors of the houses. They tend to occur under platforms at the northern part of the houses. One of the most remarkable finds was a skull that had been coated with several layers of plaster, each of which had been painted red.

The internal use of space within the houses was highly structured. There were specific places where activities could or could not happen, where items could or could not be stored. Thus ovens, artwork, obsidian caches, and buried ancestors all had their specific places. Even the parts of the house in which people could sit and work might have been restricted by age and sex.

Çatalhöyük is often described as 'the world's first city', but other than its size, it has few attributes of a city or town. Unlike Levantine sites going back to the PPNA, there are no granaries or other communal storage facilities. There is also no evidence for public buildings like those at Çayönü Tepesi and other sites; no public spaces, administrative buildings, elite quarters, or any specialised functional spaces, other than on the edge of the site. From both an economic and social point of view, the house was the basic unit of production. Houses had bins for storing agricultural produce such as wheat and lentils. Later, with the introduction of pottery, fat and grease from sheep and goats was stored in pots.

Society was therefore probably fairly egalitarian. There was no chieftain or headman, and decisions were probably made by a group of elders. Seniority – such as it was – was by ancestral tradition. Although the houses were largely autonomous, the size of the settlement would have necessitated community decisions about drainage, water supply, waste disposal and so on. A degree of collective organisation must also have been involved in such matters as hunting and allocation of land for farming and herding. It is been suggested that the Neolithic settlement was divided into two equivalent paired halves and that each functioned as a moiety, in which members of one half were obliged to marry into the other. The two moieties might also have taken turns at providing leadership roles, thus helping to retain an egalitarian social structure at the site.

The people of Çatalhöyük needed to exploit resources over a wide area. Many of the materials required for building and tool-making could not be obtained locally. The timbers used for house building were pines and junipers, obtained from mountainous regions to the south and to the west. Obsidian, which was used for tool-making and was also widely traded, could only be obtained from the mountains of Cappadocia, about 125 km (78 miles) away. It is also likely that at least some farmland was located some distance from the marshy lands around the site. Irrigated crops tend to produce larger phytoliths than those grown in dry-farming, rain-fed conditions. Those recovered from wheat remains at Çatalhöyük are mainly small, suggesting that they were cultivated in well-drained soils.

Domesticated crops included emmer and einkorn wheat, peas, lentils and vetch. However, wild vetch was still collected, and other wild foods included almonds, acorns and hackberries. The Çatalhöyük people kept sheep and goats and might also have kept ducks and geese, but not in large numbers. They hunted wild boar, aurochs and deer. Both animal remains and stable isotope analysis of human remains show that cattle were not a major part of the diet, but they were important element of communal feasting. Notably, while images, reliefs and plastered skulls of bulls form a major part of the artwork, sheep and goats are rare, suggesting an ideological distinction between the wild and the domesticated.

There is certainly no doubt that ritual played a major role in life at Çatalhöyük, but the belief systems of its inhabitants might have had its roots in much earlier times. We saw in Chapters 11 and 14 that David Lewis-Williams has proposed that the universal belief in a multi-tiered cosmos is rooted in the very structure of the human brain, and that painted caves such as Lascaux were seen as the entrails of a nether realm. Lewis-Williams and David Pearce[88] have suggested that at Çatalhöyük, descent into houses, limited light, and the need to crawl through small openings between chambers were akin to the experience of moving through limestone caves, such as those used for rituals in the Upper Palaeolithic. Limestone caves do occur in the Taurus Mountains not far to the south, and stalactite and limestone concretion have been found at Çatalhöyük. Some have been partially carved, others, resembling breasts, udders and human figures, were left un-carved. The settlement might have been a 'built cosmos' reflecting beliefs based on a three-tiered cosmos. Ladders, used to access the houses, might have been associated with trans-cosmological travel, while burials below the floor were associated with the subterranean realm. The plastered skulls of bulls and other animals might have been shamanistic spirit helpers. Walls were 'permeable' boundaries beyond which other realms lay, the 3d imagery reflecting that of Upper Palaeolithic caves. This may explain why the houses were clustered together, with no streets.

Steven Mithen[8] believes that every aspect of life in Çatalhöyük had become over-ritualised. To him, the bulls and other artwork suggest an ideology so oppressive that it stifled any independence of thought and behaviour. In stark contrast to the Natufians, the people of Çatalhöyük seemed to have feared and despised the wild.

Boom-to-bust

As the PPNB wore on, so the dependency on animal herding grew. The wild gazelle, predominant for so long, was finally supplanted by domesticated sheep and goats.[144] The period witnessed the laying of the foundations of the later Mesopotamian Halaf and Ubaid periods, leading ultimately to the emergence of the world's first city-states. The Mesopotamian lowlands, where the Sumerian civilisation later developed, were colonised by Ubaid irrigation farmers around 5900 BC, with an economic and cultural tradition that owed much to the PPNB.[21,145]

The growth in the size of the human population, the animal population upon which it now depended, and the complexity of the economy required to support this growth came with a downside – the world's first boom-to-bust. During the Final PPNB, between 6750 and 6500 BC, many sites in the Levant either shrank in size or were abandoned altogether. Abu Hureyra, which had reached 160 ha (400 acres) by the Middle PPNB, shrank to half this size, and the housing became less dense. There was widespread site abandonment in the Balikh Valley of northern Syria, especially in dryer regions. In Jordan, the settlement of Ba'ja, near Petra, was established after nearby Beidha and possibly two other Middle PPNB sites were abandoned. Ba'ja is a much smaller site than Beidha, with an extent of just 6,000 sq. m. (64,500 sq. ft.). It was home to an estimated 400 to 500 people, and might have been a last-ditch attempt at keeping sedentary life going in a region where it was becoming untenable.[146,147,21]

Kenyon attributed the apparent downturn to *"the lights of progress flickering out"* as the occupants of Jericho and other settlements lapsed into decadence and were overrun by their less progressive cousins to the north. In the 1950s and 1960s, when similar factors were widely supposed to have brought about the fall of Rome, such a view seemed highly feasible. However, as noted above, there is little evidence for destruction on the scale that could be expected from an invasion by hostile groups. Another possibility is an abrupt period of adverse climatic conditions around 6200 BC. Known as the 8.2ka event, the reduced rainfall and severe aridity might have rendered uninhabitable the already marginal environments in which many PPNB settlements were located.[148] The effects are recorded in Greenland ice cores, and in stalagmites of Soreq Cave, Israel.[33] The major problem, though, is that 6200 BC is several centuries too late for the aridity to be associated with the PPNB collapse.[26]

While less severe climate change preceding the 8.2ka event might well have exacerbated matters,[21] the most likely cause of the crisis is that the intensive mixed farming economy degraded an already fragile environment, causing a progressive drop in productivity. The effects would have been particularly severe in the southeastern 'Marginal Zone', a region of low rainfall that is only marginally suited to agriculture without the use of irrigation. The region includes most of the Jordanian sites, including Jericho, 'Ain Ghazal, Beidha and Basta. The cultivation of cereals and legumes was at the expense of deep-rooted perennials, and the lack of these soil-binding roots for much of the year left the fertile topsoil vulnerable to erosion. In the meantime, tree cover was being lost, as trees were felled to provide building materials, and fuel for domestic fires and for the production of lime plaster. Use of trees for fuel for making plaster accounted for an estimated 40,000 oaks in 1,500 years at 'Ain Ghazal; while a further 14,000 were used for construction purposes. The decreasing size of postholes in Final PPNB buildings suggests that ever younger trees were being used.[149] The depredations of the large numbers of goats now kept by the farmers were sufficient to prevent the forests from properly regenerating, leading to further soil erosion.[6]

During this period, as other sites were being abandoned, 'Ain Ghazal experienced a phenomenal population growth. The site is located on the west bank of the River Zarqa, a major tributary of the River Jordan. The settlement was less affected by the environmental degradation affecting other large sites such as Jericho and Beidha, and there was a reliable supply of food and water. Rotating crops between cereals and legumes might also have helped to keep the settlement viable. In the Late PPNB, 'Ain Ghazal covered no more than 4 to 5 ha (10 to 12 acres), but during the Final PPNB it grew to about 9 ha (22 acres), its population swollen by migrants from the many failed settlements in the region. It spread across onto the eastern bank of the river, and eventually reached a size of 12 ha (30 acres).[149,150] A large number of clay discs have been found at 'Ain Ghazal. It has been suggested that these are tokens, early precursors of accounting systems or even writing systems. If this was the case, the use of these tokens is evidence that managing the affairs of such a large population had become a complex undertaking.[21]

The northern Levant was less affected by the crisis than southern and central regions, and fewer sites were abandoned. In many parts of Syria, mixed farming remained possible. The Syrian landscape is either flat or gently rolling, and is less susceptible to soil erosion. Another factor is that sheep rather than the more destructive goats were predominant in the north.

In the south, with its rapidly changing elevations, there is a mosaic of ecological zones suitable for human exploitation, and these provided opportunities for villagers to adapt to the adverse conditions. Some populations simply dispersed to form much smaller farming communities. A more radical solution was to adopt either nomadic or semi-nomadic pastoralism, where livestock are moved between grazing pastures by groups of mobile herders. Notably, what large sites did persist all had access to arid regions unsuitable for farming, but ideal for pasturing. Such sites included 'Ain Ghazal, Basta, Tell Ramad and Wadi Shu'eib. All these sites are at the boundary between Mediterranean and desert/steppe zones. At 'Ain Ghazal, a substantial part of the population adopted a semi-nomadic existence, leaving the settlement with their flocks of sheep and goats to pastures in the semi-arid steppe for large parts of the year, and returning to the village after the grain harvest. Villagers could thus separate pastoral activities from farming, easing the pressure on the environment. The nomadic pastoralists also established a symbiotic relationship with the sedentary farmers, trading animal products for cereals, textiles and manufactured goods.[149,150,144,151]

Occupation of 'Ain Ghazal continued without a break into the Yarmoukian period, one of a number of regional pottery-using cultures that arose in the Levant after 6500 BC. Other Jordanian sites, such as Wadi Shu'eib, also show continuity between the Final PPNB and the Early Pottery Neolithic, suggesting that the appearance of pottery was a local development and did not represent the reoccupation of these sites from elsewhere. At 'Ain Ghazal, the earliest potsherds lack the decoration characteristic of Yarmoukian pots, but are otherwise very similar. They are thought to represent 'transitional' pottery from a society that would go on to develop the full range of the Yarmoukian ceramic tradition. It is likely that the relatively rapid adoption of ceramic technology for cookware and storage vessels was just one of many cultural adaptations that emerged during the period of upheaval that followed the Late PPNB. It could be argued that the transition from PPNB to Early Pottery Neolithic is somewhat arbitrary, with the real discontinuity lying between the Late and Final PPNB. For this reason, some prefer to refer to the latter as the PPNC.[152]

In summary, the Pre-Pottery Neolithic and early ceramic periods saw the gradual assembly of a potent and adaptable agricultural package of animals, cereals and legumes, and the spread of early agricultural economies from the Levant into the adjacent regions of Anatolia, Iran and Cyprus. These developments were only the beginning of a dispersal process in four major directions: to Europe, Central Asia, the Indian subcontinent and North Africa. It had taken two and a half millennia or thereabouts for the package to be assembled, but now the agricultural juggernaut was well and truly on the move.

19: Waves and lurches

Mesolithic and Neolithic Europe

Did hunter-gatherers take up farming, or were they displaced from their ancestral lands by intrusive farming communities? There has been much debate as to whether it was farmers or merely farming that spread out from the primary centres where agriculture first arose, and Europe plays a central role in this debate. What is not disputed is that the spread of agriculture from Southwest Asia was very rapid. The first farming settlements appeared in Southeast Europe between 7000 and 6500 BC, and by 4000 BC agriculture had reached Britain and Ireland. In the meantime, the four-way expansion reached the Indian subcontinent by 7000 BC, Central Asia by 6000 BC, and North Africa by 5000 BC.

As the Neolithic agricultural package was taking shape in Southwest Asia, it is important to realise that pre-agricultural Europe was certainly not a cultural backwater. In the millennia since the Last Glacial Maximum, hunter-gatherer populations had expanded from their refugia, and were now firmly established across much of Europe. Mesolithic is the term given to the pre-agricultural period in Holocene Europe, and it ended at different times in different places. It is often seen as a period of transition between the Upper Palaeolithic and Neolithic, but it was a period of significant achievement in its own right. There were considerable advances in technology and means of subsistence, and increases in population and social complexity.[1]

Innovations included increased use of microliths for a diverse range of applications, ranging from weapon tips to vegetable graters and drill bits. Experiments have shown that microlith-tipped arrows have great penetrating power,[2] and such weaponry reflected the changed needs of hunting in a Europe where tundra was replaced by woodland. The forested landscapes favoured red deer, roe deer, pigs, aurochs and elk. Unlike the reindeer and horses, these animals were less migratory, and lived in either small herds, or as solitary individuals.[3] Instead of mass killings of migrating herds, hunting methods now emphasised the stalking and shooting of single animals.[4] Dogs were probably also used to help track animals. Smaller animals, such as rabbits and hares, were probably caught in snares.[2]

In coastal regions, fishing was an important activity. In addition to substantial boats, fishing technologies included leisters for spearing fish, bone fish hooks, wicker baskets for trapping eels, and fishing nets. Contents of middens suggest that both freshwater and saltwater species were caught.[2] Remains of deep water species at settlements in western Sweden have been interpreted as evidence for deep sea fishing, although such claims have been challenged. Such evidence only occurs in regions where deep water is found close to the shore, and based on ethnographic evidence it has been suggested that the time and danger involved made deep water fishing unattractive to Mesolithic fishers.[5]

Plant foods also formed an essential part of the Mesolithic diet, and postglacial forests provided rich variety of edible plant foods including berries, fungi, nuts and root vegetables.[2] At Franchthi Cave in southern Greece, Mesolithic levels dating from 9500 to 9000 BC were found to contain over 28,000 seeds from 27 different plant species.[6] The Franchthi people collected a similar range of plant foods to those favoured by the Natufian people some millennia previously, including lentils, oats, barley, pears, pistachios, almonds and walnuts. Like the Natufians, they used grindstones and might have cultivated some of these plants.[3] Another Mesolithic plant-management practice was the burning of vegetation to stimulate plant growth; the practice was particularly widespread in the northeast of England. Such methods yielded highly productive feeding environments for game animals, and encouraged the growth of edible plant foods.[7]

Although the age of cave painting had passed, it is clear that Mesolithic people retained the sense of aesthetic so evident in Upper Palaeolithic Europe. Even purely utilitarian objects such as boat paddles, antler axes, and elk bone knives and daggers were often elaborately decorated. Animals carved from amber might have been symbols of wealth or power, or involved in regional exchange networks.[2] Some art objects are of completely unknown function. Painted schist pebbles have been found at a number of sites, principally in France and Spain. They are associated with the Azilian, a Mesolithic culture from the Franco-Cantabrian region, and date to around 9000 BC. The pebbles are decorated with dots, lines, chevrons and crosses, but there are no representational figures. A total of 16 specific motifs have been identified. Only 41 of the many possible combinations were ever used, suggesting that only certain combinations were considered valid. The implication is that the pebbles contain a symbolic code, with permitted combinations governed by a set of syntactic rules. There is little doubt that meaningful data is encoded in the pebbles, but just what that data was remains unknown.[8]

Mesolithic sites vary greatly in size and complexity. The well-studied British site of Star Carr in Yorkshire, first occupied around 8770 BC, was probably no more than a hunting camp, used for a few days or weeks each spring or summer.[3] Other sites, such as Skateholm, on the coast of southern Sweden, were much larger. The site is associated with the Late Mesolithic Ertebølle culture, and is located by a now dried-up lagoon. People were attracted by its immense diversity of plants, fish, seabirds and marine mammals, together with an adjacent forest in which deer and pigs could be hunted.[4] Despite its size, Skateholm was not a year-round settlement. Ages at death for wild boar suggest that the animals were killed during the winter only.[9] Although fish remains are abundant, there are very few cod, mackerel, or garfish. These fish come inshore to breed during the summer months, and would have been caught in large numbers if people were present at that time of year.[4]

However, some Mesolithic sites did support sedentary or near-sedentary communities. A number of these have been found along the Iron Gates, a series of gorges situated on the Danube between the Carpathian Mountains and the Dinaric Alps. At the sites of Lepenski Vir, Padina and Vlasac, fishers exploited migratory sturgeon, catfish, carp and other species. The earliest deposits at Lepenski Vir date to between 8200 and 7600 BC, but between 6200 and 5400 BC there was a settlement comprising a number of semi-subterranean trapezoidal, flat-roofed dwellings on the banks of the Danube.[10] They varied in size from 5 to 30 sq. m. (54 to 320 sq. ft.), with the wider ends facing the river. The floors were dug 0.5 to 1.5 m (1 ft. 8 in. to 3 ft. 3 in.) into the terraced slopes of the river bank, and were surfaced with reddish limestone plaster. Inside, elongated pits lined with limestone blocks served as hearths.[2,10] Many houses contained burials, although burials were also placed outside houses.[11] Human/fish anthropomorphic sculptures carved from boulders were also found in many of the houses. These have been interpreted as evidence of a belief system characterised by a totemic relationship between humans and the fish that were so vital to their subsistence economy.[12]

A significant feature of the Mesolithic is the appearance of dedicated cemeteries for the first time in Europe. They are predominantly found in regions capable of supporting large populations, such as in coastal areas, or near lakes and rivers.[2] From the cemeteries, something of the social complexity and diversity of Mesolithic Europe may be inferred. For example, at the cemetery on the island of Téviec in the Bay of Quiberon, Brittany, some child burials are accompanied by grave goods, but not others. This may be evidence of a hereditary, ranked society, in which status was acquired by virtue of birth. In such a society, one would expect to find that 'high-born' children had richer burials than those of ordinary parentage.[13] By contrast, child burials are rare at Oleneostrovski Mogilnik ('Red Deer Island'), an island site at Lake Onega in Russian Karelia. Where children are buried at all, it is in multiple graves along with adults.[14]

Oleneostrovski Mogilnik has been extensively studied.[14] The site has revealed 170 burials in two burial clusters, one northern and one southern, but the actual number might have been as high as 500. The site was previously a quarry, and many graves are thought to have been lost. Graves were typically rectangular, aligned east-west, with bodies facing east. However, four individuals – two men and two women – were interred in vertical graves consisting of a funnel-shaped shaft, and these graves have been interpreted as belonging to shamans. Oleneostrovski Mogilnik was originally excavated in the 1950s and over 7,000 artefacts were recovered from the burials, including pendants, sculptured effigies, hunting implements, and other tools. The pendants were made from the pierced teeth of bears, beavers and elks. No other animal teeth were used, suggesting that this troika of animals was of particular symbolic importance to the Oleneostrovski Mogilnik people.

Considerable variation in grave goods leaves little doubt that the Oleneostrovski Mogilnik people lived in a large, socially-complex society. Sculptured effigies, made from stone, wood, or bone, are found in many graves. Those in the northern cluster are carvings of elks, but those in the southern cluster are of either snakes or humans. The two burial clusters might have represented a division of the Oleneostrovski Mogilnik society, possibly a moiety like the one proposed for Çatalhöyük (see Chapter 18).

While some graves contained over 400 items of grave goods, around 20 percent contained none at all. Some items were gender-specific: bone points, pins and harpoons, and stone adzes were regularly associated with males, while ornaments made from carved beaver teeth characterised female burials. A few graves contained slate knives and daggers, which are thought to have been prestige items. The Oleneostrovski Mogilnik people used flint as their principle raw material, and slate was presumably obtained by trade with slate-producing regions. The knives and daggers might have highlighted the role of the deceased as middlemen in a regional exchange network. The pierced-tooth pendants might have been an indication of an individual's 'wealth'. Those made from bear teeth were found with the prestigious slate knives and daggers, suggesting that they had a higher 'value' than those of beaver and elk teeth.

It was found that individuals in the prime of life were 'better off' in terms of numbers of pendants than were the young and the old. In addition to commodities such as slate, the system might also have reflected an individual's ability to procure food. As hunting abilities declined with age, individuals became less able to hold on to their wealth. Unlike Téviec, Oleneostrovski Mogilnik was a meritocracy, but there was apparently no way to save for one's retirement.

In summary, the Mesolithic was far more than a hiatus period between the ending of the Ice Age and the coming of agriculture. The ability to adjust to the new post-glacial environments, the increase in social complexity, and the constant presence of finely-decorated artefacts demonstrate the richness and diversity of Mesolithic Europe. The disappearance of this way of life in the face of the spread of agriculture did not reflect any failings by Mesolithic communities. Rather it was a measure of the demographic strength of the new farming economies.[1]

Europe transformed

Disappear, though, it did. The transformation of Europe into a landscape of farming communities took just three and a half millennia – barely a fifth of the time that spanned the age of cave art. The first farming settlements appeared in Crete and the Greek mainland between 7000 and 6500 BC. Radiocarbon dates show that farming then spread westwards along the Mediterranean coast to Italy and Iberia, and northwards through the Balkans to Central, Western and Northern Europe, reaching Britain and Ireland by 4000 BC. Only in colder forested regions did hunter-gathering persist as a way of life.[15] What remains hotly disputed is just how all this occurred. Were the often highly-sophisticated Mesolithic peoples simply replaced by incoming farmers from Southwest Asia in all cases; or did they at least sometimes learn about agriculture from farmers, and adopt it themselves? As noted in Chapter 17, these viewpoints are known respectively as demic diffusion and cultural diffusion.

The demic diffusion view, in which farmers from Southwest Asia colonised Europe and replaced the indigenous hunter-gatherers, was first proposed by V. Gordon Childe in the 1920s, and in his 1958 work *The Prehistory of European Society*.[16] Childe was in line with the then-prevalent view that social changes in prehistoric times were largely the result of migrations and conquests, but this view later fell out of favour. While it was apparent that many components of the Southwest Asian agricultural package must have been imported into Europe, it could be argued that there is no *a priori* reason to assume that migrating farmers spread with them. Interestingly, recent computer simulations attempting to hindcast (i.e. forecast with hindsight) the spread of agriculture have suggested that the Neolithic transition to agriculture in Europe can be explained equally well by either cultural or demic diffusion.[17]

However, in the 1970s the demic diffusion model was taken up by Italian geneticist Luigi Luca Cavalli-Sforza and his collaborator, American archaeologist Albert Ammerman. The pair used mathematical models to show that the archaeological record was consistent with a continuous 'wave of advance' of Neolithic farmers across Europe. As population pressures grew, farmers spread out into previously-unfarmed regions. Further expansion occurred as these regions in turn filled up, and so on. Based on the radiocarbon data available at the time, Cavalli-Sforza and Ammerman proposed an average rate of expansion of 1 km (0.62 miles) per year, though this ranged from as little as 0.7 km (0.43 miles) per year in the Balkans to as much as 5.6 km (3.5 miles) per year in Central Europe.[18,19]

Genetic data, too, appeared to suggest that at the broad scale, farming spread through Europe by demic diffusion. Cavalli-Sforza and Ammerman[19] backed up their conclusions about a 'wave of advance' with blood group data. This showed a genetic gradient or cline running from southeastern to northwestern Europe. The gradient gave a startling match to the radiocarbon-tracked spread of agriculture through Europe and arose from intermarriage between the incoming farmers and indigenous Mesolithic hunter-gatherers.

However, in the mid-1990s, these conclusions were thrown into doubt. Early studies using mitochondrial DNA suggested that 80 percent of the mitochondrial gene pool of present-day Europe was of Upper Palaeolithic origin, whereas the Neolithic had contributed just 20 percent.[20] The implication was that the great majority of modern Europeans can trace their genetic heritage back to the Upper Palaeolithic rather than the Neolithic. On the face of it, this is the complete opposite of what may be expected on the 'wave of advance' picture, where one would expect to see predominantly Neolithic ancestry. At the time, many geneticists were still sceptical about the use of mitochondrial data,[21] although subsequent Y-chromosomal studies drew a similar conclusion.[22]

In fact, as supporters of the demic diffusion model pointed out, even a small degree of intermarriage between the Mesolithic hunter-gatherers and the incoming Neolithic farmers would gradually dilute the Neolithic genes with those of the Mesolithic hunter-gatherers. This would be seen as a genetic gradient running from southeastern to northwestern Europe, similar to that reported by Cavalli-Sforza and Ammerman for their blood group data.[23] In broad terms, this view has been backed up by subsequent studies involving mitochondrial, Y-chromosomal and autosomal DNA, which have confirmed the existence of the genetic gradient.[24,25,26,27,28] Researchers have also found that during the agricultural transition, mitochondrial haplogroups associated with farmers underwent significant expansion, whereas indigenous European lineages did not.[29]

However, the genetic evidence is far from unequivocal. Y-chromosomal studies have linked branches of the haplogroup R1b (M343) to Neolithic dispersals into Europe,[28,30] but others argue that there is insufficient data about the present-day distribution of this haplogroup to draw meaningful inferences about Neolithic dispersals.[31,32] Successful recoveries of ancient Y-chromosomal DNA are rare, but the results that have so far been published indicate a Neolithic connection with the now-uncommon haplogroup G2a (P15) rather than R2b (M343).[31,33,34,35] More recently, genome sequencing of ancient DNA obtained from 7,000 to 8,000-year-old hunter-gatherers and farmers has indicated that both populations derived part of their ancestry from ancient northern Eurasian populations related to Upper Palaeolithic Siberians such as the Mal'ta MA-1 boy.[36]

These results show that inferences drawn from the genetics of present-day populations, while useful, are not bulletproof. Conversely, genetic material from individuals who lived at the times in question is too scarce to draw safe conclusions about Neolithic dispersals. An alternative approach is to use skull metric data instead of ancient genetic data. Studies have shown that minute variations in skull shape can reliably track genetic relationships between populations, and the method has the advantage that there are far more skulls from the Neolithic period than there are DNA samples. A statistical analysis of Neolithic and Mesolithic skull data from Europe and Southwest Asia supports the demic diffusion model, and suggests that there was a continuous dispersal of farmers from Southwest Asia into Southeast Europe followed by onward migrations into Central Europe.[37]

It is clear, though, that this is not the whole picture. A recent reassessment of the radiocarbon data, using the larger body of information now available, gives an average expansion rate of 1.3 km (0.8 miles) per year. While this is broadly consistent with the earlier data, there is considerable local variation in the rate at which the Mesolithic to Neolithic transition occurred. In some places it was rapid, suggesting that one population did replace another, but in others the Mesolithic radiocarbon record tends to tail off gradually, with a significant overlap with that of the early Neolithic. In such places, it is likely that change was brought about by the spread of ideas rather than people.[15]

Archaeologist Peter Rowley-Conwy[38,39] suggests the movement of farmers was sporadic and punctuated rather than continuous. Often it involved 'leapfrog' migrations, in which farming groups moved into available space just beyond their neighbours. The incoming farmers interacted with local hunter-gatherers in a variety of ways. Sometimes the hunter-gatherers simply disappeared as a separate group, with varying numbers being assimilated into the Neolithic farming communities. On other occasions, the farmers were themselves ultimately assimilated into an indigenous or 'local' Neolithic. Such interactions would have meant that onward-migrating farmers carried to varying degrees a mixture of European and Southwest Asian genes. Overall, Rowley-Conwy suggests replacing the concept of a wave of advance with a series of local and disparate 'lurches of advance'.

While populations increased as agriculture spread across Europe, the demographic growth did not continue indefinitely. In a recent study, researchers used two sets of data from the period 6000 to 2000 BC to investigate the demographics of the transition to agriculture in Europe. They first considered data from over two hundred cemeteries, weighted by settlement size. From this they calculated juvenility index, which is the proportion of a population aged between 5 and 19 years old: in an increasing population, this is high; in a declining population it is low. They then considered over eight thousand radiocarbon dates from 24 well-documented archaeological regions across Europe to obtain a statistical quantity known as the Summed Calibrated Radiocarbon Date Probability Distribution (SCDPD), which can be used as a proxy for population density and indicate whether populations are rising or falling at a given time.

Both sets of data gave similar results. The transition from Mesolithic to Neolithic in each region was accompanied by a sharp increase in the population, but after a period of stability there was a decline. The cemetery data indicated a period of growth lasting for about 720 years, a period of stability lasting for just under 1,000 years, followed by a decline. The radiocarbon dates indicated that the period of growth had lasted for 420 years before a decline set in, which lasted for 840 years for a complete boom to bust cycle of 1,260 years. The reasons for this demographic cycle remain unclear but are probably related to the new way of life amplifying a pre-existing tendency for population fluctuation.[40]

The Neolithic in Europe was an extraordinarily diverse phenomenon, and it is unlikely that all the cultures all arose from a single cause. Accordingly, we must examine them on a case-by-case basis in five separate zones of the continent: Southeast Europe; the central and western Mediterranean; Central Europe; Atlantic Europe; and Northern Europe.

Agriculture reaches Southeast Europe

The spread of the Neolithic into Europe was in all probability driven by ever-increasing population levels in Anatolia, leading farmers to seek out new land. The earliest Neolithic dispersal predates 6500 BC, but evidence for it is sparse and it was soon followed by a more substantial expansion. It has been suggested that there are a few early aceramic sites in Thessaly, although it is possible that these are actually Mesolithic rather than Neolithic.[41] Most Greek Neolithic sites postdate 6500 BC and contain pottery.[42]

The absence of early Neolithic settlements in Greece north of Thessaly suggests that the first farmers reached mainland Greece by sea,[1,43] a conclusion that is supported by ancient DNA studies.[44] Seafaring in the Aegean is thought to date back at least as far as the Late Upper Palaeolithic. Obsidian found in Mesolithic levels at Franchthi Cave has been shown to have originated on the volcanic island of Melos,[45] and dates obtained for obsidian finds from a number of other Greek mainland and island sites range back as far as 12,500 BC.[46] However, it cannot be ruled out that some farming groups also took the overland route through Anatolia into Greece.[41]

It is unlikely that there was widespread indigenous adoption of agriculture in Southeast Europe. Greece has very few recorded Mesolithic sites, suggesting that the indigenous population was small and lived in scattered communities,[42] although some sites may remain undiscovered.[15] On the other hand, the larger Mesolithic communities at Franchthi Cave might have successfully made the switch. Possibly the Franchthi Cave people acquired agricultural staples and technology through maritime contacts with farming communities in Anatolia.[47]

Such possible exceptions apart, incoming farmers were free to move between the best pockets of potential farming land,[48] favouring the fertile alluvial floodplains of lakes and rivers. Thessaly is fairly rich in such environments[49] and if a long Aegean maritime tradition is accepted, then it is likely that prospective colonists were aware of the potential farming lands there, and planned their colonising expeditions accordingly. During the early Neolithic, the region supported a large number of farming communities, sometimes located just 2 to 3 km (1.2 to 1.8 miles) apart, of sizes ranging from several tens to several hundred inhabitants.[3] Thessaly was just one of a number of regions that eventually became key centres for early Neolithic farming communities in Southeast Europe. Farming communities were also established in Greek Macedonia, Thrace, Bulgaria, Serbia, Slovenia and Croatia. These include Nea Nikomedeia in Greek Macedonia, which might have been home to as many as 250 villagers.[1]

The transition to agriculture along the Danubian Iron Gates has been investigated using strontium and nitrogen isotope analysis of human remains from burials at Lepenski Vir, Padina, Vlasac, and other sites in the region. Strontium isotope data from dental enamel indicate that burials of non-local first generation migrants increased significantly after 6200 BC. The newcomers arrived in a series of migrations over a period of time, originating from several distinct regions. Dietary data inferred from carbon and nitrogen isotope analysis of bone collagen suggests a shift from the strong Mesolithic reliance on fish to a cereal-based diet at around this time.[50]

For the first two centuries, migrants were buried in an extended supine position characteristic of the Mesolithic mortuary tradition, albeit accompanied by Neolithic-style beads as grave goods. However, by 6000 BC Neolithic crouched burials, with the legs drawn up, had begun to predominate. The implication is that there was a period of coexistence between the hunter-gatherers and the farmers before the former were completely absorbed into the farming communities.[50]

Farming settlements in Southeast Europe sometimes remained occupied for centuries. Over time, mounds known as tells were formed as houses either collapsed or were demolished, and fresh ones built on top of the rubble. Some tells grew to a considerable size, for example Karanovo in southern Bulgaria reached a height of 12 m (40 ft.), and covered an area of 150 by 250 m (490 by 820 ft.). Other large tells include Argissa, Sesklo and Sitagroi in Greece, Azmak, Ezero and Yasatepe in Bulgaria, and Starčevo and Vinča in Serbia.[47]

The central and western Mediterranean

The spread of farming along the Mediterranean basin was aided by a climate very similar to that of Southwest Asia, making the domesticated crops fairly easy to transplant. In the western Mediterranean, the arrival of farming was marked by the appearance of an unpainted pottery style known as Impressed Ware, which was decorated by impressing objects into the wet clay prior to firing. Impressed Ware was followed around 5600 BC by Cardial Ware, where the decoration was applied with cardium shells.[1]

In Italy, late Mesolithic sites are found in the north, while virtually all the earliest Neolithic sites are located in the south. Thus the Neolithic sites are more likely to represent colonisation by farmers who arrived by sea than indigenous adoption by hunter-gatherers.[15] Some 500 Neolithic sites are known on the Tavoliere plain, located on the Adriatic coast of northern Apulia. The Tavoliere has a very similar topography and agricultural potential to that of Thessaly and the earliest Neolithic settlements there date to around 6000 BC.[1] Almost certainly, Neolithic groups on the other side of the Adriatic had long been aware of the favourable prospects there.

By around 5400 BC, farming had spread north to Perugia. The subsequent spread of farming to the south of France, Spain and Portugal was extraordinarily rapid, and took no more than 100 to 200 years.[51] Farming settlements with Cardial pottery took the form of enclaves, set up in favourable locations around the French and Iberian coastline.[1,43] The rapidity of this dispersal is best explained by the colonising farmers travelling by sea,[51] although it is likely that the movements from one enclave to the next were relatively short in distance.[1]

Pioneer farming groups might have been around forty strong. They would have required five to ten breeding pairs of each animal species and around 250 kg (¼ ton) of grain to start up a fresh settlement. Between ten and fifteen boats with a payload of one to two tonnes would have been necessary for such an undertaking, assuming a single voyage. Boats might have been constructed from logs or possibly from animal hides stretched over a frame, similar to the Irish curragh. Such craft are light enough to be carried by their crew, yet have a considerable cargo capacity.[39]

In Portugal, Mesolithic hunter-gatherers continued to thrive for some 500 years after the first arrival of the farmers. Isotope analysis of skeletal remains indicates a diet that remained heavily reliant on seafood rather than cereals, and their material culture remained unchanged throughout that period.[51] Ancient mitochondrial DNA has been used to show that Portuguese Mesolithic and Neolithic populations were genetically distinct from one another.[52]

The Neolithic Revolution

It is likely that the subsequent spread of the Neolithic into the interior of the Iberian Peninsula entailed a combined process of colonist expansion, indigenous adoption of Neolithic technologies, and the integration of colonist and indigenous populations. A similar scenario is likely in the north and the interior of Italy, where the onset of the Neolithic trailed southern and central coastal regions by several hundred years.[43]

The Linearbandkeramik Culture

From Greece, farming also spread northwards into the Balkans and Central Europe. In time, there arose a cultural phenomenon known as the Linearbandkeramik (Linear Pottery) Culture, or LBK. The LBK is named for its distinctive pottery with incised banded decoration, and characterised by settlements of massive timber-built longhouses sometimes up to 70 m (230 ft.) in length. It first appeared in western Hungary about 5600 BC, spreading rapidly to the Rhineland by 5300 BC and the Paris Basin thereafter. The LBK also spread eastwards as far as Ukraine and Moldova.[1] Farmers may well have dispersed by using boats along the rivers of Central Europe.[39]

LBK longhouses were grouped in twos and threes in forest clearings on river terraces, providing access to water and easily tilled loess soil. The settlements themselves were grouped in clusters, such as at Langweiler, in the Merzbach Valley, western Germany. There, eight distinct settlements have been found, together with special enclosures that might have been the setting for social or ritual activities by the whole community. Longhouses were rebuilt in the same place over long periods of time; for example Langweiler 8 spanned 14 generations of rebuilding in an uninterrupted occupation sequence of 400 years – a period of time comparable to the length of the Roman occupation of Britain. Settlement groups might have depended on contacts with similar clusters for exchange of breeding stock, and for social exchanges including marriage.[1]

Overall, the rapid expansion of LBK and its cultural homogeneity is suggestive of colonising farmers rather than indigenous hunter-gatherer adoption. In Germany, the Mesolithic population actually went into decline before 6000 BC, a pattern that does not fit the suggestion that the German LBK represent indigenous adoption of Neolithic culture.[15] In many cases, local hunter-gatherer populations were assimilated into the farming communities. Strontium isotope analysis of dental enamel of skeletons from LBK cemeteries at the German sites of Flomborn, Schwetzingen and Dillingen has indicated that some of those buried were of non-local origin. The tooth enamel of the inferred non-locals had a higher $^{87}Sr/^{86}Sr$ isotopic ratio than that of locals, indicating that a proportion of their diet was from upland regions, where $^{87}Sr/^{86}Sr$ ratios were higher. In many cases, burial orientation and grave goods differed from those of local people, hinting at social differentiation. Notably, the majority of these outsiders were women, suggesting that men from the farming communities were taking wives from indigenous hunter-gatherer groups. This would be consistent with ethnographically-recorded cases of forager women marrying into farming communities.[53]

A slightly different picture was found at Vaihingen near Stuttgart. Again, there were hints of social differentiation, with some burials taking in a ditch near the site rather than within the settlement itself. Although there was no gender distinctions between the two burial sites, significantly more of these buried in the ditch had lower $^{87}Sr/^{86}Sr$ ratios than those buried within the settlement, implying that the former were non-locals. The lower $^{87}Sr/^{86}Sr$ ratios may be indicative of nomadic pastors, who ranged cattle in neighbouring limestone regions where the $^{87}Sr/^{86}Sr$ ratio was lower than around the site itself.[54]

Contact between farmers and hunter-gatherers did not always result in the latter coming off second-best. By about 5000 BC, the LBK had begun to differentiate into a number of regional successor groups, defined mainly on the basis of their pottery types. Although environmental settings were now more diverse, the longhouse settlements were retained.[1] One of these successor groups was the Villeneuve-Saint-Germain (VSG) culture, located on the western fringes of the expansion in northwestern France. Instead of giving rise to later cultures, it disappeared within 200 to 300 years, to be replaced by a more general and widespread Neolithic that had arisen among indigenous hunter-gather communities. Thus in this case, the pioneer farmers were eventually assimilated by indigenous people who had adopted agriculture themselves.[55]

Some post-LBK groups simply failed. One of these was located on Poland's Baltic coast near the mouth of the Vistula. Sites associated with the Stroke Ornamented Pottery culture suggest agriculture was present around 5000 BC, but the colonisation was apparently unsuccessful and the area soon reverted to a hunter-gatherer economy.[39]

Despite the evidence of long-term continuity at many sites, violence during the LBK was not unknown. A mass grave known as the Death Pit has been discovered at Talheim, Germany. Archaeologists found the remains of 36 individuals including sixteen children and adolescents, and seven women. Most of the bodies showed traces of violence, and analysis of the injuries allowed the murder weapons to be identified. These included axes, blunt instruments and arrows. Most of the victims received head injuries on the rear of the skull, suggesting that they were attempting to flee from their killers. They were probably killed by raiders from a neighbouring LBK settlement, though the motive for the attack remains unknown. Talheim is not the only LBK site with evidence for violence. A similar discovery was made at Schletz in Austria, where the remains of 67 individuals were found in the ditch of an LBK enclosure. As at Talheim, they were mainly killed with blows to the head. The enclosure might have been a defensive structure, and the discovery of further skeletons in a well inside the settlement suggests that it was eventually overrun. Again, this appears to have been an internecine conflict between LBK communities rather than a clash with local hunter-gatherers.[1]

The mystery of haplogroup N1a

Genetic material from human remains at LBK settlements dating from 5650 to 4900 BC and at German Mesolithic sites confirms that the farming populations were intrusive. Mitochondrial haplogroups U4 and U5 predominated among the Mesolithic populations, whereas these haplogroups were rare in the LBK populations. Many of the haplogroups found among the farmers were those that are now common among European populations, including H, V, K, J, T and W. What is notable is that the now-rare haplogroup N1a occurred among the farmers with a frequency of around 15 percent. It was absent from the Mesolithic populations, and its present-day occurrence is just 0.2 percent.[56,57,35]

N1a has also been found in western France, where a megalithic passage grave at Prissé-la-Charrière dating to around 4200 BC yielded one individual (from three) with this haplogroup.[58] However, it has not been found at Neolithic sites lying further south. These include a Late Neolithic necropolis at Treilles in southern France, dating to around 3000 BC;[33] Avellaner Cave in northeast Spain, dating to around 5000 BC;[34] and the Camí de Can Grau necropolis at Granollers, near Barcelona, dating to around 3000 to 3500 BC.[59]

With the caveat that Treilles and Granollers are more recent than Prissé-la-Charrière and the LBK sites, N1a appears to be associated with Neolithic populations in Central Europe and western France but not those in the western Mediterranean region. If N1a was brought to Europe by Southwest Asian Neolithic farmers, then presumably two genetically-distinct populations were involved, one with N1a and the other without.[35]

On the other hand, the assumption that N1a is necessarily of Neolithic origin has been challenged. A detailed study of the phylogeny of N1a has determined that six LBK farmers with this haplogroup can be assigned to four different subhaplogroups of differing geographical origins. It was suggested that only three of the six could trace their origins back to Southwest Asia and the other three were probably of Central or Eastern European ancestry.[60] As we saw above, it is likely that some Mesolithic people did join the farming communities. The main problem with this view is that N1a has not been found at any of 22 Central and Northern European Mesolithic sites from which genetic material has been recovered.[57]

Regardless of its origin, an explanation must still be sought for the subsequent near-disappearance of N1a. Computer simulations have shown that genetic drift over the course of 7,500 years could not drastically reduce the incidence of N1a in Europe to present-day levels.[56] However, the effects of natural selection were not considered which, as noted in Chapter 9, may influence haplogroup distribution. It has been suggested that a combination of genetic drift and increased susceptibility to disease might have all but eliminated N1a from the present-day European mitochondrial gene-pool.[61]

Another possibility is that farmers carrying the N1a haplogroup 'leapfrogged' into Mesolithic territory. The surrounding hunter-gatherers subsequently adopted agriculture, and grew in numbers. Eventually, they outnumbered the immigrant farmers and the N1a signature of the latter was largely drowned out.[56] The fate of the VSG culture discussed above demonstrates that such a scenario is perfectly feasible. However, it still necessary to explain why the mitochondrial haplogroup composition of modern Europeans more closely resembles that of the LBK people (albeit lacking N1a) than it does their Mesolithic neighbours. It is clear that more data is required before we can reach any firm conclusions about N1a.

The Baltic region

In the Baltic region, the Trægtbægerkultur (Funnel-necked Beaker Culture) or TRB emerged around 4000 BC, and was characterised by globular beakers with a flared funnel-like rim.[1] Its origins have been much debated over the years, but it seems likely that it emerged when Ertebølle hunter-gatherer groups in southern Scandinavia came into contact with post-LBK farming groups to the south.[62,63] It is likely that the transition to agriculture involved the three-stage process outlined by Peter Rowley-Conwy,[38] and Marek Zvelebil[64] as described in Chapter 17.

More specifically, Zvelebil[64] suggested that during the earlier phases of the transition, the relationship between the Ertebølle hunter-gatherers and the farmers was cooperative. However, as time progressed, opportunistic farmers began to hunt and farm in the hunter-gatherer territory, and exploit it for other resources such as furs, honey and amber. The status of the hunter-gatherers became diminished in relation to the farmers. This led to many hunter-gatherer women marrying into farming communities, resulting in a shortage of potential marriage partners for the men. Eventually, the benefits of hunter-gathering reduced to the point at which those remaining took up agriculture.

The model is supported by data from both skull metrics and ancient DNA. A study involving over 500 Mesolithic and Neolithic skulls from sites across Europe and Southwest Asia showed that in the Baltic region, the two populations remained biologically distinct, with only limited intermarriage between them;[65] a similar conclusion was reached by a study that considered ancient DNA of hunter-gatherers and farmers from Scandinavian Mesolithic and Neolithic sites.[66]

The Atlantic coast: Megalithic Europe

On the Atlantic coast, the transition to agriculture was influenced by Cardial Ware groups from the south, and by LBK farmers of the Rhineland and the Paris basin. The process probably involved indigenous adoption by hunter-gatherers after contact with pioneering farming groups, as was the case with the VSG culture described above. By 4500 BC, farming had been adopted across the whole of the region, and by 4000 BC it had spread to Britain and Ireland.[55,1]

Here, the view has long been one of indigenous adoption,[67] but in recent years this view has changed. Stable isotope analysis suggests that there was an abrupt change in diet the start of the Neolithic, rather than the gradual change that may be expected on the indigenous view.[68] Accordingly, it is now suggested that the dominant process was colonisation, probably involving several different migrations from continental Europe. Among the immigrants was the Orkney vole, the ancestry of which has been traced to the Bay of Biscay region. One or more pairs of voles must have been stowaways on a colonising voyage from Biscay to Orkney. It is thought that a curragh-type boat could have made the trip from Brittany around the west of Ireland to Orkney in less than two weeks.[38,39]

The arrival of agriculture in Brittany, Britain, and Ireland was marked by the most visible manifestation of the Neolithic transition in Europe: the appearance of megalithic monuments including stone circles, standing stones, and chambered tombs. They range considerably in size and scope, ranging from single standing stones known only to enthusiasts to world-famous sites such as Stonehenge, Avebury and Carnac.

The smaller circles and rows were probably erected by and served local farming communities, but the larger monuments would have involved major construction projects. It has long been supposed that these required a political hierarchy. For example, in the 1970s, Colin Renfrew[69] suggested that Neolithic Wessex was controlled by a number of chiefdoms, with powerful individuals who could muster the manpower and resources needed bring these projects to fruition. More recently however, doubts have been cast on this view. Archaeologist Mike Pitts[70] has suggested that political hierarchies are not a precondition for complex projects, and that people might have provided their labour freely, in the context of rituals, traditions and social customs.

It is popularly assumed that these great monuments have an astronomical connotation, and innumerable attempts have been made to interpret them thus. We can be fairly certain that the movements of sun, moon and stars were of interest to prehistoric societies. Ethnographic accounts suggest that astronomical movements are associated with mythological events and cosmological understanding of the universe. In particular, the daily and annual movements of the sun provide an obvious symbol and metaphor for birth, death and rebirth.[1] But to what extent were these concerns associated with the construction of the megalithic monuments?

The well-known alignment of the Heel Stone at Stonehenge to the summer solstice was noted by the antiquarian William Stukeley in the 1720s.[1] Stonehenge has a complex history spanning the period from 3000 to 1600 BC, during which there were three major phases of construction.[70] The Heel Stone was probably erected early in the final phase. The alignment is not exact and the summer solstice sunrise, as viewed from the geometrical centre of the monument, actually occurs just to the left of the Heel Stone. During the third millennium BC, the sun would have risen even further to the left.[71] Many other astronomical phenomena have been linked to Stonehenge. Surely the most speculative idea is that it served as an early warning system against incoming meteorites that supposedly threatened Earth in Neolithic times.[72] Rather more plausibly, astronomers Gerald Hawkins[73] and Sir Fred Hoyle[74] proposed that the 56 Aubrey Holes that surround the monument were used to predict eclipses. Their method entailed moving markers around the holes in accordance to given rules. When certain configurations occurred, an eclipse was likely to occur. While the methods proposed by Hawkins and Hoyle do work, it is unlikely that the Aubrey Holes were ever used for such a purpose. Named for the seventeenth century author John Aubrey, they originally held timber posts or possibly bluestones. Many of them were later used for cremation burials.[70]

Recent work at Stonehenge[75] has shown that the monument was sited near a pair of naturally-occurring parallel ridges that happen to align on the summer solstitial sunrise in one direction and the winter solstitial sunset in the other. The ridges, formed by meltwater at the end of the last Ice Age, would have been seen as auspicious. Post holes dating back to around 8000 BC suggest that this natural alignment had been noticed in Mesolithic times, millennia before any monument-building began.

The monument was originally an elite graveyard, but by 2500 BC it was hosting ritual winter feasts attended by as much as four or five thousand people, which at that time would have represented around ten percent of the British population. Strontium isotope analysis of cattle remains found at the nearby site of Durrington Walls indicated that some had come from as far afield as the Scottish Highlands. Analysis of growth patterns of cattle teeth suggest that most were slaughtered nine months after birth, i.e. in the winter. Durrington Walls was served as a camp for the attendees, and it was also the location of two more circular monuments – constructed from timber rather than stone. There are however no burials at Durrington Walls. The whole ensemble has been interpreted as a ritual landscape, of which Stonehenge was only a part. It was a place of the dead, whereas Durrington Walls was a place of the living.

Stonehenge was constructed on Salisbury Plain because of a naturally-occurring astronomical alignment rather than to serve as a Neolithic observatory. At Newgrange, a passage grave in County Meath, Ireland, an alignment was intentionally built into the monument. Above the entrance is a roof-box that allows the rising sun to penetrate the back of the chamber for a few days either side of the winter solstice. While it could be argued that the alignment is coincidental, the roof-box serves no other obvious function. Furthermore, it was left open after the entrance to the tomb was blocked, suggesting that although the living could no longer enter, the midwinter sun was still permitted to do so. Again, Newgrange was not intended as an observatory, but powerful astronomical symbolism was incorporated into its design.[71]

It does seem likely that there were many other less high-profile monuments with astronomical connotations. A large majority of the tombs face east. The natural symbolism of the rising sun might have been particularly important and significant for places where the remains of the dead were deposited.[76,1] In northeastern Scotland, there are a large number of so-called recumbent stone circles, distinguished by the presence of a single large stone placed on its side between two tall uprights. In all cases, this 'recumbent' stone is placed on the SSW side of the circle. A possibility is that the intended alignment was on the setting of the midsummer full Moon. As it set over the recumbent stone and shed light into the stone circle, the Moon might have provided the backdrop for sacred ceremonials. Also common in Scotland are rows of between three to six stones. The stone rows are quite modest in size, mostly under 10 m (33 ft.) in length and rarely longer than 25 m (82 ft.). As such, they could have been erected by relatively small groups of people. Here, again, a lunar connection has been suggested. The stone rows might have tracked the lunar node cycle, which causes the southerly and northerly limits of the Moon's rising and setting to increase and decrease cyclically over the course of 18.6 years.[71]

It will be clear even from this brief summary that the Neolithic transition in Europe was a very complex process. At various times and places, it involved combinations of migration by farmers, indigenous adoption by hunter-gatherers, and varying degrees of integration between farming and hunter-gatherer communities. In some cases, hunter-gatherers were assimilated into farming communities; in others, such the VSG, migrant farmers were absorbed into former hunter-gatherer communities that had adopted agriculture. While cultural diffusion can be ruled out at a pan-European level, the spread of agriculture was far more complex than a monolithic wave of advance that either assimilated or eliminated all in its path.

We turn now to another possible consequence of farming migrations, and how they may provide the answer to a problem that has baffled linguists since the late eighteenth century.

20: Spreading the word

Where do they put it now?

In 1786, a 40-year-old English judge by the name of Sir William Jones made a remarkable observation suggesting far-reaching events many millennia previously. These events had left an eerie footprint upon languages spoken by diverse people living thousands of miles apart, between which absolutely no link existed in the historic record. The son of a mathematician, Jones was a linguistic prodigy who learned Greek, Latin, Persian and Arabic at an early age. After studying at Oxford, he worked as a tutor, and then took up the legal profession. In 1783, he went out to India to serve as a judge. There he became interested in Sanskrit, the classical language of India, which dates to around 1500 BC and possibly earlier. Although Sanskrit has not been spoken for many centuries, it is still used in religious texts, and to this day it remains one of India's 23 official languages.

Jones noted that Sanskrit shares many similarities of both grammatical structure and vocabulary with Ancient Greek and Latin. Both are also 'dead' languages, current at roughly the same time as Sanskrit. In a famous address to the Asiatic Society in Calcutta, he claimed that these similarities could not be dismissed as chance and suggested that all might have arisen "*…from some common source, which, perhaps no longer exists*". Jones also speculated that Gothic (the precursor of German), Celtic and Old Persian may also share the same common origin. The idea that languages spoken in places as far apart as Iceland and India may be linked was startling to say the least, but the connection seemed real. Furthermore, what was soon dubbed the Indo-European language family grew rapidly, and no fewer than nine major language groups were identified as members during the first half of the nineteenth century. The total now stands at twelve major language groups (Celtic, Italic, Germanic, Baltic, Slavic, Albanian, Anatolian, Greek, Armenian, Indo-Iranian (or Indo-Aryan), Iranian and Tocharian), and ten minor groups (Lusitanian, Rhaetic, Venetic, South Picene, Messapic, Illyrian, Dacian, Thracian, Macedonian and Phrygian).[1]

What does all this mean? During the course of his 1786 lectures, Jones also put forward the idea that the various ancient languages could all be traced back to "*some central country*", which he argued was Iran. He set in motion a debate that has continued ever since, during which the 'central country' has been located at just about every point on Earth. The American scholar J.P. Mallory[2] has commented "*One does not ask 'where is the Indo-European homeland?' but rather 'where do they put it now?'*".

That groups of languages can arise from a common origin was already accepted in Sir William Jones' day. It had long been realised that many European languages including French, Spanish, Portuguese, Italian and Romanian had all diverged from Latin and from each other after the fall of the Roman Empire in the fifth century AD. Following the same chain of reasoning, it was logical to assume that similarities between the Indo-European languages could be explained by divergence from a single ancestral language, originally spoken by people from a single region. This hypothetical language was termed 'Ursprache' by German scholars, or Proto-Indo-European (often abbreviated to PIE). The supposed speakers of the language became known as the 'Urvolk', and their original homeland the 'Urheimat'. The term 'Sprachbund' (speech union) was introduced in the 1920s to describe a region in which a group of closely related languages, such as those diverging from PIE, may be spoken. The question was, who were the inhabitants of this homeland, and when did they live? Above all, how did the languages descended from their ancestral tongue come to be spoken across an area far greater in extent than the Roman Empire?

How languages spread and change

In the English-speaking world, we are so used to the idea that European languages mostly resemble one another that we think nothing of it. In fact, such a lack of linguistic diversity is unusual. In the New Guinea highlands, for example, nearly a thousand mutually unintelligible languages are spoken. The difference is that before European colonisation, no significant part of the island had ever been unified politically, and the region is inhabited by groups that largely keep themselves to themselves.[3] By contrast, when the Roman Empire was at its maximum extent, Latin was spoken across large areas of Europe.

The spread of Latin is a classic example of what is known as elite dominance.[4] When one group conquers another, the subjugated people will eventually come to speak the language of the invaders. There will be a period of maybe several generations when people are bilingual, but in time the outsider tongue will become dominant. The old language will by this time be used chiefly for conversing with elderly relatives, and eventually it will die out altogether.[5]

Latin, of course, is no longer spoken anywhere in the world. Instead, we have the closely related and widely spoken languages known as the Romance group, including French, Spanish, Portuguese, Italian and Romanian. How did this come about? Part of the answer is because languages are not static, unchanging entities, but evolve over time.[5] To see that such change is discernible over the course of only a few centuries, one needs to look no further than the King James Bible:

The Lord is my shepherd; I shall not want.
He maketh me to lie down in green pastures:
He leadeth me beside the still waters.
He restoreth my soul:
He leadeth me in the paths of righteousness for his name's sake.
Yea, though I walk through the valley of the shadow of death, I shall fear no evil:
For thou art with me; thy rod and thy staff they comfort me.
Thou preparest a table before me in the presence of mine enemies:
Thou anointest my head with oil; my cup runneth over.
Surely goodness and mercy shall follow me all the days of my life:
And I will dwell in the house of the Lord for ever. – The 23rd Psalm.

Although the 'biblical' feel of the text may seem familiar, it only reflects the way people actually spoke in the early seventeenth century. Forms such as 'thou art' (you are) were still in everyday use, and the -eth, -est inflections had yet to give way to the modern -s form (for example 'makes' rather than 'maketh'). Such changes come about as one generation's sloppy speech becomes the next generation's received version. English was once a fully-inflected language, and both nouns and pronouns used grammatical cases. Although pronouns retain cases (for example he/him), those for nouns fell into disuse.[5] In addition, plurals were simplified. For example, the plurals of 'fox', 'tongue' and 'book' were once 'foxas', 'tungan' and 'bec'. Some of these archaic forms do survive, such as ox/oxen, sheep/sheep, man/men, woman/women and child/children.

Words can also acquire additional meanings, or change their meaning entirely. An obvious example is 'gay', a word that originally meant 'carefree'. Not until the twentieth century did it gradually came to mean homosexual. Other examples include 'silly' (original meaning 'glorious'), 'villain' (a peasant farmer in feudal times) and 'husband' (which originally meant the manager of a house). The process continues: it has been some time since the word 'cool' simply meant the opposite of 'warm', and the word 'wicked' is apparently in the process of completely reversing its meaning. Pronunciations also change over time; for example the silent 'k' in words such as 'knife', 'knee' and 'knight' was once pronounced. Another example is the planet Uranus, once commonly pronounced with the stress on the second syllable. Finally, words can be 'borrowed' from other languages. Since 1066, English has borrowed heavily from French, and such 'loanwords' include 'ability', 'finance', 'rendezvous' and 'theatre'. English also contains loanwords from other languages including 'hinterland' (German), 'bazaar' and 'bungalow' (from Hindi), and 'alcohol', 'algebra' and 'arsenal' (from Arabic).

This all seems fairly straightforward, but how can a group of languages arise from a common origin? Why are the French, Spanish, Portuguese, Italians and Romanians not still speaking Latin, even if it is not identical to the version that was spoken in Roman times? The answer is that in a sense they are. Just as a language is not fixed in time, so it also varies across regions. In reality there is no such a thing as a language, only dialects. English, for example, was a collection of dialects until the fifteenth century. What became known as 'Standard' English was no more than the mixture of Essex and Middlesex dialects that happened to be spoken in London. However, after 1400, London became the hub of the newly-established manuscript printing industry, and so written English was more likely to be this version. Combined with London's influence, this resulted in it becoming accepted as the 'standard' version, although the other dialects were equally valid language systems. Similarly in France, the Paris dialect came to predominate, and others were dismissed as 'patois'.[5]

Even in Roman times, different dialects of Latin were spoken in different parts of the Empire. After the fall of Rome, contacts between the various peoples reduced, and these differences became ever more marked. Eventually, the Latin dialects spoken in Italy, France, Spain, etc. diverged to such an extent that they became distinct languages, forming the present-day Romance group of languages. The problem for linguists was what could have caused a process of linguistic spread and divergence, in prehistoric times, and on a vastly greater scale to the Roman Empire?

Reconstructing PIE

During the nineteenth century, linguists attempted to reconstruct PIE. On the face of it, trying to piece together a long-dead language that was never written down may seem to be impossible. In fact, by following a number of rules, it is possible to reconstruct a disused mother tongue from its successors. Take for example the word for 'man' in various Romance languages. This is *uomo* (Italian), *l'homme* (French), *hombre* (Spanish), *homem* (Portuguese) and *om* (Romanian). As can be seen, they are all very similar to one another. The similarity reflects the common etymological origin of these words, all of which arose from the Latin word *homo*. Such words are said to be cognates (the English words 'man' and 'men' are cognate with the German words *Mann* and *Mensch*). Latin, of course, was spoken well after prehistoric times, but even had it not it would still have been possible for linguists to use cognates to reconstruct the Latin word as *homo*, by what is known as the comparative method.

In the early nineteenth century, linguists discovered that phonetic features in one language differ from those of another in a consistent way. For example, in Latin the 'f' sound in many words corresponds to the 'b' sound in Germanic languages. Thus *frater* in Latin becomes *brother* in English and *Bruder* in German. Another example is 'th-' in English, which becomes 'd-' in German. Thus 'thank' becomes *danke* in German. Similarly, '-ou-' in English becomes '-u-' in German, as in *gefunden* (found), *pfund* (pound), and *wunde* (wound). If it is known what sound shifts have occurred among a group of daughter languages (such as the Romance languages), it is possible to work backwards from a group of cognates to reconstruct a word in the original mother tongue.

It is interesting (though not very useful) to reconstruct Latin words with this method, but it can also be applied to PIE. The task got underway in the mid-nineteenth century, but first it was necessary to form a better understanding of the relationships between the various daughter languages. Two models were put forward. The first, by August Schliecher in 1862 was the genealogical or 'family tree' model of languages. Languages with strong similarities such as French and Italian were grouped together. These groups were in turn linked to produce larger groups. It is assumed languages give rise to daughter languages. For example, Italo-Celtic split to give Celtic and Italic; Italic then split to give Oscan, Umbrian and Latin. The model has a number of weaknesses. It assumes the different daughter languages remain isolated, whereas in practice this is not the case. For example, English (a Germanic language) was heavily influenced by Medieval French and Latin (both Italic). It also fails to explain similarities that cut across different language branches. These similarities are known as isoglosses. The best-known example of an isogloss is the so-called centum/satem division, named for the words for one hundred, *centum* in Latin and *satem* in Avestan (a liturgical Old Iranian language used to compose the sacred hymns and texts of the Zoroastrian Avesta). Another model, known as the wave hypothesis, was proposed by Johannes Schmidt in 1872. This assumes that language changes spread out over a speech area like ripples on a pond. A weakness is that it assumes that all the languages under consideration are all being spoken at the same time, whereas in reality some may be separated from others by thousands of years. Despite their drawbacks, no widely accepted alternative to these two models has ever been proposed.[4,2]

Nevertheless, nineteenth century linguists were able to begin reconstructing PIE. For example, the word 'sheep' is *avis* (Lithuanian), *ovis* (Latin), *ois* (Greek), *oveja* (Spanish) and *ewe* (English). Application of the comparative method gives the reconstructed PIE word *owis*, the asterisk denoting reconstruction. Other reconstructed words include *mehter* (mother), *phator* (father), *swesor* (sister), *bhrater* (brother), *dhughater* (daughter), *suhnus* (son), *tauros* (bull), *gwous* (cow), *uksen* (ox), *porkos* (pig), *kapros* (goat) and *kwon* (dog). One thing that stands out about these words is their familiarity. Even where the meaning isn't immediately obvious, it doesn't take much working out. For example, *kwon* is cognate with the English word 'hound'.

Much of the work of reconstruction was completed during the nineteenth century, though refinement has continued ever since. New information has been incorporated as lost languages such as Hittite and Tocharian have come to light. Hittite was deciphered by the Czech linguist Bedřich Hrozný in 1917 from cuneiform tablets excavated in Anatolia some years earlier, and it and other related languages in the region are now recognised as making up the Anatolian group. The Tocharian languages, once spoken in the Tarim Basin in Central Asia, were identified from a fifth century AD manuscript procured from a Buddhist monastery by the Hungarian-British archaeologist Sir Marc Aurel Stein. Not all the reconstructed words are regarded as equally secure. Ideally, a reconstructed word should have a shared correspondence between a European language and a non-adjacent Asian language, but this is not always possible.[2]

Linguistic palaeontology and PIE

The next step was for linguists to attempt to make inferences about the Proto-Indo-Europeans, their homeland, and their way of life. A number of methodologies have been used with varying degrees of success to try and tease clues out of the linguistic data. In the mid-nineteenth century, an approach was set out known as linguistic palaeontology. The basic assumption is that if a PIE word exists for something, then the Proto-Indo-Europeans must have been familiar with it, and inferences can therefore be made about their material culture, social organisation and the geography of their homeland. PIE has words pertaining to wheeled vehicles including 'wheel', 'axle', 'shaft' and 'hub'. The wheel was invented around 3300 BC and if the existence of PIE words for it is taken at face value, then we get a date for when the language was spoken that is no earlier than 3300 BC. This is consistent with the observation that Mycenaean Greek, Indo-Iranian and Anatolian separated from one another well before 2000 BC, but is it safe to accept that the Proto-Indo-Europeans had wheeled vehicles?

We cannot be certain that it is. In the 1960s, linguist and classicist Calvert Watkins[6] suggested that terms pertaining to wheeled vehicles were chiefly metaphorical extensions of older Indo-European words with different meaning. For example *nobh (wheel-hub) meant 'navel', and the word for wheel itself, *kwekwlo, is derived from the root *kwel- 'to turn' or 'to revolve'. A problem with this suggestion is that there are actually at least four different PIE verbs that mean 'to turn' or 'to revolve', any one of which could have been used. For the word 'wheel' to have emerged thus, we must assume that each branch of Indo-European independently adopted *kwel rather than one of the other possibilities. The word *kwel would also have to have remained current from the time when the Proto-Indo-Europeans lived through to 3300 BC, when the wheel was invented.[7]

However, Colin Renfrew[4,8] has suggested the universality of words pertaining to wheels results from widespread borrowing. He believes that innovations such as the wheel and wheeled vehicles spread so rapidly that that the relevant vocabulary spread with them as loanwords. Subsequent sound-shifts in the borrowing languages would create the illusion that borrowed words were part of the proto-lexicon.

Conversely, we cannot assume that because we lack a reconstructed word for a thing, it was unknown to the Proto-Indo-Europeans. For example, there are reconstructed words for 'eye' and 'eyebrow', but not 'eyelid'. We can safely assume that the Proto-Indo-Europeans had eyelids, and that the word for them has been lost. Absence of evidence, as ever, is not evidence of absence.[3]

We also run into uncertainties when reconstructed words are used to make inferences about the economic and social systems of the Proto-Indo-Europeans. PIE contains words for domestic animals, including sheep, goats, cattle, pigs and horses; but there are fewer words pertaining to farming. This led some to suppose that the Proto-Indo-Europeans were nomadic pastors rather than farmers. The problem is that, as we saw in Chapter 18, many nomadic pastors were familiar with farming and interacted with farmers. The lack of farming terminology thus proves nothing.[4]

There is a cognate word for 'king' in many Indo-European languages, for example Sanskrit *raj*, Latin *rex* and Old Irish *ri*. Some have taken this to imply that the Proto-Indo-Europeans were ruled by a king, implying a complex stratified society. It has even been suggested that the absence of a word for 'king' in some Indo-European languages is evidence for a prehistoric revolution, in which the king was driven out and the word was forgotten. In fact we need look no further than English to see that the whole notion of Proto-Indo-European kingship is highly suspect. The true cognate in English is 'ruler' (the word 'king' comes from the Old English *cyning*). The verb 'to rule' can indeed mean to reign, but it also possible to rule on other matters, such as a point of law. Nearly all forms of sport are governed by rules, such as the offside rule in association football. Things can be 'ruled out'. Finally, it is possible to rule a straight line. The correspondence between straight lines and rules can be seen in the expression 'to keep on the straight and narrow', and this correspondence is also found in other Indo-European languages. Rather than a king, the reconstructed PIE word *reg might have referred to a tribal head, or simply an arbiter of right and wrong.[4,1]

Another field of study that has long attracted Indo-European scholars is the religion of the Proto-Indo-Europeans. The word for 'god' is widely attested, for example *devas* (Sanskrit), *deus* (Latin), *dievas* (Lithuanian), *dia* (Old Irish) and *deity* (English). The reconstructed PIE word is *deiwos. Rather more striking is the word *dyeus phater (sky father), better known to anybody familiar with Greek or Roman mythology as Zeus (Greek), or Jupiter (Roman). Can we therefore assume that the chief deity of the Proto-Indo-European pantheon was a brash thunderbolt-hurling alpha male? The answer is 'no'. The same god seems less prominent in other religions such as Indic. It has been suggested that the pre-eminence of Zeus/Jupiter in Mediterranean religions was a later phenomenon involving the conflation of the Indo-European god with local weather deities.[2]

Linguistic palaeontology has also been used in attempts to locate the Proto-Indo-European homeland itself. PIE words exist for hills, mountains and swift-running rivers, leading some to suppose that the homeland was mountainous. However, one need not actually live in mountainous terrain to be familiar with mountains. There are PIE words for hot, cold, snow and ice. These may be taken to imply a seasonally-varying, temperate climate, but really only rule out a homeland in the tropics.[3,2] Much effort has been devoted to the distribution of trees and animals, for example the beach tree and the salmon. Unfortunately, we cannot be sure that the reconstructed word for the beach tree actually referred to it and not the elder, oak, or elm. Similarly with the salmon; did the PIE word refer to the Atlantic salmon, or the salmon trout?[2]

Other linguistic methods have also been used in attempts to locate the homeland, but again the results are inconclusive and often contradictory. One such method is to consider the relationship between the Indo-European languages and those of neighbouring language families. The idea is that one showing the strongest affinities may serve as a pointer. Many loanwords and grammatical loans have in fact been discerned. For example, Uralic has been used to support a homeland in the Eurasian steppe lands. Links with Afroasiatic and Kartvelian (South Caucasus) have been used to locate the homeland in either eastern Anatolia or Central Asia.[2,1] Another approach is to assume that the first groups to diverge from PIE were located in or close to the homeland. The earliest-known split is that of Anatolian, suggesting a location for the homeland in or close to Anatolia.[1] On the other hand, the conservation principle assumes that languages closer to the homeland will be less influenced by loanwords from earlier languages, and undergo less change, than those further away. There are many loanwords in Greek and Hittite, suggesting that the homeland was *not* Anatolia. Instead, the modern language most similar to PIE is Lithuanian.[3]

The Kurgan hypothesis

The purely linguistic considerations discussed above provided tantalising but rather tentative insights into the possible worlds of the Proto-Indo-Europeans. Clearly, the problem could not be solved with linguistic data alone, and by the end of the nineteenth century archaeological evidence was also being considered.

In 1926, V. Gordon Childe published *The Aryans, a study of Indo-European origins*[9] in which he proposed a homeland on the Pontic-Caspian steppes north of the Black Sea and Caspian Sea. The word 'Aryan' came to be applied to the Proto-Indo-European people during the nineteenth century. It comes from the Sanskrit word *arya*, meaning 'noble'. Iran literally means 'Land of the Aryans'. Unfortunately, the term 'Aryan' is now so indelibly associated with the Nazis that post-war scholars have tended to avoid it. Childe, for his part, later repudiated his work.

However, in the second half of the last century, the Pontic-Caspian steppes option was taken up by Lithuanian émigré Marija Gimbutas. In a series of papers published between 1956 and 1979,[10] she identified the Proto-Indo-Europeans with the Kurgan culture, which takes its name from the Russian word for their trademark barrows or burial mounds. Gimbutas introduced the name as a blanket term for a number of Chalcolithic steppe cultures in eastern Ukraine and southern Russia, originating in the lower Volga basin and the lower Dnieper region around 4500 BC. They lived as nomadic pastors, with an economy based on sheep, goats, cattle and pigs. Drawing on both linguistic and archaeological evidence, Gimbutas envisaged the Kurgan people as a warlike male-dominated society, worshipping masculine sky-gods. They were a highly mobile society, using ox-drawn wagons and horses for transport. Only a few permanent settlements have been found, as could be expected for mobile people. They are known mainly from their mortuary practices, whereby the dead were interred in earthen or stone chambers, above which a burial mound was frequently erected. By contrast, the people of what Gimbutas termed 'Old Europe' were settled farmers, living in small family-based communities. Gimbutas characterised them as peaceful, matriarchal and possessing a mother goddess-centred religion. Geographically, Old Europe encompassed the Balkan and Danube regions, the Adriatic coast of Italy, and Sicily.[11]

Gimbutas claimed that between 4400 and 2800 BC, the Kurgan people mounted three hostile incursions from the steppes, moving into Old Europe, Anatolia and the Caucasus. They then moved onwards towards India, and they also moved eastwards along the steppe into Central Asia. The female-centric culture of Old Europe disappeared, and was replaced by that of Kurgan warriors. Fine ceramics and painted wares gave way to cruder Kurgan material. Kurgan burials appeared, generally confined to males and accompanied by arrows, spears, knives and horse-headed sceptres. Evidence is claimed for the atrocious practice of suttee, whereby women are killed on the deaths of their husbands. Stone stelae have been found in the Alpine region depicting horses, wagons, axes, spears and daggers, all of which are valued by a warlike society. Similar evidence is seen in the South Caucasus, Anatolia and southern Siberia.[2]

The Kurgan hypothesis, as it became known, has been widely though not uncritically accepted. As we have seen, the notion that the Proto-Indo-European gods can be equated with the Greco-Roman pantheon is suspect, as are purely linguistic inferences about their social systems. J.P. Mallory[2] questions an explanation that places so much emphasis on the warlike nature of the steppe intruders, and suggests that other factors must have been involved. Mallory and scholars including anthropologist David Anthony[7] nevertheless favour a homeland on the Pontic-Caspian steppes.

The Anatolian hypothesis

In 1987, Colin Renfrew put forward an entirely different model in a book entitled *Archaeology and Language*.[4] According to Renfrew, the Indo-European languages were spread by Neolithic farmers dispersing from Anatolia. The date from around 7000 to 6500 BC is far earlier than that proposed for the Kurgan hypothesis. Renfrew summarised and then rejected all attempts to date to solve the Proto-Indo-European problem. His first target was linguistic palaeontology. We have already seen that this approach has its pitfalls, in particular the assumption that the Proto-Indo-Europeans must have been nomadic pastors. Renfrew then went on to challenge the assumption that the appearance in a region of new pottery styles or new mortuary practices such as the kurgans can be seen as evidence of migrations. He saw the spread of new cultural traits and material objects as the result of peer polity interaction (see Chapter 17) rather than evidence for hostile invaders.

Drawing on the work of Luigi Luca Cavalli-Sforza and Albert Ammerman as discussed in Chapter 19, Renfrew suggested that the Proto-Indo-Europeans were Neolithic farmers. It was the spread of agriculture that had distributed their language over such an enormous area. Renfrew proposed that the Proto-Indo-European expansion had begun in Anatolia before 6500 BC. From Anatolia, the expansion had moved into Greece and from there in a northwesterly direction across Europe. He also offered a choice of two scenarios as to the spread of the Indo-Iranian languages, referred to as Hypotheses A and B. Hypothesis A proposed a simple wave of advance similar to that proposed for Europe. Hypothesis B, on the other hand, invoked a modification of the steppe-invader model. Once the European wave of advance reached the steppe, nomadic pastoralism developed and the pastors moved swiftly east across the steppes and into Iran and northern India. Renfrew[8] later came down in favour of this second scenario.

Renfrew's theory attracted a lot of interest, but it was also criticised for its apparent dismissal of much of the linguistic evidence. Jared Diamond[3] suggested that the date of the Neolithic expansion was far too early to account for PIE. Based on the assumption that PIE speakers had the wheel, he notes that this came into use no earlier 3300 BC. He cited an estimate based on glottochronology of no earlier than 5000 BC for when PIE began to differentiate into daughter languages. He also cited the linguistic conservation principle which, as discussed above, argues against an Anatolian homeland – although as we have seen, cases can be made against many of these linguistic objections.

Other criticisms of Renfrew's model focused on archaeological evidence for cultural diffusion. As we saw in Chapter 19, the original wave of advance model proposed by Cavalli-Sforza and Ammerman has been replaced by models based on 'leapfrog' migrations, in which both demic and cultural diffusion play a part. In addition to taking these points on board, Renfrew[8] felt that Gimbutas' 'Old Europe' could be interpreted as an interaction zone, and thus incorporated into a revised model. Accordingly, he proposed a three-phase model, based on the Indo-Hittite (or Indo-Anatolian) hypothesis. This view states that the Anatolian languages split away from PIE considerably earlier than any other language group, and was first put forward by the American linguist Edgar H. Sturtevant in 1926.

According to Renfrew's revised scheme, the farmers living in Anatolia spoke a language that has been termed Pre-PIE, or Proto-Indo-Hittite. Phase I of the Renfrew scheme began around 6500 BC as farmers started to migrate into Greece. From there, they dispersed into the Balkans and the Danube Valley, and possibly to the edge of the Pontic-Caspian steppes. These migrations gave rise to a number of well-documented cultures, including the Bug-Dniester Culture and the Linearbandkeramik (Linear Pottery) Culture, or LBK. As we saw in Chapter 19, the latter first appeared in western Hungary about 5600 BC. It subsequently spread across whole of Central Europe from Austria and Hungary to the Rhineland and the Paris Basin in the west, and Ukraine and Moldova in the east.[12] The language of these farmers was termed Archaic PIE. Other groups dispersed to Italy and Sicily, giving rise to Early West Mediterranean PIE. Beyond these limits, local Mesolithic farmers might have adopted agriculture, acquiring the domesticated species and technology necessary for farming from their neighbours, as outlined by Peter Rowley-Conwy and Marek Zvelebil in Chapters 17 and 19.

Phase I lasted until 5000 BC, the beginning of the Balkan Chalcolithic, when copper started to come into use alongside stone. By this time, a range of dialects were being spoken within a region corresponding geographically to Marija Gimbutas' Old Europe. Renfrew referred to these as Balkan PIE and saw the region itself as an interaction zone involved in a series of peer polity interactions. These resulted in the widespread distribution of painted pottery, the copper industry, and other aspects of the rich material culture Gimbutas had identified. Within this region, a Sprachbund developed, in which the various dialects converged, or began to share linguistic features, including innovations of both form and lexicon. These dialects might have included Proto-Greek and Proto-Indo-Iranian, accounting for the similarities between Greek and Sanskrit noted by Sir William Jones. Proto-Indo-Iranian probably emerged in Ukraine, which lies in the east of the region. However, not all of the Phase I Archaic PIE regions fell within this Phase II Balkan PIE Sprachbund. Peripheral areas included the LBK region, Mediterranean coastal areas beyond the heel of Italy, and steppe lands east of Crimea. To the north and west, the Archaic PIE of Phase I persisted and expanded, laying the foundations for Proto-Celtic, Proto-Germanic and Proto-Baltic.

Also within the Archaic PIE zone, settlers moved onto the steppe lands. Renfrew suggests that early agro-pastoral adaptions in steppe lands might have been influenced by the Bug-Dniester economy. During the fourth millennium BC or possibly earlier, there was an eastward dispersal of a steppe adapted economy. This was based on many of the domesticated plant and animal species that originally came to the Archaic PIE zone from Anatolia, with the addition of the horse. The latter was still a food animal; its use for traction would only come later. The language of these steppe people was an offshoot of Archaic PIE, termed Early Steppe PIE, and they came to occupy quite a wide area of central Eurasia during the subsequent Phase II. This could help account for some archaic features later seen in Tocharian.

After 3000 BC, as documented by Marija Gimbutas, the cultural richness of Phase II disappeared. However, what she interpreted as a hostile invasion from the steppes is attributed by Renfrew to a system collapse, occurring through purely internal factors. Just what these factors might have been remain uncertain. One possibility is that the introduction of plough agriculture brought about the social changes that Gimbutas attributed to conquest. Ethnographic studies suggest that that with simple hoe agriculture, the major subsistence contribution comes from female labour in sowing, weeding and harvesting. Such societies tend to be matrilocal (where women, rather than men, remain in their place of birth after marriage) and matrilineal (descent through the female line). By contrast, plough agriculture is associated with male dominance of subsistence activities, patrilocality (men remain in their place of birth after marriage) and patrilineal descent (descent through the male line).[13]

During the ensuing Phase III, the languages in the constituent regions of the former Sprachbund became more distinct from one another. It is probably at this time that Proto-Greek began to take on the form and lexicon recognised in the Mycenaean Greek of the Linear B tablets 1,700 years later. The development of Greek came about not from the arrival of a new population in Greece, but from the existing population losing contact with the other regions in the Balkans.

Shortly after 3000 BC, a second migration took place onto the Pontic-Caspian steppes, probably from Ukraine. This led to an eastwards dispersal of Proto-Indo-Iranian, bringing the Indo-Iranian languages to the Iranian plateau no later than 1500 BC. A southward dispersal into the Indian subcontinent around 1700 BC gave rise to the Indic sub-branch of Indo-Iranian. This was probably an episode of elite dominance leading to language replacement, and was the only dispersal not primarily driven by agricultural considerations. The horse-drawn chariot, as featured prominently in the *Hymns of the Rig Veda* (a collection of ancient Hindu hymns), might have played a significant role.

This updated model has not escaped criticism, and remains controversial to this day. David Anthony[7] has put forward a number of objections. He disputes that Renfrew's Sprachbund could have held together from 6500 BC to 3000 BC over such a large area, where the only means of transport was to walk. He notes that among most tribal farmers, the documented size of language families is usually less than 200,000 sq. km. (76,000 sq. miles). Even if a figure of 250,000 to 500,000 sq. km. (95,000 to 190,000 sq. miles) is assumed, this would still result in a figure of 20 to 40 language families in an area the size of Neolithic Europe. In Central Africa and South Africa, Proto-Bantu has differentiated into 500 languages in 19 branches over 2,000 years. Anthony believes that within two to three thousand years of the initial Anatolian farming dispersal, the linguistic diversity of Europe was comparable to that of Bantu Africa. In particular, there would be no common vocabulary from which to derive words pertaining to wheels and wheeled vehicles. Accordingly, Anthony concludes, the original PIE-speakers must have been already familiar with these things, and must have lived thousands of years after the farming dispersal from Anatolia. However, as previously noted, Renfrew attributed the presence of reconstructed words for wheels and wheeled vehicles in PIE to widespread borrowing, rather than to the reuse of a pre-existing vocabulary as suggested by Calvert Watkins.

In the last decade, Bayesian inference has been applied to the PIE problem in attempts to distinguish between the two rival hypotheses. Studies have come down on the side of the Anatolian hypothesis. An early study obtained dates between 7800 and 5800 BC for when the various Indo-European languages began to diverge from one another,[14] rather earlier than the figure obtained using glottochronology. More recent work has refined the date range to between 7500 and 6000 BC.

In addition, it suggests that the geographical homeland of PIE is Anatolia. Thus both the timing and root location of the Indo-European languages fit with an agricultural expansion from Anatolia.[15]

Nostratic and the Natufians

Anatolia, as we saw in Chapter 18, represented only one of the four directions in which the agricultural expansion proceeded out of Southwest Asia. Other dispersals took place into Central Asia, the Indian subcontinent and North Africa. Might these, too, have left their linguistic mark? Peter Bellwood[16] has suggested that the Southeast Asian expansion as a whole may be linked to a controversial grouping known as Nostratic. Just as languages may be grouped into families, so families can be arranged into higher-order assemblages known as macro-families. The name Nostratic comes from the Latin *nostrates* meaning 'our countrymen'. From Nostratic arose a number of languages, including PIE. Like Indo-European, Nostratic is assumed to have arisen from a single language or tight grouping of languages termed Proto-Nostratic. If PIE can be thought of as a mother tongue of the Indo-European language group, then Proto-Nostratic is the grandmother tongue. Accordingly, its origins must be sought even further back in time, and the problems of reconstruction are correspondingly greater. Many linguists reject the concept altogether, claiming that it is not possible to go so far back in time.

Nostratic was first proposed by the Danish linguist Holger Pedersen in 1903, and developed by Soviet linguists in the 1960s. Under the scheme proposed by American linguist Allan R. Bomhard, it includes Indo-European, Afroasiatic (North and East Africa, Arabia), Kartvelian (South Caucasus), Uralic (Finland, Estonia and Hungary), Altaic (Central Asia through to Japan and Korea) and Dravidian (Indian subcontinent, mainly the south). All these families are said to share some degree of common origin, or at least a degree of inter-family contact. Bellwood associates Dravidian with a larger, hypothetical grouping, Elamo-Dravidian, which links it with the extinct Elamite languages of southwestern Iran. He notes that not all these language families can be associated with an agriculturally-driven dispersal out of Southwest Asia: Uralic is believed to be derived from Mesolithic hunter-gatherer dispersals across northern Eurasia, originating in the Ural region, and Altaic probably originated in Mongolia or Manchuria. If the farming/language dispersal model is correct, the similarities between these families and the other Nostratic members must be due to convergences arising from geographical proximity.

Although a pre-agricultural African origin for Afroasiatic cannot be ruled out, reconstruction of early vocabulary for cultural and environmental referents suggests a Levantine origin during the early Neolithic.[17] Similarly, there are good grounds to associate Elamo-Dravidian with an agricultural dispersal into the Indian subcontinent. Today, the Dravidian languages are largely confined to central and southern India and the Tamil-speaking regions of Sri Lanka, but there are isolated pockets elsewhere, most notably Brahui, spoken in Baluchistan. This distribution fits a model in which these languages were once spoken across the whole of the subcontinent, but were replaced by Indo-Iranian during Renfrew's Phase III dispersal south from the Eurasian steppes. Kartvelian is confined to the mountainous and remote regions of the Caucasus. It also fits the model, though too little is known about the grouping to draw any conclusions. Bellwood accepts that some linguists may not be happy about so picking and choosing which groups should be included in Nostratic, but claims that from an archaeological point of view, linking its distribution to the agricultural dispersal out of Southwest Asia is very appealing. Invariably, there have been attempts to identify a homeland and date for Proto-Nostratic. Bellwood admits that these will remain elusive, but speculates on a connection with the Natufian and its contemporaries.

Winning the Lottery

Although his original 1987 work mainly concerned the Indo-European problem, Renfrew also considered the possibility that other language families might have been spread by agricultural dispersals. Despite the lack of universal acceptance for its applicability to the Indo-European problem, the farming/language dispersal hypothesis has been successfully applied to other major language families. These include the Niger-Congo languages, which have been associated with the Bantu dispersal from Cameroon around 1000 BC[18] (see Chapter 21) and the Uto-Aztecan language family, which may owe its distribution to the dispersal of maize farmers from Mexico to the Southwestern United States between 3400 and 1000 BC[19,20] (see Chapter 24). In Chapter 22, we shall see how a number of language families are associated with the spread of rice farming.

If the farming/language dispersal hypothesis is correct, then the languages now spoken in much of the world are descended from the winners of linguistic lotteries that took place thousands of years ago. These were the languages that just happened to be spoken by people living in the very few parts of the world where there were indigenous plant and animal species suitable for domestication. Some of these lotteries paid out bigger 'prizes' than others, and Proto-Indo-European was by far the biggest winner. Originally spoken by no more than a few tens of thousands, it gave rise to languages now spoken by 45 percent of the world's population.[21] It did of course undergo further expansion after 1492, with the European colonisation of the New World. We should also note that Neil Armstrong's first words from the surface of the Moon were spoken in a language that may trace its origins to the Anatolian farming dispersal almost nine millennia earlier.

21: A continent divided

Predynastic foundations

Africa saw two transitions to agriculture, one in North Africa and one in sub-Saharan Africa. The transition in the north laid the foundations of pharaonic Egypt; in sub-Saharan Africa, the transition triggered an agricultural expansion that would spread farming across most of the southern half of this vast continent in just three and a half millennia.

It remains uncertain the extent to which these developments were independent of one another, or of agricultural developments elsewhere in the world. Our understanding of the transition to agriculture in Africa is limited in comparison to those in other parts of the world. Africa is far larger than either Southwest Asia or Europe, and there is no focal point of agricultural development corresponding to the Fertile Crescent. Poor preservation conditions and the general difficulties of conducting fieldwork in the equatorial forests have hampered archaeological research. These problems have been compounded by political unrest in many parts of the continent.[1,2]

Food production in Africa had its beginnings when Early Holocene hunter-gatherers re-established themselves in the Sahara, which had been uninhabitable during the Last Glacial Maximum. High rainfall brought about a greening of the Sahara, and much of what is now desert became covered with grasslands. Water levels were high in lakes and rivers, and the mountain ranges supported Mediterranean vegetation. The hunter-gatherers, concentrated in relatively well-watered lake basins across North Africa, were distinguished by their use of pottery with wavy-line decorative motifs. Some groups were fairly sedentary, and harvested wild cereals.[3]

The climate was still liable to fluctuations: colder, dryer climatic events occurred around 7500, 6600 and 5800 BC,[4] and rainfall was sufficient to support wild cattle only periodically. In order to guarantee a predictable food supply, some groups might have turned to herding cattle. They adopted a highly-mobile lifestyle, sometimes moving their herds over long distances to locations offering water and good grazing land. It is likely that knowledge of such locations was shared through cooperative links between the far-flung pastoralists. Such inter-group relationships could have developed through sharing of resources such as water and grazing pastures, and loans of livestock.[3]

The most important evidence for the development of cattle herding in North Africa has come from the site of Nabta Playa in southern Egypt, where cattle remains dating from 9000 to 7000 BC have been found.[5] It is believed that these cattle remains represent a domesticated herd, because the local environment was too marginal for cattle to have survived without human intervention.[6] Rock paintings of cattle herds and pastoral scenes attest to the emergence of mature nomadic pastoral societies from the later part of the Early Holocene in at least some parts of the Sahara.[7] Thus mobile herding rather than sedentary crop farming became the earliest form of food production in North Africa.

Genetic evidence suggests that the cattle were independently domesticated in Africa and not imported from Southwest Asia. Data from mitochondrial DNA indicates that African and Southwest Asian cattle diverged from one another between 22,000 and 26,000 years ago; this is long before cattle were domesticated in Southwest Asia, making an origin there unlikely for African cattle.[8] Although conclusive fossil evidence for differentiation of domesticated from wild African cattle is lacking, early stages of animal domestication can be difficult to identify in the fossil record, and it is generally accepted that domesticated cattle were present in the central Sahara by 5000 BC.[9] By this time, African cattle were also being herded for dairy products as well as meat.[10]

Sheep and goats from Southwest Asia appeared at a number of locations throughout Egypt after 5800 BC, and wheat, barley and legumes reached the Nile Valley no later than 5000 BC. The incoming Levantine farmers probably mixed with local foragers and fishers; these people had had no need for agriculture, but now agriculture had come to them.[4,1,11] The Nile Valley is ideal for agriculture: the annual floods reach southern Egypt from mid-August and the Nile Delta six weeks later. The waters dampen the soil for about two months in autumn and winter, allowing crops to be grown without irrigation.[1]

Early Neolithic sites in the Lower Nile region include Merimde Beni Salama, on the western edge of the Nile Delta, which dates from 4880 BC.[4] The 18 ha (44.5 acres) site comprised small mud-walled dwellings, set out along narrow lanes. It remained occupied for almost 1,000 years, although it was abandoned for a while. A number of broadly-contemporary Neolithic sites have been identified in the Fayum Depression, west of the Lower Nile. These sites were not occupied for as long, but numerous storage pits for grain have been found, often lined with matting.[4,9] Sheep and goats were the predominant domestic animals in the Fayum; cattle were less common. Remains of pigs have also been found at some sites, though it is unclear whether these were domesticated or wild. Despite the presence of livestock, fish predominated in the animal assemblages at the sites of Kom K and Kom W; this reflected the local availability of fish from the nearby Lake Qarun.[12]

Meanwhile, the desiccation of the Sahara Desert continued, and by 4700 BC the Egyptian Sahara was as hyper-arid as today.[4] Only the Nile Valley and some oases such as the Fayum Depression remained capable of sustaining a human presence. This forced the abandonment of Nabta Playa and other Saharan settlements, possibly leading to a refugee movement into the Nile Valley. There, the Saharan pastoralists encountered the farmers now firmly established in the region. In this long, narrow strip of productive farmland, surrounded on both sides by desert, a fusion of African and Levantine traditions would eventually give rise to the great civilisation of Ancient Egypt. South of Egypt, the Southwest Asian cereals hit a barrier as they encountered the monsoonal summer-rainfall climate of Sudan, in which they could not flourish. They did eventually reach the climatically more suitable Ethiopian highlands, but not until after 1000 BC.[1]

The origins of agriculture in sub-Saharan Africa

To the south of the Sahara Desert lie three vegetation zones of progressively increasing annual rainfall. The first of these, known as the Sahel, comprises semi-desert scrub and seasonal grasslands, with an annual rainfall of 100 to 400 mm. This gives way to grassland savannah, with an annual rainfall of 400 to 1,000 mm; and then to mixed savannah-woodland, where annual rainfall exceeds 1,000 mm. Although strictly speaking it applies to only the first of these three zones, the term Sahel is often used to describe the entire region lying between the Sahara Desert, the tropical rainforests of West Africa, and the region around Lake Victoria.[2]

No major crops were ever domesticated south of the Equator, but a number were domesticated in the Sahel. The most important were pearl millet and sorghum in the dry grassland and savannah zones, and African rice and Guinea yam on the fringes of the tropical rainforest in West Africa. Other crops include oil palm, cowpea and groundnut in West Africa, and finger millet, tef (a cereal used for making flat bread) and ensete (a member of the banana family that provides an edible pulp from the base of its leaves) in Ethiopia. In addition, Southeast Asian crops such as banana, taro and greater yams reached sub-Saharan Africa by sea. Some of these might have arrived with the Austronesian colonists who settled Madagascar around AD 500,[1] but the discovery of banana phytoliths dated to 500 BC in Cameroon suggests that Southeast Asian crops were reaching Africa from a much earlier date.[13]

It seems likely that food production reached the Sahel zone around 3000 BC when the increasing desiccation of the Sahara forced the Saharan pastoralists to move southwards.[14,15] Domesticated pearl millet dating to around 1800 BC is known from the sites of Dhar Tichitt in southern Mauretania and Birimi in northern Ghana,[16,17] but domesticated sorghum and African rice did not appear until late in the first millennium BC.[9]

Pastoralism reached the Lake Turkana in Northern Kenya around 2500 BC, but it did not spread further south into the Great Rift Valley for over another millennium. It is likely that this delay was due to tsetse-borne trypanosome diseases affecting livestock. Tsetse flies thrive in shady brush environments, which are avoided by contemporary African herders.[18]

By 2000 BC, populations associated with the Kintampo culture of Ivory Coast and Ghana had established a mixed farming economy. They herded sheep, goats, and possibly cattle; they grew domesticated pearl millet and possibly cowpeas, and they also made use of oil palm nuts and canarium nuts. The Kintampo culture is named for a site in Ghana, and is associated with villages of wattle-and-daub houses, pottery, ceramic human and animal figurines and ground stone tools. Kintampo-style pottery has been found across a large area, suggesting the existence of widespread exchange networks.[1,9]

By 1500 BC, though agriculture was now widespread in the savannah zone of the Sahel, the population of the whole of the southern half of Africa were still living as hunter-gatherers. This situation was about to be transformed by one of the most dramatic agricultural expansions in world prehistory.[1]

Ironworking and the Bantu expansion

Similarities between languages spoken in widely separated regions of sub-equatorial Africa were first noticed by early Portuguese navigators, who commented that languages spoken on the East African coast could be understood by anybody familiar with Angolan speech. The strong similarities between many local African languages was recognised by South African colonists in the early nineteenth century, and recognised as a language family by the German linguist Wilhelm Bleek in the 1860s. Bleek coined the term 'Bantu' from the plural of a word meaning 'people' or 'humans' in many Bantu languages, and linguists subsequently recognised Bantu as a subgroup of the Niger-Congo linguistic family. In terms of numbers of languages, Niger-Congo is the largest in the world, with 1,436 reported languages and 300 million speakers.[19] Bantu is just one of the 177 subgroups that make up the Niger-Congo family, but it is one of the largest with around 500 languages.[20]

Like Indo-European, it is generally assumed that the Bantu family arose from a single language, known as Proto-Bantu. Other languages, closely related to Bantu, are found in the Grasslands of western Cameroon that lie to the north of the tropical rainforests, and linguists believe that this is the location of the Proto-Bantu homeland.[21,22] Bantu is traditionally divided into West and East Bantu branches, and a study using a statistical technique known as maximum parsimony analysis has found that this division appeared fairly early on. It was also found that maximum linguistic diversity occurs in West Africa, supporting this region as the Proto-Bantu homeland. However, it was suggested that only East Bantu is a genuine subfamily. The East Bantu languages all descend from a single ancestral West Bantu language, whereas the West Bantu languages apparently do not all share a common ancestor. The division between East and West Bantu languages, while a convenient approximation, is not the whole picture.[23]

Proto-Bantu has words for pottery and the cultivation of root crops in fields, suggesting that these things were present when the expansion began. The archaeological record suggests that root crop agriculture and pottery appeared in the western Cameroon Grasslands around 3000 BC, suggesting that the Bantu expansion began after then.[22] Unfortunately, there still large gaps in the genetic picture for populations in East, Central and South Africa, making it difficult for firm conclusions to be drawn about the demographic processes involved.[24,25] However, the Y-chromosomal haplogroup E1b1a (M2) and its subgroup E1b1a7 (M191) appear to be associated with the Bantu expansion, and occur at high frequency among Bantu-speaking populations.[26,27,28,29] Estimates for the ages of these haplogroups suggest that the expansion began somewhere between 3000 and 1000 BC.[30,31,32]

Migrating Bantu farmers proceeded initially in two directions from their homeland. Some groups began to spread eastwards along the northern fringes of the equatorial rainforests. In the meantime, others moved southwards into the West African rainforest, eventually reaching the savannahs of Angola around 500 BC.[1,9] Eastern groups reached the African Great Lakes between 1000 and 500 BC,[1] and came into contact with farmers and herders who might have been speakers of Central Sudanic and Cushitic languages.[33] Through a relatively prolonged period of contact with them, the East Bantu acquired domesticated cattle and sheep, and also added sorghum, pearl millet and finger millet to a crop roster hitherto dominated by tubers. During this period, too, they acquired knowledge of ironworking techniques. It is surely no coincidence that this development was followed by one of the most rapid agricultural expansions on record.[34,1]

The origins of iron metallurgy in Africa are uncertain. It is disputed as to whether it diffused from Southwest Asia or Mediterranean Europe, or whether it was a purely indigenous African development. In Africa, bronze metallurgy was largely confined to Egypt. Most of the continent bypassed the Bronze Age, and progressed from stone tools directly to ironworking. On the face of it, this may not sound unduly surprising, as iron ore is far more abundant than copper and tin. The problem is that iron smelting is a far more complex process than producing bronze. In Africa, iron was smelted by the bloomer process, in which ore is heated with charcoal in a clay furnace. Air enters the furnace through openings near the bottom, either by natural updraft or with the aid of bellows. Incomplete combustion of the charcoal produces carbon monoxide, and in turn this reduces the iron ore to native iron. The process requires high temperatures of 1,150 to 1,200 degrees Celsius. In addition, the amount of air admitted is critical to ensure the correct balance between burning the charcoal fuel to reach the required temperatures, and reducing the iron ore. Too much oxygen will halt or reverse the reduction of the ore. The conventional view is that only people with experience of copper smelting would be able to master the more complex technologies associated with ironworking. It is argued, therefore, that they must have diffused to sub-Saharan Africa via the Nile or the North African coast; Meroe on the Middle Nile in Sudan has often been suggested as a staging point for the hypothetical spread of ironworking into sub-Saharan Africa.[9,35]

Against this, however, there is tentative evidence for the independent development of iron smelting at a number of locations in sub-Saharan Africa. Furnace remains excavated at Do Dimi in Niger, Taruga in Nigeria and Otumbi in Gabon all date to first millennium BC, and seem to be as early as the evidence for ironworking at Meroe. Sites in Rwanda, Burundi and the Central African Republic have produced dates said to push the introduction of ironworking technology back as far as 2000 BC, though these have been questioned. While it seems likely that iron smelting was developed indigenously in several places in sub-Saharan Africa, conclusive evidence is lacking.[9,35]

Regardless of how the East Bantu acquired the technology, it was a potent addition to their agricultural package. Iron tools are superior to those of stone, bone and wood, and would have greatly facilitated forest clearance for agriculture. The impact could have been immediate: ironworking and agriculture might have been responsible for a significant reduction in forest vegetation in the Lake Victoria region around 500 BC, as implied by pollen evidence from the lake sediments.[9]

It is not surprising that among ethnographically-recorded Bantu people, ironworking is strongly associated with ritual. The ability to transform naturally-occurring iron ore into tools and other artefacts through the use of fire confers high status on master ironworkers, comparable to that of chiefs or shamans. Furnaces were often given female anthropomorphic attributes, and their siting was driven as much by ritual and symbolic considerations as by practicality. While we cannot be certain that this was the case in prehistoric times, it is highly likely that it was.[36]

Although there is no universal agreement on the number of migrating 'streams' involved, or their sources, the overall picture is reasonably clear. The East Bantu farmers spread rapidly southwards, reaching Natal by AD 500.[1] Pottery from sites throughout this enormous region shows sufficient similarity to be grouped together as the Chifumbaze complex.[37] On the basis of stylistic variation, a number of subcultures have been identified within the Chifumbaze. The earliest of these is the Urewe group, dating from 500 BC to the beginning of the first century AD. Urewe pottery has been found in the region of Lake Victoria: in Uganda, southwestern Kenya, Rwanda, Burundi and adjacent parts of the Democratic Republic of the Congo, and in northwestern Tanzania.[9]

 Groupings further south demonstrate the speed of the expansion. Kwale ware dates to around the first century AD and is named for a site in the coastal region of southeastern Kenya. Broadly contemporary with the Kwale are the Nkope of Malawi and Zambia, and the Matola of Mozambique. Other groupings include the Gokomere/Ziwa of Zimbabwe and the Kalundu and Dambwa of Zambia. By AD 500, Chifumbaze ceramics had reached Natal, having covered the distance of 3,500 km (2,175 miles) from Lake Victoria in in just a few centuries. In the meantime, the East and West Bantu had come into contact on the savannahs to the south of the equatorial rainforests, although it remains uncertain where this occurred. East Bantu groups might have skirted the flanks of the equatorial rainforest to the southern savannah before moving westwards, and eventually coming into contact with their western cousins. Alternatively, movement might have been the other way, with an eastern spread of West Bantu from the lower Congo basin and Angola after AD 100. On this view, the westerners encountered East Bantu migrants as the latter spread down through East Africa from Tanzania.[34,1,9]

By AD 500, the dispersal of agricultural societies through East Africa had reached limits of the summer-rainfall belt of Natal. Further south, the climate is Mediterranean rather than monsoonal, and the Bantu summer-rainfall crops could spread no further. By 1652, when the Dutch settlers arrived, they found the southernmost limits of the expansion represented by the Xhosa, on the northern side of the Great Fish River in Eastern Cape Province.[38,1]

Even in southwest Africa, where agriculture failed to take hold, the indigenous Khoisan hunter-gatherers did not remain unaffected. They acquired sheep and pottery as early as 150 BC, although it is uncertain as to whether the two arrived simultaneously as a 'package'. The pottery is unrelated to the Chifumbaze complex, and in any case reached South Africa several centuries ahead of the Bantu expansion. These developments are thought to have come about through contact with herders in Angola or southern Zambia, although archaeological evidence is lacking. The Khoisan did not adopt cultivation or ironworking, and livestock herding was basically an add-on to their hunter-gather economy.[39,40]

It should be appreciated that the development of agriculture in sub-Saharan Africa was separate to that of Egypt and the Levant. Even in the warmer, wetter conditions of the Early Holocene, the Sahara Desert was an immense barrier through which farming groups and agricultural packages could spread only with difficulty. This conclusion is underlined by the linguistic evidence. Afroasiatic languages are found in the north, and Niger-Congo languages in the south. These two groups are separated along the southern fringes of the Sahara by the Nilo-Saharan languages that might have been spoken by early indigenous herders.[1] The association of the Niger-Congo languages with the Bantu expansion provides further support for the farming/language dispersal hypothesis as outlined in the previous chapter. The rapidity of the Bantu expansion demonstrates once again the economic and demographic strength of farming and herding communities in comparison to those of hunter-gatherers.

22: Of rice and men

An even bigger bang

The agricultural expansion that arose in China was even more far-reaching, geographically-speaking, than that of Southwest Asia. From the valleys of the Yellow and Yangtze Rivers, farming spread across East and Southeast Asia and out into the Pacific, eventually reaching places as widely separated as Easter Island, Madagascar and New Zealand. Unlike the Southwest Asian agricultural package, which spread more or less unchanged, crops were dropped and others added to the roster as farmers moved into environments very different to those from where the expansion began.

Driving the initial expansion were two grain crops: rice and millet. Today, rice is one of the world's most important staple crops. It provides a fifth of the world's caloric intake, and is the predominant staple food for almost 2.5 billion people.[1] There are 22 wild and two cultivated species of rice, and over 100,000 varieties are recognised. The cultivated species are *Oryza sativa* (Asian rice) and *Oryza glaberrima* (African rice), which originated from wild forms in two parts of the humid tropics: those of South and East Asia, and of West Africa.[2] Asian rice is grown world-wide, but African rice is grown mainly in West Africa. African rice has lower yields than its Asian counterpart, but it is hardier and faster-maturing.[3]

Asian rice was domesticated from a wild precursor, *Oryza rufipogon*, and has two principle varieties, *japonica* (short grained) and *indica* (long grained). It is uncertain as to whether or not these varieties were domesticated independently, and differing interpretations have been put upon the genetic data. One suggestion is that there were two entirely separate domestications: *japonica* in southern China and *indica* within a region south of the Himalaya mountain range, probably eastern India, Myanmar, or Thailand.[4] Alternatively, early semi-domesticated varieties of *indica* might have been hybridised with domesticated *japonica* varieties in northern India to produce the modern white-grained *indica* variety.[5,6] On the other hand, it has also been claimed that *japonica* and *indica* both arose from the same domestication event.[7] On this view, early domesticated rice might then have been hybridised with local wild *rufipogon* rice populations, leading eventually to the present-day *japonica* and *indica* varieties.[8] Genome variation mapping supports the latter possibility and suggests that the domestication of rice occurred in the middle reaches of the Zhu Jiang (Pearl) River, in Guanchi Province.[9] This lies well to the south of the Lower Yantze region, where the earliest archaeological evidence for domesticated rice has been found.[10]

Rice is a marsh plant, relying on nutrient from water as much as soil, so harvests can be obtained even on poor, sandy soils provided there is sufficient rainfall.[11] In Asia, rice is typically grown 'wet' in lowland fields that are either irrigated or reliant on monsoon rains. In many areas, irrigated hill-slope terraces are used to extend 'wet' cultivation high into the mountains. Rice is also grown 'dry' in upland swidden ('slash-and-burn') systems, using temporary forest clearings.[2,12]

The millets are a group of unrelated cereals that were prominent in a number of early agricultural systems in Eurasia and Africa. The most widely grown type today is pearl millet (*Pennisetum glaucum*), a species that is tolerant of drought and poor soil conditions. Pearl millet production is concentrated in the developing world, where it remains an important staple crop. However, it is now used increasingly for other purposes such as animal fodder, alcohol production, and for brewing beer.[13]

The Neolithic Revolution

Two types of millet were associated with the Chinese Neolithic: broomcorn (or common) millet (*Panicum miliaceum*), and foxtail millet (*Setaria italica*).

Pre-Neolithic roots

As was the case in in Southwest Asia, the transition to agriculture in China was a gradual process, stretching over many millennia and with roots going back to latter stages of the Pleistocene. Between 10,500 and 7000 BC, hunter-gatherers established sedentary villages in four distinct but interconnected regions: northeastern China, the North China Plain, and the Middle and Lower Yangtze River regions. However, variations in the annual monsoon cycle during the Younger Dryas and Early Holocene had a greater climatic impact in the north of China than in the south. This led to a north/south technological divide that would persist into the Neolithic. In the north, tools reflected specialised adaptations to the more extreme and unstable climate, and included microliths, polished bone tools, grinding stones, and stone axes and adzes. In the warmer, wetter and more stable climate of the south, tool technology was far more conservative.[14]

It was, however, in the south that pottery – possibly the first anywhere in the world – appeared. Potsherds found at Yuchanyan Cave in Hunan Province have been dated to between 16,300 and 13,430 BC.[15] Pottery subsequently spread to northern China, Japan and Russian East Asia, probably via social networks rather than by repeated re-invention.[14] This early emergence of pottery further refutes V. Gordon Childe's view that it was inextricably linked with the emergence of agriculture, but unlike in Southwest Asia, it preceded agriculture. The fairly basic and undecorated ceramic vessels were likely intended for the storage and cooking of plant foods,[12] although Brian Hayden[16] has suggested that early pottery was a 'prestige technology' intended to impress guests at 'competitive feasts' (see Chapter 17). Conversely, Canadian archaeologist Richard Pearson[17] believes that there is little evidence for social differentiation in pre-Neolithic China. He suggests that the plain, undecorated pottery was purely utilitarian, and would not have been used in a competitive context.

Nanzhuangtou (Hebei Province), on the western edge of the North China Plain, shows significant transitional steps toward the Neolithic. Occupation began around 10,500 BC during the Younger Dryas, and continued into the Holocene. Finds include pottery, cobble-lined pit hearths, seed-processing equipment including querns and rollers, and evidence of woodworking. Some of the pottery was smoke-blackened, suggesting that it had been used as cookware. Areas were set aside for butchering and cooking game, and two natural ditches were filled with midden deposits; these features would later be seen at Neolithic sites. Similar 'transitional' features have been found at the sites of Zhuannian and Donghulin, both located near Beijing.[14]

The Early Neolithic in China

Agriculture arose in two regions in China: in the Middle and Lower Yellow River valleys to the north, where millet was cultivated; and in the Middle and Lower Yangtze River valleys to the south, where rice was cultivated. The Yellow and Yangtze rivers are areas with a strong, reliable monsoon. The rainfall is higher than in Southwest Asia, though the temperatures are similar, with hot summers and cool to cold winters. In the Yellow River valley are terraces of fertile loess (wind-blown silt) that are ideal for rain-fed millet cultivation, and floodplain lakes in the Yangtze basin are ideal for the cultivation of rice.[18] Given the rather different techniques involved, an independent origin has been suggested for millet and rice agriculture.[11] However, as we shall see presently, it is more likely that the two developments were linked, and that northern and southern China formed a single interaction sphere.[14] A third centre of agricultural development might have been located in the southernmost part of China, along the Zhu Jiang (Pearl) River. Major crops there included roots and tubers, including taro.[19] Given genetic evidence for the possible domestication of rice in Guanchi Province,[9] it could well be that the importance of this third centre has been underestimated.

The earliest domesticated animals in East Asia were chickens and pigs. Genetic studies suggest that chickens were originally domesticated from the Red Jungle fowl in Southeast Asia, though for the next thousand years they continued to be cross-bred with the wild ancestor. Subsequently, they were taken north and were established in China by 6000 BC.[20,21] Chinese pigs were domesticated independently of Southwest Asian pigs around 7000 BC, and were widespread in both northern and southern China by no later than 6000 BC.[22] Domesticated sheep, goats and cattle followed rather later: sheep and goats did not appear until after 4000 BC,[23] and cattle until around 2000 BC.[24] Domesticated animals were at first no more than a supplementary source of meat and it was not until around 4000 BC that domesticated pigs started to become the dominant source of meat in the Yellow Valley. In the Yangtze Valley, fish and wild animals, particularly deer, remained more important than domesticated animals until around 2000 BC. It is likely that the relative abundance of diverse wild herbivores and fish in southern China reduced the incentive for animal husbandry.[23]

Early in the Neolithic, a number of cultural clusters emerged in China. Along the reaches of the Middle and Lower Yellow River were located the related cultures of the Peiligang cluster: the Peiligang itself (Henan Province), the Cishan (Hebei Province), the Houli (Shandong Province), and the Dadiwan (Gansu and Shaanxi Provinces). The first of these to appear was the Cishan, which might have emerged as early as 8300 BC. It was followed by the Peiligang and Houli between 6200 and 6000 BC; the Dadiwan was a slightly later expansion of the Peiligang to the westward reaches of the Wei River around 5900 BC. The Peiligang was linked by the Huai River system to two Yangtze cultures: the Pengtoushan (Hunan Province) of the Middle Yangtze and the Shangshan (Zhejiang Province) of the Lower Yangtze, both emerging around 8000 BC. Finally, well to the north, was the Xinglongwa of the Xiliaohe River in Inner Mongolia, which emerged around 6300 BC.[14]

These cultures were characterised by ditch-enclosed settlements with distinct areas for houses, storage facilities and cemeteries. The settlements varied considerably in size: the smallest were under 1 ha (2.5 acres), but others ranged from 2 to 10 ha (5 to 25 acres). The much-studied Peiligang site of Jiahu (Henan Province) was 5.5 ha (14 acres), but the largest Peiligang site, Tanghu (Henan Province), might have been as much as 20 ha (50 acres). Generally speaking, settlements in southern China were smaller than their northern counterparts. Houses were frequently arranged in rows or clusters, with as many as one or two hundred at the largest sites. The earlier houses were typically small, round, semi-subterranean, and sometimes double-roomed; later houses were rectangular. They were usually entered by steps or a narrow slope, and they contained a hearth. Within any village, houses tended to be similar in size.[14]

Cemeteries were located at the edges of settlements and sometimes contained several hundred burials, generally uniform in size. Xinglongwa burials commonly took place below the floors of houses rather than in cemeteries. Grave goods were not extensive and usually included a few pottery jars. Many sites of the Peiligang culture had two or more cemeteries that might have served separate social groups. At Jiahu, there were initially two cemeteries, but the number eventually increased to six. This suggests that some form of social distinction, possibly by clan, emerged over a period of time. The amount of grave goods in Jiahu burials varies, but there is a continuum from richest to poorest, and the richest graves are randomly distributed. Jiahu society apparently remained egalitarian. Overall, there is little evidence for social stratification at either household or individual level during the early part of the Chinese Neolithic.[14]

As noted above, the pre-Neolithic technological north/south divide persisted into the Neolithic. Peiligang sites have yielded large numbers of adzes, tongue-shaped spades, toothed sickles and large four-footed stone querns with rollers. Bone tools included elaborate barbed spears, points and needles. The wide variety of pottery vessel types included jars, bowls, tripod vessels, platters and pedestal serving stands. By contrast, Pengtoushan and Shangshan sites retained the southern China pre-Neolithic technology, featuring mainly retouched flakes and cobble tools. Only a few adzes and chisels have been found. In the northeast, the Xinglongwa retained pre-Neolithic elements, such as flake, blade and microlith tools, but added polished tools to their technological repertoire. Early examples of carved jades have been found at Xinglongwa sites, also at Cishan and, a little later, at Dadiwan. Jades did not appear at Yangtze sites until rather later.[14]

Millet: an ancient crop

It is within this context, close to the Pleistocene/Holocene boundary, that millet farming arose in northern China. Fine details, however, remain vague. Few plant remains have been recovered from the period between 8000 and 5500 BC in northern China, and there is no data pertaining to the onset of millet domestication there.[25] Another problem is that unlike most domesticated cereals, the wild ancestor of broomcorn millet is not known.[26] All broomcorn millet in the archaeological record is therefore domesticated, and the domestication process must have occurred earlier.

There has been some debate as to whether it was broomcorn or foxtail millet that was domesticated first. In the 1970s, excavations at Cishan revealed several hundred storage pits, of which 88 were found to contain badly-decomposed millet remains. The remains, now dated to between 8300 and 6700 BC, were for a long time thought to be foxtail millet, but analysis of phytoliths and molecular signatures has since identified them as broomcorn millet. Foxtail millet does not appear at Cishan until after 6700 BC, and then only in small quantities.[27,25] A pattern of foxtail millet appearing after broomcorn millet, and then in small quantities only, has also been reported from other sites.[14] It has been suggested that earlier use of broomcorn millet was due to its lower water requirements than those of any other grain crop, including foxtail millet. This would have been an advantage in the dry conditions prevailing in northern China during the Early Holocene, whereas foxtail millet does better in warmer and wetter conditions.[27]

That broomcorn millet had been domesticated by 8300 BC means, of course, that the beginnings of millet domestication lie further back in time. Just how much further remains unknown, but it must be at least 1,200 years. What is currently the earliest evidence for millet cultivation in China comes from Nanzhuangtou and Donghulin. Starch grains recovered from potsherds and grinding tools at the two sites have been identified as foxtail millet. The grains date to the period from 9500 to 7500 BC, and are predominantly domesticated. Notably, the proportion of the domesticated type increases over time from around 65 percent to 85 percent in later phases.[26] We must conclude that in all probability, both foxtail and broomcorn millet were domesticated before the onset of the Holocene, perhaps during the Younger Dryas. It is possible that early farmers cultivated both foxtail and broomcorn millet, but eventually found that the latter was the more reliable crop in the dry climate. Later, when the climate improved, they switched to foxtail.

Systematic work at the site of Xinglonggou (Heilongjiang Province) has provided archaeologists with an insight into the early stages of the transition from hunter-gathering to agriculture in northern China. Millet dating from 5650 BC has been identified as domesticated, with a very strong preponderance of broomcorn over foxtail. However, millet accounted for only five percent of the seed remains obtained from over 1,200 soil samples taken at the site. Xinglonggou also yielded a number of pig skulls and while most were wild, a few showed some domesticated characteristics. Thus it appears that while millet and pig farming was practiced at Xinglonggou, it was only a supplement to a subsistence strategy that still relied mainly on hunting and gathering.[19]

Another site that has yielded valuable data is Dadiwan (Gansu Province), which gives its name to the Dadiwan culture, and was occupied in two phases. During the first, lasting from 5900 to 5200 BC, the site was only intermittently occupied. The abundant remains of large wild animals, makeshift dwellings, and sparse archaeological assemblages suggest that it was at this point no more than a seasonal camp. Broomcorn millet farming seems to have made a fairly small contribution to the economy. After 5200 BC, there was a 700 year hiatus before the site was reoccupied around 4500 BC. At this point, a more substantial moat-enclosed village appeared, comprising 156 rectangular semi-subterranean houses arranged around a central plaza. The site also featured a separate cemetery, and occupation continued up until 2900 BC.[28,14]

Carbonised broomcorn remains are present at Dadiwan, but have provided little in the way of information about domestication or usage. Researchers therefore turned to carbon and nitrogen stable isotope analysis of animal remains found at the site. Increased levels of ^{13}C in skeletal remains would indicate a diet of millet, whereas reduced levels would indicate a diet based on the local vegetation. ^{15}N levels provide a second line of evidence. These increase the higher an animal is in the food chain, so animals that rely more on domestic sources of protein, such as table scraps and offal, will have higher ^{15}N levels than those living in the wild.[28]

From the first phase at Dadiwan, remains of three dogs (out of a total of five) were found to have high levels of both ^{13}C and ^{15}N, suggesting that they had been fed a diet of millet and meat. These dogs must have lived on the site, and were probably used for hunting. On the other hand, remains of four pigs found in the first phase displayed low ^{13}C levels, suggesting that they had been hunted.[28] As we saw in Chapter 18, genetic evidence suggests that dogs were domesticated from the Eurasian Grey Wolf in East Asia, south of the Yangtze. Dogs have been found at many Chinese Neolithic sites, some in ritual burials.[14,19]

The evidence from second phase suggests that a far more intensive farming economy was now operating, involving both broomcorn and foxtail millet. Stable isotope analysis was carried out on the remains of six humans, in addition to six dogs and 29 pigs. The humans had high levels of both ^{13}C and ^{15}N, suggesting that by now the subsistence economy depended heavily on millet and domestic animals. The same results were obtained for all the dogs and most of the pigs. However, four of the pigs had low levels of ^{13}C and ^{15}N, and several had intermediate levels. These suggested that some pigs were either wild animals that raided millet fields, or free-range animals that were only occasionally fed millet and meat. The implication is that while dogs had been fully incorporated into the domestic farming sphere, this was not yet the case for pigs.[28]

Two other cultures emerged in northern China at around this time: the Yangshao and the slightly later Dawenkou. The Yangshao dates from 5200 to 3000 BC and many thousand sites are known, especially along the major tributaries of the Yellow River. The best-known is Yangshao site is Banpo (Shaanxi Province), a large village enclosed by a moat, with a cemetery outside the settlement. Finds include large quantities of pottery, and stone tools for farming, harvesting and food preparation. Together with the remains of domesticated pigs and millet, this evidence suggests that agriculture had now fully replaced hunter-gathering in northern China. At another Yangshao site, Liuwan (Qinghai Province), over 1,500 graves have been examined; among the later burials the numbers of grave goods ranges from just a few to over 90 ceramic vessels. It may be supposed that social stratification was steadily increasing.[11,19]

The Dawenkou dominated the Lower Yellow River valley from 4300 to 2400 BC. There is evidence for increases in both population densities and social stratification. At the early Dawenkou site of Liulin (Shanxi Province) there is a five-lobed cemetery where each lobe was reserved for members of different lineal groups. Although none stands out from any of the others in terms of grave goods, men were interred with stone adzes and burins and women with spindle whorls. At the principal site of Dawenkou in Tai'an (Shandong Province), jade ornaments appeared increasingly as grave goods during the middle phase between 3500 and 2900 BC. By the late phase, there is evidence for the emergence of specialist potters and jade workers. By 2400 BC, the Dawenkou culture had developed seamlessly into the succeeding Longshan.[11]

The rise of rice

The domestication of rice was likely a later development than that of millet, although cultivation might have begun as early as 8000 BC in the Middle and Lower Yangtze Valley. As with millet, there was a lengthy period of low-level food production before a wholly-agricultural economy was established around 4500 BC. This is several centuries after the transition was completed in northern China.[19] It is notable that the Yangtze area is located right on the northern edge of the range of wild rice. For local hunter-gatherers, the food supply was more susceptible to climatic fluctuations; the need to make up potential shortfalls provided the motive to begin cultivation.[29,11] Against this, we should note the genetic evidence suggesting that rice was domesticated further south, along the Middle Zhu Jiang (Pearl) River in Guanchi Province.[9]

Seasonally-inhabited caves site such as Diaotonghuan (Jiangxi Province) were once thought to provide evidence for an early date for rice domestication. Phytolith studies were used to infer the shape of husk cells, and it was claimed that changes in these implied that both domesticated and wild rice were present during the period from 8000 to 6000 BC.[30] However, the correlation between changes in husk cell shape and domestication has since been questioned; this feature is not one of changes that have been linked to the domestication of other cereals.[31] Regardless of which, as we saw in Chapter 17, domestication is not an intentional process, nor is it a pre-requisite for the cultivation of a crop. Accordingly, early rice cultivation could have been practiced without domesticated rice.[19]

Sites with evidence for early rice usage – if not necessarily cultivation – include Bashidang (Hunan Province) and Shangshan (Zhejiang Province). The 3 ha (7.5 acres) Bashidang site dates to around 6800 BC and is one of the largest and best-preserved sites associated with the Pengtoushan culture of the Middle Yangtze. Prolific rice grains were among 67 species of plants identified at Bashidang, but it was probably only a secondary food and it remained wild. Animal remains included deer, fish, chickens and pigs; the latter possibly domesticated.[18,31,14] At the Lower Yangtze site of Shangshan, pottery tempered with rice husks has been found, suggesting that rice was at least gathered from the wild. The site dates to around 8000 BC.[19]

However, the earliest site at which rice cultivation has been definitely identified is Jiahu, occupied from 7000 to 5800 BC. Plant remains include tubers, nuts and rice,[19] but it is disputed as to whether or not the rice was domesticated. Claims that the rice grains are too small to be domesticated are based on data reported in 1999;[31] more recently-reported data, based on a larger sample size, suggests that the grains vary considerably in size and that the majority are indistinguishable in both shape and size from domesticated grains taken from later sites.[32]

Jiahu is located in the Upper Huai River region, well to the north of the Yangtze, and beyond the range of wild rice.[32,19] Thus regardless of whether the Jiahu rice was domesticated, it was certainly being cultivated. However, wild plant food appears to have been rather more important than rice at Jiahu, and while domesticated pigs were present, they were far less important than hunting and fishing. Thus it appears that rice and pork were only dietary supplements, and that the people of Jiahu, like their northern counterparts at Xinglonggou, relied predominantly on wild foods.[19]

Jiahu provides strong evidence for the view that the cultural clusters of the Yellow and Yangtze River systems were part of a single interaction sphere. Artefact finds are similar to those of the millet-using Peiligang culture, despite the use of rice rather than millet. Jiahu also shares certain pottery forms with the Middle Yangtze Pengtoushan culture, to which it is linked by the Huai River system. The shared ceramic styles include double-eared, round-bellied, high-neck, and small-mouth *hu* jugs; *ding* tripod vessels; and three-leg cooking stands. It is highly unlikely that all three forms were independently developed in both regions.[14]

The Pengtoushan and Shangshan cultural phases had ended by around 6500 to 6400 BC, and a number of later cultures document the next stage in the transition to agriculture in the Yangtze Valley. In the Middle Yangtze these include the Tangjiagang (5400 to 5200 BC) and the later Daxi (4400 to 3500 BC). In the Lower Yangtze, the Kuahuqiao (5900 to 5000 BC) was followed by the Hemudu (4900 to 4600 BC), and then the Majiabang (4300 to 4000 BC). The earliest site associated with these successor cultures is Kuahuqiao itself, located in Zhejiang Province. The site is located near a coastal swamp marsh at the mouth of the Qiantang River, and it was occupied between 5900 and 5000 BC. This diverse habitat provided easy access to deer, water buffalo, fish, waterfowl and turtles, and domesticated pigs were also present in small numbers. Preserved organic remains show that crafts such as woodwork and basketry were now highly developed. Mortise and tenon joinery were in use, and examples of woodwork include ladders, a 121 cm (4 ft.) mulberry bow, and a dugout canoe with oars. The latter provides direct evidence of the importance of water transport in the Yangtze region. Tool-making was significantly more advanced than that of the Shangshan: the majority of stone tools were now polished, including adzes, axes, chisels, arrow points, rollers and grinding stones. Ceramic technology was also more sophisticated: the number of vessel types increased over the Shangshan, and the pottery was more finely made. Iron-containing slips were used to produce red, grey, or black surfaces, and red and white patterns and abstract motifs were painted over the slip. These innovations represented not only technological improvements, but also new roles for pottery. In addition to processing, cooking, serving and storing food, it was now used for ritual purposes and for demonstrating social status. There were similar developments in the Middle Yangtze, where pottery with intricate geometric surface patterns was produced by the Tangjiagang culture and the later Daxi culture.[14]

During the period from 6000 to 4500 BC, the evidence for domesticated rice becomes stronger, though still not without controversy. At Kuahuqiao, rice grains and phytoliths have been interpreted as being in an early stage of domestication, with 41.7 percent of the spikelet bases identified as domesticated *japonica* type and the remaining 58.3 percent as wild.[33] However, it has been noted that a significant number of the spikelets were immature, implying that the rice was being harvested before it was ripe. This may suggest rice was not yet domesticated,[31] though it could simply be that the Kuahuqiao farmers were continuing to follow ancient harvesting practices, unaware that they were now no longer necessary. In any case, the small amount of rice as a percentage of all plant material found at the site suggests that cultivated rice was still only a supplementary food.[14]

The site of Tianluoshan (Zhejiang Province) is associated with the Hemudu, the Lower Yangtze culture that followed on from the Kuahuqiao. The site provides evidence for the oldest-known paddy fields – a technology that would eventually revolutionise rice agriculture. A study of rice spikelet bases dated from 4900 to 4600 BC shows that the Tianluoshan rice consisted of a high proportion of the shattering wild type. During that time, however, the percentage of non-shattering variety increased from 27 to 39 percent. Rice as a percentage of all plant remains increased from 8 to 24 percent. While rice was clearly increasing in importance, the process of domestication was still incomplete as late as 4600 BC.[10] Rice was still only part of more general subsistence activities at Tianluoshan, and hunting and gathering remained important.[34,19] Although they were still in the process of transition to full-blown agriculture, the Hemudu farmers had apparently begun to utilise paddy field farming. Among the Tianluoshan rice spikelet remains were found the seeds of a number of plants, including some known to be associated with wet rice cultivation. These include sedges, rushes and a number of annual grasses, all of which are present as weeds in present-day paddy fields.[10]

Direct archaeological evidence for paddy fields in both the Middle and Lower Yangtze emerges shortly after the Tianluoshan evidence. At the Lower Yangtze sites of Ciaoxieshan and Chuodun (Jiangsu Province), excavations have revealed small fields, connecting channels, and reservoirs dug into the soil. Dating to the Majiabang culture period (4300 to 4000 BC), the fields comprised small dugout features, with variable square or rectangular shapes, ranging in size from 1 to 15 sq. m (10 to 160 sq. ft.). These were connected by channels to deeper reservoirs in which water was retained. Water could be moved from the reservoirs into the field by bucket lifting, and surplus water could be allowed to flow into and out of fields through the interconnecting channels. There is slightly earlier evidence from the Middle Yangtze site of Chengtoushan (Hunan Province), dating to 4400 BC and associated with the Daxi culture. Here, rather larger fields have been identified. Measuring 2.7 by 20 m (9 by 65 ft.), they are delimited by long embankments.[5]

During the Daxi culture period, Middle Yangtze sites increased in size, and were now surrounded by permanently filled moats rather than ditches. These connected the settlements to an extensive network of natural and artificial waterways that in turn interlinked communities and fields.[14] Chengtoushan is one of the most important Daxi sites, and is China's earliest-known walled settlement. The 8 ha (20 acres) circular site is surrounded by a massive 6 m (19 ft. 8 in.) high wall. Initially, the site was surrounded by a 10 m (33 ft.) wide, 4 m (13 ft.) deep moat, but during subsequent rebuilding of the walls this was replaced by a larger 35 m (115 ft.) wide moat dug between 10 to 20 m (33 to 66 ft.) from the walls. The construction of the walls and moats occurred in four phases from around 4000 to 2800 BC, continuing throughout the Daxi and into the following Qujialing period. Within the original moat were found the remains of wooden agricultural tools, bamboo and reed baskets, linen cloth and paddles and rudders for boats.[35]

The considerable planning that must have gone into construction projects at Chengtoushan is also seen inside the walled enclosure, where houses were provided with kitchens, living-rooms and corridors. The degree of planning hints at the existence of some form of central authority, and the site does present evidence for social ranking. Burial position differed between elite and ordinary individuals: the elite were buried in a supine position, whereas the ordinary individuals were flexed. Some 700 burials have been excavated, the majority of which contained little or no grave goods. However, a few were accompanied by a significant number of items of the finest quality. For example, Burial M678 contained two jade pendants and almost 30 red polished funerary ceramic vessels. M678 held the remains of six individuals; a main burial with an additional flexed burial at all four corners of the central pit. A severed skull was also found beside the main burial. The neighbouring burials M679 and M681 also contained large amounts of funerary ceramics and jades.[35]

Also of note is a large pottery manufacturing facility with seven or eight kilns, including one capable of firing very large pieces. Such large-scale production suggests that some individuals at the site were spending at least a part of their time working as specialist potters.[35] As we shall see in later chapters, the presence of labour specialisation is a hallmark of increasing social complexity and status differentiation.

The development of the more productive 'wet' rice farming system marked a major turning point in the Chinese Neolithic.[14] Rice farming spread rapidly thereafter, with an expansion southwards reaching Fujian Province around 3500 BC, and Thailand from around 2300 BC.[11] Rice crossed the water to Taiwan by 2800 BC, where it eventually triggered the Austronesian dispersal.[36] It moved north into the millet heartlands of the Yellow River by 3000 BC,[14] and reached Korea around 1100 BC.[37] Finally, rice farming spread to Japan, where the Jōmon people had flourished for more than 10,000 years.

The Jōmon

For all but the last 2,500 years of the Holocene, Japan was the home of the Jōmon culture. The term refers to the characteristic cord marks with which their pottery was decorated. The first evidence for the Jōmon came to light in 1877, when the American antiquarian Edward S. Morse excavated a shell midden at the site of Ōmori, near Tokyo. Further discoveries followed when Japanese archaeologists trained by Morse began to excavate further sites, finding dwellings, pottery, and other artefacts. The sheer age of the pottery was not appreciated until the 1960s, and then caused widespread disbelief. Distinguished Japanese academics refused to accept that pottery could have been present in Japan thousands of years before it appeared in Southwest Asia and Europe.[38] Yet, as we have seen, we now know that pottery was present in China even earlier, possibly as long as ago as 16,300 BC.

The Jōmon followed a Preceramic period characterised by mobile hunter-gathering, and the use of ground stone tools – the latter usually a Neolithic hallmark.[39] The two periods are generally distinguished from one another by the first appearance of pottery, but the transition from the Preceramic to the Jōmon culture was very gradual and the 'boundary' between the two is ill-defined. The Jōmon is divided into six phases: the Incipient (10,000 to 7800 BC); Initial (8500 to 4000 BC); Early (4000 to 3500 BC); Middle (3500 to 2500 BC); Late (2500 to 1000 BC); and Final (1000 to 400 BC). These dates are only approximate, and there are regional variations that reflect the considerably-varying environmental conditions of Japan.[12,40]

During the Incipient Jōmon, life was little changed from the Preceramic period. The climate of the Japanese islands was cool and temperate, with vegetation dominated by deciduous broad-leafed forests of chestnut, walnut and hazelnut.[12] Settlements were small scale, and what dwellings there lacked firm structures. Many sites were located in caves and rock-shelters rather than in the open. Tool assemblages were dominated by hunting tools such as spearheads and tanged points, with relatively few tools for processing plant foods. There was at this stage very little pottery, as it was of limited use and practicality to people whose lifestyle was still largely nomadic.[39]

Towards the end of the Incipient Jōmon, a new lifestyle began to emerge in southern Kyushu, in which there is evidence for the growing importance of plant foods. At the site of Sojiyama (Kagoshima Prefecture) are remains of two semi-subterranean pit dwellings, with hearths and ventilation shafts. Artefacts included extensive pottery and plant food processing equipment, quite different to the assemblages at contemporary Incipient Jōmon sites in more northerly locations. The change was linked to an improving climate, the consequent growth of temperate and evergreen forest, and the gradual retreat of the deciduous forests to northeastern Japan. As the effects of the warmer, wetter climate gradually spread northwards, so did the new lifestyle. Both the size and the number of sites increased. Plant food processing implements have been found in large numbers, and for the first time there was evidence for marine fishing. Jōmon fishers caught tuna, moray, bream and mackerel, in addition to dolphin and marine turtle. A new type of pottery known as Yoriitomon came into widespread use, making its first appearance in Honshu. The term Yoriitomon refers to the use of cord-wrapped dowels to cord-mark the pottery, and the appearance of Yoriitomon pottery is taken to mark the beginning of the Initial Jōmon.[39,40]

By the middle of the Initial phases, the economic basis of the Jōmon culture was established. Features included marine fishing, the use of plant foods, hunting with dogs and bows and arrows, the common use of pottery, and large settlements of semi-subterranean pit dwellings. It is not a coincidence that the Jōmon economy was established at around the same time as agriculture emerged in China. The Jōmon demonstrates that agriculture was not the only adaptive strategy to the changing conditions of the Holocene; far from being 'primitive', the Jōmon economy was very successful. The stable, sedentary settlements and developments in material culture were very similar to those associated with Neolithic communities elsewhere.[39]

The number and size of settlements suggests that a peak of prosperity was reached in the Middle Jōmon phase in northeastern Japan,[39] where 80 percent of Jōmon sites are located.[41] By now, the Jōmon were exploiting acorns, walnuts, sweet chestnuts and horse chestnuts.[39] Jōmon cuisine included an unusual type of biscuit made from chestnut and walnut flour, animal meat and blood, bird's egg, salt and yeast.[39,11] Wood remains from Jōmon sites suggest that chestnut wood was also used as a construction material. It is likely that chestnut trees were managed; woodland management not only increased the supply of nuts, but also provided construction material.[41] The Jōmon also cultivated and probably domesticated barnyard grass and soybean,[42,41] and possibly buckwheat (a relation of rhubarb).[42,39]

Fish hooks, harpoons, fish-spears and nets were used to exploit the abundant fish in bays and inland waters, and fish weirs were constructed in small streams. Deer and wild pigs were hunted, often with the use of pit traps.[39] Despite the importance of pigs, however, age and sex distributions suggest that the populations were not managed.[41] Stable isotope evidence suggests that there were regional differences in the diet of the Jōmon. In southwestern Japan, there was more of an emphasis on plant foods; fish and other marine foods were of greater importance in the northeast.[43]

The Jōmon are conventionally described as hunter-gatherers, but are better thought of as low-level food producers.[44] Given that they might have also managed trees in order to produce construction materials, the broader term 'resource producers' may be appropriate.[41] The stability of the Jōmon way of life facilitated the development of fine crafts; the Jōmon produced lacquer ware, elaborately-decorated pottery, and cult objects such as ceramic female figurines and stone phalluses.[39]

The climatic optimum of the Early Holocene gave way to a downturn after 3000 BC, the effects of which intensified in Japan around 2400 BC. This might have led to a shift to roots and tubers during the Late and Final Jōmon periods. Such foods are high in starch and would have been attractive sources of food after the climate cooled, because of their ability to withstand cooler temperatures. During this period, there was a considerable increase in the incidence of dental caries, as might have been expected to accompany a shift to a starch-rich diet. Dental enamel hypoplasias suggest that Jōmon people were now suffering from food shortages. The effects were worse in the southwest, where there was a greater dependence on seasonally-available plant foods.[43]

Although prosperity would never return to Middle Jōmon levels, the Jōmon way of life continued for another two millennia before the spread of highly developed wet rice agriculture around 400 BC. On the grounds of geographical proximity, it is almost certain that wet rice farming reached Japan from Korea.[39] Although broomcorn and foxtail millet farming was adopted by the Chulmun culture in Korea around 3500 BC,[45] rice did not reach Korea until 1100 BC. It took time for varieties to arise that could flourish in a climate and day-length regime quite different to those of the Yangtze River valley.[37] The appearance of rice in Japan is associated with the Yayoi culture, divided by archaeologists into Initial, Early, Middle and Late phases. The Initial is seen only in southwestern Japan, beginning around 800 BC. Elsewhere, the Final Jōmon persisted until the onset of the Early Yayoi. Even then, the Jōmon way of life continued in the northernmost island of Hokkaido, where the climate was too cool for rice agriculture.[39,41]

The spread of agriculture in Japan cannot be explained in terms of a simple replacement of the Jōmon populations by immigrant Yayoi farmers. Instead, the Yayoi represents a fusion of cultures. Even though 80 percent of the Jōmon population resided in northeastern Japan, the newcomers still encountered significant Jōmon populations. This is reflected in pottery styles throughout Japan, where there is continuity between Final Jōmon and Early Yayoi. Only the Initial Yayoi pottery, originating in northern Kyushu, shows any Korean influence.[39,41] Y-chromosomal studies of present-day Japanese populations suggest that both the Jōmon and the Yayoi contributed to the current genetic landscape of Japan, though the levels of each vary regionally.[46]

Wet rice farming is very well adapted to the warm, humid climate of southwestern Japan. It was an agricultural 'killer app', productively far superior to the dry land systems that had previously given the Jōmon little incentive to adopt agriculture. Once established, however, wet rice farming rapidly brought an end to a way of life that had endured without fundamental change to its economic base for 10,000 years. It set off a chain reaction of increased production, increased population, the development of new rice fields, leading to further increased production. Presently, conflict arose over cultivable land and access to water. By 100 BC, there is evidence of frequent warfare in the form of defensive settlements encircled by moats, hilltop forts, and the mass production of large arrowheads intended for fighting rather than hunting. Grave goods and the establishment of separate burial areas provide evidence for the emergence of distinct social classes, followed soon after by the establishment of powerful ruling elites. By the late third century AD, coalitions of powerful clans had achieved the political unification of Japan; a dramatic example of enormous social change brought about in little over a millennium by rice agriculture.[39]

Rice and language

As a leading proponent of the farming/language distribution hypothesis, Peter Bellwood[18] believes that the linguistic impact of the rice farming expansion was second only to that of the Proto-Indo-Europeans. Within the expansion zone, three language families appear to represent primary agricultural dispersals into regions previously occupied by hunter-gatherers: Sino-Tibetan, Austroasiatic and Austronesian. Today, Sino-Tibetan languages are spoken in much of China, Burma, Bhutan, and in parts of Nepal and northeastern India. There are many views on its origin, but Bellwood sees a connection with the Yellow River Neolithic. The spread of Han Chinese populations occurred within the past 2,500 years, following the Eastern Zhou and Qin conquests of what is now China south of the Yangtze. This expansion has erased the earlier linguistic landscape in what is a classic case of elite dominance. In pre-Han times however, Sino-Tibetan might have been confined to the region north of the Austroasiatic linguistic zone.

Austroasiatic has two main branches, Mon-Khmer (Khmer, Vietnamese and Mon) and Munda (spoken in northwestern India and Bangladesh). It is the most widespread family in Mainland Southeast Asia, but its distribution is very fragmented. This suggests it represents the earliest major language dispersal in Mainland Southeast Asia, but was overlain by later expansions involving speakers of Sino-Tibetan and Austronesian languages. Reconstructed Proto-Austroasiatic contains terms for rice cultivation, suggesting that it was once spoken widely in southern China, with a homeland as far north as the Yangtze. It seems highly plausible that Austroasiatic was spread southwards by early rice farmers. Other possibilities are that the homeland lay further south, either in southern China or the north of Mainland Southeast Asia.

However, it is the Austronesian language family that is the most geographically widespread in the world. Austronesian is widely believed to have originated in Taiwan, but Bellwood suggests that the ultimate homeland was on the southern coast of the Chinese mainland, where it was later erased by the spread of Sino-Tibetan. Elsewhere, however, it continued to spread. In addition to Taiwan, Austronesian languages are spoken in Madagascar, parts of southern Vietnam, Malaysia, the Philippines, all of Indonesia except the Papuan regions of New Guinea, and right across the Pacific to Easter Island. They thus span 210 degrees of longitude, or more than half way around the world. Although rice dropped out of the picture as the Austronesians moved out into the Pacific, 'Out of Taiwan' can be seen as continuation of the expansion that began in the Middle and Lower Yangtze over four millennia earlier. It is to the Austronesian expansion that we now turn.

23: Out of Taiwan

A maritime expansion

In terms of cause and demographics, the Austronesian expansion was little different from other early farming dispersals, although it was unique in its maritime nature.[1] As noted in the last chapter, it was more a continuation of the expansion that began in China rather than a primary development. However, for the most part it utilised domesticated crops unknown to the first Chinese farmers, and in geographical scope it dwarfed anything that had come before. Aside from the equatorial rainforests of Borneo and in southern New Zealand (where it was too cold), the Austronesian economy was based on food production. However, the intensity probably varied and many Austronesians were probably better classified as low-level food producers.[2]

According to the Out of Taiwan model, a farming expansion from Taiwan eventually encompassed Island Southeast Asia, Madagascar, and the vast region known as Oceania.[2] The latter is defined as the Pacific islands from New Guinea eastwards, which in turn is divided into three regions: Melanesia, Micronesia and Polynesia. Melanesia comprises the archipelago to the north and northeast of Australia, from New Guinea to Fiji. To the north of this is Micronesia, a region containing Palau, the Mariana Islands, the Caroline Islands, the Marshall Islands and Kiribati. To the east of Melanesia and Micronesia lies Polynesia, a triangular region bounded by Hawaii, Easter Island and New Zealand. In addition, the term Near Oceania is often used for islands lying as far to the east as the Solomon Islands, with Remote Oceania referring to those lying beyond.

As with other secondary agricultural dispersals, the Austronesian expansion did not take place into a vacuum. It is believed that Austronesian speakers intermarried with indigenous Papuan speakers throughout Island Southeast Asia, before dispersing into Remote Oceania.[3] However, human populations had spread through the region to as far to the east as the Solomon Islands by 40,000 years ago, if not earlier.[4] Anthropologists have long been aware that there are two distinct native peoples in Oceania, historically referred to as Polynesians (including Micronesians) and Melanesians, though the terms Austronesian and Papuan are now often used instead. The Papuans are dark-skinned whereas the Austronesians are lighter-skinned, and by the early twentieth century, linguists had categorised the languages spoken as falling into two divisions, now known as Austronesian and Papuan. Papuan speakers are confined largely to New Guinea and the surrounding islands, though some are also found in parts of eastern Indonesia and in the Solomon Islands. These observations led to the view that two peoples had arrived at different times, in two separate migrations.[5,6]

In fact, it is now clear that the real picture must be more complex than 'two peoples, two periods'. Polynesians, Filipinos, Malays, Island Melanesians and Luzon Negritos do not share a recent common origin;[4] and the correlation between ethnicity and language breaks down in some coastal areas of New Guinea and throughout Melanesia, where Austronesian rather than Papuan languages are spoken.[5] While genetic studies confirm the existence of a pre-Neolithic component to the ancestry of the present-day populations of Island Southeast Asia,[7,8] there is no firm correlation between linguistic and genetic relationships. It is likely that this reflects Papuan speakers marrying into Austronesian groups, or vice versa. It is also possible that groups who now speak Austronesian languages once spoke Papuan languages, or vice versa.[6]

The settlement of Taiwan

Once known as Formosa ('beautiful island'), Taiwan is located 180 km (112 miles) off the southeastern coast of mainland China, from which it is separated by the Taiwan Strait. It is the world's 38th largest island, and its politics have remained a bone of contention since late 1949, when Chinese Nationalist forces retreated there following the communist takeover on the mainland. The earliest Taiwanese Neolithic culture is the Dabenkeng, named for a coastal site in the northern part of the island, although the human occupation of Taiwan goes back to the Upper Palaeolithic.[9] The Dabenkeng culture was characterised by a fairly uniform style of incised and cord-marked pottery. Similar pottery has been found in the coastal mainland provinces of Fujian and Guangdong, suggesting that the Dabenkeng originally migrated to Taiwan from mainland China. Other characteristic elements of Dabenkeng material culture included barkcloth beaters, projectile points, basalt stone adzes, baked clay spindle whorls, tanged shell reaping knives, and shell bracelets. Nephrite jade from eastern Taiwan and slate were also used for making adzes and knives. Dabenkeng sites dating from 3500 to 2500 BC occur all around coastal Taiwan, and in the Penghu Islands in the Taiwan Strait. The earliest evidence for agriculture in Taiwan comes from the site of Nanguanli, near Tainan, where rice and foxtail millet remains have been recovered from waterlogged deposits dating to around 2800 BC.[4,2]

Following the establishment of the Dabenkeng culture, there is no evidence of any island-wide population replacement in Taiwan until major Chinese settlement began in the seventeenth century AD, and the more-or-less continuous history of cultural development suggests that Taiwan was occupied by Austronesian speakers up until that time.[1] Reconstruction of the Proto-Austronesian language suggests that the early Austronesians had an extensive terminology for rice and rice cultivation, together with words for foxtail millet and sugarcane. The only root crop attested in the reconstructed Proto-Austronesian lexicon is taro, but it was regarded as a 'famine food' rather than a staple. Domesticated animals included pigs, chickens and dogs.[10] Though not attested in Proto-Austronesian, it is likely that the settlers also cultivated yams.[4] Proto-Austronesian also contains terms for fishing with hooks, bait, and traps, and for weaving with looms. There are terms pertaining to boats, such as sails and paddles, but it is not known if the outrigger canoe, a hallmark of later Polynesian culture, had yet been invented.[10]

Within eastern Taiwan, there is a marked increase in the number of archaeological sites after 2500 BC. A Middle Neolithic tradition of red slipped and cord-marked pottery emerged out of the earlier Dabenkeng tradition; by 2200 BC this had given way to a tradition of red-slipped plain ware pottery.[2] Meanwhile, the Proto-Austronesian language of the original settlers broke up into ten subgroups, nine of which remained confined to Taiwan. The tenth, known as Malayo-Polynesian, was carried further afield by the first migrants to the northern Philippines.[11,10] That this did not happen until at least a millennium after the initial colonisation of Taiwan suggests the earliest settlers lacked the nautical technology to make the 350 km (215 miles) sea crossing.[10] Proto-Malayo-Polynesian contains words for fishnets, floats, and spears, and for outrigger canoes, implying advances in fishing and sailing technologies.[12] The Austronesian expansion was about to get underway in earnest.

Spread through Island Southeast Asia

Between 2200 and 2000 BC, the first settlers from Taiwan reached the northern Philippines. With them went the associated material culture, in particular the red-slipped plain ware pottery. After 2000 BC, pottery with an incised and stamped decorative style appeared alongside the plain ware. While the plain ware is unambiguously associated with Taiwan, the origin of the decorated style is unknown;

possibly the tradition was introduced from the Chinese mainland. By around 1500 BC, combinations of red-slipped plain and decorated pottery had spread through much of Island Southeast Asia. The increasingly far-flung communities kept in touch: nephrite jade continued to be exported from Taiwan and obsidian from New Britain in the Bismarck Archipelago was found at the site of Bukit Tengkorak in Sabah, Malaysian Borneo, some 3,500 km (2,175 miles) away.[2] The pre-existence of Austroasiatic farming communities in Mainland Southeast Asia limited the Austronesian impact there, though they did settle the coastal areas of Peninsular Malaysia after 500 BC. The final westwards extension of the Austronesian world occurred around AD 500, when settlers from Borneo crossed the Indian Ocean to Madagascar.[4]

As the settlers moved south from Taiwan, new crops were added to their agricultural roster, probably in the more tropical locations of the Philippines and Indonesia. The additions included taro, breadfruit, coconut, sago and bananas.[4] Notably, other than bananas, none of these crops will grow well in Taiwan. Words exist for them in Proto-Malayo-Polynesian, but not in Proto-Austronesian.[10] As populations settled islands east of the Philippines and Borneo, rice gradually fell out of use[1] and disappeared from the vocabulary.[12] Rainfall is fairly predictable in Southeast Asia, but it is less dependable moving eastwards into the Pacific, making rice farming problematic. Another problem is that rice is very sensitive to the variations in the length of day throughout the year; near the Equator the annual day-length cycle differs considerably from that in regions where rice grows wild. Farmers began to cultivate tree crops and perennials such as yams and taro, all of which are more drought-resistant than annual cereals.[13,14] In fact, as we shall now see, such crops had been cultivated in New Guinea for thousands of years before the arrival of the Austronesians.

Independent developments in New Guinea – and Australia

Humans have lived in the highlands of New Guinea for nearly 50,000 years, with the only pause in occupation coming during the Last Glacial Maximum. With an area more than three times that of Great Britain, New Guinea is the second largest island in the world. Unlike the discontinuous highland areas of Borneo and Java, those of New Guinea form a continuous spine almost 2,000 km (1,250 miles) long. The broad, fertile highlands, with their large valleys, lie mostly between 1,300 and 2,300 m (4,250 and 7,550 ft.) above sea level, below the frost level at 2,600 m (8,500 ft.). The highlands thus comprise a large region of equable, non-tropical climate, environmentally very different from the equatorial lowlands of Island Southeast Asia and the western Pacific.[15] The earliest settlers based their subsistence around yams and pandanus nuts, all of which remain important staples to this day. Stone tools found at early sites might have been used to clear forest patches in order to promote the growth of useful plants.[16] It is within this setting that an indigenous transition to agriculture occurred, as early as any in the world.

The most important evidence comes from the site of Kuk Swamp in the Upper Wahgi Valley. The site is located on a wetland margin at an altitude of 1,560 m (5,120 ft.) above sea level, and archaeologists have identified six separate phases of activity. The earliest human activity occurred around 8200 BC, when there is evidence for fire-starting and land clearance. Pits, stake-holes, and narrow drainage channels have been interpreted as evidence for shifting cultivation on wetland margins. Stone tools have yielded starch grains of yam (*Dioscorea* sp.) and of *Colocasia esculenta*, a taro plant that normally grows lowland regions. The presence of the latter at Kuk suggests that the plant was intentionally transplanted from the lowlands. In the second phase of development, around 5000 BC, a series of mounds were constructed to create better aerated soils along the poorly-drained wetland margins. This more intensive land use suggests an increasing reliance on agriculture. In addition to taro, phytolith evidence suggests that bananas were now being cultivated. Further refinements occurred between 2350 and 2000 BC, when an extensive network of drainage ditches came into use. These dates are well before the Austronesian expansion reached the region, ruling out any connection.[17,18] Such developments are unlikely to have been confined to Upper Wahgi Valley region and were probably widespread, if variable, across the whole of the New Guinea highlands.[19]

The New Guinea highlands are close to the altitude limits above which crops such as taro, yams and bananas will not grow.[20] Nevertheless, it is probable that agriculture began there, rather than spreading from the lowlands. There is a virtual absence of sites at an altitude of 500 to 1,300 m (1,640 to 4,265 ft.) above sea level, and very few along the coast – and none of these show any signs of agriculture. Overall, there is no hard evidence for agriculture in the lowlands prior to the arrival of the Austronesians. The edge-of-range factor associated with rice agriculture in China might have also applied in New Guinea, as people sought to mitigate fluctuations in availability that resulted from frost and drought.[15]

The absence of cereals and domestic animals from the New Guinea package meant that the potential for expansion was small in comparison to those of the Eurasian mainland. Pigs did not reach New Guinea until around 1000 BC, when they were introduced by Austronesian farmers. The New World tuber sweet potato, now a major highland food source, might not have arrived until as late as AD 1550. Another factor was the isolation of the highlands by inhospitable terrain. In consequence, farming communities remained small and scattered. However, the New Guinea highlanders were still sufficiently numerous and sedentary by 1000 BC to make problematic any incursions by Austronesian settlers, who remained restricted to the lowlands.[1,4] One consequence is that in contrast to the rest of the region, New Guinea contains some of the highest linguistic diversity in the world, with nearly one thousand mutually unintelligible languages.[21]

Farming never reached Australia from New Guinea, despite the close proximity of the two landmasses. The main problem was the extreme climatic variability of the Cape York region, and the attendant risk of crop failure. This, combined with the low expansion potential of the New Guinea package ensured that agriculture never crossed the Torres Strait.[14] Despite the conventional view that Aboriginal Australians remained hunter-gatherers, however, it is possible that agriculture did arise in the Murray Valley between Victoria and New South Wales. British archaeologist Graeme Barker[22] has noted that at the time of European contact, most hunter-gatherer groups were small and mobile, but those in the central and lower Murray Valley were larger, more complex, and more sedentary. They practiced effective horticulture of a variety of tubers and rhizomes: yields were increased by burning of vegetation, and staple plants were cultivated in fertile river alluvium. While this could be classed as low-level food production, Barker believes that some pre-contact groups might have created food production systems that could be described as agricultural. He notes that the diet of the Murray Valley people was so similar to that of New Guinea agriculturalists that their tooth pathologies are virtually identical. The fact that they left so little trace in the ethnographic record is unsurprising given the disastrous effects of European contact. Disease rapidly destroyed 90 percent of Aboriginal societies, sometimes within a year. Their staple plants either reverted to natural state, or were overwhelmed by European farming and sheep grazing.

Into Oceania

The Austronesians could not penetrate into the highlands of New Guinea, and they no longer had rice; but the Austronesian expansion had certainly not run out of steam. From around 1400 BC, boat-loads of settlers headed out into the Pacific, taking with them their pottery and their updated roster of crops. The settlement of Oceania took place in three main waves of colonising activity. The first, beginning around 1400 BC, involved two unrelated migrations: one into western Micronesia;

the other into the central Pacific as far as Samoa, and associated with the Lapita culture. The Micronesian settlers colonised the Mariana Islands and Palau; radiocarbon dates from the site of Bapot-1 in Saipan suggest an arrival between 1400 and 1200 BC, and Palau is thought to have been settled between 1300 and 1100 BC. It is thought that the Micronesian and Lapita migrations were unrelated, as there were differences in material culture and economy: the simple tool-impressed pottery of the Micronesians contrasts with the more elaborate Lapita style; and pigs did not form part of the Micronesian economy. In all probability, the Micronesian settlers came from the northern Philippines, 2,100 km (1,300 miles) away; a sea voyage of astonishing length.[23]

The Lapita dispersal, between 1400 and 800 BC, led to the settlement of the islands of central and eastern Melanesia and western Polynesia. The word 'Lapita' is a Western mispronunciation of *Xapeta'a*, the native Kanak name for the site in New Caledonia that gave its name to the culture.[24] The Lapita economy was based on pigs, chickens, dogs, the new roster of crops, and the abundant seafood available to them in their maritime environment. Proto-Oceanic – the reconstructed Malayo-Polynesian branch associated with the expansion – hints that Lapita fishing technology contained several innovations. There are words for draglines, fish weirs, and pronged spears, but these are not found in Proto-Malayo-Polynesian.[12]

Stable isotope data obtained from human remains from the Lapita cemetery at Teouma, on Efate Island, Vanuatu suggests that the earliest settlers there relied on reef fish, marine turtles and fruit bats as well as the animals that they had brought with them. These results are consistent with the view that a newly-established colony would not be able to produce enough food to support itself, and would have to rely to an extent on foraging. In addition, an analysis of the remains of domestic pigs and chickens suggested that they were reared as free range animals. Such a system of husbandry would reduce demand for the limited amount of plant food that was available.[25]

The principle hallmark of the Lapita culture was its distinctive pottery. Lapita pottery was tempered with sand or crushed shells, often red-slipped, and decorated with incised and dentate-stamped motifs of rectilinear, curvilinear, and sometimes anthropomorphic forms; the latter may reflect concerns with human ancestors. The dentate stamping may reflect the present-day Polynesian body tattooing that is carried out with a small-toothed ('dentate') bone or shell chisel. Lapita potters thus 'tattooed' their pots with complex design. It is likely that the Lapita dentate tradition evolved from earlier, less elaborate dentate styles that have been found in the Philippines, Taiwan and southern coast of mainland China.[4]

By around 1300 to 1200 BC, Early Lapita communities were established over a wide area of the Bismarck Archipelago. The dispersed communities formed a network of societies that maintained regular contact with one another, and were probably related by kinship and marriage. The clearest evidence for these long-distance interactions is the trade in obsidian from New Britain and the Admiralty Islands, and parallel changes in pottery styles over the region up until around 1000 BC. After that time, inter-island contacts seem to have dropped off markedly. In the meantime, by around 1200 to 1100 BC, Lapita people had moved beyond the Bismarck Archipelago and settled parts of Remote Oceania.[12] In just 600 years, the Lapita people spread through Melanesia to the central Pacific, reaching Vanuatu by 1000 BC, Fiji and Tonga by 900 BC, and Samoa by 700 BC.[26] It was here that the migration paused after covering some 5,500 km (3,400 miles), one of the fastest movements of a prehistoric colonising population on record.[1]

The pause probably reflected the lengthy sea voyages that were required to go further, and the limitations of the Lapita peoples' sailing technology. For example, from Samoa to the Cook Islands is 1,200 km (750 miles), and to the Society Islands is 2,000 km (1,250 miles). In addition, around 1000 BC, sea levels in the mid-Pacific were higher than those of today, and many atolls were submerged. In all probability, it was the invention of the double-hulled sailing canoe that ended the hiatus. While we only know about these vessels from post-contact times, it is likely that they came into use prior to the voyages into the archipelagos of eastern Polynesia. With them, colonists could now travel long distances, together with a full complement of crops and animals.[4] The second phase of the expansion lasted roughly from 500 BC to AD 1, during which the islands of Micronesia were settled, apart from the previously-settled western groups of Mariana and Palau.[1] The final push took settlers into the archipelagos of eastern Polynesia, and did not begin until around AD 1025. There were two phases of migration: to the Society Islands between AD 1025 and 1120; and to the remote islands and New Zealand between AD 1200 and 1290.[27] Easter Island was reached at around the same time.[28] Sweet potato has been reported from the Cook Islands and Hawaii from about AD 1200, implying that there was contact between Polynesians and native South Americans by this date.[27] Sweet potato had a major impact in the Pacific, becoming the dominant crop in highland New Guinea, leeward Hawaii, Easter Island and New Zealand,[14] while Polynesian chickens might have moved in the other direction.[29]

During the period after the first expansion, the Lapita pottery gradually became less ornate, and dentate stamping went out of fashion after 750 BC. Plain ware of increasing thickness replaced it in western Polynesia, though other styles of incised, appliqué, and carved paddle-impressed pottery continued until late prehistory in many of the Melanesian archipelagos. By 300 AD, pottery had died out altogether in Samoa and southern Melanesia, meaning the final phase of expansion was aceramic. It is not clear why pottery fell out of use. Although clay is lacking on coral islands, it is abundant on the many volcanic islands in Remote Oceania. It could be that that with a diet based on fish, meat and tubers, there was no need for pottery, as earth ovens will suffice.[4]

Linguistics and genetics supports Out of Taiwan

A number of independent studies broadly support the Out of Taiwan model. Researchers have applied Bayesian analysis to the Austronesian language group in order to construct a linguistic family tree. The results placed the Formosan languages at the base of the tree, confirming that Taiwan was the Proto-Austronesian homeland. The age of the Austronesian family was estimated by calibrating the tree with archaeological date estimates and known settlement times, and a date of approximately 5,230 years old was obtained. Rates of language diversification were then used to identify pulses and pauses in the expansion. When populations are expanding and fragmenting, languages will diversify faster than when they are static. Short branches will be seen in the family trees, because there is little time for linguistic changes to accumulate before speech communities break up. Conversely, pauses in the expansion should show up as long branches. The researchers noted pauses corresponding to the periods preceding the initial dispersal from Taiwan, and the expansion into the central Pacific; pulses were found corresponding to the two expansions themselves, and also to the expansion into Micronesia.[30]

Linguistic data has also been used to infer that Austronesian society was matrilocal, i.e. one where men move to the homes of their new wives upon marriage (see Chapter 20). Linguistic trees were combined with ethnographic data to estimate the probable ancestral type of post-marital residency at four points in Austronesian prehistory where distinct speech communities emerged: namely Proto-Austronesian, Proto-Malayo-Polynesian, Proto-Central-Eastern-Malayo-Polynesian, and Proto-Oceanic. It was found that Proto-Austronesian and Proto-Malayo-Polynesian societies were very likely to have been matrilocal, and that Central-Eastern-Malayo-Polynesian and Proto-Oceanic societies probably were, though with a lower degree of confidence.[31]

A matrilocal society has also been inferred on generic grounds. Polynesian mitochondrial data is dominated by Austronesian lineages, but Y-chromosomal data is dominated by Papuan lineages. The implication is that more indigenous men than women married into Austronesian communities: a result consistent with a matrilocal society, as more local men than women would be incorporated into expanding Austronesian groups.[32,33]

Results from autosomal DNA data suggest that a sharp transition from Austronesian to Papuan ancestry occurs over a narrow geographical region in eastern Indonesia. Austronesian ancestry predominates in Sulawesi, but drops off rapidly in the islands further east: it is 81 percent on Sumba, 66 percent on Flores, and 51 percent on Alor. In the Austronesian-speaking coastal regions of New Guinea, the Austronesian genetic component falls to 14 percent, and on Vanuatu it is just 6 percent. As with Europe, this result may be interpreted as a dilution of the original Neolithic genome through intermarriage between incoming farmers and indigenous hunter-gatherers, although the European genetic gradient is gentler. The steepness may reflect a slowing of the Austronesian expansion as it reached the geographical limits of rice agriculture. The delay while the incoming farmers switched to a tuber-based economy gave the two populations more time to interbreed before the expansion continued into Remote Oceania.[33]

Finally, the broad picture of two prehistoric migrations into the Pacific was supported by a study featuring the bacterium *Helicobacter pylori*, which is found in the stomach and can sometimes cause gastric complaints. The bacterium was carried by the first migrants from Africa, and is present in much of the world's population. It was found that the Pacific migrations were associated with two distinct strains of the bacterium, hpSahul and hspMaori. The hpSahul strain split with Asian strains of *H. pylori* 32,000 to 33,000 years ago, and is associated with the initial peopling of New Guinea and Australia. The hspMaori strain split with mainland Asian strains 5,000 years ago, and is associated with Austronesian populations. The maximum genetic diversity of hspMaori occurs in Taiwan, suggesting that this was the Austronesian homeland.[34] Like the body louse study described in Chapter 10, this study is another example of how even unwanted passengers can shed light on our prehistoric past.

24: Limited options and tilted axes

A very different trajectory

The transition to agriculture in the New World was very different to that in Eurasia. As we have seen, highly-expansive agricultural packages emerged in Southwest Asia and China fairly early on in the Holocene. From well-defined primary centres in the Fertile Crescent and the valleys of the Yellow and Yangtze Rivers, these packages eventually spread across Eurasia, North Africa and Oceania. By contrast, agricultural origins were far more diffuse in the New World.[1] The three core regions of domestication are usually taken to be the Pacific Lowlands and Andean Highlands of northern South America, Mesoamerica (a region extending from central Mexico to Costa Rica), and the Eastern Woodlands of the United States.[2]

Within these broad regions, crop origins were geographically widespread. In South America, there are probably at least three regions where food production arose independently. In Mexico, many crops were domesticated in different and environmentally-dissimilar parts of the country. Possibly some plants were domesticated when groups learned about food production through long-distance contacts, and then tried cultivating their own native plants.[3] Agriculture spread from Mexico to the Southwestern United States, but in general its spread was far less complete than in Eurasia. Around half of the land area of the New World was still occupied by hunter-gatherers at the time of European contact.[1]

The transition to agriculture also occurred rather later than in Eurasia: the earliest domesticated species in the Eastern Woodlands do not occur until around 3000 BC.[4] Domestication occurred earlier in Mexico and South America, where plants were cultivated from the Early Holocene. However, large sedentary villages are not found anywhere in the New World until after 4000 BC. Early horticulturalists lived in small communities, and combined plant cultivation with hunting and gathering.[3]

One likely factor in these differences is that there were a relatively limited number of plant and animal species that could be incorporated into an agricultural package. Few New World large mammal species are suitable for domestication, and farmers continued to obtain meat mostly from hunting. Llamas, alpacas and guinea pigs were domesticated in the Andes and Peru, and in Central America turkeys were domesticated and dogs were bred for food: but none of these animals became widespread meat staples.[1] In comparison to Eurasia, there was also a lack of cereals. Only maize became a major staple, and then not until fairly late.[5] Furthermore, north of Mexico, there were no indigenous staples comparable to maize, manioc or sweet potato.[1]

However, Jared Diamond[6,7] has suggested that this may not be the whole picture. He notes the limited number of species suitable for domestication, but has also suggested that it is easier for agriculture to spread in an east-west direction than north-south. Locations at the same latitude share similar day-length, seasonality, rainfall and temperature regimes, biomes and growing seasons; but these all vary considerably with latitude. For example southern Italy, northern Iran and Japan are all at the same latitude; and although they are thousands of miles apart, they are more similar in climate than places 1,000 miles due south.

Plants and animals are finely tuned to latitude and do not do so well when farmers attempt to spread north or south rather than east or west. A look at a map of the world will show that the major axis of Eurasia lies east-west, stretching from the Bering Strait to the Bay of Biscay. By contrast, the major axes of Africa and the Americas are aligned in a north-south direction. From the Boothia Peninsula in northern Canada to Cape Froward in Chilean Patagonia is roughly 14,000 km (8,700 miles), whereas the maximum east-west width is 4,800 km (3,000 miles), narrowing to just 65 km (40 miles) at the Isthmus of Panama. The same is true for Africa, though to a lesser extent.

Accordingly, Diamond argues, the spread of agriculture in the New World was far slower and less complete than in Eurasia. Furthermore, the tropics were a barrier through which many domesticated species could not pass. Thus the domestic turkeys of Mexico and sunflowers of the Eastern Woodlands never reached the Andes, where they would have flourished. Similarly, llamas, guinea pigs and potatoes were unable to spread north from the Andean highlands to the cool highlands of Mexico.

Crop planting in South America and Mesoamerica began at the start of the Holocene, for the most part in humid tropical forests. This period is known as the Archaic Period, a period that ended at different times in different places from around 2500 BC (the Late Archaic is often referred to as the Preceramic). Among the first crops to be domesticated were the squashes (marrows); other early crops included avocado, leren (*Calathea allouia*), bottle gourd (*Lagenaria siceraria*), arrowroot (*Maranta arundinacea*), and quinoa (*Chenopodium quinoa*). Leren and arrowroot are root crops grown for their tubers, and quinoa is a grain-like crop grown for its seeds, although it is not a true cereal. Between 7500 and 6500 BC, the roster grew to include what are now major staples: maize, beans and manioc.[8,3] Maize, beans and squashes are often referred to as the 'Three Sisters', in reference to their key role in early New World agricultural systems,[2] although they were not domesticated in the same place, or at the same time.

Squashes: an early success

Squashes were first of the 'Three Sisters' to be brought under cultivation, and they were domesticated fairly early on in the Holocene. Although wild squashes have hard rind and thin, bitter flesh, the seeds are edible and nutritious, and New World hunter-gatherers would have found it advantageous to cultivate them. The closely related bottle gourd was also cultivated, though for use as net floats or containers rather than for food. Squashes and gourds require little care as crops, and thus fitted readily into a mobile lifestyle. In the event of a group moving, seeds could simply be planted at the new campsite.[8]

Genetic studies suggest that the squashes have a complex domestication history. *Cucurbita pepo* (summer squashes, acorn squash and courgette) was domesticated twice, once in southern Mexico (*Cucurbita pepo* ssp. *pepo*) and once in the Eastern United States (*Cucurbita pepo* ssp. *ovifera*). Overall, there were six separate domestications of squashes from distinct wild ancestors. In addition to *Cucurbita pepo*, these included *Cucurbita maxima* (warty squash), *Cucurbita moschata* (butternut squash), *Cucurbita argyrosperma* (cushaw pumpkin) and *Cucurbita ecuadorensis*. With the exception of the latter, all are now widely cultivated in the New World.[9]

Currently, the earliest evidence for squash domestication comes from two terminal Pleistocene/Early Holocene sites on the Santa Elena Peninsula in southwestern Ecuador. The sites, known as OGSE-80 and M5 A4-57, are associated with the Las Vegas culture. The location offered a wide range of food sources from mangrove swamps and river estuaries, and the sites were occupied by fairly sedentary hunter-gatherers over a lengthy period from about 11,800 BC to as late as 5300 BC. Although no plant remains and only a few pollen grains were recovered at either site, phytoliths from the native Ecuadorian squash *Cucurbita ecuadorensis* were abundant. The earliest phytoliths were small, indicating that the plants were still of the wild variety, but those from after 8000 BC were larger, suggesting that a semi-domesticated form of *Cucurbita ecuadorensis* was now present, probably resulting from cultivation of the local wild variety.[10]

In Mesoamerica, the earliest evidence for domesticated squash comes from the cave site of Guilá Naquitz, in the highlands of Oaxaca, Mexico. Here, squash seeds, peduncles (stalks), and fruit rind fragments from layers dating from 8000 BC have been identified as *Cucurbita pepo*, and larger seed sizes suggest that domestication was underway by then. After 6200 BC, peduncles were displaying the alternating large and small ridges that are diagnostic of domesticated *Cucurbita pepo* ssp. *pepo*; and by 5900 BC rind fragments were orange, similar to modern domesticated varieties, rather than the white rind of a wild gourd.[11] By this time, domesticated *Cucurbita pepo* was also present at Coxcatlán Cave in the Tehuacán Valley, Puebla.[12]

Cucurbita pepo was also domesticated in the Eastern Woodlands, independently of the Mexican domestication. Genetic studies suggest that the North American form (*Cucurbita pepo* ssp. *ovifera*) was domesticated from the Ozark wild gourd (*Cucurbita pepo* ssp. *ovifera* var. *ozarkana*). The earliest evidence for domestication is at the site of Phillips Spring in Missouri, dating to 3000 BC. Around half the seeds recovered exceeded size limits for the wild variety, but rind fragments remained thin, and fruit-end peduncle scars showed no change from the wild variety. The Phillips Spring *Cucurbita pepo* squash was clearly in the early stage of domestication – unlike its Mesoamerican counterpart that was by that time fully-domesticated. Over the next 4,000 years, there was a gradual increase in seed size, fruit size, peduncle size, and rind thickness of *Cucurbita pepo* squash in the archaeological record of the Eastern Woodlands. This illustrates clear development over time from an early, large-seeded, small-fruited form to later larger-fruited forms; this trend would not have been seen had fully-domesticated plants been imported from Mesoamerica.[13]

Beans, tubers and peppers

In addition to squashes, other early New World staples included beans and a number of tubers. Of the latter, Europeans are most familiar with the potato, but curiously the 'humble spud' was something of a latecomer. Instead, early cultivators grew leren, arrowroot, manioc and the yam *Dioscorea trifida*. Many of these crops were domesticated more than once, underlining the problems of trying to view New World agriculture in terms of distinctive centres of domestication.

Beans are the name given to the large seeds of certain leguminous plants. They are rich in protein, vitamins, minerals and fibre, and are widely cultivated around the world. Globally, the most important is the common bean (*Phaseolus vulgaris*). In the wild, its distribution encompasses a large geographical area from northern Mexico to northwestern Argentina.[14] Other New World beans include the Lima bean (*Phaseolus lunates*), tepary bean (*Phaseolus acutifolius*), runner bean (*Phaseolus coccineus*), and jack bean (*Canavalia ensiformis*).

Currently, the earliest evidence we have for beans in the New World are starch grains from *Phaseolus* beans at sites in the Ñanchoc Valley of northern Peru. The grains date from as early as 7400 BC (8210 radiocarbon years BP), though the exact species of bean is uncertain, as is the domestication status.[15] Firm evidence for domesticated beans is rather later: these are the remains of domesticated Lima beans dating to around 4400 BC at Chilca Canyon, southern coastal Peru, and common beans dating to 3000 BC at Guitarrero Cave, central highland Peru. Domesticated beans do not occur in Mesoamerica until 500 BC.[16]

Genetic data suggests that the common bean was domesticated at least twice: once in the Andean region (possibly in southern or central Peru) and on one or more occasions in Mesoamerica.[17,14] The

Lima bean was domesticated twice: on the western slopes of the Andes in Ecuador or northern Peru, and in Mesoamerica and the Caribbean islands.[18]

Manioc (*Manihot esculenta* ssp. *esculenta*), also known as cassava, is now a major staple in the tropics and in the developing world. It is highly drought-tolerant, and capable of growing on marginal soils. It was once thought to have been domesticated from a multiplicity of species, but genetic data suggests that it probably arose from a single progenitor, wild *Manihot esculenta*, along the southern border of the Amazon basin.[19] The earliest evidence for manioc is the fossilised remains recovered at Ñanchoc Valley dating to 6500 BC.[20,3] Domesticated manioc rapidly spread to Mesoamerica: it has been identified from starch grains dating to 5700 BC, recovered from milling stones at Aguadulce Rock Shelter, Panama,[21,3] and from pollen grains dating to 3400 BC in northern Belize.[22]

The (white) potato (*Solanum tuberosum*) is the world's fourth most important agricultural crop, after maize, rice and wheat.[23] Surprisingly, evidence for its early exploitation is scarce. Fossilised tubers from Chilca Canyon, dating to 8000 BC, have been reported as potatoes and sweet potatoes.[24] However, it is not clear if these were deliberately cultivated, or merely gathered in the wild. The earliest evidence for domesticated potato is far more recent, and comes from four sites near coastal desert city of Casma in central Peru. Here, potato starch granules have been isolated and studied from preserved tubers dating from 2000 to 1200 BC.[25] Starch grains dating from 2000 to 1600 BC at Waynuna, southern Peru, may be from potato, but this is uncertain.[26] The potato was once thought to have been domesticated from a multiplicity of species,[27] but genetic data has now traced its origins to a single wild progenitor tuber, *Solanum bukasovii*. Domestication apparently occurred only once, in southern Peru.[28]

Sweet potato or camote (*Ipomoea batatas*) is only distantly related to the (white) potato. It is another latecomer, although it went on to become a major staple for the Polynesians after they contacted the New World. Genetic data suggests that it was domesticated in Central America before spreading to Peru and Ecuador.[29] However, the earliest archaeological evidence for domesticated sweet potato comes from South America, at the site of Caral in the Supe Valley, Peru, dating to 2600 BC.[30]

In addition to these staples, the New World has contributed one of the world's most important condiments to global cuisine: peppers were widely cultivated throughout the New World for thousands of years before European contact. There are five economically-important species of domesticated capsicum pepper. The genus *Capsicum* is thought to have originated in Bolivia, but little is known about where domestication first occurred and the subsequent dispersal of domesticated species. Starch grains have been identified from milling stones, sediment samples at a number of sites in Mesoamerica, the Caribbean, Venezuela, and Peru at dates ranging from 4100 BC to AD 1550. The presence of domesticated plants used as condiments rather than as staples during the later Archaic Period indicates that sophisticated agriculture and complex cuisines arose early throughout the New World.[31]

Maize: cereal 'killer app'

Maize (*Zea mays* L. ssp. *mays*) is the most widely produced cereal crop in the world. Worldwide production was 831,358,000 tonnes for the period 2010-11, according to figures released by the US Department of Agriculture. Of this, the United States accounted for 316,165,000 tonnes, or just below 40 percent.[32] An increasing amount of maize production is now used for biofuel production rather than as a staple, especially in the United States where the figure exceeds 40 percent.[33] Other maize products include corn oil, corn syrup and animal feed.

It is now generally accepted that maize was domesticated from teosinte,[34] which is the name given to a number of annual and perennial grasses native to Mesoamerica. The name is from the indigenous

Mexican Nahuátl language, and has been interpreted to mean 'grain of the gods'. In 1990, enzyme sequence data was used to try to identify the type ancestral to domesticated maize, and hence the region where domestication occurred. It was found that only the teosinte subspecies *Zea mays* L. ssp. *parviglumis* gave a molecular overlap with maize. The best match was found with populations from the Central Balsas River watershed, a region in southwestern Mexico that is characterised by deciduous tropical forests. It was also concluded that maize was only domesticated once.[35]

Later studies, using genetic data, support these results. They suggest that maize was domesticated from *Zea mays* L. ssp. *parviglumis* after 7000 BC, and that there was a single domestication from a small but genetically diverse founding population. The most closely related wild population is that of the Central Balsas region, making it a strong candidate for the 'cradle of maize domestication'. However, it cannot be ruled out that an as yet undiscovered population may turn out to be even more closely related.[36,37,38] The domestication process was fairly slow,[37] and the modern form might only have emerged within the last 2,000 years.[39] The late emergence of a highly productive large-seeded cereal staple might have been a factor in the delayed arrival of agriculture in the New World.[5]

Wild teosinte is almost indistinguishable from maize, except in one important respect – the ears. The contrast between a many-rowed 1,000-grained ear of maize and a two-rowed, five to twelve-grained ear of teosinte could not be greater. In comparison to other wild cereals, teosinte is a most unpromising candidate for domestication. Not only are the number of grains limited, but they are enclosed in a hard, woody shell known as the cupulate fruitcase. As a grain crop, it offers such limited rewards that the question has to be asked as to why it was domesticated at all. One possibility is that that it was originally domesticated not for its grain but for its sugar-rich stems. Maize is closely related to sugarcane, and a maize stem typically contains 15 to 50 gm. (0.5 to 1.75 oz.) of sugars (sucrose, fructose, and glucose), or two to sixteen percent by weight. The sugar would have had many uses, including the making of alcoholic beverages. Plant remains found at a number of dry cave sites in Mesoamerica suggest that maize was on occasion chewed as a sugary snack. The practice declined after around 1500 BC, possibly as cobs became larger and maize became an increasingly important food staple.[5,40]

Unfortunately, there is no evidence for large-scale sugar extraction in the archaeological record. Evidence for intensive juice extraction for making maize beer would take the form of large masses of crushed and discarded stems. Proponents argue that the chances of finding such remains are extremely low. It is far more likely that such activities would take place out in the open than in dry caves where discarded maize stems might be preserved. In any case, it is probable that they were dried and used for fuel.[40]

The earliest evidence for domesticated maize is starch grains and phytoliths from the Central Balsas watershed, strengthening the case that domestication occurred there. Archaeological work near the Iguala Valley in the Central Balsas region has revealed a long sequence of human occupation and plant exploitation reaching back to the early Holocene. At the Xihuatoxtla rock shelter site, stone tools dating to around 6700 BC have been recovered, including flaked points, simple flake tools, and numerous milling stones.[41] Maize starch grains have been recovered from the milling stones and other stone tools, and account for 90 percent of the grains recovered. The average grain size is larger than the size range of wild teosinte grains, consistent with domesticated maize. The grains are irregular in shape, similar to maize but unlike the oval or bell shapes found with teosinte grains. Phytoliths, recovered from sediment samples, are also consistent with those from domesticated maize. However, the phytolith evidence fails to support the sugar stem theory. No phytoliths of the type found in both maize and teosinte stems were found, suggesting that the emphasis was on the cobs.[42]

With the domestication of maize, a highly productive cereal was finally available to New World cultivators. It matures quickly, can easily be stored, and has evolved many high yielding varieties.

Although it was preceded by other domesticated crops, maize would revolutionise food production in many regions, particularly in Mesoamerica and the United States.[1]

Early maize agriculture in Mesoamerica

Until the discoveries in the Central Balsas region, the earliest evidence for domesticated maize was thought to be at the site of San Andrés, Tabasco. The site is located 15 km (9 miles) inland from Mexico's southernmost Gulf coast and 5 km (3 miles) northeast of the later Olmec site of La Venta. Here, pollen data has been used to chart the development of early Mesoamerican agriculture over the course of over two and a half millennia.

Maize pollen first appeared around 5100 BC, but the earliest grain sizes are consistent with wild teosinte. Larger grains, consistent with domestication, first appeared around 5000 BC and were common by 4000 BC; but small pollen grains did not finally disappear until around 2500 BC. Teosinte is not native to the region, so these plants must have been introduced. Other crops soon followed: pollen that may be from domesticated manioc appeared around 4600 BC; then domesticated sunflower seeds and cotton pollen around 2500 BC. Charcoal and other pollen evidence suggests that the initial appearance of maize coincided with the clearance of forests to make way for agriculture.[43]

The earliest remains of domesticated maize cobs are rather later than this pollen evidence. These are three cob fragments from Guilá Naquitz Cave, dating to 4250 BC, and possibly all from the same harvest.[44] All three possessed non-shattering rachis, and were thus dependent on humans for dispersal and propagation. One of the cobs had four rows of grain rather than just the two seen in wild teosinte. Although the many-rowed arrangement of modern maize was not present in any of the specimens, it is clear that farmers were selecting for ears with four or more rows of grain.[45]

Maize phytoliths did not occur at Guilá Naquitz until 4250 BC, but they were frequent thereafter, and suggest that neither maize nor wild teosinte were harvested for food during earlier occupation phases of the cave. Given that the maize cobs were unquestionably domesticated (if not of the modern form), the implication is that maize arrived at Guilá Naquitz as a domesticated crop – almost four millennia after *Cucurbita pepo* squash was first cultivated there.[44] These findings are nevertheless consistent with much earlier presence of maize in the Central Balsas region. At the Tehuacán Valley cave sites of San Marcos and Coxcatlán, maize cob fragments date from around 3500 BC, again much later than the earliest domesticated *Cucurbita pepo* squash.[46]

Although maize was apparently not grown at Guilá Naquitz Cave prior to 4250 BC, it had spread southwards into Panama well before this date. Analysis of starch grains recovered from plant processing tools document its presence at rock shelter and cave sites by 5800 BC, together with locally-growing wild yams. Arrowroot and manioc from South America have also been identified from starch grains. The Isthmus of Panama forms a relatively narrow land-bridge between North and South America, and through it domesticated crops spread in both directions. Hearths and middens suggest that the Panamanian sites were used as dwellings; thus it appears that cave-dwelling groups were practicing food production long before they began to live in villages.[47]

However, by 2500 BC, maize production was becoming more intensive. Pollen data from sites in the Maya Lowlands of northern Belize has revealed evidence for forest clearance and widespread maize and manioc cultivation, although projectile points and animal remains suggest that food production still took place as part of a mixed economy that also included hunting and fishing. The more complex societies of the Maya did not start to emerge until after 1000 BC, as we shall see in Chapter 30.[22]

From Mesoamerican origins, maize spread south with some rapidity. Phytolith data has been claimed to indicate its presence at Real Alto in Ecuador around 4400 BC,[48] although this evidence has been disputed.[49] The earliest undisputed evidence for maize in Ecuador are starch grains from charred cooking-pot residues at Loma Alta, dating from between 3300 and 2950 BC.[50] Starch grain and phytolith evidence show that maize reached Waynuna in the highlands of southern Peru between 2000 and 1600 BC, where varieties suitable for making flour were cultivated. Arrowroot and possibly potatoes were also cultivated at this site; the former probably arrived from the Amazon rainforest to the east.[26]

By this time, maize cultivation had also spread east to Uruguay, where starch grains and phytoliths indicate its presence at the site of Los Ajos around 2800 BC. Beans and squashes have also been identified at this site.[51] It is clear, then, that maize was an important addition to already diverse agricultural packages all over South America. Meanwhile, in the northwards direction, fossil remains from open air sites and rock shelters in New Mexico and Arizona show that maize reached the United States no later than 2100 BC.[52]

Cultivators of the Ñanchoc Valley

Slightly later than the Ecuadorian Las Vegas data, evidence for squash domestication has been recovered from house floors and hearths at a number of sites in the Ñanchoc Valley in northern Peru. The sites are located in tropical dry forest, 500 m (1,640 ft.) above sea level, on the lower western slopes of the Andes. Excavations span three aceramic cultural phases, spanning much of the Archaic Period: the Paiján, Las Pircas and Tierra Blanca. During the late Paiján, hunter-gatherers lived in dispersed, semi-sedentary communities. From this period, dating to 8250 BC, a charred and desiccated squash seed has been identified as a domesticated form of *Cucurbita moschata*.[20]

The Las Pircas phase, following the Paiján, lasted from around 8000 to 6000 BC, and was characterised by more closely knit communities, living 200 to 400 m (0.125 to 0.25 miles) apart. The small settlements were sited near springs or along the banks of small streams, 1 to 3 km (0.6 to 1.8 miles) from the valley floor, and comprised elliptical-shaped houses built on stone foundations, together with storage facilities. Squash, manioc, quinoa and peanuts were grown in furrowed garden plots. Starch grains, recovered from the calculus of human teeth dating over a one thousand year period, have provided direct evidence for the regular consumption of *Cucurbita moschata* squash, peanuts, *Phaseolus* sp. beans, and pacay (*Inga feuillei*). The latter is a tree crop, which yields large edible pods with a sweet, white pulp. It is probably native to the lowland eastern slopes of the Andes, but can be grown at much higher elevations. It would later become important to the Inca. Most of the cultivated plants are not native to the region, implying that the Ñanchoc Valley cultivators obtained them through long-distance exchange.[20,15]

During the latter part of the final Tierra Blanca phase, the Ñanchoc Valley people began to exploit cotton and gourds as 'industrial' (non-food) crops. Cotton bolls, dating to around 4200 BC, have been recovered from a house floor. Cotton was probably used for hunting and fishing nets and storage bags, as well as for clothing.[20] By this time, it is likely that gourds were being used as fishing floats and containers.[53]

The Ñanchoc Valley people also constructed South America's earliest-known irrigation system. Three canals dating to 3400 BC and a possible fourth dating to 4700 BC have been reported. Although the full extent of the canal system is not known, they were probably between 2.0 and 2.5 km (1.25 to 1.5 miles) in length, carrying water from upstream inlets of the Ñanchoc River to the fields.[54]

Site CA-09-04 features a pair of small, stone-faced flat mounds each measuring around 30 m (100 ft.) in length and 1.5 m (5 ft.) high. The mounds date to 5770 BC and are associated with a small elliptical hut and an area for lime processing, presumably for use in coca chewing. The mounds remained in use for two millennia, undergoing periodic rebuilding. It is suggested that they served a ritual function, and that ritual evolved along with agricultural practices over time. The existence of furrowed plots, canals and ritual mounds suggests that social organisation in the Ñanchoc Valley extended beyond the level of individual households.[8,20]

Early ceramics in Amazonia

The Amazon rainforest is the largest rainforest in the world, accounting for more than half the planet's surviving rainforest. It covers most of the Amazon Basin of South America, with a total extent of 5.5 million sq. km (2.12 million sq. miles) or 40 percent of the South American landmass. Around 60 percent of the rainforest lies within the borders of Brazil, with 13 percent in Peru and 10 percent in Columbia. Smaller portions lie within the territories of Venezuela, Ecuador, Bolivia, Guyana, Suriname, and French Guiana.

We tend to assume that Amazonia remained a pristine forest throughout pre-Columbian times, but archaeological work has shown that this was not the case. There is evidence of complex regional settlement patterns and significant human-induced impact on the landscape well before European contact. These include cultivation areas, roads, hamlets, bridges, weirs, causeways, ponds and canals. Far from being surrounded by dense forest, it is likely that later prehistoric settlements were set in parkland landscapes.[55]

The earliest evidence for human presence in Amazonia dates to the Late Pleistocene. Plant and animal remains, stone tools, and red iron oxide pigment have been recovered from deposits at a Paleoindian campsite in the Caverna da Pedra Pintada, Monte Alegre in the Brazilian Amazon, and date to before 8500 BC. Rock paintings, made with red iron oxide, depict concentric circles, hand prints, and an inverted human figure with rays extending from their head. The broad-spectrum economy was based on tropical forest and riverine foraging, and the cave was periodically visited for more than 1,200 years before being abandoned.[56]

Remarkably, pottery makes an appearance in Amazonia as early as 5600 BC, earlier than anywhere else in the New World. It is first attested at the site of Taperinha, near Santarim in the Lower Amazon, where shards of an incised, sand-tempered ware have been excavated from a 6 m (19 ft. 6 in.) high shell midden. The size of the midden suggests that the Taperinha people lived a relatively sedentary existence. Other artefacts recovered included stone flake tools, hammerstones, unshaped grinding and cooking stones, and bone and shell implements. Animal remains include turtle, catfish, characins and mussels, suggesting suggest an economy based on intensive riverine foraging.[57]

The early archaeological record for Amazonia is less detailed than for the Andes. The spread of agriculture through Amazonia and the Orinoco Basin might have been associated with the domestication of manioc, but this is uncertain.[1] Squash, leren and bottle gourd dating to 7000 BC have been recovered at Peña Roja in Middle Caquetá region of Columbian Amazonia, and there is evidence for slash and burn cultivation around 4500 BC at Geral in eastern Brazilian Amazonia.[3] Overall, though, evidence for early agriculture in this vast region is elusive.

Social complexity in the Norte Chico Preceramic

By the Late Archaic (or Preceramic) Period, more complex societies were beginning to emerge in the Andean region. An extensive aceramic cultural system, reaching across an area of 1,800 sq. km (700 sq. miles) arose in the Norte Chico region on the coast of Peru, 200 km (125 miles) north of Lima. The region consists of four adjacent river valleys: the Huaura, Supe, Pativilca and Fortaleza.

The environment is considerably affected by the Humboldt Current, a cold ocean current that flows along the Pacific Coast from the southern tip of Chile to northern Peru. Named for the nineteenth century geographer Alexander von Humboldt, it is responsible for the aridity of coastal Peru, and in the river valleys, agriculture is generally not possible without irrigation. However, the Humboldt Current is also one of the major upswelling systems of the world. Nutrient-rich water is driven to the surface, supporting an abundance of marine life. To Archaic Period people capable of exploiting easily-netted schooling fish, the Peruvian coastal habitat offered exceptional opportunities.

The site of Aspero, at the mouth of the Supe, was investigated by archaeologists on a number of occasions during the first half of the twentieth century. A number of mounds were noted, but they were not recognised as constructed platforms until the 1970s. The Aspero site consists of six major platforms and eleven smaller mounds, and is surrounded by 15 ha (37 acres) of middens. The large platforms were topped by ceremonial complexes of chambers and courtyards, which were periodically filled in and rebuilt. The largest platform, known as Huaca de los Idolos ('House of the Idols'), measures 40 by 30 m (130 by 100 ft.) and is 10 m (33 ft.) high. At the summit is a large enclosed courtyard leading into a series of chambers, which contain a series of human figurines that have been interpreted as idols. The later phases date to between 3000 and 2500 BC. Another of the large mounds, the Huaca de los Sacrificios ('House of Sacrifice'), dates to 2800 BC. Within this complex has been discovered the burial of a two-month old child wrapped in cotton textile, with a headdress adorned by 500 shell, clay and plant beads. The body was placed in a basket and covered with a stone basin. It is not clear whether this represents the burial of an infant born into an elite family or group – or a human sacrifice. Those who named the complex evidently believed the latter.[58]

In 1994 a team led by Peruvian archaeologist Ruth Shady Solis began studies upstream in the Supe Valley. They identified 18 settlements with monumental and domestic architecture between the coast and 40 km (25 miles) upstream, all of which all lacked pottery indicating that they are Preceramic.[59] They include Caral, located 23 km (14 miles) inland and occupied between 2600 and 2000 BC. Its inland location and the lack of an accessible arable floodplain imply a dependency on irrigation agriculture. It is thought that a present-day irrigation canal masks the site of a prehistoric canal that served Caral, but remains recovered from the site confirm that irrigation agriculture was practiced there. Domesticated plant remains include squash, beans, guava, pacay, sweet potato and cotton – but no maize. Animal remains indicate an almost exclusive focus on seafood, and include anchovies, sardines, clams and mussels.[30]

The most notable feature of Caral is sheer scale, both of the site itself and of its monumental architecture. It contains a central zone of monumental, residential and non-residential architecture covering an area of 65 ha (160 acres). This central zone alone is larger than any other contemporary Andean site, and within are six large platform mounds, a number of smaller mounds, two sunken circular courts, and residential buildings. The largest of the platform mounds, known as the Piramide Mayor, measures 160 by 150 m (525 by 490 ft.) at the base and is 18 m (59 ft.) high. The structure is fronted by a small sunken circular court, with two staircases leading to the ritual complex at the summit. Although the platform underwent considerable remodelling of its superstructure over the course of the site's occupation, the mound itself was largely built in two major phases of construction. The smallest of the other large platform mounds is 60 by 45 m (195 by 150 ft.) at the base and 10 m (33 ft.) high. Even this was as large as anything else in the Andean world at that time. The platform mounds were constructed by filling stone retaining walls with river cobble and stone rubble contained in shicra bags (open mesh bags made from reeds). The retaining walls were then faced and covered with multiple layers of coloured plaster.[60,30]

Each of the six large mounds is associated with a large, formally-planned residential neighbourhood. There are large elite residential complexes with plastered stone walls that range in size from 450 to 800 sq. m (4,850 to 8,600 sq. ft.). However, the bulk of the accommodation was far more modest, and was constructed with walls and roofs of mats, reeds and thatch. Away from the central zone are a number of smaller long mound complexes. These include a 23 ha (57 acres) plaza and platform complex known as Chupacigarro. Although not yet investigated in detail, aerial photography suggests that they are integral parts of the site.[30]

Ruth Shady Solis[60,59] believes that Caral and the 17 other settlements in the Supe Valley were autonomous communities, but they shared cultural traits and on occasions pooled manpower. Without the ability to draw on personnel from other sites, the monumental architecture at Caral and the other sites could not have been built and maintained. Shady Solis suggested that cotton grown on the inland sites was traded for fish from the coastal sites. She also proposed that the Supe region participated in a wider interaction sphere. Support for this view came from survey work carried out between 2002 and 2003 on 13 additional large sites in the river valleys of the Fortaleza and Pativilca, lying to the north of the Supe. It was found that large-scale communal construction projects commenced between 3200 and 2500 BC, followed by a proliferation of inland sites between 2500 and 2000 BC. The sites all share certain features, including monumental architecture and extensive residential complexes.[61]

It is likely that Preceramic society in the Norte Chico was hierarchical, with centralised decision making, a formalised religion and a multifaceted economy based on inland irrigation agriculture of both cotton and food crops, and coastal fisheries.[61] The autonomous communities were probably organised at the level of simple chiefdoms.[62] Norte Chico fits well with proposals going back to the 1960s that the rich fisheries of the South American Pacific coast sustained early sedentism and population growth, and promoted rise of social complexity. This theory, now referred to as the Maritime Foundations of Andean Civilisation (MFAC) theory, was refined by anthropologist Michael Moseley in the 1970s. The theory proposes that as fishing intensified in response to population growth, requirements increased for materials including fibres for lines, floats for fishing tackle, boat-building materials, and materials for housing, clothing and fuel. Thus agriculture focussed heavily on industrial crops such as cotton, gourds and trees, together with peppers for marinating fish, whereas food crops were restricted to low-maintenance items such as beans and squash. As demand increased, so cultivators moved upstream into easily-irrigated locations such as Caral.[63,58]

Preceramic developments in Columbia and Ecuador

To the north of the Pacific fisheries, there was a rapid growth of more complex societies along the coasts of Ecuador and Columbia, as sedentary villages appeared and pottery came into use. Pottery dating from 4800 to 3000 BC has been found at the Columbian sites of San Jacinto I, Monsù, Puerto Chaco and Puerto Hormigo.[64] These ceramics differ from the earlier Amazonian pottery, and are tempered with organic fibre. The earliest examples come from San Jacinto I where ornately-decorated fibre-tempered ware has been recovered. Cooking pits and stone implements for pounding and grinding have also been excavated. The hunter-gatherer economy was based around processing wild grass seeds with grindstones prior to cooking, and meat was obtained by hunting deer and tapir. The pottery does not appear to have been used for cooking, and most of the daily cooking activities used earth ovens or fire pits for roasting. It is likely that the role of pottery was related to social activities such as serving and feasting rather than the mundanities of cooking.[65]

In coastal Ecuador, there is evidence for experimentation with clay firing in late aceramic times before useful ceramic artefacts were produced. The earliest actual pottery with reasonably secure dating has been recovered from the site of Loma Alta, and dates to around 4000 BC.[64] Loma Alta is associated with the Valdivia culture, named for a site at the small town of Valdivia. The Valdivia culture lasted from 4400 to 1450 BC[66] and is spread widely throughout coastal Ecuador. It represents the transition to settled village life in Ecuador, and is associated with early agriculture, ceramics and increasing social complexity.[58] It has been suggested that the Valdivia people learned about ceramics from Jōmon fishers from Japan, who became lost at sea and eventually found their way to South America.[67] As intriguing as this possibility sounds, a local origin for Valdivia pottery seems far more likely. Key sites include Valdivia itself, Loma Alta, Real Alto and La Emerenciana. All but the latter are located on the Santa Elena Peninsula, where the earlier Las Vegas culture flourished.

The Real Alto settlement was occupied between 4400 and 1800 BC, from the Valdivia I to Valdivia VII phases.[66] Beginning as a small village, it initially comprised small, elliptically-shaped single-roomed houses measuring around 4.5 by 3 m (15 by 10 ft.). It is thought that these housed nuclear families, and that many day-to-day activities were conducted immediately outside the house. Burials took place either under the walls or just outside.[68] During the Valdivia III phase between 2800 and 2400 BC, Real Alto grew considerably in size to 12.4 ha (30.6 acres).[66,69] By now, it contained two ceremonial mounds, arranged with houses in a U-shape around a central plaza. The two mounds are known as the Charnel House and the Fiesta House. As the names imply, the former was a funerary mound and the latter was where feasting and drinking took place. Houses were now far larger, measuring around 12 by 8 m (40 by 25 ft.), and they probably housed extended families. The framework of the houses was supported by a centre post in conjunction with posts at each end.[68,58]

Recovered starch grains and phytoliths from various artefacts have provided an insight into the agricultural economy of the Valdivia culture.[50] At Loma Alta, they have been recovered from charred cooking-pot residues and grinding stones residues, and demonstrate that maize was first cultivated at the site between 3300 and 2950 BC. Two distinct varieties of maize have been identified from the starch grains: soft endosperm (used for making flour) and hard endosperm (used for making hominy and popcorn). The existence of more than one type of maize suggests that it played a complex role in an overall broad-based cuisine. Other plants identified from starch grains include manioc, arrowroot, chilli peppers and jack beans, and squash, leren, arrowroot, beans, ginger and palm fruit have been identified from phytolith data.

Jack beans are toxic and must be cooked with salt to detoxify them; evidently the Valdivia people mastered this technique. Saline cooking increases the temperature at which starches gelatinise. The use of saline cooking may also explain why root and tuber starches occur at low frequency in the charred cooking-pot residues compared with maize, jack beans and chilli pepper starches. Maize is deficient in niacin (vitamin B3) and the essential amino acids lysine and tryptophan. Beans contain these essential dietary components, and chilli peppers contain vitamin C. Cooking all three together would facilitate a balanced diet – and explain the preferential survival of their starch grains. The implication is that the Valdivia people had a good understanding of human nutritional needs.

Similar studies were conducted at Real Alto involving phytoliths and starch grains recovered from stone tools.[69,70] The tools were found in the floor of Valdivia III phase houses, and date from 2800 to 2400 BC. Phytoliths from manioc, arrowroot, leren, squash, beans and maize were identified. The manioc was probably cultivated, as it does not occur in the wild on the Ecuadorian coast. Starch grains of maize, manioc, arrowroot were identified, in addition to gelatinised starch indicative of cooking. Phytoliths are unaffected by cooking, and are more common than the starch grains of manioc and leren, which suggests that these plants were cooked before processing with the tools. On the other hand, undamaged arrowroot and maize starch grains recovered from the tools suggests that these plants were processed raw.

Although arrowroot and leren were also in use, manioc produces more carbohydrates per edible portion than other lowland root crops and tubers. The introduction of manioc to coastal Ecuador, and its combination with maize, might have supported population expansions out of southwest Ecuador in late Valdivia times. Overall, the findings provide support for the agricultural basis of Valdivia society.

Agriculture reaches the Southwestern United States

Until the 1990s, it was believed that the Southwestern United States underwent a fairly gradual transition to agriculture. It was thought that indigenous hunter-gatherers initially incorporated small numbers of domesticated crops into a largely forager-based pattern of subsistence, and low-level food production was thought to have persisted until the first century AD or later.[71] Evidence emerging since that time suggests that that the process was far more rapid, and that the transition began fairly abruptly with the arrival of maize from Mesoamerica around 2100 BC.

In geographical terms, the Southwestern United States comprises Nevada, Utah, Arizona, western Colorado and western New Mexico. It includes the Great Basin and is a region of semi-desert steppe and high altitude forest, interspersed with bands of fertile riverine alluvium. For early farmers, irrigation was essential in most regions, apart from those at high altitude. In many upland regions, agriculture was limited to the summer months by winter frost and snow.[1]

The major crops were the 'Three Sisters' of maize, beans and squash, although they did not all arrive at the same time. Maize was present by no later than 2100 BC at sites in New Mexico and Arizona.[52] *Cucurbita pepo* squash first appears around 1500 BC, followed by beans around 200 BC.[72] Butternut squash, cushaw and cotton arrived after AD 500. The tepary bean is indigenous to the Sonoran Desert and might have been domesticated locally. It is known from the late first millennium AD, but might have been present earlier.[8]

In the 1990s, evidence for early maize agriculture dating to 2100 BC was found at a number of sites in Arizona and western New Mexico.[52] Construction projects in the Tucson area also led to some important discoveries: sites excavated include Milagro, Santa Cruz Bend and Las Capas. Milagro, located in the Tucson Basin, is a settlement of oval semi-subterranean pit-houses with outside storage pits. The bell-shaped underground storage pits are in some cases large enough to have held enough maize to feed a family of four for four months. Maize cob remains date from 1200 to 1000 BC. Other finds include projectile points and fired clay figurines, although pottery did not appear until around AD 100.[1]

Las Capas and Santa Cruz Bend are located in the Santa Cruz River Valley to the north of Tucson. Maize remains at Las Capas date to 2050 BC.[52] A significant discovery at this site is a series of irrigation canals dating to 1400 BC.[73] Similar irrigation canals have been found at Zuni Pueblo on the Colorado Plateau in New Mexico, dating to 1000 BC,[74] demonstrating that irrigation agriculture had spread beyond southern Arizona by this stage. At Santa Cruz Bend, an area of 1.2 ha (3 acres) has been excavated, revealing 183 house floors, together with storage pits. One of the floors was 8.5 m (28 ft.) in diameter, and was probably a communal building. The settlement itself might have been as large as 8 ha (20 acres), and was occupied between 1200 BC and AD 550. Remains of maize, squash, tobacco and cotton indicate an agricultural economy. Over time, there was a decrease in large hunted animals; a possible indication that population growth was damaging the environment. Pottery, crude at first, appeared after 800 BC, with polished *tecomates* (neckless jars) appearing after AD 150. The earliest pottery was not used as cookware, and might have been used for storage.[1]

Another large, complex site is Cerro Juanaqueña, located just south of the present-day US/Mexican border, in northern Chihuahua, and dating to around 1200 BC. The 10 ha (25 acre) site was constructed on the slopes and summit of a steep 140 m (460 ft.) basalt hill that juts above the Rio Casas Grandes floodplain. It comprises 468 *trincheras* (stone terraces) that originally supported houses. The *trincheras* averaged 18 m (60 ft.) in length and 7 m (23 ft.) in width, and it has been estimated that the construction of the site required 16 man-years of labour. The residents grew maize, but local seed plants might also have been of importance. Animals exploited include deer, antelope and rabbits, but despite the proximity of the Rio Casas Grandes, the rarity of fish bones and other aquatic remains suggest that the river was not greatly exploited.[75]

Such large construction projects imply the emergence of more complex forms of society and labour organisation,[52] and the abundant maize remains leave little doubt about its key role in these developments.[76] Overall, this recent evidence indicates that the transition to agriculture in the Southwestern United States was far less gradual than was once believed.[8]

Who were the Proto-Uto-Aztecans?

Uto-Aztecan is a widespread Native American language family that includes the Nahuátl language. The family extends to Idaho in the north, El Salvador in the south, California in the west and Texas in the east. Until recently, it was generally accepted that it arose from an ancestral community of hunter-gatherers, living in the uplands of Arizona and northwestern Mexico around 3000 BC. It was thought that after the original Proto-Uto-Aztecan (PUA) speech community broke up, maize spread north from Mesoamerica by a process of cultural diffusion and was adopted by southern Uto-Aztecan groups, and also the Hopi in northeastern Arizona. Hunter-gathering continued among northern groups, including the Takic and Tubatulabal of California, and the Numic of the Great Basin.[77]

However, the discoveries since the 1990s have forced a rethink. Peter Bellwood[1] and linguist Jane Hill[77] have suggested a demic diffusion model, similar to that proposed for Europe. They suggest that PUA-speaking maize farmers spread northwards from Mesoamerica into the Southwestern United States, although the northernmost groups of this expansion later reverted to hunter-gathering. A ten-item lexicon for maize cultivation and processing has been reconstructed for PUA. Hill notes that this displays regular sound correspondence among daughter languages, and is attested in both northern and southern languages. By contrast, words for beans and squash among daughter languages are later loanwords. This is consistent with the archaeological evidence suggesting that beans and squash reached the Southwestern United States after maize – and after the breakup of the PUA community. On linguistic grounds, it is thought that the latter occurred between 2000 and 1000 BC.

An issue the model must address is the return to hunter-gathering by the northern groups. Hill notes archaeological evidence showing that maize and squash were cultivated on the northern Colorado Plateau and eastern Great Basin from as early as 1300 BC; but by AD 1000, the climatic episode known as the Medieval Warm Period was shifting the northern limits of summer rains to the south. Without these, maize cultivation was not possible with the cultivation techniques then in use.

Hill suggests that Numic and Takic groups were originally divided between high-ranking clans who had access to arable land, and low-ranking ones who were relegated to marginal lands. These 'have-nots' were forced to rely to an extent on foraging. When conditions deteriorated, they were already well-adapted to a lifestyle that emphasised foraging and nomadism over cultivating and sedentism. The originally better-off groups, on the other hand, were forced to retreat south – where they found most potential refugia were already occupied. Those who remained now required larger home ranges, resulting in the spread of Numic people into their attested range across the whole of the Great Basin. Their hunter-gatherer subsistence was still in use throughout much of the Great Basin into historical times. Practices such as intensive management of wild plants and the use of seed beaters to harvest wild seeds are often described as 'proto-agricultural', but Hill regards them as vestiges from a fully-agricultural past.

Bellwood, while in agreement with this model, suggests that maize cultivation could also have been adopted by some indigenous hunter-gatherers as well. He notes that Cortaro and Gypsum projectile points from the Tucson Basin are similar to Mesoamerican points found in Coxcatlán Cave and at Tlatilco in the Valley of Mexico, and that they may be evidence for a population movement associated with the initial spread of maize farming into Arizona. However, Bellwood also notes that maize and pottery have also been found in the Tucson region with Armijo projectile points; and these appear to be indigenous to Arizona.

The Bellwood/Hill model is not without its problems. It does not explain why squash reached the Southwestern United States well after maize, despite two crops being cultivated together in central and southern Mexico as early as 3500 BC. Another issue is the assumption that the northwards expansion was driven by population increases arising from maize agriculture. In fact, population estimates for various parts of Mesoamerica are quite low throughout the period when maize agriculture was spreading to the Southwestern United States. For example, in the Valley of Oaxaca, a three-lobed region of around 2,000 sq. km (770 sq. miles), the Preceramic population is estimated to never have exceeded 75 to 150 individuals, even though maize had been cultivated there for 2,000 years or more. If these estimates are correct, then demographic pressures of the type postulated for agricultural expansions in other parts of the world were not applicable to Mesoamerica. This leaves unexplained why an expansion of maize farmers from Mesoamerica should happen in the first place.[52]

Researchers have found that maize did trigger a baby boom in the Southwestern United States – eventually. They found evidence that population increases did not occur until long after the arrival of maize. One approach was to look for evidence of a young population in the archaeological record: it was assumed that the number of juveniles (taken to be aged five to nineteen) would be high in an increasing population, and low if the population was decreasing. By considering human remains recovered from archaeological sites, researchers found that a significant population increase did not begin until around AD 500, 2,600 years after maize was first introduced to the Southwestern United States. A number of further developments were suggested as prerequisites to a population expansion, including the introduction of pottery, the bow and arrow, and of fresh races of maize amenable to dry-farming. A lack of meat animals may also have been a factor in the delay. The most significant Southwestern United States meat animal is the turkey, and it remained largely unimportant until around AD 1100.[78]

A delayed population expansion was also indicated by a genetic study that considered both mitochondrial and Y-chromosomal DNA. A date of around the first century BC was suggested for the expansion, albeit with a fair degree of uncertainty. The researchers also set out to test a prediction of the Bellwood/Hill model: as dispersing populations separate from one another, it is to be expected that both their genes and their languages would start to diverge from one another. Accordingly, it would be expected that speakers of more distantly-related languages within the Uto-Aztecan language family would show greater genetic differences than those speaking more closely related ones, reflecting the greater time of separation. It was found that the relationship only holds good for Y-chromosomal DNA. For mitochondrial DNA, the degree of divergence between populations was related to separation by geographical distance. One admittedly unlikely possibility is that the dispersing Mesoamerican farming groups consisted largely of men, or that the men predominantly married local hunter-gatherer women. A more likely possibility is that the later population expansion blurred the ancient mitochondrial signal.[79]

In response to these issues, a modified version of the cultural diffusion model has been proposed that locates the Proto-Uto-Aztecan homeland in the Great Basin.[52] The authors of this report noted that PUA lacks a reconstructed term for oaks and pinyon. The latter is a tree that yields edible nuts and is indigenous to the Southwestern United States and Mexico. Pinyon nuts were a staple of Native Americans and are still widely eaten. It was reasoned that the Proto-Uto-Aztecan homeland was located in a place and at a time where oaks and pinyon trees were absent – in the west/central Great Basin during the Early Holocene.

The break-up of this founding PUA community came when dryer conditions set in around 6900 BC, leading some groups to migrate to better-watered lands further south. Some groups eventually reached central Mexico, where they acquired maize. As the climate improved again after 3900 BC, maize diffused northwards from one Uto-Aztecan speaking group to another, reaching the Southwestern United States around 2100 BC. However, maize was not adopted by the northern groups, and these spread further northwards after the climate improved.

The main problem with this model is that the date of 6900 BC for the break-up of PUA is far earlier than many linguists are prepared to accept.[80] In response to this and other criticisms,[81] the authors of the original report expressed doubts about the reliability of glottochronology used to obtain the later and more generally-accepted dates for the break-up of PUA.[82] It should also be noted that 6900 BC is no earlier than the dates that have been proposed for the breakup of Proto-Indo-European (see Chapter 20). Conversely, as we saw in Chapter 20, the absence of a reconstructed word for something does not necessarily mean that the thing itself was also absent, and it is possible that the words for oaks and pinyon trees have been lost.

All in all, considerable uncertainty remains regarding the transition to agriculture to the Southwestern United States and the origin and spread of the Uto-Aztecan language family. The domesticated crops, for the most part, came from Mesoamerica. The process must therefore have been one of either demic or cultural diffusion, or quite possibly a combination of both. However, at this stage we do not have enough evidence to decide which model is correct.

Independent development in the Eastern Woodlands

The last of the New World's three centres of independent plant domestication was the Eastern Woodlands of the United States. In contrast to the southwest, the transition to agriculture in the east was seamless, as hunter-gatherers added agriculture to an already successful river valley economy.[83]

The Eastern Woodlands comprises the drainage basins of the Mississippi, the Arkansas, the Missouri, the Tennessee and the Ohio Rivers, and the Great Lakes and New England regions. In the Early Holocene, forests retreated north and temperate woodlands were established across a landscape characterised by woods, glades, lakes and rivers. Broad-based foraging systems were developed by indigenous Archaic groups, not unlike those of contemporary European Mesolithic populations. The region offered abundant staples in the form of forest plants such as hickory, and the seeds of plants growing in open habitats by rivers; animals hunted included the white-tailed deer.[84]

However, Bruce Smith[4] has long been of the opinion that plant domestication could not get underway in the Eastern Woodlands until after around 4500 BC, when alluvial deposits began to build up in river valleys across the interior of eastern North America as the flow rate of post-glacial river systems stabilised. The result was a significant increase in the abundance and diversity of floodplain plant and animal species available for human exploitation, which encouraged sedentism and set the stage for the appearance of agriculture. The sites of Koster, Watson Brake and Poverty Point document the gradual shift to more sedentary pre-agricultural societies.

Koster, an open-air site on the eastern edge of the lower Illinois River floodplain, saw no fewer than 19 phases of occupation from around 7000 to 1000 BC. The region would have been very attractive to hunter-gatherers, with hickory nuts, plentiful fish, shellfish and deer, and in spring and autumn, the wetlands hosted migratory waterfowl in large numbers. Initially, Koster was used as a camp to exploit seasonally-available food as part of a highly-mobile lifestyle, but after around 5500 BC the environment had become rich enough to sustain year-round occupation. The remains of houses have been found, marked by postholes and platforms. The houses measured about 5 by 4.5 m (16 by 14 ft.), and contained hearths, mussel steaming-pits, and circular storage pits. The building of permanent shelters would have represented a substantial investment in labour and materials, and imply a gradual shift to sedentism at the site.[85]

Watson Brake is a large site, overlooking the floodplain of the Ouachita River in northeastern Louisiana. Radiocarbon and thermoluminescence dates suggest that it was constructed between 3400 and 3300 BC. It comprises eleven mounds with connecting ridges, forming an oval-shaped enclosure with a maximum diameter of 280 m (920 ft.) in diameter. The largest mound is 7.5 m (24 ft.) high, and others range from 4.5 to 1 m (15 to 3 ft.) in height; the connecting ridges average about 1 m (3 ft.) in height.[86]

What is remarkable is that this large-scale earthworks was not constructed by a socially-complex, hierarchical society. The builders of Watson Point were seasonally-mobile hunter-gatherers. Like Koster, the site benefitted from a landscape made up of resource-rich gravel and sand shoal habitats, backwater swamps and small-stream habitats, in addition to the main channel of the river. These provided easy access to a wide range of aquatic foods, including fish, mussels, aquatic snails, turtle and duck, and deer and turkey were also plentiful. The ages of the fish suggest that they were mostly caught in the period from spring to early summer, suggesting a seasonal occupation of the site corresponding to the spawning season of the freshwater drum. Plant foods included goosefoot, marshelder and knotweed. All three were later domesticated, but the seeds found at Watson Brake show no signs of domestication. However, their presence may reflect the early development of processes that eventually led to domestication.[86]

Poverty Point, located on the west bank of the Bayou Macon river, is rather later than Watson Brake, and dates to around 1500 BC.[86] It is also much larger, but again there is no evidence for agriculture. It comprises six concentric semi-circular ridges, with a maximum diameter of 1.2 km (0.7 miles), with five aisles radiating through the ridges. Just outside the area formed by the ridges are five mounds, the largest of which is 21.5 m (70 ft.) tall. The role of Poverty Point is debated. Some see it as a sizable town that was occupied year-round and possibly ruled by a powerful chief, although the absence of agriculture makes this unlikely. Another theory is that it was a trading centre. Artefacts found at Poverty Point came from up to 1,100 km (660 miles) away and include beads, pendants and weights, worked from materials including galena, copper, chert and steatite. The truth is we really do not know why Watson Break, Poverty Point and other less elaborate mounds in Louisiana were constructed. No burials appear to be associated with the mounds, so a mortuary function seems unlikely. They suggest that complex construction projects do not necessarily require complex societies, but just why such projects were undertaken in the first place remains a mystery.[8]

The first domestications in the Eastern Woodlands were those of *Cucurbita pepo* squash and sunflower. As we have seen, partially-domesticated *Cucurbita pepo* squash first appeared at Phillips Spring in Missouri around 3000 BC. Domesticated sunflower seeds are first recorded around 2840 BC, at Hayes in Tennessee. However, neither formed part of an integrated suite of crops, as in each case no other domesticated species was present. Similarly, the site of Napoleon Hollow in Illinois documents the first appearance of domesticated marshelder at 2400 BC, but no other crops. It is not until 1800 BC that domesticated crops started to come together to form an agricultural package.[13,83]

Indigenously-domesticated species eventually included *Cucurbita pepo* squash, sunflower, the goosefoot species *Chenopodium berlandieri* (a close relative of quinoa), and marshelder (*Iva annua* var. *macrocarpa*). Three other plants, while never displaying the changes associated with domestication, occur with such abundance in seed assemblages as to suggest deliberate cultivation. These are little barley (*Hordeum pusillum*), maygrass (*Phalaris caroliniana*) and knotweed (*Polygonum erectum*).[83]

Along with *Cucurbita pepo* squash, the sunflower (*Helianthus annuus* var. *macrocarpus*) remains economically important do this day as one of the world's major oil-seed crops. It has long been recognised that it was a staple in the Eastern Woodlands of the United States, and it is generally believed that it was domesticated there. As noted, the earliest-known domesticated sunflower seeds from the Hayes site in Tennessee date to 2840 BC.[13] Genetic research suggests that all existent domesticated sunflowers arose from a wild population in the eastern-central United States. These were then spread by human cultivators into the Eastern Woodlands, and were eventually brought under domestication. This result has confirmed a long-standing view based on the similarities between domesticated sunflowers and wild populations in this region.[87]

However, there might have been more than one domestication event. Sunflower cultivation was also widespread in Mesoamerica, albeit less so than in the Eastern Woodlands. Nevertheless, by 400 BC, cultivation extended as far south as El Salvador. Domesticated sunflower seeds have been identified at the site of San Andrés, Tabasco, dating back to around 2700 BC. This date is more or less contemporary with the one from Hayes, and it is difficult to believe that two could represent the same domestication event. The case for independent domestication has been strengthened by the recovery of sunflower achenes (fruits) in excellent condition from the site of Cueva del Gallo, Morelos. Dating to around 300 BC, they are considerably larger than contemporary sunflower achenes from the Eastern Woodlands. The difference cannot be accounted for in terms of growing seasons, as these are more than adequate for both varieties to mature successfully. The difference does suggest that the Mexican examples represent a separate lineage.[88]

Despite this finding, genetic data suggests that wild Mexican sunflowers did not contribute to the gene pool of the present-day domesticated sunflower. The Mexican domesticated form, if it existed, must now be extinct. One possibility is that the Spanish Catholics tried to suppress it because of its association with the sun-worshipping rituals of the Aztecs. Alternatively, it might have been replaced as a result of far more recent seed imports from the United States under the North American Free Trade Agreement.[89]

The final emergence of an Eastern Woodlands agricultural package is documented at Riverton, a site located on a floodplain terrace along the Wabash River in southeastern Illinois, which was first excavated in the 1960s. The 140 by 67 m (470 by 220 ft.) site comprises a number of rectangular clay floors with an area of roughly 9 to 18 sq. m (100 to 200 sq. ft.). These are believed to be platforms, upon which houses once stood, and they are associated with pits, hearths, various artefacts and extensive midden deposits. The site was occupied for a fairly short time, beginning around 1800 BC, and was probably home to a small-scale society of half a dozen or so related extended family units. There is no evidence at Riverton for any level of social organisation beyond the extended family, nor of social differentiation. There are no signs of communal buildings or a central plaza, nor are there any indications of storage facilities above extended-family level.[83,4]

The Riverton plant assemblage is dominated by nutshells from walnuts, hickory, hazelnut and acorn. Seeds were apparently less important, but included three domesticated crops: *Chenopodium berlandieri*, sunflower and marshelder. In addition, little barley was tentatively identified from a single seed. Rind from bottle gourd and *Cucurbita pepo* squash was also recovered, though the rind from the latter was still too thin to determine whether or not it belonged to the semi-domesticated Phillips

Spring variety. Of the 641 seeds recovered, 605 were from *Chenopodium berlandieri*, suggesting that it played a central role in the economy; the Riverton seeds represent the earliest domestication of the species. The establishment of this agricultural package was not accompanied by major social or economic change, and represents instead a seamless extension to an already-successful river valley hunter-gatherer economy.[83]

The indigenous Eastern Woodlands agricultural package remained in use for many centuries. Maize did not arrive until around 200 BC, having spread from the Southwestern United States. Even then, it did not become an important staple until AD 800.[90,91] Eventually, though, the greater productivity of the 'Three Sisters' won out. Of the founder Eastern Woodlands crops, only *Cucurbita pepo* squash and sunflowers are still of importance. *Chenopodium berlandieri* survives as a minor crop in northern Mexico, where it might have been domesticated after the sixteenth century AD.[13]

The others disappeared long before Europeans reached the New World. Cultivation of little barley, maygrass and knotweed was never intensive enough for changes associated with domestication to occur. On the other hand, domesticated marshelder seeds are recorded at Napoleon Hollow in Illinois around 2400 BC.[13] At a first glance, marshelder is an attractive crop, with seeds that contain 45 percent oil and 32 percent protein. Unfortunately, the seeds are small and yields in consequence are very low.[6] Notably, although the range of the wild plant extends to Mexico, nobody ever bothered to cultivate it there.[13] The domesticated form is now considered to be an 'extinct minor cultigen'.[87]

There is no doubt that the transition to agriculture in the New World differed considerably from those in China and Southwest Asia. It was clearly delayed while the only highly productive cereal reached its full potential, but once this had happened, the New World had as strong a suite of crops as any in the world. It included, in addition to the 'Three Sisters', the potato (and its close relative, the tomato), sweet potato, manioc, sunflower, avocado, peanut, cotton and tobacco. What the New World lacked, of course, was any large domesticated mammal beyond the llama and alpaca – which in any case remained confined to the Andes. This meant a continued reliance on hunting for large meat animals, and no dairy products. While llamas can be used as beasts of burden, they are limited in comparison to the ox or horse. Geography clearly influenced the rise of agriculture, but regional considerations were likely influential factors as well as the overarching consideration of the tilted axes of the Americas.

Towards a second revolution

In these last eight chapters, we have seen just some of the ways in which agricultural packages were assembled and spread, and their impact on the languages and generics of present-day populations. In just a few millennia, human societies around the world were transformed. Instead of a mobile lifestyle, many people now lived in permanent settlements with populations in some cases numbered in the several thousands. For the first time, human populations were making a significant impact on the environment, as crops and animals were farmed beyond their natural ranges. These developments had set the scene for the second of V. Gordon Childe's two 'revolutions'.

PART IV:

THE
FIRST CITIES

6000 BC TO AD 1519

25: The Urban Revolution

The rise of civilisation

The 'Urban Revolution', as V. Gordon Childe termed it, led to the rise of what is conventionally known as 'civilisation'. The first state-level societies – the distant forerunners of today's nation states – arose as a consequence of the social changes brought about by the Neolithic Revolution. By 3000 BC, people in Mesopotamia and Egypt were living in societies almost as complex as those existing today, complete with ruling elites, social differentiation, and of course taxation. Many of the refinements of Western twenty-first century life were absent, but the rudiments were in place.

The Neolithic Revolution was a combination of technological breakthroughs and consequent social change, but the Urban Revolution was predominantly a transformation of social institutions and practices. Childe used the term 'Urban Revolution' to refer to a series of interconnected social changes, from which emerged ruling elites, social stratification, specialist professions, and a major increase in all forms of economic activity. Although the first cities appeared at this time, Childe regarded their appearance as just one aspect of the changes from which state-level societies emerged.[1] Childe developed his ideas in the 1920s and 1930s[2] and finally, in a seminal paper entitled *The Urban Revolution*,[3] he identified many of the traits now regarded as characteristic of states and not present in less complex societies. These include a hierarchical, stratified society with a centralised ruling authority; the levying of taxes; formal systems of record-keeping; and a complex division of labour, with full-time specialists such as craftsmen, transport workers, merchants, officials and priests. Childe characterised the first cities as substantially larger and more densely-populated than earlier settlements, with public works, temples, and other monumental buildings.

All of these developments were a consequence of the preceding Neolithic Revolution: without substantial food surpluses, it would not be possible for a society to support large numbers of full-time specialists who were not directly involved with food production. Greater numbers of full-time specialists led in turn to the development of increasingly complex societies, with correspondingly greater divisions of labour and wealth. These complex societies eventually became the first states. Although the term 'Urban Revolution' has since fallen into disuse, and methods and concepts have advanced considerably since 1950, Childe's basic model can be seen as influencing most of the later theories of early state formation.[1]

Bands, tribes, chiefdoms and states

The appearance of the first states was, obviously, preceded by less complex societies. In the 1960s and 1970s, anthropologists began to favour typographic schemes in which societies were classified as bands, tribes, chiefdoms and states, according their degree of social, political and economic complexity.[4,5] Bands and tribes are kin-based groups, led by an informal headman rather than a hereditary chief or king. Tribes differ from bands in that they are larger, less mobile, and more likely to practice agriculture or low-level food production. However, both bands and tribes are essentially egalitarian.[6]

By contrast, chiefdoms are ranked societies, where individuals are from birth of 'chiefly' or 'commoner' descent, regardless of their personal abilities. Lineages also hold property, and higher-ranking lineages tend to hold the best agricultural land and fishing rights. Chiefdoms often have elaborate rituals and full-time priests, with the chief sometimes serving as a priest themselves. The office of chief exists apart from the actual chief, and must be filled by somebody of comparable high status upon their death. The power of the chief typically rests upon control of access to prestige goods, made from exotic materials including jade, turquoise, alabaster, gold and lapis lazuli. Such items reinforce the status of the chief, and may be distributed to subordinates as rewards for service. Craft specialisations exist in chiefdoms, but these are not full-time occupations; craft workers are required to combine their activities with the day-to-day business of food production. Populations are often very large, exchange networks highly developed, and warfare frequent.[6] Chiefdoms are broadly characterised as either simple or complex. In complex chiefdoms, such as those of traditional Hawaiian society, communities are organised into districts under the control of lesser chiefs; these in turn are ruled over by a paramount chief.[7]

States are stratified, occupationally-diverse societies with a strong, centralised government. They have a legal system in which wrongdoing is punished in accordance with the law, rather than by offended parties and their kin. They can wage war, draft soldiers, levy taxes and exact tribute.[6] Obligations to the state, such as military service or taxation generally override obligations of kinship. Despite the reduced importance of kinship in state-level societies, the elite stratum is usually hereditary. This group largely controls the economy, enjoying preferential access to goods and services. It is from this group too that high-ranking state officials are usually recruited.[6,8]

States generally have large populations, not all of whom are engaged in food production. Many are full-time craft workers, artisans, architects, engineers and bureaucrats. States have various public buildings, works and services, the construction or implementation of which provide a constant demand for the services of these specialists. Public buildings generally include palaces and temples, which can thus provide archaeological indications of a state. Royal palaces usually comprise a residential component for the ruler and their family, and a governmental component for official duties. Temples, usually built to a standard design, indicate a state religion, and also employ full-time specialists – in this case the priesthood.[6,9] States can also be identified archaeologically by a multi-tiered settlement hierarchy, i.e. there are several distinct categories of settlement size. A four-tier hierarchy is considered to be the benchmark of a state-level society.[10] These may be interpreted as a top tier corresponding to cities, followed by second-tier regional centres, then large villages, and finally small villages.[11]

A characteristic feature of early states was the institutionalised appropriation by an elite stratum of most of the wealth produced by the lower classes. The most common and economically important forms of wealth were agricultural surpluses, although bullion, cloth and exotic raw materials such as obsidian were also important. Farmers and artisans did not accumulate large amounts of wealth themselves, but they created virtually all the wealth that existed in these societies. The main form of appropriation was the taxation levied on agricultural surpluses. In addition, taxes were frequently collected on craft production, market sales, and goods being transported from one place to another.[7] Taxation on just about everything bar breathing is nothing new.

Appropriation was not confined to taxation, and surpluses were also transferred to individual members of the upper classes in the form of rents paid to owners for the use of land. Commoners could be required to perform corvée labour for the state, which could take the form of working on government constriction projects and mining operations, cleaning and maintaining public thoroughfares, or working plots of land belonging to temples, the state, or state officials. Corvée labour could be performed either in lieu of or in addition to other forms of taxation.[7]

As in chiefdoms, offices of state exist apart from their current incumbents.[6] The difference is that while authority is also centralised within chiefdoms, they lack the administrative bureaucracies that are characteristic of states. While even a complex chiefdom will have only two levels of decision-making (local and central), states will have at least four levels. Furthermore, lower-level decision-making is divided up into specialised processes, so that nobody lower down the chain of command ever has enough power for insubordination to become a problem. By contrast, in a chiefdom society any delegation of chiefly authority to a subordinate entails a major handover of power, and the chief runs the risk of being deposed.[12] Notably, in ethnographically or historically-documented chiefdoms, relatively few terms exist to describe administrators. By contrast, a plethora of such terms exist even in small states.[13]

The origins of inequality

Prior to the Holocene, it is likely that most of the world's population was organised as bands. A few – such as some of the larger Natufian groups – may be classified as tribes. In fact, as we have seen, Palaeolithic and Epipalaeolithic societies were probably not all strictly egalitarian, and in some cases social stratification and even descent-group ranking might have occurred (see Chapter 10). At present, however, we lack convincing evidence that social complexity greater than that of the tribe level existed during this period. Indeed, among early Neolithic farming communities there is only limited evidence for social stratification – for example, the large houses around the central plaza at Çayönü Tepesi. Even large Neolithic communities such as Çatalhöyük appear to have been fairly egalitarian. A key question, therefore, is how and why did inequality become so widely institutionalised in human societies?

The search for a mechanism by which tribes become chiefdoms and chiefdoms become states has long preoccupied social scientists, and a full discussion is beyond the scope of this book. A recent study considered a number of possible evolutionary pathways from egalitarian to state-level society, using ethnographic and linguistic data from Austronesian societies. Statistical analysis of this data suggested that egalitarian societies must pass through simple and complex chiefdom stages before they can reach state-level.[14] At the risk of oversimplifying matters, our question can be reformulated as firstly, how did the first stratified societies come about; and secondly, how did these evolve into states?

There are innumerable models based around factors such as trade, or the impact of new technologies. Typically, these cause a significant dislocation in society, either through the need to manage the technology or through greed. The problem is that it is very difficult to argue that such factors must invariably lead to the rise of an initial 'petty elite' that then progressively monopolises wealth and power.[11] Furthermore, many ethnographically-recorded tribal societies have 'levelling mechanisms' in the form of social or religious institutions that regulate inequalities in landholding, wealth or power before they exceed the norms of an egalitarian society. In many societies, the accumulation of excessive amounts of private property by individuals or groups triggers a ceremony in which they are obliged to give it all away or lose face.[6]

An alternative view has been proposed by anthropologist Peter Bogucki,[11] who suggests that the roots of inequality may lie in the shift from the community to the household as the basic unit of production (see Chapter 18). Bogucki describes each household as a self-interested economic unit. As such, it seeks to acquire resources, property, favours and obligations that can provide economic and social security, and possible scope for advancement. A major goal of this activity is to establish the households of one's children as viable economic units. Households will go through a developmental cycle from establishment and dependence on parental households, through to when children marry and set up their own households.

It is of course inevitable that different households will have differing levels of success. Wise decision making, initiative, resourcefulness and luck were undoubtedly as important in Neolithic times as they are today. However, Bogucki suggests that while households were in competition with one another, the priority was simply keeping up with the others rather than getting ahead in terms of wealth and status. From an initial position of relative equality, elite individuals and households did not rise to the top. Rather, the less successful households sank below the existing norms of wealth and status. A crucial point came when these inequalities were carried over to succeeding generations, leaving children responsible for the debts and obligations of their parents and even grandparents. From this point onward, inequality was institutionalised. Meanwhile, more and more households sank below the baseline, until only a few remained with wealth and prestige. This model has the advantage that it eliminates the need to postulate individuals or groups being brought to the fore by trade monopolies or the control of new technologies.

Primary state formation

This 'residual elite' model gives us a plausible mechanism for tribes to become chiefdoms. It must be stressed that it is only one of many theories, and must not be regarded as a definitive answer. Regardless of which, it only answers one half of the question. No less important is how chiefdoms subsequently evolved into states. It is this transformation that Childe described as the Urban Revolution, although anthropologists now prefer the term 'primary state formation'. Specifically, the term refers to the process by which first generation states evolve from less complex societies, without contact with any pre-existing states.[13] Primary state formation occurred in only a few parts of the world:

1. Southern Mesopotamia – The Sumer civilisation emerged during the Late Uruk period, from 3500 BC;[15]
2. Egypt – a unified Egyptian state emerged by 3100 BC ;[16]
3. The Indus Valley – Mature Harappan, 2600 BC;[17]
4. China – the Xia Dynasty, 2070 BC;[18]
5. Mesoamerica – earliest state formation occurred at Monte Albán, in the Valley of Oaxaca, Mexico, 300 to 100 BC;[9]
6. The Andean zone – Moche Valley, northern Peru, AD 200 to 400,[13] or possibly earlier. Primary states might also have emerged in the central Andean highlands and in the Lake Titicaca basin.[19]

Unsurprisingly, these developments all occurred in regions with highly-productive agriculture, capable of supporting large, concentrated populations. Indeed, all were located in regions where agriculture had either arisen independently, or had been combined with indigenous developments. They were usually located in fertile basins or river valleys, such as the Nile, the Tigris and Euphrates, the Yangtze and Yellow Rivers, and the Indus. They relied heavily on irrigation, either by utilising receding floodwater (for example, the annual flooding of the Nile), or by systems of canals (for example, in southern Mesopotamia).[8]

These conditions are necessary for states to form, but do not answer the question of why they did so. As with agriculture, there is a tendency to assume that states are a 'good thing', bringing great benefits to their citizens, and again such a view is debatable. It could be argued that states only really bring benefits to a few. As we have seen, the earliest states were characterised by an elite that become rich and powerful at the expense of everybody else. Fast forward to the early twenty-first century, and it is hard to see that anything much has changed. On the other hand, only with centralised state control can large populations be supported. The collapse of a state is invariably followed by a population decline.[8]

Childe's theories, as we have seen, lie at the heart of many modern explanations, but later writers sought to identify more precisely the circumstances under which primary state formation occurred. One of these was the 'hydraulic' model proposed by Karl Wittfogel.[20] As previously noted, many early states developed in regions where irrigation was essential. Accordingly, Wittfogel proposed that the construction of irrigation systems led to the rise of a ruling elite who controlled access to the water supply. The main problem with this theory is that in the Nile and Indus Valleys, communities made use of the annual river flooding rather than systems of irrigation canals. Another problem is that in Mesopotamia, China and Mesoamerica, fully-fledged states developed well before the introduction of large-scale irrigation systems. In Mesopotamia, earlier systems involved relatively small-scale feeder canals, which were locally-organised. Although irrigation works might have increased state power in some cases, they did not by themselves bring about state formation.[21,22]

Another suggestion is that a lack of essential raw materials in agriculturally productive regions might have been a factor in state formation. For example, the lowland plains of Mesopotamia, while ideal for agriculture, lacked building materials such as stone and wood. Similarly, for the Mayan cities of Mesoamerica, salt, obsidian, and stone for tool-making were scarce. William Rathje[23] proposed that it was the need to acquire these materials at a distance that led to the establishment of states. Those communities that established secure supplies gained an advantage over their neighbours, consequently growing in size and power. However, the model fails to explain the appearance of states in central Mexico, where raw materials were not in short supply. Furthermore, in Mesopotamia, increased trade volumes followed rather than preceded the formation of states, and hence could not have been a factor in their appearance.[6]

American anthropologist Robert Carneiro[22] has proposed warfare as a cause of state formation. Carneiro's 'circumscription' theory defines two types of circumscription. The first is 'environmental circumscription', where an agriculturally productive region is surrounded by mountains or deserts, or is fronted by the sea; the second is 'social circumscription', where people living in the region are hemmed in by other groups. In either case, the losers in a war cannot simply migrate elsewhere, but must submit to the demands of their conquerors. Carneiro suggests environmental circumscription played a role in state formation in coastal Peru, where narrow river valleys are backed by mountains and flanked by deserts. Increasing demand for land led to conflict between Neolithic villages, and defeated villages were absorbed into polities controlled by the victors. As warfare continued, so the warring units grew in size and complexity. In time they became chiefdoms, and eventually entire valleys were unified by the strongest chiefdom. The polities so formed were large enough and sufficiently complex and centralised to warrant the description of states. The process did not stop there, and stronger valley states went on to conquer their weaker neighbours, forming larger multi-valley states. Similarly, 'social circumscription' may be used to account for state formation in northern China, and possibly Mesoamerica.

More recent theories have also emphasised the possible role of warfare in state development. Anthropologist Charles Spencer[24,13] has suggested that chiefdoms are prone to cycles of growth and decline and they must expand in order to avoid ultimate collapse. A chief's power and prestige are related to the availability of surpluses that are dissipated through elaborate ceremonies, feasting, and the acquisition and distribution of luxury goods. However, the risk of delegation of chiefly powers (see above) means that there is a limit to the amount of territory a chief can effectively control. This limits the resource base of the chief, and hence in turn limits the scope for increasing power and prestige. Once these limits have been reached, there is downward pressure on the chiefdom. By this time the cost of even maintaining the status quo has become quite high and a succession of lean years can prove disastrous.

The solution is territorial expansion by conquest of neighbouring polities, coupled with regular extraction of tribute. For such a strategy to work the chief will have to dispatch components of administration to the subjugated polities, in order to maintain control and to manage the extraction of tribute. To limit the potential for independent action by the dispatched and newly-empowered officials, the chief needs to promote internal administrative specialisation as a way of restricting their authority. The cost of maintaining this new bureaucracy is more than offset by the new resources made available by conquest. In other words, the need for territorial expansion by the chiefdom forces its internal reorganization into a state.

Closely related to Spencer's model is a proposal by archaeologist Joyce Marcus[25] that early states underwent cycles of expansion and decline. She suggested that state-level polities emerged through the absorption of smaller polities into a settlement hierarchy of four or more tiers. However, these expansive states were not stable. Once its expansion peaked, a polity would start to wane as distant subordinate settlements began to assert their independence. In time, these breakaway polities began a fresh cycle of expansion and decline.

As we shall see in the following chapters, evidence from the New World in particular does support these models. Nevertheless, it is difficult to believe that warfare and territorial expansion were the only factors involved in the rise of elites and the formation of states. Trade in essential raw materials, and access to critical resources such as water likely played a part as well. While early states may be characterised in terms of the general factors outlined above, they do not all confirm to a standard pattern that is amenable to a universal explanation. Rather each was a product of its own unique circumstances.[8]

While bearing in mind that innumerable learned volumes have been written on the subject, let us move on to review in comparative brevity the circumstances in which civilisation arose in the six regions listed above.

26: Early adopters in Mesopotamia and Egypt

Sumerian precursors: the Halaf and Ubaid

The world's first urban societies emerged in Mesopotamia from around 3500 BC, closely followed by the emergence of a unified Egyptian state along the Nile. These developments were in both cases accompanied by the invention of writing systems: cuneiform script in Mesopotamia and hieroglyphic script in Egypt. Although the ancient Mesopotamians and Egyptians were the earliest adopters of both cities and writing, there were significant differences between the two civilisations, and the process of state formation appears to have been independent in each case.

The rise of the Sumerian city-states of Mesopotamia was firmly rooted in two precursor cultures, the Halaf and the Ubaid. The Halaf was a northern Mesopotamian culture, and lasted from 6000 to 5400 BC. The slightly later Ubaid was current between 5900 and 4200 BC, starting in southern Mesopotamia and later spreading into adjacent regions. These cultures were in turn based on the agricultural package that had been assembled during the PPNA and PPNB periods as described in Chapter 18. Tools were still made principally of stone, but copper implements were starting to come into use. This transitional period between Neolithic and Bronze Age lasted from around 6000 to 3000 BC and is known as the Chalcolithic or Æneolithic, both terms meaning 'copper-stone'. However, the most important breakthrough came with the development of irrigation agriculture, so opening up the plains of what is now southern Iraq to extensive settlement by farming communities. This was a critical step in the early development of the complex societies from which the first city-states ultimately arose.[1]

The Halaf period is named for the type site of Tell Halaf in northern Syria. Sites are known from western Iran, northern Iraq, southern Turkey, and Lebanon. They were typically located in rolling hilly country with sufficient rainfall for rain-fed agriculture. Many settlements were established on virgin territory, suggesting that populations were increasing as farming techniques improved. Settlements were generally small, from 0.5 to 3 ha (1.2 to 7.5 acres), and occupied by 20 to 150 people. A few sites are apparently much larger, up to 20 ha (50 acres), but these may represent the periodic shifting around of smaller sites over a larger footprint over a period of time.[1] Another possibility is that the large sites represent loose clusters of smaller settlements; possibly kin-related groups each occupied a territory distinct from that of their neighbours.[2]

Halaf sites are characterised by rectangular dwellings accompanied by beehive-shaped circular buildings known as *tholoi* (not to be confused with the later beehive tombs of Bronze Age Greece), which probably served as storage or kitchen units. The *tholoi* were constructed from small mud bricks, with an interior diameter of about 3 m (10 ft.). The exteriors of buildings were whitewashed, while the interiors were lined with 2 cm (0.8 in.) thick hard burnt plaster.[2] The material culture of the Halaf period included fine painted pottery, female figurines and stone stamp seals. There is evidence for weaponry in the form of flat pierced wrist guards for archers and clay sling missiles. It is not known if these were used for warfare or hunting or both.[1]

Halaf communities participated in regional trading networks that probably originated with the obsidian trade of previous millennia:[3] obsidian from Turkey continued to be an important trade item, and was used to make tools, weapons and jewellery. The site of Tilkitepe in eastern Turkey is thought to have specialised in the sourcing and preliminary working of obsidian prior to its shipment to other Halaf sites.[1] The distinctive painted Halaf pottery was meticulously decorated with fine geometric designs, and in contrast to the domestic production of earlier wares, it was probably made by specialist potters. Analysis of the clays used indicates that some sites functioned as regional production centres, producing pottery that was traded over a wide area. These include Arpachiyah in Iraq and Chagar Bazar in Syria.[4]

Clay tokens, stamped clay sealings and stone stamp seals have been found at Halaf sites. Sealings are lumps of clay that are impressed with a stamp seal and used to secure pots, baskets and other containers against unauthorised opening. Several hundred sealings were found at Tell Sabi Abyad in northern Syria, in what presumably functioned as storerooms. The sealings define the property of individuals or groups, and deny access to others. Thus they imply an unequal distribution of goods, i.e. that the sealed items were not available to all and sundry. Although such a system of control over goods and people would be useful to a ruling elite, there is no additional evidence for social differentiation at Tell Sabi Abyad. It is possible that the sealed goods belonged to nomadic pastors, who spent much of the time away from the site. A more radical suggestion is that the sealed containers held tokens rather than actual goods, and that these were redeemed against goods and services at a later date. Around 200 plain clay tokens have been found at the site; and ten different types have been distinguished, including small spheres, discs, cones and cylinders. Each might have stood for a different product or service – for example, the spheres might have represented specific amounts of cereals. The cereals themselves were stored in bulk elsewhere in the building, facilitating their protection from rot, insect infestation or fungi.[5]

The social organization of Halaf society remains uncertain. Overall, there is little convincing evidence for stratification, although the so-called 'Burnt House' at Arpachiyah might have been the residence of a village headman.[1] Again, though, it might have functioned as premises where formal transactions involving the exchange of obsidian and other commodities took place. This would be consistent with Arpachiyah's role as a centre of regional trade and exchange. As its name implies, the Burnt House was burned down at the end of its life, possibly in a deliberate, ritual act.[6]

The slightly-later Ubaid period is named for Tell al-Ubaid in southern Iraq. The earliest sites are found throughout southern Mesopotamia, but from around 5400 BC, the Ubaid spread to northern Mesopotamia, where it replaced the Halaf, and beyond to southeastern Anatolia. Late Ubaid sites have also been found along shores of the Persian Gulf. The Ubaid differed in character from the Halaf, with settlements initially located on the resource-poor alluvial plains of southern Mesopotamia. The region could only be made productive by irrigation agriculture, entailing the construction of a network of canals and channels to bring the waters of the Euphrates to the otherwise dry fields.[1]

Ubaid settlements include Eridu and Tell Awayli in southern Iraq, and the more northerly site of Tell Abada. Sites were characterised by rectangular mud brick houses, varying in size from 70 to 240 sq. m. (750 to 2,600 sq. ft.). Rooms were grouped symmetrically on both sides of a large central hall, which was frequently T-shaped or cruciform. It has been suggested that these houses were occupied by groups comprising one or more families, or an extended family household.[7]

Painted pottery from excavations at Eridu enabled the Ubaid to be divided into phases named Ubaid 1 to 4, but the subsequent discovery of earlier material at Tell Awayli necessitated the introduction of an Ubaid 0. The entire scheme may have to be reconsidered should still earlier Ubaid material come to light. Given that many early settlements along the Tigris and Euphrates are now buried by modern alluvial deposits, this possibility cannot be ruled out.[1]

At Tell Abada, the centrally-located structure known as Building A has been cited as evidence of social differentiation.[8] It is three time the size of the smallest house on the site, with gypsum-plastered walls. There are 57 child burials beneath its floor in two phases, and it contains artefacts made from exotic raw materials. It stands in a group with two other large buildings that also contain child burials and exotic artefacts. Other buildings on the site are smaller, with fewer burials and exotic artefacts.[7,9] The differences persist through all three phases of occupation at the site, suggesting economic differentiation that persisted over several generations.[8] It has been suggested that Building A was the home of the community leader, and the other large buildings were occupied by his relatives.[7] However, it is also possible that the complex was a community centre rather than an elite residence.[3]

Later in the Ubaid period, there was a switch from burying the dead within buildings to cemetery burial.[9] One large cemetery has been partially excavated at Eridu, and is estimated to contain between 800 and 1,000 plain or mud brick lined pit graves. Each grave contained one or sometimes two adults, with or without children. Presumably these were family graves that were reopened as required. Grave goods typically include ceramics, tools and jewellery. Figurines with lizard-like heads sometimes found in Ubaid period graves were probably of religious significance. Some graves also contained the remains of a dog; in one such grave, the dog lay across its owner with a bone in its mouth. No individuals seem to have been singled out for special mortuary treatment, suggesting a largely egalitarian society.[4,1]

In a possible contradiction to this view, a sequence of temples has been excavated at Eridu. These mud brick structures are built on top of one another in a chronological sequence spanning the whole Ubaid period, apart from Ubaid 0. The first phase structure comprises a single room containing an altar and offering table, but over a period of several centuries a series of far larger tripartite-plan structures were built on platforms. These structures anticipate the architecture of later Sumerian temples, but at the same time resemble the domestic buildings at Tell Abada; this resemblance reflects the belief that temples were the residences of gods. Temples might have been key elements in the origins of complex society in the region: it is believed that they were a focal point for communities not just as a place of worship, but also in terms of the effort going into their construction and upkeep. They served as the home of priests and administrators who, in addition to overseeing religious rites and rituals, were probably involved with land and labour management, and distribution of food.[1,4]

As with the Halaf, Ubaid society has been interpreted as a series of chiefdoms, but again the evidence is inconclusive. Archaeologist Gil Stein[8] notes a two-level hierarchy settlement pattern consisting of a few large sites of 10 ha (25 acres) or more, such as Eridu, surrounded by clusters smaller subordinate village communities of about 1 ha (2.5 acres). Stein also notes the distinctively large Tell Abada Building A described above, and the emergence of public architecture in the form of temples. On the basis of these observations, he concludes that Ubaid society comprised a series of small, localised chiefdoms. The problem, as Stein concedes, is that there is no evidence for chiefly burials, or for warfare, or the instability and tendency to collapse associated with chiefdoms.

Accordingly, Stein proposes that Ubaid chiefly power was based on the control of cereal surpluses rather than access to prestige goods. He suggests that elites emerged when large families gained control over prime farmland. In southern Mesopotamia, there was a scarcity of good agricultural land with easy access to irrigation water. Once access to such land was secured, the next requirement was to mobilise labour to work the land and maintain the irrigation canals. Kin can provide a good source of labour, so large kin groups had an advantage. The next step was to extend the labour pool to the broader social group. Stein suggests that the key to labour mobilisation was for chiefs to manipulate religious institutions. The widespread presence of Ubaid temples implies the existence of a broadly-shared belief system. Such an ideology would have enabled the chief to mobilise labour for the construction of a temple, and to work land whose produce was theoretically allocated to its upkeep. In practice, a portion was kept back by the chief, and used for periodic status-enhancing tribal feasts. The temple also doubled as a granary, where surpluses were stored for distribution in times of food shortages. Stein argues that such communities were more stable than those where the chief relied on prestige goods to hold power. They were not vulnerable to any disruption to exchange networks through which the prestige goods are obtained, and they were less expansive and thus less prone to warfare. Furthermore, by using the relative lack of prestige goods to downplay inequality, the chief could promote the 'all in this together' ethic so popular with present-day British politicians. Stein admits that his model is speculative, but maintains that it is consistent with the archaeological evidence from Mesopotamia.

Peter Bogucki[3] characterises Halaf and Ubaid society as 'trans-egalitarian', that is to say they were neither egalitarian nor politically stratified. Such societies were moving beyond the constraints of the egalitarian households of late hunter-gatherers and early farmers, but differences had not yet solidified into rigid hierarchies. Leadership was on the way to becoming hereditary power, but the transformation was not yet complete. Nevertheless, many features of the Halaf and Ubaid periods presage developments associated with later Mesopotamian society, including temples; the use of seals and sealings in economic administration; extensive long-distance trade and exchange; and the sharing over a large region of material culture attributes including pottery and architectural style. It is upon these foundations that the final steps to urban living were taken over the following centuries.[1]

Uruk: an early city-state

During the course of the fourth millennium BC, southern Mesopotamia was transformed into the most densely-populated region in Southwest Asia, and the Uruk period (4200 to 3100 BC) saw a shift from rural to urban living. During the Early and Middle Uruk periods (4200 to 3500 BC), large settlements of up to 70 ha (170 acres) appeared. A major shift in population distribution then followed in the Late Uruk Period (3500 to 3100 BC), as many small farming communities were abandoned and their populations absorbed by the towns. By 3200 BC, people were living in societies that on the basis of size and complexity could be described as urban.[1] The early Mesopotamian cities were city-states comprising an urban core surrounded by farmland. They differed from territorial states, which have a far larger hinterland, and are governed from a capital through a hierarchy of smaller provincial administrative centres.[10]

The transition to urban society in Mesopotamia is best appreciated by a consideration of the city of Uruk. This city became the dominant settlement in the region, and gave its name to the period. The modern name of the site is Warka, and it appears in the Bible as the city of Erech. It was first settled around 4800 BC, probably beginning as two villages centred on shrines that later became the two major religious precincts of Anu and Eanna. By the Uruk period, these villages had coalesced into a single settlement that continued to expand, reaching a size of around 100 ha (250 acres) by 3100 BC – more than eight times the size of Çatalhöyük. It would have been an imposing sight with its tall buildings visible from far away. Unlike Çatalhöyük, Uruk was a genuine city – the first in the world. The population probably ran to tens of thousands, and in contrast to the generalised layout of Çatalhöyük, there were specific structures and spaces where specific activities were carried out. These included temples, public spaces for gathering and worship, craft production workshops, and housing. Uruk continued to grow, and by 2900 BC it had attained a size of 400 ha (990 acres, or 1.5 sq. miles) – rather larger than the financial district of present-day London.[1,4]

The city was dominated by two major religious complexes, which later texts suggest were dedicated to the Sumerian deities Anu (the sky god) and Inanna (goddess of war and love). In the Anu area, a series of successive temples spanning several centuries were built on terraces. The best preserved is the gypsum-plastered White Temple, set on a 13 m (42 ft.) high platform, a forerunner of the ziggurats that subsequently became prominent in Mesopotamia. The Eanna precinct contains several monumental structures, built with mud bricks. The size and layout suggests that they were used as temples, although they were not built on raised platforms. As previously noted, temples were regarded as residences of the gods and were often constructed on the same general plan as a domestic residence, though on a much larger scale. Some of the buildings might have served as communal meeting places, or as the residences of priests and officials. In the Late Uruk phase of the Eanna precinct, the largest structure, Temple D, measured 80 by 50 m (260 by 165 ft.), comparable in size to a medium-sized present-day cathedral.[1]

The exact nature of the prevailing political system remains uncertain, but texts and artistic representations attest to both priests and kings. Although there was a degree of competition between the two, Mesopotamian kings were recognised as the chief stewards and agents of their cities' patron gods, and ruled in their name.[10,4] Every aspect of life in Uruk and other early Sumerian city-states was tightly controlled by a highly-bureaucratic administrative system. The stamp seals of the Halaf period gave way to cylinder seals, mostly representing officials or institutions. Their function was to impress the clay tablets used for administrative record-keeping, and the sealings that secured storerooms, containers and bales of commodities. The scenes portrayed on the cylinder seals give an overall impression of control and order. A frequently depicted subject is one of bound captives brought before a skirted figure carrying a spear. Portrayals of warriors armed with spears further underline the impression that life in Sumerian times was far from peaceful. The Warka Vase, a large carved stone vessel found in the Eanna precinct at Uruk, portrays a procession of naked men bringing votive offerings of agricultural produce before the goddess Inanna.[1,4]

Mass-produced bevelled-rim bowls have also been interpreted as evidence of the growth of state control. They are of a standard size that closely matches the volume of the daily food ration issued in later times to state-employed workers. It is likely that the bowls served as containers for the daily rations issued to individuals working for the Uruk authorities, including craft workers, potters, metallurgists, farmers and corvée labourers.[11,4]

Anthropologist Guillermo Algaze[12] has claimed that the emergence of the Sumerian city-states was combined with a process of aggressive expansion as settlers began to exercise control over trade routes. Southern Mesopotamia lacked stone, timber and metals, all of which were vital to the powerful elite groups in order to maintain their grip on power. Algaze believes that a complex network of outposts was established in order to ensure the flow of these materials. The archaeological record shows that settlements were established at key locations in northern Mesopotamia, northern Syria, southeastern Anatolia, in the Zagros and Taurus highlands, and on the plains of southwest Iran. The latter region, previously dominated by the chiefdom of Susa, was rapidly absorbed into the Sumerian heartland. The transformation is reflected in artefact assemblages largely identical to those of southern Mesopotamia, and iconography suggests similar architectural and religious traditions.

In the peripheral regions to the north, outposts were established in northern Syria and southeastern Anatolia. They were strategically placed at important hubs of communication, and the largest were urban in size. The 18 ha (45 acres) site of Habuba Kabira on the Euphrates was constructed to a single masterplan, with carefully laid-out streets and well-differentiated residential, administrative and industrial quarters. The material culture was wholly Sumerian, leaving no doubt that the inhabitants were colonists. Smaller settlements might have served as way stations between the larger outposts and Sumerian city-states to the south. Others, beyond the range of the large outposts, might have been intended to facilitate relations with local communities.

Later written records suggest trade was based on the export of manufactured goods (mainly fine textiles) in exchange for raw materials. Imports were a mixture of luxury and essential commodities, including copper, tin, gold, silver, precious and non-precious stones, bitumen and timber. The strategic position of the outposts suggests that they succeeded in tapping into pre-existing trade networks, and funnelling some of the trade into a more extensive long-distance exchange structure aimed at fulfilling the needs of Sumerian city-states.

Charles Spencer[13] believes that the fundamentals of Algaze's model are sound and that the expansion of political-economic territory to distant regions was an integral part of the process of primary state formation in southern Mesopotamia (see Chapter 25). This process continued through the relatively brief Jemdet Nasr period (3100 to 2900 BC) and into the Early Dynastic period (2900 to 2350 BC). By now, southern Mesopotamia hosted a large number of independent city-states, each controlling a hinterland of productive agricultural territory. The period is known as the Early Dynastic because for the first time, written sources provide a list of kings and dynasties that ruled over the Sumerian city-states.[1] It is the invention of writing that brings us, via semi-mythical figures such as Gilgamesh, to the earliest dawning of recorded history.

The rise of Ancient Egypt

The emergence of the unified Egyptian state occurred slightly later than that of the Sumerian city-states. Although there is little doubt that the two regions were in contact, state formation in Egypt was a purely African phenomenon, uninfluenced by developments in Mesopotamia.[14] The unusual geography of Egypt undoubtedly affected the process. As we saw in Chapter 21, the Egyptian Sahara was entirely arid by 4700 BC, leaving only the Nile Valley and a few oases as capable of sustaining a human presence. South of the Nile Delta, Neolithic settlements were constrained to a narrow strip of moist, fertile land that was thousands of kilometres in length, yet no more than a few kilometres in width. Robert Carneiro's 'circumscription' theory (see Chapter 25) seems to be particularly applicable to this case. The losers in any conflict would not have been able to migrate elsewhere and would have had no choice but to submit to the demands of the victors. We also saw that agriculture reached the Nile Valley after 5000 BC, when farmers arrived from Southwest Asia, bringing their distinctive package of crops and animals. These were probably combined with indigenous African developments, laying the Predynastic foundations from which pharaonic Egypt arose.

Social and political change was rapid, and after 4500 BC an increasingly sophisticated material culture began to develop among numerous settlements clustered along the Nile. Gold, silver and copper working was probably introduced via trading contacts with Southwest Asia, and at the same time, social stratification increased.[14] During the Naqada I period (3700 to 3400 BC), three chiefdoms arose along the Upper Nile, with paramount centres at the sites of Naqada, Hierakonpolis and Thinis. Initially, Naqada appears to have been the dominant chiefdom; its wealth evident in the grave goods found in cemeteries there, which included items of gold, silver, ivory, and lapis lazuli. That Naqada society was unequal is strongly indicated by burials such as that of a young girl found interred with a Mesopotamian cylinder seal, ivory bangles, a slate cosmetic palette, a bone comb, a stone vase, and a Sudanese pottery dish; it is most unlikely that she could have warranted such a luxurious burial in her own right.[15]

As we saw in Chapter 25, chiefdoms are prone to cycles of growth and decline, and inevitably Naqada fell into eclipse as its rival at Hierakonpolis rose to prominence. Hierakonpolis probably began as a collection of small farming settlements around 4000 BC, with an overall population in the low hundreds; but within a few centuries the main settlement had attained a size of 32 to 37 ha (80 to 90 acres), with an estimated population of around 5,000 to 10,000. There were a number of smaller villages on its borders, some of which were quite large themselves, up to 7 ha (17 acres) in extent. Within the settlements, separate residential and industrial zones appeared, along with cemeteries. In addition to its large population and sprawling settlements, Hierakonpolis developed a complex division of labour – an important component of proto-urbanism. Fine craft items produced included stone vases, basketry, linen and pottery. Pottery was the major industry, and large numbers of kilns were sited in natural wind tunnels in the desert hills, where prevailing northerly winds could fan hotter flames and so produce a harder ceramic. In addition to utilitarian wares, a distinctive, high-status black-topped Plum Red Ware was produced, primarily intended for use as grave goods.[16]

Large rectangular mud brick-lined tombs appeared during the Naqada II period (3400 to 3200 BC), including a painted tomb that might have belonged to an early king. There are themes suggestive of foreign contacts, warfare and conquest, the beginnings of a state religion, and pharaonic-like royal regalia. The Naqada III period (3200 to 3100 BC), saw large palace and temple complexes constructed and an isolated royal necropolis established in the desert; all these features were characteristic of later pharaonic capitals. Most of the region's population now resided in the densely-packed main centre, and the settlements in the desert were largely abandoned. The economy was now heavily dependent on intensive floodplain agriculture. As regional elites competed with one another, the demand for prestige goods grew. Carnelian beads, faience vases and statuettes, carved ivories, inlaid wood and ceremonial slate palettes were locally produced, and luxury materials including lapis lazuli, turquoise, obsidian and gold were imported.[16]

During this period, Hierakonpolis gained control over the whole of Upper Egypt, before extending its power downstream. By 3000 BC, it controlled the Nile Delta, thus completing the unification of the whole of Egypt and ushering in the 1st Dynasty of the Early Dynastic period. A carved slate palette depicts a ruler with the hieroglyphic name of Narmer. He is wearing a double crown that combines the white crown of Upper Egypt and the red crown of the Nile Delta, confirming him as the first ruler of a unified Egyptian state. Subsequently, the capital was moved to Memphis, because Hierakonpolis lay too far upstream to administer the whole of Egypt.[15]

Archaeological evidence from the Sinai Peninsula and southern Israel suggests that the new Egyptian state did not delay projecting its presence into the regions that lay on its periphery. In addition to participating in long-distance exchange, it established a network of outposts in regions beyond its immediate borders. These controlled the strategically-important northern Sinai corridor, and there are also at least a dozen in southern Canaan. There were four main types of outpost: firstly, small way stations across northern Sinai; secondly, small trading posts close to the sites of local peoples; thirdly, small Egyptian enclaves within sites of local peoples; and fourthly, larger colonies, for example at Tell 'Erani, where locally-manufactured Egyptian-style ceramics have been found. There was also an expansion of influence into Lower Nubia, albeit on a smaller scale. Through these networks flowed Canaanite wine, oil, resin, honey, bitumen, turquoise and copper. From Lower Nubia came slaves, exotic fruits, tropical woods, animal skins and cattle, with Egyptian luxury goods going the other way.[12] Charles Spencer[13] has little doubt that territorial expansion played a key role in primary state formation in ancient Egypt (see Chapter 25).

The Early Dynastic period lasted until about 2575 BC. It is during this period that the Step Pyramid of Saqqara was constructed by the 3rd Dynasty king Djoser. This stone-built 60 m (200 ft.) high monument was the first of the great pyramids that are now virtually synonymous with Ancient Egypt. The technical skills, economic power and administrative organisation involved were obviously immense. Architect Imhotep faced numerous changes of design – a problem that has bedevilled large construction projects ever since. Nevertheless, it is clear that by the end of the Early Dynastic period, the foundations had been laid for the prosperity and economic stability of the Old Kingdom that followed it.[14]

Writing systems: a primer

The writing systems of Mesopotamia and Ancient Egypt are the earliest in the world, but before looking at them in detail we must pause to consider some of the underlying concepts and terminology associated with writing. American classicist Barry Powell[17] defines writing as "*a system of markings with a conventional reference that communicates information*". He divides writing systems into two basic categories: semasiography and lexigraphy. Semasiography ('meaning') is the use of symbols that are not linked to specific words to convey information. Such symbols are commonly referred to as pictograms, although Powell prefers the term sematogram. Examples of semasiographic systems include computer icons and much road and other public signage. Unlike lexigraphy, semasiography is independent of language. Thus a 'No Entry' sign is read as *'Entrée Interdite'* by a French-speaker, *'Kein Eintrag'* by a German-speaker, and so on. Lexigraphy is what we conventionally regard as 'writing', i.e. the use of written words.

There are two divisions of lexigraphy: logography and phonography. Logography uses symbols to represent words (strictly speaking, 'significant segments of speech'). The symbols are known as logograms and they have a semantic value, but not a phonetic value. For example, a picture of a cow may be used to represent a cow, but not the sound /cow/ (by convention, phonetic sounds are enclosed in slashes). The difference is illustrated by the logographic Arabic numerals 1, 2 and 3, representing in English the words 'one', 'two' and 'three'. However, in French, they represent the words 'un', 'deux' and 'trois' – these are not of course pronounced /one/, /two/ and /three/. Logograms can be complex, comprising more than one sign. The additional signs can add various types of information, for example the logogram £100 means 'one hundred pounds'. Such additional signs are known as determinatives, because they determine the category in which the accompanying signs are to be understood. Note that the verbal equivalent does not necessarily follow the order in which the signs appear; £100 is not pronounced 'pounds one hundred' despite being written that way.

Phonography uses symbols to represent sounds. In this case the symbols are known as phonograms. Unlike logograms, they do not have a semantic value, i.e. when pronounced they do not signify words even if they happen to be meaningful. For example, a symbol pronounced /go/ does not signify the word 'go'. There is a one-to-one correspondence between the order in which phonograms are arranged and in which they are pronounced. Phonograms can be of two types: syllabic (where the symbols represent one or syllables) or alphabetic (where they represent vowels and consonants). The symbols are referred to, respectively, as syllabograms and alphabetic signs (or letters).

Record-keeping and writing in Mesopotamia

As we saw in Chapter 18, semasiographic systems in Southwest Asia might go back to the pre-pottery Neolithic, but were these the forerunners of lexigraphy-based systems? In simple terms, did writing come from pictures? Barry Powell[17] and Canadian anthropologist Bruce Trigger[10] believe that it did not. Citing the work of archaeologist Denise Schmandt-Besserat,[18] they argue that the origins lie with Halaf era tokens that, as we also saw, might also have their origins in the pre-pottery Neolithic. During the Early and Middle Uruk periods (4200 to 3500 BC), the tokens became increasingly widespread and some featured incised markings. On the basis of later cuneiform script, these 'complex' tokens have been interpreted as representing sheep, oil, metal ingots, honey, garments and other commodities, whereas plain tokens might have been used to represent the quantities involved. After around 3500 BC, the tokens were secured against tampering by enclosing them in a spherical clay envelope known as a bulla. A cylinder seal was used to identify the official or place involved with the transaction. At some stage, the practice arose of recording the contents of the bulla by impressing the tokens into its surface before sealing them up inside. It must soon have been realised that this rendered the actual tokens redundant, and bullae were replaced by clay tablets as a means of recording transactions.

Over 5,000 clay tablets have been found at Uruk, dating to the Late Uruk period. They contain incised or impressed signs, made with a stylus while the clay was still soft, that were grouped together in rectangular boxes known as cases. The script is known as proto-cuneiform, and is the precursor of the cuneiform ('wedge shaped') writing that remained in use in Mesopotamia for thousands of years. The tablets are records of economic and administrative data rather than lexigraphic text. They record the commodities in question (barley, sheep, fields, etc.), quantities, accounting periods, nature of the transaction, parties involved, and names of officials and institutions. Possibly the 'complex' tokens formed the basis for the proto-cuneiform signs for commodities, and the plain tokens the amounts involved. Different numerical counting systems were used for different functions: a sexagesimal system (units of 1, 10, 60, 600) was used for counting discrete objects such as animals, people, fish, or implements; a bisexagesimal system (units of 1, 10, 60, 120, 1,200) was used for grain and other items distributed as part of a rationing system; and a time system of 1, 10, 30 was used to form a calendar of ten-day weeks, three of which comprised a month.[1,17]

Although around 90 percent of the Uruk tablets were accounting records, some word lists have also been found: these include lists of fish, birds, other animals, textiles and vessels. They reflect the need of Sumerian officials to classify their world into various categories and to teach scribes the contents of these categories.[17] The best-known is the Standard Profession List, a catalogue of professions practiced at the time, ranked according to status. The earliest version dates to the Jemdet Nasr period (3100 to 2900 BC). It is damaged and therefore cannot be read completely, but its format is followed in later versions and most of its contents have been deduced. The Standard Professions List gives an insight into the hierarchical nature of Sumerian society, not only showing how the various professions were ranked within society, but also rankings within many of the professions themselves. The catalogue evolved over time, reflecting changes in society. The profession of tax collector first appears during the Early Dynastic III period (2600 to 2334 BC), where it is recorded in the archives of the city of Shuruppak.[4]

Such recording systems were obviously still very limited, and could do little more than record transactional data. Furthermore, large numbers of symbols were required; around 1,200 different signs have been recorded. The shift to a lexigraphic system capable of recording the spoken word might have begun when somebody hit on the idea of encoding sounds with what is known as the rebus, or visual pun. Examples in English include the pronoun I (eye) and the prefix be- (bee). The earliest example of the use of rebus in Mesopotamia is found on tablets from Uruk dating to the Jemdet Nasr period. The sign for an arrow (known as TI and pronounced /ti/ in Sumerian) was used to represent the Sumerian words /til/ ('life') and /ti/ ('rib'). Another early example, commonly used in archaic texts, is the sign for 'reed', GI, used to express the Sumerian verb /gi/ ('to render'). Essentially, logograms were transformed into syllabograms by using their phonetic rather than semantic values. The system evolved over the course of several centuries as Sumerian administrators sought to extend the range of concepts that could be represented. Names were being rendered phonetically by 2700 BC, with grammatical affixes soon after. By 2400 BC, letters and other texts were being recorded.[10,17]

The ancient Sumerian language is what is known as 'agglutinative', as is modern Turkish. In an agglutinative language, words are expressed by a single syllable, and may then be built up by the addition of suffixes or prefixes as required. Agglutinative constructions also occur in English: for example, the word 'manliness' is built up from the base word 'man' with the suffixes '-ly' (like) and '-ness' (the quality of) to form 'the quality of being like a man'. For this reason, Sumerian phonetic signs mainly consist of monosyllabic syllabograms of the simple form V (vowel), CV (consonant + vowel), VC (vowel + consonant) or CVC (consonant + vowel + consonant). Only four vowel sounds were used: /a/ /e/ /i/ and /u/, with /o/ omitted.[17]

The Mesopotamian writing system as it finally evolved was logosyllabic; that is to say it was a combination of logograms, syllabograms and determinatives. Logograms were used to express nouns, verbs and adjectives; phonetic signs were used for affixes, particles, and to spell out foreign names. Over time, the number of symbols required fell. Only 600 were in use by 2800 BC, a number which remained fairly constant thereafter. At the same time, the symbols themselves became progressively more stylised. Use of a wedge-shaped stylus encouraged a style in which the symbols were made up of combinations of wedges and straight lines, and they eventually bore little resemblance to their original form. This was now the classic Mesopotamian cuneiform that remained in use for the next 2,500 years. Cuneiform writing was adapted for the Akkadian Empire some time before the reign of Sargon of Akkad (2334 to 2279 BC). Later variants are found on Babylonian and Assyrian tablets, and cuneiform only fell into disuse after the conquests of Alexander the Great between 336 and 323 BC. The last-known text dates to AD 75.[17]

Egyptian hieroglyphic writing systems

It is unclear to what extent – if any – early Egyptian writing systems were influenced by their Mesopotamian counterparts. It is sometimes claimed that the two are sufficiently different from one another as to make independent development likely.[14] However, Barry Powell[17] downplays these differences and argues that they are small in comparison to the indisputably independent developments in China and Mesoamerica. He believes that the Mesopotamian system was re-engineered for conditions in Egypt. Fully-fledged hieroglyphic writing appears at the start of the pharaonic period, 3100 BC, or slightly earlier. Unlike Mesopotamia, there are no antecedents such as an Egyptian equivalent of proto-cuneiform. Another difference is that for the first six hundred years, Egyptian writing was primarily used for veneration of the pharaohs rather than accountancy. This does suggest that somebody saw the Mesopotamian system in use and adopted it as the basis of a writing system intended for an entirely different purpose. It is possible that ivory and bone plaques excavated in 1991 were economic texts, but this cannot be confirmed. Another issue is that many early texts have undoubtedly been lost. From the beginning the Egyptians recorded texts on papyrus, a far more ephemeral medium than the Mesopotamian clay tablet.

There are definite differences between the Mesopotamian and Egyptian systems. Powell notes that hieroglyphic writing was indivisibly bound up with Egyptian art. The two share conventions of representation, and paintings, statues and decoration are normally accompanied by hieroglyphic writing. Hieroglyph means 'sacred carving', and hieroglyphic script is highly iconic, consisting mostly of stylised pictures. Hieroglyphs were often treated with great attention to detail, almost as miniature works of art. They were used on temples, tombs, sarcophagi and stelae. The *Book of the Dead*, a New Kingdom funerary text, is also inscribed in hieroglyphs. In addition to these formal hieroglyphs, the hieroglyphic system incorporates two other types of writing, hieratic and demotic. Hieratic ('priestly') script is more stylised than hieroglyphic script. It was a 'fast hand' script, providing a quicker way of recording text on papyrus. It is analogous to long-hand ('joined-up') writing in comparison to formal typeface. Demotic ('of the people') was a later development, appearing around 650 BC. Demotic was a linear script (i.e. non-iconic and consisting of abstract lines). Although it was later used for religious purposes, the initial usage was secular and included business accounts, wills and letters.[17]

Like cuneiform, Egyptian writing is logosyllabic, consisting of logograms, syllabograms and determinatives. There are a similar number of signs (around six or seven hundred) to cuneiform, working in similar ways. However Egyptian phonetic signs omit vowels: they represent syllables, but only a native speaker can pronounce them through their knowledge of the language. Unlike cuneiform, there are neither pure signs for vowels, nor are vowels encoded in any of the syllabograms.

The syllabograms are of three types, representing one, two or three consonants. They are known respectively as uniliterals, biliterals and triliterals. Vowels are implied, and must be supplied by the reader. For example the Swallow (bird) hieroglyph may be transliterated (i.e. expressed in the Roman alphabet) as the consonants '*wr*' and pronounced /*wer*/, with the implied vowel 'e' inserted by the reader. The Swallow hieroglyph means 'great' or 'important'. There were 24 uniliterals that in theory could have described all the basic sounds of Egyptian speech if used with implied vowels. In practice, this never happened, and the Egyptians never distinguished the uniliterals from the biliterals and triliterals. Many of the biliterals and all of the triliterals represented whole words, and were thus in effect logograms.[19,17]

The rise of cities and states in Mesopotamia and Egypt mark the beginnings of V. Gordon Childe's Urban Revolution, and these ancient civilisations have been intensely studied by European scholars for many centuries. Consequently, many Westerners will have been familiar with them since their childhood. The Harappan civilisation of the Indus Valley is far less well known to the general public in the West; it is to this enigmatic civilisation that we turn next.

27: An enigmatic civilisation

The Indus Valley civilisation

In contrast to the early civilisations of Mesopotamia and Ancient Egypt, there is little public awareness of the civilisation that emerged in the floodplains of the Indus and now-dry Ghaggar-Hakra Rivers around 2600 BC. Although centred on the two great urban sites of Harappa and Mohenjo-daro, the Indus Valley (or Harappan) civilisation extended over a wide area of Pakistan, southern Afghanistan and northwest India. Like the Tigris, the Euphrates and the Nile, the Indus and Ghaggar-Hakra watered large regions that would otherwise be desert, but in terms of both land area and population, the Indus Valley civilisation dwarfed the contemporary Sumerian and Egyptian Old Kingdom civilisations. Part of the reason for its relatively low profile is its late discovery. Only in 1924 was the discovery of Mohenjo-daro and Harappa announced, more than a century after the first excavations in Egypt and Mesopotamia. Furthermore, post-war investigations have been hampered by the on-going tensions between India and Pakistan.[1] To this day, the Indus Valley civilisation remains enigmatic. We have samples of what is thought to be a logosyllabic writing system, in the form of stamp seals, sealings, amulets and small tablets, but the script remains undeciphered.[2] Even the language spoken remains uncertain. Dravidian is the most obvious possibility, but Peter Bellwood[3] has suggested that it might have been a relative of Elamite. As noted in Chapter 20, Bellwood believes that Elamite and Dravidian are part of a single hypothetical language family known as Elamo-Dravidian.

The conventional chronology of the Indus Valley civilisation recognises the Early (3200 to 2600 BC), Mature (2600 to 1900 BC) and Late (1900 to 1300 BC) Harappan periods, preceded by a lengthy Pre-Harappan period. This scheme is based on a traditional view of a rise, zenith and decline, and is now seen as an oversimplification. It also fails to recognise the continuity between the Pre-Harappan and later periods. Accordingly, some scholars prefer to think in terms of four eras defined in terms of social and economic structure. Thus the Early Food Producing Era (before around 6500 to 5000 BC) had an economy based on food production but lacking pottery. During the following Era of Regionalisation (5000 to 2600 BC), distinct pottery styles appeared at particular times and places, corresponding to distinct regional cultures that interacted with one another through exchange networks. The Era of Integration (2600 to 1900 BC) saw the emergence of a widespread homogeneity in material culture. Finally, the Era of Localisation (1900 to 1300 BC) is marked by a return to the cultural differentiation of the Era of Regionalisation. The chronology is only approximate, as transitions from one era to another did not happen everywhere at the same time, and in some cases they did not happen at all. However, in the Indus Valley region, the Eras of Integration and Localisation correspond to the traditional Mature and Late Harappan periods.[4]

Mehrgarh

As with the Mesopotamian and Egyptian civilisations, the Indus Valley civilisation has indigenous roots. The 1950s view that it was brought about by diffusion from Mesopotamia was abandoned with the discovery of Mehrgarh in 1971. This settlement is located at the foot of the Bolan Pass in the mountainous region of Baluchistan. The Bolan Pass is one of the major communication routes between the Iranian Plateau, Central Asia, and the Indus Valley. Mehrgarh dates to around 7000 BC, roughly when the Southwest Asian package of crops and animals reached the Indian subcontinent. It is now widely accepted that the Neolithic occupations of Mehrgarh and the later sites of Kili Gul Mohammad Rana Ghundai were precursors to the Indus Valley civilisation.[1,5]

Mehrgarh was continuously occupied up until around 2600 BC, when the Indus Valley civilisation appeared. The vast site covers 300 ha (740 acres), although the whole of that area was never all in use at the same time. Period I, lasting from around 7000 to 6000 BC, was aceramic. Coarse ceramics first appear in Period IIA, followed by fine, lustrous red pottery in the subsequent Period IIB around 5800 BC. Buildings from the Neolithic phases were built with double rows of mud bricks, which had a herringbone pattern of thumbprints to provide keying for mud-mortar. The walls were plastered inside and out, and might have been painted on the outside. Buildings were rectangular, with fireplaces and as many as ten rooms, though four was more usual. The larger buildings were probably used as granaries rather than dwellings. Grave goods have provided much information about craft activities at the site during Period I, and include figurines, copper beads and a wide range of ornaments made from marine shells, lapis lazuli, turquoise and black steatite. More utilitarian objects found include sickles made from microliths set with bitumen into wooden hafts.[6]

Six-row barley accounts for 90 percent of the cereal remains during Period I; the barley was cultivated, but probably not fully domesticated. However, domesticated emmer and einkorn wheat were also present in small quantities. There was a strong focus on hunting wild game, and domestic animals were initially limited to goats. Later in Period I, sheep and cattle became increasingly dominant. The latter were the indigenous humped zebu cattle (*Bos indicus*) rather than the Southwest Asian non-humped (*Bos taurus*) variety. Over time, the animals decreased in size; a clear indicator of local domestication.[6] It is also possible that the second independent domestication of barley, noted in Chapter 18, occurred at Mehrgarh.[7] On the other hand, wild emmer and einkorn have not been found in South Asia,[6] so an indigenous domestication for these is less likely.

Despite the obvious differences, such as the breeding of zebu cattle, Mehrgarh displays many similarities with early Neolithic settlements in the eastern borders of Mesopotamia. Although houses were rectangular rather than round, the use of herringbone pattern of thumbprints for mortar keying has been seen at a number of aceramic sites in Zagros; and there are similarities in tool-making traditions, mortuary practices, and certain types of figurines. It is apparent that there were interactions between Neolithic sites all the way from Mesopotamia to the western margins of the Indus Valley; equally, however, Balochistan cannot be interpreted as the cultural backwater of the Southwest Asian Neolithic.[6]

Baluchistan origins

Our knowledge of the Early Food Producing Era comes largely from Mehrgarh. Only a few other aceramic farming settlements have come to light in the in the Indo-Iranian borderland region, and these do not appear until much later. It is possible, however, that settlements contemporary with Period I Mehrgarh still lie buried beneath alluvial deposits.[8] The presence at Mehrgarh of artefacts made from non-local raw materials is evidence that long-distance exchange networks were operating during Period I.[9]

The Era of Regionalisation may be said to have begun with the appearance of pottery at Period II Mehrgarh, but farming settlements do not become widespread in Baluchistan until around the mid-sixth or early fifth millennium BC. These include Kili Gul Mohammad and Rana Ghundai. From the start of the Chalcolithic around 4300 BC, there was a considerable increase in both the number and size of settlements in Baluchistan and in the adjacent lowlands. Fine pottery, often wheel-thrown, became widespread. Stylistic differences suggest the emergence of regional groups, but the wares also showed similarities. They were decorated with geometric patterns, or with stylised animal designs of sheep, goats, cranes and snakes. A spindle whorl found at Sheri Khan Tarakai suggests that there was also a flourishing textile industry. Interestingly, the geometric ceramic designs are reminiscent of those later seen in woven fabric and carpets. Stylised terracotta figurines of humans and bulls have also been found at Sheri Khan Tarakai; the use of the bull as a ceramic motif later became widespread.[8]

At this time, there was an increase in the import of raw materials from distant sources. Sites such as Period III Mehrgarh become regional centres of ceramic and other craft production. Imported raw materials were processed into luxury goods for local and regional consumption, and large quantities of fine pottery were produced for exchange to the hinterlands.[9] Workshops were sited in domestic courtyards, suggesting that craft production was organised by independent family groups rather than being centrally controlled.[10] Eventually, during the later fourth millennium BC, settlements were established at key points along the long-distance trade routes on the Indo-Iranian Plateau, and in locations where raw materials could be obtained. They included Shahr-i Sokhata in Iranian Baluchistan, an important regional centre that reached a size of 12 to 15 ha (30 to 37 acres) by 2800 BC.[11,8]

Stamp seals make an appearance during the Era of Regionalisation. They were stamped onto clay or bitumen to seal containers and bundles of goods. As with Mesopotamia, the implication is a society in which individuals or elite groups controlled access to and distribution of these goods. Seals have been found at many sites, including Mehrgarh, Rehman Dheri and Damb Sadaat. The concept of property was clearly gaining in importance. Abstract graphic symbols or graffiti occur in almost all sites from the Era of Regionalisation, primarily on fired clay objects or pottery. The graffiti are simple signs scratched into the wet clay before or after firing to identify ownership and vessel contents.[9]

Towards integration

Evidence for the colonisation of the Indus and Ghaggar-Hakra basin has not been found prior to the fourth millennium BC, thus the Era of Regionalisation does not begin there until that time. It is possible earlier settlements remain undiscovered, lying buried under thousands of years of alluvial deposit,[11] but it could be that prior to the large-scale migrations into the greater Indus region, it received only seasonal visitation by nomadic pastors.[12] The region was attractive to settlers, because it offered vast expanses of well-watered prime agricultural and grazing land. Wild game and fish were abundant, as was timber for construction and fuel.[8]

Four regional phases were originally recognised for the Era of Regionalisation in the greater Indus region, named for key sites and identified by pottery styles: the Balakot, Amri, Hakra and Kot Diji.[4] These phases were regional phenomena and not subdivisions of a single archaeological period, and as such, they could overlap in time. Subsequent archaeological investigations have since added further phases, for example the Ravi Phase.[5] Technologies and crafts were developed and refined. Although microlith sickles remained in use, copper was beginning to replace stone for heavy-duty tool-making. Wheel-thrown pottery now predominated, and there were advances in kiln technologies. Firing conditions could be controlled to produce a red (oxidised) or grey (reduced) colour. Figurines had become more detailed, and depicted a greater variety of postures than those of earlier periods. From Harappa, for example, there is a skirted standing female figurine, holding a bowl, with details of the weave of the skirt and her jewellery painted on. Features were also incised or added to figurines by appliqué. Many figurines depict women adorned with jewellery and head ornaments, who may represent Mother Goddesses, and turbaned male figurines are also known. Bulls remained a common animal subject, though rams were also depicted.[8]

The later fourth millennium BC saw the appearance of increasingly complex proto-urban settlements, presaging the full-blown urban settlements of the Era of Integration, and characterised by formally-planned street layouts enclosed by massive mud brick walls. Examples include Rehman Dheri and Kalibangan. The walled settlement of Rehman Dheri, in the Gomal Valley, was first occupied around 3300 BC and eventually attained a size of 22 ha (54 acres). Aerial photography has revealed a grid street pattern within its walls and even the remains of individual buildings. Kalibangan is located at the confluence of the Drishadvati and Saraswati Rivers, where a 4.5 ha (11 acres) settlement enclosed by a 1.9 m (6 ft.) thick wall has been identified, lying beneath a later Harappan citadel. Excavations have revealed mud brick buildings, laid out with courtyards.[11]

Further evidence for formal construction standards can be seen in standardisation of bricks, although at first there were competing standards. At Kalibangan, brick dimensions were fixed in the ratio 1:2:4, but at Harappa – at this stage still a small settlement – the ratio was 1:2:3.[8] Another hint of cultural convergence is the spread of Kot Diji pottery, named for the central Indus Valley site of Kot Diji. It has been found at sites in the region bounded by Kalibangan in the east, Rehman Dheri in west and Amri in the south. The style was current from 3200 to 2600 BC, and is usually identified by wheel-thrown globular jars of red ware with flanged rims. It was decorated with abstract geometric designs of fish-scale patterns and intersecting circles, and figurative depictions of fish, the heads of bulls, and pipal leaves.[11] Ironically, these developments never reached Baluchistan, where regional cultural traditions persisted. There was no Era of Integration in Baluchistan, and it remained a borderland on the periphery of the urban world it had spawned.[9,11]

A multi-tier settlement hierarchy

The transition to the Era of Integration lasted for about a century, beginning around 2600 BC. It appears to have been a time of considerable upheaval and there is evidence for extensive burning at the sites of Kot Diji, Gumla, Naushero and Amri, coinciding with the end of the Era of Regionalisation occupation. Although occupation continued uninterrupted at some settlements, including Harappa, a large number were abandoned. However, an even greater number of new settlements were established on virgin territory.[12] The process of urbanisation in the Indus and Ghaggar-Hakra basin was closely followed by the colonisation of neighbouring Gujarat, and the establishment of outposts at remote strategic locations. Some of these small settlements controlled long-distance trade routes, and others were close to sources of raw materials not available in the Indus Valley.[13]

At its maximum extent, the Indus Valley civilisation included five cities of at least 80 ha (200 acres) in extent: Mohenjo-daro, Harappa, Dholavira, Rakhigarhi and Ganweriwala.[11] These cities stood at the apex of a four-tier settlement hierarchy. The second tier settlements were regional centres, rather smaller at 10 to 50 ha (25 to 125 acres), and include Kalibangan and Judeirjo-daro. Below this was a third tier of large villages of 5 to 10 ha (12.5 to 25 acres), including Amri, Lothal, Chanhu-daro and Rojdi. Finally, there was a fourth tier of small villages ranging from 1 to 5 ha (2.5 to 12.5 acres), such as Balakot, Nageshwar, and Shortugai.[9] This type of four-tier settlement hierarchy, as we saw in Chapter 25, is consistent with a state-level society.

From the largest to the smallest, these settlements generally shared a number of features including formal planning, workshops and other industrial facilities, and well-appointed housing.[8] There was an efficient provision of water and sanitation though brick-lined wells and carefully designed, well-maintained drainage systems. Domestic drains carried water to larger street drains that were equipped with sump-pits. Bins were provided in the streets for non-liquid waste that was presumably collected and dumped outside the settlement. The streets were set out in a network, albeit not a strict north-south and east-west grid plan.[9] Settlements were typically walled, although in some cases there might also have been exterior suburbs. There was usually a separately-walled, raised citadel, where public buildings were located. Brick sizes were further standardised and the dimensional ratio of 1:2:4 was now generally adopted, with sizes of 7 by 14 by 28 cm (2.75 by 5.5 by 11 in) for houses and 10 by 20 by 40 cm (4 by 8 by 16 in) for city walls.[8]

The two best-known sites are Mohenjo-daro and Harappa, which are located 400 km (250 miles) apart and, as noted above, were excavated in the 1920s. Mohenjo-daro, located in the Lower Indus Valley in the Pakistan province of Sindh, is the better-preserved of the two, and might have covered over 250 ha (620 acres) with a population as high as 100,000. The city comprises a walled citadel to the west and a residential lower town to the east. It is possible that there were also extensive suburbs beyond the limits of the lower town, now buried below the alluvium of the surrounding plain. The citadel measures 200 by 400 m (660 by 1,320 ft.), and stands on an enormous platform of sand and silt within a 7 m (23 ft.) thick mud brick retaining wall.[8] It contains a number of buildings including the Great Bath, a large watertight tank set within a complex of rooms. Located close to the Great Bath are the massive foundations of a structure that is often described as a granary. In truth these interpretations are speculative and their true function is unknown.[9] The citadel also holds residential buildings and, at the southern edge, a pillared hall indicated by four rows of five brick pillars.[8]

The lower town was also constructed on a mound, though it is unwalled. It is divided into residential blocks by main streets running in a north-south direction, bisected by smaller lanes running east-west.[11] Private houses varied in size, but most were from 50 to 150 sq. m. (540 to 1,620 sq. ft.). This size variation may relate to more to the number of occupants than to differences in wealth.[14] All houses shared the same general plan, with a central courtyard providing access to the street, as well as to rooms and bathing areas that were not always interconnected. Groups of houses formed neighbourhoods that were often associated with one or more private wells. This association could indicate a need for relatively private water sources of the type necessary in later Hindu caste society to maintain ritual purity in an urban environment. Although there is no evidence for a caste society in the Harappan cities, the wells may reflect a perceived need for water purity in a congested urban environment.[9] The apparent importance attached to sanitation has led to speculation that the Great Bath at Mohenjo-daro and the fire altars found at a number of other sites were associated with purification rituals, and were symbolic reproductions of domestic bathing facilities and hearths.[14]

Harappa is rather smaller than Mohenjo-daro, but still covers an area of over 150 ha (370 acres), and the population might have been around 60,000. As we have seen, the first occupation of the site predates the Era of Integration; the city grew organically around the earlier settlement. Unfortunately, the site was plundered for bricks during the nineteenth century, so the architecture is only known from foundations, wall stubs and 'robber trenches' backfilled after the original building materials had been scavenged. What remains of the city comprises a number of walled mounds, the westernmost of which has been identified as the citadel. The mounds are clustered around a central depression that might have held water and served as a reservoir.[8] As such, Harappa differs from the 'classic' Harappan plan of a walled citadel to the west and an unwalled lower town to the east, as seen at Mohenjo-daro.[11]

The second tier of settlements were walled and formally planned along similar lines to their larger counterparts. Kalibangan, for example, comprised a rectangular 3 ha (8 acres) citadel to the west of a walled lower town of 9 ha (22 acres). The citadel, as noted above, was built over an earlier settlement.[11] The third and fourth-tier sites specialised in particular economic activities: for example, Chanhu-daro was engaged in the production of luxury items, including steatite stamp seals and carnelian beads. Smaller sites with local access to raw materials produced items for trade to the large centres and external markets. Examples include the coastal settlements of Balakot and Nageshwar, which specialised in shell working. Shortugai, in the north of Afghanistan, was a trading colony near major sources of lapis lazuli, copper and tin.[9]

Harappan craft and trade

Craft working and trade were of central importance to Harappan society, and widely dispersed settlements were linked by a hierarchical trade and exchange network. An interregional network connected the major cities to one another and to regions external to the Indus Valley; intraregional networks connected the cities to towns and villages. Local exchange systems redistributed locally-produced items and essential commodities to villages and nomadic pastoralists, and at the other end of the scale, Harappan manufactured goods were traded to regions as far away as Mesopotamia and possibly even Egypt.[9]

Craft workers were now employing more complex technologies, and working with a greater variety of materials. Very high levels of expertise were attained as workshops produced stoneware bangles, elaborately-decorated ceramics, inlaid woodwork, agate beads and steatite seals. Other complex craft techniques included copper and bronze metallurgy, shell working, gold working and faience manufacture.[9] The most commonly-found artefacts are pottery, beads, bangles and various metal tools and ornaments, but the production of perishable goods including textiles, leather, woodwork and basketry was undoubtedly of importance.[15] Figurines and seal carvings indicate that ornaments were worn in large numbers by men, women and children alike. They were produced in a variety of materials, ranging from terracotta to gold. Bangles were worn on one or both arms, from the wrist to the shoulder. Women wore torques with as many as seven massive strands of beads, and necklaces that stretched down to the waist. Though some ornaments have been found as grave goods, these do not reflect the quantity and variety apparently worn in life. In particular, only bangles made from white shell have been found. Presumably the majority of ornaments were passed on to living relatives.[16]

In an urban society, one might have expected craft production to shift from the small-scale family-based workshops seen in the Era of Regionalisation to larger-scale operations. In fact, it seems that Harappan craft production was organised on both large and small scales. Early excavations of Mound F at Harappa revealed a number of houses of uniform design, associated with a metalworking area. The houses were interpreted as 'workmen's quarters' and evidence of an administratively-controlled workshop. More recently, a pottery-producing area has been identified on the northwest side of Mound E with a kiln that was capable of firing 200 pieces at a time. Ceramic remains found in the kiln area show that the unit specialised in a fairly small range of luxury pottery. Products included ledge-shouldered jars, fluted cooking-pots, and large storage jars of 60 to 70 cm (24 to 27.5 in.) in height. In contrast to some of the more basic jars common at Harappan sites, these wares required the use of complex, multi-stage techniques. Techniques must have been standardised, as they were maintained uniformly over the period that the kiln was in use. However, much craft production remained on a smaller scale. At Mohenjo-daro, 60 percent of the workshops were below 100 sq. m (1,075 sq. ft.), and the average size was 25 to 30 sq. m (270 to 320 sq. ft.). These small, isolated units were scattered throughout the city, and many were found in residential buildings, suggesting family control. It seems that in many cases, businesses were able to resist assimilation into larger concerns and it is possible that some were operated by many generations of the same family.[10]

The Mound E pottery workshop findings are consistent with a general observation that standardisation is more evident in craft production involving prestige raw materials, and/or complex technologies, whereas regional variation is more evident in craft production involving common raw materials and simpler technologies. It would seem, therefore, that large, administratively-controlled workshops produced luxury goods for export or elite domestic markets, while smaller, family-owned businesses concentrated on the production of more mundane items for local markets.[9]

The widespread presence of clay sealings and standardised weights at major sites is evidence for extensive internal trade within Harappan society. As elsewhere, clay sealings were used to seal storage vessels or bales of commodities. Many have multiple impressions, indicating the beginnings of a bureaucracy. Standardised, cubical, stone weights have been found at all major sites. They range from 0.871 gm. (0.3 oz.) to 10.865 kg (23 lb. 15 oz.), so anything from gold and gemstones to bulk commodities could be accurately weighed. The consistency of specific weights indicates rigid control. Evidence for internal trade is also provided by the distribution of items made from raw materials only available from specific regional source. Artefacts can also be traced to particular specialised manufacturing centres, for example the shell-working sites of Balakot and Nageshwar, or carnelian beads from Chanhu-daro.[9]

There is evidence for long-distance trade contacts with Afghanistan, Iran, Central Asia, Peninsular India, the Persian Gulf, Oman and Mesopotamia. Trading outposts were established in Baluchistan and Afghanistan to ensure supplies of copper, tin and lapis lazuli. Mesopotamian texts refer to trade with a region called Meluhha, thought to be the Indus Valley. Curiously, there is little evidence for Mesopotamian manufactured goods in the Indus Valley, and imports must have taken the form of raw materials and perishable goods. Goods were probably transported by ox carts and river boats on the plains or by porters with pack animals in the hills. Depictions of boats on seals indicate that the Indus Valley people were familiar with large river and seagoing vessels. Goods were transported from the river systems to the coasts of Gujarat and the Makran, from whence seagoing craft crossed the Gulf of Oman to Arabia.[9]

Social organisation of Harappan society

Harappan society has been widely characterised as peaceful. Archaeologist and author Jane McIntosh,[8] for example, claims that it avoided the conflicts and militarism that bedevilled other early civilisations. McIntosh believes that the abundant resources of the Indus region were more than adequate for the Harappan population, so eliminating intercommunity competition. Furthermore, the Indus Valley civilisation enjoyed good relations with is neighbours, who had more to gain by peaceful trade and cooperation than by raiding. Warfare therefore played no part in either its emergence or its subsequent cohesion. Rather, the state was held together by ties of economic cooperation and shared ideology.

Such views go back to the initial discovery of the Indus Valley civilisation, and are based on the absence of displays of armed conflict from seals, figurines or pottery designs. It is claimed that there is no evidence for the accumulation of weapons, and that the integration of the Indus polities was achieved without military coercion. While walls and raised platforms at Harappan settlements have been interpreted as defensive fortifications, they might instead have served as protection against monsoon flooding and erosion. Furthermore, Harappan sites also fail to provide clear evidence for social stratification of the type so apparent in Mesopotamia and Egypt. No monumental palaces or temples have been found; there are no sumptuous royal tombs, and grave goods are confined to pottery and personal ornaments.[9] Was Harappan society not only peaceful, but also egalitarian?

The answer to both questions is 'not necessarily'. We have already seen that the period prior to the establishment of the Indus Valley civilisation was one of disruption, characterised by the abandonment and in some cases burning of existing settlements. Furthermore, Guillermo Algaze[13] has characterised the subsequent period of expansion as following the Mesopotamian pattern. He suggests that the establishment of remote settlements to control trade routes and access to raw materials were directly linked to the needs of the growing urban bureaucracies in the Indus core region. Charles Spencer[17] sees this expansion as once again linked to the process of primary state formation (see Chapter 25).

However, the Harappan bureaucracies seem to have been rather less 'showy' than their Mesopotamian counterparts. The power structure of the Indus Valley civilisation might have been dispersed, with political and religious power not restricted to a particular group or class.[14] Harappan society might have had a puritan outlook, eschewing ostentatious displays of wealth. In the light of this, it is unsurprising that conspicuous martial displays are also absent. While warfare was not celebrated as in Mesopotamia, it might have been as prevalent.[11]

Harappan society does present some evidence of inequality. The fine ceramics produced by the Mound E pottery workshop at Harappa were not available to all, neither were the stoneware bangles, nor the carefully-worked ornaments and beads of gold, lapis lazuli and carnelian. It could be that symbols on stamp-seals reflect clans or moieties. Such lineages or kin relations might have been important for trade relations, and for economic and political alliances. Without genealogical texts that we can translate, it is not possible to show that these groups were hereditary elites, but they must have been an exclusive segment of society.[9]

The Indus Valley civilisation endured with little change for 600 years before going into eclipse around 1900 BC. Most of the characteristic features of Harappan society disappeared, as the great cities were largely abandoned. Long-distance trade ended, and writing fell out of use. The Era of Localisation saw the uniform culture of the previous era replaced by a number of regional cultures, whose populations lived in far smaller communities. Early attempts to explain the collapse focused on invading Aryan warriors, supposedly responsible for a massacre at Mohenjo-daro. The case was further made by references in the *Hymns of the Rig Veda* to the destruction of the cities of the Dasas by the gods of the Aryans. It later turned out that the 'massacre' was a ritual burial, and that the *Rig Veda* referred to events much later than 1900 BC. Later theories invoked factors such as the breakdown of trade with Mesopotamia, epidemics of malaria, and the drying up of the Ghaggar-Hakra River.[11] Recent work suggests that the latter was indeed a factor. The Ghaggar-Hakra River was fed primarily by monsoonal rainfall, which began to weaken after around 3000 BC. Ironically, the resulting decrease in seasonal flooding probably stimulated intensive agriculture and hence urbanisation in the first place, but as the monsoon continued to weaken, monsoonal rivers gradually dried or became seasonal. The agricultural production that supported Harappan society was vulnerable to these changes, leading to settlement downsizing, diversification of crops, and an increase of settlements in the moister monsoon regions of the upper Punjab, Haryana and Uttar Pradesh.[18]

Eventually, between 1200 and 500 BC, urban complexity re-emerged. Fortified, formally-planned cities reappeared, writing returned, as did the mass production of ceramics and other artefacts. Like its predecessor, the second urban era is now thought to have been an indigenous development. The state-level societies that now emerged show little evidence of external contacts, but they do show continuity with many post-Harappan communities.[11] Thus while the Indus Valley civilisation may represent the first urban, state-level society in South Asia, it was only the beginning of a longer process of social and political development that affected the entire Indian subcontinent.[9]

28: Interesting times

The early civilisations of China

Classical texts place the earliest Chinese civilisations on central plains of the Yellow River. The semi-mythological Five Emperors and the Xia, Shang and Zhou Dynasties are described by the historian Sima Qian in a work entitled the *Shiji* or *Records of the Grand Historian*, compiled between 109 and 91 BC. The era of these potentates would certainly qualify as 'interesting times', as in the (supposed) ancient Chinese proverb. The Five Emperors reigned during a remote period characterised by walled cities and recurrent warfare among rival chiefdoms for supremacy in key areas of the middle-lower Yellow River Valley and coastal areas.[1,2]

This period was followed by the emergence of the Xia Dynasty, traditionally regarded as China's first dynasty. The Xia gave way to the Shang, who in turn fell to conquest by Wuwang, king of the Zhou. The defeat of the last Shang king, Dixin, is vividly described in classical texts. Wuwang assembled an army comprising 300 chariots, 3,000 'tiger warriors', and troops sent by his allies. Dixin hastily raised a large but badly-organised army in defence, but it was no match for Wuwang's forces and was comprehensively beaten. Many of the Shang troops switched sides in the heat of battle; Dixin fled to his Deer Terrace pavilion and set himself on fire, bringing an end to the Shang Dynasty.[3]

Chinese classical texts depict the Xia, Shang and Zhou Dynasties as powerful hegemonic states, and they are often referred to collectively as the Three Dynasties. While early written records are concerned mainly with these three states, they were not the only states in China at that time. There are references to other kingdoms in the south, and inscriptions on bronze vessels and other archaeological evidence suggest that there were dozens if not hundreds of polities in China during the Three Dynasties era.[3,2]

The generally-accepted chronology of Chinese history begins in 841 BC. Sima Qian was unable to construct an accurate chronology for prior events due to the inadequacy of the material available to him. The date corresponds to the first year of the Gonghe Regency, an interregnum during the Zhou Dynasty that lasted until 828 BC. For the earliest part of the Zhou Dynasty, and for the preceding Shang and Xia Dynasties, Sima Qian was able to provide only a list of kings. Many attempts were subsequently made to establish a full chronology of the first three dynasties, but these were often contradictory. At least 44 dates were proposed for the Zhou conquest, ranging from 1130 to 1018 BC.[3] Consequently, prior to the 1950s, the events of the Five Emperors and Three Dynasties eras were thought to be no more than a series of legends.

The archaeological study of early Chinese civilisation did not really begin until the 1930s, and was soon interrupted by World War II and the subsequent rise of communism. The results of Chinese investigations carried out in the 1950s and 1960s did not become available to Western scholars until East-West tensions eased in the 1970s, and it has since become widely accepted that the pre-dynastic Five Emperors period and the Xia Dynasty correspond to the archaeological cultures known respectively as the Longshan and the Erlitou.[4,1]

In 1996, in an attempt to establish a reliable chronology of the early dynastic era, the Chinese government launched the Xia-Shang-Zhou Chronology Project. Researchers used radiocarbon dating to reduce the uncertainties in dates to around thirty years. In many cases, it was possible to

The first cities

make use of meticulously-recorded astronomical events including solar eclipses, phases of the Moon, and the positions of planets to obtain precise dates. The Xia Dynasty has been dated from 2070 to 1600 BC and the Shang from 1600 to 1046 BC. King Wuwang's victory over Dixin and the latter's self-immolation have been pinpointed to 20 January 1046 BC.[3] The Longshan dates from around 2800 BC, and is divided into Early (2800 to 2600 BC) and Late (2600 to 2000 BC) phases.[5]

The Jade Age

The Longshan is conventionally termed Chalcolithic, lying chronologically as it does between the Chinese Late Neolithic and Early Bronze Age. However, it has been argued that the traditional Three Ages system of stone, bronze and iron were devised within the tradition of Western prehistory, and its application to the Longshan underplays the existence of a sophisticated jade-working technology dating to this period and slightly earlier. Accordingly, it has been suggested that the term 'Jade Age' be used instead.[1]

The roots of the Longshan are to be found in the increasing cultural and social complexity of the Late Neolithic. We saw early examples of this in Chapter 22 in the form of elite burials, craft specialisation and the construction of defensive walls. From around 3500 BC, these trends became increasingly apparent.[1] Two important cultures of this time are the Liangzhu (3300 to 2250 BC), with sites located in Jiangsu and Zhejiang Provinces, and the Hongshan culture (4700 to 2900 BC) of Liaoning Province and Inner Mongolia. Both are noted for elite burials with extensive jade grave goods.[2]

Elite Liangzhu burials typically featured jade *cong* tubes. *Cong* are square in cross-section with a circular hole, and are often embellished with human or animal masks. Their function is unknown, but they are thought to have been associated with mortuary rituals.[6,2] Their use persisted into the Three Dynasties era, with many examples known from the Shang and Zhou Dynasties.[1] The Liangzhu economy was fairly typical of the Yangtze Late Neolithic, based on paddy field rice agriculture and livestock. Settlements were located close to rivers, and the remains of wooden boats and oars attest to the importance of water transport. The sites lacked walls, but appear to have been protected by systems of large, deep canals. The rich material culture included silk, lacquer ware, basket making, and fine ceramics and jades. Hongshan grave goods included jade coiled dragons, animal masks and turtles, anticipating later Shang and Zhou art. A ritual temple has also been found at Niuheliang (Liaoning Province). The wooden-framed temple measured 22 by 9 m (72 by 30 ft.) and was built on stone foundations. It was surrounded by stone mounds raised over stone-lined elite graves.[1,2]

Thus social complexity and stratification had early beginnings in several regions of China. The final steps to state formation occurred in the Chinese Central Plain – the Middle to Lower Yellow River Valley area in Henan and southwest Shandong Provinces. The Longshan was a diverse cultural phenomenon: in addition to the traditional Longshan of Shandong Province, identified at the type site of Longshan Chengziyai in the 1930s, subcultures further west along the Middle and Upper Yellow River Valley are now included. Other cultures, located in Inner Mongolia and the Yangtze River Valley, also formed part of the same broad interaction sphere. These constituent cultures shared several traits. They each showed comparable evidence of social complexity and stratification, and emerging urbanisation. Specialised crafts and technologies appeared, including copper and bronze metallurgy, jade carving, the production of fine wheel-thrown hard-fired pottery of standardised forms, and the manufacture of silk and other textiles. At some sites in Shandong Province, there are indications of early writing in the form of inscribed pottery and oracle bones.[1]

Some features characteristic of the later Three Dynasties era first appeared during the Longshan. These included the use of rammed earth (*hangtu*) for city walls and platforms for public buildings, and the use of oracle bones for divination. Rammed earth is a mixture of earth, sand, gravel and clay, with lime as a stabiliser. The material is externally supported in a frame or mould until it sets. Oracle bones are either animal shoulder blades or the undersides of turtle shells upon which questions are carved with a sharp instrument prior to heating until the bone cracks. The crack patterns are then interpreted and the prognostication written on the piece. Questions typically concerned decisions about warfare, hunting, rainfall, agriculture and the health of royal family members. Another practice also featuring widely in later times was that of human sacrifice. At many sites, the remains of both adults and children have been found in sacrificial pits or beneath the foundations of large buildings.[1,2]

The beginning of the Longshan period saw a general increase both in population numbers and density of sites in the Middle and Lower Yellow River Valley, and in coastal areas. In Shandong Province, sites almost quadrupled in numbers in comparison to the Neolithic Dawenkou period (see Chapter 22). From the network of largely self-sufficient villages of the Neolithic, the Longshan saw the emergence of internally-differentiated settlements with a distinct two or three-tier settlement hierarchy.[5,1] *Hangtu* walled towns appeared around 2600 BC, mostly along the Middle and Lower Yellow River Valley. Others are found in Inner Mongolia and Sichuan Province, and along the Yangtze and its tributaries. Walls were anything up to 6 m (19 ft. 8 in.) high and 10 to 20 m (32 ft. 9 in. to 65 ft. 6 in.) wide. The enclosed area varied in size, reaching 38 ha (94 acres) at Jingyanggang (Shandong Province). Settlements were often surrounded by a defensive moat in addition to walls. Within the walled areas are found *hangtu* platforms, thought to have been the foundations for temples and elite residences. Jade and pottery workshops and bronze foundries occur either within the walls or just outside. Water wells up to 11 m (36 ft.) deep have also been found. In addition to providing drinking water, these supplied water for pottery workshops and for irrigation. At Pingliangtai (Henan Province), there was an underground system of terracotta pipes for draining purposes.[1]

Longshan cemeteries provide clear evidence of social stratification. At Chengzi (Shandong Province) and Taosi (Shanxi Province), graves were arranged in clusters. Within these clusters, the graves of the rich or well-to-do were surrounded by a far greater number of poorer ones. The richest burials contained up to 200 items of grave goods including jade axes, *cong* tubes and rings, musical instruments and painted pottery, but the vast majority of the burials had few if any grave goods.[4,2]

Long-distance trade occurred along networks established by the latter part of the Late Neolithic. While the presence of walled cities along later-recognised land routes confirms the importance of these, it is likely that goods also went by boat, especially along the lower and middle reaches of the Yellow River and in coastal areas. Pottery and carved jade were among the most important traded items. Other material included ivory, alligator skins, feathers, shells, turquoise and agate. Much traded goods came from peripheral areas of the Longshan interaction sphere, especially from southern regions such as the Yangtze Valley.[1]

The archaeological record suggests that the recurrent warfare referred to in the *Shiji* was a reality. Settlements, as we have seen, were fortified. Larger and heavier spear-points and arrow-heads have been found, and it has been suggested that these were for use as weapons of war rather than for hunting. There is evidence for large-scale killings and the burning of villages. At Jiangou (Hebei Province), a well was filled with skeletons, some of which had been decapitated and others apparently buried alive. Elsewhere, several skulls were found that bore evidence of scalping. There is also evidence of violent deaths at Dinggong (Shandong Province), where human remains were found in disused storage pits.[4,1]

Archaeologist Li Liu[5,7] has considered settlement sizes and hierarchies of Longshan sites in Shanxi and Henan Provinces, using an approach known as rank-size analysis. The so-called rank-size rule was derived by geographers from empirical observation of the distribution of city sizes. When cities and towns are ranked in order of size, and rank is then plotted against size (actually the logarithms of rank and size) on a graph, then a straight line is often obtained. The reason for the rule is not known, but in the late 1940s, the American linguist George Kingsley Zipf proposed the existence of two opposing forces – a 'Force of Unification' and a 'Force of Diversification'. These forces act to either encourage settlement in a single centre or disperse it throughout the region. When the two forces are in balance, cities and towns conform to the rank-size rule, and the straight-line relationship is seen. However, if the 'Force of Unification' predominates, the plot takes a concave shape. Conversely, if the 'Force of Diversification' predominates, the shape is convex.[8] One may think of either the unification forces pulling the line inwards, or the diversification forces pushing it outwards. The forces can be equated to the effects of a ruling bureaucracy versus those of resistance to centralised control.

When Liu applied the rank-size rule to regional clusters of Longshan sites, she found that all three forms were represented, and concluded that they represented three distinct types of chiefdom. She labelled these centripetal, centrifugal and competing, corresponding respectively to concave, straight-line and convex rank-size distributions. She found that the first two types followed a three-tier settlement hierarchy and the third a two-tier hierarchy. Centripetal chiefdoms are the most complex societies and competing chiefdoms the simplest; centrifugal chiefdoms lie between the two extremes.

Liu also noticed that the centripetal chiefdoms were located in regions tightly circumscribed by geographical barriers such as mountains and rivers. These included site clusters in the Linfen Basin (southern Shanxi Province) and in the hilly Sanliqiao region of western Henan Province. The centrifugal chiefdoms were located in regions only partially circumscribed, and included site clusters in the Yi-Luo basin (western Henan Province) and the Qin River Valley (northern Henan Province). The competing chiefdoms were located in non-circumscribed regions that lacked geographical barriers, and included clusters in central and northern Henan Province.

Two cultures have been associated with possible early state formation. The first is the Erlitou, a culture that emerged in a region that includes western and central Henan and southwestern Shanxi Provinces. The second is the Xiaqiyuan, contemporary with the Erlitou, and located in northern Henan and southern Hebei Provinces. These cultures are thought to be associated with the Xia Dynasty and the earliest stages of the Shang Dynasty (proto-Shang) respectively. They emerged in regions that did not host any of the complex centripetal polities, from which on the face of it one might have expected the first states to emerge. Instead, they contained only the centrifugal and decentralised polities. Liu argues that it was the competition and constant jockeying for power among these smaller chiefdoms that led to the emergence of China's first states.

The Xia Dynasty – legend or reality?

The first hints that the Xia Dynasty might have been more than just a legend came in 1959 with the discovery of the large site of Erlitou in Henan Province. The site is located on the southern bank of the Luo River, just west of its confluence with the Yi. Over 170 sites are now associated with the Erlitou culture, mainly located within 50 km (30 miles) of Erlitou itself.[7] There are small sites at Erlitou dating to the Neolithic Yangshao and the Longshan periods, but the Erlitou culture site dates to 1900 BC and follows an occupational hiatus of 600 years. At its maximum extent, it covered an area of around 300 ha (740 acres). Occupation spanned four phases, although the duration of each has not been accurately determined; the most recent date for Phase IV is 1521 BC. Erlitou was later reduced in size to an ordinary village of around 30 ha (75 acres), and subsequently it was abandoned altogether.[9]

During Phase I, the site reached a size of at least 100 ha (250 acres). Elite items recovered from this phase include white pottery, ivory and turquoise artefacts and bronze tools. However, the later occupations severely disturbed the Phase I deposits, so the layout of the settlement at this stage remains unclear. The expansion of the site to 300 ha (740 acres) occurred during Phase II, and during this period a 12 ha (30 acre) palatial complex was built in the southeastern part of the site. Four intersecting roads, running east-west and north-south, meet at the complex. Ruts in the roads suggest use of wheeled vehicles, but distance between the tracks was only 1 m (3 ft. 3 in.) and the vehicles must have been much smaller than later Shang Dynasty chariots.[9]

The palace building measured 150 by 50 m (490 by 165 ft.), and included three courtyards containing elite burials. Grave goods from these included bronzes, jades, lacquer ware, white pottery, porcelain, turquoise artefacts, and shell and cowrie ornaments. One burial contained a bronze bell and a dragon made from over 2,000 pieces of jade and turquoise. Immediately to the south of the palatial complex were a turquoise workshop and a bronze foundry, which produced tools, weapons and ritual bronze drinking vessels. The close proximity of these craft shops to the palatial complex suggests that the elite exerted tight control over the production of prestige goods and that the craft-workers might have been state employees. The palatial complex was rebuilt during Phases III and IV, and the earlier buildings were replaced by a number of structures aligned on a north-south axis. The largest of these, known as Palace No. 1, was constructed during Phase III. Located in a large walled courtyard with roofed galleries, it was almost 1 ha (2.5 acres) in size, and comprised a single wattle-and-daub building standing upon a 3 m (10 ft.) high *hangtu* platform.[9]

Over the years, there has been considerable debate regarding the attribution of the four phases. The Xia-Shang-Zhou Chronology Project concluded that all four phases belong to the Xia Dynasty. Other scholars argue for a transition to the Shang Dynasty at the end of Phase III, or even at the end of one of the first two phases. Most Chinese scholars now accept that Erlitou was at some stage the capital of the Xia Dynasty,[3] but in its early days it is unlikely to have been a state. There is no evidence for palace building during Phase I, and it is likely that social organisation at that time resembled that of the Longshan period.[5]

Ceramic data indicates that the Erlitou culture developed from the Longshan via an intermediate culture known as the Xinzhai, dating from 2000 to 1900 BC, and mainly known from sites in central Henan Province. Thus we can see that the roots of the Erlitou culture may lie with the competing, decentralised chiefdoms of that region. Interestingly, the Xinzhai heartland coincides with the location of the more complex late Longshan subcultures in a region of otherwise decentralised chiefdoms. It suggests the process that would lead to state formation was underway by that time, with some groups already to the fore. Expansion of the Erlitou culture into the northwest is documented by the appearance of sites in southern Shanxi and the Qin River Valley, dating to Erlitou Phase II. By this time, Erlitou itself had emerged as a regional centre, and settlement patterns in its hinterland show a four-tier hierarchy and a concave rank-size curve. These developments represent a transformation of the regional political structure from one of multiple competing polities with medium-sized centres to one where a single very large centre dominated many smaller centres and villages.[7] They are consistent with the emergence of a primary state with a capital at Erlitou and territorial expansion into regions 100 to 250 km (62 to 155 miles) away.[10] Again, this supports the territorial expansion/state formation model proposed by Charles Spencer (see Chapter 25).

A significant development is that the emergence of the Erlitou culture was accompanied by a sharp drop in number of settlements from 700 in Longshan times to the 170 or so noted above. The implication is of a population decline greater in extent than can be accounted for by warfare between competing chiefdoms, leaving disease or a natural disaster as possible explanations. The latter possibility is the most likely: the channels of the Lower Yellow River are prone to silting up, and periods of high rainfall can lead to the flooding of the eastern parts of the Central Plain and an alteration of the course of the river on its way to the sea. Such an episode might have occurred around 2000 BC, a date that coincides fairly closely to that of the legendary first king of the Xia Dynasty, Yu the Great. Yu is popularly supposed to have controlled the floodwaters after his father was either banished or put to death for failing to do so. If there is any truth in the legend, the floods might have been responsible for the fall in population. Yu might have been a charismatic individual who became influential during those troubled times, and who led the pre-state Xia to establish political domination over other polities in the region.[5,7]

The Shang Dynasty

At the end of Phase IV, Erlitou became a small settlement of around 30 ha (75 acres), mainly located in the area of the former palatial complex. What exactly happened remains unclear. There is no evidence for an earlier decline, or that the collapse was related to fire or warfare. All that is certain is that the production of bronzes and other elite goods completely came to an end after Phase IV.[9] However, it cannot be a coincidence that the latter days of Erlitou overlap with the rise of a large fortified town just 6 km (3.7 miles) to the northeast, at Shixianggou near the present-day city of Yanshi. By end of Erlitou Phase III, Yanshi Phase I had started to emerge, and two co-existed during Erlitou Phase IV. Shixianggou is just under 200 ha (495 acres) in extent and comprises an outer wall containing a smaller, inner enclosure. The latter contains ten *hangtu* platforms, and was presumably the elite quarter. Crucially, the predominant pottery style at Shixianggou belongs to the Erligang culture, which differs from Erlitou ware. The Erligang culture is named for Erligang, near Zhengzhou, a city that lies 85 km (53 miles) to the east of Erlitou. Archaeologists commonly accept that the Erligang culture represents the material remains of the Shang Dynasty. Discovered in 1951, the Zhengzhou site is part of an ancient walled settlement that may be the legendary city of Bo, the first Shang capital.[3,11]

The *hangtu* walls, which probably date to 1650 BC, are 36 m (118 ft.) wide at the base, 10 m (33 ft.) high, and enclose an area of 335 ha (828 acres). The extramural area of the city covers 25 sq. km. (9.7 sq. miles). Excavations within the walls have revealed the *hangtu* foundations of what might have been a palace precinct. The enclosed area also included evidence of both human and animal sacrifice in the form of pits containing human skulls and the skeletons of dogs. Elite – probably royal – graves contained bronze ritual vessels and jade and bronze ornaments. The extramural area incorporated a series of specialist workshop areas, including a bronze foundry where large ceremonial vessels and weapons were cast. The skill of the bronze casters can be judged from the sheer size of a ritual *ding* vessel, weighing 86.4 kg (190 lb.), which was recovered there. Other areas were used for the production of ceramics and for the working of bone to produce hairpins and arrowheads. The homes of the specialist craft workers were also located in the extramural area, as were cemeteries for the ordinary people. Four cemeteries have been investigated, and grave goods found include bronzes, ceramics and jade ornaments.[2]

Zhengzhou did not remain the capital throughout the Shang Dynasty, although it remained a town of some importance.[2] The Shang capital was relocated during the Middle Shang period (1400 to 1200 BC). The new capital, Xiang, is believed to be the site of Huanbei in the far north of Henan Province, which lies north of the Huan River and close to the present-day city of Anyang. The recently-discovered city comprises a central walled area of 470 ha (1.8 sq. miles) holding a palatial complex that may be as much as 20 ha (50 acres) in extent. Within the complex, *hangtu* foundations of at least 30 buildings have been identified.[12] The largest of these, a monumental building known as Palace No. 1, was built around a courtyard and measures 173 by 90 m (567 by 295 ft.). The main palace hall was situated on the north side, facing south. Situated on the opposite side of the courtyard was an entrance hall and gate house, and on the east and west side of courtyard were subsidiary buildings. The building is thought to be too large to have been a residential palace. The main hall was divided evenly into rooms, nine of which have been excavated although there were probably eleven in all. The rooms are thought to be ritual *shi* chambers, which according to oracle bone inscriptions were used as ancestral temples and for sacrificial activity, as well as for more mundane administrative activity. The west wing of the building might have been a granary. More than 20 sacrificial pits containing both human and animal remains have been found in the vicinity of the gatehouse.[13] Huanbei was apparently abandoned after only 50 years of use.[14] There is evidence that buildings were destroyed by fire, although the circumstances are unclear. It is quite possible that the buildings were deliberately burned prior to the relocation of the royal household to a new capital a short distance away on the other side of the Huan River.[12]

Yin - the final capital of the Shang Dynasty - was the first to be identified, with early hints of its existence coming right at the end of the nineteenth century. In 1899, scholars in Beijing identified archaic texts inscribed upon bones that were intended for use in traditional Chinese medicine; the bones were subsequently traced to a small village outside Anyang. The site became the most thoroughly-studied in China: excavations commenced in 1928 and have been ongoing ever since. A combination of ancient records, oracle bone inscriptions and archaeological investigation has identified it as the ancient city of Yin, the last Shang capital. The site is now known as Yinxu ('ruins of Yin'), and has been a World Heritage Site since 2006.[3,2]

The city covered at least 25 sq. km (9.7 sq. miles), but no surrounding walls have been found. The royal necropolis at Yinxu contains twelve subterranean tombs up to 13 m (43 ft.) deep, each containing a wooden burial chamber approached by four descending ramps. Grave goods include huge bronze vessels and fine jades. Two bronze cauldrons were found in the central pit of one tomb, 2 m (6 ft. 6 in.) above the burial chamber. The tomb also contained 360 spear heads, 141 helmets, and jade figures of turtles, frogs and monsters. Other graves contained the skeletons of beheaded young men; others contained only the skulls. Other human sacrificial victims included children who were apparently buried alive. Fu Hao, consort of King Wu Ding was accompanied in death by 16 slaves; her tomb also contained hundreds of objects in bronze, jade and bone, around 7,000 cowrie shells, and three ivory cups inlaid with turquoise.[2]

The Shang Dynasty may be an example of secondary state formation, where the presence of a powerful state catalyses state formation in neighbouring non-state polities. The origins of the Shang Dynasty are thought to lie with the Xiaqiyuan culture of northern Henan and southern Hebei Provinces. Xiaqiyuan ceramic types share similarities with those of the Erligang culture, but not with those of the Erlitou. The two cultures are separated by the Qin and Yellow Rivers: the Erlitou lies west of the Qin River and south of the Yellow River, and the Xiaqiyuan lies east of the Qin River and north of the Yellow River. This archaeological boundary seems to coincide with the territory of the late Xia Dynasty, as recorded in the ancient texts.[5]

The early phases of the Xiaqiyuan were contemporary with Phases II and III at Erlitou. This suggests that the Xiaqiyuan came into existence when the Erlitou culture began to expand its cultural influence to the northeast. If we accept that the Erlitou culture represents the Xia Dynasty and that Xiaqiyuan equates to proto-Shang, the implication is that the proto-Shang was a reaction to the warlike nature of Xia expansionism. When the proto-Shang culture developed into a state-level society is unclear, but it was probably no earlier than Phase II of the Erlitou culture. Notably, as with the Xinzhai, the core region of the Xiaqiyuan overlapped that of one of the more complex late Longshan chiefdoms, in a region of otherwise decentralised polities.[5]

The Shang rulers probably controlled an area of 230,000 sq. km. (89,000 sq. miles), making their realm slightly smaller than the United Kingdom.[15] Supplies of copper, tin and jade were strategically important to the regime and the nearest source of the latter was nearly 400 km (250 miles) from

Yinxu. Cowrie shells used for currency could only be obtained from the tropical seas far to the south, and turtle shells for oracle bone divination were also imported from the south.[2] Despite these long range contacts, there is no evidence for Chinese contact with Mesopotamia prior to 1300 BC.[15]

Oracle bone inscriptions suggest that warfare with neighbouring polities was a recurring theme, though many of these rivals lay on the periphery of Shang territory and were probably only minor players. However, recent archaeological work has confirmed that there were contemporary states in the rice-growing lands to the south that were apparently unknown to Sima Qian and other early Chinese historians. The findings include a 450 ha (1,200 acres) walled city at Sanxingdui (Sichuan Province). The city was accompanied by an extramural area covering 15 sq. km (6 sq. miles) and including workshops that manufactured bronzes, lacquer ware, ceramics and jade. Sanxingdui has been assigned to the newly-named Changjiang culture. Other Changjiang cities include Wucheng (Jiangxi Province), which is associated with necropolis containing a royal tomb comparable in wealth to that of Fu Hao. These new discoveries indicate that our knowledge of early Chinese civilisation is far from complete.[2]

Chinese writing systems

As we have seen, the earliest indications of writing systems in China date back to Longshan times, and indeed it is possible that simple recording systems were in use even earlier.[1] The attested origins of present-day Chinese writing are more recent, but still date back to the late Shang Dynasty around 1200 BC. Although evidence for writing from that period is confined to oracle bones and bronze vessels, it is probable that the bulk of Shang written material has been lost. Around ten percent of early Sumerian tablets are school exercises with lists of words, and literary texts copied by or dictated to student scribes. By contrast, no equivalent texts are known for China. The ordinary medium for Chinese written texts must have been a material far more ephemeral than bone or bronze, with the consequence that most have been lost. Oracle bones and bronzes may represent but one category of writing, and the one that happened to survive. Accordingly, we cannot assume that writing was invented in China for recording oracles.[16]

Spoken Chinese is not a difficult language to learn. There are no cases, tenses, gender or moods. Root vowels do not change, unlike for example *sing*, *sang* and *song* in English. Written Chinese, by contrast, includes a mind-boggling 50,000 different signs. Needless to say, nobody knows every single one. Around 1,500 will suffice to read 90 percent of a Chinese newspaper and 3,000 will cover most of it. Even those with a university education will only know around 4,000 signs. Part of the problem is that the meaning of Chinese signs cannot obviously be discerned from their shape. The Chinese writing system is not logosyllabic like Sumerian or Egyptian. More than 80 percent of Chinese signs are phono-semantic compounds, comprising two elements. The first element is a determinative (known as the 'radical') and the second element contains phonetic information. For example, 河 *hé* (river), 湖 *hú* (lake), 流 *liú* (stream), 冲 *chōng* (riptide or flush), 滑 *huá* (slippery) all include a radical of three short strokes on the left-hand side. This represents a river, indicating that the character has a semantic connection with water. The right-hand side contains the phonetic information. The phonetic information is not supplied directly as in logosyllabic or syllabic systems, but is implied by rebus. The two elements combine to form a unitary logogram tied to a specific word. To read the signs, the reader must guess the word firstly through knowledge of the radical, and secondly through knowledge of the sound suggested by the rebus of the phonetic component. Unfortunately, in most cases the original relevance of the radical has been lost, even if it can be identified from within the complex grapheme. The sound of the phonetic has also typically changed from the original. In most cases, the sign must be learned by rote. To all intents and purposes, written Chinese is a full logography, with each sign representing a different syllable. A problem for would-be reformers of the system is the extent of homophony in written Chinese. Homophony is when multiple meanings are attached to the same pronunciation, for example 'there' and 'their' in English. In Chinese, homophones commonly have dozens of different meanings – in one case, 146.[16]

Cumbersome though this venerable writing system is, it has served the Chinese well and made possible the great Chinese Empire. While many dialects were spoken across a vast area, scribes could all understand the writing and remain in contact with the imperial centre in northern China. Barry Powell[16] further notes that to significantly change written Chinese would be to lose the ancient Chinese culture encoded therein and the aesthetic opportunities afforded by calligraphy. Chinese poetry relies on sequences of beautifully drawn symbols to convey emotion. Unlike Shakespeare's sonnets, it is a multi-media experience that cannot be separated from the graphic symbols and exist purely as sounds. Rendering into an alphabetic system would lose a whole dimension. This of course happens when a Chinese poem is translated into English. The result is flat, uninteresting and unrecognisable as any form of poetry – a classic case of 'lost in translation'.

29: Mexican superpowers

Convergent evolution

The Aztec, Maya and Inca are as familiar to the general public as the Romans and Ancient Egyptians. These were the three main civilisations of the New World at the time of the Spanish conquest, and their sophistication was not lost on the Conquistadors. There was much that the Spanish recognised from the Old World and Hernán Cortés was probably aided in his conquest of Mexico by his familiarity with the general features and institutions of Aztec society.[1] While the civilisations of Mesopotamia, Ancient Egypt, the Indus Valley and China arose independently of one another, we cannot dismiss the possibility that long-distance trade between them influenced some aspects of their development. Although there have been suggestions of cultural influences from China and Japan,[2,3] most believe that there were no significant contacts between the emerging civilisations in the New World and their Old World counterparts. That they have much in common is thought to be the result of convergences, suggesting that there are certain universals in social evolution.[1]

What puzzled Cortés was the contrast between the rich, dynamic culture of Mesoamerica and its technological backwardness. In Chapter 24, we noted the absence of beasts of burden; there were no horses, donkeys, mules or oxen. However, the differences extended beyond a lack of animals for transport. There was no technology to augment manpower: no pulleys, wheeled vehicles, large sailing ships, or any form of complex machinery. Tools were largely made from wood and stone, and were crude and ineffective by European standards.[1]

Gold, copper and even meteoric iron was used to make hammered artefacts from as early as 2000 BC,[4,5,6] but smelting of metal ore was a much later development. The technique did not come into use in South America until 500 BC,[7] and did not reach Mesoamerica until as late as AD 650.[8] Even then, metals were almost entirely used to make ritual objects and jewellery rather than tools or weapons. The technology of pre-Columbian Mesoamerica was to all intents Stone Age.[1]

Timeline of pre-Columbian Mesoamerica

It is generally accepted that primary state formation occurred in two regions of the New World: Mesoamerica and the Central Andes. Following the end of the Preceramic Period (see Chapter 24), separate timelines apply to the two regions. In Mesoamerica, the Late Archaic/Preceramic ended around 2500 BC and was followed by the Preclassic (or Formative) Period (2500 BC to AD 250). This period is subdivided into an Early (2500 to 900 BC), a Middle (900 to 400 BC), a Late (400 BC to AD 100), and a Terminal (AD 100 to 250). The first settlements that could reasonably described as 'cities' did not appear until the Middle Preclassic, and earliest states did not emerge until the Late Preclassic. The Preclassic was followed by the Classic (AD 250 to 925), comprising and Early (AD 250 to 600), Late (AD 600 to 750) and Terminal (AD 750 to 925). During the Classic Period, large expansive states flourished in the Valley of Oaxaca and Valley of Mexico. This period also saw the zenith of Maya civilisation. The Classic was followed by Postclassic (AD 925 to 1519), but the Aztec Empire did not arise until the last century of the Postclassic.

Early Preclassic communities in Mesoamerica

At the close of the Preceramic Period, Mesoamerican populations were still very small, and communities were only partially dependent on agriculture. The earliest pottery appeared in Mexico at about this time, at the sites of Puerto Marqués and La Zanja on the Pacific coast of Guerrero, and in the Tehuacán Valley. These early ceramic traditions were fairly crude and undecorated, and were modelled on gourds. Over the next few hundred years, ceramic styles gradually became more sophisticated and were decorated with complex designs. After 1500 BC, pottery was widely manufactured throughout Mesoamerica.[9] Ceramic styles suggest that there were long-distance interactions between cultures on the Pacific coast of Mexico, in Honduras, El Salvador and Guatemala.[10]

At least two separate ceramic style zones existed. The Valley of Mexico, Morelos, Puebla, the Tehuacán Valley, the Valley of Oaxaca, Valley of Nochixtlán and the Cañada de Cuicatlán all shared red-on-buff pottery; but east of Tehuacán and Oaxaca, this red-on-buff style gradually gave way to one linking southern Veracruz, Tabasco, and Chiapas. This lowland complex featured *tecomates* or neckless jars with bichrome slips, fluting or crosshatching.[11] Interestingly, the boundary between the two style zones corresponds fairly closely to the boundary between the distribution of the Oto-Manguean language family to the west and the Mixe-Zoque and Maya families to the east. The first zone has uncertain western boundaries, but the second extends as far as Honduras and El Salvador, and correlates well to the eastern boundary of the Maya languages. The Oto-Manguean languages are spoken mainly in Oaxaca and in central Mexico and include the Zapotec and Mixtec groupings, and the Mixe-Zoque languages are spoken in and around the Isthmus of Tehuantepec.[12,13]

It was not until almost a millennium after the first appearance of pottery that reasonably-permanent agricultural communities became widespread. Villages typically consisted of small clusters of simple houses with earthen floors, wattle-and-daub walls and thatched roofs.[1] However, more complex societies also began to emerge. Paso de la Amada, in the Soconusco coastal region of state of Chiapas, was occupied between 1850 and 1200 BC. The 50 ha (124 acres) site is located on ancient alluvial fan, 6 km (3.75 miles) from the modern estuary and 8 km (5 miles) from the Pacific coast. As such, it was well situated for exploiting both riverine and coastal environments. More than 50 residences have been identified. A notable feature of the site is the presence of a Mesoamerican ball court (see below), a level area measuring 80 by 7 m (262 by 23 ft.) delimited by two parallel mounds.[14,1] The ball court dates to 1600 BC, and is the earliest-known structure of its kind.[15]

Much attention has centred on Mound 6, located close to the southwest periphery of the site. It is apsidal in shape and measures 22 by 10 m (72 by 33 ft.), the largest such mound on the site. It was topped by structures that were rebuilt six times, on each occasion adding to the height of the mound. The role of Mound 6 is uncertain. Rather than being arranged around a central space, large buildings at Paso de la Amada were scattered around the site, and each appears to have been surrounded by settlement clusters of smaller, residential buildings. During the early Barra and Locona ceramic phases, these clusters might have formed autonomous neighbourhoods within a decentralised community. The large buildings might have served as residences for neighbourhood leaders, or as public meeting places. However, around 1500 BC, during the later Ocós phase, the social organisation of Paso de la Amada became more centralised. At this point, the functions of the neighbourhood centres were transferred to Mound 6, which then served as a chiefly residence or a council house for village elders.[14]

The degree of ranking and social stratification at Paso de la Amada remains uncertain. The settlement was the largest of a number of villages in the region, and might have functioned as a chiefly capital or regional centre. Artefacts recovered include ornate serving bowls and dishes, suggesting regular feasting took place. Some artefacts were made using materials such as obsidian and jade, imported from distant sources. Yet despite the presence of these prestige items, and of architecture that hints at emerging elites, burials reveal no evidence of social distinction or accumulated wealth. Instead, all received the same, simple mortuary treatment.[1]

The Olmec

The processes of interaction and agricultural expansion in Mesoamerica culminated around 1400 BC with the emergence of the Olmec culture, often described as the New World's first civilisation. Their heartland was located along the Gulf Coast of the Isthmus of Tehuantepec, a lowland region comprising southern Veracruz and western Tabasco. In this hot, humid region of tropical rainforest, swamp and savannah, the Olmec thrived between 1400 and 400 BC. Several hundred sites are known, including the major settlements of Tres Zapotes, Laguna de los Cerros, San Lorenzo and La Venta.[13] The Olmec are best known for their trademark colossal stone heads, the first of which was found in 1862 at the site of Tres Zapotes in Veracruz. Seventeen carved stone head are currently known, measuring up to 3.4 m (11 ft.) in height and weighing up to 50 tonnes. Other monumental stone carvings include felines, thrones and stelae.[16,13] Olmec artisans also produced carvings from obsidian and blue-green jade, and mirrors from polished haematite and other iron ores.[1] The word 'Olmec' means 'rubber people' in the Aztec language Nahuátl. It was the term the Aztec applied to sixteenth century latex-tapping people of the Mexican Gulf Coast although we now know that the Olmec lived much earlier.

The earliest major Olmec centre was San Lorenzo, a cluster of three settlements located at the confluence of the Rio Coatzacoalcos and a tributary, the El Chiquito. Its location meant that it was ideally positioned to control traffic along the two waterways. San Lorenzo was at its peak between 1400 and 1000 BC, but suffered a decline thereafter. The main site is 700 ha (1,730 acres) in extent and was laid out around a natural plateau. The plateau was reshaped by addition of a number of artificial extensions, and is surrounded by artificial terracing supporting thatched wattle-and-daub housing. Atop the plateau stood a large building that might have been an elite residence, known as the Red Palace. Also sited on the plateau was an elaborate system of pools, aqueducts and drains.[13] The system might have been intended to provide water not only for drinking but for ritual purposes. Control over the construction, maintenance and use of the system might well have been central to the power of the ruling elite.[16]

A large number of large basalt carvings have been recovered, including ten of the stone heads. Though some of the stone heads have been moved from their original locations, they lie approximately along two parallel lines crossing the centre of the plateau. Carved stone thrones also lie along and help to define these lines. The spacing of the heads would prevent more than one being seen at a time and it might have been intended that they be viewed as a procession of ancestral rulers. The basalt was quarried from Los Tuxtlas, 60 km (37 miles) from the settlement, and to transport it over such a distance was a massive undertaking. Consequently, old monuments were frequently recycled into smaller sculptures.[16,13]

Obsidian is another high-quality material that did not occur naturally in the Olmec heartland. Trace element analysis indicates that obsidian found at San Lorenzo was sourced from locations up to 800 km (500 miles) away in Guatemala and Hidalgo. Such distances make it unlikely that the material was obtained through mining expeditions. Instead, the San Lorenzo Olmec must have participated in a long distance trade network.[17]

Lying 15 km (9 miles) southeast of San Lorenzo is the site of El Manatí, discovered in 1987 when local residents were digging a fish pond close to a spring emerging from the base of the nearby Cerro Manatí. They recovered carved wooden busts, stone axes, ceramics and human remains. The wooden busts, dated to 1200 BC, were in an exceptional state of preservation, and were attributed to the Olmec period. The ceramics were typical of those found at San Lorenzo. Archaeological excavations subsequently identified three phases between 1600 and 1200 BC. The earliest phase, Manatí A, predates San Lorenzo and may push back the start of Olmec tradition to an earlier date than the commonly-cited 1400 to 1200 BC. Finds from this phase included jade beads, ground stone tools, and fourteen rubber balls that ranged in diameter from 8 to 30 cm (3.7 to 11.8 in.). It is believed that these various artefacts were thrown into the spring as offerings, possibly to appease water gods who might otherwise have allowed devastating floods to occur during the long, tropical rainy season.[18]

San Lorenzo eventually suffered a dramatic population collapse and its stone monuments were defaced, most likely by a rival chiefdom.[11] The decline coincided with the rise of another large settlement at La Venta, 88 km (55 miles) to the northeast. The site is located in the swampland of western Tabasco, close to the Rio Tonalá, and is dominated by a 33 m (108 ft.) high earthen pyramid. On each side, lower earthen structures with associated courtyards are laid out along a central axis. These include a massive raised platform known as the Stirling Acropolis, named for American archaeologist Matthew Stirling. The site is also noted for spectacular mosaic pavements made from blocks of imported green serpentine, which depict animals or gods. Elite burials in richly-carved sarcophagi attest to a ranked society, and the presence of inherited wealth and status is underlined by the discovery of an elaborate basalt tomb containing two infants and extensive grave goods. La Venta was once envisaged as purely a ceremonial centre, but domestic refuse and the remains of houses has confirmed that it was the home to a permanent population. Unfortunately, little is known about the settlement's ordinary residents.[1,13]

Opinion is divided as to how Olmec heartland polities such as San Lorenzo and La Venta are to be classified. Some claim that they are true urban centres within a state-level society; others that Olmec societal organisation was on the simpler chiefdom level. La Venta reached its apogee between 800 and 500 BC, during which it was at the centre of a three-tier settlement hierarchy.[19] Neither San Lorenzo nor La Venta presents clear evidence for palaces, or for temples built to a standard design.[20] These results suggest that they were chiefly capitals rather than urban centres. The Olmec do have much in common with other chiefly societies. For example, some Polynesian groups also built earthen mounds. Olmec carved stone heads recall those set up by chiefdoms on Easter Island. Wooden statues and jade carvings are also associated with chiefdoms, including those of the Maori. The collapse of San Lorenzo and coincident rise of La Venta is a pattern typical of chiefdoms as they compete for labour and other resources. The size of these two settlements exceeds that of a typical Bronze Age city, again consistent with chiefdoms. As we saw in Chapter 25, chiefdoms lack a devolved administrative hierarchy. Accordingly, chiefly authority cannot be projected over a long distance, and many chiefs therefore kept their subjects as close to home as possible. When all the evidence is considered, the Olmec appear to have been a chiefdom-level rather than a state-level society.[11]

Eventually, around 400 BC, Olmec society collapsed and large settlements such as La Venta went into decline. The reasons are not well understood; one possibility is that overpopulation led to environmental degradation of the fragile tropical river valley. There may be a parallel with Easter Island, coincidentally also noted for its large carved stone heads. Here, the complex Polynesian chiefdoms collapsed as a result overexploitation of the island's natural resources. The environment was particularly fragile, and the felling of trees for timber led to massive deforestation and consequent soil erosion.[21]

The first cities

The mother culture controversy

A major controversy centres on the extent the Olmec influenced later developments in Mesoamerica. Some argue that the Olmec were the 'mother culture' of later Mesoamerican civilisations, others that they were just one of a number of comparable 'sister cultures' that arose in Mesoamerica during the Early to Middle Preclassic. The former view proposes that the Olmec dominated, inspired, and ultimately raised other regions of Mesoamerica to the level of civilisation. This they achieved through the diffusion of an art style in which Olmec cosmology, religion, ideology and iconography was encoded.[22]

Although the Olmec stone heads are confined to the Gulf Coast, much Olmec art is scattered throughout Mesoamerica. For example, sculptures found as far away as El Salvador resemble monuments from La Venta and cave paintings at the rock shelter of Oxtotitlan in Guerrero show human and animal figures sitting on La Venta-style thrones. Smaller portable objects in Olmec style appear to have been exported from the Gulf Coast region and locally-made ones feature Olmec designs. Not only is there this evidence for widespread influence, there is also the precocity of San Lorenzo and La Venta in terms of public architecture, large stone monuments, art and iconography. These factors have led some to believe that the Olmec were great innovators who invented many elements and institutions of Mesoamerican civilisation, and transmitted them to less developed societies via trade, religion and war.[1]

Critics point out that this view downplays evidence that each region contributed its own repertoire of ceramic motifs. They point out that widespread regional ceramic styles existed in Mexico before the rise of the Olmec. They also note that a number of Mesoamerican traits appeared elsewhere before their adoption by the Olmec. These include the first use of lime plaster, adobe brick, and stone masonry, all of which were in use in the Valley of Oaxaca centuries before they reached the Olmec. The Olmec also trailed the Valley of Oaxaca in the use of solar and other astronomical alignments.[11,22]

In 2005, in an attempt to address these issues, researchers used a technique known as instrumental neutron activation analysis (INAA) to compare Olmec-style ceramic artefacts with clay samples so as to identify the origin of the pottery. Neutron activation analysis is used to identify trace elements present in a sample, which is bombarded with neutrons to form radioisotopes of the constituent elements. The characteristic decay signatures of these are then used to determine what trace elements are present. From a statistical analysis of the differing proportions of trace elements in the ceramic artefacts, the researchers hoped to identify the provenance of the clays used to make them.

The ceramics dated to the period between 1350 and 1000 BC, the time when Olmec-style pottery and figurines first spread across Mesoamerica. 944 Olmec-style ceramics were analysed, and 725 were assigned to seven regional groups: San Lorenzo, Mazatán, Valley of Oaxaca, Etlatongo, Tlapacoya, San Isidro and Tehuantepec. The remainder could not be assigned by the statistical techniques used. The findings suggested that the bulk of the ceramics were made from local clays. However, ceramics made from non-local clays were exclusively from San Lorenzo, suggesting that it was the only region to export pottery.[23] It was claimed that the study documents the export to foreign communities of Olmec pottery, together with an ideology reflected in its decoration. Olmec icons, beliefs and practices were integrated into local indigenous cultural systems, and the later imitation of Olmec pottery by local potters in local clays reflects the consolidation of these exported ideas.[24]

However, critics have pointed out that INAA detects constituent elements rather than minerals, and that particular elements can occur in many kinds of parent rock. They also note that ceramics contain minerals from sources other than the clay used in their manufacture. These include tempering materials, minerals absorbed from water used to moisten the clay, and substances from items that the ceramics were used to store or cook. Buried ceramics also may absorb substances from soil over the course of millennia. Neutron activation analysis cannot distinguish between any of these sources. An alternative approach is petrographic thin slice analysis, in which thin sections of the material in question are examined under a microscope to determine the mineral content. When this technique is applied to ceramics, results can differ from those obtained by neutron activation analysis. For example, neutron activation analysis cannot distinguish between grey ware from Valley of Oaxaca and San Lorenzo Olmec pottery, despite the tempering used in the two being entirely different. Petrographic thin slice analysis, on the other hand, can readily distinguish the two. It was claimed that the technique demonstrated that San Lorenzo had received pottery from other regions after all.[25]

The INAA study was further criticised on the grounds that a consistent sampling methodology had not been applied across all the archaeological sites considered, and because many of the ceramic pieces were left unassigned to a particular region.[22] When alternative statistical methods were applied to the samples, it was claimed that all the regions except Mazatán had exported pottery to at least one other region, and that most received pottery from several areas. San Lorenzo received pottery from every region apart from Mazatán. Nor was San Lorenzo the highest percentage exporter – that distinction was claimed by Etlatongo, a site that exported over half of its wares.[25]

A final criticism was the notion that the Olmec would export pottery and receive nothing in return. It was noted that ethnographic and ethnohistoric data indicates that unreciprocated trade among chiefdoms is uncommon. Native American chiefs welcomed gifts from other regions. In the Mexican highlands, the largest chiefly centres invariably received the most foreign goods. It was suggested that if San Lorenzo really had received none, then it could not have been very important.[22]

The authors of the INAA study vigorously defended their methodologies and conclusions. They noted that only a small number of pieces were examined in the petrographic study, versus almost one thousand in their own study. However, the most obviously valid point was that San Lorenzo might simply have received something other than ceramics in exchange for its own wares. Tlapacoya, for example, had easy access to sources of obsidian, a valuable material not locally available on the Gulf Coast.[26] Both sides continued to defend their conclusions in subsequent articles.[27,28] The moral, perhaps, is that even highly advanced analytical techniques and statistical methods can be used to make a case for either point of view.

Not a matter of life and death, but something much more important

The rubber balls at El Manatí are the earliest known example of the use of rubber in Mesoamerica. Rubber was also used to make figurines and bands for hafting axe heads, and in liquid form it was used for painting and for medicinal purposes. It was obtained by tapping the indigenous *Castilla elastica* tree. Latex from this source dries into a brittle substance that is of little use, but Mesoamerican people improved its elastic properties by adding an extract from the vine *Ipomoea alba* to produce a solid white mass. Modern researchers have found that a ball formed from such material exhibits typical rubbery behaviour, and can bounce to a height of 2 m (6 ft. 6 in.). The technique alters the mechanical properties of latex and predates the modern vulcanising process by 3,500 years. Its discovery led to the emergence of the Mesoamerican ballgame, a key element in ancient Mesoamerican religious, ritual and political life.[29]

The term 'ballgame' refers to a wide variety of ball sports widely played in ancient Mesoamerica. At least three variants of the ballgame continue to be played to this day, although the rules of the original pre-Columbian games are not known. The pivotal role of the ballgame in ancient Mesoamerican life is reflected in the large number of known ball courts – almost 1,300 – located at around 1,000 sites. The earliest-known ball court, as we saw above, is that at Paso de la Amada, dating to 1600 BC.[15]

Much early evidence of the game comes from ceramic figurines and other images of ballplayers. The earliest such figurines date to 1700 BC and were recovered from a tomb at El Opeño, Michoacan. An arranged scene portrays five male ballplayers and three female spectators. Three of the ballplayers are equipped with bats. All five are wearing shin-pads and short helmets, and some wear mitts over their hands. A small yoke-shaped basalt piece was also found in the tomb. It was probably worn on the hand to protect it or for hitting the ball, and is the earliest example of ballgame equipment found so far. However, the ballplayers lack the elaborate costumes that characterise later depictions. It is likely that the ballgame had yet to assume its later significance.[15] Notably, the ball court at Paso de la Amada predates the emergence of a hierarchical society there by about a century.[14] Perhaps at this stage, the ballgame was still primarily a recreational activity.

Soon however, it would become linked to conflict, completion, hereditary leadership, and emerging political inequality. Ballgame costume is present on several pieces of monumental sculpture from San Lorenzo. Monument 34 depicts a half-kneeling male figure wearing shorts, with a thick protective belt and loincloth. The monument has been interpreted as an Olmec ruler in his role as a ballplayer. At one of the San Lorenzo satellite towns, a monument features a similarly-clad ballplayer straddling a bound captive probably destined for sacrifice. Figurines from San Lorenzo depict ballplayers equipped with headdresses and helmets that mask the whole of the face, except for the eyes. They are wearing wide, thick padded belts and loincloths, and round pendants interpreted as mirrors. Similar imagery is seen with ballplayer figurines recovered at Etlatongo in Oaxaca and Cantón Corralito in Chiapas.[15] The latter site has been interpreted as an Olmec colony due to the similarity of its ceramic assemblage with that of San Lorenzo.[30]

Figurines from the central Mexican sites of Tlatilco and Tlapacoya show distinct differences to Olmec figurines. The differences may reflect regional variations of either the game itself or the attendant rituals. Some examples from Tlapacoya wear a protective yoke supported by vertical or crossed suspenders on the front torso, probably related to the thick padded belts from San Lorenzo and Cantón Corralito. Some central Mexican figurines also wear tall, elaborate headdresses and ear flares, again distinct from their Olmec counterparts. These elaborate costumes were probably worn during ceremonies taking place before or after the game, rather than during the game itself.[15]

It is generally accepted that the ballgame was closely associated with elite power. It represented institutionalised ritual combat, possibly serving as an alternative to actual warfare. The ballgame might also have served a role in local dispute resolution. Some versions of the game were associated with human sacrifice and others were of great cosmological significance. The Maya text *Popol Vuh* describes the ballgame as a contest between mortals and sinister underworld deities. The play of the ball in the court symbolised the movements of the sun and moon, in turn representing the regeneration of life and the maintenance of cosmic order; the ball court itself represented a portal to the underworld.[15] The former Liverpool F.C. manager Bill Shankly allegedly described football as much more important than life and death: the same, apparently, was true of the Mesoamerican ballgame.

The Mesoamerican calendar

Mesoamerican calendrical systems have become well-known to the general public in recent years as a result of the Maya Long Count, which ended on 21 December 2012. There is no reason to suppose that the Maya expected anything untoward to occur on that day, but that did not stop the doomsday industry from working overtime. As the supposed day of reckoning approached, groups camped out by a mountain in southern France to await rescue by aliens. There was much nonsense about a rogue planet called Nibiru and other supposed perils. The cinema industry cashed in on the hoo-hah with the disaster movie *2012* and Lars von Trier's rather more thoughtful *Melancholia*. Neither film paid much heed to the laws of physics. In fact, periodic end of the world 'scares' are nothing new, and go back at least a thousand years.[31]

The Long Count was actually only one of three calendars in use in pre-Columbian Mesoamerica. For day-to-day reckoning, there was a solar calendar or *haab* cycle of 365 days, and there was a ritual calendar of 260-days known as the *tzolkin* or sacred almanac. All three calendars made use of the vigesimal or base-20 system of counting, rather than our familiar decimal or base-10 system; this might have come about through the practice of counting the digits on the feet as well as on the hands. The system employed a place-value notation and a zero, long before the Hindu-Arabic system introduced these concepts. Numbers were represented by combinations of ones (dots), fives (bars) and zeros (various characters) stacked vertically, with place value increasing from bottom to top.[32] The other number that featured prominently in Mesoamerican calendrical systems was 13, representing the number of levels of heaven in Mesoamerican cosmology (*cf.* the seven levels of heaven in the Jewish, Islamic and Hindu traditions).

The *haab* cycle comprised 18 'months' of 20 days each, plus 5 intercalary days. Each date was denoted by one of 20 day names paired with one of 18 month names. Like the pre-Ptolemaic Egyptian calendar, it did not take leap years into consideration, and thus did not accurately track the solar year. Days in the *tzolkin* were denoted by a number from 1 to 13 and one of 20 names, for a total of 260 days. The *haab* and *tzolkin* cycles were combined into the Calendar Round, a cycle that repeats every 18,980 days (about 52 years). The 52-year cycle was a period of great significance throughout Mesoamerica. The termination was celebrated by the New Fire ceremony, in which fires everywhere were extinguished and domestic implements and statues were discarded.[32]

The Long Count calendar generated dates from a fixed start point that were to all intents and purposes unique (as are Gregorian dates). The basic unit of time was the *tun* of 360 days, which was subdivided into 18 *uinals* of 20 *kins* (days) each. The *tun* was multiplied by successive powers of 20 (the vigesimal equivalent of decades and centuries) named *katuns* and *baktuns*. Thus a *katun* is 360 x 20 = 7200 days or just under 20 years, and a *baktun* is 360 x 20 x 20 = 144,000 days or just over 394 years. The Maya did not invent the Long Count, but by Classic times, only they were using it.[1] The Maya implementation of the Long Count began on a date corresponding to 11 August 3114 BC in the Gregorian calendar, and the 13th *baktun* from that date (13.0.0.0.0) ended on 21 December 2012. There is some dispute as to what was supposed to follow. The usual view is that 13 *baktuns* (just over 5,125 years) represents a creation epoch and the count returns to zero.[32] However, there is some evidence that the Maya intended the count to continue. There may be higher-order units beyond the *baktun*, which modern scholars (in the absence of the original Maya terms) have named the *piktun*, *kalabtun*, *kinchiltun* and *alautun*.

The reason for a 260-day ritual count remains uncertain. One suggestion is that it originated at a location between 14°42' and 15° N., where the Sun crosses the zenith at 260 and 105-day intervals. A possible candidate is the Late Preclassic site of Izapa, located on the Pacific Coast of Mexico.[33] One objection to this interpretation is that the 260-day cycle simply repeats and does not factor in the concomitant 105-day cycle.[34] Another problem is that the 260-day cycle might have been in use at the site of Monte Albán in the Valley of Oaxaca before its use at Izapa.[34] There are also Olmec inscriptions that suggest that the cycle may date to as early as 650 BC.[35,36]

Other suggestions are a link to the average human gestation period of 266 days, or to various astronomical cycles. Two *tzolkin* (520 days) corresponds closely to three eclipse half-years (519.93 days). The eclipse half-year of 173.31 days is the period between successive eclipse seasons, i.e. a period of around 33 days when the Earth, Moon and Sun can line up to produce an eclipse. There is also a close correspondence between the *tzolkin* and the average of 263 days that Venus remains visible as either a morning or evening object, before it disappears into the dawn or twilight skies.

The first cities

Links to Mars have also been suggested: the Martian synodic period (i.e. the interval between successive close approaches to Earth) is almost exactly three *tzolkin*, or 780 days.[32]

The Maya were proficient astronomers, and were able to predict the movements of Mars in some detail.[37] There is evidence for astronomical tables dating to around AD 800,[38] and it is highly likely that the Maya sought to rationalise planetary motions and other astronomical phenomena in terms of their (long-established) calendrical systems. However, it does not necessarily follow that such phenomena were responsible for the 260-day period in the first place. Given the importance of the numbers 13 and 20 in Mesoamerican culture, then 260 could represent nothing more significant than 13 multiplied by 20.

Writing in Mesoamerica

While a case could be made that the development of the Mesopotamian, Egyptian, Harappan and Chinese writing systems were not entirely independent of one another, the same cannot be said of the New World. Nevertheless, Mesoamerican writing systems mimicked their Old World counterparts in many ways.[39]

Most pre-Columbian written records are Maya, but unfortunately only a very few of their books have survived. These include the Dresden, Madrid and Paris Codices, named for the cities in which they are now kept. Most Maya books were destroyed on the orders of Diego de Landa, a Spanish bishop tasked with bringing the Roman Catholic faith to the Maya. De Landa was considered over-zealous even for the Spanish Inquisition, and he was eventually recalled to Spain. To give him his due, he was appalled by the practice of human sacrifice, and on one occasion he physically intervened to prevent the sacrifice of a young boy. De Landa also attempted to describe how the Maya writing system works. With the help of Maya interlocutors, he attempted to match Maya glyphs with the letters of the alphabet. He published his findings in a book entitled *Relación de las cosas de Yucatán*, but nineteenth century attempts to translate Maya texts with his 'alphabet' met with little success. The problem was that Mesoamerican writing systems are not alphabetic and the glyphs de Landa had recorded represented syllables rather than letters. For example, the glyph he had recorded for the letter 'B' had the phonetic value of /bay/, corresponding to the Spanish pronunciation of 'B'.

Progress was not made until the 1950s, when the Soviet scholar Yuri Knorozov proposed treating de Landa's 'letters' as syllables. However, the major breakthrough came with his suggestion that Maya script followed a rule known as synharmony. According to this, a word ending in a consonant will be written with a glyph representing a syllable whose vowel sound is the same as the vowel sound of the preceding glyph. When spoken, the vowel sound is silent. For example, the Maya word for 'turkey' is 'kutz'. Knorozov suggested that it would be made up of glyphs with the values /ku/ and /tzu/. De Landa's book provided a glyph for 'C', pronounced 'cu' in Spanish, and the same glyph appears in the Madrid Codex in conjunction with a picture of a turkey. According to the Knorozov theory, the glyph following it should have the value /tzu/. Knorozov found an example of this second glyph in the Dresden Codex, associated with a picture of a dog. The Maya word for 'dog' is 'tzul', and this not only confirmed the value of the glyph, it also suggested that the one following it should have the value /lu/. He had thus deciphered the phonetic value of two previously-unknown signs. This principle has since been used to decipher a large number of signs, though many remain unknown.

In comparison to Mesopotamian cuneiform or Egyptian hieroglyphic script, Maya script is incompletely understood. Only rarely can a pictorial origin be recognised for a particular glyph. Like the Mesopotamian writing system, Maya script is logosyllabic, but it is far more confusing. Different glyphs can have the same value, and many values can be attached to the same glyph. There are about 800 to 1,000 basic glyphs, about the number that may be expected in a logosyllabic system, but probably only two or three hundred were in regular use at any one time. The same glyph can function as a syllabogram or a logogram, depending on the context. Maya text is structured around glyphs and glyph groups. The latter comprise a central main glyph with up to four subsidiary elements affixed above (superfix), below (subfix) or on either side (prefix or postfix). Main glyphs can be compounded from two or more elements.

The origins of Mesoamerican writing are uncertain, but certainly predate the Maya. By the Late Preclassic, related glyphic scripts and calendrical systems were in use in the Isthmus of Tehuantepec and the Valley of Oaxaca, in addition to the Maya region. The similarities between the three writing and calendrical systems suggest that they all probably developed from a common ancestral script during the preceding Middle Preclassic.[35]

The Olmec are credited with what is currently claimed to be the earliest writing system in the New World. The Cascajal Block is a tablet-sized serpentine block with shallow incisions of a previously-unknown script. The block was recovered by builders in 1999 in a pile of rubble at a gravel quarry near the village of Lomas de Tacamichapa. Associated ceramic shards suggest that it dates to transition between the Early and Middle Preclassic, around 900 BC. The Olmec iconography that must have given rise to the script is consistent with that date. The 12 kg (26 lb. 8 oz.) block measures 36 by 21 cm (14 by 8 in.) and is 13 cm (5 in.) thick. There is little doubt that it is a written text. On it are inscribed a total of 62 glyphs. The script remains undeciphered, but it contains 28 distinct glyphic elements, all but seven of which occur at least twice in the text. Of course there could be further glyphic elements that do not occur in the text. The text does not appear to be related to any later writing system. The Cascajal writing system might have been devised locally, or it could have been in widespread use. In either case it must have fallen out of use before the spread of later systems. It is possible that many texts from the period were recorded on wood carvings that have not survived the tropical conditions.[40]

It has been suggested that the Cascajal block is an elaborate hoax. Concerns have been raised about its recovery by non-archaeologists. It has also been suggested that many of the supposed glyphs occur in a non-writing context on a wide range of small artefacts.[41] These claims are dismissed by the block's describers. They note that its provenance is no less secure than that of many *bona fide* examples of ancient writing. They also point out that all known glyphic systems in the world were derived from pre-existing iconography.[42]

A second Olmec artefact claimed to demonstrate a writing system was recovered at San Andrés, a subsidiary Olmec centre 5km (3 miles) northeast of La Venta. A cylinder seal and fragments of a greenstone plaque with glyphs provide evidence for early logographic writing. Both date to around 650 BC. The seal shares certain conventions with later Mesoamerican writing systems: firstly, the use of speech scrolls. These are lines or other device that connects speaker to speech, and are identical in function to the 'speech bubbles' used in comics and cartoon strips; secondly, the use of a cartouche to encircle calendrical day names; and thirdly, the use of affixes as described above. The seal depicts two speech scrolls emanating from the beak of a bird, each followed by a column of grouped glyphic elements. On the basis of comparison to later Maya glyphs, the first column has been interpreted as 'king' and the second as '3 Ajaw', a date in the Mesoamerican 260-day ritual calendar. Many Mesoamerican groups named children for their birth date in the 260-day ritual calendar; a child born on 6 Monkey, for example, would be given that name. Thus the seal may read 'King 3 Ajaw'.[35]

Ajaw is also the word for 'king' in Maya script, but in this context it is simply one of the twenty names used in the 260-day ritual calendar. In Mesoamerican iconography, birds often represent kings or gods. The seal might have been the personal seal of an Olmec ruler. Note that we cannot necessarily assume that 3 Ajaw was a king rather than a chief. As we saw in Chapter 20, the existence of a word cognate with 'king' cannot necessarily be used to draw implications about social complexity. This argument could also be applied to the Olmec world of 650 BC.

Some are sceptical about the interpretation of the seal as evidence for Olmec writing, and Mesoamerican epigrapher Stephen Houston claims that the evidence is insufficient. The supposed speech scrolls could simply be another example of the sophisticated iconography of the time.[43] More substantive evidence for writing in the Isthmus of Tehuantepec did not occur until over half a millennium after the Olmec collapse, by which time the former Olmec heartland was occupied by a culture known as the Epi-Olmec. The La Mojarra Stela 1 was recovered in 1986 from a river near the former Olmec centre of Tres Zapotes. The 2 m (6 ft.) 4 tonne basalt monument is inscribed with 520 glyphs surrounding an elaborately-carved image of a king. It was initially believed to be a forgery and remained locked away in the basement of the Xalapa Museum of Anthropology for some years, until it was finally accepted as genuine.[44] Two Long Count dates are mentioned, corresponding to AD 143 and 156.[44] Although not widely accepted,[45] a decipherment of the script has been claimed. The language represented in the La Mojarra text is said to be an early form of Zoquean, a branch of the Mixe-Zoque language family still spoken in the region.[46,47]

Roughly contemporary with the San Andrés cylinder seal is Monument 3, a carved stone relief from the Zapotec site of San Jose Mogote in Valley of Oaxaca. The monument depicts the naked corpse of a captive whose heart has been cut out and genitals mutilated. This gruesome image apparently depicts the sacrifice of a captured rival chief, and is accompanied by glyphs that may be his name. Monument 3 cannot be directly radiocarbon dated, but its context and associated ceramics have been used to assign a date range of between 700 and 500 BC.[48] It has been suggested on iconographic grounds that it is more recent,[49] but if the older date range is correct then Monument 3 is the earliest example of Zapotec writing.

The earliest evidence for Maya written scripts was until recently thought to date back to no earlier than between 100 BC and AD 100, but discoveries at San Bartolo in northeastern Guatemala have now pushed back the date range to between 200 and 300 BC. Writing has been found on murals and plaster fragments buried inside a pyramidal structure known as Las Pinturas that was constructed in discrete phases over the course of several centuries. It proved possible to obtain radiocarbon dates from samples of carbonised wood associated with the writing.[50] San Bartolo was identified in 2001, and is a relatively small Maya site. It is therefore possible that similar texts await discovery in some of the much larger Maya sites.[51]

The rise and fall of Monte Albán

If we accept that Olmec society was not at state level, then the Zapotec can probably claim to be the first civilisation to emerge in the New World. The roots of the Zapotec state can be traced to San Mogote in the northern part of Valley of Oaxaca. Early farmers in this region almost certainly spoke early forms of modern Zapotec languages.[1] San José Mogote was first occupied around 1600 BC. The site overlooks a river in one of the richest environments in the valley, surrounded on three sides by high water-table alluvium. There were at least 18 other villages in the valley, but San José Mogote was the largest, with a population in the hundreds. The settlement comprised wattle-and-daub family houses, subterranean storage pits and ritual buildings known as 'men's houses'.[48]

This first phase of occupation is known as the Tierras Largas phase. During this phase, House 19, one of the earliest on the site, was burned, possibly during a raid from a rival village. At the same time, the western periphery of the settlement was protected by a palisade formed by a double line of posts, although it is not known whether or not it surrounded the whole village. Sections of the palisade, too, were burned.[48]

Men's houses are known ethnographically and are seen in societies where groups of families claim descent from a real or mythical common ancestor. Although such societies are egalitarian, membership of the men's houses is usually restricted to men who have passed a series of ritual tests that demonstrate their value to the community. At San Mogote, they comprised single-room lime-plastered buildings measuring around 4 by 6 m (13 by 20 ft.). All are oriented 8° north of due east, suggesting an alignment with the sun's path at the equinox. This suggests that some rituals were now scheduled around dates defined by solar events, something that was possible once villages were occupied year-round. Some men's houses featured a pit built into the floor, filled with powdered lime. It is likely that this was for use with a ritual plant such as tobacco, jimson weed, or morning glory. The historic Zapotec are known to have chewed a mixture of powdered tobacco and lime to cure illness or to increase physical strength before raids.[52]

During the subsequent San José phase (1200 to 900 BC), San José Mogote experienced considerable growth as the population grew from the hundreds to over 1,000, and buildings were constructed outside the palisade. The village was now apparently large enough to deter raiders. An elite ruling class emerged, its presence announced by the appearance of elite residences and luxury goods of jade, magnetite and mother-of-pearl.[48,52] This period also saw the appearance of residential wards or hamlets within the village, each with its own set of public buildings. They were built on low, natural rises on the site and were separated by ancient erosion gullies. There were at least three wards, each comprising eight to twelve households. Area A lies on what was the eastern edge of the village; Area B lies 300 m (985 ft.) to the west; and Area C lies at the western edge of the village, a further 100 m (330 ft.) to the west.[53] The Guadalupe phase (900 to 700 BC) saw the ritual 'men's houses' gave way to platforms of wattle-and-daub, where public or ceremonial activities were conducted. However, true temples of monumental proportions did not appear until the Rosario phase (700 to 500 BC). By this time, San José Mogote was the capital of a chiefdom that incorporated 28 other villages located up to about 12 km (6 miles) away.[52,54] The sites formed a three-tier settlement hierarchy.[20]

Warfare resumed during the Guadalupe phase. Other chiefly centres had emerged in the region, some of which were only a day's journey away. None were strong enough to challenge San José Mogote directly, but some of its satellite villages were attacked. At Fábrica San José, 5 km (3 miles) to the east of San José Mogote, at least three houses were burned by raiders. The conflict, presumably intensified by completion between rival chiefdoms for land, water and labour, reached its peak during the Rosario phase. By now, each of the three main lobes of the three-lobed Valley of Oaxaca was controlled by a single chiefly centre, though at 60 to 65 ha (148 to 160 acres), San José Mogote in the northern valley was still the largest. Its main rival was probably San Martín Tilcajete, in the southern valley, with an extent of 25 ha (62 acres). The three rival chiefdoms were separated by an 80 sq. km (30 sq. mile) neutral zone in the centre of the valley that was left virtually unoccupied.[48]

Midway through the Rosario phase, San José Mogote itself was attacked and the main temple, Structure 28, was destroyed. It was never rebuilt, but a new temple was built soon after, a short distance away from the original. At some point after the construction of the new temple, the carving known as Monument 3 was set up. As noted above, it depicts the sacrifice of a captured rival chief. While it cannot be dated by radiocarbon methods, its context and associated ceramics place it in the Rosario phase. Assuming this assignment is correct, it is the earliest record of captive taking and the earliest example of Zapotec writing.[48]

Around 500 BC, at the end of the Rosario phase, San José Mogote and its outlying villages were abandoned. The inhabitants, who by this time numbered around 2,000, relocated to a more defensible settlement on Monte Albán, a previously-uninhabited mesa (flat-topped hill) lying within the former central neutral zone. They strengthened its natural defences by erecting 3 km (1.85 miles) of walls along the more easily-climbed western slopes of the mountain. From this redoubt, wars of conquest would be waged until well into the Christian era.[48]

Little time was wasted in providing a public reminder of the likely fate of anybody who resisted this emerging superpower. Located in the southwest corner of the summit complex, Building L contains 300 carved stones depicting contorted naked men. The sculptures are known as the *danzantes* because they were once thought to represent dancers. The current, rather grimmer view is that they represent sacrificed enemy captives, many of whom suffered genital mutilation. It is likely that they were the chiefs or elite members of conquered polities. Holes depicted in their earlobes probably relate to the removal of ear spools after capture. Such ornaments were probably made from luxury materials such as jade or obsidian. Some of the carvings bear glyphs which in some cases include calendrical markings in the 260-day ritual calendar. These might have been the birth date names of the defeated chiefs.[55]

Prior to 300 BC (Monte Albán I phase), there is no firm evidence for state-level organisation at Monte Albán. The transition seems to have occurred in the period from 300 to 100 BC, during which the population might have grown to as much as 20,000. The city now covered about 442 ha (1.7 sq. miles) and was at the centre of a large cluster of smaller settlements. Outside this inner ring were more distant settlements, many of which were fortified. There was a four-tier settlement hierarchy, indicating that the Monte Albán polity had now become a state-level society.[1,20]

Despite this growth, Monte Albán did not yet control the whole of the Valley of Oaxaca. A day's journey away to the south, the old enemy San Martín Tilcajete remained unyielding. The site doubled in size to 52.8 ha (130 acres), and a civic plaza was constructed. Shortly before 300 BC, it was attacked by Monte Albán and the plaza was burned, but San Martín Tilcajete refused to surrender. Between 300 and 100 BC, it grew to 71.5 ha (177 acres). A new plaza was constructed in a more defensible location, along with defensive walls. What is the oldest currently-known Zapotec royal palace was also constructed. San Martín Tilcajete was now in all probability the capital of a small secondary state, its ability to resist enhanced by its ability to draw on manpower from satellite villages. In the long term, however, resistance was futile. A more concerted attack was eventually launched, and San Martín Tilcajete fell. The royal palace and a nearby palace were destroyed and the site was abandoned. On a nearby mountaintop, a second-tier administrative centre was built by its conquerors. Monte Albán was now the capital of a unified Zapotec state;[48,56,20] its rise provides strong support for the role of territorial expansion in primary state formation[20,57] (see Chapter 25).

With San Martín Tilcajete finally defeated, the new Zapotec state expanded its realm 150 km (90 miles) beyond the Valley of Oaxaca. Building J at Monte Albán displays over 40 carved slabs with glyphs representing the names of places claimed as provinces. Only a few have been identified, but these do provide evidence of Zapotec expansion. They include the Cañada de Cuicatlán, an arid tropical river canyon 80 km (50 miles) north of Monte Albán. Zapotec forces destroyed settlements in the river floodplain, and forcibly relocated the inhabitants to make way for irrigation canals. Little resistance was encountered. Evidence of the fate of those who did resist has been found at the village La Coyotera, where the Zapotec set up a wooden rack displaying the skulls of 61 defeated enemy.[48]

At Monte Albán itself, development continued. Between 200 BC and AD 100 the summit of the mesa was levelled off and a new complex of massive buildings was laid out around a 300 m (985 ft.) long Main Plaza. To the north of the plaza was a palace complex was built on a large platform. It housed the Monte Albán royal family, together with administrative and ritual facilities. Below the floors were elaborate tombs with carved and painted chambers. On either side of the plaza were temples and a ball court. A second large platform was located at its south end. By now, the entire population of the unified valley numbered 41,000 individuals, living in 518 settlements.[1] During this period, San José Mogote was reoccupied and grew to 60 ha (148 acres). It now possessed a number of impressive temples, and served as a second-tier administrative centre.[52]

Between AD 300 and 700, some 2,000 terraces were built on the slopes of the hill to accommodate the growing population. Nearly 3,000 separate residences have been identified: most were simple adobe structures built around central courtyards, but there are also some larger, more elaborate elite residences. These final centuries of expansion represented the pinnacle for Monte Albán, and after AD 700 it went into decline. Large-scale construction ceased and ritual activity in the Main Plaza was diminished. The site was not abandoned and thousands of people continued to live there, but it never regained its former pre-eminence. For many centuries, small Zapotec and Mixtec kingdoms lived in uneasy coexistence, until the region came under the hegemony of the Aztec in the fifteenth century.[1]

Teotihuacán

The Valley of Mexico is a potentially attractive region to farmers. Its volcanic soils are fertile, and its extensive system of lakes offers abundant aquatic foods. The drawback is that tropical crops took time to adapt to the cold environment and the altitude of 2,250 m (7,400 ft.); the first farmers did not settle in the region until around 1600 BC. By 1200 BC, however, the population was about 10,000, and by the time of the Olmec collapse around 400 BC, it had increased to about 80,000. Around half-a-dozen polities existed in the relatively humid southwest part of the valley,[1] some of which were fairly large. Cuicuilco, for example, might have been 400 ha (1.5 sq. miles), with a population of 20,000.[20]

Very few farmers lived in the more arid northeast until the rise of Teotihuacán. Located 45 km (28 miles) northeast of present-day Mexico City, Teotihuacán rapidly became the largest urban settlement in the New World. It emerged between 200 and 100 BC, and by AD 1 it had attained a size of 8 sq. km (3 sq. miles) with a population of 20,000 to 40,000.[58] By this time, both Teotihuacán and Cuicuilco had evolved into states, with four-tier settlement hierarchies. At this stage, neither controlled the whole of the Valley of Mexico, and it is likely that there was ongoing confrontation between the two polities.[20] The rivalry was ended when the volcano Xitle erupted around AD 280, and devastated Cuicuilco.[59]

Teotihuacán was already very large before any monumental construction began. The monumental layout of the city began around AD 1 and was completed in around two centuries. It is possible that the major elements of the layout were envisaged as a masterplan from the beginning. The main ceremonial avenue is known as the known as the Street of the Dead, the northern part of which was laid out first, along with the Pyramid of the Moon at the northernmost extent. Subsequently, the 63 m (207 ft.) high Pyramid of the Sun was constructed in two main stages over the course of 50 years. The Street of the Dead was extended south and two large enclosures built: the Great Compound, which was probably a marketplace; and the Ciudadela ('Citadel'), which contained the Pyramid of the Feathered Serpent. The latter was constructed around AD 200, and building works were accompanied by the sacrifice of two hundred individuals. Many of the victims wore military costumes and were accompanied by weapons. It is not known if they were enemy captives, low-status Teotihuacán soldiers, or elite guardsmen of the royal household accompanying a recently-deceased ruler. By AD 250, the start of the Classic Period, the population had reached about 100,000. The growth was bolstered by movement into the city of most of the population of the Valley of Mexico. Meanwhile, the extent of the city had reached 20 sq. km (7.75 sq. miles). The population increase slowed thereafter, possibly because of limitations of the food supply. Most agricultural activities were concentrated in and near to the city.[58,1]

The residential part of the city was laid out on a grid plan of rectangular house compounds along narrow streets and alleys. Within the grid were many walled stone-built apartment complexes, but much of the accommodation might have comprised unwalled groups of more modest housing. The apartment compounds varied considerably. Some were spacious, others cramped and barracks-like. Some were beautifully decorated, others far more basic. The largest housed up to 100 people, and even the smaller ones could accommodate four to six families. Sub-floor burials were numerous, and in some cases were located under elaborate courtyard shrines. We don't fully understand this variation, but it is apparent that many Teotihuacános lived in social groups larger than the nuclear family, and that there were considerable differences in the wealth and status of the city's inhabitants.[1]

The scale and organisation of craft production in Teotihuacán are still poorly understood. Some craft specialists might have worked full time for state institutions, and many might have provided periodic labour services. However, much craft production was household-based rather than state controlled. The state's role was for the most part restricted to regulation and taxation rather than outright control. The absorption of so much of the rural population meant that many inhabitants must have worked as farmers. Commerce in obsidian was important, although estimates of 400 obsidian workshops in the city have been revised downwards. Teotihuacán controlled a number of obsidian sources, including a high-quality green variety which was widely exported.[58]

With Cuicuilco out of the way, Teotihuacán established direct control over the Valley of Mexico. It is thought that it eventually gained control over a much larger region of 25,000 sq. km (9,600 sq. miles) that included large portions of the adjoining states of Hidalgo, Tlaxcala, Puebla and Morelos. Studies within this hinterland suggest an adoption of Teotihuacán culture. For example, in the Rio Amatzinac Valley of eastern Morelos, local ceramic traditions were replaced by Teotihuacán-derived styles, and local elites seem to have adopted ritual paraphernalia associated with elite groups at Teotihuacán itself.[60] Possibly 500,000 to 750,000 people lived in this core region.[1]

What remains uncertain is how much further the administrative control of Teotihuacán extended, though evidence of its impact is undisputed. Typical ceramics, obsidian implements, iconography and even Teotihuacán-style ceremonial architecture are found across a wide area beyond central Mexico, particularly to the south. Many artefacts appear within indigenous sites, and represent little more than the vast extent of Teotihuacán's commercial and other contacts. However, some sites, mostly dating from between AD 400 and 550 show very high and on occasion segregated concentrations of Teotihuacán-related artefacts. Such sites probably represent Teotihuacán outposts and enclaves, at great distance from the core area. Three basic types have been identified: firstly, outposts sited along trade and communication routes; secondly, enclaves within native polities controlling important resources; and thirdly, outposts near resources in relatively undeveloped areas.[60]

The first type are typically small, unfortified sites that probably served as way stations on long-distance trade routes, for instance between Teotihuacán and Monte Albán. However, some of these sites are far larger. Matacapan, in the Sierra de los Tuxtlas on the Gulf Coast of Veracruz, is located 400km (250 miles) from Teotihuacán. This location commands trade routes into central Mexico, the Maya Lowlands, the Pacific Coast, and Guatemala. The 6 sq. km (2.3 sq. mile) site is dominated by a central plaza with ceremonial and public architecture. Communal residential buildings resemble the apartment complexes at Teotihuacán and many artefacts, though manufactured locally, are stylistically of Teotihuacán derivation. The site has been interpreted as a distant colonial outpost.[60]

Even further afield is the Maya city of Kaminaljuyu in Guatemala, some 700 km (430 miles) from Teotihuacán. It is located within the Maya highlands, with easy access to the Maya lowlands and the Pacific Coast. Teotihuacán imported material from all three regions, and the Teotihuacán presence at the site dates from the period between AD 400 and 550. It took the form of an enclave, segregated from the rest of the settlement. Only a limited range of Teotihuacán elite ceramics and architectural styles have been found, and utilitarian objects are exclusively of local origin. The enclave was initially located at the periphery of the site, but later moved to a more central location. This suggests that Teotihuacán eventually gained a significant degree of political control over the settlement.[60]

Possibly the new ruling elite was made up of intrusive Teotihuacános and local nobility, linked by marital ties.[45] Oxygen isotope analysis has been carried out on bone and dental enamel taken from tomb occupants. Results suggest that both elite occupants and accompanying sacrificial victims were in some cases local and in others from at least two different foreign regions. One region might have been Teotihuacán, but the other has not been identified. One individual appears to have been born near Kaminaljuyu, but spent his early teenage years at Teotihuacán.[61]

Examples of the third outpost type are scattered across mineral-rich regions of northern and western Mexico, commonly in association with mines. In some cases, Teotihuacán-style ceremonial structures have been found in addition to artefacts. These sites are at minimum evidence of contact between local polities and Teotihuacán, but in some cases they might have been run by small groups of Teotihuacán colonists. Examples may include the Rio Súchil basin in northwest Mexico, where extensive mining activity was carried out for cinnabar, hematite, limonite, malachite, chert and semiprecious stones. Around AD 400 to 450, a control complex was established at the site of Alta Vista, which incorporated architecture of a recognisably Teotihuacán style.[60,1]

The overall picture seems to be that Teotihuacán's direct rule did not extend very far outside its core region, a radius of about 90 km (56 miles). Notably, the polities of Cholula and Cantona, lying at or just beyond that distance, seem to have retained their independence. Beyond the core region, the settlement pattern suggests that Teotihuacán sought control over key routes and settlements rather than extended territory. Rather than imperial power like that of the Romans, Teotihuacán control might have been hegemonic,[58] and Teotihuacán might have been forced into a more equal relationship with states powerful enough to resist its hegemony. Ceramic evidence suggests that Monte Albán maintained an enclave within Teotihuacán.[58]

The presence at Kaminaljuyu may be an example of Teotihuacán gradually gaining political control over a distant state, but on occasions it was apparently prepared to resort to more direct measures to assert its authority. The Maya city of Tikal in the Petén Department of northern Guatemala is 1,000 km (620 miles) from Teotihuacán, even further away than Kaminaljuyu. According to Maya records, an emissary 'from the west' named Sihyaj K'ahk ('Fire is born') arrived at Tikal on 14 January AD 378, eight days after his arrival at the site El Peru. On the same day, the Tikal king Chak Toc Ich'aak I ('Great Jaguar Paw') died.[45]

Sihyaj K'ahk was apparently under the command of a shadowy figure identified by the non-Maya glyph of an atlatl conjoined with an owl – a common Teotihuacán motif. Within a year, Sihyaj K'ahk had installed the young son of 'Spear-thrower Owl', Yax Nuun Ahiin ('First Crocodile'), as king of Tikal. It is unlikely that the death of Chak Toc Ich'aak I was unrelated to the 'arrival' of Sihyaj K'ahk. In all probability, the latter 'arrived' at the head of a Teotihuacán invasion force.[45] In this instance, it seems, Teotihuacán was prepared to impose regime change. A possible twentieth century parallel is the relatively bloodless Soviet invasion of Czechoslovakia in 1968, where military intervention was used to remove the reform-minded Alexander Dubček and re-impose Marxist-Leninist orthodoxy.

Between the fourth and sixth centuries AD, Teotihuacán was at its zenith of power and influence. Its inhabitants by now numbered 125,000, making it one of the largest cities anywhere in the world. However, Teotihuacán's days as a major power were numbered. Somewhere between AD 500 and 550, the city's elite residences and the temples along the Street of the Dead were burned, and idols were smashed. It is possible that an internal conflict resulted in the destruction of the major symbols and facilities of the *ancien regime*. Another possibility is that a declining Teotihuacán state was defeated by a coalition of outsiders, perhaps aided by disaffected elements within the city. Teotihuacán survived the upheaval, albeit with a drastically reduced population of around 30,000 to 40,000. Like Monte Albán, it never regained its former glory, but it remained a small kingdom with a population of around 10,000 at the time of the Spanish conquest.[58,1]

Postclassic developments

The Early Postclassic saw the emergence of the Toltec, a people prominent in later Aztec legend. Like Olmec, Toltec is an Aztec term, in this case meaning 'skilled artisan'. The Toltec are supposed to have inhabited the fabulous city of Tollan and worshipped the god Quetzalcoatl. The historical Toltec were inhabitants of the city of Tula, located on the fringe of the Valley of Mexico, 80 km (50 miles) from Teotihuacán. The region was originally colonised by people from Teotihuacán, but ceramics from around AD 700 suggest that people with other ethnic backgrounds might also have been present. Beginning as a modest settlement at around this time, Tula developed into a huge city between AD 900 and 1200. The population might have been as large as 60,000, living in an area of around 16 sq. km (6 sq. miles). By now, Tula was a cosmopolitan city, with many of its inhabitants from regions to the north and east of the Valley of Mexico, and possibly the northern Gulf Coast. However, most of the inhabitants were probably Nahuátl-speakers.[1]

The Toltec established an extensive trade network throughout Mesoamerica and beyond, with links to places as far apart as El Salvador and Casas Grandes in northern Mexico. They undoubtedly came into contact with the Postclassic Maya at Chichén Itzá, though the exact nature of the relationship is uncertain. Tula's hegemony probably covered the whole of the Valley of Mexico, but its power never matched that of Teotihuacán. Tula collapsed sometime between AD 1150 and 1200, and there are signs that buildings were burned and looted. The outlying settlements remained inhabited, and eventually the city was reoccupied before coming under the sway of the Aztec in the early sixteenth century.[1]

The Aztec civilisation was at the zenith of its power at the time of the Spanish conquest. As such, a full discussion lies outside the scope of this work. Very briefly, the Aztec emerged right at the end of the Postclassic. 'Aztec' is a rather loose term for a number of Nahuátl-speaking groups from which a powerful empire emerged less than a century before the arrival of the Conquistadors. It is not a term they ever used to describe themselves. People 'lumped' as Aztec include the Acolhua, Tepaneca, Chalca and Mexica-Tenochca. In around AD 1325, the latter founded the city of Tenochtitlán on reclaimed land in the Valley of Mexico. Originally just one of several dozen warring polities in the Valley of Mexico, the Mexica-Tenochca formed a triple alliance with the city-states of Texcoco and Tlacopan in AD 1428, and during the next 91 years they gained control of around 400 previously independent polities over an area of some 200,000 sq. km (77,250 sq. miles). The capital, Tenochtitlán, covered an area of 12 to 15 sq. km (4.6 to 5.8 sq. miles) with a population of around 125,000.[1] By comparison, the population of sixteenth century London was around 85,000.[62] This was how things stood in AD 1519, in the reign of Moctezuma II, when Hernán Cortés arrived at the head of his small but effective army.

30: The Maya

Wars and monuments

Maya civilisation, like that of the Aztec and Inca, was still existent when the Conquistadors arrived. Unlike the other two, however, the Maya were never unified into a single polity, and none of their more powerful city-states survived up until the time of the Spanish conquest. The reasons for the Classic Maya collapse are disputed: drought and destruction of forest cover are often cited, but it is also possible that the root causes were ruling elites that were more preoccupied with waging wars and building monuments than they were with controlling infrastructure and agricultural production.

Although they did not invent either writing or the Mesoamerican calendar, the Maya are the only Mesoamerican civilisation that has left us a significant volume of texts that can be assembled into a historical record. Around 15,000 texts have been recovered, although they mostly date to the Late Classic Period after AD 600. Earlier texts are less abundant and informative. Some texts are carved on monuments or buildings, but most are recorded on pottery found in tombs or elite residences. Unfortunately, as noted in Chapter 29, only a very few books have survived. The texts and associated calendrical data provide us with excellent data about the elite of Maya society, including births, deaths and ascensions of kings, wars, alliances and rituals, and we also know that the Maya were excellent astronomers. However, Maya texts are far less informative when it comes to more mundane matters, and there are no formal accounting records like those associated with other early literate cultures.[1,2]

The Maya inhabited the southeast corner of Mesoamerica, to the east of the Olmec heartland. The Maya lands comprise the region from the Yucatán Peninsula to the Pacific Coast. They include the Mexican states of Yucatán, Quintana Roo, Campeche and the eastern portions of Tabasco and Chiapas, together with Guatemala, Belize, and the western portions of Honduras and El Salvador. Indigenous Maya live there to this day, and languages of the Maya family are widely spoken. 68 languages are currently recognised, with over six million speakers.[3]

The region may be broadly divided into three zones: the Pacific Coast and highlands of Chiapas and Guatemala, the central lowlands, and the northern lowlands of the Yucatán Peninsula. In the interior of the lowlands is an elevated region ranging from 40 to 300 m (130 to 330 ft.) in elevation, often delimited by geologic scarps. The lowlands are dominated by tropical vegetation. The wet season lasts from May through to December, but rainfall is not particularly abundant by tropical standards: in the Petén Department of northern Guatemala, the annual rainfall is only around 178 to 229 cm (70 to 90 in.), and in Yucatán it is even less. The highland wet season is well-defined, lasting May though to early November, with peaks in June and October. The overall rainfall for the highlands is no greater than that of Northern Europe. In the lower-lying central areas, there is year-round access to water from springs and perennial streams; and in the north there are sinkholes known as cenotes that breach the groundwater table. However, within the elevated interior region, springs and lakes are scarce. Consequently, the Maya constructed underground cisterns to catch and hold the rain falling during the wet season.[4,5]

Preclassic florescence

The Maya, in common with other complex societies, arose from earlier agricultural populations: maize agriculture, as noted in Chapter 24, was practiced in this region from as early as 2500 BC. Around 1000 BC, the region was populated with Maya-speaking peasant societies, with social organisation at the tribal level. There was no writing, and little in the way of architecture. In comparison to the neighbouring Olmec heartland, the Maya region was still a backwater. However, by 900 BC, more complex societies were starting to emerge. Seibal, in lowland Guatemala, was laid out as a ceremonial centre, with large platforms and pyramids. Another early ceremonial centre was Izapa, on the Pacific Coast. Middle Preclassic Maya culture was now taking on some of the characteristics of later Maya civilisation.[6,4]

Among these early settlements was Nakbé, located in the densely-forested Mirador Basin in Petén. The earliest occupation comprised only wattle-and-daub residences, with packed clay floors, external stone retaining walls, and posts set into the bedrock. However, by 800 BC, Nakbé was beginning to take on the appearance of a city, and a complex society was beginning to emerge. Between 800 and 600 BC, the first major architectural complexes were built. These were formal stone platforms with vertical walls, 2 to 3 m (7 to 10 ft.) high of roughly-hewn stone, covered with lime and clay plaster. The floors were of packed clay, limestone marl and thin lime plaster.[7]

During the later Middle Preclassic between 600 and 400 BC, the settlement grew to 50 ha (124 acres) in extent. Formal platforms were now constructed with long, linear rows of stones paved with carefully-placed stone blocks, upon which stood pyramids up to 18 m (59 ft.) high. Architectural features were linked by causeways, ranging from 18 to 24 m (60 to 80 ft.) in width, and 1 to 4 m (3 to 13 ft.) in height. The causeways pass through what are now poor-quality seasonal swamps, but in Middle and Late Preclassic times were rich wetland marshes suitable for intensive agriculture. The centre of Nakbé was arranged around two groups of monumental buildings, an eastern and a western group. This east-west alignment differs from the north-south alignment of Olmec sites and suggests that monumental architecture in the Maya lowlands developed independently, without outside influence. Nevertheless, there is evidence for contact between the rulers of Nakbé and the Olmec. A carved stone monument known as Stela 1 depicts two standing figures in full regalia, facing one another. One wears a headdress and an Olmec-style mask with flat nose, widely opened mouth, and the teeth of a beast of prey.[8,7]

The largest building at Nakbé, known as Structure 1, is located in the western group. It was erected between 300 and 200 BC over the remains of at least nine earlier buildings. It rests on a 7 m (23 ft.) high platform, and rises 48 m (158 ft.) above the ground. The building was designed in triadic form, where a dominant structure is flanked by two inward-facing mounds of equal size. The triadic form became a standard feature of Late Preclassic Maya architecture, but is not found before then. This suggests that architecture was standardised by an emerging elite, probably on religious grounds.[8,9]

With the advent of the triadic building plan, the art adorning monumental architecture also became standardised, with deity masks flanking stairways, entablatures and walls. This indicates the fundamental importance of the triadic pattern to Classic Period Maya rulers in accession ritual, ideology, cosmology, and the fusion of sacred concepts with secular construction programs. The triad may be an architectural reference to the Three Hearthstones of Maya creation mythology. The myth has been associated with the stars Rigel, Bellatrix and Saiph in the constellation of Orion. The nebula M42, lying at the centre of this triangular grouping, was thought to be the fire and smoke at the centre of the hearthstones. Triadic architecture persisted for the remainder of the Maya era.[8,7]

During the Late Preclassic, a number of new cities were established in the Mirador Basin. The three largest were El Mirador (for which the basin is named), Tintal and Wakna. El Mirador grew to be even larger than Nakbé and was dominated by two massive temple complexes. The platforms of La Danta, on the eastern side of the site, measure 500 by 350 m (1,640 by 1,150 ft.), and its main pyramid tops out at 72 m (236 ft.). On the western side of the site, the El Tigre pyramid covers an area of just under 2 ha (5 acres) and rises to 55 m (180 ft.). No less impressive were the causeways that linked El Mirador to Wakna (25 km (15.5 miles) away) and Nakbé (13 km (8 miles) away). These construction projects represent some of the most impressive engineering accomplishments anywhere in the world at that time.[8] It is unclear, though, as to whether El Mirador and other large polities of this period had developed into fully-fledged states. As yet, there is no convincing evidence for long-distance territorial expansion, or of a four-tier settlement hierarchy.[10]

Away from the Mirador Basin, the Late Preclassic saw the emergence of cities throughout the Maya region. Some of these sites were first settled during the Early Preclassic, such as Izapa. However, the bulk of its 80 temples and probably all of its carved monuments date to the Late Preclassic. In the Maya highlands, Kaminaljuyu rivalled Izapa in size and splendour, and is notable for its complex system of irrigation canals and reservoirs. Two elaborate tombs hint at the luxury lifestyle of the city's elite. The dead were accompanied by extensive, rich grave goods – and sacrificed adults and children. In one tomb, over 300 finely-worked objects accompanied the body.[4]

Meanwhile, in the densely-forested central lowlands, major construction works were underway at the great sites of Tikal, Uaxactun and Calakmul. Uaxactun, a short distance south of Nakbé, is noted for a cluster of buildings known as E-Group that might have functioned as a solar observatory. It comprises an open plaza with a single pyramid on its western side and a north-south aligned platform on its eastern side. Upon the latter stand three small equally-spaced buildings designated E-I, E-II and E-III. From the point of view of an observer standing on the western pyramid, the small buildings line up with the rising of the sun over the horizon at the summer solstice (just to the left of E-I), equinoxes (above E-II) and winter solstice (just to the right of E-III). What became known as 'E-Group' architecture was subsequently identified at a number of other sites, mostly located within a 100 km (62 mile) radius of Uaxactun. The alignment seems to have worked better in the earlier phases of its history. Later phases added to the height of the western pyramid. To an observer at its summit, the horizon now lay above the level of the eastern trio, so they were no longer able to accurately pinpoint solstitial or equinoctial sunrises. It is likely that by this time the function of E-Group had changed, and that it was no longer used as a solar observatory.[11]

Tikal, half a day's walk further south, would go on to become a major centre in Classic times, but by Late Preclassic times, its rulers were already being interred in a monumental complex known as the North Acropolis (which might better have been named 'North Necropolis'). Investigating the early history of the complex has proved difficult, as it was rebuilt almost from scratch on perhaps 20 occasions. The earliest floors date back to between 300 and 200 BC, and overlay the remains of still earlier construction. It is nevertheless apparent that by Late Preclassic times, the complex was as elaborate and imposing as it was in its final Classic Period guise.[12] The Late Preclassic also saw the construction of a highly sophisticated system of reservoirs and sand filtration beds at Tikal.[13] Just north of the border with Mexico, Tikal's future nemesis Calakmul was already a major city.[4]

Other important sites from this period included Cerros, Lamanai and Edzna. At the latter, located in a valley in central Campeche, instead of underground cisterns, an elaborate hydraulic system was constructed. The system took the form of a network of more than 20 km (12.5 miles) of radiating canals, and an extensive array of surface reservoirs. The largest of these extends 12 km (7.5 miles) south of Edzna and is 50 m (164 ft.) wide for much of its length. The entire system collected and held rainwater and the canals might additionally have served as drain channels for surrounding fields. Average annual rainfall is currently around 1,000 mm (39 in.), and the system held around two billion litres (440 million gallons) of water. The system also included a 2.7 km (1.7 miles) diameter moat, up to 110 m (360 ft.) wide in places. At the centre of the moat was a complex interpreted as a fortress, though the reason for its construction is not known.[14] The large-scale architecture, and elaborate sculpture and iconography suggest a coherent and controlling ideology.[15] To muster the workforces required for these massive projects implies a powerful centralised authority.[2]

The site of Cuello in northern Belize, though probably of no great importance in Maya times, has yielded important evidence of mortuary practices that document the gradual establishment of a ruling elite. During the Middle Preclassic, the majority of interments took place in graves cut into house platform floors, indicative of family-type residential burials. Towards the end of this period, these floors ceased to be used for other domestic activities, suggesting that they were now the focus of ritual activity in the form of ancestor worship. At the same time, differences in the quantity and types of grave goods hint at emerging social differentiation. This trend continued during the Late Preclassic. Prominent males were now buried in the city's public plaza area, and were accompanied by significantly more grave goods than individuals interred in a residential setting. Similarly, grave goods were far more likely to include items obtained by long-distance trade. These ceremonial interments also included sacrificial mass burials of 'human grave goods'. The sacrificial victims were decapitated and/or partially or wholly dismembered, though whether this was the cause of death or the result of post-mortem ritual is not known. Mass sacrificial burials were introduced just as the construction of monumental architecture was beginning to reflect the emergence of elite political power.[15]

It has been suggested that the Maya religion of the Preclassic Period arose out of ancestor worship, which had initially became established with individual family lineages. As populations increased, cults arose that transcended the bounds of lineage worship and created a broader religious movement. This underpinned and legitimised the ruling elite, manifesting itself in the enormous investment in ritual architecture seen early in the Late Preclassic at Nakbé, and subsequently at many other sites.[16] The burial evidence from Cuello may trace the early stages of this process.[15]

The Terminal Preclassic brought an end to the flowering of Maya civilisation in the Mirador Basin. By AD 150, the great cities lay desolate. While the reasons are not entirely clear, it is likely that overpopulation and environmental factors played a part. Stalagmite data suggests that the region suffered from a period of reduced rainfall between AD 100 and 300, and sediments from lakes and swamps in the Mirador Basin indicate that the area experienced widespread deforestation and soil erosion. These changes were associated with land clearing and quarrying in the preceding centuries. Evidently anthropogenic environmental degradation was at least as important as drought in bringing about the demise of cities of the Mirador Basin. The cities were not re-occupied for hundreds of years, and never regained their former splendour.[5,17]

East of the Mirador Basin, abandonment was more sporadic. San Bartolo was abandoned around AD 150, yet just 8 km (5 miles) to the south, Xultun remained occupied and became an important centre during the Classic Period. The wetlands of the region show evidence of climatic drying and anthropogenic soil loss, sedimentation, and hydrologic changes. A large-scale reservoir system was constructed at Xultun that apparently enabled it to survive. By contrast, San Bartolo, lacking a reservoir system, was not re-occupied until AD 700.[5,17] The water management system at Tikal might also have been instrumental in ensuring its survival.[13] However, possession of such a system was apparently no guarantee of survival. A huge monument complex and elaborate reservoir system was constructed at the city of Xcoch in Yucatán, but the site was nevertheless abandoned around AD 150 and not re-occupied until AD 400.[5]

Eventually, aridity gave way to a period of high rainfall. Intensively-farmed seasonal wetlands were now sustained by the rainfall, and the underground cisterns were recharged. Cities that had survived the period of crisis thrived. Tikal, an important regional centre during the Late Preclassic, now emerged as a dominant force.[17] In all probability, Tikal was well-placed to capitalise on the power vacuum left by the demise of Nakbé and El Mirador.[2] The Maya Classic Period was an era of splendour during which it attained intellectual and artistic heights unmatched in the New World at that time, and with few rivals anywhere else. It was an era of large populations, trade and prosperity. It has been described as a Golden Age, although it was by no means an era of peace.[4]

Maya civilisation in the Classic Period

Even during the Classic Period, the Maya were never politically unified into a single state. Several Maya languages or dialects were spoken; polities differed in terms of ceramic and tool traditions; and ruling dynasties were associated with differing sets of patron gods. The Maya nevertheless shared similar art, architecture, rituals and belief systems.[2] It remains disputed just how many distinct Maya polities there were. Many Classic-period sites are identified by so-called 'Emblem Glyphs', which are actually royal titles rather than place names, and read k'uhul ajaw ('holy lord') of such-and-such a kingdom.[4] A modern-day equivalent, combining title with realm, are the words 'Britannic Majesty', which appear on British passports. If one assumes that each independent polity was identified by its own emblem glyph, then by Late Classic times there were at least 60 city-states, each controlling a territory with an average size of 2,500 sq. km (965 sq. miles).[1]

Such a statistic ignores the considerable variation in size of Maya polities. The larger ones exhibit a state-like four-tier settlement hierarchy. In the course of their development, they appear to have subordinated smaller neighbouring polities rather than allow them to exist as tributary states. The number of genuine state-level polities might only have been 30 or fewer. Smaller independent polities were probably chiefdoms rather than kingdoms. What seems not to have occurred is for large Maya states to have incorporated other large states into even larger polities. Instead, states sought to reduce defeated rivals to self-governing tributaries for as long as possible. Even during periods of subjugation, states continued to be ruled by their own kings. That such states regularly freed themselves from such domination by others suggests that control by their victorious neighbours was weak and indirect.[1] It is likely that Maya state formation was cyclical, with tributaries reasserting themselves and expanding as their former overlords entered a period of decline.[18]

In an often threatening environment, it is unsurprising that some states took steps to defend their realms. The major centre of Yaxchilán maintained a fortified settlement at Tecolote, close to the frontier between its domain and that of its rival, Piedras Negras. The purpose, though, might not have been solely defensive. It is possible that Tecolote and other secondary Yaxchilán settlements also served as staging points for launching attacks into the territory of Piedras Negras.[19]

Maya cities were not dense urban settlements like Teotihuacán or Monte Albán. Instead they comprised dispersed populations, with houses gradually thinning out as one moved away from the centre. It is difficult to gauge where they end and outlying farming communities begin. Estimating populations is also problematic. Estimates for Tikal, which is around 15.5 sq. km (6 sq. miles) in extent, range from 10,000 to 90,000. There are about 3,000 structures mapped at Tikal, ranging from temples and palaces to humble thatched-roofed huts, but there is little evidence of overall planning or formal grid layouts of the type seen in other early cities.[4] Some argue that Maya cities were not true cities at all. Instead, it is suggested they are better thought of as regal and ritual centres from which the ruling elite wielded power.[2]

At the centre of a Maya city was a precinct of temples, royal palaces and other elite residences, ball courts, elite tombs, and public plazas with stelae and altars. Precincts typically grew by accretion as elite tombs and other monuments were added. In addition, monuments and indeed entire complexes were frequently rebuilt. The palace complexes housed the king, his family, the royal staff and administrators.[2,4]

Craft production was associated with residential groups rather than the specialist districts seen elsewhere.[1] It was conducted on a small-scale, and not as a full-time occupation. Even elite sculptors and painters combined craft work with a day job as a warrior, diplomat or administrator. The production of luxury items was conducted in elite households, and might have involved women as well as men. These households also manufactured weapons and utilitarian items.[20] Some of the most talented craftsmen occasionally carried out work for more than one polity, and might have been free to move between kingdoms.[1,2]

Market places have also been found at a number of Maya cities, typically located near the end of roads or causeways.[4] They include a 2.5 ha (6.2 acre) complex at Calakmul, known as Chiik Nahb. It is located to the north of the city's central precinct and contains a much-modified pyramid known as Structure 1. Within one of the building's earlier phases, fine murals have been found portraying scenes of daily life in a bustling market place. Men, women and a single child are depicted engaging in a number of activities. Individuals are wearing a variety of costumes that probably reflect differing social status. Most of the scenes include images of ceramic vessels, baskets, or various types of bound sacks and packages. A number show people preparing and dispensing foodstuffs to customers. Other individuals are shown carrying pots and baskets containing merchandise. In many cases, glyphs identify the type of goods sellers are offering, for example *aj waaj* ('maize-grain person') and *aj ixi'm* ('maize-bread person'). Other scenes feature a tobacco vendor (*aj mahy*), a woman selling pottery (*aj jaay*) and a man with a basket and spoon who is selling salt (*aj atz'aam*).[21]

Salt was a vital commodity to the Maya. As tropical farmers, they required 8 gm. (0.28 oz.) of salt per day to maintain their sodium balance. A large city such as Tikal had to import over 130 tonnes of salt per year.[4] Over forty saltworks have been identified on the southern coast of Belize, where salt was obtained by boiling seawater in pots. From there, it was probably transported inland by canoe. This possibility is supported by the discovery of a large wooden paddle at one of the saltworks. The saltworks were run by people living at nearby coastal settlements, and are an example of a private enterprise that was not controlled by the ruling elite of the cities.[22]

Star Wars

As we saw in Chapter 29, in the fourth century AD, Tikal came under the influence of Teotihuacán. Following the events of AD 378, and presumably backed by the central Mexican superpower, Tikal rapidly began to dominate Petén. At Uaxactun, a short distance to the north, a mural has been found that portrays a warrior in central Mexican attire and a Maya chief in a submissive pose. Close by, three women are seated in a flat-roofed building. It is possible that Uaxactun was subdued by Sihyaj K'ahk even before the young Yax Nuun Ahiin was enthroned at Tikal, and the mural may allude to the takeover. At the same site, Stela 5 depicts a Teotihuacán warrior armed with an atlatl. The stela marks a tomb containing five bodies, including that of a pregnant woman. It is unlikely that their deaths were natural, and they may be the family of Uaxactun's defeated king. If so, the king himself was presumably sacrificed.[23]

Sihyaj K'ahk might have continued to act as a regent for the young king. Excavations at Rio Azul to the northeast of Tikal suggest that it fell under the control of the latter. There is a reference to Sihyaj K'ahk dating to AD 393. Inscriptions on three altars depict the sacrifice of eight or more elite individuals, probably following their defeat and capture. Sihyaj K'ahk's name also appears, retrospectively, at Palenque, where he might have been instrumental in the founding of a long-lived ruling dynasty.[23] Tikal's expansion continued after Sihyaj K'ahk's time, by which time Yax Nuun Ahiin was old enough to rule in his own right. At the city of Yaxhá, a stela has been found depicting a masked Teotihuacán warrior-goddess; and at the small site of La Sufricaya, murals depict the accession of a local Maya ruler in the presence of five well-armed seated men in central Mexican attire.[4]

Yax Nuun Ahiin died in AD 411 and was succeeded by his son, Sihyaj Chan K'awiil II. Sihyaj Chan K'awiil I was a Tikal king who had reigned a hundred years earlier, and by taking his regnal name, Sihyaj Chan K'awiil II signalled a return to Maya tradition despite his foreign ancestry. Stela 31, dedicated 34 years after his ascension, contains a text providing an account of Tikal's dynastic history to date. Sihyaj Chan K'awiil II is depicted in traditional Maya regalia, holding aloft a headdress with bearing his name glyph. He is flanked by depictions of his father as a Teotihuacán warrior, complete with atlatls, feathered darts, and shields emblazoned with the central Mexican rain god Tlaloc.[23]

The reign of Sihyaj Chan K'awiil II saw the continuation of Tikal's expansionist policies. In AD 426, in an episode mirroring the regime change at Tikal 48 years earlier, an individual named K'inich Yax K'uk' Mo' ('Great Sun Quetzal-Macaw') 'arrived' at the city of Copán in western Honduras, on the very periphery of the Maya world. According to later texts, Copán's ruling dynasty was founded in AD 426 by K'inich Yax K'uk' Mo' and persisted in an unbroken line until AD 820, when the sixteenth king died. A square monument known as Altar Q depicts the final king, Yax Pasaj Yopaat and his fifteen predecessors. Yax Pasaj Yopaat is depicted receiving the baton of office from K'inich Yax K'uk' Mo', who wears Teotihuacán regalia. Among the earliest structures of the acropolis at Copán is a small temple in classic Teotihuacán architectural style containing the tomb of a 50-year-old male believed to be K'inich Yax K'uk' Mo' himself, complete with Teotihuacán-style ceramic grave goods. He had suffered a severe, deforming fracture of his right forearm – and in the depiction on Altar Q, K'inich Yax K'uk' Mo's right forearm is hidden from view by a small shield. Isotopic analysis of his teeth suggests that he spent most of his youth in Petén, possibly at Tikal, but by adolescence he had moved closer to Copán.[4]

While Tikal was undergoing this rapid rise, a second Maya superpower was emerging to the north of Petén. Located across the present-day border in the Mexican state of Campeche, Calakmul can also trace its history back to Late Preclassic times. Its history is recorded on the largest number of stelae known for any Maya site, but they were mostly carved from low-quality limestone and are badly eroded. Consequently, the early history of the city is difficult to reconstruct. The earliest date we can read is AD 435 from Stela 114, referring to an inauguration 24 years earlier in AD 411. Unfortunately, the name of the ruler is illegible. Another monument, Stela 43 dates to AD 514, but again the name cannot be read. We must rely on data from other sites for references to Calakmul and its rulers.[23,4]

These indicate that during the sixth century AD, Calakmul embarked upon its own policy of expansion that inevitably put it on a collision course with Tikal. Early ventures might not have been particularly successful; Calakmul was defeated by K'inich Tarb'u Skull II of Yaxchilán in AD 537. However, this was no more than a temporary setback, and Calakmul's kings were soon installing client rulers in other cities. These include Naranjo in AD 546 and Los Alacranes in AD 561. The latter date is the earliest reference to a Calakmul king known as Sky Witness, who set about encircling Tikal by building alliances with its neighbours. A key component of his strategy was Caracol, a large city to the southeast of Tikal. The king of Caracol, Yajaw Te' K'inich II, was inaugurated in AD 553 under the authority of Wak Chan K'awiil, king of Tikal. Caracol appeared to be firmly in the Tikal sphere of influence, but in AD 556 war broke out between the two cities and in AD 562 Tikal was defeated.[23]

The circumstances of the falling-out between Caracol and Tikal, and the subsequent defeat of the latter are unclear. Maya tradition called for an outright conquest to be marked with a glyph representing the planet Venus above one representing the defeated polity. To the Maya, Venus played a role similar to that of Mars in European tradition, and its appearance in the sky was seen as a propitious date for military action.[4] The conquest glyph has become known as the 'star war glyph', and such a glyph is recorded on the badly-eroded Altar 21 at Caracol. The name of the victorious king is unclear, but seems to be Sky Witness rather than Yajaw Te' K'inich II. Evidently Tikal was defeated by the combined forces of Calakmul and its former ally. Sky Witness presumably either engineered or took advantage of the split between Caracol and Tikal. What happened to Wak Chan K'awiil is not known, although he probably suffered the customary fate of a defeated ruler.[23]

Tikal was not sacked, but its power and influence were curtailed. Many of its monuments were destroyed by the victors, and no new ones were constructed for 130 years. A new king, nicknamed Animal Skull, was enthroned. He might have been descended, on his mother's side, from the kings who had ruled Tikal before the arrival of Sihyaj K'ahk. For the next century, much of the central lowlands were embroiled in a series of wars, a period of crisis sometimes referred to as the Hiatus. During this period, Calakmul faced problems keeping its allies in line, and keeping Tikal in check. During his 50 year reign, Yuknoom the Great maintained Calakmul's hegemony over a number of strategically-important cities. He also won a number of battles against a now-resurgent Tikal, but outright victory eluded him. His son and successor Yich'aak K'ahk' ('Fiery Claw') carried on the fight, but in AD 695 Calakmul was defeated. The defeat terminated Calakmul's influence in the central lowlands, and it turned its attention to the cities to the north. By now, though, the age of the superpowers was over. Never again would any Maya state become powerful enough to establish an extensive hegemony over its neighbours.[23,4]

Downfall

Although Tikal remained in eclipse for over a century following its defeat in AD 562, the early decades of the seventh century AD saw Classic Maya life continue much as before. A number of new ruling dynasties might have been established, but the principle difference was the absence of Teotihuacán from Maya affairs. As we saw in Chapter 29, the central Mexican city's days as a superpower were over by no later than AD 550. The impact of its demise on Maya society is uncertain, but it certainly came too early to be implicated in the later crisis. Nevertheless, over the course of around 175 years, Maya civilisation in the central lowlands disintegrated and most of the great cities in the region were abandoned. These events are often referred to as the Classic Maya collapse. However, the northern lowlands were relatively unaffected and civilisation endured there until the Spanish conquest.[2,4]

The first signs of political fragmentation occurred in the Petexbatún region of southwest Petén in AD 760. The city of Dos Pilas was founded in AD 629 by an offshoot of the ruling Tikal dynasty, in order to control the Rio Pasión basin. This was a crucial trade route between the lowlands and the highlands, through which passed jade, hard stone, quetzal feathers and other high-status materials. Dos Pilas later became caught up in the power struggle between Tikal and Calakmul, and came under the influence of the latter. In the wake of Calakmul's defeat in AD 695, Dos Pilas emerged as a major power in its own right. During the decades that followed, it gained control of many of its Rio Pasión neighbours, including the cities of Aguateca, Tamarindito, Arroyo de Piedra and Punta de Chimino. Aguateca became the second city of this hegemony. In AD 735 Dos Pilas attacked and subdued Seibal, a much larger and longer-established city.[24,4]

Yet within a quarter of a century, a series of conflicts erupted that all but destroyed the entire fabric of society in the Petexbatún region. Between AD 760 and 761, Tamarindito rebelled against its overlord and Dos Pilas was besieged. Defensible enclaves were hastily established within portions of the city. They were protected by palisaded walls, constructed with blocks taken from temples and palaces. It was all to no avail, and Dos Pilas was eventually razed. By the close of the eighth century AD, settlement patterns in the Petexbatún region had become dictated largely by defensibility. By now, Aguateca was the only city remaining under the control of the former Dos Pilas elite. Over 5 km (3 miles) of defensive walls were constructed to supplement the city's natural defences, including high cliffs to the west, and a deep gorge to the east. Despite these measures, soon after AD 800, Aguateca was overrun and set on fire. Large numbers of artefacts have been found on the floors of houses as their occupants fled. By AD 830, the population of the Petexbatún region was largely reduced to scattered households and small hamlets, sited near water sources. Only the now heavily-fortified Punta de Chimino survived as a major centre.[24]

The emigration of tens of thousands of refugees from the Petexbatún region and the disruption to the Rio Pasión trade route had a destabilising effect on polities elsewhere. In the Usumacinta region to the west, hegemonic states fragmented, construction of monuments ceased, and one by one the great centres declined and were depopulated: first Palenque, then Piedras Negras, Yaxchilán and other centres. In southeastern Guatemala, the borderland states of Copán and Quirigua followed the same pattern of fragmentation and then collapse. Elsewhere, the one-time superpowers of Tikal and Calakmul declined. By AD 900, the population of the latter might have been no more than a tenth of what it had been when the city was at its zenith little over a century earlier.[24]

At the city of Bonampak, an ally of Yaxchilán, the local ruler Yajaw Chan Muwaan commissioned a mural to commemorate a battle fought in AD 792. Scenes depict a battle fought in the jungle; the humiliation, torture, and killing of enemy captives; and finally the victory celebrations. The latter prominently feature the king and his Yaxchilán-born wife. The murals are among the finest known examples of Maya art, yet they symbolise the pinnacle before the fall: Bonampak was abandoned before the murals were even completed.[4]

Dated texts on monuments clearly document the decline. In the period from AD 750 to 775, new monuments were dedicated in at least 39 centres. Numbers fell off steeply in the period AD 775 to 800, and dropped by a further 50 percent between AD 800 and 825.[17] The *katan* ending date of 10.3.0.0.0 (AD 889) was celebrated by inscriptions at only five sites; the *katan* ending date of 10.4.0.0.0 (AD 909) appears on just one monument at the site of Tonina. The most recent date from Petén was carved on a stela at Izimte, corresponding to 15 January AD 910.[4]

Whether or not such a protracted decline constitutes a collapse is perhaps debatable. That life was profoundly disrupted in the central lowlands is beyond dispute. Jared Diamond[25] suggests that a combination of four factors was responsible for the downfall of the Classic Maya. These were firstly, that they caused damage to their environment by deforestation and soil erosion; secondly, the impact of climate change in the form of recurring drought; thirdly, the effects of constant internecine wars; and fourthly, ruling elites that placed the emphasis on war and erecting monuments rather than trying to solve underlying problems.

It is widely believed that forest cover declined as Classic Maya populations grew. Trees were felled for timber and fields cleared for agriculture. The loss of forest cover would leave land on slopes vulnerable to soil loss by erosion, although in places this was alleviated by the use of terracing. On the other hand, at Copán, pollen evidence suggests that forest cover actually increased between AD 400 and 900.[26] It is possible that the Maya practiced sustainable forest management, and did not damage their environment to the extent that Diamond has suggested.[27]

The evidence for recurring drought during the Terminal Classic is fairly secure:[28,29] the decrease in annual rainfall might have been as much as 40 percent, and was probably due to a reduction in the frequency and intensity of summer season tropical storms.[30] Recent work has identified a lengthy drought between AD 820 and 870, which was part of a longer-term drying trend that began around AD 640.[17]

Archaeologist Arthur Demarest[24] believes that the third and fourth factors highlighted by Diamond were consequences of the structural problems in Maya society. The Maya system of kingship was based around charismatic *ajaw* leadership in ritual and war. The basis of their power was access to and control over the distribution of status-reinforcing luxury goods and a considerable investment in art and monumental architecture for ritual and status-reinforcing purposes. However, there was minimal central control over infrastructure, and the local and regional economies were not under state control. Thus a king might have been able to buy the support of potential allies by lavishing rich gifts upon the rulers of neighbouring cities, but his options when faced with drought-induced agricultural shortfalls were very limited.

Essentially, the elite response to any crisis was restricted to making war, intensifying rituals and building monuments. Rituals, feasting and construction projects took their toll on the economy, while actually contributing very little to the efficient running of the states. The wars disrupted trade routes and restricted agriculture to defensible locations, leading to over-exploitation of such farmland. Such counterproductive responses to drought only exacerbated matters, leading to further conflict. In short, it is not difficult to see how the extended periods of drought and other environmental problems triggered a vicious circle of conflict and instability that eventually spread through the whole of the central lowlands. So great was the breakdown in social complexity that even areas with good access to groundwater were not necessarily spared. In the wetlands of northwest Belize, fields were not tended and irrigation canals fell into disuse.[31]

In the northern part of the Yucatán Peninsula, Maya society was less affected by the turmoil. Societal collapse nevertheless occurred, albeit delayed into the Postclassic Period. The Puuc Hills region at the northernmost part of the elevated interior region is noted for its deep, fertile soils, and during the eighth and ninth centuries AD, it experienced a very rapid growth in population. During this period, the distinctive Puuc style of architecture emerged, noted for its use of limestone veneer, round columns in doorways, and elaborate stone mosaics. The city of Uxmal emerged as the major power in the region, gaining ascendancy between AD 875 and 900. Uxmal is the site of some of the most spectacular architecture in the Maya world, and is noted for its two great temple pyramids and a palace complex known bizarrely as the Nunnery. However, the Puuc prosperity was short-lived. Around AD 1000 or a little later, the Puuc centres collapsed and the surrounding countryside heavily depopulated.[2,4]

The Puuc region was not spared the decreased rainfall, and experienced eight periods of drought between AD 806 and 935. The strong population growth that continued through this period probably owed to the extensive use of both urban reservoirs and household cisterns for water capture and storage. In the end, though, the people of Uxmal and other cities in the region might have been undone by over-exploitation of their prime farming land. The fertile soils that underpinned the late Puuc fluorescence are thought to have only been capable of supporting maximal yields for 75 years.[5]

Coinciding with the Puuc florescence was the rise of Chichén Itzá, one of the most famous of all Maya sites. It is located 130 km (80 miles) northeast of Uxmal, close to a major cenote that supplied its water needs. During the Terminal Classic, it was involved in long-distance trade by land and sea, and by AD 1000 it was the dominant power in northern Yucatán.[24] Again, though, Chichén Itzá's prosperity was short-lived. Between AD 1020 and 1100, an even dryer period occurred, and Chichén Itzá also went into decline.[17]

The collapse did not bring about an end to Maya civilisation, but it never regained its former vitality. Chichén Itzá was never completely abandoned, and remained an important pilgrimage centre. Sacrifices were still taking place there at the time of the Spanish conquest. To the west of Chichén Itzá, the city of Mayapán rose to prominence for a couple of centuries before it too declined. No great power arose to replace it, and Yucatán fragmented into smaller, independent polities. The cycle of wars and alliances continued much as before, albeit on a smaller scale. These northern societies were still fairly complex, and retained much of the Classic tradition right up until the Spanish conquest.[2]

The eventual reoccupation of the depopulated central regions was slow, even when it happened at all. The cisterns and other water capture systems necessary to sustain large populations had been developed *in situ*. To restore them to use would have required an enormous initial investment in labour, but the will to do so was not there. The failed states were seen as places of ill fortune. People shunned the ancient cities. With easy strides, the jungle came back into its own.[5]

31: Before the Inca

Civilisations of the pre-Columbian Central Andes

While Mesoamerica is usually described as a single locus of primary state formation, the same may not be true of the Central Andes. The region stretches a distance of 4,000 km (2,500 miles) from north to south. This distance is comparable to the east-west distance from the Nile to the Indus Valley, an area that covers three regions of primary state formation: in Egypt, Mesopotamia and the Indus Valley. By around AD 600, there were three relatively distinct cultural, linguistic and political regions in the Central Andes: the northern coast of Peru, the central Andean highlands and the south central Andean altiplano. It has been argued that primary state formation occurred in each of these regions.[1]

In the Central Andes, the Late Archaic/Preceramic ended around 1800 BC. The subsequent timeline is Initial Period (1800 to 900 BC), Early Horizon (900 to 200 BC), Early Intermediate Period (200 BC to AD 650), Middle Horizon (AD 650 to 1000), Late Intermediate Period (AD 1000 to 1476), and Late Horizon (AD 1476 to 1533). The start of the Initial Period is defined by the initial use of pottery, and the Early Horizon refers to period marked by the Chavín culture. There are considerable uncertainties associated with the dates involved; some authorities place the Initial Period from between 2100 and 1400 BC and the Early Horizon from 1400 to 400 BC.[2]

The earliest Andean societies widely accepted to have been states did not emerge until fairly late in the Early Intermediate Period. These are the Moche culture on the northern coast of Peru, the Wari in the central Andean highlands and Tiwanaku (older spelling Tiahuanaco) in the south central Andean altiplano.[1] However, as we shall see, claims have been made for much earlier Andean state formation.

Like the Aztec, the Inca emerged as a major power fairly late in pre-Columbian times. Although their origins go back to around AD 1000, the Inca Empire existed only during the Late Horizon.[3] No Andean state ever developed writing, but formal records were kept using knotted threads known as *quipu*.[4]

Preceramic antecedents

The Pacific coastal region of Peru is characterised by narrow river valleys, backed by mountains and flanked by deserts. During the Late Archaic/Preceramic Period, the subsistence economy of Peruvian coastal communities was based largely upon fishing. The dominant plants cultivated were cotton and gourd rather than food crops. Beans, squash, tubers and tree fruits were consumed only in minor quantities.[3] The irrigation agriculture practiced at Caral (see Chapter 24) and at some other valley sites was at this stage still uncommon.

The Initial Period saw the spread of the two-pronged economy of inland irrigation agriculture and coastal fisheries first seen in the Norte Chico region. With the adoption of this 'package', growing populations moved inland and major settlements appeared in the valleys. Coastal settlements diminished in status, becoming subsidiaries of the inland centres.[5] Innovations of the Initial Period included pottery and the use of the loom for weaving cloth.[3] Ironically, the Norte Chico region was by now losing its primacy as much larger polities arose to the north along the coast, and in the highlands.[6]

Monumental architecture became widespread. The dominant structures at any site were symmetrical U-shaped platform mound ritual complexes, with large facing plazas. The open end of the U almost always faced up-valley, towards the river's mountain headwaters. Such an orientation may suggest an association with agricultural concerns. Against this, it has been claimed that the U-shaped mound tradition began at the Preceramic site of El Paraiso, the economy of which was based more on fishing than on agriculture. The mound complexes often featured sunken circular courts of the type first seen at Caral. The concept of a mound fronted by a plaza is first seen at the Preceramic coastal site of Huaynuna. A hillside structure was constructed 8 m (26 ft.) above the surrounding terrain, comprising four stone-faced terraces divided by a central stairway. These face an open plaza area at the base of the hillside, some 500 sq. m (5,400 sq. ft.) in area. From the elevated terraces, prominent individuals could conduct ritual or ceremonial activities for the benefit of a sizable audience assembled in the plaza area. Though small-scale in comparison to the later U-shaped mound and plaza complexes, the Huaynuna structure was clearly a forerunner of these.[7,4,5]

Huaynuna and Caral both feature early examples of ventilated hearth structures thought to be associated with private rituals involving small groups. These structures are found at many Initial Period sites. They comprise a small circular or square room with a centrally-ventilated hearth. They measure from 1.5 to 9 m (5 to 30 ft.) across and are often sited on a larger rectangular platform. The hearths were ventilated by up to four subfloor shafts. The rituals might have involved burnt offerings. Another possibility is that the rooms served a similar purpose to the ceremonial and ritual 'sweat lodges' found in some Native American societies. The structures were first identified at the highland site of Kotosh in the 1960s, giving rise to the term Kotosh Religious Tradition.[7,5]

It is likely that the growing dependency on agriculture (see Chapter 24) stimulated new concerns with the cosmos and religion. Andean reverence of *Pacha Mama* (mother earth) probably dates to this period. Prominent mountain peaks (*apu*) are seen as influential spiritual forces, in all likelihood because of the link with rain and water runoff. Similarly, agricultural activities were scheduled around astronomical phenomena such as the appearance of prominent constellations in the evening skies. It is not difficult to see how such considerations became integral to Andean belief systems.[4]

Sechín Alto and the Moxeke culture

As we saw in Chapter 25, the northern coast of Peru featured in Robert Carneiro's 'circumscription' theory, where groups in agriculturally-productive regions are hemmed in either geographically or by their neighbours, leading to conflict and, ultimately, to state formation. A candidate for the first Andean state emerged in the Casma Valley early in the Initial Period. Close to the confluence of the Rio Casma and the Rio Sechín are two site complexes, Sechín Alto and Pampa de los Llamas-Moxeke. The latter gives its name to the Moxeke, a culture that is associated with a ceramic style of neckless jars decorated with deep gouges. In common with other river valley cultures, their economy was based around irrigation agriculture and seafood. The main crops were squash, beans, potato, sweet potato, peanuts, avocado and cotton. Maize was absent. The Moxeke culture has been extensively studied by anthropologists Shelia and Thomas Pozorski for many years.[8,7,9,5]

The larger of the two site complexes, Sechín Alto, is located along the Rio Sechín branch of the river system. It comprises a main site and four subsidiary sites: Taukachi-Konkan, Cerro Sechín and Sechín Bajo on the Rio Sechín, and Pampa de los Llamas-Moxeke on the Rio Casma. The main site is a massive U-shaped ritual complex, with a 300 by 250 m (985 by 820 feet) platform facing a series of rectangular plazas flanked by smaller mounds. This complex was the largest structure in the New

World at the time. Cerro Sechín is a temple with stone carvings depicting club-bearing warriors and dismembered human bodies. At Pampa de los Llamas-Moxeke, the U-shaped main mound complex is decorated with huge mud friezes, depicting humanlike figures over 3 m (10 ft.) high. The friezes face onto enormous plazas capable of holding thousands of people.

State-like features claimed for the Moxeke culture include a four-tier or even five-tier settlement hierarchy, and a royal palace at Taukachi-Konkan. It is claimed that various sites served differing functions. For example, at Pampa de los Llamas-Moxeke a structure known as Huaca A served as a warehouse for storing and redistributing food. The royal palace was located at Taukachi-Konkan, and the main ritual centre was at Sechín Alto. A number of small coastal sites are believed to have been fisheries that provided the inland sites with seafood. These differing functions imply many differing specialised roles for people, with differing levels of status and power.

The sites share many architectural features, including sunken circular courts and alignment along a central axis established by a principle mound. A notable common feature is the 'square-room unit', a square room with rounded corners. These are found within warehouses and administrative buildings. At the best-preserved site, Pampa de los Llamas-Moxeke, completed, incomplete and marked-off areas indicate that a site masterplan was followed over the course of 500 years. Large-scale works were carried out in very few phases, rather than growing by accretion over the course of many phases. All of these factors suggest a strong central leadership with the ability to see through construction projects over the course of many generations.

Four major phases of occupation have been defined at Sechín Alto. The first two phases saw the initial construction and expansion of the site. The third phase suggests that the site had come under the control of the Las Haldas culture. Las Haldas is a coastal site located 20 km (12.5 miles) south of the Casma Valley. While the two polities were doubtless aware of one another, there is no evidence for significant interaction prior to 1400 BC. Subsequently, Las Haldas-style architecture and punctate-decorated ceramics appeared at Sechín Alto and other Casma Valley sites.

It seems likely that Las Haldas took advantage of a weakening of the Moxeke polity to occupy the Casma Valley. The Moxeke decline might have been triggered by El Niño events that severely affected the agricultural economy. At around the same time, Pampa de los Llamas-Moxeke might have attempted unsuccessfully to secede from Sechín Alto. The 'victims' on the Cerro Sechín carvings wear clothing that is very similar to that worn by full-figure depictions among the Pampa de los Llamas-Moxeke friezes, and the carvings may commemorate the suppression of the revolt. The second occupation phase at Sechín Alto was fairly brief. The main mound there was greatly expanded, but most other sites including Pampa de los Llamas-Moxeke were abandoned. The implication is that an internal crisis was followed by an attempt to regroup around the polity's major site.

Only a minority of Andean archaeologists accept that Sechín Alto was a state, or that state formation occurred as early as the Initial Period. The Casma sites lack craft workshops, and there is little in the way of goods that could not be made at household level. Thus there was little opportunity for individuals to become wealthy, and there are no obviously high-status burials. The existence of palaces, warehouses and occupational specialisation is disputed.[10] There is no evidence for a multi-valley polity of the type described by Robert Carneiro.[1]

Nevertheless anthropologist Jonathan Haas[11] supports the Pozorskis' view that Sechín Alto was a state. In addition, he believes that Initial Period state-level polities arose at La Florida in the Rimac Valley, Caballo Muerto in the Moche Valley, and possibly Garagay in the Chillon Valley. All these sites contain elaborate ceremonial complexes and architecture on a significantly greater scale than anything previously seen in the region. Haas does not believe that these were the only early states on the Peruvian coast, but they are the best-described sites in the literature.

The ascendancy of Las Haldas was short-lived. By the Early Horizon, its monuments had fallen out of use and the site was occupied by 'squatters', living in small, temporary dwellings.[9] Many other coastal river valley sites declined and were abandoned at around this time.[12,10] The semi-arid coastal environments were always fragile and vulnerable to overexploitation. The considerable population growth of the Initial Period might eventually have triggered a degree of environmental collapse.[13]

Chavín de Huántar: state capital or religious centre?

The Chavín culture is named for the site of Chavín de Huántar in the Peruvian highlands. The site is located at an altitude of 3,150 m (10,335 feet), at the confluence of the Rio Mosna and Rio Huachesca, and it covers an area of approximately 50 ha (125 acres), of which 10 ha (25 acres) is public architecture. The main ceremonial complex comprises two conjoined U-shaped platform mounds known as the Old Temple and the New Temple. The latter is the larger of the two, and is fronted by a spacious sunken rectangular plaza measuring 105 by 85 m (345 by 280 ft.). There are also two much smaller sunken plazas, one circular and one square. Built into the architecture of the complex is an elaborate system of passageways, chambers, staircases, ventilation shafts and drainage canals. Experiments have shown that when rainwater drains through the stone-lined drainage system, a loud roaring sound is produced that may be heard both inside and outside the complex.[14,15]

During the first half of the twentieth century, the site was excavated by Peruvian archaeologist Julio Tello, who put forward the view that the Chavín was the Andean mother culture – a role similar to that suggested for the Olmec in Mesoamerica. From it, he claimed, widespread similarities in architecture, art and ceramics had spread across the Andes; a cultural phenomenon termed the Chavín Horizon, or Early Horizon. The model was elaborated by archaeologist John Rowe in the 1960s, who also proposed that Chavín de Huántar was developed in three phases. The New Temple and its sunken plaza were built onto the original U-shaped Old Temple, and further additions were made in the third phase. However, by the 1970s, as more radiocarbon dates became available, it was becoming clear that the coastal sites did not fit the Tello/Rowe model.[14,15,5] As we have seen, many of these sites date to the Initial Period or earlier, and are far older than Chavín de Huántar. The new dates showed that the U-shaped platform mound, then considered to be a Chavín motif, was unrelated to the Chavín phenomenon.[10] It was postulated that the Chavín culture had come to the fore only after the Initial Period settlements went into decline. The maximum extent of its pan-regional influence was estimated to have been during the fairly brief period between 400 and 200 BC, marked archaeologically by the spread of Janabarriu black ware pottery.[12]

This compressed timescale was problematic for archaeologists as it left a hiatus of several centuries between the collapse of the Initial Period coastal valley polities and the rise of Chavín.[5] However, extensive work at Chavín de Huántar in the 1990s by anthropologists Silvia Kembel and John Rick revised the picture again.[14,16] Their results suggested that Chavín de Huántar neither preceded nor followed the coastal valley sites, but overlapped with them in time. Instead of just three phases of construction, there were fifteen, spread over many centuries. Just when construction first began at Chavín de Huántar remains uncertain, but it was probably well before the end of the Initial Period. The site reached its maximum around 850 BC, declining thereafter. Rituals ceased there around 600 BC.

Anthropologist Richard Burger[10,15] believes that Chavín de Huántar was a religious centre of great prestige. He argues that its location was auspicious from the perspective of sacred geography. It is situated at the confluence of two rivers and in sight of the snow-capped peak of Huantsan, a mountain that rises 6,400 m (21,000 ft.) above sea level. It is also close to hot springs. All of these were of powerful spiritual and symbolic importance in later pre-Columbian times, and remain so among traditional Quechua speakers in the Peruvian highlands.

While the ceremonial complex itself was undoubtedly awe-inspiring to visitors, early historic accounts suggest that what impressed the most were the site's stone sculptures. Greater in number than those at any other contemporary Peruvian site, the stone sculptures were intended to communicate the power of the esoteric knowledge represented by the temple and its priests. Supernatural beings draw upon the features of the jaguar, anaconda, harpy eagle and caiman alligator. These dangerous carnivores inhabited the forested slopes and tropical lowlands to the east, an environment very different to the highlands in which Chavín de Huántar is located. Often, features were combined to produce unnatural hybrids. For example, the feathers of a harpy eagle were depicted as snakes and its ankles as fanged jawless heads. The supreme Chavín deity might have been an anthropomorphic being usually depicted with large fangs, long hair and elaborate ear ornaments. The best-known portrayal of the deity is on the Raimondi Stela, where the god holds a staff in each hand. The Raimondi Stela is a 2 m (6 ft. 6 in.) high stela named for its nineteenth century discoverer, Antonio Raimondi. Often known as the Staff God, the deity appears to have been the principal focus of Chavín worship. The Staff God might have been associated with the forces that control the weather or with creation, as were later Inca deities.

Chavín iconography is incomprehensible to the uninitiated and was probably intended only to be understood by those who participated in the rituals or underwent religious training. Ethnographic and experimental data suggest a connection between the imagery and the use of psychotropic drugs. It is therefore likely that the Chavín religious system was shamanistic and involved the use of psychotropic drugs. Friezes in the sunken circular plaza depict processions of anthropomorphic beings wearing elaborate headdresses. Some are blowing into conch-shell trumpets; others are holding stalks of the psychotropic San Pedro cactus (*Echinopsis pachanoi*), and some of the figures bear weapons. Below this precession is a second precession of jaguars, probably representing a shamanistic transformation of the figures parading above.

Conch-shell trumpets of the type depicted have been found on the site. They were cut and drilled to serve as musical instruments, and showed heavy traces of use. When played, they make a sound similar to an instrument known as a *pututu* that is used in present-day traditional ceremonies. Music, processions and dance probably all played a role in ceremonial life at Chavín de Huántar. Ritual battles might also have taken place. Contests involving the ritual shedding of blood were an important part of highland festivals until recently.

The evidence for use of the mescaline-bearing San Pedro cactus is circumstantial, but other lines of evidence suggest that psychotropic substances were utilised in rituals. Small mortars and snuff spoons have been found at Chavín de Huántar. These are believed to have been used for the preparation and inhalation of hallucinogenic snuff. Dozens of tenon stone heads adorning the central mound illustrate the shamanistic transformation of humans into jaguars and crested eagles. They depict mucus flowing from the nostrils, as would accompany the inhalation of snuff. In the present-day Amazon region, many shamans view felines as alter egos into which they transform themselves for the purpose of supernatural intervention.

Burger believes that Chavín de Huántar was a place of pilgrimage. He notes the remarks of seventeenth century writer Vasquez de Espinoza, who likened it to Rome or Jerusalem; Berger suggests that this was an astute observation. From its earliest days, the temple at Chavín de Huántar attracted people from beyond the immediate area. This is reflected in artefacts presumably brought as offerings, including ceramics from many distant cultures. It is also reflected in architectural and artistic conventions that quote a wide variety of regional traditions. These include the U-shaped mound complexes of the coastal valleys, the built-in gallery systems of the highlands, and the religious iconography of many cultures. Burger suggests that this was a deliberate attempt to create an 'international style' that blended many diverse traditions so as to appeal to a cosmopolitan audience of pilgrims.

The permanent residential population of Chavín de Huántar was initially probably no more than a few hundred, but grew to around 2,000 to 3,000 individuals as the centre's influence increased. The non-ceremonial part of the site now covered some 40 ha (100 acres), and spilled onto the east bank of the Mosna. The subsistence economy shifted from an emphasis on hunted llama and deer to herded llama. Potato and other high-altitude crops predominated over maize. Much food was imported, including seafood from the coast and llama meat from neighbouring higher-altitude villages. At the same time, what was now a proto-urban settlement became internally specialised. The zone to the west of the ceremonial centre contains gold jewellery, *Spondylus* shells and fine pottery, but these are largely absent from the overflow zone to the east. It is thought that jewellery was made in the high-status area, while the low-status area specialised in hide preparation. The difference in social status shows up in the food consumed by the two groups: while both relied heavily on llama meat, the younger animals were reserved for the high-status group. Overall, this increase in population size and social complexity probably reflected the increasing number of pilgrims visiting the site, and the attendant stimulus for long-distance trade.

Burger does not believe that Chavín de Huántar was an expansive state. Instead its relations with other polities are best-described by Colin Renfrew's peer polity interaction model (see Chapters 17 and 18). There is no evidence that the Chavín culture was spread by force, and warfare played only a very minor role in Chavín affairs. Shelia and Thomas Pozorski[5] disagree. To them, Chavín de Huántar was an aggressively-colonising state, albeit one whose power was grounded in ritual and religious symbolism. Regardless of which view is correct, Chavín de Huántar was undoubtedly a centre of exceptional wealth, power and influence for much of the Early Horizon.

State formation in the Virú and Moche valley.

The Gallinazo was a cultural phenomenon that emerged on the northern coast of Peru during the first part of the Early Intermediate Period. It was centred on the Virú Valley and lasted from around 100 BC to AD 200. The appearance and spread of the Gallinazo is marked by a distinctive black-on-orange ceramic style known as Gallinazo Negative. So-called negative-resist decoration is achieved by painting the design with a protective substance such as pitch or tallow before colour is applied to the rest of the pot. The protective substance burns off during firing, to leave a decorative design rendered in negative.

The social and cultural organisation of the Gallinazo period is not well understood, and indeed many archaeologists are reluctant to classify it as a culture, society or style. The traditional view is that it lacked strong internal cohesion. However, arguments have also been advanced that a state-level polity emerged in the Virú Valley during Gallinazo period.[17]

In 1946, the American archaeologist Gordon Willey carried out extensive fieldwork in the Virú area. He studied settlement patterns and found that during the Gallinazo period, populations increased, and virgin land was brought under cultivation by substantially expanding the irrigation canal system.[18] Stable isotope analysis of dental remains confirms that maize consumption increased, and it is possible that the intensification of maize production was an important precursor to state formation.[19] The entire valley became a unified polity, with a four-tier settlement hierarchy.[18] At the apex was a large urban centre known as the Gallinazo Group, a cluster of 30 mound sites scattered over 600 ha (1,500 acres) in the lower part of the valley, although the total occupied area was only 40 ha (100 acres).[20] The sites also contain dense aggregations of residential accommodation made up of thousands of small rooms.[21] Only six of the mounds contain civic architecture; the others are purely residential zones of varying sizes.[20]

The first cities

The largest site of the group, Huaca Gallinazo, is an 8.2 ha (20 acre) complex dominated by a towering platform and an adjacent terrace fronting a wide plaza. The overall population is estimated to have ranged from 14,400 to 28,800 based on comparisons with other 'agglutinative' settlements such as Çatalhöyük.[20] Other Virú sites apparently served specialised functions. They included Huaca San Juan, a site that is located at the take-off point for irrigation canals and probably managed the distribution of water. The site of Huaca Santa Clara has been interpreted as a medium-sized administrative centre. Elsewhere, a group of four sites at Castillo de Tomaval likely served as military garrisons.[18]

Charles Spencer[22] believes that the overall settlement pattern is consistent with the emergence of a state-level polity in the Virú Valley during the Gallinazo period. He also notes that there are hints that the Virú Valley state subsequently attempted to expand its territory northwards into the Moche and Chicama Valleys. The Moche Valley lies 35 km (22 miles) to the north of the Virú. The Gallinazo period there was characterised by warfare and population dislocation: large areas of the valley were abandoned and there was an increasing tendency to aggregate populations, fortify settlements, and locate these in defensible locations. In pre-Gallinazo times, there were eight clusters of settlements, but this reduced to just two: at Cerro Oreja in the valley neck upstream, and at the coastal location of Pampa Cruz. The two are 24 km (15 miles) apart and were probably separate polities. The Cerro Oreja polity could have commanded key take-off points for irrigation canals, and it might have coalesced – possibly even as a secondary state – in response to the threat posed by the Virú Valley state.

The Chicama Valley lies 80 km (50 miles) north of the Virú Valley. Here the Gallinazo period again saw populations aggregated and some fortification of sites. It also saw the establishment of a site at Huaca Prieta overlaying an earlier occupation. Huaca Prieta is located at the mouth of the Chicama, but numerous shards of Gallinazo Negative pottery suggest a close relationship to the Virú Valley state. Clay-lined pits and a large jar have been found in association with a large number of maize cobs from which the kernels had been removed. Ethnographic comparisons suggest that this facility was a brewery used for the production of chicha (maize beer). Charles Spencer[22] suggests that a Virú Valley outpost was established at Huaca Prieta early in the Gallinazo period, although the full extent of the presence in the Chicama Valley is far from fully understood. The relationship between the Virú Valley state and the coastal Pampa Cruz polity is unknown, but the polity at the inland Cerro Oreja site apparently resisted foreign incursions from the south.

As with Sechín Alto and Chavín de Huántar, and some of their contemporaries, the case for a Virú-Gallinazo state remains controversial. Nevertheless, many of the cultural patterns seen in the later Moche culture have direct antecedents to Gallinazo.[1] If the Virú-Gallinazo state is accepted, then we must consider the possibility that it was not the only early state to emerge on the northern coast of Peru around the turn of the Christian era.[20]

It is not until later in the Early Intermediate Period that widely accepted evidence for state formation is seen on the Peruvian coast. The Moche culture emerged around AD 200. It is named for the Moche Valley, but Moche sites are present in coastal valley sites from the Nepeña Valley in the south to the Lambayeque Valley in the north.[23] The Moche present clear evidence of palaces, royal tombs, temples, economic specialisation, an urban capital, a road system, a warrior-based elite, and a regional polity extending beyond a single valley.[1]

The Moche is known by a distinctive ceramic style, rich in images depicting many aspects of cultural life. Five consecutive ceramic phases were originally recognised, but the Moche style is not as uniform as once believed. Only three phases are present in the north and there are differences in form and iconographic content between the north and the south.[23] The Moche also made elaborate gold ornaments and both ornamental and utilitarian items from copper and bronze. The gold was probably obtained locally, as the rivers are rich in ore. Despite their good knowledge of metallurgy, the Moche for the most part did not rely on metal for weaponry.[24]

The primary site of the Moche culture, Huacas de Moche, is located in the Moche Valley, a short distance south of Peru's second city, Trujillo. The site is dominated by two large mounds, Huaca del Sol (Temple of the Sun) and Huaca de la Luna (Temple of the Moon), lying 500 m (1,640 ft.) apart. The plains separating the two mounds were occupied by an unequivocally urban settlement, characterised by a system of streets, canals, plazas, residential compounds housing expended families, and specialist workshops where elite ceramics and other fine arts were produced.[4,1]

The Huaca del Sol was a palace complex measuring 340 by 160 m (1,115 by 525 ft.) and 40 m (130 ft.) high. It is one of the largest mound complexes ever built in South America, but unfortunately much of it was destroyed when the Conquistadores mined it for gold. As with so many other New World monuments, it grew by accretion as pre-existing summit chambers and courts were repeatedly built over. Millions of mud bricks were used in the construction, many bearing impressed marks. Possibly these identified the various communities of workers who worked on assigned sections of the project.[1,3]

To the east, the smaller Huaca de la Luna was a ceremonial complex, comprising three interconnected platforms on the flanks of a hill. It was enclosed by high adobe walls richly ornamented with polychrome friezes and murals. The large central mound is topped by courts ornamented with huge depictions of the head of a supernatural being with canine teeth. Other panels depict spider-like creatures, anthropomorphic beings and the parading of prisoners of war. A short distance away, a small platform was built over a prominent rocky outcrop facing a court below. This was used for sacrificing prisoners, who were then flung downhill. The remains of twenty young males have been found, all of whom had died a violent death. The importance of human sacrifice is attested to in Moche ceramic artwork: the so-called Presentation Theme or Sacrifice Ceremony depicts elaborately-clad figures cutting the throats of naked prisoners whose hands are bound behind their backs; their blood was collected in a chalice and presented to a high-ranking priest.[1,3]

Moche political organisation has been interpreted as anything from a single territorial state to a series of single-valley kingdoms or even chiefdoms.[24] In fact, a north/south divide seems likely, with Huacas de Moche as the capital of an expansive multi-valley state-level polity. Initially, it comprised a heartland in the Moche and Chicama Valleys, and then it expanded south to incorporate the Virú, Chao, Santa and Nepeña Valleys.[1,23] The Moche presence in the latter two valleys appears to be intrusive: Moche pottery overlay earlier local ceramic styles, particularly Gallinazo, and Moche-style platform mounds also appear.[24] It is likely that the Moche rulers controlled their territory through an administration based on a settlement pattern of provincial valley capitals and local centres. The emphasis was on tight elite control of the territory and centralisation of its resources.[23]

Ties between Huacas de Moche and Moche-occupied valleys further north were probably looser. The Jequetepeque and Lambayeque Valleys are multi-river systems, each with more agricultural land and available water than several of the valleys further south combined. Consequently, intra-valley relationships are more important than inter-valley relationships. In both regions, the emphasis seems to have been on extending territory by means of larger and more efficient irrigation systems rather than by conquest. Major centres included Sipán and Pampa Grande in the Lambayeque Valley and Dos Cabezas in the Jequetepeque Valley. Extremely wealthy burials at some northern sites may be associated with royalty. Such evidence strengthens the view that these centres were independent polities.[23]

Although the existence of at least one state-level Moche polity is widely accepted, it is not without its problems. Moche iconography, like its ceramic traditions, may not be entirely uniform, and might represent different deities in different regions. This would suggest that if the Moche shared a religious system, there were local variations. The absence of a state-wide standardised religion would undermine the concept of a Moche state. Other issues are the lack of evidence for large-scale storage facilities, or a state bureaucracy. It has been suggested that the Moche society was organised at chiefdom level, and that the huaca temples were the focus of Moche life. Each huaca was built and controlled by a different chiefdom, and variations in size might have been linked to the rise and fall of kin groups and their leaders. Some huacas might have been repeatedly remodelled and grown in size over many centuries, while others might have fallen out of use after only a few decades.[25]

Regardless of their level of societal organisation, the Moche culture existed for around six centuries. Its eventual downfall has been linked to El Niño events and a period of drought between AD 562 and 594. These natural disasters threatened the agricultural and irrigation systems, thereby undermining the authority of the elite and triggering revolts against its rule. Although the Moche ceramic style endured for a while, it gradually disappeared between AD 700 and 800.[24,3]

Settlement patterns reveal that Moche people of later times responded to the environmental uncertainty by decentralisation. The emphasis shifted from urban centres to smaller-scale sites distributed across a variety of environmental settings. There was a lack of investment in large-scale projects such as major road networks, aqueducts and complex irrigation systems. Instead, there was an emphasis on low-cost agricultural systems and infrastructure that could be swiftly rebuilt or relocated in response to flooding and other environmental problems.[26]

The Nazca

The Nazca style and culture were partially contemporary with the Moche, and flourished between 200 BC and AD 650. The Nazca region is a system of valleys on the southern coast of Peru, where Nazca weavers and potters produced vibrant polychrome art, with a wide range of imagery including plants, animals, people and supernatural beings. Much of the arable land of the Nazca region is split among separate headwater streams, and it sustained a population of under 25,000, mostly living in simple farming communities. There was a ceremonial centre at Cahuachi, with around 40 mounds comprised of natural hills faced with adobe. Mostly, these were no more than medium-sized, although there was a 20 m (66 ft.) high Great Temple. There was little in the way of residential accommodation, indicating that the site was used by for ritual purposes by people who lived elsewhere. It appears to have been used by a number of separate groups, each of whom erected their own mound complex.[3]

Nazca 'headhunting' practices have been widely studied. Decapitation and the subsequent ritual use of human heads was a common practice in Peruvian cultures as early as Preceramic times. Iconographic depictions of the practice can be seen in the art of the Chavín, Moche, Wari and Inca among others, but it was on the southern coast of Peru that head removal was most common and where the best-preserved examples of such heads are found. The majority of heads are adult males aged between 20 and 45 years old, and people aged over 50 are very rare. Nazca ceramics frequently depict elaborately costumed warriors decapitating enemies on the battlefield, which is consistent with the demographic profile of the heads. Specimens are usually referred to as 'trophy heads', although Nazca iconography shows that they were primarily used in rituals rather than as trophies.[27]

The Nazca are best known for the lines and drawings picked out on the dry rocky plains between the river tributaries. Known as geoglyphs, they were created by removing dark-coloured rock and sediment to expose lighter-coloured underlying surfaces. More than 1,000 km (620 miles) of straight lines are known, some exceeding 20 km (12 miles) in length. There are also more than 300 geometric figures, and a number of figures including birds, killer whales, monkeys, humans and plants. Their purpose remains unknown. As many new drawings intrude upon earlier ones, they cannot have formed part of any master plan.[3]

The scale of the drawings means that their details cannot be made out from the ground. Needless to say, it has been suggested that they were used as runways for alien spacecraft. More plausibly, it has been proposed that the Nazca surveyed them from the air in hot air balloons. In the 1970s, a hot air balloon was constructed using materials thought to be available to the Nazca. The craft flew, but like the exploits of Thor Heyerdahl, really proves very little. Just because something is theoretically possible and can be accomplished with modern hindsight, it doesn't mean that it actually happened. More or less any society capable of making fabrics could theoretically construct a passenger-carrying hot air balloon, yet there is no reliable evidence that any actually did before the second half of the eighteenth century. The ancient Chinese used small hot air balloons for military signalling as early as the third century AD, but they never built a passenger-carrying craft.

Early developments in the Titicaca Basin

Located in the Andean altiplano on the border between Bolivia and Peru, Lake Titicaca is 3,812 m (12,507 ft.) above sea level; one the highest large bodies of water in the world. It is fed by 27 inflow rivers and has a surface area of 8,372 sq. km (3,232 sq. miles), making it the largest lake in South America. The Titicaca basin is a vast area, stretching for more than 50,000 sq. km (20,000 sq. miles). Lake edge-dwelling Aymara and Quechua farmers practice a subsistence base on a on a combination of potato and quinoa cultivation, herding llama, fishing, and intensive gathering of wild lake resources. Archaeological evidence suggests that this pattern is little altered since prehistoric times. Farmers practiced a technique known as raised field agriculture. Raised fields are constructed by excavating parallel canals and piling soil between them to form raised mounds in which crops are planted. This method improves drainage and soil conditions, and decreases the risk of frost damage. Water in the canals provides moisture during periods of drought. The method gradually fell out of use after the collapse of Tiwanaku and consequent decline in population, but it was probably never entirely abandoned until the arrival of the Spanish.[28]

Autonomous villages grew up close to the lake or its inflow rivers from around 1400 BC. Over the next 900 years, some of these became regional centres, characterised by sunken court complexes. They hosted feasts, markets and rituals and integrated people from smaller, allied villages. They were not generally located in defensible locations, and prior to 500 BC, there is little evidence for organised warfare. After that time, however, the iconography of ceramics and carved stone stelae becomes martial in tone. The trophy head motif suddenly makes an appearance in the northern Titicaca repertoire of images. Actual trophy heads have been recovered, and there was a shift to more defensible locations.[29,30]

By 400 BC, multi-tiered settlement systems, with major centres spaced 20 to 25 km (12 to 15 miles) apart, were established in the north Titicaca basin. There were also a large number of smaller centres, with subsidiary villages and hamlets. The political landscape at this time was in a state of flux, as a number of autonomous polities competed for power. Over next few centuries, sites became fewer in number, but substantially larger in size as the dominant polities absorbed or eliminated their competitors. Eventually, only a small number of powerful centres remained. By AD 50, only two dominant polities remained in the north Titicaca basin: Taraco and Pukara. Both centres had expanded to at least 100 ha (250 acres) by this time.[30]

At about this time, the two must have come into conflict. A high-status residential compound at Taraco was deliberately destroyed by fire. The site was not abandoned, but the compound was not rebuilt. Subsequent archaeological evidence from the site indicates a significant decline in the economic status of Taraco. The percentage of tools made from high-quality obsidian declined from more than 80 percent to under 50 percent. Obsidian artefacts became much smaller, suggesting that the raw material had become scarce; smaller artefacts are more economical in terms of raw material wasted. It is also likely that old, worn-out tools were reworked into smaller but still usable items. Conversely, agricultural activity increased. While farming was undoubtedly an important activity before the attack, the increase suggests that non-agricultural activities declined thereafter.[30]

With its rival defeated, Pukara began to adopt many characteristics of a state-level polity. Populations as far away as 100 km (62 miles) to the south and southeast fell under its influence. By AD 300, Pukara was a proto-urban settlement some 150 ha (370 acres) in extent. The civic centre was located on a hillside terrace and comprised three large sunken courts and about a dozen smaller ones. A large residential zone was spread across the plain below the civic centre. Pukara artisans produced standardised 'Pukara-style' ceramics, incised and slip-painted in red, yellow and black. Stylised and realistic decorative motifs were combined, the latter including birds, llamas, felines and humans. Pukara's rise is another demonstration of the link between organised warfare and state formation. However, its ascendancy was fairly short-lived and it lasted only until around AD 400.[4,31,30]

Tiwanaku: an altiplano empire

Similar developments occurred in the southern Titicaca Basin, but it was not until after Pukara went into decline that Tiwanaku emerged as the new dominant power in the region; another example of the cyclical rise and fall of large polities.[1] Tiwanaku is located on the Bolivian side of the border, 15 km (9 miles) east of Lake Titicaca. The earliest phases of Tiwanaku are contemporary with Pukara, though there is no evidence that it ever came under the latter's control.[4] By AD 800, it had attained a size of at least 6.5 sq. km (2.5 sq. miles), with a conservatively-estimated population of between 10,000 and 20,000.[32,33] Tiwanaku is noted for its fine stonework, imposing monuments, and ornate megalithic portals, including the iconic Gateway of the Sun. Unfortunately, the site has suffered from centuries of looting, non-systematic excavations, and ill-advised restoration projects.

Five phases of construction have been identified at Tiwanaku. The first two cover the period from around 400 BC to AD 100, during which time the settlement remained undistinguished. During Tiwanaku III (AD 100 to 375), the first large-scale construction and agricultural projects were undertaken. Tiwanaku IV (AD 375 to 700) saw the city attain regional hegemony and establish a hierarchy of administrative settlements around the southern Titicaca region. During Tiwanaku V (AD 700 to 1100), the city's influence was at its greatest, and distant colonies were established. Thereafter, protracted drought set in and Tiwanaku collapsed soon after.[4] It should be noted that these dates are only approximate. The chronology of Tiwanaku is complex and remains poorly understood.[34]

Many 'alternative archaeology' websites claim that Tiwanaku is anything up to 20,000 years old and link it to theories involving lost civilisations, alien astronauts and the like. Before the introduction of radiocarbon dating, Austrian-born researcher Arthur Posnansky spent many years studying astronomical alignments at Tiwanaku and after considering cyclical changes in the Earth's axial tilt (see Introduction), he calculated that the alignments matched the solstitial sunrise and sunset in around 15,000 BC. The problem with this approach is that so many statues, stelae and monoliths have been moved around the site or removed altogether that it is more or less impossible to reconstruct accurate sightlines and identify solstitial markers.

Posnansky also claimed that Tiwanaku was once a port on the shores of a Lake Titicaca more than 30 m (100 ft.) deeper than it is today. To the southwest of the Kalasasaya, he excavated structures that he believed were piers or wharfs. According to Posnansky, Tiwanaku served as a port for around 5,000 years until a violent earthquake overwhelmed it in the eleventh millennium BC. Subsequent quakes caused Lake Titicaca to drain, leaving Tiwanaku high and dry. Here it is probably simpler to assume that Posnansky's 'wharfs' were actually something entirely different than to postulate a geological upheaval that seems to have left no other evidence.

Tiwanaku comprised a moated urban core of stelae and monumental architecture, surrounded by sprawling residential districts of adobe brick houses and compounds. The urban core was 90 ha (220 acres) in extent. Within the urban core, the largest structure was the Akapana, a stepped T-shaped platform mound measuring roughly 200 m (650 ft.) on a side and 15 m (50 ft.) high. The structure dates to the Early Tiwanaku IV phase, and was probably built in stages. The platform sides were terraced with stone-faced retaining walls, rising in six steps. The two lowest walls were constructed from massive sandstone blocks whereas the higher walls were built with smaller, finely-finished andesite blocks. The top was flat, with a sunken court at the centre. This was drained by a complex system of conduits that carried runoff water to vents along the sides, and allowed it to cascade down the platform steps. The presence of numerous dismembered adult male corpses suggests that human sacrifice occurred at the Akapana. The Pumapunku, located about a kilometre (0.62 miles) from the Akapana, is roughly contemporary with it. Smaller but otherwise similar, it was built from fine andesite and sandstone masonry. It measures 150 by 150 m (490 by 490 ft.), stands 5 m (16 ft.) high, and is entered through grand portals each carved from a single slab of andesite.[4,32]

200 m (650 ft.) to the north of the Akapana is a sunken court known as the Sunken Temple, an early structure dating to Tiwanaku I. The walls of the court are ornamented by tenoned stone heads, and a number of stelae are set into the floor. These include the Bennett monolith, named for archaeologist Wendell Bennett. A short distance to the west of the Sunken Temple, stairs surmounted by a prominent gateway provide access to the summit of another platform. This is the Kalasasaya, a massive rectangular earthen platform measuring 115 by 130 m (380 by 425 ft.), and bounded by a revetment of monolithic stone pilasters and smaller finely-dressed stones. Atop is a walled inner court holding the Ponce monolith, named for Bolivian anthropologist Carlos Ponce. The Kalasasaya was probably built in stages during Tiwanaku III and IV.[4,32]

In the northwest corner of the Kalasasaya stands the ornately-carved Gateway of the Sun, a megalithic portal hewn from a single block of andesite. It measures 3 m (10 ft.) in height, 4 m (13 ft.) in width, and weighs an estimated 10 tonnes. Nineteenth century photographs and etchings show it partially buried and broken in two. It has since been reconstructed, although a crack is still clearly visible. It was apparently moved to the Kalasasaya from elsewhere on the site, possibly the Pumapunku. The portal is a showcase for Tiwanaku iconography: the lintel is ornamented with an incised frieze of figures dominated by a central 'Gateway God', an anthropomorphic figure wearing an elaborate rayed headdress. Flanked by rows of smaller human or bird-headed attendants, he stands upon a pyramid mound holding a staff in each hand, each of which is tipped with the heads of condors. This Tiwanaku Gateway God appears to be a revival of the Chavín Staff God.[4]

To the west of the Kalasasaya is the Putuni complex, comprising a low rectangular platform with a sunken court and two residential compounds. The Putuni was a fairly late structure, dating to Tiwanaku V, and built over an earlier mortuary. Again, it appears to have been built in stages. The court is surrounded by a series of panelled niches that might once have held the mummified bodies of deceased ancestors. As such, they might have served a similar function to later Aymara *chullpa* funerary towers. Associated with the platform are two residential compounds known as the East and West Palaces, which are built on stone foundations and face each other across a paved plaza. The adobe brick wall interiors of the East Palace were elaborately painted in brilliant hues of red, yellow, orange, green and blue. Residential features include a hearth, four refuse pits and three private wells. Luxury items recovered include beads of lapis lazuli, sodalite, obsidian and bone, copper pins, carved shells, gold sheets, and a wrought silver tube filled with blue pigment; it is clear that the East Palace residents were of high status. The West Palace seems to have been a later addition, and its construction was of a generally lower quality. Ceramic remains of large storage jars suggest that the main activity in the West Palace was the brewing, storing and consumption of fermented drinks.[32] The Putuni is generally supposed to have been a royal palace, but this is by no means certain. The monuments in the central core might have changed their function over time, and it is possible that different monuments or combinations of monuments served as royal palaces at different times.[34]

The stone used for these construction projects was in many cases obtained from distant sources. Analysis of andesite used in some Tiwanaku III phase constructions indicates that it was quarried in the Copacabana area to the north. Massive blocks weighing 10 to 15 tonnes were rafted some 95 km (59 miles) across Lake Titicaca to the prehistoric port of Iwawe, and then dragged another 22 km (13.5 miles) overland to Tiwanaku. Unloading the blocks without capsizing the rafts was difficult and, to judge from the number of abandoned blocks found around the quay and pier of Iwawe, not always successful.[35]

Prior to around AD 600, residential accommodation was largely concentrated in and around the core area bounded by the moat. Over the next 200 years, the settlement expanded way beyond this limit as the urban population increased. High-status residential groups, identified by the fine quality of their ceramics, remained concentrated around the urban core. Nevertheless, the expansion was not a random process of accretion of individual household units. Instead, it entailed the planned construction and occupation of large, uniformly-aligned residential compounds. Each comprised a large perimeter wall enclosing one or more domestic dwellings and associated activity areas. Compounds varied in size and internal layout, suggesting a considerable variation in the nature of resident social groups. Streets and canals ran between the compounds, providing arterial routes for the movement of people and water. All residential units shared a common alignment of between 6° to 8° east of due north: an orientation that approximates visual pathways to major local peaks, including Kimsa Chata to the south and Mount Illimani to the east. Entrances to residential compounds and primary stairways and portals to ceremonial platforms faced east or west, reflecting the daily east-west passage of the Sun.[32]

Craft production in Tiwanaku took two forms: that under elite control and for elite consumption; and that organised by residential groups under local management. Many elaborately-crafted objects were apparently made by specific skilled individuals under state control as a form of taxation. Such objects included chert and obsidian projectile points. Procurement and distribution of these high quality raw materials was centrally controlled. However, some pottery-producing groups in Tiwanaku appear to have operated as private enterprises. The wide range of styles produced indicates that production was conducted and managed locally rather than by the ruling elite.[32]

The agricultural hinterland of Tiwanaku comprised the south of the Titicaca basin and enclaves in the north. The mixed-farming economy relied on raising crops and herding llamas and alpacas. These animals supplied meat and wool, but llamas also served as pack animals for caravans used to transport commodities over long distances. There was a considerable state-controlled investment of corvée labour in improving agricultural yields and opening up new farmland. Farmers used raised field techniques, particularly around the margins of the lake where the water table was high. Fields measured anything up to 15 by 200 m (50 by 650 ft.) and they were often constructed by excavating parallel trenches and piling the soil in the middle. In some cases, permeable footings of cobbles were capped by a layer of good soil brought in from elsewhere.[4] An estimated total of 190 sq. km (73 sq. miles) of raised fields were in production during Tiwanaku times.[36] Notwithstanding these efforts, certain crops do not do well in the altiplano. Maize, for example, must be imported. Maize was also produced at distant colonies established for the purpose.[32]

It was during the Tiwanaku IV phase that Tiwanaku began to emerge as an expansive state. Settlement density increased dramatically, and a four-tier settlement hierarchy emerged. In addition to Tiwanaku itself, this included towns of 3 to 10 ha (7.5 to 25 acres), villages of 1 to 3 ha (2.5 to 7.5

acres), and a range of smaller hamlets of up to 1 ha (2.5 acres). However, rank-size analysis reveals a 'convex' pattern (see Chapter 28), suggesting that the ruling bureaucracy in Tiwanaku was weak, and communities might have enjoyed a fair degree of autonomy. In the more northerly parts of the Titicaca basin, Tiwanaku control was restricted to enclaves near roads, fields and the lake margins.[32,37]

Tiwanaku was the primary centre of settlement networks stretching over a vast heartland. Unlike Uruk (see Chapter 26) and Teotihuacán (see Chapter 29), its rise did not did not lead to a wide-scale rural abandonment. Instead, it led to the creation of a local landscape densely populated with clusters of smaller towns, villages and hamlets. Red, orange or black-slipped Tiwanaku-style serving and ceremonial wares became ubiquitous throughout the heartland after AD 500. These displayed a high degree of uniformity in terms of form and presented a notably standardised iconography of mythical, anthropomorphic and geometric designs. For example, most *escudillas* (flaring ceremonial serving bowls) were wide rimmed and decorated with stylised mythical imagery, while *sahumadores* (domestic and ritual lamps) typically portrayed stylised condor wings and feathers. The pervasiveness of these wares suggests the spread and acceptance of a common system of beliefs and practices.[32,33]

The influence of Tiwanaku was widespread, and extended across southern Peru, Bolivia, and the north of Chile and Argentina. Tiwanaku artefacts have been found over an area of around 400,000 sq. km (150,000 sq. miles), an area approximately the size of California.[37] However, to the north another great empire held sway. The rise of Wari had coincided with that of Tiwanaku. A 100 km (62 mile) wide buffer zone separated these two Andean superpowers.[3]

The innovators

The Wari (or Huari) culture is named for its capital, located at an elevation of 2,800 m (9,200 ft.) in the central sierra of Peru, 25 km (15 miles) north of the modern city of Ayacucho. A common convention is to use the term 'Wari' for the culture and 'Huari' for the city. Wari origins are rooted in the Early Intermediate Huarpa culture from around AD 200. Huarpa ceramics were strongly influenced by the Nazca, with whom they traded wool and possibly copper for salt, seafood and other lowland produce. The region lacks flatland, and steep terrain is subject to erosion. Accordingly, the Huarpa employed terraces for both rain-fed and irrigation farming. The narrow contour terraces were laid out as integrated flights of farmland, with as many as 100 terraces from the top of a hill to the valley below. Irrigation systems included rain-fed cisterns and spring-fed reservoirs sited at different levels to supply different terraces. Clay-lined canals up to 1.6 m (5 ft.) in width and several kilometres in length were also used to supply water. Such large-scale works were in all probability some form of corporate undertakings. Terraced agriculture supported a large but dispersed population. Most people lived in small farmsteads, often located on hilltops. There was also an urban centre at Nawinpukio, near Ayacucho, complete with platforms, administrative buildings, elite residences, and a system of canals that supplied water to residents.[4]

Throughout this period, Huari was a modest settlement with little political influence. The upturn in its fortunes was linked to the period of drought noted above, from AD 562 to 564. While this brought about the downfall of the Moche, Huari prospered. The key to their success was a very large and innovative irrigation system. Up until now, the Huarpa had not farmed steep mountain slopes to a significant degree, but the people of Huari constructed a long primary canal from a spring located high above their settlement. This was routed across high-elevation contours to feed secondary canals at lower levels, which in turn irrigated steep mountain-side terraced fields. The labour cost of such systems was high, but they enabled vast amounts steep, underexploited and often entirely unexploited terrain to be brought into agricultural production. Furthermore, by utilising elevated spring and streams, the vicissitudes of rainfall could be moderated.[4]

The initial priority must have been to compensate for reduced yields in traditional farming areas, but once rainfall levels returned to normal it became a powerful means of expanding agricultural economies. It was found possible to grow maize in the high terraces, and the Wari soon added new high-yield varieties of this crop to their agricultural repertoire. Having developed such 'killer app' technology, the Wari set about exporting it to populations elsewhere: a package of technology, ideology, iconography and organisational methods. A period of expansion began. Nawinpukio and many other sites were abandoned, their populations relocating to Huari and the nearby site of Conchopata.[4]

Huari is located on a ridge midway up the eastern flank of the Ayacucho Valley and coalesced between AD 500 and 600 from at least four earlier villages. Between AD 600 and 900, it developed into an urban centre comparable in size to Tiwanaku, but it was very unlike that great southern metropolis. Instead of pyramidal mounds and wide plazas, the city was dominated by rectangular compounds enclosed by high walls. The streets were few and narrow, less than 2 m (6 ft. 6 in.) wide, with high walls on both sides. Pedestrians would felt that they were walking along the bottom of a deep trench. In places there might have been nothing but the gaps between compound walls. It would certainly have been difficult for people to get about.[38] Michael Moseley[4] believes that the architecture of Huari emphasised segregation, presumably based on kin, social class and rank, and occupation.

Temples, palaces and residential houses alike were enclosed within high walls of rough stone, differing only in scale and ranging in size from 40 to 100 m (130 to 330 ft.) on a side. The walls were between 8 and 10 m (26 to 33 ft.) high and usually well over 1 m (3 ft. 3 in.) thick. The compounds were typically subdivided into a number of rectangular patios, each surrounded by long, narrow buildings of two or three storeys. Some compounds were specialist craft production workshops for ceramics, jewellery and the manufacture of projectile points. A large number of serving bowls and libation cups were found in one compound, suggesting that it was used for ritual feasting and drinking.[4,38]

D-shaped single-room temples have been found in some of the compounds. They measure 10 to 20 m (33 to 66 ft.) in diameter, with a doorway in the flat side. They were not stand-alone structures and were usually associated with other buildings. One example was found at Vegachayoc Moqo, a large complex containing burial niches; grave goods suggest that many of the deceased were not of high status. Vegachayoc Moqo was evidently a public cemetery, although the compound might have been a repurposed temple or even royal residence.[38]

A short distance from Vegachayoc Moqo is a three-storey underground burial complex known as Monjachayoq. The complex may be a royal tomb, but unfortunately it has been badly looted. Cut stone was employed in its construction, a building technique more typical of Tiwanaku. Megalithic building techniques were also employed for the semi-subterranean burial chambers at the Cheqo Wasi enclosure. The tombs are made of carefully dressed stone slabs, but again have been looted – though the looters did miss gold and other luxury items. Cheqo Wasi was probably intended for individuals of just below royal rank. Luxury goods from it and elsewhere show that the Wari imported raw materials and finished goods from great distances. These included pottery from Cajamarca in the northern Peruvian highlands, *Spondylus* shell ornaments from Ecuador, cowrie and other shells from various coastal locations, gold, silver, copper, and ornamental stones including chrysocolla, lapis lazuli and greenstone.[4,38]

Was stone cutting a building technology imported from Tiwanaku? In contrast to Tiwanaku architecture, Wari use of the technique seems to have been for underground construction.[38] Nevertheless, Michael Moseley[4] claims that elements of Tiwanaku ritual art and architecture reached Huari and Conchopata. These include a rectangular sunken court constructed around AD 580. The court might have been a temple, although it was later filled in and built over. The Wari also borrowed the Tiwanaku Gateway God, who as we have seen was a revival of the earlier Chavín Staff God. They transformed it into an agricultural symbol by replacing the rayed headdress and condor-tipped staffs with maize-bearing equivalents. This staff-bearing deity features prominently in Wari ceramics. Several centuries of interaction may explain how the Wari came to adopt central elements of the Tiwanaku religion, though they were probably as divergent as the various branches of Christianity or Islam are today.[3]

Trophy heads also played a part in Wari ritual practices. Wari trophy heads were standardised in appearance, with carefully-drilled and similarly-sized holes to insert carrying cords. One hole was nearly always drilled at the top of the skull. When suspended by a cord, the trophy head was thus displayed upright and facing forward. A hole was also frequently drilled into the occipital bone at the lower rear of the skull, possibly to display it as a separate trophy after it was detached from the skull. The regularity of both the size and placement of the holes differs from Nazca practice. Nazca trophy heads are typically drilled through the frontal bone at the front of the skull, but the holes vary in size and placement. It has been suggested, therefore, that there were rigid and possibly state-mandated rules regarding the production of Wari trophy heads.[39]

Cut-marks associated with de-fleshing suggest that the trophy heads were made from the newly-deceased. Of 31 trophy heads recovered at Conchopata, seven were children and two were female. This suggests that women and children were considered fair game, and that at least some of the heads were taken by raiding parties rather than on the battlefield. The remainder were adult males, of whom nearly half showed signs of healed cranial injuries presumably sustained in earlier battles. Iconography depicting the Staff God and other deities with bound captives and trophy heads suggests that the heads were taken from prisoners of war rather than from those killed in battle.[39] Analysis of strontium isotope ratios of dental samples from the trophy heads in comparison to those from formal Conchopata burials suggests that the majority of the trophy heads were of non-local origin.[40,41]

What the Wari did for us

Wari cultural influence became widespread: ceramics of Wari style and iconography, those of closely related provincial styles, and locally-made copies occur throughout the Central Andes north of the region dominated by Tiwanaku; and sites with rectangular Wari-style enclosures are also widespread. The enclosures measured anything from 25 to 800 m (80 to 2,600 ft.) on a side; interior buildings included open courts, storage areas, elite quarters and what might have been barracks for people rendering mit'a (corvée) labour. These centres have been interpreted as storage facilities, way stations, fortresses or administrative centres. The largest was Pikillacta, near the present-day city and one-time Inca capital of Cuzco. Although no two centres are exactly alike, the similarity in style and layout suggests that their construction was supervised by Wari architects. Many of these facilities are associated with long-distance roads; the Wari evidently built and maintained a long-distance road network.[42,4] A four-tier settlement hierarchy has been proposed, although only limited site size data is available.[43]

Three possible mechanisms have been proposed for the spread of Wari influence beyond the Ayacucho Valley: religion, trade and political expansion or conquest. The first two would have been unlikely to have led to the widespread construction of large secular facilities and an associated road network. On the other hand, these things are very likely to be associated with a political expansion.[42] The question, though, is did political control necessarily entail conquest? While the trophy head evidence shows that the Wari had enemies, their arrival was often followed by a beneficial transformation of the local economy.

A good example is Jincamocco in the Carahuarazo Valley, located about six days travel on foot from Huari. The Wari established a medium-sized site there that eventually grew to 27 ha (67 acre). Much of the valley was subsequently terraced, irrigation systems were developed, and paved roads and a bridge were constructed. People abandoned high-altitude hamlets close to zones suitable for growing tubers and herding, relocating to where they could grow maize. The major construction projects involved could not have been accomplished unaided by local groups. The likeliest scenario is a political takeover by the Wari, followed by the deployment of the additional manpower and other resources needed.[42] What is lacking from the Carahuarazo Valley is any evidence for fortified settlements or military activity. The relationship might have been co-operative rather coercive, as the local groups had everything to gain from the construction of irrigated terraces and other infrastructure projects.[4]

Embassies in Moquegua

Cooperative or not, Wari expansion southwards was limited by the presence of Tiwanaku. As noted above, the two polities were separated by a wide buffer zone. The one exception was in the Moquegua region of southern Peru, where Wari and Tiwanaku settlements were established within sight of one another. Cerro Baúl is a 600 m (1,950 ft.) high mesa that stands above the Rio Torata, a major tributary within the Rio Moquegua basin. It is regarded as a sacred *apu* by Andean people today, and temples around its base suggest that this was the case in Wari times, if not earlier.[3] 20 km (13 miles) to the south of the mesa is the Omo site complex, a 38 ha (94 acres) group of sites located close to the Rio Moquegua. The region was settled by colonists from Tiwanaku around AD 500. Initially, though, ties to Tiwanaku were fairly loose and it was more or less independent of the mother state. There was little in the way of public architecture, although the local elite enjoyed access to high-end Tiwanaku ceramics.[44]

Shortly before AD 600, in what can only be described as a bold statement of intent, the emerging Wari state occupied Cerro Baúl and the adjacent hills of Cerro Mejia and Cerro Petroglifo. While the Tiwanaku farmers at Omo remained confined to the valley bottom, the Wari colonists set about using their irrigation technology to exploit the vacant slopes. A 10 km (6.2 mile) long canal was constructed to draw water from a high-altitude tributary and feed it to terraces on the slopes of Cerro Mejia and Cerro Petroglifo. An impressive flow rate of up to 400 litres (88 gallons) per second could be achieved, and the irrigated fields could support a population of around 2,000. A ceremonial complex was constructed atop Cerro Baúl, together with elite residences, accommodation for craft workers, and a brewery complex. The latter was one of the largest of pre-Inca times, with 12 vats each capable of holding 150 litres (33 gallons) of chicha beer. Elite quarters were built at the summit of the other hills, albeit less elaborate than the facilities on Cerro Baúl. The accommodation of the lower-status colonists was located on the flanks of the three hills.[4,3]

Tiwanaku seems to have responded to this move. By AD 725, Omo had been incorporated as a province of the Tiwanaku imperium. At the site designated Omo M10, a temple complex was built comprising three courts rectangular built on a stepped terreplein ascending a small hill. The large Lower Court appears to have been a public space; from it steps led to the smaller but more elaborate Middle Court, with walled galleries on either side. This in turn led to the Upper Court, a complex of rooms arranged around a central court and entered through an antechamber. At the centre of the latter was a smaller, sunken court in which stood a single stela. To the rear stood a multi-storey building from which the entire complex could have been viewed. Notably, this vantage point affords a good view of Cerro Baúl. Radiocarbon dates indicate that the Upper Court was constructed around

AD 890, during the Tiwanaku V period when Tiwanaku's influence was at its greatest.[44] It was the only Tiwanaku platform mound to be constructed outside of the Titicaca basin.[4]

There is no reason to suppose that Cerro Baúl and Omo ever came into conflict.[4] The two settlements might have served as embassies where diplomatic exchanges were conducted between high-ranking officials. However, their ultimate fate differed. The Omo M10 complex appears to have suffered intentional destruction, possibly at the hands of rebels who rejected Tiwanaku domination while retaining many Tiwanaku cultural traditions. The process was certainly violent, also involving the destruction of canals, razing of housing and desecration of cemeteries.[44,3] By contrast, Cerro Baúl was decommissioned in an orderly fashion. The brewery was even used to prepare a final batch of chicha to mark the occasion. At the end of the festivities, the brewery was torched and large ceremonial drinking vessels cast into the flames. There is no question of this being a 'leaving do' that got out of hand. After the embers had cooled, necklaces and bracelets were carefully placed atop the ashes.[45]

The fall of two empires

The closure of Cerro Baúl might have been a response to the destruction of Omo M10. With the Tiwanaku presence in the region at an end, there was no need to keep up the expense of maintaining an embassy,[3] but by AD 1100, the fortunes of both empires had begun to wane. Tiwanaku's fate was sealed by a severe El Niño followed by a period of drought that continued for 400 years. The levels of Lake Titicaca dropped by 12 m (40 ft.), and the water table fell accordingly. The raised fields dried up. Shorn of its agricultural base, Tiwanaku declined and was eventually abandoned. Its inhabitants gradually dispersed to farm moister, higher elevations, and there was an increased emphasis on herding llama and alpaca.[4] In the meantime, the irrigation technology of the Wari did not save them, and their empire fragmented into smaller polities.[3] It is possible that the Wari economy was geared to continuing expansion. Once it had reached the limits of expansion, as bounded by Tiwanaku to the south and other, smaller polities to the north, the Wari imperium was unable to maintain itself and its collapse was inevitable.[42]

Following the collapse of the Tiwanaku and Wari empires, a number of small polities emerged in their place. In the Titicaca region, the drought-enforced shift to higher altitudes required terracing to control erosion. Throughout the altiplano and as far south as San Pedro de Atacama, competition for scarce resources meant that most people now lived in fortified settlements. A few settlements were 150 ha (370 acres) or more, but most were far smaller. The old traditions of sunken courts, platform mounds, stelae and polychrome arts were abandoned. A new tradition of interment in *chullpa* funerary towers arose. This period is referred to as the time of the Aymara kingdoms, though it is possible that Aymara-speakers only moved into the region from the north after the fall of Tiwanaku. This way of life endured throughout the four centuries of drought. With the return of wetter conditions around AD 1500, people re-colonised the lower elevations. It was at this time that the Titicaca region was conquered by the Inca, though local rulers probably found a new role as provincial administrators.[4]

The penultimate empire

The Late Intermediate period saw two major polities arise on the northern coast of Peru: the Chimú Empire (AD 900 to 1400) and the Lambayeque polity (AD 800 to 1350). The former eventually conquered the latter to establish the largest pre-Inca empire in South America. Both polities arose in the wake of the Moche collapse and were heirs to its tradition. A third polity arose further south in the Casma Valley; 'Casma Incised' ceramics spread to several neighbouring valleys, but it remains poorly understood. The three polities coexisted for around 300 years before the Chimú consolidation, an event that came fairly late in their rule. At the time of its eventual defeat by the Inca around AD 1470, Chimú settlements occupied a contiguous valley region from the Motupe Valley in the north to the Casma Valley in the south. According to contemporary Spanish accounts, the Chimú Empire was founded by a man named Taycanamu, who arrived by boat having been sent from afar to govern. Taycanamu established a dynasty that took control of the Moche Valley and then began a process of inter-valley expansion.[46,47]

The Chimú capital, Chan Chan, was located on a flat plain 7 km (4.3 miles) north of the Rio Moche. It comprised a walled area around 20 sq. km. (7.7 sq. miles) of the valley mouth, much of which was empty and set aside for future urban expansion. At the centre was a densely-packed urban core of enclosures and other buildings spread over an area of 6 sq. km (2.3 sq. miles). Within, class and occupational distinctions can clearly be seen in the architecture.[4] The city was dominated by ten palatial rectangular enclosures known as *ciudadelas* ('citadels'), built at different times throughout the city's history and ranging in size from 21.2 to 6.73 ha (52.4 to 16.6 acres). The largest contained 907 rooms and interior spaces, the smallest 113. The surrounding adobe brick walls were up to 9 m (29 ft. 6 in.) high; inside were large, elaborately-ornamented plazas, wells, storerooms, servants' quarters, and small U-shaped buildings set in courtyards known as *audiencias*.[4,47] The storerooms probably held food, drink and gifts for ceremonial feasts that were held in the plazas.[46] It has been suggested that the *audiencias* were used by city administrators as offices, control points and places for the receipt and distribution of goods. The presence of similar structures at rural sites hints at a highly-centralised system of control and authority.[48]

The *ciudadelas* probably served as royal palaces, each being associated with a different ruler or ruling lineage. Each went through an initial period of use, during which it was extensively remodelled. Subsequently, construction work ceased and the rituals carried on within focused more on the dead than the living. Most *ciudadelas* contained large mortuary mounds set in secluded courtyards, which were probably mausoleums for the rulers who built the associated *ciudadela* and important heirs. Thus the one-time palaces were transformed into funerary complexes.[4,49]

The lower-ranking elite were housed in much smaller compounds, with fewer storerooms and *audiencias*, and no large plazas or burial mounds.[46] The city's elite population might have numbered 6,000 or fewer.[4] Craft workers lived and worked in fairly modest quarters of cane construction, comprising small patios and irregular rooms. Excavations show that the predominant concerns were metallurgy and weaving, although wood and lapidary work was also carried out. Around 26,000 craft workers resided in the densely-packed neighbourhoods along the southern and western margins of the civic centre. Another 3,000 lived directly adjacent to the various royal households they served directly. People in other occupations, such as farming and fishing, were not permitted to live in the city.[4]

While Chimú was highly-centralised, with a massive urban centre at Chan Chan, the Lambayeque polity was a complex but non-state polity composed of dispersed ceremonial centres. These were never brought under a single political authority, but instead formed a loose confederation united by kin ties.[46] Again, tradition refers to a traveller from afar who had been sent to govern. In this case the traveller, whose name was Naymlap, arrived with his wife and a large entourage in a flotilla of boats and established a palatial centre at Chotuna, 4 km (2.5 miles) inland. All twelve of his grandsons are supposed to have founded important centres. Although there is no evidence for a seaborne invasion after the Moche collapse, highlanders from Cajamarca migrated into the Lambayeque region and introduced new artistic elements. Aspects of Wari iconography were also adopted. The resulting combination of these with older Moche traditions is known as the Sican tradition, which became a sharply defined style between AD 900 and 1100. It is noted for paddle-impressed black ware ceramics and a bird-like male design motif known as the Sican Lord.[4]

Batán Grande emerged as the region's largest centre after the abandonment of the Moche centre at Pampa Grande. By AD 1000, it was a major metropolis with a civic centre of over 4 sq. km (1.5 sq. miles). Local copper mines and seafaring trade undoubtedly contributed to its prosperity. Many other major centres, including Chotuna, arose during this period. A complex system of inter-valley irrigation canals carried water from the Rio Lambayeque to dryer regions. However, the good times did not last. Around AD 1100, the region was devastated by exceptionally severe El Niño floods. The badly-damaged Batán Grande was abandoned, as was reverence of the Sican Lord. Presumably the latter fell into disfavour after he had failed to prevent the disaster. Pre-eminence in the Lambayeque region then shifted to Tucume Viejo, where one of the largest platform mounds in the Andes, the Huaca Larga, was constructed. The irrigation systems were rebuilt, but recovery was hampered by the same drought that brought about the downfall of Tiwanaku.[4]

Chan Chan was also affected by the El Niño floods, but a vigorous process of reconstruction was put in hand. Irrigation canals were repaired and upgraded with stone linings, though the drought meant that the water supply was drastically reduced. An attempt build a 70 km (43 mile) canal to the Rio Chicama was unsuccessful. Deep wells and large sunken gardens were excavated in order to reach the depressed water table. Unfortunately, these projects could only partially mitigate the loss of agricultural land. It is possible that this was the trigger for the relatively late Chimú expansion, and that its purpose was to obtain land by force.[4] The Chimú arrived in the Jequetepeque Valley around AD 1310. They seized the strategically-placed Lambayeque centre of Farfán, and established further centres at Talambo and Algarrobal de Moro. Between AD 1360 and 1400, the remainder of the Lambayeque region was conquered. Meanwhile, the Casma Valley was taken around AD 1350.[47]

Unlike the great Moche, Tiwanaku and Wari civilisations, the Chimú fell to conquest rather than suffering a system collapse. The Chimú resisted the Inca, but were eventually defeated. Their administrative structure was largely dismantled. Lower-level administrators kept their jobs, albeit after some reorganisation. There was at least one rebellion against Inca rule, but the execution of the rebel leaders brought about the end of all organised resistance. The Inca did not occupy Chan Chan, but they constructed a regional centre on the road linking it to the neighbouring Chicama Valley. A major centre was established in the highland Cajamarca Valley. Many elements of Chimú culture were retained by the Inca, including fine textiles and ceramics. Indeed, these now enjoyed a broader distribution under the Inca than they had under the Chimú. The Inca undoubtedly appreciated the prestige of Chimú culture.[47]

The Spanish Conquest of the New World

Like the Aztec, a full account of the Inca is beyond the scope of this work. Although the expansion of the Inca occurred quite late in pre-Columbian times, Inca origins go back to around AD 1000 and the collapse of the Wari. Originally, over a dozen ethnic minorities were present in a 100 km (62 mile) radius of the future Inca capital of Cuzco. Over time, these rival polities either allied themselves peacefully with the Inca, or were conquered. Some groups, such as the Mohena, came into repeated conflict with the Inca before they were defeated. Having gained control over their heartland, the Inca began a period of aggressive expansion. The Titicaca region was occupied, followed by the sierra to the north and the coastal regions. Able to draw on a vast labour force, the Inca embarked on major engineering projects, including the construction of up to 40,000 km (24,800 miles) of major roads in order to link up their empire.[4,3]

By the time of the Spanish conquest, the Tahuantinsuyu ('Land of the Four Quarters') was probably the largest nation in the world. The Inca realm extended more than 5,500 km (3,400 miles) down the Andean spine of South America, roughly the distance from London to New York. It included northern Chile, the uplands of Argentina, Bolivia, Peru, Ecuador and southern Columbia. No present-day Andean state approaches it in size. Conquistador accounts claim that the splendour of the Inca capital Cuzco was unmatched in Europe.[4,3]

We can but speculate as to how the Aztec and Inca empires might have fared had the New World remained isolated from the Old for just a few more centuries. Possibly they would have suffered ultimate collapse as did their predecessors; conceivably the two empires might have come into conflict. In the event, their fate was to be very different. With the arrival of the Spanish, the Aztec faced invaders that were equipped with horses, steel armour, swords, lances and firearms.[50] The technological gulf was comparable to that between late Victorian armed forces and Martian fighting machines. Tenochtitlán fell in August 1521, just 2 ½ years after Cortés and his modest invasion force of eleven ships had sailed from Cuba. The Inca fared no better. In November 1532, Francisco Pizarro and his force of just 168 Spaniards prevailed against 80,000 Inca, capturing the Inca ruler Atahuallpa in the process. Atahuallpa was later executed, despite a substantial ransom being paid for his release. The following year, Cuzco was taken by the Spaniards.

H.G. Wells' invading Martians were finally vanquished by Terrestrial diseases to which they had no immunity. In the New World, it was the other way round. A single infected slave brought smallpox to Mexico in 1520, triggering epidemics that reduced an initial population of 20 million to just 1.6 million within a century. After spreading overland, smallpox reached Peru in 1526. The resulting epidemic killed much of the Inca population, including the emperor Huayna Capac and his designated successor. The resulting war of succession considerably aided the cause of the Conquistadors.[50]

In the last seven chapters, we have reviewed how V. Gordon Childe's 'Urban Revolution' occurred in various places around the world. Today, more or less the whole of the Earth's habitable landmass is under the jurisdiction of state-level governments, although in many cases this is more theoretical than actual. To those of us who have spent our lives in the developed world, the idea of living in a particular 'country' – Britain, France, the United States, etc. – is so normal that it is difficult to appreciate that states did not exist until 6,000 years ago, and that they did not become widespread until much later. Just as Hernán Cortés found he was able to relate to Aztec society, so we would probably feel more at home in any of the early states we have reviewed than in a present-day hunter-gatherer group. It is for this reason that that states are generally viewed as being the natural order of things, that 'civilised' is good, and 'uncivilised' bad. In an increasingly precarious world, we urgently need to adopt a more critical perspective.

32: Humans: the future

The technological ape

In this brief journey through human prehistory, we have followed the human story from our primate origins to the rise of state-level societies. In many ways, we have changed very little since we diverged from the chimpanzees. We are, like them, gregarious apes living in a hierarchical society. In both cases, those at the top enjoy privileges not available to others. The main difference is that humans use symbols and chimpanzees do not.

There is little doubt that archaic humans were capable of symbolic thought, though the extent is disputed, and the ability may not even be entirely absent from chimpanzees. However, its expression in modern humans is not found elsewhere and it sets us apart from the rest of the animal kingdom past and present. From the point at which they became behaviourally modern, humans could adapt their technology to the widely differing environments far more rapidly than evolution could adapt their bodies. They could also adapt environments to their needs: the practice of burning vegetation to promote the growth of useful plants may well predate the dispersal of modern humans from Africa.

The consequences of this extraordinary adaptability were that by the end of the last Ice Age, modern humans were established in every continent on Earth barring Antarctica. No other single species of large mammal has ever achieved a near-global distribution. Furthermore, it was achieved in the face of the climatic instability of the Late Pleistocene, when even staying in the same place offered no guarantee that radically different environmental conditions would not at some stage have to be faced.

With the end of the Ice Age and the spread of V. Gordon Childe's two 'revolutions', rising populations, greater social complexity, greater competition and better communications led to increased innovation. The rate of innovation increased dramatically after the Industrial Revolution: for the first time, significant technological changes were occurring within a single lifetime. Probably the most dramatic example was the first landing on the Moon in 1969 – just 66 years after the Wright Brothers first flew a powered aircraft at Kitty Hawk.

We live in an age where hardly a month goes by without the high-profile release of the latest must-have consumer gadget. When I was at university back in the 1970s, digital wristwatches and electronic calculators were considered hi-tech. A hand-held electronic organiser known as a 'minisec' was featured in Sir Arthur C. Clarke's 1975 science fiction novel *Imperial Earth*, set in the year 2276.[1] I never expected to see such devices in my lifetime – but it did not take 30 years, much less 300, for them to become commonplace. By 2010, they were obsolete, superseded by the smartphone.

Within the same timescale, the relentless logic of Moore's Law[2] transformed computers from room-filling cabinets found only at the offices of large companies to standard household appliances, as unremarkable as television sets, cookers and vacuum cleaners. Computer networking developed from pioneer systems such as ARPANET, used by universities and government agencies, to the present-day World Wide Web.

There is little doubt that *Homo sapiens* are a very successful species; equally, nobody would doubt that our position is now as precarious as that of our distant African ancestors, five million years ago. The difference is that our troubles are largely of our own making.

Breaking the glass ceiling

Throughout the Pleistocene, world-wide human populations were undoubtedly fairly low, and such population growth that did occur was probably due to the colonisation of previously uninhabited regions. Humans at this point were still just one of many species of large mammal inhabiting the Earth, and notwithstanding their use of symbols they were subject to the same carrying capacity-related constraints on population growth as everything else. All this changed with the Late Quaternary mass extinctions, when much of this biodiversity was lost (see Chapter 16).

The exponential growth in the world's human population began in the latter part of the last Ice Age.[3] By 8000 BC, early in agricultural times, the world population stood at around five million, and by the start of the Christian era the total had increased to around 300 million.[4] These estimates are doubtless highly inaccurate, but if taken at face value they represent a 60-fold increase in 8,000 years, or a doubling every 1,350 years. Taking a generation in that era to be approximately 20 years, this represents about 65 to 70 generations.

Such a rate of growth for a population of large mammals can only happen in the presence of abundant resources and the absence of natural enemies. In the human case, of course, much food was now being produced by agriculture and the only dangerous predators faced by humans were other humans. Surprisingly, this rate of growth was not maintained for much of the Christian era, despite the civilisations by then present in much of the world. By AD 1650, the population had reached just 500 million.[4] It has been suggested that the slowdown was due to the devastating bubonic plague pandemics that repeatedly swept Eurasia during this period.[4] However, there may be another explanation.

All living things rely on the Sun for energy and growth, either directly in the case of plants and other photosynthesising organisms, or indirectly in the case of animals. In essence, solar energy is converted into biomass, and thus Earth's total biomass is limited by the amount of energy it receives from the Sun. Before the extinctions, the solar energy available for conversion to biomass by megafauna was shared between many species. With the extinctions, megafaunal biomass crashed, creating an energy surplus. In past extinctions, such as that of the dinosaurs, crashes have been followed by explosions in biodiversity, as new species evolve to exploit the energy surplus.[3] The aftermath of the Late Quaternary extinction saw a very different outcome.

As we have seen, the end of the Ice Age saw the rise and spread of agriculture in many places around the world, which enabled far larger human populations to be supported than could be sustained by hunter-gathering. Humans were not the first animal species to produce their own food; ants are thought to have learned the trick 45 to 65 million years ago.[5] The consequences, though, were far more significant. Instead of remaining available to support reestablishment of megafaunal biodiversity, solar energy was co-opted by humans to raise crops and livestock. In effect, the energy surplus was being converted into human biomass. The Earth's large animal biomass regained pre-crash levels just before the Industrial Revolution, but now it was dominated by just one species – *Homo sapiens*. However, the same energetic constraints still applied. It is likely that the population slowdown occurred as the total human biomass approached the glass ceiling that had hitherto limited the size of Earth's megafauna population.[3]

The Industrial Revolution began in Britain between 1760 and 1780.[6] With it, Earth's human populations began to rocket, reaching one billion in 1804; two billion by 1927; three billion by 1960;[7]

and seven billion in 2013. Thanks to increasing availability of family planning and contraception, the global fertility rate (i.e. the average number of children per woman) has fallen from a peak of 5.02 for the period from 1960 to 1965 to 2.53 for the period from 2005 to 2010. Even if this decline continues, however, the UN estimates that the world's population will stand at 9.6 billion by 2050 and 10.9 billion by 2100.[8] Some believe the figure could exceed 12 billion.[9]

Biologist Anthony Barnosky[3] has suggested that the addition of fossil fuels to the global energy budget enabled the human population to break through the glass ceiling. The use of fossil fuels for heating goes back to Roman times,[10] but their use for mechanical power had to await the invention of the steam engine. Without mechanical power, the food production and distribution that supports current global populations would not be possible. If Barnosky is correct, a global population more than an order of magnitude greater than Earth's natural carrying capacity is being supported by a non-renewable resource. Even without the deleterious effects of CO_2 emissions, this is a worrying prospect.

Close to a tipping point

As we have seen, climate change has been the constant companion both of our species and of earlier hominins. One must strongly resist the temptation to think that because we came though it in the past, we should not be overly worried. We simply cannot draw parallels between today and the relatively low-tech societies that existed in an era when the world population was at a fraction of today's level.

So-called 'greenhouse gases' absorb energy from the Sun that would otherwise be reflected back into space. While this effect is highly beneficial up to a point, an excess of greenhouse gases results in global warming. The most important greenhouse gases are water vapour (H_2O), carbon dioxide (CO_2), methane (CH_4), nitrous oxide (N_2O), and ozone (O_3). Anthropogenic CO_2 emissions arise principally from the use of fossil fuels and from deforestation, with a smaller amount arising from the manufacture of cement. Deforestation and forest degradation contribute to CO_2 emissions through combustion of forest biomass and decomposition of remaining plant material and soil carbon. Especially in the tropics, deforestation may account for up to a third of all anthropogenic CO_2 emissions. Anthropogenic methane largely arises from wet rice agriculture, the herding of cattle, sheep and goats, and from landfill waste disposal sites. Nitrous oxide is also a product of agricultural activities. Ozone levels in the troposphere (lower atmosphere) have increased by 38 percent since pre-industrial times as a result of atmospheric reactions involving short-lived anthropogenic pollutants.[11,12]

The effect of anthropogenic emissions has been a warming trend unprecedented since the end of the last Ice Age. After the climatic optimum of the Early Holocene, a long-term cooling trend began after 3000 BC, and this continued right up to the beginning of the last century. Average global temperatures for the decade from 1900 to 1909 were cooler than those prevalent for 95 percent of the Holocene. The situation 100 years later shows a dramatic reversal. Average global temperatures for the decade from 2000 to 2009 did not exceed Early Holocene peaks, but were still warmer than for about 72 to 82 percent of the Holocene.[13] Global temperatures increased by 0.75 degrees Celsius during the last century.[14]

The 2009 Copenhagen Accord recognised that global temperature increases should be kept to below 2 degrees Celsius relative to pre-industrial levels, but it is unlikely that this limit will be achievable. Rises of between 3 and 4 degrees Celsius are more realistic, possibly by as early as the 2070s.[15,16] It should be noted that these figures represent average global temperatures. There will be regional variations, and greater than average increases will occur in many continental interiors. Higher latitudes will see increased rainfall; regions such as Central America, the Mediterranean, North Africa, India and parts of Southeast Asia will see rainfall decrease.[17]

Even a 2 degrees Celsius rise is now thought to be dangerous,[15] but the consequence of a 4 degrees Celsius increase will be far-reaching. Water shortages will become common in dryer parts of the world[18] and there will be a significant impact on agriculture, particularly in sub-Saharan Africa.[19] Meanwhile, sea-level rises could displace up to 187 million people by 2100.[20] Extreme weather events and water shortages could also lead to population displacements.[21]

Another serious consequence of anthropogenic CO_2 emissions is ocean acidification. Approximately half of the anthropogenic CO_2 emissions of the last 200 years have been absorbed by Earth's oceans. When CO_2 dissolves in water, it forms carbonic acid. This is a weak acid, and in seawater its effects are partly buffered. It is nevertheless responsible for lowering the pH of the oceans by 0.1 (in chemistry, a lower pH corresponds to greater acidity), and this could reach 0.5 by 2100. Even if atmospheric CO_2 was to return to pre-industrial levels, it would take thousands of years for natural processes to remove the excess CO_2 from the oceans. Marine ecosystems are highly sensitive to oceanic pH and even small changes could affect biodiversity and impact the total productivity of the oceans. Coral reefs, phytoplankton, zooplankton, molluscs, and even large marine animals are liable to be adversely affected, with potentially serious consequences for the entire marine food chain.[22]

Worryingly, anthropogenic emissions may be only part of the problem facing Earth's biosphere. Anthony Barnosky and his colleagues[23] note that intentional environment modification has now converted 43 percent of the Earth's land surface to urban or agricultural use. This is a greater change than the 30 percent that became free of ice at the end of the last Ice Age. Even without global warming and other anthropogenic effects, such a change would be likely to have significant consequences. As things stand, Barnosky and his colleagues warn that Earth's biosphere is on the brink of an irreversible 'state shift' or tipping point that would see it undergo massive and unpredictable changes. The last such shift was the transition from the Pleistocene to Holocene. Others include the 'Big Five' mass extinctions. The largest of these, the Permian, brought about the extinction of up to 90 percent of the species then living.[24]

What is to be done?

It is not difficult to see, indeed it is fairly obvious what is required if a global crisis is to be averted or at least mitigated. We must reduce anthropogenic greenhouse gas emissions to below dangerous levels, and we must preserve the planet's remaining biodiversity and undamaged ecosystems. To these ends, we must aim to eliminate the use of fossil fuels; use only sustainable resources (food, timber, etc.); and make no further encroachment into parts of the world not yet converted to human use (forests, etc.). We must make more efficient use of the resources at our disposal (agricultural land, energy, etc.). The most pressing questions are how do we sustainably feed a still-increasing global population, and how do we curb fossil fuel use? Unfortunately, there are no 'magic bullet' answers to either question.

To meet the demands of an increasing population, the world's food supply must roughly double within the next few decades. Access and distribution must be improved, and the food system must be made more resilient to climatic disturbances, diseases and economic disruption. At the same time, steps must be taken to reduce agriculture-related greenhouse emissions, unsustainable water usage for irrigation, and the impact of fertilisers on water quality, aquatic ecosystems and marine fisheries. All of this must be accomplished without further losses of habitat and biodiversity.[25]

On the face of it, this may sound like trying to square the circle. In fact, there are many ways in which agricultural productivity could be sustainably improved. In a report published in the journal *Nature*, a group of 21 environmentalists[25] suggest that four basic strategies must be adopted. Firstly, agricultural expansion must be halted. The benefits of tropical deforestation are limited, as regions cleared for agriculture are less productive than their temperate counterparts. Secondly, studies have identified 'yield gaps' in many parts of the world, where crop yields fall significantly below their potential. Effort should be focused on trying to eliminate or at least reduce these gaps. Thirdly, there is a clear need for better management of water and fertiliser use. In places where water is scarce, crops that require less water should be grown and evaporation losses reduced by mulching and reduced tillage. In many parts of the world, there is a shortage of fertiliser, leading to yield gaps; yet in other parts, over-use of fertiliser leads to widespread environmental damage. Fourthly, inefficiency and waste must be tackled. Livestock feed currently accounts for 35 percent of the world's crop production. Simple measures could reduce this figure, such as a shift from grain-fed beef to poultry, pork or pasture-fed beef. Enormous food wastage occurs due to inadequate storage and transportation facilities, destruction by pests, and other causes. It has been suggested than anything from a third to a half of all food grown is never eaten.

The report suggests that if all four strategies were adopted simultaneously, global food availability would be increased by anything between 100 and 180 percent, a figure that would meet projected demands while lowering greenhouse gas emissions, biodiversity losses, water use, and water pollution. The report warns that all four strategies will be required, and that no single strategy will be sufficient on its own. To put them into action will not be easy. Fortunately, many of the required tactics exist, including precision agriculture, drip irrigation, organic soil remedies, buffer strips and wetland restoration, new crop varieties that reduce needs for water and fertiliser, perennial grains and tree-cropping systems, and paying farmers for environmental services. The challenges facing agriculture are unprecedented, but the emphasis must be on systems that maximise the benefit to those most in need, while at the same time minimising environmental damage.

The second major challenge to curb fossil fuel use in a world that is as hungry for energy as it is for food. Here again, no all-embracing solution exists – at least not with our current technology. After World War II, there was a widespread view that nuclear power would be the solution to the world's energy needs. There was much talk about 'taming' the terrible energies that had been unleashed upon Hiroshima and Nagasaki, but to date these hopes have not been realised. All present-day nuclear power is derived from fission, where heavy elements such as enriched uranium are used as fuel. The well-publicised issues with fission include core meltdown, radioactive waste, end-of-life decommissioning, nuclear proliferation, and the threat of terrorism. Fusion – basically the same process that occurs in the Sun – is far more promising. The energy output is far greater and in radiological terms it is far cleaner. Unfortunately, despite decades of research, practical fusion power is likely to still be some decades away, making it too far off to play any significant role in climate stabilisation.[26]

In recent years, there has been much interest in biofuel. Obtaining ethanol and diesel fuel from plants is on the face of it very appealing. These fuels emit CO_2 like their non-bio counterparts, but this is balanced by the CO_2 taken up by the precursor plants. The problem with using food plants to produce fuel is that they are no longer available for use as food. Sharp increases in global food prices have been blamed on the use of maize and sugar cane for biofuel production.[27] Newer 'second generation' biofuels hold more promise. Woody plants and prairie grasses are more expensive to process, but they can be produced on agriculturally-marginal land and have minimal needs in terms of fertilisers and pesticides.[28] The use of algae as a precursor is promising, but could still be some years away from being commercially viable.[29] Ultimately, the problem with biofuel is that the energy density of photosynthesis (i.e. the amount of solar energy absorbed by photosynthesising plants per unit area of land) is too low to make a major contribution to climate stabilisation.[26]

Wind and solar power are both mature technologies, and have been used to generate electricity for decades. Wind turbines are now a major provider of electricity in many parts of the world. In 2012, the installed capacity throughout the European Union stood at 11.9 GW – enough to supply seven percent of the EU's electricity.[30] In recent years, solar power has come of age. The price of photovoltaic panels has fallen dramatically, with the result that the cost per watt of solar power is now competitive with conventional sources of electricity.[31] In addition to solar power stations, many homes, offices and factories now use roof-mounted solar panels to augment the grid-based supply. The main problem with these technologies is what to do if the wind isn't blowing or the sun isn't shining. One solution is to link together national grids into a 'super-grid' to smooth out local shortfalls. In the case of solar power, another solution may be to use solar energy to produce hydrogen rather than electricity. The hydrogen is then used in a fuel cell to generate electricity at night or on cloudy days.

Other well-proven technologies include hydroelectric, tidal and geothermal power – all requiring fairly specific geographic and geologic conditions. In fact, there is no renewable technology that represents a 'one size fits all' solution. Different solutions will be appropriate to different local conditions. A concern is that vested interests and political considerations can all too easily get in the way of the bigger picture. For example, it does not make sense to cover prime agricultural land with solar panels. For any scheme, the impact on wildlife and other environmental considerations must be fully taken into account.

We must accept that fossil fuels are not going to go away overnight, and much emphasis has been placed on mitigating the impact of CO_2 emissions. Schemes such as carbon trading are widely used to enable nations to meet their emission reduction targets specified by the Kyoto Protocol. Stabilising atmospheric CO_2 concentration at 500 parts per million is thought likely to avoid the worst effects of climate change.[32] This is less than double the pre-industrial concentration of 280 ppm, but it might not be achievable. The psychological 400 ppm milestone was passed in May 2013.

The Carbon Mitigation Initiative at Princeton University has proposed a series of 'stabilisation wedges' aimed at reducing carbon emissions by 200 billion tonnes over the next fifty years. Fifteen 'wedges' or measures were listed, of which seven needed to be adopted to meet the target. The measures are firmly based on existing technologies and include more fuel-efficient vehicle engines, reduced vehicle use, more energy-efficient buildings, the use of various renewables (including nuclear), carbon capture (where CO_2 emissions are captured at source and stored), and reduced deforestation.[32]

How hopeful can we be that a global crisis will be averted? All of the measures outlined above can be adopted with our existing technology. What is required is the will to do so. It will be necessary for governments, trade blocs and multinationals to look beyond their own vested interests. This means reviewing tariffs, subsidies and trade agreements. Ideally, the UN should take a paramount role, for which it will require more authority than it presently has.

Dyson Spheres and other speculations

If – and it's a big 'if' – humanity makes it through the twenty-first century, what may the future hold? One must bear in mind at this point that there is a fine dividing line between speculation and science fiction. Nevertheless, it seems reasonable to suppose that by the end of the century, access to space will have become as commonplace as air travel is now. There is likely to be a permanent presence on the Moon and quite possibly on Mars also. Mining asteroids for industrial metals and other resources is also likely to become a reality. Almost certainly private enterprise will play a key role in these developments, as it did with aviation in the last century. Already, the privately built and operated reusable Dragon spacecraft is being used to resupply the International Space Station, and a crew-carrying version is planned.

Some believe that we should go beyond setting up bases on other planets and establish colonies on these worlds. They argue that humanity cannot afford to put its eggs in one basket and remain confined to Earth. Within the Solar System, the only possibility is Mars. The planet lies on the outer edge of the Sun's habitable zone, i.e. it is neither too close to the Sun and thus too hot, nor too far away and thus too cold. Mars might once have supported life and it is possible that it could be 'terraformed', i.e. given oceans and a breathable atmosphere.

Eventually, human colonies may be established on habitable planets beyond the Solar System. Interstellar travel will obviously be very difficult, especially if (as seems almost certain) it turns out that Einstein was right and faster-than-light travel is impossible. In which case, one solution is the 'generation ship' where space travellers embark on a voyage that will be completed by their descendants, centuries later. Another possibility is the 'sleeper ship', where the colonists are put into suspended animation for the duration of the voyage. Alternatively, a purely robotic spacecraft may carry human genomic data stored as computer files. Human colonists would then be reared *in vitro* when the spacecraft reached its target planet.

Ambitious as these proposals may sound, they are dwarfed by the suggestion that sufficiently advanced civilisations will capture much of the energy output of their parent stars by surrounding them with a spherical shell or a ring of artificial planets. The construction material required for such a project would be obtained by dismantling Jupiter-sized planets. The concept can be traced back to the 1937 science fiction novel *Star Maker*, by Olaf Stapledon,[33] but was elaborated by British-born physicist Freeman Dyson in the 1960s.[34,35] What is now known as the Dyson Sphere is probably no more fantastical than a modern skyscraper would have seemed to the hunter-gathers of Ice Age Europe. A detailed proposal for constructing a Dyson Sphere was put forward by astronomer Iain Nicolson and journalist Adrian Berry in 1974, and it was suggested that construction could begin in as little as a thousand years.[36] Berry[37] suggests that humanity will not remain confined to the Solar System and will spread from star to star: planets and indeed stars will be dismantled in order to provide the construction materials for more Dyson Spheres, and within ten million years humanity could have spread across the entire galaxy.

What could our species become within these timescales? Some believe that profound changes may occur within decades rather than centuries. Inventor and Google director Ray Kurzweil[38] has predicted that during the first half of this century, revolutions in genetics and nanotechnology will enable aging to be postponed more or less indefinitely. The body's organs will be augmented and eventually replaced by these technologies. Within the same timescale, machine intelligence will advance to the point where it far outstrips human intelligence. What Kurzweil terms the Singularity will occur by around 2045. Eventually, humans will become non-biological entities that will go on to fill not just the galaxy but the entire universe. Even if the advances Kurzweil envisages for 2045 are not actually realised for several centuries, this is still a breathtakingly short period of time in evolutionary terms.

The main problem with the above speculations is that they raise a question. If it is possible for an advanced civilisation to spread across the galaxy and beyond, why has one not already done so?

Where are they?

In 1950, while working at Los Alamos National Laboratory, the Italian physicist Enrico Fermi is said to have posed the question *"Where are they?"* The argument is that a spacefaring civilisation would be able to colonise the entire galaxy within a comparatively short period of time, 'planet hopping' in a manner analogous to the Austronesian expansion into the Pacific (see Chapter 23). The Sun is a fairly young star, little over a third of the age of the galaxy. There has been plenty of time for an alien expansion to take place. Yet aliens have not colonised Earth, nor have they made any attempt to contact us. Dyson Spheres cannot be particularly common, much less galaxy-filling. Dyson[34] noted that they would be visible in the far infrared and readily detectable from Earth. None have been found, not even with the latest orbital infrared space telescopes.

Logically, there are only few explanations for why we have not heard from ET:

1. The zoo hypothesis (popularised in *Star Trek* as the Prime Directive). Aliens are aware of our existence, but Earth has been placed out of bounds until humans reach a certain level of technical and/or ethical attainment;
2. We are alone. Earth is the first and only planet (at least in this galaxy and its neighbourhood) to have hosted a technological civilisation;
3. Any technological civilisation must invariably wipe itself out before interstellar travel can develop;
4. Long-lived alien civilisations exist, but rarely undertake interstellar travel, and have no desire to fill the galaxy with their presence.

We cannot categorically rule out the zoo hypothesis, but my feeling is that it is not very likely. Without faster-than-light travel, it would be more or less impossible to impose a central authority on a civilisation that had spread across the galaxy. There can be no star empires or federations when it can take tens of thousands of years for the constituents to communicate. Again, there is an analogy with the Pacific islands, which were independent chiefdoms and kingdoms. The distances involved precluded any form of empire, or contact other than between closer neighbours. While some groups within range of Earth may have a Prime Directive, others possibly may not.

Could Earth be the first and only planet where intelligent life has arisen? It seems unlikely. We now know that planetary systems are commonplace in the galaxy. As of 2014, the definite existence of almost 900 extra-solar planets has been confirmed. The robotic Kepler Space Observatory has found over 3,000 candidate planets, though most have yet to be confirmed. Increasingly-sensitive observation techniques are now turning up Earth and 'super Earth'-sized planets that lie within the habitable zone of their parent star. These include Gliese 581 g, one of six planets orbiting the red dwarf Gliese 581.[39] The smallest component of the triple system Gliese 667, also a red dwarf, has no fewer than three planets in its habitable zone.[40] Gliese 581 is located just 20.3 light-years from Earth and Gliese 667 is only slightly further away at 22 light-years. Red dwarfs are much smaller than the Sun, but a recent study of the Kepler data indicated that almost a quarter of Sun-like stars may have Earth-sized planets orbiting within their habitable zones. If this figure is correct, the nearest such planet may lie within 12 light-years of Earth.[41] While we do not know if any of these planets are actually inhabited, the results suggest that habitable planets are not uncommon and that there is nothing particularly unusual about Earth.

Also, life on Earth arose very soon after the planet had cooled from its initially molten state. Cyanobacteria-like microorganisms were existent and diverse by 3,465 million years ago.[42] It took longer for eukaryotic (nucleated) organisms to arise, but both fossil and molecular evidence suggest that they were present by around 1,800 million years ago,[43] and tentative fossil evidence may push this date back to over 3,000 million years ago.[44] It could be that if a planet can support life, it will invariably arise there.

Intelligence and technological civilisation may be another matter. British physicist Paul Davies[45] suggests that if the Darwinian view of evolution is correct, then intelligence is purely a chance phenomenon, unlikely to arise more than once. The problem with this view is that if a feature is sufficiently useful, it will arise more than once. Wings have arisen four times in Earth's history (insects, pterosaurs, birds and bats). As we have seen, human intelligence arose out of primate sociality. Given that social behaviour is very common in the animal kingdom, it seems perfectly reasonable to suppose that intelligence could arise repeatedly.

The next possibility is that technological civilisations, by their very nature, are short-lived. Could this be so? Even if our own civilisation permanently collapses, does this mean that the same will happen everywhere else? The so-called Doomsday Argument, proposed among others by astrophysicist Brandon Carter and philosopher John Leslie, suggests that it probably will. The basic premise is that if the total number of humans that will ever exist is N, then we are most likely to find ourselves living at a point in time where roughly ½ N humans have already been born. Given that the world population is now increasing at a very rapid rate, it will only be a few centuries before the remaining ½ N have also been born, and humanity's day will be done. If the argument is correct, then the countdown to doomsday began at the end of the last Ice Age, when populations began to increase as agriculture spread. The same fate would befall any alien species that discovers agriculture.

In fact, more detailed formulations of the Doomsday Argument rely on probability and statistics. They do not state that doom is inevitable, only highly likely. Nevertheless, I am highly sceptical about an argument that completely ignores the facts on the ground. Let us suppose that Earth had had far fewer fossil fuel deposits. The Industrial Revolution would never have happened, and human society would have remained predominantly agrarian. As we have seen, prior to the Industrial Revolution, the population increase looked to be bottoming out. Such a society would avoid most of the perils we now face, yet the Doomsday Argument would still apply. Doom would be postponed, but only by a few millennia at most. Another question is what would have happened if somebody had pondered the problem much earlier, say around 8000 BC, when the total number of humans that had ever been born (½ N) was probably not much more than a billion? By the start of the Christian era, the total had increased almost fifty-fold[4] – but if ½ N was only just over a billion, humanity should by that time have been long extinct.

The Doomsday Argument has been around for thirty years now, during which time nobody appears to have convincingly refuted it. I nevertheless think it is better seen as an interesting philosophical problem rather than a genuine threat to our future, or to the existence of extraterrestrial intelligence. All in all, it does not seem unreasonable to conclude that extraterrestrial civilisations have arisen elsewhere in the galaxy, and at least some of them are still in existence. This leaves us with only the last possibility. Long-lived alien civilisations simply do not embark on galaxy-spanning colonisation programs. Possibly aggressive, expansive civilisations are the very ones that self-destruct before they get very far. It could be that once a mature civilisation has survived the issues that we are now facing, it loses any desire for large-scale expansion.

Conclusion

The message could not be clearer. If we are to survive as a species, we should concentrate on the many problems we face here on Earth. Even at current population levels, much of the world does not have enough to eat. Around 870 million people in the developing world are chronically undernourished.[46] According to World Bank figures for 2010, around 1,220 million people lived on less than US$ 1.25 per day and 2,400 million on less than US$ 2.00 per day. The latter figure is considered to be the average poverty line in the developing world.[47]

Nobody would dispute that eliminating these evils must be the aim of any responsible global society. Furthermore, it is hardly unreasonable that people in the developing world should aspire to a moderately-comfortable developed world standard of living. From an ecological point of view, can the economic growth required to make this a reality be sustained? The answer, probably, is 'no'. If the world's population stabilises at 10 billion or so, most will have to accept a much lower standard of living. The 'population optimum' may be no more than two or three billion. A managed (as opposed to catastrophic) reduction to these levels is unlikely to be achieved for at least two centuries.[48]

It is important to realise that we are not the end-product of over three billion years of evolution. We are just one of innumerable evolutionary outcomes, and in that respect we are no more 'advanced' than birds, bees or bacteria. Our ability to use symbols should be seen as just another evolutionary adaptation. We must accordingly see ourselves in the context of the millions of other species with which we share this planet, and realise that is not our exclusive domain. It will certainly not be easy to tackle the many problems we face as a species, but tackle them we must if we are not to follow our hominin forbears into extinction.

Maps, infographics and plates

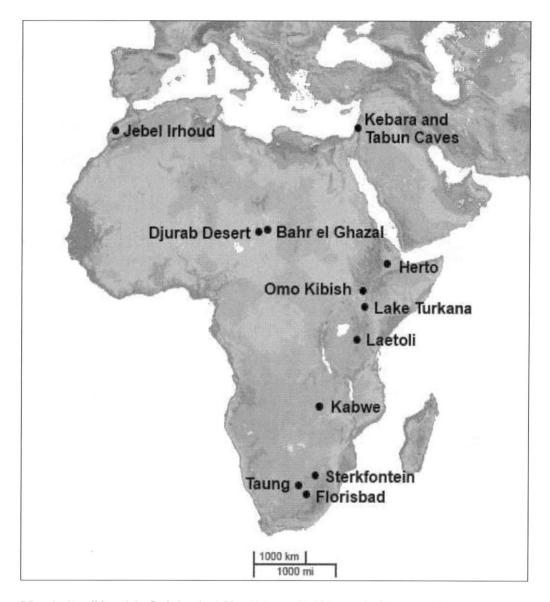

Map 1: Fossil hominin find sites in Africa (7.4m to 50,000 years before present)

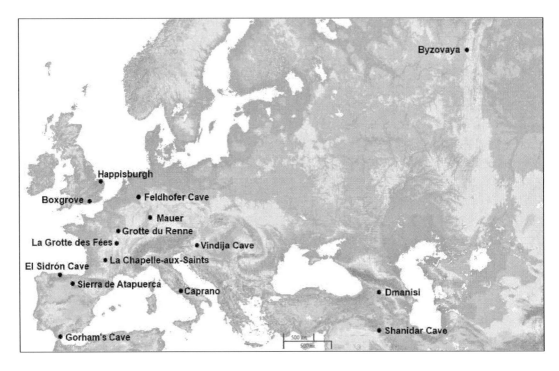

Map 2: Fossil hominin find sites in western Eurasia (850,000 to 30,000 years before present)

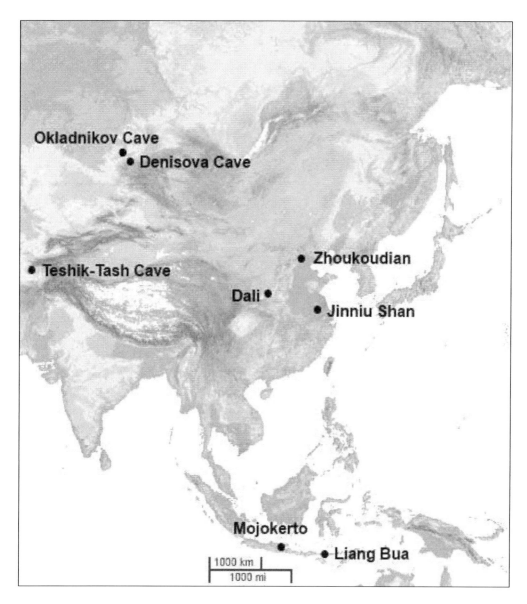

Map 3: Fossil hominin find sites in eastern Eurasia (1.81m to 50,000 years before present)

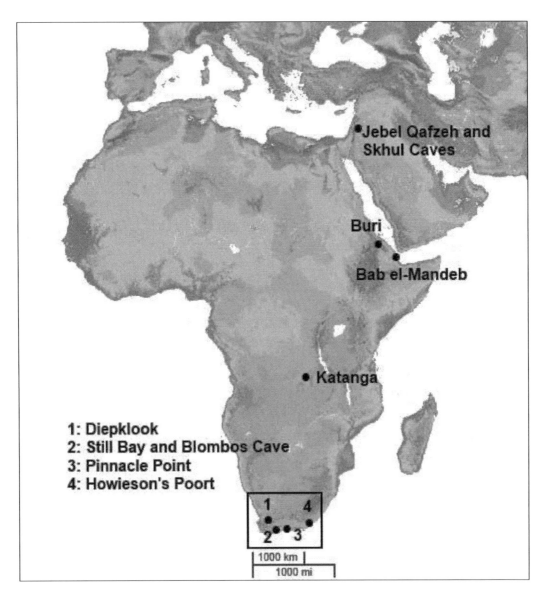

Jebel Qafzeh and Skhul Caves

Buri

Bab el-Mandeb

Katanga

1: Diepklook
2: Still Bay and Blombos Cave
3: Pinnacle Point
4: Howieson's Poort

1
4
2
3

1000 km
1000 mi

Map 4: Early modern human sites in Africa (165,000 to 60,000 years before present)

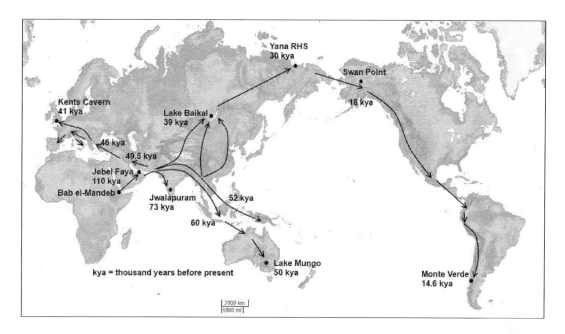

Map 5: Dispersal of modern humans around the world (110,000 to 14,600 years before present)

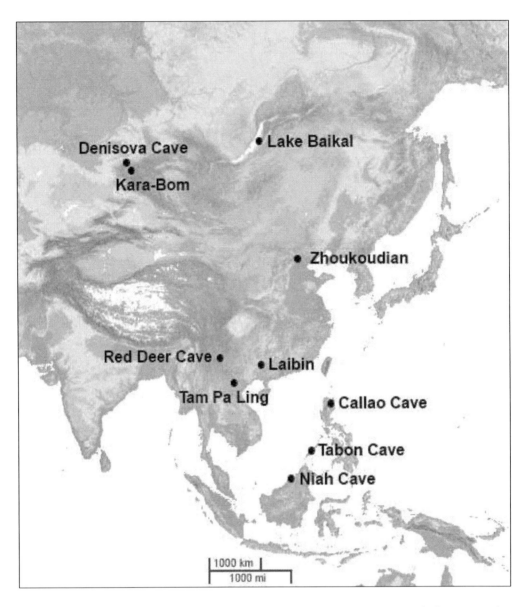

Map 6: Dispersal of modern humans into East Asia (60,000 to 20,000 years before present)

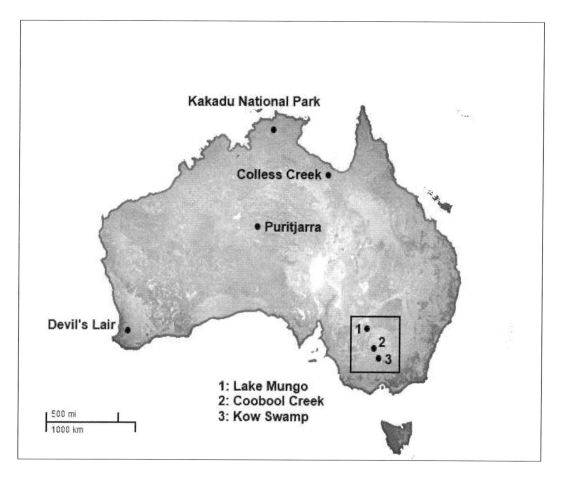

Map 7: Dispersal of modern humans into Australia (60,000 to 20,000 years before present)

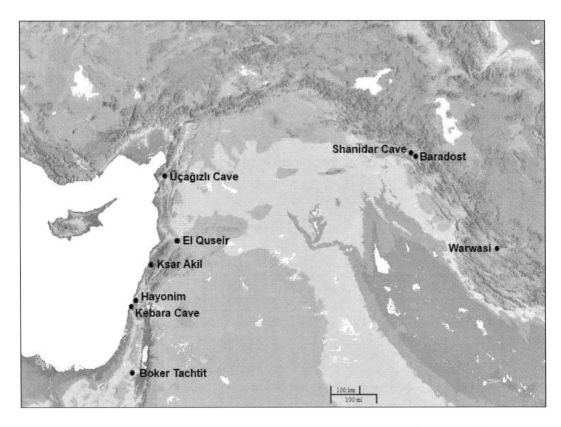

Map 8: Dispersal of modern humans into Southwest Asia (50,000 years before present)

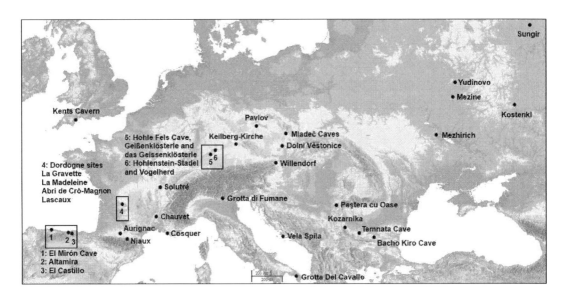

Map 9: Dispersal of modern humans into Europe (46,000 years before present)

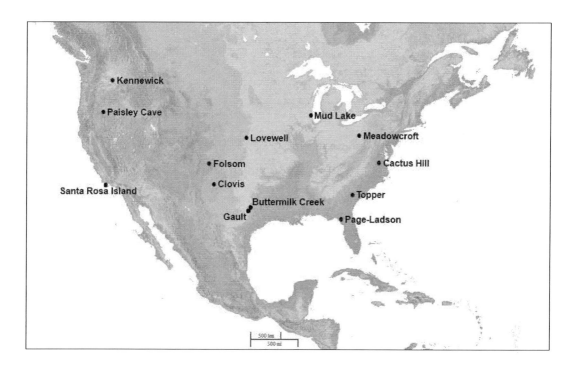

Map 10: Dispersal of modern humans into the United States (18,000 years before present)

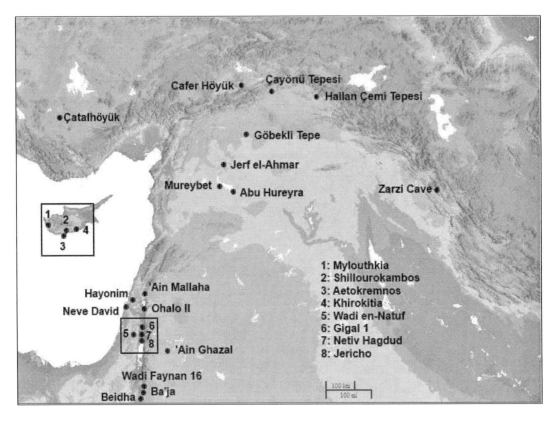

Map 11: Epipalaeolithic and Neolithic sites in Southwest Asia (21,000 to 6500 BC)

Maps, infographics and plates

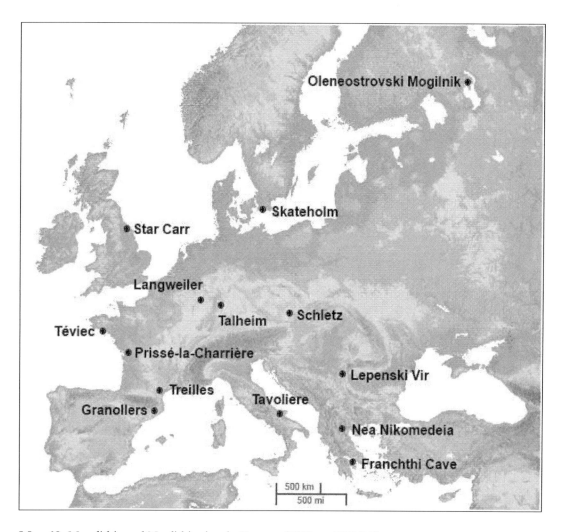

Map 12: Mesolithic and Neolithic sites in Europe (9500 to 4000 BC)

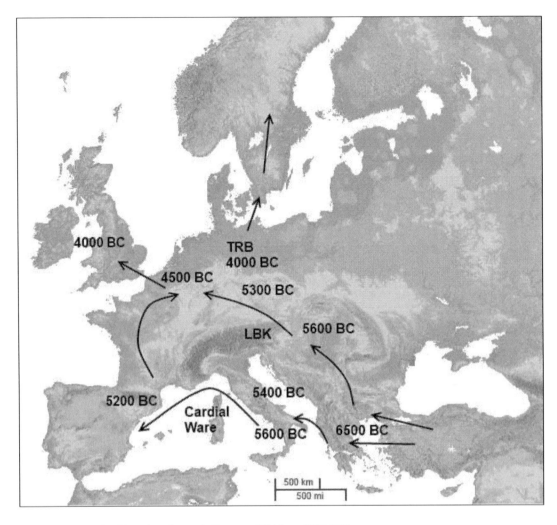

Map 13: Spread of farming through Europe (6500 to 4000 BC)

Maps, infographics and plates

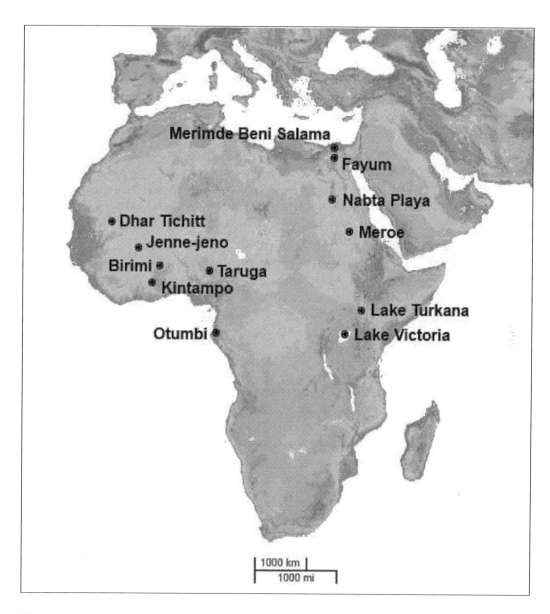

Map 14: Early agricultural and ironworking sites in Africa (9000 to 1200 BC)

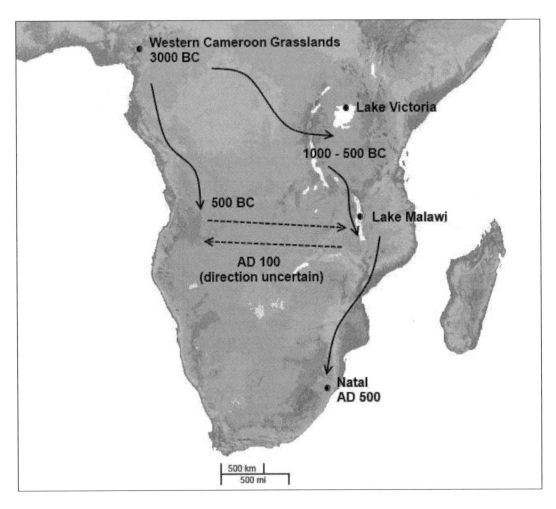

Map 15: Bantu expansion (3000 BC to AD 500)

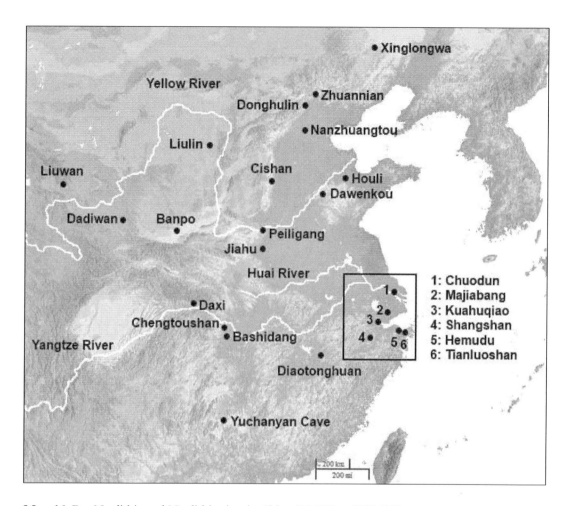

Map 16: Pre-Neolithic and Neolithic sites in China (16,300 to 3000 BC)

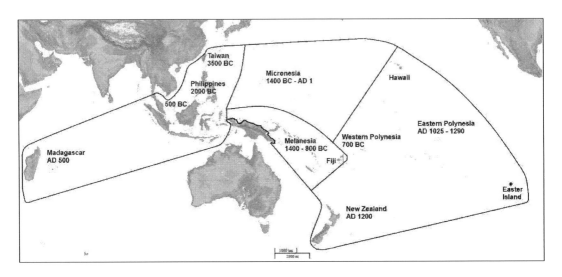

Map 17: Austronesian expansion (3500 BC to AD 1290)

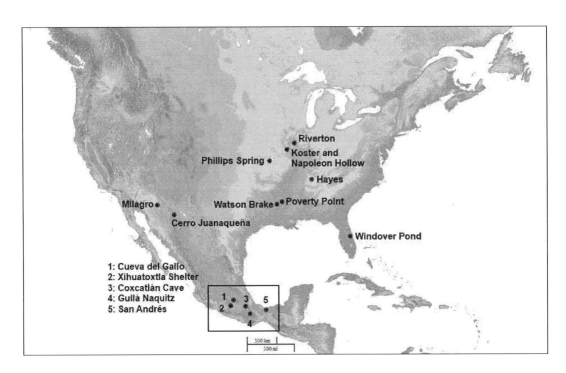

Map 18: Early agricultural sites in the United States and Mexico (8000 to 1500 BC)

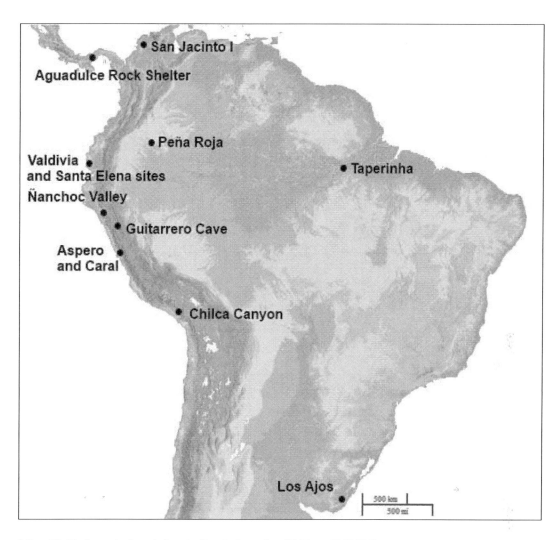

Map 19: Early agricultural sites in South America (9300 to 2000 BC)

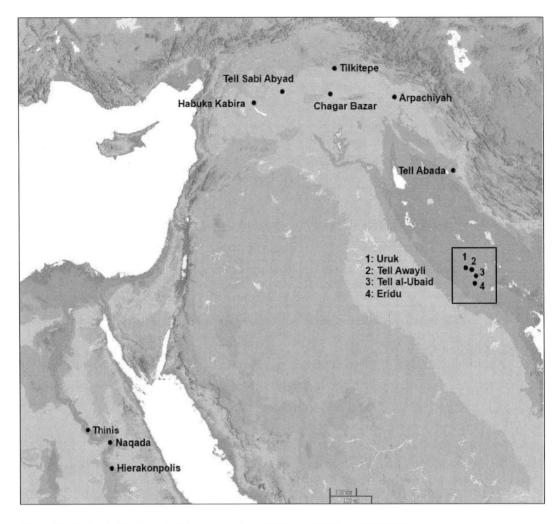

Map 20: Early civilisations in Mesopotamia and Egypt (6000 to 3100 BC)

Maps, infographics and plates

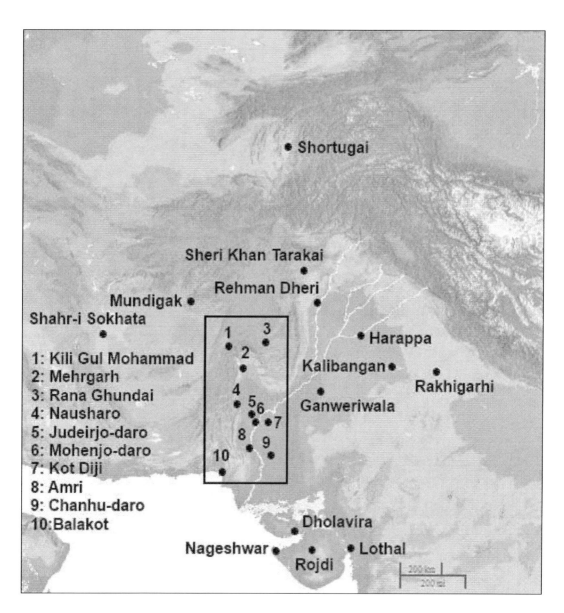

Map 21: The Indus Valley civilisation (7000 to 1300 BC)

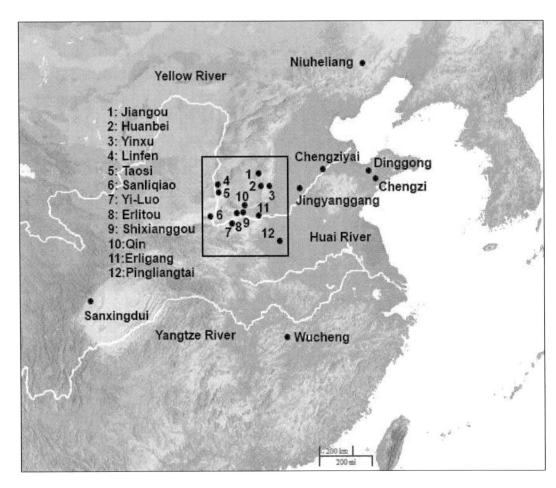

Map 22: Early civilisations in China (2800 to 1046 BC)

Maps, infographics and plates

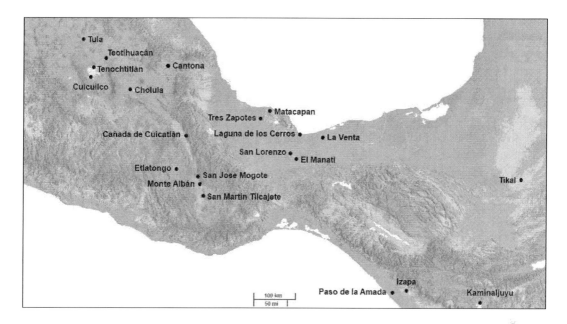

Map 23: Early civilisations in Mexico (2500 BC to AD 1519)

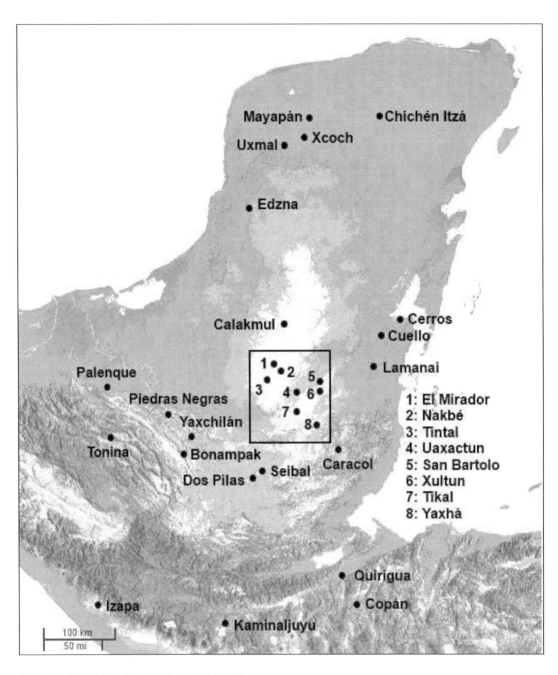

Map 24: The Maya (2500 BC to AD 1100)

Maps, infographics and plates

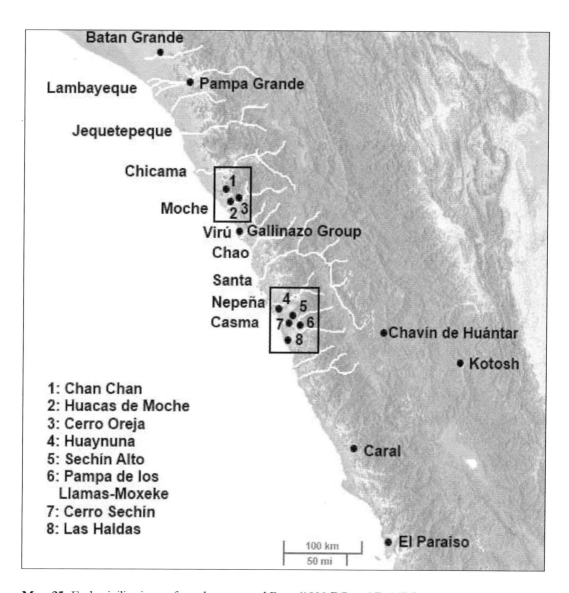

Batan Grande

Lambayeque

Pampa Grande

Jequetepeque

Chicama

1

Moche

2 3

Virú ● **Gallinazo Group**

Chao

Santa

Nepeña 4 5

Casma 7 6

8

●**Chavín de Huántar**

● **Kotosh**

1: Chan Chan
2: Huacas de Moche
3: Cerro Oreja
4: Huaynuna
5: Sechín Alto
6: Pampa de los
   Llamas-Moxeke
7: Cerro Sechín
8: Las Haldas

● **Caral**

100 km

50 mi

● **El Paraiso**

Map 25: Early civilisations of northern coastal Peru (1800 BC to AD 1476)

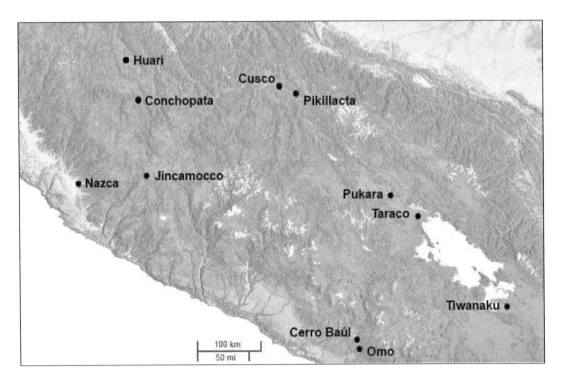

Map 26: Early civilisations of the Andean highlands and altiplano (1400 BC to AD 1100)

Maps, infographics and plates

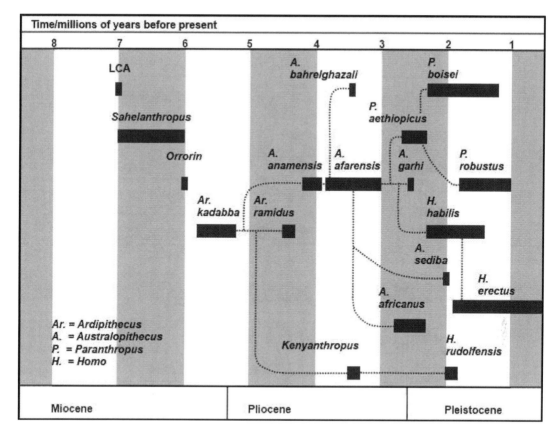

Fig. 1: Early hominin evolutionary timeline

1. Possible evolutionary relationships between species are indicated by dotted lines, but these are tentative and often disputed;
2. The Last Common Ancestor of chimpanzees and humans (LCA) has not been identified in the fossil record;
3. The relationships of *Sahelanthropus* and *Orrorin* to later hominins are unknown;
4. *Homo rudolfensis* is shown as descended from *Kenyantropus*. If this relationship is accepted then the correct name is *Kenyantropus rudolfensis*;

Homo erectus is widely believed to have evolved from *Homo habilis*, but *Australopithecus sediba* has recently been claimed as a more plausible ancestor.

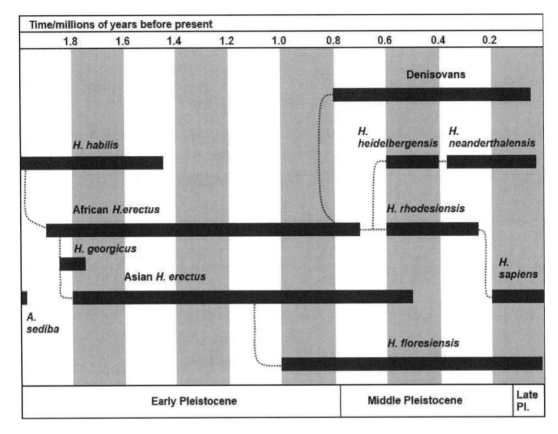

Fig. 2: Later hominin evolutionary timeline

1. *Homo erectus* is widely believed to have evolved from *Homo habilis*, but *Australopithecus sediba* has recently been claimed as a more plausible ancestor;

2. African *Homo erectus*, *Homo georgicus* and Asian *Homo erectus* are all probably variants of the same species;

3. It is uncertain as to whether *Homo rhodesiensis* and *Homo heidelbergensis* are separate species;

4. The existence of the Denisovans as a separate species is inferred from genetic data.

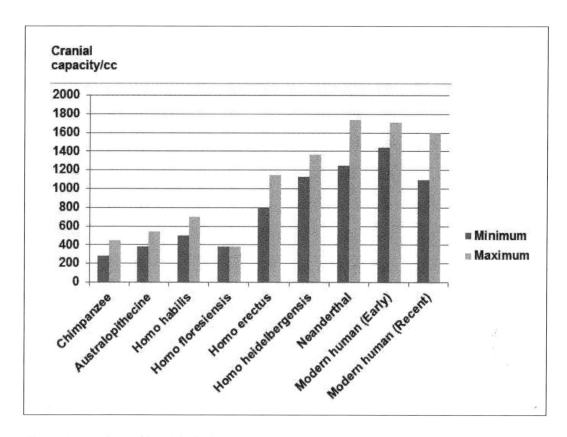

Fig. 3: Comparison of hominin brain sizes

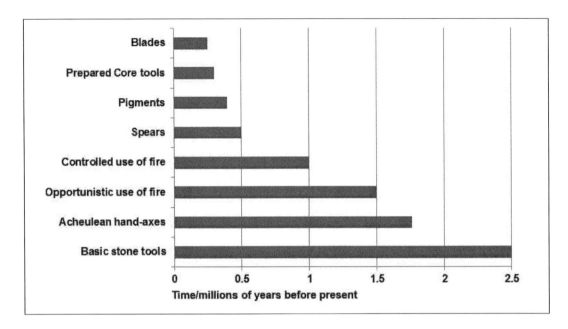

Fig. 4: Timeline of human innovation from 2.5 million years before present

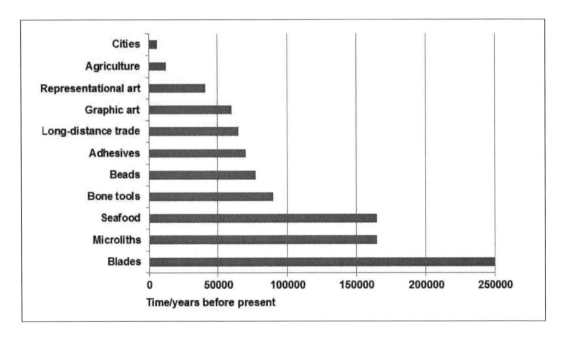

Fig. 5: Timeline of human innovation from 250,000 years before present

Maps, infographics and plates

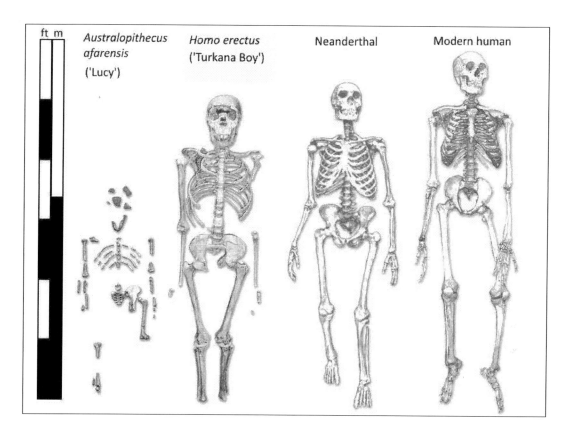

ft m | *Australopithecus afarensis* ('Lucy') | *Homo erectus* ('Turkana Boy') | Neanderthal | Modern human

Plate 01: Skeletons of Lucy, Turkana Boy, Neanderthal and modern human. Lucy (*Australopithecus afarensis*) and the Turkana Boy (*Homo erectus*) are two of the most complete early hominin skeletons ever found. Nevertheless, it can be seen that a significant number of bones are missing in both cases.

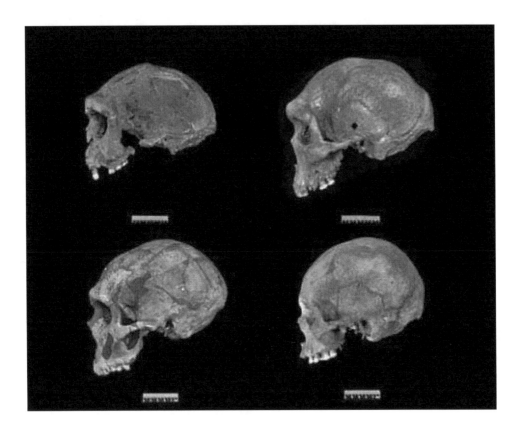

Plate 02: Skulls of archaic and modern humans compared

1. *Homo erectus* (top left) Sangiran;
2. *Homo heidelbergensis* (top right) Broken Hill;
3. *Homo neanderthalensis* (bottom left) La Ferrassie;
4. Modern *Homo sapiens* (bottom right) Polynesia.

Note the globular shape of the modern skull in comparison to the long, low braincases of the archaic humans.

Plate 03: 800,000 to 600,000-year-old Acheulean hand-axe. Found by a dog-walker in 2000 on the beach at Happisburgh, Norfolk, UK.

Plate 04: Middle Stone Age silcrete bifacial points, engraved ochre and bone tools from the c. 75,000 to 80,000-year-old M1 and M2 phases at Blombos Cave, South Africa. The engraved ochre is believed to be the earliest example of abstract art anywhere in the world and suggests that the thought-processes of people from that era were not too dissimilar to our own.

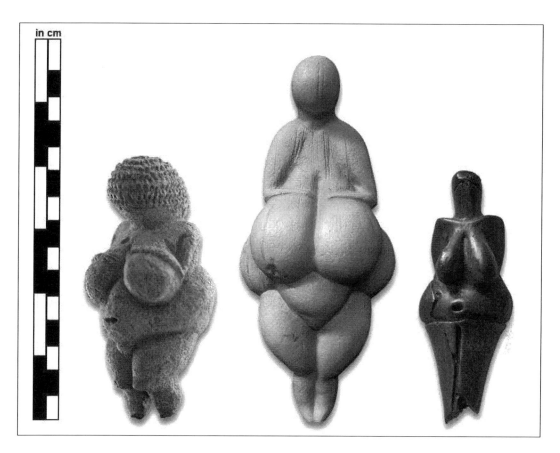

Plate 05: Gravettian period Venus figurines

1. The Willendorf Venus (left) is carved from limestone and tinted with red ochre. It was discovered in 1908 near Willendorf, Austria and now resides in the Museum of Natural History, Vienna;
2. The ivory Lespugue Venus (centre) was discovered in 1922 at the Rideaux cave of Lespugue (Haute-Garonne) in the foothills of the Pyrenees, and is now displayed in the Musée de l'Homme in Paris;
3. The ceramic Dolní Věstonice Venus (right) was discovered in 1925 in Moravia (now part of the Czech Republic). It is not currently on permanent display to the public.

The figurines are between 22,000 to 29,000 years old.

Plate 06: Upper Palaeolithic cave art at Lascaux, France. Discovered by four teenage boys in 1940, the Lascaux Caves have been described as the Sistine Chapel of Prehistory. The cave art is around 18,000 years old, dating to the later stages of the Upper Palaeolithic.

Plate 07: Neolithic pottery fragment from Llobrega Cave, Spain. From the former collection of Edouard and Louis Lartet, now on display in the Museum of Toulouse.

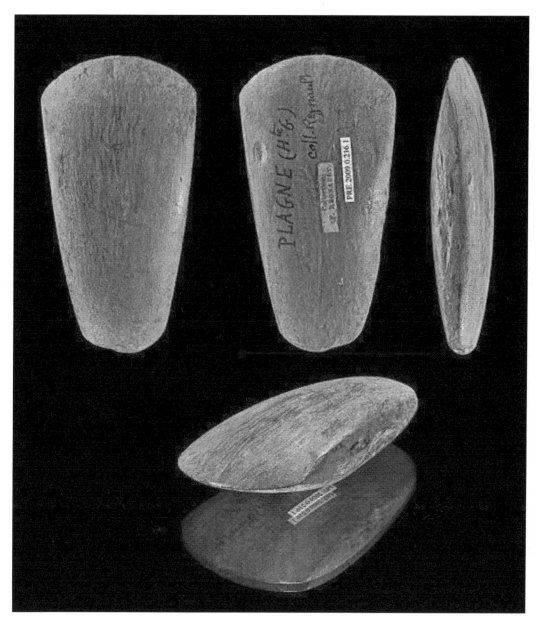

Plate 08: Neolithic polished stone axe from Plagne, Haute-Garonne, France. Found at Plagne, Haute-Garonne, France and on display in the Museum of Toulouse.

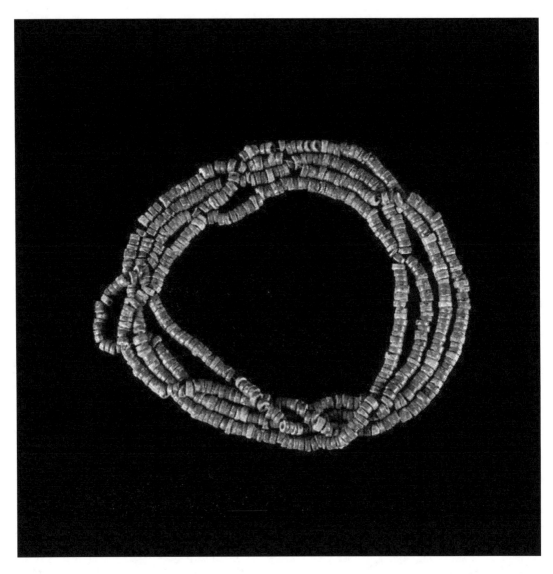

Plate 09: Neolithic talc bead necklace from Aveyron, France. Found at Aveyron, France and on display in the Museum of Toulouse.

Plate 10: Neolithic chert arrowhead from Saint-Léon, Aveyron, France. Found at Dolmen de la Glène, Saint-Léon, Aveyron, France and on display in the Museum of Toulouse.

Picture acknowledgments

Book cover design: Vici MacDonald

Book cover image: *NMS-ECAA52 A PALAEOLITHIC HANDAXE* (2012) Webpage available at: http://finds.org.uk/database/artefacts/record/id/512140 Licence: CC by Share Alike

Glanville logo design: Vici MacDonald

Plate 02: Skulls of *Homo erectus* (Sangiran); *Homo heidelbergensis* (Broken Hill); *Homo neanderthalensis* (La Ferrassie) and Modern *Homo sapiens* (Polynesia): Copyright The Natural History Museum, London

Plate 03: *NMS-ECAA52 A PALAEOLITHIC HANDAXE* (2012) Webpage available at: http://finds.org.uk/database/artefacts/record/id/512140 Licence: CC by Share Alike

Plate 04: *Image copyright held by author, Chris Henshilwood. Photo by Henning* (2007) Webpage available at: http://commons.wikimedia.org/wiki/File:BBC-artefacts.jpg Licence: CC by Share Alike 3.0 unported

Plate 06: *Photograph by Prof. Saxx* (2007) Webpage available at: http://commons.wikimedia.org/wiki/File:Lascaux_painting.jpg Licence: CC by Share Alike 3.0 unported

Plate 07: *MHNT.PRE.2010.0.102.2 Museum of Toulouse photograph by Didier Descouens (Projet Phoebus)* (2012) Webpage available at: http://commons.wikimedia.org/wiki/File:Poterie_N%C3%A9olithique_MHNT.PRE.2010.0.102.2.jpg Licence: CC by Share Alike 3.0 unported

Plate 08: *MHNT PRE.2009.0.216.1 Museum of Toulouse photograph by Didier Descouens (Projet Phoebus)* (2010) Webpage available at: http://commons.wikimedia.org/wiki/File:Hache_Plagne_Global.jpgLicence: CC by Share Alike 3.0 unported

Plate 09: *MHNT PRE.2009.0.237.1 Museum of Toulouse photograph by Rama, Wikimedia Commons (Projet Phoebus)* (2010) Webpage available at:http://commons.wikimedia.org/wiki/File:Neolithic_talc_necklace_-_PRE.2009.0.237.1.IMG_1833-black.jpg Licence: CC by Share Alike 2.0 France

Plate 10: *MHNT PRE 2009.0.923.2 Museum of Toulouse photograph by Didier Descouens (Projet Phoebus)* (2010) Webpage available at:http://commons.wikimedia.org/wiki/File:Fleche_Cartailhac_MHNT_PRE_2009.0.9232.1.jpg Licence: CC by Share Alike 3.0 unported

Glossary

Acheulean (Mode 2)

Acheulean (Mode 2) tool technology is characterised by the Acheulean hand-axe, which is named for Saint-Acheul in northern France. These hand-axes were flat cobbles or large flakes that were flaked over on both sides to produce a sharp edge. Many were teardrop-shaped, narrowing from a broad base at one end to a rounded point at the other. The hand-axes, unlike Oldowan artefacts, were the first tools to be clearly beyond the abilities of non-human apes. Tool makers now needed to concern themselves with overall shape of the finished artefact. Rather than simply producing sharp flakes, it was necessary to trim the hand-axe to produce cutting edges, and sides that converged to a pointed tip.

Allele

Variant form of a gene. For example, there are three alleles of the gene associated with blood groups: A, B and O.

Ardipithecus

Ardipithecus was a genus of bipedal apelike hominins that lived from 5.8 to 4.3 million years ago. Unlike any later hominins, *Ardipithecus* retained an opposable big toe for climbing. It was capable of walking on two legs, but it also spent time in the trees. It lacked the more advanced adaptations to bipedality that were present in later hominins, and was a less efficient walker than a human. *Ardipithecus* is currently known only from Ethiopia and probably lived in a woodland setting. Dental evidence suggests that the *Ardipithecus* diet was that of a generalised omnivore, eating fruit, nutritious plants, mushrooms, invertebrates and possibly small vertebrates. Two species have been described; *Ardipithecus ramidus* and *Ardipithecus kadabba*. It is probable that the later australopithecines evolved from *Ardipithecus*.

Argon-argon dating

Argon-argon dating is a variant of potassium-argon dating (*q.v.*) in which irradiation is used to convert non-radioactive ^{39}K to ^{39}Ar, and the ratio of ^{39}Ar to ^{40}Ar is then measured. Unlike the potassium-argon method, where the amounts of potassium and argon have to be measured separately, the argon-argon method requires a single measurement and is hence less susceptible to errors. See *Radiomentric dating*.

Australopithecine

The australopithecines were a grouping of bipedal apelike hominins that lived between 4.2 and 1.2 million years ago. Although they were bipeds, they probably retained adaptations for tree-climbing. Their brains were only slightly larger than those of chimpanzees and barely a third the size of a modern human brain. In stature they ranged from 1.0 to 1.5m (3 ft. 6 in. to 5 ft. 0 in.). The australopithecines are usually grouped into two genera: *Australopithecus* ('southern ape') and *Paranthropus* ('alongside man'). Informally, the two genera are known respectively as gracile and robust australopithecines. The graciles might have eaten a seasonally-varying diet alternating between meat and plant food while the robusts were probably vegetarians who occasionally fell back on tough seeds, roots and tubers when more favoured plant foods were unavailable. The australopithecines were not dentally-adapted for meat-eating and may have used tools for processing meat. They were adaptable and evidently lived in a wide range of habitats. The australopithecines are not known to have left Africa, although this cannot be ruled out.

Australopithecus africanus

Australopithecus africanus ('Southern ape of Africa') is an australopithecine species that lived 2.8 to 2.3 million years ago. The species is known only from four sites, all in South Africa. Its habitat ranged from wet forest with high rainfall to dry partially-wooded savannah. It might have evolved from the earlier *Australopithecus afarensis* though this is by no means certain. Its relationship (if any) to later hominins is also uncertain. *Australopithecus africanus* is a puzzling mixture of humanlike and apelike characteristics. The skull and dentition are more humanlike than those of *Australopithecus afarensis*; but *Australopithecus africanus* is more apelike in its limb proportions, with its arms longer than its legs. This suggests that it was a more proficient tree climber than the earlier species. Even at this comparatively late stage, it seems, hominins were spending a significant amount of time in the trees.

Australopithecus afarensis

Australopithecus afarensis ('Southern ape of Afar') is an australopithecine species known in the fossil record from 3.9 to 3.0 million years ago from sites in Ethiopia, Kenya and Tanzania. The species was discovered in the 1970s in Ethiopia at Hadar, a village on the southern edge of the Afar Triangle. Finds include 'Lucy', one of the most complete early hominin skeletons ever found. It gained its nickname from the Beatles song *Lucy in the Sky with Diamonds*, played at a party held to mark its discovery. The diminutive female was 1.1 m (3 ft. 8 in.) tall and weighed about 30 kg (66 lb.). *Australopithecus afarensis* was capable of occupying a range of habitats. At Hadar, Lucy and her folk apparently lived in woodland, but others occupied much more open grassland savannah. *Australopithecus afarensis* is often claimed as a human ancestor, though this remains uncertain.

Australopithecus anamensis

Australopithecus anamensis ('Southern ape of the lake') is an australopithecine species that lived from 4.2 to 3.9 million years ago and is known from sites in Kenya and Ethiopia. It favoured forest conditions, although remains have also been found in areas containing wooded, bushland, grassland and open environments. Though classed as a separate species, it was probably an earlier form of *Australopithecus afarensis*.

Australopithecus bahrelghazali

Australopithecus bahrelghazali is an australopithecine species known from a single 3.5-million-year-old find in the Bahr el Ghazal valley in northern Chad. It shows some dental differences from the contemporary *Australopithecus afarensis*, but is probably a western offshoot of that species.

Australopithecus garhi

Australopithecus garhi ('garhi' means 'surprise' in the Afar language) is an australopithecine species known from 2.5-million-year-old remains found in Ethiopia. It is claimed to be descended from *Australopithecus afarensis*, but distinct from it on the basis of the positioning of its cheekbones and of its larger back teeth. Like the earlier species, it is has been claimed as a human ancestor.

Australopithecus sediba

Australopithecus sediba ('sediba' means 'fountain' in the Sotho language) is an australopithecine species discovered in 2010 at Malapa, South Africa. The fossil remains of two individuals recovered at that time are just under 2 million years old. It has been claimed that *Australopithecus sediba* is a more plausible ancestor to *Homo erectus* than the more commonly-recognised *Homo habilis*.

Band

Bands are the least complex type of social organisation. They are egalitarian, kin-based groups, led by an informal headman rather than a hereditary chief or king. Bands generally live as mobile hunter-gatherers.

Bayesian inference

Bayesian inference is named for the eighteenth century mathematician Rev. Thomas Bayes. It is a powerful but computational-intensive statistical method that has been brought to the fore by the increased 'number-crunching' abilities of modern computers.

Blade-based tools (Mode 4)

Mode 4 tools are characterised by a predominance of blades over flakes. A blade is defined as a flake struck from a prepared prismatic stone core and that is more than twice as long as is broad. Blades can be retouched (*q.v.*) to produce a wide range of tools including knives, awls, points and scrapers. The term 'bladelet' is used to describe small blades 1 to 4 cm (0.4 to 1.6 in.) in length. Mode 4 tools became widespread during the Upper Palaeolithic in Europe and tend to be more finely-made than earlier stone tools. However, blades first appeared 280,000 years ago in East Africa and were also produced by Neanderthals.

Burin

Chisel, used for working wood, bone and antler.

Chiefdom

Chiefdoms are ranked societies, where individuals are from birth of 'chiefly' or 'commoner' descent, regardless of their personal abilities. Lineages also hold property, and higher-ranking lineages tend to hold the best agricultural land and fishing rights. Chiefdoms often have elaborate rituals and full-time priests, with the chief sometimes serving as a priest themselves. The office of chief exists apart from the actual chief, and must be filled by somebody of comparable high status upon their death. The power of the chief typically rests upon control of access to prestige goods, made from exotic materials including jade, turquoise, alabaster, gold and lapis lazuli. Such items reinforce the status of the chief, and may be distributed to subordinates as rewards for service. Craft specialisations exist in chiefdoms, but these are not full-time occupations. Craft workers are required to combine their activities with the day-to-day business of food production. Populations are often very large, exchange networks highly developed, and warfare frequent. Chiefdoms are broadly characterised as either simple or complex. In complex chiefdoms, such as those of traditional Hawaiian society, communities are organised into districts under the control of lesser chiefs; these in turn are ruled over by a paramount chief.

Cladistics

Palaeoanthropologists often make use of a technique known as cladistic analysis. In evolutionary biology, cladistics is a method of analysing evolutionary relationships between organisms. It entails identifying one or more characteristics that are unique to an evolutionary lineage, for example the vertebrate backbone. A group of organisms are said to form a 'clade' if they all share a common ancestor that itself possessed these characteristics. The term 'clade' comes from the Greek word *klados*, meaning a branch. A clade can include many species (for example vertebrates, mammals and primates all represent clades), or a group within a single species sharing a particular characteristic, such as a specific genetic lineage.

Characteristics are said to be either primitive or derived. 'Primitive' in this context does not mean a characteristic is backward or poorly-adapted. It simply means that it is shared by all members of a clade, having arisen before the clade's common ancestor. 'Derived', on the other hand, refers to traits that are unique to a particular clade. Thus the five-digit limbs of humans and other primates are primitive, because they are shared with the earliest mammals. Conversely, toe and finger nails are derived, because early mammals had claws rather than nails. Similarly, a horse's hooves are derived. Horses have shed all but the third digit of each of their limbs. Most species possess a mosaic or mixture of primitive and derived traits. It is important to note that characteristics are primitive and derived only in relation to the group under consideration. The five-digit limb is derived when considering all vertebrates, because it was not present in the earliest vertebrates. Similarly, toe and finger nails are primitive when considering hominins, because they appeared much earlier on in primate evolution.

Cladistics is based on the assumption that the appearance of derived characteristics reflects evolutionary relationships. For example, apes and humans lack the characteristic primate tail, hinting at the existence of a common ancestor that lost its tail. In order to unpick the strands that make up the hominin 'bush', palaeoanthropologists must work at much finer resolutions than presence or absence of gross anatomical features such as tails or toenails. Subtle metrical differences between fossilised bones and teeth from different hominin species must be considered. Specialist computer software is then used to construct a diagram known as a 'cladogram', which is best thought of as an evolutionary family tree of the lineage under consideration.

Corvée
Compulsory labour performed for the state as a form of taxation.

Cosmogenic radionuclide dating
A technique that relies on radioactive isotopes (*q.v.*) in an artefact arising in minute quantities through exposure to cosmic rays. Isotopes are produced at a known rate, but production will cease if the artefact becomes buried. By measuring the amounts present of various isotopes, and exploiting their known decay rate, the time since burial can be determined.

Cranial capacity
The cranial capacity of a primate is defined as the internal volume of its braincase and is as such a measure of the size of its brain.

Cranial vault
The part of the skull containing the brain.

Debitage
Waste material left over from stone tool production.

Deme
A regional population of a species exhibiting morphological differences from other, similar populations.

Denisovan

Denisovan is the provisional name assigned to a human species identified by genetic material obtained from a 48,000-year-old little finger bone found at Denisova Cave in the Altai Mountains of southern Siberia. The Denisovans diverged from modern humans 800,000 years ago; too recently to have been *Homo erectus* and too long ago to have been Neanderthals. Later work indicated that the Denisovans interbred with modern humans in Papua New Guinea, suggesting that the species was very widespread.

Dental hypoplasia

A deficiency in dental enamel formation, occurring when growth is arrested due to dietary stress.

Denticulate

Tooth-edged stone tool, possibly used as a plane or scraper for shaping wooden stakes or shafts. Some might also have been used on skins, meat or soft plant material.

Determinative

A sign used to add various types of information to a logogram (*q.v.*). For example the logogram £100 means 'one hundred pounds'. Such additional signs are known as determinatives, because they determine the category in which the accompanying signs are to be understood. Note that the verbal equivalent does not necessarily follow the order in which the signs appear; £100 is not pronounced 'pounds one hundred' despite being written that way.

Domestication

Domesticated plants and animals are raised in a human-managed environment. Often, they have undergone biological change in comparison to their wild counterparts. These changes make them more suitable for human exploitation, but in the case of plants, can also make them unable to reproduce without human intervention. It remains contentious the degree to which human intentionality played a role in such changes; also whether changes can be attributed solely to the process of domestication; and indeed whether the process of domestication necessarily involves any biological change at all. There is no universally-agreed definition of domestication, although ongoing human intervention is regarded as a key feature. It is generally accepted that agricultural societies have a degree of dependency on domesticated species, though it is disputed just how dependent a society must be before it is considered agricultural.

Ecotone

The transitional region between two ecologically-differing habitats, for example woodland and steppe regions.

End scraper

Elongated flake or blade, retouched (*q.v.*) at one end and used for working animal hide.

Encephalization quotient (EQ)

Absolute brain size of an animal is not a wholly-reliable guide to its 'braininess'. Elephants and whales are far larger than humans and need larger brains to co-ordinate body movements and perform various 'housekeeping' tasks such as breathing and maintaining correct body temperature. There isn't any capacity left over for more advanced behaviours. A more reliable guide to brainpower is the encephalization quotient (EQ), a function of brain size in relation to the size of the animal as a whole. Various formulae are used to calculate the EQ and some calculations are based on the neocortex or 'grey matter' rather than total brain mass. Regardless of the method used, mammals tend to have higher EQs than other vertebrates such as fish and reptiles; and primates in turn tend to have higher EQs than other mammals.

Endocast of brain
A cast of the inside of the braincase.

Faunal dating
Faunal dating is a low-tech but effective method that relies on finding faunal remains in the same context of the artefacts or fossils under consideration. Knowing the dates a species or a characteristic feature of a species (for example dentition) were current implies a date range for the artefacts or fossils.

Foramen magnum
The hole in the base of the skull through which the spinal column enters. In present-day apes, it is positioned at the rear, but with humans and other hominins, it is centrally-placed as an adaptation for walking upright.

Genetic diversity
Genetic diversity is the amount of genetic variation within a species or population and is measured in terms of the proportion of polymorphic loci across the genome. A genetic locus (plural loci) is the location of a particular gene on a chromosome, and if there are two or more alleles (variant forms) of the gene, it is said to be polymorphic. An example of a polymorphism in humans is the blood group-determining ABO locus, which has three alleles: A, B and O. The simplest form of polymorphism is known as a Single Nucleotide Polymorphism (SNP), where the variation involves a single nucleotide. Nucleotides are the 'building block' molecules of which strands of DNA and RNA are composed.

Genetic drift
Genetic drift refers to random changes in the relative frequency in which an allele (*q.v.*) occurs in a population. In small populations, over a number of generations, the effect can result in some alleles becoming fixed and others disappearing altogether, even if the prevailing alleles confer no particular selective advantage on their possessors. An analogy for genetic drift is seen in small isolated villages where everybody ends up with the same surname. If for example Mr and Mrs Smith are the only Smiths in the village and they have only daughters, then the surname Smith will disappear from the next generation. Over enough generations, the villagers will 'drift' to just one surname.

Geological timescale
Geologists originally divided geological time into four periods, although only the two most recent remain in use, the Tertiary and the Quaternary. The Tertiary began approximately 65 million years ago, with the extinction of the dinosaurs. The start of the Quaternary is far more recent, beginning with the onset of the Quaternary Ice Age 2,588 million years ago. The preceding age of the dinosaurs is divided into the Triassic, Jurassic and Cretaceous periods. The names of many of the earlier periods reflect British pre-eminence in the early days of geology. These include the Devonian (Devon), the Cambrian (Wales), the Ordovician and the Silurian. The latter two are named for Celtic tribes that lived in Wales before the Roman conquest of Britain.

We are largely concerned with the Tertiary and Quaternary periods. Geologists further divide these two periods into epochs, respectively the Palaeocene ('Ancient'), Eocene ('Dawn'), Oligocene

('Few'), Miocene ('Less Recent') and Pliocene ('More Recent'); and the Pleistocene ('Most Recent') and Holocene ('Wholly Recent'). Modern humans did not appear until near the end of the Middle Pleistocene.

Glottochronology

Glottochronology is a technique used by linguists to estimate the age of age of a language family; in other words when a mother tongue differentiated into its daughter languages. The method was first devised in the 1950s by the American linguist Morris Swadesh, and relies on two assumptions. The first is that in any language there will be a core vocabulary of commonly-used words (now known as the Swadesh List). The second is that words are lost from this vocabulary at a constant rate over time; a figure of 86 percent word retention over 1,000 years is commonly used. Unfortunately, there are a number of problems with the method. Certain types of word, such as personal pronouns, are retained for much longer than others. There are difficulties in deciding which words should be included in the lists themselves. Even if these difficulties are overcome, there are limits to how far back in time one can go. After around 10,000 years, the number of retained words is too small for a meaningful judgement.

Haplogroup

A haplogroup is any genetic lineage that can be defined in terms of particular genetic markers.

Hominin

The hominins include modern humans and all species that are more closely related to modern humans than they are to chimpanzees.

Homo

The genus containing *Homo sapiens* and a number of extinct human species.

Homo antecessor

Homo antecessor ('pioneer man') is a possible human species known only from Sierra de Atapuerca in northern Spain. It lived from around 1.2 million to 800,000 years ago and is claimed to be distinct from African *Homo erectus* (*q.v.*) on the basis of dental and facial characteristics. The brain size is over 1,000 cc, compared to the 900 cc of *Homo erectus*. Despite this, *Homo antecessor* lacked Acheulean hand-axes (*q.v.*) and used only simple Oldowan tools (*q.v.*). It is probable that *Homo antecessor* represents a migration into Europe by Asian *Homo erectus*, which also lacked Acheulean tool technology.

Homo ergaster

Homo ergaster ('working man') is a variant term for African *Homo erectus* (*q.v.*), believed by some to be a separate species to Asian *Homo erectus*.

Homo erectus

Homo erectus ('erect man') is the first human species known to have left Africa. Fossil remains first appear around 1.9 million years ago in East Africa, but are seen in East Asia by around 1.8 million years ago. Unlike *Homo habilis* (*q.v.*), *Homo erectus* closely resembles modern humans in its limb proportions, suggesting that it had entirely abandoned any apelike climbing abilities. However, its brain was still only about two-thirds that of a modern human at around 900 cc. Tool-making abilities were nevertheless an advance on those of *Homo habilis* and Mode 2 Acheulean hand-axes soon replaced Oldowan stone tools in Africa, though not in East Asia. The ancestry of *Homo erectus* is uncertain. The conventional view is that it evolved from *Homo habilis* in East Africa, but the South African *Australopithecus sediba* (*q.v.*) has recently been proposed as an ancestor.

Homo floresiensis

Homo floresiensis ('Flores man') is a species of hominin known only from the Indonesian island of Flores. Popularly known as the 'hobbit people', *Homo floresiensis* survived on Flores until just 12,000 years ago. The largely-complete skeleton LB1 belonged to a 30-year-old female who stood no more than 1.06 m (3 ft. 6 in,) tall. Her weight was estimated anything from 16 to 36 kg (35 to 79 lb.). She had a cranial capacity of just 380 cc, no larger than that of an australopithecine, but she lacked the large back teeth of an australopithecine, the proportions of her facial skeleton were those of a human, and her postcranial (*q.v.*) anatomy was consistent with her being a humanlike fully-committed biped. The origin of *Homo floresiensis* is disputed. It is usually regarded as a 'downsized' offshoot of *Homo erectus* (*q.v.*) that underwent dwarfing as a result of the insular conditions, but it has also been suggested that *Homo floresiensis* are the descendants of an earlier hominin migration from Africa.

Homo georgicus

Homo georgicus ('Georgian man') is known from 1.77-million-year-old hominin remains found at Dmanisi, Georgia. They ranged in height from 1.45 to 1.66 m (4 ft. 9 in. to 5 ft. 5 in.) tall, making them rather shorter than *Homo erectus* (*q.v.*) and, with a cranial capacity of 600 to 775 cc, rather smaller-brained. It has nevertheless been proposed that the species is a downsized and less-lanky form of *Homo erectus*, adapted to the Georgian climate. More controversially, it has been suggested that they evolved in Asia from an as yet unidentified australopithecine ancestor.

Homo heidelbergensis

Homo heidelbergensis ('Heidelberg man'), formerly known as Archaic *Homo sapiens* was a widespread human species known from Africa and Eurasia between 600,000 and 250,000 years ago. It brain size was around 90 percent that of modern humans and its Mode 3 prepared-core (*q.v.*) tool technologies were an advance on the venerable Acheulean hand-axe (*q.v.*). It is unclear as to whether the Eurasian and African populations were both the same species, but at all events from these populations eventually arose Neanderthals (*q.v.*) in Europe and modern humans in Africa.

Homo helmei

Homo helmei ('Helme's man') was the name given to a 259,000-year-old partial skull discovered by Thomas F. Dreyer and Alice Lyle at Florisbad, South Africa in 1932. The find was named for expedition sponsor Captain Robert E. Helme. The skull is intermediate in form between early *Homo sapiens* and *Homo heidelbergensis* (*q.v.*), but is generally classed with the latter rather than a separate species.

Homo habilis

Homo habilis ('handy man') is the earliest hominin species generally accepted as belonging to Genus *Homo* and the earliest known that definitely made and used Oldowan stone tools. Compared to modern humans, *Homo habilis* was small-brained, with a cranial capacity ranging from 500 to 700 cc, although it was better-endowed than the australopithecines (*q.v.*). *Homo habilis* retained a number of australopithecine-like features such as proportionately long arms and short legs. While these could have been rarely-needed vestigial relics of an australopithecine past, the long arms, together with hand bones do suggest *Homo habilis* might have retained some apelike tree-climbing ability. The species is reliably known from 1.9 to 1.44 million years ago, though a 2.33-million-year-old upper jawbone from Hadar, Ethiopia could be from *Homo habilis*. It is not clear whether *Homo habilis* was one species or two, and some authorities recognise *Homo rudolfensis* as a second human species that existed alongside *Homo habilis*. It is widely believed that *Homo habilis* was the ancestor of *Homo erectus* (*q.v.*) though recently this view has been questioned (see *Australopithecus sediba*).

Homo neanderthalensis
Formal name for Neanderthals (*q.v.*).

Homo sapiens
Formal name for modern humans, meaning (some would say ironically) 'wise man'.

Ice Age
2,588 million years ago, at the start of the Pleistocene, the Earth entered an Ice Age. It followed 50 million years of climatic downturn, and was the first full-blown ice age for a quarter of a billion years. Cooler, arid conditions alternated with warm, wet conditions as ice sheets ebbed and flowed in higher latitudes. The ice sheets alternately locked up vast amounts of fresh water, then released it again as temperatures rose. This alternation between a cooler and a warmer climate has continued right up to the present day. The cold spells are often referred to as 'ice ages'. In particular the end of the most recent glacial period 11,600 years ago, is popularly known as the end of the last Ice Age. In fact the warm spells – interglacial periods – are no more than breaks in an on-going ice age. The current Holocene epoch, that followed the last glacial period, is such a break. In theory, glacial conditions will one day return, though the effects of anthropogenic (human caused) global warming make this uncertain. Glacial periods are not necessarily periods of unremitting cold, but alternate between colder and warmer intervals known respectively as stadials and interstadials.

The idea that there were periods when glaciers extended beyond their present-day limits gradually emerged during the first half of the nineteenth century. Geologists sought to explain such phenomena as rock scouring and scratching, the cutting of valleys, the existence of whale-shaped hills known as drumlins and the presence of erratic boulders and ridges of rocky debris known as moraines. The term Eiszeit ('ice age') was coined in 1837 by the German botanist Karl Friedrich Schimper.

The two most recent glacial periods were the Riss Glacial from 190,000 to 126,000 years ago and the Würm Glacial or last glacial period ('the last Ice Age') from 110,000 to 11,650 years ago. Between the two was a warm interval known as the Eemian Interglacial. The latter stages of the Würm Glacial were particularly cold, and the period from 22,000 to 18,000 years ago is referred to as the Last Glacial Maximum (LGM). See *Marine Isotope Stages (MIS)*, *Milanković cycles*.

Isotope
Naturally-occurring variant forms of atoms that are chemically identical, but have slightly different masses. Radioactive isotopes of predominantly stable elements (for example carbon) are known as radioisotopes.

Last Common Ancestor (LCA)
The Last Common Ancestor or LCA was an as-yet undiscovered species of African ape that was the progenitor of both humans and chimpanzees. Molecular evidence suggests that it lived five to seven million years ago.

Last Glacial Maximum (LGM)
The coldest period of the last Ice Age (*q.v.*), between 22,000 and 18,000 years ago.

Locus (genetics)
A genetic locus (plural loci) is the location of a particular gene on a chromosome.

Logogram
A written symbol used to represent a word. Logograms have a semantic value, but not a phonetic value. For example, a picture of a cow may be used to represent a cow, but not the sound /cow/. The difference is illustrated by the logographic Arabic numerals 1, 2 and 3, representing in English the words 'one', 'two' and 'three'. However, in French, they represent the words 'un', 'deux' and 'trois' – these are not of course pronounced /one/, /two/ and /three/. Logograms can be complex, comprising more than one sign. The additional signs can add various types of information, for example the logogram £100 means 'one hundred pounds'. Such additional signs are known as determinatives, because they determine the category in which the accompanying signs are to be understood. Note that the verbal equivalent does not necessarily follow the order in which the signs appear; £100 is not pronounced 'pounds one hundred' despite being written that way.

Logosyllabic
A writing system utilising a combination of logograms (*q.v.*), syllabograms (*q.v.*) and determinatives (*q.v.*).

Low-level food production
Societies classed as low-level food producers are hunter-gatherers who also rely to an extent on farming and/or herding. Though rare in the ethnographic record, such societies are thought to have been more common in prehistoric times, and included the Jōmon culture of Japan.

Lumping (taxonomy)
The tendency to cram fossils into existing species or genera.

Luminescence dating
Luminescence dating is used for samples containing crystalline materials. Buried objects gradually accumulate a radiation 'dose' from the weak, naturally-occurring radioactivity of surrounding materials. The dose takes the form of electrons trapped by defects in the material's crystalline lattice. The technique depends on measuring the quantity of trapped electrons. If background radiation levels are known or can be measured, then by measuring the number of trapped electrons, the time it has taken for them to accumulate can be estimated. This can be done by one of three methods, the choice of which will depend on the type of material to be dated. Thermoluminescence (TL) involves heating a sample to expel the trapped electrons. As they escape, they emit light; this provides a measure of their quantity. Optically Stimulated Luminescence (OSL) works on the same principle except the electrons are expelled by an intense light source. Electron Spin Resonance (ESR) involves direct measurement of the magnetic 'signal' of the trapped electrons.

TL is used mainly for materials such as ceramics and bricks, in which any initially trapped electrons were driven off by the intense heat of firing, so setting the 'clock' running. OSL is used for quartz and sand grains, in which exposure to sunlight drove off any initially trapped electrons; here the 'clock' starts running when the material is buried or otherwise ceases to be exposed to sunlight. ESR is mainly used for dental enamel, which is precipitated during life and accumulates very few trapped electrons during that period.

Marine Isotope Stages (MIS)

One of the more important pieces of evidence for past glacial periods comes from changes in oxygen isotope (*q.v.*) ratios. The two commonest isotopes of oxygen are ^{16}O and ^{18}O. Water containing the lighter isotope ^{16}O evaporates more rapidly than that containing the heavier ^{18}O; conversely when water vapour condenses, water containing ^{18}O will condense out more rapidly. When water vapour evaporated from sea surfaces in equatorial regions moves towards the poles, it is progressively enriched in ^{16}O, as the ^{18}O condenses out. As a result, ice sheets at high latitudes are enriched in ^{16}O. When ice sheets increase in volume during glacial periods, the world's ocean waters become enriched in ^{18}O.

Crucially, we can determine past changes to oceanic oxygen isotope ratios from ice cores taken from the icecaps of Greenland and Antarctica. Such data can also be obtained from the shells of long-dead marine microorganisms such as *Foraminifera*. The oxygen content of the calcium carbonate of which these shells are largely composed reflects the oxygen isotope ratio prevailing at the time of formation. When changes in oxygen isotope ratios are plotted on a graph, distinct peaks and troughs can be seen to have occurred over the course of several hundred thousand years. These peaks and troughs correspond to past episodes of warming and cooling and are known as marine isotope stages (MIS). These are numbered, with MIS 1 being the most recent. Some stages are subdivided with a suffixed letter, for example MIS 5e.

Microlith (Mode 5) tool technology

Mode 5 is the most advanced lithic technology on Sir Grahame Clark's scale. Mode 5 tools are characterised by microliths, which are small blades with a width of less than 10 mm (0.375 in.) commonly used in composite hafted tools and weapons. They were set into bone or wooden handles, or the shafts or tips of spears and arrows. Rather than having to repair or discard an entire tool when worn or damaged, only the affected microlith would need to be repaired or replaced. Archaeologist Steven Mithen has described microliths as the 'plug-in pull-out' technology of the Stone Age. Microliths did not come into widespread use until the Epipalaeolithic and Neolithic, though they appeared sporadically in Africa from 165,000 years ago.

Milanković cycles

That ice ages (*q.v.*) might have an astronomical cause was first suggested by the Scottish scholar and businessman James Croll in the 1860s, but while attracting some interest, his theories were generally disbelieved. The astronomical theory was revived between 1912 and 1920 by the Serbian civil engineer Milutin Milanković, who carried out much of his research while interned in Budapest during World War I. Milanković proposed that changes in the Earth's climate were driven cyclical variations in the eccentricity of its orbit around the Sun (the extent to which the orbit is elliptical rather than circular) and axial tilt (the extent to which the Earth's axis of day-night rotation is tilted in relation to the Sun), together with the precession of its axis of rotation (in addition to spinning on its axis, the Earth also 'wobbles' slowly like a gyroscope or a spinning-top). These cyclical variations became known as the Milanković cycles and are of long duration. The precessional cycle is 26,000 years, the obliquity cycle is 41,000 years and the orbital eccentricity cycle comprises a number of components ranging in duration from 413,000 to 95,000 years.

Each of the Milanković cycles has its own subtle effects: the seasons are caused by the Earth's axial tilt (for example, midwinter in the Northern Hemisphere occurs in December because at that time of the year, it is tipped away from the direction of the Sun), and when the angle of axial tilt is high, the seasons will be accentuated. Similarly, eccentricity determines the extent to which the Earth's distance from the Sun varies over the course of the year and the seasons will be again be accentuated when the eccentricity is high.

Finally, the precessional cycle dictates when summer and winter occur. If these coincide with time of the year when the Earth is at its maximum or minimum distance from the Sun, then the seasons will be accentuated in the hemisphere in which summer coincides with minimum distance (and winter with maximum distance) and ameliorated in the hemisphere in which summer coincides with maximum distance (and winter with minimum distance). Currently, Earth reaches its minimum distance from the Sun early in January, ameliorating Northern Hemisphere seasons, but accentuating those in the Southern Hemisphere.

Prior to the Pleistocene these variations had little effect, but on a now generally cooler Earth they were crucial. If the energy received from the Sun in higher latitudes during the summer months was insufficient to melt snow accumulating during the previous winter, glaciers would advance as the ice built up. At other times, though, energy received from the Sun levels would increase and the ice would melt. The theory, like its predecessor, was largely ignored for decades and did not begin to gain acceptance until the late 1960s. By that time, evidence had begun to accumulate that the timing of glacial periods matched those predicted by Milanković. Unfortunately, Milanković did not live to see his theory vindicated, having died in 1958.

Mitochondrial DNA (mtDNA)
Mitochondrial DNA occurs in bodies known as mitochondria and is separate from the main genome. Humans inherit their mitochondrial DNA exclusively from the maternal line, making it easier to track genetic markers over time than with recombining DNA.

Modern human behaviour
There is no universally-accepted definition of modern human behaviour, but it generally associated with the ability to make use of symbols (i.e. sounds, images or objects) to convey meaning. Symbols can take many forms. They range from those referring directly to the object or idea to be signified (such as a representational image) to the totally abstract (such as spoken or written words). Syntactic language is a system of communication that enables an infinite range of meanings to be conveyed, but it is only one component of our ability to use symbols – an ability we do not share with our fellow apes. We use symbols all the time – whenever we read a newspaper, check the time, consult a map or admire a painting or sculpture. It is disputed as to what extent this ability was shared with earlier hominins, in particular with Neanderthals.

Moiety
A society divided into two equal halves in which members of one half are obliged to marry into the other half.

Molecular clock
In all living organisms, genetic material undergoes occasional mutations or random changes, often as a result of DNA copying errors during cell division. Any mutation affecting reproductive cells will be passed onto the next generation; thus over many generations, both DNA sequences and the proteins they produce will accumulate random mutations. The mutations occur at a roughly constant rate and hence the 'genetic distance' between two species (the differences between equivalent DNA sequences or their corresponding proteins) will be related to the 'divergence time', i.e. time since these species last shared a common ancestor. For species where actual divergence times are known from the fossil record, these can be compared with genetic distances to obtain the rate at which the latter increases with time. This 'molecular clock', as it is known, can then be used to calculate divergence times for other species. In practice calibrating the molecular clock is far from easy, and is a major source of uncertainty in genetic studies. The molecular clock principle can also be used to

determine the lengths of time that particular modern human populations (for example Khoisan and non-Khoisan populations in Africa) were isolated from one another during prehistory.

Mousterian
A prepared-core (*q.v.*) stone tool industry associated with the Neanderthals (*q.v.*).

Neanderthal
Common name for *Homo neanderthalensis*; all too often used as a pejorative. Neanderthals were short, stocky large-brained humans that emerged in Eurasia at roughly the same time as modern humans emerged in Africa. *Homo neanderthalensis* is regarded as a separate species to *Homo sapiens*, although it is now thought that the two interbred. While they were certainly not the dimwitted brutes of popular imagination, they probably lacked the behavioural flexibility of *Homo sapiens* and were unable to compete effectively when the latter entered Europe 46,000 years ago.

Notch
Stone tool with single indentation. The function is unclear, but they might have been used as a planes or scrapers for shaping wooden stakes or shafts.

Oldowan (Mode 1)
Oldowan (Mode 1) is the most basic stone tool technology on a scale of 1 to 5 devised by archaeologist Sir Grahame Clark. Oldowan-type tools are characterised by simple core forms created from river-worn cobbles or angular blocks of stone; the sharp-edged, angular flakes and fragments detached from such cores; often battered hammerstones; and occasional retouch (*q.v.*) pieces, usually flakes, the edges of which were further modified by striking off tiny chips to reshape or sharpen the edge. Such tools were made and used by early humans and possibly by australopithecines.

Palaeomagnetic dating
Palaeomagnetic dating relies on periodic changes in polarity of the Earth's magnetic field. During intervals of 'reversed' (as opposed to 'normal') polarity, a compass needle will point south rather than north. The frequency with which reversals occur has varied considerably: at times the same polarity has been maintained for tens of millions of years; at others a change has occurred after just 50,000 years. There is no preferred polarity and the present state of affairs is only considered normal because the last switch occurred 780,000 years ago – long before the invention of the compass. Ancient polarities can be detected in volcanic rock and fine-grained sediments that settled into place relatively slowly. Ferromagnetic particles in these materials will preserve a record of the polarity at the time of cooling or settling. The sequence of polarity changes is well known, especially over the last five million years, by means of paired potassium-argon (*q.v.*) and palaeomagnetic readings on volcanic rocks. Geomagnetic reversals are infrequent and the resolution of dates obtained by this method is fairly low. It is therefore generally used in conjunction with other methods.

Paranthropus
A genus of australopithecine (*q.v.*), *Paranthropus* contains three species of 'robust' australopithecine that lived between 2.7 and 1.0 million years ago.

Peer polity interaction
Peer polity interaction is a model in which a number of polities (*q.v.*) interact, none of which more prominent than any of the others. Within a given region, the highest-order social units in terms of scale and organisational complexity are considered to be polities. The peer polity interaction model

states that if significant organisational change or increase in complexity occurs within one polity, it will likely be reflected in some neighbouring polities. In addition to innovations such as agriculture, changes may include building styles, objects deemed to be of high status and burial customs. Such innovations will not be attributable to any particular site, but will appear within several different polities at about the same time. Innovations may be transmitted by a number of mechanisms, including trade, competitive emulation and warfare. The model came to the fore after earlier models based on migrations and conquest fell out of favour in the 1960s.

Polity
Any politically-autonomous community.

Phonogram
A phonogram is a symbol used to represent a sound. Unlike logograms (*q.v.*), they do not have a semantic value, i.e. when pronounced they do not signify words even if they happen to be meaningful. For example, a symbol pronounced /go/ does not signify the word 'go'. There is a one-to-one correspondence between the order in which phonograms are arranged and in which they are pronounced. Phonograms can be of two types: syllabic (where the symbols represent one or syllables) or alphabetic (where they represent vowels and consonants). The symbols are referred to, respectively, as syllabograms and alphabetic signs (or letters).

Phytoliths
Microscopic silica bodies occurring in plants. They improve the structural rigidity of the plant and also make it distasteful to predators. Phytoliths differ in size and shape between different plant species and between wild and domesticated plant varieties, and are thus a useful diagnostic tool for archaeologists.

Postcranial
The part of a skeleton that excludes the skull.

Prepared-core techniques (Mode 3)
Prepared-core techniques entail shaping a stone core to a pre-planned form, from which flakes of a desired size and shape are then struck. Depending on the shape of the core, the resulting flakes may be oval or triangular. They may then require retouching (*q.v.*) to improve their cutting edge. Such techniques are economical in their use of raw materials, because many flakes may be struck from the same core. Unlike the multi-purpose Acheulean hand-axe (*q.v.*), they enable tools to be fashioned for specific purposes. Prepared-core industries are classified as Mode 3 in Sir Grahame Clark's scheme: third generation industries lying midway in complexity between the earliest stone tools and those of late prehistory. Prepared-core industries might have arisen when it was realised that flakes produced as a by-product of hand-axe manufacture could sometimes be useful as tools in their own right. Gradually, the emphasis shifted to the flakes themselves becoming the main product. Such techniques include the Levallois technique, named for the Parisian suburb of Levallois-Perret where examples of such prepared cores were discovered in the nineteenth century. It involves at least five or six clearly separate stages, each of which requires careful preplanning. Flakes so produced were fashioned into as many as forty distinct tool types, each with its own specific cutting, scraping or piercing function. There was a much greater standardisation in the form of the tools made, indicating a clearer mental template and greater manipulative skill applied to their manufacture.

Potassium-Argon dating

Potassium-argon dating relies on the decay of the potassium isotope (*q.v.*) ^{40}K to ^{40}Ar, and it is particularly useful for dating volcanic lava flows and tuffs (ash). Before rocks solidify from a molten state, any ^{40}Ar will be driven off, but ^{40}Ar produced after they crystallize will remain trapped. The ratio of ^{40}K to trapped ^{40}Ar in the sample can thus be used to determine when the sample crystallised from the molten state. These methods are particularly useful for dating fossil remains or stone tools; the age can be estimated from the position in relation to underlying and/or overlying volcanic material. See *Radiometric dating*.

Primary state formation

The process whereby a first generation state (*q.v.*) evolves from a less complex society uninfluenced by the presence of neighbouring state-level societies (*cf.* Secondary state formation).

Processual archaeology

Processual archaeology or New Archaeology is a theoretical movement in archaeology that emerged in the 1960s. Processual archaeologists look to interpret cultures in terms of systems of social and economic behaviour. Explanations for culture change are sought in terms of either external factors such as environmental change or the impact of new technologies, or in terms of internal factors such as population stress. Great emphasis is placed on testability, whereby hypotheses are proposed and then tested against archaeological evidence. Much use is made of quantitative methods such as statistical and computational techniques, and ethnographic parallels are often used to interpret features found in the archaeological record.

Processualism remained to the fore of archaeological theory until the late 1980s, when a rival school of thought emerged. Post-processual archaeologists rejected the view that we can ever gain an objective view of the past, believing instead that there may be several equally valid interpretations that can be put on archaeological data. Emphasis is placed the importance of symbolism and belief systems in human societies. The name notwithstanding, post-processualism has not replaced processualism and many archaeologists draw on both schools of thought.

Rachis

Ears of wild cereals are held together by small, brittle structures known as rachis that shatter when ripe, so that the grains can disperse. Unless wild cereals are harvested before they fully ripen, much of the grain will be lost, but in domesticated cereals the rachis is toughened and the ear remains intact until it is harvested and threshed. Such variants occur in the wild from time to time as a result of genetic mutation, but they invariably fail to reproduce, as evidenced by the lack of feral domestic cereals. On the other hand, they would be more likely to have been successfully harvested by early farmers than the normal shattering varieties.

Radiocarbon years before present (BP)

Radiocarbon years do not coincide exactly with calendar years, and the latter must be estimated using calibration data. Not all journal articles do this, and many leave the dates uncalibrated. Where this is the case, a computer program has been used to calibrate the dates, but the original uncalibrated figures have also been supplied in brackets. See *Radiometric dating*.

Radiometric dating

Before the introduction of radiometric dating in the 1950s, dating was a rather haphazard affair, commonly involving assumptions about the diffusion of ideas and artefacts from places where written records were kept and reasonably accurate dates were known. For example, it was assumed

– quite incorrectly as it later turned out - that Stonehenge was more recent than the great civilisation of Mycenaean Greece.

The idea behind radiometric dating is that radioactive material present in a fossil, artefact or other sample can be used as a 'clock' to determine its age. The material decays at a known rate and by measuring the amount present in the sample, its age can be calculated. Decay rates are usually quoted as 'half-lives', i.e. the time it will take half of the material in question to decay. Often, the material under consideration is an unstable isotope (*q.v.*) of an element that is normally stable; for example, radiocarbon dating relies on the unstable carbon isotope, ^{14}C.

^{14}C has a half-life of 5730 years, decaying to nitrogen. This is an infinitesimally short time in comparison to the age of the Earth, and one might have expected all the ^{14}C to have long since decayed. In fact, the terrestrial supply is constantly being replenished from the action of cosmic rays upon the upper atmosphere, and so atmospheric carbon dioxide (CO_2) contains a small percentage of ^{14}C. All living things absorb carbon, either directly (by photosynthesis) or indirectly (via the food chain); thus they will also contain a small percentage of ^{14}C. Once a plant or animal dies, it ceases to absorb fresh carbon, and the percentage of ^{14}C begins to fall in comparison to living organisms. By comparing this figure with the percentage present in living things, the time since death occurred can be established.

The technique was developed by the American chemist Willard Libby in 1949 and revolutionised archaeology, earning Libby the Nobel Prize for Chemistry in 1960. However, there are limitations. Firstly, it can only be used for human, animal or plant remains – the ages of tools and other artefacts can only be inferred from organic remains, if any, that are buried in the same archaeological context. Secondly, it only has a limited 'range'. Beyond 45,000 years, the ^{14}C remaining is too small to be measured, even with modern techniques such as accelerator mass spectrometry (AMS). Another problem is the cosmic ray flux that produces ^{14}C in the upper atmosphere is not constant as was once believed, and variations have to be compensated for by using charts known calibration curves. These are based on samples that have an age that can be measured by independent means, such as by dendrochronology (counting tree-rings). Calibration curves are constantly being refined, so dates are often left uncalibrated in scientific literature and quoted as radiocarbon years before present (BP), or YBP uncalibrated. 'Present' is taken to be 1950, and readers can obtain calibrated dates using calibration curves compiled long after the article was published. In this book, where literature is cited that gives only the uncalibrated dates, these have been calibrated using a computer program and the uncalibrated literature dates added in brackets.

If it is necessary to go back beyond the range of radiocarbon dating, then other radiometric methods must be used. These include the potassium-argon (*q.v.*), argon-argon (*q.v.*) and uranium series (*q.v.*) methods.

Relative dating
Relative dating of artefacts along the lines of 'x' is older than 'y' is reasonably straightforward. Provided an archaeological site has remained undisturbed (which is not always the case), artefacts and remains that are buried deeper are usually older. But to provide absolute values for the ages of x and y is harder. Before the introduction of radiometric dating in the 1950s, dating was a rather haphazard affair. It commonly involved assumptions about the diffusion of ideas and artefacts from centres of civilisation, where written records were kept and reasonably accurate dates were known. For example, it was assumed – quite incorrectly as it later turned out - that Stonehenge was more recent than the great civilisation of Mycenaean Greece.

Retouch
Intentional reshaping of a stone flake.

Robust

Big-boned; of powerful, muscular build.

Secondary state formation

The process whereby a state evolves from a less complex society in response to the presence of neighbouring state-level societies (*q.v.*) (*cf.* Primary state formation).

Settlement hierarchy

Complex societies can also be identified archaeologically by a multi-tiered settlement hierarchy, i.e. there are several distinct categories of settlement size. A four-tier hierarchy is considered to be the benchmark of a state-level society (*q.v.*). These may be interpreted as a top tier corresponding to cities, followed by second-tier regional centres, then large villages, and finally small villages.

Sexual dimorphism

In a sexually-reproducing species, the term sexual dimorphism refers to the physical differences between the two sexes. The classic example is the angler fish: the tiny male attaches itself to the much larger female, and lives out the remainder of its life as a parasite. It becomes incapable of independent existence, serving only to fertilise the female. Sexual dimorphism is common in primates, and typically manifests itself not just in body size but also in dental differences. In many species males have enlarged canine teeth, used for threat displays in order to gain social dominance. Among the living primates, a strong correlation between mating strategy and sexual dimorphism has been found. This in turn is related to male-on-male aggression. In species that are monogamous, such as gibbons, inter-male aggression is fairly limited. Other than their primary sexual characteristics, there is not much difference between males and females. On the other hand, in polygamous species, there is a tendency for male-on-male aggression when competing for access to females.

Side scraper

Flake that has been retouched (*q.v.*) on one side and used for cutting and slicing of wood, meat or skin, as well as for scraping hide or bone.

Social brain hypothesis

A theory stating that the large brains of primates enable them to use knowledge about the social behaviour of their fellows for predicting their likely future behaviour. They then base relationships upon these predictions.

Splitting (taxonomy)

The tendency to assign new species or genera to fossil finds.

Stable isotope analysis

Many elements have more than one stable isotope (*q.v.*), for example carbon (^{12}C and ^{13}C), oxygen (^{16}O and ^{18}O) and nitrogen (^{14}N and ^{15}N). The ratios in which isotopes of various elements occur in fossil remains are dependent on factors while these individuals were alive, including their diet and the geology of where they spent the early part of their lives.

State

States are stratified, occupationally-diverse societies with a strong, centralised government. They have a legal system in which wrongdoing is punished in accordance with the law, rather than by offended parties and their kin. They can wage war, draft soldiers, levy taxes and exact tribute. Obligations to the state, such as military service or taxation generally override obligations of kinship. Despite the reduced importance of kinship in state-level societies, the elite stratum is usually hereditary. This group largely controls the economy, enjoying preferential access to goods and services. It is from this group too that high-ranking state officials are usually recruited.

States generally have large populations, not all of whom are engaged in food production. Many are full-time craft workers, artisans, architects, engineers and bureaucrats. States have various public buildings, works and services, the construction or implementation of which provide a constant demand for the services of these specialists. The public buildings will generally include palaces and standardised temples that may be detected archaeologically. Royal palaces usually comprise a residential component for the ruler and their family, and a governmental component for official duties. Temples indicate a state religion, and also employ full-time specialists – in this case the priesthood.

State-level societies may be described as either city-states or territorial states. City-states comprise an urban core surrounded by farmland. They differ from territorial states, which have a far larger hinterland, and are governed from a capital through a hierarchy of smaller provincial administrative centres.

Syllabogram
A phonogram (*q.v.*) representing one or more syllables.

Three Age system
Archaeologists still use the familiar Three Age system, devised by Christian Jürgensen Thomsen in the early nineteenth century. Archaeological eras are denoted by the technology predominantly used, thus the Stone Age was followed by the Bronze Age and finally the Iron Age. However, the system has been extended to reflect the fact that the Stone Age lasted around 2.5 million years and encompasses all but the last five or six millennia. In the 1860s, Sir John Lubbock subdivided the Stone Age into the Palaeolithic ('Old Stone Age') and Neolithic ('New Stone Age') with the latter following the transition to farming. Later workers split the Palaeolithic into Lower, Middle and Upper periods and also introduced the Mesolithic ('Middle Stone Age') between the Palaeolithic and Neolithic. In addition, the terms Epipalaeolithic and Chalcolithic ('Copper and Stone') are sometimes used, to cater for early adopters of agriculture and metallurgy respectively. In Africa, a rather simpler system of Early, Middle and Late Stone Ages is used.

Tribe
Tribes are larger and less mobile than bands (*q.v.*), but are also kin-based groups, led by an informal headman rather than a hereditary chief or king. Like bands, tribes are essentially egalitarian. However, they are more likely to practice agriculture or low-level food production than are bands.

Uranium series dating
The uranium series method relies on the decay of ^{234}U to the thorium isotope (*q.v.*) ^{230}Th. The method is used to date calcium carbonate materials such as speleothem (stalagmites and stalactites), which precipitate from natural water. Uranium is slightly soluble in water, and such materials contain uranium in small amounts; but thorium is insoluble, and will not be present in freshly-precipitated speleothem. The amount of thorium present in a sample will, therefore, serve as a measure of how much time has passed since it was precipitated. See *Radiometric dating*.

Writing systems

Writing may be thought of as a system of markings with a conventional reference that communicates information and divided into two basic categories: semasiography and lexigraphy. Semasiography ('meaning') is the use of symbols that are not linked to specific words to convey information. Such symbols are commonly referred to as pictograms. Examples of semasiographic systems include computer icons and much road and other public signage. Unlike lexigraphy, semasiography is independent of language. Thus a 'No Entry' sign is read as *'Entrée Interdite'* by a French-speaker, *'Kein Eintrag'* by a German-speaker, and so on. Lexigraphy is what we conventionally regard as 'writing', i.e. the use of written words.

There are two divisions of lexigraphy: logography and phonography. Logography uses symbols to represent words (strictly speaking, 'significant segments of speech'). The symbols are known as logograms and they have a semantic value, but not a phonetic value. For example, a picture of a cow may be used to represent a cow, but not the sound /cow/ (by convention, phonetic sounds are enclosed in slashes). The difference is illustrated by the logographic Arabic numerals 1, 2 and 3, representing in English the words 'one', 'two' and 'three'. However, in French, they represent the words 'un', 'deux' and 'trois' – these are not of course pronounced /one/, /two/ and /three/. Logograms can be complex, comprising more than one sign. The additional signs can add various types of information, for example the logogram £100 means 'one hundred pounds' rather than the cardinal 'one hundred'. Such additional signs are known as determinatives, because they determine the category in which the accompanying signs are to be understood. Note that the verbal equivalent does not follow the order in which the signs appear; £100 is not pronounced 'pounds one hundred' despite being written that way.

Phonography uses symbols to represent sounds. In this case the symbols are known as phonograms. Unlike logograms, they do not have a semantic value, i.e. when pronounced they do not signify words even if they happen to be meaningful. For example, a symbol pronounced /go/ does not signify the word 'go'. There is a one-to-one correspondence between the order in which phonograms are arranged and in which they are pronounced. Phonograms can be of two types: syllabic (where the symbols represent one or syllables) or alphabetic (where they represent vowels and consonants). The symbols are referred to, respectively, as syllabograms and alphabetic signs (or letters).

Some writing systems are logosyllabic, i.e. a combination of logograms, syllabograms and determinatives. In the writing systems of ancient Mesopotamia, for example, logograms were used to express nouns, verbs and adjectives; phonetic signs were used for affixes, particles, and to spell out foreign names. Others are phono-semantic, for example Chinese, where signs comprise two elements. The first element is a determinative (known as the 'radical') and the second element contains phonetic information.

Y-chromosomal DNA

The Y-chromosome is the male sex-determining chromosome and is passed exclusively down the male line. Like with mitochondrial DNA, Y-chromosomal genetic markers are easier to track over time than those from recombining DNA.

Younger Dryas

The Younger Dryas was a cold snap that reversed global warming towards the end of last Ice Age. It takes its name from the arctic-alpine flowering plant *Dryas octopetala* that flourished in the northern tundra at that time, and lasted from 12,900 to 11,600 years ago before conditions again improved.

References

Technical primer

1. Severinghaus, J., Sowers, T., Brook, E., Alley, R. & Bender, M., Timing of abrupt climate change at the end of the Younger Dryas interval from thermally fractionated gases in polar ice. *Nature* **391**, 141-146 (1998).
2. Wilson, R., Drury, S. & Chapman, J., *The Great Ice Age* (Routledge, London, 2000).
3. Martinson, D., Pisias, N., Hays, J., Imbried, J. & Moore, T., Age dating and the orbital theory of the ice ages: Development of a high-resolution 0 to 300,000-year chronostratigraphy. *Quaternary Research* **27** (1), 1-29 (1987).
4. Ridley, M., *Genome* (Fourth Estate Limited, London, 1999).
5. Dawkins, R., *The Ancestor's Tale* (Weidenfeld & Nicholson, London, 2004).

1: A very remote period indeed

1. Morris, D., The Naked Ape: A Zoologist's Study of the Human Animal (Vintage Books, London, 1967).
2. Diamond, J., The Third Chimpanzee (Random, London, 1991).

2: The rise and fall of the Planet of the Apes

1. Sarich, V. & Wilson, A., Immunological time scale for hominid evolution. *Science* **158**, 1200-1203 (1967).
2. Takahata, N. & Satta, Y., Evolution of the primate lineage leading to modern humans: Phylogenetic and demographic inferences from DNA sequences. *PNAS* **94**, 4811-4815 (1997).
3. Chen, F. & Li, W., Genomic Divergences between Humans and Other Hominoids and the Effective Population Size of the Common Ancestor of Humans and Chimpanzees. *American Journal of Human Genetics* **68**, 444-456 (2001).
4. Stauffer, R., Walker, A., Ryder, O., Lyons-Weiler, M. & Blair Hedges, S., Human and Ape Molecular Clocks and Constraints on Paleontological Hypotheses. *The Journal of Heredity* **92** (6), 469-474 (2001).
5. Kumar, S., Filipski, A., Swarna, V., Walker, A. & Hedges, B., Placing confidence limits on the molecular age of the human–chimpanzee divergence. *PNAS* **102** (52), 18842-18847 (2005).
6. Patterson, N., Richter, D., Gnerre, S., Lander, E. & Reich, D., Genetic evidence for complex speciation of humans and chimpanzees. *Nature* **441**, 1103-1108 (2006).
7. Langergraber, K. *et al.*, Generation times in wild chimpanzees and gorillas suggest earlier divergence times in great ape and human evolution. *PNAS* **109** (39), 15716-15721 (2012).
8. Scally, A. *et al.*, Insights into hominid evolution from the gorilla genome sequence. *Nature* **483**, 169-175 (2012).
9. Groves, C., *Primate Taxonomy* (Smithsonian Institution Scholarly Press, Washington, DC, 2001).
10. Perelman, P. *et al.*, A Molecular Phylogeny of Living Primates. *PLoS Genetics* **7** (3) (2011).
11. Klein, R., *The Human Career*, 2nd ed. (University of Chicago Press, Chicago, 1999).
12. Dunbar, R., *Grooming. Gossip and the Evolution of Language*, 2nd ed. (Faber and Faber Ltd., London, 2004).
13. De Waal, F., Attitudinal reciprocity in food sharing among brown capuchin monkeys. *Animal Behaviour* **60**, 251-261 (2000).

14.	Aiello, L. & Dunbar, R., Neocortex Size, Group Size and the Evolution of Language. *Current Anthropology* **34** (2), 184-193 (1993).

15.	Mitani, J. & Watts, D., Why do chimpanzees hunt and share meat? *Animal Behaviour* **61**, 915–924 (2001).

16.	Hockings, K. *et al.*, Chimpanzees Share Forbidden Fruit. *PLoS One* **2** (9) (2007).

17.	Duffy, K., Wrangham, R. & Silk, J., Male chimpanzees exchange political support for mating opportunities. *Current Biology* **17** (15), R586–R587 (2007).

18.	Wroblewski, E. *et al.*, Male dominance rank and reproductive success in chimpanzees, Pan troglodytes schweinfurthii. *Animal Behaviour* **77** (4), 873-885 (2009).

19.	Wittig, R. & Boesch, C., Food Competition and Linear Dominance Hierarchy among Female Chimpanzees of the Tai National Park. *International Journal of Primatology* **24** (4), 847-867 (2003).

20.	Byrne, R. & Whiten, A., *Machiavellian Intelligence* (Oxford University Press, Oxford, 1988).

21.	Dunbar, R., The Social Brain Hypothesis. *Evolutionary Anthropology* **6** (5), 178-190 (1998).

22.	Dunbar, R., *The Human Story* (Faber and Faber, London, 2004).

23.	Dunbar, R., in *Rethinking the human revolution*, edited by Mellars, P., Boyle, K., Bar-Yosef, O. & Stringer, C. (McDonald Institute, Cambridge, 2007), pp. 91-105.

24.	Archibald, J. & Deutschman, D., Quantitative Analysis of the Timing of the Origin and Diversification of Extant Placental Orders. *Journal of Mammalian Evolution* **8** (2), 107-124 (2001).

25.	Springer, M., Murphy, W., Eizirik, E. & O'Brien, S., Placental mammal diversification and the Cretaceous–Tertiary boundary. *PNAS* **100** (3), 1056-1061 (2003).

26.	Miller, E., Gunnell, G. & Martin, R., Deep Time Depth and the search for Anthropoid Origins. *Yearbook of Physical Anthropology* **48**, 60-95 (2005).

27.	Tavaré, S., Marshall, C., Will, O., Soligo, C. & Martin, R., Using the fossil record to estimate the age of the last common ancestor of extant primates. *Nature* **416**, 726-729 (2002).

28.	Ni, X. *et al.*, The oldest known primate skeleton and early haplorhine evolution. *Nature* **498**, 60-64 (2013).

29.	Tan, Y., Yoder, A., Yamasita, N. & Li, W., Evidence from opsin genes rejects nocturnality in ancestral primates. *PNAS* **102** (41) (2005).

30.	Beard, K. C., Krishtalka, L. & Stucky, R. K., First skulls of the early Eocene primate Shoshonius cooperi and the anthropoid–tarsier dichotomy. *Nature* **349**, 64-67 (1991).

31.	Williams, B., Kay, R. & Kirk, C., New perspectives on anthropoid origins. *PNAS* **107** (11), 4797-4804 (2010).

32.	Gebo, D., Dagosto, M., Beard, C., Qi, T. & Wang, J., The oldest known anthropoid postcranial fossils and the early evolution of higher primates. *Nature* **404**, 276-278 (2000).

33.	Seiffert, E. *et al.*, Basal Anthropoids from Egypt and the Antiquity of Africa's Higher Primate Radiation. *Science* **310**, 300-304 (2005).

34.	Jaeger, J. *et al.*, Late middle Eocene epoch of Libya yields earliest known radiation of African anthropoids. *Nature* **467**, 1095-1099 (2010).

35.	Miller, E. & Simons, E., Dentition of Proteopithecus sylviae, an archaic anthropoid from the Fayum. *PNAS* **94**, 13760–13764 (1997).

36.	Glazko, G. & Nei, M., Estimation of Divergence Times for Major Lineages of Primate Species. *Molcular Biology and Evolution* **20** (3), 424-434 (2003).

37.	Steiper, M., Young, N. & Sukarna, T., Genomic data support the hominoid slowdown and an Early Oligocene estimate for the hominoid–cercopithecoid divergence. *PNAS* **101** (49), 17021-17026 (2004).

38.	Zalmout, I. *et al.*, New Oligocene primate from Saudi Arabia and the divergence of apes and Old World monkeys. *Nature* **466**, 360-364 (2010).

39.	Stringer, C. & Andrews, P., *The Complete World of Human Evolution* (Thames & Hudson, London, 2005).

40.	Conroy, G., *Reconstructing Human Origins: A Modern Synthesis* (W. W. Norton & Company, Inc., New York, NY, 1997).

41.	Lewin, R. & Foley, R., *Principles of Human Evolution*, 2nd ed. (Blackwell Science Ltd, Oxford, 2004).

42.	Cameron, D. & Groves, C., *Bones, Stones and Molecules: "Out of Africa" and Human Origins* (Elsevier Academic Press, London, 2004).

43.	Scher, H. & Martin, E., Timing and Climatic Consequences of the Opening of Drake Passage. *Science* **312**, 428-430 (2006).

44. Zachos, J., Pagani, M., Sloan, L., Thomas, E. & Billups, K., Trends, Rhythms, and Aberrations in Global Climate 65 Ma to Present. *Science* **292**, 686-693 (2001).
45. Harrison, T., Apes Among the Tangled Branches of Human Origins. *Science* **327**, 532-534 (2010).
46. Moya-Sola, S., Kohler, M., Alba, D., Casanovas-Vilar, I. & Galindo, J., Pierolapithecus catalaunicus, a New Middle Miocene Great Ape from Spain. *Science* **306**, 1339-1344 (2004).
47. Moya-Sola, S. *et al.*, A unique Middle Miocene European hominoid and the origins of the great ape and human clade. *PNAS* **109** (24), 9601-9606 (2009).
48. Toth, N. & Schick, K., in *The Human Past*, edited by Scarre, C. (Thames & Hudson, London, 2005), pp. 46-83.
49. Stewart, C. & Disotell, T., Primate evolution — in and out of Africa. *Current Biology* **8** (16), 582-588 (1998).
50. Suwa, G., Kono, R., Katoh, S., Asfaw, B. & Beyene, Y., A new species of great ape from the late Miocene epoch in Ethiopia. *Nature* **448**, 921-924 (2007).
51. Kunimatsu, Y. *et al.*, A new Late Miocene great ape from Kenya and its implications for the origins of African great apes and humans. *PNAS* **104** (49), 19220-19225 (2007).
52. Wilson, R., Drury, S. & Chapman, J., *The Great Ice Age* (Routledge, London, 2000).
53. Garcia-Castellanos, D. *et al.*, Catastrophic flood of the Mediterranean after the Messinian salinity crisis. *Nature* **462**, 778-781 (2009).
54. Aiello, L. & Collard, M., Our Newest Oldest Ancestor. *Nature* **410**, 526-527 (2001).
55. Wood, B. & Harrison, T., The evolutionary context of the first hominins. *Nature* **470**, 347-352 (2011).
56. McBrearty, S. & Jablonski, N., First Fossil Chimpanzee. *Nature* **437**, 105-108 (2005).
57. Caswell, J. *et al.*, Analysis of Chimpanzee History Based on Genome Sequence Alignments. *PLoS One* **4** (4) (2008).
58. Richmond, B. & Strait, D., Evidence that humans evolved from a knuckle-walking ancestor. *Nature* **404**, 382-385 (2000).
59. Richmond, B., Begin, D. & Strait, D., Origin of Human Bipedalism: The Knuckle-Walking Hypothesis Revisited. *Yearbook of Physical Anthropology* **44**, 70-105 (2001).
60. Kivell, T. & Schmitt, D., Independent evolution of knuckle-walking in African apes shows that humans did not evolve from a knuckle-walking ancestor. *PNAS* **106** (34), 14241-14246 (2009).
61. Lovejoy, O., Reexamining Human Origins in Light of Ardipithecus ramidus. *Science* **326**, 74 (2009).

3: Down from the trees

1. White, T., Suwa, G. & Asfaw, B., Australopithecus ramidus, a new species of early hominid from Aramis, Ethiopia. *Nature* **371**, 306-312 (1994).
2. Gibbons, A., A New Kind of Ancestor: Ardipithecus Unveiled. *Science* **326**, 36-40 (2009).
3. Haile-Selassie, Y., Late Miocene hominids from the Middle Awash, Ethiopia. *Nature* **412**, 178-181 (2001).
4. Semaw, S. *et al.*, Early Pliocene hominids from Gona, Ethiopia. *Nature* **433**, 301-305 (2005).
5. Pickford, M. & Senut, B., The geological and faunal context of Late Miocene hominid remains from Lukeino, Kenya. *Comptes Rendus de l'Académie des Sciences* **332** (2), 145-152 (2001).
6. Senut, B. *et al.*, First hominid from the Miocene (Lukeino Formation, Kenya). *Comptes Rendus de l'Académie des Sciences* **332** (2), 137-144 (2001).
7. Galik, K. *et al.*, External and Internal Morphology of the BAR 1002'00 Orrorin tugenensis Femur. *Science* **305**, 1450-1453 (2004).
8. Gibbons, A., Oldest Human Femur Wades into Controversy. *Science* **305**, 1885 (2004).
9. Ohman, J., Lovejoy, O. & White, T., Questions about Orrorin femur. *Science* **307**, 845 (2005).
10. Richmond, B. & Jungers, W., Orrorin tugenensis Femoral Morphology and the Evolution of Hominin Bipedalism. *Science* **319**, 1662-1665 (2008).
11. Almecija, S., Moya-Sola, S. & Alba, D., Early Origin for Human-Like Precision Grasping: A Comparative Study of Pollical Distal Phalanges in Fossil Hominins. *PLoS One* **5** (7) (2010).
12. Brunet, M. *et al.*, A new hominid from the Upper Miocene of Chad, Central Africa. *Nature* **418**, 145-151 (2002).

13. Vignaud, P. *et al.*, Geology and palaeontology of the Upper Miocene Toros-Menalla hominid locality, Chad. *Nature* **418**, 152-155 (2002).

14. Wolpoff, M., Hawks, J., Senut, B., Pickford, M. & Ahern, J., An Ape or the Ape: Is the Toumaï Cranium TM 266 a Hominid? *PaleoAnthropology*, 36-50 (2006).

15. Guy, F. *et al.*, Morphological affinities of the Sahelanthropus tchadensis (Late Miocene hominid from Chad) cranium. *PNAS* **102** (52), 18836–18841 (2005).

16. Brunet, M. *et al.*, New material of the earliest hominid from the Upper Miocene of Chad. *Nature* **434**, 752-755 (2005).

17. Zollikofer, C. *et al.*, Virtual cranial reconstruction of Sahelanthropus tchadensis. *Nature* **434**, 755-758 (2005).

18. Patterson, N., Richter, D., Gnerre, S., Lander, E. & Reich, D., Genetic evidence for complex speciation of humans and chimpanzees. *Nature* **441**, 1103-1108 (2006).

19. Langergraber, K. *et al.*, Generation times in wild chimpanzees and gorillas suggest earlier divergence times in great ape and human evolution. *PNAS* **109** (39), 15716-15721 (2012).

20. Aiello, L. & Collard, M., Our Newest Oldest Ancestor. *Nature* **410**, 526-527 (2001).

21. Wood, B. & Harrison, T., The evolutionary context of the first hominins. *Nature* **470**, 347-352 (2011).

22. Haile-Selassie, Y., Suwa, G. & White, T., Late Miocene Teeth from Middle Awash, Ethiopia, and Early Hominid Dental Evolution. *Science* **303**, 1503-1505 (2004).

23. White, T. *et al.*, Ardipithecus ramidus and the Paleobiology of Early Hominids. *Science* **326**, 75-86 (2009).

24. Suwa, G. *et al.*, The Ardipithecus ramidus Skull and Its Implications for Hominid Origins. *Science* **326**, 68 (2009).

25. White, T. *et al.*, Macrovertebrate Paleontology and the Pliocene Habitat of Ardipithecus ramidus. *Science* **326**, 87-93 (2009).

26. Louchart, A. *et al.*, Taphonomic, Avian, and Small-Vertebrate Indicators of Ardipithecus ramidus Habitat. *Science* **326**, 66e1-66e4 (2009).

27. WoldeGabriel, G. *et al.*, The Geological, Isotopic, Botanical,Invertebrate, and Lower Vertebrate Surroundings of Ardipithecus ramidus. *Science* **326**, 65e1-65e5 (2009).

28. Suwa, G. *et al.*, Paleobiological Implications of the Ardipithecus ramidus Dentition. *Science* **326**, 94-99 (2009).

29. Lovejoy, O., Suwa, G., Simpson, S., Matternes, J. & White, T., The Great Divides: Ardipithecus ramidus Reveals the Postcrania of Our Last Common Ancestors with African Apes. *Science* **326**, 100-106 (2009).

30. Lovejoy, O., Suwa, G., Spurlock, L., Asfaw, B. & White, T., The Pelvis and Femur of Ardipithecus ramidus: The Emergence of Upright Walking. *Science* **326**, 71 (2009).

31. Lovejoy, O., Latimer, B., Suwa, G., Asfaw, B. & White, T., Combining Prehension and Propulsion: The Foot of Ardipithecus ramidus. *Science* **326**, 72e1-72e8 (2009).

32. Lovejoy, O., Simpson, S., White, T., Asfaw, B. & Suwa, G., Careful Climbing in the Miocene: The Forelimbs of Ardipithecus ramidus and Humans Are Primitive. *Science* **326**, 70e1-70e8 (2009).

33. McHenry, H., How Big Were Early Hominids? *Evolutionary Anthropology*, 15-20 (1992).

34. Klein, R., *The Human Career*, 2nd ed. (University of Chicago Press, Chicago, 1999).

35. Stokes, E., Parnell, R. & Olejniczak, C., Female dispersal and reproductive success in wild western lowland gorillas (Gorilla gorilla gorilla). *Behavioral Ecology and Sociobiology* **54**, 329-339 (2003).

36. De Waal, F. & Lanting, F., *Bonobo: The Forgotten Ape* (University of California Press, Berkley & Los Angeles, CA, 1997).

37. Diamond, J., *The Third Chimpanzee* (Random, London, 1991).

38. Burt, A., Concealed Ovulation and Sexual Signals in Primates. *Folia Primatologica* **58**, 1-6 (1992).

39. Lewin, R. & Foley, R., *Principles of Human Evolution*, 2nd ed. (Blackwell Science Ltd, Oxford, 2004).

40. Reno, P., Meindl, R., McCollum, M. & Lovejoy, O., Sexual dimorphism in Australopithecus afarensis was similar to that of modern humans. *PNAS* **500** (16), 9404-9409 (2003).

41. Jablonski, N. & Chaplin, G., Origin of habitual terrestrial bipedalism in the ancestor of the Hominidae. *Journal of Human Evolution* **23**, 259-280 (1993).

42. Hunt, K., The evolution of human bipedality: ecology and functional morphology. *Journal of Human Evolution* **23**, 183-202 (1994).

43. Rodman, P. & McHenry, H., Biogenetics and the Origin of Hominid Bipedalism. *American Journal of Physical Anthropology* **52**, 103-106 (1980).
44. Wheeler, P., The Evolution of Bipedality and Loss of Functional Body Hair in Hominoids. *Journal of Human Evolution* **13**, 91-98 (1984).
45. Lovejoy, O., The Origins of Man. *Science* **211**, 341-350 (1981).
46. Lovejoy, O., Reexamining Human Origins in Light of Ardipithecus ramidus. *Science* **326**, 74e1-74e8 (2009).
47. Hughes, J. *et al.*, Conservation of Y-linked genes during human evolution revealed by comparative sequencing in chimpanzee. *Nature* **437** (2005).
48. Hughes, J. *et al.*, Chimpanzee and human Y chromosomes are remarkably divergent in structure and gene content. *Nature* **463**, 536-539 (2010).

4: The southern apes

1. Bryson, B., *A Short History of Nearly Everything* (Doubleday, London, 2003).
2. Leakey, M., Feibel, C., McDougall, I., Ward, C. & Walkerk, A., New specimens and confirmation of an early age for Australopithecus anamensis. *Nature* **393**, 62-66 (1998).
3. White, T. *et al.*, Asa Issie, Aramis and the origin of Australopithecus. *Nature* **440**, 883-889 (2006).
4. White, T. *et al.*, Ardipithecus ramidus and the Paleobiology of Early Hominids. *Science* **326**, 64 (2009).
5. Eldridge, N. & Gould, S., in *Models in Paleobiology*, edited by Schopf, T. (Freeman, Cooper and Company, San Francisco, 1972), pp. 82-115.
6. Dawkins, R., *The Blind Watchmaker* (Longman, London, 1986).
7. Haile-Selassie, Y. *et al.*, A new hominin foot from Ethiopia shows multiple Pliocene bipedal adaptations. *Nature* **483**, 565-570 (2012).
8. Klein, R., *The Human Career*, 2nd ed. (University of Chicago Press, Chicago, 1999).
9. Conroy, G., *Reconstructing Human Origins: A Modern Synthesis* (W. W. Norton & Company, Inc., New York, NY, 1997).
10. Lewin, R. & Foley, R., *Principles of Human Evolution*, 2nd ed. (Blackwell Science Ltd, Oxford, 2004).
11. DeSilva, J., Functional morphology of the ankle and the likelihood of climbing in early hominins. *PNAS* **106** (16), 6567-6572 (2009).
12. Ward, C., Kimbel, W. & Johanson, D., Complete Fourth Metatarsal and Arches in the Foot of Australopithecus afarensis. *Science* **331**, 750-753 (2011).
13. Lovejoy, O., Latimer, B., Suwa, G., Asfaw, B. & White, T., Combining Prehension and Propulsion: The Foot of Ardipithecus ramidus. *Science* **326**, 72e1-72e8 (2009).
14. Haile-Selassie, Y. *et al.*, An early Australopithecus afarensis postcranium from Woranso-Mille, Ethiopia. *PNAS* **107** (27), 112121-12126 (2010).
15. Schmid, P. *et al.*, Mosaic Morphology in the Thorax of Australopithecus sediba. *Science* **340** (2013).
16. Quam, R. *et al.*, Early hominin auditory ossicles from South Africa. *PNAS* **110** (22), 8847-8851 (2013).
17. DeSilva, J., A shift toward birthing relatively large infants early in human evolution. *PNAS* **108** (3), 1022-1027 (2011).
18. Teaford, M. & Ungar, P., Diet and the evolution of the earliest human ancestors. *PNAS* **97** (25), 13506-13511 (2000).
19. Ungar, P., Dental topography and diets of Australopithecus afarensis and early Homo. *Journal of Human Evolution* **46**, 605-622 (2004).
20. Strait, D. *et al.*, The feeding biomechanics and dietary ecology of Australopithecus africanus. *PNAS* **106** (7), 2124-2129 (2009).
21. Constantino, P. *et al.*, Tooth chipping can reveal the diet and bite forces of fossil hominins. *Biology Letters* **6**, 826-829 (2010).
22. Sponheimer, M. & Lee-Thorp, J., Isotopic Evidence for the Diet of an Early Hominid, Australopithecus africanus. *Science* **238**, 368-370 (1999).
23. Balter, V., Braga, J., Télouk, P. & Thackeray, F., Evidence for dietary change but not landscape use in South African early hominins. *Nature* **489**, 558–560 (2012).

24.   Copeland, S. *et al.*, Strontium isotope evidence for landscape use by early hominins. *Nature* **474**, 76-78 (2011).

25.   Leakey, M., Feibel, C., McDougall, I. & Walker, A., New four-million-year-old hominid species from Kanapoi and Allia Bay, Kenya. *Nature* **376**, 565-571 (1995).

26.   Stringer, C. & Andrews, P., *The Complete World of Human Evolution* (Thames & Hudson, London, 2005).

27.   Cameron, D. & Groves, C., *Bones, Stones and Molecules: "Out of Africa" and Human Origins* (Elsevier Academic Press, London, 2004).

28.   Crompton, R. P. T. *et al.*, Human-like external function of the foot, and fully upright gait, confirmed in the 3.66 million year old Laetoli hominin footprints by topographic statistics, experimental footprint formation and computer simulation. *Journal of the Royal Society Interface* **9**, 707-719 (2012).

29.   Macho, G. *et al.*, An Exploratory Study on the Combined Effects of External and Internal Morphology on Load Dissipation in Primate Capitates: Its Potential for an Understanding of the Positional and Locomotor Repertoire of Early Hominins. *Folia Primatologica* **81**, 292-304 (2010).

30.   McHenry, H., How Big Were Early Hominids? *Evolutionary Anthropology*, 15-20 (1992).

31.   Reno, P., Meindl, R., McCollum, M. & Lovejoy, O., Sexual dimorphism in Australopithecus afarensis was similar to that of modern humans. *PNAS* **500** (16), 9404-9409 (2003).

32.   Brunet, M. *et al.*, The first australopithecine 2,500 kilometres west of the Rift Valley (Chad). *Nature* **378**, 273-275 (1995).

33.   Leakey, M. *et al.*, New hominin genus from eastern Africa shows diverse middle Pliocene lineages. *Nature* **410**, 433-440 (2001).

34.   White, T., Early Hominids--Diversity or Distortion? *Science* **229**, 1994-1997 (2003).

35.   Derricourt, R., The enigma of Raymond Dart, the Australian discoverer of Man's African origins, Available at http://www.abc.net.au/radionational/programs/ockhamsrazor/the-enigma-of-raymond-dart-the-australian/3212188 (2007).

36.   Dart, R., Australopithecus africanus: The Man-Ape of South Africa. *Nature* **115** (2884), 195-199 (1925).

37.   Asfaw, B. *et al.*, Australopithecus garhi: A New Species of Early Hominid from Ethiopia. *Science* **284**, 629-635 (1999).

38.   Berger, L. *et al.*, Australopithecus sediba: A New Species of Homo-Like Australopith from South Africa. *Science* **328**, 195-204 (2010).

39.   Balter, M., Candidate Human Ancestor From South Africa Sparks Praise and Debate. *Science* **328**, 154-155 (2010).

40.   Dirks, P. *et al.*, Geological Setting and Age of Australopithecus sediba from Southern Africa. *Science* **328**, 205-208 (2010).

41.   Pickering, R. *et al.*, Australopithecus sediba at 1.977 Ma and Implications for the Origins of the Genus Homo. *Science* **333**, 1421-1423 (2011).

42.   MacKnight, H., Experts reject new human species theory, Available at http://www.independent.co.uk/news/science/experts-reject-new-human-species-theory-1939512.html (2010).

43.   Wood, B. & Harrison, T., The evolutionary context of the first hominins. *Nature* **470**, 347-352 (2011).

44.   Carlson, K. *et al.*, The Endocast of MH1, Australopithecus sediba. *Science* **333**, 1402-1407 (2011).

45.   Irish, J., Guatelli-Steinberg, D., Legge, S., de Ruiter, D. & Berger, L., Dental Morphology and the Phylogenetic "Place" of Australopithecus sediba. *Science* **340**, 1233062-1-1233062-4 (2013).

46.   De Ruiter, D. *et al.*, Mandibular Remains Support Taxonomic Validity of Australopithecus sediba. *Science* **340**, 1232997-1-1232997-4 (2013).

47.   Williams, S. *et al.*, The Vertebral Column of Australopithecus sediba. *Science* **340**, 1232996-1-1232996-5 (2013).

48.   Churchill, S. *et al.*, The Upper Limb of Australopithecus sediba. *Science* **340**, 1233477-1-1233477-6 (2013).

49.   Kivell, T., Kibii, J., Churchill, S., Schmid, P. & Berger, L., Australopithecus sediba Hand Demonstrates Mosaic Evolution of Locomotor and Manipulative Abilities. *Science* **333**, 1411-1417 (2011).

50.   Kibii, J. *et al.*, A Partial Pelvis of Australopithecus sediba. *Science* **333**, 1407-1411 (2011).

51.   Zipfel, B. *et al.*, The Foot and Ankle of Australopithecus sediba. *Science* **333**, 1417-1420 (2011).

52.   DeSilva, J. *et al.*, The Lower Limb and Mechanics of Walking in Australopithecus sediba. *Science* **340**, 1232999-1-1232999-5 (2013).

53.   McCollum, M., The Robust Australopithecine Face: A Morphogenetic Perspective. *Science* **284**, 301-305 (1999).

54.   Rak, Y., Ginzburg, A. & Geffen, E., Gorilla-like anatomy on Australopithecus afarensis mandibles suggests Au. afarensis link to robust australopiths. *PNAS* **104** (16), 6568-6572 (2007).

55.   Toth, N. & Schick, K., in *The Human Past*, edited by Scarre, C. (Thames & Hudson, London, 2005), pp. 46-83.

56.   Sponheimer, M. *et al.*, Isotopic Evidence for Dietary Variability in the Early Hominin Paranthropus robustus. *Science* **314**, 980-982 (2006).

57.   Ungar, P., Grine, F. & Teaford, M., Dental Microwear and Diet of the Plio-Pleistocene Hominin Paranthropus boisei. *PLoS One* **3** (4) (2008).

58.   Sanz, C., Call, J. & Morgan, D., Design complexity in termite-fishing tools of chimpanzees (Pan troglodytes). *Biology Letters* **5**, 293-296 (2009).

59.   Panger, M., Brooks, A., Richmond, B. & Wood, B., Older Than the Oldowan? Rethinking the Emergence of Hominin Tool Use. *Evolutionary Anthropology* **11** (6), 235-245 (2002).

60.   Hobaiter, C., Poisot, T., Zuberbühler, K., Hoppitt, W. & Gruber, T., Social Network Analysis Shows Direct Evidence for Social Transmission of Tool Use in Wild Chimpanzees. *PLoS Biology* **12** (9), e1001960 (2014).

61.   Semaw, S. *et al.*, 2.5-million-year-old stone tools from Gona, Ethiopia. *Nature* **385**, 333-336 (1997).

62.   Semaw, S., The World's Oldest Stone Artefacts from Gona, Ethiopia: Their Implications for Understanding Stone Technology and Patterns of Human Evolution Between 2·6–1·5 Million Years Ago. *Journal of Archaeological Science* **27**, 1197–1214 (2000).

63.   De Heinzelin, J. *et al.*, Environment and Behavior of 2.5-Million-Year-Old Bouri Hominids. *Science* **284**, 625-629 (1999).

64.   McPherron, S. *et al.*, Evidence for stone-tool-assisted consumption of animal tissues before 3.39 million years ago at Dikika, Ethiopia. *Nature* **466**, 857-860 (2010).

65.   Domínguez-Rodrigo, M., Pickering, T. & Bunn, H., Reply to McPherron et al.: Doubting Dikika is about data, not paradigms. *PNAS* **108** (21), E117 (2011).

66.   Ferraro, J. *et al.*, Earliest Archaeological Evidence of Persistent Hominin Carnivory. *PLoS One* **8** (4) (2013).

67.   Toth, N., The Oldowan reassessed: a close look at early stone artefacts. *Journal of Archaeological Science* **20**, 101-120 (1985).

68.   Wynn, T. & McGrew, W., An ape's view of the Oldowan. *Man* **24**, 383-398 (1989).

69.   Toth, N., Schick, K. & Savage-Rumbaugh, E., Pan the toolmaker: investigations into the stone tool-making and tool-using abilities of a bonobo (Pan paniscus). *Journal of Archaeological Science* **20**, 81-91 (1993).

70.   Dennell, R. & Roebroeks, W., An Asian perspective on early human dispersal from Africa. *Nature* **438**, 1099-1104 (2005).

5: Becoming human

1.   Leakey, L., Tobias, P. & Napier, J., A new species of the genus Homo from Olduvai Gorge. *Nature* **202** (4927), 7-9 (1964).

2.   Cameron, D. & Groves, C., *Bones, Stones and Molecules: "Out of Africa" and Human Origins* (Elsevier Academic Press, London, 2004).

3.   Klein, R., *The Human Career*, 2nd ed. (University of Chicago Press, Chicago, 1999).

4.   Kimbel, W., Johanson, D. & Rak, Y., Systematic Assessment of a Maxilla of Homo From Hadar, Ethiopia. *American Journal of Physical Anthropology* **103**, 235-262 (1997).

5.   Spoor, F. *et al.*, Implications of new early Homo fossils from Ileret, east of Lake Turkana, Kenya. *Nature* **448**, 688-691 (2007).

6.   Lieberman, D., Homing in on early Homo. *Nature* **449**, 291-292 (2007).

7.   Wood, B., Reconstructing human evolution: Achievements, challenges, and opportunities. *PNAS* **107** (Suppl. 2), 8902-8909 (2010).

8. Conroy, G., *Reconstructing Human Origins: A Modern Synthesis* (W. W. Norton & Company, Inc., New York, NY, 1997).

9. Johanson, D. *et al.*, New partial skeleton of Homo habilis from Olduvai Gorge, Tanzania. *Nature* **327**, 205-209 (1987).

10. McHenry, H., How Big Were Early Hominids? *Evolutionary Anthropology*, 15-20 (1992).

11. Berger, L. *et al.*, Australopithecus sediba: A New Species of Homo-Like Australopith from South Africa. *Science* **328**, 195-204 (2010).

12. Bromage, T. *et al.*, Craniofacial architectural constraints and their importance for reconstructing the early Homo skull KNM-ER 1470. *The Journal of Clinical Pediatric Dentistry* **33** (1), 43-51 (2008).

13. Groves, C., *A Theory of Human and Primate Evolution* (Oxford University Press, Oxford, 1989).

14. Leakey, M. *et al.*, New fossils from Koobi Fora in northern Kenya confirm taxonomic diversity in early Homo. *Nature* **488**, 201-204 (2012).

15. Stringer, C. & Andrews, P., *The Complete World of Human Evolution* (Thames & Hudson, London, 2005).

16. Wade, N., *Before the Dawn* (Penguin, London, 2006).

17. Aiello, L. & Collard, M., Our Newest Oldest Ancestor. *Nature* **410**, 526-527 (2001).

18. Dennell, R. & Roebroeks, W., An Asian perspective on early human dispersal from Africa. *Nature* **438**, 1099-1104 (2005).

19. Wood, B. & Collard, M., The Human Genus. *Science* **284**, 65-71 (1999).

20. Gonzalez-Jose, R., Escapa, I., Neves, W., Cuneo, R. & Pucciarelli, H., Cladistic analysis of continuous modularized traits provides phylogenetic signals in Homo evolution. *Nature* **453**, 775-779 (2008).

21. Wood, B., Did early Homo migrate "out of " or "in to" Africa? *PNAS* **108** (26), 10375-10376 (2011).

22. Tobias, P., The brain of Homo habilis: a new level of organization in cerebral evolution. *Journal of Human Evolution* **16**, 741-761 (1987).

23. Mithen, S., *The Singing Neanderthal* (Weidenfeld & Nicholson, London, 2005).

24. Coolidge, F. & Wynn, T., *The Rise of Homo sapiens* (Wiley-Blackwell, Hoboken, NJ, 2009).

25. Aiello, L. & Dunbar, R., Neocortex Size, Group Size and the Evolution of Language. *Current Anthropology* **34** (2), 184-193 (1993).

26. Toth, N. & Schick, K., in *The Human Past*, edited by Scarre, C. (Thames & Hudson, London, 2005), pp. 46-83.

27. Lewin, R. & Foley, R., *Principles of Human Evolution*, 2nd ed. (Blackwell Science Ltd, Oxford, 2004).

28. Toth, N., The Oldowan reassessed: a close look at early stone artefacts. *Journal of Archaeological Science* **20**, 101-120 (1985).

29. Aiello, L. & Wheeler, P., The expensive tissue hypothesis: the brain and the digestive system in human and primate evolution. *Current Anthropology* **36**, 199-221 (1995).

30. Navarrete, A., van Schaik, C. & Isler, K., Energetics and the evolution of human brain size. *Nature* **480**, 91-93 (2011).

31. Isaac, G., The food sharing behaviour of protohuman hominids. *Scientific American* **238**, 90-108 (1978).

32. Binford, L., *Bones: Ancient Men and Modern Myths* (Academic Press, New York, 1981).

33. Potts, R., Temporal span of bone accumulations at Olduvai Gorge and implications for early hominid foraging behaviour. *Paleobiology* **12**, 25-31 (1986).

34. Potts, R., *Early Hominid Activities at Olduvai Gorge* (Aldine de Gruyter, New York, 1988).

35. Blumenschine, R., Characteristics of an early hominid scavenging niche. *Current Anthropology* **28**, 283-407 (1986).

36. Mithen, S., *The Prehistory of the Mind* (Thomas & Hudson, London, 1996).

6: The first Diaspora – or was it?

1. Dean, C. *et al.*, Growth processes in teeth distinguish modern humans from Homo erectus and earlier hominins. *Nature* **414**, 628-631 (2001).

2. Klein, R., in *The Human Past*, edited by Scarre, C. (Thames & Hudson, London, 2005), pp. 84-123.

3. Cameron, D. & Groves, C., *Bones, Stones and Molecules: "Out of Africa" and Human Origins* (Elsevier Academic Press, London, 2004).
4. Bennett, M. *et al.*, Early Hominin Foot Morphology Based on 1.5-Million-Year-Old Footprints from Ileret, Kenya. *Science* **323**, 1197-1201 (2009).
5. Klein, R., *The Human Career*, 2nd ed. (University of Chicago Press, Chicago, 1999).
6. MacLarnon, A. & Hewitt, G., The Evolution of Human Speech: The Role of Enhanced Breathing Control. *American Journal of Physical Anthropology* **109**, 341-363 (1999).
7. Smith, H., Dental development as a Measure of Life History in Primates. *Evolution* **43** (3), 683-688 (1989).
8. Risnes, S., Growth tracks in dental enamel. *Journal of Human Evolution* **35** (4-5), 331-350 (1998).
9. Smith, T., Experimental determination of the periodicity of incremental features in enamel. *Journal of Anatomy* **208**, 99-113 (2006).
10. Smith, T. *et al.*, Earliest evidence of modern human life history in North African early Homo sapiens. *PNAS* **104** (15), 6128-6133 (2007).
11. Rightmire, P., Human Evolution in the Middle Pleistocene: The Role of Homo heidelbergensis. *Evolutionary Anthropology* **6** (6), 218-227 (1998).
12. Wood, B., Reconstructing human evolution: Achievements, challenges, and opportunities. *PNAS* **107** (Suppl. 2), 8902-8909 (2010).
13. Wood, B., Did early Homo migrate "out of" or "in to" Africa? *PNAS* **108** (26), 10375-10376 (2011).
14. Rosenberg, K. & Trevathan, W., Birth, obstetrics and human evolution. *BJOG: an International Journal of Obstetrics and Gynaecology* **109**, 1199-1206 (2002).
15. Dunsworth, H., Warrender, A., Deacon, T., Ellison, P. & Pontzer, H., Metabolic hypothesis for human altriciality. *PNAS* **109** (38), 15212-15218 (2012).
16. Walker, A., Zimmerman, M. & Leakey, R., A possible case of hypervitaminosis A in Homo erectus. *Nature* **296**, 248-250 (1982).
17. McHenry, H., How Big Were Early Hominids? *Evolutionary Anthropology*, 15-20 (1992).
18. Lordkipanidze, D. *et al.*, Postcranial evidence from early Homo from Dmanisi, Georgia. *Nature* **449**, 305-310 (2007).
19. Joordens, J. *et al.*, Homo erectus at Trinil on Java used shells for tool production and engraving. *Nature* (2014).
20. Crawford, M. *et al.*, Evidence for the unique function of docasahexaenoic acid during the evolution of the modern human brain. *Lipids* **34** (Supplement), S39-S47 (1999).
21. Bramble, D. & Lieberman, D., Endurance running and the evolution of Homo. *Nature* **432**, 345-352 (2004).
22. Asfaw, B. *et al.*, Remains of Homo erectus from Bouri, Middle Awash, Ethiopia. *Nature* **416**, 317-320 (2002).
23. Trauth, M., Maslin, M., Deino, A. & Strecker, M., Late Cenozoic Moisture History of East Africa. *Science* **309**, 2051-2053 (2005).
24. Spoor, F. *et al.*, Implications of new early Homo fossils from Ileret, east of Lake Turkana, Kenya. *Nature* **448**, 688-691 (2007).
25. Lepre, C. *et al.*, An earlier origin for the Acheulian. *Nature* **477**, 82-85 (2011).
26. Pappu, S. *et al.*, Early Pleistocene Presence of Acheulian Hominins in South India. *Science* **331**, 1596-1598 (2011).
27. Coolidge, F. & Wynn, T., *The Rise of Homo sapiens* (Wiley-Blackwell, Hoboken, NJ, 2009).
28. Kohn, M. & Mithen, S., Handaxes: products of sexual selection?. *Antiquity* **73**, 518-526 (1999).
29. Swisher, C. *et al.*, Age of the earliest known hominids in Java, Indonesia. *Science* **263**, 1118-1121 (1994).
30. Lycett, S. & von Cramon-Taubadel, N., Acheulean variability and hominin dispersals: a model-bound approach. *Journal of Archaeological Science* **35**, 553-562 (2008).
31. Roberts, A., *The Incredible Human Journey* (Bloomsbury, London, 2009).
32. Lewin, R. & Foley, R., *Principles of Human Evolution*, 2nd ed. (Blackwell Science Ltd, Oxford, 2004).
33. Dennell, R., in *Living in the Landscape: Essays in honour of Graeme Barker*, edited by Boyle, K., Rabett, R. & Hunt, C. (McDonald Institute for Archaeological Research, 2014), pp. 11-34.
34. Wrangham, R., *Catching Fire: How Cooking Made Us Human* (Basic Books, New York, NY, 2009).

35. Pickering, T., What's new is old: Comments on (more) archaeological evidence of one-million-year-old fire from South Africa. *South African Journal of Science* **108** (5/6), 1-2 (2012).

36. Brain, C. & Sillen, A., Evidence from the Swartkrans cave for the earliest use of fire. *Nature* **336**, 464-466 (1988).

37. Berna, F. *et al.*, Microstratigraphic evidence of in situ fire in the Acheulean strata of Wonderwerk Cave, Northern Cape province, South Africa. *PNAS* **109** (20), E1215-E1220 (2012).

38. Roebroeks, W. & Villa, P., On the earliest evidence for habitual use of fire in Europe. *PNAS* **108** (13), 5209-5214 (2011).

39. Weiner, S., Xu, Q., Goldberg, P., Liu, J. & Bar-Yosef, O., Evidence for the Use of Fire at Zhoukoudian, China. *Science* **281**, 251-253 (1998).

40. Goren-Inbar, N. *et al.*, Evidence of Hominin Control of Fire at Gesher Benot Ya'aqov, Israel. *Science* **304**, 725-727 (2004).

41. Gabunia, L. *et al.*, Earliest Pleistocene Hominid Cranial Remains from Dmanisi,Republic of Georgia: Taxonomy, Geological Setting, and Age. *Science* **228**, 1019-1025 (2000).

42. Ferring, R. *et al.*, Earliest human occupations at Dmanisi (Georgian Caucasus) dated to 1.85–1.78 Ma. *PNAS* **108** (26), 10432-10436 (2011).

43. Vekua, A. *et al.*, A New Skull of Early Homo from Dmanisi, Georgia. *Science* **297**, 85-89 (2002).

44. Lordkipanidze, D. et al., A Fourth Hominin Skull From Dmanisi, Georgia. The Anatomical Record Part A: Discoveries in Molecular, Cellular, and Evolutionary Biology **288A**, 1146-1157 (2006).

45. Lordkipanidze, D. *et al.*, A Complete Skull from Dmanisi, Georgia, and the Evolutionary Biology of Early Homo. *Science* **342**, 326-331 (2013).

46. Lordkipanidze, D. *et al.*, The earliest toothless hominin skull. *Nature* **434**, 717-718 (2005).

47. Lieberman, D., Homing in on early Homo. *Nature* **449**, 291-292 (2007).

48. Gabunia, L., de Lumley, M.-A., Vekua, A., Lordkipanidze, D. & de Lumley, H., Découverte d'un nouvel hominidé à Dmanissi (Transcaucasie, Géorgie). *C.R. Palévol.* **1**, 243-253 (2002).

49. Bermúdez de Castro, J., Martinón-Torres, M., Sier, M. & Martín-Francés, L., On the Variability of the Dmanisi Mandibles. *PLoS One* **9** (2), e88212 (2014).

50. Curtis, G., Swisher, C. & Lewin, R., *Java Man* (Little, Brown and Company, New York, NY, 2000).

51. Coqueugniot, H., Hublin, J., Veillon, F., Houet, F. & Jacob, T., Early brain growth in Homo erectus and implications for cognitive ability. *Nature* **431**, 299-302 (2004).

52. Berger, L., Liu, W. & Wu, X., Investigation of a credible report by a US Marine on the location of the missing Peking Man fossils. *South African Journal of Science* **108** (3/4) (2012).

53. Morwood, M., O'Sullivan, P., Susanto, E. & Aziz, F., Revised age for Mojokerto 1, an early Homo erectus cranium from East Java, Indonesia. *Australian Archaeology* (57) (2003).

54. Larick, R. *et al.*, Early Pleistocene 40Ar-39Ar ages for Bapang Formation hominins, Central Jawa, Indonesia. *PNAS* **98** (9), 4866-4871 (2001).

55. Zhu, Z. *et al.*, New dating of the Homo erectus cranium from Lantian (Gongwangling), China. *Journal of Human Evolution* (2014).

56. Zhu, R. *et al.*, Earliest presence of humans in northeast Asia. *Nature* **413**, 413-417 (2001).

57. Zhu, R. *et al.*, New evidence on the earliest human presence at high northern latitudes in northeast Asia. *Nature* **431**, 559-562 (2004).

58. Brown, P. *et al.*, A new small-bodied hominin from the Late Pleistocene of Flores, Indonesia. *Nature* **431**, 1055-1061 (2004).

59. Morwood, M. *et al.*, Archaeology and age of a new hominin from Flores in eastern Indonesia. *Nature* **431**, 1087-1091 (2004).

60. Morwood, M. *et al.*, Further evidence for small-bodied hominins from the Late Pleistocene of Flores, Indonesia. *Nature* **437**, 1012-1017 (2005).

61. Aaronovitch, D., Big little man, Available at http://www.guardian.co.uk/science/2004/oct/31/comment.columnists (2004).

62. Jacob, T. *et al.*, Pygmoid Australomelanesian Homo sapiens skeletal remains from Liang Bua, Flores: Population affinities and pathological abnormalities. *PNAS* **103** (36), 13421-13426 (2006).

63. Martin, R. *et al.*, Comment on "The Brain of LB1, Homo floresiensis". *Science* **312**, 999b (2006).

64. Eckhardt, R., Henneberg, M., Weller, A. & Hsüc, K., Rare events in earth history include the LB1 human skeleton from Flores, Indonesia, as a developmental singularity, not a unique taxon. *PNAS* **111** (33), 11961-11966 (2014).

65. Henneberg, M., Eckhardt, R., Chavanaves, S. & Hsüe, K., Evolved developmental homeostasis disturbed in LB1 from Flores, Indonesia, denotes Down syndrome and not diagnostic traits of the invalid species Homo floresiensis. *PNAS* **111** (33), 11967-11972 (2014).

66. Argue, D., Donlon, D., Groves, C. & Wright, R., Homo floresiensis: Microcephalic, pygmoid, Australopithecus, or Homo? *Journal of Human Evolution* **51**, 360-374 (2006).

67. Falk, D. *et al.*, The Brain of LB1, Homo floresiensis. *Science* **308**, 624-628 (2005).

68. Falk, D. *et al.*, Brain shape in human microcephalics and Homo floresiensis. *PNAS* **104** (7), 2513-2518 (2007).

69. Tocheri, M. *et al.*, The Primitive Wrist of Homo floresiensis and Its Implications for Hominin Evolution. *Science* **317**, 1743-1745 (2007).

70. Lyras, G., Dermitzakis, M., Van der Geer, A., Van der Geer, S. & De Vos, J., The origin of Homo floresiensis and its relation to evolutionary processes under isolation. *Anthropological Science* (2008).

71. Jungers, W. *et al.*, The foot of Homo floresiensis. *Nature* **459**, 81-84 (2009).

72. Lieberman, D., Homo floresiensis from head to toe. *Nature* **459**, 41-42 (2009).

73. Montgomery, S., Capellini, I., Barton, R. & Mundy, N., Reconstructing the ups and downs of primate brain evolution: implications for adaptive hypotheses and Homo floresiensis. *BMC Biology* **8** (9), 1-19 (2010).

74. Kubo, D., Kono, R. & Kaifu, Y., Brain size of Homo floresiensis and its evolutionary implications. *Proceedings of the Royal Society B* **280** (1760) (2013).

75. Gibbons, A., Ancient Island Tools Suggest Homo erectus Was a Seafarer. *Science* **279**, 1635-1637 (1998).

76. Brumm, A. *et al.*, Early stone technology on Flores and its implications for Homo floresiensis. *Nature* **441**, 624-628 (2006).

77. Brumm, A. *et al.*, Hominins on Flores, Indonesia, by one million years ago. *Nature* **464**, 748-753 (2010).

78. Dennell, R. & Roebroeks, W., An Asian perspective on early human dispersal from Africa. *Nature* **438**, 1099-1104 (2005).

79. Carbonell, E. *et al.*, Lower Pleistocene Hominids and Artifacts from Atapuerca-TD6 (Spain). *Science* **269**, 826-830 (1995).

80. Carbonell, E. *et al.*, The TD6 level lithic industry from Gran Dolina, Atapuerca (Burgos, Spain): production and use. *Journal of Human Evolution* **37**, 653-693 (1999).

81. Bermúdez de Castro, J. *et al.*, A new early Pleistocene hominin mandible from Atapuerca-TD6, Spain. *Journal of Human Evolution* **55**, 729-735 (2008).

82. Bermúdez de Castro, J. *et al.*, A Hominid from the Lower Pleistocene of Atapuerca, Spain: Possible Ancestor to Neandertals and Modern Humans. *Science* **276**, 1392-1395 (1997).

83. Carbonell, E. *et al.*, An Early Pleistocene hominin mandible from Atapuerca-TD6, Spain. *PNAS* **102** (16), 5674-5678 (2005).

84. Falguères, C. *et al.*, Earliest humans in Europe: the age of TD6 Gran Dolina, Atapuerca, Spain. *Journal of Human Evolution* **37** (3-4), 343-352 (1999).

85. Carbonell, E. *et al.*, The first hominin of Europe. *Nature* **452**, 465-470 (2008).

86. Martinon-Torres, M. *et al.*, Dental evidence on the hominin dispersals during the Pleistocene. *PNAS* **104** (33), 13279-13282 (2007).

87. Gomez-Robles, A. *et al.*, Geometric morphometric analysis of the crown morphology of the lower first premolar of hominins, with special attention to Pleistocene Homo. *Journal of Human Evolution* **53**, 272-285 (2007).

88. Martinón-Torres, M., Dennell, R. & Bermúdez de Castro, J., The Denisova hominin need not be an out of Africa story. *Journal of Human Evolution* **60**, 251-255 (2011).

89. Fernandez-Jalvo, Y., Diez, J., Caceres, I. & Rosell, J., Human cannibalism in the Early Pleistocene of Europe (Gran Dolina, Sierra de Aterpuerca, Burgos, Spain). *Journal of Human Evolution* **37**, 591-622 (1999).

90. Clarke, R., A corrected reconstruction and interpretation of the Homo erectus calvaria from Ceprano, Italy. *Journal of Human Evolution* **39**, 433-442 (2000).

91. Lahr, M. & Foley, R., Towards a Theory of Modern Human Origins: Geography, Demography, and Diversity in Recent Human Evolution. *Yearbook of Physical Anthropology* **41**, 137-176 (1998).

92. Baxter, S., *Evolution* (Gollancz, London, 2002).

93. Groves, C., *A Theory of Human and Primate Evolution* (Oxford University Press, Oxford, 1989).

94.   Scott, G. & Gibert, L., The oldest hand-axes in Europe. *Nature* **461**, 82-85 (2009).

95.   Parfitt, S. *et al.*, The earliest record of human activity in northern Europe. *Nature* **438**, 1008-1012 (2005).

96.   Parfitt, S. *et al.*, Early Pleistocene human occupation at the edge of the boreal zone in northwest Europe. *Nature* **466**, 229-233 (2010).

97.   Ashton, N. *et al.*, Hominin Footprints from Early Pleistocene Deposits at Happisburgh, UK. *PLoS One* **9** (2) (2014).

98.   Roberts, A. & Grun, R., Early human northerners. *Nature* **466**, 189 (2010).

99.   Swisher, C. *et al.*, Latest Homo erectus of Java: Potential Contemporaneity with Homo sapiens in Southeast Asia. *Science* **274**, 1870-1874 (1996).

100.   Indriati, E. *et al.*, The Age of the 20 Meter Solo River Terrace, Java, Indonesia and the Survival of Homo erectus in Asia. *PLoS One* **6** (6) (2011).

7: The archaics

1.   Wagner, G. *et al.*, Radiometric dating of the type-site for Homo heidelbergensis at Mauer, Germany. *PNAS* **107** (46), 19726-19730 (2010).

2.   Stringer, C. & Andrews, P., *The Complete World of Human Evolution* (Thames & Hudson, London, 2005).

3.   Coolidge, F. & Wynn, T., *The Rise of Homo sapiens* (Wiley-Blackwell, Hoboken, NJ, 2009).

4.   Cameron, D. & Groves, C., *Bones, Stones and Molecules: "Out of Africa" and Human Origins* (Elsevier Academic Press, London, 2004).

5.   Manzi, G., Mallegni, F. & Ascenzi, A., A cranium for the earliest Europeans: Phylogenetic position of the hominid from Ceprano, Italy. *PNAS* **98** (17), 10011-10016 (2001).

6.   Mallegni, M. *et al.*, Homo cepranensis sp. nov. and the evolution of African-European Middle Pleistocene hominids. *C. R. Palevol 2* , 153-159 (2003).

7.   Clarke, R., A corrected reconstruction and interpretation of the Homo erectus calvaria from Ceprano, Italy. *Journal of Human Evolution* **39**, 433-442 (2000).

8.   Muttoni, G., Scardia, G., Kent, D., Swisher, C. & Manzi, G., Pleistocene magnetochronology of early hominin sites at Ceprano and Fontana Ranuccio, Italy. *Earth and Planetary Science Letters* **286** (1-2), 255-268 (2009).

9.   Manzi, G. *et al.*, The new chronology of the Ceprano calvarium (Italy). *Journal of Human Evolution* **59** (5), 580-585 (2010).

10.   Mounier, A., Condemi, S. & Manzi, G., The Stem Species of Our Species: A Place for the Archaic Human Cranium from Ceprano, Italy. *PLoS One* **6** (4) (2011).

11.   Roksandic, M. *et al.*, A human mandible (BH-1) from the Pleistocene deposits of Mala Balanica cave (Sicevo Gorge, Nis, Serbia). *Journal of Human Evolution* **61** (2), 186-196 (2011).

12.   Rink, W. *et al.*, New Radiometric Ages for the BH-1 Hominin from Balanica (Serbia): Implications for Understanding the Role of the Balkans in Middle Pleistocene Human Evolution. *PLoS One* **8** (2) (2013).

13.   Clark, J. *et al.*, African Homo erectus: Old Radiometric Ages and Young Oldowan Assemblages in the Middle Awash Valley, Ethiopia. *Science* **264**, 1907-1910 (1994).

14.   Bae, C., The Late Middle Pleistocene Hominin Fossil Record of Eastern Asia: Synthesis and Review. *Yearbook of Physical Anthropology* **53**, 75-93 (2010).

15.   Rightmire, P., Human Evolution in the Middle Pleistocene: The Role of Homo heidelbergensis. *Evolutionary Anthropology* **6** (6), 218-227 (1998).

16.   Manzi, G., Human Evolution at the Matuyama-Brunhes Boundary. *Evolutionary Anthropology* **13**, 11-24 (2004).

17.   Brauer, G., The Origin of Modern Anatomy: By Speciation or Intraspecific Evolution? *Evolutionary Anthropology* **17**, 22-37 (2008).

18.   Harvati, K., 100 years of Homo heidelbergensis - life and times of a controversial taxon. *Mitteilungen der Gesellschaft für Urgeschichte* **16**, 85-94 (2007).

19.   Rightmire, P., Homo in the Middle Pleistocene: Hypodigms, Variation, and Species Recognition. *Evolutionary Anthropology* **17**, 8-21 (2008).

20.   Dennell, R., Martinón-Torres, M. & Bermúdez de Castro, J., Hominin variability, climatic instability and population demography in Middle Pleistocene Europe. *Quaternary Science Reviews* **30**, 1511-1524 (2011).

21.   Gonzalez-Jose, R., Escapa, I., Neves, W., Cuneo, R. & Pucciarelli, H., Cladistic analysis of continuous modularized traits provides phylogenetic signals in Homo evolution. *Nature* **453**, 775-779 (2008).

22.   Klein, R., in *The Human Past*, edited by Scarre, C. (Thames & Hudson, London, 2005), pp. 84-123.

23.   Aiello, L. & Dunbar, R., Neocortex Size, Group Size and the Evolution of Language. *Current Anthropology* **34** (2), 184-193 (1993).

24.   Wilson, R., Drury, S. & Chapman, J., *The Great Ice Age* (Routledge, London, 2000).

25.   Pettitt, P., in *The Human Past*, edited by Scarre, C. (Thames & Hudson, London, 2005), pp. 124-173.

26.   Dunbar, R., *Grooming, Gossip and the Evolution of Language*, 2nd ed. (Faber and Faber Ltd., London, 2004).

27.   Scott, G. & Gibert, L., The oldest hand-axes in Europe. *Nature* **461**, 82-85 (2009).

28.   Wilkins, J., Schoville, B., Brown, K. & Chazan, M., Evidence for Early Hafted Hunting Technology. *Science* **338**, 942-946 (2012).

29.   Thieme, H., Lower Paleolithic hunting spears from Germany. *Nature* **385**, 807-810 (1997).

30.   Sahle, Y. *et al.*, Earliest Stone-Tipped Projectiles from the Ethiopian Rift Date to 279,000 Years Ago. *PLoS One* **8** (11) (2013).

31.   McBrearty, S. & Brooks, A., The revolution that wasn't: a new interpretation of the origin of modern human behaviour. *Journal of Human Evolution* **39**, 453-563 (2000).

32.   Clark, J. *et al.*, Stratigraphic, chronological and behavioural contexts of Pleistocene Homo sapiens from Middle Awash, Ethiopia. *Nature* **423**, 747-752 (2003).

33.   Klein, R., *The Human Career*, 2nd ed. (University of Chicago Press, Chicago, 1999).

34.   Shimelmitz, R., Kuhn, S., Ronen, A. & Weinstein-Evron, M., Predetermined Flake Production at the Lower/Middle Paleolithic Boundary: Yabrudian Scraper-Blank Technology. *PLoS One* **9** (9), e106293 (2014).

35.   Lewin, R. & Foley, R., *Principles of Human Evolution*, 2nd ed. (Blackwell Science Ltd, Oxford, 2004).

36.   Adler, D. *et al.*, Early Levallois technology and the Lower to Middle Paleolithic transition in the Southern Caucasus. *Science* **345** (6204), 1609-1612 (2014).

37.   Mellars, P., *The Neanderthal Legacy* (Princeton University Press, 1996).

38.   Roebroeks, W. & Villa, P., On the earliest evidence for habitual use of fire in Europe. *PNAS* **108** (13), 5209-5214 (2011).

39.   Stringer, C., *Homo Britannicus* (Penguin, London, 2006).

40.   Marshack, A., The Berekhat Ram figurine: a late Acheulian carving from the Middle East. *Antiquity* **71** (272), 327-333 (1997).

41.   Klein, R. & Edgar, B., *The Dawn of Human Culture* (John Wiley & Sons, Inc., New York, NY, 2002).

42.   Diamond, J., *The Third Chimpanzee* (Random, London, 1991).

43.   Barham, L., Systematic Pigment Use in the Middle Pleistocene of South-Central Africa. *Current Anthropology* **43** (1), 181-190 (2002).

44.   Himelfarb, E., Prehistoric Body Painting. *Archaeology* **53** (4) (2000).

45.   Henderson, Z., Florisbad, South Africa: Over 120,000 years of human activity. *Nyame Akuma* (44), 53-56 (1995).

46.   Grün, R. *et al.*, Direct dating of the Florisbad hominid. *Nature* **382**, 500-501 (1996).

47.   Brauer, G., Yokoyama, Y., Falgueres, C. & Mbuer, E., Modern Human Origins Backdated. *Nature* **386**, 337-338 (1997).

48.   Rightmire, P., Middle and later Pleistocene hominins in Africa and Southwest Asia. *PNAS* **106** (38), 16046-16050 (2009).

8: The other people

1.   Cameron, D. & Groves, C., *Bones, Stones and Molecules: "Out of Africa" and Human Origins* (Elsevier Academic Press, London, 2004).

2.   Klein, R., *The Human Career*, 2nd ed. (University of Chicago Press, Chicago, 1999).

3.   Bahn, P., Neandertal Finds. *Archaeology* **52** (2) (1999).

4.   Schmitz, R. *et al.*, The Neandertal type site revisited: Interdisciplinary investigations of skeletal remains from the Neander Valley, Germany. *PNAS* **99** (20), 13342-13347 (2002).

5.   Pearce, E., Stringer, C. & Dunbar, R., New insights into differences in brain organization between Neanderthals and anatomically modern humans. *Proceedings of the Royal Society B* **280** (1758) (2013).

6.   Helmuth, H., Body height, body mass and surface area of the Neanderthals. *Zeitschrift für Morphologie und Anthropologie* **82** (1), 1-12 (1998).

7.   Coolidge, F. & Wynn, T., *The Rise of Homo sapiens* (Wiley-Blackwell, Hoboken, NJ, 2009).

8.   Gomez-Olivencia, A., Eaves-Johnson, L., Franciscus, R., Carretero, J. & Arsuaga, J., Kebara 2: new insights regarding the most complete Neandertal thorax. *Journal of Human Evolution* **57**, 75-90 (2009).

9.   Conroy, G., *Reconstructing Human Origins: A Modern Synthesis* (W. W. Norton & Company, Inc., New York, NY, 1997).

10.   Pettitt, P., in *The Human Past*, edited by Scarre, C. (Thames & Hudson, London, 2005), pp. 124-173.

11.   Rak, Y., Ginzburg, A. & Geffen, E., Does Homo neanderthalensis play a role in modern human ancestry? The mandibular evidence. *American Journal of Physical Anthropology* **119**, 199-204 (2002).

12.   Shaw, C., Hofmann, C., Petraglia, M., Stock, J. & Gottschall, J., Neandertal Humeri May Reflect Adaptation to Scraping Tasks, but Not Spear Thrusting. *PLoS One* **7** (7) (2012).

13.   Trinkaus, E., Neandertal pubic morphology and gestation length. *Current Anthropology* **25**, 509-514 (1984).

14.   Anderson, C., Neandertal Pelves and Gestation Length: Hypotheses and Holism in Paleoanthropology. *American Anthropologist* **91**, 327-340 (1989).

15.   Dunsworth, H., Warrender, A., Deacon, T., Ellison, P. & Pontzer, H., Metabolic hypothesis for human altriciality. *PNAS* **109** (38), 15212-15218 (2012).

16.   Rosenberg, K., Neandertal Birth Canals. *American Journal of Physical Anthropology* **66**, 222 (1985).

17.   Dean, M., Stringer, C. & Bromage, T., Age at death of the Neanderthal child from Devil's Tower, Gibraltar and the implications for studies of general growth and development in Neanderthals. *American Journal of Physical Anthropology* **70** (3), 301-309 (1986).

18.   Rak, Y. & Arensburg, B., Kebara 2 Neanderthal pelvis: first look at a complete inlet. *American Journal of Physical Anthropology* **73** (2), 227-231 (1987).

19.   Ponce de Leon, M. *et al.*, Neanderthal brain size at birth provides insights into the evolution of human life history. *PNAS* **105** (37), 13764-13768 (2008).

20.   Weaver, T. & Hublin, J., Neandertal birth canal shape and the evolution of human childbirth. *PNAS* **106** (20), 8151-8156 (2009).

21.   Gunz, P., Neubauer, S., Maureille, B. & Hublin, J., Brain development after birth differs between Neanderthals and modern humans. *Current Biology* **20** (21), 921-922 (2010).

22.   Rozzi, F. & Bermúdez de Castro, J., Surprisingly rapid growth in Neanderthals. *Nature* **428**, 936-939 (2004).

23.   Macchiarelli, R. *et al.*, How Neanderthal molar teeth grew. *Nature* **444**, 748-751 (2006).

24.   Smith, T. *et al.*, Dental evidence for ontogenetic differences between modern humans and Neanderthals. *PNAS* **107** (49), 20923-20928 (2010).

25.   Braun, D., Neanderthal Model Is First Replica of Extinct Human Species Based on DNA, Available at http://newswatch.nationalgeographic.com/2008/09/17/neanderthal_woman_is_first_rep/ (2008).

26.   Lalueza-Fox, C. *et al.*, A Melanocortin 1 Receptor Allele Suggests Varying Pigmentation Among Neanderthals. *Science* **318**, 1453-1455 (2007).

27.   Green, R. *et al.*, A Complete Neandertal Mitochondrial Genome Sequence Determined by High-Throughput Sequencing. *Cell* **134**, 416-426 (2008).

28.   Noonan, J. *et al.*, Sequencing and Analysis of Neanderthal Genomic DNA. *Science* **314**, 1113-1118 (2006).

29.   Hublin, J., The origin of Neandertals. *PNAS* **106** (38), 16022-16027 (2009).

30.   Weaver, T., The meaning of Neandertal skeletal morphology. *PNAS* **106** (38), 16028–16033 (2009).

31.   Weaver, T., Roseman, C. & Stringer, C., Close correspondence between quantitative- and molecular-genetic divergence times for Neandertals and modern humans. *PNAS* **105** (12), 4645–4649 (2008).

32.   Bischoff, J. *et al.*, The Sima de los Huesos Hominids Date to Beyond U/Th Equilibrium (>350 kyr) and Perhaps to 400–500 kyr: New Radiometric Dates. *Journal of Archaeological Science* **30** (3), 275-280 (2003).

33.   Bischoff, J. *et al.*, High-resolution U-series dates from the Sima de los Huesos hominids yields 600 +/-66 kyrs: implications for the evolution of the early Neanderthal lineage. *Journal of Archaeological Science* **34**, 763-770 (2007).

34.   Arsuaga, J. *et al.*, Neandertal roots: Cranial and chronological evidence from Sima de los Huesos.

Science **344** (6190), 1358-1363 (2014).

35.   Martinson, D., Pisias, N., Hays, J., Imbried, J. & Moore, T., Age dating and the orbital theory of the ice ages: Development of a high-resolution 0 to 300,000-year chronostratigraphy. *Quaternary Research* **27** (1), 1-29 (1987).

36.   Severinghaus, J., Sowers, T., Brook, E., Alley, R. & Bender, M., Timing of abrupt climate change at the end of the Younger Dryas interval from thermally fractionated gases in polar ice. *Nature* **391**, 141-146 (1998).

37.   Shackleton, N., Sanchez-Goni, M., Pailler, D. & Lancelot, D., Marine Isotope Substage 5e and the Eemian Interglacial. *Global and Planetary Change* **36**, 151-155 (2003).

38.   van Kolfschoten, T., The Eemian mammal fauna of central Europe. *Netherlands Journal of Geosciences* **79** (2/3), 269-281 (2000).

39.   Van Andel, T. & Tzedakis, P., Palaeolithic landscapes of Europe and environs 150,000-25,000 years ago: an overview. *Quaternary Science Reviews* **15** (5-6), 481-500 (1996).

40.   Wilson, R., Drury, S. & Chapman, J., *The Great Ice Age* (Routledge, London, 2000).

41.   Roche, D., Paillard, D. & Cortijo, E., Constraints on the duration and freshwater release of Heinrich event 4 through isotope modelling. *Nature* **432**, 379-383 (2004).

42.   Krause, J. *et al.*, Neanderthals in central Asia and Siberia. *Nature* **449**, 902-904 (2007).

43.   Prufer, K. *et al.*, The complete genome sequence of a Neanderthal from the Altai Mountains. *Nature* **505**, 43-49 (2014).

44.   Gamble, C., in *The Oxford Illustrated History of Prehistoric Europe*, edited by Cunliffe, B. (Oxford University Press, Oxford, 1994), pp. 5-41.

45.   Fabre, V., Condemi, S. & Degioanni, A., Genetic Evidence of Geographical Groups among Neanderthals. *PLoS One* **4** (4) (2009).

46.   Briggs, A. *et al.*, Targeted Retrieval and Analysis of Five Neandertal mtDNA Genomes. *Science* **325**, 318-321 (2009).

47.   Dalén, L. *et al.*, Partial genetic turnover in neandertals: continuity in the east and population replacement in the west. *Molecular Biology and Evolution* **29** (8), 1893-1897 (2012).

48.   Rosas, A. *et al.*, Paleobiology and comparative morphology of a late Neandertal sample from El Sidron, Asturias, Spain. *PNAS* **103** (51), 19266-19271 (2006).

49.   Lalueza-Fox, C. *et al.*, Genetic evidence for patrilocal mating behavior among Neandertal groups. *PNAS* **108** (1), 250-253 (2011).

50.   De Torres, T. *et al.*, Dating Of The Hominid (Homo Neanderthalensis) Remains Accumulation From El Sidron Cave (Pilona, Asturias, North Spain): An Example Of A Multi-Methodological Approach To The Dating Of Upper Pleistocene Sites. *Archaeometry* **52**, 680-705 (2010).

51.   Mellars, P., *The Neanderthal Legacy* (Princeton University Press, 1996).

52.   Vallverdu, J. *et al.*, Sleeping Activity Area within the Site Structure of Archaic Human Groups Evidence from Abric Romanı Level N Combustion Activity Areas. *Current Anthropology* **51** (1), 137-145 (2010).

53.   Roebroeks, W. & Villa, P., On the earliest evidence for habitual use of fire in Europe. *PNAS* **108** (13), 5209-5214 (2011).

54.   Oppenheimer, S., *Out of Eden* (Constable & Robinson Ltd, London, 2003).

55.   Soressi, M. *et al.*, Neandertals made the first specialized bone tools in Europe. *PNAS* **110** (35), 14186-14190 (2013).

56.   Sørensen, B., Energy use by Eem Neanderthals. *Journal of Archaeological Science* **36** (10), 2201-2005 (2009).

57.   Hoffecker, J., Innovation and Technological Knowledge in the Upper Paleolithic of Northern Eurasia. *Evolutionary Anthropology* **14**, 186-198 (2005).

58.   Richards, M. *et al.*, Neanderthal diet at Vindija and Neanderthal predation: The evidence from stable isotopes. *PNAS* **97** (13), 7663-7666 (2000).

59.   Richards, M. & Trinkaus, E., Isotopic evidence for the diets of European Neanderthals and early modern humans. *PNAS* **106** (38), 16034-16039 (2009).

60.   Faivre, J. *et al.*, Middle Pleistocene Human Remains from Tourville-la-Rivière (Normandy, France) and Their Archaeological Context. *PLoS One* **9** (10), e104111 (2014).

61.   Sahle, Y. *et al.*, Earliest Stone-Tipped Projectiles from the Ethiopian Rift Date to.279,000 Years Ago. *PLoS One* **8** (11) (2013).

62.   Lieberman, D. & Shea, J., Behavioral Differences between Archaic and Modern Humans in the Levantine Mousterian. *American Anthropological Association* **96** (2), 330-332 (1994).

63.   Cortes-Sanchez, M. *et al.*, Earliest Known Use of Marine Resources by Neanderthals. *PLoS One* **6** (9) (2011).

64.   Stringer, C. *et al.*, Neanderthal exploitation of marine mammals in Gibraltar. *PNAS* **105** (38), 14319-

14324 (2008).

65.   Blasco, R. *et al.*, The earliest pigeon fanciers. *Nature Scientific Reports* **online** (2014).

66.   Fiorenza, L. *et al.*, Molar Macrowear Reveals Neanderthal Eco-Geographic Dietary Variation. *PLoS One* **6** (3) (2011).

67.   Sistiaga, A., Mallol, C., Galván, B. & Everett Summons, R., The Neanderthal Meal: A New Perspective Using Faecal Biomarkers. *PLoS One* **9** (6), e101045 (2014).

68.   Henry, A., Brooks, A. & Piperno, D., Microfossils in calculus demonstrate consumption of plants and cooked foods in Neanderthal diets (Shanidar III, Iraq; Spy I and II, Belgium). *PNAS* **108** (2), 486-491 (2011).

69.   Solecki, R., Shanidar IV, a Neanderthal flower burial in northern Iraq. *Science* **190**, 880–881 (1975).

70.   Sommer, J., The Shanidar IV 'flower burial': A reevaluation of Neanderthal burial ritual. *Cambridge Archæological Journal* **9**, 127-129 (1999).

71.   Roebroeks, W. *et al.*, Use of red ochre by early Neandertals. *PNAS* **109** (6), 1889-1894 (2012).

72.   Klein, R. & Edgar, B., *The Dawn of Human Culture* (John Wiley & Sons, Inc., New York, NY, 2002).

73.   Hublin, J., Spoor, F., Braun, M., Zonneveld, F. & Condemi, S., A late Neanderthal associated with Upper Palaeolithic artefacts. *Nature* **381**, 224-226 (1996).

74.   D'Errico, F., Zilhao, J., Julien, M., Baffier, D. & Pelegrin, J., Neanderthal Acculturation in Western Europe? *Current Anthropology* **39**, S1-S44 (1998).

75.   Mellars, P., A new radiocarbon revolution and the dispersal of modern humans in Eurasia. *Nature* **493**, 931-935 (2006).

76.   Mellars, P., in *The Speciation of Modern Homo sapiens*, edited by Crow, T. (Oxford University Press, Oxford, 2002), pp. 31-47.

77.   Mellars, P., The Impossible Coincidence. A Single-Species Model for the Origins of Modern Human Behavior in Europe. *Evolutionary Anthropology* **14**, 12-27 (2005).

78.   Mithen, S., *The Singing Neanderthal* (Weidenfeld & Nicholson, London, 2005).

79.   Gravina, B., Mellars, P. & Ramsey, C., Radiocarbon dating of interstratified Neanderthal and early modern human occupations at the Chatelperronian type-site. *Nature* **438**, 51-56 (2005).

80.   Zilhão, J. *et al.*, Analysis of Aurignacian interstratification at the Châtelperronian -type site and implications for the behavioral modernity of Neandertals. *PNAS* **103** (33), 12643-12648 (2006).

81.   Mellars, P., Gravina, B. & Ramsey, C., Confirmation of Neanderthal/modern human interstratification at the Chatelperronian type-site. *PNAS* **104** (9), 3657-3662 (2007).

82.   Higham, T. *et al.*, Chronology of the Grotte du Renne (France) and implications for the context of ornaments and human remains within the Châtelperronian. *PNAS* **107** (47), 20234-20239 (2010).

83.   Mellars, P., Neanderthal symbolism and ornament manufacture:The bursting of a bubble? *PNAS* **107** (47), 20147-20148 (2010).

84.   Caron, F., d'Errico, F., Del Moral, P., Santos, F. & Zilhão, J., The Reality of Neandertal Symbolic Behavior at the Grotte du Renne, Arcy-sur-Cure, France. *PLoS One* **6** (6) (2011).

85.   Hublin, J. *et al.*, Radiocarbon dates from the Grotte du Renne and Saint-Césaire support a Neandertal origin for the Châtelperronian. *PNAS* **109** (46), 18743-18748 (2012).

86.   Higham, T. *et al.*, The timing and spatiotemporal patterning of Neanderthal disappearance. *Nature* **512**, 306-309 (2014).

87.   Zilhão, J. *et al.*, Symbolic use of marine shells and mineral pigments by Iberian Neandertals. *PNAS* **107** (3), 1023-1028 (2010).

88.   BBC, Neanderthal 'make-up' containers discovered, Available at http://news.bbc.co.uk/1/hi/sci/tech/8448660.stm (2010).

89.   Peresani, M., Fiore, I., Gala, M., Romandini, M. & Tagliacozzo, A., Late Neandertals and the intentional removal of feathers as evidenced from bird bone taphonomy at Fumane Cave 44 ky B.P., Italy. *PNAS* **108** (10), 3888-3893 (2011).

90.   Finlayson, C. *et al.*, Birds of a Feather: Neanderthal Exploitation of Raptors and Corvids. *PLoS One* **7** (9) (2012).

91.   Rodríguez-Vidal, J. *et al.*, A rock engraving made by Neanderthals in Gibraltar. *PNAS* (Early edition) (2014).

92.   Benazzi, S. *et al.*, Early dispersal of modern humans in Europe and implications for Neanderthal behaviour. *Nature* **479**, 525-528 (2011).

93.   Higham, T. *et al.*, The earliest evidence for anatomically modern humans in northwestern Europe. *Nature* **479**, 521-524 (2011).

94.   D'Errico, F., The Invisible Frontier. A Multiple Species Model for the Origin of Behavioral Modernity. *Evolutionary Anthropology* **12**, 188-202 (2003).

95.   D'Errico, F. & Vanhaeren, M., in *Rethinking the human revolution*, edited by Mellars, P., Boyle, K., Bar-Yosef, O. & Stringer, C. (McDonald Institute, Cambridge, 2007), pp. 275-286.

96. D'Errico, F. & Stringer, C., Evolution, revolution or saltation scenario for the emergence of modern cultures? *Philosophical Transactions of the Royal Society B* **366**, 1060-1069 (2011).

97. D'Errico, F. *et al.*, Archaeological Evidence for the Emergence of Language, Symbolism, and Music – An Alternative Multidisciplinary Perspective. *Journal of World Prehistory* **17** (1), 1-70 (2003).

98. Arensburg, B., Tillier, A., Vandermeersch, B., Duday, H. & Rak, Y., A middle Palaeolithic human hyoid bone. *Nature* **338**, 758-760 (1989).

99. Arensburg, B., Schepartz, L., Tillier, A., Vandermeersch, B. & Rak, Y., A reappraisal of the anatomical basis for speech in Middle Palaeolithic hominids. *American Journal of Physical Anthropology* **83** (2), 137-146 (1990).

100. D'Anastasio, R. *et al.*, Micro-Biomechanics of the Kebara 2 Hyoid and Its Implications for Speech in Neanderthals. *PLoS One* **8** (12) (2013).

101. Barney, A., Martelli, S., Serrurier, A. & Steele, J., Articulatory capacity of Neanderthals, a very recent and human-like fossil hominin. *Philosophical Transactions of the Royal Society B* **367**, 88-102 (2012).

102. MacLarnon, A. & Hewitt, G., The Evolution of Human Speech: The Role of Enhanced Breathing Control. *American Journal of Physical Anthropology* **109**, 341-363 (1999).

103. Kay, R., Cartmill, M. & Balow, M., The hypoglossal canal and the origin of human vocal behavior. *PNAS* **95**, 5417-5419 (1998).

104. DeGusta, D., Gilbert, H. & Turner, S., Hypoglossal canal size and hominid speech. *PNAS* **96**, 1800-1804 (1999).

105. Volpato, V. *et al.*, Hand to Mouth in a Neandertal: Right-Handedness in Regourdou 1. *PLoS One* **7** (8) (2012).

106. Trinkaus, E., European early modern humans and the fate of the Neandertals. *PNAS* **104** (18), 7367-7372 (2007).

107. Duarte, C. *et al.*, The Early Upper Paleolithic Human Skeleton from the Abrigo do Lagar Velho (Portugal) and Modern Human Emergence in Iberia. *PNAS* **96**, 7604-7609 (1999).

108. Tattersall, I. & Schwartz, J., Hominids and hybrids: The place of Neanderthals in human evolution. *PNAS* **96**, 7117-7119 (1999).

109. Condemi, S. *et al.*, Possible Interbreeding in Late Italian Neanderthals? New Data from the Mezzena Jaw (Monti Lessini, Verona, Italy). *PLoS One* **8** (3) (2013).

110. Longo, L. *et al.*, Did Neandertals and anatomically modern humans coexist in northern Italy during the late MIS 3? *Quaternary International* **259**, 102-112 (2012).

111. Caramelli, D. *et al.*, Evidence for a genetic discontinuity between Neandertals and 24,000-year-old anatomically modern Europeans. *PNAS* **100** (11), 6593-6597 (2003).

112. Serre, D. *et al.*, No Evidence of Neandertal mtDNA Contribution to Early Modern Humans. *PLoS Biology* **2** (3), 0313-0317 (2004).

113. Caramelli, D. *et al.*, A 28,000 Years Old Cro-Magnon mtDNA Sequence Differs from All Potentially Contaminating Modern Sequences. *PLoS One* **3** (7) (2008).

114. Currat, M. & Excoffier, L., Modern Humans Did Not Admix with Neanderthals during Their Range Expansion into Europe. *PLoS Biology* **2** (12), 2264-2274 (2004).

115. Evans, P., Mekel-Bobrov, N., Vallender, E., Hudson, R. & Lahn, B., Evidence that the adaptive allele of the brain size gene microcephalin introgressed into Homo sapiens from an archaic Homo lineage. *PNAS* **103** (48), 18178-18183 (2006).

116. Pennisi, E., Tales of a Prehistoric Human Genome. *Science* **323**, 866-871 (2009).

117. Lari, M. *et al.*, The Microcephalin Ancestral Allele in a Neanderthal Individual. *PLoS One* **5** (5) (2010).

118. Plagnol, V. & Wall, J., Possible Ancestral Structure in Human Populations. *PLoS Genetics* **2** (7), 972-979 (2006).

119. Wall, J., Lohmueller, K. & Plagnol, V., Detecting Ancient Admixture and Estimating Demographic Parameters in Multiple Human Populations. *Molecular Biology and Evolution* **26** (8), 1823-1827 (2009).

120. Green, R. *et al.*, Analysis of one million base pairs of Neanderthal DNA. *Nature* **444**, 330-336 (2006).

121. Green, R. *et al.*, A Draft Sequence of the Neandertal Genome. *Science* **328**, 710-722 (2010).

122. Eriksson, A. & Manica, A., Effect of ancient population structure on the degree of polymorphism shared between modern human populations and ancient hominins. *PNAS* **109** (35), 13956-13960 (2012).

123. Yotova, V. *et al.*, An X-Linked Haplotype of Neandertal Origin Is Present Among All Non-African Populations. *Molecular Biology and Evolution* **28** (7), 1957-1962 (2011).

124. Sankararaman, S., Patterson, N., Li, H., Pääbo, S. & Reich, D., The Date of Interbreeding between Neandertals and Modern Humans. *PLoS Genetics* **8** (10) (2012).

125. Fu, Q. *et al.*, Genome sequence of a 45,000-year-old modern human from western Siberia. *Nature* **514**, 445-450 (2014).

126. Seguin-Orlando, A. *et al.*, Genomic structure in Europeans dating back at least 36,000 years. *Science* (2014).

127. Yang, M., Malaspinas, A., Durand, E. & Slatkin, M., Ancient Structure in Africa Unlikely to Explain Neanderthal and Non-African Genetic Similarity. *Molecular Biology and Evolution* **29** (10), 2987-2995 (2012).

128. Meyer, M. *et al.*, A High-Coverage Genome Sequence from an Archaic Denisovan Individual. *Science* **338**, 222-226 (2012).

129. Wall, J. *et al.*, Higher levels of Neanderthal ancestry in East Asians than in Europeans. *Genetics* **194**, 199-209 (2013).

130. Vernot, B. & Akey, J., Resurrecting Surviving Neandertal Lineages from Modern Human Genomes. *Science* **343**, 1017-1021 (2014).

131. Sánchez-Quinto, F. *et al.*, North African Populations Carry the Signature of Admixture with Neandertals. *PLoS One* **7** (10) (2012).

132. Olivieri, A. *et al.*, The mtDNA Legacy of the Levantine Early Upper Palaeolithic in Africa. *Science* **314**, 1757-1770 (2006).

133. González, A. *et al.*, Mitochondrial lineage M1 traces an early human backflow to Africa. *BMC Genomics* **8** (223) (2007).

134. Sankararaman, S. *et al.*, The genomic landscape of Neanderthal ancestry in present-day humans. *Nature* **507**, 354-357 (2014).

135. Ding, Q., Hu, Y., Xu, S., Wang, J. & Jin, L., Neanderthal Introgression at Chromosome 3p21.31 Was Under Positive Natural Selection in East Asians. *Molecular Biology and Evolution* **31** (3), 683-695 (2013).

136. Currat, M. & Excoffier, L., Strong reproductive isolation between humans and Neanderthals inferred from observed patterns of introgression. *PNAS* **108** (37), 15129-15134 (2011).

137. Neves, A. & Serva, M., Extremely Rare Interbreeding Events Can Explain Neanderthal DNA in Living Humans. *PLoS One* **7** (10) (2012).

138. Krause, J. *et al.*, The complete mitochondrial DNA genome of an unknown hominin from southern Siberia. *Nature* **464**, 894-897 (2010).

139. Reich, D. *et al.*, Genetic history of an archaic hominin group from Denisova Cave in Siberia. *Nature* **468**, 1053-1060 (2010).

140. Reich, D. *et al.*, Denisova Admixture and the First Modern Human Dispersals into Southeast Asia and Oceania. *American Journal of Human Genetics* **89**, 1-13 (2011).

141. Skoglund, P. & Jakobsson, M., Archaic human ancestry in East Asia. *PNAS* **108** (45), 18301-18306 (2011).

142. Abi-Rached, L. *et al.*, The Shaping of Modern Human Immune Systems by Multiregional Admixture with Archaic Humans. *Science* (2011).

143. Trinkaus, E., Milota, S., Rodrigo, R., Mircea, G. & Moldovan, O., Early modern human cranial remains from the Peştera cu Oase, Romania. *Journal of Human Evolution* **45**, 245-253 (2003).

144. Trinkaus, E. *et al.*, An early modern human from Peştera cu Oase, Romania. *PNAS* **100** (20), 11231-11236 (2003).

145. Hawks, J., The Denisova genome FAQ, Available at http://johnhawks.net/weblog/reviews/neandertals/neandertal_dna/denisova-nuclear-genome-reich-2010.html (2010).

146. Meyer, M. *et al.*, A mitochondrial genome sequence of a hominin from Sima de los Huesos. *Nature* **505**, 403-406 (2014).

147. Stringer, C., What makes a modern human. *Nature* **485**, 33-35 (2012).

148. Smith, F., Trinkaus, E., Pettitt, P., Karavanic, I. & Paunovic, M., Direct radiocarbon dates for Vindija G1 and Velika Pecina Late Pleistocene hominid remains. *PNAS* **96** (22), 12281-12286 (1999).

149. Higham, T., Ramsey, C., Karavanic, I., Smith, F. & Trinkaus, E., Revised direct radiocarbon dating of the Vindija G1 Upper Paleolithic Neandertals. *PNAS* **103** (3), 553-557 (2006).

150. Pinhasi, R., Higham, T., Golovanova, L. & Doronichev, V., Revised age of late Neanderthal occupation and the end of the Middle Paleolithic in the northern Caucasus. *PNAS* **108** (21), 8611-8616 (2011).

151. Finlayson, C. *et al.*, Late survival of Neanderthals at the southernmost extreme of Europe. *Nature* **443**, 850-853 (2006).

152. Finlayson, C. *et al.*, Gorham's Cave, Gibraltar - The persistence of a Neanderthal population. *Quaternary International* **181**, 74-71 (2008).

153. Slimak, L. *et al.*, Late Mousterian Persistence near the Arctic Circle. *Science* **332**, 841-845 (2011).

154. Fedele, F., Giaccio, B. & Hajdas, I., Timescales and cultural process at 40,000 BP in the light of the

Campanian Ignimbrite eruption, Western Eurasia. *Journal of Human Evolution* **55**, 834-857 (2008).

155. Lowe, J. *et al.*, Volcanic ash layers illuminate the resilience of Neanderthals and early modern humans to natural hazards. *PNAS* **109** (34), 13532-13537 (2012).

156. Sepulchre, P. *et al.*, H4 abrupt event and late Neanderthal presence in Iberia. *Earth and Planetary Science Letters* **258**, 283-292 (2007).

157. Wood, R. *et al.*, Radiocarbon dating casts doubt on the late chronology of the Middle to Upper Palaeolithic transition in southern Iberia. *PNAS* **110** (8), 2781-2786 (2013).

158. Wade, N., *Before the Dawn* (Penguin, London, 2006).

159. Churchill, S., Franciscus, R., McKean-Peraza, H., Daniel, J. & Warren, B., Shanidar 3 Neandertal rib puncture wound and paleolithic weaponry. *Journal of Human Evolution* **57**, 163-178 (2009).

160. Zollikofer, C., Ponce de Leon, M., Vandermeersch, B. & Leveque, F., Evidence for interpersonal violence in the St. Cesaire Neanderthal. *PNAS* **99** (9), 6444-6448 (2002).

161. Diamond, J., *The Third Chimpanzee* (Random, London, 1991).

162. Villa, P. & Roebroeks, W., Neandertal Demise: An Archaeological Analysis of the Modern Human Superiority Complex. *PLoS One* **9** (4), e96424 (2014).

163. Banks, W. *et al.*, Neanderthal Extinction by Competitive Exclusion. *PLoS One* **3** (12) (2008).

164. Mellars, P. & French, J., Tenfold Population Increase in Western Europe at the Neandertal–to–Modern Human Transition. *Science* **333**, 623-627 (2011).

9: Enter *Homo sapiens*

1. Lieberman, D., McBratney, B. & Krovitz, G., The evolution and development of cranial form in Homo sapiens. *PNAS* **99** (3), 1134-1139 (2002).

2. Balter, M., What Made Humans Modern? *Science* **295**, 1219-1225 (2002).

3. Lieberman, D., Sphenoid shortening and the evolution of modern human cranial shape. *Nature* **393**, 158-162 (1998).

4. Conroy, G., *Reconstructing Human Origins: A Modern Synthesis* (W. W. Norton & Company, Inc., New York, NY, 1997).

5. Pettitt, P., in *The Human Past*, edited by Scarre, C. (Thames & Hudson, London, 2005), pp. 124-173.

6. Day, M., Early Homo sapiens Remains from the Omo River Region of South-west Ethiopia: Omo Human Skeletal Remain. *Nature* **222**, 1135-1138 (1969).

7. McDougall, I., Brown, F. & Fleagle, J., Stratigraphic placement and age of modern humans from Kibish, Ethiopia. *Nature* **433**, 733-736 (2005).

8. Shea, J., Fleagle, J. & Assefa, Z., in *Rethinking the human revolution*, edited by Mellars, P., Boyle, K., Bar-Yosef, O. & Stringer, C. (McDonald Institute, Cambridge, 2007), pp. 153-162.

9. Rightmire, P., Middle and later Pleistocene hominins in Africa and Southwest Asia. *PNAS* **106** (38), 16046-16050 (2009).

10. White, T. *et al.*, Pleistocene Homo sapiens from Middle Awash, Ethiopia. *Nature* **423**, 742-747 (2003).

11. Clark, J. *et al.*, Stratigraphic, chronological and behavioural contexts of Pleistocene Homo sapiens from Middle Awash, Ethiopia. *Nature* **423**, 747-752 (2003).

12. Smith, T. *et al.*, Earliest evidence of modern human life history in North African early Homo sapiens. *PNAS* **104** (15), 6128-6133 (2007).

13. Cameron, D. & Groves, C., *Bones, Stones and Molecules: "Out of Africa" and Human Origins* (Elsevier Academic Press, London, 2004).

14. Klein, R., *The Human Career*, 2nd ed. (University of Chicago Press, Chicago, 1999).

15. Marean, C. *et al.*, Early human use of marine resources and pigment in South Africa during the Middle Pleistocene. *Nature* **449**, 905-909 (2007).

16. Osborne, A. *et al.*, A humid corridor across the Sahara for the migration of early modern humans out of Africa 120,000 years ago. *PNAS* **105** (43), 16444-16447 (2008).

17. Lahr, M. & Foley, R., Towards a Theory of Modern Human Origins: Geography, Demography, and Diversity in Recent Human Evolution. *Yearbook of Physical Anthropology* **41**, 137-176 (1998).

18. Wells, S., *The Journey of Man* (London, Penguin, 2002).

19. Shen, G. *et al.*, U-Series dating of Liujiang hominid site in Guangxi, Southern China. *Journal of Human Evolution* **43** (6), 817-829 (2002).

20. Curnoe, D. *et al.*, Human Remains from the Pleistocene-Holocene Transition of Southwest China Suggest a Complex Evolutionary History for East Asians. *PLoS One* **7** (3) (2012).

21. Liu, W. *et al.*, Human remains from Zhirendong, South China,and modern human emergence in East Asia. *PNAS* **107** (45), 19201-1920 (2010).

22. Dennell, R., Early Homo sapiens in China. *Nature* **468**, 512-513 (2010).

23. Bowler, J. *et al.*, New ages for human occupation and climatic change at Lake Mungo, Australia. *Nature* **421**, 837-840 (2003).

24. Thorne, A. *et al.*, Australia's oldest human remains: age of the Lake Mungo 3 skeleton. *Journal of Human Evolution* **36** (6), 591-612 (1999).

25. Demeter, F. *et al.*, Anatomically modern human in Southeast Asia (Laos) by 46 ka. *PNAS* **109** (36), 14375-14380 (2012).

26. Détroit, F. *et al.*, Upper Pleistocene Homo sapiens from the Tabon cave (Palawan, The Philippines): description and dating of new discoveries. *C. R. Palevol* **3** (8), 705-712 (2004).

27. Benazzi, S. *et al.*, Early dispersal of modern humans in Europe and implications for Neanderthal behaviour. *Nature* **479**, 525-528 (2011).

28. Higham, T. *et al.*, The earliest evidence for anatomically modern humans in northwestern Europe. *Nature* **479**, 521-524 (2011).

29. Trinkaus, E. *et al.*, An early modern human from Peştera cu Oase, Romania. *PNAS* **100** (20), 11231-11236 (2003).

30. Soares, P. *et al.*, Correcting for Purifying Selection: An Improved Human Mitochondrial Molecular Clock. *American Journal of Human Genetics* **84**, 740-759 (2009).

31. Ruiz-Pesini, E., Mishmar, D., Brandon, M., Procaccio, V. & Wallace, D., Effects of Purifying and Adaptive Selection on Regional Variation in Human mtDNA. *Science* **303**, 223-226 (2004).

32. Kivisild, T. *et al.*, The Role of Selection in the Evolution of Human Mitochondrial Genomes. *Genetics* **172**, 373-387 (2006).

33. Levy-Coffman, E., We Are Not Our Ancestors: Evidence for Discontinuity between Prehistoric and Modern Europeans. *Journal of Genetic Genealogy,* **2**, 40-50 (2006).

34. Cann, R., Stoneking, M. & Wilson, A., Mitochondrial DNA and human evolution. *Nature* **325**, 31-36 (1987).

35. Vigilant, L., Stoneking, M., Harpending, H., Hawkes, K. & Wilson, A., African Populations and the Evolution of Human Mitochondrial DNA. *Science* **253**, 1503-1507 (1991).

36. Ingman, M., Kaessmann, H., Pääbo, S. & Gyllensten, U., Mitochondrial genome variation and the origin of modern humans. *Nature* **408**, 708-713 (2000).

37. Jorde, L. *et al.*, The Distribution of Human Genetic Diversity: A Comparison of Mitochondrial, Autosomal, and Y-Chromosome Data. *American Journal of Human Genetics* **66**, 979-988 (2000).

38. Alexe, G. *et al.*, PCA and Clustering Reveal Alternate mtDNA Phylogeny of N and M Clades. *Journal of Molecular Evolution* **67**, 465-487 (2008).

39. Hammer, M. *et al.*, Out of Africa and Back Again: Nested Cladistic Analysis of Human Y Chromosome Variation. *Molecular Biology and Evolution* **15** (4), 427-441 (1998).

40. Underhill, P. *et al.*, Y chromosome sequence variation and the history of human populations. *Nature Genetics* **26**, 358-361 (2000).

41. Underhill, P. *et al.*, The phylogeography of Y chromosome binary haplotypes and the origins of modern human populations. *Annual of Human Genetics* **65**, 43-62 (2001).

42. Ke, Y. *et al.*, African Origin of Modern Humans in East Asia: A Tale of 12,000 Y Chromosomes. *Science* **292**, 1151-1153 (2001).

43. Shi, W. *et al.*, A Worldwide Survey of Human Male Demographic History Based on Y-SNP and Y-STR Data from the HGDP–CEPH Populations. *Molecular Biology and Evolution* **27** (2), 385-393 (2010).

44. Ramachandran, S. *et al.*, Support from the relationship of genetic and geographic distance in human populations for a serial founder effect originating in Africa. *PNAS* **102** (44), 15942-15947 (2005).

45. Jakobsson, M. *et al.*, Genotype, haplotype and copy-number variation in worldwide human populations. *Nature* **451**, 998-1003 (2008).

46. Li, J. *et al.*, Worldwide Human Relationships Inferred from Genome-Wide Patterns of Variation. *Science* **319**, 1100-1104 (2008).

47. Tishkoff, S. *et al.*, The Genetic Structure and History of Africans and African Americans. *Science* **342**, 1035-1044 (2009).

48.   Forster, P., Ice Ages and the mitochondrial DNA chronology of human dispersals: a review. *Philosophical Transactions of the Royal Society B* **359**, 255-264 (2004).

49.   Behar, D. *et al.*, The Dawn of Human Matrilineal Diversity. *American Journal of Human Genetics* **82**, 1130-1140 (2008).

50.   Henn, C. *et al.*, Hunter-gatherer genomic diversity suggests a southern African origin for modern humans. *PNAS* **108** (13), 5154-5162 (2011).

51.   Stringer, C., in *The Speciation of Modern Homo sapiens*, edited by Crow, T. (Oxford University Press, Oxford, 2002), pp. 23-30.

52.   Stringer, C., Modern human origins: progress and prospects. *Philosophical Transactions of the Royal Society B* **357**, 563-579 (2002).

53.   Stringer, C., Out of Ethiopia. *Nature* **423**, 692-695 (2003).

54.   Stringer, C., in *Rethinking the human revolution*, edited by Mellars, P., Boyle, K., Bar-Yosef, O. & Stringer, C. (McDonald Institute, Cambridge, 2007), pp. 13-20.

55.   Brauer, G., The Origin of Modern Anatomy: By Speciation or Intraspecific Evolution? *Evolutionary Anthropology* **17**, 22-37 (2008).

56.   Garrigan, D., Mobasher, Z., Kingan, S., Wilder, J. & Hammer, M., Deep Haplotype Divergence and Long-Range Linkage Disequilibrium at Xp21.1 Provide Evidence That Humans Descend From a Structured Ancestral Population. *Genetics* **170**, 1849-1856 (2005).

57.   Hammer, M., Woerner, A., Mendez, F., Watkins, J. & Wall, J., Genetic evidence for archaic admixture in Africa. *PNAS* **108** (37), 15123-15128 (2011).

58.   Oppenheimer, S., *Out of Eden* (Constable & Robinson Ltd, London, 2003).

10: The long African dawn

1.   Behar, D. *et al.*, The Dawn of Human Matrilineal Diversity. *American Journal of Human Genetics* **82**, 1130-1140 (2008).

2.   Cohen, A. *et al.*, Ecological consequences of early Late Pleistocene megadroughts in tropical Africa. *PNAS* **107** (42), 16422-16427 (2007).

3.   Scholz, C. *et al.*, East African megadroughts between 135 and 75 thousand years ago and bearing on early-modern human origins. *PNAS* **104** (42), 16416-16421 (2007).

4.   Stager, C., Ryves, D., Chase, B. & Pausata, F., Catastrophic Drought in the Afro-Asian Monsoon Region During Heinrich Event 1. *Science* **331**, 1299-1302 (2011).

5.   Marean, C. *et al.*, Early human use of marine resources and pigment in South Africa during the Middle Pleistocene. *Nature* **449**, 905-909 (2007).

6.   McBrearty, S. & Stringer, C., The coast in colour. *Nature* **449**, 793-794 (2007).

7.   Mithen, S., *After the Ice: A Global Human History 20,000 - 5,000 BC* (Weidenfield & Nicholson, London, 2003).

8.   Brown, K. *et al.*, Fire As an Engineering Tool of Early Modern Humans. *Science* **325**, 859-862 (2009).

9.   Crawford, M. *et al.*, Evidence for the unique function of docasahexaenoic acid during the evolution of the modern human brain. *Lipids* **34** (Supplement), S39-S47 (1999).

10.   Walter, R. *et al.*, Early human occupation of the Red Sea coast of Eritrea during the last interglacial. *Nature* **405**, 65-69 (2000).

11.   Yellen, J., Brooks, A., Cornelissen, E., Mehlman, M. & Stewart, K., A middle stone age worked bone industry from Katanda, Upper Semliki Valley, Zaire. *Science* **268**, 553-556 (1995).

12.   McBrearty, S. & Brooks, A., The revolution that wasn't: a new interpretation of the origin of modern human behaviour. *Journal of Human Evolution* **39**, 453-563 (2000).

13.   Henshilwood, C. & Marean, C., The Origin of Modern Human Behavior. *Current Anthropology* **44** (5), 627-651 (2003).

14.   Henshilwood, C., d'Errico, F., Marean, C., Milo, R. & Yates, R., An early bone tool industry from the Middle Stone Age at Blombos Cave, South Africa: implications for the origins of modern human behaviour, symbolism and language. *Journal of Human Evolution* **41**, 631-678 (2001).

15.   Klein, R. & Edgar, B., *The Dawn of Human Culture* (John Wiley & Sons, Inc., New York, NY, 2002).

16.   Henshilwood, C., in *From Tools to Symbols. From Early Hominids to Modern Humans*, edited by d'Errico, F. & Backwell, L. (Witwatersrand University Press, Johannesburg, 2005), pp. 441-458.

17. Henshilwood, C. *et al.*, Emergence of Modern Human Behavior: Middle Stone Age Engravings from South Africa. *Science* **295**, 1278-1280 (2002).

18. Jacobs, Z., Duller, G., Wintle, A. & Henshilwood, C., Extending the chronology of deposits at Blombos Cave,South Africa, back to 140 ka using optical dating of single and multiple grains of quartz. *Journal of Human Evolution* **51**, 255-273 (2006).

19. Tribolo, C. *et al.*, TL dating of burnt lithics from Blombos Cave (South Africa): further evidence for the antiquity of modern human behaviour. *Archaeometry* **48** (2), 341-357 (2006).

20. Henshilwood, C., in *Rethinking the human revolution*, edited by Mellars, P., Boyle, K., Bar-Yosef, O. & Stringer, C. (McDonald Institute, Cambridge, 2007), pp. 123-132.

21. Henshilwood, C. *et al.*, A 100,000-Year-Old Ochre-Processing Workshop at Blombos Cave, South Africa. *Science* **334**, 219-222 (2011).

22. Henshilwood, C., Identifying the Collector: Evidence for Human Processing of the Cape Dune Mole-Rat, Bathyergus suillus, from Blombos Cave, Southern Cape, South Africa. *Journal of Archaeological Science* **24**, 659-662 (1997).

23. Henshilwood, C. *et al.*, Blombos Cave, Southern Cape, South Africa: Preliminary Report on the 1992–1999 Excavations of the Middle Stone Age Levels. *Journal of Archaeological Science* **28**, 421-448 (2001).

24. Mellars, P., in *Prehistoric Europe*, edited by Cunliffe, B. (Oxford University Press, Oxford, 1994), pp. 42-78.

25. Wadley, L., Hodgskiss, T. & Grant, M., Implications for complex cognition from the hafting of tools with compound adhesives in the Middle Stone Age, South Africa. *PNAS* **106** (24), 9590-9594 (2009).

26. Wynn, T., Hafted spears and the archaeology of mind. *PNAS* **16** (24), 9544-9545 (2009).

27. Mourre, V., Villa, P. & Henshilwood, C., Early Use of Pressure Flaking on Lithic Artifacts at Blombos Cave, South Africa. *Science* **330**, 659-662 (2010).

28. Henshilwood, C., d'Errico, F., Vanhaeren, M., van Niekerk, K. & Jacobs, Z., Middle Stone Age Shell Beads from South Africa. *Science* **304**, 404 (2004).

29. D'Errico, F., Henshilwood, C., Vanhaeren, M. & van Niekerke, K., Nassarius kraussianus shell beads from Blombos Cave: evidence for symbolic behaviour in the Middle Stone Age. *Journal of Human Evolution* **48**, 3-24 (2005).

30. Vanhaeren, M. *et al.*, Middle Paleolithic Shell Beads in Israel and Algeria. *Science* **312**, 1785-1788 (2006).

31. Bouzouggar, A. *et al.*, 82,000-year-old shell beads from North Africa and implications for the origins of modern human behavior. *PNAS* **104** (23), 9964-9969 (2007).

32. D'Errico, F. *et al.*, Additional evidence on the use of personal ornaments in the Middle Paleolithic of North Africa. *PNAS* **106** (38), 16051-16056 (2009).

33. Texier, P. *et al.*, A Howiesons Poort tradition of engraving ostrich eggshell containers dated to 60,000 years ago at Diepkloof Rock Shelter, South Africa. *PNAS* **107** (14), 6180-6185 (2010).

34. Henshilwood, C., d'Errico, F. & Watts, I., Engraved ochres from the Middle Stone Age levels at Blombos Cave, South Africa. *Journal of Human Evolution* **57**, 27-47 (2009).

35. Barham, L., in *Rethinking the human revolution*, edited by Mellars, P., Boyle, K., Bar-Yosef, O. & Stringer, C. (McDonald Institute, Cambridge, 2007), pp. 163-176.

36. Roscoe, P., The hunters and gatherers of New Guinea. *Current Anthropology* **43**, 153-162 (2002).

37. Kuhn, S. & Stiner, M., in *Rethinking the human revolution*, edited by Mellars, P., Boyle, K., Bar-Yosef, O. & Stringer, C. (McDonald Institute, Cambridge, 2007), pp. 45-54.

38. Wynn, T. & Coolidge, F., in *Rethinking the human revolution*, edited by Mellars, P., Boyle, K., Bar-Yosef, O. & Stringer, C. (McDonald Institute, Cambridge, 2007), pp. 79-90.

39. Wadley, L., Announcing a Still Bay industry at Sibudu Cave, South Africa. *Journal of Human Evolution* **52** (6), 681-689 (2007).

40. Jacobs, Z. *et al.*, Ages for the Middle Stone Age of Southern Africa: Implications for Human Behavior and Dispersal. *Science* **322**, 733-735 (2008).

41. Wurtz, S. & Lombard, M., 70 000-year-old geometric backed tools from the Howiesons Poort at Klasies River, South Africa: were they used for hunting? *Southern African Humanities* **19**, 1-11 (2007).

42. Lombard, M. & Pargeter, J., Hunting with Howiesons Poort segments: pilot experimental study and the functional interpretation of archaeological tools. *Journal of Archaeological Science* **35**, 2523-2531 (2008).

43. Mellars, P., Why did modern human populations disperse from Africa ca. 60,000 years ago? A new model. *PNAS* **103** (25), 9381-9386 (2006).

44. Jacobs, Z. & Roberts, R., Catalysts for Stone Age innovations. *Communicative & Integrative Biology* **2** (2), 191-193 (2009).

45. Oppenheimer, S., *Out of Eden* (Constable & Robinson Ltd, London, 2003).

46. Powell, A., Shennan, S. & Thomas, M., Late Pleistocene Demography and the Appearance of Modern Human Behavior. *PNAS* **324**, 1298-1301 (2009).

47. Villa, P., Soriano, S., Teyssandier, N. & Wurz, S., The Howiesons Poort and MSA III at Klasies River main site, Cave 1A. *Journal of Archaeological Science* **37**, 630-655 (2010).

48. Brown, K. *et al.*, An early and enduring advanced technology originating 71,000 years ago in South Africa. *Nature* **491**, 590-593 (2012).

49. Mackay, A., Nature and significance of the Howiesons Poort to post-Howiesons Poort transition at Klein Kliphuis rockshelter, South Africa. *Journal of Archaeological Science* **38**, 1430-1440 (2011).

50. Clarke, J. & Plug, I., Animal exploitation strategies during the South African Middle Stone Age: Howiesons Poort and post-Howiesons Poort fauna from Sibudu Cave. *Journal of Human Evolution* **54** (6), 886-898 (2008).

51. Will, M., Bader, G. & Conard, N., Characterizing the Late Pleistocene MSA Lithic Technology of Sibudu, KwaZulu-Natal, South Africa. *PLoS One* **9** (5), e98359 (2014).

52. Wells, S., *The Journey of Man* (London, Penguin, 2002).

53. Roberts, A., *The Incredible Human Journey* (Bloomsbury, London, 2009).

54. Tishkoff, S. *et al.*, History of Click-Speaking Populations of Africa Inferred from mtDNA and Y Chromosome Genetic Variation. *Molecular Biology and Evolution* **24** (10), 2180-2195 (2007).

55. Salas, A. *et al.*, The Making of the African mtDNA Landscape. *American Journal of Human Genetics* **71**, 1082-1111 (2002).

56. Semino, O., Santachiara-Benerecetti, S., Falaschi, F., Cavalli-Sforza, L. & Underhill, P., Ethiopians and Khoisan Share the Deepest Clades of the Human Y-Chromosome Phylogeny. *American Journal of Human Genetics* **70**, 265-268 (2002).

57. Knight, A. *et al.*, African Y Chromosome and mtDNA Divergence Provides Insight into the History of Click Languages. *Current Biology* **13**, 464-473 (2003).

58. Quintana-Murci, L. *et al.*, Maternal traces of deep common ancestry and asymmetric gene flow between Pygmy hunter–gatherers and Bantu-speaking farmers. *PNAS* **105** (5), 1596-1601 (2008).

59. Soares, P. *et al.*, The Expansion of mtDNA Haplogroup L3 within and out of Africa. *Molecular Biology and Evolution* **29** (3), 915-927 (2012).

60. Watson, E., Forster, P., Richards, M. & Bandelt, H., Mitochondrial Footprints of Human Expansions in Africa. *American Journal of Human Genetics* **61**, 691-704 (1997).

61. Atkinson, Q., Gray, R. & Drummond, A., Bayesian coalescent inference of major human mitochondrial DNA haplogroup expansions in Africa. *Proceedings of the Royal Society B* **276**, 367-373 (2009).

62. Soares, P. *et al.*, Correcting for Purifying Selection: An Improved Human Mitochondrial Molecular Clock. *American Journal of Human Genetics* **84**, 740-759 (2009).

63. Kittler, R., Kayser, M. & Stoneking, M., Molecular Evolution of Pediculus humanus and the Origin of Clothing. *Current Biology* **13**, 1414-1417 (2003).

11: The making of the modern mind

1. Renfrew, C., in *Archaeological Theory Today*, edited by Hodder, I. (Polity Press, Cambridge, 2001), pp. 122-140.

2. Renfrew, C., *Prehistory: Making of the Human Mind* (Weidenfeld & Nicholson, London, 2007).

3. Renfrew, C., Neuroscience, evolution and the sapient paradox: the factuality of value and of the sacred. *Philosophical Transactions of the Royal Society B* **363**, 2041-2047 (2008).

4. Diamond, J., *The Third Chimpanzee* (Random, London, 1991).

5. Klein, R. & Edgar, B., *The Dawn of Human Culture* (John Wiley & Sons, Inc., New York, NY, 2002).

6. Lai, C., Fisher, S., Hurst, J., Vargha-Khadem, F. & Monaco, A., A forkhead-domain gene is mutated in a severe speech and language disorder. *Nature* **413**, 519-523 (2001).

7.   Enard, W. *et al.*, Molecular evolution of FOXP2, a gene involved in speech and language. *Nature* **418**, 869-872 (2002).

8.   Krause, J. *et al.*, The Derived FOXP2 Variant of Modern Humans Was Shared with Neandertals. *Current Biology* **17**, 1908-1912 (2007).

9.   McBrearty, S. & Brooks, A., The revolution that wasn't: a new interpretation of the origin of modern human behaviour. *Journal of Human Evolution* **39**, 453-563 (2000).

10. McBrearty, S., in *Rethinking the human revolution*, edited by Mellars, P., Boyle, K., Bar-Yosef, O. & Stringer, C. (McDonald Institute, Cambridge, 2007), pp. 133-151.

11. Coolidge, F. & Wynn, T., *The Rise of Homo sapiens* (Wiley-Blackwell, Hoboken, NJ, 2009).

12. D'Errico, F., The Invisible Frontier. A Multiple Species Model for the Origin of Behavioral Modernity. *Evolutionary Anthropology* **12**, 188-202 (2003).

13. D'Errico, F. *et al.*, Early evidence of San material culture represented by organic artifacts from Border Cave, South Africa. *PNAS* **109** (33), 13214-13219 (2012).

14. Powell, A., Shennan, S. & Thomas, M., Late Pleistocene Demography and the Appearance of Modern Human Behavior. *Science* **324**, 1298-1301 (2009).

15. Henshilwood, C. & Marean, C., The Origin of Modern Human Behavior. *Current Anthropology* **44** (5), 627-651 (2003).

16. Henshilwood, C., in *Rethinking the human revolution*, edited by Mellars, P., Boyle, K., Bar-Yosef, O. & Stringer, C. (McDonald Institute, Cambridge, 2007), pp. 123-132.

17. Lieberman, D., Speculations About the Selective Basis for Modern Human Craniofacial Form. *Evolutionary Anthropology* **17**, 55-68 (2008).

18. Pinker, S., *The Language Instinct* (Penguin, London, 1994).

19. Mithen, S., *The Singing Neanderthal* (Weidenfeld & Nicholson, London, 2005).

20. Dunbar, R., *Grooming. Gossip and the Evolution of Language*, 2nd ed. (Faber and Faber Ltd., London, 2004).

21. Aiello, L. & Dunbar, R., Neocortex Size, Group Size and the Evolution of Language. *Current Anthropology* **34** (2), 184-193 (1993).

22. Bickerton, D., *Adam's Tongue* (Hill & Wang, New York, 2009).

23. Bickerton, D., *Language & Species* (University of Chicago Press, Chicago, 1990).

24. Bickerton, D., in *The Speciation of Modern Homo sapiens*, edited by Crow, T. (Oxford University Press, Oxford, 2002), pp. 103-120.

25. Bickerton, D., in *Rethinking the human revolution*, edited by Mellars, P., Boyle, K., Bar-Yosef, O. & Stringer, C. (McDonald Institute, Cambridge, 2007), pp. 99-105.

26. Bickerton, D., Language evolution: A brief guide for linguists. *Lingua* **117**, 510-526 (2007).

27. Wray, A., Protolanguage as a holistic system for social interaction. *Language and Communication* **18**, 47-67 (1998).

28. Kirby, S., in *Linguistic Evolution through Language Acquisition: Formal and Computational Models*, edited by Briscoe, E. (Cambridge University Press, Cambridge, 2002), pp. 173-204.

29. Mithen, S., in *Rethinking the human revolution*, edited by Mellars, P., Boyle, K., Bar-Yosef, O. & Stringer, C. (McDonald Institute, Cambridge, 2007), pp. 107-120.

30. Baron-Cohen, S., Leslie, A. & Frith, U., Does the autistic child have a 'theory of mind'? *Cognition* **21**, 37-46 (1985).

31. Mithen, S., *The Prehistory of the Mind* (Thomas & Hudson, London, 1996).

32. Fodor, J., *The Modularity of Mind* (MIT Press, Cambridge, MA, 1983).

33. Gardner, H., *Frames of Mind: The Theory of Multiple Intelligences* (Basic Books, New York, NY, 1983).

34. Karmiloff-Smith, A., *Beyond Modularity: a Developmental Perspective on Cognitive Science* (MIT Press, Cambridge, MA, 1992).

35. Boden, M., *The creative mind: myths and mechanisms*, 2nd ed. (Routledge, Abingdon, 2004).

36. Jaynes, J., *The Origin of Consciousness in the Breakdown of the Bicameral Mind* (Mariner Books, New York, 1976).

37. Wynn, T. & Coolidge, F., in *Rethinking the human revolution*, edited by Mellars, P., Boyle, K., Bar-Yosef, O. & Stringer, C. (McDonald Institute, Cambridge, 2007), pp. 79-90.

38. Stout, D. & Chaminade, T., Stone tools, language and the brain in human evolution. *Philosophical Transactions of the Royal Society B* **367**, 75-87 (2012).

39. Stout, D. & Chaminade, T., The evolutionary neuroscience of tool making. *Neuropsychologia* **45**, 1091-1100 (2007).

40. Stout, D., Toth, N., Schick, K. & Chaminade, T., Neural correlates of Early Stone Age toolmaking: technology, language and cognition in human evolution. *Philosophical Transactions of the Royal Society B* **363**, 1939-1949 (2008).

41. Faisal, A., Stout, D., Apel, J. & Bradley, B., The Manipulative Complexity of Lower Paleolithic Stone Toolmaking. *PLoS One* **5** (11) (2010).

42. Bowyer, P., *Religion Explained* (William Heinemann, London, 2001).

43. Dawkins, R., *The God Delusion* (Bantam Press, London, 2006).

44. Dunbar, R., *The Human Story* (Faber and Faber, London, 2004).

45. Dunbar, R., in *Rethinking the human revolution*, edited by Mellars, P., Boyle, K., Bar-Yosef, O. & Stringer, C. (McDonald Institute, Cambridge, 2007), pp. 91-105.

46. Durkheim, *The Elementary Forms of Religious Life (translated Cosman, C., 2001)* (Oxford University Press, Oxford, 1912).

47. Lewis-Williams, D. & Pearce, D., *Inside the Neolithic Mind* (Thames & Hudson, London, 2005).

48. Lovejoy, R. (personal communication).

49. Lewis-Williams, D., *The Mind in the Cave:Consciousness And The Origins Of Art* (Thames & Hudson, London, 2002).

50. Lewis-Williams, D., *Conceiving God: The Cognitive Origin and Evolution of Religion* (Thames & Hudson, London, 2010).

12: Going global

1. Field, J. & Lahr, M., Assessment of the Southern Dispersal: GIS-Based Analyses of Potential Routes at Oxygen Isotopic Stage 4. *Journal of World Prehistory* **19** (1), 1-45 (2005).

2. Derricourt, R., Getting "Out of Africa": Sea Crossings, Land Crossings and Culture in the Hominin Migrations. *Journal of World Prehistory* **19**, 119-132 (2005).

3. Lahr, M. & Foley, R., Towards a Theory of Modern Human Origins: Geography, Demography, and Diversity in Recent Human Evolution. *Yearbook of Physical Anthropology* **41**, 137-176 (1998).

4. Wells, S., *The Journey of Man* (London, Penguin, 2002).

5. Castaneda, I. *et al.*, Wet phases in the Sahara/Sahel region and human migration patterns in North Africa. *PNAS* **106** (48), 20159-20163 (2009).

6. Osborne, A. *et al.*, A humid corridor across the Sahara for the migration of early modern humans out of Africa 120,000 years ago. *PNAS* **105** (43), 16444-16447 (2008).

7. Drake, N., Blench, R., Armitage, S., Bristow, C. & White, K., Ancient watercourses and biogeography of the Sahara explain the peopling of the desert. *PNAS* **108** (2), 458-462 (2011).

8. Oppenheimer, S., *Out of Eden* (Constable & Robinson Ltd, London, 2003).

9. Oppenheimer, S., The great arc of dispersal of modern humans:Africa to Australia. *Quaternary International* **202**, 2-13 (2008).

10. Rose, J., The Arabian Corridor Migration Model:archaeological evidence for hominin dispersals into Oman during the Middle and Upper Pleistocene. *Proceedings of the Seminar for Arabian Studies* **37** (2007).

11. Dennell, R. (personal communication).

12. Pettitt, P., in *The Human Past*, edited by Scarre, C. (Thames & Hudson, London, 2005), pp. 124-173.

13. Rightmire, P., Middle and later Pleistocene hominins in Africa and Southwest Asia. *PNAS* **106** (38), 16046-16050 (2009).

14. Roberts, A., *The Incredible Human Journey* (Bloomsbury, London, 2009).

15. Grün, R. *et al.*, U-series and ESR analyses of bones and teeth relating to the human burials from Skhul. *Journal of Human Evolution* **49** (3), 316-334 (2005).

16. Vanhaeren, M. *et al.*, Middle Paleolithic Shell Beads in Israel and Algeria. *Science* **312**, 1785-1788 (2006).

17. Bar-Yosef Mayer, D., Vandermeersch, B. & Bar-Yosef, O., Shells and ochre in Middle Paleolithic Qafzeh Cave, Israel: indications for modern behavior. *Journal of Human Evolution* **56**, 307-314 (2009).

18. Klein, R., *The Human Career*, 2nd ed. (University of Chicago Press, Chicago, 1999).

19. Schwarcz, H. *et al.*, ESR dates for the hominid burial site of Qafzeh in Israel. *Journal of Human Evolution* **17** (8), 733-737 (1988).

20.   Rose, J. *et al.*, The Nubian Complex of Dhofar, Oman: An African Middle Stone Age Industry in Southern Arabia. *PLoS One* **6** (11) (2011).

21.   Grun, R. & Stringer, C., Tabun revisited: revised ESR chronology and new ESR and U-series analyses of dental material from Tabun C1. *Journal of Human Evolution* **39**, 601-612 (2000).

22.   Shea, J., in *Rethinking the human revolution*, edited by Mellars, P., Boyle, K., Bar-Yosef, O. & Stringer, C. (McDonald Institute, Cambridge, 2007), pp. 219-232.

23.   Cameron, D. & Groves, C., *Bones, Stones and Molecules: "Out of Africa" and Human Origins* (Elsevier Academic Press, London, 2004).

24.   Pope, K. & Terrell, J., Environmental setting of human migrations in the circum-Pacific region. *Journal of Biogeography* **35**, 1-21 (2008).

25.   Klein, R. & Edgar, B., *The Dawn of Human Culture* (John Wiley & Sons, Inc., New York, NY, 2002).

26.   Shen, G. *et al.*, U-Series dating of Liujiang hominid site in Guangxi, Southern China. *Journal of Human Evolution* **43** (6), 817-829 (2002).

27.   Curnoe, D. *et al.*, Human Remains from the Pleistocene-Holocene Transition of Southwest China Suggest a Complex Evolutionary History for East Asians. *PLoS One* **7** (3) (2012).

28.   Liu, W. *et al.*, Human remains from Zhirendong, South China,and modern human emergence in East Asia. *PNAS* **107** (45), 19201-1920 (2010).

29.   Dennell, R., Early Homo sapiens in China. *Nature* **468**, 512-513 (2010).

30.   Mellars, P., Why did modern human populations disperse from Africa ca. 60,000 years ago? A new model. *PNAS* **103** (25), 9381-9386 (2006).

31.   Mellars, P., Gori, K., Carr, M., Soares, P. & Richards, M., Genetic and archaeological perspectives on the initial modern human colonization of southern Asia. *PNAS* **110** (26), 10699-10704 (2013).

32.   Bowler, J. *et al.*, New ages for human occupation and climatic change at Lake Mungo, Australia. *Nature* **421**, 837-840 (2003).

33.   Thorne, A. *et al.*, Australia's oldest human remains: age of the Lake Mungo 3 skeleton. *Journal of Human Evolution* **36** (6), 591-612 (1999).

34.   Demeter, F. *et al.*, Anatomically modern human in Southeast Asia (Laos) by 46 ka. *PNAS* **109** (36), 14375-14380 (2012).

35.   Détroit, F. *et al.*, Upper Pleistocene Homo sapiens from the Tabon cave (Palawan, The Philippines): description and dating of new discoveries. *C. R. Palevol* **3** (8), 705-712 (2004).

36.   Benazzi, S. *et al.*, Early dispersal of modern humans in Europe and implications for Neanderthal behaviour. *Nature* **479**, 525-528 (2011).

37.   Higham, T. *et al.*, The earliest evidence for anatomically modern humans in northwestern Europe. *Nature* **479**, 521-524 (2011).

38.   Trinkaus, E. *et al.*, An early modern human from Peştera cu Oase, Romania. *PNAS* **100** (20), 11231-11236 (2003).

39.   Mellars, P., A new radiocarbon revolution and the dispersal of modern humans in Eurasia. *Nature* **493**, 931-935 (2006).

40.   Hiscock, P., *Archaeology of Ancient Australia* (Routledge, Abingdon, 2008).

41.   Macaulay, V. *et al.*, Single, Rapid Coastal Settlement of Asia Revealed by Analysis of Complete Mitochondrial Genomes. *Science* **308**, 1034-1036 (2005).

42.   Atkinson, Q., Gray, R. & Drummond, A., Bayesian coalescent inference of major human mitochondrial DNA haplogroup expansions in Africa. *Proceedings of the Royal Society B* **276**, 367-373 (2009).

43.   Soares, P. *et al.*, Correcting for Purifying Selection: An Improved Human Mitochondrial Molecular Clock. *American Journal of Human Genetics* **84**, 740-759 (2009).

44.   Soares, P. *et al.*, The Expansion of mtDNA Haplogroup L3 within and out of Africa. *Molecular Biology and Evolution* **29** (3), 915-927 (2012).

45.   Salas, A. *et al.*, The Making of the African mtDNA Landscape. *American Journal of Human Genetics* **71**, 1082-1111 (2002).

46.   Forster, P., Torroni, A., Renfrew, C. & Rohl, A., Phylogenetic Star Contraction Applied to Asian and Papuan mtDNA Evolution. *Molecular Biology and Evolution* **18** (10), 1864-1881 (2001).

47.   Atkinson, Q., Gray, R. & Drummond, A., mtDNA Variation Predicts Population Size in Humans and Reveals a Major Southern Asian Chapter in Human Prehistory. *Molecular Biology and Evolution* **25** (2), 468-474 (2008).

48.   Torroni, A., Achilli, A., Macaulay, V., Richards, M. & Bandelt, H., Harvesting the fruit of the human mtDNA tree. *Trends in Genetics* **22** (6), 339-345 (2006).

49.   Metspalu, M. *et al.*, Most of the extant mtDNA boundaries in South and Southwest Asia were likely shaped during the initial settlement of Eurasia by anatomically modern humans. *BMC Genetics* **5** (26) (2004).

50.   Kivisild, T. *et al.*, Ethiopian Mitochondrial DNA Heritage: Tracking Gene Flow Across and Around the Gate of Tears. *American Journal of Human Genetics* **75**, 752-770 (2004).

51.   Abu-Amero, K., Larruga, J., Cabrera, V. & González, A., Mitochondrial DNA structure in the Arabian Peninsula. *BMC Evolutionary Biology* **8** (45) (2008).

52.   Cerny, V. *et al.*, Regional Differences in the Distribution of the Sub-Saharan, West Eurasian, and South Asian mtDNA Lineages in Yemen. *American Journal of Physical Anthropology* **136**, 128-137 (2008).

53.   Kittler, R., Kayser, M. & Stoneking, M., Molecular Evolution of Pediculus humanus and the Origin of Clothing. *Current Biology* **13**, 1414-1417 (2003).

54.   Forster, P. & Matsumura, S., Did Early Humans Go North or South. *Science* **308**, 965-966 (2005).

55.   Liu, H., Prugnolle, F., Manica, A. & Balloux, F., A Geographically Explicit Genetic Model of Worldwide Human-Settlement History. *American Journal of Human Genetics* **79**, 230-237 (2006).

56.   Thangaraj, K. *et al.*, Reconstructing the Origin of Andaman Islanders. *Science* **308**, 996 (2005).

57.   Stringer, C., Coasting out of Africa. *Nature* **405**, 24-27 (2000).

58.   Mellars, P., Going East: New Genetic and Archaeological Perspectives on the Modern Human Colonization of Eurasia. *Science* **313**, 796-800 (2006).

59.   Bulbeck, D., Where River Meets Sea: A Parsimonious Model for Homo sapiens Colonization of the Indian Ocean Rim and Sahul. *Current Anthropology* **48** (2), 315-321 (2007).

60.   Field, J., Petraglia, M. & Lahr, M., The southern dispersal hypothesis and the South Asian archaeological record: Examination of dispersal routes through GIS analysis. *Journal of Anthropological Archaeology* **26**, 88-108 (2006).

61.   Petraglia, M., Groucutt, H. & Blinkhorn, J., in *Changing Deserts: Integrating People and their Environment*, edited by Mol, L. & Sternberg, T. (The White Horse Press, Isle of Harris, 2012), pp. 61-82.

62.   Burns, S., Fleitmann, D., Matter, A., Neff, U. & Mangini, A., Speleothem evidence from Oman for continental pluvial events during interglacial periods **7**, 623-626 (2001).

63.   Fleitmann, D. & Matter, A., The speleothem record of climate variability in Southern Arabia. *C. R. Geoscience* **341**, 633-642 (2009).

64.   Rose, J., New Light on Human Prehistory in the Arabo-Persian Gulf Oasis. *Current Anthropology* **51** (6), 849-883 (2010).

65.   Fleitmann, D. *et al.*, Holocene and Pleistocene pluvial periods in Yemen, southern Arabia. *Quaternary Science Reviews* **30** (7-8), 783-787 (2011).

66.   Petraglia, M. & Alsharekh, A., The Middle Palaeolithic of Arabia: Implications for modern human origins, behaviour and dispersals. *Antiquity* **77** (298), 671-684 (2003).

67.   Armitage, S. *et al.*, The Southern Route "Out of Africa": Evidence for an Early Expansion of Modern Humans into Arabia. *Science* **331**, 453-456 (2011).

68.   Lawler, A., Did Modern Humans Travel Out of Africa Via Arabia? *Science* **331**, 387 (2011).

69.   Delagnes, A. *et al.*, Inland human settlement in southern Arabia 55,000 years ago. New evidence from the Wadi Surdud Middle Paleolithic site complex, western Yemen. *Journal of Human Evolution* **63**, 452-474 (2012).

70.   Chesner, C., Westgate, J., Rose, W., Drake, R. & Deino, A., Eruptive history of Earth's largest Quaternary caldera (Toba, Indonesia). *Geology* **19**, 200-203 (1991).

71.   Rose, W. & Chesner, C., Dispersal of ash in the great Toba eruption, 75 ka. *Geology* **15**, 913-917 (1987).

72.   Acharyya, S. & Basu, P., Toba ash on the Indian subcontinent and its implications for correlation of Late Pleistocene alluvium. *Quaternary Research* **40**, 10-19 (1993).

73.   Williams, M. *et al.*, Environmental impact of the 73 ka Toba super-eruption in South Asia. *Palaeogeography, Palaeoclimatology, Palaeoecology* **284**, 295-314 (2009).

74.   Bühring, C., Sarnthein, M. & Party, L. 1. S. S., Toba ash layers in the South China Sea: Evidence of contrasting wind directions during eruption ca. 74 ka. *Geology* **28** (3), 275-278 (2000).

75.   Rampino, M. & Self, S., Volcanic winter and accelerated glaciation following the Toba super-eruption. *Nature* **359**, 50-52 (1992).

76.   Zielinski, G. *et al.*, Potential atmospheric impact of Toba mega-eruption ~71,000 years ago. *Geophysical Research Letters* **23** (8), 837-840 (1996).

77.   Ambrose, S., Late Pleistocene human population bottlenecks, volcanic winter, and differentiation of modern humans. *Journal of Human Evolution* **34**, 623-651 (1998).

78.   Robock, A. *et al.*, Did the Toba volcanic eruption of ~74 ka B.P. produce widespread glaciation. *Journal of Geophysical Research* **114** (2009).

79.   Oppenheimer, C., Limited global change due to the largest known Quaternary eruption, Toba ≈74 kyr BP? *Quaternary Science Reviews* **21** (14-15), 1593-1609 (2002).

80.   Gathorne-Hardy, F. & Harcourt-Smith, W., The super-eruption of Toba, did it cause a human bottleneck? *Journal of Human Evolution* **45**, 227-230 (2003).

81.   Petraglia, M. *et al.*, Middle Paleolithic Assemblages from the Indian Subcontinent Before and After the Toba Super-Eruption. *Science* **317**, 114-116 (2007).

82.   Petraglia, M., Ditchfield, P., Jones, S., Korisettar, R. & Pal, J., The Toba volcanic super-eruption, environmental change, and hominin occupation history in India over the last 140,000 years. *Quaternary International* **238**, 119-134 (2011).

83.   Kivisild, T. *et al.*, The Genetic Heritage of the Earliest Settlers Persists Both in Indian Tribal and Caste Populations. *American Journal of Human Genetics* **72**, 313-332 (2003).

84.   Thangaraj, K. *et al.*, In situ origin of deep rooting lineages of mitochondrial Macrohaplogroup 'M' in India. *BMC Genomics* **7** (151) (2006).

85.   Rajkumar, R., Banerjee, J., Gunturi, H., Trivedi, R. & Kashyap, V., Phylogeny and antiquity of M macrohaplogroup inferred from complete mt DNA sequence of Indian specific lineages. *BMC Evolutionary Biology* **26** (5) (2005).

86.   Dennell, R. & Petraglia, M., The dispersal of Homo sapiens across southern Asia: how early, how often, how complex? *Quaternary Science Reviews* **47**, 15-22 (2012).

87.   Ridl, J., Reply to: New Light on Human Prehistory in the Arabo-Persian Gulf Oasis. *Current Anthroplogy* **51** (6), 849-883 (2012).

88.   Reyes-Centeno, H. *et al.*, Genomic and cranial phenotype data support multiple modern human dispersals from Africa and a southern route into Asia. *PNAS* **111** (20), 7248-7253 (2014).

13: Two waves

1.   Lambeck, K. & Chappell, J., Sea Level Change Through the Last Glacial Cycle. *Science* **292**, 679-686 (2001).

2.   Rasmussen, M. *et al.*, An Aboriginal Australian Genome Reveals Separate Human Dispersals into Asia. *Science* **334**, 94-98 (2011).

3.   Curnoe, D. *et al.*, Human Remains from the Pleistocene-Holocene Transition of Southwest China Suggest a Complex Evolutionary History for East Asians. *PLoS One* **7** (3) (2012).

4.   Gunz, P. *et al.*, Early modern human diversity suggests subdivided population structure and a complex out-of-Africa scenario. *PNAS* **106** (15), 6094-6098 (2009).

5.   Rabett, R. & Barker, G., in *Rethinking the human revolution*, edited by Mellars, P., Boyle, K., Bar-Yosef, O. & Stringer, C. (McDonald Institute, Cambridge, 2007), pp. 411-424.

6.   Roberts, A., *The Incredible Human Journey* (Bloomsbury, London, 2009).

7.   Birdsell, J., A reassessment of the age, sex and population affinities of the Niah cranium. *American Journal of Physical Anthropology* **50**, 419 (1979).

8.   Demeter, F. *et al.*, Anatomically modern human in Southeast Asia (Laos) by 46 ka. *PNAS* **109** (36), 14375-14380 (2012).

9.   Détroit, F. *et al.*, Upper Pleistocene Homo sapiens from the Tabon cave (Palawan, The Philippines): description and dating of new discoveries. *C. R. Palevol* **3** (8), 705-712 (2004).

10.   Mijares, A. *et al.*, New evidence for a 62000-year-old human presence at Callao Cave, Luzon, Philippines. *Journal of Human Evolution* **59**, 123-132 (2010).

11.   Aubert, M. *et al.*, Pleistocene cave art from Sulawesi, Indonesia. *Nature* **514**, 223-227 (2014).

12.   O'Connell, J. & Allen, J., in *Rethinking the human revolution*, edited by Mellars, P., Boyle, K., Bar-Yosef, O. & Stringer, C. (McDonald Institute, Cambridge, 2007), pp. 395-410.

13.   Stringer, C., Coasting out of Africa. *Nature* **405**, 24-27 (2000).

14. Oppenheimer, S., *Out of Eden* (Constable & Robinson Ltd, London, 2003).

15. Summerhayes, G. *et al.*, Human Adaptation and Plant Use in Highland New Guinea 49,000 to 44,000 Years Ago. *Science* **330**, 78-81 (2010).

16. Bowler, J., Willandra Lakes Revisited: environmental framework for human occupation. *Archaeology in Oceania* **33**, 120-155 (1998).

17. Bowler, J. *et al.*, New ages for human occupation and climatic change at Lake Mungo, Australia. *Nature* **421**, 837-840 (2003).

18. Thorne, A. *et al.*, Australia's oldest human remains: age of the Lake Mungo 3 skeleton. *Journal of Human Evolution* **36** (6), 591-612 (1999).

19. Adcock, G. *et al.*, Mitochondrial DNA sequences in ancient Australians: Implications for modern human origins. *PNAS* **98** (2), 537-542 (2001).

20. Smith, C., Chamberlain, A., Riley, M., Stringer, C. & Collins, M., The thermal history of human fossils and the likelihood of successful DNA amplification. *Journal of Human Evolution* **43**, 203-217 (2003).

21. Roberts, R., Jones, R. & Smith, M., Thermoluminescence dating of a 50,000-year-old human occupation site in northern Australia. *Nature* **345**, 153-156 (1990).

22. Roberts, R. *et al.*, The human colonisation of Australia: optical dates of 53,000 and 60,000 years bracket human arrival at Deaf Adder Gorge, Northern Territory. *Quaternary Science Reviews* **13** (5-7), 575-583 (1994).

23. Roberts, R. *et al.*, Single-aliquot and single-grain optical dating confirm thermoluminescent age estimates at Malakunanja rock shelter in northern Australia. *Ancient TL* **16** (1), 19-24 (1998).

24. Gillespie, R., Dating the first Australians. *Radiocarbon* **44** (2), 455-472 (2002).

25. O'Connell, J. & Allen, J., Dating the colonization of Sahul (Pleistocene Australia–New Guinea): a review of recent research. *Journal of Archaeological Science* **31**, 835-853 (2004).

26. Allen, J. & O'Connell, J., The long and the short of it: Archaeological approaches to determining when humans first colonised Australia and New Guinea. *Australian Archaeology* **57**, 5-19 (2003).

27. Hiscock, P., *Archaeology of Ancient Australia* (Routledge, Abingdon, 2008).

28. Stone, T. & Cupper, M., Last Glacial Maximum ages for robust humans at Kow Swamp, southern Australia. *Journal of Human Evolution* **45**, 99-111 (2003).

29. Thorne, A., Australia's human origins - how many sources. *American Journal of Physical Anthropology* **63**, 227 (1984).

30. Birdsell, J., Preliminary data on the trihybrid origin of the Australiam aborigines. *Archaeology and Physical Anthropology in Oceania* **2**, 100-155 (1967).

31. Hudjashov, G. *et al.*, Revealing the prehistoric settlement of Australia by Y chromosome and mtDNA analysis. *PNAS* **104** (21), 8726-8730 (2007).

32. Reich, D. *et al.*, Denisova Admixture and the First Modern Human Dispersals into Southeast Asia and Oceania. *American Journal of Human Genetics* **89**, 1-13 (2011).

33. Ingman, M. & Gyllensten, U., Mitochondrial Genome Variation and Evolutionary History of Australian and New Guinean Aborigines. *Genome Research* **13**, 1600-1606 (2003).

34. Merriwether, A. *et al.*, Ancient mitochondrial M haplogroups identified in the Southwest Pacific. *PNAS* **102** (37), 13034-13039 (2005).

35. Cameron, D. & Groves, C., *Bones, Stones and Molecules: "Out of Africa" and Human Origins* (Elsevier Academic Press, London, 2004).

36. Lewin, R. & Foley, R., *Principles of Human Evolution*, 2nd ed. (Blackwell Science Ltd, Oxford, 2004).

37. Veth, P., Islands in the interior: a model for the colonization of Australia's arid zone. *Archaeology in Oceania* **24**, 81-92 (1989).

38. Hiscock, P. & Wallis, L., in *Desert Peoples: Archaological Perspectives*, edited by Veth, P., Smith, M. & Hiscock, P. (Blackwell, Oxford, 2005), pp. 34-57.

39. Atkinson, Q., Gray, R. & Drummond, A., mtDNA Variation Predicts Population Size in Humans and Reveals a Major Southern Asian Chapter in Human Prehistory. *Molecular Biology and Evolution* **25** (2), 468-474 (2008).

40. Guthrie, D., Origin and causes of the mammoth steppe: a story of cloud cover, woolly mammal tooth pits, buckles, and inside-out Beringia. *Quaternary Science Reviews* **20**, 549-574 (2001).

41. Goebel, T., Derevianko, A. & Petrin, V., Dating the Middle-to-Upper Paleolithic Transition at Kara-Bom. *Current Anthropology* **34** (4), 452-458 (1993).

42. Brantingham, J., Krivoshapkin, A., Jinzeng, L. & Tserendagva, Y., The Initial Upper Paleolithic in Northeast Asia. *Current Anthropology* **42** (5), 735-745 (2001).

43. Vasil'ev, S., Kuzmin, Y., Orlova, L. & Dementiev, V., Radiocarbon-Based Chronology Of the Paleolithic in Siberia and its Relevance to the Peopling of The New World. *Radiocarbon* **44** (2), 503-530 (2002).

44. Pope, K. & Terrell, J., Environmental setting of human migrations in the circum-Pacific region. *Journal of Biogeography* **35**, 1-21 (2008).

45. Meltzer, D., Peopling of North America. *Development in Quaternary Science* **1**, 539-563 (2003).

46. Pitulko, V. *et al.*, The Yana RHS Site: Humans in the Arctic Before the Last Glacial Maximum. *Science* **303** (52), 52-56 (2004).

47. Graf, K., in *Sourcebook of Paleolithic Transitions*, edited by Camps, M. & Chauhan, P. (George Washington University, Washington, DC, 2009), pp. 479-501.

48. Fu, Q. *et al.*, Genome sequence of a 45,000-year-old modern human from western Siberia. *Nature* **514**, 445-450 (2014).

49. Shang, H., Tong, H., Zhang, S., Chen, F. & Trinkaus, E., An early modern human from Tianyuan Cave, Zhoukoudian, China. *PNAS* **104** (16), 6573-6578 (2007).

50. Shen, G., Wang, W., Cheng, H. & Edwards, L., Mass spectrometric U-series dating of Laibin hominid site in Guangxi, southern China. *Journal of Archaeological Science* **34** (12), 2109-2114 (2007).

51. Jin, L. & Su, B., Natives or immigrants: modern human origin in East Asia. *Nature Reviews Genetics* **1**, 126-133 (2000).

52. Kivisild, T. *et al.*, The Emerging Limbs and Twigs of the East Asian mtDNA Tree. *Molecular Biology and Evolution*. **19** (10), 1737-1751 (2002).

53. Ballinger, S. *et al.*, Southeast Asian Mitochondrial DNA Analysis Reveals Genetic Continuity of Ancient Mongoloid Migrations. *Genetics* **130**, 139-152 (1992).

54. Li, H. *et al.*, Mitochondrial DNA Diversity and Population Differentiation in Southern East Asia. *American Journal of Physical Anthropology* **134**, 481-488 (2007).

55. Yao, Y., Kong, Q., Bandelt, H., Kivisild, T. & Zhang, Y., Phylogeographic Differentiation of Mitochondrial DNA in Han Chinese. *American Journal of Human Genetics* **70**, 635-651 (2002).

56. Su, B. *et al.*, Y-Chromosome Evidence for a Northward Migration of Modern Humans into Eastern Asia during the Last Ice Age. *American Journal of Human Genetics* **65**, 1718-1724 (1999).

57. Karafet, T. *et al.*, Paternal Population History of East Asia: Sources, Patterns, and Microevolutionary Processes. *American Journal of Human Genetics* **69**, 615-628 (2001).

58. Xue, Y. *et al.*, Male Demography in East Asia: A North–South Contrast in Human Population Expansion Times. *Genetics* **172**, 2431-2439 (2006).

59. Shi, H. *et al.*, Y-Chromosome Evidence of Southern Origin of the East Asian–Specific Haplogroup O3-M122. *American Journal of Human Genetics* **77**, 408-419 (2005).

60. Shi, H. *et al.*, Y chromosome evidence of earliest modern human settlement in East Asia and multiple origins of Tibetan and Japanese populations. *BMC Biology* **6** (45) (2008).

61. Ding, Y. *et al.*, Population structure and history in East Asia. *PNAS* **97** (25), 14003-14006 (2000).

14: An inaccessible peninsula

1. Clottes, J., *Cave Art* (Phaidon, New York, 2008).

2. Pike, A. *et al.*, U-Series Dating of Paleolithic Art in 11 Caves in Spain. *Science* **336**, 1409-1413 (2012).

3. Mellars, P., A new radiocarbon revolution and the dispersal of modern humans in Eurasia. *Nature* **493**, 931-935 (2006).

4. Mellars, P., Neanderthals and the modern human colonization of Europe. *Nature* **432**, 461-465 (2004).

5. Mellars, P., Origins of the female image. *Nature* **439**, 176-177 (2009).

6. Mellars, P., *The Neanderthal Legacy* (Princeton University Press, 1996).

7. Pettitt, P., in *The Human Past*, edited by Scarre, C. (Thames & Hudson, London, 2005), pp. 124-173.

8. Mellars, P., in *Prehistoric Europe*, edited by Cunliffe, B. (Oxford University Press, Oxford, 1994), pp. 42-78.

9. Klein, R., *The Human Career*, 2nd ed. (University of Chicago Press, Chicago, 1999).

10. Conard, N., Grootes, P. & Smith, F., Unexpectedly recent dates for human remains from

Vogelherd. *Nature* **430**, 198-201 (2004).

11. Benazzi, S. *et al.*, Early dispersal of modern humans in Europe and implications for Neanderthal behaviour. *Nature* **479**, 525-528 (2011).

12. Higham, T. *et al.*, The earliest evidence for anatomically modern humans in northwestern Europe. *Nature* **479**, 521-524 (2011).

13. Trinkaus, E., Milota, S., Rodrigo, R., Mircea, G. & Moldovan, O., Early modern human cranial remains from the Peştera cu Oase, Romania. *Journal of Human Evolution* **45**, 245-253 (2003).

14. Trinkaus, E. *et al.*, An early modern human from Peştera cu Oase, Romania. *PNAS* **100** (20), 11231-11236 (2003).

15. Zilhão, J. *et al.*, in *Rethinking the human revolution*, edited by Mellars, P., Boyle, K., Bar-Yosef, O. & Stringer, C. (McDonald Institute, Cambridge, 2007), pp. 249-261.

16. Mellars, P., Archeology and the Dispersal of Modern Humans in Europe: Deconstructing the "Aurignacian". *Evolutionary Anthropology* **15**, 167-182 (2006).

17. Wild, E. *et al.*, Direct dating of Early Upper Palaeolithic human remains from Mladeč. *Nature* **435**, 332-335 (2005).

18. Higham, T. *et al.*, The timing and spatiotemporal patterning of Neanderthal disappearance. *Nature* **512**, 306-309 (2014).

19. Mellars, P. & French, J., Tenfold Population Increase in Western Europe at the Neandertal–to–Modern Human Transition. *Science* **333**, 623-627 (2011).

20. Longo, L. *et al.*, Did Neandertals and anatomically modern humans coexist in northern Italy during the late MIS 3? *Quaternary International* **259**, 102-112 (2012).

21. Mellars, P., in *The Speciation of Modern Homo sapiens*, edited by Crow, T. (Oxford University Press, Oxford, 2002), pp. 31-47.

22. Mellars, P., The Impossible Coincidence. A Single-Species Model for the Origins of Modern Human Behavior in Europe. *Evolutionary Anthropology* **14**, 12-27 (2005).

23. Mithen, S., *The Singing Neanderthal* (Weidenfeld & Nicholson, London, 2005).

24. Oppenheimer, S., *Out of Eden* (Constable & Robinson Ltd, London, 2003).

25. Otte, M., in *Rethinking the human revolution*, edited by Mellars, P., Boyle, K., Bar-Yosef, O. & Stringer, C. (McDonald Institute, Cambridge, 2007), pp. 359-366.

26. Hoffecker, J., The spread of modern humans in Europe. *PNAS* **106** (38), 16040-16045 (2009).

27. Martinson, D., Pisias, N., Hays, J., Imbried, J. & Moore, T., Age dating and the orbital theory of the ice ages: Development of a high-resolution 0 to 300,000-year chronostratigraphy. *Quaternary Research* **27** (1), 1-29 (1987).

28. Bond, G. *et al.*, Correlations between climate records from North Atlantic sediments and Greenland ice. *Nature* **365**, 143-147 (1993).

29. Dansgaard, W. *et al.*, Evidence for general instability of past climate from a 250-kyr ice-core record. *Nature* **364**, 218-220 (1993).

30. Shackleton, N., Fairbanks, R., Chiu, T. & Parrenin, F., Absolute calibration of the Greenland time scale: implications for Antarctic time scales and for D14C. *Quaternary Science Reviews* **23**, 1513-1522 (2004).

31. Atkinson, Q., Gray, R. & Drummond, A., mtDNA Variation Predicts Population Size in Humans and Reveals a Major Southern Asian Chapter in Human Prehistory. *Molecular Biology and Evolution* **25** (2), 468-474 (2008).

32. Anikovich, M. *et al.*, Early Upper Paleolithic in Eastern Europe and Implications for the Dispersal of Modern Humans. *Science* **315**, 223-226 (2007).

33. Pavlov, P., Svendsen, J. & Indrelid, S., Human presence in the European Arctic nearly 40,000 years ago. *Nature* **413**, 64-67 (2001).

34. Hemming, S., Heinrich events: Massive late Pleistocene detritus layers of the North Atlantic and their global climate imprint. *Review of Geophysics* **42** (2004).

35. Higham, T. *et al.*, Testing models for the beginnings of the Aurignacian and the advent of figurative art and music: The radiocarbon chronology of Geißenklösterle. *Journal of Human Evolution* **62** (6), 664-676 (2012).

36. Conard, N. & Bolus, M., Radiocarbon dating the appearance of modern humans and timing of cultural innovations in Europe: new results and new challenges. *Journal of Human Evolution* **44**, 331-371 (2003).

37. Olszewski, D. & Dibble, H., The Zagros Aurignacian. *Current Anthropology* **35** (1), 68-75 (1994).

38. Olszewski, D. & Dibble, H., in *Towards a definition of the Aurignacian*, edited by Bar-Yosef, O. & Zilhão, J. (Trabalhos de Arqueooga, Lisbon, 2002), pp. 355-373.

39. Bergman, C. & Stringer, C., Fifty years after: Egbert, an early Upper Paleolithic juvenile from Ksar Akil, Lebanon. *Paléorient* **15**, 99-111 (1989).

40.   Kuhn, S., Stiner, M., Reese, D. & Gulec, E., Ornaments of the earliest Upper Paleolithic: New insights from the Levant. *PNAS* **98** (13), 7641-7646 (2001).

41.   Svoboda, J., in *Rethinking the human revolution*, edited by Mellars, P., Boyle, K., Bar-Yosef, O. & Stringer, C. (McDonald Institute, Cambridge, 2007), pp. 329-339.

42.   Kuhn, S. *et al.*, The early Upper Paleolithic occupations at Üçağızlı Cave (Hatay, Turkey). *Journal of Human Evolution* **56**, 87-113 (2009).

43.   Belfer-Cohen, A. & Goring-Morris, N., in *Rethinking the human revolution*, edited by Mellars, P., Boyle, K., Bar-Yosef, O. & Stringer, C. (McDonald Institute, Cambridge, 2007), pp. 199-205.

44.   Kuhn, S., Paleolithic Archaeology in Turkey. *Evolutionary Anthropology* **11**, 198-210 (2002).

45.   Kozlowski, J., in *Rethinking the human revolution*, edited by Mellars, P., Boyle, K., Bar-Yosef, O. & Stringer, C. (McDonald Institute, Cambridge, 2007), pp. 317-328.

46.   Clark, P. *et al.*, The Last Glacial Maximum. *Science* **325**, 710-714 (2009).

47.   Hoffecker, J., Innovation and Technological Knowledge in the Upper Paleolithic of Northern Eurasia. *Evolutionary Anthropology* **14**, 186-198 (2005).

48.   Straus, L., The Upper Palaeolithic of Europe: An Overview. *Evolutionary Anthropology* **4**, 4-16 (1995).

49.   Richards, M., Pettitt, P., Stiner, M. & Trinkaus, E., Stable isotope evidence for increasing dietary breadth in the European mid-Upper Paleolithic. *PNAS* **98** (11), 6528-6532 (2001).

50.   Richards, M. & Trinkaus, E., Isotopic evidence for the diets of European Neanderthals and early modern humans. *PNAS* **106** (38), 16034-16039 (2009).

51.   Formicola, V., From the Sunghir Children to the Romito Dwarf: Aspects of the Upper Paleolithic Funerary Landscape. *Current Anthropology* **48** (3), 446-453 (2007).

52.   Schulting, R., Antlers, bone pins and flint blades: the mesolithic cemeteries of Teviec and Hoedic, Brittany. *Antiquity* **70** (268), 335-350 (1996).

53.   Svoboda, J., The Gravettian of the Middle Danube. *Paléoanthropologie* **19**, 203-220 (2007).

54.   Conard, N., Palaeolithic ivory sculptures from southwestern Germany and the origins of figurative art. *Nature* **426**, 830-832 (2003).

55.   Conard, N., Malina, M. & Munzel, S., New flutes document the earliest musical tradition in southwestern Germany. *Nature* **460**, 738-740 (2009).

56.   Conard, N., A female figurine from the basal Aurignacian of Hohle Fels Cave in southwestern Germany. *Nature* **459**, 248-252 (2009).

57.   Vandiver, P., Soffer, O., Klima, B. & Svoboda, J., The Origins of Ceramic Technology at Dolní Věstonice, Czechoslovakia. *Science* **246**, 1002-1008 (1989).

58.   McDermott, L., Self-Representation in female figurines. *Current Anthropology* **37** (227-275) (1996).

59.   McCoid, C. & McDermott, L., Towards Decolonizing Gender: Female Vision in the Upper Palaeolithic. *American Anthroplogist* **98** (2), 319-326 (1996).

60.   Morales, M. & Straus, L., Extraordinary Early Magdalenian finds from El Mirón Cave, Cantabria (Spain). *Antiquity* **3**, 267-281 (2009).

61.   Marshack, A., *The Roots of Civilization* (McGraw-Hill, New York, 1972).

62.   Lewis-Williams, D., *The Mind in the Cave:Consciousness And The Origins Of Art* (Thames & Hudson, London, 2002).

63.   Barton, M., Clark, G. & Cohen, A., Art as information: explaining Upper Palaeolithic art in western Europe. *World Archaeology* **26** (2), 185-207 (1994).

64.   Yokoyama, Y., Lambeck, K., De Deckker, P., Johnston, P. & Field, K., Timing of the Last Glacial Maximum from observed sea-level minima. *Nature* **406** (2000).

65.   Gamble, C., Davies, W., Pettitt, P. & Richards, M., Climate change and evolving human diversity in Europe during the last glacial. *Philosophical Transactions of the Royal Society B* **349**, 243-254 (2004).

66.   Hewitt, G., The genetic legacy of the Quaternary ice ages. *Nature* **405**, 907-913 (2000).

67.   Hewitt, G., Genetic consequences of climatic oscillations in the Quaternary. *Philosophical Transactions of the Royal Society B* **359**, 183-195 (2004).

68.   Farbstein, R., Radic, D., Brajkovic, D. & Miracle, P., First Epigravettian Ceramic Figurines from Europe (Vela Spila, Croatia). *PLoS One* **7** (7) (2012).

69.   Banks, W. *et al.*, Eco-cultural niches of the Badegoulian: Unraveling links between cultural adaptation and ecology during the Last Glacial Maximum in France. *Journal of Anthropological Archaeology* **30** (3), 359-374 (2011).

70.   Gamble, C., Davies, W., Pettitt, P., Hazelwood, L. & Richards, M., The Late Glacial ancestry of Euopeans: combining genetic and archaeological evidence. *Documenta Praehistorica* **23** (2006).

71.   Terberger, T. & Street, M., Hiatus or continuity? New results for the question of pleniglacial settlement in Central Europe. *Antiquity* **76**, 691-698 (2002).

72.   Liu, Z. *et al.*, Transient Simulation of Last Deglaciation with a New Mechanism for Bølling-Allerød Warming. *Science* **325**, 310-314 (2009).

73.   Torroni, A. *et al.*, Classification of European mtDNAs From an Analysis of Three European Populations. *Genetics* **144**, 1835-1850 (1996).

74.   Richards, M. *et al.*, Tracing European Founder Lineages in the Near Eastern mtDNA Pool. *American Journal of Human Genetics* **67**, 1251-1276 (2000).

75.   Achilli, A. *et al.*, Saami and Berbers—An Unexpected Mitochondrial DNA Link. *American Journal of Human Genetics* **76**, 883-886 (2005).

76.   Malyarchuk, B. *et al.*, The Peopling of Europe from the Mitochondrial Haplogroup U5 Perspective. *PLoS One* **5** (4) (2010).

77.   Soares, P. *et al.*, The Archaeogenetics of Europe. *Current Biology* **20**, R174-R183 (2010).

78.   Semino, O. *et al.*, The Genetic Legacy of Paleolithic Homo sapiens sapiens in Extant Europeans: A Y Chromosome Perspective. *Science* **290**, 1155-1159 (2000).

79.   Underhill, P. *et al.*, The phylogeography of Y chromosome binary haplotypes and the origins of modern human populations. *Annual of Human Genetics* **65**, 43-62 (2001).

80.   Olivieri, A. *et al.*, The mtDNA Legacy of the Levantine Early Upper Palaeolithic in Africa. *Science* **314**, 1757-1770 (2006).

81.   González, A. *et al.*, Mitochondrial lineage M1 traces an early human backflow to Africa. *BMC Genomics* **8** (223) (2007).

82.   Hammer, M. *et al.*, Out of Africa and Back Again: Nested Cladistic Analysis of Human Y Chromosome Variation. *Molecular Biology and Evolution* **15** (4), 427-441 (1998).

83.   Cruciani, F. *et al.*, A Back Migration from Asia to Sub-Saharan Africa Is Supported by High-Resolution Analysis of Human Y-Chromosome Haplotypes. *American Journal of Human Genetics* **70**, 1197-1214 (2002).

84.   Krause, J. *et al.*, A Complete mtDNA Genome of an Early Modern Human from Kostenki, Russia. *Current Biology* **20**, 231-236 (2010).

85.   Kivisild, T. *et al.*, Deep common ancestry of Indian and western-Eurasian mitochondrial DNA lineages. *Current Biology* **9**, 1331-1334 (1999).

86.   Palanichamy, M. *et al.*, Phylogeny of Mitochondrial DNA Macrohaplogroup N in India, Based on Complete Sequencing: Implications for the Peopling of South Asia. *American Journal of Human Genetics* **75**, 966-978 (2004).

87.   Richards, M., Macaulay, V., Bandelt, H. & Sykes, B., Phylogeography of mitochondrial DNA in western Europe. *Annual of human genetics* **62**, 241-260 (1998).

88.   Sykes, B., The molecular genetics of European ancestry. *Philosophical Transactions of the Royal Society B* **354**, 131-139 (1999).

89.   Richards, M., Macaulay, V., Torroni, A. & Bandelt, H., In Search of Geographical Patterns in European Mitochondrial DNA. *American Journal of Human Genetics* **71**, 1168-1174 (2002).

90.   Achilli, A. *et al.*, The Molecular Dissection of mtDNA Haplogroup H Confirms That the Franco-Cantabrian Glacial Refuge Was a Major Source for the European Gene Pool. *American Journal of Human Genetics* **75**, 910-918 (2004).

91.   Loogvali, E. *et al.*, Disuniting Uniformity: A Pied Cladistic Canvas of mtDNA Haplogroup H in Eurasia. *Molecular Biology and Evolution* **21** (11), 2012-2021 (2004).

92.   Alvarez-Iglesias, V. *et al.*, New Population and Phylogenetic Features of the Internal Variation within Mitochondrial DNA Macro-Haplogroup R0. *PLoS One* **4** (4) (2009).

93.   Kivisild, T. *et al.*, in *Genomic Diversity: Applications in Human Population Genetics*, edited by Papiha, D., Chakraborty, K. & Kluwer, S. (Academic/Plenum Publishers, New York, NY, 1999), pp. 135-152.

94.   Maca-Meyer, N. *et al.*, Y Chromosome and Mitochondrial DNA Characterization of Pasiegos, a Human Isolate from Cantabria (Spain). *Annals of Human Genetics* **67**, 329-339 (2003).

95.   García, O. *et al.*, Using mitochondrial DNA to test the hypothesis of a European post-glacial human recolonization from the Franco-Cantabrian refuge. *Heredity* **106**, 37-45 (2011).

96.   Torroni, A. *et al.*, mtDNA Analysis Reveals a Major Late Paleolithic Population Expansion from Southwestern to Northeastern Europe. *American Journal of Human Genetics* **62**, 1137-1152 (1998).

97.   Torroni, A. *et al.*, A Signal, from Human mtDNA, of Postglacial Recolonization in Europe. *American Journal of Human Genetics* **69**, 844-852 (2001).

98.   Pereira, L. *et al.*, High-resolution mtDNA evidence for the late-glacial resettlement of Europe from an Iberian refugium. *Genome Research* **15**, 19-24 (2005).

99.   Ottoni, C. *et al.*, Mitochondrial Haplogroup H1 in North Africa: An Early Holocene Arrival from Iberia. *PLoS One* **5** (10) (2010).

100.   Pala, M. *et al.*, Mitochondrial Haplogroup U5b3: A Distant Echo of the Epipaleolithic in Italy and the Legacy of the Early Sardinians. *American Journal of Human Genetics* **84**, 814-821 (2009).

101.   Malyarchuk, B. *et al.*, Mitochondrial DNA Phylogeny in Eastern and Western Slavs. *Molecular Biology and Evolution* **25** (8), 1651-1658 (2008).

102. Rootsi, S. *et al.*, Phylogeography of Y-Chromosome Haplogroup I Reveals Distinct Domains of Prehistoric Gene Flow in Europe. *American Journal of Human Genetics* **75**, 128-137 (2004).

103. Pala, M. *et al.*, Mitochondrial DNA Signals of Late Glacial Recolonization of Europe from Near Eastern Refugia. *American Journal of Human Genetics* **90**, 915-924 (2012).

104. Gómez-Carballa, A. *et al.*, Genetic Continuity in the Franco-Cantabrian Region: New Clues from Autochthonous Mitogenomes. *PLoS One* **7** (3) (2012).

105. Behar, D. *et al.*, The Basque Paradigm: Genetic Evidence of a Maternal Continuity in the Franco-Cantabrian Region since Pre-Neolithic Times. *American Journal of Human Genetics* **90** (2012).

106. Barbujani, G., Bertorelle, G. & Chikhi, L., Evidence for Paleolithic and Neolithic Gene Flow in Europe. *American Journal of Human Genetics* **62**, 488-491 (1998).

107. Barbujani, G. & Dupanloup, I., in *Examining the farming/language dispersal hypothesis*, edited by Bellwood, P. & Renfrew, C. (McDonald Institute, Cambridge, 2002), pp. 421-433.

108. Levy-Coffman, E., We Are Not Our Ancestors: Evidence for Discontinuity between Prehistoric and Modern Europeans. *Journal of Genetic Genealogy*, **2**, 40-50 (2006).

109. Izagirre, N. & Rúa, d. l., An mtDNA Analysis in Ancient Basque Populations: Implications for Haplogroup V as a Marker for a Major Paleolithic Expansion from Southwestern Europe. *American Journal of Human Genetics* **65**, 199-207 (1999).

110. Sampietro, M. *et al.*, The Genetics of the Pre-Roman Iberian Peninsula: A mtDNA Study of Ancient Iberians. *Annals of Human Genetics* **69**, 535-548 (2005).

111. Chandler, H., Sykes, B. & Zilhão, J., in *Actas del III Congreso del Neolítico en la Península Ibérica. Santander*, edited by Arias-Cabal, P., Ontañón, R. & García-Moncó, C. (Instituto Internacional de Investigaciones Prehistóricas de Cantabria, Santander, 2005), pp. 781-786.

112. Bramanti, B. *et al.*, Genetic Discontinuity Between Local Hunter-Gatherers and Central Europe's First Farmers. *Science* **326**, 137-140 (2009).

113. Seguin-Orlando, A. *et al.*, Genomic structure in Europeans dating back at least 36,000 years. *Science* (2014).

114. Raghavan, M. *et al.*, Upper Palaeolithic Siberian genome reveals dual ancestry of Native Americans. *Nature* **505**, 87-94 (2014).

15: The final frontier

1. Hoffecker, J., Powers, R. & Goebel, T., The Colonization of Beringia and the Peopling of the New World. *Science* **259**, 46-53 (1993).

2. Guthrie, D., Origin and causes of the mammoth steppe: a story of cloud cover, woolly mammal tooth pits, buckles, and inside-out Beringia. *Quaternary Science Reviews* **20**, 549-574 (2001).

3. Zazula, G. *et al.*, Vegetation buried under Dawson tephra (25,300 14C years BP) and locally diverse late Pleistocene paleoenvironments of Goldbottom Creek, Yukon, Canada. *Palaeogeography, Palaeoclimatology, Palaeoecology* **242**, 253-286 (2006).

4. Goebel, T., Waters, M. & O'Rourke, D., The Late Pleistocene Dispersal of Modern Humans in the Americas. *Science* **319**, 1497-1502 (2008).

5. Dillehay, T., Probing deeper into first American studies. *PNAS* **106** (4), 971-978 (2009).

6. Dyke, A. *et al.*, Quaternary Science Reviews 21 (2002) 9-31 The Laurentide and Innuitian ice sheets during the Last Glacial Maximum. *Quaternary Science Reviews* **21**, 9–31 (2002).

7. Clague, J., Froese, D., Hutchinson, I., James, T. & Simon, K., Early growth of the last Cordilleran ice sheet deduced from glacio-isostatic depression in southwest British Columbia, Canada. *Quaternary Research* **63**, 53-59 (2005).

8. Meltzer, D., Peopling of North America. *Development in Quaternary Science* **1**, 539-563 (2003).

9. Kelly, R., Maybe we do know when people first came to North America; and what does it mean if we do? *Quaternary International* **109-110**, 133-145 (2003).

10. Derenko, M. *et al.*, Phylogeographic Analysis of Mitochondrial DNA in Northern Asian Populations. *American Journal of Human Genetics* **81**, 1025-1041 (2007).

11. Torroni, A. *et al.*, mtDNA Variation of Aboriginal Siberians Reveals Distinct Genetic Affinities with Native Americans. *American Journal of Human Genetics* **53**, 591-608 (1993).

12. Torroni, A. *et al.*, Asian Affinities and Continental Radiation of the Four Founding Native American mtDNAs. *American Journal of Human Genetics* **53**, 563-590 (1993).

13. Torroni, A. *et al.*, Native American Mitochondrial DNA Analysis Indicates That the Amerind and the Nadene Populations Were Founded by Two Independent Migrations. *Genetics* **130**, 153-162 (1992).

14. Kolman, C., Sambuughin, N. & Bermingham, E., Mitochondrial DNA Analysis of Mongolian Populations and Implications for the Origin of New World Founders. *Genetics* **142**, 1321-1334 (1996).

15. Eshleman, J., Malhi, R. & Smith, D., Mitochondrial DNA Studies of Native Americans: Conceptions and Misconceptions of the Population Prehistory of the Americas. *Evolutionary Anthropology* **18**, 7-18 (2003).

16. Derenko, M. *et al.*, Complete Mitochondrial DNA Analysis of Eastern Eurasian Haplogroups Rarely Found in Populations of Northern Asia and Eastern Europe. *PLoS One* **7** (2) (2012).

17. Forster, P., Harding, R., Torroni, A. & Bandelt, H., Origin and Evolution of Native American mtDNA Variation: A Reappraisal. *American Journal of Human Genetics* **59**, 935-945 (1996).

18. Torroni, A. *et al.*, Classification of European mtDNAs From an Analysis of Three European Populations. *Genetics* **144**, 1835-1850 (1996).

19. Derenko, M. *et al.*, The Presence of Mitochondrial Haplogroup X in Altaians from South Siberia. *American Journal of Human Genetics* **69**, 237-241 (2001).

20. Reidla, M. *et al.*, Origin and Diffusion of mtDNA Haplogroup X. *American Journal of Human Genetics* **73**, 1178-1190 (2003).

21. Zegura, S., Karafet, T., Zhivotovsky, L. & Hammer, M., High-Resolution SNPs and Microsatellite Haplotypes Point to a Single, Recent Entry of Native American Y Chromosomes into the Americas. *Molecular Biology and Evolution* **21** (1), 164-175 (2004).

22. Karafet, T. *et al.*, New binary polymorphisms reshape and increase resolution of the human Y chromosomal haplogroup tree. *Genome Research* **18** (5), 830-838 (2008).

23. Raghavan, M. *et al.*, Upper Palaeolithic Siberian genome reveals dual ancestry of Native Americans. *Nature* **505**, 87-94 (2014).

24. Kitchen, A., Miyamoto, M. & Mulligan, C., A Three-Stage Colonization Model for the Peopling of the Americas. *PLoS One* **3** (2) (2008).

25. Mulligan, C., Kitchen, A. & Miyamoto, M., Updated Three-Stage Model for the Peopling of the Americas. *PLoS One* **3** (9) (2008).

26. Fagundes, N. *et al.*, Mitochondrial Population Genomics Supports a Single Pre-Clovis Origin with a Coastal Route for the Peopling of the Americas. *American Journal of Human Genetics* **82**, 583-592 (2008).

27. Fagundes, N., Kanitz, R. & Bonatto, S., A Reevaluation of the Native American MtDNA Genome Diversity and Its Bearing on the Models of Early Colonization of Beringia. *PLoS One* **3** (9) (2008).

28. Bandelt, H. *et al.*, Identification of Native American Founder mtDNAs Through the Analysis of Complete mtDNA Sequences:Some Caveats. *Annals of Human Genetics* **67**, 512-524 (2003).

29. Tamm, E. *et al.*, Beringian Standstill and Spread of Native American Founders. *PLoS One* (9) (2007).

30. Perego, U. *et al.*, The initial peopling of the Americas: A growing number of founding mitochondrial genomes from Beringia. *Genome Research* **20**, 1174-1179 (2010).

31. Atkinson, Q., Gray, R. & Drummond, A., mtDNA Variation Predicts Population Size in Humans and Reveals a Major Southern Asian Chapter in Human Prehistory. *Molecular Biology and Evolution* **25** (2), 468-474 (2008).

32. Bonatto, S. & Salzano, F., A single and early migration for the peopling of the Americas supported by mitochondrial DNA sequence data. *PNAS* **94**, 1866-1871 (1997).

33. Hey, J., On the Number of New World Founders: A Population Genetic Portrait of the Peopling of the Americas. *PLoS One* **3** (6), 965-975 (2005).

34. Hamilton, M. & Buchanan, B., Archaeological Support for the Three-Stage Expansion of Modern Humans across Northeastern Eurasia and into the Americas. *PLoS One* **5** (8) (2010).

35. Waters, M. & Stafford, T., Redefining the Age of Clovis: Implications for the Peopling of the Americas. *Science* **315**, 1122-1126 (2007).

36. Waters, M. *et al.*, The Buttermilk Creek Complex and the Origins of Clovis at the Debra L. Friedkin Site, Texas. *Science* **331**, 1599-1603 (2011).

37. Waters, M. *et al.*, Pre-Clovis Mastodon Hunting 13,800 Years Ago at the Manis Site, Washington. *Science* **334**, 351-353 (2011).

38.   Gilbert, T. *et al.*, DNA from Pre-Clovis Human Coprolites in Oregon, North America. *Science* **320**, 786-789 (2008).

39.   Jenkins, D. *et al.*, Clovis Age Western Stemmed Projectile Points and Human Coprolites at the Paisley Caves. *Science* **337**, 223-228 (2012).

40.   Dillehay, T., *The Archaeological Context, vol. II of Monte Verde: A Late Pleistocene Settlement in Chile* (Smithsonian, Washington, DC, 1997).

41.   Dillehay, T. *et al.*, Monte Verde: Seaweed, Food, Medicine, and the Peopling of South America. *Science* **320**, 784-786 (2008).

42.   Keefer, D. *et al.*, Early Maritime Economy and El Nino Events at Quebrada Tacahuay, Peru. *Science* **281** , 1833-1835 (1998).

43.   Sandweiss, D. *et al.*, Quebrada Jaguay: Early South American Maritime Adaptations. *Science* **281**, 1830-1832 (1998).

44.   Jackson, D., Mendez, C., Seguel, R., Maldonado, A. & Vargas, G., Initial Occupation of the Pacific Coast of Chile during Late Pleistocene Times. *Current Anthropology* **48** (5), 725-731 (2007).

45.   Wang, S. *et al.*, Genetic Variation and Population Structure in Native Americans. *PLoS One* **3** (11), 2049-2067 (2007).

46.   Mithen, S., *After the Ice: A Global Human History 20,000 - 5,000 BC* (Weidenfield & Nicholson, London, 2003).

47.   Waguespack, N. & Surovell, T., Clovis hunting strategies, or how to make out on plentiful resources. *American Antiquity,* **68** (2), 333-352 (2003).

48.   Grayson, D. & Meltzer, D., Clovis Hunting and Large Mammal Extinction: A Critical Review of the Evidence. *Journal of World Prehistory* **15** (4), 313-359 (2002).

49.   Grayson, D. & Meltzer, D., A requiem for North American overkill. *Journal of Archaeological Science* **30**, 585-593 (2003).

50.   Hamilton, M. & Buchanan, B., Spatial gradients in Clovis-age radiocarbon dates across North America suggest rapid colonization from the north. *PNAS* **104** (40), 15625-15630 (2007).

51.   Bradley, B. & Stanford, D., The North Atlantic ice-edge corridor: a possible Palaeolithic route to the New World. *World Archaeology* **36** (4), 459-478 (2004).

52.   Straus, L., Meltzer, D. & Goebel, T., Ice Age Atlantis? Exploring the Solutrean-Clovis 'Connection'. *World Archaeology* **37** (4), 507-532 (2005).

53.   Waters, M. & Stafford, T., Response to Comment on "Redefining the Age of Clovis: Implications for the Peopling of the Americas". *Science* **317**, 320c (2007).

54.   Haynes, G. *et al.*, Comment on "Redefining the Age of Clovis: Implications for the Peopling of the Americas". *Science* **317**, 320b (2007).

55.   Oppenheimer, S., *Out of Eden* (Constable & Robinson Ltd, London, 2003).

56.   Hubbe, M., Neves, W. & Harvati, K., Testing Evolutionary and Dispersion Scenarios for the Settlement of the New World. *PLoS One* **5** (6) (2010).

57.   Perez, I., Bernal, V., Gonzalez, P., Sardi, M. & Politis, G., Discrepancy between Cranial and DNA Data of Early Americans: Implications for American Peopling. *PLoS One* **4** (5) (2009).

58.   Jantz, R. & Owsley, D., Variation Among Early North American Crania. *American Journal of Physical Anthropology* **114**, 144-156 (2001).

59.   Gonzalez-Jose, R., Bortolini, M., Santos, F. & Bonatto, S., The Peopling of America: Craniofacial Shape Variation on a Continental Scale and its Interpretation From an Interdisciplinary View. *American Journal of Physical Anthropology* **137**, 175-187 (2008).

60.   Greenberg, J., Turner, C. & Zegura, S., The Settlement of the Americas: A Comparison of the Linguistic, Dental, and Genetic Evidence. *Current Anthropology* **27** (5), 477-497 (1986).

61.   Stone, A. & Stoneking, M., mtDNA Analysis of a Prehistoric Oneota Population: Implications for the Peopling of the New World. *American Journal of Human Genetics* **62**, 1153-1170 (1998).

62.   Karafet, T. *et al.*, Ancestral Asian Source(s) of New World Y-Chromosome Founder Haplotypes. *American Journal of Human Genetics* **64**, 817-831 (1999).

63.   Lell, J. *et al.*, The Dual Origin and Siberian Affinities of Native American Y Chromosomes. *American Journal of Human Genetics* **70**, 192-206 (2002).

64.   Bortolini, M. *et al.*, Y-Chromosome Evidence for Differing Ancient Demographic Histories in the Americas. *American Journal of Human Genetics* **73**, 524-539 (2003).

65.   Reich, D. *et al.*, Reconstructing Native American population history. *Nature* **488**, 370-374 (2012).

66. Raghavan, M. *et al.*, The genetic prehistory of the New World Arctic. *Science* **345** (620), 1020,1255832 (2014).

67. Rasmussen, M., Anzick, S., Waters, M., Skoglund, P. & DeGiorgio, M., The genome of a Late Pleistocene human from a Clovis burial site in western Montana. *Nature* **506**, 225-229 (2014).

68. Chatters, J. *et al.*, Late Pleistocene Human Skeleton and mtDNA Link Paleoamericans and Modern Native Americans. *Science* **344**, 750-754 (2014).

16: Humanity in the dock

1. Barnosky, A., Koch, P., Feranec, R., Wing, S. & Shabel, A., Assessing the Causes of Late Pleistocene Extinctions on the Continents. *Science* **306**, 70-75 (2004).

2. Lyons, K., Smith, F. & Brown, J., Of mice, mastodons and men: human-mediated extinctions on four continents. *Evolutionary Ecology Research* **6**, 339-358 (2004).

3. Koch, P. & Barnosky, A., Late Quaternary Extinctions: State of the Debate. *The Annual Review of Ecology, Evolution, and Systematics* **37**, 215-250 (2006).

4. Barnosky, A., Megafauna biomass tradeoff as a driver of Quaternary and future extinctions. *PNAS* **105** (Suppl. 1), 11543-11548 (2008).

5. Grayson, D., in *Quaternary Extinctions: A Prehistoric Revolution*, edited by Martin, P. & Klein, R. (University of Arizona Press, Tucson, AZ, 1984), pp. 5-39.

6. Martin, P., The Discovery of America. *Science* **179**, 969-974 (1973).

7. Martin, P., in *Quaternary Extinctions: A Prehistoric Revolution*, edited by Martin, P. & Klein, R. (University of Arizona Press, Tucson, AZ, 1984), pp. 354-403.

8. Whittington, S. & Dyke, B., in *Quaternary Extinctions: A Prehistoric Revolution*, edited by Martin, P. & Klein, R. (University of Arizona Press, Tucson, AZ, 1984), pp. 451-465.

9. Wroe, S., Field, J., Fullagar, R. & Jermin, L., Megafaunal extinction in the late Quaternary and the global overkill hypothesis. *Alcheringa: An Australasian Journal of Palaeontology* **1**, 291-331 (2004).

10. Olson, S. & James, H., in *Quaternary Extinctions: A Prehistoric Revolution*, edited by Martin, P. & Klein, R. (University of Arizona Press, Tucson, AZ, 1984), pp. 768-780.

11. Cassels, R., in *Quaternary Extinctions: A Prehistoric Revolution*, edited by Martin, P. & Klein, R. (University of Arizona Press, Tucson, AZ, 1984), pp. 741-767.

12. Dewar, P., in *Quaternary Extinctions: A Prehistoric Revolution*, edited by Martin, P. & Klein, R. (University of Arizona Press, Tucson, Az, 1984), pp. 574-593.

13. Miller, G. *et al.*, Ecosystem Collapse in Pleistocene Australia and a Human Role in Megafaunal Extinction. *Science* **309**, 297-290 (2005).

14. Innes, J. & Blackford, J., The Ecology of Late Mesolithic Woodland Disturbances: Model Testing with Fungal Spore Assemblage Data. *Journal of Archaeological Science* **30**, 185-194 (2003).

15. Diamond, J., in *Quaternary Extinctions: A Prehistoric Revolution*, edited by Martin, P. & Klein, R. (University of Arizona Press, Tucson, AZ, 1984), pp. 824-862.

16. MacPhee, R. & Marx, P., in *Natural Change and Human Impact in Madagascar* (Smithsonian Institute Press, Washington, DC, 1997), pp. 169-217.

17. King, J. & Saunders, J., in *Quaternary Extinctions: A Prehistoric Revolution*, edited by Martin, P. & Klein, R. (University of Arizona Press, Tucson, AZ, 1984), pp. 315-339.

18. Guthrie, D., in *Quaternary Extinctions: A Prehistoric Revolution*, edited by Martin, P. & Klein, R. (University of Arizona Press, Tucson, AZ, 1984), pp. 259–298.

19. Graham, R. & Lundelius, E., in *Quaternary Extinctions: A Prehistoric Revolution*, edited by Martin, P. & Klein, R. (University of Arizona Press, Tucson, AZ, 1984), pp. 223-249.

20. Gingerich, P., in *Quaternary Extinctions: A Prehistoric Revolution*, edited by Martin, P. & Klein, R. (University of Arizona Press, Tucson, AZ, 1984), pp. 211-222.

21. Firestone, R. *et al.*, Evidence for an extraterrestrial impact 12,900 years ago that contributed to the megafaunal extinctions and the Younger Dryas cooling. *PNAS* **104** (41), 16016-16021 (2007).

22. Haynes, V., Younger Dryas "black mats" and the Rancholabrean termination in North America. *PNAS* **105** (18), 6520-6525 (2008).

23. Kennett, D. *et al.*, Nanodiamonds in the Younger Dryas Boundary Sediment Layer. *Science* **323**, 94 (2009).

24. Israde-Alcántara, I. *et al.*, Evidence from central Mexico supporting the Younger Dryas extraterrestrial impact hypothesis. *PNAS* **109** (13), E738-E747 (2012).

25. Bunch, T. *et al.*, Very high-temperature impact melt products as evidence for cosmic airbursts and impacts 12,900 years ago. *PNAS* **109** (28), E1903-E1912 (2012).

26. Petaev, M., Huang, S., Jacobsen, S. & Zindler, A., Large Pt anomaly in the Greenland ice core points to a cataclysm at the onset of Younger Dryas. *PNAS* **110** (32), 12917-12920 (2013).

27. Taylor, K. *et al.*, The Holocene–Younger Dryas Transition Recorded at Summit, Greenland. *Science* **278**, 825-827 (1997).

28. Severinghaus, J., Sowers, T., Brook, E., Alley, R. & Bender, M., Timing of abrupt climate change at the end of the Younger Dryas interval from thermally fractionated gases in polar ice. *Nature* **391**, 141-146 (1998).

29. Murton, J., Bateman, M., Dallimore, S., Teller, J. & Yang, Z., Identification of Younger Dryas outburst flood path from Lake Agassiz to the Arctic Ocean. *Nature* **464**, 740-743 (2010).

30. Moreno, P., Jacobson, G., Lowell, T. & Denton, G., Interhemispheric climate links revealed by a late-glacial cooling episode in southern Chile. *Nature* **409** , 804-808 (2001).

31. Daulton, T., Pinter, N. & Scott, A., No evidence of nanodiamonds in Younger–Dryas sediments to support an impact event. *PNAS* **107** (37), 16043-16047 (2010).

32. Gill, J. (personal communication).

33. Marlon, J. *et al.*, Wildfire responses to abrupt climate change in North America. *PNAS* **106** (8), 2519-2524 (2009).

34. Surovell, T. *et al.*, An independent evaluation of the Younger Dryas extraterrestrial impact hypothesis. *PNAS* **106** (43), 18155-18158 (2009).

35. Gill, J. *et al.*, Paleoecological changes at Lake Cuitzeo were not consistent with an extraterrestrial impact. *PNAS* **109** (34), E2243 (2012).

36. Beck, R., Godthelp, H., Weisbecker, V., Archer, M. & Hand, S., Australia's Oldest Marsupial Fossils and their Biogeographical Implications. *PLoS One* **3** (3) (2008).

37. Miller, G. *et al.*, Pleistocene Extinction of Genyornis newtoni: Human Impact on Australian Megafauna. *Science* **283**, 205-208 (1999).

38. Hiscock, P., *Archaeology of Ancient Australia* (Routledge, Abingdon, 2008).

39. Flannery, T., Pleistocene faunal loss: implications of the aftershock for Australia's past and future. *Archaeology in Oceania*, 45-67 (1990).

40. Grayson, D. & Meltzer, D., A requiem for North American overkill. *Journal of Archaeological Science* **30**, 585-593 (2003).

41. Roberts, R. *et al.*, New Ages for the Last Australian Megafauna: Continent-Wide Extinction About 46,000 Years Ago. *Science* **292**, 1888-1892 (2001).

42. Rule, S. *et al.*, The Aftermath of Megafaunal Extinction: Ecosystem Transformation in Pleistocene Australia. *Science* **335**, 1483-1486 (2012).

43. Field, J., Australia's Megafauna Extinctions: Cause and Effect, Available at http://www.australasianscience.com.au/article/issue-may-2012/australias-megafauna-extinctions-cause-and-effect.html (2012).

44. EPICA, One-to-one coupling of glacial climate variability in Greenland and Antarctica. *Nature* **444**, 195-198 (2006).

45. Cohen, T. *et al.*, Continental aridification and the vanishing of Australia's megalakes. *Geology* **39** (2), 167-170 (2011).

46. Kershaw, P., in *Quaternary Extinctions: A Prehistoric Revolution*, edited by Martin, P. & Klein, R. (University of Arizona Press, Tucson, AZ, 1984), pp. 691-707.

47. Horton, D., in *Quaternary Extinctions: A Prehistoric Revolution*, edited by Martin, P. & Klein, R. (University of Arizona Press, Tucson, AZ, 1984), pp. 639-680.

48. Bird, R., Bird, D., Codding, B., Parker, C. & Jones, J., The fire stick farming hypothesis: Australian Aboriginal foraging strategies, biodiversity, and anthropogenic fire mosaics. *PNAS* **39**, 14796-14801 (2008).

49. Mooney, S. *et al.*, Late Quaternary fire regimes of Australasia. *Quaternary Science Reviews* **30**, 28-46 (2011).

50. Wroe, S. & Field, J., A review of the evidence for a human role in the extinction of Australian megafauna and an alternative interpretation. *Quaternary Science Reviews* **25**, 2692-2703 (2006).

51. Field, J. & Dodson, J., Late Pleistocene megafauna and human occupation at Cuddie Springs, southeastern Australia. *Preceedings of the Prehistoric Society* **65**, 275-301 (1999).
52. Field, J. & Fullagar, R., Archaeology and Australian Megafauna. *Science* **294**, 7a (2001).
53. Field, J., Dodson, J. & Prosser, I., A Late Pleistocene vegetation history from the Australian semi-arid zone. *Quaternary Science Reviews* **21**, 1023-1037 (2002).
54. Trueman, C., Field, J., Dortch, J., Charles, B. & Wroe, S., Prolonged coexistence of humans and megafauna in Pleistocene Australia. *PNAS* **102** (23), 8381-8385 (2005).
55. Field, J., Fillios, M. & Wroe, S., Chronological overlap between humans and megafauna in Sahul (Pleistocene Australia-New Guinea): A review of the evidence. *Earth-Science Reviews* **89**, 97-115 (2008).
56. Roberts, R. *et al.*, Archaeology and Australian megafauna - Response. *Science* **294**, 7a (2001).
57. Prideaux, G. *et al.*, An arid-adapted middle Pleistocene vertebrate fauna from south-central Australia. *Nature* **445**, 422-425 (2007).
58. Prideaux, G. *et al.*, Extinction implications of a chenopod browse diet for a giant Pleistocene kangaroo. *PNAS* **106** (28), 11646-11650 (2009).
59. Prideaux, G. *et al.*, Timing and dynamics of Late Pleistocene mammal extinctions in southwestern Australia. *PNAS* **107** (51), 22157-22162 (2010).
60. Alroy, J., A Multispecies Overkill Simulation of the End-Pleistocene Megafaunal Mass Extinction. *Science* **292**, 1893-1896 (2001).
61. Guthrie, D., Rapid body size decline in Alaskan Pleistocene horses before extinction. *Nature* **426**, 169-171 (2003).
62. Robinson, G., Burney, L. & Burney, D., Landscape Paleoecology and Megafaunal Extinction in Southeastern New York State. *Ecological Monographs* **75** (3), 295-315 (2005).
63. Gill, J., Williams, J., Jackson, S., Lininger, K. & Robinson, G., Pleistocene Megafaunal Collapse, Novel Plant Communities, and Enhanced Fire Regimes in North America. *Science* **326**, 1100-1103 (2009).
64. Moreno, P., Climate, Fire, and Vegetation between About 13,000 and 9200 14C yr B.P. in the Chilean Lake District. *Quaternary Research* **54**, 81-89 (2000).
65. Faith, T. & Surovell, T., Synchronous extinction of North America's Pleistocene mammals. *PNAS* **106** (49), 20641-20645 (2009).
66. Stuart, A., Kosintsev, P., Higham, T. & Lister, A., Pleistocene to Holocene extinction dynamics in giant deer and woolly mammoth. *Nature* **431**, 684-413 (2004).
67. Vartanyan, S., Garrut, V. & Sher, A., Holocene dwarf mammoths from Wrangel Island in the Siberian Arctic. *Nature* **382**, 337-340 (1993).
68. Guthrie, D., Radiocarbon evidence of mid-Holocene mammoths stranded on an Alaskan Bering Sea island. *Nature* **429**, 746-749 (2004).
69. Klein, R., in *Quaternary Exinctions: A Prehistoric Revolution*, edited by Martin, P. & Klein, R. (University of Arizona Press, Tucson, AZ, 1984), pp. 553-573.

17: Feed the World

1. Scarre, C., in *The Human Past*, edited by Scarre, C. (Thames & Hudson, London, 2005), pp. 176-199.
2. Oppenheimer, S., *Eden in the East* (Weidenfield & Nicholson, London, 1998).
3. Childe, G., *Man Makes Himself* (Watts and Co., London, 1936).
4. Zeder, M., Central Questions in the Domestication of Plants and Animals. *Evolutionary Anthropology* **15**, 105-117 (2006).
5. Harris, D., in *The Origins and Spread of Agriculture and Pastoralism in Eurasia*, edited by Harris, D. (Routeledge, London, 1996), pp. 1-9.
6. Smith, B., in *Keeping It Living, Traditions of Plant Use and Cultivation on the Northwest Coast of North America*, edited by Deur, D. & Turner, N. (UBC Press and Seattle: University of Washington Press, Vancouver, 2005), pp. 37-66.
7. Smith, B., Low-Level Food Production. *Journal of Archaeological Research* **9** (1), 1-43 (2001).
8. Hillman, G. & Davies, S., Dornestication rates in wild-type wheats and barley under primitive cultivation. *Journal of the Linnaean Society* **39**, 39-78 (1990).

9.   Zeder, M., The Origins of Agriculture in the Near East. *Current Anthropology* **52** (S4) (2011).

10. Lu, H. *et al.*, Phytoliths Analysis for the Discrimination of Foxtail Millet (Setaria italica) and Common Millet (Panicum miliaceum). *PLoS One* **4** (2) (2009).

11. Yang, X. *et al.*, Early millet use in northern China. *PNAS* **109** (8) (2012).

12. Zhang, J., Lu, H., Wu, N., Yang, X. & Diao, X., Phytolith Analysis for Differentiating between Foxtail Millet (Setaria italica) and Green Foxtail (Setaria viridis). *PLoS One* **6** (5) (2011).

13. Lu, H. *et al.*, Earliest domestication of common millet (Panicum miliaceum) in East Asia extended to 10,000 years ago. *PNAS* **106** (18), 7367-7372 (2009).

14. Diamond, J., *Guns, Germs and Steel* (Chatto & Windus, London, 1997).

15. Diamond, J., *The Third Chimpanzee* (Random, London, 1991).

16. Zeder, M., A Metrical Analysis of a Collection of Modern Goats (Capra hircus aegargus and C. h. hircus) from Iran and Iraq: Implications for the Study of Caprine Domestication. *Journal of Archaeological Science* **28**, 61-79 (2001).

17. Zeder, M., Domestication and early agriculture in the Mediterranean Basin: Origins, diffusion, and impact. *PNAS* **105** (33), 11597-11604 (2008).

18. Özdoğan, M., Archaeological Evidence on the Westward Expansion of Farming Communities from Eastern Anatolia to the Aegean and the Balkans. *Current Anthropology* **52** (S4) (2011).

19. Bellwood, P., *First Farmers* (Blackwell Publishing, Oxford, 2005).

20. Barker, G., *The Agricultural Revolution in Prehistory: Why did Foragers become Farmers* (Oxford University Press, Oxford, 2006).

21. Dewar, R., Rainfall Variability and Subsistence Systems. *Current Anthropology* **44** (3), 369-388 (2003).

22. Harris, D., in *Examining the farming/language dispersal hypothesis*, edited by Bellwood, P. & Renfrew, C. (McDonald Institute, Cambridge, 2002), pp. 31-39.

23. Harris, D., Reply to: Rainfall Variability and Subsistence Systems. *Current Anthropology* **44** (3), 379-380 (2003).

24. Richerson, P., Boyd, R. & Bettinger, R., Was agriculture impossible during the Pleistocene but mandatory during the Holocene: a climate change hypothesis. *American Antiquity* **6** (3), 387-411 (2001).

25. Braidwood, R., The Agricultural Revolution. *Scientific American* **203**, 138-140 (1960).

26. Lee, R., in *Man the Hunter*, edited by Lee, R. & de Vere, I. (Aldine, Chicago, 1968), pp. 30-48.

27. Cohen, M., in *Examining the farming/language dispersal hypothesis*, edited by Bellwood, P. & Renfrew, C. (McDonald Institute, Cambridge, 2002), pp. 41-47.

28. Wood, J., Milner, G., Harpending, H. & Weiss, K., The Osteological Paradox: Problems of Inferring Prehistoric Health from Skeletal Samples. *Current Anthropology* **33** (4), 343-370 (1992).

29. Scarre, C., in *The Human Past*, edited by Scarre, C. (Thames & Hudson, London, 2005), pp. 25-43.

30. Renfrew, C., *Before Civilization* (Jonathon Cape, London, 1973).

31. Renfrew, C., in *Peer-polity interaction and socio-political change*, edited by Renfrew, C. & Cherry, J. (Cambridge University Press, Cambridge, 1986), pp. 1-18.

32. Burgess, C. & Shennan, S., in *Settlement and Economy in the Third and Second Millennia B.C. (B. A. R. 33)*, edited by Burgess, C. & Miket, R. (British Archaeological Reports, Oxford, 1976), pp. 309-326.

33. Rowley-Conwy, P., How the West Was Lost: A Reconsideration of Agricultural Origins in Britain, Ireland, and Southern Scandinavia. *Current Anthropology* **45** (Supplement, August–October), S83-S113 (2004).

34. Binford, L., in *New Perspectives in Archaeology*, edited by Binford, S. & Binford, L. (Aldine, Chicago, 1968), pp. 313-341.

35. Diamond, J., Evolution, consequences and future of plant and animal domestication. *Nature* **418**, 700-707 (2002).

36. Flannery, K., in *The Domestication and Exploitation of Plants and Animals*, edited by Ucko, P. & Dimbleby, G. (Duckworth, London, 1969), pp. 73-100.

37. Cohen, M., *The Food Crisis in Prehistory: Overpopulation and the Origins of Agriculture* (Yale University Press, New Haven, CT, 1977).

38. Hillman, G., in *The Origins and Spread of Agriculture and Pastoralism in Eurasia*, edited by Harris, D. (Routledge, London, 1996), pp. 159-201.

39. Hillman, G., Hedges, R., Moore, A., Colledge, S. & Pettitt, P., New evidence of Lateglacial cereal cultivation at Abu Hureyra on the Euphrates. *The Holocene* **11** (4), 382-393 (2001).

40. Bar-Yosef, O., in *Examining the farming/language dispersal hypothesis*, edited by Bellwood, P. & Renfrew, C. (McDonald Institute, Cambridge, 2002), pp. 113-126.
41. Hayden, B., in *Transitions to Agriculture in Prehistory*, edited by Gebauer, A. & Price, T. (Prehistory Press, Madison, WI, 1992), pp. 11-19.
42. Rindos, D., *The Origins of Agriculture: An Evolutionary Perspective* (Academic Press, Orlando, 1984).
43. Hodder, I., *The Domestication of Europe* (Basil Blackwell, Oxford, 1990).
44. Zvelebil, M., in *The Origins and Spread of Agriculture and Pastoralism in Eurasia*, edited by Harris, D. (Routledge, London, 1996), pp. 323-345.
45. Crawford, G., in *Transitions to Agriculture in Prehistory*, edited by Gebauer, A. & Price, D. (Prehistory Press, Maduson, WI, 1992), pp. 117-132.

18: Assembling the package

1. Belfer-Cohen, A. & Goring-Morris, N., Becoming Farmers: The Inside Story. *Current Anthropology* **52** (S4) (2011).
2. Barker, G., *The Agricultural Revolution in Prehistory: Why did Foragers become Famers* (Oxford University Press, Oxford, 2006).
3. Goring-Morris, N. & Belfer-Cohen, A., Neolithization Processes in the Levant The Outer Envelope. *Current Anthropology* **52** (S4) (2011).
4. Garrard, A., Colledge, S. & Martin, L., in *The Origins and Spread of Agriculture and Pastoralism in Eurasia*, edited by Harris, D. (Routledge, London, 1996), pp. 204-226.
5. Hillman, G., in *The Origins and Spread of Agriculture and Pastoralism in Eurasia*, edited by Harris, D. (Routledge, London, 1996), pp. 159-201.
6. Watkins, T., in *The Human Past*, edited by Scarre, C. (Thames & Hudson, London, 2005), pp. 200-233.
7. Nadel, D. *et al.*, New Dates From Submerged Late Pleistocene Sediments in the Southern Sea of Galilee, Israel. *Radiocarbon* **43** (3), 1167-1178 (2001).
8. Mithen, S., *After the Ice: A Global Human History 20,000 - 5,000 BC* (Weidenfield & Nicholson, London, 2003).
9. Davis, S., Why domesticate food animals? Some zoo-archaeological evidence from the Levant. *Journal of Archaeological Science* **32**, 1408-1416 (2005).
10. Nadel, D. & Werker, E., The oldest ever brush hut plant remains from Ohalo II, Jordan Valley, Israel. *Antiquity* **73** (282), 755-764 (1999).
11. Weiss, E., Wetterstrom, W., Nadel, D. & Bar-Yosef, O., The broad spectrum revisited: Evidence from plant remains. *PNAS* **101** (26), 9551-9555 (2004).
12. Hershkovitz, L. *et al.*, Ohalo II man - unusual findings in the anterior rib cage and shoulder girdle of a 19000-year-old specimen. *International Journal of Osteoarchaeology* **3** (3), 177-188 (1993).
13. Nadel, D., Levantine Upper Palaeolithic - Early Epipalaeolithic Burial Customs: Ohalo II as a case study. *Paléorient* **20** (1), 113-121 (1994).
14. Hershkovitz, L. *et al.*, Ohalo II H2: A 19,000-Year-Old Skeleton From a Water-Logged Site at the Sea of Galilee, Israel. *American Journal of Physical Anthropology* **96**, 215-234 (1995).
15. Nadel, D. *et al.*, Stone Age hut in Israel yields world's oldest evidence of bedding. *PNAS* **101** (17), 6821-6826 (2004).
16. Weiss, E., Kislev, M., Simchoni, O., Nadel, D. & Tschauner, H., Plant-food preparation area on an Upper Paleolithic brush hut floor at Ohalo II, Israel. *Journal of Archaeological Science* **35**, 2400-2414 (2008).
17. Piperno, D., Weiss, E., Holst, I. & Nadel, D., Processing of wild cereal grains in the Upper Palaeolithic revealed by starch grain analysis. *Nature* **450**, 670-673 (2004).
18. Kislev, M., Nadel, D. & Carmi, I., Epipalaeolithic (19,000 BP) cereal and fruit diet at Ohalo II, Sea of Galilee, Israel. *Review of Palaeobotany and Palynology* **73** (1-4), 161-166 (1992).
19. Lieberman, D., The rise and fall of seasonal mobility among hunter-gatherers. *Current Anthropology* **34** (5), 599-631 (1993).

20.   Simmons, T. & Nadel, D., The avifauna of the early Epipalaeolithic site of Ohalo II (19,400 BP), Israel: species diversity, habitat and seasonality. *International Journal of Osteoarchaeology* **8** (2), 79-96 (1998).

21.   Bellwood, P., *First Farmers* (Blackwell Publishing, Oxford, 2005).

22.   Kislev, M., Weiss, E. & Hartmann, A., Impetus for sowing and the beginning of agriculture: Ground collecting of wild cereals. *PNAS* **101** (9), 2692-2695 (2004).

23.   Bar-Oz, G. & Dyan, T., The Epipalaeolithic Faunal Sequence in Israel: A View from Neve David. *Journal of Archaeological Science* **26**, 67-82 (1999).

24.   Maher, L. *et al.*, A Unique Human-Fox Burial from a Pre-Natufian Cemetery in the Levant (Jordan). *PLoS One* **6** (1) (2011).

25.   Liu, Z. *et al.*, Transient Simulation of Last Deglaciation with a New Mechanism for Bølling-Allerød Warming. *Science* **325**, 310-314 (2009).

26.   Maher, L., Banning, E. & Chazan, M., Oasis or Mirage? Assessing the Role of Abrupt Climate Change in the Prehistory of the Southern Levant. *Cambridge Archaeological Journal* **21** (1), 1-29 (2011).

27.   Wright, K., Ground-stone tools and hunter-gatherer subsistence in Southwest Asia: implications for the transition to farming. *American Antiquity* **59** (2), 238-263 (1994).

28.   Belfer-Cohen, A., in *The Natufian Culture in the Levant*, edited by Bar-Yosef, O. & Valla, F. (University of Michigan, International Monographs in Prehistory, Ann Arbor, MI, 1991), pp. 369-388.

29.   Noy, T., in *The Natufian Culture in the Levant*, edited by Bar-Yosef, O. & Valla, F. (University of Michigan, International Monographs in Prehistory, Ann Arbor, MI, 1991), pp. 557-568.

30.   Bar-Yosef, O. & Belfer-Cohen, A., in *Transitions to Agriculture in Prehistory*, edited by Gebaur, A. & Price, D. (Prehistory Press, Madison, WI, 1992), pp. 21-48.

31.   Bar-Yosef, O. & Belfer-Cohen, A., Encoding information: unique Natufian objects from Hayonim Cave, western Galilee, Israel. *Antiquity* **75**, 402-410 (1999).

32.   Garrod, D., The Natufian Culture: the life and economy of a Mesolithic people in the Near East. *Proceedings of the Prehistoric Society* **43**, 211-227 (1957).

33.   Bar-Yosef, O., in *Examining the farming/language dispersal hypothesis*, edited by Bellwood, P. & Renfrew, C. (McDonald Institute, Cambridge, 2002), pp. 113-126.

34.   Moore, A., in *The Natufian Culture in the Levant*, edited by Bar-Yosef, O. & Valla, F. (University of Michigan, International Monographs in Prehistory, Ann Arbor, MI, 1991), pp. 277-294.

35.   Valla, F., in *The Natufian Culture in the Levant*, edited by Bar-Yosef, O. & Valla, F. (University of Michigan, International Monographs in Prehistory, Ann Arbor, MI, 1991), pp. 111-122.

36.   Bar-Yosef, O., The Natufian Culture in the Levant, Threshold to the Origins of Agriculture. *Evolutionary Anthropology* **6** (5), 159-177 (1998).

37.   Anderson, P., in *The Natufian Culture in the Levant*, edited by Bar-Yosef, O. & Valla, F. (University of Michigan, International Monographs in Prehistory, Ann Arbor, MI, 1991), pp. 521-556.

38.   Unger-Hamilton, R., in *The Natufian Culture in the Levant*, edited by Bar-Yosef, O. & Valla, F. (International Monographs in Prehistory, Ann Arbor, MI, 1991), pp. 483-520.

39.   Hillman, G., Colledge, S. & Harris, D., in *Foraging and farming: Evolutoin of plant exploitation*, edited by Harris, D. & Hillman, G. (Unwin and Hyman, London, 1989), pp. 240-268.

40.   Smith, B., Low-Level Food Production. *Journal of Archaeological Research* **9** (1), 1-43 (2001).

41.   Cope, C., in *The Natufian Culture in the Levant*, edited by Bar-Yosef, O. & Valla, F. (University of Michigan, International Monographs in Prehistory, Ann Arbor, MI, 1991), pp. 341-358.

42.   Bar-Oz, G. & Munro, N., Gazelle bone marrow yields and Epipalaeolithic carcass exploitation strategies in the southern Levant. *Journal of Archaeological Science* **34** (6), 946-956 (2007).

43.   Legge, A. & Rowley-Conwy, P., Gazelle killing in Stone Age Syria. *Scientific American* **257** (2), 88-95 (1987).

44.   Tchernov, E. & Valla, F., Two New Dogs, and Other Natufian Dogs, from the Southern Levant. *Journal of Archaeological Science* **24** (1), 65-95 (1997).

45.   Vila, C. *et al.*, Multiple and Ancient Origins of the Domestic Dog. *Science* **276**, 1687-1689 (1997).

46.   Savolainen, P., Zhang, Y., Luo, J., Lundeberg, J. & Leitner, T., Genetic Evidence for an East Asian Origin of Domestic Dogs. *Science* **298**, 1610-1613 (2002).

47.   Germonpré, M. *et al.*, Fossil dogs and wolves from Palaeolithic sites in Belgium, the Ukraine and Russia: osteometry, ancient DNA and stable isotopes. *Journal of Archaeological Science* **36** (2), 473-490 (2009).

48. Boyko, A. *et al.*, Complex population structure in African village dogs and its implications for inferring dog domestication history. *PNAS* **106** (33), 13903-13908 (2009).

49. Ding, Z. *et al.*, Origins of domestic dog in Southern East Asia is supported by analysis of Y-chromosome DNA. *Heredity* **108**, 507-514 (2012).

50. Driscoll, C., Macdonald, D. & O'Brien, S., From wild animals to domestic pets, an evolutionary view of domestication. *PNAS* **106**, 9971-9978 (2009).

51. Tchernov, E., in *The Natufian Culture in the Levant*, edited by Bar-Yosef, O. & Valla, F. (International Monographs in Prehistory, Ann Arbor, MI, 1991), pp. 315-340.

52. Tchernov, E., Of mice and men. Biological markers for long-term sedentism : a reply. *Paléorient* **17** (1), 153-160 (1991).

53. Wyncoll, G. & Tangri, D., Of mice and men : is the presence of commensal animals in archaeological sites a positive correlate of sedentism ? *Paléorient* **15** (2), 85-94 (1989).

54. Valla, F., in *Seasonality and Sedentism: Archaeological Perspectives from Old and New World Sites*, edited by Rocek, T. & Bar-Yosef, O. (Peabody Museum of Archaeology and Ethnology, Cambridge, MA, 1998), pp. 93-108.

55. Byrd, B. & Monahan, C., Death, Mortuary Ritual, and Natufian Social Structure. *Journal of Anthropological Archaeology* **14** (3), 251-287 (1995).

56. Mithen, S., in *Prehistoric Europe*, edited by Cunliffe, B. (Oxford University Press, Oxford, 1994), pp. 79-135.

57. Bar-Yosef, D., in *The Natufian Culture in the Levant*, edited by Bar-Yosef, O. & Valla, F. (International Monographs in Prehistory, Ann Arbor, MI, 1991), pp. 629-636.

58. Reese, D., in *The Natufian Culture in the Levant*, edited by Bar-Yosef, O. & Valla, F. (International Monographs in Prehistory, Ann Arbor, MI, 1991), pp. 613-628.

59. Belfer-Cohen, A., Schepartz, A. & Arensburg, B., in *The Natufian Culture in the Levant*, edited by Bar-Yosef, O. & Valla, F. (International Monographs in Prehistory, Ann Arbor, MI, 1991), pp. 411-424.

60. Mahoney, P., Dental Microwear From Natufian Hunter-Gatherers and Early Neolithic Farmers: Comparisons Within and Between Samples. *American Journal of Physical Anthropology* **130**, 308-319 (2006).

61. Smith, P., in *The Natufian Culture in the Levant*, edited by Bar-Yosef, O. & Valla, F. (International Monographs in Prehistory, Ann Arbor, MI, 1991), pp. 425-432.

62. Kuijt, I., Negotiating Equality through Ritual: A Consideration of Late Natufian and Prepottery Neolithic A Period Mortuary Practices. *Journal of Anthropological Archaeology* **15**, 313-336 (1996).

63. Grosman, L., Munro, N. & Belfer-Cohen, A., A 12,000-year-old Shaman burial from the southern Levant (Israel). *PNAS* **105** (46), 17665-17669 (2008).

64. Munro, N. & Grosman, L., Early evidence (ca. 12,000 B.P.) for feasting at a burial cave in Israel. *PNAS* **107** (35), 15362-15366 (2010).

65. Sillen, A. & Lee-Thorp, J., in *The Natufian Culture in the Levant*, edited by Bar-Yosef, O. & Valla, F. (University of Michigan, International Monographs in Prehistory, Ann Arbor, MI, 1991), pp. 399-410.

66. Goring-Morris, N., in *The Natufian Culture in the Levant*, edited by Bar-Yosef, O. & Valla, F. (University of Michigan, International Monographs in Prehistory, Ann Arbor, MI, 1991), pp. 173-216.

67. Crabtree, P., Campana, D., Belfer-Cohen, A. & Bar-Yosef, D., in *The Natufian Culture in the Levant*, edited by Bar-Yosef, O. & Valla, F. (University of Michigan, International Monographs in Prehistory, Ann Arbor, MI, 1991), pp. 161-172.

68. Ronen, A. & Lechevallier, M., in *The Natufian Culture in the Levant*, edited by Bar-Yosef, O. & Valla, F. (University of Michigan, International Monographs in Prehistory, Ann Arbor, MI, 1991), pp. 149-160.

69. Rosenberg, M., Nesbitt, R., Redding, R. & Peasnall, B., Hallan Çemi, pig husbandry, and post-Pleistocene adaptations along the Taurus-Zagros Arc (Turkey). *Paléorient* **24** (1), 25-41 (1998).

70. Rosenberg, M., Nesbitt, M., Redding, R. & Strasser, T., Hallan Çemi Tepesi: Some Preliminary Observations Concerning Early Neolithic Subsistence Behaviors in Eastern Anatolia. *Anatolica* **21**, 3-12 (1995).

71. Hillman, G., Hedges, R., Moore, A., Colledge, S. & Pettitt, P., New evidence of Lateglacial cereal cultivation at Abu Hureyra on the Euphrates. *The Holocene* **11** (4), 382-393 (2001).

72. Severinghaus, J., Sowers, T., Brook, E., Alley, R. & Bender, M., Timing of abrupt climate change at the end of the Younger Dryas interval from thermally fractionated gases in polar ice. *Nature* **391**, 141-146 (1998).

73. Bar-Yosef, O., The Walls of Jericho: An Alternative Interpretation. *Current Anthropology* **27** (2), 157-162 (1986).

74. Zeder, M., The Origins of Agriculture in the Near East. *Current Anthropology* **52** (S4) (2011).

75. Bar-Yosef Mayer, D. & Porat, N., Green stone beads at the dawn of agriculture. *PNAS* **105** (25), 8548-8551 (2008).

76. Weiss, E., Kislev, M. & Hartmann, A., Autonomous Cultivation Before Domestication. *Science* **312**, 1608-1610 (2006).

77. Kuijt, I. & Finlayson, B., Evidence for food storage and predomestication granaries 11,000 years ago in the Jordan Valley. *PNAS* **106** (27), 10966-10970 (2009).

78. Finlayson, B. *et al.*, Dhra', Excavation Project, 2002 Interim Report. *Levant* **35** (2003).

79. Willcox, G., Evidence for plant exploitation and vegetation history from three Early Neolithic pre-pottery sites on the Euphrates (Syria). *Vegetation History and Archaeobotany* **5**, 143-152 (1996).

80. Stordeur, D., New Discoveries in Architecture and Symbolism at Jerf el Ahmar (Syria), 1997-1999. *Neo-Lithics* (1/00), 1-4 (2000).

81. Ladizinsky, G., Identification of the lentil's wild genetic stock. *Genetic Resources and Crop Evolution* **46**, 115-118 (1999).

82. Kislev, M., Hartmann, A. & Bar-Yosef, O., Early Domesticated Fig in the Jordan Valley. *Science* **312**, 1372-1374 (2006).

83. Schmidt, K., Investigations in the early Meospotamian Neolithic: Göbekli Tepe and Gürcütepe. *Neo-Lithics* (2/95), 9-10 (1995).

84. Schmidt, K., Beyond Daily Bread: Evidence of Early Neolithic Ritual from Göbekli Tepe. *Neo-Lithics* (2/98), 1-5 (1998).

85. Schmidt, K., Göbekli Tepe, Southeastern Turkey A Preliminary Report on the 1995-1999 Excavations. *Paléorient* **26** (1), 45-54 (2000).

86. Schmidt, K., The 2003 Campaign at Göbekli Tepe (Southeastern Turkey). *Neo-Lithics* (2/03), 3-8 (2003).

87. Peters, J. & Schmidt, K., Animals in the symbolic world of Pre-Pottery Neolithic Göbekli Tepe, south-eastern Turkey: a preliminary assessment. *Anthropozoologica* **39** (1), 179-218 (2004).

88. Lewis-Williams, D. & Pearce, D., *Inside the Neolithic Mind* (Thames & Hudson, London, 2005).

89. Kromer, B. & Schmidt, K., Two Radiocarbon Dates from Göbekli Tepe, South Eastern Turkey. *Neo-Lithics* (3/98), 8-9 (1998).

90. Pustovoytov, K., 14 C Dating of Pedogenic Carbonate Coatings on Wall Stones at Göbekli Tepe (Southeastern Turkey). *Neo-Lithics* (2/02), 3-4 (2002).

91. Ex Oriente eV Scientific Society, PPND - the platform for Neolithic Radiocarbon Dates, Available at http://www.exoriente.org/associated_projects/ppnd.php (2011).

92. Stordeur, D., Jammous, B., Helmer, D. & Willcox, G., Jerf el-Ahmar: a New Mureybetian Site (PPNA) on the Middle Euphrates. *Neo-Lithics* **2/96**, 1-2 (1996).

93. Finlayson, B. *et al.*, Architecture, sedentism, and social complexity at Pre-Pottery Neolithic A WF16, Southern Jordan. *PNAS* **108** (20), 8183-8188 (2011).

94. Kuijt, I., People and Space in Early Agricultural Villages: Exploring Daily Lives, Community Size, and Architecture in the Late Pre-Pottery Neolithic. *Journal of Anthropological Archaeology* **19**, 75–102 (2000).

95. Price, D. & Bar-Yosef, O., The Origins of Agriculture: New Data, New Ideas. *Current Anthropology* **52** (S4) (2011).

96. Kuijt, I., The Regeneration of Life: Neolithic Structures of Symbolic Remembering and Forgetting. *Current Anthropology* **49** (2), 171-197 (2008).

97. Weiss, E. & Zohary, D., The Neolithic Southwest Asian Founder Crops Their Biology and Archaeobotany. *Current Anthropology* **52** (S4) (2011).

98. Heun, M. *et al.*, Site of Einkorn Wheat Domestication Identified by DNA Fingerprinting. *Science* **278**, 1312-1314 (1997).

99. Heun, M., Haldorsen, S. & Vollan, K., Reassessing domestication events in the Near East: Einkorn and Triticum urartu. *Genome* **51** (6), 444-451 (2008).

100. Ozkan, H., Brandolini, A., Schafer-Preg, R. & Salamini, F., AFLP Analysis of a Collection of Tetraploid Wheats Indicates the Origin of Emmer and Hard Wheat Domestication in Southeast Turkey. *Molecular Biology and Evolution* **19** (10), 1797-1801 (2002).

101. Badr, A. *et al.*, On the Origin and Domestication History of Barley (Hordeum vulgare). *Molecular Biology and Evolution* **17** (4), 499-510 (2000).

102. Kilian, B. *et al.*, Molecular Diversity at 18 Loci in 321 Wild and 92 Domesticate Lines Reveal No Reduction of Nucleotide Diversity during Triticum monococcum (Einkorn) Domestication: Implications for the Origin of Agriculture. *Molecular Biology and Evolution* **24** (12), 2657-2668 (2007).

103. Feldman, M. & Kislev, M., Century of Wheat Research-From Wild Emmer Discovery to Genome Analysi. *Israel Journal of Plant Sciences* **55** (3-4), 207-221 (2007).

104. Morrell, P. & Clegg, M., Genetic evidence for a second domestication of barley (Hordeum vulgare) east of the Fertile Crescent. *PNAS* **104** (9), 3289-3294 (2007).

105. Ervynck, A., Dobney, K., Hongo, H. & Meadow, R., Born free? new evidence for the Status of Sus scrofa at Neolithic Çayônu Tepesi (Southeastern Anatolia, Turkey). *Paléorient* **27** (2), 47-73 (2001).

106. Larson, G. *et al.*, Worldwide Phylogeography of Wild Boar Reveals Multiple Centers of Pig Domestication. *Science* **307**, 1618-1621 (2005).

107. Larson, G. *et al.*, Ancient DNA, pig domestication, and the spread of the Neolithic into Europe. *PNAS* **104** (39), 15276-15281 (2007).

108. Zeder, M., Animal Domestication in the Zagros : A Review of Past and Current Research. *Paléorient* **25** (2), 11-25 (1999).

109. Luikart, G. *et al.*, Multiple maternal origins and weak phylogeographic structure in domestic goats. *PNAS* **98** (10), 5927-5932 (2001).

110. Naderi, S. *et al.*, Large-Scale Mitochondrial DNA Analysis of the Domestic Goat Reveals Six Haplogroups with High Diversity. *PLoS One* **2** (10) (2007).

111. Naderi, S. *et al.*, The goat domestication process inferred from large-scale mitochondrial DNA analysis of wild and domestic individuals. *PNAS* **105** (46), 17659-17664 (2008).

112. Arbuckle, B. & Ozkaya, V., Animal exploitation at Körtik Tepe: an early Aceramic Neolithic site in southeastern Turkey. *Paléorient* **32** (2), 113-136 (2006).

113. Peters, J., Helmer, D., Von Den Driesch, A. & Segui, M., Early Animal Husbandry in the Northern Levant. *Paléorient* **25** (2), 27-48 (1999).

114. Hiendleder, S., Kaupe, B., Wassmuth, R. & Janke, A., Molecular analysis of wild and domestic sheep questions current nomenclature and provides evidence for domestication from two different subspecies. *Proceedings of the Royal Society B* **269**, 893-904 (2002).

115. Pedrosa, S. *et al.*, Evidence of three maternal lineages in near eastern sheep supporting multiple domestication events. *Proceedings of the Royal Society B* **272**, 2211-2217 (2005).

116. Troy, C. *et al.*, Genetic evidence for Near-Eastern origins of European cattle. *Nature* **410**, 1088-1091 (2001).

117. Beja-Pereira, A. *et al.*, The origin of European cattle: Evidence from modern and ancient DNA. *PNAS* **103** (21), 8113-8118 (2006).

118. Achilli, A. *et al.*, The Multifaceted Origin of Taurine Cattle Reflected by the Mitochondrial Genome. *PLoS One* **4** (6) (2009).

119. Sherratt, A., in *Pattern of the past: studies in honour of David Clarke*, edited by Clarke, D., Hodder, I., Isaac, G. & Hammond, N. (Cambridge University Press, Cambridge, 1981), pp. 261-305.

120. Vigne, J. & Helmer, D., Was milk a "secondary product" in the Old World Neolithisation process? Its role in the domestication of cattle, sheep and goats. *Anthropozoologica* **40** (2), 9-40 (2007).

121. Evershed, R. *et al.*, Earliest date for milk use in the Near East and southeastern Europe linked to cattle herding. *Nature* **455**, 528-531 (2008).

122. Bersaglieri, T. *et al.*, Genetic Signatures of Strong Recent Positive Selection at the Lactase Gene. *American Journal of Human Genetics* **74**, 1111–1120 (2004).

123. Lacan, M. *et al.*, Ancient DNA reveals male diffusion through the Neolithic Mediterranean route. *PNAS* **108** (24), 9788-9791 (2011).

124. Bar-Yosef, O. & Belfer-Cohen, A., in *People and culture in change: proceedings of the Second Symposium on Upper Palaeolithic, Mesolithic and Neolithic Populations of Europe and the Mediterranean Basin, Volume 1 (BAR International Series 508)*, edited by Hershkovitz, I. (BAR, Oxford, 1989), pp. 59-72.

125. Braidwood, R., Çambel, H. & Schirmer, W., Beginnings of Village-Farming Communities in Southeastern Turkey: Çayönü Tepesi, 1978 and 1979. *Journal of Field Archaeology* **8**, 251-258 (1981).

126. Hongo, H., Meadow, R., Öksuz, B. & Ilgezdi, G., in *Archaeozoology of the Near East V*, edited by Buitenhuis, H., Choyke, A., Mashkour, M. & Al-Shiyab, A. (ARC Publication, Groningen, 2002), pp. 153-165.

127. Özdogan, A. & Özdogan, M., Çayönü. A Conspectus of Recent Work. *Paléorient* **15** (1), 65-75 (1989).

128. Schirmer, W., Some aspects of building at the 'aceramic-neolithic' settlement of Çayönü Tepesi. *World Archaeology* **21** (3), 363-387 (1990).

129. Loy, T. & Wood, A., Blood Residue Analysis at Çayönü Tepesi, Turkey. *Journal of Field Archaeology* **16** (1989).

130. Hongo, H., Pearson, J., Öksüz, B. & İlgezdi, G., The Process of Ungulate Domestication at Çayönü, Southeastern Turkey: A Multidisciplinary Approach focussing on Bos sp. and Cervus elaphus. *Anthropozoologica* **44** (1), 63-78 (2009).

131. Legge, T., in *The Origin and Spread of Agriculture and Pastoralism in Eurasia*, edited by Harris, D. (Routledge, London, 1996), pp. 238-262.

132. Vigne, J., Carrère, I., Briois, F. & Guilaine, J., The Early Process of Mammal Domestication in the Near East New Evidence from the Pre-Neolithic and Pre-Pottery Neolithic in Cyprus. *Current Anthropology* **52** (S4), 255-271 (2011).

133. Vigne, J. *et al.*, Pre-Neolithic wild boar management and introduction to Cyprus more than 11,400 years ago. *PNAS* **106** (38), 16135-16138 (2009).

134. Simmons, A., Extinct pygmy hippopotamus and early man in Cyprus. *Nature* **333**, 554–557 (1988).

135. Peltenburg, E., Cyprus: A Regional Component of the Levantine PPN. *Neo-Lithics* (1/04), 3-7 (2004).

136. Croft, P., in *The Colonization and Settlement of Cyprus: Investigations at Kissonerga-Mylouthkia, 1976-1996*, edited by Peltenburg, E. (Studies in Mediterranean Archaeology, Sävedalen, Sweden, 2003), pp. 3-10.

137. Peltenburg, E., in *The Colonization and Settlement of Cyprus: Investigations at Kissonerga-Mylouthkia, 1976-1996*, edited by Peltenburg, E. (Studies in Mediterranean Archaeology, Sävedalen, Sweden, 2003), pp. 83-103.

138. Vigne, J., Guilaine, J., Debue, K., Haye, L. & Gerard, P., Early Taming of the Cat in Cyprus. *Science* **304**, 259 (2004).

139. Driscoll, C. *et al.*, The Near Eastern Origin of Cat Domestication. *Science* **317**, 519-523 (2007).

140. Willcox, G., in *Le néolithique de Chypre : actes du colloque international organisé par le Département des antiquités de Chypre et l'Ecole Française d'Athènes, Nicosie, 17-19 mai 2001: Bulletin de Correspondance Hellénique, supplément 43*, edited by Guilaine, J. & Le Brun, A. (Ecole Française d'Athène, Athens, 2003), pp. 231-238.

141. Le Brun, A., in *The earliest prehistory of Cyprus: from colonization to exploitation: Cyprus American Archaeological Research Institute Monograph Series, Volume 2*, edited by Swiny, S. (American Schools of Oriental Research, Boston, MA, 2001), pp. 109-118.

142. Todd, I., in *The earliest prehistory of Cyprus: from colonization to exploitation: Cyprus American Archaeological Research Institute Monograph Series, Volume 2*, edited by Swiny, S. (American Schools of Oriental Research, Boston, MA, 2001), pp. 95-108.

143. Hodder, I., *Çatalhöyük the Leopard's Tale* (Thames & Hudson, London, 2006).

144. Zarins, J., Early Pastoral Nomadism and the Settlement of Lower Mesopotamia. *BASOR* **280**, 31-65 (1990).

145. Matthews, R., in *The Human Past*, edited by Scarre, C. (Thames & Hudson, London, 2005), pp. 432-471.

146. Gebel, H. & Bienert, H., The 1997 Season at Ba'ja Southern Jordan. *Neo-Lithics* (3/97), 14-18 (1997).

147. Gebel, H. & Hermansen, B., Ba'ja Neolithic Project 1999 : Short Report on Architectural Findings. *Neo-Lithics* (3/99), 18-21 (1999).

148. Staubwasser, M. & Weiss, H., Holocene climate and cultural evolution in late prehistoric-early historic West Asia. *Quaternary Research* **66** (3), 372-387 (2006).

149. Köhler-Rollefson, I., The Aftermath of the Levantine Neolithic Revolution in the Light of Ecological and Ethnographic Evidence. *Paléorient* **14** (1), 87-93 (1988).

150. Rollefson, G., The Aceramic Neolithic of the Southern Levant : The View from 'Ain Ghazal. *Paléorient* **15** (1), 135-140 (1989).

151. Rollefson, G. & Köhler-Rollefson, I., PPNC adaptations in the first half of the 6th millennium B.C. *Paléorient* **19** (1), 33-42 (1993).

152.   Rollefson, G., The Origins of the Yarmoukian at 'Ain Ghazal. *Paléorient* **19** (1), 91-100 (1993).

19: Waves and lurches

1.   Scarre, C., in *The human past*, edited by Scarre, C. (Thames & Hudson, London, 2005), pp. 392-431.
2.   Mithen, S., in *Prehistoric Europe*, edited by Cunliffe, B. (Oxford University Press, Oxford, 1994), pp. 79-135.
3.   Barker, G., *The Agricultural Revolution in Prehistory: Why did Foragers become Farmers* (Oxford University Press, Oxford, 2006).
4.   Mithen, S., *After the Ice: A Global Human History 20,000 - 5,000 BC* (Weidenfield & Nicholson, London, 2003).
5.   Pickard, C. & Bonsall, C., Deep sea fishing in the European Mesolithic: Fact or Fantasy? *European Journal of Archaeology* **7** (3), 273-290 (2004).
6.   Hansen, J. & Renfrew, J., Palaeolithic–Neolithic seed remains at Franchthi Cave, Greece. *Nature* **271**, 349-352 (1978).
7.   Innes, J. & Blackford, J., The Ecology of Late Mesolithic Woodland Disturbances: Model Testing with Fungal Spore Assemblage Data. *Journal of Archaeological Science* **30**, 185-194 (2003).
8.   Bahn, P. & Couraud, C., Azilian pebbles: An unsolved mystery. *Endeavour* **8**, 156-158 (1984).
9.   Rowley-Conwy, P., in *Harvesting the sea, farming the forest: the emergence of Neolithic societies*, edited by Zvelebil, M., Domańska, L. & Dennell, R. (Sheffield Academic Press, Sheffield, 1998), pp. 193-202.
10.   Borić, D., The Lepenski Vir conundrum: reinterpretation of the Mesolithic and Neolithic sequences in the Danube Gorges. *Antiquity* **76** (294), 1026-1039 (2002).
11.   Radovanovic, I., Houses and burials at Lepenski Vir. *European Journal of Archaeology* **3** (3), 330-349 (2000).
12.   Borić, D., Body Metamorphosis and Animality: Volatile Bodies and Boulder Artworks from Lepenski Vir. *Cambridge Archaeological Journal* **15** (1), 35-69 (2005).
13.   Schulting, R., Antlers, bone pins and flint blades: the Mesolithic cemeteries of Téviec and Hoëdic, Brittany. *Antiquity* **70** (268), 335-350 (1996).
14.   O'Shea, J. & Zvelebil, M., Oleneostrovski Mogilnik: Reconstructing the Social and Economic Organization of Prehistoric Foragers in Northern Russia. *Journal of Anthropological Archaeology* **3**, 1-40 (1984).
15.   Gkiasta, M., Russell, T., Shennan, S. & Steele, J., Neolithic transition in Europe: the radiocarbon record revisited. *Antiquity* **77**, 45-62 (2003).
16.   Childe, G., *The Prehistory of European Society* (Russell Press, Nottingham, 1958).
17.   Lemmen, C., Gronenborn, D. & Wirtz, K., A simulation of the Neolithic transition in Western Eurasia. *Journal of Archaeological Science* **38** (12), 3459-3470 (2011).
18.   Ammerman, A. & Cavalli-Sforza, L., in *The Explanation of Culture Change: Models in Prehistory*, edited by Renfrew, C. (Duckworth, London, 1973), pp. 343–358.
19.   Ammerman, A. & Cavalli-Sforza, L., *The Neolithic Transition and the Genetics of Populations in Europe* (Princeton University Press, Princeton, NJ, 1984).
20.   Sykes, B., The molecular genetics of European ancestry. *Philosophical Transactions of the Royal Society B* **354**, 131-139 (1999).
21.   Sykes, B., *The Seven Daughters of Eve* (Bantam Press, London, 2001).
22.   Semino, O. *et al.*, The Genetic Legacy of Paleolithic Homo sapiens sapiens in Extant Europeans: A Y Chromosome Perspective. *Science* **290**, 1155-1159 (2000).
23.   Renfrew, C., in *Examining the farming/language dispersal hypothesis*, edited by Bellwood, P. & Renfrew, C. (McDonald Institute, Cambridge, 2002), pp. 3-16.
24.   Chikhi, L., Destro-Bisol, G., Bertorelle, G., Pascali, V. & Barbujani, G., Clines of nuclear DNA markers suggest a largely Neolithic ancestry of the European gene pool. *PNAS* **95**, 9053-9058 (1998).
25.   Simoni, L., Calafell, F., Pettener, D., Bertranpetit, J. & Barbujani, G., Geographic Patterns of mtDNA Diversity in Europe. *American Journal of Human Genetics* **66**, 262-278 (2000).
26.   Chikhi, L., Nichols, R., Barbujani, G. & Beaumont, M., Y genetic data support the Neolithic demic diffusion model. *PNAS* **99** (17), 11008-11013 (2002).

27.   Dupanloup, I., Bertorelle, G., Chikhi, L. & Barbujani, G., Estimating the Impact of Prehistoric Admixture on the Genome of Europeans. *Molecular Biology and Evolution* **21** (7), 1361-1372 (2004).

28.   Balaresque, P. *et al.*, A Predominantly Neolithic Origin for European Paternal Lineages. *PLoS Biology* **8** (1) (2010).

29.   Gignouxa, C., Henn, B. & Mountain, J., Rapid, global demographic expansions after the origins of agriculture. *PNAS* **108** (15), 6044-6049 (2011).

30.   Myres, N. *et al.*, A major Y-chromosome haplogroup Rb Holocene era founder effect in Central and Western Europe. *European Journal of Human Genetics* **19**, 95-101 (2011).

31.   Battaglia, V. *et al.*, Y-chromosomal evidence of the cultural diffusion of agriculture in southeast Europe. *European Journal of Human Genetics* **17**, 820-830 (2009).

32.   Busby, G. *et al.*, The peopling of Europe and the cautionary tale of Y-chromosome lineage R-M269. *Proceedings of the Royal Society B* **279**, 884-892 (2012).

33.   Lacan, M. *et al.*, Ancient DNA reveals male diffusion through the Neolithic Mediterranean route. *PNAS* **108** (24), 9788-9791 (2011).

34.   Lacan, M. *et al.*, Ancient DNA suggests the leading role played by men in the Neolithic dissemination. *PNAS* **108** (45), 18255-18259 (2011).

35.   Haak, W. *et al.*, Ancient DNA from European Early Neolithic Farmers Reveals Their Near Eastern Affinities. *PLoS Biology* **8** (11) (2010).

36.   Lazaridis, I. *et al.*, Ancient human genomes suggest three ancestral populations for present-day Europeans **513**, 409-413 (2014).

37.   Pinhasi, R. & von Cramon-Taubade, N., Craniometric Data Supports Demic Diffusion Model for the Spread of Agriculture into Europe. *PLoS One* **4** (8) (2009).

38.   Rowley-Conwy, P., How the West Was Lost: A Reconsideration of Agricultural Origins in Britain,Ireland, and Southern Scandinavia. *Current Anthropology* **45** (Supplement, August–October), S83-S113 (2004).

39.   Rowley-Conwy, P., Westward ho! *Current Anthropology* **52** (S4) (2011).

40.   Downey, S., Bocaege, E., Kerig, T., Edinborough, K. & Shennan, S., Correlation with Juvenility Index Supports Interpretation of the Summed Calibrated Radiocarbon Date Probability Distribution (SCDPD) as a Valid Demographic Proxy. *PLoS One* **9** (8), e105730 (2014).

41.   Özdoğan, M., Archaeological Evidence on the Westward Expansion of Farming Communities from Eastern Anatolia to the Aegean and the Balkans. *Current Anthropology* **52** (S4) (2011).

42.   Perlès, C., *The Early Neolithic in Greece* (Cambridge University Press, Cambridge, 2001).

43.   Zeder, M., Domestication and early agriculture in the Mediterranean Basin: Origins, diffusion, and impact. *PNAS* **105** (33), 11597-11604 (2008).

44.   Fernández, E. *et al.*, Ancient DNA Analysis of 8000 B.C. Near Eastern Farmers Supports an Early Neolithic Pioneer Maritime Colonization of Mainland Europe through Cyprus and the Aegean Islands. *PLoS One Genetics* **10** (6), e1004401 (2014).

45.   Durrani, S., Khan, H. & Renfrew, C., Obsidian Source Identification by Fission Track Analysis. *Nature* **233**, 242-245 (1971).

46.   Laskaris, N., Sampson, A., Mavridis, F. & Liritzis, I., Late Pleistocene/Early Holocene seafaring in the Aegean: new obsidian hydration dates with the SIMS-SS method. *Journal of Archaeological Science* **38** (9), 2475-2479 (2011).

47.   Whittle, A., in *The Oxford Illustrated History of Prehistoric Europe*, edited by Cunliffe, B. (Oxford University Press, Oxford, 1994), pp. 136-166.

48.   Bellwood, P., *First Farmers* (Blackwell Publishing, Oxford, 2005).

49.   Van Andel, T. & Runnels, C., The earliest farmers in Europe. *Antiquity* **69** (264), 481-500 (1995).

50.   Borić, D. & Price, D., Strontium isotopes document greater human mobility at the start of the Balkan Neolithic. *PNAS* **110** (9), 3298-3303 (2013).

51.   Zilhão, J., Radiocarbon evidence for maritime pioneer colonization at the origins of farming in west Mediterranean Europe. *PNAS* **98** (24), 14180-14185 (2001).

52.   Chandler, H., Sykes, B. & Zilhão, J., in *Actas del III Congreso del Neolítico en la Península Ibérica. Santander*, edited by Arias-Cabal, P., Ontañón, R. & García-Moncó, C. (Instituto Internacional de Investigaciones Prehistóricas de Cantabria, Santander, 2005), pp. 781-786.

53.   Bentley, A. *et al.*, Prehistoric Migration in Europe: Strontium Isotope Analysis of Early Neolithic Skeletons. *Current Anthropology* **43** (5), 799-804 (2002).

54. Bentley, R., Krause, R., Price, T. & Kaufmann, B., Human mobility at the Early Neolithic settlement of Vaihingen, Germany: evidence from strontium isotope analysis. *Archaeometry* **45**, 471-486 (2003).

55. Scarre, C., in *Examining the farming/language dispersal hypothesis*, edited by Bellwood, P. & Renfrew, C. (McDonald Institute, Cambridge, 2002), pp. 395-407.

56. Haak, W. *et al.*, Ancient DNA from the First European Farmers in 7500-Year-Old Neolithic Sites. *Science* **310**, 1016-1018 (2005).

57. Bramanti, B. *et al.*, Genetic Discontinuity Between Local Hunter-Gatherers and Central Europe's First Farmers. *Science* **326**, 137-140 (2009).

58. Deguilloux, M. *et al.*, News From the West: Ancient DNA From a French Megalithic Burial Chamber. *American Journal of Physical Anthropology* **144**, 108-118 (2011).

59. Sampietro, L. *et al.*, Palaeogenetic evidence supports a dual model of Neolithic spreading into Europe. *Proceedings of the Royal Society B* **274**, 2161-2167 (2007).

60. Palanichamy, M. *et al.*, Mitochondrial haplogroup N1a phylogeography, with implication to the origin of European farmers. *BMC Evolutionary Biology* **10** (304) (2010).

61. Levy-Coffman, E., We Are Not Our Ancestors: Evidence for Discontinuity between Prehistoric and Modern Europeans. *Journal of Genetic Genealogy,* **2**, 40-50 (2006).

62. Thomas, J., in *The Origins and Spread of Agriculture and Pastoralism in Eurasia*, edited by Harris, D. (London, Routledge, 1996), pp. 312-322.

63. Price, D., in *The Origins and Spread of Agriculture and Pastoralism in Eurasia*, edited by Harris, D. (Routledge, London, 1996), pp. 346-362.

64. Zvelebil, M., in *The Origins and Spread of Agriculture and Pastoralism in Eurasia*, edited by Harris, D. (Routledge, London, 1996), pp. 323-345.

65. Von Cramon-Taubadel, N. & Pinhasi, R., Craniometric data support a mosaic model of demic and cultural Neolithic diffusion to outlying regions of Europe. *Proceedings of the Royal Society B* **278**, 2874-2880 (2011).

66. Skoglund, P. *et al.*, Genomic Diversity and Admixture Differs for Stone-Age Scandinavian Foragers and Farmers. *Science* (2014).

67. Pryor, F., *Britain B.C.* (HarperCollins, London, 2003).

68. Cramp, L. *et al.*, Immediate replacement of fishing with dairying by the earliest farmers of the northeast Atlantic archipelagos. *Proceedings of the Royal Society B* **281** (2014).

69. Renfrew, C., *Before Civilization* (Jonathon Cape, London, 1973).

70. Pitts, M., *Hengeworld* (Century, London, 2000).

71. Ruggles, C., *Astronomy in Prehistoric Britain and Ireland* (Yale University Press, New Haven, CT, 1999).

72. Steel, D., *Rogue asteroids and doomsday comets* (John Wiley & Sons, Inc., New York, 1993).

73. Hawkins, G., *Stonehenge Decoded* (Souvenir Press, London, 1966).

74. Hoyle, F., *On Stonehenge* (W. H. Freeman and Co., San Francisco, CA, 1977).

75. Parker Pearson, M., Rewriting Stonehenge's history, Available at http://www.meograph.com/ucl/33276/rewriting-stonehenges-history (2012).

76. Hoskin, M., *Tombs, Temples and their Orientations* (Ocarina Books, Bognor Regis, 2001).

20: Spreading the word

1. Mallory, J. & Adams, D., The Oxford Introduction to Proto-Indo-European and the Proto-Indo-European world (Oxford University Press, New York, NY, 2006).

2. Mallory, J., In Search of the Indo-Europeans: Language, Archaeology and Myth (Thames & Hudson, London, 1989).

3. Diamond, J., The Third Chimpanzee (Random, London, 1991).

4. Renfrew, C., Archaeology & Language (Jonathon Cape, London, 1987).

5. McWhorter, J., The Power of Babel: a Natural History of Language (William Heinemann, London, 2002).

6. Watkins, C., in The American Heritage Dictionary of the English Language (Houghton Mifflin Company, Boston, MA, 1969).

7. Anthony, D., The Horse the Wheel and Language: how Bronze-Age riders from the Eurasian steppes shaped the modern world (Princeton University Press, Princeton, NJ, 2007).

8.   Renfrew, C., in Languages in Prehistoric Europe, edited by Bammesberger, A. & Vennemann, T. (Universitätsverlag Winter, Heidelberg, 2004), pp. 17-48.

9.   Childe, G., The Aryans, a Study of Indo-European Origins (Kegan Paul, Trench & Trubner, London, 1926).

10.   Gimbutas, M., in Journal of Indo-European Studies Monographs No. 18, edited by Dexter, M. & Jones-Bley, K. (Institute of the Study of Man, Washington, DC, 1997).

11.   Gimbutas, M. & Dexter, M., The Living Goddesses (University of California Press, Berkeley & Los Angeles, CA, 1999).

12.   Scarre, C., in The human past, edited by Scarre, C. (Thames & Hudson, London, 2005b), pp. 392-431.

13.   Sherratt, A., in Pattern of the past: studies in honour of David Clarke, edited by Clarke, D., Hodder, I., Isaac, G. & Hammond, N. (Cambridge University Press, Cambridge, 1981), pp. 261-305.

14.   Gray, R. & Atkinson, Q., Language-tree divergence times support the Anatolian theory of Indo-European origin. Nature **426**, 435-439 (2003).

15.   Bouckaert, R. et al., Mapping the Origins and Expansion of the Indo-European Language Family. Science **337**, 957-960 (2012).

16.   Bellwood, P., First Farmers (Blackwell Publishing, Oxford, 2005).

17.   Diamond, J. & Bellwood, P., Farmers and Their Languages: The First Expansions. Science **300**, 597-603 (2003).

18.   Phillipson, D., in Examining the farming/language dispersal hypothesis, edited by Bellwood, P. & Renfrew, C. (McDonald Institute, Cambridge, 2002), pp. 177-187.

19.   Hill, J., in Examining the farming/language dispersal hypothesis, edited by Bellwood, P. & Renfrew, C. (McDonald Institute, Cambridge, 2002), pp. 331-340.

20.   Matson, R., in Examining the farming/language dispersal hypothesis, edited by Bellwood, P. & Renfrew, C. (McDonald Institute, Cambridge, 2002), pp. 341-356.

21.   Lewis, P., http://www.ethnologue.com/web.asp, Available at http://www.ethnologue.com/ethno_docs/distribution.asp?by=family (2009).

21: A continent divided

1.   Bellwood, P., *First Farmers* (Blackwell Publishing, Oxford, 2005).

2.   Barker, G., *The Agricultural Revolution in Prehistory: Why did Foragers become Famers* (Oxford University Press, Oxford, 2006).

3.   Marshall, F. & Hildebrand, E., Cattle Before Crops: The Beginnings of Food Production in Africa. *Journal of World Prehistory* **16** (2), 99-143 (2002).

4.   Hassan, F., in *Examining the farming/language dispersal hypothesis*, edited by Bellwood, P. & Renfrew, C. (McDonald Institute, Cambridge, 2002), pp. 127-133.

5.   Marshall, F. & Weissbrod, L., Domestication Processes and Morphological Change Through the Lens of the Donkey and African Pastoralism. *Current Anthropology* **52** (S4) (2011).

6.   Wendorf, F. & Schild, R., Nabta Playa and Its Role in Northeastern African Prehistory. *Journal of Anthropological Archaeology* **17**, 97-123 (1998).

7.   Holl, A., The Dawn of African Pastoralisms: An Introductory Note. *Journal of Anthropological Archaeology* **17**, 81-96 (1998).

8.   Bradley, D., Machugh, D., Cunningham, P. & Loftus, R., Mitochondrial diversity and the origins of African and European cattle. *PNAS* **93**, 5131-5135 (1996).

9.   Connah, G., in *The human past*, edited by Scarre, C. (Thames & Hudson, London, 2005), pp. 350-391.

10.   Dunne, J. et al., First dairying in green Saharan Africa in the fifth millennium BC. *Nature* **486**, 390-394 (2012).

11.   Madella, M., García-Granero, J., Out, W., Ryan, P. & Usai, D., Microbotanical Evidence of Domestic Cereals in Africa 7000 Years Ago. *PLoS One* **9** (10), e110177 (2014).

12.   Linseele, V. et al., New Archaeozoological Data from the Fayum "Neolithic" with a Critical Assessment of the Evidence for Early Stock Keeping in Egypt. *PLoS One* **9** (10), e108517 (2014).

13. Mbida, C., van Neer, W., Doutrelepont, H. & Vrydaghs, L., Evidence for Banana Cultivation and Animal Husbandry During the First Millennium BC in the Forest of Southern Cameroon. *Journal of Archaeological Science* **27**, 151-162 (2000).

14. McIntosh, S. & McIntosh, R., From Stone to Metal: New Perspectives on the Later Prehistory of West Africa. *Journal of World Prehistory* **2** (1), 89-133 (1988).

15. McIntosh, S., Changing Perceptions of West Africa's Past: Archaeological Research Since 1988. *Journal of Archaeological Research* **2** (2), 165-187 (1994).

16. D'Andrea, A., Klee, M. & Kasey, J., Archaeobotanical evidence for pearl millet (Pennisetum glaucum) in sub-Saharan West Africa. *Antiquity* **75** (288), 341-348 (2001).

17. Harris, D., in *Examining the farming/language dispersal hypothesis*, edited by Bellwood, P. & Renfrew, C. (McDonald Institute, Cambridge, 2002), pp. 31-39.

18. Gifford-Gonzalez, D., Early Pastoralists in East Africa: Ecological and Social Dimensions. *Journal of Anthropological Archaeology* **17**, 166-200 (1998).

19. Williamson, K. & Blench, R., in *African Languages: an Introduction*, edited by Heine, B. & Nurse, D. (Cambridge University Press, Cambridge, 2000), pp. 11-42.

20. Diamond, J. & Bellwood, P., Farmers and Their Languages: The First Expansions. *Science* **300**, 597-603 (2003).

21. Blench, R., in *Datation et Chronologie dans le Bassin du Lac Tchad*, edited by Barreteau, D. & Graffenried, C. (ORSTOM, Paris, 1993), pp. 147-160.

22. Vansina, J., New Linguistic Evidence and 'the Bantu Expansion'. *The Journal of African History* **36** (2), 175-195 (1995).

23. Holden, C., Bantu language trees reflect the spread of farming across sub-Saharan Africa: a maximum-parsimony analysis. *Proceedings of the Royal Society B* **269**, 793-799 (2002).

24. Pakendorf, B., Bostoen, K. & de Filippo, C., Molecular Perspectives on the Bantu Expansion: A Synthesis. *Language Dynamics and Change* **1**, 50-88 (2011).

25. Montano, V. *et al.*, The Bantu expansion revisited: a new analysis of Y chromosome variation in Central Western Africa. *Molecular Ecology* **20**, 2693-2708 (2011).

26. Underhill, P. *et al.*, The phylogeography of Y chromosome binary haplotypes and the origins of modern human populations. *Annual of Human Genetics* **65**, 43-62 (2001).

27. Cruciani, F. *et al.*, A Back Migration from Asia to Sub-Saharan Africa Is Supported by High-Resolution Analysis of Human Y-Chromosome Haplotypes. *American Journal of Human Genetics* **70**, 1197-1214 (2002).

28. Beleza, S., Gusmao, L., Amorim, A., Carracedo, A. & Salas, A., The genetic legacy of western Bantu migrations. *Human Genetics* **117**, 366-375 (2005).

29. Wood, E. *et al.*, Contrasting patterns of Y chromosome and mtDNA variation in Africa: evidence for sex-biased demographic processes. *European Journal of Human Genetics* **13**, 867-876 (2005).

30. Zhivotovsky, L. *et al.*, The Effective Mutation Rate at Y Chromosome Short Tandem Repeats, with Application to Human Population-Divergence Time. *American Journal of Human Genetics* **74**, 50-61 (2004).

31. Berniell-Lee, G. *et al.*, Genetic and Demographic Implications of the Bantu Expansion: Insights from Human Paternal Lineages. *Molecular Biology and Evolution* **26** (7), 1581-1589 (2009).

32. De Filippo, C. *et al.*, Y-Chromosomal Variation in Sub-Saharan Africa: Insights Into the History of Niger-Congo Groups. *Molecular Biology and Evolution* **28** (3), 1255-1269 (2011).

33. Ehret, C., in *Examining the farming/language dispersal hypothesis*, edited by Bellwood, P. & Renfrew, C. (McDonald Institute, Cambridge, 2002), pp. 163-176.

34. Phillipson, D., in *Examining the farming/language dispersal hypothesis*, edited by Bellwood, P. & Renfrew, C. (McDonald Institute, Cambridge, 2002), pp. 177-187.

35. Pringle, H., Seeking Africa's First Iron Men. *Science* **323**, 200-202 (2009).

36. Childs, T., Style, Technology, and Iron Smelting Furnaces in Bantu-Speaking Africa. *Journal of Anthropological Archaeology* **10**, 332-359 (1991).

37. Phillipson, D., *African Archaeology*, 2nd ed. (Cambridge University Press, Cambridge, 1993).

38. Diamond, J., *Guns, Germs and Steel* (Chatto & Windus, London, 1997).

39. Bousman, B., The Chronological Evidence for the Introduction of Domestic Stock into Southern Africa. *African Archaeological Review* **15** (2), 132-150 (1998).

40. Sadr, K., The First Herders at the Cape of Good Hope. *African Archaeological Review* **15** (2), 101-132 (1998).

22: Of rice and men

1. FAO, *Rice is life*. Rome: Food and Agriculture Organisation of the United Nations (2004).
2. Glover, I. & Higham, C., in *The Origins and Spread of Agriculture and Pastoralism in Eurasia*, edited by Harris, D. (Routledge, London, 1996), pp. 413-441.
3. Linares, O., African rice (Oryza glaberrima): History and future potential. *PNAS* **99** (25), 16360-16365 (2002).
4. Londo, J., Chiang, Y., Hung, K., Chiang, T. & Schaal, B., Phylogeography of Asian wild rice, Oryza rufipogon, reveals multiple independent domestications of cultivated rice, Oryza sativa. *PNAS* **103** (25), 9578-9583 (2006).
5. Fuller, D. & Qin, L., Water management and labour in the origins and dispersal of Asian rice. *World Archaeology* **41** (1), 88-111 (2009).
6. Fuller, D., Finding Plant Domestication in the Indian Subcontinent. *Current Anthropology* **52** (S4), S347-S362 (2011).
7. Gao, L. & Innan, H., Nonindependent Domestication of the Two Rice Subspecies, Oryza sativa ssp. indica and ssp. japonica, Demonstrated by Multilocus Microsatellites. *Genetics* **179**, 965-976 (2008).
8. Molina, J. *et al.*, Molecular evidence for a single evolutionary origin of domesticated rice. *PNAS* **108** (20), 8351-8356 (2011).
9. Huang, X. *et al.*, A map of rice genome variation reveals the origin of cultivated rice. *Nature* **490**, 497-502 (2012).
10. Fuller, D. *et al.*, The Domestication Process and Domestication Rate in Rice: Spikelet Bases from the Lower Yangtze. *Science* **323**, 1607-1610 (2009).
11. Higham, C., in *The Human Past*, edited by Scarre, C. (Thames & Hudson, London, 2005), pp. 234-263.
12. Barker, G., *The Agricultural Revolution in Prehistory: Why did Foragers become Famers* (Oxford University Press, Oxford, 2006).
13. Basavaraj, G., Rao, P., Bhagavatula, S. & Ahmed, W., Availability and utilization of pearl millet in India. *Journal of SAT Agricultural Research* **8** (2010).
14. Cohen, D., The Beginnings of Agriculture in China: A Multiregional View. *Current Anthropology* **52** (S4), S273-S293 (2011).
15. Boaretto, E. *et al.*, Radiocarbon dating of charcoal and bone collagen associated with early pottery at Yuchanyan Cave, Hunan Province, China. *PNAS* **106** (24), 9595-9600 (2009).
16. Hayden, B., in *The emergence of pottery: technology and innovation*, edited by Barnett, W. & Hoopes, J. (Smithsonian Institution Press, Washington, DC, 1995), pp. 257-266.
17. Pearson, R., The social context of early pottery in the Lingnan region of south China. *Antiquity* **79** (306), 819-828 (2005).
18. Bellwood, P., *First Farmers* (Blackwell Publishing, Oxford, 2005).
19. Zhao, Z., New Archaeobotanic Data for the Study of the Origins of Agriculture in China. *Current Anthropology* **52** (S4) (2011).
20. West, B. & Zhou, B., Did chickens go north? New evidence for domestication. *World's Poultry Science Journal* **45**, 205-218 (1989).
21. Wong, G. *et al.*, A genetic variation map for chicken with 2.8 million single-nucleotide polymorphisms. *Nature* **432**, 717-722 (2004).
22. Larson, G. *et al.*, Patterns of East Asian pig domestication, migration, and turnover revealed by modern and ancient DNA. *PNAS* **107** (17), 7686-7691 (2010).
23. Yuan, J., Flad, R. & Yunbing, L., Meat-acquisition patterns in the Neolithic Yangzi river valley, China. *Antiquity* **82** (316), 351-366 (2008).
24. Yuan, J., The Problem of the Origin of Domestic Animals in Neolithic China. *Chinese Archaeology* **3**, 154-156 (2003).
25. Crawford, G., Agricultural origins in North China pushed back to the Pleistocene–Holocene boundary. *PNAS* **106** (18), 7271-7272 (2009).
26. Yang, X. *et al.*, Early millet use in northern China. *PNAS* **109** (10), 3726-3730 (2012).
27. Lu, H. *et al.*, Earliest domestication of common millet (Panicum miliaceum) in East Asia extended to 10,000 years ago. *PNAS* **106** (18), 7367-7372 (2009).
28. Barton, L. *et al.*, Agricultural origins and the isotopic identity of domestication in northern China. *PNAS* **106** (14), 5523-5528 (2009).
29. Bellwood, P., in *The Origins and Spread of Agriculture and Pastoralism in Eurasia*, edited by Harris, D. (Routledge, London, 1996), pp. 465-498.
30. Zhao, Z., The Middle Yangtze region in China is one place where rice was domesticated: phytolith

evidence from the Diaotonghuan Cave, Northern Jaingxi. *Antiquity* **72**, 885-897 (1998).

31. Fuller, D., Qin, L. & Harvey, E., A critical assessment of early agriculture in East Asia, with emphasis on Lower Yangtze rice domestication. *Pradghara (Journal of the Uttar Pradesh State Archaeology Department)* **18**, 17-52 (2008).

32. Liu, L., Lee, G., Jiang, L. & Zhang, J., The earliest rice domestication in China. *Antiquity* **81** (313) (2007).

33. Zheng, Y., Guoping, S. & Xugao, C., Characteristics of the short rachillae of rice from archaeological sites dating to 7000 years ago. *China Science Bulletin (English edition)* **52** (12), 1654-1660 (2007).

34. Zheng, Y. *et al.*, Rice fields and modes of rice cultivation between 5000 and 2500 BC in East China. *Journal of Archaeological Science* **36**, 2609-2616 (2009).

35. Jiejun, H., Excavations at Chengtoushan in Li County, Hunan Province, China. *Bulletin of the Indo-Pacific Prehistory Association* **18**, 101-103 (1999).

36. Bellwood, P., Holocene Population History in the Pacific Region as a Model for Worldwide Food Producer Dispersals. *Current Anthropology* **52** (S4), 363-378 (2011).

37. Harris, D., in *Examining the farming/language dispersal hypothesis*, edited by Bellwood, P. & Renfrew, C. (McDonald Institute, Cambridge, 2002), pp. 31-39.

38. Mithen, S., *After the Ice: A Global Human History 20,000 - 5,000 BC* (Weidenfield & Nicholson, London, 2003).

39. Imamura, K., in *The origins and spread of agriculture and pastoralism in Eurasia*, edited by Harris, D. (Routledge, London, 1996), pp. 442-464.

40. Keally, J., Jomon Culture, Available at http://www.t-net.ne.jp/~keally/jomon.html (2010).

41. Crawford, G., Advances in Understanding Early Agriculture in Japan. *Current Anthropology* **52** (S4) (2011).

42. Crawford, G., in *Transitions to Agriculture in Prehistory*, edited by Gebauer, A. & Price, D. (Prehistory Press, Maduson, WI, 1992), pp. 117-132.

43. Temple, D., Dietary Variation and Stress Among Prehistoric Jomon Foragers From Japan. *American Journal of Physical Anthropology* **133**, 1035-1046 (2007).

44. Smith, B., Low-Level Food Production. *Journal of Archaeological Research* **9** (1), 1-43 (2001).

45. Lee, G., The Transition from Foraging to Farming in Prehistoric Korea. *Current Anthropology* **52** (S4), 307-329 (2011).

46. Hammer, M. *et al.*, Dual origins of the Japanese: common ground for hunter-gatherer and farmer Y chromosomes. *Journal of Human Genetics* **51**, 47-58 (2006).

23: Out of Taiwan

1. Bellwood, P., *First Farmers* (Blackwell Publishing, Oxford, 2005).

2. Bellwood, P., Holocene Population History in the Pacific Region as a Model for Worldwide Food Producer Dispersals. *Current Anthropology* **52** (S4), 363-378 (2011).

3. Diamond, J. & Bellwood, P., Farmers and Their Languages: The First Expansions. *Science* **300**, 597-603 (2003).

4. Bellwood, P. & Hiscock, P., in *The human past*, edited by Scarre, C. (Thames & Hudson, London, 2005), pp. 264-305.

5. Terrell, J., Kelly, K. & Rainbird, P., Foregone Conclusions? In Search of "Papuans" and "Austronesians". *Current Anthropology* **42** (1), 97-124 (2001).

6. Mona, S. *et al.*, Genetic Admixture History of Eastern Indonesia as Revealed by Y-Chromosome and Mitochondrial DNA Analysis. *Molecular Biology and Evolution* **26**, 1865-1877 (2009).

7. Karafet, T. *et al.*, Balinese Y-chromosome perspective on the peopling of Indonesia: genetic contributions from pre-neolithic hunter-gatherers, Austronesian farmers, and Indian traders. *Human Biology* **77** (1), 93-114 (2005).

8. Hill, C. *et al.*, A Mitochondrial Stratigraphy for Island Southeast Asia. *American Journal of Human Genetics* **80**, 29-43 (2007).

9. Chang, K., The Neolithic Taiwan Strait. *Kaogu* **6**, 541-550,569 (1989).

10. Pawley, A., in *Examining the farming/language dispersal hypothesis*, edited by Bellwood, P. & Renfrew, C. (McDonald Institute, Cambridge, 2002), pp. 251-273.

11.   Blust, R., in *Selected papers from the eighth international conference on Austronesian linguistics*, edited by Zeitoun, E. & Li, P. (Academia Sinica, Taipai, Taiwan, 1999), pp. 31–94.

12.   Pawley, A., in *Oceanic Explorations: Lapita and Western Pacific Settlement (Terra Australis 26)*, edited by Bedford, S., Sand, C. & Connaughton, S. (ANU ePress, Canberra, Australia, 2007), pp. 17-49.

13.   Paz, V., in *Examining the farming/language dispersal hypothesis*, edited by Bellwood, P. & Renfrew, C. (McDonald Institute, Cambridge, 2002), pp. 275-285.

14.   Dewar, R., Rainfall Variability and Subsistence Systems. *Current Anthropology* **44** (3), 369-388 (2003).

15.   Bellwood, P., in *The Origins and Spread of Agriculture and Pastoralism in Eurasia*, edited by Harris, D. (Routledge, London, 1996), pp. 465-498.

16.   Summerhayes, G. *et al.*, Human Adaptation and Plant Use in Highland New Guinea 49,000 to 44,000 Years Ago. *Science* **330**, 78-81 (2010).

17.   Denham, T. *et al.*, Origins of Agriculture at Kuk Swamp in the Highlands of New Guinea. *Science* **301**, 189-193 (2003).

18.   Fullagar, R., Field, J., Denham, T. & Lentfer, C., Early and mid-Holocene processing of taro (Colocasia esculenta) and yam (Dioscorea sp.) at Kuk Swamp in the Highlands of Papua New Guinea. *Journal of Archaeological Science* **33**, 595-614 (2006).

19.   Denham, T., Early Agriculture and Plant Domestication in New Guinea and Island Southeast Asia. *Current Anthropology* **52** (S4), S379-S395 (2011).

20.   Bayliss-Smith, T., in *The Origins and Spread of Agriculture and Pastoralism in Eurasia*, edited by Harris, D. (Routledge, London, 1996), pp. 499-523.

21.   Diamond, J., *The Third Chimpanzee* (Random, London, 1991).

22.   Barker, G., *The Agricultural Revolution in Prehistory: Why did Foragers become Famers* (Oxford University Press, Oxford, 2006).

23.   Clark, G., Petchey, F., Winter, O., Carson, M. & O'Day, P., New Radiocarbon Dates from the Bapot-1 Site in Saipan and Neolithic Dispersal by Stratified Diffusion. *Journal of Pacific Archaeology* **1** (1), 21-35 (2011).

24.   Mortagne, V., Lapita: Oceanic Ancestors – review, Available at http://www.guardian.co.uk/culture/2010/dec/14/lapita-oceanic-ancestors-paris-review (2010).

25.   Kinaston, R. *et al.*, Lapita Diet in Remote Oceania: New Stable Isotope Evidence from the 3000-Year-Old Teouma Site, Efate Island, Vanuatu. *PLoS One* **9** (3), e90376 (2014).

26.   Addison, D. & Matisoo-Smith, E., Rethinking Polynesian origins: a West Polynesia triple-I model. *Archaeology in Oceania* **45**, 1-12 (2010).

27.   Wilmshurst, J., Hunt, T., Lipo, C. & Anderson, A., High-precision radiocarbon dating shows recent and rapid initial human colonization of East Polynesia. *PNAS* **108** (5), 1815-1820 (2010).

28.   Hunt, T. & Lipo, C., Late Colonization of Easter Island. *Science* **311**, 1603-1606 (2006).

29.   Storey, A. *et al.*, Radiocarbon and DNA evidence for a pre-Columbian introduction of Polynesian chickens to Chile. *PNAS* **104** (25), 10335-10339 (2007).

30.   Gray, R., Drummond, A. & Greenhill, S., Language Phylogenies Reveal Expansion Pulses and Pauses in Pacific Settlement. *Science* **323**, 479-483 (2009).

31.   Jordan, F., Gray, R., Greenhill, S. & Mace, R., Matrilocal residence is ancestral in Austronesian societies. *Proceedings of the Royal Society B* **276**, 1957-1964 (2009).

32.   Kayser, M. *et al.*, Melanesian and Asian origins of Polynesians: mtDNA and Y chromosome gradients across the Pacific. *Molecular Biology and Evolution* **23**, 2234-2244 (2006).

33.   Cox, M., Karafet, T., Lansing, S., Sudoyo, H. & Hammer, M., Autosomal and X-linked single nucleotide polymorphisms reveal a steep Asian–Melanesian ancestry cline in eastern Indonesia and a sex bias in admixture rates. *Proceedings of the Royal Society B* **277**, 1589-1596 (2010).

34.   Moodley, Y. *et al.*, The Peopling of the Pacific from a Bacterial Perspective. *Science* **323**, 527-530 (2009).

24: Limited options and tilted axes

1.   Bellwood, P., *First Farmers* (Blackwell Publishing, Oxford, 2005).

2.   Scarre, C., in *The Human Past*, edited by Scarre, C. (Thames & Hudson, London, 2005), pp. 176-199.

3.   Piperno, D., The Origins of Plant Cultivation and Domestication in the New World Tropics Patterns, Process, and New Developments. *Current Anthropology* **52** (S4) (2011).

4.   Smith, B., Plant Domestication in Eastern North America. *Current Anthropology* **52** (S4) (2011).

5.   Iltis, H., Homeotic sexual translocations and the origin of maize (zea mays, poaceae): a new look at an old problem. *Economic Botany* **54** (1), 7-42 (2000).

6.   Diamond, J., *Guns, Germs and Steel* (Chatto & Windus, London, 1997).

7.   Diamond, J., Evolution, consequences and future of plant and animal domestication. *Nature* **418**, 700-707 (2002).

8.   Browman, D., Fritz, G., Watson, P. & Meltzer, D., in *The Human Past*, edited by Scarre, C. (Thames & Hudson, London, 2005), pp. 306-349.

9.   Sanjur, O., Piperno, D., Andres, T. & Wessel-Beaver, L., Phylogenetic relationships among domesticated and wild species of Cucurbita (Cucurbitaceae) inferred from a mitochondrial gene: Implications for crop plant evolution and areas of origin. *PNAS* **99** (1), 535-540 (2002).

10.   Piperno, D. & Stothert, K., Phytolith Evidence for Early Holocene Cucurbita Domestication in Southwest Ecuador. *Science* **99** (16), 10923-10928 (2003).

11.   Smith, B., The Initial Domestication of Cucurbita pepo in the Americas 10,000 Years Ago. *Science* **276**, 932-934 (1997).

12.   Smith, B., Reassessing Coxcatlan Cave and the early history of domesticated plants in Mesoamerica. *PNAS* **102** (27), 9438-9445 (2005).

13.   Smith, B., Eastern North America as an independent center of plant domestication. *PNAS* **103** (33), 12223-12228 (2006).

14.   Bitocchi, E. *et al.*, Mesoamerican origin of the common bean (Phaseolus vulgaris L.) is revealed by sequence data. *PNAS* **109** (14), E788-E796 (2012).

15.   Piperno, D. & Dillehay, T., Starch grains on human teeth reveal early broad crop diet in northern Peru. *PNAS* **105** (50), 19622-19627 (2008).

16.   Kaplan, L. & Lynch, T., Phaseolus (Fabaceae) in Archaeology: AMS Radiocarbon Dates and their significance for Pre-Colombian Agriculture. *Economic Botany* **53** (3), 261-272 (1999).

17.   Chacón, M., Pickersgill, S. & Debouck, D., Domestication patterns in common bean (Phaseolus vulgaris L.) and the origin of the Mesoamerican and Andean cultivated races. *Theoretical and Applied Genetics* **110**, 432-444 (2005).

18.   Fofana, B., du Jardin, P. & Baudoin, J., Genetic diversity in the Lima bean (Phaseolus lunatus L.) as revealed by chloroplast DNA (cpDNA) variations. *Genetic Resources and Crop Evolution* **48**, 437-445 (2001).

19.   Olsen, K. & Schaal, B., Evidence on the origin of cassava: Phylogeography of Manihot esculenta. *PNAS* **96**, 5586-5591 (1999).

20.   Dillehay, T., Rossen, J., Andres, T. & Williams, D., Preceramic Adoption of Peanut, Squash, and Cotton in Northern Peru. *Science* **316** (2007).

21.   Piperno, D., Ranere, A., Holst, I. & Hansell, P., Starch grains reveal early root crop horticulture in the Panamanian tropical forest. *Nature* **407**, 894-897 (2000).

22.   Pohl, M. *et al.*, Early Agriculture in the Maya Lowlands. *Latin American Antiquity* **7** (4), 355-372 (1996).

23.   FAO, *International Year of the Potato 2008*. Rome: International Year of the Potato Secretariat, Food and Agriculture Organization of the United Nations (2008)

24.   Engel, F., Exploration of the Chilca Canyon, Peru **11**, 55-58 (1970).

25.   Ugent, D., Pozorski, S. & Pozorski, T., Archaeological Potato Tuber Remains from the Casma Valley of Peru. *Economic Botany* **32** (2), 182-192 (1982).

26.   Perry, L. *et al.*, Early maize agriculture and interzonal interaction in southern Peru. *Nature* **440**, 76-79 (2006).

27.   Ugent, D., The potato: What is the botanical origin of this important crop plant and how did it first become domesticated? *Science* **170** (3963), 1161-1166 (1970).

28.   Spooner, D., McLean, K., Ramsay, G., Waugh, R. & Bryan, G., A single domestication for potato based on multilocus amplified fragment length polymorphism genotyping. *PNAS* **102** (41), 14694-14699 (2005).

29.   Zhang, D., Cervantes, J., Huamán, Z.., Carey, E. & Ghislain, M., Assessing genetic diversity of sweet potato (Ipomoea batatas (L.) Lam.) cultivars from tropical America using AFLP. *Genetic Resources and Crop Evolution* **47**, 659-665 (2000).

30.   Shady Solis, R., Haas, J. & Creamer, W., Dating Caral, a Preceramic Site in the Supe Valley on the Central Coast of Peru. *Science* **292**, 723-726 (2001).

31.   Perry, L. *et al.*, Starch Fossils and the Domestication and Dispersal of Chili Peppers (Capsicum spp. L.) in the Americas. *Science* **315**, 986-988 (2007).

32.   USDA, World Corn Production, Consumption, and Stocks, Available at http://www.fas.usda.gov/psdonline/psdgetreport.aspx?hidReportRetrievalName=BVS&hidReport RetrievalID=459&hidReportRetrievalTemplateID=7 (2012).

33.   Wise, T., 2012.

34.   Bennetzen, J. *et al.*, Genetic evidence and the origin of maize. *Latin American Antiquity* **12** (1), 84-86 (2001).

35.   Doebley, J., Molecular Evidence and the Evolution of Maize. *Economic Botany* **44** (3 Supplement), 6-27 (1990).

36.   Eyre-Walker, A., Gaut, R., Hilton, H., Feldman, D. & Gaut, B., Investigation of the bottleneck leading to the domestication of maize. *PNAS* **95**, 4441-4446 (1998).

37.   Wang, R., Stec, A., Hey, J., Lukens, L. & Doebley, J., The limits of selection during maize domestication. *Nature* **398**, 236-239 (1999).

38.   Matsuoka, Y. *et al.*, A single domestication for maize shown by multilocus microsatellite genotyping. *PNAS* **99** (9), 6080-6084 (2002).

39.   Jaenicke-Després, V. *et al.*, Early Allelic Selection in Maize as Revealed by Ancient DNA. *Science* **302**, 1206-1208 (2003).

40.   Smalley, J. & Blake, M., Sweet Beginnings Stalk Sugar and the Domestication of Maize. *Current Anthropology* **44** (5), 675-703 (2003).

41.   Ranere, A., Piperno, D., Holst, I., Dickau, R. & Iriarte, J., The cultural and chronological context of early Holocene maize and squash domestication in the Central Balsas River Valley, Mexico. *PNAS* **106** (13), 5014-5018 (2009).

42.   Piperno, D., Ranere, A., Holst, I., Iriarte, J. & Dickau, R., Starch grain and phytolith evidence for early ninth millennium B.P. maize from the Central Balsas River Valley, Mexico. *PNAS* **106** (13), 5019-5024 (2009).

43.   Pope, K. *et al.*, Origin and Environmental Setting of Ancient Agriculture in the Lowlands of Mesoamerica. *Science* **292**, 1370-1373 (2001).

44.   Piperno, D. & Flannery, K., The earliest archaeological maize (Zea mays L.) from highland Mexico: New accelerator mass spectrometry dates and their implications. *PNAS* **98** (4), 2101-2103 (2001).

45.   Benz, B., Archaeological evidence of teosinte domestication from Guila Naquitz, Oaxaca. *PNAS* **98** (4), 2104-2106 (2001).

46.   Long, A., Benz, B., Donahue, D., Jull, A. & Toolin, L., First Direct Ams Dates On Early Maize From Tehuacan, Mexico. *Radiocarbon* **31** (3), 1035-1040 (1989).

47.   Dickau, R., Ranere, A. & Cooke, R., Starch grain evidence for the preceramic dispersals of maize and root crops into tropical dry and humid forests of Panama **104** (9), 3651-3656 (2007).

48.   Pearsall, D., Maize is Still Ancient in Prehistoric Ecuador: The View from Real Alto, with Comments on Staller and Thompson. *Journal of Archaeological Science* **29** (1), 51-55 (2002).

49.   Staller, J., An Examination of the Palaeobotanical and Chronological Evidence for an Early Introduction of Maize (Zea mays L.) into South America: A Response to Pearsall. *Journal of Archaeological Science* **30** (3), 373-380 (2003).

50.   Zarrillo, S., Pearsall, D., Raymond, S., Tisdale, M. & Quon, D., Directly dated starch residues document early formative maize (Zea mays L.) in tropical Ecuador. *PNAS* **105** (13), 5006-5011 (2008).

51.   Iriarte, J. *et al.*, Evidence for cultivar adoption and emerging complexity during the mid-Holocene in the La Plata basin. *Nature* **432**, 614-617 (2004).

52.   Merrill, W. *et al.*, The diffusion of maize to the southwestern United States and its impact. *PNAS* **106** (50), 21019-21026 (2009).

53.   Erickson, D., Smith, B., Clarke, A., Sandweiss, D. & Tuross, N., An Asian origin for a 10,000-year-old domesticated plant in the Americas. *PNAS* **102** (51), 18315-18320 (2005).

54.   Dillehay, T., Eling, H. & Rossen, J., Preceramic irrigation canals in the Peruvian Andes. *PNAS* **102** (47), 17241-17244 (2005).

55.   Heckenberger, M. *et al.*, Amazonia 1492: Pristine Forest or Cultural Parkland? *Science* **301**, 1710-1714 (2003).

56. Roosevelt, A. *et al.*, Paleoindian Cave Dwellers in the Amazon: The Peopling of the Americas. *Science* **272**, 373-394 (1996).

57. Roosevelt, A., Housley, R., Imazio da Silveira, M., Maranca, S. & Johnson, R., Eighth Millennium Pottery from a Prehistoric Shell Midden in the Brazilian Amazon. *Science* **254**, 1621-1624 (1991).

58. Moseley, M. & Heckenberger, M., in *The human past*, edited by Scarre, C. (Thames & Hudson, London, 2005), pp. 640-677.

59. Shady Solis, R., Open Letter from Ruth Shady, Available at http://caralperu.typepad.com/caral_civilization_peru/2005/01/open_letter_fro.html (2005).

60. Shady Solis, R., La Ciudad Sagrada de Caral - Supe en los Albores de la Civilización en el Perú, Lima: Universidad Nacional Mayor de San Marco (1997).

61. Haas, J., Creamer, W. & Ruiz, A., Dating the Late Archaic occupation of the Norte Chico region in Peru. *Nature* **432**, 1020-1023 (2004).

62. Stanish, C., The origin of state societies in South America. *Annual Review of Anthropology* **30**, 41-64 (2001).

63. Moseley, M., *The Incas and Their Ancestors: The Archaeology of Peru*, 2nd ed. (Thames & Hudson, London, 2001).

64. Hoopes, J., Ford Revisited - A Critical-Review Of Chronology And Relationships Of. The Earliest Ceramic Complexes In The New-World, 6000-1500-BC. *Journal of World Prehistory* **8** (1), 1-49 (1994).

65. Oyuela-Caycedo, A., The Study of Collector Variability in the Transition to Sedentary Food Producers in Northern Colombia. *Journal of World Prehistory* **10** (1), 49-93 (1996).

66. Marcos, J. & Michczynski, A., Good dates and bad dates in Ecuador - radiocarbon samples and archaeological excavations: A commentary based on the "Valdivia Absolute Chronology". *Andes: Boletın de la Mision Arqueolo gica Andina (Warsaw)* **1**, 93-114 (1996).

67. Meggers, B., Evans, C. & Estrada, B., The Early Formative Period of the coast of Ecuador: the Valdivia and Machillia Phases. *Smithsonian Contributions to Anthropology* (1965).

68. Damp, J., Architecture of the Early Valdivia Village. *American Antiquity* **49** (3), 573-585 (1984).

69. Pearsall, D., Chandler-Ezell, K. & Zeidler, J., Maize in ancient Ecuador: results of residue analysis of stone tools from the Real Alto site. *Journal of Archaeological Science* **31**, 423-442 (2004).

70. Chandler-Ezell, K., Pearsall, D. & Zeidler, J., Root and Tuber Phytoliths and Starch Grains Document Manioc (Manihot esculenta), Arrowroot (Maranta arundinacea), and Llerén (Calathea sp.) at the Real Alto Site, Ecuador. *Economic Botany* **60** (2), 103-120 (2006).

71. Minnis, P., in *The Origins of Agriculture: An International Perspective*, edited by Cowan, C. & Watson, P. (Smithsonian Institution Press, Washington, DC, 1992), pp. 121-142.

72. Smith, B., Documenting plant domestication: The consilience of biological and archaeological approaches. *PNAS* **98** (4), 1324-1326 (2001).

73. Mabry, J., Las Capas and early irrigation farming. *Archaeology Southwest* **13** (1), 14 (1999).

74. Damp, J., Hall, S. & Smith, S., Early Irrigation on the Colorado Plateau near Zuni Pueblo, New Mexico. *American Antiquity* **67**, 665-676 (2002).

75. Hard, R. & Roney, J., A Massive Terraced Village Complex in Chihuahua, Mexico,3000 Years Before Present. *Science* **279**, 1661-1664 (1998).

76. Matson, R., in *Examining the farming/language dispersal hypothesis*, edited by Bellwood, P. & Renfrew, C. (McDonald Institute, Cambridge, 2002), pp. 341-356.

77. Hill, J., in *Examining the farming/language dispersal hypothesis*, edited by Bellwood, P. & Renfrew, C. (McDonald Institute, Cambridge, 2002), pp. 331-340.

78. Kohler, T., Glaude, M., Bocquet-Appel, J. & Kemp, B., The Neolithic Demographic Transition in the U.S. Southwest. *American Antiquity* **73** (4), 645-669 (2008).

79. Kemp, B. *et al.*, Evaluating the Farming/Language Dispersal Hypothesis with genetic variation exhibited by populations in the Southwest and Mesoamerica. *PNAS* **107** (15), 6759-6764 (2010).

80. Brown, C., Lack of linguistic support for Proto- Uto-Aztecan at 8900 BP. *PNAS* **107** (11), E34 (2010).

81. Hill, J., New evidence for a Mesoamerican homeland for Proto-Uto-Aztecan. *PNAS* **107** (11), E33 (2010).

82. Merrill, W. *et al.*, Reply to Hill and Brown: Maize and Uto-Aztecan cultural history. *PNAS* **107** (11), E35-E36 (2010).

83. Smith, B. & Yarnell, R., Initial formation of an indigenous crop complex in eastern North America at 3800 B.P. *PNAS* **106** (16), 6561-6566 (2009).

84.   Barker, G., *The Agricultural Revolution in Prehistory: Why did Foragers become Famers* (Oxford University Press, Oxford, 2006).

85.   Brown, J. & Vierra, R., in *Archaic Hunters and Gatherers in the American Midwest*, edited by Phillips, J. & Brown, J. (Academic Press, New York, NY, 1993), pp. 165-195.

86.   Saunders, J. *et al.*, A Mound Complex in Louisiana at 5400–5000 Years Before the Present. *Science* **277**, 1796-1799 (1997).

87.   Harter, A. *et al.*, Origin of extant domesticated sunflowers in eastern North America. *Nature* **430**, 201-205 (2004).

88.   Lentz, D., Pohl, M., Alvarado, J., Tarighat, S. & Bye, R., Sunflower (Helianthus annuus L.) as a pre-Columbian domesticate in Mexico. *PNAS* **105** (17), 6232-6237 (2008).

89.   Blackman, B. *et al.*, Sunflower domestication alleles support single domestication center in eastern North America. *PNAS* **108** (34), 14360-14365 (2011).

90.   Doebley, J., Goodman, M. & Stuber, C., Exceptional Genetic Divergence of Northern Flint Corn. *American Journal of Botany* **73** (1), 64-69 (1986).

91.   Riley, T., Edging, R. & Rossen, J., Cultigens in prehistoric Eastern North America: changing paradigms. *Current Anthropology* **31** (5), 525-541 (1990).

25: The Urban Revolution

1.   Smith, M., V. Gordon Childe and the Urban Revolution: a historical perspective on a revolution in urban studies. *Town Planning Review* **80** (1), 3-29 (2009).

2.   Childe, G., *Man Makes Himself* (Watts and Co., London, 1936).

3.   Childe, G., The Urban Revolution. *The Town Planning Review* **21** (1), 3-17 (1950).

4.   Service, E., *Primitive Social organization* (Random House, New York, NY, 1962).

5.   Fried, M., *The Evolution of Political Society* (Random House, New York, NY, 1967).

6.   Flannery, K., The Cultural Evolution of Civilizations. *Annual Review of Ecology and Systematics* **3**, 399-426 (1972).

7.   Trigger, B., *Understanding early civilizations* (Cambridge University Press, New York, NY, 2003).

8.   Scarre, C., in *The Human Past*, edited by Scarre, C. (Thames & Hudson, London, 2005a), pp. 176-199.

9.   Spencer, C. & Redmond, E., Primary state formation in Mesoamerica. *Annual Review of Anthropology* **33**, 173-199 (2004).

10.   Wright, H. & Johnson, G., Population, exchange, and early state formation in Southwestern Iran. *American Anthropologist* **77**, 267-289 (1975).

11.   Bogucki, P., *The Origins of Human Society* (Blackwell Publishing, Oxford, 1999).

12.   Wright, H., Recent research on the origin of the state. *Annual Review of Anthropology* **6**, 379-397 (1977).

13.   Spencer, C., Territorial expansion and primary state formation. *PNAS* **107** (16), 7119-7126 (2010).

14.   Currie, T., Greenhill, S., Gray, R., Hasegawa, T. & Mace, R., Rise and fall of political complexity in island South-East Asia and the Pacific. *Nature* **467**, 801-804 (2010).

15.   Matthews, R., in *The Human Past*, edited by Scarre, C. (Thames & Hudson, London, 2005), pp. 432-471.

16.   Connah, G., in *The human past*, edited by Scarre, C. (Thames & Hudson, London, 2005), pp. 350-391.

17.   Coningham, R., in *The human past*, edited by Scarre, C. (Thames & Hudson, London, 2005), pp. 518-551.

18.   Lee, Y., Building the Chronology of Early Chinese History. *Asian Perspectives* **41** (1), 15-42 (2002).

19.   Stanish, C., The origin of state societies in South America. *Annual Review of Anthropology* **30**, 41-64 (2001).

20.   Wittfogel, K., *Oriental Despotism* (Yale University, New Haven, CT, 1957).

21.   Adams, R., *The evolution of urban society* (Aldine, Chicago, IL, 1966).

22.   Carneiro, R., A Theory of the Origin of the State. *Science* **169**, 733-738 (1970).

23.   Rathje, W., The Origin and Development of Lowland Classic Maya Civilization. *American Antiquity* **36**, 275-285 (1971).

24. Spencer, C., A Mathematical Model of Primary State Formation. *Cultural Dynamics* **10** (1), 5-20 (1998).

25. Marcus, J., in *Archaic States*, edited by Feinman, G. & Marcus, J. (School of American Research Press, Santa Fe, NM, 1998), pp. 59-94.

26: Early adopters in Mesopotamia and Egypt

1. Matthews, R., in *The Human Past*, edited by Scarre, C. (Thames & Hudson, London, 2005), pp. 432-471.

2. Akkermans, P., A Late Neolithic and Early Halaf village at Sabi Abyad, northern Syria. *Paléorient* **13** (1), 23-40 (1987).

3. Bogucki, P., *The Origins of Human Society* (Blackwell Publishing, Oxford, 1999).

4. McIntosh, J., *Ancient Mesopotamia: New perspectives* (ABC-CLIO, Santa Barbara, CA, 2005).

5. Akkermans, P. & Duistermaat, K., Of storage and nomads: the sealings from Late Neolithic Sabi Abyad, Syria. *Paléorient* **22** (2), 17-44 (1997).

6. Campbell, S., The Burnt House at Arpachiyah: A Reexamination. *Bulletin of the American Schools of Oriental Research* **318**, 1-40 (2000).

7. Jasim, S., *The Ubaid period in Iraq: recent excavations in the Hamrin region (Issue 267, Parts 1-2)* (British Archaeological Reports, Oxford, 1985).

8. Stein, G., in *Chiefdoms and Early States in the Near East: the Organizational Dynamics of Complexity*, edited by Stein, G. & Rothman, M. (Prehistory Press, Madison, WI, 1994), pp. 35-46.

9. Hole, F., in *Upon this foundation: the 'Ubaid reconsidered*, edited by Henrickson, E. & Thuesen, I. (Carsten Niebuhr Institute, Copenhagen, 1989), pp. 149-180.

10. Trigger, B., *Understanding early civilizations* (Cambridge University Press, New York, NY, 2003).

11. Wright, H. & Johnson, G., Population, exchange, and early state formation in Southwestern Iran. *American Anthropologist* **77**, 267-289 (1975).

12. Algaze, G., Expansionary dynamics of some early pristine states. *American Anthropologist* **95**, 304-333 (1993).

13. Spencer, C., Territorial expansion and primary state formation. *PNAS* **107** (16), 7119-7126 (2010).

14. Connah, G., in *The human past*, edited by Scarre, C. (Thames & Hudson, London, 2005), pp. 350-391.

15. Marcus, J., The archaeological evidence for social evolution. *Annual Review of Anthropology* **37**, 251-266 (2008).

16. Hoffman, M., Hamroush, H. & Allen, R., A Model of Urban Development for the Hierakonpolis Region from Predynastic through Old. *Journal of the American Research Center in Egypt* **23**, 175-187 (1986).

17. Powell, B., *Writing: Theory and History of the Technology of Civilization* (Wiley-Blackwell, Chichester/Malden, MA, 2009).

18. Schmandt-Besserat, D., *Before Writing (2 vols.)* (University of Texas Press, Austin, TX, 1992).

19. Collier, M. & Manley, B., *How to read Egyptian (revised edition)* (British Museum Press, London, 1998).

27: An enigmatic civilisation

1. Lawler, A., Boring no more, a trade-savvy Indus emerges. *Science* **320**, 1276-1281 (2008).

2. Rao, R. *et al.*, Entropic Evidence for Linguistic Structure in the Indus Script. *Science* **324**, 1165 (2009).

3. Bellwood, P., *First Farmers* (Blackwell Publishing, Oxford, 2005).

4. Schaffer, J., in *Chronologies in Old World Archaeology*, edited by Ehrich, R. (University of Chicago Press, Chicago, IL, 1992), pp. 441-446.

5. Manuel, M., in *Sirinimal Lakdusinghe Felicitation Volume*, edited by Gunawardhana, P., Adikari, G. & Coningham, R. (Neptune, Battaramulla, 2010), pp. 145-152.

6. Jarrige, J., Mehrgarh Neolithic. *Pragdhara* **18**, 135-154 (2006).

7. Morrell, P. & Clegg, M., Genetic evidence for a second domestication of barley (Hordeum vulgare) east of the Fertile Crescent. *PNAS* **104** (9), 3289-3294 (2007).

8.   McIntosh, J., *The Ancient Indus Valley: New Perspectives* (ABC-CLIO, Inc., Denver, CL, 2008).

9.   Kenoyer, J., The Indus Valley Tradition of Pakistan and western India. *Journal of World Prehistory* **5** (4), 331-385 (1991).

10.   Wright, R., in *Monographs in World Archaeology No.3*, edited by Meadow, R. (Prehistory Press, Madison, WI, 1991), pp. 71-88.

11.   Coningham, R., in *The human past*, edited by Scarre, C. (Thames & Hudson, London, 2005), pp. 518-551.

12.   Possehl, G., *The Indus Civilization: A Contemporary Perspective* (AltaMira Press, Lanham, MD, 2002).

13.   Algaze, G., Expansionary dynamics of some early pristine states. *American Anthropologist* **95**, 304-333 (1993).

14.   Miller, D., Ideology and the Harappan Civilization. *Journal of Anthropological Archaeology* **4**, 34-71 (1985).

15.   Kenoyer, J., Craft Traditions of the Indus Civilization and their Legacy in Modern Pakistan. *Lahore Museum Bulletin* **IX** (2) (1996).

16.   Kenoyer, J., Ornament Styles of the Indus Valley Tradition : Evidence from Recent Excavations at Harappa, Pakistan. *Paléorient* **71** (2), 79-98 (1991).

17.   Spencer, C., Territorial expansion and primary state formation. *PNAS* **107** (16), 7119-7126 (2010).

18.   Giosan, L. *et al.*, Fluvial landscapes of the Harappan civilization. *PNAS* **109** (26), 10138-10139 (2012).

28: Interesting times

1.   Dematte, P., Longshan-Era Urbanism: The Role of Cities in Predynastic China. *Asian Perspectives* **38** (2), 119-153 (1999).

2.   Higham, C., in *The human past*, edited by Scarre, C. (Thames & Hudson, London, 2005), pp. 552-593.

3.   Lee, Y., Building the Chronology of Early Chinese History. *Asian Perspectives* **41** (1), 15-42 (2002).

4.   Bogucki, P., *The Origins of Human Society* (Blackwell Publishing, Oxford, 1999).

5.   Liu, L., Settlement patterns, chiefdom variability, and the development of early states in North China. *Journal of Anthropological Archaeology* **15**, 237-288 (1996).

6.   Higham, C., in *The Human Past*, edited by Scarre, C. (Thames & Hudson, London, 2005), pp. 234-263.

7.   Liu, L., The Development and Decline of Social Complexity in North China: Some Environmental and Social Factors. *Indo-Pacific Prehistory Association Bulletin* **20**, 14-34 (2000).

8.   Savage, S., Accessing Departures from Log-Normality in the Rank-Size Rule. *Journal of Archaeological Sizes* **24**, 233-244 (1997).

9.   Liu, L. & Xu, H., Rethinking Erlitou: legend, history and Chinese archaeology. *Antiquity* **81** (314), 886-901 (2007).

10.   Spencer, C., Territorial expansion and primary state formation. *PNAS* **107** (16), 7119-7126 (2010).

11.   Liu, L. & Chen, X., Settlement Archaeology and the Study of Social Complexity in China. *The Review of Archaeology* **22** (2), 4-22 (2001).

12.   Tang, J., Jing, Z., Liu, Z. & Yue, Z., Survey and Test Excavation of the Huanbei Shang City in Anyang. *Kaogu* **5**, 3-16 (2003).

13.   Du, J., A Preliminary Investigation of Place Foundation No.1 at the Huanbei Shang City. *Chinese Archaeology* **5** (1), 192-199 (2004).

14.   Jarus, O., Human sacrifices discovered at torched Shang Dynasty city Huanbei, Available at http://www.independent.co.uk/life-style/history/human-sacrifices-discovered-at-torched-shang-dynasty-city-huanbei-1975492.html (2010).

15.   Trigger, B., *Understanding early civilizations* (Cambridge University Press, New York, NY, 2003).

16.   Powell, B., *Writing: Theory and History of the Technology of Civilization* (Wiley-Blackwell, Chichester/Malden, MA, 2009).

29: Mexican superpowers

1. Webster, D. & Evans, S., in *The human past*, edited by Scarre, C. (Thames & Hudson, London, 2005), pp. 594-639.
2. Meggers, B., Evans, C. & Estrada, B., The Early Formative Period of the coast of Ecuador: the Valdivia and Machillia Phases. *Smithsonian Contributions to Anthropology* (1965).
3. Meggers, B., The Origins of Olmec Civilization. *Science* **309**, 556 (2005).
4. Rickard, T., The Use of Meteoric Iron. *The Journal of the Royal Anthropological Institute of Great Britain and Ireland* **71** (1/2), 55-66 (1941).
5. Burger, R. & Gordon, R., Early Central Andean Metalworking from Mina Perdida, Peru. *Science* **282**, 1108-1111 (1998).
6. Aldenderfer, M., Craig, N., Speakman, R. & Popelka-Filcoff, R., Four-thousand-year-old gold artifacts from the Lake Titicaca basin, southern Peru. *PNAS* **105** (13), 5002-5005 (2008).
7. Cooke, C., Abbott, M. & Wolfe, A., in *Encyclopedia of the History of Science, Technology, and Medicine in Non-Western Cultures Vol. 2*, edited by Seline, H. (Kluwer Science, Dordrecht, 2008), pp. 1658-1662.
8. Hosler, D. & Macfarlane, A., Copper Sources, Metal Production, and Metals Trade in Late Postclassic Mesoamerica. *Science* **273**, 1819-1824 (1996).
9. Hoopes, J., Ford Revisited - A Critical-Review Of Chronology And Relationships Of. The Earliest Ceramic Complexes In The New-World, 6000-1500-BC. *Journal of World Prehistory* **8** (1), 1-49 (1994).
10. Joyce, R. & Henderson, J., Beginnings of village life in eastern Mesoamerica. *Latin American Antiquity* **12** (1), 5-24 (2001).
11. Flannery, K. & Marcus, J., Formative Mexican Chiefdoms and the Myth of the "Mother Culture". *Journal of Anthropological Archaeology* **19**, 1-37 (2000).
12. Bellwood, P., *First Farmers* (Blackwell Publishing, Oxford, 2005).
13. Pool, C., *Olmec Archaeology and Early Mesoamerica* (Cambridge University Press, Cambridge, 2007).
14. Lesure, R., Early Formative Platforms at Paso de la Amada, Chiapas, Mexico. *Latin American Antiquity* **8** (3), 217-235 (1997).
15. Blomster, J., Early evidence of the ballgame in Oaxaca, Mexico. *PNAS* **109** (21), 8020–8025 (2012).
16. Cypher, A., in *Social Patterns in Pre-Classic Mesoamerica*, edited by Grove, D. & Joyce, R. (Dumbarton Oaks Research Library and Collection, Washington, DC, 1999), pp. 155-181.
17. Cobean, R., Coe, M., Perry, E., Turekian, K. & Kharkar, D., Obsidian Trade at San Lorenzo Tenochtitlan, Mexico. *Science* **174**, 666-671 (1971).
18. Ortíz, M. & Rodríguez, M., in *Social Patterns in Pre-Classic Mesoamerica*, edited by Grove, D. & Joyce, R. (Dumbarton Oaks Research Library and Collection, Washington, DC, 1999), pp. 225-254.
19. Rust, W. & Sharer, R., Olmec Settlement Data from La Venta, Tabasco, Mexico. *Science* **242**, 102-104 (1988).
20. Spencer, C. & Redmond, E., Primary state formation in Mesoamerica. *Annual Review of Anthropology* **33**, 173-199 (2004).
21. Diamond, J., *Collapse: how societies choose to fail or survive* (Viking Penguin, New York, NY, USA, 2005).
22. Flannery, K. *et al.*, Implications of new petrographic analysis for the Olmec 'mother culture' model. *PNAS* **102** (32), 11219-11223 (2005).
23. Blomster, J., Neff, H. & Glascock, M., Olmec Pottery Production and Export in Ancient Mexico Determined Through Elemental Analysis. *Science* **307**, 1068-1072 (2005).
24. Diehl, R., Patterns of Cultural Primacy. *Science* **307**, 1055-1056 (2005).
25. Stoltman, J., Marcus, J., Flannery, K., Burton, J. & Moyle, R., Petrographic evidence shows that pottery exchange between the Olmec and their neighbors was two-way. *PNAS* **102** (32), 11213-11218 (2005).
26. Neff, H. *et al.*, Methodological Issues in the Provenance Investigation of Early Formative Mesoamerican Ceramics. *Latin American Antiquity* **17** (1), 54-76 (2006).
27. Sharer, R. *et al.*, On the Logic of Archaeological Inference: Early Formative Pottery and the Evolution of Mesoamerican Societies. *Latin American Antiquity* **17** (1), 90-103 (2006).
28. Neff, H. *et al.*, Smokescreens in the Provenance Investigation Of Early Formative Mesoamerican Ceramics. *Latin Antiquity* **17** (1), 104-118 (2006).
29. Hosler, D., Burkett, S. & Tarkanian, M., Prehistoric Polymers: Rubber Processing in Ancient Mesoamerica. *Science* **284**, 1988-1991 (1999).

30. Cheetham, D., Cantón Corralito: Objects from a Possible Gulf Olmec Colony, Crystal River, FL:Foundation for the Advancement of Mesoamerican Studies Inc. (2007).

31. Moore, P., *Countdown!. or how nigh is the end?* (Pan, London, 1999).

32. Aventi, A., *Skywatchers* (University of Texas Press, Austin, TX, 2001).

33. Malmstrom, V., Origin of the Mesoamerican 260-Day Calendar. *Science* **181**, 939-940 (1973).

34. Henderson, J., Origin of the 260-Day Cycle in Mesoamerica. *Science* **185**, 542 (1973).

35. Pohl, M., Pope, K. & von Nagy, C., Olmec Origins of Mesoamerican Writing. *Science* **298**, 1984-1987 (2002).

36. Stokstad, E., Oldest New World Writing Suggests Olmec Innovation. *Science* **298**, 1873-1874 (2002).

37. Bricker, H., Aventi, A. & Bricker, V., Ancient Maya documents concerning the movements of Mars. *PNAS* **98** (4), 2107-2110 (2001).

38. Saturno, W., Stuart, D., Aveni, A. & Rossi, F., Ancient Maya Astronomical Tables from Xultun, Guatemala. *Science* **336**, 714-717 (2012).

39. Powell, B., *Writing: Theory and History of the Technology of Civilization* (Wiley-Blackwell, Chichester/Malden, MA, 2009).

40. Del Carmen Rodríguez Martínez, M. *et al.*, Oldest Writing in the New World. *Science* **313**, 1610-1614 (2006).

41. Bruhns, K. & Kelker, N., Did the Olmec Know How to Write? *Science* **315**, 1365 (2007).

42. Del Carmen Rodríguez Martínez, M. *et al.*, Did the Olmec Know How to Write? *Science* **315**, 1365-1366 (2007).

43. Popson, C., Earliest Mesoamerican Writing?, Available at http://archive.archaeology.org/0303/newsbriefs/olmec.html (2003).

44. Morell, V., New Light on Writing in the Americas. *Science* **251**, 268-270 (1991).

45. Coe, M., *The Maya*, 8th ed. (Thames & Hudson, London, 2011).

46. Justeson, J. & Kaufman, T., A Decipherment of Epi-Olmec Hieroglyphic Writing. *Science* **259**, 1703-1711 (1993).

47. Justeson, J. & Kaufman, T., A Newly Discovered Column in the Hieroglyphic Text on La Mojarra Stela 1: A Test of the Epi-Olmec Decipherment. *Science* **277**, 207-210 (1997).

48. Flannery, K. & Marcus, J., The origin of war: New 14C dates from ancient Mexico. *PNAS* **100** (20), 11801-11805 (2003).

49. Cahn, R. & Winter, M., The San José Mogote Danzante. *Indiana* **13**, 39-64 (1993).

50. Saturno, W., Stuart, D. & Beltrán, B., Early Maya Writing at San Bartolo, Guatemala. *Science* **311**, 1281-1283 (2006).

51. Houston, S., An Example of Preclassic Mayan Writing? *Science* **311**, 1249-1250 (2006).

52. Marcus, J. & Flannery, K., The coevolution of ritual and society: New 14C dates from ancient Mexico. *PNAS* **101** (52), 18257-18261 (2004).

53. Flannery, K., in *The Early Mesoamerican Village*, edited by Flannery, K. (Left Coast Press, Walnut Creek, CA, 1976), pp. 72-75.

54. Drennan, R. & Peterson, C., Patterned variation in prehistoric chiefdoms. *PNAS* **103** (11), 3960–3967 (2006).

55. Orr, H., Danzantes of Building L at Monte Albán, Available at http://www.famsi.org/reports/93003/93003Orr01.pdf (1994).

56. Spencer, C., War and early state formation in Oaxaca, Mexico. *PNAS* **100** (20), 11185-11187 (2003).

57. Spencer, C., Territorial expansion and primary state formation. *PNAS* **107** (16), 7119-7126 (2010).

58. Cowgill, G., State and society at Teotihuacan, Mexico. *Annual Review of Anthropology* **26**, 129-161 (1997).

59. Siebe, C., Age and archaeological implications of Xitle volcano, southwestern Basin of Mexico-City. *Journal of Volcanology and Geothermal Research* **104**, 45-64 (2000).

60. Algaze, G., Expansionary dynamics of some early pristine states. *American Anthropologist* **95**, 304-333 (1993).

61. White, C., Teotihuacán at Kaminaljuyú? The Evidence from Oxygen Isotopes in Human Bone, Available at http://www.famsi.org/reports/95084/95084White01.pdf (1996).

62. Ackroyd, P., *London: the biography* (Chatto & Windus, London, 2000).

References

30: The Maya

1. Trigger, B., *Understanding early civilizations* (Cambridge University Press, New York, NY, 2003).
2. Webster, D. & Evans, S., in *The human past*, edited by Scarre, C. (Thames & Hudson, London, 2005), pp. 594-639.
3. Lewis, P., http://www.ethnologue.com/web.asp, Available at http://www.ethnologue.com/ethno_docs/distribution.asp?by=family (2009).
4. Coe, M., *The Maya*, 8th ed. (Thames & Hudson, London, 2011).
5. Dunning, N., Beach, T. & Luzzadder-Beach, S., Kax and kol: Collapse and resilience in lowland Maya civilization. *PNAS* **109** (10), 3652-3657 (2012).
6. Pohl, M. *et al.*, Early Agriculture in the Maya Lowlands. *Latin American Antiquity* **7** (4), 355-372 (1996).
7. Hansen, R., in *Maya: Divine Kings of the Rain Forest*, edited by Grube, N. (Konemann Press, Verlag, Germany, 2001), pp. 50-65.
8. Hansen, R., in *Function and Meaning in Classic Maya Architecture*, edited by Houston, S. (Dumbarton Oaks, Washington, DC, 1998), pp. 49-122.
9. Hansen, R., The Architectural Development of an Early Maya Structure at Nakbé, Petén, Guatemala, Available at http://www.famsi.org/reports/95113/95113Hansen01.pdf (2002).
10. Spencer, C. & Redmond, E., Primary state formation in Mesoamerica. *Annual Review of Anthropology* **33**, 173-199 (2004).
11. Aventi, A., *Skywatchers* (University of Texas Press, Austin, TX, 2001).
12. Coe, M., Tikal, Guatemala, and Emergent Maya Civilization. *Science* **147** (3664), 1401-1419 (1965).
13. Scarborough, V. *et al.*, Water and sustainable land use at the ancient tropical city of Tikal, Guatemala. *PNAS* **109** (31), 12408-12413 (2012).
14. Matheny, R., Maya Lowland Hydraulic Systems. *Science* **193** (4254), 639-646 (1976).
15. Hammond, N., in *Social patterns in Pre-classic Mesoamerica*, edited by Grove, D. & Joyce, R. (Dumbarton Oaks, Washington, DC, 1999), pp. 49-66.
16. Hansen, R., in *V Simposio de investigaciones arquelógicas en Guatemala, Museo Nacional de Arqueología y Etnología, 15–18 de Julio de 1991*, edited by Laporte, J., Escobedo, A. & de Brady, S. (Ministerio de Cultura y Deportes, Instituto de Antropología e Historia, Asociación Tikal, Guatemala City, 1992), pp. 81-87.
17. Kennett, D. *et al.*, Development and Disintegration of Maya Political Systems in Response to Climate Change. *Science* **338**, 788-791 (2012).
18. Marcus, J., in *Archaic States*, edited by Feinman, G. & Marcus, J. (School of American Research Press, Santa Fe, NM, 1998), pp. 59–94.
19. Scherer, A. & Golden, C., Tecolote, Guatemala: Archaeological Evidence for a Fortified Late Classic Maya Political Border. *Journal of Field Archaeology* **34**, 285-305 (2009).
20. Aoyama, K., Elite artists and craft producers in Classic Maya society: Lithic evidence from Aguateca, Guatemala. *Latin American Antiquity* **18** (1), 3-26 (2007).
21. Vargas, R., López, V. & Martin, S., Daily life of the ancient Maya recorded on murals at Calakmul, Mexico. *PNAS* **106** (46), 19245–19249 (2009).
22. McKillop, H., Finds in Belize document Late Classic Maya salt making and canoe transport. *PNAS* **102** (15), 5630-5634 (2005).
23. Sharer, R. & Traxler, L., *The Ancient Maya (6th Edition)* (Stanford University Press, Stanford, CA, 2005).
24. Demarest, A., *Ancient Maya: The Rise and Fall of a Rainforest Civilization* (Cambridge University Press, Cambridge, 2004).
25. Diamond, J., *Collapse: how societies choose to fail or survive* (Viking Penguin, New York, NY, USA, 2005).
26. McNeil, C., Burney, D. & Burney, L., Evidence disputing deforestation as the cause for the collapse of the ancient Maya polity of Copan, Honduras. *PNAS* **107** (3), 1017-1022 (2010).
27. Fedick, S., The Maya Forest: Destroyed or cultivated by the ancient Maya? *PNAS* **107** (3), 953-954 (2010).
28. Hodell, D., Brenner, M., Curtis, J. & Guilderson, T., Solar Forcing of Drought Frequency in the Maya Lowlands. *Science* **292**, 1367-1370 (2001).

29.   Medina-Elizalde, M. *et al.*, High resolution stalagmite climate record from the Yucatán Peninsula spanning the Maya terminal classic period. *Earth and Planetary Science Letters* **298**, 255-262 (2010).
30.   Medina-Elizalde, M. & Rohling, E., Collapse of Classic Maya Civilization Related to Modest Reduction in Precipitation. *Science* **335**, 956-959 (2012).
31.   Luzzadder-Beach, S., Beach, T. & Dunning, N., Wetland fields as mirrors of drought and the Maya abandonment. *PNAS* **109** (10), 3646-3651 (2012).

31: Before the Inca

1.   Stanish, C., The origin of state societies in South America. *Annual Review of Anthropology* **30**, 41-64 (2001).
2.   Pozorski, T. & Pozorski, S., in *The Origins and development of the Andean state*, edited by Haas, J., Pozorski, S. & Pozorski, T. (Cambridge University Press, Cambridge, 1987), pp. 36-46.
3.   Moseley, M. & Heckenberger, M., in *The human past*, edited by Scarre, C. (Thames & Hudson, London, 2005), pp. 640-677.
4.   Moseley, M., *The Incas and Their Ancestors: The Archaeology of Peru*, 2nd ed. (Thames & Hudson, London, 2001).
5.   Pozorski, S. & Pozorski, T., in *Handbook of South American Archaeology*, edited by Silverman, H. & Isbell, W. (Springer, New York, NY, 2008), pp. 602-632.
6.   Haas, J., Creamer, W. & Ruiz, A., Dating the Late Archaic occupation of the Norte Chico region in Peru. *Nature* **432**, 1020-1023 (2004).
7.   Pozorski, T. & Pozorski, S., Early Complex Societies and Ceremonialism on the Peruvian North Coast. *Senri Ethnological Studies* **37**, 45-68 (1993).
8.   Pozorski, S., in *The Origins and development of the Andean state*, edited by Haas, J., Pozorski, S. & Pozorski, T. (Cambridge University Press, Cambridge, 1987), pp. 15-30.
9.   Pozorski, S. & Pozorski, T., Las Halidas: An Expanding Initial Period Polity of Coastal Peru. *Journal of Anthropological Research* **62**, 27-52 (2006).
10.   Burger, R., *Chavin: And the Origins of the Andean Civilization* (Thames & Hudson, London, 1992).
11.   Haas, J., in *The origins and development of the Andean state*, edited by Haas, J., Pozorski, S. & Pozorski, T. (Cambridge University Press, Cambrisge, 1987), pp. 31-35.
12.   Burger, R., The Radiocarbon Evidence for the Temporal Priority of Chavín de Huántar. *American Antiquity* **46** (2), 592-602 (1981).
13.   Bellwood, P., *First Farmers* (Blackwell Publishing, Oxford, 2005).
14.   Kembel, S., *Architectural sequence and chronology at Chavin de Huantar, Peru*. PhD dissertation, Department of Anthropological Sciences, Stanford University (2001).
15.   Burger, R., in *Handbook of South American Archeology*, edited by Silverman, H. & Isbell, W. (Springer, New York, NY, 2008), pp. 681-706.
16.   Kembel, S. & Rick, J., in *Andean Archaeology*, edited by Silverman, H. (Blackwell Publishing, Oxford, 2004), pp. 51-75.
17.   Butters, L., in *Gallinazo: An Early Cultural Tradition on the Peruvian North Coast*, edited by Millaire, J. & Morlion, M. (Cotsen Institute of Archaeology at UCLA, Los Angeles, CA, 2009).
18.   Willey, G., *Prehistoric Settlement Patterns in the Virú Valley, Perú* (Smithsonian Institution Press, Washington, DC, 1953).
19.   Lambert, P. *et al.*, Bone chemistry at Cerro Oreja: a stable isotope perspective on the development of a regional economy in the Moche Valley, Peru during the Early Intermediate Period. *Latin American Antiquity* **23** (2), 144-166 (2012).
20.   Millaire, J., Primary State Formation in the Virú Valley, North Coast of Peru. *PNAS* **107** (14), 6186-6191 (2010).
21.   Bennett, W., *The Gallinazo Group, Viru Valley, Peru* (Yale University, New Haven, CT, 1950).
22.   Spencer, C., Territorial expansion and primary state formation. *PNAS* **107** (16), 7119-7126 (2010).
23.   Butters, L. & Castillo, S., in *Handbook of South American Archaeology*, edited by Silverman, H. & Isbell, W. (Springer, New York, NY, 2008), pp. 707-729.
24.   Quilter, J., Moche Politics, Religion, and Warfare. *Journal of World Prehistory* **16** (2), 145-195 (2002).

25.   Quilter, J. & Koons, M., The fall of the Moche: a critique of claims for South America's first state. *Latin American Antiquity* **23** (2), 127-143 (2012).

26.   Dillehay, T. & Kolata, A., Long-term human response to uncertain environmental conditions in the Andes. *PNAS* **101** (12), 4325-4330 (2004).

27.   Proulx, D., in *Nasca: Geheimnisvolle Zeichen im Alten Peru*, edited by Rickenbach, J. (Museum Rietberg Zürich, Zurich, 1999), pp. 79-87.

28.   Erickson, C., Raised field agriculture in the Lake Titicaca basin: putting ancient agriculture back to work. *Expedition* **30** (3), 8-16 (1988).

29.   Hastorf, C., in *Advances in Titicaca Basin Archaeology-1*, edited by Stanish, C., Cohen, A. & Aldenderfer, M. (Cotsen Institute of Archaeology Press, Los Angeles, CA, 2005), pp. 65-94.

30.   Stanish, C. & Levine, A., War and early state formation in the northern Titicaca Basin, Peru. *PNAS* **108** (34), 13901-13906 (2011).

31.   Plourde, A. & Stanish, C., in *Andean Archaeology III: North and South*, edited by Isbell, W. & Silverman, H. (Springer, New York, NY, 2006), pp. 237-257.

32.   Janusek, J., *Identity and Power in the Ancient Andes: Tiwanaku Cities through Time* (Routledge, London, 2004).

33.   Janusek, J., in *Advances in Titicaca Basin Archaeology-1*, edited by Stanish, C., Cohen, A. & Aldenderfer, M. (Cotsen Institute of Archaeology Press, Los Angeles, CA, 2005), pp. 143-171.

34.   Isbell, W., in *Palaces of the Ancient New World*, edited by Evans, S. & Pillbury, J. (Dumbarton Oaks, Washington, DC, 2004), pp. 191-246.

35.   Browman, D., Lithic provenience analysis and emerging material complexity at Formative Period Chiripa, Bolivia. *Andean Past* **8**, 301-324 (1998).

36.   Kolata, A., The Technology and Organization of Agricultural Production in the Tiwanaku State. *Latin American Antiquity* **2** (2), 99-125 (1991).

37.   Stanish, C., Frye, K., de la Vega, E. & Seddon, M., in *Advances in Titicaca Basin Archaeology-1*, edited by Stanish, C., Cohen, A. & Aldenderfer, M. (Cotsen Institute of Archaeology Press, Los Angeles, CA, 2005), pp. 103-114.

38.   Isbell, W. & Vranich, A., in *Andean Archaeology*, edited by Silverman, H. (Blackwell Publishing, Oxford, 2004), pp. 167-181.

39.   Tung, T., Dismembering bodies for display: a bioarchaeological study of trophy heads from the Wari site of Conchopata, Peru. *American Journal of Physical Anthropology* **136** (3), 294-308 (2008).

40.   Tung, T. & Knudson, K., Social Identities and Geographical Origins of Wari Trophy Heads from Conchopata, Peru. *Current Anthropology* **49** (5), 915-925 (2008).

41.   Tung, T. & Knudson, K., Identifying locals, migrants, and captives in the Wari Heartland: A bioarchaeological and biogeochemical study of human remains from Conchopata, Peru. *Journal of Anthropological Archaeology* **30**, 247-261 (2011).

42.   Schreiber, K., in *The Origins and Development of the Andean State*, edited by Haas, J., Pozorski, S. & Pozorski, T. (Cambridge University Press, Cambridge, 1987), pp. 91-96.

43.   Isbell, W. & Schreiber, K., Was Huari a state? *American Antiquity* **43**, 372-389 (1978).

44.   Bernstein, P., Tiwanaku temples and state expansion: a Tiwanaku sunken-court temple in Moquegua, Peru. *Latin American Antiquity* **41** (1), 22-47 (1993).

45.   Moseley, M. *et al.*, Burning down the brewery: Establishing and evacuating an ancient imperial colony at Cerro Baúl, Peru. *PNAS* **102** (48), 17264-17271 (2005).

46.   Conlee, C., Dulanto, J., Mackey, C. & Stanish, C., in *Andean Archaeology*, edited by Silverman, H. (Blackwell Publishing, Oxford, 2004), pp. 209-236.

47.   Moore, J. & Mackey, C., in *Handbook of South American Archaeology*, edited by Silverman, H. & Isbell, W. (Springer, New York, NY, 2008), pp. 783-808.

48.   Andrews, A., The U-shaped structures at Chan Chan, Peru. *Journal of Field Archaeology* **1** (3/4), 241-264 (1974).

49.   Pillsbury, J. & Leonard, B., in *Palaces of the Ancient New World*, edited by Evans, S. & Pillbury, J. (Dumbarton Oaks Research Library and Collection, Washington, DV, 2004), pp. 247-298.

50.   Diamond, J., *Guns, Germs and Steel* (Chatto & Windus, London, 1997).

32: Humans: the future

1.   Clarke, A., *Imperial Earth* (Victor Gollancz, London, 1975).
2.   Moore, G., Cramming more components onto integrated circuits. *Electronics* **38** (8) (1965).
3.   Barnosky, A., Megafauna biomass tradeoff as a driver of Quaternary and future extinctions. *PNAS* **105** (Suppl. 1), 11543-11548 (2008).
4.   Haub, C., How Many People Have Ever Lived? *Population Today* **38** (8), 3-4 (2002).
5.   Mueller, U., Schultz, T., Currie, C., Adams, R. & Malloch, D., The origin of the attine ant-fungus mutualism. *Quarterly Review of Biology* **76** (2), 169-197 (2001).
6.   Porter, R., *England in the Eighteenth Century*, 2nd ed. (Penguin, London, 1990).
7.   UN, The World at Six Billion, Available at http://www.un.org/esa/population/publications/sixbillion/sixbilpart1.pdf (1999).
8.   UN, World Population Prospects: The 2012 Revision, New York, NY: UN Population Division (2013).
9.   Gerland, P. *et al.*, World population stabilization unlikely this century. *Science* (published online) (2014).
10.   Smith, A., Provenance of Coals from Roman Sites in England and Wales. *Britannia* **28**, 297-324 (1997).
11.   Denman, K. *et al.*, in *Climate Change 2007: The Physical Science Basis. Contribution of Working Group I to the Fourth Assessment Report of the Intergovernmental Panel on Climate Change*, edited by Solomon, S. *et al.* (Cambridge University Press, Cambridge, 2007), pp. 501-587.
12.   Van der Werf, G. *et al.*, CO2 emissions from forest loss. *Nature Geoscience* **2**, 737-738 (2009).
13.   Marcott, S., Shakun, J., Clark, P. & Mix, A., A Reconstruction of Regional and Global Temperature for the Past 11,300 Years. *Science* **339**, 1198-1201 (2013).
14.   Met Office, How has our climate changed?, Available at http://www.metoffice.gov.uk/climate-change/guide/how#Increasing-temperatures.
15.   Anderson, K. & Bows, A., Beyond 'dangerous' climate change: emission scenarios for a new world. *Philosophical Transactions of the Royal Society A* **369**, 20-44 (2011).
16.   Betts, R. *et al.*, When could global warming reach 4°C? *Philosophical Transactions of the Royal Society A* **269**, 67-84 (2011).
17.   Sanderson, M., Hemming, D. & Betts, R., Regional temperature and precipitation changes under high-end (≥4°C) global warming. *Philosophical Transactions of the Royal Society A* **369**, 85-98 (2011).
18.   Fung, F., Lopez, A. & New, M., Water availability in +2°C and +4°C worlds. *Philosophical Transactions of the Royal Society A* **369**, 99-116 (2011).
19.   Thornton, P., Jones, P., Ericksen, P. & Challinor, A., Agriculture and food systems in sub-Saharan Africa in a 4°C+ world. *Philosophical Transactions of the Royal Society A* **369**, 117-136 (2011).
20.   Nicholls, R. *et al.*, Sea-level rise and its possible impacts given a 'beyond 4°C world' in the twenty-first century. *Philosophical Transactions of the Royal Society A* **369**, 161-181 (2011).
21.   Gemenne, F., Climate-induced population displacements in a 4°C+ world. *Philosophical Transactions of the Royal Society A* **369**, 182-195 (2011).
22.   The Royal Society, Ocean Acidification Due to Increasing Atmospheric Carbon Dioxide, London:The Royal Society (2005).
23.   Barnosky, A. *et al.*, Approaching a state shift in Earth's biosphere. *Nature* **486**, 52-58 (2012).
24.   Benton, M., *When Life Nearly Died* (Thames & Hudson, London, 2003).
25.   Foley, J. *et al.*, Solutions for a cultivated planet. *Nature* **478**, 337-342 (2011).
26.   Hoffert, M. *et al.*, Advanced Technology Paths to Global Climate Stability: Energy for a Greenhouse Planet. *Science* **298**, 981-987 (2002).
27.   Rosegrant, M., Biofuels and Grain Prices: Impacts and Policy Responses, Washington, DC: International Food Policy Reasearch Unit (2008).
28.   Hill, J., Nelson, E., Tilman, D., Polasky, S. & Tiffany, D., Environmental, economic, and energetic costs and benefits of biodiesel and ethanol biofuels. *PNAS* **103** (30), 11206-11210 (2006).
29.   Carroll, J., Exxon at Least 25 Years Away From Making Fuel From Algae, Available at http://www.bloomberg.com/news/2013-03-08/exxon-at-least-25-years-away-from-making-fuel-from-algae.html (2013).

30. Wilkes, J. & Moccia, J., Wind in power: 2012 European statistics, European Wind Energy Association (2013).

31. Swanson, R., Photovoltaics Power Up. *Science* **324**, 891-892 (2009).

32. Pacala, S. & Socolow, R., Stabilization Wedges: Solving the Climate Problem for the Next 50 Years with Current Technologies. *Science* **305**, 968-972 (2004).

33. Stapledon, O., *Star Maker* (Methuen, London, 1937).

34. Dyson, F., Search for Artificial Stellar Sources of Infrared Radiation. *Science* **131**, 1667 (1960).

35. Dyson, F., in *Perspectives in Modern Physics*, edited by Marshak, R. (Interscience Publishers, New York, NY, 1966), pp. 641-655.

36. Nicolson, I. & Berry, A., in *The next ten thousand years*, edited by Berry, A. (Jonathan Cape, London, 1974), pp. 187-196.

37. Berry, A., *The next ten thousand years* (Jonathan Cape, London, 1974).

38. Kurzweil, R., *The Singularity is Near* (Viking Books, New York, NY, 2005).

39. Vogt, S. *et al.*, A 3.1 Me Planet in the Habitable Zone of the Nearby M3V Star Gliese 581, s.l.: The Lick-Carnegie Exoplanet Survey (2010).

40. Anglada-Escudé, G. *et al.*, A dynamically-packed planetary system around GJ 667C with three super-Earths in its habitable zone. *Astronomy & Astrophysics* **201** (2013).

41. Petigura, E., Howard, A. & Marcy, G., Prevalence of Earth-size planets orbiting Sun-like stars. *PNAS* **110** (48), 19273-19278 (2013).

42. Schopf, W., Microfossils of the Early Archean Apex Chert: New Evidence of the Antiquity of Life. *Science* **260**, 640-646 (1993).

43. Wegener Parfrey, L., Lahr, D., Knoll, A. & Katz, L., Estimating the timing of early eukaryotic diversification with multigene molecular clocks. *PNAS* **108** (33), 13624-13629 (2011).

44. Buick, R., Early life: Ancient acritarchs. *Nature* **463**, 885-886 (2010).

45. Davies, P., *Are we alone?* (Penguin, London, 1995).

46. FAO, The State of Food Insecurity in the World 2012, Rome: Food and Agriculture Organization of the United Nations (2012).

47. World Bank, Poverty Overview, Available at http://www.worldbank.org/en/topic/poverty/overview (2010).

48. Smail, K., Global Population Reduction: Confronting the Inevitable. *World Watch Magazine* **17** (5), 58-59 (2004).

Index

Abu Hureyra, 237-40, 244-5, 264

Acheulean tool industry, 66-8, 76-9, 82-4, 86, 98-9, 118, 147, 459, 469, 475-6, 482

Afroasiatic languages, 284, 288, 294

agriculture, 7, 12, 109, 114, 140, 196, 205, 213, 224-33, 234, 243-8, 251-9, 260-1, 263-6, 268-78, 283, 285-8, 290-1, 294-5, 296-7, 299-306, 307-10, 312-3, 314-21, 323-6, 328-31, 338, 341, 346-7, 353, 359, 361, 370, 387, 394-5, 397-8, 406, 409, 411, 413, 419-22, 478

Ahmarian tool industry, 182-4, 186

Aleut-Eskimo languages, 205-7

Amerind languages, 205-6

Ammerman, Albert, 269, 285-6

Amri, 354-5

Anatolian hypothesis of Indo-European origins, 285-7

Ardipithecus, 8, 31-4, 36-45, 118, 469

Ardipithecus kadabba, 8, 32-3, 40, 469

Ardipithecus ramidus, 8, 32-3, 40, 469

Arlington Springs, 198

Aspero, 322

Aurignacian, 103-4, 113, 115, 178-86, 188, 194

australopithecine, 8-9, 31-4, 36, 38-44, 46-51, 53-8, 62, 68, 70, 73-4, 76, 147, 469, 470, 476, 481

Australopithecus afarensis, 31, 36, 41, 43-9, 56, 457, 470

Australopithecus africanus, 31, 36, 41, 43, 45-9, 54, 56, 470

Australopithecus anamensis, 40, 43-5, 470

Australopithecus bahrelghazali, 45, 470

Australopithecus garhi, 47-8, 50-1, 56, 74, 470

Australopithecus sediba, 7, 47-8, 54, 56, 66, 453-4, 470, 476-7

Austroasiatic languages, 306, 309

Austronesian languages, 168, 291, 303, 306-10, 312-13, 337, 425, 444

Aztec, 369, 371, 382, 385-6, 397, 416-7

Bab el-Mandeb Strait, 74, 153-4, 157, 160

Bachokirian tool industry, 184

Badegoulian tool industry, 193, 195

Balakot, 354-5, 357-8

Bantu, 132-3, 232, 287, 289, 292-5, 442

Baradostian tool industry, 181, 183-4

Barham, Larry, 86, 130

Barker, Graeme, 231, 310

barley, 101, 224, 226, 234-5, 238, 244, 247, 252, 257, 260, 267, 291, 330-1, 349, 353

Barnosky, Anthony, 420-1

Bashidang, 301

Bayesian inference, 135, 287, 312, 471

beads, 103, 116, 128, 130, 138-9, 154, 178-9, 183-6, 236-7, 240, 246, 256-7, 272, 322, 329, 347, 353, 356-9, 372, 408, 464

beans, 224, 226, 315-6, 320, 322-6, 397-8

Bellwood, Peter, 232-3, 288, 306, 327, 352

Berekhat Ram pebble, 86

Berger, Lee, 47-8, 401

Beringia, 197-200, 223

Bickerton, Derek, 141-3

Bilzingsleben, 84

bipedalism, 30, 36-8, 48, 64

Blombos Cave, 126-30, 134, 138-9, 460

boats and watercraft, 74-5, 144, 154, 159, 169, 198, 202-3, 266-7, 272-3, 276, 302-3, 308, 310-1, 323, 358, 361-2, 391, 415

Bogucki, Peter, 337-8

Bølling-Allerød Interstadial, 193, 203, 211, 218, 230, 237, 240

Bonampak, 394

bone tools, 99, 115, 126, 127, 202, 237, 240, 297, 299, 460

bonobos (*Pan paniscus*), 19, 23, 25, 30, 33, 35, 44, 51

Boucher de Perthes, Jacques, 21, 66

bow wave effect, 103-6, 237

Bowler, Jim, 169

Boxgrove, 84-5

Braidwood, Robert, 227

Brooks, Alison, 138

Broom, Robert, 46, 49, 87

broomcorn millet, 297, 299-300, 305

Bulbeck, David, 159, 169

Buri Peninsula, 125

Buttermilk Creek, 199

Cactus Hill, 199-200

Cafer Höyük, 252-4, 257

Calakmul, 388, 391-4

Callao Cave, 168

Cann, Rebecca, 120

cannibalism, 77, 95, 97, 119

Caracol, 392

Caral, 317, 322-3, 397-8

Cardial Ware culture, 272, 276

Carneiro, Robert, 339, 346, 398-9

Cascajal Block, 378

Çatalhöyük, 251, 261-3, 268, 337, 344, 403

cats, 19, 27, 208-9, 259-60

cattle, 93, 99, 118, 127, 177, 225-6, 228, 242, 254-5, 258, 260, 262-3, 273, 277, 283-4, 290-3, 298, 347, 353, 420

Cavalli-Sforza, Luigi Luca, 269, 285, 286

Çayönü Tepesi, 252-3, 255-62, 337

cereals, 101, 224-6, 230, 235-8, 241-4, 246-7, 250, 252, 255, 257, 264-5, 272, 290-1, 296, 299, 301, 309-10, 314-5, 317-8, 331, 342-3, 353, 483

Cerro Juanaqueña, 326

Chak Toc Ich'aak I, 384

Chanhu-daro, 355-6, 358

Châtelperronian tool industry, 103-5, 114, 116

Chavín de Huántar, 400-3

Chengtoushan, 303

Chichén Itzá, 385, 395

chickens, 225, 298, 301, 308, 311-2

Child, V. Gordon, 223-4, 227, 245, 249, 269, 284, 297, 331, 335, 338-9, 351, 417-8

chimpanzees (*Pan troglodytes*), 7-8, 16, 19, 23-5, 27-30, 31-9, 41-4, 50-1, 56, 72, 106, 137, 140, 142, 144-5, 418, 453, 469, 475, 477

Chimú Empire, 414-6

Chuodun, 303

Ciaoxieshan, 303

Cishan culture, 298, 299

clades and cladistics, 10, 48, 55, 81, 471-2

Clark, Sir Grahame, 57, 66, 83, 98, 125, 178, 479, 481-2

Clarke, Sir Arthur C., 418

click languages, 133-4

climate change, 7, 10, 23, 27, 37-8, 58, 82, 100, 113, 115, 124, 150, 156, 159, 172, 198, 208-17, 219, 230, 252, 258, 264, 394, 420, 423

Clottes, Jean, 186

Clovis, 199-204, 207, 210, 215-7

cognitive fluidity, 144-6

Copán, 392, 394

Copenhagen Accord, 420

corvée labour, 336, 345, 409, 412, 472

Linnaeus, Carl, 24

logograms, 348-50, 367, 378, 473, 478, 482, 487

Longshan, 301, 360-4, 366-7

Lothal, 355

Lovejoy, Owen, 5, 33-4, 36, 38

Löwenmensch figurines, 186-7

low-level food production, 233, 238, 248, 255, 257, 260, 301, 305, 307, 310, 325, 336, 478, 486

Lucy (*Australopithecus afarensis*), 31, 33, 40-1, 43-4, 54, 61, 457, 470

Lyell, Sir Charles, 20

Magdalenian, 177-8, 188-9, 193, 196

maize, 224, 226, 244, 289, 314-5, 317-20, 322, 324-8, 331, 387, 391, 398, 402-3, 409, 411-3, 422

Majiabang culture, 302-3

Mammoth Steppe, 174-6

manioc, 224, 226, 314-7, 319-21, 324-5, 331

Manis, 199-200

Marean, Curtis, 125, 138-9

Marine isotope stages, 12, 96, 135, 153-56, 160-2, 164, 166, 180, 199, 213, 477, 479

Marshack, Alexander, 188

Martin. Paul, 208, 212, 215-6

Mauer Mandible, 80

Maya Long Count, 375-6, 379

Maya script, 377-8

McBrearty, Sally, 137-8

Meadowcroft Rockshelter, 199, 204

Mehrgarh, 352-4

Mellars, Sir Paul, 104, 161, 184

Mesoamerican ballgame, 374-5

metallurgy, 12, 293, 357, 361, 404, 415, 486

microliths, 125, 130-2, 139, 155, 197, 200, 236, 238, 246, 266, 297, 299, 353-4, 479

Micronesian, 311

Milagro, 325

Mithen, Steven, 107, 115, 143-6, 240, 242, 252-3, 479

Mitochondrial Eve, 121-2, 170

Mladeč Caves, 179

Moche culture, 338, 397, 399, 402-5, 410, 415-6

modern human (*Homo sapiens*), 7-9, 12-3, 15-6, 19, 24, 29, 31, 35-9, 41-2, 44, 48, 54, 56, 57, 61-4, 70, 73-5, 76, 77, 79, 80-2, 84, 86-8, 89-94, 96, 99-101, 103-116, 117-123, 136-50, 432-7, 457-8, 467, 469, 473, 477, 481

modern human behaviour, 19, 86, 103, 119, 123, 125-6, 130, 136-50, 155, 480

Mohenjo-daro, 352, 355-7, 359

Mojokerto Child (*Homo erectus*), 71-2

Monte Albán, 338, 376, 379-84, 390

Monte Verde, 201-2

mortuary practices, 98, 118-9, 185, 236, 241-2, 251, 272, 285, 329, 343, 353, 361, 371, 389, 408, 415

Mousterian, 98, 103-5, 113-4, 184, 481

Mrs Ples (*Paranthropus robustus*), 33, 46

Mugharet es-Skhul, 119, 136, 146, 154-6

multiregional continuity model, 9, 112, 120

Mureybet, 237, 240, 245-6, 254

Nabta Playa, 290-1

Na-Dene languages, 205-7

Nageshwar, 355, 357-8

Nakbé, 387-89

Ñanchoc Valley, 316-17, 320-1

Naqada, 346, 347

Natufian, 234, 236-46, 253, 259, 266, 288, 337

Nazca culture, 405-6, 410, 412

Neanderthal, 7, 9, 23, 29, 64, 69, 76-7, 80-1, 88, 89-116, 120, 122, 124, 136-8, 143, 145-6, 155-6, 160, 162, 164, 176, 178-80, 236, 457-8, 467, 471, 473, 476-7, 480-1

Netiv Hagdud, 245, 247

Nevali Çori, 249, 254, 257, 259

24218010R00318

Made in the USA
San Bernardino, CA
20 September 2015